a Wolters Kluwer business

Family Foundation Handbook

2007 Edition

by Jerry J. McCoy and Kathryn W. Miree

The *Family Foundation Handbook* provides ongoing practical advice on how to operate a family foundation. It helps the foundation director set and meet personal goals, learn how to avoid liability, and make the most effective grants. This book provides forms, checklists, questionnaires, training forms, and other items to help provide the professional assistance every foundation needs.

> Immediately following the highlights is a Special Alert on the Pension Protection Act of 2006.

Highlights of the 2007 Edition

The 2007 Edition of the *Family Foundation Handbook* incorporates the changes in tax law and practice that have occurred in this complex and constantly changing field. Highlights include:

- The most recent statistics of family foundation trends and profiles from The Foundation Center, the Council on Foundations, and the Internal Revenue Service.

- Many new court cases and foundation missteps from the Tax Courts, the IRS, and the news media that illustrate issues and highlight pitfalls.

- Expanded sections on personal liability of board members, including up-to-date references for state Volunteer Liability laws.

- The latest data on staff salaries and guidelines for review and implementation of salary policies.

- The most current list of resources for international grants, charitable trade groups, online research sites, socially responsible investment options, and much more.

- An expanded section on researching and enforcing the use of grant funds.

- The latest news on possible changes to the Uniform Management of Institutional Funds Act.

- A new section dealing with the problems encountered when foundation managers, younger generations, or others attempt to "hijack" the family foundation by taking it into areas the founder(s) would not approve. More important, the new edition discusses preventive measures that can help keep a foundation on course.

- Updated tables listing resources, contacts, and other information for family foundations.

- Newly expanded discussion of the excise tax on net investment income of foundations (IRC §4940).

- Review of pertinent private letter rulings and other IRS announcements.

- Discussion of non-tax cases involving family foundation issues.

8/06

Special Alert
2006 Legislation

NOTICE – On August 17, 2006, just as this edition of the *Family Foundation Handbook* was going to print, President Bush signed the Pension Protection Act of 2006 ("the Act"), which included a number of sweeping changes affecting family foundations and other tax-exempt organizations. While these developments emerged too late to be included in the body of the text, we are including a summary of the most important items here in this special alert. In an attempt to make it as useful as possible, we have included references to the primary portions of the handbook to which the changes relate.

Chapter 2 [§ 2.03[B]]

Even a cursory reading of this book will demonstrate that private foundations are second-class citizens from the standpoint of their tax treatment. Contributions to foundations do not qualify for much of the more favorable tax treatment granted to similar contributions made to public charities.

This unfortunate tradition is continued in the Act, which expands this category of second-class tax citizens. An important new charitable giving incentive created by the Act is expressly denied for private foundation contributions. Section 1201 of the Act permits certain older taxpayers (aged 70½ or more) to have amounts up to $100,000 per year transferred from their individual retirement accounts to charity. The provision is often referred to as a rollover, since it permits such a transfer to be made tax free — the individual has no income tax on a distribution from his account and receives no charitable deduction for the amount passing to charity. The Act makes this tax break available for contributions made during 2006 and 2007.

This treatment is available only if the charity receiving the distribution is a public charity *other than* a supporting organization or a donor-advised fund. Since private foundations are not public charities, they are automatically excluded. Moreover, as will be seen from the sections that follow, supporting organizations and donor-advised funds are disadvantaged by the Act in many respects. As a result, many of the former tax advantages of these organizations, compared with private foundations, have been reduced or eliminated.

Chapter 2 [§ 2.05]

Foundation Alternatives

Individuals considering the creation of a family foundation are urged to consider other alternatives, which might be more economical or efficient for some situations, particularly those involving smaller contributions. Two of those alternatives, donor-advised funds and supporting organizations, are the subject of new regulatory schemes under the Act. In general, the new restrictions are less severe than those initially proposed, and are generally workable, although they will require some adjustments.

In addition to the actual changes described below, the Act directed the Treasury Department to conduct a study of these two types of organizations and report back to the Congress within a year. That study is specifically to consider the following items:

- Whether income tax, gift tax or estate tax charitable deductions are appropriate for these entities in view of (1) the use of the contributed assets including the type, extent and timing of such use, and (2) the use of the assets of the organization for the benefit of the person making the charitable contribution;

- Whether donor-advised funds should be required to distribute a specified amount based on income or assets in order to ensure that the sponsoring organization is operating consistently with its exempt purposes and its status as a public charity;

- Whether the retention by donors of rights or privileges with respect to contributions to such organizations (including advisory rights or privileges with respective grants or investments) is consistent with such contributions as completed transfers for deduction purposes; and

- Whether such issues also arise with respect to other forms of charities or charitable contributions.

That study could, of course, result in an additional legislation affecting donor-advised funds and supporting organizations. Readers are urged to remain alert to the possibility of additional changes and to watch for the issuance of this Treasury report, probably in 2007.

NEW RULES FOR DONOR ADVISED FUNDS

In recent years, donor-advised funds have proliferated, becoming a very popular alternative for a person considering a private foundation. Neither the Internal Revenue Code nor the Regulations, however, have heretofore provided any specific rules governing donor-advised funds. As with any situation in which the rules are unstated or unclear, this absence of specific rules led to abuse by some organizations. The vast majority of U.S. donor-advised funds, including those operated by community foundations or by mutual funds or other financial institutions, were not involved in such abuses and will be only minimally affected by the changes.

To set the stage, a donor-advised fund is normally a program offered by a public charity to facilitate charitable gifts by individual donors. In the discussion that follows, that public charity is referred to as the "sponsoring organization." It may be a community foundation or other public charity with an independent charitable program of its own, or it may have no program aside from the donor-advised fund operation. See § 2.05[C] of the text for more on donor-advised funds.

The Act starts out by creating a statutory definition for donor-advised funds, then proceeds to impose a number of special rules on the organizations falling within that definition. While the definition must be kept in mind when considering these new rules, as a practical matter in most cases, the organizations under consideration as alternatives to private foundations will clearly be donor-advised funds (under the new statutory definition). In other words, you will know one when you see it.

A. Definition — A donor-advised fund is defined as a fund or account that is:

1. Separately identified by reference to contributions of a donor or donors;

2. Owned and controlled by a sponsoring organization; and

3. With respect to which a donor (or a person appointed by the donor as a "donor advisor") has, or reasonably expects to have, advisory privileges with respect to the distribution or investments of the amount held in the separately identified fund or account by reason of the donor's status as a donor.

There are several exceptions to the definition. A donor-advised fund does not include a fund or account making distributions only to a single identified organization (e.g., an endowment fund owned and controlled by a college that is held exclusively for the benefit of the college, even if the fund is named after its principal donor and that donor has advisory privileges over fund distributions).

Exceptions are also provided for several types of funds operated on a committee basis. These apply to a fund or account with respect to which a donor or donor advisor provides advice as to grantees selected for travel, study or similar grants, provided:

1. The advisory privileges of the donor or advisor are performed exclusively in his/her capacity as a member of the committee, all the members of which are appointed by the sponsoring organization;

2. No combination of a donor, donor advisor, or related persons has direct or indirect control of the committee; and

3. All the funds grants are awarded on an objective and nondiscriminatory basis under procedures approved in advance by the Board of Directors of the supporting organization, under procedures that conform to the

requirements of Code Section 4945(g)(1), (2), or (3), governing private foundation grants to individuals.

The IRS is also authorized to exempt funds from treatment as a donor-advised fund in other situations, provided the fund is advised by a committee which is not controlled directly or indirectly by a donor, donor advisor or related persons. The technical explanation of the Act indicates that where a donor is able to exercise effective control, indirect control will be deemed to be present. For example, if a donor, a donor advisor, and an attorney hired by the donor constitute three members on the five-member committee, the donor will be deemed to have indirect control. The Act authorizes the IRS to establish rules regarding committee-advised funds, and rules excepting certain types of committee-advised funds, such as a fund established exclusively for disaster relief from the donor-advised fund definition.

The IRS is also authorized to provide an exemption for a fund or an account benefiting "a single identified charitable purpose" from the donor-advised fund definition. Neither the technical explanation nor the Act itself provides any insight into exactly how this would apply.

Deductions for Contributions to Donor Advised Funds

In accordance with general rules, the Act provides that no deductions will be allowed for contributions to donor-advised funds unless the sponsoring organization is a qualified charitable organization described in Code Section 170(c), other than a private foundation. Thus, contributions to donor-advised funds operated by other types of exempt organizations will not qualify for charitable deductions for income tax, gift tax, or estate tax purposes. If the sponsoring organization is a type 3 supporting organization, deductions for contributions will be denied unless the sponsor is a functionally integrated type 3 supporting organization as discussed below.

Additional substantiation requirements, beyond those applicable to charitable contributions generally under Code Section 170(f), apply for contributions to donor-advised funds under new Section 170(f)(18). The contemporaneous written acknowledgment provided by the sponsoring organization must state specifically that the sponsoring organization has exclusive legal control over the assets contributed.

Excess Business Holdings

The private foundation rules governing excess business holdings (Code Section 4943) will apply to donor-advised funds. In applying those rules, the term "disqualified person" will include donors, donor advisors, members of the family of either, or a 35 percent controlled entity of any such person. The excess business holdings rules are described in § 6.05 of the text.

Transition rules similar to those in Code Section 4943(c)(4)-(6) will be applied to the present holdings of the donor or advised fund.

Automatic Excess Benefit Transactions

The Act effectively prevents any grant, loan, compensation, expense reimbursement or other similar payment from a donor-advised fund to a donor, donor advisor, or related persons. Any such payment will be automatically treated as an excess benefit transaction under the intermediate sanction rules (Code Section 4958). (The intermediate sanctions rules are described in § 5.05[A][3][e] of the text.) Regardless of the facts, the full amount of the payment will be treated as the amount of the excess benefit.

Payments pursuant to a bona fide sale or lease of property will not be subject to this special rule, but will instead be subject to the general arm's-length rules of Code Section 4958, with the special disqualified person definition described above applicable. The technical explanation of the Act makes it clear that a substance-over-form analysis will apply to determine whether a purchase is made from a donor-advised fund (in which case the full amount involved will be deemed the excess benefit) or from the sponsoring organization (in which case an arm's-length standard will apply).

For example, if a donor contributes securities to a donor-advised fund, the donor-advised fund distributes them to the sponsoring organization, and the donor purchases the securities from the sponsoring organization, the distribution to the sponsoring organization will be ignored. Thus, the purchase from the sponsoring organization will be subject to tax under Code Section 4958.

A person who is a donor to a donor-advised fund will not be treated as a disqualified person with respect to the sponsoring organization by virtue of that fact alone. Thus, if the donor to a donor-advised fund is a service provider to the sponsoring organization, the general rules of Code Section 4958 will generally apply to the payment received for such services. Similarly, an investment adviser (and related persons) will be treated as a disqualified person with respect to the sponsoring organization.

Taxable Distributions

Certain types of distributions are in effect forbidden and will be subject to a new excise tax under new Code Section 4966. These "taxable distributions" include any distributions paid to a natural person, or to any other person for a noncharitable purpose. Even if the distribution is made for a charitable purpose, the tax will apply if the sponsoring organization does not exercise expenditure responsibility in accordance with Code Section 4945(h). The expenditure responsibility rules are described in § 6.07[D] of the text.

A distribution to a public charity or to the sponsoring organization of the fund, or to another donor organized fund, will not normally be a taxable distribution, except in the case of a distribution to a "disqualified supporting organization." Disqualified supporting organizations include any Type 3 supporting organization other than one that is "functionally integrated" (as discussed below), or any other supporting organization if the donor or a donor advisor of the donor-advised fund has direct or indirect control; the IRS is authorized to determine by regulation that other distributions to supporting organizations are inappropriate.

More Than Incidental Benefit

If the distribution results in a more-than-incidental benefit to a donor or a donor advisor, or any related person who provided advice regarding the distribution, the Act imposes an excise tax equal to 125 percent of the amount of the benefit against both the person who advised the distribution and the recipient of the benefit. This is provided in new Code Section 4967. If a manager of the sponsoring organization agreed to the making of the distribution knowing that it would confer such a benefit, the manager is subject to a 10 percent excise tax (not to exceed $10,000). These taxes are subject to abatement under the general rules of existing law.

The existence of a more than incidental benefit is determined under the same rules as are used to determine when the receipt of the benefit would reduce or eliminate a charitable deduction. For example, if a donor advises a distribution from his donor-advised fund to the Girl Scouts of America, the mere fact that the donor or his daughter is a member of the local Girl Scout unit would not be sufficient to incur the new excise tax. Such a benefit would be incidental.

Reporting and Disclosure

The Act imposes new requirements for the information returns filed by sponsoring organizations. Such organizations must report the total number of donor-advised funds owned, the aggregate value of the assets of those funds, and the aggregate contributions to, and grants made from, those funds during the year.

In addition, a new sponsoring organization seeking recognition of its tax-exempt status must disclose whether it intends to maintain the donor-advised funds. It would also be required to provide information regarding its planned operation of such funds, including, for example, the procedures it intends to use to notify donors and others that assets held in donor-advised funds are the property of the sponsoring organization, and how it intends to ensure that distributions from donor-advised funds do not result in more than incidental benefit to any person.

Effective Dates

The Pension Protection Act of 2006 became law on August 17, 2006. The new rules for donor-advised funds are generally effective for taxable years beginning after the date of enactment. Some of the new penalties, however, take effect earlier than that. The provision relating to excess benefit transactions takes effect for transactions occurring after the date of enactment. The requirements concerning charitable contributions to donor-advised funds are effective for contributions made more than 180 days from the date of enactment of the Act.

NEW RULES FOR SUPPORTING ORGANIZATIONS

Supporting organizations are often used when a person who might otherwise choose to create a private foundation finds that some aspect of the private foundation rules makes that impractical. A supporting organization may resemble a private foundation in many respects, but because of its relationship with one or more public charities, which serve as its beneficiaries, it treats itself as a public charity rather than a private foundation. (In the discussion that follows, those public charities are referred to as the supported organizations.)

There are three separate types of supporting organizations. They are generally referred to by number as "Type 1," "Type 2," or "Type 3." Type 1 and Type 2 supporting organizations have a particularly close relationship with their supported organizations. However, the Type 3 organization is merely "operated in connection with" its supported organizations, which gives more leeway for independence. It is the Type 3 supporting organization that is most often proposed as an alternative to a family foundation, precisely because it does offer this leeway. As is so often the case, however, that leeway has often led to abuses, and it is those abuses that the Act seeks to stop.

See § 2.05[D] of the text for more background on supporting organizations. The Act imposes a number of new requirements for supporting organizations, aimed primarily, but not exclusively, at Type 3 supporting organizations.

Type 3 Supporting Organizations

The following are the new rules for Type 3 supporting organizations:

1. A Foreign Charity May Not Be the Supported Organization — Beginning with the date of enactment, a Type 3 supporting organization can no longer support a foreign charity. (A Type 3 supporting organization that is already established to support a foreign public charity will not be subject to this rule until its third taxable year beginning after the date of enactment.)

2. "Functionally Integrated" Type 3 Supporting Organizations — One of the key concepts in the new type 3 supporting organization rules is that of a "functionally integrated" organization; though it is central to several of the new provisions, this concept remains a bit unclear. The Joint Committee Technical Explanation of the Act suggests that a functionally integrated organization is one which, rather than simply providing funds to its supported organization,

conducts activities that relate to the performance of the supported organization's functions or carrying out its purposes. For example, a blood bank operated by hospital would presumably be considered as functionally integrated with its parent organization. In many cases, however, the presence or absence of this relationship would not be entirely clear, so regulations or perhaps even a clarifying amendment may be necessary to enable planners to work with and apply this provision.

3. <u>Minimum Payout</u> — The Act directs the Treasury Department to promulgate new regulations that impose a minimum payout requirement on Type 3 supporting organizations that are not functionally integrated with their supported organizations. Thus, functionally integrated Type 3 supporting organizations will not be subject to the new payout requirement when it appears. The payout requirement will be expressed in terms of a percentage on either income or assets of the supporting organization. Under prior law, because a supporting organization was classified as a public charity rather than a private foundation, and hence was not subject to the specific minimum payout requirement of Code Section 4942, it had no minimum distribution requirement.

4. <u>Excess Business Holdings</u> — Formerly, supporting organizations were sometimes used as a means of holding family business interests in situations where Code Section 4943 would prevent a family foundation from doing so. (The excess business holdings rules are described in § 6.05 of the text.)

To prevent that, the Act provides that excess business holdings rules of Code Section 4943 will apply to Type 3 supporting organizations *except* those that are functionally integrated as discussed above, effective for transactions occurring after July 25, 2006. Transition rules will apply to the present holdings of a Type 3 supporting organization, paralleling those provided in Code Sections 4943(c)(4) through (6). The IRS will have authority to waive the application of the excess business holding rules if the organization can establish that its holdings are consistent with its charitable purpose or function; the rule contemplates that the findings of the applicable state attorney general would be taken into account in exercising this authority.

The excess business holdings rules will also apply to Type 2 supporting organizations if they accept a contribution from a person (other than a public charity) having direct or indirect control of its supported organization. Moreover, if a Type 1 or Type 3 supporting organization accepts a gift from such a person, it will be treated as a private foundation for all purposes, until it demonstrates to the satisfaction of the IRS that it qualifies as a public charity, other than as a supporting organization.

5. <u>Reporting Requirement</u> — The Act requires a Type 3 supporting organization to provide detailed information to each of the organizations it supports. An organization's failure to comply with this requirement will be deemed an important factor in determining whether it meets the responsiveness test of prior law.

6. Distributions to Supporting Organizations — In general, private foundations may not count distributions to Type 3 supporting organizations as qualifying distributions for purposes of the minimum distribution requirement imposed on foundations under Code Section 4942. This rule does not apply if the recipient is a functionally integrated Type 3 supporting organization.

Foundation distributions to any other supporting organizations (i.e., Type 1 and Type 2 supporting organizations, and Type 3 supporting organizations which are functionally integrated) are likewise disqualified under Section 4942 if anyone who is a disqualified person with respect to the distributing foundation indirectly controls either the supporting organization grantee or its supported organization. And this rule goes even further: if a distribution does not count as a qualifying distribution under this rule, it is treated as a taxable expenditure under Code Section 4945.

7. Other Requirements — If a Type 3 supporting organization is organized as a trust, it must also demonstrate to the satisfaction of the IRS that it has a close and continuous relationship with its supported organization, so that the trust is responsive to the needs and demands of the supported organization. For existing trusts, this rule is not effective until a year after the date of enactment of the Act.

The Act will require a closer relationship between a supported organization and public charities it supports. For example, for taxable years beginning after the date of enactment, a Type 3 supporting organization must supply additional information (to be prescribed by the Treasury Department) to each of its supported organizations, to ensure that it is responsive to the needs or demands of the supported organizations.

Types 1, 2, and 3 Supporting Organizations — Generally, the foregoing rules apply only to Type 3 supporting organizations. In addition, however, the Act provides a number of new rules that apply to all supporting organizations, Type 1, Type 2, and Type 3.

1. Automatic Excess Benefit Transactions — Since they are not private foundations, by definition, supporting organizations have not been subject to the intermediate sanctions rules, which provide penalty excise taxes on so-called "excess benefit transactions" under Code Section 4958. (The intermediate sanctions rules are described in § 5.05[A][3][e] of the text.) The Act greatly expands the application of those penalty taxes to supporting organizations.

Under the new rules, if any supporting organization, Type 1, Type 2, or Type 3, makes a grant, loan, compensation payment, or other similar payment to a substantial contributor of the supporting organization (or a related person), the payment is automatically treated as an excess benefit transaction with a disqualified person. Moreover, the entire amount of the payment is treated as the taxable excess benefit. This is stricter than the general rule applicable to other public charities, where the excess benefit is only the amount by which the benefit provided exceeds the value of the consideration received.

In addition, a loan by any supporting organization to a disqualified person (applying the existing definition in Code Section 4958) is treated as an excess benefit transaction. For purposes of that provision, the entire amount of the loan, rather than interest element alone, is the taxable excess benefit.

2. Disclosure Requirements — Most public charities are excused from filing annual information returns on Form 990 if their gross receipts are less than $25,000. Under the Act, however, all supporting organizations must file returns regardless of their gross receipts. Moreover, the Act requires supported organizations to indicate on their returns, whether they are a Type 1, Type 2, or Type 3 supporting organization, and in addition they must identify their supported organizations.

Many of the problems in applying the prior law on supporting organizations arose from the exercise of indirect control by disqualified persons. To correct this situation, the Act requires supporting organizations to demonstrate annually that they are not controlled by disqualified persons by means of a certification to this effect on their Forms 990. The explanation expresses an intention that supporting organizations be able to certify that the majority of their governing body is comprised of individuals selected on the basis of their special knowledge or expertise in the particular field in which the organization operates, or because they represent a particular community that is served by the supported public charities.

3. Disqualified Person — The Act provides that, for purposes of the excess benefit transaction rules in Code Section 4958, a disqualified person of a supporting organization will be treated as a disqualified person of the supported organization.

Effective Dates for Supporting Organization Changes

Most of the provisions described above take effect on the date of enactment, August 17, 2006. The excess benefit transaction rules apply to transactions occurring after July 25, 2006. The excess business holdings requirements are effective for taxable years beginning after the date of enactment. The provision relating to distributions by nonoperating private foundations to supporting organizations takes effect for distributions and expenditures made after the date of enactment.

The return requirements are effective for returns filed for taxable years ending after the date of enactment, and thus will apply to returns for calendar 2006.

Chapter 6

The rates of tax applied under the private foundation penalty provisions in Chapter 42 of the Code (Code Sections 4941, 4942, 4943, 4944, and 4945), and under the intermediate sanction provisions applicable to public charities (Code Section 4958) are all doubled under the Act. The dollar limitations on the amounts that may be assessed against foundation managers and organization managers are likewise doubled. The following table demonstrates the levels of various private foundation excise taxes under prior law and under the Pension Reform Act of 2006:

	Former Law	New Law
Self-dealing (§ 4941)		
Initial tax on self dealer	5%	10%
Initial tax on foundation manager	2 ½ %	5%
Failure to distribute income (§ 4942)		
Initial tax	15%	30%
Excess business holdings (§ 4943)		
Initial tax	5%	10%
Limits on foundation managers (per investment)		
Initial tax	$ 5,000	$10,000
Additional tax	$10,000	$20,000
Taxable expenditures (§ 4945)		
Initial tax on foundation	10%	20%
Initial tax on foundation managers	2 ½ %	5%
Limits on foundation managers		
Initial tax	$ 5,000	$10,000
Additional tax	$10,000	20,000

This provision is effective for taxable years beginning after the date of enactment. A similar provision appeared in S. 2020, which passed the Senate last year, but that provision also included an additional increase in the tax on acts of self-dealing regarding the payment of compensation by a foundation to disqualified persons, and provided that the additional portion would, unlike the tax on other acts of self-dealing, be subject to abatement. The Act includes no such special treatment for compensation transactions.

Chapter 7 [§ 7.02]

In connection with the discussion of qualifying distributions for purposes of the minimum distribution requirement imposed on foundations by Code Section 4942, note that the Act changes the rules governing distributions to supporting organizations. In general, distributions to Type 3 supporting organizations will no longer count as qualifying distributions for purposes of the minimum distribution requirement imposed on foundations under Code Section 4942. This rule does not apply if the recipient is a "functionally integrated" Type 3 supporting organization, as discussed above in connection with Chapter 2.

Foundation distributions to any other supporting organizations (i.e., Type 1 and Type 2 supporting organizations, and Type 3 supporting organizations which are functionally integrated) are likewise disqualified under Section 4942 if anyone who is a disqualified person with respect to the distributing foundation indirectly controls either the supporting organization grantee or its supported organization. In addition, if a distribution is disqualified under this rule, it is also treated as a taxable expenditure under Code Section 4945.

Distributions from foundations to donor-advised funds are not affected by the Act.

Chapter 8 [§ 8.04]

Section 4940(a) imposes a two-percent excise tax on the net investment income of a private foundation. The two-percent rate is reduced to 1 percent, if the foundation meets certain distribution requirements. The Act makes several changes affecting this excise tax.

First, the Act amends the definition of gross investment income subject to the tax to include items of income that are similar to the items presently enumerated in the statute. This change, effective for taxable years beginning after the date of enactment, overrides several cases the IRS lost in litigation, and primarily affects hedging transactions, notional principal contracts, and annuities.

In addition, the Act expands the tax under Section 4940 to apply to gains realized on the sale of property devoted to a charitable use by the foundation. Examples would include artwork or buildings used by the foundation in conducting its charitable operations.

Both of these changes apply to taxable years beginning after the date of enactment.

FAMILY FOUNDATION HANDBOOK

Jerry J. McCoy
Kathryn W. Miree

CCH
a Wolters Kluwer business

ISBN: 0-8080-9051-8

To Alex, Maddy, Alli, and Jon
— JJM

To my family—Ben, Kyser, and Harry—
the most patient people on the planet

I greatly appreciate the help of my colleagues and clients in this field who continue to teach me more about the world of family foundations. This book contains the results of many collaborative efforts over the years.

I would also like to thank Marty Carter of Family Communications and David Hobbs of Hilb, Rogal & Hamilton Company of Alabama for their review of and input on segments of the manuscript.
— KWM

ABOUT THE AUTHORS

Jerry J. McCoy, Esq. is an independent attorney in Washington, D.C., specializing in charitable tax planning, tax-exempt organizations, and estate planning. He holds law degrees from Duke University and New York University.

A member of the American Law Institute and a fellow of both the American College of Trust and Estate Counsel (ACTEC) and the American College of Tax Counsel, Mr. McCoy is listed in *Who's Who in America*, *Who's Who in American Law*, and *The Best Lawyers in America*. A frequent presenter at planned giving, tax, and estate planning seminars, he serves on the adjunct faculties at the Georgetown University Law Center and the University of Miami Law School. He is chairman of the Charitable Planning and Exempt Organizations Committee of ACTEC.

Mr. McCoy is co-founder and co-editor of *Charitable Gift Planning News,* a monthly newsletter.

Kathryn W. Miree, Esq. is president of Kathryn W. Miree & Associates, Inc., a consulting firm that works with nonprofits to develop planned giving programs. She received her undergraduate degree from Emory University and her law degree from The University of Alabama School of Law. She spent 15 years in various positions, including manager of the Personal Trust Department, in the Trust Division of a large southeastern bank. During her tenure with the bank, Ms. Miree handled the foundation administration and grant administration for more than 40 foundations. She joined a regional brokerage firm in 1994 to start its trust company. She established Kathryn W. Miree & Associates, Inc. in 1997.

Ms. Miree is a past president of the National Committee on Planned Giving, the founding president of the Alabama Planned Giving Council, a past president of the Estate Planning Council of Birmingham, Inc., and a past member of the Board of the National Association of Estate Planners & Councils. In addition to those professional associations, she currently serves on a number of foundation and nonprofit boards. She is a graduate of both Leadership Birmingham and Leadership Alabama.

Ms. Miree is a frequent lecturer on nonprofit management and fundraising. Her clients include a variety of nonprofit organizations across the nation.

TABLE OF CONTENTS

Chapter 3
HOW TO CREATE A FAMILY FOUNDATION

Chapter 4
USING CHARITABLE TRUSTS TO FUND THE FAMILY FOUNDATION

Chapter 6
OPERATING RESTRICTIONS. **6-1**

Chapter 7
GRANTMAKING **7-1**

Chapter 9
SPECIAL ISSUES

PREFACE

Like most children, neither of us grew up hoping to work with foundations. We both ended up there by accident, following different routes to a similar destination. Here are our stories and how we hope this book may make the reader's journey a bit easier.

Kathryn's Story:

> *I became a foundation administrator by accident — like so many of us find our roles in life. I was an attorney, involved in estate and trust administration, and was asked to take a management role administering charitable trusts and foundations. It seemed like a great idea (because it was a step up), but I had no idea of how to define, much less manage, a charitable foundation. So I asked a simple question: What books can I read to help me learn how to make grants, manage finances, invest money, and keep the foundations on track? I was referred to the Internal Revenue Code and the regulations.*
>
> *I spent weeks reading the Code and regulations and was as lost at the end of the exercise as when I began. I felt that there must be better resources, so I called my friends who practiced in this area and asked them to refer me to an English version of the rules. They also referred me to the Code and the regulations. I kept reading the Code, and still do so today. But the best advice I received came through talking with other foundation administrators and combining their wisdom with resources found in the for profit sector.*

Jerry's Story:

> *Like Kathryn, I likewise became involved in foundation matters by accident, even involuntarily. Congress began work on the Tax Reform Act of 1969 in February of that year and, as the newest attornehy in a Washington tax boutique law firm, I was sent off to Capitol Hill too watch the proceedings. The firm had a number of charitably inclined clients, including a number of private foundations, and my assignment was to let them know through overnight bulletins just what was going on in the hearings. This turned out to be a historic time for private foundations, as Congress put together what remains almost unchanged as our federal law on this subject over the course of that year. A few years later I was privileged to serve on the staff of the Commission on Private Philanthropy and Public Needs, named the "Filer Commission" after its chairman. John H. Filer. This landmark study of the nonprofit sector included a detailed review of the law governing private foundations.*

With these two experiences under my belt, my fate was sealed. Like it or not, I was a specialist in charitable tax planning, with a subspecialty in private foundations. My practice in this area brought me into contact with a number of lawyers around the country who sought assistance in this increasingly specialized field. Along the way I was surprised over and over to see how many people, lawyers and clients alike, got so caught up in the many complications and complexities in this area that they missed the bigger and more important part of the picture — how useful a family foundation can be and how those complications often don't matter at all. In many cases, these complications discouraged the advisers so much that they in turn discouraged their clients from creating foundations.

Family Foundation Handbook is designed to save you from some of the struggles we encountered by giving you answers to the most frequently asked questions and practical solutions for both common and uncommon problems. It will be a valuable tool for advisors and clients and will help them harness the tremendous potential that the family foundation offers. While the Code and regulations are available, there are few practical resources that provide quick, understandable answers to these questions. This book is designed to bring practical, understandable answers and solutions to these commonly asked questions. We have taken our 45 (plus) year of hands-on experience, combined it with the technical directives of the Internal Revenue Code, and reduced it to practical guide for the professional.

The questions are practical but require precise answers:

- Should I create a family foundation, or is there a more effective way to involve my family in charitable giving?

- How does creation of the foundation impact my estate plan?

- How do I handle grant administration? Do you have a sample form?

- What are the administrative obligations of a family foundation?

- Am I required to file tax returns?

- Can I pay myself or a member of my family a salary for foundation work?

- Can I lease my property to the foundation?

- How do I manage foundation investments?

Foundation boards may answer these questions in different ways. Founders establish foundations with different goals, varying levels of assets, and diverse objectives. This book provides the tools to help the professional coach the foundation board through the steps to find the answers.

Moreover, as our experience has too often shown us, the creator of the family foundation is left at the starting line with a new foundation and little direction about how to move forward. The accountant analyzes the tax impact of creating the foundation and gives the go-ahead. The financial planner helps fit the foundation into the family's overall financial picture. The attorney prepares the documents and qualifies the foundation with the Internal Revenue Service. But no one is there to provide ongoing, practical advice on how to operate the new entity. The new foundation director needs help to set and meet personal goals and to learn how to avoid liability, how to make the most effective grants, and how and when to hire an executive director. This book provides forms, checklists, questionnaires, training forms, and other items to help you provide the professional assistance that the foundation needs.

Kathryn Miree

July 2006

Jerry McCoy

CHAPTER 1

INTRODUCTION

§ 1.01   THE PHILANTHROPIC IMPULSE

[A]   Growth of U.S. Philanthropy

Despite some appearances to the contrary, Americans are at heart a generous, caring people who have for centuries routinely put aside their self-interest to provide assistance and relief to others who need it. They enthusiastically support the greatest network of schools, colleges and universities, cultural institutions, and other nonprofit organizations the world has ever known. This enthusiasm is backed up with annual contributions amounting to $260.28 billion in 2005, about 2.1 percent of gross domestic product.[1]

From the earliest times, a spirit of community helping and cooperation has been a characteristic of North American residents and immigrants alike. The first explorers to arrive here were aided by the generous Native Americans they found already in residence. Later, of necessity, a culture of cooperation and mutual assistance grew up. Early settlers left their homes in Europe and elsewhere in search of not just a different life here, but a better one as well. They arrived in America to find a heavily forested, sparsely populated continent, with harsh living conditions that forced them to help one another build homes, schools, houses of worship, and other public facilities. This acceptance of mutual interdependence continued as Americans moved across the prairies and mountains to settle this new nation. Many vignettes of early American life bear out a spirit of cooperation and common efforts aimed at providing a better life for all; from the Minutemen rushing to the defense of their villages, to the pioneers attending barn-raising parties on the prairies, to the residents forming volunteer fire brigades, our traditions are steeped in this spirit.

Although born of necessity, community helping soon became a basic feature of the American way of life. The initial help provided directly by one resident to another soon became institutionalized, with the growth of mutual entities to undertake such help on a larger scale. Alexis de Tocqueville, in *Democracy in America*, his insightful report of observations as a visitor from Europe in the early nineteenth century, noted this tendency:

> Americans of all ages, all conditions, and all dispositions constantly form associations. They have not only commercial and manufacturing companies, in which all take part, but associations of a thousand other kinds, religious, moral, serious, futile, general or restricted, enormous or diminutive. The Americans make associations to give entertainments, to found seminaries, to build inns, to construct churches, to diffuse books, to send missionaries to the antipodes; in this manner they found hospitals, prisons, and schools. If it is proposed to inculcate some truth or to foster some feeling by the encouragement of a great example, they form a society. Wherever at the

---

[1] *Giving USA* (2006), Giving USA Foundation, *www.aafrc.org*; gross domestic product based on 2005 GDP of $12,487.1 billion.

head of some new undertaking you see the government in France, or a man of rank in England, in the United States you will be sure to find an association.[2]

Modern Americans have continued to participate in these endeavors up to the present time through contributions and volunteer activities. Some have gone even farther and made charitable activity a family priority through the creation of family foundations.

[B] Growth of American Foundations

Although participation in collective activities has always involved a commitment of financial resources as well as time, the United States has perfected a new type of nongovernmental institution designed primarily to help distribute funds toward the solution of societal problems and other charitable and religious undertakings. Ironically, this altruistic form of organization grew out of the seemingly self-centered and acquisitive age of the Robber Barons — industrialists who amassed huge, unprecedented amounts of wealth in the late nineteenth century. Philosophically, these fortunes were not always deployed to charitable purposes out of a spirit of providing aid to those less fortunate, who were the traditional objects of charity. Rather, they resulted from the various personal motivations that moved the early leaders of that age.

For Andrew Carnegie, who had come to this country as a penniless immigrant in his childhood and had struggled to better himself, the objective was to provide a helping hand to youths who, like himself, evidenced a willingness to work toward personal improvement. Carnegie felt it was a disgrace to die rich and in his essay entitled "Wealth," published in the *North American Review* in June 1889, proposed that millionaires should administer their fortunes as a public trust during their lifetimes, rather than amassing a fortune to pass along to heirs, or even to benevolent causes, upon their deaths.

The modern private foundation was advocated by John D. Rockefeller, the first American billionaire, as a means of more effectively organizing what he called "this business of benevolence." Although skeptics speculated that he was moved to charitable endeavors by some combination of guilt over his business methods and a desire for positive public relations, the truth is that deep-seated religious beliefs played a larger role in leading him to this service. Rockefeller believed that his wealth was the result of divine influence and that the wise application of it to the betterment of humanity was his solemn duty. He had benefited from the use of business combinations, including the use of corporations, in amassing his wealth, and it was only natural that he would turn to similar tools and techniques in order to give money away more effectively.

Thus was born the first corporation aimed at providing an orderly and businesslike approach to philanthropy. Rockefeller attempted without success

---

[2] A. de Tocqueville, *Democracy in America* 2d pt., 2d bk., ch.V, at 106 (Knopf 1994).

to obtain from Congress a federal charter for what would become the Rockefeller Foundation and in the end settled for a New York corporation, which he formed in 1913. Given the important role of taxes as an incentive to modern U.S. philanthropy, it is interesting to note that efforts to form the Rockefeller Foundation were under way several years before the modern federal income tax was enacted. Other foundations created at about this same time, well before the enactment of the federal income tax, were the Rockefeller Institute for Medical Research (1901), Carnegie Foundation for the Advancement of Teaching (1905), Russell Sage Foundation (1907), and Carnegie Corporation of New York (1911).

The suspicious and distrusting attitude of Congress in denying Rockefeller's efforts to secure a federal charter reflects a recurring theme in the attitude of the U.S. public toward charitable undertakings and philanthropists — the social reformers' antipathy toward the wealthy and skepticism about their motivations in giving money away. Initially, there was a reluctance on the part of many church groups and other elements in society to accept foundation grants on grounds that this was somehow tainted money that should not be welcomed, lest the recipient be deemed to acquiesce in the giver's acts in earning the fortune wherein it originated.

Similar waves of suspicion and adverse public reaction to organized philanthropy occurred periodically in the twentieth century, and it was such a sentiment that led to consideration and passage of our modern tax rules for private foundations in the Tax Reform Act of 1969. The leadoff witness at the initial hearings on that Act was Texas Congressman Wright Patman, who had held a series of investigative hearings through the 1960s depicting various actual and perceived abuses by foundations and sounding a populist call for restrictions reining in these agents of wealth.

[C]   Private Foundations Today

The Foundation Center estimates that there were 31,347 family foundations in the United States in 2004 (the latest year for which there are statistics), and their number seems to be on the rise again after an abrupt drop-off following the passage of the Tax Reform Act of 1969.[3] Indeed, the restrictions imposed under that legislation have proved to be a good thing for foundations in general in that they have eliminated most of the practices that generated legitimate criticism of foundations. This is borne out by Internal Revenue Service (IRS) personnel, who have reported that private foundations have by and large become the model citizens of the exempt organization community, rather than its bad boys. Virtually all of the widely reported charitable abuses and scandals of the 1980s and the 1990s involved public charities, rather than private foundations. Examples include the televangelist abuses, the excesses of the Bishop Estate trustees and the

---

[3] *Key Facts on Family Foundations,* The Foundation Center (January 2006), *http://fdncenter.org/research/trends_analysis/pdf/key_facts_fam.pdf.*

Adelphi College administration, and the Ponzi scheme of the Foundation for New Era Philanthropy.

The booming economy of the late 1990s and its new technology wealth created a climate eerily evocative of the time a century earlier when new industrial fortunes gave rise to a new age of private philanthropy. Increasingly, the holders of this new wealth are turning to the same sorts of outlets for their personal passions and concerns as their counterparts of a hundred years earlier.

§ 1.02   THE PURPOSE OF THE BOOK

The number of family foundations in this country is growing rapidly as families amass wealth, understand options in disposition of wealth, and focus on values. As interest in foundations grows, professionals must be able to offer advice to clients about the role of foundations in estate planning and wealth transfer planning. More important, the professional must be able to support the client in the ongoing management of the foundation, including administration, tax filings, grantmaking, and investment management.

Foundation management, like any area of tax practice, is detailed and unforgivingly exact. Many professionals do not have the tax training or practical experience to move through the issues easily. This book is designed to fill the gap.

The goal of the handbook is to provide forms and checklists to guide the most important activities, provide warnings for the most dangerous activities, add effectiveness to grantmaking, and answer common questions. The authors understand that most administrators and managers are less interested in understanding the details of an IRS letter ruling or regulation than they are in understanding what they need to do to get the job done correctly. The details of the Internal Revenue Code (IRC), the regulations, and the rulings are reduced to an easy-to-read format, accompanied by citations necessary to do additional research. The handbook provides guidelines for efficient and effective administration, direction on grantmaking, and answers to common questions. In short, this book is designed to shortcut the learning process and provide the benefits of experience to those who have not worked extensively in the field.

[A]   Resource for the Legal Practitioner

Attorneys are called on to provide advice to family foundations in several situations. A client may approach the firm to create the foundation, to guide the client through the transfer of a family business to heirs, or to execute an estate plan that includes a philanthropic component. The legal practitioner must be able to do more than simply create the foundation and qualify it with the Internal Revenue Service; he or she must also advise the family on ongoing management.

As an attorney, there are five ways that this book will help you in your practice:

1. *It will help you understand your client's goals and objectives in establishing a foundation.* You will learn how family foundations are used to further family values as well as philanthropy and the role that these foundations play in binding generations.

2. *It will help you provide guidance on the decision to create the foundation.* You will learn how to determine whether a family foundation is appropriate or whether the donor should consider other philanthropic alternatives.

3. *It will help you explain the long-term implications of the decision to create a foundation to your client.* You will learn more about the daily management duties of the foundation — administration, tax filings, public disclosure — and how to find resources to handle these tasks. Forms, checklists, and guidelines are provided in the event that you want to take a more active role in this process.

4. *It will save you time.* You will find answers to commonly asked questions, ranging from leasing property from family members and paying salaries to family members, to meeting minimum distribution requirements, devising investment strategies, and handling other administrative issues.

5. *The insights provided will help you expand your practice.* You will understand more about why donors create foundations, why they succeed, why they fail, and what the options are upon dissolution so that you can position your practice to serve this growing market.

[B] Resource for the Accountant

This book is also an excellent resource if you have an accounting practice. The donor's accountant provides the income tax perspective for gifts and is one of the first contacts made by the donor when he or she is considering a foundation. The client's questions may initially center on the deduction and the impact on the current year's return, but may quickly evolve into broader issues. Many donors have done extensive reading on the issues and will have questions relating to the use of the foundation to make gifts, limitations of the IRS rules on investments or self-dealing, reporting requirements, and resources available to meet operating requirements.

While the accounting firm may have a segment devoted to nonprofit practice, many of the questions raised by the client may be more practical in nature:

- Can I select a fiscal tax-year end?

- What impact does selection of the tax year have on grants made by the foundation?

- Is there an easy way to calculate required annual distributions?
- Can I pay myself, or a family member, a salary?
- Are there restrictions on the organizations that can receive grants?
- Can I make grants to individuals?

This book provides quick answers to these questions. It provides practical guidance on how to advise the client in making the decision to create a foundation, how to file Form 1023 for nonprofit status, and how and when to file the appropriate tax returns. Most important, it will broaden your perspective on the more practical issues of foundation administration that are faced by your family foundation client on a daily basis.

[C]   Resource for the Financial Planner

Financial planners will find that this book provides valuable perspectives for the growing interest in charitable planning. Financial planning involves much more than budgeting finances, planning for retirement, or maximizing estate distributions. More often, clients use financial planners as master planners for individual and family asset management. Clients may seek services as basic as financial planning or investment management or as sophisticated as business succession planning, family office management, or family foundation management. This book provides the planner with the detail necessary to understand this important area of family financial planning.

Families may seek a financial planner's advice on several aspects of family foundations:

- Is there a tool that we can use to teach our family members, especially the younger generation, our values?
- Is there a way to make a significant charitable gift, but to stay involved in the disposition of those assets?
- Is there a way to maximize the sale of the family business by using a family foundation?
- How do I involve my family in the management of the foundation and in grantmaking?
- Can you provide investment management for our foundation assets in the same way that you provide investment management for our individual assets?
- Are there any special rules or restrictions that we should be aware of in investment management?

The family foundation may figure prominently in the client's desire to improve family communication, to centralize investments, to maintain control of the family business, and to shape the long-term distribution of family assets. The financial planner must understand how to analyze the appropriateness of a family foundation, when to recommend exploration of that option, and the steps involved in creation. Then the planner must know how the foundation will be managed once it is established. Who will handle the day-to-day duties? What is required in managing daily operations? What will it require from the family members?

Often, the financial planner will remain a primary advisor, and perhaps administrator, of the foundation and will need tools to guide the foundation through organization, strategic planning, grantmaking, and tax reporting. While the planner does not serve as legal counsel, it is important to have the answers to basic questions and to know where to find resources. This book is designed to support the financial planner in providing this service.

[D] Resource for the Foundation Administrator

Administration of family foundations is a growth business for banks, trust companies, financial planning firms, and consultants. Many of these financial services firms make contact with family foundations for investment management purposes, but find that the foundation board also needs help with accounting, reporting to the Internal Revenue Service, and meeting expenditure responsibilities. Few families have the time and expertise to manage these administrative functions, and the administrator's ability to handle these duties may distinguish his or her firm from others handling only investment management. Many banks, trust companies, and brokerage firms have created special nonprofit administrative teams to meet the demand.

However, training an employee to fill this administrative role is challenging. This book is organized as a how-to guide for those responsible for administering the daily activities of the foundation. It gives the foundation manager practical tools such as checklists, sample forms, sample policies, and other useful worksheets. In addition, it provides answers for the most commonly asked questions related to distributions, self-dealing, tax reporting, and the other activities where penalties are assessed for failure to comply.

[E] Resource for the Potential Donor and Director

This book is also designed to serve as a source of information for the donor who is interested in establishing a family foundation and the donor who wants to improve the effectiveness of the foundation's operation and grantmaking. The book takes the prospective donor through the process of analyzing the advantages and disadvantages of establishing a family foundation as well as discussing how the foundation fits into the donor's and the family's estate plans. Once the decision is made to move forward, the book provides a step-by-step guide to establishing, funding, and managing the foundation. Many donors want some of the advantages of a family foundation — such as input in the distribution of funds — but do not want the regulatory responsibilities and administrative work required for management. For those individuals, the book suggests other options. Finally, in the event that the foundation no longer serves the role it was created to play, this book provides help on foundation dissolution or merger with another charitable entity.

Practical issues of governance and operation are addressed. There is specific focus on family dynamics, how those dynamics affect the effectiveness of the foundation, and how to resolve the most common problems. Suggestions are made for getting younger generations involved, finding appropriate roles for family members, and creating an atmosphere that encourages effective communication. Grantmaking, tax filing, and record keeping are discussed in detail and augmented with sample forms and checklists to make implementation simple.

Finally, the book sets out the foundation rules. The "prohibited transaction" rules, the restrictions on self-dealing and personal benefit, are discussed in language that is simple to understand. Fiduciary obligations, investment management, and liability insurance are among the many important topics covered in this manual. The goal of this book is to create a single, complete resource for the donor that allows him or her to move from creation to ongoing management.

§ 1.03   RESOURCES FOR FAMILY FOUNDATIONS

One of the most difficult tasks for those new to foundation management is the identification of resources. Tables 1-1 through 1-5 provide a list of family foundation trade associations and vendors providing services, including publications, software, and administrative management. These lists contain only a sampling of the resources available but should provide foundation managers and advisors with a solid place to start.

TABLE 1-1
Trade or Resource Organizations for Foundations

Name	*Contact Information*	*Comments*
Association of Small Foundations	4905 Del Ray Avenue Suite 200 Bethesda, MD 20814 301-907-3337 (phone) 888-212-9922 (toll free) 301-907-0980 (fax) *www.smallfoundations.org*	This membership organization serves foundations with little or no staff regardless of asset size.
BBB Wise Giving Alliance	4200 Wilson Boulevard Suite 800 Arlington, VA 22203-1838	This organization is a merger of the National Charities Information Bureau and

TABLE 1-1.   CONTINUED

Name	Contact Information	Comments
	703-276-0100 (phone) 703-525-8277 (fax) *www.give.org*	the Council of BBB's Foundation and its Philanthropic Advisory Services. Its mission is to promote informed giving and to enable more contributors to make sound giving decisions.
Board Source (formerly the National Center for Nonprofit Boards)	1828 L Street, NW Suite 900 Washington, DC 20036-5114 800-883-6262 or 202-452-6262 (phone) 202-452-6299 (fax) *www.boardsource.org*	This membership organization provides resources to increase the effectiveness of nonprofit boards. Resources include publications, workshops, and consultants.
Center on Nonprofits & Philanthropy	The Urban Institute 2100 M Street, NW Washington, DC 20037 202-833-7200 *www.urban.org/content/ PolicyCenters/ Nonprofitsand Philanthropy/ Overview.htm* *Paffairs@ui.urban.org*	This division of The Urban Institute (a nonpartisan economic and social policy research organization) conducts research and provides information to the public about nonprofits to address the roles and relationships of nonprofits, government, and the market.
Charity Navigator	1200 MacArthur Boulevard Second Floor Mahwah, NJ 07430 201-818-1288 (phone) 201-818-4694 (fax) *www.charitynavigator.org* *info@charitynavigator.org*	The organization maintains a searchable database of over 3,700 charities and provides ratings.
Conference of Southwest Foundations	3102 Maple Avenue Suite 260 Dallas, TX 75201 214-740-1787 (phone) 214-740-1790 (fax) www.c-s-f.org	This regional association represents corporate, independent, family, and public foundations in the Southwest.
Council on Foundations	1828 L Street, NW Washington, DC 20036	This membership organization provides

TABLE 1-1. CONTINUED

Name	Contact Information	Comments
	202-466-6512 (phone) 202-785-3926 (fax) *www.cof.org* *webmaster@cof.org*	support for all types of foundations, including family foundations. COF has a large staff available to answer members' questions. It conducts annual conferences, provides links to affinity groups, conducts research, and provides links to grantmaking associations with specific interests.
Evangelical Council for Financial Accountability	440 West Jubal Early Drive Suite 130 Winchester, VA 22601 800-323-9473 (phone) 540-535-0533 (fax) *www.ecfa.org* *info@ecfa.org*	ECFA's mission is to improve accountability for Christian organizations to improve public trust. The site has guidelines for giving, information on its more than 1,000 members, and news.
Family Office Exchange LLC	100 S. Wacker Drive Suite 900 Chicago, IL 60606 312-327-1200 (phone) 312-327-1212 (fax) *www.foxexchange.com*	Family Office Exchange serves as an independent advisor to families of exceptional wealth, offering an education on complex financial issues and guidance on the selection of appropriate advisors.
Forum of Regional Association of Grantmakers	1111 19th Street, NW Suite 650 Washington, DC 20036 202-467-1120 (phone) 202-467-0055 (fax) *www.givingforum.org* *info@givingforum.org*	This trade group, referred to as RAGS, is a network of geographically focused associations of grantmakers in cities, states, and regions across the country. Within this grantmaking group, grantmakers collaborate to promote philanthropy.
The Foundation Center	79 Fifth Avenue New York, NY 10003-3076 212-620-4230 (phone) 800-424-9836 (phone)	The Foundation Center is a clearinghouse for information on grantmaking and maintains libraries in a

TABLE 1-1.   CONTINUED

Name	Contact Information	Comments
	212-691-1828 (fax) *www.fdncenter.org*	number of cities across the country. It conducts research on foundations and is a good source of information on grantmaking organizations, the types of grants that are made, and the recipient charities.
Grantmakers Without Borders	Boston office: P.O. Box 181282 Boston, MA 02118 617-794-2253 (phone) 617-266-0497 (fax) West Coast Office 1009 General Kennedy Ave. #2 San Francisco, CA 94129 415-730-0367 (phone) *www.internationaldonors. org*	This is a collaborative project of the international Donors' Dialogue and the International Working Group of the National Network of Grantmakers with the objective of expanding and enriching global social change philanthropy.
Grantsmanship Center	1125 West Sixth Street Fifth Floor P.O. Box 17220 Los Angeles, CA 90017 213-482-9860 (phone) 213-482-9863 (fax) *www.tgci.com*	The Grantsmanship Center offers training in grantmaking and produces publications for the nonprofit sector. It conducts 200 workshops per year.
Independent Sector	1200 Eighteenth Street, NW Suite 200 Washington, DC 20036 202-467-6100 (phone) 202-467-6101 (fax) *www.independentsector.org*	Independent Sector conducts extensive research on the nonprofit sector, donor giving habits, volunteers, and other topics of interest to philanthropists. The web site contains good information and links for those researching philanthropic issues.
National Center for Charitable Statistics	The Urban Institute 2100 M Street, NW, 5th Floor Washington, DC 20037 866-518-3874 (phone) 202-833-6231 (fax) *http://nccsdataweb.urban.*	This organization develops and distributes data on nonprofits and their activities. The Center is a program of the Center on Nonprofits and

TABLE 1-1.   CONTINUED

Name	Contact Information	Comments
	org/FAQ/index.php? category=31	Philanthropy and is the former research arm of Independent Sector.
National Center for Family Philanthropy	1818 N Street, NW Suite 300 Washington, DC 20036 202-293-3424 (phone) 202-293-3395 (fax) ncfp@ncfp.org www.ncfp.org	NCFP conducts seminars and workshops for groups interested in family philanthropy, conducts research on family philanthropy issues, provides referrals for consultants and services, and maintains a library of information of interest to donors.
National Committee for Responsive Philanthrophy	2001 S Street, NW Suite 620 Washington, DC 20009 202-387-9177 (phone) 202-332-5084 (fax) www.ncrp.org info@ncrp.org	NCRP's mission is to make philanthropy more responsive, relevant, and accountable. It produces a number of publications reflecting its mission and goals.
National Council of Nonprofit Associations	1030 15th Street, NW Suite 870 Washington, DC 20005 202-962-0322 (phone) 202-962-0321 (fax) www.ncna.org ncna@ncna.org	The National Council of Nonprofit Associations is a network of 37 state and regional nonprofit associations representing more than 21,000 nonprofits across the country. The goal of the association is to collaborate and exchange information to strengthen local nonprofits.
National Network of Grantmakers	2801 21st Avenue South Suite 132 Minneapolis, MN 55407 612-724-0702 (phone) 612-724-0705 (fax) www.nng.org nng@nng.org	This membership organization consists of individuals involved in funding social and economic justice. Members include donors, foundation staff, board, and grantmaking committee members.
Philanthropy Roundtable	1150 Seventeenth Street, NW Suite 503	The Philanthropy Roundtable is a national association

TABLE 1-1.   CONTINUED

Name	Contact Information	Comments
	Washington, DC 20036 202-822-8333 (phone) 202-822-8325 (fax) *www.philanthropyroun- dtable.org* *main@philanthropy roundtable.org*	of more than 600 individual donors, corporate giving representatives, foundation staff, and trustees and trust and estate officers.
Social Venture Partners	1601 Second Avenue Suite 605 Seattle, WA 98101 206-374-8757 (phone) 206-728-0552 (fax) *www.svpseattle.org*	This is a philanthropic organization that uses a venture capital model. The organization provides guidance, training, and resources to promote philanthropy.
Southeastern Council of Foundations	50 Hurt Plaza SE Suite 350 Atlanta, GA 30303-2914 404-524-0911 (phone) 404-523-5116 (fax) *www.secf.org* *info@secf.org*	This association represents corporate, independent, family, and public foundations across the Southeast.
Support Center for Nonprofit Management	305 Seventh Avenue 11th Floor New York, NY 10001-6008 212-924-6744 (phone) 212-924-9544 (fax) *www.supportctr.org* *info@supportctr.org*	This association provides management training and consulting, information, and resources to nonprofit organizations.
Worldwide Initiatives for Grantmaker Support (WINGS)	c/o European Foundation Centre 51 rue de la Concorde Brussels B-1050 Belgium 32.2.512.8938 (phone) 32.2.512.3265 (fax) *www.wingsweb.org/index. html* *wings@efc.bc*	This organization is a network of more than 95 membership associations serving grantmakers and support organizations working for philanthropic causes.

TABLE 1-2
Family Advisory Services

Resource	Contact Information
Family Philanthrophy Advisors Diane Neimann, President	1818 Oliver Avenue South Minneapolis, MN 55405-2208 612-377-8400 (phone) 612-377-8407 (fax) *www.fpadvisors.com* *general@fpadvisors.com*
Family Firm Institute	200 Lincoln Street #201 Boston, MA 02111 617-482-3045 (phone) 617-482-3049 (fax) *ffi@ffi.org*
IFF Advisors, LLC	Doug Freeman, Chairman and National Managing Partner 2 Park Plz, Suite 1245 Irvine, CA 92614-2582 866-833-1112 (toll free) 949-833-1112 (phone) 949-833-9584 (fax)

TABLE 1-3
Balance Sheet Software Resources

Vendor	Contact Information	Comments
Blackbaud	2000 Daniel Island Drive Charleston, SC 29492-7541 800-443-9441 (phone) 843-216-6111 (fax) *www.blackbaud.com* *solutions@blackbaud.com*	This software manages general ledger, financial accounting, budget preparation, payroll, and fundraising management.
CYMA Systems, Inc.	2330 West University Drive Suite 7 Tempe, AZ 85281 800-292-2962 or 480-303-2962 (phone) 480-303-2969 (fax) *www.cyma.com* *info@cyma.com*	This software manages general ledger, financial accounting, budget preparation, and payroll.
Data Pro, Inc.	P.O. Box 457 108 South Main Street Plainwell, MI 49080	This software manages general ledger, financial accounting,

TABLE 1-3.   CONTINUED

Vendor	*Contact Information*	*Comments*
	269-685-9214 (phone) 269-685-5660 (fax) *www.data-pro.com*	budget preparation, and payroll.
Executive Data Systems, Inc.	1640 Powers Ferry Road Building 14, Suite 300 Marietta, GA 30067 800-272-3374 (phone) 770-995-1975 (fax) *www.execdata.com* *sales@execdata.com*	This software manages general ledger, financial accounting, budget preparation, payroll, and fundraising management.
FUND E-Z	106 Corporate Park Drive White Plains, NY 10604 914-696-0900 (phone) 914-696-0948 (fax) *www.fundez.com* *sales@fundez.com*	This software manages general ledger, financial accounting, budget preparation, payroll, and fundraising management.
Kintera FundWare	6430 S. Fiddlers Green Circle Suite 500 Greenwood Village, CO 80111 800-551-4458 (phone) 303-756-3514 (fax) *www.fundware.com* *information@publicsector.* *intuit.com*	This software manages general ledger, financial accounting, budget preparation, and payroll.
Mirasoft, Inc.	865F Cotting Lane Vacaville, CA 95688 707-453-8300 or 800-414-3863 (phone) 707-453-8303 (fax) *www.mirasoft-inc.com*	This software manages general ledger, financial accounting, budget preparation, and payroll.
NPO Solutions	89 North State Street Concord, NH 03301 603-224-3400 (phone) 603-228-5718 (fax) *www.nposolutions.com* *info@nposolutions.com*	This firm has two products: Foundation Information Management Systems (FIMS) and Foundation Power. This software offers an integrated system for financial accounting, balance

TABLE 1-3.   CONTINUED

Vendor	Contact Information	Comments
		sheet, donor management, funds management, grants management, and a report writer.
Sage Software	12301 Research Blvd. Bldg IV, Suite 350 Austin, TX 78759 800-647-3863 (phone) 512-454-1246 (fax)	This product has three levels, from basic to high transaction. The software manages general ledger, financial accounting, budget, and payroll.

TABLE 1-4
Publications of Interest to Family Foundations

Publication	Contact Information	Comments
The Chronicle of Philanthropy	1255 Twenty-Third Street, NW Suite 700 Washington, DC 20037 202-466-1200 (phone) *http://philanthropy.com* *help@philanthropy.com*	This newspaper is published biweekly except the last two weeks in June and the last two weeks in December.
Contributions Magazine	P.O. Box 338 Medfield, MA 02052 508-359-0019 (phone) 508-359-2703 (fax) *www.contributionsmagazine.com*	This publication deals with broad philanthropic issues such as direct mail, trends in philanthropy, and management.
Foundations Today Series 2006 Edition	Foundation Center Department SN 79 Fifth Avenue New York, NY 10003-3076 800-424-9836 (phone) 212-807-3691 (fax) *www.fdncenter.org*	This three-report annual series provides comprehensive data on foundation grantmaking and statistics.
The Nonprofit Times	201 Littleton Road Second Floor Morris Plaius, NJ 07950 973-401-0202 (phone) 973-401-0404 (fax) *www.nptimes.com*	This newspaper provides information on donors, technology, current events in the charitable world, and nonprofit management.

TABLE 1-5
Grantmaking Software

Vendor	Contact Information	Comments
CyberGrants, Inc.	Two Dundee Park Suite 100 Andover, MA 01810 978-824-0300 (phone) 978-824-0301 (fax) *www.cybergrants.com* *info@cybergrants.com*	This product is an Internet-based grants management system.
Digital Footbridge	7301 RR 620 North Suites 155-168 Austin, TX 78726 512-699-7644 (phone) www.digitalfootbridge.org	This software provides Internet-based grantmaking software and includes features such as an online grant application process.
Dyna-Quest Technologies, Inc.	77 Court Street Suite 1028 Laconia, NH 03246 603-267-1845 (phone) 603-267-1846 (fax) *www.Dyna-Quest.com*	This product (Grant Administrator) handles fund accounting for grants, projects, contracts, proposals, and clinical trials. It also tracks expenditures, salary, and income and generates audit trails.
Arlington Group	1750 Old Meadow Rd. Suite 200 McLean, VA 22102 703-893-9353, ext. 117 (phone) 703-893-9363 (fax) *www.arlingtongroup.com* *info@arlgroup.com*	The Easygrants grant management system streamlines the grant application process, administration, and reporting and can be customized to fit foundation needs.
MicroEdge	619 West 54th Street 10th Floor New York, NY 10019 800-899-0890 (phone) *www.microedge.com* *info@microedge.com*	This firm provides Internet-based grantmaking software.
NPO Solutions A Division of MicroEdge	89 North State Street Concord, NH 03301 603-224-3400 (phone) 603-228-5718 (fax) *www.nposolutions.com* *info@nposolutions.com*	This firm has two products: Foundation Information Management Systems (FIMS) and Foundation Power. This software

TABLE 1-5.   CONTINUED

Publication	Contact Information	Comments
		offers an integrated system for financial accounting, balance sheet, donor management, funds management, grants management, and a report writer.

CHAPTER 2
FAMILY FOUNDATION BASICS

§ 2.01   WHAT IS A FAMILY FOUNDATION?

The term "family foundation" is not a legal term, but rather a phrase used to describe a foundation that is established and run by family members. A family foundation is a form of private foundation because it is funded through family contributions and investment income, rather than contributions from the general public. In addition, it is controlled by a group of individuals selected by the donor. The family members, and individuals selected by the family, determine the charitable distributions to be made from the foundation. These distributions generally reflect the goals, objectives, and values of the family and carry the family name.

Though there is no established description of a family foundation, most have several of the following characteristics:

- A founder that is an individual, rather than a corporation;

- A name that incorporates the founder's family name;

- A board, the majority of which are family members;

- A grantmaking committee, the majority of which are family members;

- A board where new appointments are made by family members;

- A board designed to incorporate multiple generations or extended family members over time;

- A foundation management role for one or more family members; and

- A purpose that reflects family values.

Determining the number of family foundations that exist in the United States is a challenge. The Internal Revenue Service (IRS) does not make such a distinction in its records. There is also little way to make a determination by physical review of the tax return, Form 990-PF. While a family foundation is easy to identify in the first generation of family involvement, the family relationship is more difficult to discern once the foundation has moved to the second or even third generation. Family members may then be in the minority or may have surnames that do not reflect the founder's surname. In truth, foundations can be classified as "family" foundations only through self-identification, and even this determination is subjective.

The Foundation Center makes an annual survey to determine the number of family foundations operating in the United States and to track growth patterns for those foundations. The 2005 survey (based on 2004 data) identified 31,347 family foundations, an increase of 28.3 percent over the 24,434 identified in 2000.[1] The Foundation Center used four criteria to classify a foundation, since there is no

---

[1] Key Facts on Family Foundations, The Foundation Center (January 2006), <http://fdncenter.org/research/trends_analysis/pdf/key_facts_fam.pdf>.

legal indicator that distinguishes a family foundation from other private foundations. These criteria were:

- self-identification on the survey instrument;
- the use of the word "family" or "families" in the foundation's legal name;
- a donor listing whose surname matched the foundation name; or
- two or more trustees whose surnames matched a living or deceased foundation donor.

For the 2004 tax year, the family foundations in the survey reported assets of $209.2 billion and grants of $12.67 billion.[2] They received $9.28 billion in additional contributions.[3]

    A special report on family foundations published in 2002 by a researcher from The Foundation Center acknowledged the difficulty of determining whether a private foundation is controlled by the family or influenced by family attitudes and policies.[4] The study estimated that 60.9 percent of all family foundations created since 1980 continue to have family involvement, while only 21 percent of those foundations created before 1940 still reflect that influence.[5] The eventual loss of family involvement should be anticipated when structuring the board appointment mechanism and granting parameters.[6]

§ 2.02   BENEFITS GAINED

[A]   Tax Benefits

    A family foundation offers almost no tax advantage or benefit beyond the benefits that are available for any charitable transfer. Those benefits are significant, of course, but the person who is seeking nothing more than a tax benefit need not undertake the considerable added upkeep and expense of a foundation. The foundation itself will qualify for exemption from tax as a section 501(c)(3) organization and will thus pay no federal income tax (and usually no state income tax) on most of its income. This is a substantial tax benefit, and its value cannot be doubted.

    However, because it is classified as a private foundation for tax purposes, a family foundation is subject to a number of restrictions and penalties (discussed

---

   [2] *Id.*

   [3] *Id.*

   [4] Lawrence, Steven, *Family Foundations: A Profile of Funders and Trends,* The Foundation Center 2000, p. xi. A copy of this report can be ordered for $19.95 from The Foundation Center, 79 Fifth Avenue, New York, NY 10003, by phone at 800-424-9836, or from the Foundation Center's web site, *www.fdncenter.org.*

   [5] *Id.*

   [6] *See* Chapter 5 for a discussion of foundation design and Chapter 7 for a discussion of the grantmaking process.

elsewhere in this volume) that other section 501(c)(3) organizations escape. Those restrictions and penalties are not always troublesome, for they tend to affect only donors and foundations that stray beyond a straightforward pattern of behavior. If a family foundation is funded with cash and publicly traded stocks and if its program consists of making grants to other section 501(c)(3) organizations that are classified as public charities for tax purposes, it may not be seriously hampered by the private foundation rules. On the other hand, those rules intrude seriously upon the donor who wishes to fund his or her family foundation with real estate or closely held business interests; likewise, if the foundation wishes to engage in transactions with members of the donor's family or embark upon a program of grants to individuals, the applicable rules must be closely followed.

Despite these restrictions and limitations, however, there is one distinct tax advantage to be obtained through the creation of a foundation, and that is the manner in which a foundation enables a donor to achieve income tax deductions for expenditures that would not be deductible if made by an individual.[7] Amounts contributed to a foundation are typically deductible, and the foundation may use those funds in any activity permissible under the foundation rules discussed in Chapter 6. Despite their generally restrictive nature, those rules do contemplate many activities and expenditures that would not give rise to a deduction if undertaken by the donor directly. For example, a foundation may make grants to individuals or to foreign charities, while comparable contributions by individuals would not be deductible. This advantage may not be sufficient alone to justify creation of a foundation, but it should not be overlooked as one factor to be considered in making this decision.

Contributions to a family foundation (or to any entity classified as a private foundation for tax purposes) are generally deductible in full, but there are several special limitations on such contributions that do not apply to other types of charitable gifts. Thus, while there are some tax advantages to be obtained by forming and funding a family foundation, on balance those may more appropriately be viewed as tax *disadvantages* in comparison with the advantages available from contributions to charitable organizations that are not classified as private foundations. These disadvantages are discussed below in § 2.03[B].

[B] Nontax Benefits

Because of the various tax limitations, it is in the nontax area that the primary benefits available from a family foundation are obtained. The benefits gained by a

---

[7] Under IRC § 170, an individual is entitled to a charitable contribution deduction only for a contribution to or for the use of a qualified donee organization, as listed in IRC § 170(c). By contrast, a foundation may make distributions for virtually any charitable purpose, provided the Chapter 42 restrictions on self-dealing, taxable expenditures, etc., are not violated. *See* IRC § 4942(g). Thus, for example, foundation grants to foreign grantees are permissible, while an individual's contribution to the same grantee would not be deductible.

given family from a family foundation will vary with the family's individual priorities and objectives, but the following are among the benefits often described.

[1] Ongoing Control of Charitable Contributions

Although contributions to public charities are deductible and are treated more favorably, as discussed above, the donor has no continuing control or use of the funds and property that are contributed to such entity. By creating a foundation, the founder and his or her family can exercise control over the programs of the foundation and its distributions permanently, from one generation to another. So long as the minimum distribution requirements described in Chapter 7 are met and the foundation's grants are permissible under the taxable expenditure rules described in Chapter 6, the founder or the family can generally exercise as much control as desired over the programs of the foundation, the selection of its grantees, and every other aspect of the foundation's operations.

The extent of this control is probably the most common reason for creation of a foundation. There is no other form of charitable organization that offers a donor the same degree of personal control over the donee and the donated funds. The alternatives to the family foundation (described and discussed in § 2.05 below) all require the donor to compromise on either the issue of control or the available tax benefits, and for some donors, that makes the foundation the organization of choice, regardless of the limitations.

[2] Family Institution or Memorial

The existence of a foundation bearing the name of the family or its founding members can serve as an enduring memorial to its founders, thereby immortalizing them through a perpetual program of good works. In this way, children can honor their parents, and the family's name can be kept alive and dignified through future generations. Institutions such as the Rockefeller Foundation established in 1913 and funded by John D. Rockefeller, or the Charles Stewart Mott Foundation established by Mr. Mott in 1926, or the Lilly Endowment, created in 1937 by J. K. Lilly, Sr., J. K. Lilly, Jr., and Eli Lilly have operated for decades beyond the founders' lifetimes and make substantive contributions memorializing the family name each year. This can be a very effective means of achieving public recognition for the achievements of a successful individual, plus a means whereby such an individual may share the fruits of his or her success by giving back to the community in the name of the family.

In addition to the element of public recognition, there is another family benefit to be obtained from creating a family foundation: The foundation itself can help perpetuate the family unit by requiring the attention and interaction of children and grandchildren on an ongoing and permanent basis. The operations of the foundation, with regular meetings and collective decisions regarding grants and projects, can thus provide a mandatory focal point for members of the family. This necessity of regular collaboration and working together in the name of the family can help strengthen family traditions and cohesiveness. This is a feature that can be particularly productive under modern living conditions, with younger-generation family members often becoming geographically scattered and less close personally.

[3] Institutionalized, Yet Flexible Giving

Through a foundation, a family can create a formal structure by which it can apply family resources to the solution of social problems and other issues of concern and can support community institutions and other charitable organizations on a regular, organized basis. This can help provide the family with enhanced access to individuals and institutions and generally can increase the credibility and legitimacy of individual opinions and actions. All of these advantages of an institution separate and apart from the individual family members are obtained without any loss of family domination, and the priorities and concerns of the institution can be directed or changed as desired.

[4] Maintaining and Endowing a Giving Program

Often a person considering creating a family foundation is personally involved with several charitable organizations and, as a result, becomes accustomed to providing them with financial support. By transferring a corpus to a private foundation, such a person can create an endowment that will produce an income stream sufficient to continue this program of charitable giving for the benefit of the organizations in which he or she is involved. Moreover, this income stream can continue indefinitely into the future, a factor that can be helpful to the donor in arranging his or her estate plan.

The existence of such an endowment can also help the beneficiary organizations by enabling them to plan more effectively for the continuation of their programs. In addition, construction of buildings and other major capital improvements can be facilitated. Moreover, the founder and his or her family can guide and influence the future of those organizations through their continuing control of the foundation and its distributions.

[5] Personal Development of Younger Family Members

Typically, families that consider creating a family foundation have achieved some degree of financial success. Children from such a background ironically are often denied many opportunities that are taken for granted in families that are less well off. As they are "spared" the burdens of part-time jobs and other responsibilities, these children may also miss out on the chance to develop self-reliance and personal responsibility. A family foundation offers a chance for children to work together with other family members to shape family priorities and use the family's resources to help others and accomplish something meaningful beyond the mere purchase of toys and satisfaction of personal desires.[8]

Even young children can be involved in the process of discussing and comparing potential grantees, evaluating projects, and making collective judgments on the basis of these considerations. This may be more beneficial for the children initially as a learning experience that teaches not only about how grantees are selected, but also about the various programs discussed and the community institutions that conduct those programs. Later, with this background, the children can become increasingly helpful in the work of the foundation. Some family foundations have junior boards for younger family members, with carefully delineated areas of responsibility.

As the children become older, the foundation can serve as an introduction to financial management and even investment principles. How the foundation handles its assets and the discussions surrounding investments, budgets, and changes in the foundation's finances can all provide a useful introduction and orientation for older children as they become younger board members.

All of these things can be accomplished more easily and with less discomfort when undertaken in the context of the foundation, rather than a child's personal needs and wants. Intergenerational frictions and deep-seated personal issues are less likely to create barriers to effective communication when the discussion can center outside the family. Particularly with money matters, the discussion can be less contentious when it concerns the foundation's funds, rather than the money to be handled by the child.

[6] Possible Asset Protection

A family foundation may even provide a means by which a family can avoid losing control of assets. Issues sometimes arise regarding the ability of creditors to reach charitable contributions made by donors who subsequently file for bankruptcy protection.

Under the Religious Liberty and Charitable Donation Act of 1998,[9] contributions of cash or "financial instruments" (stocks, bonds, options, and certain financial derivatives) made before the donor files a bankruptcy petition will be protected from creditors to the extent they did not exceed 15 percent of the donor's gross annual income for the year of the contribution. A transfer in excess

---

[8] *See* Chapter 9 for more detail on engaging younger generations in foundation work. For a thoughtful discussion on family wealth generally, including the role and benefits of family philanthropy, *see Wealth in Families* by Charles W. Collier, Senior Philanthropic Advisor at Harvard University ($15.00 per copy), available from Harvard University, 617-495-5040.

[9] Pub. L. No. 105-183 (1998).

of this 15 percent figure may still be protected where it can be shown that such contribution "was consistent with the practices of the debtor in making charitable contributions."[10] This protection is available only for individual donors; contributions by corporations are unaffected. After the filing of a bankruptcy petition, an individual donor's charitable contributions will still be protected to the extent of 15 percent of gross income for the year.

While it is not clear that family foundations were among the entities Congress wanted to protect by this Act, it does seem clear that they are within the protection afforded. The Act protects contributions to any "qualified religious or charitable entity or organization." This category is defined as including all entities described in § 170(c)(1) or (2) of the Internal Revenue Code. Family foundations are definitely included in IRC § 170(c)(2).

§ 2.03 DISADVANTAGES

In a nutshell, the costs of a foundation can be greater and the tax benefits more limited than for the available alternatives.[11]

[A] Expense

It should be obvious that creating a charitable organization will be more costly and less convenient than providing comparable support to an existing entity. The family that creates a foundation must pay all the costs of forming the entity and obtaining recognition of its tax exemption and, thereafter, the ongoing expenses of operation. If an existing entity is used, the family is spared these costs. These costs are not necessarily unique to the family foundation, but rather reflect the expense inherent in choosing to create a charitable entity of one's own, rather than merely providing support to one that is already in existence.

As discussed in Chapter 3, formation of a foundation requires that a trust or nonprofit corporation be formed. If this is to be done with assurance of its legality, a lawyer's assistance is recommended, and there are governmental fees involved if a corporation is formed. Next, an exemption application must be filed with the Internal Revenue Service to confirm the foundation's tax-exempt status. This step also requires the founders to bear costs — a fee must be paid to the IRS, and, in most cases, there will also be the expense of a lawyer's services in preparing and filing Form 1023.

Once the foundation is up and running, there are ongoing expenses of operation. These include the preparation of the foundation's annual tax return (Form 990-PF) at a minimum, plus any additional accounting services needed

---

[10] *See* 11 U.S.C. § 548(d)(3).
[11] *See* § 2.05 *infra.*

and routine expenses involved in administering the foundation, such as postage and clerical expenses, plus costs of managing the foundation's investments.

None of these costs is necessarily prohibitive, but they can be substantial for a person who contemplates devoting only a limited amount of money to the project. It will probably cost in the range of $5,000 to form a foundation and secure IRS recognition of its tax exemption. If the founder will be devoting as much as $2 million to the foundation, this is not a significant cost factor. If, on the other hand, only $25,000 will be involved, the cost of creating the foundation is so large relative to the total that the founder would be well advised to consider pursuing one of the alternatives described below.[12]

[B] Tax Disadvantages

Charitable deductions for contributions to foundations are subject to several limitations that do not apply to other contributions. Lower percentage-of-adjusted-gross-income limitations apply to such contributions, and, in addition, contributions of property other than publicly traded stock are limited to the donor's tax basis.[13]

In some instances, these limitations create a serious disadvantage to the prospective donor. In many cases, however, they have little or no impact. Consider, for example, the donor who contemplates a family foundation that will be created currently, but not fully funded until later, by means of a bequest at the founder's death. In this situation, these limitations are unlikely to pose a problem for the founder. The same would be true for the donor who uses publicly traded stock for the foundation's initial funding and makes transfers in amounts that do not substantially exceed 20 percent of his or her adjusted gross income.

A far greater tax disadvantage is the effect on a private foundation of the system of excise taxes imposed under Chapter 42 of the Internal Revenue Code (IRC), discussed in Chapter 6. These include a two percent tax on investment income,[14] a minimum distribution requirement,[15] investment restrictions,[16] and limitations on permissible grants, expenditures, and activities.[17]

The principal tax limitations on contributions to private foundations are lower percentage limitations and reduced deductions for property contributions, and these are discussed below. Note that these are income tax limitations; by contrast, there are no comparable restrictions on estate tax deductions for amounts passing to private foundations at death.

---

[12] *See* § 2.05 *infra.*
[13] IRC §§ 170(b)(1)(B) and 170(e)(1)(B)(ii).
[14] IRC § 4940.
[15] IRC § 4942.
[16] IRC §§ 4943 and 4944.
[17] IRC § 4945.

[1]   Lower Percentage Limitations

There are limitations on the percentage of an individual's income that he or she may give to charity and deduct in any one taxable year. These limitations differ depending on the nature of the charitable recipient and the type of property given. The limitations are higher in every case for gifts to public charities (such as churches, colleges, and organizations like the American Red Cross and The Nature Conservancy) than for gifts to family foundations or other organizations classified as private foundations for tax purposes. Similarly, the applicable limitations are higher for cash gifts than for gifts of property. An individual may deduct cash gifts made to public charities up to 50 percent of his or her adjusted gross income and property gifts up to 30 percent.[18] For gifts to private foundations, the limitations are 30 percent of adjusted gross income for cash gifts and 20 percent for property gifts.[19] See Table 2-1. Any contributions in excess of the limitation carryover and may be deducted in each of the five subsequent years.[20]

TABLE 2-1
Percentage Limitations for Charitable Contributions by Individuals
(Expressed as a Percentage of Adjusted Gross Income)

Type of Property Given	*Nature of Donee Organization*	
	Public Charity	*Private Foundation*
Cash	50%	30%
Property	30%	20%

Note: The limitations affect only the total amount of charitable contributions an individual may deduct in any one taxable year. There is no limitation on the amount an individual may give to charity, and a person is free to give all of his or her income or more to charity if that is what he or she wants to do.

A separate percentage limitation is provided for charitable contributions of corporations. These are deductible up to 10 percent of the corporation's *taxable* income, regardless of the nature of the donee organization or the gift property.[21] As with individual contributions, any excess may be carried over for up to five more years.[22]

---

[18] We have referred to the limitations as percentages of adjusted gross income for convenience, but the actual limitation is expressed in terms of an individual's *contribution base*, which is his or her adjusted gross income computed without regard to any net operating loss carryback. Since few individuals have net operating loss carrybacks, one may safely think of the limitation in terms of adjusted gross income alone. Adjusted gross income is defined in IRC § 62 as gross income less certain deductions, such as trade and business deductions, alimony, moving expenses, and certain retirement plan contributions, to name just a few.

[19] IRC §§ 170(b)(1)(B)(i) and 170(b)(1)(D)(i).

[20] IRC §§ 170(d)(1)(A) and 170(b)(1)(D)(ii).

[21] IRC § 170(b)(2).

[22] IRC § 170(d)(2).

[2] Special Carryover Problems

The percentage limitations on charitable deductions are interrelated and can become quite complex under some circumstances. Several of these situations can have practical implications for family foundations. The first and most important of these occurs in the context of the *30 percent limitation*, which applies to contributions of cash to private foundations. That limitation is usually understood and remembered as limiting deductions for such contributions in any one year to a straight 30 percent of the donor's adjusted gross income for the year.[23] In fact, however, the Internal Revenue Code defines this limitation in more complicated terms, and a close reading of the literal language of the Code is required to understand it. The actual limitation amount is defined by the Code[24] as whichever of the following two amounts is the *smaller* —

1. 30 percent of the taxpayer's adjusted gross income for the taxable year or

2. The excess of —

   a. 50 percent of the taxpayer's adjusted gross income for the taxable year over
   b. The amount of charitable contributions allowable under the fifty percent limitation of § 170(b)(1)(A) (determined without regard to the separate thirty percent limitation on deductions for appreciated property gifts under § 170(b)(1)(C)).[25]

This means that the limitation will be less than 30 percent of AGI under certain circumstances. To determine the actual limitation on a given set of facts requires one to go through all of this labyrinth, filling in the actual amounts. In most cases, the 30-percent-of-AGI amount will be the limitation, but there are exceptions. This will always be the result when a donor, in a single taxable year, makes contributions falling into two categories:[26]

1. Contributions of cash to a private foundation and

2. Appreciated capital gain property to public charities, where the amount of such contributions exceeds the separate 30 percent limitation that governs these contributions, as described above.

---

[23] Here, again, the actual limitation is based not on adjusted gross income (AGI) alone, but rather on the donor's contribution base. This term is defined in IRC § 170(b)(1)(F) as the donor's AGI computed without regard to any net operating loss carryback to the taxable year in question. Because net operating loss carrybacks are relatively uncommon for individual taxpayers, we will refer to the limitation here in terms of AGI alone.

[24] IRC § 170(b)(1)(B)(ii).

[25] *See* IRC § 170(b)(1)(B)(ii) and the regulations thereunder.

[26] This results from the interplay between IRC §§ 170(b)(1)(B) and 170(b)(1)(C), and the fact that the limitation amount specified in IRC § 170(b)(1)(B)(ii) disregards the separate 30 percent limitation on appreciated property gifts. *See* the Example in the text at footnote 30 *infra*, for a demonstration of this effect.

Under these circumstances, the excess of the property contribution over the separate 30 percent limitation in category 2 may reduce (or even eliminate) the amount deductible for category 1.

> **Example:** Dan Donor has a contribution base (adjusted gross income) of $100,000 and makes two contributions, as follows:
>
> > $50,000 worth of listed stocks to a university and
> > $20,000 in cash to The Donor Foundation, a private foundation.
>
> Dan's overall limitation is 50 percent of contribution base, or $50,000.
>
> *Step 1:* The property contribution to the university is subject to a general 30 percent limitation, so only $30,000 of this $50,000 contribution is deductible, and the $20,000 excess carries over to the next taxable year.
>
> *Step 2:* Since Dan has deducted only $30,000 of his $50,000 overall limitation, one might logically expect that he would be able to deduct the $20,000 cash contribution to The Donor Foundation, but that is not correct. This cash contribution to a private foundation is subject to the general limitation of 30 percent of his AGI applicable under IRC § 170(b)(1)(B). On these facts, however, as explained above, this limitation is actually limited to the *lesser* of (item 1) 30 percent of AGI ($30,000 here) or (item 2) the excess of (a) 50 percent of AGI ($50,000 here) over (b) the amount of all deductible contributions to 50 percent-style charities, *determined without regard to the 30 percent limitation for property contributions* ($50,000 here[27]). The excess of $50,000 over $50,000 is zero, and this is less than $30,000, so there is no deduction allowable for the gift to the private foundation.

Amounts disqualified from a current deduction under this rule (including Dan Donor's $20,000 cash contribution in the foregoing example), like all amounts that exceed the applicable percentage limitation, carry over to the next five taxable years and are deductible subject to the same percentage limitation in such years until fully deducted.

One might wonder why this seemingly needless complication is included in what should be a straightforward provision. There is no clear answer, except that one must resist the tendency of writers and politicians to conclude that it flows

---

[27] Why is this amount $50,000? Dan gave $50,000 to the university, and this full amount is deductible even though his deduction for the year of contribution is limited to $30,000 (and the balance carries over to the following year). At this point, we must look at the amount of all deductible contributions to 50 percent-style charities, *determined without regard to the 30 percent limitation for property contributions*, and, in Dan's case, his deductible contributions to 50 percent-style charities (i.e., public charities) are $50,000. This precisely equals 50 percent of his AGI, so there is no excess of (a) over (b) in item 2 above; thus, item 2 is zero, and this is less than the $30,000 amount in item 1.

from some failure of judgment on the part of IRS officials. That is clearly not the case, since this rule was placed in the Internal Revenue Code by Congress and the IRS is required by law to apply the Code as enacted by Congress. This rule probably resulted from the unquestionable intention of Congress that the provisions governing private foundations be clearly more limited than those governing other public charities. Note that this rule is less harsh in its application now than it was when originally passed, for as originally enacted the law provided no carryover of contributions to private foundations in excess of the applicable percentage limitations; the law was changed in 1984 to permit such carryovers, thus rendering this rule less onerous in its operation.

A similar, but less drastic, situation exists with respect to the 20-percent-of-AGI limitation that applies to contributions of capital gain property to private foundations. (Remember, the only contributions of this type that are fully deductible in any event are contributions of publicly traded stock.) This limitation, too, is more complicated than the shorthand version that most people remember. The Internal Revenue Code provides that the deduction limitation for such gifts is not a straight 20 percent of AGI, but rather the lesser of two amounts:[28]

1. 20 percent of the taxpayer's contribution base (AGI) for the taxable year, or

2. The *excess* of —

   a. 30 percent of the taxpayer's contribution base (AGI) for the taxable year over

   b. The amount of the contributions of capital gain property to public charities.

For purposes of this rule, contributions of capital gain property to private foundations are taken into account after all other charitable contributions.[29] And, remember, the overall limitation of 30 percent may also limit the donor's overall deduction for private foundation contributions.

The effect of this rule is to assure that the overall limitation for all gifts to private foundations in a single taxable year is 30 percent of AGI (contribution base) and that foundation gifts are deductible only after gifts to public charities have been taken into account.

> **Example:** Mark Sosa contributes $50,000 to the Sosa Family Foundation in a year for which his AGI (contribution base) is $100,000. This consists of $25,000 in cash and publicly traded stock worth $25,000, and he makes no other charitable contributions for the year. His cash contribution ($25,000) is taken into account first, and because it is less than the 30-percent-of-AGI overall limit, it is deductible in full in the year of the contribution. The

---

[28] *See* IRC § 170(b)(1)(D)(i).

[29] IRC § 170(b)(1)(D)(i)(II) (last sentence).

deductibility of his remaining contribution of stock worth $25,000 is determined by two different limitations:

1. The remaining amount of the 30 percent overall limitation and

2. The more complex formula in IRC § 170(b)(1)(D)(i), described above.

The latter provision limits Mark's deduction to the lesser of (item 1) 20 percent of AGI ($20,000 here) or (item 2) the excess of (a) 30 percent of AGI ($30,000 here) over (b) the amount of the contributions of capital gain property to public charities (zero here).[30] Item 1 ($20,000) is less than item 2 ($30,000), so Mark may potentially deduct $20,000 of his stock contribution. However, for this year, Mark has an overall limitation of 30 percent of AGI, or $30,000, for all contributions to private foundations. Because he has already used $25,000 of this for his cash contribution to the Sosa Family Foundation, only the remaining $5,000 of his overall limitation is available, so only $5,000 of his property contribution is deductible currently; the rest, or $20,000, will carry over to the next taxable year for the next five years.

[3] Reduced Deductions for Property Contributions

In general, the amount deductible for a charitable contribution of property is the fair market value of the property on the date of the gift.[31] Many people, even some tax lawyers, have the misconception that the Tax Reform Act of 1986 changed this rule and limited all property contributions to the donor's basis. This is not true, although there are several important exceptions. One of those exceptions provides that deductions for most contributions of appreciated capital gain property to private foundations will be limited in amount to the donor's basis in the contributed property. Gifts of publicly traded stocks to private foundations, however, are deductible at their full fair market value, as provided in IRC § 170(e)(5).

The starting point for any charitable contribution of property other than cash is the fair market value of the property. That is the amount of the deduction allowable for most property contributions, but there are several exceptions.

First, the property must be capital gain property if a deduction is to be allowed for its full value. This requires a determination of what sort of income would be produced if the property were sold, instead of contributed, on the date of contribution. If the contributed property would produce a gain or profit that is taxed as anything other than long-term capital gain, the donor's deduction is reduced by the amount of that non-long-term capital gain.[32]

---

[30] *See* IRC § 170(b)(1)(D)(i).
[31] Reg. § 1.170-1(c)(1).
[32] IRC § 170(e)(1)(A).

Example: Sarah, a furniture dealer, contributes beds to a local relief agency to assist flood victims. The beds have a retail value of $500, and they cost Sarah $200. If Sarah sold the beds in her furniture store, she would realize a profit of $300, and that profit would be taxed as ordinary income. Sarah's deduction for this contribution is $200 ($500 market value less the $300 ordinary income she would have realized upon selling the property).

Even if the contributed property is capital gain property, the donor's deduction is still reduced in two additional situations. The first involves contributions of tangible personal property. Such property will produce a deduction equal to its fair market value only if the donee organization's use of the property is related to its charitable purposes.[33] Thus, a gift of artwork to an art museum by a collector who is not a dealer would generally produce a deduction equal to the fair market value of the artwork. A contribution of the same artwork by the same donor would be limited to the donor's cost basis if the donee institution were a day-care center rather than a museum because the day-care center would not use artwork in its charitable program.

The second of these situations is more pertinent for our purposes. A gift of capital gain property to an organization classified as a private foundation for tax purposes will generally be limited to the donor's cost basis.[34] There is an important exception to this rule where the gift property consists of "qualified appreciated stock."[35] Qualified appreciated stock is publicly traded stock for which market quotations are readily available on an established securities market. Any donor may contribute up to 10 percent of the stock in any one corporation under this rule.

Note: Such contributions are subject to a special 20-percent-of-adjusted-gross-income limitation under IRC § 170(b)(1)(D)(i), but may be reduced (and carried over) if the donor has also made contributions subject to the general 30 percent limitation on appreciated property contributions.

This rule places practical limitations on the types of property normally used to fund contributions to family foundations. Corporate stock can be used for this purpose, but only if it is publicly traded stock, and not more than 10 percent of the stock of any corporation can be used. Although stock in a corporation may qualify under this rule, if bonds or any other securities of the same corporation are used, the donor's deduction will be limited to basis. Contributions of closely held stocks or partnership interests will likewise be limited to basis, as will gifts of real estate or any property other than publicly traded stocks.

---

[33] IRC § 170(e)(1)(B)(i).
[34] IRC § 170(e)(1)(B)(ii).
[35] IRC § 170(e)(5).

[4] Special Rules for Certain Types of Private Foundations

The foregoing rules, which limit the applicable percentage limitations and reduce the amount of deductions for property contributions to private foundations, do not apply in the case of certain categories of private foundations. Contributions of capital gain property to the following types of private foundation (described in IRC § 170(b)(1)(E)) are deductible on the same basis as contributions to public charities:

1. Private operating foundations;[36]

2. Foundations that distribute all of the contributions received for a given year by the 15th day of the third month of the following year (the conduit or pass-through foundation);[37] and

3. Pooled fund foundations.[38]

These specially treated types of private foundation offer much planning potential for donors.[39]

[5] Possible State Income Tax Issues

As discussed in § 2.09, a family sometimes considers relocating a foundation when family members move to another state upon retirement or otherwise. Sometimes relocation allows a foundation to escape burdensome reporting rules, intrusive state supervision, or other legal obstacles in the old location. The decision to move a foundation, like the family members' personal decision to relocate, requires a careful consideration of all the surrounding circumstances. A recent Minnesota case underscores the importance of carefully thinking through all the potential implications of "moving" your family to a new location — including state income taxes.

Between 1994 and 1996, Minneapolis insurance executive R. Austin Chapman contributed some $1.6 million to a donor-advised fund based in Massachusetts. (A donor-advised fund is a charity that accepts contributions, creates a "fund" in the name of the donor, then makes grants from the fund to other public charities, usually acting in response to the donor's nonbinding recommendations.) Beginning in 1997, acting on Mr. Chapman's recommendations, the donor-advised fund made a number of grants from his account to charities located in Minnesota. The Minnesota Tax Court held that contributions to this out-of-state charity were not deductible for purposes of the Minnesota alternative minimum tax (AMT), even though the funds in question

---

[36] Private operating foundations are defined in IRC § 4942(j)(3).

[37] *See* IRC § 170(b)(1)(E)(ii).

[38] *See* IRC § 170(b)(1)(E)(iii).

[39] *See* § 2.06 *infra.*

were eventually distributed to Minnesota charities. This may seem like a complex technicality, but the result for Mr. Chapman was a $145,000 tax bill.

This decision of the Minnesota Tax Court was subsequently affirmed by the Minnesota Supreme Court, in a somewhat confusing decision. The Supreme Court agreed with the Chapmans that the statute limiting deductible contributions to in-state charities was unconstitutional (violating the Commerce Clause of the U.S. Constitution), but found that it lacked authority to allow the Chapmans' deductions. Instead, it sent the case back to the Minnesota Tax Court for further action.

Although this case did not involve a foundation, the implications for foundation gifts were obvious. For a Minnesota resident who moved a Minnesota-based family foundation to Florida or some other vacation/retirement home, the result could be equally extreme. The moral: Do not jump to the conclusion that a foundation should be relocated without considering all the potential problems under the law of the destination state.

> **Note:** Minnesota has since taken steps to eliminate this AMT problem. Effective for 2002 and later years, Minnesota law allows an AMT charitable deduction for all charitable gifts to either Minnesota or non-Minnesota charities, but only to the extent that the total charitable deduction exceeds 1.3 percent of federal adjusted gross income. Subsequently, the Minnesota Department of Revenue issued Revenue Notice 03-03, allowing individual taxpayers an AMT deduction for charitable contributions made to non-Minnesota charities in earlier tax years.

Is this just a Minnesota problem? Frankly, that is a question you will have to address to a knowledgeable tax professional in the state or states where you or your donor pay state income taxes. If your state tax law does include a similar tax trap (or any other provision affecting deductions for contributions to family foundations), we invite you to let us know so that we may share your thoughts with other readers.

§ 2.04   FACTORS TO CONSIDER WHEN CREATING A FAMILY FOUNDATION

A donor generally understands why he or she creates a family foundation: there are the income, gift, and estate tax benefits; the foundation serves as a perpetual representative of the family in the community; and the grantor's family can continue to control the distribution of funds after contribution. However, few donors move beyond the benefits of creation to consider what happens after the foundation is created. The decision to create the foundation should be based on a careful review of issues related to its size, the donor's commitment to management, the donor's goals in its creation, and the ability to discharge administrative responsibilities.

[A] Size

The ultimate size of the foundation is an important consideration in deciding to create a family foundation or to make an alternative form of charitable gift. Although there is no minimum size prescribed by law, the costs of administration and the need for substantive dollars for grantmaking suggest a minimum size of $1 million and a recommended size of $5 million or more.

Many foundations are dramatically larger. One familiar family foundation — the Bill and Melinda Gates Foundation in Seattle, Washington — reported assets of $28.8 billion at the end of calendar year 2004.[40] The Gateses have steadily funded the Foundation during their lives and will add assets at their deaths.[41] The size of the Foundation and funds available for distribution have allowed the Gates Foundation to make substantial contributions to libraries, global health projects, vaccine development, and other areas of personal interest. Grants in 2004 totalled 1.26 billion and ranged from a grant of $10,000 to one for $50 million.[42] The scale of the Foundation's grantmaking means the Gateses can create significant positive results for targeted projects. And while the Foundation spent $68.3 million on program and administrative expenses in 2004, this figure was only 4.51 percent of the $1.26 billion in grants and $25.3 million in direct charitable expenses paid by the Foundation in that year.[43]

In contrast, consider the grantmaking of a fictitious $10,000 foundation, the Blanchard Family Foundation. The distribution requirement for the Blanchard Foundation is only $500 per year. While there are many charities that would appreciate a grant of $100 or even the full $500, the foundation cannot make a short-term or long-term impact with such limited funds. In addition, the Blanchards should expect to spend $5,000 or more to create the foundation, to file Form 1023 to qualify the Foundation as a tax-exempt entity, and to order the basic stationery, envelopes, and office supplies. The Foundation may then spend up to $1,500 or more each year for tax return preparation, investment management, and other administrative costs. As a practical matter, such expenditures do not make economic sense for an entity funded with $10,000 because these costs represent a drain on earnings and funds available for grants. The family should consider one of the alternatives to a family foundation that are discussed in more detail later in this chapter.[44]

---

[40] Bill and Melinda Gates Foundation, *www.gatesfoundation.org*.

[41] The Gates Foundation's financials, posted on the web site at *www.gatesfoundation.org,* show contributions of $5 billion in 2000, $1.18 billion in 2001, $82.5 million in 2002, $81.9 million in 2003, and $711.4 million in 2004.

[42] *www.gatesfoundation.org/.*

[43] *Id.*

[44] *See* § 2.05 *infra.*

[B]   Commitment

A second consideration in creating a foundation is the willingness to make a commitment to the process and to the perpetual nature of the foundation. Foundations cost money to create, to manage, and to disassemble. They also require the donor's attention on an ongoing basis. Therefore, foundations are best suited for individuals who want to create a long-term or perpetual grantmaking mechanism and for those who are willing to commit the time and resources for that period. In short, the donor should balance the desire to maintain control of grants for himself or herself, and for family that follows, with the time and effort required to keep a foundation operating effectively, efficiently, and legally.

These comments should not imply foundations cannot be created for a term. For example, John M. Olin created the John M. Olin foundation in 1953 with the goal that the foundation—which had assets of $118 million at one point and funded conservative research and causes—would be distributed within a generation. Following the death of Mr. Olin's wife, the foundation distributed its assets and closed its doors in December 2005. In this case, the commitment was for a generation extending 52 years.[45]

[C]   Goals

Take the time to ensure that the donor articulates his or her goals in creating the foundation. Too often foundations are recommended to donors without an honest assessment of the donor's objectives. The checklist found in Table 2-2 provides a way to identify specific objectives that point to creation of a family foundation. Donors who enjoy the idea of a named charitable entity, but who have no interest in handling the details of administration, may be best served by another giving option.

TABLE 2-2
Goal Checklist Indicating Need for Family Foundation

Objective	Indicates Private Foundation	Indicates Alternative to Private Foundation
You want to create a permanent fund for charitable giving.	X	
You want to create a temporary fund (less than 10 years) for charitable giving.		X

---

[45] For more information on the John M. Olin Foundation's termination, see the foundation profile on the International Relation Center's Right Web, <http://rightweb.irc-online.org/profile/653>, the funder profile on Media Transparency's website at <http://www.mediatransparency.org/funderprofile.php?funderID=7>, and Roger William's article, Sustaining Ideas on the Right, in Foundation News and Commentary (Vol. 47, No. 1, January/February 2006), <http://www.nationalreview.com/miller/miller200504060758.asp>.

TABLE 2-2. CONTINUED

Objective	Indicates Private Foundation	Indicates Alternative to Private Foundation
You and your family want to be actively involved in the decision making on distributions to be made from the charitable fund.	X	
You prefer to have others who are more qualified make decisions on how funds are spent.		X
You intend to have staff or advisors who can file the necessary tax returns and public disclosure forms.	X	
You intend to fund the foundation at a level of $1,000,000 or greater and to add to it over time.	X	
You do not anticipate the foundation size exceeding $1,000,000.		X
Your family members want to be involved in the initial year of operation; after that, they prefer that someone else take care of administration and grant making.		X
Either you or your family wants to continue to be involved in foundation management for as long as possible.	X	

[D] Administration

Foundations must answer to a variety of observers, including the IRS, the state attorney general, and the general public. This means that there are a variety of administrative duties for which the foundation manager is responsible. These duties are listed below and described in greater detail in Chapter 8.

1. *Tax filings.* Perhaps the most obvious duty is to file an annual tax return, the Form 990-PF, and related returns where necessary.

2. *Filings with the state attorney general.* Copies of the annual 990-PF must generally be filed with the state attorney general. The office may require additional filings as well.

3. *Public disclosure.* The law requires that private foundations share copies of Form 1023 (the document filed for tax-exempt status), the 990-PFs for the last three years, and the names and addresses of the donors.

4. *Grantmaking.* Grantmaking is one of the most interesting and the most burdensome aspects of foundation management. Grant recipients must be qualified; files must be built to document grantmaking. Receipt and use of the funds must be verified. While many of these functions can be outsourced to third parties, the foundation board is responsible for ensuring that grants are handled responsibly.

5. *Investment management.* The foundation board is responsible for effective and responsible management of the assets of the foundation.

6. *Structural management.* There is a certain amount of energy required to ensure that the board operates in an effective manner. Board members must be contacted for meetings, assembled for committees, and receive copies of minutes, tax filings, and investment statements. New members must be selected periodically and educated about the work of the foundation.

While any or all of these duties can be assigned to third parties, the foundation board is responsible for ensuring that these duties are handled correctly and on a timely basis. This means that the foundation board must meet regularly to receive reports of activities and that it must review and report those activities. There is no reason to take on these responsibilities without a strong desire to make decisions on the grants to be made from the foundation.

[E] Stock Market Declines May Pose Special Difficulties for Some Family Foundations

When stock values decline substantially over prior years' levels, some family foundations may encounter an unexpected tax problem on top of their investment losses. Here is how this dilemma arises.

When a foundation's investment assets decline in value, its grantmaking capacity is often impaired as a result. When significant declines are experienced, this effect can be quite dramatic. For example, a foundation that has experienced a 50 percent drop in the value of its assets will find it difficult to continue making grants in the same amounts as it did when it had twice the assets. For some foundations, however, it is not just enough to maintain existing grant levels. Foundations that seek to qualify for a reduced rate of tax on their investment income under IRC § 4940 must increase their charitable distributions over prior distribution levels.

Under the general rule, a foundation must pay an excise tax amounting to two percent of its net investment income. A special rule added in 1986 provides a reduced rate of one percent for a foundation that meets certain requirements. One of those requirements is that its current charitable distributions must at least equal the sum of (1) its current assets multiplied by its average percentage payout over the last five taxable years, plus (2) one percent of its current year's net investment income. Thus, in effect, relief is available only if the foundation maintains the same percentage rate of distributions and pays out an amount equal to the tax relief to be achieved. A foundation that has been using this rule to reduce its tax is thus choosing to apply its resources to make charitable distributions rather than to pay tax. When asset levels decline, however, this choice becomes more difficult, as shown in the example below.

This is unfortunate, since it has the effect of penalizing a foundation that has taken the constructive approach of making distributions to charity at a level consistently higher than the five percent minimum. When asset levels decline, the financially prudent step may be to curtail grants, but this will cause a higher tax liability for foundations that have been qualifying for the one percent rate. This effect will obviously be greater for larger foundations, for which the one percent tax savings can be a significant amount. The bottom line effect of this tax "benefit" is to penalize a foundation that has already established a record of distributing more than the minimum amount required vis-È-vis a comparably situated foundation that has distributed the five percent minimum.

It is worth noting that legislation pending in Congress would help eliminate this problem by simplifying the present two-tier tax on foundation investment income to impose a flat one percent rate on all foundations, regardless of their distributions to charity. These provisions are being considered by Congress as this goes to press in 2006.

Example: The Ambitious Foundation currently has investment assets amounting to $1 million, and its net investment income for the year is expected to total $50,000. Five years ago, when its assets were in the $4 million range, it adopted a policy of paying out charitable distributions equal to six percent of assets, or about $240,000 annually, and made grant commitments in that amount. For each of the five preceding taxable years, it has honored those commitments and distributed $240,000 annually. As the value of its assets declined over that period, but grants continued at the same level, its percentage payouts increased as indicated below:

Year	Grants	Assets	Percentage Payout
1	$240,000	$4,000,000	6.0%
2	240,000	3,750,000	6.4%
3	240,000	3,000,000	8.0%
4	240,000	3,000,000	8.0%
5	240,000	2,000,000	12.0%

Thus, for the preceding five-year period the foundation's average percentage payout was 8.08 percent. By maintaining its grantmaking level at the same rate for five years notwithstanding the declining market value of its investments, The Ambitious Foundation has greatly increased its percentage payout. This in turn increases the amount it must distribute to reduce its excise tax on investment income to one percent for the current year. Despite the 75 percent reduction in assets it has suffered over the last five years, The Ambitious Foundation must make charitable distributions of at least $81,300, computed as follows, to lower its tax by qualifying for the one percent rate for Year 6:

(1)   Average percentage payout of 8.08% $80,800
        × $1,000,000 current assets =

PLUS

(2)   1% of current year's net investment income   500
        1% of $50,000 =

        Total distribution required = $81,300

Since its anticipated investment income for Year 6 is only $100,000 in any event, the tax saving achieved by distributing this amount is only $500. Is it financially worthwhile for The Ambitious Foundation to distribute at the 8.13 percent level to save only $500? Alternatively, would it be better off paying the full $1,000 in tax but distributing only $50,000 (the five percent minimum amount)? Only its board of directors can make that determination, but one can certainly understand that the board may decide to save the foundation's assets by reducing the distributions to $50,000 for Year 6 so that it will be more likely to have a sufficient asset base for future years' distributions.

§ 2.05   ALTERNATIVES TO THE FAMILY FOUNDATION

[A]   In General

A family considering a family foundation should be aware of other alternatives that could be well suited for its particular situation. All of these devices allow the family to conduct a program of charitable contributions or similar activities. Whatever the proponents of a particular alternative approach may contend, however, remember that only a foundation will give the family complete and unrestricted control over its charitable program. This may be an important consideration, as many people who create a family foundation do so at least in part out of a desire to retain continued dominion over their charitable contributions.

Some of these alternatives are simpler and more economical than family foundations, and these should be carefully considered where relatively small amounts of money are to be devoted to the project or where costs are a factor for other reasons. Typically, for situations of this type, the trade-off is one between the control offered by a foundation and the economy of the alternative device. Other alternatives, such as the supporting organization, are no less expensive to create and operate, but offer freedom from the self-dealing rules and other private foundation restrictions. Still others use the foundation format, but qualify for special, more liberal income tax treatment for contributions.

Clients sometimes go to a lawyer or other advisor with a very specific request: "I want to create a family foundation." In such a situation, the advisor should be prepared to discuss the alternatives and, where appropriate, advise the client that one of the other alternatives would be a better fit.

[B] Outright Contributions

If the family envisions its proposed foundation simply as a means for providing contributions to other charitable organizations, it should consider carefully whether the foundation is necessary or desirable at all. Perhaps the same effect could be accomplished simply by making direct contributions to such other organizations in lieu of the family foundation.

We have already discussed a number of reasons why the foundation might be desired, and the family should consider how important these reasons are to them. Once funds are contributed to the charity, the donor necessarily gives up control and dominion over the contribution. It may be possible for the donor to enter into a gift agreement with the donee organization that specifies how the funds will be used, what reports will be given, and so on, but the security provided by such an agreement is probably less effective than the ongoing ability of foundation to advance and withhold funds. Nevertheless, direct contributions may be preferable in some situations.

[C] Donor-Advised Funds

[1] In General

One charitable gift device that closely resembles a private foundation in many respects is the *donor-advised fund*. This is an arrangement with a publicly supported charitable organization that allows an individual or family to establish a fund from which distributions will be made to other charitable organizations. For tax purposes, the donor has made a gift to the public charity sponsoring the fund. Because that donee is a public charity, such a gift qualifies for the most favorable tax treatment possible.

The donor and his or her family retain only the right to make nonbinding recommendations or give advice to the sponsoring charity as to how their fund will be applied. The sponsoring charity is free to accept or reject that advice, and the donor is thus left with no real legal control over his or her fund. As a practical matter, the donor's advice is typically followed unless the recommended grantees are not properly qualified organizations, but this may not satisfy the donor who wants to call the shots personally, without consulting with or advising anyone else. This is offset to some extent by a principal advantage of the donor-advised fund: All administrative matters — such as record keeping, preparation of checks, tax returns, and so on — are handled by the sponsoring charity. Thus, there is no expense to the donor for such items, and the donor need not be bothered.

The defining characteristic of the donor-advised fund is the requirement that the donor not have control over contributed funds. If control is necessary to a particular donor, the family foundation remains the vehicle of choice. With this important exception, however, the donor-advised fund can offer many of the advantages of a private foundation. Where a relatively small foundation is envisioned, including eventual bequests and contributions as well as immediate funding, the donor should consider a donor-advised fund as a more efficient and economical means of proceeding. What amount is "relatively small" for this purpose?[46]

[2] In a Community Foundation

Traditionally, community foundations have been the principal suppliers of donor-advised funds, and virtually every community foundation offers this option. We can include within this group all organizations such as United Jewish Appeal (UJA) affiliates and other similar units serving nongeographic communities. Most community foundations offer grantmaking assistance to their donor-advised funds as well as insight into charitable needs in the community. A particular donor may or may not welcome such grantmaking assistance, but the community foundation's familiarity with prospective grantee organizations can help the donor avoid mistakes and accomplish the desired goals more easily.

Some community foundations have operating rules that limit the types of grantees to which distributions may be made from donor-advised funds. For example, geographical restrictions may apply, so that all distributions must be made within the community served by the foundation. Grants to individuals may or may not be permitted. The potential impact of any such restrictions can and should be ascertained by a donor who is considering the creation of a donor-advised fund at a community foundation. In this manner, the donor can make certain that his or her anticipated grantees are permissible under the governing rules.

[3] Other Sponsors

In recent years, donor-advised funds have been offered by public charities beyond the traditional community foundation/UJA sponsors. A number of traditional charities, such as colleges and universities, churches, and the like, now offer such funds as a service to their donor constituencies. It is not unusual for such funds to have restrictions requiring that at least some minimum portion (e.

---

[46] *See* § 2.07, "The Standby Foundation," for a discussion of this question.

g., one-half) of all distributions from the donor-advised funds maintained by the charity be distributed to that charity or some affiliated entity.

Another new type of charitable entity has grown rapidly in popularity in the last few years—the commercially sponsored donor-advised fund or, as it is sometimes called, "gift fund." These funds are typically formed by a mutual fund group or similar financial institution. One such entity, the Fidelity Charitable Gift Fund, has become one of the largest charitable organizations, in the United States in terms of contributions received. Commercially sponsored donor-advised funds may offer some grantmaking assistance to donors, but their principal selling point is that they function much like a private foundation, but at a lower cost, and provide all the tax benefits available for contributions to a public charity. Because they do not have other charitable operations of the sort conducted by a community foundation, university, or other donor-advised fund sponsor, gift funds may be less likely to question a donor's advice or otherwise attempt to exert influence. Whatever the differences may be in a particular situation, these entities are like the similar funds offered by community foundations in that they cannot provide the unlimited donor control that is inherent in a private foundation.

Nevertheless, with this important exception in mind, it can be seen that the donor-advised fund offers the tax advantages of a public charity, external administration, and involvement (if not control) by the donor's family. If desired, the family can institute grantmaking procedures comparable to those outlined in Chapter 7 to determine what grantee organizations to recommend to the donor-advised fund sponsor. In this fashion, younger family members can be involved in the process, and the family can realize most of the nontax benefits that a foundation would provide. The major difference is that the grants would be made by "The Simpson Family Fund of the Amalgamated Gift Fund," rather than "The Simpson Family Foundation." That distinction may or may not be important to the family, and only the family can make that determination. Whatever choice is ultimately made, the donor-advised fund should be carefully considered by the family contemplating a foundation.

> **Caution:** There are some donor-advised funds with a national scope that purport to offer exceptionally broad programs and an ability to make grants that other organizations would decline to make. These are not affiliated with any major financial institution or firm, and may have names suggesting a patriotic focus. Some of these permit donors to use their fund accounts to pay themselves or their family members for their charitable volunteer work, or to take deductible vacation trips under the guise of investigating potential grantees. They may suggest that they can channel contributions to entities that are precluded from receiving tax-deductible contributions (foreign organizations or noncharitable entities, for example), thereby circumventing the applicable rules. These should be approached with caution. As our mothers told us, anything that sounds too good to be true

is quite likely to be so. As this goes to press, legislation is pending in Congress to provide clearer guidance for all donor-advised funds and to rein in these aggressive organizations.

[D] Supporting Organization

When Congress created the present tax rules governing private foundations in 1969, it had to define the various categories of charitable entities that would be subject to those rules. Public charities — colleges, churches, publicly supported entities, and the like — were viewed as not needing the special scrutiny these rules produce, so these categories were excluded. The necessary involvement of the public in charities of this type was viewed as providing sufficient checks and balances to avoid the abuses with which Congress was concerned. A university, for example, is subject to scrutiny by its alumni, students, and the interested public, one or more of whom will be likely to call attention to any improper actions attempted by the university administration. By contrast, Congress concluded that purely private entities (i.e., private foundations) had no such public oversight, so they were viewed as needing the oversight the new rules provided.

Those extremes at one end of the scale or the other left some organizations in the middle. They had a special relationship with one or more charities, but were still formed and funded by private individuals outside the charities. Congress decided in 1969 that an entity of this sort would be allowed to qualify as a public charity, but only if its relationship with its beneficiary organization(s) was sufficiently close and it was not "controlled" by private interests. These entities are known as *supporting organizations* and are described in section 509(a)(3) of the Internal Revenue Code. A more complete technical discussion of the requirements for qualification as a supporting organization is included in Appendix 2-A.

For our purposes, it is sufficient to think of the supporting organization as a charitable entity that is closely involved with one or more publicly supported charities in one way or another. In some cases, the board of directors of the supporting organization is appointed by its beneficiary public charity (known as the *supported organization*) or is appointed in the same manner as the governing board of the supported organization. In other cases, the board of the supporting organization is selected in some other manner involving less direct control and supervision by the supported organization. Where such a relationship exists, the supporting organization is said to be "operated in connection with" its supported organization(s). It is this latter sort of supporting organization arrangement that is often proposed as a substitute for a family foundation.

The names used in this context can be confusing, so much so that the casual observer may wonder if confusion is a part of the program. The type of supporting organization that operates on this basis has been called "entrepreneurial," "Type 3" (because it is the third of the three types of supporting organizations described in the Treasury Regulations), "Category Two" (because it is different from the other two varieties, which the IRS lumps together as Category One organizations in its publication on this topic),[47] and simply a supporting organization "operated in connection with" its supported organization. This confusion will not be compounded here because here we will be discussing *only* this type of supporting organization.

This type of supporting organization, which is "operated in connection with" the public charity it supports, remains a strong alternative to the family foundation in practice. Because this "Type 3 (or III)" supporting organization has the least restrictive relationship with its supported entity, it has more appeal to the client who wishes to remain as independent as possible.

The technical requirements for qualification of this sort of supporting organization are set forth below and in Appendix 2-A in detail, and it should be evident that problems may be encountered where the creator of such an entity seeks to retain excessive influence over it. Where this occurs, and a donor is found to "control" the organization, it cannot qualify as a supporting organization. Under Code § 509(a)(3)(C), one of the three tests for qualification as a Type 3 supporting organization is that it "is not controlled directly or indirectly by one or more disqualified persons . . . other than foundation managers and other than one or more [public charities]."

This control issue and other qualification questions for supporting organizations have become a serious issue for supporting organizations, and several different steps are being taken to block abuses in their use. There have been reports of various abuses in which donors form supporting organizations in order to avoid the restrictions applicable to private foundations, but operate them in an inappropriate manner. For example, one widely reported scheme involved donors who contributed appreciated property to such organizations, sold it, and then borrowed the proceeds back from the organization.

As one might expect, the result of these reports has been subject to heightened scrutiny. As this goes to press, legislation originating in the Senate Finance Committee staff would impose an array of new restrictions and limitations on supporting organizations. The reader is cautioned to check the status of that legislation before attempting to evaluate a supporting organization.

In addition, The IRS has an audit initiative underway, and the regulations defining supporting organizations are reportedly being reexamined. Moreover, as discussed below, several recent cases have taken a strict view of the applicable requirements. As a result, the Type 3 supporting organization should be approached with caution until these legislative and administrative actions have reached a point where the outcome is evident.

Some of these issues were addressed by the Internal Revenue Service in its Exempt Organizations Continuing Professional Education Text for Fiscal 2001, Topic G, "Control and Power: Issues Involving Supporting Organizations, Donor

---

[47] *See* IRS Publication 557 (5-97), *Tax-Exempt Status for Your Organization*, and Appendix 2-A, which is adapted therefrom.

TABLE 2-3

SOCHECK

(CHECKSHEET QUESTIONNAIRE FOR IRC 509(a)(3) SUPPORTING ORGANIZATIONS DETERMINATIONS)

<u>Selected Regs.; Readings; and Notes</u>

Legend

SO = Supporting Organization
    SO1 = "operated, supervised or controlled by" SO
    SO2 = "supervised or controlled in connection with" SO
    SO3 = "operated in connection with" SO
SD = Supported Organization described in IRC 509(a)(1) or (2)
DP = Disqualified Person
    ("s" for plural form; e.g., "SOs, "SDs")

[Caveat: SOCHECK may not include and/or sketch all possible facts and circumstances tests. Please refer to the Regulations.]

Note: SOCHECK contains <u>5</u> parts. <u>All</u> SO applicants must satisfy <u>all</u> parts.

1. THRESHOLD REQUIREMENT

2001 CPE Topic G. <u>Note:</u>
No exemption for organizations primarily operated to carry on UTB for unrelated SDs.

A. Is the SO claiming IRC 501(c)(3) status, organized and operated exclusively for charitable purposes?

(1) [ ] Yes—go to Part 2
(2) [ ] No—Organization is not eligible for SO status.

B. Is trust entity SO, not claiming IRC 501(c)(3) status, described in IRC 4947(a)(1)?

Rev. Proc. 72-50

(1) [ ] Yes—go to Part 2
(2) [ ] No—Organization is not eligible for SO status.

2. RELATIONSHIP TESTS. . . . [Including relationships with IRC 501(c)(4), (c)(5), or (c)(6) entities treated like IRC 509(a)(2)s]

A. Is the SO a SO1?

(1) Do the SD(s) officials select a majority of Directors or Trustees of SO?

Reg. 1.509(a)-4(g)

    a. [ ] Yes—go to Part 3
    b. [ ] No—go to B.

B. Is the SO a SO2?

Reg. 1.509(a)-4(h)

(1) is control of the management of the SO vested in the same persons who control or manage the SD(s)?
    a. [ ] Yes—go directly to Part 3
    b. [ ] No—go to C.

Reg. 1.509(a)-4(i)

C. Is the SO a SO3 because it meets <u>both</u> the **Responsiveness test** (in either (1) or (2) below) <u>and</u> the **Integral Part test** (in (3) below)?

Reg. 1.509(a)-4(i)(2)(ii)

(1) <u>Responsiveness test</u>—The SO must meet a, b, <u>or</u> c <u>and</u> also must meet item d <u>OR</u> meet <u>Alternative Responsiveness</u> test at (2) below.

   a. Do the officers, directors, trustees, or membership of the SDs elect or appoint one or more of the officers, directors o trustees of the SO? <u>Or</u>
   b. Are one or more members of the governing bodies of the SDs also officers, directors or trustees or hold other important offices of the SO? <u>Or</u>
   c. Do officers, directors or trustees of the SO maintain a close and continuous working relationship with the officers, directors, or trustees of the SDs?

   <u>AND</u>

In <u>Windsor Foundation</u>, 77-2 USTC 9709, Tax Court held that SO failed Responsiveness Test for failure to meet (d). 1982 CPE, p. 28.

   d. By reason of the relationship described above, does the SD have a significant voice in the SO's investment policies, timing of grants, manner of making grants, and selection of recipients of grants, etc.?

      i. [ ] Yes—go to (3)
      ii. [ ] No—go to (2)

(2) <u>Alternative Responsiveness test</u>—If Responsiveness test (1) above is not met, the organization must meet a, b, <u>and</u> c below.

Reg. 1.509(a)-4(I)(2)(iii) <u>Note</u>: More common for SO to meet (2) than (1).

   a. Is the SO a charitable trust under State law or an entity treated as a trust)? <u>and</u>
   b. Is each specified SD(s) a named beneficiary under the SO's governing instrument? <u>and</u>

1982 CPE, p. 29.

   c. Do the specified SD(s) have the power to enforce the trust and compel an accounting under State law?

      i. [ ] Yes—go to (3).
      ii. [ ] No—organization fails to meet SO3 relationship test

(3) <u>Integral Part test</u>—The SO must meet requirement a <u>or</u> b below.

1997 EO CPE, Topic I; IRM 7.8.3 (5.2)

Reg. 1.509(a)-4(i)(3)(ii) <u>Note</u>: "FS Test" rarely satisfied. Grantmaking not considered supportive enough. TAM 9730002. Grant making to other public charities <u>may</u> be supportive if SD is a community trust. G.C.M. 38417. 1997 CPE, p. 108.

   a. The <u>"Functional Support" test</u>. Does the SO engage <u>in activities</u>, not including grant making, for or on behalf of SD(s) which perform the functions of or carry out purposes of the SD(s) and which the SD(s) would otherwise normally undertake, but for the involvement of the SO?

      i. [ ] Yes—go to Part 3.
      ii. [ ] No—go to b

   <u>OR</u>

b. The "Attentiveness" test: Requires satisfaction of tests i;
    ii(a), (b), or (c); and iii, below.

Reg. 1.509(a)-4(i)(3)(iii)
Note: Most SO3s meet this test
because they distribute to SDs.

(i). Does the SO make payments of substantially all (85%) of its
      income (including short term capital gain) to or for the use
      of the designated SD(s)? and

IRM 7.8.3 (5.2.4.2)

G.C.M. 36379

(ii). (a). Does the SO's support of the SD (within the meaning of
            IRC 509(d)) constitute at least 10% of the SD's total support?
            (Or, if SO supports multiple SDs, 10% of the total support o
            one of the SDs?) or

Note: See Reg. 1.509(a)-
4(i)(3)(iii) examples; G.C.M.
36326 looks favorably on
significant program with 50%
SO support.

(b). Does the SO earmark its support for a significant
      particular program or activity of the SD and, if so, can the
      SO demonstrate that if its funding of such program or
      activity is discontinued, the SDs operation of such program
      or activity will be interrupted?

Reg. 1.509(a)-4(i)(3)(iii)(d);
G.C.M. 36379
Note: New organizations do
not have a history. Special
5 year rule with H & C at
Reg. 1.509(a)-4(i)(1)(iii);
1982 CPE, p. 32.

(c). Is the SD attentive based on all pertinent facts and
      circumstances often involving a historic and continuing
      relationship?

and

G.C.M. 36326

(iii) Does the SO's support which meets (ii) above, consistently
      constitute 33 1/3% of the SO's total support?

(a) [ ] Yes — go to Part 3.
(b) [ ] No — organization fails SO3 test.

3. ORGANIZATIONAL TEST

Reg. 1.509(a)-4(c)(1). IRM
7.8.3 (5.3)

A. Does the SO's organization instrument limit its purposes to
    those for the benefit of, to perform the functions of, or to carry
    out the purposes of one or more specified SDs, and does not
    expressly empower the SO to engage in activities which are not
    in furtherance of such purposes?

    (1) Are purposes limited appropriately?

         a. [ ] Yes — go to (2).
         b. [ ] No — organization fails Organizational Test

    (2) Do SO1s, SO2s, and SO3s meet specificity requirements?

         a. SO1s and SO2s — Are beneficiary SDs specified or or
Reg. 1.509(a)-4(d)(2)(iii);   designated by class or purpose in governing instrument?
Special community trust rule–
Rev. Rul. 81-43
             (i) [ ] Yes — go to c.
             (ii) [ ] No — Is there an historic and continuing
                  relationship with the SD? If yes, go to c
Reg. 1.509(a)-4(d)(2)(iv);   Otherwise, SO fails the organization test.
IRM 7.8.3 (5.4.3)
         b. Specificity requirements for SO3s — Are SDs specified by
             name?

             (i) [ ] Yes — go to c.
             (ii) [ ] No — SO fails organization test.

c. <u>Governing Instrument Provisions</u>—Are there governing instrument provisions involving substitutions, etc.? If so, are there conflicts with the specificity requirements?

SO1s & SO2s—Reg. 1.509(a)-4(d)(3); SO3s—Reg. 1.509(a)-4(d)(4) IRM. 7.8.3 (5.3); 2001 CPE, Topic G.

(i) If there are no conflicts, SO meets Organization Test Go to 4. If there are conflicts, SO does not meet Organization Test.

4. OPERATIONAL TEST

A. Is the SO operated exclusively for the benefit of, to perform the functions of, or carry out the purposes of one or more specified SDs?

Reg. 1.509(a)-4(e)(I); IRM 7.8.3 (5.5); 2001 CPE, Topic G.

(1) Does the SO support or benefit only the specified SDs meeting the Organization Test in 3 above?

a. [ ] Yes—go on to (2)
b. [ ] No—organization fails Operational Test.

Special permissible activities include fundraising, alumni activity, etc. Reg. 1.509(a)-4(e)(2); 1982 CPE, p. 36.

(2) Does SO support or benefit SD through disbursements to SD or other permissible activities?

a. [ ] Yes—go on to 5.
b. [ ] No—SO fails Operational Test

5. CONTROL TEST—Often the Most Critical Factor

A. Is the SO controlled directly or indirectly by DPs other than foundation managers and other than one or more SDs?

Reg. 1.509(a)-4(j); 2000 CPE, p. 222; 2001 CPE, Topic G; IRM 7.8.3 (5.6)

(1) <u>SO1s and SO2s</u>

By nature of meeting these relationship tests, SOs are generally controlled by the SDs. There should be an analysis to discover whether SDs select or designate SO board members that may be DPs, for a reason in addition to being foundation managers, or are connected to DPs through family or economic associations. Otherwise go to (3).

(2) <u>SO3s</u>

DP power to annually designate charitable recipients is control. Rev. Rul. 80-305.

a. Do DPs control SO?

(i) <u>Directly</u> through majority presence on the Board, or positions of authority, veto power, etc.?

(ii) <u>Indirectly,</u> through board nomination process, or manipulation of board structure, or through presence of board members or persons of authority that have family or economic association with DPs?

Rev. Rul. 80-207

(iii) Indirectly, through control of SO assets or other facts and circumstances?

[ ] If Yes, SO fails Control Test.
[ ] If No, go to (3).

(3) If SO1 or SO2 or SO3 is not controlled by DPs, Control Test is met and if all SOCHECK parts have been met, SO qualifies as a IRC 509(a)(3).

SOs may not support IRC
509(a)(3) but see G.C.M. 39508.
2% rule — Reg. 1.170A-9(e)(6)(i).
Domestic Government entity is
a good SD- IRC 170(b)(1)(A)(v);
G.C. 36523; foreign
nongovernment SD is o.k. Rev.
Rul. 74-229; Rev. Proc. 92-94.
Lobby election restriction — IRC
501(h)(4)(F); 1997 CPE, p. 126.

COLLATERAL NOTES:

1. There should be a representation that SD organization is a valid IRC 501(c)(3) and IRC 509(a)(1) (including a government entity) or 509(a)(2) organization. Note that an IRC 509(a)(3) is not excepted from the 2 percent source limit for IRC 170(b)(1)(A)(vi), thus, SO support may affect the public charity status of its SD.
2. SOs that support an IRC 501(c)(4), (c)(5), or (c)(6) can not make the lobbying election under IRC 501(h).
3. ALL 509(a)(3)s are subject to IRC 6104(d) disclosure rules.

Advised Funds, and Disqualified Person Financial Institutions" (CPE), available on the IRS website, *www.irs.gov*). A complete discussion of supporting organizations is beyond the scope of this book, but the interested reader is referred to this CPE Text for a full discussion of current issues as viewed by the Internal Revenue Service. Of particular interest is the "SOCheck" Checklist developed by the IRS National Office Exempt Organizations Unit for use by its personnel in determining whether organizations qualify as supporting organizations. This checklist is set forth below as Table 2-3.

There is a good reason why the Type 3 of supporting organization is often discussed as an alternative to the private foundation. As described above, this relationship requires a looser and less direct connection between the supporting organization(s) and the organization it supports than the other varieties of supporting organizations. This in turn suggests a lesser degree of supervision by the supported organization(s). It is for this reason that the Regulations go into far more detail in describing this relationship than for the other types of supporting organizations. The following discussion will summarize the requirements they impose on this type of supporting organization.

First, the Regulations impose a *responsiveness test* to ensure that the beneficiary organizations will be able to influence the activities of the supporting organization.[48] This may be met in either of several ways:

1. The officers, directors, trustees, or membership of the supported organization(s) may either select one or more officers, directors, or trustees of the supporting organization or may actually serve in such capacity themselves or hold other important offices in the supporting organization.[49] Or, even more indirect, the officers, directors, or trustees of the supporting

---

[48] *See* Reg. § 1.509(a)-4(i)(1)(i).
[49] Reg. § 1.509(a)-4(i)(2)(ii).

organization may merely "maintain a close and continuous working relationship with the officers, directors, or trustees of the publicly supported organizations."[50] Whichever approach is used, the result must be that "the officers, directors or trustees of the publicly supported organizations have a significant voice in the investment policies of the supporting organization, the timing of grants, the manner of making them, and the selection of recipients by such supporting organization, and in otherwise directing the use of the income or assets of such supporting organization."[51]

2. Alternatively, the responsiveness test will be met where the supporting organization is a charitable trust under state law, with each beneficiary organization being specifically named in the governing instrument of the trust and each named beneficiary organization having the power to enforce the trust and to compel an accounting under state law.[52]

Second, the Regulations impose an *integral part test* to ensure that a supporting organization that is "operated in connection with" its beneficiary organization(s) maintains a "significant involvement" in the operations of its beneficiary organization and that the beneficiary or supported organizations in turn are dependent upon the supporting organization for the type of support it provides them.[53] Here, again, as with the responsiveness test, there are two alternatives for satisfying this test:[54]

1. The supporting organization may support its beneficiary organizations by conducting activities that would otherwise normally be undertaken by the beneficiary organizations themselves.[55]

2. In the alternative, the integral part test may be satisfied if the supporting organization pays substantially all (85 percent) of its income to or for the use of one or more of its beneficiary organizations *and* if the amount of support received by one or more of such beneficiary organizations is sufficient to ensure their attentiveness to the operations of the supporting organization.[56] (If this alternative is used, the support received by the supported organization must represent a sufficiently large part of the its total support so as to ensure such attentiveness.)

---

[50] Reg. § 1.509(a)-4(i)(2)(ii)(c).
[51] Reg. § 1.509(a)-4(i)(2)(ii)(d).
[52] Reg. § 1.509(a)-4(i)(2)(iii).
[53] Reg. § 1.509(a)-4(i)(3)(i).
[54] Reg. § 1.509(a)-4(i)(3).
[55] Reg. § 1.509(a)-4(i)(3)(ii).
[56] Reg. § 1.509(a)-4(i)(3)(iii)(a).

Several recent cases have rejected organizations' claims to qualify as so-called Type 3 supporting organizations "operated in connection with" the public charities they supported. In late 2002, the Tax Court issued not just one but two important cases on this point, and one has already been affirmed on appeal. In both cases the Tax Court found that the *integral part* test was failed. In effect, the court held in each case that the amount of support supplied by the supporting organization was insufficient to ensure that the supported charity would be attentive to the supporting organization. This being the case, the facts did not justify granting the supporting organization public charity status. The opinions are lengthy and go into great detail in analyzing the complex regulations governing Type 3 supporting organizations.

The Lapham Foundation Case

In *Lapham Foundation Inc. v. Commissioner*,[57] the Tax Court held that a purported supporting organization failed to satisfy the integral part test, and was thus a private foundation, where its supported organization was a donor-advised fund. The organization's stated purpose was to provide support to a donor-advised fund for charitable organizations and activities in a designated area of southeastern Michigan. It claimed status as a so-called Type 3 supporting organization "operated in connection with" the donor-advised fund it supported. The Tax Court found that it did not qualify because it failed to meet the *integral part* test. The Sixth Circuit affirmed the Tax Court's decision based upon essentially the same reasoning.[58]

The integral part test consists of two alternative subtests, the "but-for" test[59] and the "attentiveness" test.[60] The integral part test is not met unless one or the other of these subtests is met. The Tax Court concluded that the Lapham Foundation failed both tests.

But-for subtest:
The but-for subtest is met where:

1. The activities engaged in for or on behalf of the supported organization are activities to perform the functions of or to carry out the purposes of the supported organization, and

2. But for the involvement of the supporting entity, such activities would normally be engaged in by the supported organization itself.

---

[57] T.C. Memo 2002-293, *aff'd,* 389 F.3d 606 (6th Cir. 2004).
[58] 389 F.3d 606 (6th Cir. 2004).
[59] Reg. § 1.509(a)-4(i)(3)(ii).
[60] Reg. § 509(a)-4(i)(3)(iii).

The Tax Court reasoned that the grantmaking activities of the Lapham Foundation could not properly be characterized as something the donor-advised fund would be engaged in but for the foundation's support. The donor-advised fund made grants in communities nationwide and will continue to do so, irrespective of the fact that the Foundation's funds provided for grants to charities in southeastern Michigan. Moreover, as a donor-advised fund, the fund's grants are made by and at the full discretion of its board of directors. The Foundation can recommend to the fund that the amounts it provides to the fund be used for activities in southeastern Michigan, but it cannot direct that they be used thus. Therefore, the requisite but-for relationship is not present.

Attentiveness subtest:

Under the attentiveness subtest:

1. The supporting organization must make payments of substantially all of its income to or for the use of the supported organization, and

2. Either:

   a. The amount of support must be sufficient to ensure the attentiveness of the supported entity, or

   b. The funds must be earmarked for a substantial program or activity of the supported entity, such that the supported organization will be attentive to avoid interruption thereof.

In addition, a substantial amount of the total support of the supporting organization must go to those publicly supported organizations that meet the attentiveness requirement.

Here again, the Tax Court found that the Lapham Foundation did not meet the applicable standard. First, for the "substantially all the income" requirement, the support provided must be significant in amount relative to the beneficiary's total support. The Foundation's expectation that it would provide grants amounting to approximately $7,600 out of more than $7 million in total annual contributions received by the donor-advised fund did not rise to the requisite level.

Second, the Lapham Foundation claimed to meet the alternative test in item (2)(b) above on the basis that its grants would be earmarked for the designated projects in southeastern Michigan. The Tax Court found this argument lacking in two respects. Because the grants in question were made to a donor-advised fund, the redistribution from the fund to the Michigan grantees recommended by the Foundation was entirely at the discretion of the donor-advised fund's board. It was a legal impossibility for the Foundation to earmark its grants to the fund for any specific grantee or project.

Note: Advisors considering the use of a supporting organization to support a public charity that conducts a donor-advised fund program should take into account the possible application of the *Lapham* rationale. In such a situation, it may be advisable to specify that a program *other than* the donor-advised fund is the beneficiary of the supporting organization.

In addition, under the regulations any such earmarked payments must be earmarked for a substantial program or activity of the supported organization. The donor-advised fund made only small grants ($5,500 in 1998) in the entire state of Michigan; thus, the small amounts to be provided by the Lapham Foundation were not sufficient to disrupt the fund's activities. Accordingly, there was no reason to believe that the support received from the Foundation would make the fund attentive to the operations of the Foundation.

The Cuddeback *Case*

In *Christie E. Cuddeback and Lucille M. Cuddeback Memorial Fund v. Commissioner,*[61] the Tax Court again addressed the integral part test, this time in the context of a testamentary trust seeking to qualify as a "Type 3" supporting organization "operated in connection with" three public charities it supported. The court held, without even citing the Lapham Foundation case, that this trust also failed the integral part test under the regulations. In effect, the court held again that the amount of support supplied by the supporting organization was insufficient to ensure that the supported charity would be attentive to the supporting organization.

As in *Lapham*, the court analyzed allegations about the projected grants the erstwhile supporting organization would make to its charity beneficiaries and found that the attentiveness test was not met. The record was too sketchy or incomplete to support some of the trust's claims, and the court simply disagreed with others. Accordingly, the trust was held not to qualify.

The cases described above reflect a growing awareness and interest on the part of the Internal Revenue Service of the problems inherent in this area and the resultant application of stricter standards in granting approval to such organizations in the determination process.

Remember, the supporting organization cannot be controlled by donors or other "disqualified persons,"[62] so the creator of a supporting organization will often seek a structure that provides the supported organization with as little control as possible. This often leads to an attempt to come as close as possible to actual control without violating the Regulations. The danger inherent in such

---

[61] T.C. Memo 2002-300 (Dec. 6, 2002).
[62] IRC § 509(a)(3)(C).

an attempt to avoid a clear statutory prohibition should be evident to a cautious observer. Nevertheless, if the family is able to fit into this pattern and accept the absence of clear legal control over the entity, a supporting organization may fit its needs and make this alternative preferable to a family foundation.

> **Note:** The "control" by disqualified persons that will disqualify a supporting organization is defined under the Regulations as the ability, by aggregating their votes or positions of authority in the organization, to require the organization to perform any acts that significantly affect its operations or to prevent it from performing any significant acts. The Regulations refer to the right of a substantial contributor or his spouse to designate recipients of the income from his contribution as an example of the sort of significant act that will violate the control prohibition. In addition, they provide that the holding of 50 percent or more of the voting power on the organization's governing body will amount to control if this conveys (as it normally would) the ability to veto proposed actions.[63]

[E] Charitable Lead Trusts

In some situations a client may not require an entity that will continue in existence indefinitely. Under these circumstances, a charitable lead trust may be sufficient. Such trusts are discussed at § 4.03.

For example, such a client may be satisfied to provide financial support for fifteen or twenty years to charities in which he or she is interested, rather than endowing them indefinitely.

This alternative offers an additional benefit in that the corpus remaining at the end of the trust term may be distributed to family members or other non-charitable beneficiaries.

[F] Foreign Organizations and Offshore Trusts

Sometimes a donor with a large proposed transfer may conclude that both the private foundation rules and the basic rules governing all section 501(c)(3) organizations are simply unacceptable and overly intrusive. Remember, such an organization must file an exemption application initially and annual tax returns thereafter, and if that is not enough to deter a prospective donor, both of these must be made available to the general public (including the press) on demand. These documents necessarily provide extensive details concerning the assets, contributions, and income of the organization as well as its board, management, and activities. What other choice is there for the family that is put off by this mandatory disclosure?

---

[63] Reg. § 1.509(a)-4(j)(1).

One press account suggests that these disadvantages may be avoided in some, admittedly rare instances by simply forgoing all U.S. tax benefits and locating the organization in another country where the rules are more accommodating. A 1997 article in the *Chronicle of Philanthropy* reports that Charles F. Feeney, an Irish-American businessman, anonymously distributed more than $600 million to charity over a 15-year period through a trust and a foundation he created in Bermuda.[64] These two entities together reportedly held assets valued at more than $3.5 billion as of that time. Their existence became known as a result of documents required to be filed in connection with the sale of his interest in Duty Free Shoppers Ltd., a chain of airport duty-free stores. The beneficiaries of Mr. Feeney's grants included Sinn Fein, the political wing of the Irish Republican Army, in addition to many conventional charities. He was described as a private person who did not want his gifts publicized. In a statement, Feeney said: "[P]eople of substantial wealth potentially create problems for future generations unless they themselves accept responsibility to use their wealth during their lifetime to help worthwhile causes."[65]

By locating his charities in Bermuda, Feeney avoided the U.S. tax rules requiring disclosure and publicity of their operations as well as grant restrictions and other constraints. But the cost of this freedom was the loss of any U.S. tax benefits for the amounts contributed to these Bermuda organizations. Moreover, if Feeney retains any personal power to direct the grants made by the Bermuda organizations, their assets may be included in his taxable estate for U.S. estate tax purposes.[66] While few prospective donors would be willing to make this trade-off, it is worth considering for those who value their privacy above the potential tax advantages.

[G] Other Special Situations

A family considering particular types of charitable contributions and activities should review several special-purpose alternatives. Some of these alternatives are discussed below, but the reader is urged to examine similar alternatives that might be available for other, parallel situations.

One familiar set of problems is that faced by a person who wishes to provide support for a charitable organization that is not a U.S. entity. One of the basic charitable contribution rules, and one that has no real exceptions, is the requirement that the recipient of a deductible charitable contribution be a domestic (U.S.) organization.[67] How can a U.S. taxpayer provide support for a foreign organiza-

---

[64] *See For Anonymous Donors, Offshore Philanthropy Can Be Appealing,* by Stephan G. Greene, Jennifer Moore, and Grant Williams, available on the *Chronicle's* web site at *http://philanthropy. com/premium/articles/v11/i23/990.*

[65] *Id.*

[66] *See* Rev. Rul. 72-552, 1972-2 C.B. 525; Rifkind v. United States, 5 Cl. Ct. 362 (1984).

[67] *See* IRC § 170(c)(2)(A).

tion? One solution may be simply to form a family foundation and have it make grants to the foreign grantee, following all of the rules governing grants to organizations, as discussed in Chapter 6.[68] In some cases, however, this may not suit the particular circumstances, and some other course must be found. In such a situation, there are at least two possible approaches to be examined.

First, many foreign charities that have supporters in the United States have already formed charitable organizations in the United States to receive such support and apply it to the needs of the foreign sponsor. These are often referred to as "American Friends" organizations, since they offer a means whereby American friends of the foreign charity may make contributions in its behalf, but still qualify for charitable contribution deductions. Thus, the first point of inquiry for the family seeking a means of providing support for a non-U.S. charity should be whether it has already formed an American Friends entity. If so, this may be all that is needed.

Another possibility for overseas charitable projects is CAF America, a U.S. charitable organization affiliated with the Charities Aid Foundation (UK) in order to support, promote, and facilitate global philanthropy. On its web site, it describes its role in the following terms:

> Our job at CAF America is to remove the obstacles to international giving in order to increase the flow of funds to charitable organizations around the world. Our services are focused on bringing together U.S. donors and non-U.S. charitable organizations by developing tax-effective giving programs and serving as an information clearinghouse for donors and international charities.[69]

It offers a wide array of options for all sorts of U.S. donors, including individuals, corporations, private foundations, and community foundations.

One of CAF America's programs resembles the donor-advised funds described earlier in this chapter, but its work is limited to international projects outside the United States. A potential contributor can propose a project and a foreign grantee to CAF America, and the CAF America staff then undertakes to review and evaluate the project and the grantee in exactly the same way any grantmaking charity would investigate a prospective grantee. This process culminates in a report that is considered by the board of CAF America, and if the grantee is approved by the board, the donor may make contributions to CAF America in support of the project.

---

[68] *See* § 6.06[D] *infra.*

[69] CAF America may be contacted as follows: CAF America, King Street Station, 1800 Diagonal Road, Suite 150, Alexandria, VA 22314-2840; telephone: 703-549-8931, fax: 703-549-8934; e-mail: *cafamerica@caf.charitynet.org.*

[H] A Comparison of the Three Most Popular Options

[1] The Choices

The three most popular vehicles for family philanthropy are a private foundation, a supporting organization, and a donor-advised fund at a public charity. See Table 2-4 for a comparison of these entities. Many philanthropists choose private foundations over other charitable forms for the express pleasure of managing the foundation and controlling its distributions. Yet some who take on this responsibility do so without carefully considering other options, foundation management, and the cost of using the private foundation form. Donors may approach their attorney, indicate an interest in controlled philanthropy, and simply execute the documents they are handed without further discussion.

While there are certainly tax benefits in creating a private foundation, the chief benefit of selecting that form over other charitable options is control. The donor controls the foundation board and the foundation's distributions—he or she may allocate funds to one organization, one sector, or one geographic area. This broad control (limited only by IRS guidelines) is the single most compelling factor distinguishing a private foundation from other charitable entities.

[2] The Penalties of Choosing the Private Foundation Form

However, using a private foundation rather than another charitable form can be costly. Consider these costs that attach to private—but not to public—foundations:

- The income tax benefits for gifts to private foundations are more limited than those to public charities. Appreciated assets—other than publicly traded stock—are deductible at cost basis rather than market value, and gifts are limited to 30 percent of adjusted gross income (for cash gifts) or 20 percent of adjusted gross income (for appreciated property);

- Private foundations must pay a two percent (reduced to one percent in some circumstances) excise tax on income and capital gains.

- Private foundations are subject to the prohibited transaction rules that limit transactions between the donor (and most of the donor's family) and the foundation.

- Private foundations are separate entities for tax purposes and must file annual tax returns, fully disclose grants, expenses, board members, and donors, and comply with all federal rules and regulations.

The best advice in selecting a form is to employ counsel to guide the decision. The advisor should be experienced with nonprofits and have worked with family foundations in the past. This area of practice is not intuitive, and practitioners

TABLE 2-4
Comparison of Private Foundation to
Supporting Organization and Donor-Advised Fund

	Private Foundation	*Supporting Organization*	*Donor-Advised Fund*
Separate entity for tax purposes?	Yes	Yes	No
Tax return required	Yes, Form 990-PF	Yes, Form 990	No (filed by sponsoring charity)
Tax paid	Yes, pays 2% excise tax on income and capital gains; reduced to 1% in come circumstances.	No	No
Creation requirements	Create nonprofit corporation or trust; file Form 1023 with IRS seeking tax-exempt status.	Create nonprofit corporation or trust; file Form 1023 with IRS seeking tax-exempt status.	Execute advised fund agreement supplied by the sponsoring charity.
Funding issues for donor	Donor may deduct amount up to 30% of adjusted gross income for cash gifts or 20% of adjusted gross income for long-term gain assets. Amounts not used may be carried forward five years. Gift of non-publicly traded stock limited to cost basis.	Donor may deduct amount up to 50% of adjusted gross income for cash gifts, or 30% of adjusted gross income for long-term gain assets. Amounts not used may be carried forward five years.	Donor may deduct amount up to 50% of adjusted gross income for cash gifts, or 30% of adjusted gross income for long-term gain assets. Amounts not used may be carried forward five years.
Annual distribution requirements	Must distribute at least 5% of average investment asset value annually.	No minimum distributions	No minimum distributions (check with sponsoring charity)
Perpetual?	Yes	Yes	No — generally designed to distribute all assets
Control of distributions	Donor can establish board and methods of	Donor can establish board and methods of	Donor, and donor's family, can make nonbinding

TABLE 2-4. CONTINUED

	Private Foundation	*Supporting Organization*	*Donor-Advised Fund*
	replacement; provides greatest degree of control over decision making and distributions.	replacement but must have nexus/ oversight of supported charity; great degree of control but not as much control as with private foundation.	recommendations; most funds follow donor advice.
Cost to operate	Investment management, record keeping, tax return, miscellaneous	Investment management, record keeping, tax return, miscellaneous	Investment management, record keeping
Public disclosure requirements	Yes	Yes	No
Restriction on investments	Yes, prohibited transaction rules prevent holding of more than 20% (35% in some circumstances) of a single business enterprise.	No	No
Self-dealing rules applicable?	Yes, rules prohibit certain transactions (primarily sales or leases) between the foundation and disqualified persons (the donor and most of the donor's family members and controlled business or trust interests).	No	No

benefit from practical experience. The rules governing creation of foundations, tax deductions for gifts, and the IRS rules may be complex, but the goals of the donor in creating the foundation are not. Once the donor has determined his or her objectives and understands the responsibilities associated with the decision, the advisor can select the appropriate form and create the entity.

§ 2.06 SPECIALLY TREATED PRIVATE FOUNDATIONS

The family that wants a foundation, but finds unacceptable the tax deduction limitations that flow from private foundation status, has several alternatives— forms of private foundations that are the equivalent of their public charity counterparts in some respects. This special treatment with regard to tax deductions is largely related to the donors' deductions for their contributions, but there can be some additional benefits.

[A] Private Operating Foundation

The *private operating foundation* is a cross between a public charity and a private foundation. It is defined in IRC § 4942(j)(3) and is treated as a public charity for purposes of donors' deductions for contributions, but it is a private foundation subject to many (but not all) of the restrictions that govern private foundations generally. Most significant, private operating foundations are not subject to the excise tax imposed on undistributed income of private foundations by section 4942. Typically, a private operating foundation does not make grants to other organizations in the manner of most private foundations, but rather engages in the active conduct of some sort of charitable operations, such as a museum or park. Often it has difficulty in meeting the support tests to qualify as a publicly supported organization, whether due to a lack of revenues from the general public or an excess of endowment income. A more complete technical discussion of the private operating foundation rules is provided in Appendix 2-B.

Qualification as a private operating foundation requires an organization to meet an *income test,* plus any one of three additional tests known as the *assets test, the endowment test,* and the *support test.*[70]

[1] The Income Test (Mandatory)

The income test requires the foundation to make "qualifying distributions ... directly for the active conduct of the activities constituting the purpose or function for which it is organized and operated equal to substantially all of the lesser of (i) its adjusted net income ... or (ii) its minimum investment return."[71] Translated and simplified, this means the foundation must spend 85 percent of its income or 4.25 percent of its investment assets (that's 85 percent of the five percent minimum investment return) in the form of direct charitable expenditures, as distinguished from grants to other organizations. This includes amounts paid to buy or maintain assets used directly in the conduct of the foundation's exempt activities, such as the operating assets of a museum, public park, or historic site.

---

[70] Reg. § 53.4942(b)-1(a)(1).
[71] IRC § 4942(j)(3)(A).

Qualifying distributions can include grants, scholarships, or other payments to individuals (including program-related investments) made directly for the active conduct of exempt activities, but only if the foundation maintains some significant involvement in the active programs in which the payments arise.[72] By contrast, if a foundation does nothing more than screen grant or scholarship applicants, the grants or scholarships will not be considered made directly for the active conduct of the foundation's exempt activities.[73]

Also, for this purpose, a private operating foundation may treat its payments of the excise tax on investment income (IRC § 4940) as qualifying distributions made directly for the active conduct of activities constituting the foundation's exempt purpose.

[2] The Three Alternative Tests

[a] Assets Test

A private foundation will meet the assets test if 65 percent or more of its assets:[74]

1. Are devoted directly to the active conduct of its exempt activity, or to a functionally related business, or to a combination of the two;

2. Consist of stock of a corporation that is 80 percent controlled by the foundation and at least 85 percent of the assets of which are so devoted; or

3. Are any combination of items 1 and 2.

Assets such as real property or objects (such as museum assets, classroom fixtures, and research equipment) and intangible assets (such as patents, copyrights, and trademarks) are directly devoted to the extent they are used by the foundation in directly carrying on its exempt activities or program. However, assets held primarily for the production of income or investment are not devoted directly to the active conduct of the foundation's exempt function, even though the income from the assets is used to carry on the foundation's exempt function.

> **Note:**   A number of private operating foundations qualify under the assets test, with major assets such as a park site or museum building comprising more than the 65 percent requirement.

[b] Endowment Test

A foundation will meet the endowment test if it normally makes qualifying distributions directly for the active conduct of its exempt activities of at least

---

[72] Reg. § 53.4942(b)-1(b)(2)(i).
[73] *Id.*
[74] IRC § 4942(j)(3)(B)(i).

two-thirds of its minimum investment return.[75] The phrase "directly for the active conduct of its exempt activities" means the same as it does for the income test discussed above.

Example: The McCoy Foundation has $400,000 of endowment funds and other assets not directly used for its exempt purpose. It makes qualifying distributions of $20,000 during the year directly for the active conduct of its exempt function. Two-thirds of the McCoy Foundation's minimum investment return is $13,333.33 (i.e., five percent of $400,000 is $20,000, and 2/3 of $20,000 is $13,333.33). Since the $20,000 distribution is greater than $13,333.33, the McCoy Foundation meets the endowment test.

Careful consideration of the endowment test and the mandatory income test above shows how easy it can be for a foundation to qualify under this alternative if its activities consist primarily of some sort of active charitable program as opposed to merely making grants to other organizations. Most foundations whose expenditures meet the income test will automatically meet the endowment test as well. For example, in the preceding example, the McCoy Foundation met the endowment test with its $20,000 in direct charitable expenditures, since that amount exceeded two-thirds of its minimum investment return; that amount also meets the income test, since it also exceeds 85% of the foundation's minimum investment return. A foundation that makes such distributions in an amount sufficient to pass the mandatory 85% test (i.e., the income test) will necessarily meet the less stringent two-thirds requirement of the endowment test in most instances.

[c] Support Test

A private foundation will meet the support test if:[76]

1. At least 85 percent of its support (other than gross investment income) is normally received from the general public and five or more unrelated exempt organizations;

2. Not more than 25 percent of its support (other than gross investment income) is normally received from any one exempt organization; and

3. Not more than 50 percent of its support is normally received from gross investment income.

In this context, the term "support" means gifts, grants, contributions, membership fees, the value of services or facilities furnished by a government unit without charge, nct income from unrelated business activities, and gross receipts from admissions, sales of merchandise, performance of services, or the provision of facilities in any activity that is not an unrelated trade or business. The support received from any one

---

[75] IRC § 4942(j)(3)(B)(ii).
[76] IRC § 4942(j)(3)(B)(iii).

exempt organization may be counted toward satisfying the 85 percent support test only if the foundation receives support from at least five exempt organizations.

For example, a foundation that normally receives 20 percent of its support (other than gross investment income) from each of five unrelated exempt organizations will meet the support test even though it receives no support from the general public. However, if a foundation normally receives 50 percent of its support (other than gross investment income) from three foundations and the balance of the support comes from sources other than exempt organizations, the foundation will not meet the 85 percent test.

[3] Changing to or from Private Operating Foundation Status

Qualification as a private operating foundation depends in general upon meeting the applicable tests (i.e., the income test and either the assets, endowment, or support tests for a four-year period — the current year, plus the preceding three years). There are two methods for qualification. The tests may be met for any three years out of the four-year period, or for the entire four-year period on the basis of income, assets, or distributions using aggregate figures for the four-year period. Whichever test is used, it must be used for purposes of all the applicable tests.[77]

A newly formed foundation will be treated as a private operating foundation from inception if it can demonstrate a good-faith determination that it is likely to meet the applicable tests for its first taxable year, based upon a suitable affidavit or opinion of counsel. However, an existing foundation that seeks to qualify must meet the tests for at least the three-out-of-four-years period before its status as a private operating foundation will be recognized.[78]

[B] Exempt Operating Foundation

In 1984, Congress amended the Internal Revenue Code to exempt some private operating foundations from the excise tax on investment income (under IRC § 4940) as well as the expenditure responsibility requirements of IRC § 4945(d)(4) and (h). The entities granted this relief are *exempt operating foundations*, as defined in IRC § 4940(d)(2). To qualify, a private foundation must meet four tests:[79]

1. It is a private operating foundation (as defined in IRC § 4942(j)(3));

2. It has been publicly supported for at least 10 taxable years;

3. Its governing body consists of individuals at least 75 percent of whom are not disqualified individuals and is broadly representative of the general public; and

4. None of its officers is a disqualified individual.

---

[77] *See* Appendix 2-B, § 2-B.01[F], *infra* for details.
[78] *See* Priv. Ltr. Rul. 9646002.
[79] IRC § 4940(d)(2).

The term "disqualified individual" for this purpose is defined in IRC § 4940(d)(3)(B) as including substantial contributors and certain related parties.[80]

A special transition rule in the 1984 legislation creating the exempt operating foundation category allowed all private operating foundations existing as of January 1, 1983, to automatically and permanently qualify without meeting the 10-year public support test.[81] Moreover, a glance at the definition makes it clear that few new operating foundations will be able to qualify. As a result, this category is of limited general interest.

[C] Conduit or Pass-Through Foundation

In defining the categories of contributions that deserve optimum treatment (higher percentage limitations and full deductibility for contributions of capital gain property), Congress included two categories of private nonoperating foundations (i.e., foundations that do not qualify as private operating foundations). The first of these is a logical candidate for such treatment, even though the Internal Revenue Code uses predictably obscure language to define it. In plain English, it seems appropriate to extend public charity tax results to a contribution that, although made to a private foundation, is promptly redistributed by that foundation to one or more public charities. Since the contributed property or cash ends up in the hands of a public charity in fairly short order and doesn't remain in the foundation for long, why not excuse it from the strict rules governing contributions to private foundations?

This type of foundation is often referred to as a *conduit* or *pass-through foundation*, for obvious reasons. It is defined in IRC § 170(b)(1)(E)(ii) as a private foundation other than a private operating foundation that, not later than the 15th day of the third month after the close of its taxable year in which contributions are received, distributes an amount equal to 100 percent of the contributions received in such year and has no remaining undistributed income for such year. Using a calendar year for simplicity, assume the Miree Foundation receives total contributions of $500,000 in 2005. By March 15, 2006, it has distributed an amount equal to this entire $500,000, plus all of its income for 2005. The Miree Foundation qualifies as a conduit foundation for 2005, which means that the individual(s) who contributed the $500,000 may deduct it up to 50 percent of their adjusted gross income for 2005 (30 percent for appreciated property contributions), rather than the 30 percent (20 percent for property) that would be applicable if the Miree Foundation did not so qualify. Moreover, and more important in many instances, capital gain property contributed to the Miree Foundation during 2005 would be fully deductible up to its full fair market value. This would be true regardless of

---

[80] For a more complete technical discussion of the exempt operating foundation rules, *see* Appendix 2-B.

[81] Pub. L. No. 98-369, § 302(c)(3).

whether the property was in the form of publicly traded stocks, real estate, or whatever.[82]

Note that the utility of the conduit foundation option may be enhanced if the foundation adopts a fiscal year ending late in the calendar year. For example, assume that the Miree Foundation in the preceding example is on a fiscal year ending November 30. In December of 2006, it receives a contribution of $200,000. This contribution is received in the first month of the foundation's taxable year, and the foundation will qualify as a conduit under the rules described above if it distributes this $200,000 (plus any undistributed income) by the 15th day of the third month after the close of its taxable year in which the contribution was received, which would be February 15, 2008. However, the donor will reflect the enhanced tax benefits of a contribution to a conduit foundation on his or her Form 1040 for 2006, the year when the contribution was made.

The donor who claims a deduction for a contribution to a conduit foundation must obtain adequate records or other sufficient evidence showing that the required distributions were made in a timely fashion and attach them to his or her income tax return for the year in which the deduction is claimed.[83]

Qualification as a conduit foundation is determined on a year-by-year basis, so the foundation can make the necessary distributions to qualify for a given year as desired. This can be a useful way out of the problem situation that arises when a donor unwittingly makes contributions that might otherwise be reduced or deferred. For example, consider the situation of an individual who, without consulting her advisors, contributes shares of stock in her closely held family corporation to her family foundation; such stock has a tax basis of $1,500 and is appraised at $35,000. Without more, her deduction for this charitable contribution will be reduced to $1,500, her basis in the stock.[84] If the foundation makes distributions sufficient to qualify as a conduit foundation for the year of her contribution (by distributing all of its income and all contributions received for the year), her deduction will be the full $35,000.

Note that a special rule is available for property contributions. If the foundation either sells the contributed property or distributes it in kind to a public charity within 30 days of the date of contribution, then, at the foundation's election, the property value for purposes of the distribution requirement is treated as equal to either (1) the gross amount received from the sale (less reasonable selling expenses incurred) or (2) the fair market value of the contributed property at the date of its distribution to the public charity.[85] This rule protects the foundation

---

[82] An exception would exist for tangible personal property the use of which is not related to the charitable function or purpose of the Miree Foundation. Such contributions of tangible personal property are reduced to the donor's basis in every instance, whether the donee is a public charity, a private foundation, or a conduit foundation.

[83] *See* IRC § 170(b)(1)(E)(ii); Reg. § 1.170A-9(g)(4).

[84] IRC § 170(e)(1)(B)(ii).

[85] Reg. § 1.170A-9(g)(2)(iv).

against the hardship that would result if the property should drop significantly in value before its sale.

One other planning option should be noted. The distribution requirement is couched in terms of the qualifying distributions made by the foundation seeking to qualify as a conduit foundation. That is, by the time in question, the foundation must make "qualifying distributions (as defined in section 4942(g), without regard to paragraph (3) thereof), which are treated, after the application of section 4942(g)(3), as distributions out of corpus (in accordance with section 4942(h)) in an amount equal to 100 percent of such contributions." This brings into play the various rules defining qualifying distributions, including the rules that permit a five-year carryover of excess qualifying distributions in prior taxable years.[86] Accordingly, a foundation that has such carryovers can use them to help it qualify as a conduit foundation for years in the carryover period. This may be useful for foundations that routinely distribute amounts significantly in excess of the minimum amounts required under section 4942. This would often be the case for corporate foundations, which frequently distribute virtually all funds received from the corporate parent, and thus customarily generate substantial carryovers.

[D] Pooled Fund Foundation

The final category of private foundation that is spared the rigors of the private foundation deduction limitations is the *pooled fund foundation*. This is a foundation that pools all of the contributions it receives in a common fund and that would be described in IRC § 509(a)(3) except that one or more donors (or their spouses) have the right to designate the public charities to receive the income and corpus attributable to their contributions to the fund.[87] There are two additional requirements to be met. All the income of the common fund must be distributed to public charities within two and one-half months after the close of the taxable year, and all of the corpus attributable to any donor's contribution to the fund must be distributed to one or more public charities within one year after his or her death (or after the death of his or her surviving spouse if such spouse has the right to designate the recipients of such corpus).[88]

Foundations of this type are sometimes created by community foundations or other umbrella charities to serve as a sort of cross between a supporting organization and a donor-advised fund.[89] Thus, a donor may create such a fund and receive all the contribution deduction benefits of a gift to a public charity, but still

---

[86] IRC § 4942(i); Reg. § 53.4942(a)-3(e).

[87] IRC § 170(b)(1)(E)(iii).

[88] *See* IRC § 170(b)(1)(E)(iii); Reg. § 1.170A-9(h) for details.

[89] *See* Rev. Rul. 80-305, 1980-2 C.B. 71, involving a pooled fund foundation operated by a community foundation. *See also* Priv. Ltr. Rul. 8212009, in which a university created such a fund and the fund documents provided that if the donors failed to designate recipients of the fund's income principal, those amounts would go to the university.

retain the right to control distributions from the fund. This permits the donor to prepay charitable contributions and receive an immediate contribution deduction (without the private foundation deduction limitations), while actual distributions to charity are made over time.

§ 2.07   THE STANDBY FOUNDATION

A family considering a family foundation is often uncertain as to both the overall desirability of such a plan and how much in the way of family resources should be committed to the proposed foundation. This need not be as troublesome an issue as it may appear at first blush. Many families create a family foundation with relatively small amounts of money or property, with a view to considering at a later date whether this has been a successful undertaking. They can decide at that time whether to continue the foundation and endow it with substantial resources or, alternatively, to distribute its assets to other charities and consider it an experiment that did not justify itself.

Indeed, this might be a logical approach for anyone who is considering a foundation. It is possible to create a foundation at death, under one's will or revocable trust, and this is often done. However, it is equally feasible to create the foundation during one's lifetime and then make major additions to its corpus at death. The foundation that is funded in this manner is sometimes referred to as a *standby foundation*. The foundation can be fully functional during the founder's lifetime, but it is not fully funded in its initial, standby phase. This allows the founder to preview how the program envisioned for the foundation is proceeding, how the family conducts itself with respect to the foundation, whether children or grandchildren evidence sufficient interest or ability to manage it, and whether on balance this particular foundation and this particular family are likely to achieve the objectives the creator envisioned. Key advisors and board members from outside the family can be selected and functioning on the board while the founder is still able to leave his or her stamp on the organization.

Most important, this approach gives the creator an opportunity to avoid making a major mistake if it should appear that the foundation is not likely to accomplish his or her objectives. It is much better to learn this early on, after committing only limited sums to the project, than to endow the fledgling foundation with a major portion of the creator's estate and let it proceed after the creator's death, when the creator's vision, judgment, and guidance are no longer available.

Beyond merely avoiding mistakes, the standby foundation can also help assure successes. It can provide the creator the opportunity to structure the foundation and guide it in its early stages. Board members can be recruited and seasoned, and key programs undertaken, while the person who envisioned them initially is still available to provide direction and leadership. Rather than merely providing money in a postdeath setting, the founder can enjoy the rare reward of seeing his or her own vision become a reality.

In presentations to advisors' groups, probably the most commonly asked question is "How large does a foundation have to be to be viable?" This is akin to asking how large a meal must be, or a house, or a pet. All of these things come in various sizes, and the important consideration is not size alone, but rather size that is appropriate to the task. Size is an important factor if we are speaking of a self-sufficient grantmaking entity that has already attained its full measure of growth. An entity of this sort must have the ability to generate income in large enough amounts to support both its grant programs and its own administrative costs. Indeed, some advisors feel that a foundation is not justified unless a corpus of at least $1 million to $2 million is involved. But few foundations start out in such a fully matured state, and the standby foundation is an example to remember when this question is raised.

Any foundation can serve as a standby foundation, for there is no real qualification standard or benchmark. The best definition is a functional one — a standby foundation is one that is under consideration for a major role in the founding family's estate plan, either as the recipient of major contributions and bequests or as the beneficiary of transfers through charitable remainder trusts or charitable lead trusts.[90] It may have endowment assets to provide part or all of its support, or it may be dependent on annual contributions from family members. Either way, its distinguishing feature is that it has not yet reached its potential for full funding. Although it is able to function as completely as the available resources allow, it is standing by for future additions as it plays out a major role in the overall estate plan(s) of its founding family.

§ 2.08   CHANGING THE FORM OF THE FOUNDATION

[A]   Reasons for Changing Form

The family that starts a foundation may eventually want to change its nature in some way, either to get out of the foundation business altogether by turning the assets of the family foundation over to another organization or to change the nature of its operations so that it is no longer a foundation. Such a decision may be prompted by a variety of reasons. The operating restrictions on private foundations may have proven too restrictive in practice to allow the foundation to continue in that form. In some cases, the deduction limitations on contributions to private foundations may have made it impossible for some planned contribution to proceed. In other situations, the organization may wish to undertake some course of action (e.g., ownership of a business interest, an aggressive grantmaking program, or some important transaction with disqualified persons) that is not possible or is too risky for a private foundation. Or the family may wish to limit its involvement or cut its costs by turning things over to another charitable entity.

Whatever the reason for the proposed change of status, there are several alternative possibilities for a family in this position. In order to understand these

---

[90] *See* Chapter 4 for a discussion of charitable trusts.

alternatives, we will begin by considering what concerns Congress had when it created the laws that define this process. As discussed in more detail in Chapter 6, the Tax Reform Act of 1969 imposed a new system of taxes and restrictions on private foundations. When this occurred, it clearly became a disadvantage for a charitable organization to be classified as a private foundation for tax purposes. Since private foundations, including those that had been in existence for some time, were brought under the new provisions, there was some concern that existing organizations would not be able to escape the new rules easily by simply surrendering their tax-exempt status and thereby slipping out of the private foundation category. In some cases, the creators of such organizations had long since reaped the benefits of the tax deductions allowable for their contributions, so that they might be able to continue as taxable entities without undue difficulty. This was thought to be too easy an escape from this new system of regulation. Accordingly, Congress also prescribed a set of rules limiting the means by which an organization could terminate its status as a private foundation and thereby cease to be subject to the various penalties and restrictions applicable to private foundations. Those rules are found in IRC § 507.

> **Note:** Changes in the form of a family foundation are not limited to smaller foundations. In 2001, two large nationally known foundations posted on their web sites explanations for major changes they had undergone during the year.
>
> The W. Alton Jones Foundation in Charlottesville, Virginia,[91] announced that its board of trustees had agreed to dissolve the foundation and to distribute its assets among three new charitable organizations that will be headed by members of the founding Jones family. The foundation, formed in 1944, characterized the change as enabling it to build upon its prior achievements while "providing the opportunity to explore additional areas of philanthropic activity."
>
> By contrast, the Charles and Helen Schwab Foundation, based in Northern California, went in the other direction. This foundation was formed in 2001 from the merger of the Schwab Foundation for Learning (established in 1998) and the Schwab Family Foundation (created in 1993). This merger was said to have grown out of a two-year strategic planning process aimed at enhancing the effectiveness and impact of the predecessor entities as they grew in resources and expertise.[92]

[B] Termination Tax

Once an organization is determined to be a private foundation, its status as such may be terminated only under the rules set forth in IRC § 507. Section 507

---

[91] *www.wajones.org.*

[92] *See* details at *www.schwabfamilyfdn.org/history.* For a technical analysis of the tax details of a transfer of assets from two private foundations to another foundation, *see* Priv. Ltr. Rul. 200139029.

(a) allows an organization's status as a private foundation to be terminated either voluntarily or involuntarily without any transfer of its assets or change of its form. A voluntary termination under section 507(a)(1) allows the terminating foundation to give up its private foundation status and pay the tax described below. An involuntary termination under IRC § 507(a)(2) results when the IRS notifies the organization that, because of willful, flagrant, or repeated acts or failures to act giving rise to the Chapter 42 excise taxes, the organization is liable for section 507(c) tax. If either of these two routes is chosen, the organization becomes liable for tax under IRC § 507(c). After an assessment of that tax is made, it is possible to have the tax abated by the IRS if certain actions are taken.

The termination tax under IRC § 507(c) imposes a horrendous burden, and in most cases, unless the tax is abated, it would result in the forfeiture of all of the foundation's assets.[93] Needless to say, this tax is something to be avoided if at all possible, and that is the focus of planning in this area. As a result, most foundations seeking to terminate their status do not pursue either of these alternatives. Instead, most choose the other primary termination route, voluntary termination under IRC § 507(b)(1). To pursue that route, the foundation must either go out of business by transferring all of its net assets to a public charity or change its own status to that of a public charity and operate as such for five years.

An organization that voluntarily terminates its status under IRC § 507(b)(1) is not subject to the termination tax under IRC § 507(c). As mentioned, such a voluntary termination may take either of two forms. First, a foundation may terminate its status under IRC § 507(b)(1)(A) by *distributing* all its net assets to one or more organizations that have been in existence and classified by the Internal Revenue Service as public charities (i.e., as described in section 509(a)(1)) for a continuous period of at least 60 months before the distribution. There is no requirement that the foundation notify the IRS of its intent to terminate if its termination is to be accomplished by transferring its assets to a public charity under section 507(b)(1)(A).

Alternatively, a foundation may terminate its status under IRC § 507(b)(1)(B) by *operating* as a public charity (i.e., meeting the requirements of IRC § 509(a)(1), (2), or (3)) for a continuous 60-month period beginning with the first day of any tax year. The foundation pursuing this route must notify its IRS district director in advance, before the beginning of the 60-month period, that it is terminating its private foundation status. Also, it must establish immediately after the end of the 60-month period that it has met the requirements of section 509(a)(1), (2), or (3).

The family that wishes to close down its foundation and cease operations has an easy path to follow. It simply chooses one or more public charities and

---

[93] The tax imposed under IRC § 507(c) on a voluntary or involuntary termination of a private foundation under section 507(a)(1) is the lesser of (1) the combined tax benefit resulting from the section 501(c)(3) status of the organization or (2) the value of the net assets of the organization. An organization's "combined tax benefit" for this purpose consists of the value of all tax benefits realized since the advent of the income tax in 1913 as a result of the organization's tax-exempt status; this includes the deductions enjoyed by substantial contributors as well as the taxes the organization would have paid if it were not tax exempt, plus interest on both.

transfers all of the foundation's assets, net of liabilities, to the selected beneficiaries. Perhaps due to the finality of that step, the termination is effective immediately, and the IRS need not even be told about the situation. The sections that follow will examine how a family that wishes to continue its foundation in a different form might change it into another type of organization, pursuant to the termination rules of IRC § 507. The reason for such conversion, and the family's perception of how the next phase of the foundation's existence will play out, may dictate the route to be followed.

[C] Converting to a Supporting Organization

As described above, one means by which a foundation may terminate its private foundation status without incurring the termination tax of IRC § 507(c) is by converting itself into a public charity and operating as such for a continuous 60-month period. Of the various types of public charities, most do not lend themselves to this approach, since a foundation is ordinarily not in a position to generate broad public support and will usually not fit into the other categories (such as hospitals, churches, and schools). There is one category, however, that is more consistent with the basic nature of a family foundation and may well be a format to which a foundation could readily adapt: the *supporting organization* described in IRC § 509(a)(3).[94] The supporting organization is a charitable entity that is closely involved in one way or another with one or more publicly supported charities. Conversion of a family foundation to supporting organization status may be attractive where the donor family already has a close relationship with one or more public charities and is willing to compromise its control of the organization. The family should be aware that it cannot legally control the supporting organization. Moreover, as discussed above in § 2.05[D], obviously, the first step in conversion to supporting organization status is to determine just what structure will be used for the new entity. Will the beneficiary public charity (known as the *supported organization*) be entitled to appoint the board of directors of the supporting organization? Will some other arrangement be utilized instead? If the board of the supporting organization is selected in some other manner involving less direct control and supervision by the supported organization, the rules get more complicated.[95] This will usually be a matter for discussion and negotiation between the terminating family foundation and the potential supported organization(s).

The actual termination process is commenced by advance notification to the IRS that the foundation intends to terminate its status under IRC § 507(b)(1)(B). The notice of termination should include:

- The name and address of the private foundation;

- Its intention to terminate its private foundation status;

---

[94] The applicable requirements are discussed in § 2.05[D] *supra.*
[95] *See* § 2.05[D] *supra.*

- The Code section under which it seeks classification (section 509(a)(1), (2), or (3));

- If section 509(a)(1) applies, the specific type of section 170(b)(1)(A) organization for which it seeks classification (not applicable if the foundation is converting to a supporting organization);

- The date its regular tax year begins; and

- The date the 60-month period begins.

The organization must revise its certificate of incorporation and bylaws (or other governing instrument) and do whatever else is necessary to conform to the requirements for a supporting organization under IRC § 509(a)(3) and the Regulations thereunder. This should be completed by the beginning of the organization's next taxable year, for the 60-month period must begin with the first day of the taxable year.[96]

The Internal Revenue Service has discretion to issue an advance ruling that the organization can reasonably be expected to terminate its private foundation status over the 60-month period, and this is something worth considering at the time the foundation files the notification required for a 60-month termination. By securing a ruling, the foundation can establish with certainty the qualification of its proposed supporting organization structure and thus eliminate doubt as to its status during the 60-month period. If an advance ruling is sought, the foundation must file a signed and dated agreement (IRS Form 872, Consent to Extend the Time to Assess Tax) with its request for the advance ruling; this gives the IRS additional time to assess the section 4940 tax on net investment income for the years in the 60-month termination period in the event the foundation fails to complete the termination successfully.

In considering the possibility of converting to supporting organization status, a family foundation may wish to think about establishing a relationship with its local community foundation as its supported organization. Such an entity may offer an advantage over either transferring the foundation assets directly to the community foundation for an advised fund[97] or selecting one or more actual operating public charities (such as a church, university, or hospital) that would be less likely to facilitate distributions to other entities suggested by the family. Virtually all community foundations offer their donors donor-advised-fund programs,[98] whereby contributions received from a donor may be held in a fund from which the sponsoring community foundation may make grants to other charities; the donor retains the right to make nonbinding suggestions as to the charities to which

---

[96] If the foundation does not wish to wait until the beginning of its next year, it may want to investigate changing its taxable year to a period starting in the near future. It would then utilize the beginning of that new taxable year as the beginning of its 60-month period.

[97] See § 2.05[C] *supra.*

such grants will be made, but the selection of grantees is entirely at the discretion of the community foundation. See the discussion of the Lapham Foundation[99] case in § 2.05[D], however, for potential difficulties where a supporting organization was intended to support a donor-advised fund. There, the fact that proposed "grants" were to be made to a donor-advised fund and the granting organization would recommend further grants to a specific project made it insufficient to qualify. Because distributions from the donor-advised fund were at the discretion of the fund's board and could not be earmarked by the contributor to the fund for redistribution to any specific grantee, the claimed relationship failed to qualify the organization as a Type 3 supporting organization.

Anyone planning to create an entity to qualify as a Type 3 supporting organization on the basis of its support of a donor-advised fund should read the *Lapham* case with care.

Because of the continuing influence (short of actual control) the supporting arrangement can afford, a donor may prefer to have his or her family foundation support a community foundation, rather than simply terminating into the community foundation by transferring all of its assets to the latter. The Internal Revenue Service has issued at least one private letter ruling approving a supporting organization that has a community foundation as its supported organization.[100] However, the IRS has begun to examine more closely the structure of supporting organizations that purport to support a large number of public charities, holding where appropriate that the requisite relationship is not present where the supported organizations (1) do not select a majority of the supporting organization's governing board and (2) do not receive a meaningful amount of financial support from the supporting organization.

[D] Terminating the Foundation into a Donor-Advised Fund

Rather than changing its structure and continuing to incur the burdens and costs of operating its own program, with all of the tax returns and other reporting requirements that would continue to apply, the foundation may prefer to cease operations and distribute all of its assets to an existing public charity. The public charity (or charities) selected must have a five-year history of operations in that mode[101] (i.e., as a public charity), and the foundation would be well advised to secure a copy of the prospective distributee's exemption letter classifying it as a public charity before distributing assets.

> **Note:** Pending legislation, the status and content of which is unclear as this edition goes to press in June, 2006, could affect the qualification of a donor-advised fund as a potential transferee or a terminating foundation. See H.R. 4297 (Senate version), 109th Congress (2006).

---

[98] *See* §§ 2.05[C]-[D] *supra*.
[99] Lapham Foundation Inc. v. Comm'r, T.C. Memo 2002-293 (Nov. 27, 2002).
[100] *See* Priv. Ltr. Rul. 9212030.

With that general requirement in mind, the foundation is free to select any sort of public charity it may desire as the entity into which it will terminate. Actually, this sort of termination is the easiest and simplest, since the foundation simply turns over its assets to the public charity or charities it has selected. There is no requirement that the Internal Revenue Service be notified, and there is no reporting requirement other than the foundation's final return. If the family that has heretofore managed the private foundation simply wishes to be rid of the job, with no further involvement on its part, it may simply relinquish its assets and go quietly out of existence. In other situations, however, the family may want a means of continuing its charitable distributions into the future without the obligations and responsibilities that managing a family foundation brings. In that case, the family may select as the terminal beneficiary of its foundation an entity that will facilitate such a continuation of the family's charitable impulses.

At this point, the family has the same choices available as when it originally chose to create the foundation.[102] In either context, the family may decide that its charitable aims may be accomplished most efficiently and at minimum cost by creating a donor-advised fund. Such an arrangement may be entered into with a community foundation or with any other public charity that sponsors such a program (provided the transferee has the required 60-month history). The family establishes a fund within the sponsor organization from which the sponsor will, after consulting with the family, make distributions to other charitable organizations. The family retains the right to make nonbinding recommendations or give advice to the sponsoring charity as to how its fund will be applied. The sponsoring charity is free to accept or reject that advice, and the family is thus left with no real legal control over its fund. This is offset to some extent by the principal advantage of the donor-advised fund: All administrative matters — such as record keeping, preparation of checks, and tax returns — are handled by the sponsoring charity. Thus, the family assumes no expense or time commitment for these steps.

This simplicity may make the donor-advised fund an attractive candidate for the family that wishes to terminate its foundation because it now finds these burdens excessive. The actual termination is quite simple to accomplish — the terminating foundation simply distributes all of its assets, after providing for payment of all of its liabilities, to the sponsoring charity. Caution must be exercised to be sure that there are no material restrictions on the latter's use of the assets. Under the Regulations, the terminating foundation may not impose any material restriction or condition on the transferee's subsequent use of the assets.[103] If any such restriction exists that would prevent the transferee organization from "freely and effectively" employing the assets in furtherance of its exempt purposes, the termination might be held not to qualify under IRC § 507

---

[101] IRC § 507(b)(1)(A).

[102] These alternatives to the family foundation are discussed in § 2.05 *supra.*

(b)(1)(A). The terms under which the typical donor-advised fund operates will normally be sufficient to meet this standard. Nevertheless, the family operating the terminating foundation must not seek any special accommodation or other specific privileges for the donor-advised fund to be created with the funds distributed by the terminating foundation.

The text suggests, as § 507(b)(1)(A) provides, that a foundation that terminates into a donor-advised fund must be sure that the fund has a 60-month history of operations.[104] Revenue Ruling 2002-28 suggested that a transfer by a foundation of all of its assets to another entity is not necessarily a "termination" for purposes of IRC § 507. In that ruling, the transferees under a variety of fact situations were all private foundations, so that the transfers there were described in § 507(b)(2). A transfer of assets described in § 507(b)(2) does not constitute a termination of the transferor's private foundation status under § 507(a)(1) unless the transferor voluntarily gives notice pursuant to § 507(a)(1).[105] Because the transferor foundation is not required to provide such notice, the transfers there were not necessarily "terminations" for tax purposes, even though the existence of the transferor came to a close and in a colloquial sense "terminated."

The Internal Revenue Service finally confirmed in Revenue Ruling 2003-13[106] that a comparable analysis applied to a transfer by a private foundation to a *public charity*. This being the case, a foundation may make a transfer to a donor-advised fund (or any other public charity) that does not have a 60-month history, without causing a "termination" for purposes of IRC § 507.[107]

[E]   Other Termination Possibilities

For the average family foundation, the foregoing alternatives are probably the most logical approaches, since the attributes of the posttermination entities discussed here (the supporting organization and the donor-advised fund) are likely to be somewhat similar to those of the foundation itself, with one major difference: The tax restrictions and limitations applicable to private foundations no longer apply. In some cases, however, there may be other alternatives worth considering.

In some cases, a foundation may be able to qualify as a public charity under IRC § 509(a)(2). This is an organization that is publicly supported on the basis of contributions and the income it receives from related business activities. This may be the case, for example, where the foundation operates a facility of some sort, such as a museum or park with a dependable stream of income from admissions, or a program of selling merchandise that is somehow related to its

---

[103] Reg. § 1.507-2(a)(8).

[104] *See* Rev. Rul. 2002-28, 2002-1 C.B. 941, however, for a possible alternative analysis.

[105] *See* Treas. Reg. §§ 1.507-1(b)(6) and 1.507-3(d).

[106] 2003-4 I.R.B. 305.

[107] *See* the discussion in § 2.08[H], "Terminating the Foundation into a Public Charity."

exempt purpose. Under IRC § 509(a)(2), an organization will be classified as a public charity if its financial support meets two tests:

1. *More than one-third* of the organization's support each tax year comes from any combination of:

   - Gifts, grants, contributions, or membership fees, and

   - Gross receipts from admissions, sales of merchandise, performance of services, or furnishing of facilities in an activity that is not an unrelated trade or business;[108] and

2. *No more than one-third* of its support in each tax year comes from gross investment income and net, after-tax unrelated business income.

If none of the termination alternatives described above is feasible in a particular family's circumstances, partial relief from the private foundation limitations may be obtained by establishing that the foundation qualifies as a private operating foundation or one of the other categories of specially treated private foundations.

[F] Dissolving the Foundation and Returning Assets to the Donor? Don't Try It

A businessperson often likes to know there will be an acceptable exit strategy for any significant action under consideration. As discussed above, those possibilities involve either continuing the foundation in a new form or distributing its assets to another charity. What about the obvious alternative of simply taking back the assets and forgetting the whole thing? While theoretically possible, as a practical matter that is so costly as to be impossible. If the family is so uncertain that it wishes to retain this option, it should probably not proceed with a family foundation.

This is one of the possibilities that concerned Congress in 1969 and led it to enact section 507 of the Code. As the Senate Finance Committee explained it:

> The committee agrees with the House that foundations should not receive substantial and continuing tax benefits in exchange for the promise of use of the assets involved for educational, charitable, religious, etc., purposes but avoid the carrying out of these responsibilities.[109]

The result was the penalty tax of IRC § 507(c), described above, which requires the foundation to repay the government all of the tax benefits realized by it and all of its donors (plus interest). This can amount to as much as the foundation's

---

[108] In computing the support received from gross receipts for this purpose, gross receipts received from any person or from any single government agency are included only to the extent they do not exceed the greater of $5,000 or one percent of the organization's total support for the year.

entire asset holdings, although it will not exceed that amount. There is also the possibility that some of the other penalty taxes discussed in Chapter 6 may apply, including the tax on acts of self-dealing and the tax on taxable expenditures. And, finally, if this is not enough to discourage such actions, the Internal Revenue Service is required to notify the appropriate state officer (usually the state attorney general) that it has issued a notice of deficiency for the tax imposed under IRC § 507(c) to a terminating foundation, raising the possibility of state law penalties or enforcement actions (even including possible criminal penalties).[110]

All in all, a family considering the possibility of simply reclaiming the assets in its family foundation would be well advised not to even think about it.

[G] Foundation-to-Foundation Transfers

With the increasing numbers of new foundations formed in recent years, it is inevitable that some of these will seek to merge, split up, or otherwise change their form. In Revenue Ruling 2002-28,[111] the Internal Revenue Service provided new guidance for some of these structural changes.

The ruling dealt with three common foundation-to-foundation transfer situations. In each of these situations, the transferee foundation was permitted to go out of existence without incurring the onerous termination tax imposed under § 507(c) of the Internal Revenue Code.[112] Advisors had complained for some time about the lack of a clear explanation of how the termination rules work, and in 1999 the Exempt Organizations Committee of the American Bar Association Section of Taxation even submitted a draft ruling on the subject to IRS. Revenue Ruling 2002-28 provided some, but by no means all, of what the clarification advisors had hoped for. The bottom line, however, is positive: Foundation professionals now have important additional guidance on how to handle these situations effectively.

The first situation dealt with in the ruling is a foundation whose directors develop "divergent charitable objectives," a euphemistic way to say that they disagree intensely and cannot go forward together. This often occurs in the context of a divorce or other family disruption. As a result, the directors want to split up their foundation and transfer all of its assets (in equal shares) to three new foundations, after which the old foundation is dissolved under state law.

The second situation in the ruling presents another familiar scenario: A foundation created in trust form decides to change to corporate form. Accordingly, the trustees create a new nonprofit corporation and transfer all of the trust's assets and liabilities to it. In the third situation, two foundations with

---

[109] S. Rep. No. 552, 91st Cong., 1st Sess. 55 (1969).

[110] IRC § 6104(c).

[111] 2002-1 C.B. 941.

[112] For a complete discussion of this tax, *see* § 2.08[B], *supra*.

identical charitable purposes achieve cost savings by merging and transferring all of their assets and liabilities to a third, newly formed foundation.

The Ruling holds that the transfers in all three situations are not terminations of the transferor foundations' private foundation status for tax purposes unless the transferor voluntarily notifies the Internal Revenue Service of its intent to terminate. If no notice is given, the transfers do not terminate the transferor foundations' private foundation status, and the dreaded termination tax is inapplicable. The transferors' private foundation status continues, even if it has been dissolved under state law. (Note the metaphysical assumption here: Even though the transferor foundation no longer exists under the applicable state law, its status as a private foundation theoretically continues, so the tax on terminations does not apply.) The transferor must file the usual tax return, Form 990-PF, for the year of termination, but not thereafter (unless it subsequently receives additional assets or engages in activities).

What if the transferor foundation does notify the Internal Revenue Service of its intention to terminate, through mistake or otherwise? Under these circumstances, the IRS says that the § 507(c) termination tax would technically apply, but this will not be a problem because if the foundation has already divested itself of all its assets, the tax would be zero.

The ruling clears up some points on which there has not been sufficient guidance to help advisors plan transactions of these types. Now the IRS has spoken on the matter, and done so in a published ruling upon which the public may rely. (A similar holding in a private letter ruling would not serve as reliable authority for anyone other than the person who sought and received the ruling.) The key holding is that a foundation that transfers all of its assets to another foundation is not required to notify the IRS that it intends to terminate its private foundation status. Moreover, even if it does give such notice, there will be no tax due if it has already transferred all of its assets. This principle and the description of the return filing requirements applicable to the transferor foundations in such circumstances provide useful direction for foundation advisors.

The implications raised in Revenue Ruling 2002-28 about other types of transfers were clarified in Revenue Ruling 2003-13, discussed in § 2.08[H] below, "Terminating the Foundation into a Public Charity." That ruling confirms that a foundation that formally dissolves under the applicable state law and thus ceases to exist will not necessarily be considered "terminated" for purposes of IRC § 507.

[H] Terminating the Foundation into a Public Charity

Although Revenue Ruling 2002-28, discussed above, showed how such foundation-to-foundation transfers could be made without incurring the onerous termination tax imposed under § 507(c) of the Code, it failed to address another, equally important question. Many family foundations prefer to wind up their operations by transferring their assets to public charities rather than to other private foundations. Revenue Ruling 2002-28 raised certain implications about such transfers but did not address them squarely. That ruling carefully distinguished between a "termination" under IRC § 507 and other events that end a foundation's legal existence without effecting such a termination, but it went no further.

The next year, in Revenue Ruling 2003-13,[113] the IRS issued another ruling, describing the tax consequences produced when a private foundation transfers all of its assets to a *public charity*. In general terms, IRC § 507 allows a foundation to escape the dreaded termination tax in either of two ways: (1) it may operate as a public charity for five years, or (2) it may transfer all of its assets to an entity that has been a public charity for five years. Revenue Ruling 2003-13 confirmed that this situation avoids undesirable consequences under the private foundation penalty taxes (as provided in the Code) and went on to deal with several other situations — transfers to a public charity that *lacks* a five-year history or to supporting organizations (described in IRC § 509(a)(3)) and § 509(a)(2) organizations. Revenue Ruling 2003-13 provides a blueprint for making such distributions without incurring the termination tax. Someone reading the Code provision (IRC § 507) literally might find these clarifications a surprise.

What does this mean for family foundations? Sometimes a family simply loses interest in the foundation. Perhaps the expense and bother of running the program, and filing tax returns and other reports, becomes more than they want to deal with. Revenue Ruling 2003-13 provides several new options for a family in such a position. First, the foundation may transfer its remaining assets to a donor-advised fund and greatly reduce the aggravation it faces. Some national donor-advised funds have been around for less than five years, but the ruling indicates that even such a fund can be the recipient of the foundation's assets. Another approach may be to create a supporting organization for a favorite charity (or use an existing supporting organization) for this purpose. Such an organization may be preferable to simply turning the assets over to the charity itself, since it can afford the family more assurance that the assets will be used as intended and not just added to the general funds of the charity. Before Revenue Ruling 2003-13, the lack of official guidance on this point could have led some advisors to question whether a supporting organization would be appropriate for this purpose.

The termination tax and all of the accompanying rules grew out of Congressional concerns that the new private foundation rules Congress passed in 1969 not be easily avoided by existing foundations that simply gave up their status as tax-exempt Section 501(c)(3) organizations. It is not clear that these rules are entirely necessary today, and this ruling provides useful guidance for many family foundations that wish to change their status without adverse tax results.

---

[113] 2003-4 I.R.B. 305.

§ 2.09   AVOIDING FUTURE CHANGES WHICH TAKE THE FOUNDATION "OFF COURSE"*

A frequent concern of individuals considering the creation of a family foundation is assuring it will continue to function, permanently, in the manner envisioned by the creator. This concern may take a variety of forms. The most often cited is the problem of "mission drift," in which a foundation's purposes and activities change over time. Many observers consider the Ford Foundation to be the classic case in this category. After the death of its founder, family members played a less important role and it undertook a number of projects that would probably have been antithetical to the founder's conservative social and political views.

A related problem is the possibility that a foundation may be "hijacked" by non-family management at some later date and operated in a fashion that the creator would deplore. Press accounts in recent years have described several instances of such hijackings. One widely-reported example is the Maddox Foundation in Memphis. When its founder and his wife died in a boating accident, leaving some $100 million to the foundation, a business associate became its president. She moved the foundation (originally a Tennessee trust) to Mississippi, where it was established as a nonprofit corporation. Mississippi law permits such a corporation to have a single director, and she assumed that role. What ensued was a series of questionable grants and investments, a shift in the foundation's grantmaking policy, and protracted litigation over the move to Mississippi—all things the founder would probably prefer to have avoided.

Such changes in foundation management may be less unusual than one might expect.[114] Where the creator of a foundation is concerned about such a possibility, there are some steps that can help prevent future hijacking.

[A]   Choice of Entity

As discussed below, a foundation may be created as either a nonprofit corporation or a trust.[115] Although there are a number of factors that must be considered in choosing the correct entity, a key consideration for preventing a hijacking is the ease with which the entity's formative documents may be changed. Of course, tax issues such as differences in tax rates if the charity recognizes unrelated taxable income[116] or has an unrelated debt financed income[117] is important as well. But a critical factor, and one of the most important in preventing a hijacking, is the choice of entity.

---

* The authors gratefully acknowledge the contribution of Douglas W. Stein, Esq., of Barris, Sott, Denn & Driker, P.L.L.C., in Detroit, Michigan, to this section.

[114] For an instructive discussion of such charitable scandals, including the Maddox Foundation situation, see *Scandal Is a Good Teacher*, by Michelle D. Monse, Trusts & Estates (Feb. 2006) at p. 56.

[115] See § 3.01 *infra*.

[116] See § 3.01 *infra*.

[117] IRC § 514.

For this purpose, the ease of changing both the charitable charter and the composition of the board is the cornerstone of planning. If these are difficult to change, the founder's preferences are more likely to prevail. As a general rule, corporate charters are easier to amend than the terms of a trust. Sometimes, but not always, changes to a nonprofit corporation charter must be approved by the attorney general. Changes to a corporate charter may include changing the situs of the corporation to a state which has a lax or inactive attorney general. Once the corporation is established in a state where the attorney general plays a minimal role in oversight, the charitable purpose of the corporation can be easily changed to accommodate the new board's desires and solidify the hijacker's control over the entity.

A trust is usually significantly more difficult to change than a corporation. The state Attorney General will usually be involved because the trust is a charitable trust, and a court proceeding is normally required to amend or modify the terms of the trust. The doctrine of cy pres can allow a court to change the purposes of a charity, but only upon a showing that the charitable purposes are impossible to achieve or unlawful — a high burden to meet. In addition, even if the doctrine of cy pres is applicable, the trustees named in the instrument are usually significantly more difficult to change thus making it very important that the creator have full confidence in the trustees.

Because irrevocable trusts are generally difficult to change, a charity formed as a trust has the distinct advantage of being difficult to hijack, unless the trustee is doing the hijacking and the charitable purpose becomes impossible to discharge. However, the risk of a trustee hijacking a trust can be minimized by carefully choosing the trustee and ensuring that sufficient safeguards are built into the trust. The safeguards described below can help minimize the chance that the trustee will be able to hijack the trust.

[B] Mandatory Distributions

The trust instrument for a charitable trust can require mandatory distributions to a specific charity or for a very narrow charitable purpose. This charitable purpose can be very detailed and should be carefully crafted. In fact, more attention should be given to describing the charitable charter and the donor's goals, than to almost any other issue. For example, a trust could require that 5 percent of the trust property be distributed to XYZ School and perhaps even direct that no other distributions may be made. In the alternative, the trust could set forth a range for the amount to be distributed.

> **Note:** This minimum distribution is separate from the minimum distribution requirement of section 4942 of the Code, discussed in Chapter 7. Care must be taken to ensure that the minimum distribution requirements of that provision are met as well, if it is applicable.

[C] Poison Pill

Another option is to include a poison pill. A poison pill could be structured such that if the required 5 percent distribution to the XYZ School is not made for a stated period of time, the trust will terminate or a new trustee is automatically appointed. In the alternative, the charity could be given the ability to remove the trustee and appoint a new successor trustee.[118] While great care must be taken when drafting these types of provisions to ensure the trust qualifies for a charitable deduction, a poison pill should chill any change effecting the distributions to the named charitable beneficiary.

[D] Trust Protector

Similar to an irrevocable trust, a charitable trust could name a trust protector. A trust protector is becoming much more common in dynastic or long term trusts, due to the length of time the trust is expected to last and a donor's desire that the trust goals be properly implemented. The same can be accomplished with a charitable trust. For example, the trust protector could be given the power to veto any change of the charitable beneficiary. The trust should also require that the trust protector be given notice of any proposed modification to the trust, including changes of situs, significant changes in distributions, and approval of any membership dues and other significant expenses.

To minimize the trustee's ability to amend the trust, the trust protector could be given the power to alter or amend the administrative provisions of the trust, as the trustee deems appropriate. It is vitally important that the trust protector not be given the power to change the charitable purpose or the charitable beneficiaries, unless such change meets some objective criteria.

Consideration should be given to when or if the trust should terminate, liquidate, or merge. It may be best to permit such changes only when it is extremely difficult or impossible to discharge the trust's charitable purpose. It is important to be mindful that the trust must also be protected from the whims and vicissitudes of the trust protector as well as the trustee. Furthermore, if a trust protector is named, it is wise to also name a successor trust protector or a method by which the trust protector can be named.

[E] Change of Trustee

Consider requiring that the appointment of new trustees must be by unanimous consent of all the trustees and the trust protector, if there is one, as well as the consent of the primary charitable beneficiary, if any. Although these provisions increase the complexity of trust administration, they also reduce the risk that a

---

[118] Great care should be taken when drafting this provision to ensure that the charity will not hijack the client's foundation.

successor trustee will have ulterior motives. Of course, there are real risks to this particular power. First, if a charitable beneficiary serves as a trustee, it is unlikely to ever consent to its own removal even if such a change is in the trust's best interest. Second, it may be very difficult to obtain unanimous consent, so some form of tie breaker needs to be devised. Lastly, care needs to be taken to make certain that the successor trustees can work together productively.

[F] Where Only a Corporation Will Work

There are times when only a corporation will do, as for example when the foundation is expected to have significant amounts of unrelated business income, or when a corporation will be a major donor. Under these circumstances, a corporation will usually result in a lower tax, due to the compressed tax rates applicable to trusts. In this situation, consideration might be given to a Michigan trustee corporation.[119]

A Michigan trustee corporation is a corporation created by the trustees of a charitable trust for the express purpose of carrying out the provisions of such trust.[120] The trustee corporation has all the powers of a corporation but is charged solely with carrying out the terms of the trust. The trust instrument is attached to the certificate of corporation and in effect becomes a part of it. Unlike a standard corporation, the officers and directors of the corporation have the same degree of responsibility with respect to the trustee corporation's assets as a trustee of the trust creating such corporation, except where a lesser degree or a particular degree of responsibility is prescribed in the trust instrument.[121] In addition, if the grantor of the trust attempts to alter, amend, enlarge, or restrict any of the terms of the trust, such change must be filed as if it were an amendment to the Articles of incorporation. Importantly, no amendment to the Articles is valid if it entirely changes the original purpose of the corporation.

In sum, a Michigan trustee corporation is a hybrid entity. It can have the flexibility and taxation of a corporation but with the limited scope that can only be provided by a trust.

By taking great care in the early stages of creating a charitable organization, one can improve the effectiveness of the organization and increase the likelihood that the organization will accomplish the donor's objectives. To minimize the likelihood that a charitable organization will be hijacked, the choice of entity should be a trust. Safeguards, like mandatory distributions and appointment of a trust protector, can be included in the trust instrument to protect the trust from the trustee. The provisions which can be included in a trust to reduce the risk of a hijacking are limited only by the diligence and imagination of the attorney.

---

[119] Michigan Comp. Laws §§ 450.148 *et. seq.*
[120] Michigan Comp. Laws § 450.148
[121] Michigan Comp. Laws § 450.153.

Of course, no measures can provide absolute protection, and the possibility of future litigation over the governance and direction of the foundation are always a possibility. Indeed, nothing in life is certain. However, prudent planning at the beginning can help give the founder greater assurance that his or her plans will be carried out.

§ 2.10   WHEN A FOUNDATION IS RELOCATED

When family members retire and/or move to a distant city in a warmer climate, what about the family foundation? Does it move with them? How does that work if the family decides it does want to relocate the foundation? A private letter ruling issued in 2001 outlines the procedures and consequences of such a decision. In a nutshell, the family would usually take the following steps to "move" the foundation:

1. Form a new foundation as a nonprofit corporation under the laws of the new state;

2. File an exemption application for the new foundation (just as any new foundation would do);

3. Merge the old foundation into the new one, so that the new foundation as the surviving entity assumes all the assets and liabilities of the old foundation.

As described in the text, termination of private foundation status can be tricky if it is not done correctly. Above all, the terminating foundation must be careful to avoid the termination tax, which can be as much as 100 percent of its net assets. In a situation like the one we just considered, where a foundation moves to a different state by merging with a new foundation formed there, the new foundation is not treated as a newly created organization. Instead it is regarded as a continuation of the old foundation, with all the tax attributes of the old foundation; and, most importantly, the termination tax does not apply.

The Internal Revenue Service discussed the technical tax rules that apply in this situation in Letter Ruling 200150031. The bottom line, however, is that for tax purposes the new foundation simply steps into the shoes of the old one and thereafter possesses all of the attributes and characteristics of the old foundation. After the merger has taken place (and not before), the old entity can voluntarily terminate its private foundation status by notifying the IRS; at that time its net assets will be zero, so no termination tax will be due.

It may or may not be necessary or even desirable to "move" the foundation when family members relocate. The family might prefer to do this if they are permanently leaving the old state and wish to be free of reporting rules, intrusive state supervision, or other legal obstacles in the old location. On the other hand, many states do not impose onerous rules upon foundations and other charitable organizations, so it may be possible simply to keep the old foundation in place. Furthermore, these problems may be less troublesome for a foundation that was created in trust form rather than as a nonprofit corporation. Since trusts are typically not required to register with the authorities in the new state, it would generally not be necessary to take any steps to relocate the foundation.

CHAPTER 2

APPENDICES

Most of the materials in the following Appendices are adapted from Internal Revenue Service Publication 578, *Tax Information for Private Foundations and Foundation Managers*. This invaluable publication has been out of print for some time, since the last edition was released in January 1989. The author has updated the materials in Publication 578 for post-1989 changes and simplified it to make it more readable. In addition, the author added commentary on practical points. These Appendices provide a thorough discussion of the extremely complex tax rules governing private foundations, and are designed to help the reader who wants a more detailed answer to a particular question.

SUPPORTING ORGANIZATIONS (IRC § 509(A)(3) ORGANIZATIONS)

§ 2-A.01   DEFINITION

IRC Section 509(a)(3) excludes from the definition of private foundation those organizations that meet all three of the following requirements:

1. The organization must be organized and at all times thereafter operated exclusively for the benefit of, to perform the functions of, or to carry out the purposes of one or more specified organizations (which can be either domestic or foreign) as described in § 509(a)(1) or (2). These §§ 509(a)(1) and 509(a)(2) organizations are commonly called publicly supported organizations.

2. The organization must be operated, supervised, or controlled by or in connection with one or more of the organizations described in § 509(a)(1) or (2).

3. The organization must not be controlled directly or indirectly by disqualified persons (defined later) other than foundation managers and other than one or more organizations described in § 509(a)(1) or (2).

This provision, § 509(a)(3), differs from the other provisions of § 509 that describe publicly supported organizations. Instead of describing an organization that conducts a particular kind of activity or that receives financial support from the general public, § 509(a)(3) describes organizations that have established certain relationships in support of § 509(a)(1) or (2) organizations. Thus, an organization may qualify as other than a private foundation even though it may be funded by a single donor, family, or corporation. This kind of funding ordinarily would indicate private foundation status, but a § 509(a)(3) organization has limited purposes and activities and gives up a significant degree of independence.

The requirement in (2) above provides that a supporting (§ 509(a)(3)) organization have one of three types of relationships with one or more publicly supported (§ 509(a)(1) or (2)) organizations. It must be:

1. Operated, supervised, or controlled by a publicly supported organization;
2. Supervised or controlled in connection with a publicly supported organization; or
3. Operated in connection with a publicly supported organization.

More than one type of relationship may exist between a supporting organization and a publicly supported organization. Any relationship, however, must insure that the supporting organization will be responsive to the needs or demands of, and will be an integral part of or maintain a significant involvement in, the operations of one or more publicly supported organizations.

The first two relationships, "operated, supervised, or controlled by" and "supervised or controlled in connection with," are based on an existence of majority control of the governing body of the supporting organization by the publicly supported organization. They have the same rules for meeting the tests under requirement (1) and are discussed as *Category One* organizations in the following discussion. The "operated in connection with" relationship requires that the supporting organization be responsive to and have operational relationships with publicly supported organizations. This third relationship has different rules for meeting the requirement (1) tests and is discussed separately as *Category Two* organizations.

> **Note:** Various sources and authors refer to these categories of supporting organization with different terminology, and this can result in unnecessary confusion. Sometimes the three categories listed in the preceding paragraph are called Type I, Type II and Type III (or Category 1, Category 2 and Category 3), respectively. This discussion will follow the terminology used by the Internal Revenue Service in the publication from which it was adapted. Thus, in this Appendix 2-A, Category One organizations are those that are either "operated, supervised, or controlled by," or "supervised or controlled in connection with," the publicly charity or charities they support, while Category Two organizations are those that are "operated in connection with" their supported organization(s).

§ 2-A.02   "CATEGORY ONE" SUPPORTING ORGANIZATIONS

This category includes organizations either "operated, supervised, or controlled by" or "supervised or controlled in connection with" organizations described in § 509(a)(1) or (2). [Reg. § 1.509(a)-4(f)(4).] These kinds of organizations have a governing body that either includes a majority of members elected or appointed by one or more publicly supported organizations or that consists of the same persons that control or manage the publicly supported organizations. If an organization is to qualify under this category, it also must meet an organizational test, an operational test, and not be controlled by disqualified persons. [Reg. §§ 1.509(a)-4(a)(2), (3) and (4).] These requirements are covered later in this discussion.

[A]   Operated, Supervised, or Controlled by

Each of these terms, as used for supporting organizations, presupposes a substantial degree of direction over the policies, programs, and activities of a supporting organization by one or more publicly supported organizations. The relationship required under any one of these terms is comparable to that of a parent and subsidiary, in which the subsidiary is under the direction of and is accountable or responsible to the parent organization. This relationship is established when a majority of the officers, directors, or trustees of the supporting organization are appointed or elected by the governing body, members of the governing body, officers acting in their official capacity, or the membership of one or more publicly supported organizations.

A supporting organization may be operated, supervised, or controlled by one or more publicly supported organizations even though its governing body is not made up of representatives of the specified publicly supported organizations for whose benefit it is operated. [Reg. § 1.509(a)-4(g)(1)(ii).] This occurs only if it can be demonstrated that the purposes of the publicly supported organizations are carried out by benefiting the specified publicly supported organizations [discussed later at § 2A.02[C][1][b]].

[B] Supervised or Controlled in Connection With

The control or management of the supporting organization must be vested in the same persons that control or manage the publicly supported organization. [Reg. § 1.509(a)-4(h)(1).] In order for an organization to be supervised or controlled in connection with a publicly supported organization, common supervision or control by the persons supervising or controlling both organizations must exist to ensure that the supporting organization will be responsive to the needs and requirements of the publicly supported organization. [Reg. § 1.509(a)-4(h)(1).]

An organization will not be considered supervised or controlled in connection with one or more publicly supported organizations if it merely makes payments (mandatory or discretionary) to the publicly supported organizations. This is true even if the obligation to make payments is legally enforceable and the organization's governing instrument contains provisions requiring the distribution. These arrangements do not provide a sufficient connection between the payor organization and the needs and requirements of the publicly supported organizations to constitute supervision or control in connection with the organizations. [Reg. § 1.509(a)-4(h)(2).]

[C] Organizational and Operational Tests

To qualify as a § 509(a)(3) organization (supporting organization), the organization must be both organized and operated for the purposes set out in requirement (1) at the beginning of this section. If an organization fails to meet either the organizational or the operational test, it cannot qualify as a supporting organization.

In the case of supporting organizations created before 1970, the organizational and operational tests apply as of January 1, 1970. Therefore, even though the original articles of organization did not limit its purposes to those in requirement (1), and even though it operated before 1970 for some purpose other than those in requirement (1), an organization will satisfy the organizational and operational tests if, on January 1, 1970, and at all times thereafter, it is so constituted as to comply with these tests. [Reg. § 1.509(a)-4(b)(2).]

[1] Organizational Test

[a] *Requirements*

An organization is organized exclusively for one or more of the purposes specified in requirement (1) only if its articles of organization:

1. Limit the purposes of the organization to one or more of those purposes;

2. Do not expressly empower the organization to engage in activities that are not in furtherance of those purposes;

3. "Specify" (as explained later under "specified organizations") the publicly supported organizations on whose behalf the organization is operated; and

4. Do not expressly empower the organization to operate to support or benefit any organization other than the ones specified in item (3).

[Reg. § 1.509(a)-4(c)(1).]

In meeting the organizational test, the organization's purposes as stated in its articles may be as broad as, or more specific than, the purposes set forth in requirement (1) at the beginning of the discussion of § 509(a)(3), "Organizations." Therefore, an organization that by the terms of its articles is formed for the benefit of one or more specified publicly supported organizations will, if it otherwise meets the other requirements, be considered to have met the organizational test.

For example, articles stating that an organization is formed to perform the publishing functions of a specified university are enough to comply with the organizational test. An organization operated, supervised, or controlled by, or supervised or controlled in connection with, one or more publicly supported organizations to carry out the purposes of those organizations, will be considered to have met these requirements if the purposes set forth in its articles are similar to but no broader than the purposes set forth in the articles of its controlling organizations. If, however, the organization by which it is operated, supervised, or controlled is a publicly supported § 501(c)(4), (5), or (6) organization, the supporting organization will be considered to have met these requirements if its articles require it to carry on charitable, etc., activities within the meaning of § 170(c)(2). [Reg. § 1.509(a)-4(c)(2).]

[b] Limits

An organization is not organized exclusively for the purposes specified in requirement (1) if its articles expressly permit it to operate, to support, or to benefit any organization other than the specified publicly supported organizations. It will not meet the organizational test even though the actual operations of the organization have been exclusively for the benefit of the specified publicly supported organizations. [Reg. § 1.509(a)-4(c)(3).]

[c] Specified Organizations

In order to meet requirement (1), an organization must be organized and operated exclusively to support or benefit one or more specified publicly supported organizations. The manner in which the publicly supported organizations must be specified in the articles will depend on whether the supporting organization is "operated, supervised, or controlled by" or "supervised or controlled in connection with" the organizations or whether it is "operated in connection with" the organizations. [Reg. § 1.509(a)-4(d)(1).]

Generally, the articles of the supporting organization must designate each of the specified organizations by name, unless:

1. The supporting organization is "operated, supervised, or controlled by" or "supervised or controlled in connection with" one or more publicly supported organizations and the articles of organization of the supporting organization require that it be operated to support or benefit one or more beneficiary organizations that are designated by class or purpose and include —

(a) The publicly supported organizations referred to above (without designating the organizations by name), or

(b) Publicly supported organizations that are closely related in purpose or function to those publicly supported organizations; or

2. An historic and continuing relationship exists between the supporting organization and the publicly supported organizations, and because of this relationship, a substantial identity of interests has developed between the organizations.

[Reg. § 1.509(a)-4(d)(2).]

If a supporting organization is operated, supervised, or controlled by, or is supervised or controlled in connection with, one or more publicly supported organizations, it will not fail the test of being organized for the benefit of specified organizations solely because its articles:

1. Permit the substitution of one publicly supported organization within a designated class for another publicly supported organization either in the same or a different class designated in the articles;

2. Permit the supporting organization to operate for the benefit of new or additional publicly supported organizations of the same or a different class designated in the articles; or

3. Permit the supporting organization to vary the amount of its support among different publicly supported organizations within the class or classes of organizations designated by the articles.

[Reg. § 1.509(a)-4(d)(3).]

[2] Operational Test

[a] *Permissible Beneficiaries*

A supporting organization will be regarded as operated exclusively to support one or more specified publicly supported organizations only if it engages solely in activities that support or benefit the specified organizations. These activities may include making payments to or for the use of, or providing services or facilities for, individual members of the charitable class benefitted by the specified publicly supported organization. [Reg. § 1.509(a)-4(e)(1).]

For example, a supporting organization may make a payment indirectly through another unrelated organization to a member of a charitable class benefitted by a specified publicly supported organization, but only if the payment is a grant to an individual rather than a grant to an organization. Similarly, an organization will be regarded as operated exclusively to support or benefit one or more specified publicly supported organizations if it supports or benefits a § 501(c)(3) organization, other than a private foundation, that is operated, supervised, or controlled directly by or in connection with a publicly supported organization, or an organization that is a publicly owned college or university. However, an organization will not be regarded as one that is operated exclusively to support or benefit a publicly supported organization if any part of its activities is in furtherance of a purpose other than supporting or benefitting one or more specified publicly supported organizations. [Reg. § 1.509(a)-4(e)(1).]

[b]   Permissible Activities

A supporting organization does not have to pay its income to the publicly supported organizations to meet the operational test. It may satisfy the test by using its income to carry on an independent activity or program that supports or benefits the specified publicly supported organizations. All such support, however, must be limited to permissible beneficiaries described earlier. The supporting organization also may engage in fund raising activities, such as solicitations, fund raising dinners, and unrelated trade or business, to raise funds for the publicly supported organizations or for the permissible beneficiaries. [Reg. § 1.509(a)-4(e)(2).]

[D]   Absence of Control by Disqualified Persons

The third requirement an organization must meet to qualify as a supporting organization requires that the organization not be controlled directly or indirectly by one or more disqualified persons other than foundation managers or one or more publicly supported organizations.

[1]   Disqualified Persons Defined

For the purposes of the rules discussed here [*see* Appendix 6-A *infra*, for a thorough discussion], the following persons are considered disqualified persons:

1.   All substantial contributors to the foundation;
2.   All foundation managers of the foundation;
3.   An owner of more than 20% of —

(a) The total combined voting power of a corporation that is (during such ownership) a substantial contributor to the foundation,

(b) The profits interest of a partnership that is (during such ownership) a substantial contributor to the foundation, or

(c) The beneficial interest of a trust or unincorporated enterprise that is (during such ownership) a substantial contributor to the foundation;

4. A member of the family of any of the individuals listed above;

5. A corporation of which more than 35% of the total combined voting power is owned by persons listed above;

6. A partnership of which more than 35% of the profits interest is owned by persons described in (1), (2), (3), or (4); or

7. A trust, estate, or unincorporated enterprise of which more than 35% of the beneficial interest is owned by persons described in (1), (2), (3), or (4).

Remember, however, that foundation managers and publicly supported organizations are not disqualified persons for purposes of the third requirement under § 509(a)(3).

If a person who is a disqualified person with respect to a supporting organization, such as a substantial contributor, is appointed or designated as a foundation manager of the supporting organization by a publicly supported beneficiary organization to serve as the representative of the publicly supported organization, that person is still a disqualified person, rather than a representative of the publicly supported organization. [Reg. § 1.509(a)-4(j)(1).]

An organization is considered controlled for this purpose if the disqualified persons, by combining their votes or positions of authority, may require the organization to perform any act that significantly affects its operations or may prevent the organization from performing the act. This includes, but is not limited to, the right of any substantial contributor or spouse to designate annually the recipients from among the publicly supported organizations of the income from his or her contribution. Except as explained under proof of independent control, below, a supporting organization will be considered to be controlled directly or indirectly by one or more disqualified persons if the voting power of those persons is 50% or more of the total voting power of the organization's governing body, or if one or more of those persons have the right to exercise veto power over the actions of the organization. [Reg. § 1.509(a)-4(j)(1).]

Thus, if the governing body of a foundation is composed of five trustees, none of whom has a veto power over the actions of the foundation, and no more than two trustees are at any time disqualified persons, the foundation is not considered controlled directly or indirectly by one or more disqualified persons by reason of this fact alone. However, all pertinent facts and circumstances (including the nature, diversity, and income yield of an organization's holdings, the length of time particular stocks, securities, or other assets are retained, and its manner of exercising its voting rights with respect to stocks in which members of its governing body also have some interest) are considered in determining whether a disqualified person does in fact indirectly control an organization. [Reg. § 1.509(a)-4(j)(1).]

[2] Proof of Independent Control

An organization is permitted to establish to the satisfaction of the IRS that disqualified persons, in fact, do not directly or indirectly control it. For example, in the case of a religious organization operated in connection with a church, the fact that the majority of the organization's governing body is composed of lay persons who are substantial contributors to the organization will not disqualify the organization under § 509(a)(3) if a representative of the church, such as a bishop or other official, has control over the policies and decisions of the organization. [Reg. § 1.509(a)-4(j)(2).]

§ 2-A.03   "CATEGORY TWO" SUPPORTING ORGANIZATIONS

This category includes organizations "operated in connection with" one or more organizations described in § 509(a)(1) or (2). This kind of § 509(a)(3) organization is one that has certain types of operational relationships. If an organization is to qualify as a § 509(a)(3) organization because it is "operated in connection with" one or more publicly supported organizations, it must not be controlled by disqualified persons (as described earlier) and it must meet an organizational test, a responsiveness test, an integral part test, and an operational test. [Reg. § 1.509(a)-4(a)(2).]

> **Note:** Such an entity is also referred to in some sources as a "Type III" (or 3) or "Category III" (or 3) organization, or even as an "entrepreneurial" supporting organization. Because this type requires the least stringent relationship with the supported organization, it is sometimes more appealing to the donor who wishes to have the least substantial relationship permissible with the latter.

[A] Organizational Test

[1] Requirements

This test requires that the organization, in its governing instrument:

1. Limit its purposes to supporting one or more publicly supported organizations;
2. Designate the organizations "operated, supervised, or controlled by"; and
3. Not have express powers inconsistent with these purposes.

These tests apply to all supporting organizations.

In the case of an organization that is "operated in connection with" one or more publicly supported organizations, however, the designation requirement under the organizational test can be satisfied using either of the following two methods.

[2] Method One — Supported Organizations Designated

If an organization is organized and operated to support one or more publicly supported organizations and it is "operated in connection with" that type of organization or organizations, then, its articles of organization must designate the specified organizations by name to satisfy the test. [Reg. § 1.509(a)-4(d)(2).] But a supporting organization that has one or more specified organizations designated by name in its articles will not fail the organizational test solely because its articles:

a. Permit a publicly supported organization, that is designated by class or purpose rather than by name, to be substituted for the publicly supported organization or organizations designated by name in the articles, but only if the substitution is conditioned upon the occurrence of an event that is beyond the control of the supporting organization, such as loss of exemption, substantial failure or abandonment of operations, or dissolution of the organization or organizations designated in the articles;

b. Permit the supporting organization to operate for the benefit of an organization that is not a publicly supported organization, but only if the supporting organization is currently operating for the benefit of a publicly supported organization and the possibility of its operating for the benefit of other than a publicly supported organization is remote; or

c. Permit the supporting organization to vary the amount of its support between different designated organizations, as long as it meets the requirements of the integral part test (discussed later) with respect to at least one beneficiary organization.

[Reg. § 1.509(a)-4(d)(4)(i).]

If the beneficiary organization referred to in (2) is not a publicly supported organization, the supporting organization will not meet the operational test. Therefore, if a supporting organization substituted a beneficiary other than a publicly supported organization and operated in support of that beneficiary, the supporting organization would not be one described in § 509(a)(3). [Reg. § 1.509(a)-4(d)(4)(i).]

[3] Method Two — Supported Organizations Not Designated

If an historic and continuing relationship exists between the supporting organization and the publicly supported organizations, and because of this relationship, a substantial identity of interests has developed between the organizations, then the articles of organization will not have to designate the specified organization by name. [Reg. § 1.509(a)-4(d)(2)(iv).]

[4] Responsiveness Test

An organization will meet this test if it is responsive to the needs or demands of the publicly supported organizations. To meet this test, either of the following must be satisfied:

1. The publicly supported organizations must elect, appoint, or maintain a close and continuing relationship with the officers, directors, or trustees of the supporting organization. (Consequently, the officers, directors, or trustees of the publicly supported organizations have a significant voice in the investment policies of the supporting organization, the timing of grants and the manner of making them, the selection of recipients, and generally the use of the income or assets of the supporting organization); or

2. The supporting organization is a charitable trust under state law, each specified publicly supported organization is a named beneficiary under the trust's governing instrument, and the beneficiary organization has the power to enforce the trust and compel an accounting under state law. [Reg. § 1.509(a)-4(i)(2).]

For an organization that was supporting or benefitting one or more publicly supported organizations before November 20, 1970, additional facts and circumstances, such as an historic and continuing relationship between organizations, may be taken into account in addition to the factors described earlier to establish compliance with the responsiveness test. [Reg. § 1.509(a)-4(i)(1)(i).]

[5] Integral Part Test

The organization will meet this test if it maintains a significant involvement in the operations of one or more publicly supported organizations and these organizations are in turn dependent upon the supporting organization for the type of support that it provides. To meet this test, either of the following must be satisfied [unless transitional rules, discussed in § 2-A.03[A][4] *supra*, apply]:

1. The activities engaged in for, or on behalf of, the publicly supported organizations are activities to perform the functions of or to carry out the purposes of the organizations, and, but for the involvement of the supporting organization, would normally be engaged in by the publicly supported organizations themselves; or

2. The supporting organization makes payments of substantially all of its income to, or for the use of, publicly supported organizations, and the amount of support received by one or more of these publicly supported organizations is enough to insure the attentiveness of these organizations to the operations of the supporting organization. [Reg. § 1.509(a)-4(i)(3).]

If item (2) is being relied on, a substantial amount of the total support of the supporting organization also must go to those publicly supported organizations that meet the attentiveness requirement with respect to the supporting organization. Except as explained in the next paragraph, the amount of support received by a publicly supported organization must represent a large enough part of the organization's total support to insure such attentiveness. In applying this, if the supporting organization makes payments to, or for the use of, a particular department or school of a university, hospital, or church, the total support of the department or school must be substituted for the total support of the beneficiary organization. [Reg. § 1.509(a)-4(i)(3)(iii)(a).]

Even when the amount of support received by a publicly supported beneficiary organization does not represent a large enough part of the beneficiary organization's total support, the amount of support received from a supporting organization may be large enough to meet the requirements of item (2) of the integral part test if it can be demonstrated that, in order to avoid the interruption of a particular function or activity, the beneficiary organization will be sufficiently attentive to the operations of the supporting organization. This may occur when either the supporting organization or the beneficiary organization earmarks the support received from the supporting organization for a particular program or activity, even if the program or activity is not the beneficiary organization's primary program or activity, as long as the program or activity is a substantial one. [*See* Reg. § 1.509(a)-4(i)(3)(iii)(b).]

All factors, including the number of beneficiaries, the length and nature of the relationship between the beneficiary and supporting organization, and the purpose to which the funds are put, will be considered in determining whether the amount of support received by a publicly supported beneficiary organization is large enough to insure the attentiveness of the organization to the operations of the supporting organization. [Reg. § 1.509(a)-4(i)(3)(iii)(d).]

Normally, the attentiveness of a beneficiary organization is motivated by the amounts received from the supporting organization. Thus, the more substantial the amount involved, in terms of a percentage of the publicly supported organization's total support, the greater the likelihood that the required degree of attentiveness will be present. However, in determining whether the amount received from the supporting organization is large enough to insure the attentiveness of the beneficiary organization to the operations of the supporting organization (including attentiveness to the nature and yield of the supporting organization's investments), evidence of actual attentiveness by the beneficiary organization is of almost equal importance. [Reg. § 1.509(a)-4(i)(3)(iii)(d).]

Imposing this requirement is merely one of the factors in determining whether a supporting organization is complying with the attentiveness test. The absence of this requirement will not preclude an organization from classification as a supporting organization if it complies with the other factors.

However, when none of the beneficiary organizations are dependent upon the supporting organization for a large enough amount of their support, the requirements of item (2) of the integral part test will not be satisfied, even though the beneficiary organizations have enforceable rights against the supporting organization under state law. [Reg. § 1.509(a)-4(i)(3)(iii)(e).]

If an organization cannot meet the requirements of item (2) of the integral part test for its current tax year solely because the amount received by one or more of the beneficiaries from the supporting organization is no longer large enough, it can still qualify under the integral part test if it can establish that it has met the requirements of item (2) of the integral part test for any five-year period and that there has been an historic and continuing relationship of support between the organizations between the end of the five-year period and the tax year in question. [Reg. § 1.509(a)-4(i)(1)(iii).]

[6]   Transitional Rule for Integral Part Test

A charitable trust created before November 20, 1970, will meet the integral part test if for tax years beginning after October 16, 1972, the trustee makes annual written reports to all publicly supported beneficiary organizations giving a description of the trust assets (including a detailed list of the assets and the income produced by them) and if the following five conditions have been met continuously since November 20, 1970.

1.   All the unexpired interests in the trust are devoted to charitable purposes;
2.   The trust did not receive any grant, contribution, bequest, or other transfer on or after November 20, 1970;
3.   The trust is required by its governing instrument to distribute all its net income currently to designated publicly supported beneficiary organizations;
4.   The trustee does not have discretion to vary either the beneficiaries or the amounts payable to the beneficiaries;
5.   None of the trustees would be disqualified persons (other than foundation managers) with respect to the trust if the trust were treated as a private foundation.

[Reg. § 1.509(a)-4(i)(4).]

[B]   Operational Test

[1]   Requirements

The requirements for meeting the operational test for organizations "operated, supervised, or controlled by" publicly supported organizations (discussed earlier) have limited applicability to organizations "operated in connection with" one or more publicly supported organizations. This is because the operational requirements of the integral part test, just discussed, generally are more specific than the general rules found for the operational test in the preceding category. However, a supporting organization can fail both the integral part test and the operational test if it conducts activities of its own that do not constitute activities or programs that would, but for the supporting organization, have been conducted by any publicly supported organization named in the supporting organization's governing instrument. [Reg. § 1.509(a)-4(i)(3)(ii).] A similar result occurs for such activities or programs that would not have been conducted by an organization with which the supporting organization has established an historic and continuing relationship.

An organization operated in conjunction with a social welfare organization, labor or agricultural organization, business league, chamber of commerce, or other organization described in § 501(c)(4), (5), or (6), may qualify as a supporting organization under § 509(a)(3) and therefore not be classified as a private foundation if both the following conditions are met:

1. The supporting organization must meet all the requirements previously specified (the organizational tests, the operational test, and the requirement that it be operated, supervised, or controlled by or in connection with one or more specified organizations, and not be controlled by disqualified persons); and

2. The § 501(c)(4), (5), or (6) organization would be described in § 509(a)(2) if it was a charitable organization described in § 501(c)(3). This provision allows separate charitable funds of certain noncharitable organizations to be described in § 509(a)(3) if the noncharitable organizations receive their support and otherwise operate in the manner specified by § 509(a)(2).

[Reg. § 1.509(a)-4(k).]

[2] Special Rules of Attribution

To determine whether an organization meets the not-more-than-one-third support test in § 509(a)(2), amounts received by the organization from an organization that seeks to be a § 509(a)(3) organization because of its support of the organization are gross investment income (rather than gifts or contributions) to the extent they are gross investment income of the distributing organization. [Reg. § 1.509(a)-5(a)(1).] (This rule also applies to amounts received from a charitable trust, corporation, fund, association, or similar organization that is required by its governing instrument or otherwise to distribute, or that normally does distribute, at least 25% of its adjusted net income to the organization, and whose distribution normally comprises at least 5% of its adjusted net income.) All income that is gross investment income of the distributing organization will be considered distributed first by that organization. If the supporting organization makes distributions to more than one organization, the amount of gross investment income considered distributed will be prorated among the distributees. [Reg. § 1.509(a)-5 (a)(1).]

Also, amounts paid by an organization to provide goods, services, or facilities for the direct benefit of an organization seeking § 509(a)(2) status (rather than for the direct benefit of the general public) shall be treated in the same manner as amounts received by the latter organization. These amounts will be treated as gross investment income to the extent they are gross investment income of the organization spending the amounts. [Reg. § 1.509(a)-5(a)(2).] An organization seeking § 509(a)(2) status must file a separate statement with its annual information return, Form 990, listing all amounts received from supporting organizations. [Reg. § 1.509(a)-5(a)(3).]

[3] Relationships Created for Avoidance Purposes

If a relationship between an organization seeking § 509(a)(3) status and an organization seeking § 509(a)(2) status is established or availed of after October 9, 1969, and one of the purposes of establishing or using the relationship is to avoid classification as a private foundation with respect to either organization, then the character and amount of support received by the § 509(a)(3) organization will be attributed to the § 509(a)(2) organization for purposes of determining whether the latter meets the support tests under § 509(a)(2). If this type of relationship is established or used between an organization seeking 509(a)(3) status and two or more organizations seeking 509(a)(2) status, the amount and character of support received by the former organization will be prorated among the latter organizations. [Reg. § 1.509(a)-5(b)(1).]

In determining whether a relationship exists between an organization seeking 509(a)(3) status (supporting organization) and one or more organizations seeking 509(a)(2) status (beneficiary organizations) for the purpose of avoiding private foundation status, all pertinent facts and circumstances will be taken into account. The following facts may be used as evidence that such a relationship was not established or availed of to avoid classification as a private foundation.

1. The supporting organization is operated to support or benefit several specified beneficiary organizations;
2. The beneficiary organization has a substantial number of dues-paying members who have an effective voice in the management of both the supporting and the beneficiary organizations;
3. The beneficiary organization is composed of several membership organizations, each of which has a substantial number of members, and the membership organizations have an effective voice in the management of the supporting and beneficiary organizations;
4. The beneficiary organization receives a substantial amount of support from the general public, public charities, or governmental grants.
5. The supporting organization uses its funds to carry on a meaningful program of activities to support or benefit the beneficiary organization and, if the supporting organization were a private foundation, this use would be sufficient to avoid the imposition of the tax on failure to distribute income;
6. The operations of the beneficiary and supporting organizations are managed by different persons, and each organization performs a different function; and

7. The supporting organization is not able to exercise substantial control or influence over the beneficiary organization because the beneficiary organization receives support or holds assets that are disproportionately large in comparison to the support received or assets held by the supporting organization.

[Reg. § 1.509(a)-5(b)(2).]

[4] Effect on § 509(a)(3) Organizations

If a beneficiary organization fails to meet either of the support tests of § 509 (a)(2) due to these provisions, and the beneficiary organization is one for whose support the organization seeking § 509(a)(3) status is operated, then the supporting organization will not be considered to be operated exclusively to support or benefit one or more § 509(a)(1) or (2) organizations and therefore would not qualify for § 509(a)(3) status. [Reg. § 1.509(a)-5(a)(2).]

[C] Absence of Control by Disqualified Persons

As with the "Category One" supporting organization, the "Category Two" supporting organization must not be controlled directly or indirectly by disqualified persons, as discussed in § 2-A.02[D] above.

§ 2-A.04   CLASSIFICATION UNDER § 509(A)

If an organization is described in § 509(a)(1), and is also described in either § 509(a)(2) or (3), it will be treated as a § 509(a)(1) organization. [Reg. § 1.509 (a)-6.]

§ 2-A.05   RELIANCE BY GRANTORS AND CONTRIBUTORS

Once an organization has received a final ruling or determination letter classifying it as an organization described in § 509(a)(1), (2), or (3), the treatment of grants and contributions and the status of grantors and contributors to the organization will generally not be affected by reason of a later revocation by the IRS of the organization's classification until the date on which notice of change of status is made to the public (generally by publication in the *Internal Revenue Bulletin*) or another applicable date, if any, specified in the public notice. In appropriate cases, however, the treatment of grants and contributions and the status of grantors and contributors to an organization described in § 509 (a)(1), (2), or (3) may be affected pending verification of the continued classification of the organization. Notice to this effect will be made in a public announcement by the IRS. In these cases, the effect of grants and contributions made after the date of the announcement will depend on the statutory qualification of the organization as an organization described in § 509(a)(1), (2), or (3). [Reg. § 1.509(a)-7(a).]

Caution: The preceding paragraph shall not apply if the grantor or contributor:

1. Had knowledge of the revocation of the ruling or determination letter classifying the organization as an organization described in § 509(a)(1), (2), or (3); or

2. Was in part responsible for, or was aware of, the act, the failure to act, or the substantial and material change on the part of the organization that gave rise to the revocation.

[Reg. § 1.509(A)-7(B).]

PRIVATE OPERATING FOUNDATIONS AND EXEMPT OPERATING FOUNDATIONS (IRC §§ 4942(J)(3) AND 4940(D)(2))

§ 2-B.01 PRIVATE OPERATING FOUNDATION (IRC § 4942(j)(3))

[A] Defined

A private foundation may qualify for treatment as a private operating foundation. These foundations generally are still subject to the tax on net investment income (under IRC § 4940), and to the other requirements and restrictions that generally apply to private foundation activity. However, operating foundations are not subject to the excise tax on failure to distribution income (under IRC § 4942). Also, contributions to private operating foundations described in § 4942(j)(3) are deductible by the donors to the extent of 50% of the donor's adjusted gross income, whereas contributions to other private foundations are generally limited to 30% of the donor's adjusted gross income. In addition, a private operating foundation may receive qualifying distributions from a private foundation if the private foundation does not control it.

A private operating foundation is any private foundation that spends at least 85% of its adjusted net income or its minimum investment return, whichever is less, directly for the active conduct of its exempt activities (the income test), and that, in addition, meets one of the following tests: the assets test, the endowment test, or the support test. Certain private foundations that provide long-term care facilities are treated as operating foundations *only* for the purposes of the excise tax on failure to distribute income.

[B] Income Test

To qualify as an operating foundation, the organization must make qualifying distributions directly for the active conduct of its exempt activities equal to substantially all (at least 85%) of the lesser of its: (1) Adjusted net income, or (2) Minimum investment return. [IRC § 4942(j)(3)(A) and Reg. § 53.4942(b)-1(c).]

If a private foundation's qualifying distributions exceed its minimum investment return for the tax year, but are less than its adjusted net income, substantially all of the total qualified distributions must be made directly for the active conduct of the foundation's exempt activities. However, if the foundation's minimum investment return is less than its adjusted net income and its qualified distributions equal or exceed the adjusted net income, only that part of the qualified distributions equal to substantially all of the foundation's adjusted net income must be made directly for the active conduct of the foundation's exempt activities. [Qualifying distributions and minimum investment return are defined in Appendix 6-D.]

[1] Adjusted Net Income

Adjusted net income is the excess of gross income for the tax year (including gross income from any unrelated trade or business) determined with certain modifications (described later) over the total deductions (including deductions directly connected with carrying on any unrelated trade or business) that would be allowed a taxable corporation determined with certain modifications (described later). [IRC § 4942(f).]

Gross income does not include gifts, grants, or contributions received by the private operating foundation but does include income from a functionally-related business. Gross income and the total deductions allowable from that income will be figured as they are normally figured for income tax purposes except as otherwise provided. In figuring adjusted net income, no exclusions, deductions, or credits are allowed except those provided under Income Modifications and Deduction Modifications, as discussed below.

[a] Income Modifications

The following modifications must be made to income:

1. Interest on government obligations normally excluded under § 103 of the Code is included in gross income.

2. When reporting capital gains and losses from the sale or other disposition of property, only net short-term capital gains are included in gross income. Long-term capital gains or losses are not included. Neither are net § 1231 gains included. But net § 1231 losses may be included in the computation if the losses are otherwise deductible under these rules. Any net short-term capital loss may not be deducted for the year in which it occurs. This loss may not be carried back or carried over to earlier or later tax years regardless of whether the foundation is a corporation or a trust. Capital gain dividends received from a regulated investment company are excluded from the foundation's adjusted net income.

3. Gross income includes:

> (a) Amounts received or accrued as repayments of amounts taken into account as qualifying distributions for any tax year,

> (b) Amounts received or accrued from the sale or other disposition of property to the extent that the acquisition of the property was considered a qualifying distribution for any tax year, and

> (c) Any amount set aside for a specific project (*see* Set-asides, in Chapter 7) to the extent the amount set aside was not necessary for the purposes for which it was set aside.

4. The excess of fair market value on the date of distribution over adjusted basis of property distributed to a state, a U.S. possession, or any political subdivision thereof, the United States, or the District of Columbia for public purposes, or to a charitable trust or corporation, will not be included in gross income.

5. The income received from an estate during the administration period will not be included in the operating foundation's gross income. However,

if the estate is considered terminated for income tax purposes because of a prolonged administration period, the income will be included in gross income.

[IRC § 4942(f)(2); Reg. § 53.4942(a)-2(d)(2).]

For purposes of item 2, in determining gain from the sale or other disposition of property, adjusted basis will be the greater of:

1. The fair market value of the property on December 31, 1969, plus or minus all adjustments to basis after 1969, using straight line depreciation and cost depletion, if the foundation held the property on December 31, 1969, and continuously thereafter to the date of sale or disposition, or

2. Adjusted basis as normally determined using straight line depreciation or cost depletion.

[Reg. § 53.4942(a)-2(d)(3).]

For determining loss from a sale or other disposition of property, the adjusted basis as normally determined using straight-line depreciation or cost depletion will apply.

> **Example:** The Morgan Foundation bought unimproved land in January 1969, for $102,000. On December 31, 1969, the fair market value of the property was $110,000 and the adjusted basis was still $102,000. The property was sold on January 2, 1983, for $105,000. Because the fair market value on December 31, 1969, was greater than the adjusted basis, the fair market value is the adjusted basis used to determine gain. However, because the adjusted basis for determining gain, $110,000, was greater than the sale price, there was no gain. Moreover, because the adjusted basis for determining loss, $102,000, was less than the sale price, there was no loss. [Reg. § 53.4942(a)-2(d)(3), Example (3).]

[b] Deduction Modifications

Deductions generally are limited to ordinary and necessary expenses paid or incurred for the production or collection of gross income, or for the management, conservation, or maintenance of property held for the production of income. These expenses include the part of a private foundation's operating expenses paid or incurred for the production or collection of gross income. Operating expenses include compensation of officers, other salaries and wages of employees, interest, rent, and taxes. When only part of the property is income producing or held for the production of income subject to the provisions of § 4942 and the remainder is used for exempt purposes, the allowable deductions must be divided between exempt and nonexempt uses. If the expenses for property used for exempt purposes are more than the income received from the property, the excess may not be deducted. [IRC § 4942(f)(3); Reg. § 53.4942(a)-2(d)(4).]

Allowances for straight line depreciation and depletion (other than percentage depletion) are deductible. Deductions will be allowed for expenses and interest paid or incurred to carry tax-exempt obligations. However, no deduction will be allowed for amounts not paid or incurred for purposes described earlier. For example, there will be no deduction for:

1. Charitable contributions;
2. Net operating losses; and
3. The special deductions for corporations.

[IRC § 4942(f)(3); Reg. § 53.4942(a)-2(d)(4).]

[2] Qualifying Distributions

[a] *Directly for the Active Conduct of Exempt Activities*

The qualifying distributions must be made "directly for the active conduct of exempt activities" means qualifying distributions a foundation makes that are used to conduct exempt activities by the foundation itself, rather than by or through one or more grantee organizations that receive the qualifying distributions directly or indirectly from the foundation. [Reg. § 53.4942(b)-1(b)(1).]

[b] *Grants Made to Other Organizations*

Grants made to other organizations to assist them in conducting their activities are considered an indirect, rather than direct, means of carrying out an exempt purpose of the private foundation, even though the activities of the grantee organization may further the exempt activities of the grantor foundation. [Reg. § 53.4942(b)-1(b)(1).]

[c] *Amounts Paid to Buy or Maintain Assets*

Amounts paid to buy or maintain assets used directly in the conduct of the foundation's exempt activities, such as the operating assets of a museum, public park, or historic site, are direct expenditures for the active conduct of the foundation's exempt activities. Likewise, administrative expenses (such as staff salaries and traveling expenses) and other operating costs necessary to conduct the foundation's exempt activities (regardless of whether they are directly for the active conduct of exempt activities) are treated as qualifying distributions expended directly for the active conduct of exempt activities if the expenses and costs are reasonable in amount. However, administrative expenses and operating costs that are not for exempt activities, such as expenses in connection with the production of investment income, are not treated as qualifying distributions.

Expenses for both exempt and non-exempt activities will be allocated to each activity on a reasonable and consistently applied basis. [Reg. § 53.4942(b)-1(b)(1).]

Any amount set aside by a foundation for a specific project, for example to buy and restore or build additional buildings or facilities that are to be used by the foundation directly for the active conduct of the foundation's exempt activities, will be treated as qualifying distributions expended directly for the active conduct of the foundation's exempt activities if the set-aside meets the requirements described in Chapter 7. [Reg.§ 53.4942(b)-1(b)(1).]

[d]   *Payments to Individuals*

If a foundation makes or awards grants, scholarships, or other payments to individual beneficiaries (including program-related investments as described in Chapter 7) to support active programs to carry out the foundation's exempt purpose, the payments will be treated as qualifying distributions made directly for the active conduct of exempt activities only if the foundation maintains some *significant involvement* in the active programs in support of which it makes the payments. A foundation will be considered as maintaining a *significant involvement* in grantmaking if:

1. The foundation operates as follows:

(a) An exempt purpose of the foundation is the relief of poverty or human distress, and its exempt activities are designed to improve conditions among the poor or distressed or in an area subject to poverty or national disaster (such as providing food or clothing to indigents or residents in a disaster area),

(b) The grants or other payments for the exempt purpose are made directly by the foundation without the help of an intervening organization or agency, and

(c) The foundation has a salaried or voluntary staff of administrators, researchers, or other personnel who supervise and direct the exempt activities on a continuing basis, or

2. The foundation has developed some specialized skills, expertise, or is involved in a particular discipline (such as scientific or medical research, social work, education, or the social sciences). It has a salaried staff of administrators, researchers, or other personnel who supervise or conduct programs or activities that support the foundation's work in its particular area of interest. As part of these programs or activities the foundation makes grants, scholarships, or other payments to individuals to encourage their involvement in the foundation's area of interest and in some segment of the activities carried on by the foundation (such as grants under which the recipients, in addition to independent study, attend classes, seminars, or conferences sponsored or conducted by the foundation, or grants to engage

in social work or scientific research projects under the general direction and supervision of the foundation). [Reg. § 53.4942(b)-1(b)(2) (i).]

Whether making or awarding grants, scholarships, or other payments constitutes qualifying distributions made directly for the active conduct of the foundation's exempt activities is determined by the facts and circumstances of each particular case. The test applied is a qualitative one. If the foundation maintains a significant involvement (as defined earlier), it will not fail to qualify solely because more of its funds are devoted to grants, scholarships, or other payments than to the active programs that such grants, scholarships, or other payments support.

However, if a foundation does not more than select, screen, and investigate applicants for grants or scholarships, under which the recipients perform their work or studies alone or exclusively under the direction of some other organization, the grants or scholarships will not be treated as qualifying distributions made directly for the active conduct of the foundation's exempt activities. The administrative expenses of screening and investigating (as opposed to the grants or scholarships themselves) may be treated as qualifying distributions made directly for the active conduct of the foundation's exempt activities. [Reg. § 53.4942(b)-1(b)(2)(i).]

[e] *Payment of Tax on Net Investment Income*

Only private operating foundations may treat the payment of the tax on net investment income [*see* Chapter 7] as a qualifying distribution made directly for the active conduct of activities constituting the foundation's exempt purpose. [Reg. § 53.4942(b)-1(b)(3).]

[C] Assets Test

A private foundation will meet the assets test if 65% or more of its assets:

1. Are devoted directly to the active conduct of its exempt activity, or to a functionally related business, or a combination of the two,
2. Consist of stock of a corporation that is controlled by the foundation (by ownership of at least 80% of the total voting power of all classes of stock entitled to vote and at least 80% of the total shares of all other classes of stock) and at least 85% of the assets of which are so devoted, or
3. Are any combination of (1) and (2).

[IRC § 4942(j)(3)(B)(i); Reg. § 53.4942(b)-2(a).]

[1] Qualifying Assets

An asset is devoted directly to the foundation's exempt purpose only if it is used by the foundation in actually carrying on the charitable, educational, or other similar function that gives rise to the exempt status of the foundation. Assets such as real property, physical facilities or objects (such as museum assets, classroom fixtures, and research equipment) and intangible assets (such as patents, copyrights, and trademarks) are directly devoted to the extent they are used by the foundation in directly carrying on its exempt activities or program. However, assets (for example, stocks, bonds, or rental property) including endowment funds, when held primarily for the production of income, for investment, or for some similar use, are not devoted directly to the active conduct of the foundation's exempt function, even though income from the assets is used to carry on the foundation's exempt function. Whether an asset is held for the production of income, for investment, or for some similar use, rather than being used for the active conduct of the foundation's exempt activities, is a question of fact. [Reg. § 53.4942(b)-2(a)(2)(i).]

For example, an office building used to provide offices for employees engaged in the management of endowment funds of the foundation is not devoted to the active conduct of the foundation's exempt activities. However, for property used both for exempt and other purposes, if the exempt use of the property represents at least 95% of the total use, the property will be considered to be used exclusively for an exempt purpose. Property acquired by a foundation to be used in carrying out its exempt purpose may be considered devoted directly to the active conduct of that purpose even though the property, in whole or in part, is leased for a limited and reasonable period of time during which arrangements are made for its conversion to the use for which it was acquired. Generally, one year is considered a reasonable period of time. Similarly, when property is leased by a foundation in carrying out its exempt purpose and when the rental income received from the property by the foundation is less than the amount that would be required to be charged to recover the cost of purchase and maintenance of the property, the property will be considered devoted directly to the active conduct of the foundation's exempt activities. [Reg. § 53.4942(b)-2(a)(2)(i).]

Fair market value must be used in determining whether 65% or more of the assets are devoted directly to exempt purposes. However, in the case of assets that are unique and for which no ready market or standard valuation method exists, such as historical objects, buildings, certain works of art, and botanical gardens, the historical cost (unadjusted for depreciation) will be considered fair market value, unless the foundation can show that fair market value is other than cost. If the foundation can show that fair market value is other than cost, this substituted valuation may be used for the tax year for which the new valuation is shown and for each of the following four tax years. [Reg. § 53.4942(b)-2(a)(4).] [See Chapter 7 for a discussion of valuation issues.]

Assets maintained for extending credit or making funds available to members of a charitable class are not considered assets devoted directly to the active conduct of exempt activities. For example, assets set aside in special reserve accounts to guarantee student loans made by lending institutions will not be considered qualifying assets. Even though amounts set aside for specific projects may qualify, as previously explained, as distributions expended directly for the active conduct of exempt activities for the income test, they do not qualify under the assets test as assets devoted directly to the active conduct of the foundation's exempt activities. [Reg. § 53.4942(b)-2(a)(2(ii).]

[2] Assets Held for Less than a Full Tax Year

In applying the assets test, assets held for only part of the tax year are taken into account for the year by multiplying the fair market value of each asset by a fraction. The numerator of the fraction is the number of days during the year that the foundation held the asset, and the denominator is the total number of days in the year. [Reg. § 53.4942(b)-2(a)(3).]

[D] Endowment Test

A foundation will meet the endowment test if it normally makes qualifying distributions (defined in Chapter 7) directly for the active conduct of its exempt activities of at least two-thirds of its minimum investment return. The term "directly for the active conduct of its exempt activities" means the same as it does for the income test discussed earlier. [IRC § 4942(j)(3)(B)(ii) and Reg. § 53.4942(b)-2(b).]

The minimum investment return for any private foundation is 5% of the excess of the combined fair market value of all assets of the foundation (other than those used or held for use directly in the active conduct of its exempt purpose) over the amount of indebtedness incurred to buy those assets. The qualifying distributions required to meet the endowment test are thus, in effect, two-thirds of this amount, or $3\frac{1}{3}$% of the foundation's endowment. In determining whether the amount of qualifying distributions is at least two-thirds of the organization's minimum investment return, the organization is not required to trace the source of the expenditures to determine whether they were received from investment income or from contributions. [Reg. § 53.4942(b)-2(b) (1).]

> **Example:** X foundation, created after May 26, 1969, has $400,000 of endowment funds and other assets not directly used for its exempt purpose. X makes qualifying distributions of $20,000 during the year directly for the active conduct of its exempt function. Two-thirds of X's minimum investment return is $13,333.33 (5% × $400,000 = $20,000; $\frac{2}{3}$ × $20,000 = $13,333.33). Since the $20,000 distribution is greater than $13,333.33, X meets the endowment test.

[E] Support Test

A private foundation will meet the support test if:

1. At least 85% of its support (other than gross investment income) is normally received from the general public and 5 or more unrelated exempt organizations;

2. Not more than 25% of its support (other than gross investment income) is normally received from any one exempt organization; and

3. Not more than 50% of its support is normally received from gross investment income.

[IRC § 4942(j)(3)(B)(iii); Reg. § 53.4942(b)-2(c)(1).]

Here the term *support* means gifts, grants, contributions, membership fees, the value of services or facilities furnished by a government unit without charge, net income from unrelated business activities, and gross receipts from admissions, sales of merchandise, performance of services, or providing facilities in any activity that is not an unrelated trade or business, as provided in IRC § 509 (d). [Reg. § 53.4942(b)-2(c)(2)(i).] The support received from any one exempt organization may be counted toward satisfying the 85% support test only if the foundation receives support from at least five exempt organizations. [Reg. § 53.4942(b)-2(c)(2)(iii).]

> **Example:** A foundation that normally receives 20% of its support (other than gross investment income) from each of five unrelated exempt organizations will meet the support test even though it receives no support from the general public. However, if a foundation normally receives 50% of its support (other than gross investment income) from three foundations and the balance of the support comes from sources other than exempt organizations, the foundation will not meet the 85% test. [Reg. § 53.4942(b)-2(c)(2) (iii).]

Support from the general public includes support received from an individual, trust, corporation, or governmental unit to the extent that the total amount received from any one individual, trust, or corporation does not exceed 1% of the foundation's total support (other than gross investment income) for the period. In applying the 1% limit, all support received from any donor and any person related to the donor is treated as received from one person. Support received from a governmental unit is not subject to the 1% limit. [Reg. § 53.4942(b)-2(c) (2)(iv).]

[F] Determination of Compliance with Operating Foundation Tests

The determination of whether the income test and one of the three remaining tests are met depends on whether the tests are met in the normal and regular operation of a foundation over a period of years, rather than on a given day during the year or on a year-by-year basis. A foundation may qualify as an operating foundation if it meets the income test and either the assets, endowment, or support test for any three years during a four-year period, or on the basis of a combination of all pertinent amounts of income or assets held, received, or distributed during the four-year period. The four-year period consists of the tax year in question and the three years immediately before the year in question. A foundation may not use one method for satisfying the income test and the other method for satisfying one of the other tests. [Reg. § 53.4942 (b)-3 (a).]

For example, if the income test is satisfied on the three-out-of-four-year basis, you may not use the four-year combination method to satisfy one of the other tests. However, the fact that the foundation uses one method to satisfy the tests in a particular year will not prevent it from using the other method to satisfy the tests in a later year. If a foundation fails to satisfy the income test and either the assets, endowment, or support test for a particular tax year under *either* the three-out-of-four-year method or the combination method, it will be treated as a nonoperating foundation for the tax year and for all later tax years until it satisfies the tests. [Reg. § 53.4942(b)-3(a).]

[G] New Organizations

A newly organized foundation generally will be treated as an operating foundation only if it has satisfied the income test and one of the three other tests for its first tax year of existence. If so, it will be treated as an operating foundation from the beginning of its first year. This status will continue for its second and third tax years of existence only if it satisfies the tests by the combination method for all tax years of existence. [Reg. § 53.4942(b)-3(b)(1).]

Before the end of its first tax year, a foundation may be treated as an operating foundation if it has made a good faith determination that it is likely to meet the tests for its first year. A good faith determination may be based on an affidavit or opinion of counsel, giving enough facts concerning the operations and support of the organization to enable the Internal Revenue Service to determine that the requirements are likely to be met. If a foundation is treated as an operating foundation for its first year, but actually fails to qualify for the first year, it will be treated as a nonoperating foundation as of the first day of its second year. However, such a foundation may establish to the satisfaction of the Service that it is likely to qualify as an operating foundation on the basis of its second, third, and fourth tax years. If so, it will be treated as an operating foundation until the first day of a tax year in which it fails to qualify. Status as a private foundation that is not an operating foundation will continue until the organization is able to satisfy these tests by either the three-out-of-four-year method or the combination method. [Reg. § 53.4942(b)-3(a)(2).]

[H] The Deductibility of Grants or Contributions

The deductibility of grants or contributions to an operating foundation will not be affected until notice of a change in the status of such an organization is made to the public (such as by publication in the Internal Revenue Bulletin) *unless:*

1. The contribution was made after the contributor acquired knowledge that the organization would be deleted by the Service from classification as an operating foundation; or

2. The contribution was made after an act or failure to act which caused the inability to satisfy the tests for qualification as an operating foundation, and the contributor was responsible for, or was aware of, the act or failure to act. A contributor will not be considered responsible for, or aware of, the act or failure to act if the contributor made the contribution relying on a written statement by the foundation that the contribution would not result in the inability to qualify as an operating foundation. This statement must be signed by a foundation manager and must give enough facts concerning the operations and support of the organization to assure a reasonably prudent person that a contribution would not result in disqualification as an operating foundation.

[Reg. § 53.4942(b)-3(d).]

§ 2-B.02   EXEMPT OPERATING FOUNDATIONS (IRC § 4940(d)(2))

[A]   Defined

Effective for tax years beginning after 1984, certain private operating foundations, known as exempt operating foundations are not subject to the tax on net investment income. To qualify as an exempt operating foundation for a tax year, a private foundation must meet all the following requirements:

1. It must be a private foundation;
2. It has been *publicly supported* for at least 10 tax years or was a private operating foundation on January 1, 1983, or for its last tax year ending before January 1, 1983;
3. Its governing body, at all times during the tax year, consists of individuals less than 25% of whom are disqualified individuals, and is broadly representative of the general public; and
4. It has no officer who is a disqualified individual at any time during the tax year.

[IRC § 4940(d)(2).]

[1]   Publicly Supported

Publicly supported means that the organization normally receives:

1. A substantial part of its support (other than income from its exempt function) from governmental units or from direct or indirect contributions from the general public; or
2. More than a third of its support from governmental units, certain publicly supported charities, and persons other than disqualified persons [*see* Chapter 5], in any combination of gifts, grants, contributions, membership fees, and gross receipts from activities that are not an unrelated trade or business (but only

including such gross receipts from any one person, or bureau or similar agency of a governmental unit, that are not more than the greater of $5,000 or 1% of the foundation's support for the tax year), and does not normally receive more than a third of its support from gross investment income [*see* Chapter 4] plus any excess of unrelated business taxable income over the tax on unrelated business income. [IRC §§ 4940(d)(2)(A), 170(b)(1)(A)(vi), and 509(a)(2).]

A "substantial part" of the foundation's support, for purposes of (1) above, generally is a third of its total support, figured on a combined basis for the four tax years immediately preceding the tax year in question. However, if the foundation does not meet this one-third support test, it may still qualify as deriving a substantial part of its support from governmental units and from the general public if it:

1. Normally receives at least 10% of its support from these sources;
2. Satisfies the "attraction of public support" requirement by being organized and operated to attract new and additional public or governmental support on a continuous basis; and
3. Satisfies some or all of five public support factors.

Substantial public support is discussed in detail in IRS Publication 557, Tax-Exempt Status for Your Organization.

[2] Disqualified Individual

For purposes of the requirements regarding composition of the governing body and officers of the foundation, the term "disqualified individual" means any of the following:

1. A substantial contributor [*see* Chapter 6];
2. An owner of more than 20% of —
    (a) The total combined voting power of a corporation;
    (b) The profits interest of a partnership; or
    (c) The beneficial interest of a trust or unincorporated enterprise, which is a substantial contributor to the foundaton; or
3. A member of the family [*see* Chapter 5] of any individual described in (1) or (2).

[IRC § 4940(d)(3)(B).]

Indirect ownership of stock in a corporation, profits interest in a partnership, or beneficial interest in a trust or unincorporated enterprise is taken into account for determining a disqualified individual under (2) above, according to the rules explained under attribution of ownership in Chapter 6.

[B]   Ruling Letter Required

A foundation wanting recognition of "exempt operating foundation" status must obtain a ruling letter from the Internal Revenue Service determining that it has met the specific requirements of this special status. To claim exemption from the tax on net investment income, the foundation should attach a copy of this ruling letter to its annual returns, Forms 990-PF, for tax years beginning after 1984 for which the claim for exemption is made. The Internal Revenue Service has centralized its processing of various types of exempt organization requests and applications in the Ohio Key District Office, Cincinnati, and requests for recognition of exempt operating foundation status are among these. To obtain such a ruling letter, the foundation should submit its request to Internal Revenue Service,

    Internal Revenue Service
    P.O. Box 192
    Covington, KY 41012-0192

Applications shipped by Express Mail or a delivery service should be sent to:

    Internal Revenue Service
    Attn: Extracting Stop 312
    201 West Rivercenter Blvd.
    Covington, KY 41011

There is no user fee charged for such a ruling letter.

Supporting documents and materials with the ruling request must demonstrate that requirements (1) through (4) listed at the beginning of this discussion are met. Specifically, for purposes of requirements (3) and (4), the foundation must list all its officers and members of its governing body for the current year and identify any that are disqualified individuals.

[Ann. 85-88, 1988-21 IRB 21; Rev. Proc. 2000-8, 2000-1 I.R.B. 230.]

CHAPTER 3

HOW TO CREATE A FAMILY FOUNDATION

§ 3.01   OPERATING FORM: CORPORATION OR TRUST

[A]   Legal Differences

A family foundation may be formed as one of two types of legal entities — a trust or a corporation. A trust and a corporation are distinctly different sorts of legal entities, and these differences have consequences that may come into play at some point in the future. The donor family should review these differences before selecting the form that is preferable for its particular family foundation.

[1]   Formation and Reporting Requirements

When the corporate form is used, the foundation is typically a nonprofit corporation organized under the nonprofit corporation laws of the state in which it is located. Such a corporation is formed by filing the proper document with the appropriate state office. This document is typically the articles of incorporation or certificate of incorporation, sometimes referred to as the corporation's "charter." Most states have separate statutory provisions governing nonprofit or not-for-profit (as distinguished from for-profit) corporations. The proper forms must be filed, and these must be in the correct form; as a result, the corporation usually cannot begin operation until the forms are filed and accepted by the appropriate state agency. Once a nonprofit corporation has been properly created, it must adopt bylaws to provide internal operating rules for the corporation. These bylaws and the statutes of the state of incorporation together provide a set of regulations that govern the foundation and form the framework for its governance.

By contrast, the creation of a trust is easier and quicker, since all that is required is the preparation and execution of a trust document and the transfer of the initial trust assets. There is usually no requirement that the trust instrument be filed or recorded with the state government. Although a foundation formed as a trust need not do so, it may adopt bylaws to form a framework of operating rules for its governance. In most states, a trust is ultimately subject to the jurisdiction of a local court — typically, the probate court — which can be petitioned to intervene when problems or disputes arise.

The corporation is subject to other governmental requirements that normally do not apply to a trust. Because a corporation is a creature of state law, it must be formed and operated in accordance with the laws of its state of incorporation. This means that, in addition to the initial filing requirements, certain formalities have to be followed on an ongoing basis. In most states, an annual report form, listing the officers and directors and other information, must be filed and an accompanying filing fee paid. Failure to file this will normally result in a penalty charge, and if several filings are missed, the corporation's charter may be revoked. Even though this is usually easily corrected by updating the filings and paying the necessary fees, it is important for the corporation to meet these requirements and keep its corporate status up to date.

One other corporate filing is normally required when the corporation is formed under the laws of one state and has its operations centered in another state. This filing may have different names in different states, but is generally referred to as an application for a certificate of authority or a registration to do business as a foreign corporation in the state other that the state of incorporation. An example might be a foundation formed under Delaware law that will have its only operations in, say, New York. This may be done for any number of reasons; one reason may be that the family's legal counsel may be familiar with Delaware law and wish to secure some benefit that is available under that law, but not under the law of New York. Sometimes Delaware or some other state is selected when the law of the family's state of residence is deemed undesirable because of some demanding regulatory requirement or other feature that may be avoided by incorporating elsewhere. Once the corporation is registered (or "qualified") in the second state, however, it will normally have to comply with annual filing requirements there as well, so be sure that the demanding requirement that is to be avoided by incorporating elsewhere is really avoided.

The legal nature of a corporation differs from that of a trust in a number of respects, so there are other considerations to be taken into account as well. For example, a trust acts through its trustee or trustees, while a corporation acts through its directors. The applicable local law may impose different standards of conduct on trustees and directors, with trustees usually held to a higher standard. Similarly, state law may provide for limited liability of corporate directors, but extend no comparable privilege to trustees.[1]

[2] Flexibility in Changing Purposes

Trusts and corporations differ also in the degree of flexibility that they offer to their creators and administrators, particularly insofar as changes to the purposes and functions of the entity are concerned. A trust is limited by its governing instrument to whatever purposes and functions its creator chooses to include in the instrument. Unless the instrument contemplates changes in future years, those purposes and functions cannot be easily changed; if they can be changed at all, this must be accomplished in a court proceeding, the outcome of which may be far from clear. Unless all parties to the trust (including the creator and, in many cases, the state attorney general's office) are before the court and join in requesting the change, the trust is unlikely to be amended. By contrast, a corporation may readily be changed, often by a simple majority vote of its board of directors to amend its certificate of incorporation. This may be an important consideration to some families creating a family foundation; depending upon the circumstances, such a family may favor one entity or the other.

Some families are intent upon creating a foundation that will serve a given set of priorities, and no others, forever. This is often the case when a foundation

---

[1] *See* Chapter 5 for a discussion of liability issues.

is created to serve religious purposes or some other deeply held views of the founders. In such an instance, the family may prefer to create a trust rather than a nonprofit corporation, thereby making it difficult for future generations to depart from the charitable purposes prescribed by the founders. On the other hand, another family may find the flexibility offered by a nonprofit corporation to be more appealing, so that future descendants will be free to pursue their own charitable goals and interests as they see fit. Depending upon how the family views such future changes, either the trust or the nonprofit corporation may be better suited to carry out the intended purposes.

While the trust is inherently less flexible than the nonprofit corporation, one should not conclude that the trust form is the only choice for a person who desires to maintain complete control of a family foundation in its initial years. Often the potential shortcomings can be offset with careful planning and drafting of the governing documents. For example, the law of most states permits formation of a membership corporation with a single member — which can be the founder. In most cases, it will even be possible to designate that person to serve as sole member for life. Acting in that capacity, he or she can select board members, control grants, and, in short, dictate every aspect of what happens with the foundation.

Conversely, a trust can be drafted to include much of the flexibility that would normally be available only via state corporation statutes. As a consequence of such planning factors, the choice between a trust and a corporation cannot be made solely on the basis of flexibility; if one form or another is desired on other grounds, it may be made to fit the client's overall needs through careful draftsmanship.

> **Note:** A related consideration is the concern of some clients that in the distant future their descendants (or worse, the foundation management) may take their foundation off course. Such clients often cite the Ford Foundation as an example of this. For measures to prevent this, see § 2.09.

[3] Flexibility of Corporate Statutes

The state statutes governing corporations, both nonprofit and for-profit, are for the most part comprehensive and provide a detailed framework of operating rules to govern the management and in general guide the affairs of the corporation. A trust, by contrast, is an inherently inflexible device that has historically operated primarily to invest its corpus and devote the income therefrom to whatever purposes the creator has designated. The management of the trust cannot be easily changed, and the trustees' discretion and decisions are subject to review by a court at the instance of an aggrieved beneficiary. Having arisen in the context of donative transfers as a means of providing ongoing support for the beneficiaries, along with a touch of supervision, the trust is not designed to meet fast-changing conditions or to react swiftly to changing conditions. If special considerations such as a mechanism for changing trustees or a method for resolving competing considerations are to be provided for in a trust, these must normally be included in the governing instrument; if no such provisions are made, the trustees may be required to seek the approval of a court for their actions. Corporation statutes in every state provide easy answers to such every-day issues.

[4] Operating an Active Program

If the family foundation will be operating a program of some sort, perhaps with a staff and an office or other facility at which active operations are conducted, as opposed to a mere funding or grantmaking function, the corporate format may be better adapted. In our system, the nonprofit corporation is the norm for such an operation, and the flexibility afforded by the state statutes governing such entities can provide a convenient structure for the conduct of this enterprise. For the reasons discussed in the immediately preceding section, the corporation and its adaptable framework can be easier to work with than the inflexible trust format.

[5] Foreign Grants or Overseas Operations

Due to an odd provision in the Internal Revenue Code (IRC), selection of a form of entity may be important for some family foundations with overseas programs. The last sentence of IRC § 170(c)(2) provides a special disallowance rule for an organization that both (1) receives contributions from donors that are corporations and (2) uses such funds outside the United States. Under that provision, the corporate donor is not entitled to deduct its contributions unless the donee organization is a nonprofit *corporation* (as opposed to a trust). Thus, the trust format should probably be avoided if overseas operations or grant programs are contemplated and contributions to the foundation may come from a family corporation.

[6] Taxation of Unrelated Business Income

Although the family foundation will be exempt from tax, at least at the federal level, under IRC § 501(c)(3), its exemption will not extend to certain types of business income. Even such a tax-exempt entity is taxable on its *unrelated business taxable income*. This refers to the income of a *trade or business* that is *regularly carried on* and is *not related to the organization's tax-exempt purpose or function*. In addition, an exempt organization's *debt-financed* income is taxable. Most family foundations have only passive investment income, which is not subject to this tax, so the unrelated business income tax is not normally a factor. Nevertheless, this can become an important consideration in some circumstances, particularly if the foundation managers are unaware of the applicable rules. This may occur, for example, if the foundation's investment managers cause it to purchase an interest in some sort of entity that produces gains or other returns by purchasing investments with borrowed funds.

If the foundation should realize unrelated business income in this or any other manner, it will be subject to tax on the resultant income as either a trust or a corporation, depending upon which form of entity is used. A foundation formed as a trust will be taxable at trust rates, which are usually higher than those applicable to corporations.

[B] A Checklist to Guide the Decision

The following factors should be considered when making a decision whether to utilize a trust or a nonprofit corporation for a family foundation:

- How important is the ability to change the purposes and programs of the foundation to meet changing conditions in the future?

- Do the founders want to lay down strict limitations to be followed permanently by future generations?

- Is it anticipated that the foundation will realize income classified as unrelated business income for tax purposes?

- Will the foundation be a passive grantmaking entity, or will it conduct active operations?

- Will there be corporate donors to the foundation? If so, does the foundation anticipate using the contributed funds outside United States?

§ 3.02   FUNDING THE FOUNDATION

The foundation will not be fully operational until it has received assets, which it may use (along with the income earned on such assets) to finance its operations, pay the expenses of its administration, and conduct its regular operations. Selection of corporate assets to fund the foundation involves a number of considerations, including both tax issues and practical realities.

One overriding consideration is the special tax limitation applicable to contributions of appreciated property to organizations that are classified as private foundations for tax purposes. The general rule is that a deduction otherwise allowable for such a contribution is limited to the donor's cost basis in the transferred property.[2] As with most tax rules, there is an exception, and in this instance, the exception is as important as the rule itself. Contributions of publicly traded stocks to private foundations are deductible in full. As a result, such contributions are the most common basis for funding a family foundation. In most cases, a donor who is contemplating creating a private foundation

---

[2] *See* IRC § 170(e)(1)(B)(ii), and the exception in IRC § 170(e)(5).

considers the availability of a contribution deduction, and the amount of that deduction, an important factor. The donor may have a variety of assets to choose from, and if this is the case, he or she will be well advised in most cases to utilize publicly traded stocks that have appreciated in value since they were acquired. For this category of asset, and this category alone, the donor's deduction will be equal to the fair market value of the property, and the donor will avoid any capital gains tax on the appreciation. If any other type property is used, the donor's deduction will be limited to basis.[3]

Note also the following special considerations for such property contributions to family foundations:

1. These deduction limitations are not applicable to some specialized categories of foundations. These organizations, although classified as private foundations for tax purposes and thus subject to many of the restrictions discussed in Chapter 6, are treated more generously for contribution deduction purposes. Examples most commonly encountered are private operating foundations and "conduit" foundations.

2. In some circumstances, the donor's basis in the property may be sufficiently high that these limitations are not a problem. This could be true, for example, where the donor contributes property that has recently been inherited and thus has received a stepped-up basis or where the property simply has not appreciated significantly in value. Although a well-informed tax planner will be properly concerned about the possible reduction of the donor's contribution deduction for a gift of property to a foundation, this factor must be evaluated in light of the precise property to be contributed.

[A] Investment Assets

The foundation obviously needs financial resources if it is to survive. Access to resources may occur in either of two ways. Some family foundations exist, and thrive, on the basis on an ongoing annual program of contributions and disbursements. Others depend upon a one-time or occasional contribution, which it uses to build an endowment fund. The term "endowment" implies a lofty concept, but it is really a very practical answer to the foundation's need for ongoing capital. Through an endowment fund, the foundation builds a more or less permanent accumulation of investment assets that will produce an income stream sufficient to support its ongoing operations.

Often the foundation will receive a contribution of stock, which it then sells in order to assemble a diversified portfolio of income-producing investments. Real estate, closely held business interests, or other assets may be contributed for

---

[3] *See* § 2.03 *supra* for a full discussion of these deduction limitations.

the same purpose, but this is less common because, as discussed above, the donor's deduction may be limited to basis.

In selecting assets to contribute to the foundation, one must look beyond the immediate consequences of the contribution itself to the practical issues that will arise from the foundation's subsequent ownership of the asset. An asset that makes perfect sense as a holding for the donor or the donor's family may pose problems for the foundation. For example, business interests are a very common form of wealth in this country, and a donor's first inclination may be to transfer such an interest to his or her foundation. However, ownership by a private foundation raises issues that are never encountered when individuals own the same interest. These issues, including the points discussed below, need not prevent the use of a business interest to fund a foundation, but they are best taken into account initially by thinking through the possible problems that could arise on the particular facts presented and by trying to anticipate and avoid them.

The excess business holdings rules, discussed in Chapter 6, limit the business ownership interest that may be held by a private foundation. While those rules can be quite complicated, they generally limit the foundation's permissible business interest to 20 percent, *reduced by* the percentages held by the donor and related interests. That is, this group as a whole can hold only 20 percent of a business corporation or partnership. (The allowable percentage is raised to 35 percent if effective control is held by persons outside the group.) A *de minimis* rule permits the foundation to hold a two percent interest in any event. And the foundation may not hold any interest whatsoever in a sole proprietorship conducting a business. These rules may make it advisable to find other property to contribute to a family foundation. (An exception may exist in situations where the business is about to be sold to an independent third-party buyer from outside the family; the foundation is entitled to hold property received by gift or bequest for at least five years, which may be sufficient to allow a well-considered sale.)

Another set of problems for the foundation-owned business can arise under the self-dealing prohibition, which is discussed in Chapter 6. When a family business is owned, even in part, by a foundation, there is a possibility that many common business situations, such as paying compensation, employing family members, and setting expense account allowances, can trigger self-dealing issues. These may not be serious, if indeed they are encountered at all, but the important thing to remember is that this is a potential problem that arises only if the foundation is given an ownership interest. Again, the planner must look past the initial contribution to anticipate what practical operating problems may arise at a later date.

The management of the foundation's investment portfolio is ultimately the responsibility of its board of directors or trustees, although investment advisors or managers normally are hired to assist in this process.[4]

---

[4] *See* Chapter 8 for a discussion of investment management.

[B] Program-Related Assets

In addition to its investment portfolio, a foundation may hold assets that are used in the conduct of its charitable program. Examples might include artworks made available to museums, medical equipment used to treat needy patients, or an automobile used to transport the elderly to obtain medical attention. Such assets play no role in the generation of income or gain to support the foundation, but are nevertheless important to the accomplishment of its charitable objectives. These assets raise several considerations that distinguish them from the other assets held by the foundation. First, as discussed above, these assets may be subject to deduction limitations, so that when contributed to the foundation they produce a deduction equal to the donor's basis in the property, rather than the fair market value. Thus, the donor may wish to consider whether this reduction in the contribution deduction available is a large enough factor to warrant selecting other property for the contribution. (Often the need for this particular piece of property will outweigh the deduction factor, but the donor should be aware of the difference.)

Also, the nature of these assets raises other implications for the donor and the donor's contribution deduction. In most cases, program-related assets are tangible personal property. While the usual rules governing tangible personal property will be met (since the donee's use of the property will be related to its exempt purposes), there are other points to consider. Since such property often has no title registration, as would be the case with art objects or office equipment, it may be necessary to document the transfer to the foundation via a notarized deed of gift (to pin down the date definitively).

Finally, program-related assets have a special status in the hands of the foundation, in that they are disregarded in computing the foundation's minimum distribution requirement. The amount the foundation must distribute annually is determined by reference to its investment assets alone, so assets used in its charitable program are disregarded for this purpose.[5]

[C] Valuation

The value of the assets of a foundation must be determined on at least two occasions. First, when assets are contributed to the foundation by the donor, the donor's deduction is determined by reference to their fair market value at the time of contribution. In general, fair market value is defined as the price at which the object would sell between a willing buyer and a willing seller, with neither under any compulsion to buy or sell and both in full possession of the facts concerning the object.

Second, the foundation's investment assets must be valued on a regular basis in order to determine the amount of the foundation's minimum distribution requirement, which is generally equal to five percent of its investment assets.[6]

---

[5] *See* § 7.04[B][2] *infra* for a complete discussion of this principle.

[6] *See id.* for a detailed discussion of minimum distribution requirements.

[D] Timing the Funding

There are as many different approaches to the timing of foundation funding as there are family foundations. Some foundations are funded in one or just a few installments so as to build an endowment that will continue on the fairly permanent basis. This would normally be the case, for example, where the foundation is created by bequest, under the creator's will. Others are funded on an in-and-out basis, with one or more contributions made each year, followed by grants or distributions in a similar overall amount. There is no right or wrong way to do this, and the appropriate approach for any given family foundation depends upon the needs and wishes of the parties.

From the donor's perspective, an important consideration is that his or her deduction will be allowable in the year in which the contribution is made. When making contributions at the end of the year (a very common situation), it is important to be sure that the transfer to the foundation is completed by December 31. The emphasis here is on *completion*. If the donee is a newly formed foundation, one must be sure that it is properly formed and its existence is not in doubt. If the foundation is a corporation, the certificate of incorporation from the applicable state official should be in hand. If it is a trust, the document should be completed and executed; the signatures should be notarized to avoid any doubt as to the date in this case.

The transfer itself must be completed and not merely started. Payments by check should be evidenced by depositing the check in the mail on or before December 31. If the check subsequently clears in due course, this is sufficient. To be absolutely certain, the check should be deposited in sufficient time to allow it to clear by year end. Stock transfers should be completed by leaving no act yet to be performed as of the end of the year. Thus, stocks should be out of the donor's brokerage account and into the foundation's account by December 31. In case of other property, the donor should follow a similar approach so that no steps remain incomplete by year end. The key to avoiding mistakes and complications here is to plan ahead and take all necessary steps well in advance of the applicable deadline.

> **Example 1:**   Mrs. Rosen decides to contribute 100 shares of IBM stock to her family foundation in December 2006. The stock is held in her brokerage account. On November 15, 2006, she sends her broker written instructions to transfer the shares from her account to the foundation's account. Her letter provides the account numbers for both accounts and indicates that she wants the transfer to be completed no later than December 15. On December 1, she calls to check on the status of the transfer and learns that it is not yet completed. She calls again on December 8 and learns that the stock was transferred to the foundation's account on December 6. Mrs. Rosen has handled the transfer properly, and she will be entitled to a deduction for the transfer on her 2006 income tax return. The amount of her deduction will be the average of the high and low trading prices on December 6, 2006.

Example 2: Mrs. Thompson decides to contribute 100 shares of IBM stock to her family foundation in December 2006. The stock is held in her brokerage account. On December 15, 2006, she calls her broker and instructs the broker to make the transfer. When she receives her January statement on January 10, 2007, she sees that the transfer was never made and the stock remains in her account. Because of the sloppy manner in which the transfer instructions were handled, she will not be entitled to a 2006 deduction.

[E]   Funding from Outside Donors

In the typical case, virtually all the funding for a family foundation comes from one or more members of a single family. This is by no means required, however, and the family foundation is free to seek and receive funding from other sources. The family corporation may make contributions, and these will be fully deductible on its income tax return. The same is true of friends, business associates, or other contributors. Persons whose employers operate matching grant programs should check the terms of those programs to determine whether private foundation donees are excluded. The substantiation requirements, which are applicable to contributions from outside donors as well as those from within the family, are discussed below.

[F]   Substantiation — No Special Exception for Foundations!

Any charitable contribution of $250 or more, *including a contribution to a family foundation*, must be properly substantiated if it is to be deductible for federal income tax purposes. The donor's deduction may be disallowed if a dated receipt from the donee charity is not obtained prior to the due date for the donor's return, including extensions (or the date the return is filed, if earlier). That receipt must include the following information:

- The date of the contribution,

- The nature and amount of the payment (for example, $5,000 in cash or 500 shares of Microsoft common stock), and

- The value of any goods or services (quid pro quo) provided the donor (if none were provided, as should always be the case with a foundation donee, the receipt must state that none were provided).

Note that while you may think you misread that last part, you probably did not. The donor who makes a contribution to his or her own family foundation is required, in effect, to issue a receipt to himself or herself. While this may seem useless and silly, it is required by law, and the donor's failure to comply can cause loss of the deduction. See § 3.02[G] below for a discussion of a case disallowing a contribution to a foundation where the donor had no receipt to substantiate his contribution. A sample substantiation form is set forth in Appendix 3-A.

[G] No Receipt, No Deduction

A 2003 Tax Court case underscores the fact that family foundation contributions must be substantiated in the same fashion as any other contribution.

The case in question, *Stussy v. Commissioner,*[7] is a memorandum decision of the United States Tax Court, which means that it is primarily a factual determination rather than a legal precedent. The taxpayer in question, Dieter Stussy, argued with the IRS over several issues on his 1998 tax return and eventually took the case to the Tax Court. Mr. Stussy and the government were unable to agree on three issues involving a total tax deficiency of $2,983.

Mr. Stussy's father had been an active professional painter and a former Dean of the School of Art at UCLA. Just before the father died in 1990, a § 501 (c)(3) organization named the Jan Stussy Foundation (Foundation) was formed to deal with his paintings and other artwork. The Foundation's collection of more than 1,000 large paintings was stored at Stussy's Los Angeles residence, and its value as of December 31, 1998, was $820,934. Mr. Stussy's father had given the Foundation a license for the exclusive use of four rooms in the residence. The rooms, totaling 900 square feet, were not used by Mr. Stussy for personal purposes during 1998, and he was not entitled to collect rent from the Foundation; the Foundation was liable for only the payment of insurance.

During 1998, Mr. Stussy paid some $4,782 in miscellaneous expenses with respect to the residence. He allocated these amounts to the Foundation using a percentage allocation and claimed a charitable contribution for the portion of the expenses allocated to the Foundation. He did not receive any written acknowledgment from the Foundation for any contributions to the Foundation during 1998, and the Foundation did not report its receipt of any contributions during 1998.

The IRS disallowed the deductions for one reason only—Mr. Stussy did not have the written acknowledgment required by IRC § 170(f)(8)(A) for all contributions of $250 or more. One might expect the IRS to quibble with the nature of these expenses or the allocations used, but the court does not mention any IRS contention other than the missing receipt. The Tax Court agreed with the IRS and disallowed the deductions in full:

> Given that petitioner does not have such a written acknowledgment from the Foundation as to the disputed expenses, we conclude that he is precluded from deducting them. . . . A contrary conclusion would contravene the statutory text and the purpose of recordkeeping for contributions in excess of $250.

---

[7] T.C. Memo 2003-232.

Admittedly, the facts in this case differ from the typical family foundation contribution of cash or securities. The deductions claimed were for an allocation of household expenses, a type of deduction that can be expected to elicit IRS scrutiny. The charitable deduction issue was one of several minor issues remaining after the parties apparently compromised on other issues. Moreover, the decision leaves open the possibility that there may have been other reasons for challenging the deduction even if proper substantiation had been obtained. Furthermore, this is only a memorandum decision, which the Tax Court does not regard as precedent for other cases. In addition, the donor did not have the assistance of an attorney, who might have mounted Stussy's argument more effectively. But despite these potentially mitigating circumstances, the fact remains that the Tax Court denied the donor's deduction in an opinion reasoned solely on the basis of the missing substantiation.

> **Note:** The *Stussy* case was appealed, partly on grounds that at least some of the expenses paid on behalf of the Foundation were paid in amounts of less than $250, such that a contemporaneous written acknowledgment would not be required. This contention may or may not have been proved on appeal. It seems likely that the case was settled, or dropped. Nevertheless, the underlying principle is worth noting. The Regulations state that a series of separate contributions will not normally be aggregated to determine whether the $250 threshold is met. Thus, for example, if Mr. Stussy had paid a $200 expense for the Foundation each month for a full year, substantiation would presumably not be required, even though the total amount paid on behalf of the Foundation would total $2,400. While this principle should not be relied upon as a planning technique, it may be helpful if it fits the particular circumstances involved.

[H] IRS Publication Makes Substantiation Easier

A 2002 revision of IRS Publication 1771, "Charitable Contributions — Substantiation and Disclosure Requirements" — available on the IRS web site at *www.irs.gov* — provided an easy means of providing substantiation for contributions to foundations. In discussing the various ways that charities may comply with the rules, the IRS states that the charity may provide the required acknowledgment electronically, such as via an e-mail addressed to the donor. The donor should not attach the acknowledgment to his or her return but rather retain it to substantiate the contribution if and when the IRS comes to call.

> **Note:** Many taxpayers seek an extension of the due date for their income tax returns rather than filing on April 15. An automatic four-month extension to August 15 is easily available, and the IRS will extend the due date even longer if the taxpayer can demonstrate a good reason. Extension of the date for filing your return also extends the deadline for getting your

charitable contributions in hand. If your return (or that of a client) is on extension, it makes good sense to check whether any necessary charity acknowledgments are still missing. If so, armed with the new information about the willingness of the IRS to accept electronic acknowledgments (i.e., e-mails), you have both the time and the opportunity to correct the situation.

An e-mail acknowledgment of a contribution can be quite simple. IRS Publication 1771 provides several examples demonstrating how simple wording in an e-mail from the donee to the donor will suffice. If the acknowledgment relates to a contribution to your own family foundation, you can simply send yourself an e-mail along the lines of the sample below; be sure to sign the e-mail in your capacity as an officer, trustee, or director of the foundation. Here is an example of what you need to say in your electronic acknowledgment:

> Thank you for your contribution of 1,000 shares of ABC Corporation common stock *or, your cash contribution of $10,000* received on December 12, 2006. No goods or services were provided in exchange for your contribution.

§ 3.03   SEEKING TAX-EXEMPT STATUS

The family foundation will not be fully functional until it has received Internal Revenue Service (IRS) recognition of its exemption from tax under IRC § 501(c)(3). Application for tax-exempt status should be made promptly after the foundation is formed, although as a matter of law it need not be done for 27 months (a 15-month initial deadline plus an automatic 12-month extension).[8] If an exemption application is filed within that period, the foundation will be regarded as tax exempt from the date of its formation. Completing, filing, and processing the exemption application is normally the most time-consuming and expensive aspect of creating the foundation and should be done promptly after the foundation is established.

[A]   Form 1023

[1]   In General

Application to the IRS for recognition of the foundation's status as a tax-exempt organization, described in IRC § 501(c)(3), is made by means of Form 1023. The form, set forth in Appendix 3-B, consists of some 28 pages, with a lengthy booklet of instructions. It should be filled out carefully, with special attention paid to providing answers that are complete and fully responsive to the questions asked. If these guidelines are followed, the processing of the form will

---

[8] Reg. § 1.508-1(a)(2) provides the 15-month period, and this is automatically extended for an additional 12-month period by Reg. § 301.9100-2(a)(2)(iv).

be greatly expedited and the foundation's exemption letter received without undue delay.

If you are setting out to prepare Form 1023, make sure you have the newest version. A major revision in 2004 rendered prior versions obsolete, and the IRS will no longer accept prior versions. The current form is available on the IRS web site (*www.irs.gov*), and is reproduced *infra* in Appendix 3-B.

It is worth noting that, under our system of government, tax-exempt status is not granted or denied on the basis of any discretion exercised by the IRS. Rather, any organization that meets the applicable standards is entitled to tax-exempt status. Form 1023 is designed merely to elicit sufficient information to allow the IRS to determine that the applicable standards have been met.

Most of the information requested on Form 1023 is readily apparent and self-explanatory. However, there are a few points that should be noted, and careful adherence to these suggestions can prevent unnecessary delay in the receipt of a foundation's exemption letter. The following suggestions relate to the parts of Form 1023 indicated.[9]

[2] Completing Form 1023

First, with regard to the entire exemption application, remember that you are filling out and filing a document that will be available to the general public on demand. That includes your friends and enemies alike, plus newspaper reporters and your nosy neighbors. So try to be complete and concise in your answers, but do not go beyond the information requested, and do not say anything you would not want to see in your local newspapers.

Answer every question, and include "not applicable" or "NA" where appropriate, rather than leaving a blank.

Remember that this is a "one size fits all" form used by all of the various types of charitable organizations to apply for recognition of their status as a section 501(c)(3) organization. Accordingly, some of the questions will have no relevance to a family foundation. For example, the questions about fund-raising activities and tax-exempt bond financing will generally be irrelevant to the family foundation.

Also worth noting is the fact that Form 1023 is the first contact your foundation will have with the IRS. The form is designed to provide the IRS with an overall picture of the organization and thus serve as a starting point for its file. For this reason, the IRS person processing the form may ask additional questions upon reviewing Form 1023, and some of these may appear to request duplicate information that was already provided in the initial filing. Here, there are several things to keep in mind. First, the IRS needs and is entitled to a full picture of the organization, and evasive or incomplete answers are likely to delay

---

[9] *See* Appendix 3-B for a copy of Form 1023 and the official instructions therefor.

the process. Second, many of the questions are there only to elicit descriptive information; there are no "trick" questions, and many have no right or wrong response. Finally, if your response to a request for additional information is arrogant or rude (such as "As we said in our original filing . . . " or "If you will simply look at Item 2 on page X of Form 1023, you will see that . . . "), you are less likely to elicit a favorable response. Review your response to be sure it conveys the impression that a responsible and businesslike adult prepared it. Your application will be processed by a knowledgeable individual who has a job to do, and you will be more likely to produce the result you want if you remember this and treat him or her with the respect you would expect yourself.

[3] Completing Form 1023 — Specific (Line-by-Line) Comments

Part I, Item 2. Include the foundation's employer identification number (EIN). If no number has been obtained, follow the official instructions that pertain to this line and Form SS-4 to obtain a number by telephone or online. In the past, if a number had been applied for, but not yet received, some practitioners would put "applied for" in this space. The Instructions to Form 1023 now state unequivocally "Do not submit this application until you have obtained an EIN." You can easily obtain an EIN without delay on the IRS website, or by fax or phone. See the instructions to Form SS-4 (available of www.irs.gov) for correct instructions.

Part III, Required Provisions in Your Organizing Documents — This set of questions attempts to ensure that your articles of incorporation or trust instrument do not omit any of the required provisions by asking you to identify the precise location of each mandatory provision.

Part IV, Narrative Description of Activities — Read the directions carefully, and do what they say. Do not merely repeat the language in your foundation's articles of incorporation or trust instrument. This item asks for your foundation's *activities*, not its purposes or other background information. Exactly what will the foundation do? For most foundations, the answer here will be fairly straightforward, for most foundations simply make grants to other organizations as determined by their boards of directors or trustees. Explain any relationships you contemplate with other organizations, and include any activities you plan to initiate at a later date. Look over your response carefully to be sure you have not raised more questions than you have answered. If you make passing references to commercial activities or other items that suggest possible noncharitable activities, you can expect a request for clarification. Accordingly, be sure Form 1023 (and especially this response) makes your foundation looks like a charitable organization and not some other sort of entity.

Part V, Compensation — Here the Form 1023 asks a number of questions about compensation and other financial arrangement with officers, directors, trustees, and independent contractors. These should be read carefully and answered completely. Item 5 asks if you have a conflict of interest policy and directs you to a sample set forth in the Instructions. Here, even though foundations are largely precluded from many of the situations addressed in that sample, it may prove expeditious to adopt the policy statement (appropriately adjusted to fit your situation) and thereby avoid a possible inquiry as to why no such policy is in place.

Part V, Items 1a-c. It is a common practice to attach a statement listing the officers, directors, trustees, and other persons on the printed Form 1023. Where this is done, the notation "See attached statement" in this block is sufficient. But pay careful attention to the instructions, which indicate that the mailing addresses of the listed individuals, and not that of the organization, should be given. Also, if you use an attached statement, do not overlook the fact that the annual compensation of each is to be listed (with "none" stated if that is the case); failure to do this may cause delay. Be complete when describing how compensation levels and other arrangements with insiders are to be determined.

Part VI. The question about members refers to active, dues-paying members. Few family foundations are organized on a membership basis.

Part VI, Items 1-3. The question about providing benefits refers to things such as meals to needy individuals, a home for the aged, or a museum. Grants to other organizations are not included here.

Part VII, Item 2. To be exempt under section 501(c)(3) from the date it is created, an organization is required to file Form 1023 within 15 months of its initial formation. The IRS has provided an automatic extension of another 12 months (for a total of 27 months) if the organization files Form 1023 within 12 months after the end of the 15-month period.[10] Beyond this time, the organization can apply for a discretionary extension if it can show that it acted reasonably and in good faith and that granting this extension will not prejudice the interests of the government. See Schedule E of Form 1023 and page 21 of the instructions for Form 1023[11] for more details on this sort of extension.

Part VIII, Items 1-4. Most family foundations will answer "no" to these questions, and certainly to Item 1 regarding political campaigns.[12]

---

[10] Reg. § 301.9100-2(a)(2)(iv).

[11] The instructions for Form 1023 are provided at Appendix 3-B.

[12] *See* §§ 6.06[A] and [B] *infra* for more details on what activities are prohibited for private foundations.

Part VIII, Item 13. Most private foundations make grants, loans, or other distributions to organizations, and so must answer all the subparts of this question. A newly formed foundation typically will not yet have sample grant agreements or grant applications to provide, and may thus state "not yet available" to the questions asking for copies of these documents.

Part IX, Financial Data. These financial schedules must be filled in as completely as possible. Use of the IRS format, as indicated on Form 1023, will increase the likelihood of acceptance, but a substitute statement can be attached if desired. For a new organization (one in existence for less than a year), revenue and expenditures are required for the current year, plus proposed budgets for the next two years. Pay careful attention to any unusual revenue or expenditure categories, and be sure that any questions raised are covered in Part IV. For example, if your budget statements indicate that significant revenue is expected from royalties or publications, but the description of activities does not include anything that would produce such revenue, a question has been raised. It is better to anticipate and answer the question than to await an inquiry from the IRS.

Part X. The typical family foundation is a private foundation for tax purposes and must thus answer "yes" to Item 1A.

Part X, Items 2-4. These questions cover private operating foundation status.[13]

Part X, Items 5a-5i. The typical family foundation will have answered "yes" to Item 7, indicating that it is a private foundation, so it will leave these items blank

Part XI, User Fee. Attach a check for the fee indicated on the form. Note that the fee for Form 1023 is subject to change, and the current amounts can be obtained on the IRS web site (*www.irs.gov*) by typing "User Fee" in the keyword box, or by phone from IRS Customer Account Services at 1-877-829-5500.

Signatures. Form 1023 is to be signed by an officer, a trustee, a director, or other official authorized to sign the application. An individual authorized by a power of attorney (Form 2848) may not sign the application unless that person is also an officer, director, trustee, or other authorized official.

Attachments. Do not forget to include all of the required attachments, or your exemption application will be delayed:

Form 1023 Checklist. The last two pages of IRS Form 1023 provide a checklist to help you assure that your Form is complete and ready for filing.

---

[13] *See* § 2.06[A] *supra* for a discussion of private foundation operating status.

(See Appendix 3-B, *infra*.) You should place a check in the box for each of the points raised on the checklist and provide the information requested. When completed, this checklist goes on the top of the package as you send it to IRS.

- *Organizing Documents.* Attach a copy of the articles of incorporation or trust agreement, plus the bylaws if they have been adopted. If bylaws have not yet been adopted, you must attach an explanation of how officers, directors, or trustees are selected.

- *Power of Attorney.* If an attorney or other agent is to file Form 1023 on behalf of the foundation, an executed copy of Form 2848, Power of Attorney and Declaration of Representative, should be included in the package.

- *Attached Statements.* If any attachments are referred to in Form 1023, as, for example, where space is inadequate for a full answer or where an attached statement is used to list officers and directors (see Part II, Item 4a, above), this should be on 8½ × 11 paper, with the organization's name, address, and employer identification number at the top of each page. Every entry on an attachment should refer to the part and item number to which it relates.

[B]   State Tax Qualification

Receipt of an exemption letter from the IRS establishes the foundation's tax-exempt status under the federal tax laws, but this leaves open the question of the foundation's tax status under the applicable state law. In some states, receipt of the IRS exemption letter will automatically qualify the foundation to be exempt under state law. In other states, a separate state exemption application must be filed with the state tax authorities. States vary in the degree to which they impose rules and regulations beyond the state tax rules affecting charitable entities within their jurisdiction.

> **Note:**   The question of the foundation's status under state *tax* laws is separate from questions involving the issuance of a certificate of incorporation for a nonprofit corporation and subsequent annual filings with the state corporation officials. A foundation that is organized as a nonprofit corporation must file two sets of documents — tax returns with the state (and federal) tax authorities and corporate filings with the corporation authorities in its home state. In addition, if the foundation is registered to do business in other states, it will probably have filing obligations there as well. A trust typically files only with the tax authorities, but the applicable law in your jurisdiction should be checked.

SAMPLE SUBSTANTIATION TRUST FORM

Every person who contributes $250 or more to any charity, including a family foundation, must be given a receipt in substantially the form shown below. Such a donor will *not* be entitled to an income tax deduction for the contribution unless he or she can produce the receipt for the IRS on demand. At one time, a canceled check was sufficient substantiation, but that is no longer the case. A donor of $250 or more must have this receipt in hand before filing IRS Form 1040 for the year of the contribution. Although this receipt requirement is somewhat silly in the case of a donor who contributes to his or her own family foundation, this is what the law requires. The receipt itself does not have to be complicated. Most donee organizations provide receipts to their donors in the form of a simple letter. Whether a letter or a separate form is used, it should include language similar to the sample below.

THE DAVID AND GOLIATH FAMILY FOUNDATION

Thank you for your contribution of $ _____ in cash [and/or insert description of property, e.g., 100 shares of ABC Stock]. The Internal Revenue Code requires us to acknowledge your contribution in writing and to state that we provided no goods or services in consideration of your gift. You should keep this letter with your tax records. YOUR INCOME TAX CHARITABLE DEDUCTION MAY BE DISAL-LOWED IF YOU ARE UNABLE TO PROVIDE THIS ACKNOWLEDGMENT TO THE INTERNAL REVENUE SERVICE UPON REQUEST.

The value of property contributions need not be included, but these contributions must be described specifically, as demonstrated above.

Alternatively, as described above in § 3.02[H], a substantiation may be sent via e-mail. This may be done via a form along the lines of the following:

To: Daniel Donor

From: Daniel Donee, Treasurer, Donee Family Foundation

Subject: Substantiation for your 200[X] contribution(s)

Thank you for your contribution of 1,000 shares of ABC Corporation common stock [*or, your cash contribution of $10,000*] received on December 12, 200[X]. No goods or services were provided in exchange for your contribution.

FORM 1023 AND INSTRUCTIONS

[*Note: A full-sized version of the following form and instructions can be viewed at* http://ftp.fedworld.gov/pub/irs-pdf/k1023.pdf.]

Instructions for Form 1023

 Department of the Treasury
Internal Revenue Service

(Rev. June 2006)

Application for Recognition of Exemption Under Section 501(c)(3) of the Internal Revenue Code

Section references are to the Internal Revenue Code unless otherwise noted.

What's New

The user fee for the initial application for recognition of exemption under IRC Section 501(c)(3) has been increased. Part XI of Form 1023 has been revised to reflect the new fee. See Rev. Proc. 2006-8, 2006-1 I.R.B. 245 for more information about user fees that may be applicable to tax-exempt organizations.

How To Get Forms and Publications

Personal Computer

You can access the IRS website 24 hours a day, 7 days a week at *www.irs.gov* to:
• Order IRS products online.
• Download forms, instructions, and publications.
• Get answers to frequently asked tax questions.
• Search publications online by topic or keyword.
• Send us comments or request help by email.
• Sign up to receive local and national tax news by email.

CD-ROM

You can order Publication 1796, IRS Tax Products CD, and obtain:
• Current-year forms, instructions, and publications.
• Prior-year forms, instructions, and publications.
• Bonus: Historical Tax Products DVD — Ships with the final release.

Cat. No. 17132z

• Tax Map: an electronic research tool and finding aid.
• Tax Law frequently asked questions (FAQs).
• Tax Topics from the IRS telephone response system.
• Fill-in, print, and save features for most tax forms.
• Internal Revenue Bulletins.
• Toll-free and email technical support.
• The CD is released twice during the year.
  o The first release will ship the beginning of January 2007.
  o The final release will ship the beginning of March 2007.

Purchase the CD from National Technical Information Service at *www.irs. gov/cdorders* $25 (no handling fee) or call 1-877-CDFORMS (1-877-233-6767) toll-free to buy the CD for $25 (plus a $5 handling fee). Price is subject to change.

By Phone and In Person

You can order forms and publications by calling **1-800-TAX-FORM** (1-800-829-3676). You can also get most forms and publications at your local IRS office.

Overview of Section 501(c)(3) Organizations

Who Is Eligible for Section 501(c)(3) Status?

Organizations organized and operated exclusively for religious, charitable, scientific, testing for public safety, literary, or educational purposes, or to foster national or international amateur sports competition, or for the prevention of cruelty to children or animals are eligible to file Form 1023 to obtain recognition of exemption from federal income tax under section 501(c)(3) of the Internal Revenue Code.

Form 1023 not necessary. The following types of organizations may be considered tax exempt under section 501(c)(3) even if they do not file Form 1023.
• Churches, including synagogues, temples, and mosques.
• Integrated auxiliaries of churches and conventions or associations of churches.
• Any organization that has gross receipts in each taxable year of normally not more than $5,000.

Even though the above organizations are not required to file Form 1023 to be tax exempt, these organizations may choose to file Form 1023 in order to receive a determination letter that recognizes their section 501(c)(3) status and specifies whether contributions to them are tax deductible.

Qualification of a Section 501(c)(3) Organization

There are two key requirements for an organization to be exempt from federal income tax under section 501(c)(3). A 501(c)(3) organization must be organized and operated exclusively for one or more exempt purposes.

Organized. An organization must be organized as a corporation (including a limited liability company), trust, or unincorporated association. The organizing document (articles of incorporation if you are a corporation, articles of organization if you are a limited liability company, articles of association or constitution if you are an association, or trust agreement or declaration of trust if you are a trust) must limit the organization's purpose(s) and permanently dedicate its assets to exempt purposes.

Operated. An organization must be operated to further one or more of the exempt purposes stated in its organizing document. Certain other activities are prohibited or restricted, including, but not limited to, the following activities. A 501(c)(3) organization must:

   a. Absolutely refrain from participating in the political campaigns of candidates for local, state, or federal office.
   b. Absolutely ensure that its assets and earnings do not unjustly enrich board members, officers, key management employees, or other insiders.
   c. Not further non-exempt purposes (such as purposes that benefit private interests) more than insubstantially.
   d. Not operate for the primary purpose of conducting a trade or business that is not related to its exempt purpose(s).
   e. Not engage in activities that are illegal or violate fundamental public policy.
   f. Restrict its legislative activities.

Legislative activity. An organization does not qualify for section 501(c)(3) status if a substantial part of its activities is attempting to influence legislation.

   Form 5768. Most public charities are eligible to elect to make expenditures to influence legislation by filing Form 5768, Election/Revocation of Election by an Eligible Section 501(c)(3) Organization To Make Expenditures To Influence Legislation. By filing Form 5768, an eligible organization's legislative activities will be measured solely by an expenditure limit rather than by the "no substantial amount" limit. For additional information on the expenditure limit or the no

substantial amount limit, see Publication 557, Tax-Exempt Status for Your Organization.

For this purpose, "legislation" includes action by Congress, a state legislature, a local council, or a similar governing body, with respect to acts, bills, resolutions or similar items (such as legislative confirmation of appointive offices). Legislation also includes action by the public in a referendum, ballot initiative, constitutional amendment, or similar procedure. Legislation generally does not include actions by executive, judicial, or administrative bodies.

Organizations may involve themselves in issues of public policy without being engaged in legislative activity. For example, organizations may conduct educational meetings, prepare and distribute educational materials, or otherwise consider public policy issues. Similarly, an organization may appear before a governmental body to offer testimony about a decision that may affect the organization's existence.

 A private foundation is not allowed to influence legislation.

Political campaign intervention. All 501(c)(3) organizations are absolutely prohibited from directly or indirectly participating or intervening in any political campaign on behalf of (or in opposition to) any candidate for elective public office. Non-partisan voter education activities (including public forums and voter education guides) are permitted. Similarly, non-partisan activities to encourage people to participate in the electoral process, such as voter registration and get-out-the-vote drives, are not prohibited political campaign activity. However, voter education or registration activities that (a) favor one candidate over another, (b) oppose a candidate in some manner, or (c) favor a group of candidates, are prohibited.

Public Charities and Private Foundations

Every organization that qualifies for tax-exempt status under section 501(c)(3) is further classified as either a public charity or a private foundation. For some organizations, the primary distinction between a public charity and a private foundation is an organization's source of financial support.

A public charity has a broad base of support, while a private foundation receives its support from a small number of donors. This classification is important because different tax rules apply to the operations of each entity.

Deductibility of contributions to a private foundation is more limited than contributions to a public charity. See Publication 526, Charitable Contributions, for more information on the deductibility of contributions. In addition, private foundations are subject to excise taxes that are not imposed on public charities.

Public charities. The following 501(c)(3) organizations are classified as public charities.
● Churches.
● Schools.
● Hospitals, medical research organizations, and cooperative hospital service organizations.
● Organizations that receive substantial support from grants, governmental units, and/or contributions from the general public.
● Organizations that normally receive more than one-third of their support from contributions, membership fees, and gross receipts from activities related to their exempt functions, and not more than one-third of their support from gross investment income and net unrelated business income.
● Organizations that support other public charities.

If an organization requests public charity classification based on receiving substantial public support, it must continue to seek significant and diversified public support contributions in later years. A new organization that cannot show it will receive enough public support may request an advance ruling of its status. After 5 years, it must file Form 8734, Support Schedule for Advance Ruling Period, showing its sources of support during the advance ruling period. If the organization does not meet the public support requirements during the 5-year advance ruling period, it could be reclassified as a private foundation.

Private foundation. A 501(c)(3) organization that cannot meet one of the specific exceptions to be classified as a public charity is a private foundation.

 *Classification as a private foundation has nothing to do with the name of the organization. There are many organizations that include the word foundation in their names that are **not** private foundations for tax purposes.*

Private operating foundations. A private foundation that lacks general public support but actively conducts exempt programs (as opposed to making grants to other organizations to conduct exempt activities) may be treated as a private operating foundation. Private operating foundations are subject to more favorable rules than other private foundations in terms of charitable contribution deductions and attracting grants from private foundations. In order to be classified as a private operating foundation, an organization must meet certain support tests.

State Registration Requirements

Tax exemption under section 501(c)(3) is a matter of federal law. After receiving federal tax exemption, you may also be required to register with one or more states to solicit for contributions or to obtain exemption from state taxes. The National Association of State Charity Officials (NASCO) maintains a website

Instructions for Form 1023

that provides informational links to the various states for these purposes. It can be accessed at *www.nasconet.org*.

General Instructions

Section references are to the Internal Revenue Code unless otherwise noted.

"You" and "Us". Throughout these instructions and Form 1023, the terms "you" and "your" refer to the organization that is applying for tax-exempt status. The terms "us" and "we" refer to the Internal Revenue Service.

Definitions. Terms in bold type in Form 1023 are defined throughout these instructions and in *Appendix C*.

Answers

Answer items completely. Where a "Yes" or "No" reply is not requested, you may answer "Not Applicable" where appropriate. If you believe you have previously answered the item, you may refer to your previous answer.

 Your answers must provide sufficient detail about your past, present, and planned activities to prove that you are an exempt organization. We will not be able to recognize you as tax exempt based on generalizations. Therefore, we need to understand the specific activities you will undertake to reach your charitable goals.

Financial data. Form 1023 asks you to answer a series of questions and provide information to assist us in determining if you meet the requirements for tax exemption under section 501(c)(3). One of the key pieces of information requested is financial data. This data, whether budgeted or actual, should be consistent with other information presented in the application.

For example, if you are requesting public charity status under one of the public support tests, the financial data should show contributions from the public or receipts from providing exempt services. Budgeted financial data should be prepared based upon your current plans. We recognize that the organization's actual financial results may vary from the budgeted amounts.

Past, present, and planned activities. Many items on Form 1023 are written in the present tense; however, your answers should be based on your past, present, and planned activities.

Language and currency requirements. Prepare Form 1023 and attachments in English. Provide an English translation if the articles of organization or bylaws are in any other language.

We may ask you to provide English translations of foreign language publications you submit with your Form 1023.

Report financial information in U.S. dollars (specify the conversion rate used). Combine amounts from within and outside the United States and report the

total for each line on the financial statements.

Purpose of Form

Completed Form 1023 required for section 501(c)(3) exemption. Form 1023 is filed by organizations to apply for recognition of exemption from federal income tax under section 501(c)(3). Upon approval, we will issue a determination letter that provides written assurance about the organization's tax-exempt status, and its qualification to receive tax-deductible charitable contributions. Every organization qualifying for exemption under section 501(c)(3) will also be classified as either a "public charity" or a "private foundation."

Other organizations that may file Form 1023. Other organizations that apply for tax-exempt status under section 501(c)(3) by filing Form 1023 include section 501(e) and (f) cooperative service organizations, section 501(k) childcare organizations, and section 501(n) charitable risk pools.

Obtaining Tax-Exempt Status

To apply for tax-exempt status, file Form 1023 and pay the appropriate user fee.

Expedite Requests

We will only approve expedited processing of an application where a request is made in writing and contains a compelling reason for processing the application ahead of others. Circumstances generally warranting expedited processing include:

• A grant to the applicant is pending and the failure to secure the grant may have an adverse impact on the organization's ability to continue operations.
• The purpose of the newly created organization is to provide disaster relief to victims of emergencies such as flood and hurricane.
• There have been undue delays in issuing a letter caused by problems within the IRS.

User Fee

The law requires payment of a user fee with each application. Submit the appropriate user fee based on your average annual gross receipts as indicated on Form 1023. Enclose payment with your application. DO NOT STAPLE or otherwise attach your check or money order to your application.

You may pay your user fee with a personal or certified check, bank check, or cashier's check. Processing your application will not be delayed by the form of payment unless your check is returned to us for insufficient funds.

Generally, a user fee will be refunded only if we decline to issue a determination. Additional guidance regarding user fees is available in Rev. Proc. 2006-8, 2006-1 I.R.B. 245, or later revision (revised in the first Internal

Revenue Bulletin (I.R.B.) issued each year).

For additional information on the user fee, see *Part XI*.

Group Exemption

Form 1023 is not used to apply for a group exemption. A group exemption is issued to a central organization that recognizes on a group basis the exemption of subordinate organizations on whose behalf the central organization has applied. See Publication 557 for information on how to apply for a group exemption.

Leaving a group exemption. If a subordinate organization in an existing group exemption wishes to apply for an individual exemption, it should notify its parent organization of its intention to leave the group ruling before filing Form 1023.

What to File

All applicants, unless otherwise noted, must complete Parts I through XI of Form 1023, plus any required schedules and attachments.

The following organizations must complete additional schedules to Form 1023.

IF your organization is a(n) . . .	THEN you must file Schedule . . .
Church	A
School, College, or University	B
Hospital or Medical Research Organization . .	C
Section 509(a) Supporting Organization	D
Organization Not Filing Form 1023 Within 27 Months of Formation	E
Home for the Elderly or Handicapped and Low-Income Housing	F
Successor to Other Organizations	G
Organization Providing Scholarships, Fellowships, Educational Loans, or Other Educational Grants to Individuals and Private Foundations Requesting Approval of Individual Grant Procedures	H

Assembly of Application Package

To assist us in processing the application, documents should be submitted in the following order.

• User fee enclosed but not attached to the application form.
• Form 1023 Checklist.
• Form 2848, Power of Attorney and Declaration of Representative (if needed).

- Form 8821, Tax Information Authorization (if needed).
- Expedite request (if needed).
- Application (Form 1023, Checklist, and Schedules A through H, as required).
- Organizing document.
- Amendments to organizing document in chronological order.
- Bylaws or other rules of operation and amendments.
- Documentation of nondiscriminatory policy for schools, as required by Schedule B.
- Form 5768, Election/Revocation of Election by an Eligible Section 501(c)(3) Organization To Make Expenditures To Influence Legislation (if filing).
- All other attachments, including explanations, financial data, and printed materials or publications.

Attachments

Use an attachment where there is insufficient space on the form for you to legibly and accurately respond to a question. For any attachments submitted with your Form 1023:
- Use 8½ x 11 inch paper.
- Provide your name and Employer Identification Number (EIN) at the top of each page.
- Identify the Part and line number to which the attachment relates.

Include any court decisions, rulings, opinions, or any other documents that will assist us in processing your Form 1023.

Generally, attachments in the form of tape, recordings or other electronic media are not acceptable unless accompanied by a transcript.

Attachments must be in English.

When to File

If you file Form 1023 within 27 months after the end of the month in which you were legally formed, and we approve the application, the legal date of formation will be the effective date of your exempt status.

If you do not file Form 1023 within 27 months of formation, you may not qualify for exempt status before the date we receive Form 1023. The date considered to be the date we receive Form 1023 is generally the postmark date. For exceptions and special rules, including automatic extensions, see Schedule E of Form 1023.

Where To File

 Send the completed Form 1023 application, with all required information, and the applicable user fee to:

Internal Revenue Service
P.O. Box 192
Covington, KY 41012-0192

If you are using express mail or a delivery service, send the completed Form 1023 application, with all required information and user fee to:

Internal Revenue Service
201 West Rivercenter Blvd.
Attn: Extracting Stop 312
Covington, KY 41011

Private Delivery Services

In addition to the United States mail, you can use certain private delivery services designated by the IRS to meet the "timely mailing as timely filing/paying" rule for tax returns and payments. The most recent list of designated private delivery services includes only the following:
- DHL Express (DHL): DHL "Same Day" Service; DHL Next Day 10:30 AM; DHL Next Day 12:00 PM; DHL Next Day 3:00 PM; and DHL 2nd Day Service.
- Federal Express (FedEx): FedEx Priority Overnight, FedEx Standard Overnight, FedEx 2Day, FedEx International Priority, and FedEx International First.
- United Parcel Service (UPS): UPS Next Day Air, UPS Next Day Air Saver, UPS 2nd Day Air, UPS 2nd Day Air A.M., UPS Worldwide Express Plus, and UPS Worldwide Express.

The private delivery service can tell you how to get written proof of the mailing date.

Filing Assistance

For help in completing this form or general questions relating to an exempt organization, call the Exempt Organization Customer Account Services toll free at 1-877-829-5500. You may also access information on our website at www.irs.gov/eo.

Listed below are a number of publications that may be helpful to your organization.

- Publication 517, Social Security and Other Information for Members of the Clergy and Religious Workers
- Publication 526, Charitable Contributions
- Publication 557, Tax-Exempt Status for Your Organization
- Publication 598, Tax on Unrelated Business Income of Exempt Organizations
- Publication 1771, Charitable Contributions Substantiation and Disclosure Requirements
- Publication 1828, Tax Guide for Churches and Religious Organizations
- Publication 3079, Gaming Publication for Tax-Exempt Organizations
- Publication 3833, Disaster Relief: Providing Assistance through Charitable Organizations
- Publication 4220, Applying for 501(c)(3) Tax-Exempt Status
- Publication 4221, Compliance Guide for 501(c)(3) Tax-Exempt Organizations
- Publication 78, Cumulative List of Organizations Described in Section 170(c) of the Internal Revenue Code of 1986 (searchable online at www.irs.gov/eo)

Philanthropic Research, Inc., aka GuideStar, a 501(c)(3) nonprofit organization, maintains information about specific section 501(c)(3) organizations (searchable online at www.guidestar.org).

Signature Requirements

An officer, director, trustee, or other official who is authorized to sign for the organization must sign Form 1023 at the end of Part XI. The signature must be accompanied by the title or authority of the signer and the date. Please clearly print the accompanying information.

Figure 1. Table of Annual Returns

Type of Annual Return	Who Should File
Form 990, Return of Organization Exempt from Income Tax	Section 501(c)(3) public charities
Form 990-EZ, Short Form Return of Organization Exempt from Income Tax	Section 501(c)(3) public charities whose gross receipts during the year were less than $100,000 and total assets at the end of the year were less than $250,000
Schedule A (Form 990 or 990-EZ), Organization Exempt under Section 501(c)(3)	Section 501(c)(3) public charities
Schedule B (Form 990, 990-EZ, or 990-PF), Schedule of Contributors	All section 501(c)(3) organizations
Form 990-PF, Return of Private Foundation	Private foundations, including private operating foundations
Form 990-T, Exempt Organization Business Income Tax Return	Public charities and private foundations that have gross unrelated business income of $1,000 or more

-4-   Instructions for Form 1023

Representation

Form 2848. Attach a completed Form 2848 if you want to authorize a representative to represent you regarding your application. An individual authorized by Form 2848 may not sign the application unless that person is also an officer, director, trustee, or other official who is authorized to sign the application.

 A centralized authorization file (CAF) number is not required to be listed on Form 2848.

Form 8821. Form 8821 authorizes us to discuss your application with the person you have appointed.

Form 8821 does not authorize your appointee to advocate your position with respect to the Federal tax laws; to execute waivers, consents, or closing agreements; or to otherwise represent you before the IRS. If you want to authorize an individual to represent you, use Form 2848.

After You Submit Form 1023

We will acknowledge receiving your application in writing. You may expect to receive this notice within 21 days of the postmark date of the Form 1023. Read the notice thoroughly because it will provide further information about the processing of your Form 1023.

No additional information needed. If our initial review shows that you qualify, we will send you a letter stating that you are exempt under section 501(c)(3) and whether you are a public charity or a private foundation.

Additional information needed. If the initial review shows that we need additional information or changes, we will assign Form 1023 to a specialist who will call or write you. Generally, we assign applications in the order we receive them. Unless the application is approved for expedited processing, it will be worked in the order received.

If the additional information indicates that you qualify, we will send you a letter stating that you are exempt under section 501(c)(3) and whether you are a public charity or a private foundation. If we conclude that you do not qualify for exemption, we will send you a letter that explains our position and your appeal rights.

Annual Filing Requirements

If an annual information return or tax return is due while the Form 1023 is pending, complete the return, mark "Application Pending" in the heading, and send the return to the address indicated in the instructions.

Information on return filing requirements and exceptions may be found in Publications 557 and 598 and in the instructions to the annual returns listed in Figure 1.

Instructions for Form 1023

 You may also be required to file other returns, such as employment tax returns or benefit plan returns, which are not discussed here.

Public Inspection

Information available for public inspection. If we approve exempt status under section 501(c)(3), the following information will be open for public inspection.
• Your complete Form 1023 and any supporting documents.
• All correspondence between you and the IRS concerning Form 1023, including Form 2848.
• The letter we issue approving your exemption.
• Annual information returns (Forms 990, 990-EZ, or 990-PF).
• Schedule A, included with Forms 990 or 990-EZ.
• Schedule B, included with Forms 990 or 990-EZ, except the names and addresses of contributors and other identifying information about contributors.
• Schedule B, included with Form 990-PF, including names, addresses and other identifying information about contributors.

Information not available for public inspection. The following items will not be open for public inspection.

• Any information relating to a trade secret, patent, style of work, or apparatus that, if released, would adversely affect you. (We must approve withholding this information.)
• Any other information that would adversely affect the national defense. (We must approve withholding this information.)
• User fee check.
• Information only applications from the United States Virgin Islands, Bureau of Internal Revenue (BIR) and related supporting documents.
• Contributors' names and addresses and identifying information about contributors included with Forms 990 or 990-EZ and the Schedule B, filed with these forms.
• Form 990-T, Exempt Organization Business Income Tax Return.

When applying for tax-exempt status, you must clearly identify any information that is not open for public inspection by separately marking it as "NOT SUBJECT TO PUBLIC INSPECTION" and attaching an explanation of why you are asking for the information to be withheld. We will decide whether to withhold the identified information from public inspection.

Making documents available for public inspection. Both you and the IRS must make the information that is subject to disclosure available for public inspection. The public may contact us toll-free at 1-877-829-5500 to request public inspection or copies of the information. The public may also request inspection of the information or a copy of the information directly from you.

An exempt organization may post the documents required to be available for public inspection on its own website. The information return and exemption application materials must be posted exactly as filed with the IRS. Only the information that is not open for public inspection may be deleted.

If an exempt organization posts the documents on its website, it must provide notice of the website address where the documents may be found, but it need not provide copies of the information. However, documents posted on an organization's website must still be made available for public inspection without charge at its main office during regular business hours.

Documents are not considered available for public inspection on a website if the otherwise disclosable information is edited or subject to editing by a third party when posted. To date, the IRS has not approved any third party websites for posting.

See Publication 557 for additional guidance on public inspection.

Foreign Organizations in General

Foreign organizations are those that were created in countries other than the United States, its territories, or its possessions. Foreign organizations may apply for tax-exempt status on income earned in the United States in the same way that domestic organizations apply for exempt status. See, *Language and currency requirements*.

A foreign organization applying for exempt status should complete all required parts of Form 1023. There are, however, special rules below for some Canadian organizations.

TIP *Contributions by U.S. residents to foreign organizations generally are not deductible. Tax treaties between the U.S. and certain foreign countries provide specific limited exceptions.*

Annual returns for foreign organizations. A foreign organization that obtains exemption as a public charity must file an information return annually (Form 990 or Form 990-EZ). A foreign organization that is a private foundation must file Form 990-PF annually. However, a foreign organization, other than a private foundation, may be relieved from filing Form 990 or Form 990-EZ in any year in which it has gross receipts from U.S. source income of $25,000 or less and has not conducted significant activity in the United States. See the Instructions for Form 990 and Form 990-EZ, and the Instructions for Form 990-PF for further information. A foreign organization that is subject to unrelated business income tax must file Form 990-T.

-5-

Canadian Organizations

Canadian organizations that have received a Notification of Registration from the Canada Customs and Revenue Agency (formerly, Revenue Canada), and whose registrations have not been revoked ("Canadian registered charities"), are automatically recognized as section 501(c)(3) organizations and are not required to file Form 1023. Canadian registered charities are also presumed to be private foundations. A Canadian registered charity may complete certain portions of the Form 1023 in order to be listed as a section 501(c)(3) organization in IRS Publication 78, or to request classification as a public charity, rather than a private foundation. A Canadian registered charity should only complete and submit the following documents.

- Copy of its Notification of Registration.
- *Part I* of Form 1023.
- *Part X* of Form 1023 (if requesting public charity classification).
- Signature line in *Part XI* of Form 1023.
- Form 8833, Treaty-Based Return Position Disclosure Under Section 6114 or 7701(b).
- No user fee is required.

Organizations Created in United States Territories and Possessions

Organizations created in possessions and territories of the United States are generally treated as domestic organizations. These organizations complete all required parts of Form 1023 to apply for exempt status under section 501(c)(3). Special rules, discussed below, apply to some Virgin Islands organizations.

Charitable contributions to organizations created in United States possessions and territories are deductible by the donors if the organization qualifies for exempt status under section 501(c)(3).

Virgin Islands Organizations

The United States Virgin Islands, Bureau of Internal Revenue (BIR) may request an information only letter concerning the exempt status under section 501(c)(3) of an organization formed in the Virgin Islands. The organization itself does not seek U.S. recognition of exempt status. The information only procedure requires the BIR to complete Form 1023 and supporting documents for the organization, but does not require a user fee payment. The application and supporting documents are not open for public inspection (see *Public Inspection,* for more information).

All other Virgin Islands organizations that seek U.S. recognition of exempt status under section 501(c)(3) must follow the normal application process.

Specific Instructions

Part I. Identification of Applicant

Line 1. Full name of organization. Enter your complete name exactly as it appears in your organizing document, including amendments.

Line 2. c/o Name. If you have an "in care of" name, enter it here.

Line 3. Mailing address. Enter your complete address where all correspondence will be sent. If mail is not delivered to the street address and you have a P.O. Box, show the box number instead of the street address.

For a foreign address, enter the information in the following order: city, province or state, and country. Follow the country's practice in placing the postal code in the address. Do not abbreviate the country name.

Line 4. Employer Identification Number (EIN). Enter the nine-digit EIN assigned to you.

 Do not submit this application until you have obtained an EIN.

An EIN is your account number with us and is required regardless of whether you have employees. If you need an EIN, you can apply for one by:
1. Calling 1-800-829-4933.
2. Calling 1-215-516-6999, if you are located outside the United States.
3. Mailing Form SS-4 to the IRS.
4. Faxing Form SS-4 to a location provided in the Instructions for Form SS-4.

You can get Form SS-4 online at *www.irs.gov,* or by calling 1-800-829-3676, to order IRS tax forms and publications.

If you previously applied for an EIN and have not yet received it, or you are unsure whether you have an EIN, please call our toll-free customer account services number, 1-877-829-5500, for assistance.

Line 5. Month the annual accounting period ends (01-12). Enter the month that your annual accounting period ends, using a two-digit number format. For example, if your annual accounting period ends December 31, enter "12." Your annual accounting period is the 12-month period on which your annual financial records are based. Your first tax year could be less than 12 months.

Check your bylaws or other rules of operation for consistency with the annual accounting period entered in line 5.

Line 6a. Primary contact. Your primary contact person may be an officer, director, trustee, or other individual who is permitted to speak with us according to your bylaws or other rules of operation. Your primary contact person may also be an "authorized representative," such as

an attorney or certified public accountant for whom you have submitted a completed Form 2848, with the Form 1023.

Line 7. If you wish to be represented by an authorized representative, a completed Form 2848 must be attached to the Form 1023.

Line 8. Provide information about persons, other than your officers, directors, trustees, employees, or authorized representative(s), whom you paid, or promised to pay, to assist you in establishing your organization, developing programs to solicit funds, or otherwise advising you about organizational, financial, or tax matters.

For example, provide information about a paid consultant who advised you about obtaining tax exemption.

Line 9a. Organization's website. Enter your complete website address if you have one. Also, list any websites maintained on your behalf. The information on your website should be consistent with the information in your Form 1023.

Line 9b. Email (optional). Enter your email address to receive educational information from us in the future. Because of security concerns, we cannot send confidential information via email. However, we can use a fax to contact you.

Line 10. Generally, organizations not required to file Form 990 (or Form 990-EZ) include churches, certain church affiliated organizations, certain affiliates of a governmental unit, and organizations with annual gross receipts normally not more than $25,000. For more information, see the Instructions for Form 990 and Form 990-EZ.

 Private foundations must file Form 990-PF regardless of the amount of their gross receipts.

Line 11. List the date you were legally created by month, day, and year (for example, 02/01/2004). The date should be consistent with your organizing document described in *Part II.*

Line 12. For purposes of completing this application, you are formed under the laws of a foreign country if you are not formed under the laws of (1) the United States, its territories and possessions, (2) federally recognized Indian tribal or Alaska Native governments, or (3) the District of Columbia.

Part II. Organizational Structure

Only trusts, unincorporated associations, or corporations (including limited liability companies) are eligible for tax-exempt status under section 501(c)(3) of the Code. Sole proprietorships, partnerships, or loosely affiliated groups of individuals are not eligible.

To qualify for tax-exempt status, you must check "Yes" on either line 1, 2, 3, or

Instructions for Form 1023

4 and submit a copy of your organizing document.

Line 1. A "corporation" is an entity organized under a Federal or state statute, or a statute of a federally recognized Indian tribal or Alaskan native government. A corporation's organizing document is its "articles of incorporation."

Certification of filing. If formed under state statute, your articles of incorporation must show certification of filing. This means your articles show evidence that on a specific date they were filed with and approved by an appropriate state authority. The document must be an exact copy of what is on file with your state.

If you do not have a copy of your articles of incorporation showing evidence of having been filed and approved by an appropriate state official, you may submit a substitute copy of your articles of incorporation. This substitute copy may be handwritten, typed, printed, or otherwise reproduced. It must be accompanied by a declaration, signed by an officer authorized to sign for you, that it is a complete and correct copy of the articles of incorporation and that it contains all the powers, principles, purposes, functions, and other provisions by which you currently govern yourself.

Line 2. A "limited liability company (LLC)" that files its own exemption application is treated as a corporation rather than a partnership. Instead of articles of incorporation, an LLC's organizing document is its state-approved "articles of organization." If it has adopted an "operating agreement," then this document is also part of its organizing document.

An LLC may only have 501(c)(3) member(s) to qualify for an exemption. An LLC should not file an exemption application if it wants to be treated as a disregarded entity by its tax-exempt member.

Line 3. An "unincorporated association" formed under state law must have at least two members who have signed a written document for a specifically defined purpose.

The articles of organization of an unincorporated association must include the name of your organization, your purpose, the date the document was adopted, and the signatures of at least two individuals. If your copy does not contain the proper signatures and date of adoption, you may submit a written declaration that states your copy is a complete and accurate copy of the signed and dated original. Your declaration should clearly indicate the original date of adoption.

 Bylaws may be considered an organizing document only if they are properly structured (includes name, purpose, signatures, and intent to form an organization).

Line 4a. A trust may be formed by a trust agreement or declaration of trust. A trust may also be formed through a will.

If your trust agreement copy does not contain the proper signatures, you may submit a written declaration that states your copy is a complete and accurate copy of the signed and dated original. Your declaration should clearly indicate the original date that it was signed.

Trust created by a will. For trusts created by a will, include a copy of the death certificate or a statement indicating the date of death, and a copy of the relevant portions of the will.

Trust agreement and non-charitable interests. If your trust agreement provided for distributions for non-charitable interests, indicate the date on which these interests expired. If your trust agreement continues to provide for these interests, you will not qualify for tax-exempt status.

Line 4b. Generally, a trust must be funded with property, such as money, real estate, or personal property to be legally created.

Line 5. "Bylaws" are generally the internal rules and regulations of an organization. If you have bylaws, you should submit a current copy.

Bylaws do not need to be signed unless they are the organizing document as described in line 3 above.

Part III. Required Provisions in Your Organizing Document

Line 1. Purpose clause. Your organizing document must limit your purposes to those described in section 501(c)(3). Those purposes are: charitable, religious, educational, scientific, literary, testing for public safety, fostering national or international amateur sports competition, and preventing cruelty to children or animals.

The generally accepted legal definition of "charitable" includes relief of the poor, the distressed, or the underprivileged; advancement of religion; advancement of education or science; erecting or maintaining public buildings, monuments, or works; lessening the burdens of government; lessening neighborhood tensions; eliminating prejudice and discrimination; defending human and civil rights secured by law; and combating community deterioration and juvenile delinquency. Therefore, the phrase "relief of the poor" in your organizing document properly limits your purposes.

If your purposes are limited in some way by referring to section 501(c)(3), your organizing document also properly limits your purposes. For example, the phrase "relief of the elderly within the meaning of section 501(c)(3)" in your organizing document also properly limits your purposes.

However, if the purposes listed in your organizing document are broader than those listed in section 501(c)(3), you should amend your organizing document before applying. A reference to section 501(c)(3) will not ensure that your purposes are limited to those described in section 501(c)(3). All of the language in your organizing document must be considered. The following is an example of an acceptable purpose clause:

The organization is organized exclusively for charitable, religious, educational, and scientific purposes under section 501(c)(3) of the Internal Revenue Code, or corresponding section of any future federal tax code.

See Publication 557 for further information and examples of how to limit your purposes.

Any amendment to your articles of organization you submit should show evidence that it was signed, dated, and certified as described in *Part II.*

Line 2a. Dissolution clause. Your organizing document must permanently dedicate your assets for a section 501(c)(3) purpose. This means that if you dissolve your organization in the future, your assets must be distributed for an exempt purpose described in section 501(c)(3), or to the federal government, or to a state or local government for a public purpose.

If your organizing document states that your assets would be distributed to members or private individuals or for any purpose other than those provided in section 501(c)(3), you must amend your organizing document to remove such statements.

If multiple amendments are required, they may be done at the same time. For example, if you are a corporation and are required to amend both your purpose and dissolution clauses, you may file a single amending document with your appropriate government authority.

The following is an example of an acceptable dissolution clause:

Upon the dissolution of this organization, assets shall be distributed for one or more exempt purposes within the meaning of section 501(c)(3) of the Internal Revenue Code, or corresponding section of any future federal tax code, or shall be distributed to the federal government, or to a state or local government, for a public purpose.

Naming a specific organization to receive your assets upon dissolution will only be acceptable if your articles state that the specific organization must be exempt under section 501(c)(3) at the time your dissolution takes place and your articles provide for an acceptable alternative if the specific organization is not exempt. See Publication 557 for further information and examples of acceptable language for dedication of assets in your organizing document.

Line 2c. Operation of state law. If you are a corporation formed in the following states, then you do not need a specific provision in your articles of incorporation providing for the distribution of assets upon dissolution.

Arkansas	Minnesota
California	Missouri
Louisiana	Ohio
Massachusetts	Oklahoma

If you are a testamentary charitable trust formed in the following states, then you do not need a specific provision in your trust agreement or declaration of trust providing for the distribution of assets upon dissolution.

Alabama	South Dakota
Louisiana	Virginia
Pennsylvania	

If you are a testamentary charitable trust formed in the states listed below and the language of your trust instrument provides for a general intent to benefit charity, then you do not need a specific provision in your trust agreement or declaration of trust providing for the distribution of assets upon dissolution.

Arkansas	Minnesota
California	Mississippi
Colorado	Missouri
Connecticut	Nebraska
Delaware	New Hampshire
District of Columbia	New Jersey
Florida	North Carolina
Georgia	Ohio
Illinois	Oklahoma
Indiana	Oregon
Iowa	Rhode Island
Kansas	Tennessee
Kentucky	Texas
Maine	Vermont
Maryland	Washington
Massachusetts	Wisconsin
Michigan	

Operation of state law is based on Rev. Proc. 82-2, 1982-1 C.B. 367.

Foreign organizations. Foreign organizations may be able to rely upon the applicable laws of their jurisdiction in a similar manner. You must provide a copy of the applicable law with an English translation.

Part IV. Narrative Description of Your Activities

Describe completely and in detail your past, present, and planned activities. Do not refer to or repeat the purposes in your organizing document. You may refer to other parts of the application rather than repeat information provided elsewhere.

For each past, present, or planned activity, include information that answers the following questions.
● What is the activity?
● Who conducts the activity?
● When is the activity conducted?
● Where is the activity conducted (for example: Los Angeles and San Francisco, California)?
● How does the activity further your exempt purposes?
● What percentage of your total time is allocated to the activity?
● How is the activity funded? (This should agree with the financial data in *Part IX*.)
● List any alternate names under which you operate, including any "aka" (also known as) or "dba" (doing business as) names.

If you have a website, you may attach a paper copy to support your narrative description of activities.

Part V. Compensation and Other Financial Arrangements With Your Officers, Directors, Trustees, Employees, and Independent Contractors

Compensation. For purposes of *Part V*, compensation includes salary or wages, deferred compensation, retirement benefits, whether in the form of a qualified or non-qualified employee plan (pensions or annuities), fringe benefits (personal vehicle, meals, lodging, personal and family educational benefits, low interest loans, payment of personal travel, entertainment, or other expenses, athletic or country club membership, and personal use of your property), and bonuses.

Example. Assume an organization compensates its director as follows:

Wages	
Director Compensation	$ 2,500
Salary as Chief Executive Officer	40,000
Deferred retirement	2,000
Health insurance policy	5,000
Use of a vehicle	5,000
Total Compensation	$ 54,500

Information in *Part V* must be consistent with the information provided in *Part IX. Financial Data.*

Line 1a. For each person listed, state their total annual compensation, or proposed compensation, for all services to the organization, whether as an officer, employee, or other position. Use actual figures, if available. Officers, directors, and trustees may use the organization's address for mailing.

Line 1b. Employees may use the organization's address for mailing. Report total compensation. For employees who are also officers, directors, or trustees,

their compensation as employees and for all other services should be reported in line 1a.

Line 1c. "Independent contractors" are persons who are not treated as employees for employment tax purposes. For information on determining if an individual is an employee or an independent contractor, see Publication 15-A, Employer's Supplemental Tax Guide.

Line 2a. Describe family or business relationships between your officers, directors, or trustees. "Related" refers to both family and business relationships.
● "Family relationships" include the individual's spouse, ancestors, children, grandchildren, great grandchildren, siblings (whether by whole or half blood), and the spouses of children, grandchildren, great grandchildren, and siblings.
● "Business relationships" include employment and contractual relationships, and common ownership of a business where any officers, directors, or trustees, individually or together, possess more than a 35% ownership interest in common. "Ownership" means voting power in a corporation, profits interest in a partnership, or beneficial interest in a trust.

Line 2b. Describe family or business relationships between you and any of your officers, directors, or trustees other than their position with you as an officer, director, or trustee.

Line 2c. Describe family or business relationships between your officers, directors, or trustees and your five highest compensated employees or five highest compensated independent contractors who will receive more than $50,000 in taxable or non-taxable compensation per year.

Line 3b. "Common control" means that you and one or more other organizations have (1) a majority of your governing boards or officers appointed or elected by the same organization(s), or (2) a majority of your governing boards or officers consist of the same individuals. Common control also occurs when you and one or more commonly controlled organizations have a majority ownership interest in a corporation, partnership, or trust. See the instructions for line 2a, above, for a definition of ownership.

Line 4. By adopting these recommended compensation-setting practices, such as by resolution of your governing board, you will be establishing procedures aimed at helping to prevent your top officials from receiving excess compensation benefits.

Line 4e. "Similarly situated organizations" means tax-exempt or taxable organizations of a comparable size, purpose, and resources. Adjustments due to geographic area, and other specific conditions are appropriate, but should be documented. The source(s) of comparable compensation data, both taxable and non-taxable, should be documented and copies retained in your permanent records.

Line 4g. "Reasonable compensation" is the amount that would ordinarily be paid for like services by like organizations under like circumstances as of the date the compensation arrangement is made. Establishing and documenting reasonable compensation is important because excessive compensation may result in excise taxes on both the individual and the organization. In addition, this may jeopardize the organization's tax exemption.

Line 5a. A "conflict of interest" arises when a person in a position of authority over an organization, such as a director, officer, or manager, may benefit personally from a decision he or she could make. A *Sample Conflict of Interest Policy* is included as *Appendix A*.

Adoption of a conflict of interest policy is not required to obtain tax-exempt status. However, by adopting the sample policy or a similar policy, you will be choosing to put in place procedures that will help you avoid the possibility that those in positions of authority over you may receive an inappropriate benefit.

Line 6a. A "fixed payment" means a payment that is either a set dollar amount or fixed through a specific formula where the amount does not depend on discretion. For example, a base salary of $200,000 that is adjusted annually based on the increase in the Consumer Price Index is a fixed payment.

A "non-fixed payment" means a payment that depends on discretion. For example, a bonus of up to $100,000 that is based on an evaluation of performance by the governing board is a non-fixed payment because the governing body has discretion over whether the bonus is paid and the amount of the bonus.

Line 7a. Do not include purchases of goods and services in your normal course of operations that are available to the general public under similar terms and conditions.

Arm's length. An arm's length standard exists where the parties have an adverse (or opposing) interest. For example, a seller wants to sell his goods at the highest possible price, while a buyer wants to buy at the lowest possible price. These are adverse interests.

In negotiating with a person, an adverse interest is assumed if that person is otherwise unrelated to you in the sense of not being in a position to exercise substantial influence over you or your affairs. If the person is in a position to exercise substantial influence over your affairs, then an arm's length standard requires additional precautions to eliminate the effect of the relationship.

Using a conflict of interest policy, information about comparable transactions between unrelated parties, and reliable methods for evaluating the transaction, are examples of precautions

that would help make the negotiation process equivalent to one between unrelated persons.

Fair market value. This is the price at which property or the right to use property would change hands between a willing buyer and a willing seller, neither being under any compulsion to buy, sell, or transfer property or the right to use property, and both having reasonable knowledge of relevant facts.

Line 7b. Do not include sales of goods and services in your normal course of operations that are available to the general public under similar terms and conditions.

Line 9a. Answer "Yes" if any of your officers, directors, or trustees:
• Is an officer, director, or trustee in another organization (other than a section 501(c)(3) organization) that has a lease, contract, loan, or other agreement with you.
• Possess more than a 35% ownership interest in any organization that has a lease, contract, loan, or other agreement with you. For example, you would answer "Yes" if one of your directors were an officer for a section 501(c)(4) organization with whom you had a lease for office space. You would also answer "Yes" if one of your directors owns more than 35% of the voting stock of a corporation to which you made a loan.

Part VI. Your Members and Other Individuals, and Organizations That Receive Benefits From You

Line 1a. Benefits to individuals. Describe any programs where you provide goods, services, or funds to individuals. For example, describe programs by which you provide food to the homeless, employment counseling to senior citizens, or grants to victims of a disaster.

Line 1b. Benefits to organizations. Describe any programs where you provide goods, services, or funds to organizations. For example, programs where you provide equipment, accounting assistance, or grants to other organizations.

Line 2. For programs that are available only for members, include a sample membership application and a schedule of membership dues. Also, describe any different membership levels and the benefits each membership level receives.

Line 3. Describe any business or family relationship between individuals who receive goods, services, or funds through your programs with any officer, director, trustee, or with any of the five-highest compensated employees or independent contractors listed in *Part V*, lines 1a, 1b, or 1c.

Part VII. Your History

Line 1. You are a "successor" if you have:
• Substantially taken over all of the assets or activities of another organization,
• Been converted or merged from another organization, or
• Installed the same officers, directors, or trustees as another organization that no longer exists and that had purpose(s) similar to your purpose(s).

 The predecessor organization may be or may not have been a tax-exempt or non-exempt organization.

Part VIII. Your Specific Activities

Line 1. You participate in a political campaign if you promote or oppose the candidacy of an individual for public office. Your explanation should include representative copies of your political literature, brochures, pamphlets, etc. Candidate debates and nonpartisan voter education are permitted.

 Organizations described in section 501(c)(3) are prohibited from supporting or opposing candidates for public office in any political campaign. If you answer "Yes," you are not qualified for tax exemption under section 501(c)(3) and should reconsider whether the filing of application Form 1023 is appropriate for your organization. See Publication 557 for a description of other Internal Revenue Code sections under which you may qualify.

Line 2a. You are attempting to "influence legislation" if you directly contact or urge the public to contact members of a legislative body for the purpose of proposing, supporting, or opposing legislation. You are also attempting to influence legislation if you advocate the adoption or rejection of legislation. If you answer "Yes," your explanation should include the percentage of your total time and total funds spent on such legislative activities. Also, submit representative copies of your legislative literature, brochures, pamphlets, etc.

Organizations described in section 501(c)(3) are prohibited from engaging in a substantial amount of legislative activities. Whether you are engaged in substantial legislative activities depends on all of the facts and circumstances.

Line 2b. By filing Form 5768 your legislative activities will be measured solely by expenditure limits under section 501(h) rather than by whether legislative activity is considered substantial. Form 5768 is included in Package 1023 for your convenience. It describes the types of organizations that are eligible to make an election. For a discussion of the requirements of section 501(h), see Publication 557. If you are an organization that elects to use

expenditure limits in influencing legislation:
• Attach a copy of Form 5768 that has already been separately filed with us, or
• Provide a completed Form 5768 with your exemption application.

 Churches and private foundations are not eligible to make this election.

Line 3a. For purposes of this application, "bingo" is a game of chance played with cards that are generally printed with 5 rows of 5 squares each on which participants place markers to form a preselected pattern to win the game. Other gaming activities include pull-tabs, raffles, keno, split-the-pot, and other games of chance.

Describe these activities, including how often your bingo or other gaming activities are conducted, where they are conducted, and who conducts them. Also describe whether your workers are compensated. If workers are compensated, describe who receives compensation and how the amount is determined.

Revenue associated with these activities means gross revenue amounts.

Expenses associated with these activities means direct and indirect expenses. The dollar value of prizes should be included in expenses.

 Gaming may be subject to unrelated business income tax. See Publication 3079 for further information about gaming.

Line 3c. Local jurisdictions include cities, counties, towns, municipalities, and similar government jurisdictions within a state. A local jurisdiction also includes an Indian Reservation.

Line 4a. "Fundraising" includes efforts to raise funds through appeals for financial support. Fundraising may be conducted by your employees or volunteers, through an agent, or through an independent contractor. If you answer "Yes," check all the boxes that apply and complete lines 4b through 4e.

Line 4d. Local jurisdictions include cities, counties, towns, municipalities, and similar government jurisdictions within a state. A local jurisdiction also includes an Indian Reservation.

Line 4e. This line is intended to obtain information from you regarding donor-advised funds that you may maintain. A "donor-advised fund" is maintained if you establish separate accounts for a donor whereby the donor may exercise a right to make a recommendation on either uses of the account, such as providing advice about how to invest, or distributions from the account, such as providing advice about how to make expenditures.

Line 5. You are "affiliated" with a governmental unit if you were created by, controlled by, or closely related to a governmental unit. Identify each governmental unit and describe your

relationship with it. Include details of any financial reports or audits required by the governmental unit. Also, describe any power or authority given to you by the governmental unit.

For purposes of this question, a "governmental unit" includes a State, a possession of the United States, or any political subdivision of a State or a possession of the United States, or the United States, or the District of Columbia.

A governmental unit would generally not qualify for exemption under section 501(c)(3). Also, if you can exercise certain sovereign powers, such as the power to tax or police powers, you would generally not qualify for exemption under section 501(c)(3).

Line 6a. "Economic development" organizations are generally formed to combat community deterioration by assisting businesses located in a particular geographic area whose economy is economically depressed or deteriorating. Their varieties of activities include grants, loans, provision of information and expertise, or creation of industrial parks. Economic development organizations may also be formed to eliminate prejudice and discrimination or lessen the burdens of government through involvement with business development.

If your exempt purpose is to combat community deterioration, describe whether the area or areas in which you will operate have been declared blighted or economically depressed by a government finding. If the area has not been declared blighted or economically depressed, a more suitable exemption may be under sections 501(c)(4) or 501(c)(6). See Publication 557 for more information.

If your exempt purpose is to eliminate prejudice and discrimination, describe how your activities further this purpose.

If your exempt purpose is to lessen the burdens of government, describe whether the government has recognized your activities as those for which it would otherwise be responsible, and any involvement you have with governmental entities that demonstrates that you are actually lessening governmental burdens.

Line 7a. "Develop" means the planning, financing, construction, or provision of similar services involved in the acquisition of real property, such as land or a building. For example, you should provide information regarding the services of a consultant who puts together an arrangement for you to acquire a nursing home through the issuance of tax-exempt bonds.

Line 7b. "Manage" means to direct or administer. For example, you would provide information about an organization hired to administer a museum gift shop. See the instructions for *Part V*, line 2a, for a description of the term business or family relationships.

Line 7c. See the instructions for *Part V*, line 2a, for a description of the term business or family relationships. See the instructions for *Part V*, line 7a, for a description of the term arm's length.

Line 8. A "joint venture" is a legal agreement in which the persons jointly undertake a transaction for mutual profit. Generally, each person contributes assets and shares risks. Like a partnership, joint ventures can involve any type of business transaction and the persons involved can be individuals, groups of individuals, companies, or corporations.

Line 9a. Childcare services provide care for children away from their homes. An organization providing childcare services may qualify for tax-exempt status as either a:
• School under IRC 170(b)(1)(A)(ii).
• Childcare organization under IRC 501(k).
Refer to the instructions for *Part VII*, line 19, to determine if you qualify as a school.

A childcare organization qualifies under IRC 501(k) if it provides care for children away from their homes; substantially all of the childcare enables individuals to be gainfully employed; and the services provided by the organization are available to the general public.

Line 9b. "Gainfully employed" includes enabling individuals to work or to seek work.

Line 9c. Section 501(k) states that to qualify as a childcare organization, substantially all of the care you provide should be to permit individuals to be gainfully employed. If less than 85% of your services are for children of working parents or caretakers:
• Describe the percentage of the children for whom you provide services to permit parents or caretakers to work, and
• Describe any efforts you are taking to increase the percentage of the children for whom you provide services to permit parents or caretakers to work.

Line 9d. Describe any eligibility requirements, such as employment with a particular employer.

Line 10. " Intellectual property" includes:
• Patents (for inventions).
• Copyrights (for literary and artistic works such as novels, poems, plays, films, musical works, drawings, paintings, photographs, sculptures, architectural designs, performances, recordings, film, and radio or television programs).
• Trade names, trade marks, and service marks (for symbols, names, images, and designs).
• Formulas, know-how, and trade secrets.

Line 12a. A "foreign country" is a country other than the United States, its territories and possessions, and the District of Columbia.

Line 13d. A "relationship" between you and the recipient organization includes the following situations:

-10-

• You control the recipient organization or it controls you through common officers, directors, or trustees, or through authority to approve budgets or expenditures.
• You and the recipient organization were created at approximately the same time and by the same persons.
• You and the recipient organization operate in a coordinated manner with respect to facilities, programs, employees, or other activities.
• Persons who exercise substantial influence over you also exercise substantial influence over the other organization.

Line 14a. Answer "Yes" if you make grants, loans, or other distributions, such as goods, to a foreign organization. For purposes of completing this application, a domestic organization is one that is formed under the laws of the United States, its territories and possessions, federally recognized Indian Tribal and Alaska Native governments (including political subdivisions), or the District of Columbia. A "foreign organization" is one that is not a domestic organization.

A list of federally recognized Indian tribes is provided in Rev. Proc. 2002-64, 2002-2 C.B. 717. A list of entities that are treated as political subdivisions of Indian tribal governments is provided in Rev. Proc. 86-17, 1986-1 C.B. 550 and Rev. Proc. 84-36, 1984-1 C.B. 510.

Line 15. A "close connection" between you and another organization includes the following situations:
• You control the organization or it controls you through common officers, directors, or trustees, or through authority to approve budgets or expenditures.
• You and the organization were created at approximately the same time and by the same persons.
   For example, you were formed within months of the time that a social welfare organization and a political action committee were established by the same persons who were instrumental in your formation.
• You and the organization operate in a coordinated manner with respect to facilities, programs, employees, or other activities.
   For example, you share rental expenses for office space and employees with a for-profit corporation.
• Persons who exercise substantial influence over you also exercise substantial influence over the other organization and (1) you either conduct activities in common or (2) have a financial relationship.
   For example, a voting member of your governing body is also a voting member of the governing body of a business league with which you intend to cooperate in planning an advertising campaign that will inform the public about the benefits of a particular program.
   For example, a voting member of your governing body is also a voting member

of the governing body of a business league that has made a loan to you.

Line 16. A "cooperative hospital service organization" described in section 501(e) is organized and operated on a cooperative basis to provide its section 501(c)(3) hospital members one or more of the following activities.
• Data processing.
• Purchasing (including purchasing insurance on a group basis).
• Warehousing.
• Billing and collection (including purchasing patron accounts receivable on a recourse basis).
• Food.
• Clinical.
• Industrial engineering.
• Laboratory.
• Printing.
• Communications.
• Record center.
• Personnel (including selecting, testing, training, and educating personnel) services.

A cooperative hospital service organization must also meet certain other requirements specified in section 501(e). For additional information, see Publication 557.

Line 17. A cooperative service organization of operating educational organizations described in section 501(f) is organized and operated to provide investment services to its members. Those members must be organizations described in section 170(b)(1)(A)(ii) or (iv), and either tax exempt under section 501(a) or whose income is excluded from taxation under section 115(a).

See Publication 557 for additional information.

Line 18. A "charitable risk pool" described in section 501(n) is organized and operated to pool insurable risks of its section 501(c)(3) members (other than risks related to medical malpractice). A section 501(n) organization must be organized under state law provisions authorizing risk pooling arrangements for charitable organizations and also meet certain other requirements provided by section 501(n).

See Publication 557 for additional information.

Line 19. "A school" is an educational organization whose primary function is the presentation of formal instruction and which normally maintains a regular faculty and curriculum and normally has a regularly enrolled body of pupils or students in attendance at the place where its educational activities are regularly carried on. A school may include a:
• Primary, secondary, preparatory, or high school.
• College or university.
• Trade or technical school.
• Nursery or pre-school.
• School that you operate as an activity, such as a school that is operated as an

activity of a museum, historical society, or church.

If you are a nursery or pre-school that meets the description of a school, you would answer "Yes" to line 19 and complete *Schedule B*. You would also answer "No" to *Part VIII*, line 9a.

If you are a nursery or pre-school that does not meet the description of a school, you would answer "No" to line 19. You would answer "Yes" to *Part VIII*, line 9a, if you are applying for exemption as a childcare organization.

See Publication 557 for additional information.

Line 20. "Hospital or medical care" includes the treatment of any physical or mental disability or condition, whether as an inpatient or outpatient. A hospital includes:
• Hospitals and rehabilitation institutions, outpatient clinics, or community mental health or drug treatment centers if the principal purpose or function is the providing of medical or hospital care or medical education or research.
• Medical research organizations, if the principal purpose or function is the continuous active conduct of medical research in conjunction with a hospital.

See Publication 557 for additional information.

Line 21. "Low-income housing" refers to rental or ownership housing provided to persons based on financial need. "Elderly housing" refers to rental or ownership housing provided to persons based on age, including retirement, assisted-living, independent living, continuous care, and life care arrangements. "Handicapped housing" refers to rental or ownership housing provided to persons based on physical or mental disabilities, including nursing homes.

If you are a skilled nursing facility, you should also complete *Schedule C*.

Line 22. Answer "Yes" if you pay monies to an individual as a scholarship, fellowship, or educational loan, for travel, study, or other similar purposes. Also answer "Yes" if you pay such amounts on behalf of an individual to a school or a tuition or educational savings program.

Travel, study, or other similar purposes include payments made to enhance a literary, artistic, musical, scientific, teaching or other similar capacity, skill, or talent of the individual recipient. For example amounts paid to:
• Vocational high school students to be used to purchase basic tools.
• Teachers to induce them to teach in an economically depressed, public school system.
• A scientific researcher to underwrite that individual's research project.

Educational grants do not include amounts you pay to an individual as compensation, such as payments made to a consultant for personal services or to produce a report for you.

Instructions for Form 1023   -11-

Educational grants do not include amounts paid to another organization that distributes your funds as a scholarship to an individual if you have no role in the selection process.

If you are a "private foundation" as described in *Part X*, you can request advance approval of your grant-making procedures by completing *Schedule H* and avoid the possible imposition of excise taxes under section 4945.

Part IX. Financial Data

A. Statement of Revenues and Expenses

Existed 4 years or more. If you have been in existence for 4 or more years, complete the *A. Statement of Revenues and Expenses* for your most recently completed year and each of the three years immediately before it for a total of four years of financial information. Place financial information for your most recently completed year in the column marked *Current tax year.*

 We may request financial information for more than four years if necessary.

Existed more than one year, less than 4 years. If you have been in existence for more than 1 year and less than 4 years, provide your actual income and expenses for each completed year you have existed and projections of your likely income and expenses based on a reasonable and good faith estimate of your future finances for your current year and each year you have not existed for a total of 3 years of financial information. Place financial information for the year you are filing this application in the column marked *Current tax year.*

Existed less than 1 year. If you have existed for less than 1 year, you must provide projections of your likely income and expenses for your current year and projections of your likely income and expenses for the next 2 years based on a reasonable and good faith estimate of

your future finances. Place financial information for the year you are filing this application in the column marked *Current tax year.*

Preparing the statement. Prepare the statements using the method of accounting you use in keeping your books and records. If you use a method other than the cash receipts and disbursements method, attach a statement explaining the method used. For example, state whether you used the accrual method of accounting to prepare the financial statements included with this application.

Prepare the statements using the accounting period entered on *Part I,* line 5. Financial information should reflect projected activities reported elsewhere in this application.

Line 1. Include funds or other items of value that you receive as gifts, grants, or contributions. For example, if one of your activities is a food drive, the value of the donated food must be included on this line. Also include on this line payments a governmental unit makes to enable you to both:
• Accomplish your exempt purpose(s), and
• Provide a service or facility directly to the general public.

See the instructions to line 9 if you are uncertain whether revenue should be included as a grant in line 1 or as gross receipts in line 9. Unusual grants are not included on this line, but are included on line 12.

Examples

1. A city pays the symphony orchestra to provide free music programs in the public schools. The programs are open to the public. This income received from a governmental unit accomplishes the orchestra's exempt purpose and directly provides a service to the general public. The income is a grant to the symphony orchestra that should be listed on line 1.

2. The symphony orchestra sells tickets to the public for its fall season. Such income is gross receipts received from the general public in performance of

the orchestra's exempt function and should be listed on line 9.

3. The public school system pays the symphony orchestra to create several musical pieces suitable for the school system's elementary music curriculum. This payment by a governmental unit for the music compositions is primarily for its (the school system's) own use, not for the direct benefit of the public. Therefore, this income is gross receipts received from a governmental unit in performance of the orchestra's exempt function that should be listed on line 9.

Line 2. Include amounts received from members to provide support to the organization. Do not include payments from members or on behalf of members to purchase admissions, merchandise, services, or use of facilities.

Line 3. Include gross income from dividends, interest, payments received on securities, loans, rents, and royalties that are held for investment purposes.

Line 4. Net income from unrelated business activities generally includes income from any trade or business activity that is regularly carried on, not conducted with substantially all (at least 85%) volunteer labor, and not related to your exempt purposes. (This amount can be taken from Form 990-T, if filed.)

Report on line 9 income from activities that are not related to the accomplishment of your exempt purposes, but are not considered unrelated business activities. For example, income from the sale of merchandise by volunteers that is not treated as an unrelated trade or business is reported on line 9.

See Publication 598 for additional information regarding unrelated business income.

Line 5. Include the amount collected by any local tax authority from the public on your behalf.

Line 6. To determine the value of services or facilities furnished by a governmental unit, use the fair market value of the services or facilities furnished to you. Do not include the value of services or facilities generally provided to the public without charge.

Line 7. Enter the total income from all sources not reported on lines 1 through 6, or lines 9, 11, and 13. Submit an itemized list showing each type and amount of income included on this line. Also, briefly describe each type of income.

Line 8. Add lines 1 through 7 and enter the amount.

Line 9. "Gross receipts" is income from activities that you conduct to further your exempt purposes (excluding amounts listed on other lines). It includes payments by a governmental unit that may be called a "grant," but that is actually payment for a service or facility for the use of the government payer, rather than for the direct benefit of the public.

Figure 2. Part IX–A. Statement of Revenues and Expenses
Line 11. Net Gain or (Loss)

	Categories		
	(A) Real Estate	(B) Securities	(C) Other
1. Gross sales price of assets (other than inventory) by category.			
2. **Less:** Cost or other basis and sales expenses.			
3. Gain or (loss). Subtract line 2 from line 1.			
4. Net gain or (loss) – Add line 3 of columns (A), (B), and (C). Enter here and on Form 1023, *Part IX - A. Statement of Revenues and Expenses*, line 11.			

Example: The state government gives a conservation group a grant to study the consequences to an ecologically significant woodland area of a new sewage treatment plan. Although the payment is called a grant, it is actually gross receipts that should be included on line 9. The payment is by a governmental unit (state) for a study for its own use, not for the direct benefit of the general public. The study could have been done by a for-profit consulting company rather than by the tax-exempt conservation group.

Submit an itemized list of payments by any governmental units showing:
• Payer (governmental unit or bureau).
• Purpose of payment.
• Amount.

Include as gross receipts the income from activity conducted:
• Intermittently (not regularly carried on), such as an occasional auction.
• With substantially all (at least 85%) volunteer labor, such as a car wash.
• For the convenience of members, students, patients, officers, or employees, such as a parking lot for a school's students and employees.
• With substantially all contributed merchandise, such as a thrift store.

See Publication 598 for additional information regarding income that is not from an unrelated trade or business.

Line 10. Add lines 8 and 9 and enter the amount.

Line 11. Attach a schedule with total amounts entered (rather than each individual transaction) for each category using the format in Figure 2.

Line 12. "Unusual grants" generally are substantial contributions and bequests from disinterested persons that by their size adversely affect classification as a public charity. They are unusual, unexpected, and received from an unrelated party.

You must fully describe your unusual grants in *Part X*, line 7. For additional information about unusual grants and a description of public charity classification see Publication 557.

Line 13. Add lines 10 through 12 and enter the amount.

Line 14. Fundraising expenses include the total expenses incurred by you for soliciting gifts, grants, and contributions included on line 1. Where you allocate a portion of your other expenses to fundraising, submit an itemized list describing the amounts allocated. Include fees paid to professional fundraisers for soliciting gifts, grants, and contributions.

Line 15. If distributions have been made, submit an itemized list showing the name of each recipient, a brief description of the purposes or conditions of payment, and the amount paid.

Colleges, universities, and other educational institutions and agencies subject to the Family Educational Rights and Privacy Act (20 U.S.C. 1232g) need not list the names of individuals who were provided scholarships or other financial assistance where such disclosure would violate the privacy provisions of the law. Instead, such organizations should group each type of financial aid provided, indicate the number of individuals who received the aid, and specify the aggregate dollar amount.

Line 16. If payments have been made, submit an itemized list showing the name of each recipient, a brief description of the purposes or condition of payment, and amount paid. Do not include any amounts on line 15.

Line 17. Enter the total amount of compensation. Be consistent with information provided in *Part V*, lines 1a, 1b, and 1c.

Line 18. Enter the total amount of employees' salaries and wages not reported on line 17, above.

Line 19. Enter the total interest expense for the year, excluding mortgage interest treated as an occupancy expense on line 20.

Line 20. Enter the amount paid for the use of office space or other facilities, heat, light, power, and other utilities, outside janitorial services, mortgage interest, real estate taxes, and similar expenses.

Line 21. If you record depreciation, depletion, and similar expenses, enter the total amount.

Line 22. Professional fees are those charged by individuals and entities that are not your employees. They include fees for professional fundraisers (other than fees listed on line 14, above), accounting services, legal counsel, consulting services, contract management, or any independent contractors.

Line 23. Submit an itemized list showing the type and amount of each significant expense for which a separate line is not provided.

Line 24. Add lines 14 through 23 and enter the amount on line 24.

B. Balance Sheet

Complete the following for your most recently completed tax year. If you have not completed a full tax year, use the most current information available. Be sure to enter the year-end date for the information provided and not the date the form is prepared.

Line 1. Enter the total cash in checking and savings accounts, temporary cash investments (money market funds, CDs, treasury bills, or other obligations that mature in less than one year), and petty cash funds.

Line 2. Enter the total accounts receivable that arose from the sale of goods and/or performance of services, less any reserve for bad debt.

Line 3. Enter the amount of materials, goods, and supplies you purchased or manufactured and held to be sold or used in some future period.

Line 4. Enter the total amount of bonds or notes that you issued that will be repaid to you. Submit an itemized list that shows the name of each borrower, a brief description of the obligation, the rate of return, the due date, and the amount due.

Line 5. Enter the total fair market value (FMV) of corporate stocks you hold. Submit an itemized list of your corporate stock holdings. For stock of closely held corporations, the statement should show the name of the corporation, a brief summary of the corporation's capital structure, the number of shares held, and their value as carried on your books. If such valuation does not reflect current fair market value, also include fair market value.

For stock traded on an organized exchange or in substantial quantities over the counter, the statement should show the name of the corporation, a description of the stock and the principal exchange on which it is traded, the number of shares held, and their value as carried on your books and their fair market value.

Line 6. Enter the total amount of loans (personal and mortgage loans) receivable. Submit an itemized list that shows each borrower's name, purpose of loan, repayment terms, interest rate, and original amount of loan. Report each loan separately, even if more than one loan was made to the same person.

Line 7. Enter the total book value of other investments. Include the total book value of government securities (federal, state, or municipal), and buildings and equipment held for investment purposes. Submit an itemized list identifying and reporting the book value of each building/item of equipment held for investment purposes.

Line 8. Enter the total book value of buildings and equipment not held for investment. This includes facilities you own and equipment you use in conducting your exempt activities. Submit an itemized list of these assets held at the end of the current tax year/period, including the cost or other basis.

Line 9. Enter the total book value of land not held for investment.

Line 10. Enter the total book value of any other category of assets not reported on lines 1 through 9. For example, you would include patents, copyrights, or other intangible assets. Submit an itemized list of each asset.

Line 11. Add lines 1 through 10 and enter the amount.

Line 12. Enter the total amount of accounts payable to suppliers and others, such as salaries payable, accrued payroll taxes, and interest payable.

Line 13. Enter the total unpaid portion of grants and contributions you have committed to pay to other organizations or individuals.

Line 14. Enter the total of mortgages and other notes payable outstanding at the end of the current tax year/period. Submit an itemized list that shows each note separately, including the lender's name, purpose of loan, repayment terms, interest rate, and original amount.

Line 15. Enter the total amount of any other liabilities not reported on lines 12 through 14. Submit an itemized list of these liabilities, including the amounts owed.

Line 16. Add lines 12 through 15 and enter the amount.

Line 17. Under fund accounting, an organization segregates its assets, liabilities, and net assets into separate funds according to restrictions on the use of certain assets. Each fund is like a separate entity in that it has a self-balancing set of accounts showing assets, liabilities, equity (fund balance), income, and expenses. If you do not use fund accounting, report only the "net assets" account balances, which include capital stock, paid-in capital, retained earnings or accumulated income, and endowment funds.

Line 18. Add lines 16 and 17 and enter the amount.

Line 19. If you answer "Yes," describe the change and explain what caused it.

Part X. Public Charity Status

Line 1a. Organizations that are exempt under section 501(c)(3) are private foundations *unless* they are:
• Churches, schools, hospitals, governmental units, entities that undertake testing for public safety; organizations that have broad financial support from the general public; or
• Organizations that support one or more other organization(s) that are themselves classified as public charities.

Section 501(c)(3) organizations excepted from private foundation status are public charities. See the instructions for *Part X*, lines 5a through 5i for a more detailed description of public charities.

Unless you meet one of the exceptions above, you are a private foundation and must answer, "Yes," on line 1a.

Line 1b. Section 508(e) provides that a private foundation is not tax exempt unless its organizing document contains specific provisions. These specific provisions require that you operate to avoid liability for excise taxes under sections 4941(d), 4942, 4943(c), 4944, and 4945(d). You can also meet these provisions by reliance on state law.

See Publication 557, Chapter 3, *Section 501(c)(3) Organizations: Private Foundations,* for samples of provisions that will meet section 508(e). Also, see *Appendix B.* for a list of states that have enacted statutory provisions that satisfy the requirements of section 508(e), subject to notations. *Appendix B.* is based on Revenue Ruling 75-38, 1975-1 C.B. 161.

Line 2. Some private foundations are private operating foundations. These are types of private foundations that lack general public support, but make qualifying distributions directly for the active conduct of their educational, charitable, and religious purposes. "Directly for the active conduct" means that the distributions are used by the foundation itself to carry out the programs for which it is organized and operated. Grants made to assist other organizations or individuals are normally considered indirect.

For additional information about private operating foundations, log on to *www.irs.gov/charities/foundations/article/ 0,,id=136358,00.html.*

Line 3. If you have existed for one year or more, you must provide financial information that demonstrates you meet the requirements to be classified as a private operating foundation.

Line 4. If you have existed for less than one year, you must ordinarily provide an affidavit or opinion of counsel that sets forth facts concerning your operations and projected support to demonstrate that you are likely to satisfy the requirements to be classified as a private operating foundation. If you have not provided an affidavit or opinion of counsel, you may provide a narrative statement that provides sufficient information to demonstrate that you are likely to satisfy the requirements to be classified as a private operating foundation.

Line 5a. Check this box if your primary purpose is operating a church or a convention or association of churches. The term "church" includes mosques, temples, synagogues, etc. If you select this box, complete and submit *Schedule A.*

Line 5b. Check this box if your primary purpose is operating a school. If you select this box, complete and submit *Schedule B.*

If you operate a school but it is not your primary purpose, do not check this box. However, you must still complete and submit *Schedule B.*

Be sure your response is consistent with *Part VIII,* line 19.

Line 5c. Check this box if your primary purpose is providing medical or hospital care, or medical education or research (performed in association with a hospital). If you select this box, complete and submit *Schedule C.*

A hospital includes a rehabilitation institution, outpatient clinic, community mental health clinic, drug treatment center, or skilled nursing facility.

A hospital does not include convalescent homes, homes for children or the aged, or institutions whose principal purpose or function is to train handicapped individuals to pursue some vocation.

Cooperative hospital service organizations described in section 501(e)

should also check this box, but do not complete *Schedule C.*

Line 5d. Check this box if you are organized and operated to support organizations described in lines 5a through 5c, 5f, 5g, or 5h, or an organization that is tax exempt under section 501(c)(4), (5), or (6). If you select this box, complete and submit *Schedule D.*

The organization(s) you support should have a significant influence over your operations.

Line 5e. Check this box if your primary purpose is to test products to determine their acceptability for use by the general public.

Contributions to organizations of this type are not deductible under section 170(c). Also, organizations that primarily test for specific manufacturers do not qualify for exemption under section 501(c)(3).

Line 5f. Check this box if you are organized and operated exclusively to benefit a college or university owned or operated by a governmental unit. You must also normally receive a substantial part of your support from a governmental unit or from contributions from the general public.

Organizations that qualify under this category would generally also qualify under section 509(a)(3), line 5d, which would be an easier public charity status to maintain.

Line 5g. Check this box if you normally receive a substantial part of your support from grants from governmental units or from contributions from the general public, or a combination of these sources. Typically, a substantial part of your income would be shown on *Part IX-A. Statement of Revenues and Expenses,* lines 1 and 2.

⚠ *If you select this public charity status, you must request either an advance ruling or a definitive ruling by completing* Part X. line 6.

Under this public charity status, you must meet the one-third public support test or the 10% facts and circumstances test.

Public support test. An organization must receive either (1) at least one-third of its total support from governmental agencies, contributions from the general public, and contributions or grants from other public charities, or (2) at least 10% of its total support from governmental agencies, contributions from the general public, and contributions or grants from other public charities and also satisfy a facts and circumstances test.

Facts and circumstances test. Facts and circumstances include (1) the amount of support you received from the general public, governmental units, or public charities, (2) whether you have a continuous and bona fide program for solicitation of funds from the general public, governmental units, or public

Instructions for Form 1023

charities, and (3) all other facts and circumstances, including the public nature of your governing board, the extent to which your facilities or programs are publicly available, the extent to which your dues encourage membership, and whether your activities are likely to appeal to persons having a broad common interest or purpose. For additional information about the 10% facts and circumstances test, see Publication 557 and Treas. Regs. section 1.170A-9(e)(3).

Line 5h. Check this box if you normally receive more than one-third of your support from contributions, membership fees, and gross receipts from activities related to your exempt functions, or a combination of these sources, and not more than one-third of your support from gross investment income and net unrelated business income. Typically, a substantial part of your income would be shown on *Part IX-A. Statement of Revenues and Expenses*, lines 1, 2, and 9.

Under this public charity status, you must meet both the "one-third public support test" and the "not-more-than-one-third investment income and net unrelated business income test". Before checking this box, consider the types of income you listed on *Part IX-A. Statement of Revenues and Expenses*, lines 1 through 13. If you select this public charity status, you must request either an advance ruling or a definitive ruling by completing *Part X*, line 6. See Publication 557 for additional information about these tests.

Line 5i. Check this box if you are unsure whether you are better described in box 5g or 5h. By checking this box, you agree to let us choose the best public charity status for you.

Request For Advance Ruling Or Definitive Ruling

If you checked the box for line 5g, 5h, or 5i, you must check either line 6a or 6b. Your request for an "advance ruling" or a "definitive ruling" depends on the following factors:
• The date you were formed or other date that your exemption would be effective;
• Whether you have completed at least one tax year (consisting of at least 8 full months) from the date you were formed or other date that your exemption would be effective; and
• The amount and type of income you have received.

Line 6a. Request for Advance Ruling. By checking the box on line 6a, you are requesting an advance ruling for your public charity status. The advance ruling gives you a 5-year period in which you can get the financial support needed to meet one of the public support tests described in line 5g or 5h. Generally, the financial information for the 5-year period is submitted at the end of your advance ruling period and a final determination is

made as to whether you are a public charity or a private foundation.

When your advance ruling period ends in 5 years, we will ask that you provide updated information about your public support by completing Form 8734.

Statute extension. To receive an advance ruling, you must agree to extend the statute of limitations for any of the 5 tax years in the advance ruling period. This agreement allows us additional time to assess federal taxes under section 4940 if you do not qualify as a public charity for any of the 5 tax years in the advance ruling period. You are not required to agree to the extension requested. However, in this situation, we will not be able to issue an advance ruling. If you agree to the extension, the statute will extend 8 years, 4 months, and 15 days beyond the end of your first tax year. By signing the consent, you are agreeing to the statute extension. If, at the end of your 5-year advance ruling period, we determine that you do not meet the public support tests and you are a private foundation, we will assess the tax under section 4940 for that 5-year period.

If you requested an advance ruling, we will return a copy of *Part X* of your application with your signed consent, also signed by an IRS official. Keep this signed document in your permanent records.

First tax year not completed. If you have not yet completed your first tax year consisting of at least 8 full months, you must check the box for line 6a to request an advance ruling. For example, if you were formed on May 15, 2003, with an accounting period that ends December 31, and you submitted your application on August 15, 2004, you must request an advance ruling since your first tax year consisted of only 7½ months and you have not completed your second tax year.

Completed first tax year. If you have completed your first tax year consisting of at least 8 full months but cannot currently meet one of the required public charity supports tests, you may still wish to request an advance ruling. This request should only be made if you reasonably expect to meet the required public charity support tests within the 5-year advance ruling period.

Completed more than 5 tax years. If you have completed more than 5 tax years from the date your exemption would be effective, do not request an advance ruling.

Line 6b. Request for Definitive Ruling. By checking line 6b, you are requesting a definitive ruling for your public charity status. The definitive ruling is given to you when you apply if you have existed at least one tax year of 8 months or more, and meet one of the public support tests described in these instructions and Publication 557.

A definitive ruling must be based on your public support computed on the cash

method of accounting. Therefore, if you use the accrual method of accounting, please use a worksheet to convert your revenue accounts from the accrual to the cash basis. Such a worksheet is provided in Instructions for Schedule A (Form 990 or 990-EZ), *Part IV-A. Support Schedule.*

If you have completed your first tax year consisting of at least 8 full months and can meet one of the required public charity support tests, you should check the box for line 6b.

To show that you meet one of the required public charity support tests, complete lines 6b(i) and/or 6b(ii).

Line 6b(i)(a). From *Part IX-A. Statement of Revenues and Expenses*, add the line 8 amounts from completed tax years only. Multiply the total by 2% (0.02) and enter the amount in the space provided.

Line 6b(ii)(b). The required list for this line should include the name of and amounts paid by each individual or organization included on line 9, *Part IX-A. Statement of Revenues and Expenses*, that were greater than the larger of 1% of line 10, of the *Part IX-A. Statement of Revenues and Expenses* or $5,000 for any completed tax year. Your list for each payer must show a year-by-year breakdown of the amounts reported for completed tax years on *Part IX-A. Statement of Revenues and Expenses*, line 9.

⚠ *Do not include disqualified persons in this list. Disqualified persons should be listed in line 6b(ii)(a).*

If you did not receive such payments, check the box for this line.

For purposes of this application, a "disqualified person" is any individual or organization that is:

1. A "substantial contributor" to you (defined below).
2. An officer, director, trustee, or any other individual who has similar powers or responsibilities.
3. An individual who owns more than 20% of the total combined voting power of a corporation that is a substantial contributor.
4. An individual who owns more than 20% of the profits interest of a partnership that is a substantial contributor.
5. An individual who owns more than 20% of the beneficial interest of a trust or estate that is a substantial contributor.
6. A member of the family of any individual described in 1, 2, 3, 4, or 5 above.
7. A corporation in which any individuals described in 1, 2, 3, 4, 5, or 6 above, hold more than 35% of the total combined voting power.
8. A trust or estate in which any individuals described in 1, 2, 3, 4, 5, or 6 above, hold more than 35% of the beneficial interests.
9. A partnership in which any individuals described in 1, 2, 3, 4, 5, or 6

Instructions for Form 1023   -15-

above, hold more than 35% of the profits interest.

Substantial contributor. A "substantial contributor" is any individual or organization that gave more than $5,000 to you from the date you were formed or other date that your exemption would be effective, to the end of the year in which the contributions were received. This total amount contributed must also be more than 2% of all the contributions you received. A creator of a trust is treated as a substantial contributor regardless of the amount contributed.

For more information regarding substantial contributors, log on to the IRS website at *www.irs.gov/charities/foundations/article/0,,id=136935,00.html.*

Family members. A "member of the family" includes the spouse, ancestors, children, grandchildren, great grandchildren, and their spouses.

For additional information concerning members of the family, go to *www.irs.gov/charities/foundations/article/0,,id=136955,00.html.*

Further information about disqualified persons, can be obtained at *www.irs.gov/charities/foundations/article/0,,id=136927,00.html.*

Line 7. "Unusual grants" generally are substantial contributions and bequests from disinterested persons that by reason of their size adversely affect classification as a public charity. They are unusual, unexpected, and received from an unrelated party. If you answer "Yes" to line 7, submit a statement for each grant. The statement should include the name of the contributor, the date and amount of the grant, a brief description of the grant, and an explanation of why it is unusual. You should include details of any additional funds you expect to receive from the contributors listed. If they qualify for unusual grant treatment, these amounts should be reported on *Part IX-A. Statement of Revenues and Expenses,* line 12.

See Publication 557 for additional information about unusual grants.

Part XI. User Fee Information

 Your application will not be processed without payment of the proper user fee.

Your user fee may be paid by a personal or certified check, bank check, or cashier's check. Your check should be made payable to the United States Treasury.

Gross receipts. The total amount listed on *Part IX-A. Statement of Revenues and Expenses,* line 10 is your gross receipts for purposes of determining your user fee.

Line 1. Compute the average of your gross receipts for a 4-year period based on either (1) the gross receipts you expect to receive over your first four years

if you have not completed a 4-year period, or (2) the gross receipts you actually received for the immediately preceding 4 years if you have completed a 4-year period.

Schedule A. Churches

General Information:

There is no single definition of the word "church" for tax purposes. When determining whether a section 501(c)(3) religious organization is also a church, we will consider characteristics generally attributed to churches and the facts and circumstances of each organization applying for public charity status as a church.

The characteristics generally attributed to churches are as follows.
• A distinct legal existence.
• A recognized creed and form of worship.
• A definite and distinct ecclesiastical government.
• A formal code of doctrine and discipline.
• A distinct religious history.
• A membership not associated with any other church or denomination.
• Ordained ministers ministering to the congregation.
• Ordained ministers selected after completing prescribed courses of study.
• A literature of its own.
• Established places of worship.
• Regular congregations.
• Regular religious services.
• Sunday schools for the religious instruction of the young.
• Schools for the preparation of ministers.

Although it is not necessary that each of the above criteria be met, a congregation or other religious membership group is generally required. A church includes mosques, temples, synagogues, and other forms of religious organizations. For more information, see Publication 1828.

The practices and rituals associated with your religious beliefs or creed must not be illegal or contrary to clearly defined public policy.

Specific Line Items

Line 1a. Provide a copy of your written creed, statement of faith, or summary of beliefs.

Line 1b. A "form of worship" refers to religious practices that express your devotion to your creed, faith, or beliefs.

Line 2a. A "code of doctrine and discipline" refers to a body of laws or rules that govern behavior.

Line 2b. Your "religious history" includes the story of your establishment and major events in your past.

Line 2c. Your literature includes any writings about your beliefs, rules, or history.

Line 3. A "religious hierarchy or ecclesiastical government" refers to

people or institutions that exercise significant influence or authority over you.

Line 4a. Indicate the regular days and times of your religious services. Describe the order of events during your regular worship service and explain how the activities conducted as part of your services further your religious purposes. Also include sample copies of church bulletins, pamphlets, or flyers that are distributed to your members or the general public.

Line 4b. Enter on the line provided, the average number of members and non-members who attend your regularly scheduled religious services.

Line 5a. An "established place of worship" is a place where you hold regularly scheduled religious services. It may be a place that you own, rent, or which is provided freely for your use. If you answer "Yes," go to line 5b. If you answer "No," describe where you meet to hold regularly scheduled religious services.

Line 6. An "established congregation" or "other religious membership group" includes individuals who regularly attend and take part in the religious services of your organization at an established location. An established congregation generally does not include members of only one family. If you answer "No" because you do not have an established congregation or other religious membership, you may be a religious organization that does not qualify as a church. If you do not qualify as a church, you will need to go back to *Part X,* line 5, to reconsider your public charity status.

TIP *You may request classification as a church at a later date after you establish a congregation or other religious membership group. For information about this option, contact our customer account service representatives at 1-877-829-5500 (toll-free).*

Line 7. Enter the total number of your current members in the line provided. If you have no members, enter zero.

Line 8a. Answer "Yes" if you have a prescribed way to become a member. Answer "Yes" even if you just keep records of who is currently a member. Describe any actions required for individuals to become members. Submit copies of any application forms used.

Line 8b. Describe any rights and benefits of members. You should include details of any levels of membership and the rights and/or benefits associated with each level.

Line 8c. If your members may be associated with another denomination or church, describe the circumstances in which your members would be members of your church and another church.

Line 8d. See *Glossary, Appendix C,* for a description of the word "family."

Line 9. Answer "Yes" if you conduct baptisms, weddings, funerals, or other religious rites.

Instructions for Form 1023

Line 10. A school for the religious instruction of the young refers to any regularly scheduled religious, educational activities for youth, such as a "Sunday school."

Line 11a. A "prescribed course of study" refers to formal or informal training. It does not include self-ordination or paying a fee for an ordination certificate without completing a course of study. Describe the course of study completed by your religious leader.

Line 12. Answer "Yes" if your religious leader is listed in *Part V*, line 1a.

Line 14. Answer "Yes" if you are part of a group of churches with similar beliefs and structures, such as a convention, association, or union of churches.

Line 16. If you answer "Yes," submit a copy of your church charter. Identify the organization that issued the charter and describe the requirements you met to receive it. Do not describe organizational charters you received from your state's Secretary of State, Franchise Tax Board, or similar administrative office.

Line 17. Attach any additional information you would like us to consider that would help us classify you as a church.

Schedule B. Schools, Colleges, and Universities

General Information:

An organization is a school if it:
• Presents formal instruction as its primary function.
• Has a regularly scheduled curriculum.
• Has a regular faculty of qualified teachers.
• Has a regularly enrolled student body.
• Has a place where educational activities are regularly carried on.

The term "school" includes primary, secondary, preparatory, high schools, colleges, and universities. It does not include organizations engaged in both educational and non-educational activities, unless the latter are merely incidental to the educational activities. Non-traditional schools such as an outdoor survival school or a yoga school may qualify.

The term "school" does not include home schools.

Section I. Operational Information

Line 1a. Answer "Yes" if you have a regularly scheduled curriculum, a regular faculty of qualified teachers, a regularly enrolled student body, and facilities where your educational activities are regularly carried on. Submit evidence establishing that you meet these factors, as described below:
• Evidence that you have a regularly scheduled curriculum includes a list of required courses of study, dates and times courses are offered, and other information about how to complete required courses.

• Evidence that you have a regular faculty of qualified teachers, includes certifications by the appropriate state authority or successful completion of required training.
• Evidence of a regularly enrolled student body includes records of regular attendance by students at your facility.
• Evidence of a place where your exclusively educational activities are regularly carried on includes a lease agreement or deed for your facility.

If you answer "No," do not complete *Schedule B*. You do not meet the requirements of a school and you will need to go back to *Part X*, line 5, to reconsider your public charity status.

Line 1b. Answer "Yes" if your primary function is the presentation of formal instruction. If you answer "No," do not complete *Schedule B*. You do not meet the requirements of a school and you will need to go back to *Part X*, line 5, to reconsider your public charity status.

Line 2a. Answer "Yes" if you are a public school. Submit documentation of your status as a public school. If you answer "Yes," do not complete the remainder of *Schedule B*.

Line 2b. Answer "Yes" if you have a signed contract or agreement with a state or local government under which you operate and receive funding. Submit a signed and dated copy of your contract or agreement. If you answer "Yes," do not complete the remainder of *Schedule B*.

Line 3. Enter the name of the public school district and county where you operate.

Line 4. Answer "Yes" if you were formed or substantially expanded during a period of time when public schools in your district or county were desegregated by court order.

 If you are unsure whether to answer "Yes," contact an appropriate public school official.

Line 5. Answer "Yes" if a state or federal administrative agency or judicial body ever determined your organization to be racially discriminatory. Identify the parties involved and the forum in which the case was presented. Explain the reason for the action, the decision reached, and provide legal citations (if any) for the decision. Also, explain in detail any changes made in response to the action against your organization or the decision reached.

Line 7. In responding to this line, you may reference information previously provided in response to *Part VIII*, line 7a, 7b, or 7c, along with any additional information to fully respond.

Line 8. Answer "Yes" if you manage or intend to manage your programs through your own employees or by using volunteers. Answer "No" if you engage or intend to engage a separate organization or independent contractor. Make sure your answer is consistent with the information provided in *Part VIII*, line 7b. In responding to this line, you may

reference information previously provided in response to *Part VIII*, line 7a, 7b, or 7c, along with any additional information to fully respond.

Section II. Establishment of Racially Nondiscriminatory Policy

A section 501(c)(3) organization that is a school must publish a notice of its racially nondiscriminatory policy as to students as follows.

The M school admits students of any race, color, national origin, and ethnic origin to all the rights, privileges, programs, and activities generally accorded or made available to students at the school. It does not discriminate on the basis of race, color, national origin, and ethnic origin in administration of its educational policies, admission policies, scholarship and loan programs, and athletic and other school-administered programs.

Every private school is subject to the provisions of Revenue Procedure 75-50, 1975-2 C.B. 587 (Rev. Proc. 75-50). See Publication 557, which sets forth the requirements of Rev. Proc. 75-50 under the section for *Private Schools.*

A private school must also certify annually that it meets the requirements of Rev. Proc. 75-50. This can be accomplished by filing Schedule A (Form 990, Form 990-EZ) Organization Exempt Under Section 501(c)(3).

Schools that do not file Form 990 must file Form 5578, Annual Certification of Racial Nondiscrimination for a Private School Exempt From Federal Income Tax.

Line 1. Answer "Yes" if your organizing document or bylaws contain a nondiscriminatory statement as to students similar to the one shown above.

Answer "No" if the nondiscrimination statement is not included. If the statement is not included in your organizing document or bylaws, you may submit a copy of your signed and dated resolution that was adopted according to your internal rules or regulations. Your resolution should approve a nondiscriminatory policy similar to the one shown above.

Line 2. Answer "Yes" if your brochures, application forms, advertisements, and catalogues dealing with student admissions, programs, and scholarships contain a statement similar to the following.

The M school admits students of any race, color, and national or ethnic origin.

Submit representative copies of each document.

If you answer "No," to line 2, but checked the box on line 2b, you are agreeing that all future printed materials,

Instructions for Form 1023   -17-

including Internet content, will contain a statement of nondiscriminatory policy as to students similar to the one provided above.

Line 3. You must demonstrate that you have made your nondiscriminatory policy known to all segments of the general community served by the school. One way of meeting this requirement is to publish the school's nondiscriminatory policy annually. If you have already published your notice, submit the actual page of the newspaper on which the notice appears. We cannot accept a photocopy, other electronic reproduction, or partial page of the newspaper.

Answer "No," if you have not attached your notice and describe how you meet the publicity requirement of Rev. Proc. 75-50.

See Publication 557 or Rev. Proc. 75-50 for guidance on the format and content of the required notice and whether any exceptions may apply to you.

 A notice published in the legal notices section or classified advertisements of your local newspaper is generally not acceptable.

Line 5. Enter the racial composition of your student body, faculty, and administrative staff in the spaces provided. Enter actual numbers, rather than percentages, for the current year and projected numbers for the next academic year. If the number is zero, then enter "0."

 Do not identify students, faculty, and staff by name.

If you are completing the table based on estimates, submit documentation that supports how you arrived at the estimated numbers. For example, if your estimates are based on the racial composition of the community in which you operate, submit current census data of the racial composition for the area. If your numbers and the census numbers differ greatly, explain why.

Line 6. Enter the racial composition of students to whom you award loans and scholarships in the spaces provided. Enter actual numbers, rather than percentages, for the current year and projected numbers for the next academic year. If the number is zero, then enter "0."

 Do not identify students by name.

Line 7a. Submit a list that identifies each individual or organization by name. Your list must include your incorporators, founders, board members, donors of land, and donors of buildings.

Line 7b. Answer "Yes" if any individuals or organizations on your list have an objective to keep public or private school education segregated by race. Explain how these individuals or organizations promote segregation in public or private schools.

Line 8. Answer "Yes" if on a continuing basis, you will maintain for a minimum period of three years the following records.

● Your racial composition (similar to the information requested in *Schedule B, Section II*, line 5).

● Evidence that your scholarships and loans are awarded on a racially nondiscriminatory basis (similar to the information requested in *Schedule B, Section II*, line 6).

● Copies of all materials used by you or on your behalf to solicit contributions.

● Copies of brochures, application forms, advertisements, and catalogues dealing with student admissions, programs, and financial aid.

Answer "No" if you do not maintain records and explain how you meet the recordkeeping requirements under Rev. Proc. 75-50.

 Failure to maintain these records or produce them upon the proper request, will create a presumption that you have not complied with the requirements of Rev. Proc. 75-50.

Schedule C. Hospitals and Medical Research Organizations

General Information:

An organization qualifies as a hospital if it is a:

● Hospital.

● Cooperative hospital service organization (*Schedule C* not required).

● Medical research organization operated in conjunction with a hospital.

Hospital. An organization is a "hospital" if its principal purpose or function is providing medical or hospital care or medical education or research. Medical care includes treatment of any physical or mental disability or condition, on an inpatient or outpatient basis. Thus, if an organization is a rehabilitation institution, outpatient clinic, or community mental health or drug treatment center, it is a hospital if its principal function is providing treatment services as described above.

A hospital does not include convalescent homes, homes for children or the aged, or institutions whose principal purpose or function is to train handicapped individuals to pursue a vocation.

Medical research organization. An organization is a "medical research organization" if its principal purpose or function is the direct, continuous, and active conduct of medical research in conjunction with a hospital. The hospital with which the organization is affiliated must be described in section 501(c)(3), a federal hospital, or an instrumentality of a governmental unit, such as a municipal hospital.

"Medical research" means investigations, experiments, and studies to discover, develop, or verify knowledge

relating to the causes, diagnosis, treatment, prevention, or control of human physical or mental diseases and impairments. For more information, see Treas. Regs. section 1.170A-9(c)(2).

If you are a hospital, check the first box on *Schedule C* and complete *Section I.*

If you are a medical research organization, check the second box on *Schedule C* and complete *Section II.*

Section I. Hospitals

Line 1. Answer "Yes" if all doctors in your community are eligible for staff privileges at your facility. You may answer "Yes" if staff privileges at your facility are limited by capacity.

Answer "No" if all doctors in your community are not eligible for staff privileges at your facility.

If you answer "No," describe in detail how you limit eligibility for staff privileges at your facility. Include details of your eligibility criteria and selection procedures for your courtesy staff of doctors.

Line 2a. Answer "Yes" if you admit all patients in your community who can pay for themselves or through private health insurance.

Answer "No" if you limit admission for these individuals in any way. If you answer "No," describe your admission policy in detail. You should explain how and why you restrict patient admission.

Line 2b. Answer "Yes" if you admit all patients in your community who participate in Medicare.

Answer "No" if you limit admission in any way for these individuals. If you answer "No," describe your admission policy in detail. You should explain how and why you restrict patient admission to exclude persons who participate in Medicare.

Line 2c. Answer "Yes" if you admit all patients in your community who participate in Medicaid.

Answer "No" if you limit admission in any way for these individuals. If you answer "No," describe your admission policy in detail. You should explain how and why you restrict patient admission to exclude persons who participate in Medicaid.

Line 3a. Answer "Yes" if you require a deposit from Medicare and/or Medicaid patients before admission. If you answer "Yes," describe in detail how you determined the amount required and explain why a deposit is needed.

Line 3b. Answer "Yes" if you require a deposit for other patients before admission and the requirement is the same as for Medicare and/or Medicaid patients.

Answer "No" if you require a deposit, but deposits for Medicare/Medicaid patients and other patients differ as to: (1) the way the amount is determined, or (2) the reason for the deposit. If you answer "No," describe the differences in detail.

-18-

Line 4a. Answer "Yes" if you offer emergency medical or hospital care at your facility on a 24-hour basis, seven days a week. If "No," explain why you do not offer an emergency room. For example, emergency care may be inappropriate for the type of services you provide. Also, describe any emergency services that you provide.

Line 4b. Answer "Yes" if you have a specific written plan or policy to accept all patients in need of emergency care without considering their ability to pay.

If you answer "Yes," submit a copy of your plan or policy.

Line 4c. Answer "Yes" if you have specific arrangements with any police, fire, or ambulance service providers to bring emergency cases to your facility.

If you answer "Yes," describe each specific agreement. For written agreements, you may submit a copy of each agreement. If it is oral, explain fully the agreement. For any oral agreements, include details of how and when the agreement was arranged.

Line 5a. Answer "Yes" if you provide free or low cost medical or hospital care services to the poor. If you answer "Yes," answer lines 5b through 5e. Do not answer 5b through 5e if you answer "No."

Line 5b. Submit a copy of your written policy or explain fully the understanding under which you operate regarding the admission and/or treatment of charity cases. Explain how you distinguish between charity care and bad debts.

 Include details of how you inform the general public about your policy. Submit copies of any documents or agreements you require charity patients to sign before being admitted and/or treated.

Line 5c. Submit information that shows the amounts you expend for treating charity care patients and the types of services you provide. Include an explanation that distinguishes charity care patient expenditures from uncollected bad debts.

Line 5d. Submit copies of any written agreements you have with municipalities or government agencies to subsidize the cost of admitting or treating charity patients.

Line 5e. A sliding fee scale establishes payments depending on financial ability to pay.

Line 6a. Answer "Yes" if you have a formal program of medical training and research. If you answer "Yes," describe your program in detail, including its length and criteria for acceptance into your program.

Line 6b. Answer "Yes" if you have a formal program of community educational programs. If you answer "Yes," describe your program in detail.

Line 7. Answer "Yes" if you provide office space to physicians conducting their own medical practices.

Line 8. Answer "Yes" if you have a board of directors that is representative of the community you serve. Include a list of each board member with the individual's name and employment affiliation. Also, for each board member, describe how that individual represents the community. Generally, hospital employees and staff physicians are not individuals considered to be community representatives.

 Answer "Yes" if an organization described in section 501(c)(3) with a community board exercises rights or powers over you, such as the right to appoint members to your governing board of directors and the power to approve certain transactions. Describe these rights and powers. In addition, describe how each of that organization's board of directors represents the community.

Answer "Yes" if you are subject to a state corporate practice of medicine law that requires your governing board to be composed solely of physicians licensed to practice medicine in the state. If you answer "Yes" on this basis, also provide the following information.

• Describe whether a hospital described in section 501(c)(3) exercises any rights or powers over you.
• Identify the corporate practice of medicine law under which you operate.
• Explain how the section 501(c)(3) hospital exercises any rights or powers over you, such as the right to appoint members to your governing board of directors and the right to approve certain transactions.
• Explain what services you provide to the section 501(c)(3) hospital.

Line 10. Answer "Yes" if you manage or intend to manage your programs through your own employees or by using volunteers. Answer "No" if you engage or intend to engage a separate organization or independent contractor. Make sure your answer is consistent with the information provided in *Part VIII,* line 7b.

Line 11. Recruitment incentives may be offered to attract or retain physicians as employees or to serve the community in which the hospital is located. Such incentives are generally offered when there is an acute shortage of such physicians in your hospital or within the community.

Line 12. Physicians who have a financial or professional relationship with you include physicians with whom you have a business relationship, such as employees, staff physicians, participants in joint ventures, or physicians with whom you contract for services.

Line 13. A business relationship includes employment, contractual relationship, or status as a member of your board of directors.

Line 14. Answer "Yes" if you have adopted a conflict of interest policy consistent with the sample conflict of

interest policy provided in these instructions or you are subject to similar conflict of interest policies under state law. Provide copies of the policies to which you are subject. Although a conflict of interest policy is not required as a matter of tax law, we encourage adoption of a substantive conflict of interest policy because it makes it more likely that you will operate for the benefit of the community and not for private interests.

An example of a substantive conflict of interest policy is available in *Appendix A.* in these instructions.

Answer "No" if you have not adopted a conflict of interest policy or you are not subject to conflict of interest policies under state law.

Section II. Medical Research Organizations

Line 1. Attach a list of hospitals with which you have relationships relating to the conduct of medical research. Describe in detail the relationship you have with each hospital. Submit copies of any written agreements.

Line 2. Describe in detail all activities that directly accomplish your conduct of medical research.

Making grants to other organizations does not directly accomplish the conduct of medical research.

Line 3. Your schedule should explain how you determine the fair market value of your assets.

Schedule D. Section 509(a)(3) Supporting Organizations

General Information:

A section 509(a)(3) organization is commonly referred to as a "supporting organization." An organization that a supporting organization benefits is commonly referred to as a "supported organization." A supporting organization may support more than one supported organization.

An organization qualifies for public charity status as a supporting organization under section 509(a)(3) if:
• It is organized and at all times thereafter is operated exclusively for the benefit of, to perform the functions of, or to carry out the purposes of one or more public charities described in section 509(a)(1) or 509(a)(2);
• It meets one of three required relationship tests with the supported organization(s); and
• It is not controlled directly or indirectly by "disqualified persons." See specific instructions for *Part X,* line 6b(ii)(b), for a definition of a "disqualified persons."

A supporting organization can also support the charitable purposes of organizations that are exempt under sections 501(c)(4), (5), or (6).

-19-

3-42

Section I. Identifying Information About Supported Organization(s)

Line 1. Enter the name, address, and EIN of each organization you support.

Line 2. Answer "Yes" if each supported organization has received a letter from the IRS recognizing it as a public charity under section 509(a)(1) or 509(a)(2). Then, go to *Section II*, line 1.

Answer "No" if any supported organization has not received a letter from us recognizing it as a public charity under section 509(a)(1) or 509(a)(2). Then, go to line 3.

Line 3. Answer "Yes" if any supported organization you listed in line 1 received a letter from us stating that it is exempt under section 501(c)(4), (5), or (6). Also, to show how the organization meets the public support test, submit the amounts and sources of revenue for the last four completed tax years for the supported organization(s). You should provide the requested financial data in the format shown on *Part IX-A. Statement of Revenues and Expenses*, for each supported organization. You must then submit the lists requested by *Part X*, line 6b(ii), which is applicable to the public support test under section 509(a)(2).

Answer "No" if no supported organization listed in line 1 has been recognized as tax-exempt under section 501(c)(4), (5), or (6).

 If any organization you intend to support has not received a letter from us recognizing it as a public charity under section 509(a)(1) or 509(a)(2), or has not received a determination recognizing that it is tax-exempt under section 501(c)(4), (5), or (6), you must demonstrate, in writing, that each organization you support is described in section 509(a)(1) or 509(a)(2). For example, if you support a church or foreign organization, you should describe how this organization qualifies as a public charity under section 509(a)(1) or 509(a)(2).

Section II. Relationship with Supported Organization(s) – Three Tests

To qualify under section 509(a)(3), you must show that you meet one of three relationship tests with the supported organization(s).

- Test I. Operated, supervised, or controlled by (comparable to a parent-subsidiary relationship);
- Test 2. Supervised or controlled in connection with (comparable to a brother-sister relationship); or
- Test 3. Operated in connection with (responsive to the needs or demands of, and having significant involvement in the affairs of, the supported organization(s)).

Line 1. Answer "Yes" if your governing document, bylaws, or other internal rules and regulations show that the majority of your governing board or officers is elected or appointed by the supported organization(s). Then, go to Section III.

Answer "No" if your governing document, bylaws, or other internal rules and regulations do not show that the majority of your governing board or officers is elected or appointed by the supported organization(s). If you answer "No" but still believe you satisfy this test, explain and go to Section III. Otherwise, go to line 2 because you do not meet the "operated, supervised, or controlled by" relationship test.

Line 2. Answer "Yes" if your governing document, bylaws, or other internal rules and regulations show that a majority of your governing board consists of individuals who also serve on the governing board of the supported organization(s). Then, go to Section III.

Answer "No" if your governing document, bylaws, or other internal rules and regulations do not show that a majority of your governing board consists of individuals who also serve on the governing board of the supported organization(s). If you answer "No" but still believe you satisfy this test, explain and go to Section III. Otherwise, go to line 3 because you do not meet the "supervised or controlled in connection with" relationship test.

Line 3. Answer "Yes" if you are a charitable trust under state law, you name each specified publicly supported organization as a beneficiary in your trust agreement, and each beneficiary organization has the power to enforce the trust and compel an accounting under state law. Then, go to *Section II*, line 5.

Line 4a. Answer "Yes" if the officers, directors, trustees, or members of the supported organization(s) elect or appoint any of your officers, directors, or trustees. If your governing document, bylaws, or other internal rules and regulations do not provide for this, explain how your officers, directors, or trustees are elected or appointed. Then, go to line 4d.

Line 4b. Answer "Yes" if any members of the governing body of the supported organization(s) also serve as your officers, directors, trustees, or hold another important office for your organization. Describe the position held and whether the position is ongoing. Then, go to line 4d.

Line 4c. Answer "Yes" if your officers, directors, or trustees maintain a close and continuous working relationship with the officers, directors, or trustees of the supported organization(s). Explain the continuous relationship in detail. Then, go to line 4d.

 If you answer "No," on line 4c and your answer to lines 3, 4a, and 4b were "No," you do not meet the "operated in connection with" relationship test. You must establish a different relationship with the supported organization or go back to Part X, to reconsider your public charity status.

Line 4d. Answer "Yes" if the supported organization has a significant involvement in your investment policies, making and timing of grants, and directing the use of your income and assets. Explain how the supported organization is involved in these matters.

Line 5. An applicant for tax exemption as a supporting organization under the "operated in connection with" relationship must satisfy either the integral part test or the alternative integral part test. If you are requesting supporting organization status by meeting the "operated in connection with" relationship, you must satisfy either the integral part test or the alternative integral part test. If you satisfy the integral part test described in line 5, then you do not have to complete line 6.

Answer "Yes" if you conduct activities that the supported organization would otherwise conduct. Describe the activities that you conduct, other than distributing funds. Then, go to *Section III*.

Line 6a. To satisfy the alternative integral part test as a supporting organization, you must distribute at least 85% of your annual "net income" to the organization(s) you support. See the *Glossary* for a description of "net income" to be used in calculating whether you meet the 85% distribution threshold.

Answer "Yes" if you distribute at least 85% of your net income to the supported organization(s). For purposes of this schedule, "net income" has the same meaning as the term "adjusted net income," which is applicable to private operating foundations.

In general, "adjusted net income" is the excess of gross income, including gross income from any unrelated trade or business, determined with certain modifications, reduced by total deductions. Gross income does not include gifts, grants, or contributions.

If you answer line 6a "No," and your answer to line 5 was "No," unless you establish that the supported organization(s) will be attentive to your operations, you do not meet the "operated in connection with" relationship test. Go back to *Part X*, to reconsider your public charity status.

Line 6b. Submit a list that shows the total amount distributed annually to each supported organization. Also, indicate how each amount will vary from year to year.

Line 6c. Submit a list that shows the total annual income for each supported organization.

Line 6d. Answer "Yes" if your funds are "earmarked" for a particular program or activity.

If you distribute your income to, or for the use of, a particular department or program of an organization, list the total annual revenue of the supported department or program in line 6c.

Line 7a. The "operated in connection with" test requires that you specify the supported organization(s) by name in your organizing document unless there has been an historic and continuing

-20-

Instructions for Form 1023

relationship between you and the supported organization(s).

Line 7b. An historic and continuing relationship depends on all the facts and circumstances that would demonstrate a substantial identity of interests between you and the supported organization.

If you answer "No" to lines 7a and 7b, you may consider amending your organizing document to specify the supported organization(s) by name so you can answer "Yes" to line 7a. Otherwise, you will need to go back to *Part X* to reconsider your public charity status.

Section III. Organizational Test

Line 1a. If you answered "No" to line 1a, you must amend your organizing document to specify the supported organization(s) by name, purpose, or class. Otherwise, you will not meet the operational test under section 509(a)(3) and you will need to go back to *Part X* to reconsider your public charity status.

Line 1b. If you answered "No" to line 1b, you must amend your organizing document to specify the supported organization(s) by name. Otherwise you will not meet the operational test under section 509(a)(3) and you will need to go back to *Part X* to reconsider your public charity status.

Section IV. Disqualified Person Test

Control. As a section 509(a)(3) supporting organization, you may not be controlled directly or indirectly by disqualified persons. You are controlled if disqualified persons can exercise 50% or more of the total voting power of your governing body. You are also controlled if disqualified persons have authority to affect significant decisions, such as power over your investment decisions, or power over your charitable disbursement decisions. You are also controlled if disqualified persons can exercise veto power. Although control is generally demonstrated where disqualified persons have the authority over your governing body to require you to take an action or refrain from taking an action, indirect control by disqualified persons will also disqualify you as a supporting organization.

See the instructions for *Part X*, line 6b for a description of the term "disqualified person."

A public charity is not a disqualified person.

A "foundation manager" means your:
● Officers, directors, or trustees, or
● An individual having powers or responsibilities similar to those of your officers, directors, or trustees.

Line 1b. See the instructions for *Part V*, line 2a, for a description of the terms "family or business relationship."

Schedule E. Organizations Not Filing Form 1023 Within 27 Months of Formation

General Information:

The questions in this schedule will help us determine the effective date of exemption for an organization that filed its application more than 27 months after the end of the month in which it was legally formed.
● If you meet exceptions for late filing, your exemption under section 501(c)(3) will be effective from the date you were legally formed.
● If you do not meet any exceptions, your exemption under section 501(c)(3) will be effective from the date you filed your application.
● Although you do not meet any exceptions, you may, nevertheless, qualify for tax exemption as an organization described in section 501(c)(4) for the period beginning with the date you were legally formed and ending with the date you are recognized under section 501(c)(3). Generally, contributions made to a section 501(c)(4) organization are not tax deductible.

Line 1. Answer "Yes" if you are a church or an association of churches. You should have also checked *Part X*, line 5a, and completed *Schedule A*. If you qualify as a church or an association of churches, your exemption will be effective from the date of your legal formation.

Answer "Yes" if you are an integrated auxiliary of a church. If you qualify as an integrated auxiliary of a church, your exemption will be effective from the date of your legal formation.

An "integrated auxiliary of a church" refers to a class of organizations that are related to a church or convention or association of churches, but are not such organizations themselves. In general, you must:
● Be described as both tax exempt under section 501(c)(3) and a public charity described in sections 509(a)(1), (2), or (3); and
● Receive financial support primarily from internal church sources as opposed to public or governmental sources.

Men's and women's organizations, seminaries, mission societies, and youth groups that satisfy the above referenced sections 501(c)(3) and 509(a)(1), (2), or (3) requirements are considered integrated auxiliaries whether or not they meet the internal support requirements. More guidance as to the types of organizations that qualify as integrated auxiliaries can be found in Treas. Regs. section 1.6033-2(h).

Line 2a. Answer "Yes" if you are a public charity and your annual gross receipts are normally $5,000 or less. For information about whether your annual gross receipts are normally $5,000 or less, see Publication 557. If you qualify as an

-21-

organization with annual gross receipts of normally $5,000 or less, your exemption would be effective from the date of your legal formation.

Answer "No" if you are a private foundation, regardless of your gross receipts.

Line 2b. Answer "Yes" if:
● Your gross receipts were normally less than $5,000 for years before your last completed tax year,
● Your gross receipts normally exceeded $5,000 for your last completed tax year, and
● You filed this application within 90 days from the end of your last completed tax year.

Line 3. Lines 3a, 3b, and 3c are applicable to subordinates included in a group exemption application. See Publication 557 for information regarding group exemptions. If you were a subordinate of a group exemption that was timely filed and you are filing for exemption within 27 months from the date you were notified by the organization holding the group exemption letter that either (1) you are no longer covered by the group exemption letter, or (2) the group exemption request was denied, answer "Yes" and do not complete the remainder of this schedule.

Line 4. Answer "Yes" if you were formed on or before October 9, 1969. If you are a corporation, your formation date is the date your articles of incorporation were filed with and approved by your state officials. If you are an association, your formation date is the date you adopted your organizing document. If you are a trust, your formation date is generally the date your trust was both adopted and funded.

⚠ *If you answer "Yes," do not complete the rest of this schedule.* As an organization formed on or before October 9, 1969, your exemption would be effective from the date of your legal formation. Answer "No" if you were formed after October 9, 1969.

Line 5. You may receive an extension of time to file Form 1023 beyond the 27-month period if you can establish that you acted reasonably and in good faith, and that granting an extension will not prejudice the interests of the government.
● You filed Form 1023 before we discovered your failure to file.
● You failed to file because of intervening events beyond your control.
● You exercised reasonable diligence but you were not aware of the filing requirements. (The complexity of your filing and experience in these matters is taken into consideration.)
● You reasonably relied on written advice from us.
● You reasonably relied on the advice of a qualified tax professional who failed to file or advise you to file Form 1023.

Answer "Yes" if you wish to request an extension of time to file under these provisions. If you answer "Yes," describe in detail the reasons for filing late based on the factors listed above. Do not complete the rest of this schedule.

Answer "No" if you do not wish to request an extension under these provisions and go to line 6a.

Line 6a. By checking "Yes," and completing *Part X*, line 6a, you are eligible for an advance ruling to be classified as a public charity from the postmark date of your application.

Do not complete line 6a, 6b, or 7 if you checked the boxes in *Part X*, lines 5a, 5b, 5c, 5d, or 5e.

Line 6b. If you anticipate significant changes in your sources of support in the future, answer "Yes," and we will base your qualification for an advance ruling on the financial information you provide in line 7. If you check "Yes," complete the financial information requested in line 7 of Schedule E.

If you answer "No," we will base your qualification for an advance ruling on the financial information you provided in *Part IX*. If you answer "No," do not complete line 7 of *Schedule E*.

Line 7. Complete projected budgets of income for the first two full tax years after the date you mailed your Form 1023. See the specific instructions for *Part IX-A. Statement of Revenues and Expenses*, lines 1 through 13, if you need guidance on what to include in the various categories.

Line 8. Check the box if you wish to request exemption under section 501(c)(4) for the period before the postmark date of your Form 1023. If you check the box, attach page 1 of Form 1024. Form 1024 is available on the IRS website at *www.irs.gov* or by calling 1-800-829-3676.

If you qualify for exemption under section 501(c)(4), you will not be liable for income tax returns as a taxable entity, but you will need to file any exempt organization returns for which you may be responsible. Contributions to section 501(c)(4) organizations are generally not deductible by donors.

Do not check the box if you do not wish to be tax exempt under section 501(c)(4) for the period before the postmark date of your Form 1023. If you do not request and obtain exemption under section 501(c)(4) for the period before the postmark date of your Form 1023, you may be liable for income tax returns as a taxable entity for that time period.

Schedule F. Homes for the Elderly or Handicapped and Low-Income Housing

General Information:

Homes for the elderly or handicapped are eligible for tax exemption as charitable

organizations only if they meet the special needs of the elderly or handicapped for residential facilities designed to meet their physical, social, recreation, health care, and transportation needs. Homes for the elderly or handicapped must also be within the financial reach of a significant segment of the elderly or handicapped in the community. Once admitted to the elderly or handicapped housing facility, the organization must have an established policy to maintain them as residents, to the extent possible, even if the residents subsequently become unable to pay the monthly charges.

Low-income housing must provide affordable housing for a significant segment of individuals in your community with low incomes. Your housing may serve a combination of purposes, such as for poor, frail, and elderly persons.

Section I. General Information about Your Housing

Line 1. The type of housing you provide should include both a description of the type of facility provided, such as apartment complex, condominium, cooperative, or private residence, and the nature of your facility, such as assisted-living facility, continuing-care facility, nursing home, low-income facility, etc.

Line 7. See the instructions for *Part V*, line 7a, for a description of the terms arm's length and fair market value.

Line 8. Answer "Yes" if you manage or intend to manage your programs through your own employees or by using volunteers. Answer "No" if you engage or intend to engage a separate organization or independent contractor. Make sure your answer is consistent with the information provided in *Part VIII*, line 7b.

Line 9. Government programs include federal, state, or local government programs.

Section II. Homes for the Elderly or Handicapped

Line 2a. Answer "Yes" if you charge a one-time fee for admission to your facility.

Line 2b. Answer "Yes" if you charge daily, weekly, monthly, or annual fees or maintenance charges.

Line 2c. A "community" refers to the area that will be served by your facility. For example, a community may be a local area or a region.

Line 3a. Describe what happens to individuals if they become unable to pay your regular charges. For example, you may have a policy whereby you have a reserve fund for maintaining residents who are having trouble in paying their regular charges. You may also have a

policy of keeping residents who are having trouble in paying their regular charges in place for a period of time to permit them to find alternative housing. Include a copy of any printed materials that informs the public about your policy.

Line 3b. Describe any arrangements you have or expect to have with welfare agencies, sponsoring organizations, or others to assist residents who become unable to afford to remain residents.

Line 4. Describe how you provide for the health care needs of residents, including the services provided. This can include providing for the activities of daily living of residents at your facilities and transporting residents to other facilities for medical services.

Line 5. Describe how living units and common areas are designed to meet the physical needs of residents (such as grab bars in bathrooms, wide doorways and hallways, design of kitchens and bathrooms, etc.). Also, include information about facilities and programs designed to meet some combination of physical, emotional, recreational, social, religious, and similar needs of residents.

Section III. Low-Income Housing

Line 2. Answer "Yes" if you charge daily, weekly, monthly, or annual fees or maintenance charges.

Schedule G. Successors to Other Organizations

General Information:

You should complete this schedule as a successor organization if any of the following situations pertain to you.
• You have taken or will take over the activities that were previously conducted by another.
• You have taken or will take over 25 percent or more of the fair market value of the net assets of another organization.
• You were established upon the conversion of an organization from for-profit to non-profit status.

The other organization is the predecessor organization. You should complete this schedule regardless of whether the predecessor (other organization) was exempt or not exempt from federal income tax.

Line 1a. For purposes of this schedule, a "for-profit" organization is one in which persons are permitted to have an ownership or partnership interest, such as corporate stock. It includes sole proprietorships, corporations, and other entities that provide for ownership interests.

-22-

Schedule H. Organizations Providing Scholarships, Fellowships, Educational Loans, or Other Educational Grants to Individuals and Private Foundations Requesting Advance Approval of Individual Grant Procedures

General Information:

Complete this schedule if you provide scholarships, fellowships, grants, loans, or other distributions to individuals for educational purposes. When answering the questions on this schedule, you should demonstrate how these distributions further your exempt purposes.

Generally, distributions made to individuals may advance educational purposes if selection is made:
• In a non-discriminatory fashion in terms of racial preference,
• Based on need and/or merit, and
• To a charitable class in terms of being available to an open-ended group, rather than to pre-selected individuals.

A scholarship or fellowship is tax free to the recipient only if he or she is:
• A candidate for a degree at an eligible educational institution; and
• Uses the scholarship or fellowship to pay qualified education expenses.

Qualified education expenses include tuition and fees; and course-related expenses such as books, supplies, and equipment. Room and board, travel, research, clerical help, and non-required equipment are not qualified education expenses. See Publication 970, Tax Benefits for Education, for additional information.

Selection of individuals using a lottery system generally has not been approved by the IRS.

Section I

Line 1b. If you have different grant programs, describe the purpose and amount of each program.

Line 1c. If you award educational loans, describe the terms of the loan (for example, interest rate, duration, forgiveness provision, etc.). Also, describe how any other loan institutions are involved in your program.

Line 1d. Explain how you will publicize your program and whether you publicize to the general public or to another group of possible recipients. Include specific information about the geographic area in which your program will be publicized and the means you will use, such as through newspaper advertisements, school district announcements, or community groups.

Line 1e. Submit sample copies of your solicitation material for applicants or materials announcing the awards. If solicitation is done orally through school counselors or others, explain fully.

Line 2. Organizations that make grants to individuals must maintain adequate records and case histories showing the name and address of each recipient pursuant to Revenue Ruling 56-304, 1956-2 C.B. 306. If you answer "No," explain how you will be able to demonstrate that your distributions serve exempt purposes.

Section II

Line 1a. Only complete lines 1a through 4 if you are a private foundation based on your answers to *Part X*, line 1a. Answer "Yes" if you are a private foundation and you are requesting advance approval of your grant-making procedures under section 4945(g). Answer "No" if you are a private foundation but do not wish to request advance approval of your grant-making procedures under section 4945(g). If you answer "No," the amounts you distribute as educational grants provided to individuals may be considered taxable expenditures under section 4945.

Answer "N/A" if you are requesting public charity status in *Part X*.

For more information about advance approval of grant-making procedures of a private foundation, log on to *www.irs.gov/charities/foundations/article/0,,id=137397,00.html*.

Line 1b. Check the box for section "4945(g)(1)" if your award qualifies as a scholarship or fellowship grant that is awarded on an objective and

nondiscriminatory basis and is used for study at a school (see the *Schedule B, General Information* for what is considered a school).

Check the box for section "4945(g)(3)" if the purpose of your award is to achieve a specific objective, produce a report or other similar product, or improve or enhance a literary, artistic, musical, scientific, teaching, or other similar capacity, skill, or talent of the recipient. Include your educational loan program under this section. You may check more than one box.

If your award qualifies as a prize or award that is subject to the provisions of section 74(b) and your recipient is selected from the general public, you do not have to request advance approval of your grant-making procedures since a prize or award is not subject to the advance approval procedure requirements because it is not a grant for travel, study, or other similar purposes. See Revenue Rulings 77-380, 1977-2 C.B. 419; 76-460, 1976-2 C.B. 371, and 75-393, 1975-2 C.B. 451.

Line 4. For additional information regarding private foundations requesting advance approval of individual grant procedures, go to *www.irs.gov/charities/foundations/article/0,,id=137396,00.html*.

Line 4a Answer "Yes" if you award scholarships on a preferential basis because you require, as an initial qualification, that the individual be an employee or be related to an employee of a particular employer.

Line 4c. Answer "N/A" if you do not provide scholarships, fellowships, or educational loans to employees of a particular employer.

Line 4d. Answer "N/A" if you do not provide scholarships, fellowships, or educational loans to children of employees of a particular employer.

Line 4e. Answer "N/A" if your answer to line 4d is "N/A."

TIP *For purposes of this schedule, a program for children of employees of a particular employer includes children and family members of employees.*

Paperwork Reduction Act Notice. We ask for the information on this form to carry out the Internal Revenue laws of the United States. If you want your organization to be recognized as tax exempt by the IRS, you are required to give us this information. We need it to determine whether the organization meets the legal requirements for tax-exempt status.

The organization is not required to provide the information requested on a form that is subject to the Paperwork Reduction Act unless the form displays a valid OMB control number. Books or records relating to a form or its instructions must be retained as long as their contents may become material in the administration of any Internal Revenue law. The rules governing the confidentiality of the Form 1023 application are covered in Code section 6104.

The time needed to complete and file these forms will vary depending on individual circumstances. The estimated average times are:

	Recordkeeping	Learning about the law or the form	Preparing the form	Copying, assembling, and sending the form to the IRS
Parts I to XI	89 hrs. 26 mins.	5 hrs. 10 mins.	9hrs. 39 mins.	48 mins.
1023 Sch. A	10 hrs. 2 mins.	6 mins.	16 mins.	—
1023 Sch. B	15 hrs. 18 mins.	12 mins.	27 mins.	—
1023 Sch. C	11 hrs. 14 mins.	12 mins.	23 mins.	—
1023 Sch. D	9 hrs. 48 mins.	42 mins.	53 mins.	—
1023 Sch. E	14 hrs. 35 mins.	1 hrs. 9 mins.	2 hrs. 22 mins.	16 mins.
1023 Sch. F	11 hrs. 28 mins.	12 mins.	23 mins.	—
1023 Sch. G	6 hrs. 42 mins.	6 mins.	12 mins.	—
1023 Sch. H	7 hrs. 53 mins.	42 mins.	51 mins.	—

If you have comments concerning the accuracy of these time estimates or suggestions for making these forms simpler, we would be happy to hear from you. You can write to the Internal Revenue Service, Tax Products Coordinating Committee, SE:W:CAR:MP:T:T:SP, 1111 Constitution Avenue, NW, IR-6406 Washington, DC 20224.

DO NOT send the application to this address. Instead, see *Where to File* on page 4.

Appendix A: Sample Conflict of Interest Policy

Note: Items marked *Hospital insert – for hospitals that complete Schedule C* are intended to be adopted by hospitals.

Article I
Purpose

The purpose of the conflict of interest policy is to protect this tax-exempt organization's (Organization) interest when it is contemplating entering into a transaction or arrangement that might benefit the private interest of an officer or director of the Organization or might result in a possible excess benefit transaction. This policy is intended to supplement but not replace any applicable state and federal laws governing conflict of interest applicable to nonprofit and charitable organizations.

Article II
Definitions

1. Interested Person

Any director, principal officer, or member of a committee with governing board delegated powers, who has a direct or indirect financial interest, as defined below, is an interested person.

[Hospital Insert – for hospitals that complete Schedule C

If a person is an interested person with respect to any entity in the health care system of which the organization is a part, he or she is an interested person with respect to all entities in the health care system.]

2. Financial Interest

A person has a financial interest if the person has, directly or indirectly, through business, investment, or family:

    a. An ownership or investment interest in any entity with which the Organization has a transaction or arrangement,

    b. A compensation arrangement with the Organization or with any entity or individual with which the Organization has a transaction or arrangement, or

    c. A potential ownership or investment interest in, or compensation arrangement with, any entity or individual with which the Organization is negotiating a transaction or arrangement.

Compensation includes direct and indirect remuneration as well as gifts or favors that are not insubstantial.

A financial interest is not necessarily a conflict of interest. Under Article III, Section 2, a person who has a financial interest may have a conflict of interest only if the appropriate governing board or committee decides that a conflict of interest exists.

Article III
Procedures

1. Duty to Disclose

In connection with any actual or possible conflict of interest, an interested person must disclose the existence of the financial interest and be given the opportunity to disclose all material facts to the directors and members of committees with governing board delegated powers considering the proposed transaction or arrangement.

2. Determining Whether a Conflict of Interest Exists

After disclosure of the financial interest and all material facts, and after any discussion with the interested person, he/she shall leave the governing board or committee meeting while the determination of a conflict of interest is discussed and voted upon. The remaining board or committee members shall decide if a conflict of interest exists.

3. Procedures for Addressing the Conflict of Interest

    a. An interested person may make a presentation at the governing board or committee meeting, but after the presentation, he/she shall leave the meeting during the discussion of, and the vote on, the transaction or arrangement involving the possible conflict of interest.

    b. The chairperson of the governing board or committee shall, if appropriate, appoint a disinterested person or committee to investigate alternatives to the proposed transaction or arrangement.

    c. After exercising due diligence, the governing board or committee shall determine whether the Organization can obtain with reasonable efforts a more advantageous transaction or arrangement from a person or entity that would not give rise to a conflict of interest.

    d. If a more advantageous transaction or arrangement is not reasonably possible under circumstances not producing a conflict of interest, the governing board or committee shall determine by a majority vote of the disinterested directors whether the transaction or arrangement is in the Organization's best interest, for its own benefit, and whether it is fair and reasonable. In conformity with the above determination it shall make its decision as to whether to enter into the transaction or arrangement.

Instructions for Form 1023   -25-

4. Violations of the Conflicts of Interest Policy

a. If the governing board or committee has reasonable cause to believe a member has failed to disclose actual or possible conflicts of interest, it shall inform the member of the basis for such belief and afford the member an opportunity to explain the alleged failure to disclose.

b. If, after hearing the member's response and after making further investigation as warranted by the circumstances, the governing board or committee determines the member has failed to disclose an actual or possible conflict of interest, it shall take appropriate disciplinary and corrective action.

Article IV
Records of Proceedings

The minutes of the governing board and all committees with board delegated powers shall contain:

a. The names of the persons who disclosed or otherwise were found to have a financial interest in connection with an actual or possible conflict of interest, the nature of the financial interest, any action taken to determine whether a conflict of interest was present, and the governing board's or committee's decision as to whether a conflict of interest in fact existed.

b. The names of the persons who were present for discussions and votes relating to the transaction or arrangement, the content of the discussion, including any alternatives to the proposed transaction or arrangement, and a record of any votes taken in connection with the proceedings.

Article V
Compensation

a. A voting member of the governing board who receives compensation, directly or indirectly, from the Organization for services is precluded from voting on matters pertaining to that member's compensation.

b. A voting member of any committee whose jurisdiction includes compensation matters and who receives compensation, directly or indirectly, from the Organization for services is precluded from voting on matters pertaining to that member's compensation.

c. No voting member of the governing board or any committee whose jurisdiction includes compensation matters and who receives compensation, directly or indirectly, from the Organization, either individually or collectively, is prohibited from providing information to any committee regarding compensation.

[Hospital Insert – for hospitals that complete Schedule C
d. Physicians who receive compensation from the Organization, whether directly or indirectly or as employees or independent contractors, are precluded from membership on any committee whose jurisdiction includes compensation matters. No physician, either individually or collectively, is prohibited from providing information to any committee regarding physician compensation.]

Article VI
Annual Statements

Each director, principal officer and member of a committee with governing board delegated powers shall annually sign a statement which affirms such person:

a. Has received a copy of the conflicts of interest policy,

b. Has read and understands the policy,

c. Has agreed to comply with the policy, and

d. Understands the Organization is charitable and in order to maintain its federal tax exemption it must engage primarily in activities which accomplish one or more of its tax-exempt purposes.

Article VII
Periodic Reviews

To ensure the Organization operates in a manner consistent with charitable purposes and does not engage in activities that could jeopardize its tax-exempt status, periodic reviews shall be conducted. The periodic reviews shall, at a minimum, include the following subjects:

a. Whether compensation arrangements and benefits are reasonable, based on competent survey information, and the result of arm's length bargaining.

b. Whether partnerships, joint ventures, and arrangements with management organizations conform to the Organization's written policies, are properly recorded, reflect reasonable investment or payments for goods and services, further charitable purposes and do not result in inurement, impermissible private benefit or in an excess benefit transaction.

Article VIII
Use of Outside Experts

When conducting the periodic reviews as provided for in Article VII, the Organization may, but need not, use outside advisors. If outside experts are used, their use shall not relieve the governing board of its responsibility for ensuring periodic reviews are conducted.

-26-   Instructions for Form 1023

Appendix B: States with Statutory Provisions Satisfying the Requirements of Internal Revenue Code Section 508(e)

The following states have adopted legislation satisfying the requirements of section 508(e) relating to private foundation governing instruments. Information derived from Revenue Ruling 75-38, 1975-1 C.B. 161.

ALABAMA — except where otherwise provided by a decree of a court of competent jurisdiction or by a provision in the private foundation's governing instrument which in either case has been entered or made after October 1, 1971, and expressly limits the applicability of State law.

ALASKA — except for such private foundations which expressly provide in their governing instruments that the applicable sections of Alaska law do not apply to them.

ARKANSAS — except for such private foundations which expressly provide in their governing instruments that the applicable sections of Arkansas law do not apply to them and except in the case of trusts where otherwise provided by decree of a court of competent jurisdiction.

CALIFORNIA — except where otherwise provided by a court of competent jurisdiction.

COLORADO — with respect to trusts that are private foundations except where otherwise provided by a court of competent jurisdiction.

CONNECTICUT — except where otherwise provided by a court of competent jurisdiction.

DELAWARE — except for such private foundations which expressly provide in their governing instruments that the applicable sections of Delaware law do not apply to them.

DISTRICT OF COLUMBIA — except for such corporations which expressly provide in their governing instruments that the applicable sections of District of Columbia law do not apply to them and except in the case of trusts where otherwise provided by a court of competent jurisdiction. (For purposes of this statute, corporations include corporations organized under any Act of Congress applicable to the District of Columbia as well as corporations organized under the laws of the District of Columbia.)

FLORIDA — except for such trusts which file a proper election not to be subject to the applicable provisions of Florida law and for such corporations as to which a court of competent jurisdiction has otherwise determined.

GEORGIA — except for such private foundations which file a proper election not to be subject to such law.

HAWAII — no exceptions.

IDAHO — except for such private foundations which expressly provide in their governing instruments that the applicable sections of Idaho law do not apply to them.

ILLINOIS — except for such corporations which have express provisions to the contrary in their articles of incorporation and except for trusts where it is otherwise provided by a court of competent jurisdiction.

INDIANA — except where otherwise determined by a court of competent jurisdiction with respect to private foundations organized before January 1, 1970.

IOWA — except for such private foundations which expressly provide in their governing instruments that the applicable sections of Iowa law do not apply to them.

KANSAS — except where otherwise provided by a court of competent jurisdiction.

KENTUCKY — except, with respect to corporations in existence on July 1, 1972, to the extent that such a corporation provides to the contrary by amendment to its articles of incorporation adopted after July 1, 1972, and, with respect to trusts in existence on July 1, 1972, where action is properly commenced on or before December 31, 1972, in a court of competent jurisdiction to excuse the trust from compliance with the requirements of section 508(e) of the Code.

LOUISIANA — except for such private foundations which expressly provide in their governing instruments that the applicable sections of Louisiana law do not apply to them.

MAINE — except where otherwise provided by a court of competent jurisdiction.

MARYLAND — except where otherwise provided by a court of competent jurisdiction.

MASSACHUSETTS — except where otherwise provided by a court of competent jurisdiction.

MICHIGAN — with respect to trusts that are private foundations except for such private foundations which file a notice of inconsistency under Michigan law.

MINNESOTA — except for private foundations that have been held by a court of competent jurisdiction not to be affected by such State statute.

MISSISSIPPI — except where otherwise provided by a court of competent jurisdiction.

MISSOURI — except for private foundations that have been held by a court of competent jurisdiction not to be affected by such State statute.

MONTANA — except in the case of trusts where otherwise provided by court decree entered after March 28, 1974, and except in the case of a corporation which has an express provision to the contrary in its articles of incorporation.

NEBRASKA — except for such trusts which effectively elect to be excluded from the applicable sections of Nebraska law, for such corporations which have governing instruments expressly providing to the contrary, and except as a court of competent jurisdiction has otherwise determined in any given case.

NEVADA — no exceptions.

NEW HAMPSHIRE — except where it is otherwise provided by a court of competent jurisdiction.

NEW JERSEY — except for such private foundations which expressly provide in their governing instruments that the applicable sections of New Jersey law do not apply to them.

NEW YORK — except where such law conflicts with any mandatory direction of an instrument by which assets were transferred prior to June 1, 1971, and such conflicting direction has not been removed legally.

NORTH CAROLINA — except for such private foundations which expressly provide in their governing instruments that the applicable sections of North Carolina law do not apply to them and except for trusts that have their governing instruments reformed by a decree of the Superior Court of North Carolina.

NORTH DAKOTA — with respect to trusts that are private foundations except where otherwise provided by a court of competent jurisdiction.

OHIO — except in the case of trusts where it is provided otherwise by a court of competent jurisdiction and except in the case of corporations in existence on September 17, 1971, which expressly adopt contrary provisions in their governing instruments after September 17, 1971.

OKLAHOMA — except for such private foundations which file a proper election not to be subject to such law.

OREGON — no exceptions.

PENNSYLVANIA — except where otherwise provided by a court of competent jurisdiction.

RHODE ISLAND — except where otherwise provided by a court of competent jurisdiction.

SOUTH CAROLINA — except for private foundations which expressly provide in their governing instruments that the applicable sections of South Carolina law do not apply to them.

SOUTH DAKOTA — except where otherwise provided by a court of competent jurisdiction.

TENNESSEE — except where otherwise provided by a court of competent jurisdiction.

TEXAS — except for such private foundations which file a proper election not to be subject to such law.

UTAH — with respect to trusts that are private foundations except where otherwise provided by a court of competent jurisdiction.

VERMONT — except where otherwise provided by a court of competent jurisdiction.

VIRGINIA — except for private foundations whose governing instruments contain express provisions to the contrary or which have filed a proper election not to be subject to such law.

WASHINGTON — except for such private foundations which expressly provide in their governing instruments that the applicable sections of Washington law do not apply to them.

WEST VIRGINIA — with respect to trusts that are private foundations except for such trusts which provide in their governing instruments that the applicable sections of West Virginia law do not apply to them.

WISCONSIN — except as may otherwise be provided by decree of a court of competent jurisdiction.

WYOMING — except where otherwise provided by a court of competent jurisdiction.

Appendix C: Glossary of Terms

Adjusted net income (for Schedule D)

Adjusted net income includes: gross income from any unrelated trade or business; gross income from functionally related businesses; interest payments received on loans; amounts received or accrued as repayments of amounts taken as qualifying distributions for any tax year; amounts received or accrued from the sale or other disposition of property to the extent acquisition of the property was treated as a qualifying distribution for any tax year; any amounts set aside for a specific project to the extent the full set aside was not necessary for the project; interest on government obligations normally excluded under section 103 of the Code; net short-term capital gains on sale or other disposition of property; and income received from an estate if the estate is considered terminated for income tax purposes because of a prolonged administration period.

It does not include: gifts, grants, and contributions received; long-term capital gains or losses; net section 1231 gains; capital gain dividends; the excess of fair market value over adjusted basis of property distributed to the U.S. or a possession or political subdivision, a state or its political subdivision, a charitable trust or corporation for public purposes, or income received from an estate during the administration period.

In computing adjusted net income, deduct the following: ordinary and necessary expenses paid or incurred for the production or collection of gross income, or for the management, conservation, or collection of gross income (includes operating expenses such as compensation of officers, employee wages and salaries, interest, rent, and taxes); straight-line depreciation and depletion (not percentage depletion); and expenses and interest paid or incurred to carry tax-exempt obligations. Do not deduct net short-term capital losses for the year in which they occur (these losses cannot be carried back or carried over to earlier or later tax years); the excess of expenses for property used for exempt purposes over the income received from the property; charitable contributions made by you; net operating losses; and special deductions for corporations.

Advance ruling

A written determination by us on your public charity status that treats you as a publicly supported organization during a 5-year period beginning, generally, from the date of your formation. At the end of the 5-year period, you will qualify for a definitive ruling (defined below) if you were publicly supported based on the support you received during the 5-year period.

Affiliated

Created by, controlled by, or closely related to a governmental unit, including a State, a possession of the United States, or any political subdivision of a State or a possession of the United States, or the United States, or the District of Columbia.

Arm's length

A transaction between parties having adverse (or opposing) interests; where none of the participants are in a position to exercise substantial influence over the transaction because of business or family relationship(s) with more than one of the parties.

Authorized representative

By submitting Form 2848, an attorney or certified public accountant who is permitted to represent you before us regarding your application for tax-exempt status.

Bingo

A game of chance played with cards that are generally printed with 5 rows of 5 squares each, on which participants place markers to form a pre-selected pattern to win the game. Bingo is gambling.

Business relationships	Employment and contractual relationships, and common ownership of a business where any officers, directors, or trustees, individually or together, possess more than a 35% ownership interest in common. Ownership means voting power in a corporation, profits interest in a partnership, or beneficial interest in a trust.
Bylaws	The internal rules and regulations of an organization.
Certification of filing	Articles of incorporation for your organization showing evidence that on a specific date they were filed with and approved by an appropriate state authority.
Charitable risk pool	An organization described in section 501(n), which is organized and operated to pool insurable risks (other than medical malpractice) of its section 501(c)(3) members.
Close connection	A relationship between organizations that may include: control of one organization by another through common governance or through authority to approve budgets or expenditures; coordination of operations as to facilities, programs, employees, or other activities; or common persons exercising substantial influence over all of the organizations.
Common control	You and one or more other organizations have (1) a majority of your governing boards or officers appointed or elected by the same organization(s), or (2) a majority of your governing boards or officers consist of the same individuals. Common control also occurs when you and one or more commonly controlled organizations have a majority ownership interest in a corporation, partnership, or trust. Ownership means voting power in a corporation, profits interest in a partnership, or beneficial interest in a trust.
Community	The local or regional geographic area to be served by an organization.
Compensation	All forms of income from working, including salary or wages; deferred compensation; retirement benefits, whether in the form of a qualified or non-qualified employee plan (for example: pensions or annuities); fringe benefits (for example: personal vehicle, meals, lodging, personal and family educational benefits, low interest loans, payment of personal travel, entertainment, or other expenses, athletic or country club membership, and personal use of your property); and bonuses.
Conflict of interest policy	A conflict of interest arises when a person in a position of authority over an organization, such as a director, officer, or manager, may benefit personally from a decision he or she could make. A conflict of interest policy consists of a set of procedures to follow to avoid the possibility that those in positions of authority over an organization may receive an inappropriate benefit.
Controlled by disqualified persons	As a section 509(a)(3) supporting organization, you may not be controlled directly or indirectly by disqualified persons. You are controlled if disqualified persons can exercise 50% or more of the total voting power of your governing body. You are also controlled if disqualified persons have authority to affect significant decisions, such as power over your investment decisions, or power over your charitable disbursement decisions. You are also controlled if disqualified persons can exercise veto power. Although control is generally demonstrated where disqualified persons have the authority over your governing body to require you to take an action or refrain from taking an action, indirect control by disqualified persons will also disqualify you as a supporting organization.

Cooperative hospital service organization	An organization described in section 501(e) is organized and operated on a cooperative basis to provide its section 501(c)(3) hospital members one or more of the following activities: data processing, purchasing (including purchasing insurance on a group basis), warehousing, billing and collection (including purchasing patron accounts receivable on a recourse basis), food, clinical, industrial engineering, laboratory, printing, communications, record center, and personnel (including selecting, testing, training, and educating personnel) services.
Cooperative service organization of operating educational organizations	An organization described in section 501(f) is organized and operated to provide investment services to its members. Those members must be organizations described in section 170(b)(1)(A)(ii) or (iv), and either tax exempt under section 501(a) or whose income is excluded from taxation under section 115(a).
Corporation	An entity organized under a Federal or state statute, or a statute of a federally recognized Indian tribal or Alaskan native government.
Definitive ruling	A written determination by us on your public charity status that classifies you as a publicly supported organization if you have completed your first tax year, consisting of at least 8 full months, and you meet one of the public support tests. A definitive ruling may also be issued at the end of your 5-year advance ruling period if you were issued an advance ruling and you meet one of the public support tests.
Develop	Develop means the planning, financing, construction, or provision of similar services involved in the acquisition of real property, such as land or a building.
Disqualified person	Any individual or organization that is: **a.** A substantial contributor to you (see *substantial contributor*). **b.** An officer, director, trustee, or any other individual who has similar powers or responsibilities. **c.** An individual who owns more than 20% of the total combined voting power of a corporation that is a substantial contributor to you. **d.** An individual who owns more than 20% of the profits interest of a partnership that is a substantial contributor to you. **e.** An individual who owns more than 20% of the beneficial interest of a trust or estate that is a substantial contributor to you. **f.** A member of the family of any individual described in a, b, c, d, or e above; **g.** A corporation in which any individuals described in a, b, c, d, e, or f above hold more than 35% of the total combined voting power; **h.** A trust or estate in which any individuals described in a, b, c, d, e, or f above hold more than 35% of the beneficial interests; and **i.** A partnership in which any individuals described a, b, c, d, e, or f above hold more than 35% of the profits interest.
Earmark	Donations or other contributions given to you to assist particular individuals or specific identified groups.
Economic development	Organizations formed to combat community deterioration by assisting businesses located in a particular geographic area whose economy is economically depressed or deteriorating. Economic development activities include grants, loans, provision of information and expertise, or creation of industrial parks. Economic development organizations may also be formed to eliminate prejudice and discrimination or lessen the burdens of government through involvement with business development.

Elderly housing	Generally, the primary beneficiaries of the tax-exempt housing are age 62 and older. The elderly are treated as appropriate charitable beneficiaries for certain purposes regardless of socio-economic status because, as a group, they face many barriers to their basic needs as they age. The elderly, as a class, face forms of distress other than financial, such as the need for suitable housing, physical and mental health care, civic, cultural, and recreational activities, and an overall environment conducive to dignity and independence.
Expenses	Financial burdens or outlays; costs (of doing business); business outlays chargeable against revenues. For purposes of this form, expenses mean direct and indirect expenses.
Fair market value	The price at which property or the right to use property would change hands between a willing buyer and a willing seller, neither being under any compulsion to buy, sell, or transfer property or the right to use property, and both having reasonable knowledge of relevant facts.
Family	Includes an individual's spouse, ancestors, children, grandchildren, great grandchildren, siblings (whether by whole or half blood), and the spouses of children, grandchildren, great grandchildren, and siblings.
Foreign country	A country other than the United States, its territories and possessions, and the District of Columbia.
For-profit	A business entity whose activities are conducted or maintained to make a profit (e.g. revenues greater than expenses).
Foundation manager	Officers, directors, or trustees, or an individual having powers or responsibilities similar to those of a foundation's officers, directors, or trustees.
Fundraising	The organized activity of raising funds, whether by volunteers, employees, or paid independent contractors.
Gainfully employed	Employed or actively looking for work.
Gaming	The term gaming includes activities such as Bingo, Beano, lotteries, pull-tabs, pari-mutuel betting, Calcutta wagering, pickle jars, punch boards, tip boards, tip jars, certain video games, 21, raffles, keno, split-the-pot, and other games of chance.
Gross investment income	As defined in section 509, gross investment income means the gross amount of income from interest, dividends, payments with respect to securities loans, rents, and royalties, but not including any such income to the extent included in computing the tax imposed by section 511.
Gross receipts	For purposes of *Part IX-A. Statement of Revenues and Expenses*, gross receipts includes monies earned from activities related to your charitable or other section 501(c)(3) activities, such as selling admissions or merchandise, performing services, or furnishing facilities.
Handicapped	Persons with physical or mental disabilities with special needs for suitable housing, physical and mental health care, civic, cultural, and recreational activities, transportation, and an overall environment conducive to dignity and independence.

Hospital	Hospital or medical care includes the treatment of any physical or mental disability or condition, whether on an inpatient or outpatient basis. A hospital includes:
	a. Hospitals and rehabilitation institutions, outpatient clinics, or community mental health or drug treatment centers if the principal purpose or function is the providing of medical or hospital care or medical education or research.
	b. Medical research organizations, if the principal purpose or function is the continuous active conduct of medical research in conjunction with a hospital.
Independent contractors	Persons who are not treated as employees for employment tax purposes.
Influence legislation	The act of directly contacting or urging the public to contact members of a legislative body for the purpose of proposing, supporting, or opposing legislation. You are also attempting to influence legislation if you advocate the adoption or rejection of legislation.
Intellectual property	A type of property (distinct from real or personal property) which includes:
	a. Patents (for inventions).
	b. Copyrights (for literary and artistic works such as novels, poems, plays, films, musical works, drawings, paintings, photographs, sculptures, architectural designs, performances, recordings, film, and radio or television programs).
	c. Trade names, trade marks, and service marks (for symbols, names, images, and designs).
	d. Formulas, know-how, and trade secrets.
Joint ventures	A legal agreement in which the parties jointly undertake a transaction for mutual profit. Generally, each person contributes assets and shares risks. Like a partnership, joint ventures can involve any type of business transaction and the "persons" involved can be individuals, groups of individuals, companies, or corporations.
Limited liability company	A limited liability company (LLC) combines attributes of both corporations and partnerships (or, for one-person LLCs, sole proprietorships). The corporation's protection from personal liability for business debts and the pass-through tax structure of partnerships and sole proprietorships.
Low-income housing	Rental or ownership housing provided to persons based on financial need.
Mailing address	Address where you wish all correspondence to be sent.
Manage	Manage means to direct or administer.
Medical care	The treatment of any physical or mental disability or condition, whether on an inpatient or outpatient basis.
Medical research organization	An organization whose principal purpose or function is the continuous active conduct of medical research in conjunction with a hospital.
Net income (for Schedule D)	See *adjusted net income*.
Non-fixed payments	A non-fixed payment means a payment that depends on discretion. For example, a bonus of up to $100,000 that is based on an evaluation of performance by the governing board is a non-fixed payment because the governing body has discretion over whether the bonus is paid and the amount of the bonus.

Organizing document	The organizing document depends on the form of the organization. For a corporation, the document is the articles of incorporation. For a limited liability company (LLC), the document is the articles of organization. For an unincorporated association, the document is the articles of association or constitution. The organizing document of a trust is the trust agreement.
Political	You participate in a political campaign if you promote or oppose, through political literature, brochures, pamphlets, hosting or participating in events, etc., the candidacy of an individual for public office. Debates and nonpartisan voter education are not considered political.
Predecessor	An organization whose activities or assets were taken over by another organization.
Private foundations	Organizations that are exempt under section 501(c)(3) are private foundations unless they are: churches, schools, hospitals, governmental units, entities that undertake testing for public safety; organizations that have broad financial support from the general public; or organizations that support one or more other organizations that are themselves classified as public charities.
Private operating foundation	A type of private foundation that lacks general public support, but makes qualifying distributions directly for the active conduct of its educational, charitable, and religious purposes. "Directly for the active conduct" means that the distributions are used by the foundation itself to carry out the programs for which it is organized and operated. Grants made to assist other organizations or individuals are normally considered indirect.
Public charity	Organizations that are exempt under section 501(c)(3) and are not private foundations because they are: churches, schools, hospitals, governmental units, entities that undertake testing for public safety; organizations that have broad financial support from the general public; or organizations that support one or more other organizations that are themselves classified as public charities. Public charity status is a more favorable tax status than private foundation status.
Reasonable compensation	Reasonable compensation is the amount that would ordinarily be paid for like services by like organizations under like circumstances as of the date the compensation arrangement is made. Reasonable compensation is important because excessive benefits in the form of compensation to disqualified persons may result in the imposition of excise taxes and jeopardize the organization's tax-exempt status.
Related	The family or business relationships between persons.
Relationship	A relationship between you and the recipient organization includes the following situations: **a.** You control the organization or it controls you through common officers, directors, or trustees, or through authority to approve budgets or expenditures. **b.** You and the organization were created at approximately the same time and by the same persons. **c.** You and the organization operate in a coordinated manner with respect to facilities, programs, employees, or other activities. **d.** Persons who exercise substantial influence over you also exercise substantial influence over the other organization.
Revenue	Revenue means gross revenue amounts.

Instructions for Form 1023   -35-

Revenue Procedure	An official statement of a procedure published in the IRS Cumulative Bulletin that either affects the rights or duties of taxpayers or other members of the public under the Internal Revenue Code and related statutes, treaties, and regulations or, although not necessarily affecting the rights and duties of the public, should be a matter of public knowledge.
Revenue Ruling	An official interpretation by the IRS of the Internal Revenue laws and related statutes, treaties, and regulations, that has been published in the Cumulative Bulletin. Revenue Rulings are issued only by the National Office and are published for the information and guidance of taxpayers, IRS officials, and others concerned.
SS-4	Application for Employer Identification Number.
School	A school is an educational organization whose primary function is the presentation of formal instruction and which normally maintains a regular faculty and curriculum and normally has a regularly enrolled body of pupils or students in attendance at the place where its educational activities are regularly carried on. A school may include a:

a. Primary, secondary, preparatory, or high school.

b. College or university.

c. Trade or technical school.

d. Nursery or preschool.

e. School that you operate as an activity, such as school that is operated as an activity of a museum, historical society, or church.

Similarly situated	Similarly situated organizations means tax-exempt or taxable organizations of a comparable size, purpose, and resources.
Substantial contributor	Any individual or organization that gave more than $5,000 to you from the date you were formed or other date that your exemption would be effective, to the end of the year in which the contributions were received. This total amount contributed must also be more than 2% of all the contributions you received. A creator of a trust is treated as a substantial contributor regardless of the amount contributed.
Successor	An organization that took over:

a. More than a negligible amount of the activities that were previously conducted by another organization;

b. Twenty-five percent or more of the fair market value of the net assets of another organization; or

c. Was established upon the conversion of an organization from for-profit to non-profit status.

Trust	A trust is an entity that may be formed by a trust agreement or declaration of trust. A trust may also be formed through a will.
Unincorporated association	An unincorporated association formed under state law must have at least two members who have signed a written document for a specifically defined purpose.
Unusual grants	Substantial contributions and bequests from disinterested persons that by their size adversely affect classification as a public charity. They are:

a. Unusual;

b. Unexpected; and

c. Received from an unrelated party.

Index

Form **1023**	**Application for Recognition of Exemption**	OMB No. 1545-0056
(Rev. June 2006) Department of the Treasury Internal Revenue Service	**Under Section 501(c)(3) of the Internal Revenue Code**	**Note:** *If exempt status is approved, this application will be open for public inspection.*

Use the instructions to complete this application and for a definition of all **bold** items. For additional help, call IRS Exempt Organizations Customer Account Services toll-free at 1-877-829-5500. Visit our website at **www.irs.gov** for forms and publications. If the required information and documents are not submitted with payment of the appropriate user fee, the application may be returned to you.

Attach additional sheets to this application if you need more space to answer fully. Put your name and EIN on each sheet and identify each answer by Part and line number. Complete Parts I - XI of Form 1023 and submit only those Schedules (A through H) that apply to you.

Part I   Identification of Applicant

1 Full name of organization (exactly as it appears in your **organizing document**)	2 c/o Name (if applicable)
3 **Mailing address** (Number and street) (see instructions) Room/Suite	4 Employer Identification Number (EIN)
City or town, state or country, and ZIP + 4	5 Month the annual accounting period ends (01 – 12)
6 Primary contact (officer, director, trustee, or **authorized representative**) a Name:	**b** Phone: **c** Fax: (optional)

7 Are you represented by an authorized representative, such as an attorney or accountant? If "Yes," provide the authorized representative's name, and the name and address of the authorized representative's firm. Include a completed Form 2848, *Power of Attorney and Declaration of Representative*, with your application if you would like us to communicate with your representative.   ☐ Yes   ☐ No

8 Was a person who is not one of your officers, directors, trustees, employees, or an authorized representative listed in line 7, paid, or promised payment, to help plan, manage, or advise you about the structure or activities of your organization, or about your financial or tax matters? If "Yes," provide the person's name, the name and address of the person's firm, the amounts paid or promised to be paid, and describe that person's role.   ☐ Yes   ☐ No

9a Organization's website:

  b Organization's email: (optional)

10 Certain organizations are not required to file an information return (Form 990 or Form 990-EZ). If you are granted tax-exemption, are you claiming to be excused from filing Form 990 or Form 990-EZ? If "Yes," explain. See the instructions for a description of organizations not required to file Form 990 or Form 990-EZ.   ☐ Yes   ☐ No

11 Date incorporated if a corporation, or formed, if other than a corporation.   (MM/DD/YYYY)   /   /

12 Were you formed under the laws of a **foreign country?**   ☐ Yes   ☐ No
If "Yes," state the country.

For Paperwork Reduction Act Notice, see page 24 of the instructions.   Cat. No. 17133K   Form **1023** (Rev. 6-2006)

Form 1023 (Rev. 6-2006)   Name: EIN: –   Page **2**

Part II — Organizational Structure

You must be a corporation (including a limited liability company), an unincorporated association, or a trust to be tax exempt. (See instructions.) **DO NOT file this form unless you can check "Yes" on lines 1, 2, 3, or 4.**

1 Are you a **corporation**? If "Yes," attach a copy of your articles of incorporation showing **certification**   ☐ **Yes**   ☐ **No**
of filing with the appropriate state agency. Include copies of any amendments to your articles and
be sure they also show state filing certification.

2 Are you a **limited liability company (LLC)**? If "Yes," attach a copy of your articles of organization showing   ☐ **Yes**   ☐ **No**
certification of filing with the appropriate state agency. Also, if you adopted an operating agreement, attach
a copy. Include copies of any amendments to your articles and be sure they show state filing certification.
Refer to the instructions for circumstances when an LLC should not file its own exemption application.

3 Are you an **unincorporated association**? If "Yes," attach a copy of your articles of association,   ☐ **Yes**   ☐ **No**
constitution, or other similar organizing document that is dated and includes at least two signatures.
Include signed and dated copies of any amendments.

4a Are you a **trust**? If "Yes," attach a signed and dated copy of your trust agreement. Include signed   ☐ **Yes**   ☐ **No**
and dated copies of any amendments.
b Have you been funded? If "No," explain how you are formed without anything of value placed in trust.   ☐ **Yes**   ☐ **No**

5 Have you adopted **bylaws**? If "Yes," attach a current copy showing date of adoption. If "No," explain   ☐ **Yes**   ☐ **No**
how your officers, directors, or trustees are selected.

Part III — Required Provisions in Your Organizing Document

The following questions are designed to ensure that when you file this application, your organizing document contains the required provisions to meet the organizational test under section 501(c)(3). Unless you can check the boxes in both lines 1 and 2, your organizing document does not meet the organizational test. **DO NOT file this application until you have amended your organizing document.** Submit your original and amended organizing documents (showing state filing certification if you are a corporation or an LLC) with your application.

1 Section 501(c)(3) requires that your organizing document state your exempt purpose(s), such as charitable,   ☐
religious, educational, and/or scientific purposes. Check the box to confirm that your organizing document
meets this requirement. Describe specifically where your organizing document meets this requirement, such as
a reference to a particular article or section in your organizing document. Refer to the instructions for exempt
purpose language. Location of Purpose Clause (Page, Article, and Paragraph): _____

2a Section 501(c)(3) requires that upon dissolution of your organization, your remaining assets must be used exclusively   ☐
for exempt purposes, such as charitable, religious, educational, and/or scientific purposes. Check the box on line 2a to
confirm that your organizing document meets this requirement by express provision for the distribution of assets upon
dissolution. If you rely on state law for your dissolution provision, do not check the box on line 2a and go to line 2c.

2b If you checked the box on line 2a, specify the location of your dissolution clause (Page, Article, and Paragraph).
Do not complete line 2c if you checked box 2a. _____

2c See the instructions for information about the operation of state law in your particular state. Check this box if   ☐
you rely on operation of state law for your dissolution provision and indicate the state: _____

Part IV — Narrative Description of Your Activities

Using an attachment, describe your *past, present,* and *planned* activities in a narrative. If you believe that you have already provided some of this information in response to other parts of this application, you may summarize that information here and refer to the specific parts of the application for supporting details. You may also attach representative copies of newsletters, brochures, or similar documents for supporting details to this narrative. Remember that if this application is approved, it will be open for public inspection. Therefore, your narrative description of activities should be thorough and accurate. Refer to the instructions for information that must be included in your description.

Part V — Compensation and Other Financial Arrangements With Your Officers, Directors, Trustees, Employees, and Independent Contractors

1a List the names, titles, and mailing addresses of all of your officers, directors, and trustees. For each person listed, state their
total annual **compensation**, or proposed compensation, for all services to the organization, whether as an officer, employee, or
other position. Use actual figures, if available. Enter "none" if no compensation is or will be paid. If additional space is needed,
attach a separate sheet. Refer to the instructions for information on what to include as compensation.

Name	Title	Mailing address	Compensation amount (annual actual or estimated)

Form **1023** (Rev. 6-2006)

Part V Compensation and Other Financial Arrangements With Your Officers, Directors, Trustees, Employees, and Independent Contractors *(Continued)*

b List the names, titles, and mailing addresses of each of your five highest compensated employees who receive or will receive compensation of more than $50,000 per year. Use the actual figure, if available. Refer to the instructions for information on what to include as compensation. Do not include officers, directors, or trustees listed in line 1a.

Name	Title	Mailing address	Compensation amount (annual actual or estimated)

c List the names, names of businesses, and mailing addresses of your five highest compensated **independent contractors** that receive or will receive compensation of more than $50,000 per year. Use the actual figure, if available. Refer to the instructions for information on what to include as compensation.

Name	Title	Mailing address	Compensation amount (annual actual or estimated)

The following "Yes" or "No" questions relate to *past, present, or planned* relationships, transactions, or agreements with your officers, directors, trustees, highest compensated employees, and highest compensated independent contractors listed in lines 1a, 1b, and 1c.

2a Are any of your officers, directors, or trustees **related** to each other through **family** or **business relationships**? If "Yes," identify the individuals and explain the relationship. ☐ Yes ☐ No

b Do you have a business relationship with any of your officers, directors, or trustees other than through their position as an officer, director, or trustee? If "Yes," identify the individuals and describe the business relationship with each of your officers, directors, or trustees. ☐ Yes ☐ No

c Are any of your officers, directors, or trustees related to your highest compensated employees or highest compensated independent contractors listed on lines 1b or 1c through family or business relationships? If "Yes," identify the individuals and explain the relationship. ☐ Yes ☐ No

3a For each of your officers, directors, trustees, highest compensated employees, and highest compensated independent contractors listed on lines 1a, 1b, or 1c, attach a list showing their name, qualifications, average hours worked, and duties.

b Do any of your officers, directors, trustees, highest compensated employees, and highest compensated independent contractors listed on lines 1a, 1b, or 1c receive compensation from any other organizations, whether tax exempt or taxable, that are related to you through **common control**? If "Yes," identify the individuals, explain the relationship between you and the other organization, and describe the compensation arrangement. ☐ Yes ☐ No

4 In establishing the compensation for your officers, directors, trustees, highest compensated employees, and highest compensated independent contractors listed on lines 1a, 1b, and 1c, the following practices are recommended, although they are not required to obtain exemption. Answer "Yes" to all the practices you use.

a Do you or will the individuals that approve compensation arrangements follow a conflict of interest policy? ☐ Yes ☐ No

b Do you or will you approve compensation arrangements in advance of paying compensation? ☐ Yes ☐ No

c Do you or will you document in writing the date and terms of approved compensation arrangements? ☐ Yes ☐ No

Form **1023** (Rev. 6-2006)

Form 1023 (Rev. 6-2006)   Name: EIN: —   Page **4**

Part V   **Compensation and Other Financial Arrangements With Your Officers, Directors, Trustees, Employees, and Independent Contractors** *(Continued)*

d Do you or will you record in writing the decision made by each individual who decided or voted on compensation arrangements?   ☐ Yes ☐ No

e Do you or will you approve compensation arrangements based on information about compensation paid by **similarly situated** taxable or tax-exempt organizations for similar services, current compensation surveys compiled by independent firms, or actual written offers from similarly situated organizations? Refer to the instructions for Part V, lines 1a, 1b, and 1c, for information on what to include as compensation.   ☐ Yes ☐ No

f Do you or will you record in writing both the information on which you relied to base your decision and its source?   ☐ Yes ☐ No

g If you answered "No" to any item on lines 4a through 4f, describe how you set compensation that is **reasonable** for your officers, directors, trustees, highest compensated employees, and highest compensated independent contractors listed in Part V, lines 1a, 1b, and 1c.

5a Have you adopted a **conflict of interest policy** consistent with the sample conflict of interest policy in Appendix A to the instructions? If "Yes," provide a copy of the policy and explain how the policy has been adopted, such as by resolution of your governing board. If "No," answer lines 5b and 5c.   ☐ Yes ☐ No

b What procedures will you follow to assure that persons who have a conflict of interest will not have influence over you for setting their own compensation?

c What procedures will you follow to assure that persons who have a conflict of interest will not have influence over you regarding business deals with themselves?

Note: A conflict of interest policy is recommended though it is not required to obtain exemption. Hospitals, see Schedule C, Section I, line 14.

6a Do you or will you compensate any of your officers, directors, trustees, highest compensated employees, and highest compensated independent contractors listed in 1a, 1b, or 1c through **non-fixed payments**, such as discretionary bonuses or revenue-based payments? If "Yes," describe all non-fixed compensation arrangements, including how the amounts are determined, who is eligible for such arrangements, whether you place a limitation on total compensation, and how you determine or will determine that you pay no more than reasonable compensation for services. Refer to the instructions for Part V, lines 1a, 1b, and 1c, for information on what to include as compensation.   ☐ Yes ☐ No

b Do you or will you compensate any of your employees, other than your officers, directors, trustees, or your five highest compensated employees who receive or will receive compensation of more than $50,000 per year, through non-fixed payments, such as discretionary bonuses or revenue-based payments? If "Yes," describe all non-fixed compensation arrangements, including how the amounts are or will be determined, who is or will be eligible for such arrangements, whether you place or will place a limitation on total compensation, and how you determine or will determine that you pay no more than reasonable compensation for services. Refer to the instructions for Part V, lines 1a, 1b, and 1c, for information on what to include as compensation.   ☐ Yes ☐ No

7a Do you or will you purchase any goods, services, or assets from any of your officers, directors, trustees, highest compensated employees, or highest compensated independent contractors listed in lines 1a, 1b, or 1c? If "Yes," describe any such purchase that you made or intend to make, from whom you make or will make such purchases, how the terms are or will be negotiated at **arm's length**, and explain how you determine or will determine that you pay no more than **fair market value**. Attach copies of any written contracts or other agreements relating to such purchases.   ☐ Yes ☐ No

b Do you or will you sell any goods, services, or assets to any of your officers, directors, trustees, highest compensated employees, or highest compensated independent contractors listed in lines 1a, 1b, or 1c? If "Yes," describe any such sales that you made or intend to make, to whom you make or will make such sales, how the terms are or will be negotiated at arm's length, and explain how you determine or will be paid at least fair market value. Attach copies of any written contracts or other agreements relating to such sales.   ☐ Yes ☐ No

8a Do you or will you have any leases, contracts, loans, or other agreements with your officers, directors, trustees, highest compensated employees, or highest compensated independent contractors listed in lines 1a, 1b, or 1c? If "Yes," provide the information requested in lines 8b through 8f.   ☐ Yes ☐ No

b Describe any written or oral arrangements that you made or intend to make.

c Identify with whom you have or will have such arrangements.

d Explain how the terms are or will be negotiated at arm's length.

e Explain how you determine you pay no more than fair market value or you are paid at least fair market value.

f Attach copies of any signed leases, contracts, loans, or other agreements relating to such arrangements.

9a Do you or will you have any leases, contracts, loans, or other agreements with any organization in which any of your officers, directors, or trustees are also officers, directors, or trustees, or in which any individual officer, director, or trustee owns more than a 35% interest? If "Yes," provide the information requested in lines 9b through 9f.   ☐ Yes ☐ No

Form **1023** (Rev. 6-2006)

Part V **Compensation and Other Financial Arrangements With Your Officers, Directors, Trustees, Employees, and Independent Contractors** *(Continued)*

b Describe any written or oral arrangements you made or intend to make.

c Identify with whom you have or will have such arrangements.

d Explain how the terms are or will be negotiated at arm's length.

e Explain how you determine or will determine you pay no more than fair market value or that you are paid at least fair market value.

f Attach a copy of any signed leases, contracts, loans, or other agreements relating to such arrangements.

Part VI **Your Members and Other Individuals and Organizations That Receive Benefits From You**

The following "Yes" or "No" questions relate to goods, services, and funds you provide to individuals and organizations as part of your activities. Your answers should pertain to *past, present,* and *planned* activities. (See instructions.)

1a In carrying out your exempt purposes, do you provide goods, services, or funds to individuals? If "Yes," describe each program that provides goods, services, or funds to individuals. ☐ **Yes** ☐ **No**

b In carrying out your exempt purposes, do you provide goods, services, or funds to organizations? If "Yes," describe each program that provides goods, services, or funds to organizations. ☐ **Yes** ☐ **No**

2 Do any of your programs limit the provision of goods, services, or funds to a specific individual or group of specific individuals? For example, answer "Yes," if goods, services, or funds are provided only for a particular individual, your members, individuals who work for a particular employer, or graduates of a particular school. If "Yes," explain the limitation and how recipients are selected for each program. ☐ **Yes** ☐ **No**

3 Do any individuals who receive goods, services, or funds through your programs have a family or business relationship with any officer, director, trustee, or with any of your highest compensated employees or highest compensated independent contractors listed in Part V, lines 1a, 1b, and 1c? If "Yes," explain how these related individuals are eligible for goods, services, or funds. ☐ **Yes** ☐ **No**

Part VII **Your History**

The following "Yes" or "No" questions relate to your history. (See instructions.)

1 Are you a **successor** to another organization? Answer "Yes," if you have taken or will take over the activities of another organization; you took over 25% or more of the fair market value of the net assets of another organization; or you were established upon the conversion of an organization from for-profit to non-profit status. If "Yes," complete Schedule G. ☐ **Yes** ☐ **No**

2 Are you submitting this application more than 27 months after the end of the month in which you were legally formed? If "Yes," complete Schedule E. ☐ **Yes** ☐ **No**

Part VIII **Your Specific Activities**

The following "Yes" or "No" questions relate to specific activities that you may conduct. Check the appropriate box. Your answers should pertain to *past, present,* and *planned* activities. (See instructions.)

1 Do you support or oppose candidates in **political campaigns** in any way? If "Yes," explain. ☐ **Yes** ☐ **No**

2a Do you attempt to **influence legislation**? If "Yes," explain how you attempt to influence legislation and complete line 2b. If "No," go to line 3a. ☐ **Yes** ☐ **No**

b Have you made or are you making an **election** to have your legislative activities measured by expenditures by filing Form 5768? If "Yes," attach a copy of the Form 5768 that was already filed or attach a completed Form 5768 that you are filing with this application. If "No," describe whether your attempts to influence legislation are a substantial part of your activities. Include the time and money spent on your attempts to influence legislation as compared to your total activities. ☐ **Yes** ☐ **No**

3a Do you or will you operate bingo or **gaming** activities? If "Yes," describe who conducts them, and list all revenue received or expected to be received and expenses paid or expected to be paid in operating these activities. **Revenue and expenses** should be provided for the time periods specified in Part IX, Financial Data. ☐ **Yes** ☐ **No**

b Do you or will you enter into contracts or other agreements with individuals or organizations to conduct bingo or gaming for you? If "Yes," describe any written or oral arrangements that you made or intend to make, identify with whom you have or will have such arrangements, explain how the terms are or will be negotiated at arm's length, and explain how you determine or will determine you pay no more than fair market value or you will be paid at least fair market value. Attach copies or any written contracts or other agreements relating to such arrangements. ☐ **Yes** ☐ **No**

c List the states and local jurisdictions, including Indian Reservations, in which you conduct or will conduct gaming or bingo.

Form **1023** (Rev. 6-2006)

Form 1023 (Rev. 6-2006)   Name: EIN: –   Page **6**

Part VIII   Your Specific Activities *(Continued)*

4a Do you or will you undertake **fundraising**? If "Yes," check all the fundraising programs you do or will   ☐ Yes   ☐ No
conduct. (See instructions.)

☐ mail solicitations   ☐ phone solicitations
☐ email solicitations   ☐ accept donations on your website
☐ personal solicitations   ☐ receive donations from another organization's website
☐ vehicle, boat, plane, or similar donations ☐ government grant solicitations
☐ foundation grant solicitations   ☐ Other

Attach a description of each fundraising program.

b Do you or will you have written or oral contracts with any individuals or organizations to raise funds   ☐ Yes   ☐ No
for you? If "Yes," describe these activities. Include all revenue and expenses from these activities
and state who conducts them. Revenue and expenses should be provided for the time periods
specified in Part IX, Financial Data. Also, attach a copy of any contracts or agreements.

c Do you or will you engage in fundraising activities for other organizations? If "Yes," describe these   ☐ Yes   ☐ No
arrangements. Include a description of the organizations for which you raise funds and attach copies
of all contracts or agreements.

d List all states and local jurisdictions in which you conduct fundraising. For each state or local
jurisdiction listed, specify whether you fundraise for your own organization, you fundraise for another
organization, or another organization fundraises for you.

e Do you or will you maintain separate accounts for any contributor under which the contributor has   ☐ Yes   ☐ No
the right to advise on the use or distribution of funds? Answer "Yes" if the donor may provide advice
on the types of investments, distributions from the types of investments, or the distribution from the
donor's contribution account. If "Yes," describe this program, including the type of advice that may
be provided and submit copies of any written materials provided to donors.

5   Are you **affiliated** with a governmental unit? If "Yes," explain.   ☐ Yes   ☐ No

6a Do you or will you engage in **economic development**? If "Yes," describe your program.   ☐ Yes   ☐ No
b Describe in full who benefits from your economic development activities and how the activities
promote exempt purposes.

7a Do or will persons other than your employees or volunteers **develop** your facilities? If "Yes," describe   ☐ Yes   ☐ No
each facility, the role of the developer, and any business or family relationship(s) between the
developer and your officers, directors, or trustees.

b Do or will persons other than your employees or volunteers **manage** your activities or facilities? If   ☐ Yes   ☐ No
"Yes," describe each activity and facility, the role of the manager, and any business or family
relationship(s) between the manager and your officers, directors, or trustees.

c If there is a business or family relationship between any manager or developer and your officers,
directors, or trustees, identify the individuals, explain the relationship, describe how contracts are
negotiated at arm's length so that you pay no more than fair market value, and submit a copy of any
contracts or other agreements.

8   Do you or will you enter into **joint ventures**, including partnerships or **limited liability companies**   ☐ Yes   ☐ No
treated as partnerships, in which you share profits and losses with partners other than section
501(c)(3) organizations? If "Yes," describe the activities of these joint ventures in which you
participate.

9a Are you applying for exemption as a childcare organization under section 501(k)? If "Yes," answer   ☐ Yes   ☐ No
lines 9b through 9d. If "No," go to line 10.

b Do you provide child care so that parents or caretakers of children you care for can be **gainfully**   ☐ Yes   ☐ No
employed (see instructions)? If "No," explain how you qualify as a childcare organization described
in section 501(k).

c Of the children for whom you provide child care, are 85% or more of them cared for by you to   ☐ Yes   ☐ No
enable their parents or caretakers to be gainfully employed (see instructions)? If "No," explain how
you qualify as a childcare organization described in section 501(k).

d Are your services available to the general public? If "No," describe the specific group of people for   ☐ Yes   ☐ No
whom your activities are available. Also, see the instructions and explain how you qualify as a
childcare organization described in section 501(k).

10 Do you or will you publish, own, or have rights in music, literature, tapes, artworks, choreography,   ☐ Yes   ☐ No
scientific discoveries, or other **intellectual property**? If "Yes," explain. Describe who owns or will
own any copyrights, patents, or trademarks, whether fees are or will be charged, how the fees are
determined, and how any items are or will be produced, distributed, and marketed.

Form **1023** (Rev. 6-2006)

Form 1023 (Rev. 6-2006)   Name: EIN: –   Page **7**

Part VIII   Your Specific Activities *(Continued)*

11   Do you or will you accept contributions of: real property; conservation easements; closely held   ☐ **Yes**   ☐ **No**
securities; intellectual property such as patents, trademarks, and copyrights; works of music or art;
licenses; royalties; automobiles, boats, planes, or other vehicles; or collectibles of any type? If "Yes,"
describe each type of contribution, any conditions imposed by the donor on the contribution, and
any agreements with the donor regarding the contribution.

12a Do you or will you operate in a **foreign country** or **countries?** If "Yes," answer lines 12b through   ☐ **Yes**   ☐ **No**
12d. If "No," go to line 13a.

  b Name the foreign countries and regions within the countries in which you operate.

  c Describe your operations in each country and region in which you operate.

  d Describe how your operations in each country and region further your exempt purposes.

13a Do you or will you make grants, loans, or other distributions to organization(s)? If "Yes," answer lines   ☐ **Yes**   ☐ **No**
13b through 13g. If "No," go to line 14a.

  b Describe how your grants, loans, or other distributions to organizations further your exempt purposes.

  c Do you have written contracts with each of these organizations? If "Yes," attach a copy of each contract.   ☐ **Yes**   ☐ **No**

  d Identify each recipient organization and any **relationship** between you and the recipient organization.

  e Describe the records you keep with respect to the grants, loans, or other distributions you make.

  f Describe your selection process, including whether you do any of the following:

    (i) Do you require an application form? If "Yes," attach a copy of the form.   ☐ **Yes**   ☐ **No**

    (ii) Do you require a grant proposal? If "Yes," describe whether the grant proposal specifies your   ☐ **Yes**   ☐ **No**
responsibilities and those of the grantee, obligates the grantee to use the grant funds only for the
purposes for which the grant was made, provides for periodic written reports concerning the use
of grant funds, requires a final written report and an accounting of how grant funds were used,
and acknowledges your authority to withhold and/or recover grant funds in case such funds are,
or appear to be, misused.

  g Describe your procedures for oversight of distributions that assure you the resources are used to
further your exempt purposes, including whether you require periodic and final reports on the use of
resources.

14a Do you or will you make grants, loans, or other distributions to foreign organizations? If "Yes,"   ☐ **Yes**   ☐ **No**
answer lines 14b through 14f. If "No," go to line 15.

  b Provide the name of each foreign organization, the country and regions within a country in which
each foreign organization operates, and describe any relationship you have with each foreign
organization.

  c Does any foreign organization listed in line 14b accept contributions earmarked for a specific country   ☐ **Yes**   ☐ **No**
or specific organization? If "Yes," list all earmarked organizations or countries.

  d Do your contributors know that you have ultimate authority to use contributions made to you at your   ☐ **Yes**   ☐ **No**
discretion for purposes consistent with your exempt purposes? If "Yes," describe how you relay this
information to contributors.

  e Do you or will you make pre-grant inquiries about the recipient organization? If "Yes," describe these   ☐ **Yes**   ☐ **No**
inquiries, including whether you inquire about the recipient's financial status, its tax-exempt status
under the Internal Revenue Code, its ability to accomplish the purpose for which the resources are
provided, and other relevant information.

  f Do you or will you use any additional procedures to ensure that your distributions to foreign   ☐ **Yes**   ☐ **No**
organizations are used in furtherance of your exempt purposes? If "Yes," describe these procedures,
including site visits by your employees or compliance checks by impartial experts, to verify that grant
funds are being used appropriately.

Form **1023** (Rev. 6-2006)

Form 1023 (Rev. 6-2006)   Name: EIN: −   Page **8**

Part VIII Your Specific Activities *(Continued)*		
15 Do you have a **close connection** with any organizations? If "Yes," explain.	☐ **Yes**	☐ **No**
16 Are you applying for exemption as a **cooperative hospital service organization** under section 501(e)? If "Yes," explain.	☐ **Yes**	☐ **No**
17 Are you applying for exemption as a **cooperative service organization of operating educational organizations** under section 501(f)? If "Yes," explain.	☐ **Yes**	☐ **No**
18 Are you applying for exemption as a **charitable risk pool** under section 501(n)? If "Yes," explain.	☐ **Yes**	☐ **No**
19 Do you or will you operate a **school**? If "Yes," complete Schedule B. Answer "Yes," whether you operate a school as your main function or as a secondary activity.	☐ **Yes**	☐ **No**
20 Is your main function to provide **hospital** or **medical care**? If "Yes," complete Schedule C.	☐ **Yes**	☐ **No**
21 Do you or will you provide **low-income housing** or housing for the **elderly** or **handicapped**? If "Yes," complete Schedule F.	☐ **Yes**	☐ **No**
22 Do you or will you provide scholarships, fellowships, educational loans, or other educational grants to individuals, including grants for travel, study, or other similar purposes? If "Yes," complete Schedule H. **Note: Private foundations** may use Schedule H to request advance approval of individual grant procedures.	☐ **Yes**	☐ **No**

Form **1023** (Rev. 6-2006)

Form 1023 (Rev. 6-2006)   Name: EIN: −   Page **9**

Part IX   **Financial Data**

For purposes of this schedule, years in existence refer to completed tax years. If in existence 4 or more years, complete the schedule for the most recent 4 tax years. If in existence more than 1 year but less than 4 years, complete the statements for each year in existence and provide projections of your likely revenues and expenses based on a reasonable and good faith estimate of your future finances for a total of 3 years of financial information. If in existence less than 1 year, provide projections of your likely revenues and expenses for the current year and the 2 following years, based on a reasonable and good faith estimate of your future finances for a total of 3 years of financial information. (See instructions.)

A. Statement of Revenues and Expenses

	Type of revenue or expense	Current tax year	3 prior tax years or 2 succeeding tax years			
		(a) From............ To	**(b)** From............ To	**(c)** From............ To	**(d)** From............ To	**(e)** Provide Total for (a) through (d)
Revenues	1 Gifts, grants, and contributions received (do not include unusual grants)					
	2 Membership fees received					
	3 Gross investment income					
	4 Net unrelated business income					
	5 Taxes levied for your benefit					
	6 Value of services or facilities furnished by a governmental unit without charge (not including the value of services generally furnished to the public without charge)					
	7 Any revenue not otherwise listed above or in lines 9–12 below (attach an itemized list)					
	8 Total of lines 1 through 7					
	9 Gross receipts from admissions, merchandise sold or services performed, or furnishing of facilities in any activity that is related to your exempt purposes (attach itemized list)					
	10 Total of lines 8 and 9					
	11 Net gain or loss on sale of capital assets (attach schedule and see instructions)					
	12 **Unusual grants**					
	13 Total Revenue Add lines 10 through 12					
Expenses	14 Fundraising expenses					
	15 Contributions, gifts, grants, and similar amounts paid out (attach an itemized list)					
	16 Disbursements to or for the benefit of members (attach an itemized list)					
	17 Compensation of officers, directors, and trustees					
	18 Other salaries and wages					
	19 Interest expense					
	20 Occupancy (rent, utilities, etc.)					
	21 Depreciation and depletion					
	22 Professional fees					
	23 Any expense not otherwise classified, such as program services (attach itemized list)					
	24 Total Expenses Add lines 14 through 23					

Form **1023** (Rev. 6-2006)

Form 1023 (Rev. 6-2006)   Name: EIN: –   Page **10**

Part IX   Financial Data *(Continued)*

B. Balance Sheet (for your most recently completed tax year)

Year End:

(Whole dollars)

Assets

1	Cash	1	
2	Accounts receivable, net	2	
3	Inventories	3	
4	Bonds and notes receivable (attach an itemized list)	4	
5	Corporate stocks (attach an itemized list)	5	
6	Loans receivable (attach an itemized list)	6	
7	Other investments (attach an itemized list)	7	
8	Depreciable and depletable assets (attach an itemized list)	8	
9	Land	9	
10	Other assets (attach an itemized list)	10	
11	Total Assets (add lines 1 through 10)	11	

Liabilities

12	Accounts payable	12	
13	Contributions, gifts, grants, etc. payable	13	
14	Mortgages and notes payable (attach an itemized list)	14	
15	Other liabilities (attach an itemized list)	15	
16	Total Liabilities (add lines 12 through 15)	16	

Fund Balances or Net Assets

17	Total fund balances or net assets	17	
18	Total Liabilities and Fund Balances or Net Assets (add lines 16 and 17)	18	

19 Have there been any substantial changes in your assets or liabilities since the end of the period shown above? If "Yes," explain.   ☐ Yes   ☐ No

Part X   Public Charity Status

Part X is designed to classify you as an organization that is either a **private foundation** or a **public charity**. Public charity status is a more favorable tax status than private foundation status. If you are a private foundation, Part X is designed to further determine whether you are a **private operating foundation**. (See instructions.)

1a Are you a private foundation? If "Yes," go to line 1b. If "No," go to line 5 and proceed as instructed. If you are unsure, see the instructions.   ☐ Yes   ☐ No

b As a private foundation, section 508(e) requires special provisions in your organizing document in addition to those that apply to all organizations described in section 501(c)(3). Check the box to confirm that your organizing document meets this requirement, whether by express provision or by reliance on operation of state law. Attach a statement that describes specifically where your organizing document meets this requirement, such as a reference to a particular article or section in your organizing document or by operation of state law. See the instructions, including Appendix B, for information about the special provisions that need to be contained in your organizing document. Go to line 2.   ☐

2 Are you a private operating foundation? To be a private operating foundation you must engage directly in the active conduct of charitable, religious, educational, and similar activities, as opposed to indirectly carrying out these activities by providing grants to individuals or other organizations. If "Yes," go to line 3. If "No," go to the signature section of Part XI.   ☐ Yes   ☐ No

3 Have you existed for one or more years? If "Yes," attach financial information showing that you are a private operating foundation; go to the signature section of Part XI. If "No," continue to line 4.   ☐ Yes   ☐ No

4 Have you attached either (1) an affidavit or opinion of counsel, (including a written affidavit or opinion from a certified public accountant or accounting firm with expertise regarding this tax law matter), that sets forth facts concerning your operations and support to demonstrate that you are likely to satisfy the requirements to be classified as a private operating foundation; or (2) a statement describing your proposed operations as a private operating foundation?   ☐ Yes   ☐ No

5 If you answered "No" to line 1a, indicate the type of public charity status you are requesting by checking one of the choices below. You may check only one box.

The organization is not a private foundation because it is:

a 509(a)(1) and 170(b)(1)(A)(i)—a church or a convention or association of churches. Complete and attach Schedule A.   ☐

b 509(a)(1) and 170(b)(1)(A)(ii)—a **school**. Complete and attach Schedule B.   ☐

c 509(a)(1) and 170(b)(1)(A)(iii)—a **hospital**, a cooperative hospital service organization, or a medical research organization operated in conjunction with a hospital. Complete and attach Schedule C.   ☐

d 509(a)(3)—an organization supporting either one or more organizations described in line 5a through c, f, g, or h or a publicly supported section 501(c)(4), (5), or (6) organization. Complete and attach Schedule D.   ☐

Form **1023** (Rev. 6-2006)

Form 1023 (Rev. 6-2006)   Name: EIN: –   Page **11**

Part X   **Public Charity Status** *(Continued)*

e 509(a)(4)—an organization organized and operated exclusively for testing for public safety. ☐

f 509(a)(1) and 170(b)(1)(A)(iv)—an organization operated for the benefit of a college or university that is owned or operated by a governmental unit. ☐

g 509(a)(1) and 170(b)(1)(A)(vi)—an organization that receives a substantial part of its financial support in the form of contributions from publicly supported organizations, from a governmental unit, or from the general public. ☐

h 509(a)(2)—an organization that normally receives not more than one-third of its financial support from gross **investment income** and receives more than one-third of its financial support from contributions, membership fees, and gross receipts from activities related to its exempt functions (subject to certain exceptions). ☐

i A publicly supported organization, but unsure if it is described in 5g or 5h. The organization would like the IRS to decide the correct status. ☐

6 If you checked box g, h, or i in question 5 above, you must request either an **advance** or a **definitive ruling** by selecting one of the boxes below. Refer to the instructions to determine which type of ruling you are eligible to receive.

a **Request for Advance Ruling:** By checking this box and signing the consent, pursuant to section 6501(c)(4) of the Code you request an advance ruling and agree to extend the statute of limitations on the assessment of excise tax under section 4940 of the Code. The tax will apply only if you do not establish public support status at the end of the 5-year advance ruling period. The assessment period will be extended for the 5 advance ruling years to 8 years, 4 months, and 15 days beyond the end of the first year. You have the right to refuse or limit the extension to a mutually agreed-upon period of time or issue(s). Publication 1035, *Extending the Tax Assessment Period,* provides a more detailed explanation of your rights and the consequences of the choices you make. You may obtain Publication 1035 free of charge from the IRS web site at *www.irs.gov* or by calling toll-free 1-800-829-3676. Signing this consent will not deprive you of any appeal rights to which you would otherwise be entitled. If you decide not to extend the statute of limitations, you are not eligible for an advance ruling. ☐

Consent Fixing Period of Limitations Upon Assessment of Tax Under Section 4940 of the Internal Revenue Code

For Organization

--   ---------------------------------------   --------------------------
(Signature of Officer, Director, Trustee, or other   (Type or print name of signer)   (Date)
authorized official)

                                                            (Type or print title or authority of signer)

For IRS Use Only

--   --------------------------
IRS Director, Exempt Organizations   (Date)

b **Request for Definitive Ruling:** Check this box if you have completed one tax year of at least 8 full months and you are requesting a definitive ruling. To confirm your public support status, answer line 6b(i) if you checked box g in line 5 above. Answer line 6b(ii) if you checked box h in line 5 above. If you checked box i in line 5 above, answer both lines 6b(i) and (ii). ☐

  (i) (a) Enter 2% of line 8, column (e) on Part IX-A. Statement of Revenues and Expenses. _____

  (b) Attach a list showing the name and amount contributed by each person, company, or organization whose gifts totaled more than the 2% amount. If the answer is "None," check this box. ☐

  (ii) (a) For each year amounts are included on lines 1, 2, and 9 of Part IX-A. Statement of Revenues and Expenses, attach a list showing the name of and amount received from each **disqualified person.** If the answer is "None," check this box. ☐

  (b) For each year amounts are included on line 9 of Part IX-A. Statement of Revenues and Expenses, attach a list showing the name of and amount received from each payer, other than a disqualified person, whose payments were more than the larger of (1) 1% of line 10, Part IX-A. Statement of Revenues and Expenses, or (2) $5,000. If the answer is "None," check this box. ☐

7 Did you receive any unusual grants during any of the years shown on Part IX-A. Statement of Revenues and Expenses? If "Yes," attach a list including the name of the contributor, the date and amount of the grant, a brief description of the grant, and explain why it is unusual.   ☐ **Yes**   ☐ **No**

Form **1023** (Rev. 6-2006)

Form 1023 (Rev. 6-2006)   Name: EIN: –   Page **12**

Part XI	**User Fee Information**

You must include a user fee payment with this application. It will not be processed without your paid user fee. If your average annual gross receipts have exceeded or will exceed $10,000 annually over a 4-year period, you must submit payment of $750. If your gross receipts have not exceeded or will not exceed $10,000 annually over a 4-year period, the required user fee payment is $300. See instructions for Part XI, for a definition of **gross receipts** over a 4-year period. Your check or money order must be made payable to the United States Treasury. *User fees are subject to change. Check our website at www.irs.gov and type "User Fee" in the keyword box, or call Customer Account Services at 1-877-829-5500 for current information.*

1	Have your annual gross receipts averaged or are they expected to average not more than $10,000?	☐ **Yes**		☐ **No**
	If "Yes," check the box on line 2 and enclose a user fee payment of $300 (Subject to change—see above).			
	If "No," check the box on line 3 and enclose a user fee payment of $750 (Subject to change—see above).			
2	Check the box if you have enclosed the reduced user fee payment of $300 (Subject to change).			☐
3	Check the box if you have enclosed the user fee payment of $750 (Subject to change).			☐

I declare under the penalties of perjury that I am authorized to sign this application on behalf of the above organization and that I have examined this application, including the accompanying schedules and attachments, and to the best of my knowledge it is true, correct, and complete.

**Please
Sign
Here** ▶

(Signature of Officer, Director, Trustee, or other authorized official)

(Type or print name of signer)

(Type or print title or authority of signer)

(Date)

Reminder: Send the completed Form 1023 Checklist with your filled-in-application.   Form **1023** (Rev. 6-2006)

Form 1023 (Rev. 6-2006)   Name: EIN: –   Page **13**

Schedule A. Churches

1a	Do you have a written creed, statement of faith, or summary of beliefs? If "Yes," attach copies of relevant documents.	☐ **Yes**	☐ **No**
b	Do you have a form of worship? If "Yes," describe your form of worship.	☐ **Yes**	☐ **No**
2a	Do you have a formal code of doctrine and discipline? If "Yes," describe your code of doctrine and discipline.	☐ **Yes**	☐ **No**
b	Do you have a distinct religious history? If "Yes," describe your religious history.	☐ **Yes**	☐ **No**
c	Do you have a literature of your own? If "Yes," describe your literature.	☐ **Yes**	☐ **No**
3	Describe the organization's religious hierarchy or ecclesiastical government.		
4a	Do you have regularly scheduled religious services? If "Yes," describe the nature of the services and provide representative copies of relevant literature such as church bulletins.	☐ **Yes**	☐ **No**
b	What is the average attendance at your regularly scheduled religious services?	_____	
5a	Do you have an established place of worship? If "Yes," refer to the instructions for the information required.	☐ **Yes**	☐ **No**
b	Do you own the property where you have an established place of worship?	☐ **Yes**	☐ **No**
6	Do you have an established congregation or other regular membership group? If "No," refer to the instructions.	☐ **Yes**	☐ **No**
7	How many members do you have?	_____	
8a	Do you have a process by which an individual becomes a member? If "Yes," describe the process and complete lines 8b–8d, below.	☐ **Yes**	☐ **No**
b	If you have members, do your members have voting rights, rights to participate in religious functions, or other rights? If "Yes," describe the rights your members have.	☐ **Yes**	☐ **No**
c	May your members be associated with another denomination or church?	☐ **Yes**	☐ **No**
d	Are all of your members part of the same **family**?	☐ **Yes**	☐ **No**
9	Do you conduct baptisms, weddings, funerals, etc.?	☐ **Yes**	☐ **No**
10	Do you have a school for the religious instruction of the young?	☐ **Yes**	☐ **No**
11a	Do you have a minister or religious leader? If "Yes," describe this person's role and explain whether the minister or religious leader was ordained, commissioned, or licensed after a prescribed course of study.	☐ **Yes**	☐ **No**
b	Do you have schools for the preparation of your ordained ministers or religious leaders?	☐ **Yes**	☐ **No**
12	Is your minister or religious leader also one of your officers, directors, or trustees?	☐ **Yes**	☐ **No**
13	Do you ordain, commission, or license ministers or religious leaders? If "Yes," describe the requirements for ordination, commission, or licensure.	☐ **Yes**	☐ **No**
14	Are you part of a group of churches with similar beliefs and structures? If "Yes," explain. Include the name of the group of churches.	☐ **Yes**	☐ **No**
15	Do you issue church charters? If "Yes," describe the requirements for issuing a charter.	☐ **Yes**	☐ **No**
16	Did you pay a fee for a church charter? If "Yes," attach a copy of the charter.	☐ **Yes**	☐ **No**
17	Do you have other information you believe should be considered regarding your status as a church? If "Yes," explain.	☐ **Yes**	☐ **No**

Form **1023** (Rev. 6-2006)

Form 1023 (Rev. 6-2006)   Name: EIN: –   Page **14**

Schedule B. Schools, Colleges, and Universities

If you operate a school as an activity, complete Schedule B

Section I	**Operational Information**

1a Do you normally have a regularly scheduled curriculum, a regular faculty of qualified teachers, a regularly enrolled student body, and facilities where your educational activities are regularly carried on? If "No," do not complete the remainder of Schedule B. ☐ Yes ☐ No

b Is the primary function of your school the presentation of formal instruction? If "Yes," describe your school in terms of whether it is an elementary, secondary, college, technical, or other type of school. If "No," do not complete the remainder of Schedule B. ☐ Yes ☐ No

2a Are you a public school because you are operated by a state or subdivision of a state? If "Yes," explain how you are operated by a state or subdivision of a state. Do not complete the remainder of Schedule B. ☐ Yes ☐ No

b Are you a public school because you are operated wholly or predominantly from government funds or property? If "Yes," explain how you are operated wholly or predominantly from government funds or property. Submit a copy of your funding agreement regarding government funding. Do not complete the remainder of Schedule B. ☐ Yes ☐ No

3 In what public school district, county, and state are you located?

4 Were you formed or substantially expanded at the time of public school desegregation in the above school district or county? ☐ Yes ☐ No

5 Has a state or federal administrative agency or judicial body ever determined that you are racially discriminatory? If "Yes," explain. ☐ Yes ☐ No

6 Has your right to receive financial aid or assistance from a governmental agency ever been revoked or suspended? If "Yes," explain. ☐ Yes ☐ No

7 Do you or will you contract with another organization to develop, build, market, or finance your facilities? If "Yes," explain how that entity is selected, explain how the terms of any contracts or other agreements are negotiated at arm's length, and explain how you determine that you will pay no more than fair market value for services. ☐ Yes ☐ No

Note. Make sure your answer is consistent with the information provided in Part VIII, line 7a.

8 Do you or will you manage your activities or facilities through your own employees or volunteers? If "No," attach a statement describing the activities that will be managed by others, the names of the persons or organizations that manage or will manage your activities or facilities, and how these managers were or will be selected. Also, submit copies of any contracts, proposed contracts, or other agreements regarding the provision of management services for your activities or facilities. Explain how the terms of any contracts or other agreements were or will be negotiated, and explain how you determine you will pay no more than fair market value for services. ☐ Yes ☐ No

Note. Answer "Yes" if you manage or intend to manage your programs through your own employees or by using volunteers. Answer "No" if you engage or intend to engage a separate organization or independent contractor. Make sure your answer is consistent with the information provided in Part VIII, line 7b.

Section II	**Establishment of Racially Nondiscriminatory Policy**

Information required by **Revenue Procedure 75-50.**

1 Have you adopted a racially nondiscriminatory policy as to students in your organizing document, bylaws, or by resolution of your governing body? If "Yes," state where the policy can be found or supply a copy of the policy. If "No," you must adopt a nondiscriminatory policy as to students before submitting this application. See Publication 557. ☐ Yes ☐ No

2 Do your brochures, application forms, advertisements, and catalogues dealing with student admissions, programs, and scholarships contain a statement of your racially nondiscriminatory policy? ☐ Yes ☐ No

a If "Yes," attach a representative sample of each document.

b If "No," by checking the box to the right you agree that all future printed materials, including website content, will contain the required nondiscriminatory policy statement. ▶ ☐

3 Have you published a notice of your nondiscriminatory policy in a newspaper of general circulation that serves all racial segments of the community? (See the instructions for specific requirements.) If "No," explain. ☐ Yes ☐ No

4 Does or will the organization (or any department or division within it) discriminate in any way on the basis of race with respect to admissions; use of facilities or exercise of student privileges; faculty or administrative staff; or scholarship or loan programs? If "Yes," for any of the above, explain fully. ☐ Yes ☐ No

Form **1023** (Rev. 6-2006)

Schedule B. Schools, Colleges, and Universities *(Continued)*

5 Complete the table below to show the racial composition for the current academic year and projected for the next academic year, of: (a) the student body, (b) the faculty, and (c) the administrative staff. Provide actual numbers rather than percentages for each racial category.

If you are not operational, submit an estimate based on the best information available (such as the racial composition of the community served).

Racial Category	(a) Student Body		(b) Faculty		(c) Administrative Staff	
	Current Year	Next Year	Current Year	Next Year	Current Year	Next Year
Total						

6 In the table below, provide the number and amount of loans and scholarships awarded to students enrolled by racial categories.

Racial Category	Number of Loans		Amount of Loans		Number of Scholarships		Amount of Scholarships	
	Current Year	Next Year	Current Year	Next Year	Current Year	Next Year	Current Year	Next Year
Total								

7a Attach a list of your incorporators, founders, board members, and donors of land or buildings, whether individuals or organizations.

b Do any of these individuals or organizations have an objective to maintain segregated public or private school education? If "Yes," explain.   ☐ **Yes**   ☐ **No**

8 Will you maintain records according to the non-discrimination provisions contained in Revenue Procedure 75-50? If "No," explain. (See instructions.)   ☐ **Yes**   ☐ **No**

Form **1023** (Rev. 6-2006)

Schedule C. Hospitals and Medical Research Organizations

Check the box if you are a **hospital**. See the instructions for a definition of the term "hospital," which includes an organization whose principal purpose or function is providing **hospital** or **medical care**. Complete Section I below. ☐

Check the box if you are a **medical research organization** operated in conjunction with a hospital. See the instructions for a definition of the term "medical research organization," which refers to an organization whose principal purpose or function is medical research and which is directly engaged in the continuous active conduct of medical research in conjunction with a hospital. Complete Section II. ☐

Section I	**Hospitals**		
1a	Are all the doctors in the community eligible for staff privileges? If "No," give the reasons why and explain how the medical staff is selected.	☐ Yes	☐ No
2a	Do you or will you provide medical services to all individuals in your community who can pay for themselves or have private health insurance? If "No," explain.	☐ Yes	☐ No
b	Do you or will you provide medical services to all individuals in your community who participate in Medicare? If "No," explain.	☐ Yes	☐ No
c	Do you or will you provide medical services to all individuals in your community who participate in Medicaid? If "No," explain.	☐ Yes	☐ No
3a	Do you or will you require persons covered by Medicare or Medicaid to pay a deposit before receiving services? If "Yes," explain.	☐ Yes	☐ No
b	Does the same deposit requirement, if any, apply to all other patients? If "No," explain.	☐ Yes	☐ No
4a	Do you or will you maintain a full-time emergency room? If "No," explain why you do not maintain a full-time emergency room. Also, describe any emergency services that you provide.	☐ Yes	☐ No
b	Do you have a policy on providing emergency services to persons without apparent means to pay? If "Yes," provide a copy of the policy.	☐ Yes	☐ No
c	Do you have any arrangements with police, fire, and voluntary ambulance services for the delivery or admission of emergency cases? If "Yes," describe the arrangements, including whether they are written or oral agreements. If written, submit copies of all such agreements.	☐ Yes	☐ No
5a	Do you provide for a portion of your services and facilities to be used for charity patients? If "Yes," answer 5b through 5e.	☐ Yes	☐ No
b	Explain your policy regarding charity cases, including how you distinguish between charity care and bad debts. Submit a copy of your written policy.		
c	Provide data on your past experience in admitting charity patients, including amounts you expend for treating charity care patients and types of services you provide to charity care patients.		
d	Describe any arrangements you have with federal, state, or local governments or government agencies for paying for the cost of treating charity care patients. Submit copies of any written agreements.		
e	Do you provide services on a sliding fee schedule depending on financial ability to pay? If "Yes," submit your sliding fee schedule.	☐ Yes	☐ No
6a	Do you or will you carry on a formal program of medical training or medical research? If "Yes," describe such programs, including the type of programs offered, the scope of such programs, and affiliations with other hospitals or medical care providers with which you carry on the medical training or research programs.	☐ Yes	☐ No
b	Do you or will you carry on a formal program of community education? If "Yes," describe such programs, including the type of programs offered, the scope of such programs, and affiliation with other hospitals or medical care providers with which you offer community education programs.	☐ Yes	☐ No
7	Do you or will you provide office space to physicians carrying on their own medical practices? If "Yes," describe the criteria for who may use the space, explain the means used to determine that you are paid at least fair market value, and submit representative lease agreements.	☐ Yes	☐ No
8	Is your board of directors comprised of a majority of individuals who are representative of the community you serve? Include a list of each board member's name and business, financial, or professional relationship with the hospital. Also, identify each board member who is representative of the community and describe how that individual is a community representative.	☐ Yes	☐ No
9	Do you participate in any joint ventures? If "Yes," state your ownership percentage in each joint venture, list your investment in each joint venture, describe the tax status of other participants in each joint venture (including whether they are section 501(c)(3) organizations), describe the activities of each joint venture, describe how you exercise control over the activities of each joint venture, and describe how each joint venture furthers your exempt purposes. Also, submit copies of all agreements. **Note.** Make sure your answer is consistent with the information provided in Part VIII, line 8.	☐ Yes	☐ No

Form **1023** (Rev. 6-2006)

Form 1023 (Rev. 6-2006)   Name: EIN: –   Page **17**

Schedule C. Hospitals and Medical Research Organizations *(Continued)*

Section I   **Hospitals** *(Continued)*

10	Do you or will you manage your activities or facilities through your own employees or volunteers? If "No," attach a statement describing the activities that will be managed by others, the names of the persons or organizations that manage or will manage your activities or facilities, and how these managers were or will be selected. Also, submit copies of any contracts, proposed contracts, or other agreements regarding the provision of management services for your activities or facilities. Explain how the terms of any contracts or other agreements were or will be negotiated, and explain how you determine you will pay no more than fair market value for services.	☐ **Yes**	☐ **No**
	Note. Answer "Yes" if you do manage or intend to manage your programs through your own employees or by using volunteers. Answer "No" if you engage or intend to engage a separate organization or independent contractor. Make sure your answer is consistent with the information provided in Part VIII, line 7b.		
11	Do you or will you offer recruitment incentives to physicians? If "Yes," describe your recruitment incentives and attach copies of all written recruitment incentive policies.	☐ **Yes**	☐ **No**
12	Do you or will you lease equipment, assets, or office space from physicians who have a financial or professional relationship with you? If "Yes," explain how you establish a fair market value for the lease.	☐ **Yes**	☐ **No**
13	Have you purchased medical practices, ambulatory surgery centers, or other business assets from physicians or other persons with whom you have a business relationship, aside from the purchase? If "Yes," submit a copy of each purchase and sales contract and describe how you arrived at fair market value, including copies of appraisals.	☐ **Yes**	☐ **No**
14	Have you adopted a **conflict of interest policy** consistent with the sample health care organization conflict of interest policy in Appendix A of the instructions? If "Yes," submit a copy of the policy and explain how the policy has been adopted, such as by resolution of your governing board. If "No," explain how you will avoid any conflicts of interest in your business dealings.	☐ **Yes**	☐ **No**

Section II   **Medical Research Organizations**

1   Name the hospitals with which you have a relationship and describe the relationship. Attach copies of written agreements with each hospital that demonstrate continuing relationships between you and the hospital(s).

2   Attach a schedule describing your present and proposed activities for the direct conduct of medical research; describe the nature of the activities, and the amount of money that has been or will be spent in carrying them out.

3   Attach a schedule of assets showing their fair market value and the portion of your assets directly devoted to medical research.

Form **1023** (Rev. 6-2006)

Schedule D. Section 509(a)(3) Supporting Organizations

Section I   **Identifying Information About the Supported Organization(s)**

1   State the names, addresses, and EINs of the supported organizations. If additional space is needed, attach a separate sheet.

Name	Address	EIN
	....	–
	....	–

2   Are all supported organizations listed in line 1 public charities under section 509(a)(1) or (2)? If "Yes," go to Section II. If "No," go to line 3.   ☐ **Yes**   ☐ **No**

3   Do the supported organizations have tax-exempt status under section 501(c)(4), 501(c)(5), or 501(c)(6)?   ☐ **Yes**   ☐ **No**

If "Yes," for each 501(c)(4), (5), or (6) organization supported, provide the following financial information:

- Part IX-A. Statement of Revenues and Expenses, lines 1–13 and
- Part X, lines 6b(ii)(a), 6b(ii)(b), and 7.

If "No," attach a statement describing how each organization you support is a public charity under section 509(a)(1) or (2).

Section II   **Relationship with Supported Organization(s)—Three Tests**

To be classified as a supporting organization, an organization must meet one of three relationship tests:

Test 1: "Operated, supervised, or controlled by" one or more publicly supported organizations, or
Test 2: "Supervised or controlled in connection with" one or more publicly supported organizations, or
Test 3: "Operated in connection with" one or more publicly supported organizations.

1   Information to establish the "operated, supervised, or controlled by" relationship (Test 1)

Is a majority of your governing board or officers elected or appointed by the supported organization(s)? If "Yes," describe the process by which your governing board is appointed and elected; go to Section III. If "No," continue to line 2.   ☐ **Yes**   ☐ **No**

2   Information to establish the "supervised or controlled in connection with" relationship (Test 2)

Does a majority of your governing board consist of individuals who also serve on the governing board of the supported organization(s)? If "Yes," describe the process by which your governing board is appointed and elected; go to Section III. If "No," go to line 3.   ☐ **Yes**   ☐ **No**

3   Information to establish the "operated in connection with" responsiveness test (Test 3)

Are you a trust from which the named supported organization(s) can enforce and compel an accounting under state law? If "Yes," explain whether you advised the supported organization(s) in writing of these rights and provide a copy of the written communication documenting this; go to Section II, line 5. If "No," go to line 4a.   ☐ **Yes**   ☐ **No**

4   Information to establish the alternative "operated in connection with" responsiveness test (Test 3)

a Do the officers, directors, trustees, or members of the supported organization(s) elect or appoint one or more of your officers, directors, or trustees? If "Yes," explain and provide documentation; go to line 4d, below. If "No," go to line 4b.   ☐ **Yes**   ☐ **No**

b Do one or more members of the governing body of the supported organization(s) also serve as your officers, directors, or trustees or hold other important offices with respect to you? If "Yes," explain and provide documentation; go to line 4d, below. If "No," go to line 4c.   ☐ **Yes**   ☐ **No**

c Do your officers, directors, or trustees maintain a close and continuous working relationship with the officers, directors, or trustees of the supported organization(s)? If "Yes," explain and provide documentation.   ☐ **Yes**   ☐ **No**

d Do the supported organization(s) have a significant voice in your investment policies, in the making and timing of grants, and in otherwise directing the use of your income or assets? If "Yes," explain and provide documentation.   ☐ **Yes**   ☐ **No**

e Describe and provide copies of written communications documenting how you made the supported organization(s) aware of your supporting activities.

Form **1023** (Rev. 6-2006)

Form 1023 (Rev. 6-2006)   Name: EIN: –   Page **19**

Schedule D. Section 509(a)(3) Supporting Organizations *(Continued)*

Section II   **Relationship with Supported Organization(s)—Three Tests** *(Continued)*

5   Information to establish the "operated in connection with" integral part test (Test 3)

Do you conduct activities that would otherwise be carried out by the supported organization(s)? If "Yes," explain and go to Section III. If "No," continue to line 6a.   ☐ **Yes**   ☐ **No**

6   Information to establish the alternative "operated in connection with" integral part test (Test 3)

a   Do you distribute at least 85% of your annual **net income** to the supported organization(s)? If "Yes," go to line 6b. (See instructions.)   ☐ **Yes**   ☐ **No**

If "No," state the percentage of your income that you distribute to each supported organization. Also explain how you ensure that the supported organization(s) are attentive to your operations.

b   How much do you contribute annually to each supported organization? Attach a schedule.

c   What is the total annual revenue of each supported organization? If you need additional space, attach a list.

d   Do you or the supported organization(s) **earmark** your funds for support of a particular program or activity? If "Yes," explain.   ☐ **Yes**   ☐ **No**

7a   Does your organizing document specify the supported organization(s) by name? If "Yes," state the article and paragraph number and go to Section III. If "No," answer line 7b.   ☐ **Yes**   ☐ **No**

b   Attach a statement describing whether there has been an historic and continuing relationship between you and the supported organization(s).

Section III   **Organizational Test**

1a   If you met relationship Test 1 or Test 2 in Section II, your organizing document must specify the supported organization(s) by name, or by naming a similar purpose or charitable class of beneficiaries. If your organizing document complies with this requirement, answer "Yes." If your organizing document does not comply with this requirement, answer "No," and see the instructions.   ☐ **Yes**   ☐ **No**

b   If you met relationship Test 3 in Section II, your organizing document must generally specify the supported organization(s) by name. If your organizing document complies with this requirement, answer "Yes," and go to Section IV. If your organizing document does not comply with this requirement, answer "No," and see the instructions.   ☐ **Yes**   ☐ **No**

Section IV   **Disqualified Person Test**

You do not qualify as a supporting organization if you are **controlled** directly or indirectly by one or more **disqualified persons** (as defined in section 4946) other than **foundation managers** or one or more organizations that you support. Foundation managers who are also disqualified persons for another reason are disqualified persons with respect to you.

1a   Do any persons who are disqualified persons with respect to you, (except individuals who are disqualified persons only because they are foundation managers), appoint any of your foundation managers? If "Yes," (1) describe the process by which disqualified persons appoint any of your foundation managers, (2) provide the names of these disqualified persons and the foundation managers they appoint, and (3) explain how control is vested over your operations (including assets and activities) by persons other than disqualified persons.   ☐ **Yes**   ☐ **No**

b   Do any persons who have a family or business relationship with any disqualified persons with respect to you, (except individuals who are disqualified persons only because they are foundation managers), appoint any of your foundation managers? If "Yes," (1) describe the process by which individuals with a family or business relationship with disqualified persons appoint any of your foundation managers, (2) provide the names of these disqualified persons, the individuals with a family or business relationship with disqualified persons, and the foundation managers appointed, and (3) explain how control is vested over your operations (including assets and activities) in individuals other than disqualified persons.   ☐ **Yes**   ☐ **No**

c   Do any persons who are disqualified persons, (except individuals who are disqualified persons only because they are foundation managers), have any influence regarding your operations, including your assets or activities? If "Yes," (1) provide the names of these disqualified persons, (2) explain how influence is exerted over your operations (including assets and activities), and (3) explain how control is vested over your operations (including assets and activities) by individuals other than disqualified persons.   ☐ **Yes**   ☐ **No**

Form **1023** (Rev. 6-2006)

Form 1023 (Rev. 6-2006)   Name: EIN: –   Page **20**

Schedule E. Organizations Not Filing Form 1023 Within 27 Months of Formation

Schedule E is intended to determine whether you are eligible for tax exemption under section 501(c)(3) from the postmark date of your application or from your date of incorporation or formation, whichever is earlier. If you are not eligible for tax exemption under section 501(c)(3) from your date of incorporation or formation, Schedule E is also intended to determine whether you are eligible for tax exemption under section 501(c)(4) for the period between your date of incorporation or formation and the postmark date of your application.

1 Are you a church, association of churches, or integrated auxiliary of a church? If "Yes," complete Schedule A and stop here. Do not complete the remainder of Schedule E.   ☐ Yes ☐ No

2a Are you a public charity with annual **gross receipts** that are normally $5,000 or less? If "Yes," stop here. Answer "No" if you are a private foundation, regardless of your gross receipts.   ☐ Yes ☐ No

b If your gross receipts were normally more than $5,000, are you filing this application within 90 days from the end of the tax year in which your gross receipts were normally more than $5,000? If "Yes," stop here.   ☐ Yes ☐ No

3a Were you included as a subordinate in a group exemption application or letter? If "No," go to line 4.   ☐ Yes ☐ No

b If you were included as a subordinate in a group exemption letter, are you filing this application within 27 months from the date you were notified by the organization holding the group exemption letter or the Internal Revenue Service that you cease to be covered by the group exemption letter? If "Yes," stop here.   ☐ Yes ☐ No

c If you were included as a subordinate in a timely filed group exemption request that was denied, are you filing this application within 27 months from the postmark date of the Internal Revenue Service final adverse ruling letter? If "Yes," stop here.   ☐ Yes ☐ No

4 Were you created on or before October 9, 1969? If "Yes," stop here. Do not complete the remainder of this schedule.   ☐ Yes ☐ No

5 If you answered "No" to lines 1 through 4, we cannot recognize you as tax exempt from your date of formation unless you qualify for an extension of time to apply for exemption. Do you wish to request an extension of time to apply to be recognized as exempt from the date you were formed? If "Yes," attach a statement explaining why you did not file this application within the 27-month period. Do not answer lines 6, 7, or 8. If "No," go to line 6a.   ☐ Yes ☐ No

6a If you answered "No" to line 5, you can only be exempt under section 501(c)(3) from the postmark date of this application. Therefore, do you want us to treat this application as a request for tax exemption from the postmark date? If "Yes," you are eligible for an advance ruling. Complete Part X, line 6a. If "No," you will be treated as a private foundation.   ☐ Yes ☐ No

Note. Be sure your ruling eligibility agrees with your answer to Part X, line 6.

b Do you anticipate significant changes in your sources of support in the future? If "Yes," complete line 7 below.   ☐ Yes ☐ No

Form **1023** (Rev. 6-2006)

Form 1023 (Rev. 6-2006)   Name: EIN: –   Page **21**

Schedule E. Organizations Not Filing Form 1023 Within 27 Months of Formation *(Continued)*

7   Complete this item only if you answered "Yes" to line 6b. Include projected revenue for the first two full years following the current tax year.

Type of Revenue	Projected revenue for 2 years following current tax year		
	(a) From .... To	**(b)** From .... To	**(c)** Total
1 Gifts, grants, and contributions received (do not include unusual grants)			
2 Membership fees received			
3 Gross investment income			
4 Net unrelated business income			
5 Taxes levied for your benefit			
6 Value of services or facilities furnished by a governmental unit without charge (not including the value of services generally furnished to the public without charge)			
7 Any revenue not otherwise listed above or in lines 9–12 below (attach an itemized list)			
8 Total of lines 1 through 7			
9 Gross receipts from admissions, merchandise sold, or services performed, or furnishing of facilities in any activity that is related to your exempt purposes (attach itemized list)			
10 Total of lines 8 and 9			
11 Net gain or loss on sale of capital assets (attach an itemized list)			
12 Unusual grants			
13 Total revenue. Add lines 10 through 12			

8   According to your answers, you are only eligible for tax exemption under section 501(c)(3) from the postmark date of your application. However, you may be eligible for tax exemption under section 501(c)(4) from your date of formation to the postmark date of the Form 1023. Tax exemption under section 501(c)(4) allows exemption from federal income tax, but generally not deductibility of contributions under Code section 170. Check the box at right if you want us to treat this as a request for exemption under 501(c)(4) from your date of formation to the postmark date.   ▶ ☐

Attach a completed Page 1 of Form 1024, Application for Recognition of Exemption Under Section 501(a), to this application.

Form **1023** (Rev. 6-2006)

Schedule F. Homes for the Elderly or Handicapped and Low-Income Housing

Section I   General Information About Your Housing

1 Describe the type of housing you provide.

2 Provide copies of any application forms you use for admission.

3 Explain how the public is made aware of your facility.

4a Provide a description of each facility.
 b What is the total number of residents each facility can accommodate?
 c What is your current number of residents in each facility?
 d Describe each facility in terms of whether residents rent or purchase housing from you.

5 Attach a sample copy of your residency or homeownership contract or agreement.

6 Do you participate in any joint ventures? If "Yes," state your ownership percentage in each joint   ☐ **Yes**   ☐ **No**
venture, list your investment in each joint venture, describe the tax status of other participants in
each joint venture (including whether they are section 501(c)(3) organizations), describe the activities
of each joint venture, describe how you exercise control over the activities of each joint venture, and
describe how each joint venture furthers your exempt purposes. Also, submit copies of all joint
venture agreements.

Note. Make sure your answer is consistent with the information provided in Part VIII, line 8.

7 Do you or will you contract with another organization to develop, build, market, or finance your   ☐ **Yes**   ☐ **No**
housing? If "Yes," explain how that entity is selected, explain how the terms of any contract(s) are
negotiated at arm's length, and explain how you determine you will pay no more than fair market
value for services.

Note. Make sure your answer is consistent with the information provided in Part VIII, line 7a.

8 Do you or will you manage your activities or facilities through your own employees or volunteers? If   ☐ **Yes**   ☐ **No**
"No," attach a statement describing the activities that will be managed by others, the names of the
persons or organizations that manage or will manage your activities or facilities, and how these
managers were or will be selected. Also, submit copies of any contracts, proposed contracts, or
other agreements regarding the provision of management services for your activities or facilities.
Explain how the terms of any contracts or other agreements were or will be negotiated, and explain
how you determine you will pay no more than fair market value for services.

Note. Answer "Yes" if you do manage or intend to manage your programs through your own
employees or by using volunteers. Answer "No" if you engage or intend to engage a separate
organization or independent contractor. Make sure your answer is consistent with the information
provided in Part VIII, line 7b.

9 Do you participate in any government housing programs? If "Yes," describe these programs.   ☐ **Yes**   ☐ **No**

10a Do you own the facility? If "No," describe any enforceable rights you possess to purchase the facility   ☐ **Yes**   ☐ **No**
in the future; go to line 10c. If "Yes," answer line 10b.

 b How did you acquire the facility? For example, did you develop it yourself, purchase a project, etc.
Attach all contracts, transfer agreements, or other documents connected with the acquisition of the
facility.

 c Do you lease the facility or the land on which it is located? If "Yes," describe the parties to the   ☐ **Yes**   ☐ **No**
lease(s) and provide copies of all leases.

Schedule F. Homes for the Elderly or Handicapped and Low-Income Housing *(Continued)*

Section II	Homes for the Elderly or Handicapped

1a Do you provide housing for the elderly? If "Yes," describe who qualifies for your housing in terms of age, infirmity, or other criteria and explain how you select persons for your housing. ☐ **Yes** ☐ **No**

b Do you provide housing for the handicapped? If "Yes," describe who qualifies for your housing in terms of disability, income levels, or other criteria and explain how you select persons for your housing. ☐ **Yes** ☐ **No**

2a Do you charge an entrance or founder's fee? If "Yes," describe what this charge covers, whether it is a one-time fee, how the fee is determined, whether it is payable in a lump sum or on an installment basis, whether it is refundable, and the circumstances, if any, under which it may be waived. ☐ **Yes** ☐ **No**

b Do you charge periodic fees or maintenance charges? If "Yes," describe what these charges cover and how they are determined. ☐ **Yes** ☐ **No**

c Is your housing affordable to a significant segment of the elderly or handicapped persons in the community? Identify your **community**. Also, if "Yes," explain how you determine your housing is affordable. ☐ **Yes** ☐ **No**

3a Do you have an established policy concerning residents who become unable to pay their regular charges? If "Yes," describe your established policy. ☐ **Yes** ☐ **No**

b Do you have any arrangements with government welfare agencies or others to absorb all or part of the cost of maintaining residents who become unable to pay their regular charges? If "Yes," describe these arrangements. ☐ **Yes** ☐ **No**

4 Do you have arrangements for the healthcare needs of your residents? If "Yes," describe these arrangements. ☐ **Yes** ☐ **No**

5 Are your facilities designed to meet the physical, emotional, recreational, social, religious, and/or other similar needs of the elderly or handicapped? If "Yes," describe these design features. ☐ **Yes** ☐ **No**

Section III	Low-Income Housing

1 Do you provide low-income housing? If "Yes," describe who qualifies for your housing in terms of income levels or other criteria, and describe how you select persons for your housing. ☐ **Yes** ☐ **No**

2 In addition to rent or mortgage payments, do residents pay periodic fees or maintenance charges? If "Yes," describe what these charges cover and how they are determined. ☐ **Yes** ☐ **No**

3a Is your housing affordable to low income residents? If "Yes," describe how your housing is made affordable to low-income residents. ☐ **Yes** ☐ **No**

Note. Revenue Procedure 96-32, 1996-1 C.B. 717, provides guidelines for providing low-income housing that will be treated as charitable. (At least 75% of the units are occupied by low-income tenants or 40% are occupied by tenants earning not more than 120% of the very low-income levels for the area.)

b Do you impose any restrictions to make sure that your housing remains affordable to low-income residents? If "Yes," describe these restrictions. ☐ **Yes** ☐ **No**

4 Do you provide social services to residents? If "Yes," describe these services. ☐ **Yes** ☐ **No**

Form **1023** (Rev. 6-2006)

Form 1023 (Rev. 6-2006)   Name: EIN: –   Page **24**

Schedule G. Successors to Other Organizations

1a Are you a **successor** to a **for-profit organization**? If "Yes," explain the relationship with the **predecessor** organization that resulted in your creation and complete line 1b. ☐ Yes ☐ No

b Explain why you took over the activities or assets of a for-profit organization or converted from for-profit to nonprofit status.

2a Are you a successor to an organization other than a for-profit organization? Answer "Yes" if you have taken or will take over the activities of another organization; or you have taken or will take over 25% or more of the fair market value of the net assets of another organization. If "Yes," explain the relationship with the other organzation that resulted in your creation. ☐ Yes ☐ No

b Provide the tax status of the predecessor organization.

c Did you or did an organization to which you are a successor previously apply for tax exemption under section 501(c)(3) or any other section of the Code? If "Yes," explain how the application was resolved. ☐ Yes ☐ No

d Was your prior tax exemption or the tax exemption of an organization to which you are a successor revoked or suspended? If "Yes," explain. Include a description of the corrections you made to re-establish tax exemption. ☐ Yes ☐ No

e Explain why you took over the activities or assets of another organization.

3 Provide the name, last address, and EIN of the predecessor organization and describe its activities.
Name: _____ EIN: ___–_____
Address: _____

4 List the owners, partners, principal stockholders, officers, and governing board members of the predecessor organization. Attach a separate sheet if additional space is needed.

Name	Address	Share/Interest (If a for-profit)

5 Do or will any of the persons listed in line 4, maintain a working relationship with you? If "Yes," describe the relationship in detail and include copies of any agreements with any of these persons or with any for-profit organizations in which these persons own more than a 35% interest. ☐ Yes ☐ No

6a Were any assets transferred, whether by gift or sale, from the predecessor organization to you? ☐ Yes ☐ No
If "Yes," provide a list of assets, indicate the value of each asset, explain how the value was determined, and attach an appraisal, if available. For each asset listed, also explain if the transfer was by gift, sale, or combination thereof.

b Were any restrictions placed on the use or sale of the assets? If "Yes," explain the restrictions. ☐ Yes ☐ No

c Provide a copy of the agreement(s) of sale or transfer.

7 Were any debts or liabilities transferred from the predecessor for-profit organization to you? ☐ Yes ☐ No
If "Yes," provide a list of the debts or liabilities that were transferred to you, indicating the amount of each, how the amount was determined, and the name of the person to whom the debt or liability is owed.

8 Will you lease or rent any property or equipment previously owned or used by the predecessor for-profit organization, or from persons listed in line 4, or from for-profit organizations in which these persons own more than a 35% interest? If "Yes," submit a copy of the lease or rental agreement(s). Indicate how the lease or rental value of the property or equipment was determined. ☐ Yes ☐ No

9 Will you lease or rent property or equipment to persons listed in line 4, or to for-profit organizations in which these persons own more than a 35% interest? If "Yes," attach a list of the property or equipment, provide a copy of the lease or rental agreement(s), and indicate how the lease or rental value of the property or equipment was determined. ☐ Yes ☐ No

Form **1023** (Rev. 6-2006)

Form 1023 (Rev. 6-2006)   Name: EIN: –   Page **25**

Schedule H. Organizations Providing Scholarships, Fellowships, Educational Loans, or Other Educational Grants to Individuals and Private Foundations Requesting Advance Approval of Individual Grant Procedures

Section I   *Names of individual recipients are not required to be listed in Schedule H.*

Public charities and private foundations complete lines 1a through 7 of this section. See the instructions to Part X if you are not sure whether you are a public charity or a private foundation.

1a Describe the types of educational grants you provide to individuals, such as scholarships, fellowships, loans, etc.

b Describe the purpose and amount of your scholarships, fellowships, and other educational grants and loans that you award.

c If you award educational loans, explain the terms of the loans (interest rate, length, forgiveness, etc.).

d Specify how your program is publicized.

e Provide copies of any solicitation or announcement materials.

f Provide a sample copy of the application used.

2 Do you maintain case histories showing recipients of your scholarships, fellowships, educational loans, or other educational grants, including names, addresses, purposes of awards, amount of each grant, manner of selection, and relationship (if any) to officers, trustees, or donors of funds to you? If "No," refer to the instructions.   ☐ **Yes**   ☐ **No**

3 Describe the specific criteria you use to determine who is eligible for your program. (For example, eligibility selection criteria could consist of graduating high school students from a particular high school who will attend college, writers of scholarly works about American history, etc.)

4a Describe the specific criteria you use to select recipients. (For example, specific selection criteria could consist of prior academic performance, financial need, etc.)

b Describe how you determine the number of grants that will be made annually.

c Describe how you determine the amount of each of your grants.

d Describe any requirement or condition that you impose on recipients to obtain, maintain, or qualify for renewal of a grant. (For example, specific requirements or conditions could consist of attendance at a four-year college, maintaining a certain grade point average, teaching in public school after graduation from college, etc.)

5 Describe your procedures for supervising the scholarships, fellowships, educational loans, or other educational grants. Describe whether you obtain reports and grade transcripts from recipients, or you pay grants directly to a school under an arrangement whereby the school will apply the grant funds only for enrolled students who are in good standing. Also, describe your procedures for taking action if the terms of the award are violated.

6 Who is on the selection committee for the awards made under your program, including names of current committee members, criteria for committee membership, and the method of replacing committee members?

7 Are relatives of members of the selection committee, or of your officers, directors, or **substantial contributors** eligible for awards made under your program? If "Yes," what measures are taken to ensure unbiased selections?   ☐ **Yes**   ☐ **No**

Note. If you are a private foundation, you are not permitted to provide educational grants to **disqualified persons.** Disqualified persons include your substantial contributors and foundation managers and certain family members of disqualified persons.

Section II   Private foundations complete lines 1a through 4f of this section. Public charities do not complete this section.

1a If we determine that you are a private foundation, do you want this application to be considered as a request for advance approval of grant making procedures?   ☐ **Yes**   ☐ **No**   ☐ **N/A**

b For which section(s) do you wish to be considered?

- 4945(g)(1)—Scholarship or fellowship grant to an individual for study at an educational institution   ☐

- 4945(g)(3)—Other grants, including loans, to an individual for travel, study, or other similar purposes, to enhance a particular skill of the grantee or to produce a specific product   ☐

2 Do you represent that you will (1) arrange to receive and review grantee reports annually and upon completion of the purpose for which the grant was awarded, (2) investigate diversions of funds from their intended purposes, and (3) take all reasonable and appropriate steps to recover diverted funds, ensure other grant funds held by a grantee are used for their intended purposes, and withhold further payments to grantees until you obtain grantees' assurances that future diversions will not occur and that grantees will take extraordinary precautions to prevent future diversions from occurring?   ☐ **Yes**   ☐ **No**

3 Do you represent that you will maintain all records relating to individual grants, including information obtained to evaluate grantees, identify whether a grantee is a disqualified person, establish the amount and purpose of each grant, and establish that you undertook the supervision and investigation of grants described in line 2?   ☐ **Yes**   ☐ **No**

Form **1023** (Rev. 6-2006)

Schedule H. Organizations Providing Scholarships, Fellowships, Educational Loans, or Other Educational Grants to Individuals and Private Foundations Requesting Advance Approval of Individual Grant Procedures *(Continued)*

Section II	Private foundations complete lines 1a through 4f of this section. Public charities do not complete this section. *(Continued)*

4a Do you or will you award scholarships, fellowships, and educational loans to attend an educational institution based on the status of an individual being an *employee of a particular employer?* If "Yes," complete lines 4b through 4f. ☐ **Yes** ☐ **No**

b Will you comply with the seven conditions and either the percentage tests or facts and circumstances test for scholarships, fellowships, and educational loans to attend an educational institution as set forth in Revenue Procedures 76-47, 1976-2 C.B. 670, and 80-39, 1980-2 C.B. 772, which apply to inducement, selection committee, eligibility requirements, objective basis of selection, employment, course of study, and other objectives? (See lines 4c, 4d, and 4e, regarding the percentage tests.) ☐ **Yes** ☐ **No**

c Do you or will you provide scholarships, fellowships, or educational loans to attend an educational institution to employees of a particular employer? ☐ **Yes** ☐ **No** ☐ **N/A**

If "Yes," will you award grants to 10% or fewer of the eligible applicants who were actually considered by the selection committee in selecting recipients of grants in that year as provided by Revenue Procedures 76-47 and 80-39? ☐ **Yes** ☐ **No**

d Do you provide scholarships, fellowships, or educational loans to attend an educational institution to children of employees of a particular employer? ☐ **Yes** ☐ **No** ☐ **N/A**

If "Yes," will you award grants to 25% or fewer of the eligible applicants who were actually considered by the selection committee in selecting recipients of grants in that year as provided by Revenue Procedures 76-47 and 80-39? If "No," go to line 4e. ☐ **Yes** ☐ **No**

e If you provide scholarships, fellowships, or educational loans to attend an educational institution to children of employees of a particular employer, will you award grants to 10% or fewer of the number of employees' children who can be shown to be eligible for grants (whether or not they submitted an application) in that year, as provided by Revenue Procedures 76-47 and 80-39? ☐ **Yes** ☐ **No** ☐ **N/A**

If "Yes," describe how you will determine who can be shown to be eligible for grants without submitting an application, such as by obtaining written statements or other information about the expectations of employees' children to attend an educational institution. If "No," go to line 4f.

Note. Statistical or sampling techniques are not acceptable. See Revenue Procedure 85-51, 1985-2 C.B. 717, for additional information.

f If you provide scholarships, fellowships, or educational loans to attend an educational institution to *children of employees of a particular employer* without regard to either the 25% limitation described in line 4d, or the 10% limitation described in line 4e, will you award grants based on facts and circumstances that demonstrate that the grants will not be considered compensation for past, present, or future services or otherwise provide a significant benefit to the particular employer? If "Yes," describe the facts and circumstances that you believe will demonstrate that the grants are neither compensatory nor a significant benefit to the particular employer. In your explanation, describe why you cannot satisfy either the 25% test described in line 4d or the 10% test described in line 4e. ☐ **Yes** ☐ **No**

Form **1023** (Rev. 6-2006)

Form 1023 Checklist

(Revised June 2006)

Application for Recognition of Exemption under Section 501(c)(3) of the Internal Revenue Code

Note. *Retain a copy of the completed Form 1023 in your permanent records. Refer to the* General Instructions *regarding Public Inspection of approved applications.*

Check each box to finish your application (Form 1023). Send this completed Checklist with your filled-in application. If you have not answered all the items below, your application may be returned to you as incomplete.

☐ Assemble the application and materials in this order:
  • Form 1023 Checklist
  • Form 2848, *Power of Attorney and Declaration of Representative* (if filing)
  • Form 8821, *Tax Information Authorization* (if filing)
  • Expedite request (if requesting)
  • Application (Form 1023 and Schedules A through H, as required)
  • Articles of organization
  • Amendments to articles of organization in chronological order
  • Bylaws or other rules of operation and amendments
  • Documentation of nondiscriminatory policy for schools, as required by Schedule B
  • Form 5768, Election/Revocation of Election by an Eligible Section 501(c)(3) Organization To Make Expenditures To Influence Legislation (if filing)
  • All other attachments, including explanations, financial data, and printed materials or publications. Label each page with name and EIN.

☐ User fee payment placed in envelope on top of checklist. DO NOT STAPLE or otherwise attach your check or money order to your application. Instead, just place it in the envelope.

☐ Employer Identification Number (EIN)

☐ Completed Parts I through XI of the application, including any requested information and any required Schedules A through H.
  • You must provide specific details about your past, present, and planned activities.
  • Generalizations or failure to answer questions in the Form 1023 application will prevent us from recognizing you as tax exempt.
  • Describe your purposes and proposed activities in specific easily understood terms.
  • Financial information should correspond with proposed activities.

☐ Schedules. Submit only those schedules that apply to you and check either "Yes" or "No" below.

Schedule A Yes ____ No ____	Schedule E Yes ____ No ____
Schedule B Yes ____ No ____	Schedule F Yes ____ No ____
Schedule C Yes ____ No ____	Schedule G Yes ____ No ____
Schedule D Yes ____ No ____	Schedule H Yes ____ No ____

☐   An exact copy of your complete articles of organization (creating document). Absence of the proper purpose and dissolution clauses is the number one reason for delays in the issuance of determination letters.

    • Location of Purpose Clause from Part III, line 1 (Page, Article and Paragraph Number)_____
    • Location of Dissolution Clause from Part III, line 2b or 2c (Page, Article and Paragraph Number) or by operation of state law _____

☐   Signature of an officer, director, trustee, or other official who is authorized to sign the application.
    • Signature at Part XI of Form 1023.

☐   Your name on the application must be the same as your legal name as it appears in your articles of organization.

Send completed Form 1023, user fee payment, and all other required information, to:

Internal Revenue Service
P.O. Box 192
Covington, KY 41012-0192

If you are using express mail or a delivery service, send Form 1023, user fee payment, and attachments to:

Internal Revenue Service
201 West Rivercenter Blvd.
Attn: Extracting Stop 312
Covington, KY 41011

 Printed on recycled paper

CHAPTER 4

USING CHARITABLE TRUSTS TO FUND THE FAMILY FOUNDATION

§ 4.01   OVERVIEW — THE FAMILY FOUNDATION IN THE ESTATE PLAN

One popular reason for forming a family foundation is the utility of the foundation as an important component of the family's overall estate plan. Other chapters have reviewed the various benefits a family can realize from a family foundation. In addition to the advantages previously discussed, a family foundation can in effect serve as an additional family member. Moreover, as a section 501(c)(3) organization, it is a family member that brings an added dimension to the table in its ability to receive deductible contributions and bequests. Such deductions are available for purposes of the gift and estate taxes as well as the income tax. In addition, a family foundation serves a nontax function as a means of carrying out family goals as a grantmaking entity, a perpetual family memorial, and a community institution.

Much of modern estate planning is concerned with saving taxes by reducing the overall tax burden on the family's assets as they pass from one generation to another. The principal taxes involved are the estate tax and the gift tax, referred to collectively as transfer taxes. The family foundation can help with several aspects of this process.

First, gifts and bequests to a family foundation are fully deductible for gift tax and estate tax purposes, as with transfers to any charitable entity. Unlike the income tax, neither the gift tax nor the estate tax imposes percentage limitations or other special restrictions on the availability of a charitable deduction for transfers to a private foundation. This is one of the few areas in which a family foundation and a public charity are true equals. Thus, if a family wished to do so, it could completely avoid gift and estate taxes by simply transferring all of its assets to the family foundation during life, at death, or by some combination of the two. However, despite the tax savings available, that plan is not a popular one because it leaves nothing for the family over and above the privilege of administering the foundation. Nevertheless, many families do choose to take advantage of the tax deduction available for transfers to the family foundation, if not for their entire estate, at least for a significant portion thereof. Charitable bequests can fit in with the estate plan and provide tax savings in the context of the overall family plan. More sophisticated arrangements, and greater tax advantages for the family, are often possible through the use of trusts. A charitable remainder trust or charitable lead trust can provide benefits that are split between family beneficiaries (private individuals) and charitable beneficiaries, as discussed below. Because of this, these trusts are often referred to as *split-interest trusts*. The family foundation can fit nicely into such a plan as the charitable beneficiary. Table 4–1 compares the charitable remainder trust with the charitable lead trust.

TABLE 4–1
Comparison of Charitable Remainder Trust and Charitable Lead Trust

	Charitable Remainder Trust	*Charitable Lead Trust*
Purpose of trust	Combine income stream for donor or other beneficiary with eventual charitable transfer; diversify investments free of tax	Combine income stream for charity with eventual transfer to family; reduce transfer tax burden on very large transfers
Trust format	Unitrust or annuity trust	Unitrust or annuity trust
Income tax charitable deduction for grantor	Yes, for actuarial value of charitable remainder interest	Generally no (deduction available if trust is grantor trust); trust entitled to deduct its charitable distributions on its own return
Gift tax and estate tax charitable deductions	Yes, for actuarial value of current charitable interest	Yes, for actuarial value of current charitable interest
Portion subject to gift tax or estate tax	Actuarial value of current beneficiaries' interests (except donor's retained interest)	Actuarial value of remainder interest (passing to family beneficiaries)
Tax treatment of trust	Tax exempt (if trust has no unrelated business taxable income)	Trust is taxable, but may deduct its distributions to charity
Self-dealing and other foundation restrictions	May apply to trust	May apply to trust
Family foundation as beneficiary	Yes, of remainder interest	Yes, of current annuity or unitrust distributions

§ 4.02   CHARITABLE REMAINDER TRUSTS

[A]   Defined

A charitable remainder trust is a trust that makes payments to individuals (usually the donor and/or the donor's family) for life or for a period of up to 20 years, after which the remaining trust property is distributed to a charitable organization.[1] That charitable organization may be a family foundation.

---

[1] *See* IRC § 664 for full details concerning qualified charitable remainder trusts.

[B] Beneficiaries

As indicated above, there are two classes of beneficiaries. The *current beneficiaries*, who receive distributions during the term of the trust, are normally individuals. They may include the donor and/or the spouse of the donor as well as any other beneficiaries named by the donor when the trust is created. These beneficiaries are sometimes referred to inaccurately as income beneficiaries, by analogy to the income beneficiaries of other types of trusts. However, because the charitable remainder trust must use either an annuity trust or a unitrust format as discussed below, the amounts they receive do not necessarily bear any direct relationship to the income received by the trust. Although all of the current beneficiaries are usually individuals or other noncharitable entities, the applicable Internal Revenue Code (IRC) and Treasury Regulation provisions require only that *at least one* of the current beneficiaries be a noncharitable entity.[2]

The *remainder beneficiary (or beneficiaries)* is the charitable organization (or organizations) that receives the remaining trust property at the end of the trust term. Note, however, that it is permissible for the trust to provide that, rather than distributing the remaining trust property directly to the charitable beneficiary, the trust may continue on for the benefit of the charitable remainder beneficiary.[3]

[C] Trust Term

The term or duration of the trust may take either of two forms. The trust may continue for the life or lives of its current beneficiaries, or it may continue for a stated number of years.[4] If the latter, term-of-years approach is selected, the trust may not have a term in excess of 20 years.[5] There is no parallel limitation, however, for a trust that runs for the life or lives of the current beneficiaries, as curious as this may seem.[6] Thus, a qualified charitable remainder trust may be created to make distributions to the donor and the donor's spouse for their lives, even though actuarial probability indicates that this trust may be expected to run for 50 years or more. On the other hand, a trust created to make distributions to the same beneficiaries for a 21-year period will not qualify. If the trust term is based on the life or lives of the current beneficiaries, every current beneficiary

---

[2] IRC § 664(d)(1)(A), (2)(A).

[3] IRC § 664(d)(1)(C), (2)(C).

[4] IRC § 664(d)(1)(A), (2)(A).

[5] IRC § 664(d)(1)(A), (2)(A).

[6] There is a practical limitation on the number and nature of potential beneficiaries, at least for trusts that continue for the lives of the beneficiaries, in the rule of IRC § 664(d)(1)(D) and (2)(D) requiring a minimum charitable share of 10 percent of the trust corpus. The value of the charitable share is determined in part by the term (or duration) of the trust, and inclusion of either a large number of beneficiaries or very young beneficiaries will cause the trust to continue for such a long period that, even if the minimum payout of five percent is used, the charitable share will fall below 10 percent.

must be alive at the time the trust is created; thus, unless the trust is to run for a stated term of years, it may not have as a current beneficiary a person who is not alive at the time the trust was created.

[D] Types of Charitable Remainder Trusts

[1] Generally

Charitable remainder trusts are substantially different from "regular" trusts in the amounts they pay out to current beneficiaries. When Congress enacted the current charitable remainder trust provisions in 1969, it was primarily concerned with abuses it felt had been possible under prior law. Under that pre-1969 law, a person could create a charitable remainder trust that would pay out to individual beneficiaries all of the trust's income, just as a regular noncharitable trust does. However, the trustee could manage the trust in such a way as to produce large amounts of current income for distribution, and, in doing so, might choose investments that would not produce safety and growth of the trust property for eventual distribution to the charitable remainder beneficiary. Thus, even though the donor received a deduction for the value of the remainder when the trust was created, that deduction might bear no resemblance to the amount eventually available for charity. The amount of the donor's charitable deduction would be calculated on the basis of actuarial tables assuming a given level of income, but, in practice, the income experience of a given charitable remainder trust would be more or less than that assumption and would be entirely subject to the discretion and control of the trustee.

The Tax Reform Act of 1969[7] restructured all the Internal Revenue Code provisions dealing with charitable contributions, including the rules governing charitable remainder trusts. Many of those changes were designed to assure more correlation between the charitable contribution deductions claimed by donors and the actual benefits to be received by the charitable donees. In the case of charitable remainder trusts, this took the form of a limitation on the type of trust that would qualify for the tax benefits afforded such trusts. The basic concept was a simple one: No trust would qualify unless it was one of a sort in which the interest of the charity was clear and predictable.

[2] Unitrust and Annuity Trusts

Congress specified two types of trusts that would meet this standard — the *unitrust* and the *annuity trust*.[8] In each of these types of trusts, the distributions out to the noncharitable beneficiaries are predetermined when the trust is established, thus preventing trustee manipulation at the expense of the charitable

---

[7] Pub. L. No. 91-172 (Dec. 30, 1969).
[8] IRC § 664(a).

remainder interest. In the case of a *unitrust*, the value of the trust assets is determined each year, and a designated percentage of that value (no less than five percent or more than 50 percent) is distributable to the income beneficiary.[9] In the case of an *annuity trust*, the amount distributable to the current beneficiaries is a fixed dollar amount determined at the time the trust is created and never changing thereafter. Such dollar amount may be no less than five percent or more than 50 percent of the *initial* trust corpus.[10] Both of these trusts make their stipulated distributions to the current beneficiaries irrespective of the amount of income or capital gain earned by the trust. Thus, trustee manipulation cannot encroach upon the value of the charitable interest in the trust.

[3] Net Income Charitable Remainder Trusts

There are several additional categories of charitable remainder trust, which are actually hybrids. The first of these is the *net income charitable remainder unitrust*, which is really nothing more than a unitrust with an additional feature. The net income unitrust is subject to all the usual rules governing charitable remainder unitrusts, but with one distinction: If it does not realize enough current income to make the required distribution, its distributions are limited to the amount of the actual income earned.[11] Thus, the interests of the remainder beneficiary are protected against erosion, since the trustee is prohibited from invading the corpus for the benefit of the current beneficiaries. An additional option permits such a trust to include a makeup clause as well; in subsequent years, when trust income exceeds the amount of current distributions, the excess can be used to make up past deficiencies. A net income unitrust with a makeup provision is sometimes known by its acronym, NIMCRUT.

[4] Flip Trusts

Another hybrid type of charitable remainder trust is the *flip trust*. This is another form of unitrust, which starts out as a net income unitrust (with or without a makeup clause); then, at a specified time, it "flips" off its net income feature and becomes a standard unitrust, paying out its specified percentage amount irrespective of trust income.[12] Such a trust can be useful as a means of dealing with illiquid or non-income-producing property. For example, consider a donor who wishes to create a charitable remainder trust for herself funded with a piece of real property that is currently producing no rental income. If this property is placed in a net income charitable remainder unitrust, the trust can

---

[9] IRC § 664(d)(2)(A).

[10] IRC § 664(d)(1)(A).

[11] IRC § 664(d)(3); Reg. § 1.664-3(a)(i)(b).

[12] *See* Reg. § 1.664-3(a)(1)(i)(c)-(f) for the detailed rules governing flip trusts.

forgo making distributions to the donor for so long as the property produces no income. The donor may be willing to have no income during this period, since, after all, she would have had no income from the property if she had continued to hold it outright. However, if the property is sold and the proceeds are reinvested, the donor may no longer be willing to forgo distributions. By structuring the trust as a flip trust, the donor can provide for distributions limited to trust income for the period up until the property is sold, but require the trust to make its standard percentage distributions thereafter.

[E] Trust Investments

An annuity or unitrust will not be treated as a qualified charitable remainder trust if there is any provision in the trust instrument restricting the trustee from "investing the trust assets in a manner which could result in the annual realization of a reasonable amount of income or gain from the sale or disposition of trust assets."[13] Often, particularly when the donor is also the current beneficiary of the trust, he or she will want to include a provision in the trust either preventing the trustee from selling some asset that was transferred to the trust or requiring the trustee to invest in some particular class of investment (e.g., tax-exempt bonds). The Internal Revenue Service (IRS) construes this requirement strictly, and such a provision will disqualify a trust not-withstanding an innocent intent or logical reason for the particular restriction imposed. A provision requiring the trustee to consult with the donor or the current beneficiary before disposing of a trust asset will be deemed to violate this provision.[14] Also, this requirement applies equally if the donor enters into an informal agreement with the trustee, rather than placing an investment limitation in the trust agreement itself.

[F] Tax Exemption

One of the major advantages of a charitable remainder trust is the fact that in general it is entirely exempt from all income taxes, including capital gains taxes.[15] This means that if such a trust is funded with property that has greatly appreciated in value, the trust may sell the property free of tax and invest the full proceeds for the benefit of the current beneficiaries. If the donor instead sold the property personally, he or she would have only the after-tax proceeds available for reinvestment. This is one reason for the popularity of charitable remainder trusts among investors and others contemplating the sale of a highly appreciated asset.

There is one simple, but nevertheless important, limitation on the tax exemption of charitable remainder trusts. They are exempt from tax only so

---

[13] Reg. § 1.664-1(a)(3).
[14] *See* Priv. Ltr. Ruls. 7928076, 8238085.
[15] IRC § 664(c).

long as they have no unrelated business taxable income.[16] If the trust has any unrelated business taxable income whatsoever, then the trust loses its full exemption and, instead of being fully exempt, is fully taxable. This is an unexpected result, for a quick reading of the statute suggests that it is only the trust's unrelated business income that is potentially taxable; instead, a trust must avoid unrelated business income altogether, or it may be taxable in full on all of its income.[17] As a practical matter, any business income earned by a charitable remainder trust (i.e., earned directly, and not through dividends paid by a corporation owned by the trust) will normally be treated as unrelated.[18] Another category of income that is automatically categorized as unrelated business income is unrelated debt-financed income.[19] For this reason, it is very important that a charitable remainder trust not borrow money for any reason other than the straight operation of its trust/distribution function.

Remember, if the trust has any unrelated business taxable income whatsoever, all of its income will be fully taxable.[20] The only leeway here lies in the definition of the term "unrelated business taxable income" in IRC § 512(a)(1). That provision makes it clear that, just like a tax-exempt organization that is subject to the unrelated business income tax, a charitable remainder trust is entitled to a $1,000 "specific deduction" under IRC § 512(b)(12). This means that a charitable remainder trust may have up to $1,000 of gross income that is categorized as unrelated business income before it will have any unrelated business *taxable* income. This is best not relied on except as a fallback position, however, since the penalty for exceeding the $1,000 amount can be so severe.

[G] Tax Treatment of Distributions to Trust Beneficiaries

Amounts distributed by a charitable remainder trust to a current beneficiary retain the same tax character in the hands of the beneficiary as they had in the trust.[21] The annuity or unitrust amount is taxed as ordinary income to the extent of the trust's ordinary income for the current year, plus any undistributed

---

[16] Reg. § 1.664-1(c).

[17] Leila G. Newhall Unitrust v. Commissioner, 104 T.C. 236 (1995), *aff'd,* 105 F.3d 482 (9th Cir. 1997).

[18] A charitable remainder trust differs from the types of tax-exempt organizations subject to the tax on unrelated business income in that its exemption from tax is based on its status as a charitable remainder trust and not its adherence to a tax-exempt purpose. Since it has no exempt purpose, it is unlikely that any business income will be related to its exempt purpose.

[19] IRC §§ 512(b)(4), 514.

[20] The unrelated business income tax (UBIT) was enacted in 1950 to limit the tax exemption of a tax-exempt organization to passive investment income and income derived from activities related to its exempt purpose. Although there are many qualifications and special rules, income of an exempt organization is potentially subject to the unrelated business income tax if it meets three tests: (1) It is derived from the conduct of a *trade or business,* (2) such business activity is *regularly carried on,* and (3) the conduct of that activity is *not substantially related* (other than through the production of funds) to the performance of the organization's exempt function.

[21] *See* IRC § 664(b); Reg. § 1.664-1(d).

ordinary income from past years.[22] If the beneficiary's distribution exceeds such current and undistributed ordinary income, the excess comes in turn from the following categories:[23]

1. Short-term capital gain to the extent of current and past undistributed short-term capital gains;

2. Long-term capital gain to the extent of current and past undistributed long-term capital gains;

3. Other income (e.g., tax-exempt income) to the extent of the trust's current and past undistributed other income; and

4. Tax-free distribution of principal.

This is sometimes referred to as a WIFO system, reflecting a "worst in, first out" approach, since more favorably taxed categories of income are not reached until all less favorably taxed categories are exhausted. This system makes it difficult to provide tax-exempt income to a beneficiary, particularly where the trust is funded with significantly appreciated property, since all recognized capital gains must be distributed before payments can be considered tax-free income.

[H] Termination of Trust upon Qualified Contingencies

Internal Revenue Code § 664(f) specifically permits a charitable remainder trust to terminate upon the happening of a specified contingency, provided that termination occurs on a date not later than the trust would otherwise terminate. This rule, enacted in 1984, reversed earlier IRS rulings that prohibited the use of contingencies and otherwise qualified charitable remainder trusts.

> **Example:** A charitable remainder trust created under Marigold Flowers's will provides for current distributions to her husband, Thornton, for his life. However, if Thornton remarries, his interest will terminate, and the property will be distributed immediately to the charitable remainder beneficiary. This is a qualified contingency under section 664(f) and accordingly does not disqualify the trust.

[I] Private Foundation Restrictions

The charitable remainder trust is one of the types of trusts referred to as a *split-interest trust* because some interests are owned by private individuals and other interests are owned by charity (and for which a charitable deduction was claimed under one or more of the charitable deduction provisions for income

---

[22] IRC § 664(b); Reg. § 1.664-1(d).
[23] IRC §§ 664(b)(2)-(4).

tax, gift tax, or estate tax purposes). The fact that it combines private and charitable interests calls for special care on the part of the trustee, the grantor, and all related interests. Under section 4947(a)(2), a split-interest trust is treated as if it were a private foundation for purposes of several of the restrictions applicable to private foundations. Those restrictions are discussed at length in Chapter 6. The restrictions applicable to charitable remainder trusts are the following:

- The prohibition on self-dealing (IRC § 4941); and

- The tax on "taxable expenditures" (IRC § 4945).

The self-dealing rules are by far the more important of these limitations, since they prohibit virtually all dealings between a charitable remainder trust and its donor (or other disqualified persons). This makes it necessary to carefully monitor all proposed transactions involving such a trust. The taxable expenditure rule, set forth in IRC § 4945, has little practical implication for charitable remainder trusts, as it is aimed primarily at prohibiting private foundations from making certain types of grants.[24] As a practical matter, a charitable remainder trust would be affected by the taxable expenditure rule only when the trust continued on after the termination of the interests of the current beneficiaries (i.e., when it would be functioning as a private foundation).

Two other private foundation provisions — the prohibition of jeopardy investments, which might jeopardize the trust's ability to carry out its charitable purposes (IRC § 4944), and the limitation on excess business holdings, which limits the ability of the trust to hold closely held stocks and interests in partnerships (IRC § 4943) — are generally inapplicable to charitable remainder trusts unless they continue on after the interests of the current (noncharitable) beneficiaries have terminated. This occurs because section 4947(b)(3)(B) makes these provisions inapplicable to a split-interest charitable trust if a charitable deduction was allowed for amounts payable under the terms of such a trust to all remainder beneficiaries, but not to any income beneficiaries. This is an intricate way to describe the ordinary charitable remainder trust.

[J] Funding Charitable Remainder Trusts — What Property to Use

The planner faces some difficult choices when it comes to the selection of property to recommend for a charitable remainder trust. Often the creation of the trust is prompted by a pending sale of some particular property or investment. The selection of which property to use raises a wide range of considerations; some categories of property are problematic.

A detailed review of the various problem assets a donor may wish to transfer into a charitable remainder trust is beyond the scope of this book.

---

[24] *See* Chapter 7 for a discussion of grantmaking.

Nevertheless, for the purposes of this book, it is sufficient to emphasize what is generally the best possible asset to use. A donor will seldom get into trouble if he or she transfers only passive investments to the trust. This is not always possible, and the planner's job may be to help the donor achieve his or her goals through the transfer of some other, more difficult asset, but remember as a starting point that the *best* alternative is a simple stock or bond, or even cash. Many problems are avoided if the planner can resist pressures to find some way to shoehorn difficult property into a charitable remainder trust and can find some other way to accomplish the donor's desires.

If the charitable beneficiary of a charitable remainder trust is a family foundation, one must remember that all the limitations applicable to private foundation contributions are applicable. In effect, the deduction allowable for a transfer to such a trust is for the transfer of the remainder interest in the trust to the foundation; the amount of the deduction is the actuarial value of that remainder interest. Thus, the lower percentage limitations (30 percent of adjusted gross income (AGI) for cash contributions and 20 percent for appreciated property) apply, and the amount of a deduction for a transfer of appreciated property is limited to the donor's tax basis in the property.[25] This is understandable, for one might logically expect the tax consequences of an indirect contribution to a foundation, made via a charitable remainder trust, to be no more favorable than the consequences of a direct contribution.

[K] Practical Uses of Charitable Remainder Trusts

The charitable remainder trust is most useful for the donor who wants to attain the very objective that such trusts were created to accomplish — combining an income stream for the donor and/or other beneficiaries with an eventual transfer to charity. Unless the charitable transfer is an important part of the donor's plan, the donor might be well advised to consider some other arrangement. With that said, however, the charitable remainder trust offers the donor a considerable array of attractive tax benefits.

Probably the most common tax strategy for the charitable remainder trust is the use of the trust to facilitate a sale of highly appreciated property and effectively diversify the donor's investment in the transferred property on a tax-advantaged basis. Consider the position of a donor holding an investment that has appreciated in value since she acquired it. She may wish to sell it and reinvest the proceeds to produce an income stream, but if she does just that, she

---

[25] IRC § 170(e)(1)(B)(ii) reaches this result by requiring the donor's deduction otherwise allowable to be reduced by "the amount of gain which would have been long-term capital gain if the property contributed had been sold by the taxpayer at its fair market value (determined at the time of such contribution)." *See* Reg. § 1.170A-4(d), example 9, which demonstrates the application of a former version of this rule. *See also* § 2.02[A] *supra.* IRC § 170(e)(5) provides an exception whereby a contribution of publicly traded stock to a foundation will produce a full fair-market-value deduction.

will incur a capital gains tax. As a result, she will have only the net after-tax proceeds left to reinvest. If, instead, she transfers the property to a charitable remainder trust, the results differ in several ways. First, she will receive an income tax charitable deduction for her transfer equal to the actuarial value of the remainder interest in the trust. Second, because the trust is exempt from tax, it can sell the property free of tax and have the full sales proceeds available for reinvestment. Third, so long as the trust conforms to the requirements for qualification under IRC § 664, she will receive distributions from the trust for whatever period, and in whatever amount, she desires. And, finally, she will be providing a transfer to whatever charitable beneficiary or beneficiaries she may choose, which may include a family foundation.

> **Example:** In 1984, Kathryn purchased stock in a New York Stock Exchange-listed company for $50,000. Now the stock is worth $750,000 and is providing Kathryn with annual income of $7,500. Assume Kathryn is 75 years old, unmarried, and interested in assuring her retirement income. Her estate plan is centered around providing for her own old age, with the balance remaining at her death passing to her family foundation.
>
> *Alternative 1* — If she sells the stock and reinvests the proceeds in securities that will provide her with more income, Kathryn will incur a capital gain of $700,000. At a 15 percent capital gains tax rate, that will result in a tax of $105,000, leaving her only $645,000 to reinvest. If she invests that amount at five percent, she will realize annual income of $32,250 from this holding.
>
> *Alternative 2* — Assume Kathryn transfers the stock to a charitable remainder unitrust that will pay her seven percent of corpus annually for her lifetime, after which the remaining trust corpus will pass to The Kathryn Foundation. Upon creating the trust and transferring her publicly traded stock to it, she will be entitled to a current income tax deduction of $389,933.[26] That deduction, which is allowable up to 20 percent of her adjusted gross income for the year she creates the trust and the five following years, will save up to $136,477 in income taxes at the maximum (35 percent) federal income tax bracket. Note that the amount of the deduction will vary, depending upon the current actuarial rate in effect under IRC § 7520, as well as the trust's payout rate, Kathryn's age, and the amount contributed. Each year Kathryn will receive a distribution from the trust equal to seven percent of trust corpus (or $52,500 for the first year); this amount will increase or decrease as the value of the corpus increases or decreases. Upon her death, the remaining trust corpus will be distributed to The Kathryn Foundation. Although the trust property will be included in

---

[26] This is based on an IRS actuarial rate of 6 percent and an annual payout 12 months after the initial valuation date. The amount of the deduction will vary with the age of the beneficiary, the number of beneficiaries, the payout percentage, the terms of the trust, and the IRS actuarial rate at the time the trust is created.

her taxable estate (under IRC § 2036, due to her retained income interest), Kathryn's estate will receive an estate tax charitable deduction that completely offsets that inclusion and renders the property free of estate tax. *Summary* — As shown above, on these facts the charitable remainder trust in alternative 2 produces more than twice as much annual income for Kathryn as alternative 1 above (and nearly eight times as much as she currently receives from the property placed in the trust), plus a substantial income tax deduction. Moreover, she and her family will realize all of the nontax benefits that normally flow from a family foundation, as discussed in Chapter 2. These benefits come at a cost, however, as Kathryn is no longer able to spend the $750,000 corpus or leave it to her heirs.

Whenever a person simultaneously wants to (1) provide himself or someone else with an income stream and (2) provide an eventual transfer to charity, a charitable remainder trust can help achieve both desires. The possible applications are limitless. For example, such a trust may prove useful when a donor wants to benefit an individual (e.g., a family employee, such as a housekeeper, or an aging, but distant, relative) without giving that individual a fund that would benefit his or her own family. Particularly when the donor has a family foundation to serve as the remainder beneficiary, the use of a charitable remainder trust can offer a convenient solution.

Another common use of the charitable remainder trust is to advance a charitable bequest. Rather than leaving a bequest for charity in her will, a donor may create a trust and thereby realize the current benefits outlined in alternative 2 above in addition to the estate tax benefits that would result from a bequest of the same property to charity.

[L]   Use of Wealth Replacement Life Insurance with a Charitable Remainder Trust

The example above (alternative 2) demonstrates how a charitable remainder trust can produce significant benefits for a charitably inclined donor. That example also demonstrates a potential drawback of such a trust — the benefits realized come at the cost of any alternative arrangements the donor and his or her family might have contemplated for the transferred property. Having put the subject property in a charitable remainder trust, the donor may no longer leave it to his or her children or other heirs. This is a problem that has a readily available solution in many instances.

A donor who contemplates putting an asset into a charitable remainder trust, but is concerned about the resultant inability to leave this portion of his or her wealth to children or other heirs, may wish to consider using a wealth replacement trust to provide a corresponding amount to such heirs upon his or her death. The latter is a simple, garden-variety irrevocable life insurance trust that takes out a policy on the life of the donor and receives the proceeds free of estate tax for the benefit of the donor's heirs. In some cases, a second-to-die policy on the lives of the donor and his or her spouse can provide the same result at a lower premium cost. As with any insurance purchase, the policy premiums should be carefully selected and alternative policies compared.

For example, the charitable remainder trust in the preceding example was able to dramatically increase the income Kathryn received from the property she placed in the trust. She could use just a part of that increase in income to buy insurance on her life through a life insurance trust. Then, when she dies and the trust property passes to her family foundation, her heirs as beneficiaries of the life insurance trust will receive the proceeds. The precise results depend on a number of factors. These include the charitable remainder trust results, the donor's personal situation (age, health, and insurability), and the insurance contract selected (no-load or standard) and the premium charged.

Although this arrangement appears to enable the donor to have her cake and eat it, too (i.e., leave the property to the foundation and still leave a corresponding amount to her heirs), do not lose sight of the fact that this is accomplished through a purchase of life insurance, and not a magic wand. Kathryn in the foregoing example may not be insurable, or the premium costs may be prohibitively high. Such premium payments are potentially subject to the gift tax and, depending on the amounts involved, may seriously impinge on the benefits she expects to derive from the charitable remainder trust. If her family's economic benefit is her primary concern, Kathryn could simply keep the property (or sell it), forgo the charitable remainder trust, and still buy the insurance policy in the life insurance trust, and the result would probably be even better for her family. Realistically, any charitable transfer is going to reduce the property available for other applications.

In addition, while this technique can produce results that seem dramatic, a closer look may be in order. The donor should consider carefully whether he or she really wants or needs life insurance and, if so, whether the plan presented is the best available from a financial standpoint. The mere fact of a charitable gift is scant justification for buying insurance. If a person spends $100,000 per year on excessive consumption (such as clothing, vacations, and the like), he or she probably would not feel compelled to "replace" for the heirs the value thereby lost to his or her estate. The same reasoning could be applied to a proposed charitable transfer. Also, any contemplated charitable transfer, to a charitable remainder trust or otherwise, that appears to distort the client's estate plan may well be too large for the donor's circumstances. In any event, the charitable transfer and the life insurance purchase are totally separate, and neither depends on the other. Notwithstanding the financial power of life insurance to produce large amounts of cash in the event of an untimely death, financial and tax considerations alone will seldom, if ever, justify a charitable transfer.

[M]   Drafting Considerations

When a charitable remainder trust is intended to benefit a private foundation, the trust must be drafted with special care to ensure that the trust assets can in fact be transferred to the foundation at the termination of the trust. This requires close attention to the language of the trust, particularly the mandatory clause dealing with substitute remainder beneficiaries. Every charitable remainder trust must include a provision dealing with the disposition of trust corpus upon the termination of the trust in the event that the charitable beneficiary or beneficiaries named in the trust instrument are not qualified charities at that time. The typical clause of this sort provides as follows:

> If the Charitable Organization is not an organization described in sections 170(c),2055(a), and 2522(a) of the Code at the time when any principal or income of the Trust is to be distributed to it, then the Trustee shall distribute the then principal or income to one or more organizations described in sections 170(c), 2055(a), and 2522(a) as the Trustee shall select, and in the proportions as the Trustee shall decides in the Trustee's sole discretion.[27]

The statutory references used must be selected very carefully to accomplish precisely what is desired. The principal problem arises in the selection of a proper reference to section 170, the income tax charitable deduction provision. The category referred to in the clause quoted above, section 170(c), is a very broad category that includes all charitable organizations, both private foundations and public charities. Some forms include section 170(b)(1)(A) here, either instead of or in addition to section 170(c). It is important to note that the category of organization referred to in section 170(b)(1)(A) includes only public charities.

The drafting of this clause raises considerations that are both substantive and tax related. From a substantive standpoint, the drafter must assure that trust assets can pass to the desired charitable beneficiary. If that beneficiary is to be a family foundation, the substitute remainder beneficiary clause must refer to section 170(c), the category that includes private foundations, and not to section 170(b)(1)(A), which does not. If section 170(b)(1)(A) is used, either instead of section 170(c) or in addition thereto, the family foundation will be excluded as a potential beneficiary, and a substitute remainder beneficiary will have to receive the assets.

On the other hand, the tax aspects may dictate the use of section 170(b)(1)(A) in this clause. We have seen that the tax treatment of contributions to private

---

[27] This sample and the others that follow in this section are taken from Rev. Proc. 2005-52, 2005-34 I.R.B. 326, which provides sample trust language for inter vivos charitable remainder unitrusts continuing for one measuring life. Other charitable remainder trust sample forms appear in Rev. Procs. 2005-53 through 2005-59, 2005-34 I.R.B. 339, *et seq.* and Rev. Procs. 2003-53, through 2003-60, 2003-31 I.R.B. 230 *et seq.*

foundations is more restrictive than that applicable where the donee is a public charity. Lower percentage limitations apply, and, more important, deductions for contributions of any property *other than* publicly traded stocks cannot exceed the donor's tax basis. Thus, a donor who transfers real estate or closely held stock to a private foundation will be entitled to deduct only an amount equal to his or her tax basis in such property even though the value of the property is much higher. If this gift is made through a charitable remainder trust and the donor wishes to deduct the full value of the transferred property, it must be clear that the ultimate taker will not be a private foundation.[28] Thus, in this instance, the substitute remainder beneficiary clause must clearly limit the beneficiary category to organizations described in section 170(b)(1)(A), as follows:

> If the Charitable Organization is not an organization described in sections 170 (b)(1)(A), 2055(a), and 2522(a) of the Code at the time when any principal or income of the Trust is to be distributed to it, then the Trustee shall distribute the then principal or income to one or more organizations described in sections 170 (b)(1)(A), 2055(a), and 2522(a) as the Trustee shall select and in the proportions as the Trustee shall decide, in the Trustee's sole discretion.

Accordingly, one must be quite careful in using form books or computerized drafting aids for situations of this type. If a family foundation is to be the beneficiary, references restricting the charitable beneficiaries to organizations described in section 170(b)(1)(A) must be avoided, or the donor's intentions may be thwarted.

§ 4.03 CHARITABLE LEAD TRUSTS

[A] Defined

For some families, another type of split-interest charitable trust may be worth considering, either alone or in conjunction with other arrangements. The *charitable lead trust* is similar in many ways to the charitable remainder trust examined in the preceding section, but it has a very different purpose. In its form, a charitable lead trust resembles a charitable remainder trust with the interests reversed. Instead of providing current distributions to individual beneficiaries with the remainder eventually passing to charity, the charitable lead trust provides current distributions to charity with the remaining trust assets passing to individual family beneficiaries when the trust terminates. As with the charitable remainder trust, a charitable lead trust must follow a unitrust or annuity trust

---

[28] *See* Priv. Ltr. Rul. 200002042, involving reformation of a charitable remainder trust to delete references to section 170(b)(1)(A), so as to ensure that the remainder interest could be distributed to a private foundation. Because the donors had funded the trust with stock that was not "qualified appreciated stock" under section 170(e)(5)(B), their deduction was limited to their adjusted basis in the stock and 20 percent of their adjusted gross income.

format, so that current distributions are either a fixed percentage of trust assets valued annually or a fixed dollar amount each year.[29] Likewise, in both types of trusts, the charitable interest qualifies for a gift tax or an estate tax charitable deduction. A comparison of charitable remainder trusts and charitable lead trusts is provided in Table 4–1 *supra.*

[B] Tax Treatment

In other ways, the two types of trusts are different. While the remainder trust normally gives rise to an income tax charitable deduction, the lead trust in most cases does not. The exception, where an income tax deduction is available, is the situation wherein the charitable lead trust is structured as a grantor trust, with the grantor treated as the owner of the trust for income tax purposes.[30] In those circumstances, the donor is entitled to an income tax charitable deduction for the charitable interest in the trust, but he or she is taxable on trust income for as long as the trust continues, and he or she is *not* entitled to any deduction for the amounts the trust distributes to charity. For most persons considering a charitable lead trust, however, the grantor trust approach is not desirable, and the discussion that follows will be limited to the much more common situation where the trust is a nongrantor trust and is intended to produce only a gift tax or an estate tax charitable deduction.

Assuming it is not structured as a grantor trust, a charitable lead trust is *not* exempt from tax. It is fully subject to the income tax and is taxed in the same manner as any other complex trust.[31] A charitable lead trust does, however, receive a charitable deduction for amounts of trust income it distributes to charity, with no limitations as to amount.[32] Often a charitable lead trust will be able to largely avoid income tax as a result, except possibly for taxes on capital gains realized by the trust.

> **Example:** The McCoy Charitable Lead Trust is required to pay an annuity to the McCoy Family Foundation amounting to $100,000 each year. For 2007, the trust receives interest and dividends (ordinary income) of $25,000 and realizes capital gains of $50,000. Assuming that under the trust instrument and local law the charitable annuity comes first from the trust's ordinary income and then from capital gain, the trust would be entitled to a charitable deduction under section 642(c) equal to $75,000, which would

---

[29] IRC § 170(f)(2)(B); Reg. § 1.170A-6(c).

[30] *See* § 170(f)(2)(B), requiring that the grantor be treated as the owner of the income interest in the trust under IRC § 671. This means the grantor is taxed on all of the income of the trust even though he or she receives none of it. If the donor ceases to be treated as the owner for any reason (including the donor's death) before the trust terminates, he or she must realize a constructive income item representing the amount of the original deduction not yet reported in income.

[31] *See* Subchapter J of the Internal Revenue Code, especially sections 661-663.

[32] IRC § 642(c).

fully offset its taxable income. If its charitable distribution had been only $60,000, the charitable deduction would likewise have been $60,000, leaving $15,000 of capital gain subject to tax.

Despite these limitations, a grantor charitable lead trust can be useful for some planning situations. One such occasion is where an individual has claimed so much in charitable contribution deductions that he or she is no longer able, under the percentage-of-AGI limitations, to realize a tax benefit from making more charitable gifts currently.[33] Even though no income tax deduction is allowable for creating the charitable lead trust, the donor can achieve a comparable effect by transferring income-producing property to the trust and thereby removing the income on the transferred property from his or her tax return. The trust can then make distributions to the same charities that the donor would otherwise be supporting via nondeductible contributions. The trust will be entitled to an income tax deduction for such distributions. Thus, the trust enables the donor to avoid the adverse impact of the percentage limitations.

A charitable lead trust can also be helpful where the grantor receives a burst of income that pushes him or her into an unusually high tax bracket for that year and needs the deduction the transfers to the trust would produce for that year, but will be in a much lower tax bracket in future trust years. In this instance, a grantor lead trust can allow the grantor to take an income tax deduction in the year when the highest tax bracket applies and then report the trust income over the years when his or her income is taxed in lower brackets.

Although the Internal Revenue Service has issued sample forms for various types of charitable remainder trusts, there are no comparable charitable lead trust forms to assist the drafter.[34] As a result, some attorneys utilize the IRS charitable remainder trust sample forms as a guide in drafting charitable lead trusts. As with any sample forms, such prototypes must be used carefully, as the applicable rules are different in many respects.

It should be noted that contributions to a charitable lead trust, regardless of whether the beneficiary is a private foundation or a public charity, are subject to reduced percentage limitations (30 percent of AGI for cash gifts and 20 percent for property contributions).[35] This is because such contributions are considered gifts "for the use of" charity, rather than gifts "to" charity.[36] Only gifts "to" public charities qualify for the higher 50 and 30 percent limitations.[37]

Finally, like the charitable remainder trust, the charitable lead trust is a split-interest trust that is subject to the self-dealing limitations and certain of the

---

[33] These percentage limitations appear in IRC § 170(b)(1).

[34] *See* note 27 *supra.* The IRS is reportedly planning to issue lead trust forms eventually.

[35] IRC § 170(b)(1).

[36] IRC § 170(b)(1)(B).

[37] IRC § 170(b)(1)(A).

other IRC Chapter 42 private foundation limitations discussed in Chapter 6. The restrictions applicable to charitable lead trusts are the following:

- The prohibition on self-dealing (IRC § 4941); and

- The tax on "taxable expenditures" (IRC § 4945).

The self-dealing rules are by far the more important of these limitations, since they prohibit virtually all dealings between a charitable lead trust and its grantor (or other disqualified persons). This makes it necessary to monitor carefully all proposed transactions involving such a trust. The taxable expenditure rule, set forth in IRC § 4945, may also be important insofar as it places limitations on the types of grants the trust may make.[38]

Two other private foundation provisions — the prohibition of jeopardy investments, which might jeopardize the trust's ability to carry out its charitable purposes,[39] and the limitation on excess business holdings, which limits the ability of the trust to hold closely held stocks and interests in partnerships[40] — apply to a charitable lead trust only if the actuarial value of the charitable interest in the trust (as of the inception of the trust) is 60 percent or more of the total value of the trust, valued at the inception of the trust.[41]

[C] Valuation and Its Effect on Trust Structure

The principal estate planning use of the charitable lead trust is to reduce the amount of gift tax or estate tax payable on large transfers, and it can be quite effective for this purpose. This result is made possible because of the split-interest nature of these trusts. The initial interest, providing current distributions to charity, is deductible for gift tax and estate tax purposes. The portion actually subject to gift tax or estate tax is thus the remainder interest, which is in effect discounted because it is delayed for the period of the current charitable interest. For gift tax and estate tax purposes, the amount subject to tax is the full amount transferred to the trust, less the actuarial value of the current charitable interest.

The actuarial values are determined primarily by the interrelationship of the amount distributable to charity, the term of the trust, and the Internal Revenue Service actuarial rates applicable at the time the trust is created.[42] The IRS actuarial rates are based on a discount rate equal to 120 percent of the applicable federal midterm rate then in effect and on mortality tables that

---

[38] *See* discussion at § 6.06 *infra.*

[39] IRC § 4944.

[40] IRC § 4943.

[41] IRC § 4947(b)(3)(A).

[42] The payout sequence of the trust (annual, semiannual, quarterly, or monthly payments to charity) and the timing of the initial distribution also affect this valuation.

are updated at least every ten years to reflect the most recent U.S. Census figures.[43]

> **Example 1:** Paul transferred $1,000,000 to a charitable lead annuity trust that will pay an annuity of six percent or $60,000 per year to charity for 15 years, with the remainder to Paul's children. Based on an IRS actuarial rate of 6 percent, the value of the charitable share under the IRS actuarial tables is $582,738. Thus, the value of the remainder interest (the amount subject to gift tax) is Paul's $1,000,000 transfer less the charitable deduction of $582,738, or $417,262.

> **Example 2:** Paul transferred $1,000,000 to a charitable lead unitrust that will pay a unitrust amount equal to six percent of trust corpus (valued annually) to charity each year for 15 years, with the remainder to Paul's children. Based on an IRS actuarial rate of 6 percent, the value of the charitable share under the IRS actuarial tables is $582,693. Thus, the value of the remainder interest (the amount subject to gift tax) is Paul's $1,000,000 transfer less the charitable deduction of $582,693 or $417,693.

If the current charitable distributions are sufficiently large or continue for a sufficiently long time, they may even reduce the value of the family's remainder interest to zero. This effect is possible only with a charitable lead annuity trust.

> **Example 3:** Raoul transfers $10,000,000 to a charitable lead annuity trust that will pay to charity an annuity of 8.75 percent, or $875,000, per year for 20 years, with the remainder to Raoul's children. Based on an IRS actuarial rate of 6 percent, the value of the charitable share under the IRS actuarial tables is just over $10,000,000, but the allowable charitable deduction cannot exceed the amount transferred to the trust, or $10,000,000. Thus, the value of the remainder interest (the amount subject to gift tax) is zero — Raoul's $10,000,000 transfer less the charitable deduction of $10,000,000. This means that the remaining trust assets, if any, will be distributed to Raoul's children in 20 years completely free of gift or estate taxes.

The net result in example 3 above (no gift or estate tax) may be obtained from other combinations of payout and trust term, as shown in Table 4–2 below. These figures should be viewed as demonstrations of the underlying principles and not as planning absolutes. Obviously, a trust that is saddled with a payout in excess of 25 percent, even for as little as five years, will be quite unlikely to produce any growth in the value of the corpus. Fluctuations in corpus value may well cause such a trust to exhaust itself prior to expiration of the five-year trust

---

[43] *See* IRC § 7520 for the applicable rules.

term, leaving nothing for the remainder beneficiaries. On the other hand, a trust with a payout in the range of nine percent may be able to produce growth in the value of its corpus and thus have a sizeable corpus to turn over to the remainder beneficiaries when it terminates; however, to produce a zero gift tax or estate tax value, a trust with a payout of this size must continue for 30 years or so. The remainder beneficiaries may then be too old to make good use of the corpus, even if they are so fortunate as to outlive the trust. And one other, very important factor is the level of the IRS actuarial rate at the time in question. Lower actuarial rates produce a beneficial tax result for the charitable lead trust and make a zero tax result easier to achieve. Higher rates have the opposite effect.

TABLE 4–2
Trust Payout/Term Combinations to Produce Zero
Remainder Value (Calculated at 6.0 percent IRS actuarial rate)

Trust Term (in Years)	Payout (as % of Initial Trust Corpus)
5	23.740%
10	13.587%
15	10.297%
20	8.719%
25	7.823%
30	7.265%
35	6.898%
40	6.647%

Note: Set forth in Table 4-2 are the figures for an IRS actuarial rate of 6.0 percent. (These are the values for the remainder of a charitable lead Annuity providing for Annual payments to charity at the End of the year.) It goes without saying that such calculations must be done for any particular trust based upon the particulars of that trust at the then-current actuarial rates and tables; the figures in Table 4-2 below are illustrative only and should not be relied upon for actual planning situations.

As appealing as a zero tax result may seem to a tax-sensitive grantor, this is not necessarily the most effective way to arrange a charitable lead trust. Computer projections can be run to show the result on a given set of assumptions of growth rates and future values, but such projections should be viewed with some caution. Any variation from the underlying assumptions used for the projections will render the results invalid. Since no one is able to predict with any degree of precision just what economic and investment conditions will be in five years, let alone 20 or 25 years, the planner should simply attempt to position a trust to make the best of whatever conditions it may experience. This will usually mean a moderate payout rate that will enable the trust to retain a portion of whatever positive investment experience it is able to achieve. An exhaustive discussion of this point is beyond the scope of this book, but it is important that the reader be aware of the elusive nature of any permanent conclusions in this area.

[D] Charitable Lead Trust with Private Foundation Beneficiary

The charitable beneficiary of a charitable lead trust may be any charitable organization, including a family foundation. One popular estate planning approach for large estates is to provide a bequest to a charitable lead trust that will make distributions to a family foundation for period of years, as outlined above, followed by the distribution of remaining trust assets to children and/or grandchildren of the grantor. The delay in the family's receipt of benefits from the charitable lead trust is offset to some extent by the resultant savings in gift tax or estate tax and the intangible benefits derived from managing the family foundation and directing its grants. This planning approach finds its most receptive audience among families whose children and grandchildren have been otherwise provided for and thus are not entirely dependent on the charitable lead trust assets. They are in a suitable position to wait out the charitable term before receiving those assets.

The receipt of distributions from a charitable lead trust can provide a family foundation with assets to form or enhance its endowment and generate investment income to fund ongoing foundation distributions in the future. Historically, the IRS position has been that a private foundation that is the beneficiary of a charitable lead trust must increase the amount of its minimum distribution for purposes of the section 4942 tax on undistributed income by the lesser of the distributions from the lead trust or five percent of the trust assets.[44] This position has been rejected by the U.S. Tax Court and a federal appeals court, both of which held the subject regulation invalid.[45] Although the IRS apparently accepts this rejection of its position, it has yet to amend the regulations.

Official acceptance of the *Ann Jackson Family Foundation* case is further indicated in the IRS Exempt Organizations Continuing Professional Education Text for Fiscal 2001, Topic G, "Control and Power: Issues Involving Supporting Organizations, Donor Advised Funds, and Disqualified Person Financial Institutions" (CPE Text). Part 5 of that chapter, entitled "Update on IRC 4940 Treatment of Distributions from Charitable Lead Trusts," states as follows:

> Topic P of the 2000 CPE Text, page 225, discussed the definition of net investment income under IRC 4940(c)(1) in the context of income

---

[44] Reg. § 53.4942(a)-2(c)(2)(iii).

[45] Ann Jackson Family Foundation v. Commissioner, 15 F.3d 917 (9th Cir. 1994), *aff'g* 97 T.C. 534 (1991).

distributions from a charitable lead trust to a private foundation (PF). The specific concern is whether the ordinary income component of distributions received by a PF from a IRC 4947(a)(2) trust should be included in the calculation of net investment income for purposes of IRC 4940. Reg. 53.4940-1(d) (2) requires that the PF include the ordinary income component of a distribution from section 4947(a)(2) trusts in the calculation of its net investment income as if the income were its own.

We believe that courts would likely hold that the Reg. 53.4840-1(d)(2) goes beyond the statutory authority. Accordingly, distinctions should not be made for purposes of IRC 4940 between distributions from taxable entities and private foundations, including trusts described in IRC 4947(a)(1) or 4947(a) (2). Similar treatment should be afforded IRC 4942 minimum investment return treatment of IRC 4947(a)(2) trust distributions following Ann Jackson Family Foundation v. Commissioner, 97 T.C. 534 (1991), aff'd 15 F.3d 917 (9th Cir. 1999).

Foundations that have paid the excise tax on investment income under IRC § 4940 on distributions from a charitable lead trust should review their situation and, if the applicable statute of limitations is still open (normally three years from the filing of the return), consider filing a refund claim. Refunds have reportedly been made on this basis despite the lack of any IRS pronouncement on the issue other than the CPE Text quoted above.

Estate Tax Issue — Where a charitable lead trust makes payments to a private foundation, it is important to be aware of the possibility that the trust corpus may be included in the estate of the person creating the trust if that person maintains control of the ultimate recipients of the funds paid, through control of the foundation distributee or otherwise. This can be an unwelcome surprise where a charitable lead trust makes distributions to a foundation in which the creator of the trust is an active participant. And the result grows increasingly serious as the taxable portion of a charitable lead trust — the family's remainder interest — grows larger each year as the trust moves onward toward its termination date.

Here is how this situation arises. Internal Revenue Code § 2036(a)(2) includes in a decedent's gross estate for estate tax purposes any transferred property in which the decedent retained the right to designate the person or persons entitled to possess the property or the income therefrom. This result is reached whether the retained power is exercisable by the decedent alone or in conjunction with others. Moreover, the capacity in which the decedent can exercise such power is immaterial.

In the case of a charitable lead trust, this rule can render the trust subject to estate tax in several ways. First, and most obviously, if the decedent creates a charitable lead trust and retains the right to designate the charitable recipients of the current distributions, he or she has obviously retained a "right to designate" that is within the rule. However, the same result is reached if the decedent retains no such right but instead makes the trust distributions payable to his or her family foundation, in which he or she has a role in selecting the recipients of grants from the foundation. Such indirect control will run afoul of the retained power rule of § 2036(a)(2) every bit as much as a direct retention of control over trust distributions. This was the result in *Rifkind v. United States.*[46]

This rule is more of a trap for the unwary than a real planning obstacle. If the creator of a charitable lead trust is willing to assume a limited role in his or her family foundation, so that he or she plays no role in the foundation's distribution of the funds it receives from the charitable lead trust, the trust can be brought beyond the reach of the estate tax. A blueprint for this planning technique is set forth in Private Letter Ruling 200138018. There, the taxpayer created a charitable lead trust paying an annuity for 10 years to a foundation created by her at some earlier date. After the 10-year trust term, the remaining principal will be paid to her descendants or trusts for their benefit. The foundation amended its bylaws to provide several safeguards:

1. While the grantor remained as a director for her life, her role was limited. At any time when the foundation is the recipient of amounts from any charitable trust created by a director or officer of the foundation, that director or officer is prohibited from acting on matters concerning funds coming to the foundation from the charitable trust;

2. An officer or director who creates a charitable trust for the benefit of the foundation is prohibited from voting on any matters relating to the funds received from or anticipated to be received from such a trust (including grants or disbursements of such funds) and may not even be counted toward a quorum for voting on such matters;

3. Any funds received by the foundation from a charitable trust are segregated into a separate fund account to be administered and distributed by a separate fund committee, and the grantor is not to possess any power over that separate fund committee;

4. These rules may not be altered, amended, or repealed.

Under these circumstances, the taxpayer who created the charitable lead trust retained no interest in the trust or any right to control its distributions. Accordingly, no portion of the trust will be included in her estate for federal estate tax purposes.

[E] Use of Charitable Lead Trust to Transfer Family Assets to Children and Grandchildren

Often clients describe their estate planning objectives in general, somewhat vague terms. One common example of this is the desire often expressed by individuals who wish to leave their principal holdings (such as real estate or family

---

[46] 5 Ct. Cl. 362 (1984).

business interests) to their children or grandchildren, make some provisions for charity, and do all this at the lowest possible estate tax cost. Often a charitable lead trust and a family foundation together can help achieve such goals.

We have seen how the charitable lead trust can reduce estate tax costs by interposing a charitable term interest between the estate of the older generation members and their children or grandchildren. This alone can accomplish much of the stated goal, except perhaps for the desire that the family's principal holdings go to children and grandchildren. The family beneficiaries of a charitable lead trust do not receive their remainder distributions for a number of years, and this may not satisfy the older generation's desire that business or real estate holdings pass directly to their offspring.

On first examination, these goals appear to create an irreconcilable conflict, one that will require the family to compromise on one point or another. After all, to leave the assets in question to family members will result in an estate tax burden, while leaving them to the charitable lead trust may require the family to wait for decades before receiving the assets. These seemingly inconsistent objectives may be reconciled in a single, multipart transaction if the family finds the necessary terms acceptable.

In a nutshell, the older generation's objectives may be met by arranging a sale of the target holdings by the estate of the older generation members to the children or grandchildren, in exchange for their personal notes. Thereafter, these notes will form the corpus of the charitable lead trust, so that amounts paid by the children or grandchildren as obligors on the notes will eventually be returned to them in their capacity as remainder beneficiaries of the charitable lead trust.

Normally, an arrangement of this sort would be impossible. The charitable lead trust is treated as a private foundation for purposes of several of the private foundation restrictions, including the prohibition on self-dealing. Accordingly, the sale of assets otherwise destined for the foundation by the estate to disqualified persons would be prohibited as an indirect act of self-dealing. Moreover, the holding of children's or grandchildren's notes by the charitable lead trust would be an extension of credit that would likewise violate the self-dealing rules. However, the Regulations under the self-dealing provisions include a specific exception that facilitates transactions of this type.

The Regulations provide a specific exception to the self-dealing rules for various types of transactions that arise during the administration of an estate (or a revocable trust).[47] Under this exception, certain transactions affecting a foundation's interest or expectancy in property held by an estate or revocable trust will not be classified as acts of self-dealing, provided the following tests are met:

1. The administrator or executor of the estate (or trustee of the revocable trust) possesses a power of sale with respect to the property, has the power to reallocate the property to another beneficiary, or is required to

---

[47] *See* Reg. § 53.4941(d)-1(b)(3).

sell the property under the terms of an option subject to which the property was acquired by the estate or revocable trust;

2. The transaction is approved by the appropriate court (either the probate court having jurisdiction over the estate or another court having jurisdiction over the estate or trust or over the foundation);

3. The transaction occurs before the estate is considered terminated for federal income tax purposes (or, in the case of a revocable trust, before it becomes a split-interest trust);

4. The amount to be received by the estate or trust equals or exceeds the fair market value of the foundation's interest or expectancy in such property at the time of the transaction, taking into account the terms of any option subject to which the property was acquired by the estate or trust; and

5. The transaction (a) results in the foundation receiving an interest or expectancy at least as liquid as the one it gave up, (b) results in the foundation receiving an asset related to the active carrying out of its exempt purposes, or (c) is required under the terms of an option that is binding on the estate or trust.[48]

A person who has created a foundation may arrange his or her estate to take advantage of this rule. The founder's will might leave the residue of his or her estate to a charitable lead trust providing distributions to the family foundation for a period of years, with the remainder to the heirs. A separate provision, either in the will or elsewhere, could give the heirs (who are disqualified persons) an option to acquire the founder's business holdings, real estate, or other assets, which would otherwise pass to the foundation. After the founder's death, the executor of the estate can sell the property in question to the heirs pursuant to the option, carefully adhering to all the terms of this exception. The heirs thus end up holding the property, while the foundation holds an equivalent value in the form of the sale proceeds.

Moreover, if the parties comply with this exception, the exemption from self-dealing applies not only to the sale of the assets in question, but also to any extension of credit involved.[49] Thus, in the preceding example, the heirs could purchase the property in question from the estate by giving their personal notes as part of the consideration paid. These notes would be distributed to and held by the foundation. Although such an extension of credit would normally be a separate act of self-dealing, the foundation's holding of the notes during their term and receipt of payments under the notes are exempt from self-dealing under this exception.[50]

---

[48] The last requirement, in item 5, applies only with respect to transactions occurring after April 16, 1973.

[49] Reg. § 53.4941(d)-2(c)(1).

[50] *See* Priv. Ltr. Ruls. 9042030 and 9108024, approving such transactions under this exception.

Upon the termination of the trust, the notes would be distributed to the heirs as remainder beneficiaries of the trust.

[F] Generation-Skipping Transfer Tax

A special planning situation arises where grandchildren are, or may become, the remainder beneficiaries of a charitable lead trust. In addition to the gift tax and/or the estate tax, a separate transfer tax known as the tax on generation-skipping transfers (GST) may be imposed upon a trust, including a charitable lead trust,[51] which has grandchildren (or more remote descendants) among its beneficiaries. This tax applies in general whenever property is transferred to or for the benefit of someone more than one generation younger than the transferor of the property (referred to as a "skip person") or when an intervening interest in property terminates in favor of such a person. This tax is imposed at the top marginal estate tax rate in effect at the time of the generation-skipping transfer, so it must not be overlooked in planning a trust.

Neither the creation of a charitable lead trust nor distributions to its charitable beneficiaries is an act that will generate any GST tax. However, when the charitable interest in such a trust terminates, a GST tax may be imposed if trust corpus is then distributable to remainder beneficiaries who are grandchildren or other "skip persons" in relation to the donor of the lead trust. Although a GST exemption may be available to shield part or all of the remainder interest from GST tax, every donor should consider the potential impact of the GST tax. This is particularly true where grandchildren or other skip persons are intentionally designated to receive a trust interest, but the GST tax may be a factor even if skip persons are not the principal beneficiaries. Consider for example the situation where the grantor's daughter is named as remainderman of a charitable lead trust, but a grandson (the daughter's son) will succeed to the trust remainder if the daughter should die before the charitable interest expires; the GST tax would apply to this trust if the daughter should fail to survive until her share is distributable.

Under IRC § 2631, every individual is granted a $1,000,000 "GST exemption," which may be allocated to lifetime and/or testamentary transfers to exclude all or part of such transfers from GST tax.[52] Allocation of the donor's GST exemption to a charitable lead *unitrust* that will result in a generation-skipping transfer (i.e., where the remainder passes to grandchildren) is relatively simple: To avoid future GST tax, the donor may allocate (on a timely filed gift or estate tax return) a portion of his or her GST exemption equal to the value of his

---

[51] A complete discussion of the GST tax is beyond the scope of this book. For full details, *see* Price, John R., *Price on Contemporary Estate Planning*, Chapter 2, Part E (2d ed. Panel Publishers 2000) and IRC Chapter 13, §§ 2601-2663.

[52] This amount is indexed for post 1997 inflation. *See* IRC § 2631(c).

or her taxable transfer(s) to "skip persons," using the Service's valuation factors in effect as of the date the unitrust is created.[53]

Allocating the donor's GST exemption upon creation of a charitable lead *annuity* trust is less straightforward. IRC § 2642(e) imposes a special rule for determining the GST exclusion ration for charitable lead annuity trusts. In effect, this rule delays the GST determination until the expiration of the charitable term, but allows interest (at the rate used in valuing the charitable annuity) on the GST exclusion applied.

As a result, some planners favor the charitable lead unitrust for situations where the GST is seen as a major factor. With the unitrust format, the full $1,000,000 exemption can be applied at the outset, making the trust fully exempt from the GST, whereas a comparable charitable lead annuity trust may or may not be fully exempt, depending upon the actual trust corpus amount when the charitable term ends.

> **Example 1 [Unitrust]:** Madeleine transfers listed stocks worth $4,000,000 to a charitable lead unitrust. The terms of the trust call for payment of eight percent of trust assets (valued annually) to her family foundation each year for 20 years, and the trust assets remaining at the termination of the trust are to be distributed to Madeleine's grandchildren. Assuming an AFR of 6% for this trust, the charitable interest would be valued at approximately $3,167,200, leaving a remainder value of $832,800 subject to gift tax. When the remainder interest is distributed to Madeleine's grandchildren in 20 years, that transfer will be potentially subject to the GST tax, calculated at the maximum marginal estate tax rate then in effect.
>
> To prevent this result, Madeleine may allocate $832,800 of her $1,000,000 GST exemption to this trust on her gift tax return reporting this transfer. This will render the trust completely exempt from the GST tax, regardless of how much the overall trust value may increase.
>
> **Example 2 [Annuity Trust]:** Allison transfers listed stocks worth $4,000,000 to a charitable lead annuity trust. The terms of the trust call for payment of a $320,000 annuity to her family foundation each year for 20 years, and the trust assets remaining at the termination of the trust are to be distributed to Allison's grandchildren. Assuming an AFR of 6% for this trust, the charitable interest would be valued at approximately $3,670,368, leaving a remainder value of $329,632 subject to gift tax. When the remainder interest is distributed to Allison's grandchildren in 20 years, that transfer will be potentially subject to the GST tax, calculated at the maximum marginal estate tax rate then in effect.
>
> Allison might be able to prevent this result by allocating all or part of her $1,000,000 GST exemption to this trust, but the precise result will

---

[53] *See* IRC § 2642(a).

depend upon the amount of trust assets remaining when the trust terminates. Moreover, the GST result will not be known until that time. On her gift tax return reporting this transfer, Allison may allocate $329,632 of her GST exemption to this trust. When the trust terminates, GST tax may or may not be due. The exemption will render a portion of the trust exempt from GST tax. That portion consists of [1] the amount of GST exemption applied by Allison upon the creation of the trust ($329,632), plus [2] interest on that amount over the 20-year trust term at the 6% AFR rate used to value the trust for tax purposes ($727,542), for a total of $1,057,174. If the trust assets remaining at the end of the trust term are valued at $1,057,174 or less, the trust will be exempt and no GST tax will be due. On the other hand, if the trust assets amount to more than $1,057,174 only that portion will be exempt and any excess will be subject to GST tax.

Thus, if the investment performance of a charitable lead annuity trust exceeds the applicable AFR rate, a portion of the trust will be subjected to the GST tax. If the trust's growth is equal to or less than the AFR rate, no GST tax will be due. What if the donor allocates a portion of his or her GST exemption to a trust and this turns out to be more than was necessary to avoid GST tax? The Regulations provide, in Reg. § 26.2642-3(b), that no portion of the GST exemption allocated to the trust is restored to the grantor or the grantor's estate under these circumstances.[54]

Many clients decide that the certainty of the charitable lead unitrust makes that choice preferable to the charitable lead annuity trust for this application.

[G]   Charitable Lead Trusts — How Not to Do It

A 2003 private letter ruling provides a useful example of some of the problems one encounters in planning a charitable lead trust.[55] The taxpayer in Private Letter Ruling 200328030 set out to create a charitable lead unitrust. As demonstrated in "Example 1 [Unitrust]" above, such a trust can be quite useful in connection with a family foundation as a means of reducing or eliminating gift taxes, estate taxes, and especially generation-skipping transfer taxes. The taxpayer (T) proposed to create an irrevocable trust, with his three children as trustees. This trust was designed to pay five percent of its principal annually to a family foundation for 20 years, at which time the remaining trust assets would be distributed to an existing trust or to T's surviving family members. T retained the right to amend or revoke any charitable beneficiary's share by adding or substituting other charities, and/or changing the shares of any charity.

---

[54] Reg. § 26.2642-3(b).
[55] Priv. Ltr. Rul. 200328030.

T's ruling request asked for several rulings. First, he asked for assurance that the trust would be treated as a charitable lead unitrust, would be considered a completed gift, and would qualify for a gift tax charitable deduction based upon the present value of the charitable lead unitrust payments. "No," said the IRS — wrong on all three points. Why? Because T's right to change the charitable beneficiaries of the trust rendered the gift to the trust an incomplete transfer. Consequently, there can be no gift tax charitable deduction, since there is no potentially taxable transfer.

Second, T asked for a ruling that the trust would not be included in his gross estate (for federal estate tax purposes) upon his death. Same answer — no — for the same reason. T's rights to change the charitable beneficiaries, and to add or substitute other charities, fall squarely within the reach of both IRC §§ 2036(a) and 2038(a)(1). Therefore, the trust property would be included in T's estate, should he die before the trust terminates.

Next issue — T hoped the trust would not be considered a grantor trust for income tax purposes, so that no portion of the trust income would be taxable to him. On this point, the IRS said, "we'll see about that later" — while nothing in the trust itself suggested that the trust would be a grantor trust, that issue would really be decided by the actual operation of the trust, so this would be determined later, if and when the trust is audited. In particular, the IRS noted that IRC § 675 would tax the grantor on trust income if under the terms of the trust agreement or the circumstances surrounding its operation administrative control is exercisable primarily for the benefit of the grantor rather than the trust beneficiaries. While the trust instrument did not appear to violate this rule, it remained to be seen how the trust would be operated. (T's retained power to change beneficiaries also had the potential to make trust income taxable to him, but there is a specific exception for a power to change *charitable* beneficiaries — see IRC § 674(b)(4).)

So far, T is 0 for 3. Readers who always favor the underdog will be glad to learn that T did get a favorable ruling on his last request — that the trust would be entitled to an annual charitable deduction for the income paid each year to charity.

One other point is always worth reviewing when speaking of a charitable lead trust making distributions to a private foundation. If the person creating the charitable lead trust controls the foundation or its distributions, the trust will be included in his or her estate for estate tax purposes even if the creator does not retain direct controls of the sort T retained in this ruling.[56] Private Letter Ruling 200328030 does not indicate whether T controlled the foundation. Chances are the IRS would have ruled the same way if the trust paid the income to the foundation and T did not have any ability to change the beneficiary but was in control of determining which charities would receive distributions from the foundation.

---

[56] *See* the discussion of *Rifkind v. United States* at § 4.03[D], N. 46 *supra*.

Note the practical problem created for T here. If he had already funded this irrevocable trust, the amount in the trust would be beyond his reach, even though his power to select and change beneficiaries rendered the trust includible in his estate for estate tax purposes. At that point, with T deceased, the trust would presumably qualify for an estate tax charitable deduction. That is good news, of course, but not as good as it might seem. The charitable deduction allowable for estate tax purposes would equal the value of the charitable interest in the trust. In the natural order of things, that value is at its highest for a charitable lead trust at the outset, when the trust is created. It goes down over the life of the trust. After 19 years, for example, T's trust would have only one year of charitable distributions left. Accordingly, its current value at that time would be minimal. Thus, if T should die at that point, almost all of the assets in the trust would be subject to estate tax. That is bad news for T and his estate plan, especially if the estate tax savings from this trust formed an important factor in his overall estate plan.

Retaining the right to control distributions from a charitable lead trust can be an important factor for many people, but this must not be undertaken in a vacuum. It is important for the grantor's entire planning team to be in on the planning. What factors are important to this client? Is the potential estate tax savings the most important element? If so, the client may be well advised to forgo the satisfaction to be gained from controlling trust distributions. On the other hand, if control over such distributions is the critical consideration, the client may want to go forward irrespective of the estate tax problems. In most cases, this is the client's call and not something that the planner should decide.

CHAPTER 5

DESIGNING THE FAMILY FOUNDATION

§ 5.01 INTRODUCTION

One of the real strengths of the family foundation is that it can be structured to meet the goals of the donor who designs it. These goals are as diverse as the individuals who create foundations. The donor may want to distribute all of the foundation assets within a set number of years or to establish a perpetual source of funding for favorite charities. The donor may want to establish a perpetual reminder of the family's generosity by incorporating the family name in the foundation's identity or to use a non-family name to preserve anonymity for its gifts. The donor may structure the foundation to allow distributions to a broad field of nonprofit organizations or to limit distributions by specific organization, geography, or purpose. All of these options are appropriate and allowable under current law.

In fact, if the donor does not have rather specific goals in establishing the foundation, he or she should consider simpler options, such as an advised fund at a community foundation.[1] Private foundations are burdened with enough penalties; the donor should not struggle with these unless there is a need for more control.

Unfortunately, some donors create foundations without giving thought to the way the organization will operate and without appreciating the impact that a carefully managed foundation can have on the community. These donors may assume that managing a foundation is no different than managing decisions relating to annual charitable gifts. In doing so, the foundation loses some of the power and impact that may be achieved through better planning.

This chapter sets forth a system or process for the creation and design of the foundation, drawing on successful models found in the corporate and public foundation field. Some donors may choose private foundations because they want to control the foundation without a governance process. This is a mistake. Using a governance process will guide the donor and his or her family through the task of setting goals, articulating the mission, operating the foundation, and keeping the foundation on track long term.

§ 5.02 A BASIC TRUTH: THE FOUNDATION IS A SEPARATE LEGAL ENTITY

[A] A New Nonprofit Citizen

A family foundation is a separate legal entity that must function effectively and efficiently on its own. There are several reasons why sound operation is important:

- The family foundation is a unique charitable giving arm of the family, reflecting its values and priorities. It is difficult to reach consensus and reflect those values without a mechanism for making decisions and resolving conflicts;

---

[1] *See* Chapter 2 for a detailed discussion of alternatives to a foundation.

- The board of the foundation has a fiduciary duty to operate that organization in compliance with state and federal laws. The rules of operation are not intuitive and require both knowledge and structure for proper navigation;

- The potential penalties for the foundation and the individuals who manage it are great. Sound foundation design will protect the foundation assets and managers from costly lawsuits and excise taxes.

Family foundation structure, therefore, reflects a unique combination of personal goals, family values, and legal principals. An excellent, example of standards to guide a foundation can be found in the Council on Foundation's Committee on Family Foundations Stewardship Principles for Family Foundations adopted in September 2004, provided in full at Appendix 5-A.

[B] Form and Function

The foundation is created in one of two ways: as a nonprofit corporation or as a nonprofit trust. Both forms can qualify as private foundations as long as the organizing documents incorporate the critical rules discussed in detail in Chapters 6 (Operating Restrictions) and 7 (Grantmaking). The advantages and disadvantages of these forms and the organizational requirements are discussed in detail in Chapter 3. This chapter addresses the more practical issues related to operating the foundation once it is established.

[1] The Bylaws

The bylaws provide the road map for the governance of the foundation. Bylaws are standard documents generally created at the inception of the foundation. Take the time to review these prior to adoption to ensure that your foundation is set up to operate effectively and in a way that accommodates the donor's goals in establishing the foundation. The bylaws generally contain the elements discussed below and should be reviewed on an annual basis to ensure they reflect the appropriate structure. Always check state law to identify and include provisions required by state law.

[a] Location of Offices

The bylaws specify the state, county, and city in which the foundation maintains its principal office. (This is also required for the articles of incorporation when the foundation is a corporation, but may be restated here.)

[b] Registered Agent

The foundation board must designate a registered agent or foundation representative for the purpose of service of process or other legal communications. (This is required for the articles of incorporation when the foundation is a corporation, but may be restated in the bylaws.)

[c] Board of Directors

The bylaws set out the general powers of the board; the number, tenure, and qualification of board members; the manner in which those members are elected (including the nominating committee process); and the manner in which vacancies are filled. The bylaws also set out the meeting schedule, the requirement for meeting notices, the standard for a quorum, the voting requirements, the manner of taking informal actions, and the procedure for dissent from an action. If ex officio members are to be named (such as the founder or the executive director), this provision is included.

The practical issues related to board selection, board diversification, terms of office, and options such as junior boards are discussed in detail later in this chapter. The board structure and operation are critical to the successful operation of the family foundation. Take the time to consider the issues carefully then incorporate those decisions in the bylaws.

[d] Committee Structure

The bylaws establish the standing committees of the board. These committees, discussed in section 5.06, may vary depending upon the size and focus of the foundation. Do not feel compelled to establish a committee that is not needed in the operation of the foundation.

Always provide for the creation of ad hoc committees. The foundation president may need to appoint committees for a limited purpose, such as preparing a strategic plan, developing a grant format, or carrying out some other periodic function.

[e] Officers and Agents

The bylaws should establish the number and titles of the permanent officers of the foundation, such as the president, vice-president, treasurer, secretary, and others. In addition, the document should describe the manner of electing officers, removal from office, terms of office, and the manner of filling vacancies. The duties of each officer are also detailed, including the authority to bind the foundation and to preside at meetings (succession in the event that the president does not attend), as are any limitations of power.

The foundation will need the ability to appoint agents to carry out duties in the name of the foundation or to conduct parts of the administrative process of the foundation. Normally, the bylaws delegate this power to the board, although the board may delegate this duty to the president or executive director (with approval by the board).

[f] Contracts, Loans, Checks, Deposits, Investments, and Expenses

The bylaws specify those officers that have the authority to bind the foundation and handle foundation assets relating to contracts, loans, checks, deposits, investments, and expenses. The foundation should specify the steps necessary to take on debt, list those with authority to handle assets, and state that no loans will be made to directors or officers.

[g] Fiscal Year

A foundation is allowed to select a fiscal or calendar tax year.[2] The bylaws set the tax year for the foundation; any change to the tax year must be approved by the board and then the Internal Revenue Service (IRS).

[h] Accounting Records and Annual Report

The bylaws simply establish the directive to maintain records of foundation activities. They may go further to name a specific officer with responsibility. If an annual report will be prepared, the bylaws may provide this directive, state the timing for the report, state who will receive the report, and name the person responsible for preparing the report.

[i] No Dividends to Individuals

Private foundations can be corporations (the most popular modern form) but may not pay dividends or profits of the corporation to or for individuals. In fact, most state non-profit corporation statutes require this language, and the entity's tax-exempt status will not be approved without this provision. Foundations may only make distributions for charitable purposes.

The foundation may, however, pay directors' fees or reasonable compensation to its directors, officers, and employees. It may also reimburse its directors, officers, and employees for reasonable expenses associated with the discharge of their foundation duties.[3]

---

[2] A full discussion of the advantages and disadvantages of this election can be found in Chapter 8.

[3] *See* Chapter 6 for more detail on compensation and expense reimbursement.

[j] Corporate Seal

A corporation generally maintains a corporate seal with its name, its state of incorporation, and the term "corporate seal." There is no requirement that the seal be specially created; a generic corporate seal with the term "corporate seal" will suffice. The seal is maintained by the secretary and is used to validate the signatures of the corporation's officers and employees.

[k] Method of Amending Bylaws

Bylaws for a nonprofit corporation are generally created when the articles of incorporation are drafted and adopted by the board in its first meeting. Bylaws for a foundation created in trust form are less common, but serve a similar purpose. The need for bylaws for a trust depends in large part on the detail provided in the governing trust document. Some trust documents provide extensive detail, especially as to the election of trustees, while others leave the operational details to the trustees or board. The bylaws represent a more flexible way to address governance issues, since bylaws can be changed through a vote of the board; trust documents almost always require a court proceeding for amendment. A sample set of bylaws is provided at Appendix 5-B.

The foundation's attorney should draft the bylaws for the foundation to ensure that all relevant requirements of the state's nonprofit corporation law are included. The founder and founder's family should be involved at the draft stage, however, to ensure that the result is practical and reflects the family's goals.

[2] Meeting Minutes

Although state law governs minimum meeting frequency for nonprofit corporations, the foundation is generally required to meet at least annually. As a practical matter, most foundations meet more frequently, on a semiannual or quarterly basis. The foundation secretary is normally responsible for recording and publishing (to the board) the minutes of these meetings.

The requirement to maintain minutes is one that is easily overlooked, especially when the parties to the meetings know each other well. It may seem foolish to record the discussions and actions at a family meeting. Minutes are important, however, for the following reasons:

- Minutes record and make official the actions of the board. These actions include adoption of bylaws, changes to bylaws, election of board members (giving them the authority to make decisions on behalf of the foundation), election of officers (giving them the authority to bind the foundation in transactions), decisions on grants, and oversight of grants;

- Minutes protect the board members and officers in the discharge of their duties. The minutes provide evidence of the authority given to, or approval of the acts of, the directors. They also provide testament to the careful exercise of fiduciary duty;

- Minutes help the memory-challenged members of the group recall decisions. A written record is useful in remembering events, conversations, or the resolution of issues through a deliberative process;

- Minutes prove compliance with operational requirements, showing that the foundation conducted regular meetings, elected officers and directors, and took other actions as required by law;

- Minutes provide future generations with a history of the foundation. Details on the purpose of the foundation, its grantmaking history, its grantmaking goals, and the roles of various family members make it easier to assemble an accurate record.

Minutes may be formal or casual, as suits the style of the secretary and the directives of the president, so long as they are clear and complete. A sample set of minutes for a family foundation meeting and a sample corporate resolution based on action taken by the board are provided at Appendix 5-C.[4]

[a] Keeping Your Minutes Private

Minutes seldom make for exciting or provocative reading. However, this is not *always* the case. Some material in the minutes or accompanying documents may be embarrassing at a minimum, and could even be potentially harmful to the foundation's interests. Consider, for example, that a proposed grant may be refused for reasons that include awkward or embarrassing personal opinions, or that background materials may relate to negotiations with potential buyers or sellers, or employees who are to be discharged. A board member who initiates, or opposes, a particular action may not wish to see that position reported in the local newspapers.

A 2002 Ohio case reminds us that the minutes of a private organization (such as a family foundation) can become available to the general public if proper precautions are not observed. As a general matter, corporate records, including minutes of board meetings, are private documents that are not required to be given out to just anyone who asks to see them. This is a rare bit of privacy for family foundations, which are required by law to disclose to the public a number of what might otherwise be considered private documents — things like tax returns, donor information, and IRS exemption applications. But if the foundation is not careful, its private documents may become public information.

---

[4] For a more detailed discussion of the protection afforded by minutes and the process of taking and preserving minutes, *see* § 8.02[B] *infra.*

In the case in question, *State of Ohio ex rel. Hunter v. City of Alliance*,[5] a nonprofit hospital in Ohio included among the members of its board of directors the mayor of the local community. When the hospital became involved in litigation concerning the use of the city's eminent domain power to condemn property for a new hospital, the opposing parties requested (pursuant to court discovery proceedings) that the mayor produce copies of various documents, including minutes of board meetings, "including all information, documents and reports submitted to the Board members" and all correspondence directed to the mayor or other city officials from the hospital. The mayor resisted, on grounds that (1) as a board member she had no responsibility to maintain such records, and (2) she had taken most of the requested documents home and shredded them.

The court specifically held that the minutes delivered to the mayor in her official capacity were public records subject to disclosure under Ohio law and imposed monetary penalties ($1,000 for each such public record she had destroyed).

That case did not, of course, involve a foundation. Nevertheless, a family foundation that has a public official of any sort serving as a director or trustee should take steps to ensure that his or her service to the foundation is separate from the public duties of his or her office. Be careful to use the official's home address on all correspondence, especially when minutes or other potentially sensitive documents are sent. If this is impractical for any reason, be sure to review what is sent and delete or redact any sensitive or potentially embarrassing information. Otherwise, items sent to the official's office address might become a part of the public records, like the materials in the Ohio case described above.

Even if the foundation does not have a public official on its board, it may have correspondence or other dealings with such an official. This may be as simple as the condemnation proceedings involved in the Ohio case above or may involve expressions of opinion on issues considered by a school board, a county council, or a state historical commission. State and local laws vary insofar as they require disclosure of official communications with such bodies, and the foundation should take steps to be sure it isn't left open to criticism or embarrassment. In this connection as well, any materials sent to a public official or quasi-governmental body should be reviewed from the standpoint of whether the foundation would want to see the contents revealed to the public, the press, or its local critics.

[3] Making Changes When Required

Bylaws establish the governance procedures for the foundation, but are meant to be reviewed and changed when necessary. They should be reviewed at least annually, and those elements that are not practical or effective should be

---

[5] 2002 Ohio 1130, 2002 Ohio App. LEXIS 1134 (Mar. 11, 2002).

changed. The bylaws will be most helpful if they are used, rather than gathering dust like many legal documents.

§ 5.03   PROVIDING FOCUS WITH A MISSION STATEMENT

[A]   The Mission Statement

Mission statements are an important part of the corporate environment and are increasingly evident in the nonprofit sector. A mission statement allows a family foundation to focus its grantmaking activities, to communicate the foundation's role in and to the community, and to make the case for support to potential donors within the family.

[1]   Why Draft a Mission Statement?

Families are made up of individuals representing a diverse group of interests. Some come to the table with focused philanthropic interests, while others understand little about charitable giving. The older generation may favor arts, education, and domestic welfare, while the younger generation may focus on global issues, environmental causes, and health issues. This diversity of interests can add strength to the foundation's giving programs, or it can create conflict. When left unfocused, the foundation may distribute funds to so many causes that the impact of smaller grants spread among many causes will be minimal.

Foundations are also besieged with requests for funds from individuals and organizations. The mission statement offers a way to broadcast the goals, limits, and attitude of the foundation board. A clearly worded statement should not only diminish the quantity and improve the quality of the unsolicited applications for grants, but may also inspire responses to targeted needs by clearly identifying the foundation's funding priorities.

Finally, family foundations can and should solicit contributions from the family members on the board and those sharing similar interests. A board member or family member who contributes is far more interested in monitoring outcomes and results. However, that individual is less likely to contribute when the long-term use of those funds is unclear.

[2]   Preparing to Draft the Mission Statement

Writing a mission statement is not easy. The best approach is to gather the board members in a strategic planning session and to prepare them before they begin. One way to prepare the group is to send them a questionnaire before the session that asks them to provide answers to the following questions. This questionnaire should be designed to provoke thought on the mission of the foundation as well as to help the board member articulate priorities and goals of the foundation.

- What is your personal vision for the long-term goals or objectives of the foundation?

- What are the funding priorities for the foundation? Should the foundation make grants to all charitable organizations, or should grants be focused on health care, religion, education, etc.?

- What is the appropriate geographic scope for the foundation? Should the foundation focus its grantmaking in the city, county, or state, or domestically? Can qualified international organizations apply for funds?

- What is the appropriate funding philosophy for grants? Should the foundation seek to augment current projects or get involved only where foundation funds make a project possible?

- What type of grants should the foundation make? Will the grants cover nonprofit operating overhead or be restricted to capital, start-up, or one-time projects? Will it make one-time or multiyear grants?[6]

- How much money should the foundation distribute?

- How will the foundation grow? Should the family members focus personal giving through the foundation?

Once the board members have completed the work, bring them together, and ask them to share the answers to each question out loud. Sharing the information as a part of the process is an effective way to make sure that all of the participants understand the vision and goals of other participants. Groups that know each other well, especially families, may assume that they know how other members of the family feel about issues when, in fact, those family members have very different opinions or priorities. Once the issues are on the table, the group can identify the key issues and reach consensus on the goals and mission of the foundation.

Use a facilitator to help manage this discussion. The facilitator should be from a firm or company outside the board so that observations about the organization can be offered without concern for political or personal connections. Experienced facilitators can be found in strategic planning firms, in some consulting firms that work with nonprofit organizations, or on the faculty of a local university.

---

[6] *See* Chapter 8 for a detailed discussion of writing grantmaking policy. The group should reach a basic consensus about the overall goals in distributing funds from the foundation.

[3]   Drafting the Mission Statement

Once the board has reached general agreement about the foundation's mission, the mission should be reduced to a clear, concise statement. Whether simple or eloquent, it should be easily understood by the board and provide guidance for decision making in awarding grants. The statement should also be easily understood and interpreted by the public.

Consider the following examples of simple mission statements:

The mission of the Miree Family Foundation is to improve the quality of health care of the citizens of the state of Alabama through grant partnerships to initiate health care facilities, to foster education, and to expand health care access for all citizens.

The McCoy Family Foundation believes in the obligation of the private sector to address community needs and is dedicated to funding qualified arts, education, health, religious, and social welfare organizations in the greater Washington, D.C. area.

It is important to note that the mission of a family foundation may change over time. The family foundation is generally a private foundation, meaning that the foundation is funded from a single source, rather than public sources. The founder may or may not be open to input on the personal goals that led him or her to make that decision. As noted earlier, some founders create a foundation for the specific purpose of teaching family members about philanthropy, while others have a particular philanthropic cause or goal in mind. Early mission statements may reflect the founder's philosophy. As younger generations gain control, this focus may change. Therefore, the mission statement should be reviewed at least every two to three years to ensure that it still reflects the guiding principles of the foundation.

Larger and more mature foundations may want to develop a mission statement as part of a strategic planning process. As the foundation moves through generations and family members drift geographically, politically, and personally, a strategic planning process provides a formal platform from which to focus on the basics. These basics include long-term goals, grantmaking philosophies, opportunities, challenges (including family structure), and method of operation. Mission statements are more easily written when significant time has been devoted to these issues.

[B]   The Strategic Planning Session

Strategic planning, one of the most important tools for effectiveness in the corporate world, is rapidly gaining importance in the nonprofit sector. As charities struggle to survive the current economy, build contributions, replace diminishing government support, and comply with new administrative requirements, the strategic plan has been the tool many use to strengthen mission focus and more effectively communicate that mission to the public. For many non-profits, the results have made the difference between survival and obsolescence.

While a family foundation may not face all of the service and contribution-related challenges experienced by a public charity, it has its own tactical hurdles. The foundation must establish a grantmaking focus, create policies that support and promote that focus, manage operational risk and administration, and incorporate family objectives in the foundation's mission. Strategic planning is not a one-time need — the discipline is required throughout the foundation's history: when it is created; when the board revisits the foundation mission and grantmaking goals; and when staff develops the annual budget and work plan.

[1] Goals of Family Foundation Strategic Planning

Strategic planning is designed to promote focus on the foundation's current activities and position the organization for future challenges. While some elements of strategic planning are common to all organizations, for family foundations, this planning must incorporate several unique elements.

- *Clarification of the foundation's mission and purpose.* The foundation should review its current mission statement, its organizing documents, the early minutes of the foundation, and its current operational focus. Is its mission statement clear? Does it accurately reflect the goals of the board and organization? Do the foundation's grantmaking policies and practices reflect that mission?

- *Examination of the most effective way to achieve the foundation's mission.* This step involves identifying needs in the foundation's service area, setting goals that address those needs, and establishing clear steps to achieve those goals.

- *Analysis of current resource use — staff, funding, and assets — to determine if those resources are being used effectively.* In some instances, the foundation may hire internal staff or purchase software that allows it to conduct its own grant review, site visits, project evaluation, and daily administration. In other cases, it may be more cost effective and practical to hire third parties to perform these services. It is easy to simply repeat each year's activities. It is much harder to raise questions about whether past practices should be discontinued and new ones initiated.

- *Review the foundation's form.* Private foundations have always (or at least since 1969) suffered from more onerous administrative requirements than public charities. Current proposed legislation would impose additional requirements on foundations, disallowing treatment of certain administrative expenses as charitable distributions and requiring those expense amounts to be replaced by direct grants to charitable organizations. In addition, the administrative requirements imposed by Executive Order 13224 and the Patriot Act put a strain on small foundations with a small compliance budget. The foundation may want to consider converting to a supporting organization or transferring its assets (within legally proscribed guidelines) to a donor-advised fund to eliminate those requirements unique to private charities.

- *Analysis of the foundation's governance structure.* Family foundations are designed to involve family members and promote family values. Examine the family representation on the board, especially if the family has entered its second or third generation since creation. Does the board appropriately reflect the current family structure? It may be time to revise the bylaws to afford equal representation to family branches, and to encourage participation by younger generations.

- *Consensus building among stakeholders — on goals, objectives, and the time-lines required to achieve those goals.* Strategic planning allows everyone involved in setting foundation policy to use the same facts, figures, and factors to make decisions, and to reach agreement about direction and priorities. This is particularly important in engaging lower family generations in the foundation's decisionmaking and grantmaking.

- *Create a vision of the organization's role and impact in the future.* Family foundations generally have two purposes: to advance the family's charitable mission and to engage and teach family members about philanthropy. Since each family has unique goals, achieving those goals requires planning and preparation.

- *Effectively communicate the organization's role to the public.* Public communication is often far down the list of priorities for family foundations. However, the public's perception of foundations would be greatly enhanced through this effort. Look for ways to make the foundation more visible. Share information about the foundation's operation, grantmaking, and assets to encourage the public to follow its charitable lead.

[2] Getting Help from a Consultant

[a] *How to Effectively Recruit a Third-Party Advisor*

Effective strategic planning requires finesse and is best handled by an experienced consultant. Begin the search by establishing the goals of the process; clearly articulate what the group hopes to achieve in the process. Next, prioritize those goals. For example, a foundation may want to focus its grantmaking, determine whether it needs internal staff or third-party services, and design a governance process that allows younger generations to begin to participate in foundation management. However, its primary goal may be to resolve the governance issues. Finally, reduce these goals and priorities to writing, share them with prospective consultants when searching, and keep them in front of the search committee when evaluating firms.

Next, determine who will participate in the strategic planning process, where those individuals reside, and an anticipated timetable for completion. Determine the product outcome. Do you want a formal strategic plan? Do you need a detailed workplan and budget?

Incorporate these goals, the timeline, and the expected outcomes in a Request for Proposal (RFP). Send the RFP to planners recommended by colleagues, local nonprofit trade organizations (such as the local Nonprofit Resource Center), or national or regional trade organizations (such as the Council on Foundations, the Association of Small Foundations, or the Southeastern Council of Foundations). Describe the essential elements of the proposal. For example, you might ask all applicants to provide:

- A brief description of the firm, including its history, its client base, and its principals;

- A biography of the firm members who will handle the work, including their experience in nonprofit strategic planning;

- The firm's experience working with family foundations;

- A description of the firm's strategic planning philosophy and practice;

- A timetable, including the number of meetings involved in the process;

- The cost for facilitating the process and producing the desired products at its conclusion;

- References from at least three nonprofits that can provide insight into the consultant's work style and success in planning (preferably family foundations); and

- Any other information relevant to the planning process.

Include a deadline for submission of the proposal with the RFP, provide an address for delivery (including electronic delivery, if acceptable), and specify the number of copies required.

[b] Selecting the Winning Bid

Once the proposals have been submitted, select the two or three proposals that best meet the foundation's needs. Invite these individuals to make a personal presentation to the selection committee. As you evaluate the candidates, look for the following qualities:

- *Experience with family foundations.* Family foundations are unique because of the human dynamics of the closely related individuals and the very personal goals of the family unit. The facilitator should understand family foundations and how they operate and be familiar with trends in the industry;

- *Training in conflict management.* A good strategic planning process encourages everyone to engage in discussion of the foundation's core values and objectives. While this does not always involve conflict, problems are more likely unless there are established ground rules and someone to monitor the process;

- *Proficiency in nonprofit strategic planning.* While the principles of corporate planning have value for charities, the nonprofit's philanthropic mission makes it distinctly different. Family foundations, especially those staffed primarily by families, are even further removed from the corporate structure. Understanding the basic principles and distinctions is important;

- *A reputation as an innovative and creative thinker.* A good planner is flexible, not formula driven. Each family is comprised of a unique blend of personalities, goals, and personal residences. The planner must help the family set goals and create a work plan fitting those factors;

- *Command the respect of all generations.* Many families engage in planning to bridge the gap between generations and find a role for younger family members. If so, it may be best to use a planner unassociated with any family member (such as the senior generation's internal corporate planner). Include representatives of each active generation on the consultant search committee to give everyone a voice;

- *A personality and work style compatible with the family.* A consultant can be nationally recognized and an established author, but if he or she does not communicate well with the family, the planning will not be effective. It is important to meet with the consultant before hiring to ensure compatibility.

Select the individual or firm that meets the foundation's requirements, has the strongest recommendations, and best fits the style of the key players. Devoting this much time and planning to consultant selection may seem burdensome, but it dramatically improves the chances that the foundation will select the right firm.

[3] The Follow-through

Once the consultant has been selected, the work is just getting started. Set aside enough time to fully engage in the planning process. Involve as many of the key family members, board members, and other community stakeholders as possible. Those involved in planning will have more incentive to ensure that the plans become reality. Develop a formal work plan following the planning to record the group's conclusions and plans.

Use the work plan and goals to measure the foundation's success. Bring the plan to the table at every board meeting to measure progress against stated goals. Periodically — every year or two — revisit the plan in a mini-planning process. If the initial planning process was successful, use the planning firm to take the board through a review of the plan and update it as necessary. Regardless of the success of a single planning meeting, family needs and goals will change over time, just as changes in the legislative and regulatory environment may compel the foundation to make changes.

§ 5.04 BOARD MEMBERSHIP AND FUNCTION

The family foundation board should be constructed so as to operate effectively and efficiently to support the foundation's mission; the board should be trained to handle its fiduciary responsibilities, and the foundation should be structured and insured to provide protection from liability. Keep in mind that the members of the board, or the trustees, are responsible for oversight of foundation management. Establish policies to guide the distribution of cash from the foundation account, and consider an annual audit to review distribution and expenditure processes.

[A] The Role of the Family

The family is the heart of the family foundation. The family — or at least one or more members of the family — organized the foundation and established its charter and bylaws. More important, a family member contributed the funds for operation. The goal of creating a family foundation, as opposed to contributing to a public foundation, is to achieve a measure of control and involvement in the distribution process not possible with public foundations.

Family foundations may have a variety of purposes, all of which are personal to the founder. Some are established to teach younger generations the duties and responsibilities of contributing to philanthropy. Other motivations may include a preference for private direction of funds rather than the more public direction through tax payments, a desire to shelter the individual and the family from multiple requests for charitable gifts, and a wish to achieve prestige in the community through control of charitable dollars. In addition, the founder may use a family foundation to teach children about budgeting, responsible spending, investment management, and project management. The foundation is a platform from which all of these goals can be met.

[B] The Role of the Board

The duties and responsibilities of a board member in both management and legal terms are often underestimated. Those asked to serve in the role may assume their role is to supervise distributions of funds to charitable organizations. In fact, the board role is much broader. The foundation board has, at a minimum, the following 11 functional roles.[7]

---

[7] These functions are patterned on the roles set out in Ten Basic Responsibilities of Nonprofit Boards, published by Board Source, 1828 L Street, NW, Suite 900, Washington, DC 20036-5114, 202-452-6262, *www.boardsource.org.*

1. *Conduct the business of the foundation in accordance with the law.* A board member has a duty to comply with corporate law, state law, and federal law. This means that the individual must be familiar not only with the governing documents of the foundation, but also with the various requirements of the regulatory agencies providing oversight.

2. *Determine the mission of the foundation.* As previously discussed, the board is responsible for establishing and reviewing the organization's mission.

3. *Secure the staff to operate the foundation.* Many family foundations do not use professional help. Most of them should. The family members who are a part of the board are generally not qualified to operate the foundation. Foundation management requires education, training, experience, and time to handle daily activities.

   Some boards may obtain this expertise through use of professional advisors. Attorneys, accountants, trust officers, financial planners, and consultants have expertise in the rules and operating procedures required to meet the stringent IRS requirements for private foundations.

   Boards may also hire one or more employees with expertise to handle the daily operating duties. If the foundation is large, the board may decide to hire an executive director. That director is then responsible for hiring and firing the remainder of the staff. The size and activities of the foundation will determine the breadth of staff required, but ultimately the board is responsible for the result.

4. *Approve a budget for the foundation.* Managing a foundation costs money. The foundation's budget should include normal operating costs such as space, furniture, equipment, and utilities as well as staff, professional assistance, grants administration, and other costs. Foundation costs are closely scrutinized, and family foundations must be particularly aware of and sensitive to issues of self-dealing, discussed in more detail in Chapter 6. Finally, board members have a fiduciary duty to control and manage costs. A formal budget is appropriate even for less formal foundation operations.[8]

5. *Manage the finances and assets of the foundation.* The foundation's assets are its greatest resource and require careful management not only to ensure effective use of those assets, but also to meet state and federal fiduciary requirements. Drafting a budget and monitoring annual expenses are the first step in this process. Proper investment management is even more important. The foundation is advised to hire a professional asset manager, adopt investment management policies, and carefully monitor the results of the process.[9]

---

[8] See § 8.03 *infra* for detail on developing a budget.
[9] See § 8.06 *infra* for more information.

6. *Ensure that IRS operating requirements are met.* This book is testament to the extent and nature of the IRS requirements for operating a private foundation. The board is charged with the duty of ensuring compliance. Again, professional help and resources may be necessary to respond adequately.[10]

7. *Report to the IRS, the state attorney general (or other designated state authority), and the public about the foundation's activities in a timely and responsive manner.* Reporting duties are a part of the overall duty to meet IRS operating requirements, to account to state regulatory authorities, and to provide public accountability for charitable funds. Private foundations must make Form 990-PF and Form 1023 or Form 1024 available for public inspection, or provide copies of these documents, upon request.[11] Board members must be familiar with the details of the 990-PF in order to ensure that the filing is accurate.[12] Failure to comply can result in penalties.

8. *Set grantmaking policy for the foundation.* The board has the discretion and the duty to set grantmaking policy for the foundation. Foundations have limited funds to distribute. The more effective the policy, the more effective the grantmaking. These policies should reflect the mission and purposes of the foundation.[13]

9. *Review and make grants from the foundation.* Most board members embrace the role of reviewing and making grants from the foundation, mistaking it for the single greatest role. This role is the most public indication of the activities of the board and requires education, study, and review to make the most effective decisions.

10. *Oversee and audit those grants to ensure effectiveness and use of the funds for the purposes intended.* Making grants is only the first step in the giving process. Auditing or monitoring those grants adds to the educational level of the grantmaking board as well as enhancing the effectiveness of those grants. Charitable organizations that receive grants from the foundation should be asked to acknowledge that the funds were used for the specified purpose and report to the board on the effectiveness of the funds' use. The board should then evaluate the effectiveness of those grants by measuring actual outcomes against expected outcomes.

11. *Select and train replacements on the board to ensure ongoing leadership.* Family foundation boards, like all boards, benefit from turnover in leadership and membership. Rotation allows new perspective and energy to be introduced to the governance and grantmaking process. New board members

---

[10] *See* Chapter 6 and § 5.05[A][3] infra for a discussion of liability issues.

[11] IRC § 6104 and the regulations thereunder.

[12] *See* the discussion in Chapter 6 on the content of Form 990-PF and the discussion in Chapter 8 on reporting duties and the elements of the return.

[13] Chapter 7 provides detail on grantmaking.

should reflect the values and goals of the foundation, while adding depth in representation in the community or in the foundation's area of interest. New board members should be trained and oriented to their duties, the foundation history, its structure and management, and fiduciary responsibilities.[14]

These roles are substantive. Ensure that board members understand their roles. Do not waste the board members' time with minor administrative details. Keep them focused on these job functions, and make the time spent in work for the board productive.

[C] Selecting the Board

Selection of the board should be undertaken with the same care used in assembling any nonprofit board. This means you should use a process that allows you to establish the jobs of the board, to list the qualities needed to perform those jobs, and then to select individuals that can best fill those roles. It should make no difference that the majority of the positions may be filled by family. Using a process will allow you to clearly communicate the board roles to family and to fill other roles with the most valuable outsiders.

Membership on the family foundation board need not be restricted to family members. Representation beyond the family allows the foundation to draw on the knowledge and resources of the community and to enhance the effectiveness of its policy making, grantmaking, and public profile.

[1] Defining the Roles and Skills Needed on the Board

Begin by listing the roles of the board, drawing on the list detailed in the previous section. Add any roles to this list that are specific to your foundation. For example, if your foundation was established to take a key role in a community development project, you may need to add an individual who has access to local and state agencies. If your foundation was established to initiate change in the educational system, you may need to add an individual who is linked with community leadership or visible in this area.

Use a checklist of the personal characteristics that define effective board members. Consider the following items for that list:

- *Interest in and knowledge of the nonprofit sector.* They should have interest in and knowledge, especially the area or areas addressed by the foundation.

- *Availability to attend meetings.* Board members must be available to attend board meetings, committee meetings, on-site reviews, and other foundation activities.

---

[14] *See* § 5.07 *infra* for information on board training.

- *Commitment to participate.* Too often board members are recruited with the assurance that they will not have to participate unless convenient. This recruitment technique sends a message that the foundation activities are not important and the member's input is inconsequential.

- *Knowledge of a board member's legal and fiduciary duties.* This quality is best evidenced by active participation on the boards of other successful nonprofit organizations.

- *Ability to work with a group.* A good board member must work well with others and have the ability to articulate ideas, listen to other ideas, and compromise.

- *Motivation to participate.* This quality is critically important to involvement, even among family members. Motivational factors are difficult to assess, but have a powerful impact on the way in which the board member approaches the role. They may include altruism, personal interest in potential outcomes, self-esteem, personal growth, status, power, family pressure, or peer pressure. Some of these motivations are positive, while others have decidedly negative overtones. Look for the positive; avoid or work to overcome the negative.

Finally, make a more specific list of those characteristics that are specific to the success of your foundation. These should be functional skills, rather than personal character traits, and may include the following:

- *Leadership.* Boards without leadership breed frustration. There are few individuals with true leadership skills. A good board will have not only current leadership, but also future leadership in its membership, allowing effective transition from year to year. This happens by design rather than chance;

- *Financial skills.* Financial management skills can be found in a variety of professionals, ranging from accountants to attorneys to consultants. Anyone who has started and successfully run a company is also likely to have this focus and discipline. The foundation will generally have an accountant that prepares tax returns and balance sheets, but this professional service does not substitute for financial leadership on the board;

- *Organizational/strategic planning skills.* It is a great luxury to have a strategic planner on the board to lead the foundation through the steps of establishing a strategy and reexamining that strategy periodically. The foundation should develop a strategic plan when created and should update that plan every three to five years or as conditions change. If the foundation does not have a strategic planner as part of the board, hire a professional to conduct the planning sessions;

- *Staff evaluation skills.* Someone on the board must be responsible for hiring internal and external staff as well as managing and evaluating that staff. Some family foundations remain small and operate only with a secretary. Others hire a director, office staff, program staff, and occasionally fund-raisers. Where an executive director or CEO is hired, that person should hire, fire, and evaluate staff, and the board's role should be to hire, fire, and evaluate the CEO. Where a family member is serving in the chief executive role and does not possess those skills, someone on the board may need to fill that role;

- *Program evaluation skills.* The most important and consistently needed skills relate to program evaluation. The foundation will be presented with scores of grant applications. Many of these applications will address the same need in the community. The board will be most effective if it has the ability to evaluate programs and results so that it can direct foundation dollars to the most effective organization. Without these skills, judgment may be based on the number of phone calls received or the attractiveness of the grant proposal;

- *Contacts with people or organizations representing the foundation's interests.* Contacts within the nonprofit community add dimension to the evaluative nature of the grantmaking process. It is always helpful to have someone with knowledge of the nonprofit community served by the foundation on the board to provide insight and information. These contacts are particularly important when the foundation focuses on a single area, such as health care, education, religion, the environment, or any narrow charitable interest;

- *Program administration experience.* Having a board member experienced with private foundation management is a luxury. When a board is educated on the rules of administration, the list is daunting and difficult to understand out of context. Experience helps in the process of prioritizing concerns and addressing record keeping and decision making;

- *Contribution and potential contribution to the foundation.* It is likely that the founding contributor will remain as a member of the board for as long as the interest prevails. However, family foundations have a unique opportunity to cultivate younger generations of the family and to get them or keep them involved on the board. Family members that contribute to the foundation are far more likely to stay actively involved in the management of the foundation;

- *Political connections or community influence.* Some of the most effective grants are collaborative in nature. That is, the grant is made in combination with one or more other nonprofits and/or government agencies to achieve a particular goal. Recruiting a board member with those contacts may be an effective strategy, especially for small to midsize foundations that can provide more through leadership in initiating such a project than through money alone.

[2] The Selection Process

The selection process begins only after the foundation founder or the nominating committee has worked through the process of identifying the critical personal traits and the skills needed on the board. With those lists in hand, create a worksheet.

The left side of the worksheet should contain the functional skills required on the board. Under each skill, leave space for three to five names of individuals that possess this skill. List the personal traits needed for an effective board across the top of the worksheet. Each trait should be entered in a separate column with a box for a checkmark if applicable. A sample worksheet is provided in Appendix 5-D.

A group with an interest in the foundation, familiar with the family, knowledgeable of the foundation's goals, and with contacts in the community should then be assembled. This group may initially consist of the donor, key members of the donor's family, and advisors, or it may be a formal nominating committee, once the foundation is established. Begin by placing involved family members on the list under the various functional categories. Often philanthropically oriented families have great experience in the nonprofit sector and may professionally possess some of the required skills.

Nominees outside of the board (if desired) should then be added. Outside directors may be indicated when specific skill sets are needed that are not represented among the family. The total number of nominees should ideally be at least double the number of directors sought for the board to allow some discrimination in selection among the group. This list should also provide two to three choices in each of the functional categories. Make sure that this list remains confidential throughout the review and selection process.

Develop information on these candidates. Read the newspapers, talk with people who know the candidates, and observe them in action. This process takes time. It is important to take the time to do the work necessary to get the best candidates and to get insight into the new members of the board.

Once information on the candidates has been fully developed, move across the worksheet, checking each personal trait possessed by the nominees and totaling the checks on the far right. This system will allow the selection group to rate potential board members and enlist those members most qualified to do the job. In addition, selecting members from each of the functional skill groups creates a strong, diverse, and more successful board.

Make sure that the individual charged with recruiting the nominated board member asks the individual to join by making a personal visit if at all possible. If geography prevents a personal visit, schedule a phone call for that purpose. When recruiting a new board member, make sure that you:

1. *Make the case to the potential board member about why participation is valuable and important.* This requires that you understand possible motivations to participate and explain the role he or she will play on the foundation board;

2. *Explain the duties of board membership.* Use the list of duties developed in the board nominating process. Stress participation, involvement, and outcomes;

3. *Ask the new member to sign a conflict of interest statement.* While asking board members to sign conflict of interest statements should be standard procedure for nonprofit board recruitment, such a statement is especially important for family foundations. Private foundations have special rules related to conflict of interest, with excise taxes imposed on disqualified persons for engaging in self-dealing activities,[15] including substantial contributors to the foundation, foundation managers, and family members of substantial contributors or foundation managers. The excise tax applies both to the foundation and to the disqualified person violating the rule. The board member may knowingly or unknowingly make a decision that advances his or her own interests over those of the nonprofit. The easiest way to avoid this is to anticipate areas of conflict and to address potential conflicts before they occur. A sample conflict of interest statement is provided at Appendix 5-E.

[3] Size of the Board

The size of the board can expand beyond the statutory requirements of the state in which the corporation is organized to as large a group as is manageable. There is no right number that guarantees success. Rather, the size of the board is more a function of the jobs to be done and the practical issues of work and management. The most common factors indicating size include:

- *Practicality.* Committees should be established for work purposes. Committees are designed to accomplish detailed work in a group small enough to get the work done. By serving on a committee, members develop expertise in the area of work. Committees should not be established if there is no substantive work to be assigned to the group. Keep in mind that committees do not have to be permanent or standing committees. The newer model is to form committees for specific purposes, dissolving those committees when the work is done.[16] This model is more likely to focus the group on the task at hand;

- *Work to be done.* Look at the key tasks of the foundation. Managing the finances of the foundation is an example of ongoing work, as is managing the grants administration. Temporary committees may review the by-laws or engage in strategic planning to guide the future of the foundation;

- *Balance.* The family will normally want to ensure that the family maintains control of the foundation's governance, mission, and purpose. This balance becomes more difficult as the family descends through generations, so that not only are there more players, but also those players are more likely to

---

[15] *See* Chapter 6 for a detailed discussion of disqualified persons.

[16] *See* Barbara E. Taylor, Richard P. Chait, and Thomas P. Holland, *The New Work of the Nonprofit Board*, Harvard Business Review 36-46 (September-October 1996).

have diverse interests. Look ahead when establishing the foundation structure, creating by-laws to anticipate issues of balance of inside and outside directors as well as ways to maintain balance among family interests.

In a study of family foundations conducted by The Foundation Center based on 2004 data, family foundations reported a median number of three trustees/directors for foundations established since the 1970s, and a median number of seven trustees/directors for foundations established before 1940, indicating that family foundation boards increase over time.[17]

[4] Terms of Office

Terms of office should be structured to allow and encourage transition on the foundation board. This is true even when considering family foundations, especially when there are many family members to be included. For example, the by-laws may provide that directors serve three-year terms, but not more than two consecutive terms. In this example, a board member might serve for six years, take a year off, and return for another six years.

The foundation founder will want to maintain a permanent seat on the board and should be treated as an exception to this rule. One of the primary reasons for establishing a private foundation is to maintain control over the distribution of charitable dollars. Make provision for the founder in the bylaws, but encourage rotation of other members to the extent possible.

Rotation serves several purposes:

- Term limits allow the circulation of new people and, with them, new ideas and priorities;

- Term limits allow those without a real interest a graceful way to remove themselves from service;

- Term limits allow board members to focus during the board term, rest during the break, and renew enthusiasm when returning to the board;

- New members add to the dynamics of the decision making. Some individuals dominate a process, and a rotation that removes the dominators, allowing the addition of new ideas, may result in a more lively distribution and management process.

Some families may be so small that all family members wish to remain in ongoing roles. In this instance, terms are still recommended. However, the document may not limit the number of consecutive terms served.

---

[17] *Key Facts on Family Foundations, The Foundation* Center (January 2006), *http://fdncenter. org/research/trends_analysis/pdf/key_facts_fam.pdf.*

Another idea is to provide limits on service for directors outside the family, while leaving open the service period of family members. This mixed model allows for ongoing family involvement and the constant movement of new people and ideas through the board from outside directors.

[5] Succession Issues

Succession issues must be viewed on two levels. First, there is the structural issue. You must look at the organizing documents for the foundation to determine how and when succession is accomplished. Trust documents may specify how members are to be appointed. The process may be as simple as self-selection, meaning that the current members select new members by majority vote. Or the process may require appointment of members by outside entities or groups, with appointment or approval by a court of local jurisdiction. Ultimately, the court in the jurisdiction where the foundation's assets are located will have authority to act to appoint or replace board members by virtue of its equity jurisdiction over the foundation.

[6] The Need for Family Succession

The foundation grantor must prepare for succession from the outset. Family dynamics have considerable impact on the effectiveness of the foundation operation. Conflicts on a personal level find a way into the grantmaking or administrative process.

In addition, some family members are leaders, while others are followers. Some members live in a location allowing input, while others may be scattered across the country and may be less interested in the process. Identify family leaders who have the ability to build consensus and are inclusive, yet have the ability and responsibility to make decisions. Teach those potential successors how to manage the process, and ensure that the succession planning incorporates those individuals at an early stage so that there is time to learn the duties of management.

Sometimes a founder finds that few or none of the descendants are interested in or prepared to serve in a foundation leadership role. While most founders anticipate that children will want to assume the responsibility and control that come with the ability to distribute large sums of money for charitable causes, some may not. It may be necessary to reach outside the family to build future leadership.

The decision of how far to reach out in the family, and when to include outsiders in positions of leadership, is subjective. Newer and smaller foundations may focus strictly on family issues and the selection of the strongest or most representative family members to take on this role. More mature or larger foundations may also consider when and how to incorporate members outside the family. The point is that some decision about succession must be made, and the earlier the decision is made, the more likely it is that the family foundation will be able to carry on its mission without interruption or discord.

[7] Board Models

Corporate succession is generally directed by the nonprofit corporation's bylaws. Careful attention is generally given to this issue when drafting the foundation documents. There are several models for family control.

[a] Immediate Family Model

The most common form of family foundation is one consisting of immediate family members only. This foundation may have been created by the parents of the family with the hope of involving children as they matured. Board selection is a matter of choice of the founder, with children assuming more responsibility with experience.

[b] Extended Family Model

The extended family model for the family foundation may seek to include brothers, sisters, aunts, uncles, and other family members in a model that pools family resources for impact. This model has the advantage of depth of membership in the decision-making process, but may suffer from the variety of priorities expressed by multiple generations in an extended family.

[c] Family Plus Outside Experts Model

A family foundation that mixes outside experts who have an interest in and knowledge of the foundation's priorities with the immediate family represents the most effective model. It allows the family to control the seats on the board of directors and benefit from the knowledge and wisdom of experts in order to be more effective in the grantmaking process.

These outsiders need not be paid for their time, although sometimes that is appropriate if the individual is a recognized expert who spends quantitative and qualitative time on the foundation's behalf. It is also possible to recruit volunteers for this role, especially where those volunteers are passionate about the foundation's area of expertise. Make the outside board member's role clear at the outset.

[d] The Junior Board

One common goal of a family foundation creator is to establish a mechanism to involve younger generations in philanthropy through the use of a junior board of the foundation. A junior board allows children to get involved in the work of the foundation at an early age. Junior board members generally have a limited, nonvoting role that allows them to learn more about making grant decisions. It works best for minors — generally ages 10 through 21 — who likely have no authority to act as directors or trustees under state law. This early involvement generally leads to a lifelong interest in the foundation and its operation.

Children easily learn the lessons of the for-profit world. They receive an allowance and learn to distinguish among computer games, music CDs, and other items on the lengthy list of "must have" items. They learn these lessons by participating in the purchasing process. The junior board affords these children the same opportunities to learn about the nonprofit sector through participation in the grantmaking process.

In most models, the junior board members are given a specific sum over which they have advisory power. Each child is asked to identify one or more areas of charitable interest and then must find two or three charities representing each of these areas. Adult involvement is recommended to explain the concept of charitable assistance, the areas of charitable interest, and familiar organizations that meet those needs.

The next step is research. Junior board members can use the Internet, the library, the phone, or personal visits to develop more information about each charity. Finally, the junior board makes a decision and recommendation to the foundation's governing board for approval and distribution.

This concept is flexible and easily incorporated into the foundation's bylaws. If the foundation structure cannot accommodate a junior board for any reason, the same principles are also easily transferred to a family-advised fund in which specific funds are set aside for younger generations, or even annual giving by the family outside of a foundation or advised fund structure.

§ 5.05   PROTECTING THE FOUNDATION AND THE BOARD FROM LIABILITY

[A]   Liability Issues

[1]   Why Should the Family Foundation Be Concerned About Liability?

Family foundations, and the individuals who govern them, must protect themselves against risk. Generally, this risk is managed in two ways: through adherence to a well-designed system of policies and procedures and through the purchase of insurance. This section focuses on the latter, while policies and procedures are addressed in more detail in Chapter 6.

Insurance protection can be provided by self-insuring the risk or purchasing one or more policies to cover exposure. It is difficult for most family members to understand the liability issues, since they perceive the family foundation as a tool for helping and doing good in the community. How can things go wrong? Easily.

Distributions may be made to unqualified organizations. A director or trustee may make distributions or sign contracts for personal benefit. A program funded exclusively by the foundation may be run in a way that causes death or injury to the participants.

The State Attorneys General may sue the foundation for breach of fiduciary duty or other violations of the foundation's mission and charitable purpose. Such problems are generally discovered through the Attorney Generals' review of the foundation's Form 990-PF, which the foundation is required to file in each state in which the foundation does business. Some states have strong charitable enforcement divisions and have taken this duty more seriously as the publicity about foundation and charity malfeasance has increased. For example, New York's State Attorney General, Eliot Spitzer, has been on a crusade for accountability in the nonprofit sector.

The public has the right to sue the foundation, and/or its managers, for damages that result from the foundation's act or failure to act. These legal causes of action may result from damages from breach of contract, accidents on the foundation's property, harm caused by grants or programs administered by the foundation, or damages resulting from the operation of motor vehicles. The amount of insurance required depends upon the type of operations of the foundation and the amount of property or assets at risk.

The process of assigning blame is complex and too large a topic for this book. Factors that impact liability include state law, common law principles, and the roles of the injured party and the responsible party. The foundation should seek advice of legal counsel as part of the initial organizational process to get a clear picture of the primary risks faced by the foundation.

Both the foundation and the governing body of the foundation need protection. Family foundations may hold assets ranging from thousands to billions of dollars. In addition, the family foundation's governing body will have personal assets at risk. Those individuals are not likely to willingly put those assets at risk to serve in a volunteer role. Nor should they be asked to do so.

By working with its attorney or a consultant, the foundation manager and board must assess the risks to which the foundation, its assets, and its managers (and board members) are exposed. Then it should protect itself by adopting policies and procedures to address risky activities. Some of the most common risk-oriented policies include investment management, grant management, financial standards, or gift acceptance (where additional contributions from family are anticipated). Foundations with employees should have personnel policies. These are especially important, to ensure that self-dealing rules are not violated, when family members assume paid staff roles. If the foundation is engaged in providing services to the public or provides the bulk of the budget for any single charity, it should have policies governing those services or have oversight of the funded organization's activities.

The foundation manager should share the results of the risk assessment, the foundation's policies, and its insurance coverage with the board, explaining the role of the policies in managing the board member's and the foundation's risk. In some cases, it may be appropriate to use an outside trainer, the foundation's advisor, or a consultant to conduct a training workshop. This will not only educate the board but also impress upon it the seriousness of its management responsibility.

The foundation's president or executive director and finance committee should also undertake an annual review of the foundation's insurance coverage and risk management policies. Consider the ways in which the foundation has changed its operation or programs over the course of the year. Add or eliminate insurance as the situation dictates. Then make changes in coverage to fit the foundation's needs, and report the adjustments to the board.

Foundations and their boards can go a long way in managing risk. However, all foundations should consider insurance as a backstop to protect foundation assets and its volunteers. In a world in which investment markets are haywire, assets are fluctuating, and attention to fraud and misfeasance is high, insurance is a necessity.

[2] Protecting the Foundation from Liability

It is important for the foundation manager, or professional resource for the foundation, to understand the risks to which the foundation and its managers are exposed and how to best provide protection from those risks.

The foundation owns both financial assets and property. The advisor to the foundation will likely be called on to help determine the types and amounts of protection required. There is no formula answer because foundations vary so widely in size, mission, and function. In addition, state law may have an impact on liability. This section provides an overview of the insurance options that are available. The foundation should work with a legal advisor and insurance professional to design the most appropriate coverage.

[a] Property Insurance

The foundation owns assets ranging from property, such as desks, computers, buildings, or fixtures, to financial assets. These assets should be protected through a basic property insurance package, which provides protection for damage from fire, flood, and theft.

[b] Casualty Insurance

In addition, the foundation may need casualty insurance, which is designed to provided protection for damage to the person or property of others. Make sure that the foundation has coverage for damage caused to others by employees or agents in motorized vehicles.

TABLE 5-1
Glossary of Insurance Terms

Bodily injury	Bodily injury is a direct injury or harm to the body.
Casualty insurance	Casualty insurance is an element of general liability insurance and covers bodily injury and damage to property of others that is not in the insured's care, custody, or control. This is a broad statement; insurance contracts can provide exceptions. The property of others over which the insured is exercising physical control is insured by obtaining direct property insurance for that item. Casualty insurance for motorized vehicles is obtained through automobile liability and physical damage insurance.
Claims made policy	A claims made policy covers claims made only during the specified policy period.
Directors and officers insurance	Directors and officers insurance provides coverage for occurrences other than damage to the property or physical injury to the person. These might include damages resulting from conflict of interest, breach of duty, mismanagement of foundation assets, discrimination in employment or administration of a grants program, libel, slander, or other common law claims.
Errors and omissions insurance	Errors and omissions insurance covers damages resulting from the conduct of a business and the offering of professional services or advice. Few family foundations serve in an operating foundation role to actively offer services (as opposed to funding services). Therefore, few family foundations have or need this insurance.
First-party insurance	First-party insurance refers to coverage for the foundation's property and assets against direct loss or harm. Examples of the types of loss protected include fire, flood, and theft.
General liability insurance	General liability insurance provides broad protection for the foundation's operations, its contracts, and accidents on its premises. This insurance does not cover property of others in the foundation's custody.
Indemnity	Indemnification is the process of restoring someone who has suffered a loss to the position he or she was in before the loss.
Negligence	Negligence is the failure to act with the degree of care that an ordinary and prudent person would use in conducting his or her business. Negligence is often an unintentional act.

TABLE 5-1   CONTINUED

Personal injury	Personal injury can extend beyond physical injury to include false arrest, detention, imprisonment, libel, slander, defamation of character, or wrongful entry or eviction. This coverage generally involves an additional premium.
Property injury	Property injury includes damage to physical assets or property.
Property insurance	Property insurance covers the foundation's property and the property of others in its custody. Property insurance may also cover claims based on the ability to generate income from those assets.
Tail coverage	Tail coverage is additional protection under a claims made policy that covers the foundation for a period beyond the claims period. This may be particularly appropriate if the foundation has been involved in a conversion or a program that may have a higher degree of liability.
Third-party insurance	Third-party insurance refers to coverage for damages or loss incurred by individuals or organizations as a result of the foundation's intentional or negligent acts or failure to act.

[c]   General Liability Insurance

The foundation should also have coverage for damages caused by the foundation's actions or failure to act. The degree of coverage that is required will depend upon the activities of the foundation. The law makes a distinction between those organizations that are actively involved in the delivery of services and those that passively fund those services. Sometimes it is difficult to know where to draw the line.

Foundations that are at greatest risk are those that are participating in the delivery of care or services. Services might include day care or child care, education, health care, shelter for the homeless, or any other direct services to the public. Where professional services are involved, such as providing medical care through doctors or nurses, or legal services through licensed attorneys, there is an even higher degree of liability, since the law imposes a higher degree of care on licensed professionals. In fact, some states impose that duty of care on all licensed professionals and do not provide exemption from liability under the volunteer statutes, even where those professionals are serving without compensation. Most family foundations do not fall within this group. However, the foundation may be considered a provider of services if it is the sole, or primary, funding agent for such a nonprofit operation.

[d] Directors and Officers Insurance

The foundation should provide directors and officers (D & O) insurance for its volunteers. D & O insurance is designed to protect directors against claims resulting from breach of duty, errors in judgment, omissions, or other wrongful acts, although it is not designed to protect directors who engaged in wilful and wanton acts in violation of the duty of a director. While general liability insurance covers physical damages, loss, and injuries of the foundation, D & O's insurance covers personal claims against the directors and officers for damages and the costs of defending against those damages, loss, and injuries. This insurance is generally obtained and paid for by the foundation to protect individuals who serve the foundation in order to protect them from any claims that may be filed against them during their term of office.

There is no "standard" D & O coverage, and the foundation must be careful to understand the type of protection that it is purchasing and providing to its directors. Always ask your insurance carrier to explain the options and check the policy carefully. Coverage may be available through a rider or additional premium payment for items not normally covered. State law may also impact the type of coverage that is permissible.

The following acts are generally covered by a D & O policy.

- *Unintentional violations of the law.* Unintentional violations may include actions filed by federal agencies, such as the Internal Revenue Service or the Securities Exchange Commission, or by state agencies.

- *Fines and penalties in third-party suits.* Fines and penalties may include excise taxes (described in this chapter), ERISA claims, and Environmental Protection Agency claims.

- *Punitive damages in third-party suits.* While general liability insurance covers physical damages to the person, physical damages to the property, and actual loss resulting from those claims, D & O insurance may cover punitive damages resulting from those claims.

- *Expenses in defending actions.* One of the costliest elements of a lawsuit is the legal cost of defending against the suit. Defense costs will exist without regard to fault and in extreme cases may run into hundreds of thousands of dollars. This coverage will either advance or reimburse the insured for these costs.

The following acts may not be covered by the D & O policy:

- *Intentional violations of the law.* Intentional violations of the law are rarely, if ever, covered by insurance, federal volunteer laws, or state volunteer laws. Dishonesty is an intentional act generally not covered by the policy.

- *Bodily or property injury.* Both bodily injury and property injury are covered by general liability insurance.

- *Professional liability.* The law distinguishes betwcen ordinary liability and the liability associated with someone trained to perform professional duties. Examples of professional duties include legal services and medical services performed by a doctor or nurse.

- *Punitive damages.* While punitive damages may be covered, these damages may also be excluded. It is important to check your policy.

- *Torts.* Torts that involve nonphysical harm done to others, such as libel and slander, may not be included under this coverage.

- *Suits or legal actions of one director against another.* Directors may file suits against each other for acts or failure to act. These suits are generally not covered.

- *Employment violations (pension laws, wrongful termination, discrimination, etc.).* Employment violations are another form of damage that may be included or excluded from D & O coverage. Foundations are most at risk in this area, according to a 1997 survey by the consulting firm of Watson Wyatt Worldwide (now a part of Tillinghast-Towers Perrin in Chicago). The firm surveyed 726 nonprofit organizations about their experience with D & O claims over the previous ten years. Thirty-six of those charities reported claims over the period. Eighty percent of those claims related to employment practices (wrongful termination, discrimination in hiring, discrimination in promotion).[18]

The insurance carries specific limits and conditions of coverage. The board member may be required to fund the defense and seek reimbursement after the proceedings. Coverage may be limited to specific dollar amounts. Some policies may cover only the activities or costs that the foundation has agreed to indemnify.

Policies may cover directors and officers only or may extend to employees and volunteers of the organization. Since policies can vary to such a great degree, make sure that someone reads and understands the coverage and that the policy covers all the elements needed to protect the foundation and its group of managers.

The foundation board must determine the level of coverage that is necessary or desirable. Begin with a general assessment of the most likely problems the foundation will encounter. Think about the scope of the grantmaking activities of the foundation, the dollar amount of those grants, the number of grants, and the foundation's role in the implementation of those grants. A large, active, and involved foundation will require more coverage than a small foundation making simple annual grants.

---

[18] Grandi, Edward, *Liability Protection for Governing Boards*, InTrust Online (Summer 1999), http://intrust.org/magazine/article_print.cfm?id=252&CFID=10123337&CFTOKEN=25957954.

Next, examine the need for protection. Many directors will carry personal umbrella policies to cover any major claims and may need only nominal protection. Others may stand to lose all of their assets in the event of disaster. Have an open dialogue with the board about the dangers and the protection provided by the foundation.

Look at the foundation assets to determine the level of protection provided. Small foundations are less help than large foundations.

Finally, look at the cost of the insurance. In a climate in which foundations are heavily assaulted with claims, insurance companies often reduce coverage and raise rates. In an environment in which the costs are relatively stable, insurance companies may offer cost-effective rates. Balance the benefits of self-insurance (indemnification) versus paid coverage (D & O insurance).

[e] Workers' Compensation Insurance

Workers' compensation insurance provides employees that have been injured on the job with a set remedy under law for those injuries. This insurance coverage is based on set compensation for injuries and is awarded without regard to fault on the part of the employer. While employees may still sue an employer for a wanton or willful violation of the law, this insurance is designed to prevent a continuous stream of lawsuits resulting from on-the-job injuries. State law will generally require that this insurance be purchased once the foundation has more than six employees. Coverage is recommended even where there are fewer employees, however, because the foundation is still responsible for on-the-job injuries.

[f] Fidelity Insurance

Fidelity insurance is designed to protect the foundation from loss by employee or officer theft or embezzlement of foundation funds. The insurance provides reimbursement to the foundation for assets stolen by a covered employee. This coverage is listed separately because coverage for theft or embezzlement is often excluded from other types of insurance coverage.

[3] Board Members' Liability

Board members have liability for wrongful acts committed by the foundation and foundation officers. Generally, this liability takes two forms: third-party liability to the general public and penalties or sanctions imposed by regulatory agencies.

[a] Comparing the Duties of Corporate Directors and Trustees

A family foundation may be formed as a corporation or a trust. The distinction is important because state law often sets a higher standard for trustees than for other fiduciaries or directors.

[i] Fiduciary duty. A board member has a fiduciary relationship to the foundation. This fiduciary relationship may be defined in one of two ways depending upon whether the board member serves as a board member of a nonprofit corporation or a nonprofit trust. If the board member serves for a nonprofit corporation, state law may define the board member's duties. If the board member serves as trustee of a nonprofit trust, state fiduciary law will define the responsibilities.

[ii] The duty to act in the best interests of the corporation or trust. Basic corporate fiduciary duties include the duty to act in good faith, the duty to act with care (often that of an ordinarily prudent person), and the duty of loyalty, which is the duty to act in the best interests of the corporation. State law generally provides that the corporate board member can rely on information presented to him or to her from sources believed to be reliable, on information presented as the result of committee work, and on opinions offered by professional counsel. Basic trust fiduciary duties are much the same. A trustee has the duty to act in good faith, the duty to act with the care of a prudent person, and the duty of loyalty.

[iii] The effect of the Volunteer Protection Act and other state laws. Liability of trustees and directors may be affected by the federal Volunteer Protection Act of 1997[19] or by the volunteer liability laws of the various states, which are discussed in more detail later in this chapter. These laws are generally found in the statutes relating to corporations and apply to directors and officers of nonprofit corporations. Some laws cover trustees and volunteers in all capacities, while others limit coverage to nonprofit directors or volunteers.

[iv] Conflict of interest. The duty of loyalty requires that the fiduciary put foundation interests before personal interests. State law, federal law, and common law define this responsibility. For private foundation directors and trustees, this duty has largely been codified through the imposition of sanctions that levy excise taxes for the violation of this duty. Examples of conflict include acts in which the individual who created the foundation, or members of his or her family, engage in transactions with the foundation that result in personal benefit. These include buying or selling property to the foundation, leasing property to

---

[19] 42 U.S.C. § 14501. *See* § 5.05[C] *infra* for a discussion of the Volunteer Protection Act and a listing of state laws providing protection for volunteers. The Volunteer Protection Act is provided at Appendix 5-G.

the foundation, taking large salaries from the foundation, and receiving higher than normal fees from the foundation for professional services.[20]

A good way to compare the duties of a trustee and a director is to examine the duties related to conflict of interest. Trustees are forbidden to engage in acts involving conflict of interest, which are actions in which the trustee has a direct or indirect interest. So, for example, trustees can not purchase trust property or sell assets to a trust or lease property to or from a trust under most state laws. Such an act involves a conflict of interest, even if conducted at market price.

Directors, however, are generally allowed to engage in transactions involving a conflict of interest so long as that transaction is disclosed and approved. The conflict must be disclosed prior to the transaction, and the transaction must be approved by a majority of the board, the attorney general, or a court. In addition, the interested director should generally abstain from the vote.[21]

Both trustees and directors are subject to the prohibited transaction rules governing private foundations.[22] This means that every transaction involving potential conflict of interest should be reviewed, although the fact that a trustee or director is involved may ultimately affect the result.

[v] Investment management. One of the most obvious duties of care is the requirement that the board member invest the assets of the foundation prudently. The modern standard of investment conduct is the prudent investor rule. The prudent investor rule is set forth in the *Restatement (Third) of Trusts* promulgated by the American Law Institute and incorporated as a part of the trust law of most states,[23] and it is also recommended in the Uniform Management of Institutional Funds Act, the model law for management of permanent charitable funds adopted by most states.[24] The prudent investor rule requires that the fiduciary (the trustee or director) make investment decisions based on the size of the portfolio, the general economic conditions at the time of investment, the portfolio's investment horizon, the beneficiaries' needs, and the portfolio's long-term goals. The rule also permits delegation of investment management to obtain expert advice.[25]

---

[20] Sanctions are discussed in § 5.05[A][3][c] *infra*. Chapter 6 address these conflicts in greater detail in the prohibited transaction analysis.

[21] This same transaction may violate the IRS self-dealing rules, however, which are equally applicable to trustees and directors.

[22] *See* Chapter 6 for a detailed discussion of the prohibited transaction rules.

[23] Restatement (Third) of Trusts § 227 (American Law Institute 1992).

[24] A copy of all Uniform and Model Acts can be obtained from the National Conference of Commissioners on Uniform State Laws, 211 East Ontario Street, Suite 1300, Chicago, IL 60611, 312-915-0195. *See www.law.upenn/edu/bll/ulc/ulc_final.htm#umifa* for text.

[25] The Uniform Management of Institutional Funds Act was approved and recommended for enactment in all states by the National Conference of Commissioners on Uniform State Laws in 1972. A copy of all Uniform and Model Acts can be obtained from the National Conference of Commissioners on Uniform State Laws, 211 East Ontario Street, Suite 1300, Chicago, IL 60611. *See www.law.upenn/edu/bll/ulc/ulc_final.htm#umifa* for text.

Under the prudent investor standard, the fiduciary's success is measured by the process employed in managing the funds rather than the investment results. For example, one court interpreting the prudent man rule held a fiduciary responsible for a concentration of bank stock in an estate, even though the family had asked the bank to retain the stock.[26] The stock had increased in value during the term of the trust, but not to the extent of the equities market as a whole. Since the fiduciary had violated the rule prohibiting a concentration of stock, the court held it strictly liable. Under the new prudent investor rule, the fiduciary would have been judged on the portfolio as a whole, and how that particular concentration fit the portfolio strategy. If the fiduciary could have shown that its analysis and strategy was appropriate at the time, it might have avoided this result.

States adhering to the older "prudent man" rule place the focus on results, while states using the prudent investor rule focus on process. It is important to be aware of the standard under which your state operates so that you will know how to effectively manage and review this process. Chapter 8 contains an extensive review of the investment management process and provides worksheets and guidelines for policy.

The dramatic downturn in the equity and bond markets of 2000-2002 caught many foundation managers unaware. Family foundation portfolios with high equity concentrations may have experienced losses of 50 percent or greater if the portfolio also held concentrations of technology stocks, or problematic stocks with bad news such as those of Enron, WorldCom, and telecommunications companies. When a foundation's portfolio takes a dramatic negative turn, foundation managers may have to answer hard questions from the Internal Revenue Service, the Congress, or the general public. Those managers that did not have an investment process in place or were not monitoring results may face personal liability. The foundation trustee or director must be aware of the applicable investment standards for the foundation's assets and get involved in the oversight of the foundation's investment management team.

The bottom line is that the fiduciary has a duty to be informed about and involved in the actions of the family foundation. Make sure that the liability issues are fully explored prior to the creation of the foundation. There may be an advantage to organizing in the corporate form rather than the trust form. The board is charged with the fiduciary responsibility to manage the foundation and is ultimately responsible when assets are improperly managed, funds diverted, or laws violated. Service without participation may result in liability.

[b] Third-Party Liability

The term "third-party liability" refers to the liability that the foundation board has to individuals or organizations that are damaged as a result of

---

[26] *First Alabama Bank of Huntsville v. Spragins*, 475 So. 2d 512 (Ala. 1985), *on rehearing*, 515 So. 2d 962 (Ala. 1987).

the wanton or willful negligence of the board in the actions or activities of the foundation. Damages may result from breach of the duty of care in handling the assets of the foundation, conflict of interest, discrimination in employment, discrimination in the administration of grants, libel, slander, breach of contract, or other common law actions that address damages.

The logical question to raise is "Who would file a third-party liability suit against the foundation and its directors?" The foundation does not have clearly identified individual beneficiaries. Rather, the potential beneficiaries include the public at large and include anyone who might receive services or benefits from organizations funded by the foundation. For example:

- Employees may file lawsuits alleging discrimination (race, sex, age, national origin, religion, disability, or sexual orientation), wrongful termination, or harassment.

- Charities may sue the foundation alleging they were denied funding they were entitled to, or did not receive sufficient funds.

- Donors may file suit alleging the foundation is no longer fulfilling the goals intended when the foundation was established.

- Members of the general public may sue claiming conflict of interest, failure to supervise employees, libel, slander, or other tortious behavior.

For the most part, oversight of directors takes place at a regulatory level through review of the foundation's annual return by the attorney general of the state in which the foundation is located, through public review of the foundation's return through public inspection, and by sanctions levied by the IRS for violation of rules designed to prevent personal benefit from charitable organizations. The fact that there is oversight does not preclude a lawsuit from someone who feels he or she has been damaged by the foundation.

The attorney general of a state may also bring suit against a foundation and its directors for malfeasance or damage. The IRS requires that foundations with assets of $5,000 or greater at any time during the tax year file a copy of the foundation's Form 990-PF with each state in which the foundation reports or is registered, in which it has a principal office, and in which it was incorporated (or created in the case of a trust).[27] In addition, the IRS is required to notify the state attorney general and chief financial officer when it has made a final determination that a foundation is denied or loses its tax-exempt status or when there is a tax deficiency. While some states do not have the staff to pursue such issues, many — such as New York, California, Minnesota and South Dakota — are taking a more active role. In New York, for example, Eliot Spitzer has aggressively pursued nonprofits that appear to have violated private inurement rules, citing instances of excessive compensation, excessive professional payments to

---

[27] Reg. § 1.6033-3(c).

individuals or firms related to disqualified persons, unsecured loans of foundation assets at below market rates to disqualified persons, improper investment
management, and failure of a charity's board to provide oversight. In some
instances, the individuals involved have been required to step down from their
foundation role and repay funds to the foundation.[28]

[c] Sanctions Imposed by the Internal Revenue Code

Sanctions, in the form of excise taxes, are imposed on foundations for a
variety of acts. The purpose of the sanctions is to discourage foundation managers
from acts of self-dealing, jeopardizing investments and taxable expenditures. The
prohibited transaction rules are discussed in great detail in Chapter 6. However, a
brief review of these three activities is included here, since a foundation manager is
jointly and severally liable for penalties imposed by these rules. A foundation
manager is defined as an officer, director, or trustee of a private foundation; a
person with powers similar to an officer, director, or trustee; or an employee having
the power to take action and represent the foundation without further approval.[29]
Table 5–2 details the sanctions imposed by the Internal Revenue Code (IRC or
Code) on board members and trustees. Table 5–2 details the sanctions imposed by
the IRC on board members and trustees. Note that sanctions are divided into "First-
tier" sanctions and "Second-tier" sanctions. First-tier sanctions are those imposed
as a penalty for the original transaction. Second-tier sanctions are those imposed
when corrective action is not taken within the time specified in the Code.

[i] Self-dealing: disqualified persons. Self-dealing, direct or indirect transactions between a disqualified person and the foundation, is strictly prohibited. A
disqualified person is basically a person that has a position of influence with the
foundation. Categories of disqualified persons include substantial contributors,[30] 20
percent owners of entities that are substantial contributors,[31] foundation managers,[32]
and family members of any of these three classes.[33] Corporations, partnerships,
trusts, and estates may also be classified as disqualified persons if 35 percent of the
ownership or beneficial ownership is held by any of the above-mentioned disqualified persons.[34] Private foundations may be considered disqualified persons under

---

[28] *See* Grant Williams, *Making Philanthropy Accountable* and *New York's Review of Nonprofit
Groups: A Sampling of Cases*, The Chronicle of Philanthropy (Vol. 15, Issue 18, June 26, 2003).

[29] IRC § 4946(b); Reg. § 53.4946-1(f).

[30] IRC § 4946(a)(1)(A).

[31] IRC § 4946(a)(1)(C).

[32] IRC § 4946(a)(1)(B).

[33] IRC § 4946(a)(1)(D).

[34] IRC § 4946(a)(1)(E), (F), (G).

certain conditions,[35] and government officials may also be defined as disqualified persons for the purposes of the self-dealing rules.[36]

TABLE 5-2
Sanctions Imposed on Board Members/Trustees by the Internal Revenue Code

Activity	First-Tier Sanction/ Trigger for Payment	Second-Tier Sanction/ Trigger for Payment
Self-Dealing IRC § 4941	2.5% of the transaction amount up to a maximum of $10,000 imposed on the manager for each year the transaction is outstanding and has not been corrected	50% of the transaction up to a maximum of $10,000 imposed on the manager if he or she refuses to resolve the situation and agree to all or part of the penalty
Jeopardizing Investments IRC § 4944	5% of the transaction amount up to $5,000 per investment transaction imposed for each year that the jeopardizing investment is held by the foundation	5% of the transaction amount up to a maximum per manager of $10,000 imposed on those managers who do not agree to remove the jeopardizing asset
Taxable Expenditures IRC § 4945	2.5% per expenditure up to $5,000 per manager imposed on those managers who knew about and agreed to make the expenditure	50% per expenditure up to $10,000 imposed on those managers who refuse to correct the expenditure
Political Expenditures IRC § 4955	2.5% of each expenditure imposed imposed on the manager agreed to making the expenditure	50% of each expenditure imposed on the manager who refuses to agree to all or part of the correction

While the Code broadly prohibits financial transactions between the foundation and the disqualified person, it also lists six specific acts that are considered self-dealing:

1. Selling, leasing, or exchanging property between the disqualified person and the foundation.[37]

2. Lending money or extending credit from the foundation to the disqualified person.[38]

3. Furnishing goods, services, or facilities to the foundation by the disqualified person.[39]

---

[35] IRC § 4946(a)(1)(H).
[36] IRC § 4946(a)(1)(I).
[37] IRC § 4941(d)(1)(A).
[38] IRC § 4941(d)(1)(B).
[39] IRC § 4941(d)(1)(C).

4. Paying compensation to (or reimbursing expenses of) the disqualified person.[40]

5. Transferring foundation income or assets to or for the benefit of a disqualified person.[41]

6. Agreeing to pay a government official with foundation assets.[42]

The regulations provide a number of exceptions to these rules.[43] For example, compensation may be paid to disqualified persons for certain services so long as that compensation is reasonable and necessary.[44] As mentioned previously, the practical aspects of these rules are discussed in detail in Chapter 6. However, for the purposes of a liability review, it is important to understand that the exceptions are narrow and the foundation managers are responsible for ensuring that the foundation activities fit within those exceptions.

[ii] Jeopardizing investments. Jeopardizing investments are broadly defined as any investment that jeopardizes the ability of the foundation to carry out its tax-exempt purpose.[45] There is no list of jeopardizing investments; rather, the manager violates the rules when he or she "fails to exercise ordinary business care and prudence, under the facts and circumstances prevailing at the time of the investment, in providing for the long and short-term financial needs of the foundation to carry out its exempt purpose."[46] This rule, which sounds very similar to the standards established in the prudent investor rule, requires that the investment manager understand the role that the investment plays in the overall portfolio, and does not automatically penalize a manager for an investment if it loses value. With that said, a manager that invests in an asset that loses most or all of its value must be able to establish its appropriateness at the time it was purchased.

The regulations list certain types of investments that represent riskier investments:[47]

*   Trading on margin

*   Trading in commodity futures

*   Investments in working interests in oil and gas wells

---

[40] IRC § 4941(d)(1)(D).
[41] IRC § 4941(d)(1)(E).
[42] IRC § 4941(d)(1)(F).
[43] Reg. § 53.4941(d)-3.
[44] Reg. § 53.4941(d)-3(c)(1).
[45] IRC § 4944(a)(1).
[46] Reg. § 53.4944-1(a)(2).
[47] *Id.*

- Use of puts, calls, and straddles
- The purchase of warrants
- Short sales

When the regulations were first published in 1972 (and subsequently amended in 1973), puts, calls, straddles, and warrants were considered far riskier than in the current investment environment. Today's investment managers may employ these tools to reduce risk in a portfolio. However, the fact that such tools are employed to reduce risk in some portfolios does not mean that the investment is appropriate. The manager must be able to explain why the investment is a necessary part of the foundation's portfolio.

The IRS will not rule that a specific asset is jeopardizing or safe.[48] The best way to avoid violating the rule is to adopt a sound set of investment management policies, use care in investing assets, and adhere to state law.

[iii] **Taxable expenditures.** Taxable expenditures encompass a broad range of activities, all of which are prohibited for private foundations. These include expenditures for lobbying, political campaigns, grants to individuals (some exceptions exist where approval is obtained in advance), and grants to otherwise nonqualified organizations.

These taxable activities, often called prohibited transactions, are part of the sweeping reform of private foundations enacted in the 1969 Tax Reform Act, designed to strictly limit the possibility of private benefit from tax-exempt organizations closely controlled by donors.[49] The penalties are in the form of taxes and are not classified as criminal acts. The taxes set out in Table 5–2 represent only the penalties on the managers. Additional penalties are imposed on the foundation. These are discussed in Chapter 6 and in the supplemental tax materials in this book.

It is important to note that it is difficult to insure directors from these penalties because the penalties are generally assessed only where the director knowingly and willfully violated the rule. Most insurance does not cover a willful violation of the law, and most state indemnification laws do not allow protection or reimbursement for such acts.

[d] *Tax Return Filings*

Foundation directors additionally have responsibility for filing the annual tax return and may be held personally liable for the failure to do so.[50] Where the failure to act is "willful and flagrant," the person is liable for a penalty equal to

---

[48] Rev. Rul. 74-316, 1974-2 C.B. 389.

[49] The prohibited transaction rules are found in IRC §§ 4941-4946.

[50] IRC § 6684.

the tax.[51] The directors and officers should take the time to fully review the form to understand its basic elements and representations.

In addition, foundations are required to file quarterly estimates reflecting excise taxes on investment income. Failure to file this tax may result in liability for the foundation manager.[52]

Finally, the foundation must provide the general public with a copy of its three most recent tax returns, as well as the application for exempt status, upon request.[53] This rule is designed to give the general public a watchdog role in overseeing the uses of funds committed to charitable purposes. More often, however, it is used to satisfy general curiosity about the operation of a foundation or to research opportunities for grants.

[e] Intermediate Sanctions

In 1996, Congress approved legislation imposing intermediate sanctions — a tax on excess benefit transactions — on individuals involved in transactions with tax-exempt organizations that result in private benefit.[54] This legislation was largely as a result of the tales of abuse regularly reported in the press. However, it was also the reflection of the frustration of the IRS, which wanted to impose meaningful punishment on individuals who received private benefit from public entities (as opposed to private foundations). Under prior law, the IRS could impose penalties for self-dealing on private foundations. Punishment of public charities was generally pursued through the revocation of tax-exempt status. While this penalty was devastating for the charity, it did little to reach the individuals who used the charity's assets for personal benefit.

This tax on excess benefit transactions penalizes the individuals who benefit from such a transaction and also assesses the board and committee members who approve the transfer of funds and the foundation managers who are parties to the transfer. Penalties are imposed jointly and severally and range from first-tier taxes of 10 to 25 percent to second-tier taxes of 200 percent.[55]

The good news for private foundations is that the intermediate sanctions apply only to Internal Revenue Code (IRC) § 501(c)(3) public charities and IRC § 501(c)(4) entities organized and operated for social benefit. Private foundations are specifically excluded from coverage.[56] Do not forget, however, that the self-dealing rules in place for private foundations since 1969 do reach transactions

---

[51] IRC § 6684.

[52] IRC § 6656.

[53] IRC § 6104(d).

[54] IRC § 4958; Temporary Regulations §§ 53.4958-0T-53.4958-8T. For an explanation of the temporary regulations, see the 2002 Continuing Professional Education text published by the IRS at www.irs.treas.gov/prod/bus_info/eo/interest.html.

[55] IRC §§ 4958(a), (b).

[56] IRC § 4958(e).

with disqualified persons. Also, the self-dealing rules adopt a general policy of prohibiting virtually all dealings between private foundations and disqualified persons, while the intermediate sanctions adopt a less restrictive standard that merely requires such dealings to be conducted at fair market value and arm's length.

[B] Protection Through Indemnification and Insurance

Members of the board of a family foundation are likely to have substantial personal assets at risk as the result of board service. These individuals must receive or obtain some form of protection for personal assets if they serve as a director or officer of the foundation. This protection can be obtained through indemnification of the board members by the foundation and through insurance obtained through the foundation and through the individual's personal carrier.

One of the easiest ways to obtain Directors and Officers Liability insurance is through a foundation trade organization such as the Council on Foundations, the Association of Small Foundations, or the Southeastern Council of Foundations.[57] Alternatively, call the foundation's property and casualty insurance carrier or the board member's insurance carriers to obtain this insurance. If your carrier does not provide coverage, ask it to put you in touch with an insurance firm that specializes in, or is familiar with, nonprofit coverage.

[1] Indemnification

The foundation may indemnify its directors, officers, and employees for acts conducted in good faith within the scope of duty. An indemnification is a promise to pay expenses and costs for litigation, legal counsel fees, or court costs associated with claims filed against the director, officer, or employee. Indemnification may provide directors with considerable protection where there are substantial foundation assets, but provide little relief where the assets are small.

Indemnification may take two forms: mandatory and permissive. Mandatory indemnification is an absolute right to indemnification that can be enforced by the board member seeking restitution. Many state laws provide for mandatory indemnification under certain circumstances, especially those involving lawsuits from parties outside the foundation board. Permissive indemnification simply allows the foundation, on a vote, to reimburse the director for certain costs.

State law generally sets out the ground rules for how much indemnification the foundation can provide. Some states limit coverage to defense costs but do not cover any money damages or fines that are assessed. Other states limit coverage to those instances in which the director is successful in defending the suit. And still other states provide expansive coverage so long as the action taken

---

[57] *See* Chapter 1 for a directory of foundation trade organizations.

was within the scope of permissible duties, the director was acting in good faith, and the director was acting in the best interests of the corporation.

The foundation should clearly determine the extent to which it will indemnify its directors and officers and should outline the circumstances under which this indemnification will occur. These guidelines may be a part of the articles of incorporation or bylaws, or the trust document, or they may be established simply by resolution of the board. The indemnification statement should reflect the maximum indemnification available under state law. Ask the foundation's counsel for the specifics of the applicable law.

[2] General Liability Insurance

General liability insurance is broad coverage protecting the foundation from bodily injury and property damage liability claims for actual injuries to an individual or to property that may result from contracts, accidents on the premises, foundation programs, fire, theft, accidental loss, or accident. It is generally separated into two forms of coverage: personal injury and property injury. This insurance does not cover costs that are not the direct result of an injury, such as the costs of litigation, mental distress, punitive damages, or other less tangible costs or claims. It can cover personal injury liability, such as false arrest, slander, or defamation of character.

[3] Personal Insurance

The board member concerned about liability should seek advice from his or her personal liability carrier to determine whether personal coverage in the form of additional umbrella coverage would be applicable and appropriate. This coverage is usually offered as an extension of the board member's automobile policy or homeowner's policy and can extend protection by $1 million, by $2 million, or to the extent required. Many wealthy individuals obtain an umbrella policy as a matter of course and may not require additional insurance.

[4] Insurance Checklist

Table 5–3 contains a checklist of the various types of insurance available to protect the foundation and its board members, officers, and directors.

[5] Taxation of Insurance Benefits

Two basic concerns may arise where a foundation provides insurance benefits to its directors and officers. The first concern is whether the insurance coverage provided by the foundation constitutes compensation that must be reported on either a 1099 or a W-2. Prior to the issuance of regulations in

1992, a portion of the insurance was generally considered taxable. Current regulations, however, provide that insurance benefits that are provided by the foundation for a manager, covering that manager's acts or failure to act within the ordinary scope of his or her duties, are not taxable as compensation to that manager.[58]

The second concern relates to the prohibition on self-dealing when the foundation makes an expenditure from its assets to provide personal protection to its directors and officers. The foundation may provide indemnification for a foundation manager for liability in civil proceedings related to his or her performance of (or the failure to perform) service for the foundation.[59] He or she may be indemnified for expenses including attorneys' fees, judgments, and settlement expenses so long as those are reasonably incurred in connection with the civil action and so long as the act in question was not willful or without reasonable cause. Indemnification for compensatory purposes, such as the payment of taxes or penalties, the expense of correcting the action that is the basis of the suit, an expense that is not reasonably incurred in the defense of the suit, or an expense incurred in the defense of an act that is willful and without cause, is considered an act of self-dealing unless the expense, when added to other compensation of the foundation manager, is considered reasonable (under the reasonable compensation test discussed in Chapter 6).[60]

TABLE 5-3
Insurance Checklist for Family Foundations

Type of Protection	*Purpose*	*Extent of Coverage*
Indemnification	Indemnification protects board members from the costs of defending legal actions brought against them by virtue of their service on the board. This coverage is provided by the foundation through its general assets.	State law directs the extent of mandatory and permissive coverage.
General Liability Insurance	This coverage protects board members from liability claims and losses for bodily injury resulting from the foundation's activities and property as well as damage to the property of others not in the custody of the insured. This insurance also provides coverage for liability claims from personal injury, including libel, slander,	This policy is a must. Without this coverage, the foundation is in a self-insured position, and protection is available able only to the extent that the foundation has assets. This coverage does not include coverage of the property of others in the foundation's custody.

---

[58] Reg. § 53.4941(d)-2(f)(3)(i).
[59] Reg. § 53.4941(d)-2(f)(3).
[60] Reg. § 53.4941(d)-2(f)(4).

TABLE 5-3.   CONTINUED

Type of Protection	*Purpose*	*Extent of Coverage*
	defamation of character, and false arrest.	
Casualty Insurance	Casualty insurance is a part of general liability insurance and covers bodily injury and damage to the property of others not in the insured's care, custody, or control.	Casualty insurance for the property of others over which the insured is exercising physical control is obtained through direct property insurance on that property.
Automobile Casualty and Physical Damage Insurance	This casualty insurance for motorized vehicles covers bodily injury or property damage to someone else arising out of the operation of motorized vehicles.	Physical damage insurance (comprehensive and collision coverage) should be purchased to cover damage to vehicles.
Property Insurance	This coverage is designed to protect the assets of the foundation and may also protect against injury that occurs on the foundation's property. The insurance covers the foundation's property and the property of others in the custody of the foundation from physical loss due to fire, theft, etc.	Property insurance is particularly important if the foundation operates from separate offices, if it owns real property, or if it has extensive equipment.
Workers' Compensation Insurance	This insurance protects the foundation from claims of employees for injuries incurred on or at the workplace.	This coverage is generally regulated by law and is required once the foundation has a specific number of permanent full-time employees.
Directors and Officers Insurance	D & O insurance protects directors and officers from claims other than those for personal injury, property damage, or loss of property. This policy provided by an insurance company, covers the costs of defending suits for directors and officers engaged in normal activities	The purchase of this insurance, and the extent of this insurance, is optional. The foundation must make sure it does not secure excessive coverage that might represent a taxable benefit to the officer or director.

TABLE 5-3. CONTINUED

Type of Protection	Purpose	Extent of Coverage
Personal Umbrella Insurance	within the scope of duty as a director or officer. Officers and directors may want to secure umbrella coverage through personal insurance policies that protect against the costs of defending actions in their role as a director or officer.	The purchase of this coverage is a personal decision and depends largely upon the size of the individual assets at risk in the event of a problem.
Environmental Liability Insurance	This coverage relates specifically to CERCLA problems on real estate owned by the foundation. The policy should cover cleanup and restoration costs, if required.	This coverage is generally provided through a rider.

The rule on insurance follows the same logic. When insurance is provided to the foundation manager to cover the liability for acts that are not willful or without cause or for actions (or the failure to act) in carrying out duties on behalf of the foundation, the provision of insurance is not self-dealing.[61] When insurance is provided to cover compensatory damages, the cost of the insurance must be added to other compensation provided to the manager to determine whether it is reasonable.[62]

[C] Federal Volunteer Protection Act of 1997

The Volunteer Protection Act of 1997 was enacted in June 1997, with an effective date of September 16, 1997.[63] That legislation is designed to protect officers, directors, trustees, and other volunteers for nonprofit organizations from civil suits resulting from acts or omissions committed in their volunteer role. It is important to note that the act protects volunteers rather than the organizations that they serve. A copy of the text of the act is provided at Appendix 5-G.

[1] Goals of the Legislation

The goals of the legislation were to reduce volunteers' concerns about liability and stem the decrease in board members and volunteers providing

---

[61] Reg. § 53.4941(d)-2(f)(3)(ii).
[62] Reg. § 53.4941(d)-2(f)(4)(ii).
[63] 42 U.S.C. § 14501.

nonprofit service. It was also designed to reduce nonprofit operating costs by encouraging volunteer work and to reduce insurance costs by clarifying the risk and liability of volunteers. The preface to the legislation specifically noted that the federal government did not have the ability to provide services currently provided by nonprofit organizations.[64]

[2] Individuals Covered by the Act

Individuals covered by the act include uncompensated directors, officers, trustees, and direct service volunteers who perform services for a 501(c)(3) organization or any organization established for charitable, civic, educational, religious, welfare, or health purposes (other than an organization involved in hate crimes) or for the state.[65] The individual is considered a volunteer because he or she does not receive compensation (other than reimbursement for actual expenses) or an item of value in excess of $500 per year.[66]

[3] Volunteer Actions Covered by the Act

Volunteers are exempted from liability for harm for an act or omission, provided:

- The volunteer is acting within the scope of his or her duties;

- If appropriate or required, the volunteer is licensed, certified, or authorized to perform the activity;

- The act or omission was not willful or criminal misconduct, gross negligence, reckless misconduct, or a flagrant indifference to the safety or rights of the individual that is harmed; and

- The harm was not caused by the volunteer operating a motor vehicle requiring a license or insurance.[67]

Volunteers are protected from punitive damages so long as the act or omission occurred within the scope of the volunteer's duties and was not willful or criminal misconduct or a "conscious, flagrant indifference to the rights or safety of the individual harmed."[68]

Where volunteers are responsible for non-economic loss, defined as physical and emotional pain, suffering, inconvenience, physical impairment, mental anguish, disfigurement, loss of enjoyment of life, loss of society and companion-

---

[64] 42 U.S.C. § 14501(a)(7)(C).
[65] 42 U.S.C. § 14505(4), (6).
[66] 42 U.S.C. § 14505(6).
[67] 42 U.S.C. § 14503(a).
[68] 42 U.S.C. § 14503(a)(3).

ship, loss of consortium, hedonic damages, and injury to reputation, the liability is to be assessed in proportion to the responsibility of the volunteer.[69] The court determines the percentage of responsibility.

[4] Relationship of State Law

The federal law "preempts the laws of any State to the extent that such laws are inconsistent with" the act unless the state law provides additional protection from liability.[70] The law specifically states that state provisions that require nonprofits or government agencies to adhere to certain risk management procedures (including mandatory training), that make an organization liable for its volunteers to the same extent it is liable for its employees, that require that an organization make provision for liability through insurance or other sources, or that limit liability if the civil action is brought by an officer of the state or local government under state or local law are not "inconsistent" with the federal law.

[D] State Volunteer Liability Laws

State volunteer liability laws, enacted in some form in all states, also offer some protection for the volunteer. These laws vary from state to state, but are generally worded to provide some immunity to the volunteer from tort claims by third parties.[71] Most of these statutes were enacted in the 1980s in an effort to provide nonprofit organizations some relief from the high insurance premiums in effect at that time.

Some state laws bar civil suits against the volunteer. Others allow the suits, but fully protect the volunteer from personal liability. Still others simply provide immunity for liability in excess of any insurance coverage carried by the individual or the corporation. It is important to check not only the extent of your state's coverage, but also the interpretation of that law by the state courts.

Individuals covered by the limited liability or immunity statutes vary from state to state. In most states, a volunteer is defined as an individual who performs services for a nonprofit organization, a nonprofit corporation, a hospital, or a governmental agency without compensation. This may include officers, directors, trustees, and any individuals who offer services to or for the nonprofit. To receive the protection of the statute, the volunteer must be acting in good faith, within the scope of his or her duties, and without wanton or willful misconduct. Note that the state laws vary widely in defining "volunteers," and some provide exceptions for specific activities or allow for prior insurance coverage.

---

[69] 42 U.S.C. § 14505(3); 42 U.S.C. § 14504(b)(1).

[70] 42 U.S.C. § 14502(a).

[71] For an excellent, comprehensive review of state volunteer liability laws and court interpretations of those statutes see State Liability Laws for Charitable Organizations and Volunteers, Nonprofit Risk Management Center, <http://www.nonprofitrisk.org/pubs/PDFs/sll.pdf>, (2001, updated January 2006).

TABLE 5-4
Summaries of State Volunteer Liability Laws

State	Code Section	Summary of Key Provisions
Alabama	Ala. Code §§ 6-5-335, 336	The Volunteer Service Act provides civil immunity for uncompensated volunteers serving as officers, directors, or trustees of nonprofit public and private organizations for acts or omissions resulting in injury as long as the volunteer acted in good faith and within the scope of official volunteer duties and the harm was not the result of willful or wanton misconduct.
Alaska	Alaska Stat. §§ 09.65.170, 21.84.045, 47.32.160, 47.62.035, 26.20.140, 44.21.450	This statute (Limited Liability of Certain Directors and Officers) protects directors and officers of nonprofit corporations, certain hospital boards, school boards, and citizens' advisory committees of municipalities and regional development corporations from tort damages for personal injury, death, or damage to property for an act or omission so long as the act occurred within the scope of official duties and did not constitute gross negligence.
Arizona	Ariz. Rev. Stat. Ann. §§ 12-981 to 12-982, 12-715, 20-867, 26-314, 32-1452(H)	The law provides that a volunteer is immune from civil liability where the volunteer caused harm if the volunteer was acting in good faith and within the scope of his or her official functions and duties for a nonprofit organization, hospital, or governmental entity so long as the damage was not caused by "willful, wanton or grossly negligent misconduct." Where the act was within the scope of the volunteer's duties, the organization has vicarious liability. A volunteer is defined as someone performing a service for a nonprofit (without compensation) and extends to directors, officers, trustees, and direct service volunteers.

TABLE 5-4.   CONTINUED

State	Code Section	Summary of Key Provisions
Arkansas	Ark. Code Ann. §§ 16-6-101 to 16-6-105, 16-6-201, 16-5-101	The Arkansas Volunteer Immunity Act protects qualified volunteers who serve without compensation for a nonprofit as long as the acts were within the scope of the volunteer program and the volunteer was not acting in bad faith or with gross negligence. The Act covers volunteers of governmental programs, community volunteer organizations, and any IRC § 501(c)(3) organizations other than those established primarily for the recreational benefit of stockholders or members. There are exceptions, however. When the volunteer is covered by insurance, liability for ordinary negligence is limited to the amount of the insurance; when the harm is caused by a volunteer who negligently operates a car, plane, boat, or other "power mode of conveyance," the liability for ordinary negligence is limited to the amount of insurance coverage that exists. The statute also provides immunity for harm caused by retired physicians and surgeons who provide services without compensation unless the harm was caused by willful misconduct or gross negligence.
California	Cal. Corp. Code §§ 7231.5, 9247; Cal. Gov. Code §§ 8657, 818.9; Cal. Health and Safety Code § 1799.107; Cal. Bus. and Prof. Code §§ 5536.27, 6706	Volunteer directors and executive directors of nonprofit organizations are not subject to monetary liability or causes of action as long as they perform their duties with care, in good faith, and in a way that they believe is in the best interests of the corporation. However, this section is not applicable if the director participates in a self-dealing transaction or if the

TABLE 5-4. CONTINUED

State	Code Section	Summary of Key Provisions
		transaction involves a distribution, loan, or guarantee. There is no personal liability to a third party for a volunteer director or volunteer executive committee officer of a nonprofit as long as the act or omission causing the harm was within the scope of duties, was performed in good faith, and was not reckless, wanton, intentional, or grossly negligent, and the organization had obtained, or had tried to obtain, liability coverage.
Colorado	Colo. Rev. Stat. Ann. §§ 13-21-115.5, 13-21-115.7, 13-21-116, 24-32-2605	Colorado's Volunteer Service Act protects volunteers — defined as uncompensated directors, officers, and trustees of nonprofit organizations or a hospital — from civil liability for acts or omissions as long as the volunteer acted in good faith and within the scope of official duties and functions, and the act was not willful or wanton misconduct or gross negligence. Harm caused in the operation of a motor vehicle is not excluded but is limited to the limit of the individual's insurance for the vehicle.
Connecticut	Conn. Gen. Stat. Ann. §§ 52-557m, 7-308, 10-235, 29-22, 52-557b	Noncompensated directors, officers, and trustees of nonprofit organizations are immune from civil liability for acts, errors, or omissions made in exercising policy or decision-making responsibilities if such actions are made in good faith and are within the scope of official duty, and so long as the acts are not the result of reckless, willful, or wanton misconduct.
Delaware	Del. Code. Ann. §§ 10-8133, 10-8135, 16-6801-6802; 11-9505	A volunteer is defined as a trustee, ex-officio trustee, director, officer, agent, or nonprofit worker serving without compensation.

TABLE 5-4. CONTINUED

State	Code Section	Summary of Key Provisions
		A nonprofit is defined as any organization exempt from federal income tax under IRC § 501(c). Volunteers are protected from lawsuits for civil damages for acts or omissions unless the act was willful and wanton or grossly negligent. There is an exception for acts relating to the operation of motor vehicles (liability is limited to the coverage of the volunteer's insurance) and for doctors and nurses (liability is limited to the coverage of the volunteer's insurance).
District of Columbia	D.C. Code Ann. §§ 29-301.113, 7-402, 1-307.22, 7-2206	D.C.'s statute defines a volunteer as an officer, director, trustee, or other person who performs services and is not paid (other than reimbursement of expenses). Such a volunteer is immune from civil liability unless the volunteer engaged in willful misconduct, an intentional violation of the law, a transaction that was self-serving (improper personal benefit of money, property, or service), activities beyond the scope of his or her corporate duties, or activities or omissions prior to the effective date of the statute on March 17, 1993. This immunity is valid, however, only if the nonprofit corporation maintains liability insurance of not less than $200,000 per individual claim and $500,000 per total claims from the same event. Nonprofits with less than $100,000 in assets are exempt from the liability insurance requirement.
Florida	Fla. Stat. Ann. §§ 768.1355, 430.204, 768.135, 768.136	The Florida Volunteer Protection Act provides that a volunteer serving without compensation is immune from civil liability if the act or omission was undertaken

TABLE 5-4.   CONTINUED

State	Code Section	Summary of Key Provisions
		in good faith, was within the scope of the volunteer's duties, and was not wanton or willful and the volunteer was acting as an ordinary reasonably prudent person would have acted. Florida's law also covers individuals who are compensated under Florida's Domestic Service Volunteer Act of 1973. The law also provides immunity for "[m]embers of elected or appointed boards, councils, and commissions of the state, counties, municipalities, authorities and special districts."
Georgia	Ga. Code Ann., §§ 51-1-20 to 51-1-20.2, 51-1-29 to 51-1-30.3; 20-2-1001; 38-3-35	Georgia law provides that uncompensated or compensated members, directors, or trustees and uncompensated officers of nonprofit organizations, nonprofit hospitals or government agencies, boards, authorities, or entities are immune from civil liability for injury so long as the person was acting in good faith, within the scope of official duties, and the act was not willful or wanton misconduct.
Hawaii	Haw. Rev. Stat. §§ 662FD-1 to 662D-4; 127-7; 663-1.5	Hawaii extends protection to a volunteer (one providing noncompensated services to a nonprofit, hospital, or governmental entity) for injury resulting from duties so long as the volunteer was acting in good faith and within the scope of function and duty. Volunteers are not protected from civil liability where the act represented willful and wanton misconduct, intentional misconduct, or gross negligence; the act was connected to the operation of a motor vehicle; the volunteer was "unreasonably interfering" with the lawful activities of someone else; the

TABLE 5-4.   CONTINUED

State	Code Section	Summary of Key Provisions
		act took place on the property of an owner that did not give consent; or the volunteer was licensed to perform the act. Hawaii requires general liability coverage of $200,000 per occurrence and $500,000 aggregate unless total assets, exclusive of grants and allocations, are less than $50,000. In 2003, Hawaii extended limited liability to volunteers who design, construct, maintain, or repair skateboard parks for governmental entities (except for harm resulting from gross negligence or intentional misconduct).
Idaho	Idaho Stat. §§ 6-1605, 5-333, 41-3208, 39-7703	Idaho extends protection from personal liability (for amounts in excess of personal coverage or nonprofit coverage) for civil suits to officers, directors, and volunteers of nonprofit organizations where those individuals are not compensated and are acting within the scope of their duties and functions and at the direction of the nonprofit organization. This statute contains a number of exceptions for coverage: willful or wanton conduct, conduct that involves fraud, intentional misconduct or a knowing violation of the law, intentional breach of fiduciary duty or duty of loyalty, or transactions involving improper personal benefit. In addition, coverage is not available for damages involving the operation of a motor vehicle.
Illinois	805 ILCS 105/108.70; 5 ILCS 350/1; 705 ILCS 405/2-17.1; 735 ILCS 5/8-802.1; 740 ILCS 75/1; 745 ILCS/49; 745 ILCS 10/2-214; 745 ILCS 80	Illinois provides that no suit may be brought against directors, officers, and persons who serve nonprofit corporations without compensation for damages related to the exercise of

TABLE 5-4.   CONTINUED

State	Code Section	Summary of Key Provisions
		judgment or discretion or acts within the scope of duties and responsibilities. Coverage is not available for actions that constitute willful or wanton misconduct. There is also limited coverage for directors who serve and earn $5,000 or less for that service. And, finally, protection is extended to those who provide services to or for the nonprofit without compensation.
Indiana	Ind. Code Ann. §§ 23-17-13-1 (d), 34-30-4-1 to 34-30-4-3; 36-8-12-8, 31-15-6-9	Directors are offered immunity from civil liability under the Civil Code. No mention is made of officers, trustees, or other volunteers. Volunteer protection has been considered. For this discussion, see the meeting minutes of October 6, 2001, of the Interim Study Committee on Civil and Family Law, *www.IN.gov/legislative/Interim/ committeeminutes/ICFL4A3.pdf.*
Iowa	Iowa Code §§ 504A.101, 613.19, 512B.9, 613.17, 28H.4, 135.24, 357A.22, 497.33, 672.1	Nonprofit corporation directors, officers, members, or other volunteers are not personally liable for acts resulting in harm as long as the individual acted in good faith and without either intentional misconduct or knowing violation of the law. The protection does not extend to individuals who breach a duty of loyalty or who receive an improper personal benefit from the transaction.
Kansas	Kan. Stat. Ann. §§ 60-3601 to 60-3611, 38-1505a, 48-915, 75-6102 to 75-6103, 65-2891	If a nonprofit carries general liability coverage, an uncompensated volunteer of that organization — defined as an officer, director, trustee, or person who performs services — is not civilly liable for acts or omissions resulting

TABLE 5-4. CONTINUED

State	Code Section	Summary of Key Provisions
		in harm as long as the conduct was not willful or wanton misconduct or intentionally tortious. Volunteers are not liable for the acts or omissions of the nonprofit's officers, directors, trustees, employees, or other volunteers unless the volunteer approves, authorizes, ratifies, or otherwise actively participates in the act and such act or omission constitutes willful or wanton misconduct of intentionally tortious conduct. If the volunteer is required to be insured, or is insured against such acts, liability exists only to the extent of such coverage.
Kentucky	Ky. Rev. Stat. §§ 411.200, 39A.280, 75.070, 311.668, 327.045	Uncompensated directors, officers, volunteers, and trustees of nonprofit organizations are immune from civil liability for acts or omissions resulting from that service as long as they acted in good faith and the act or omission was not willful or wanton.
Louisiana	La. Rev. Stat. Ann. §§ 9:2792 to 9:2793.2, 9:2798, 9:2798.2, 9:2799.5, 29:5, 37:1735	Louisiana's statutes make separate provision for uncompensated directors, officers, or trustees of nonprofit organizations (so long as the actions were in good faith and unless the harm was caused by willful or wanton misconduct); uncompensated members, directors, trustees, or officers of nonprofit hospitals; board members of downtown development districts; directors, officers, trustees, or volunteer workers for nonprofits with civic or historical purpose (with or without compensation); members of boards, commissions, or political subdivision authorities; uncompensated officers of federal or state credit unions;

TABLE 5-4.   CONTINUED

State	Code Section	Summary of Key Provisions
		trustees of self-insurance trust funds (compensated or uncompensated); uncompensated directors, officers, or trustees of certain homeowners' associations; employees of nonprofits supervising or coordinating community services; and volunteers of agencies on aging.
Maine	14 M.R.S. §§ 158-A, 158-B, 164, 8102, 8111; 4 M.R.S. § 1506; 22 M.R.S. 1063	Uncompensated directors, officers, or volunteers of charitable organizations are immune from civil liability for personal injury, death, or property damage arising from acts or omissions within the scope of activities of the organization.
Maryland	Md. Code Ann. Cts. & Jud. Proc. §§ 5-407, 5-603, 5-605, 5-606, 5-607, 5-518, 4-106	The Maryland Volunteer Service Act limits damages of uncompensated officers, directors, trustees, or other volunteers performing services for an association or organization (broadly defined to include charitable organizations; business leagues; civic leagues; clubs; labor, agricultural, or horticultural organizations; or local associations of employees) to the individual's personal insurance levels unless the act or omission was gross negligence, reckless willful or wanton misconduct, or intentionally tortious conduct.
Massachusetts	Mass. Gen. Laws 231 §§ 85W, 85V, 85K, 19A § 33A, 38; 112 § 12B, 58A	Uncompensated officers, directors, or trustees of nonprofit charitable organizations are not liable for civil damages relating to the performance of duties as long as the acts or omissions were not intentional or grossly negligent. The law does not affect or modify the liability for acts or omissions committed in the course of activities

TABLE 5-4.   CONTINUED

State	Code Section	Summary of Key Provisions
		"primarily commercial in nature" or for damages resulting from the operation of a motor vehicle. Uncompensated volunteers in sports programs (including umpires and referees who receive a modest honorarium) have no individual liability for harm so long as the action was not intentional or grossly negligent.
Michigan	M.C.L.S. §§ 450.2209, 450.2556, 324.20301, 324.20302	If the nonprofit corporation's articles of incorporation provide the nonprofit corporation assumes liability for acts or omissions of a volunteer director, officer, or other volunteer if the volunteer was acting within the scope of authority, acting in good faith, the conduct was not willful, wanton or intentionally tortious, and did not arise from the ownership, use, or maintenance of a motor vehicle, then claims for monetary damages must be filed against the nonprofit corporation rather than the volunteer.
Minnesota	Minn. Stat. Ann. §§ 317A.257, 604A.01, 604.11, 604.12, 256.9742	Unpaid directors, officers, trustees, members, or agents of organizations exempt from state income tax are not civilly liable for acts or omissions so long as the act was in good faith, was within the scope of duty, and was not willful or reckless. There are exceptions to the act, including actions brought by the attorney general for breach of fiduciary duty, federal causes of action, actions based on a contract, or actions based on breach of fiduciary duty for a public pension plan.

TABLE 5-4.   CONTINUED

State	Code Section	Summary of Key Provisions
Mississippi	Miss. Code Ann. §§ 95-9-1, 95-9-3, 95-9-5, 73-25-38	Uncompensated "qualified volunteers" are not liable for the negligence of another or for personal actions within the scope of volunteer duties unless the act or omission was intentional, willful, wanton, reckless, or grossly negligent or unless the act or omission was related to the operation of a motor vehicle, aircraft, boat, or other powered vehicle.
Missouri	R.S. Mo. §§ 537.117, 537.118, 160.261, 252.245, 217.055, 260.545, 660.608, 44.023	Volunteers — defined as uncompensated individuals performing services for nonprofit or governmental organizations — are immune from personal liability for acts or omissions if the act was in good faith and within the scope of official duties and the damage was not caused by intentional or malicious conduct or negligence.
Montana	Mont. Code Ann. (2005) §§ 27-1-732, 27-1-733, 10-3-111, 10-3-207, 27-1-714, 27-1-736, 27-1-716, 41-3-1010	Officers, directors, or volunteers of nonprofit corporations are not individually liable for acts or omissions within the scope of duties unless the act or omission was willful or wanton misconduct. There are special provisions for sponsors of rodeo and similar events.
Nebraska	Neb. Rev. Stat. §§ 25.21,191, 25-21,192, 25-21, 193, 35-107, 43-3716, 81-1568	Individuals who serve as directors, officers, or trustees of most tax-exempt organizations and who are not compensated are immune from civil liability for damages that occur within the scope of duty so long as the act was not willful or wanton. This immunity is not applicable if the harm occurred while operating a motor vehicle, plane, or boat or if the volunteer was impaired by alcohol or a controlled substance.

TABLE 5-4.   CONTINUED

State	Code Section	Summary of Key Provisions
Nevada	N.R.S. §§ 41.485, 41.0308, 41.0309, 41.491, 41.500, 41.507, 414.110	Uncompensated officers, directors, trustees, or other persons volunteering for a nonprofit are immune from liability for civil damages resulting from personal acts or omissions so long as those acts were not supervisory; were not part of duties or responsibilities he or she may have had as an officer, director, or trustee; and were not intentional, willful, wanton, or malicious.
New Hampshire	N. H. Rev. Stats. Ann. §§ 508:16, 508:17, 508:12, 508:12-b, 154:1-d, 188-F:32-c	Directors and officers of charitable organizations are not liable for damages for bodily injury, personal injury, or property damage as long as the act causing the damage was committed in good faith and was an activity to further the charitable purposes of the organization. Volunteers of nonprofit organizations and governmental entities are immune from civil liability so long as the organization has a record showing the person was a volunteer; the act was in good faith and within the scope of volunteer duties; and the damage was not willful, wanton, or grossly negligent. Nonprofits have a limitation on the liability for the acts of their volunteers.
New Jersey	N.J. Stat. Ann. §§ 2A:53-A-7 to 2A:53-A-7.3, 2A:53A-12, 2A:53A-13, 2A:62A-1	The Charitable Immunity Act provides protection from liability for uncompensated trustees, officers, or voluntary members of boards, councils, or governing bodies of nonprofit corporations, societies, or associations (including cemetery or burial corporations and economic development organizations) for acts or omissions resulting from the exercise of judgment or

TABLE 5-4.   CONTINUED

State	Code Section	Summary of Key Provisions
		discretion within the scope of duty as long as the individual's conduct did not constitute a willful, wanton, or grossly negligent act or omission and the damage was not the result of negligent operation of a motor vehicle.
New Mexico	N.M. Stat. Ann. §§ 53-8-25.3, 41-12-1	Nonprofit board members are not personally liable for damages resulting from negligent acts or omissions of employees of the corporation, negligent acts or omissions of other directors, or personal acts or omissions unless the director breached his or her duties of office or the act or a failure to act was willful misconduct or recklessness.
New York	N.Y.C.L.S. Not-For-Profit Corp. § 720-a, N.Y.C.L.S. Educ. § 6205, N.Y.C.L.S. Gen. Mun. § 205-b	Uncompensated directors, officers, or trustees of nonprofit entities are liable to others for duties relating to service unless their conduct was intentional or grossly negligent, except certain actions related to fiduciary duties and accountability, including actions brought by the Attorney General; actions brought by the beneficiaries of a charitable trust against the trustees; actions of directors related to private inurement (see N.Y. Not-for-Profit Corp. Law § 719); or actions brought against one or more corporate directors or officers to compel the defendant to account for conduct for negligence, transfer, or waste of assets, or to set aside or enjoin unlawful conveyances of corporate assets.
North Carolina	N.C. Gen. Stat. §§ 1-539.10, 1-539.11, 83A-13.1, 89C-19.1, 143-215.104,	North Carolina provides immunity from civil liability for volunteers, defined as individuals providing direct service for organizations

TABLE 5-4. CONTINUED

State	Code Section	Summary of Key Provisions
	55A-8-60, 58-80-45, 58-82-5, 7B-1204	that have charitable purposes and are exempt from taxation. This immunity is available only where the volunteer was not compensated; the volunteer was acting in good faith; the services were reasonable under the circumstances; and the act was not intentional, was not the result of gross negligence, was not wanton, and did not occur while the volunteer was operating a motorized vehicle.
North Dakota	N.D. Cent. Code §§ 10-33-47, 10-33-48, 32-03-44, 32-03-45, 32-03.1-02, 32-03.1-02.2, 32-03-46, 23-27-04.1, 61-35-27	Officers, directors, and trustees of nonprofit organizations (incorporated or unincorporated) are immune from civil liability as long as the person was acting in good faith, within the scope of duty, the act was not willful misconduct or gross negligence, and reimbursed expenses did not exceed $2,000. Volunteers for nonprofits are immune from civil liability as long as they were acting in good faith, within the scope of duty, the act was not willful misconduct or gross negligence, and the individual did not cause the harm while operating a motor vehicle.
Ohio	Ohio Rev. Code Ann. §§ 2305.38, 1702.55, 5502.30, 2305.234, 2305.23, 2305.231	Volunteers are defined as uncompensated officers, trustees, or other persons who perform services for a charitable organization within the scope of their duties. A nonprofit volunteer is not liable for civil damages for acts or omission in general unless the volunteer had prior knowledge of the act or omission of an officer, employee, trustee, or volunteer and the volunteer authorizes, approves, or actively participates, or after an act or omission the volunteer (with full knowledge) ratifies

TABLE 5-4.   CONTINUED

State	Code Section	Summary of Key Provisions
		the act or omission. In addition, supervisory volunteers are not covered if the act or omission constitutes willful or wanton misconduct or intentional tortious conduct, and nonsupervisory volunteers are not covered if the act or omission was negligent, willful, or wanton misconduct, or intentionally tortious conduct.
Oklahoma	Okla. Stat. Ann. §§ 76-31, 18-866, 18-867, 22-1367	Volunteers are immune from civil liability as long as the act was in good faith and within the scope of their duties, and was not negligent, willful, or wanton misconduct. Volunteers are defined as individuals who provide service without compensation (as long as that individual does not provide the same service to the public for a fee). This immunity does not extend to harm caused in the operation of a motor vehicle.
Oregon	Or. Rev. Stat. §§ 65.369, 30.492, 30.495, 30.497, 30.792, 30.800, 30.803, 419A.170, 419A.110	Nonprofit officers, directors, and executive board members as well as state and governmental board members serving without compensation have protection from civil liability for performance or nonperformance of duties unless the act or failure to act was the result of gross negligence or intentional misconduct. More comprehensive volunteer liability bills filed in 1995 and 1997 failed.
Pennsylvania	42 Pa. C.S. §§ 8331 to 8332.4, 8334, 8336, 8338; 35 Pa. C.S. 6022.301	Any person serving as officer, director of trustee of a § 501(c)(3) organization without compensation shall not be liable for civil damages resulting from acts or omissions

TABLE 5-4.   CONTINUED

State	*Code Section*	*Summary of Key Provisions*
		unless the conduct falls below standards for a like person and that individual knew there was substantial risk the act or omission would result in harm. (Conduct falling below ordinary standards alone is not sufficient to void the protection.) A similar standard applies to volunteers who render public service for a nonprofit organization under IRC § 501(c)(3), (4) or (6) or for a Commonwealth or local government agency conducting or sponsoring a public service program or project.
Rhode Island	R.I. Gen. Laws §§ 7-6-9, 9-1-27, 9-1-27.2, 9-1-34, 9-1-48, 16-19-10, 30-15-15, 401-26-6.1, 42-73-11, 45-57-12	The Rhode Island Nonprofit Corporation Act provides that uncompensated volunteers, directors, officers, or trustees of nonprofit organizations are exempt from liability for "conduct in the execution of the office or duty" unless the activity constituted malicious, willful, or wanton misconduct.
South Carolina	S.C. Code Ann. §§ 33-31-834, 20-7-545, 38-38-130, 8-25-40, 44-29-210	South Carolina provides immunity from suit for directors, trustees, or members of nonprofit governing bodies when the act was part of the operation of that organization, unless the act causing the injury was willful, wanton, or grossly negligent.
South Dakota	S.D. Codified Laws §§ 47-23-28 to 47-23-32, 47-23.21, 20-9-4.1	South Dakota provides immunity for directors, officers, trustees, or direct service volunteers of nonprofits, governmental agencies, and certain free clinics and hospitals so long as the individual was acting in good faith and within the scope of official duties and functions and the action was not grossly negligent, willful, or wanton, and the injury was not the result

TABLE 5-4.   CONTINUED

State	*Code Section*	*Summary of Key Provisions*
		of the negligent operation of a motor vehicle. To the extent the volunteer participates in a risk-sharing pool or has liability insurance, the immunity is not valid to the extent of that coverage.
Tennessee	Tenn. Code Ann. §§ 45-58-601, 29-20-201, 29-20-102, 16-20-105, 37-5-106, 63-6-707, 63-6-218, 62-2-109	Directors, trustees, and members of the governing bodies of nonprofits, whether compensated or not, are immune from lawsuits arising from conducting the business of the organization unless the conduct was willful, wanton, or grossly negligent. Where the nonprofit is a cemetery association, corporation, or organization, there is coverage only where the organization carries liability insurance (this last provision affects counties of a certain size only — see statute).
Texas	Tex. Civ. Prac. & Rem. Code Ann. §§ 84.001 to 84.008, 78.001, 76.004, 154.055; Tex. Educ. Code Ann. § 51.937; Tex. Fam. Code Ann. §§ 261.106, 264.407; Tex. Hum. Res. Code Ann. §§ 40.061, 48.054, 61.096	The Charitable Immunity and Liability Act provides immunity from civil liability to officers, directors, and trustees of nonprofit organizations (other than health care providers) who were serving within the scope of duty (unless that harm occurred because of the operation of motor-driven equipment) to the extent insurance was available, and to direct service volunteers if acting in good faith and in the course and scope of duty unless the act was intentional, willful, or wanton, or undertaken with conscious indifference or reckless disregard for the safety of others.
Utah	Utah Code Ann. §§ 78-19-1, 78-19-2, 78-11-22, 26-8A-601, 58-13-2, 17a-2-1830, 53A-3-402,	Volunteers — defined as uncompensated directors, officers, trustees, or direct service volunteers of nonprofits

TABLE 5-4. CONTINUED

State	Code Section	Summary of Key Provisions
	53A-6-502, 58-13-3, 62A-14-108	(other than public entities) — are not personally liable for acts or omissions so long as the volunteer causing the injury was acting in good faith; believed the act was within the scope of official duties; and the conduct was not illegal, willful, or wanton and did not involve the operation of a motorized vehicle for which a pilot's or operator's license was required. The statute does not provide coverage where the nonprofit does not have a ''financially secure source of recovery'' for those that were injured. Where the nonprofit has falsely led the volunteer to believe it did have coverage, the volunteer may sue the nonprofit.
Vermont	Vt. Stat. Ann., §§ 12-201-5781, 12-201-5782, 12-201-5783, 3-29-1101, 20-175-2922, 20-175-2962, 20-175-2964, 20-193-3812, 24-71-2687, 12-197-5762	Uncompensated nonprofit directors, officers, and trustees are not personally liable for damages resulting from acts or omissions as long as the act was within the scope of the person's functions or duties, was in good faith, and did not constitute gross negligence or an intentional tort. The protection is not extended when the damages result from the operation of a motor vehicle.
Virginia	Va. Code Ann. §§ 8.01-220.1:1 through 8.01-220.1:4, 13.1-870.1, 27-23.6, 32.1-122.10:005, 8.01-225, 8.01-225.01, 8.01-225.1, 8.01-225.2, 8.01-226.2, 8.01-226.4, 8.01-226.5, 2.2-3605, 9.1-154, 15.2-1132, 22.1-258	Uncompensated directors, trustees, and officers of §§ 501 or 528 organizations are immune from civil liability for actions taken in the capacity of their positions. Compensated directors, trustees, or officers of §§ 501 or 528 organizations are limited in liability to an amount equal to their compensation in the 12 months preceding the damaging act or omission. This protection is not available if the individual's act was willful

TABLE 5-4. CONTINUED

State	Code Section	Summary of Key Provisions
		misconduct, a knowing violation of the criminal law, resulted from the operation of a motor vehicle, or was a violation of a fiduciary obligation. Civil immunity is also provided for officers and directors of entities related to the implementation of the national tobacco trust unless actions constitute gross negligence, willful misconduct, or a knowing violation of criminal law.
Washington	Rev. Code Wash §§ 4.24.264, 4.24.300, 4.92.060, 7.75.100, 43.150.080, 72.09.320	A member of the board of directors or an officer of a nonprofit corporation is not individually liable for discretionary decisions or performance or failure to make a decision within the scope of that position, unless the act constituted gross negligence. This limitation of liability does not modify the obligations of the director or officer to the corporation or its members.
West Virginia	W. Va. Code §§ 55-7C-1 to 55-7C-4, 55-7C-3, 30-3-10a, 55-7-19, 15-5-11, 20-3-4	Qualified directors (uncompensated officers, members, or directors of a nonprofit entity rendering personal services) are not personally liable for negligence for acts or omissions when performing managerial functions for volunteer organizations within the scope of the director's duties. The section does not exempt qualified directors from liability where there is gross negligence in performance of duties or when operating a motor vehicle. The nonprofit is not exempt from liability of volunteers.
Wisconsin	Wis. Stat. §§ 181.0670, 184.06, 895.48, 895.51, 187.33, 187.43, 118.29, 118.295	Uncompensated volunteers (defined as all individuals other than an employee) are not liable for damages as long as the act

TABLE 5-4. CONTINUED

State	*Code Section*	*Summary of Key Provisions*
		or omission causing the harm did not violate the law (unless there was a reason to believe the conduct was not criminal), was not willful, and did not represent negligence in the practice of a trade or profession. When the volunteer is a director or officer, the act or omission must also be within the scope of his or her duty.
Wyoming	Wyo. Stat. §§ 1-1-125, 1-1-120, 3-2-112, 17-19-830	Uncompensated officers, directors, trustees, or other persons performing services for nonprofit organizations are immune from civil liability if the act was within the scope of their duties and was not willful or wanton misconduct or gross negligence. The section does not grant immunity for the negligent operation of a motor vehicle.

These statutes protect only the individual, and not the nonprofit. In cases where damage has occurred as a result of the volunteer's actions, the nonprofit itself is then responsible.

Where the state law provides statutory protection for volunteers, do not rely on the statute for absolute protection. While these laws were enacted to encourage and support volunteerism, there are still issues of fact and law that must be determined before the statute's protection attaches. For example, these laws will not protect volunteers acting outside the scope of duty. Moreover, since there has been little judicial interpretation of these rules, it is difficult to know how the law will be applied when tested. When state law provides protection, use the existence of the statute to negotiate a lower rate for such coverage, since the insurance will serve as a supplement to the statutory protection.

The states listed in Table 5-4 (beginning on page 5-51) have specific volunteer liability laws, which are summarized and referenced. The reader is cautioned that state laws are frequently amended, repealed, or added. These select references are to be used as an aid in your review of state law and to quickly locate the applicable statute, rather than as an accurate and current interpretation of the law. The reader should check the actual statute in his or her jurisdiction.

[E] Safeguards from Liability

Scrutiny of nonprofit organizations, including foundations, is increasing as state and federal legislation designed to dictate nonprofit accountability is put in place. Generally speaking, more and more attention is being paid to directors' oversight responsibility — and how well they fulfill it — with hefty personal liability assessments in recent corporate cases (e.g., Enron). In short, fiduciary knowledge is a necessity, not a luxury.

The best protections against liability are active participation and informed involvement in the activities of the foundation. This involvement is best achieved in an environment structured to achieve consistent results by a board that participates, reads materials, questions results, and oversees activities. Knowledge of the foundation and its activities is the best protection.

[1] The 20 Questions

One of the ways to engage board members and challenge them to develop the requisite knowledge is to assess current operating skills. As an annual review or retreat exercise, assess the board's knowledge of their board responsibilities and oversight by asking them to answer the following 20 questions. When scoring the results, allow one point for each question, with bonus points, as noted, for detail.

1. *Provide a brief review of the foundation's history, including the date founded, its founders, and any changes in direction that have occurred since inception.* The foundation's history has enormous impact on its goals, grantmaking, board composition, and board relationships.

2. *State the foundation's mission and purpose.* The mission and purpose can be paraphrased but should reflect the foundation's role and primary goals.

3. *What is the foundation's current market value?* You cannot be an effective fiduciary if you do not know how much money you have to disburse. (Award an extra half point if the board member can correctly state the foundation's ending market value for the previous two years as well.)

4. *What is the foundation's grant spending policy?* Express the foundation's annual grantmaking target in dollars or as a percentage of the foundation's investment assets.

5. *How much does the foundation pay in operating expenses?* Operating expenses include salaries, administrative costs, excise taxes, investment management costs, and similar costs.

6. *What is the ratio of the foundation's operating expenses to grants?* The expense ratio should be determined by dividing the foundation's grants by expenses as reported on the most recent 990-PF. (Award an extra half point if the board member can explain how the foundation's expense ratio compares to other foundations of similar size and purpose.)

7. *What was the foundation's return on assets last year?* Managing the investment of the foundation's charitable assets is one of the most visible and easily analyzed responsibilities. (Award an extra half point if the board member knows how the foundation's return compared to market indices for the period in the same asset allocation, and an additional extra half point if he or she knows how the foundation's investment return compared to other foundations of similar size.)

8. *What is the foundation's current asset allocation?* The mix of equities, fixed income, cash, and alternative investments (such as hedge funds or real estate) is the greatest determinant of performance and the key to risk management.

9. *How much is the foundation's chief executive paid?* Include salary, deferred salary, retirement benefits, health benefits, paid memberships, and other personal benefits.

10. *How much are other staff members and board members paid?* Salaries and benefits should be set annually, considering the individual's job responsibilities, hours of work, and comparable salaries in the field. (Add an extra half point if the individual can correctly state the average annual increase in salary and benefits for all paid staff.)

11. *Does the foundation have a conflict of interest policy applicable to board actions, foundation transactions, and grants?* If so, describe the key elements of the policy as they affect board and staff. If not, describe why those policies are not in place.

12. *Are the conflict of interest policy statements executed annually?* If so, where are those documents stored and who is responsible for initiating and following through on the process? Describe, if possible, how this process and its completion are reported to the board.

13. *Describe the foundation's grantmaking parameters and goals.* Go into as much detail as possible about grant forms, the geographic scope, and grant size.

14. Describe the foundation's follow-up, review, and analysis of its grants.

15. *Have you read each of the foundation's 990-PFs for the last five years and raised questions about any items you did not understand?* Even if you have served on the board for fewer than five years, you need to have this broad understanding. Never "let slide" items that don't make sense to you; if something doesn't seem right, it may not be right.

16. *Does the foundation have an annual audit?* If yes, describe the process of selecting the audit firm. Also, is there an independent audit committee? If not, detail the foundation's reasoning in not obtaining an annual audit.

17. *Which individuals have authority to conduct financial transactions?* Who can make deposits, write checks, buy assets, sell assets, and enter into contracts?

18. *Who approves and reviews the foundation's financial transactions?* This response should include not only the individuals authorized by resolution to write checks, approve asset purchases and sales, and execute contracts on behalf of the foundation, but also the committee or individual who regularly reviews transactions. Award an extra half point if the individual knows whether these financial management policies are reduced to writing in the foundation's policies and procedures.

19. *How much and what forms of insurance does the foundation maintain for its officers, directors, staff, and assets?* This information is not only critical to good foundation management, it may have direct personal bearing if the foundation board is ever sued.

20. *Does the foundation maintain minutes of its board and committees?* This response should also include detail about how the board reviews and approves those minutes, as well as where those documents are archived.

[2] The Scorecard

Tally the correct answers for each participant and compare the results to the scorecard below. There were 20 questions, with a possible perfect score of 23 if the participant answered all questions and half-point bonuses.

Number of Questions You Can Answer	Scoring
17–23 Excellent	Congratulations! The individual is well prepared and will serve as a fiduciary model for other board members.
13–16 Good	The board member is moderately prepared for a role as a board member — he or she will be able to contribute to foundation management and address the foundation's major issues. However, he or she will do a better job if you fill in some of the blanks.
9–12 Fair	The board member has only a basic knowledge of the essentials and should work to improve his or her knowledge base.
5–8 Poor	The board member has great vulnerability for liability. The foundation may be at risk if the knowledge of all board members is limited to this base.
1–4 Abysmal	How could this happen? Provide the individual with answers to these questions and think about how to keep that information current through board meetings and the agenda for those meetings.

[3] How to Improve Results

The questions raised in this survey are core competencies related to basic board responsibilities. While some are more technical than others, all are important. If board member scores fall short of the "excellent" mark, look for ways to improve the results. The most common solutions include the following.

- *Institute annual board training sessions.* Training is critical for new board members, but valuable for all. A good training program should cover the foundation's history, structure, purpose, and goals; board responsibilities; state and federal laws impacting foundations; and asset and liability management.

- *Set regular meetings with complete agendas.* Consider meeting at least quarterly. Two of the meetings may be devoted largely to grants, but the remaining meetings should be devoted to administration, staff, budget, and policies. Strongly encourage attendance. Distribute written materials, including minutes, budgets, grant requests, bylaw changes, and any other matter requiring a vote, prior to the meeting. Encourage all members to read and raise questions about the written materials prior to the meeting so that knowledgeable decisions are made at meetings. As a corollary to this practice, the meetings should be documented by careful minutes with the operating details and reports.

- *Create active committees to conduct work and make recommendations.* One of the most effective ways for a board member to roll up his or her sleeves and get involved in decision making is through committee work. Active committees—for finance, investment management, grantmaking, audit, and personnel— ensure that the board gets involved in substantive work and provides required oversight of staff and third-party professionals.

- *Keep a checklist of "need to know" items and make sure you have answers on an annual basis.* Use a year-end checklist (you can use the 20 questions listed here as a start) and make sure you have the answers you need. It's difficult to know when information is overlooked or omitted without comparing it to a specific list.

- *Create policies and procedures.* These policies should cover decisionmaking, acceptance of gifts, and distribution of grants that highlight issues that need the most consideration and provide a process to reach informed decisions. These should also address investment management, conflict of interest, distribution of funds, and audit of results, that ensure oversight of the spending of funds.

- *Adopt conflict of interest statements.* Have all board members sign a conflict of interest statement that ensures they will reveal all transactions in which they have a direct or indirect interest, and will place the interests of the foundation above personal interests in making decisions.[72]

- *Create a board manual.* Provide all board members with a board management book that contains the organizing documents of the foundation, the tax determination letter, policies and procedures, forms and grant distribution rules, the latest tax return, and any other information relevant to the governance process.

- *Create a process to address issues.* Develop a process to follow up and report back on questions and concerns.

- *Hire good help when needed.* Hire professional assistance, when needed, to clarify legal and procedural issues.

[F] Checklists to Manage Board Liability

Board members control family foundations and are charged with responsibility under federal and state law for the effective operation of those foundations. Anyone joining a nonprofit board, whether a family foundation or a public charity, should be concerned about personal liability. One of the best ways to manage liability is to use a checklist. The checklists provided in Appendix 5-H outline questions to ask before joining the foundation board, an annual analysis of the board member's participation in foundation governance, and a list of annual questions to raise with the foundation administrator.

§ 5.06   BOARD COMMITTEES

The committees of the board should address functional, necessary roles. This means that some foundations will need many committees, while others will

---

[72] *See* sample at Appendix 5-E.

need only a few. If there is no role or meaningful function for the committee, do not create it.

[A] The Role and Function of Committees

The purpose of a committee is to divide the detailed work of the board into manageable portions and to assign those portions to individuals with the knowledge and expertise to render judgments and recommendations on that area of the foundation's work. Sometimes the knowledge and expertise are developed in the process of the committee work, and sometimes the committee members are assigned because of that expertise.

The committees should focus on the essential work or governance of the foundation. Committees should do substantive work in a way that adds value to the effectiveness of their operation. Committee work should be reported from the committee to the board in the form of a recommendation, proposal, or motion. The board should fully understand the recommendation or proposal, ask questions, and even return the matter to committee for more work if necessary. The board should not visit the issue de novo, arbitrarily change the basics of the proposal, or second-guess the conclusions. Where major changes are required to the proposal, the matter should be returned to committee for further work. Committees serve no useful role if the work is reassembled and reconstituted by the full board.

There are two types of committees of a board. There are standing committees, which are committees that have an ongoing role in the life of the foundation, generally of a functional nature. There are also "ad hoc" committees, which are committees that are appointed for a specific purpose, generally for a limited amount of time.

The four functional committees that should be a part of every foundation include (1) the executive committee, (2) the finance committee, (3) the grants committee, and (4) the nominating committee. These are discussed in greater detail in the sections that follow.

In addition to these functional committees, the foundation may periodically establish goal-oriented committees. In the operational area, ad hoc committees may include a Strategic Planning Committee, or a Board Training Committee assembled to accomplish a one-time task. On the programmatic side, ad hoc committees or task forces may be created to research an issue or accomplish a specific objective. For example, if the foundation is focused on environmental issues, and specifically on reducing ozone levels in the community, a committee to "Identify Factors Contributing to Ozone Levels" or to "Develop Collaborative Solutions" may be appropriate. In larger, multi-interest foundations, committees may be established to focus on each charitable sector to which grants are made. There may be committees on "Social Welfare Issues," "Health Care Issues," "Education Issues," and so on.

Membership on committees may be restricted to the board, or it may include individuals outside the board membership. Using outside volunteers may be one solution to building expertise and diversity for the foundation without diluting the family's control of the governance. It may also represent a way to put potential outside board candidates through a trial run to test interest, cooperation, and value to the process.

Keep the size of committees as a reasonable level. "Reasonable" will vary depending upon the number of hands required to get the work done, but should generally be in the five- to 10-person range. Larger committees may not be effective. When a committee grows in size, the chance of working effectively diminishes proportionately as the committee spends most of its time just trying to accommodate group governance and to reach consensus.

[B] Executive Committee

The role of the executive committee is to provide oversight and direction to the activities of the foundation and, when necessary, to make between-meeting decisions about issues delegated to the executive committee. Too often the committee is used to make all of the substantive decisions, so that the remaining board members are disenfranchised.

[C] Finance Committee

This committee manages most of the fiduciary and regulatory operations of the foundation, making it critical to the organization's long-term viability. The finance committee is responsible for recommending a budget, recommending changes to that budget, overseeing and reporting on foundation spending relative to budget, reporting on grantmaking, overseeing the management of foundation assets, and overseeing and reporting on required filings.

This committee is also charged with oversight of the most rigorous of the IRS requirements. Investment management requires not only prudence, but also care to comply with the rules on excess business holdings,[73] jeopardizing investments,[74] taxable expenditures,[75] and unrelated business taxable income.[76] The committee must also ensure that the foundation complies with the mandatory distribution rules, does not distribute to disqualified organizations, and complies with the public inspection laws.

---

[73] IRC § 4943.
[74] IRC § 4944.
[75] IRC § 4945.
[76] IRC § 512.

[D] Grants Committee

The grants committee is considered to be the seat of power in most foundations, especially in family foundations. This committee is responsible for developing grant guidelines, including the scope of foundation grants both geographically and in terms of areas of interest, and a way for the foundation to express and prioritize the grantmaking. The committee should develop the application for grant and the policies and procedures for accepting, reviewing, and selecting grant applications. The group should also develop a system to audit the effectiveness of grants, measuring this effectiveness in terms of both compliance with the terms of the funding and the outcome of the fund use. The mechanics of the grants process are discussed in detail in Chapter 7.

[E] Nominating Committee

The nominating committee has the responsibility of developing profiles of new board members, identifying potential candidates for those positions, and then cultivating and recruiting those members. It is a yearlong job that is too often carried out on one day.

[F] Investment Committee

The investment committee has the responsibility of managing the assets of the foundation. While investment management is discussed more fully in Chapter 8, a summary of the duties will be outlined here. The investment committee should develop investment guidelines, set investment goals in accordance with the distribution goals of the foundation, select an investment manager, monitor investment results, and make changes to policies, goals, and managers when appropriate. While the investment committee does not generally manage investments on its own, it is helpful to have experienced members who are comfortable with and knowledgeable about the process to select investment managers and oversee the results. Experience is often developed through personal investment management, through corporate or employee benefit management, or through experience with other foundations.

§ 5.07   TRAINING THE BOARD

People are not born with a special gene for board service. Good board members are the product of training, experience, and applied knowledge. Training is an especially important issue for family foundations, since training in philanthropy, decision making, and money management may be central to the decision to create the foundation.

[A]   Board Retreats

Board retreats have been used so much that the very mention of a retreat causes anguish in the experienced board member. The whole idea of the retreat is to take the group to a location where there can be an extended period of uninterrupted consideration of issues that are important to the future of the foundation.

There are a number of benefits to a retreat:

• The act of committing to the retreat allows the board to set aside time devoted to foundation management issues. Without this commitment, members may come late, leave early, take calls during the meeting, and never fully disengage from the corporate world.

• The board members have time to get to know each other in both a formal and an informal setting. Retreats always involve more than formal meetings and may include meals, activities, cocktail hours, and other activities that allow interaction. Once members get to know each other, they are far more likely to freely express opinions. This is true even among family members who may not take the time to get together.

• The foundation can set the agenda for the next year, or the next five years.

• The foundation can consider policies and procedures. This is a time not only to review current policies, but also to suggest changes and modifications that may be appropriate.

• Attention can be devoted to housekeeping issues, such as audit reports, financial reports, and insurance coverage (where the word "liability" is mentioned often as a way to keep the group focused).

Since the purpose is to set aside a block of time, announce the retreat well in advance, stress the importance of attendance, and take the group far enough away so that they quit doing corporate business and turn attention to foundation business. Use professional meeting facilitators to make sure that the meeting is focused and goal oriented. Make sure that there is a follow-up report after the meeting that provides a summary of the key decisions and the list of "to do" items requiring follow-up.

Cost and time represent restraints on this process. Make sure that time that is spent is spent well. Consider retreats annually, or semiannually, so that new members are pulled into the process as quickly as possible.

[B]   Mentoring

One method of ongoing training, suggested by Barbara E. Taylor, Richard P. Chait, and Thomas P. Holland in their *Harvard Business Review* article entitled "The New Work of the Nonprofit Board,"[77] is to establish a mentoring program. Assign new board members to experienced board members for the first year, matching interests and personalities where possible. Assign training or review of training to that member. Then seat the paired board members together at meetings so that the long-term members can explain to the newer members the operation of the board and its committees, the influence of various board members, and less-than-obvious interests and habits.

This concept is particularly effective within a family foundation because it creates a natural and supportive structure with which to involve younger generations or new family members and to make them a part of the process as quickly as possible. Many of the donors who create family foundations do so with the goal of teaching family members the value and process of philanthropy as well as educating them on management of funds.

[C] Specialized Training

Some foundations use a formal training program, much like those employed by large corporations, to indoctrinate new board members. The goal of the training is to expose the incoming board member to every aspect of foundation management. It involves spending time with the foundation's chief executive officer, its program officer, and its financial officer. If the foundation is too small to staff these positions, the training may consist of spending time with the foundation's accountant, administrator, or consultant. In some cases, training may involve an internship with the local United Way or community foundation in order to develop a deeper knowledge of the charities operating in the area.

The training period should encompass active participation in the grantmaking process. This may require site visits, application review, or follow-up report administration. If the foundation focuses in a specific area of need, the new board member may be asked to do research in that area, to identify program resources regionally, nationally, or to internationally, or to engage in some other hands-on activity designed to stimulate interest and build his knowledge base. The best training will involve time spent in each of the critical areas of foundation management.

[D] Conferences and Focus Groups

Another effective way to train family members is to attend conferences or focus groups involving other foundations. These events allow board members to learn more about trends in administration and grantmaking, to talk to individuals with similar interests, and to focus their personal interest in

---

[77] Taylor, Barbara E., Chait, Richard P. and Holland, Thomas P., *The New Work of the Nonprofit Board*, vol. 74, no. 5 Harvard Business Review 36-46 (September-October 1996).

foundation involvement. The growing number of family foundations has resulted in events catering to the needs of large foundations, small foundations, or those with regional interests. A sampling of ongoing conferences is detailed in Table 5–5. In addition to these annual conferences, there are any number of wealth management, investment management, and specialty conferences open to family foundation members. Contact any of these sponsoring organizations for more information on specialty events.

TABLE 5-5
Conferences and Events of Interest to Family Foundation Trustees and Directors

Events	*Sponsor Contact Information*
• National Conference for Small Foundations • Foundations 101 • Next Generation • Trustee Leadership • Family Foundation Succession	Association of Small Foundations 4905 DelRay Avenue Suite 200 Bethesda, MD 20814 310-907-3337 (phone) 888-212-9922 (phone) www.smallfoundations.org
• Annual Family Foundation Conference • Trustee Leadership	Council on Foundations 1828 L Street, NW Washington, DC 20036 www.cof.org
• Creating Change Through Family Philanthropy Retreat	Resource Generation 24 Thorndike Street 2nd Floor Cambridge, MA 02141 617-225-3939 (phone) www.resourcegeneration.org
• The Philanthropy Roundtable Annual Meeting	The Philanthropy Roundtable 1150 Seventh Street, NW Suite 503 Washington, DC 20036 202-822-8333 (phone) 202-822-8325 (fax) www.philanthropyroundtable.org
• Southeastern Council of Foundations Annual Meeting	Southeastern Council of Foundations 50 Hurt Plaza SE Suite 350 Atlanta, GA 30303-2914 404-524-0911 (phone) 404-523-5116 (fax) www.secf.org

§ 5.08 A CALENDAR OF FOUNDATION ACTIVITIES

Effective management of the foundation requires that the president, the executive director, or staff keep an eye on the critical events during the year. These events include governance matters, tax filings, grants cycles, exercise of expenditure responsibility/gathering data, and other activities mandated by the board. A sample annual calendar for the Miree Foundation is set out in Table 5–6.

§ 5.09   STAFFING THE FOUNDATION

The increased pressure for accountability and the probability of greater IRS oversight may drive more foundations to hire staff. Hiring a foundation employee, whether full time or part time, can be a daunting experience for the uninitiated. Hiring the right employee to manage a family foundation is difficult. As with any hiring process, experience is the key to defining that staff member's role, locating the right person, and putting them to work.

[A]   Does the Foundation Need Staff?

Family foundations are established to make charitable grants, not to create opportunities for tedious paperwork. When a donor creates a foundation, he may assume that administration is comprised primarily of tax filings, legal actions, or investment management, all of which will be handled by professional advisors. Therefore, little attention is given to the more mundane (and frankly more important) day-to-day details of reviewing grant requests, responding to inquiries, compliance, and governance. Answer the following questions to determine if you might need assistance:

TABLE 5-6
Sample Annual Calendar of Activities for Miree Foundation —
Calendar-Year Foundation

JANUARY

Collect remaining grant follow-up reports not received in December. Obtain year-end valuation of foundation assets from custodian; obtain transaction statement for full year from accounting firm or bank; get valuations on nonmarketable assets as necessary.

Prepare estimate of grant distributions that must be made/should be made in current year.

Mail grant worksheet, pregrant inquiry summaries, and new grant applications to grants committee/board.

Send meeting notice for grant meeting, board meeting; check attendance to ensure quorum.

Prepare and mail 1099s for foundation.

Collect and mail all tax information for 990-PF to accountant to prepare return.

Review minutes from board meetings to determine if the foundation changed its articles of incorporation or bylaws to an extent requiring that the IRS be notified about a change in mission or purpose. Use legal counsel for review if necessary.

File monthly estimates or tax filings with appropriate federal, state, or local authorities (employee tax deposits, federal and state

TABLE 5-6   CONTINUED

tax estimates). File quarterly reports for employees and other required tax returns. File 8283 if gift of more than $5,000 involving nonmarketable property was sold or otherwise disposed of during quarter.

FEBRUARY

Conduct first grant meeting of the year; have decisions approved by board; notify recipients; notify those rejected; make distributions.

Make serial grant payments due in first quarter.

Conduct quarterly board meeting; approve grants; approve other actions, as required.

Appoint nominating committee for new officers and directors; charge with bringing slate to May board meeting.

Conduct annual review of investment performance; manager(s) make personal presentation; review investment policies for critical changes.

Obtain January month-end valuations.

File monthly estimates or tax filings with appropriate federal, state, or local authorities (employee tax deposits, federal and state tax estimates).

MARCH

Review bylaws to determine if changes are needed. Ask attorney to draft changes for board approval at May meeting.

Obtain February month-end valuations.

File monthly estimates or tax filings with appropriate federal, state, or local authorities (employee tax deposits, federal and state tax estimates). File annual employee reports.

APRIL

Update estimate of grant distributions that must be made/should be made in current year.

Mail grant worksheet, pregrant inquiry summaries, and new grant applications to grants committee/board.

Send meeting notice for grant meeting, board meeting; check attendance to ensure quorum.

Obtain March month-end valuations.

File monthly estimates or tax filings with appropriate federal, state, or local authorities (employee tax deposits, federal and state tax estimates). File quarterly reports for employees and other required tax returns. File 8283 if gift of more than $5,000 involving nonmarketable property was sold or otherwise disposed of during quarter.

MAY

Conduct second grant meeting of the year; have decisions approved by board; notify recipients; notify those rejected; make distributions.

Make serial grant distributions due in second quarter.

Conduct annual meeting of the foundation; include grants for approval; include changes to bylaws if necessary; elect new officers; elect directors.

TABLE 5-6   CONTINUED

File 990-PF; send copy of 990-PF to appropriate state officials; post 990-PF on web site, and send to national clearinghouses that post returns.

Obtain April month-end valuations.

File monthly estimates or tax filings with appropriate federal, state, or local authorities (employee tax deposits, federal and state tax estimates).

JUNE

Prepare and publish annual report of the foundation; update on-line information (remove any 990-PF older than three years).

Obtain May month-end valuations.

File monthly estimates or tax filings with appropriate federal, state, or local authorities (employee tax deposits, federal and state tax estimates).

JULY

Update estimate of grant distributions that must be made/should be made in current year.

Mail grant worksheet, pregrant inquiry summaries, and new grant applications to grants committee/board.

Send meeting notice for grant meeting, board meeting; check attendance to ensure quorum.

Obtain June month-end valuations.

File monthly estimates or tax filings with appropriate federal, state, or local authorities (employee tax deposits, federal and state tax estimates). File quarterly reports for employees and other required tax returns. File 8283 if gift of more than $5,000 involving nonmarketable property was sold or otherwise disposed of during quarter.

AUGUST

Conduct third grant meeting of the year; have decisions approved by board; notify recipients; notify those rejected; make distributions.

Make serial grant distributions due in third quarter.

Conduct quarterly board meeting; approve grants; review investment performance; approve other actions, as required.

Obtain July month-end valuations.

File monthly estimates or tax filings with appropriate federal, state, or local authorities (employee tax deposits, federal and state tax estimates).

SEPTEMBER

Obtain August month-end valuations.

File monthly estimates or tax filings with appropriate federal, state, or local authorities (employee tax deposits, federal and state tax estimates).

TABLE 5-6   CONTINUED

OCTOBER

    Prepare worksheet showing grants that must be made in current year, grants that may be made in current year.

    Mail grant worksheet, pregrant inquiry summaries, and new grant applications to grants committee board.

    Send meeting notice for final grant meeting, final board meeting; check attendance to ensure quorum.

    Obtain September month-end valuations.

    File monthly estimates or tax filings with appropriate federal, state, or local authorities (employee tax deposits, federal and state tax estimates). File quarterly reports for employees and other required tax returns. File 8283 if gift of more than $5,000 involving nonmarketable property was sold or otherwise disposed of during quarter.

NOVEMBER

    Review, renew liability insurance for foundation.

    Conduct final grant meeting of the year; have decisions approved by board; notify recipients; notify those rejected. Prepare and mail grant agreements with grant checks.

    Make serial grant payments due in fourth quarter. Update serial grant payment file (chart) to reflect payments completed in current year; add payments awarded during grant meetings in current year.

    Conduct final quarterly board meeting; approve grants; approve other actions, as required.

    Obtain October month-end valuations.

    File monthly estimates or tax filings with appropriate federal, state, or local authorities (employee tax deposits, federal and state tax estimates).

    Pay property tax for real and intangible property.

DECEMBER

    Make grant distributions necessary for qualifying distributions for year. (Have accountant check outstanding qualified distributions from prior year and update estimate for current year; prepay serial grants for following year if necessary.)

    Obtain November month-end valuations.

    File monthly estimates or tax filings with appropriate federal, state, or local authorities (employee tax deposits, federal and state tax estimates).

    Check to make sure grant expenditure reports from all recipients have been received and are in file.

      Develop a calendar for your foundation, using the worksheet provided at Appendix 5-F to list required activities.

- Do you have the time (and commitment) to comply with the governance procedures described in the bylaws? The foundation should have minutes of meetings, resolutions adopting grant recommendations, documentation of board member elections, and regular meetings. Evidence of compliance is important for state nonprofit requirements and is legal evidence of the exercise of fiduciary duties.

- Does the board have the information they need to make decisions on grants? The most effective grant review process involves researching applicants, considering the role of the grant in discharging the foundation's mission, talking with applicants about proposed projects (and making site visits for larger grants), mailing grant applications and research results to the grants committee prior to the meeting, recording decisions, making grant distributions, and analyzing results.

- Is there appropriate follow-up with grant awards? The demand for accountability makes it more important than ever to send grant award letters outlining the use of the grant and requiring a grant report when the funds are expended.

- Do grant seekers receive quick responses to their queries? This communications role can be time consuming, but it is a critical element of establishing communication with the nonprofit community.

If these administrative details have become burdensome or irritating — or worse, have been left undone — it may be time to consider hiring a full- or part-time employee.

[B] Creating a Job Description

The scope of the staff position will be different for every foundation. Some may need a true foundation manager who assumes responsibility for the daily operation of the foundation and oversees additional staff, while others may have a limited role such as grantmaking management. Begin the staff needs assessment by writing a formal job description. The basic elements include the following:

- *Job title*. The title should be as generous as possible while accurately describing the position. For example, if the position is an administrative assistant, the title of "Foundation Administrator" may be more appealing than "Secretary," without misleading the applicant about the responsibilities.

- *Job summary*. The job summary should provide a broad description of the job requirements including the job purpose and general responsibilities. (The specific elements of the job are detailed later.)

- *Reporting lines*. Who's the boss? The applicant should report to a single individual with responsibility for work assignment and oversight. Experienced employees will run from a position requiring them to report to the full board, each of whom may issue instructions. If the staff position has responsibility for supervision of other employees, those responsibilities should be noted.

- *Educational requirements.* Consider the employee's responsibilities to determine the minimum educational level required for the position. The educational break points are generally a high school degree (or GED equivalent), a college degree, or a graduate degree of some form. If you are willing to compromise, you can always specify a high school degree is required, but a college degree is preferred.

- *Personal skills.* Basic skills might include the ability to use common software programs including spreadsheets, word processing, and database programs. If the foundation maintains its financial and grant data on a specific company's database, reference this in the job description, noting that experience with that software is a plus. Applicants may also need to have organizational skills, the ability to interact with the public, to manage projects, to work with limited supervision, and to meet deadlines.

- *Work experience.* Although every foundation would prefer to have an employee with prior family foundation experience, such individuals are rare. Think realistically about alternative employment experiences that might be equivalent. Such experience might include clerical experience, volunteer or work time with a nonprofit, or experience as an administrative assistant.

- *Work Responsibilities.* Make a detailed list of job responsibilities. The job may require acknowledging grant applications, reviewing applications for sufficiency, responding to grantseekers or the press, keeping grant records, preparing the annual report, preparing grant agendas for meetings, scheduling board meetings, paying foundation bills, keeping foundation minutes, etc. List these responsibilities in order of importance in the job description. If possible, indicate the percentage of time each is estimated to require. Detailing the job requirements is the best way to communicate responsibilities to potential applicants, to determine whether you need a full- or part-time employee, and to assess the types of personal skills, educational background, and experience that are required of the successful applicant.

Once the job description is complete, make it available to potential applicants by posting it on the foundation's web site, or by mailing, faxing, or e-mailing the document to qualified applicants. (I have always been inclined to favor applicants who asked for a copy of the job description on the assumption the candidate was making a realistic assessment of his ability to perform those duties.)

[C] Setting Time Requirements, Work Options, and Salary Requirements

The next step is to determine the number of hours required to do the work. The foundation may need help one or two days a week or on a full-time basis. In determining the work schedule, include practical considerations such as where the employee will work and how he or she will be supervised.

Also consider the practical implications of hiring an employee, such as where he or she will work. Does the foundation have a physical office, or will the records be maintained at the foundation president's corporate office or home? Some foundation administrators work from a home office. If so, consideration should be given to how the integrity of the foundation records will be maintained and how the employee's work will be supervised.

Finally, set salary bands for the position. Using a range allows you to adjust the salary offered to a candidate based on his or her experience, reserving the high end for those with exceptional skills. The Council on Foundations, Association of Small Foundations, and The Foundation Center are resources for determining appropriate salaries.

[D] Hiring Staff

[1] Advertising the Position

Advertise the open position as widely as possible, spreading the word among the corporate and nonprofit communities using friends, board connections, and family members. Also contact the state's Nonprofit Resource Center, Association of Fundraising Professionals (AFP), local university job boards, and state job banks. The Internet has opened job searches to an international field of candidates and made interaction with applicants faster and easier. Many membership groups, trade groups, and universities have Internet job boards that allow immediate position postings and facilitate quick responses. The ad should include the job title, job summary, educational and personal skill requirements, and time requirements (full- or part-time), and offer applicants a copy of the job description upon request. (I recommend omitting the salary in the job posting, though you should be prepared to share the salary ranges with interested candidates who are trying to determine their interest in the position.) The ad should also tell applicants how to apply and what to include in the application. Generally, the candidate should submit a resume that includes work experience, three to five contacts for recommendations, and salary expectations. Allow applicants to submit this information by e-mail, fax, or mail.

[2] Interviewing Candidates

Review applications to weed out individuals who do not meet the job requirements. (You may be surprised to see how many people ignore the published education or experience requirements.) Then narrow the field to the applicants who look promising. If the pool is too large for personal interviews, conduct a brief phone interview to make an assessment of the candidate's conversational skills, ability to think on his or her feet, and basic qualifications.

When you have narrowed the field to a group of viable candidates, arrange personal interviews. Interviews generally open with a discussion of topics that put candidates at ease. This is also a good time to give the interviewee an overview of the foundation's history, purpose, and operation. The best candidates will come to the interview having researched the foundation through community resources or the Internet, and will ask questions designed to clarify their findings. Candidates who arrive without a clue about the foundation and express no interest in your overview should be considered with caution.

Spend most of the interview focusing on the candidate's skills and interests. You will learn more about an applicant if you ask open-ended questions rather than those requiring "yes" or "no" answers. For example:

- How did you learn about this position?

- What interests you most about this position?

- What do you know about family foundations?

- What are your greatest strengths?

- What are your greatest weaknesses?

- What are the three most important things you're looking for in your next job?

- What would be the two or three things that would tell you this was not the right job for you?

- Why are you interested in leaving your current position?

- Where do you see yourself five years from now?

Some of these questions are fairly standard, and candidates may come with prepared answers. Prepare a list of interview questions in advance, adding less standard questions to the mix. The goal is to get the individual to talk about priorities, goals, strengths, and weaknesses so that you can evaluate his or her intelligence, organizational skills, and priorities.

While you may be curious, there are certain questions you may not raise in the hiring process. By law, employers may not ask questions related to age, race, marital status, or disability (although there may be questions related to the ability to perform a specific task) since answers to those queries may lead to discrimination. Ask your foundation counsel to provide guidelines for the questions that must be avoided.

[3] Steps to Take After Hiring an Employee

Once you've selected the perfect employee (and that employee has accepted the position), clarify his or her duties, salary, benefits, and supervision in writing. It is also best to establish written goals as quickly as possible after the hire so that both the employee and his or her manager will know the evaluation standards.

Once the new employee begins work, schedule regular meetings to assign and review work. Also set dates for performance and salary review. Employees need regular feedback on performance and affirmation that they are doing a good job. Employees who work in a more traditional work setting are often easier to manage than those working from home or satellite offices, but meeting and review schedules are recommended for both.

[E] Recent Statistics on Foundation Staff Salaries

[1] The Council on Foundations

The Council on Foundations' 2005 Grantmakers Salary and Benefits Report provides the most comprehensive data on foundation salaries.[78] In the 2005 survey, the Council received responses from 742 foundations across the country, 69 of which were corporate foundations, 673 of which were community foundations, family foundations, private independent foundations, or public foundations. The median salaries for the most highly compensated officers are set out in Table 5–7.

---

[78] *2005 Salary and Benefits Report*, Chapter Six, Council on Foundations (Washington, D.C.:2006).

TABLE 5-7
Median U.S. Compensation Results for Top Private Foundation
(Independent and Family) Officers for 2004

Position	Median Salary
Chief Executive Officer	$158,415
Associate Director/Executive Vice President	$135,000
Vice President (Administration)	$154,577
Vice President (Program)	$184,128
Chief Financial Officer	$150,000
Chief Investment Officer	$275,460
Program Director	$129,896
Senior Program Officer	$108,000
Director of Communications	$102,772

While the survey analysis contains much of interest to foundation managers, several findings were of particular interest:

- *Median CEO Salary.* The median salary for a CEO was $115,000 for 2004. For the CEOs for whom deferred compensation figures were available, the median reported deferred compensation in 2004 was $12,000. The median bonus reported for CEOs who reported receiving a bonus was $12,000.

- *Salary Increases.* The vast majority (88.5 percent) of the foundations surveyed awarded salary increases in 2004 and 94.7 percent planned to award salary increases in 2005. The median increases for community, family, independent and public foundations were 4 percent.

- *Staff Benefits.* Of the foundations surveyed, 97.9 percent provided benefits (other than those required by law) to full-time employees. The median cost of those benefits was 26 percent. Of those foundations offering retirement benefits, 2.3 percent offered defined benefit plans, 92.3 percent offered defined contribution plans, and 5.4 percent offered both defined benefit and defined contribution plans.

- *Family Foundation Staff Size.* Staff size varied dramatically, depending on foundation size and practice. Family foundations as a group reported a median of 3 staff with a range of 1 ($10 million to $24.9 million) to 11 ($250 million or greater).

- *Family Foundation Gender and Race.* Staff of family foundations was predominantly female, representing 73.6 percent of all full-time staff. This compares to a 76.2 percent of full-time staff for all surveyed foundations. Family foundation full-time staff was comprised 19.2 percent of minorities and 80.8 percent white.[79]

[2] The Foundation Center

The most recent detailed analysis of family foundation staffing was conducted by The Foundation Center, examining statistics from 2002. The number of staffed foundations and total foundation employees increased in 2002, according to the latest report published by The Foundation Center.[80] The report, *Foundation Staffing*, surveyed 20,716 foundations with at least $1 million in assets, and grants of $100,000 or more. Of the group surveyed, 3,360 (16.22 percent) reported paid staff members, a total of 17,821. Key findings are summarized below.

- *Growth trends.* The percentage of foundations engaging paid staff has steadily decreased, from 23 percent in 1993 to 16.2 percent in 2003. During the same period, the average number of staff per foundation increased from 4.6 in 1993 to 5.3 in 2003. (The average number of employees peaked at 5.5 in 2001, dropped to 5.4 in 2002, and to 5.3 in 2003.)

- *Size matters.* The size of the foundation correlates to the likelihood of paid staff. The study found paid staff at 75.6 percent of the foundations with $100 million or more in assets, 62.3 percent of the foundations with assets of $50 million to $100 million, and 29.9 percent of the foundations in the $10 million to $50 million range. See also Table 5–8. The age of the foundation also correlated to staff levels. Foundations created before 1950 employed an average of 9.8 individuals, those founded between 1950 and 1979 had an average of 5.7, and those created after 1979 had only 3.2 staff members.

- *Type also matters.* The grantmaking foundations surveyed by The Foundation Center were segmented into four groups: independent foundations; corporate foundations; community foundations; and operating foundations. The data reflected the fact that community foundations were the most likely to employ staff, with 81.6 percent of the group surveyed reporting an average of 7.4 staff members. Corporate foundations were the next most likely to have staff; the 23.9 percent staffed corporate foundations reported an average employee pool of 3.4. Operating foundations — those foundations that actually deliver charitable services — were next, with 16.8 percent of the group reporting staff, at an average of 24.5 employees. Finally, independent foundations (a group that includes family foundations) had the lowest incidence of staff, with 13.7 percent of the group reporting an average of 4.3 workers.

---

[79] *2005 Salary and Benefits Report*, Council on Foundations (Washington, D.C.:2006).

[80] Lawrence, Steven, Josefina Atienza and Leslie Marino, *Foundation Staffing*, Foundations Today Series 2003 Edition, The Foundation Center (2003).

- *Shared staff.* A number of the foundations in the survey reported they had joined forces to share staff, allowing a more strategic use of expensive employees to avoid duplication of basic services. Most foundations electing to share full-time employees had a family or mission nexus.

- *Foundation trustees.* The group surveyed reported an average of 4.2 trustees and a median of 3. These figures also varied by foundation type. Community foundations reported an average of 12.4, corporate foundations an average of 5.6, operating foundations an average of 4, and independent foundations an average of 3.8.

These results were updated in January 2006 with The Foundation Center's online publication of "Key Facts on Family Foundations."[81] This snapshot revealed a 28.3 percent growth in family foundations from 2000 (24,434 family foundations) to 2004 (31,347 family foundations). The Foundation Center's survey found 63 percent of these foundation reported assets of less than $1,000,000 and 51 percent reported grants of less than $50,000. Thirteen percent of those surveyed had staff, an increase from the 12.5 percent reported in the prior year.

[F] Paying Salaries to Disqualified Persons

One of the most frequently raised questions in family foundation management is whether family members can receive a salary or other compensation for serving as an officer, director, or employee of the family foundation. The answer is yes.

TABLE 5-8
Median Annual Salaries of Private Foundation CEOS by Foundation Asset Size – Council on Foundations 2005 Survey[82]

Foundation Asset Value (in Millions)	2001	2002	2003	2004	2005
$250+	$288,688	$307,500	$320,000	$335,000	$350,004
$100-$249	$170,000	$177,500	$180,000	$189,500	$200,000
$50-$99.9	$119,750	$123,138	$126,126	$125,000	$130,000
$25-$49.9	$ 86,063	$ 95,000	$ 93,950	$ 98,940	$102,500
$10-$24.9	$ 81,600	$ 84,048	$ 78,000	$ 89,167	$ 91,396
Less than $10	$ 64,125	$ 65,375	$ 67,000	$ 68,924	$ 70,172
All	$156,619	$167,932	$171,200	$185,000	$190,000

---

[81] *Key Facts on Family Foundations*, The Foundation Center (January 2005), at *http://fdncenter. org/research/trends_analysis/pdf/key_facts_fam.pdf.*

[82] *2005 Salary and Benefits Report*, Table 2.22, Council on Foundations (Washington, D.C.:2006), p. 34.

Salaries may be paid to family members on staff so long as the salary is paid for personal services, the services are reasonable and necessary for the operation of the foundation, and the payment is not excessive. The latter is relatively easy to analyze using the salary ranges reported by The Foundation Center and the Council on Foundations.

There is a second test, however, that some family staff members have difficulty meeting. The salary must be reasonable and necessary for the operation of the foundation. That means that the staff member receiving a salary must perform substantive (and necessary) work for the foundation. This may range from providing administrative management, to visiting potential grantees, to reviewing and awarding grants, to providing investment management. Smaller foundations making a few grants a year would have a harder time justifying a $100,000 salary for a chief executive officer than a large foundation that maintains an active community profile and operates a sophisticated grants program.[83]

§ 5.10   SECURING PROFESSIONAL ADVICE FOR THE FOUNDATION

Foundation management is a rapidly expanding field. In the past, a few specialists guided families in goal setting, grantmaking, and in following all the rules. Most families chose to manage the foundation themselves and used outside assistance only when they needed help responding to the Internal Revenue Service, the state attorney general, the press, or the public. Foundation managers used legal counsel to create the foundation and to solve operating problems created by lack of experience, such as self-dealing, disclosure, potential loss of investments, or failure to distribute. They used accountants to file tax returns. And they used banks or investment management firms to manage invested funds. If they could find them, they employed philanthropic consultants to advise on grantmaking.

For the first few decades after the massive changes occasioned by the 1969 tax law changes, professional advisors — attorneys, accountants, financial planners, bankers, and philanthropic consultants — devoted little of their practice to this area. This environment has changed for both foundations and professionals as family foundations have increased in number and asset size. Now there are many resources for family foundations designed to help even small foundations operate like their better-funded counterparts with extensive staff. Professional firms not only perform basic services; they also provide ongoing management advice that helps foundations avoid problems and maximize grant resources.

[A]   Professional Advisors

Most foundations understand the need for an attorney to create the foundation and an accountant to file the annual return. Their needs extend beyond

---

[83] For more information on the self-dealing rules, *see* Chapter 6.

singular activities to a broader range of advisors. Advisors involved, and the roles they play, include the following.

[1] Attorneys

The attorney has a greater role than to simply create the foundation. Too often, foundations are established and clients are sent on their way without any sense of the difficulties of complying with IRS rules and regulations. Attorneys may provide the following services:

- *Probing the potential founder to determine goals and objectives.* This conversation is critical in exploring the potential tax and operating benefits of a foundation as well as the ongoing obligations of foundation management.

- *Selecting the foundation form.* The client should always consider philanthropic alternatives to the creation of a foundation — such as the use of donor-advised funds or a supporting organization — that may more effectively meet his or her goals. (Attorneys, accountants, financial planners, and philanthropic consultants should consider all alternatives.)

- *Establishing the foundation.* This service includes providing the legal documents representing the framework for the foundation.

- *Providing oversight of ongoing foundation management.* Although this duty may also be filled by other professionals, the attorney may review meeting minutes, serve as a resource for questions on unusual grants, analyze potential self-dealing transactions (such as salaries paid to family members, professional service fees paid to family members, sales of property by disqualified persons to the foundation, or personal real estate leased to the foundation), and monitor minimum distributions.

[2] Accountants

Accountants may also provide a variety of services. Some of these services are critical to the ongoing operation of the foundation, whereas others may be specific to the foundation size or function:

- *Making periodic tax filings.* A brief review of the tax filings required for foundations is provided in Chapter 8. It is important to retain an accountant familiar with private foundation requirements.

- *Providing ongoing foundation management and oversight.* An accounting firm may be an effective place to get ongoing oversight and management advice, especially if the firm manages a number of foundations, has seen the most common problems, and is equipped to put disaster-prevention measures in place.

- *Assist in designing a grants management system or manage audit of grants.* This outside review may be particularly important if the foundation makes grants requiring expenditure responsibility, such as grants to individuals, grants to non-501(c)(3) organizations, foreign grants to nonqualified organizations, or program-related investments.

[3] Financial Planners

Financial planners may offer special services to large families, including their foundations. Specific services may include:

- *Facilitation of family and foundation meetings.* Some financial planning firms specialize in family office management. These firms may provide meeting services and coordinate family attendance.

- *Coordination of additions to the foundation.* Financial planning firms offer one-stop planning services that include budgeting and investment management, retirement planning, and estate planning. The firm may coordinate additions to the foundation from the founder and other family members as part of a broader tax and philanthropic plan.

- *Management of board activities.* The firm may also offer services that include keeping minutes and financial records.

[4] Investment Managers

Most foundations are well advised to employ professional investment counsel. The basic services offered by investment managers include:

- *Investment of the foundation's assets.* The manager may specialize in specific equity or fixed income styles or offer balanced portfolio management. The foundation may employ one or more firms depending on its size and investment strategy.

- *Develop and annually review the foundation's investment policies.* The investment management firm may assist the foundation in drafting its investment and spending policies and reviewing the documents at least annually to adjust for economic, market, or grantmaking changes. The investment manager with experience in foundation management can provide solid insight into the practices of other similar foundations.

[5] Administrative Firms

There are an increasing number of administrative firms, some centered in banks and financial firms, others established as independent entities, that provide assistance with day-to-day foundation management. Check the resources provided in Chapters 1 and 8 for firm names. Consulting services cover every aspect of foundation administration, including the following:

- *Developing forms, checklists, and guidelines to provide structure for foundation management.* These lists should help managers manage daily matters such as purchase and sale of assets, making minimum distributions, avoiding self-dealing in business transactions and grantmaking, and providing follow-up. (Attorneys, accountants, and philanthropic consultants)

- *Integrating personal estate and family planning goals with future foundation funding.* Often the foundation is the central element of an estate plan, the recipient on the sale of a family business, or the charitable beneficiary in a high-tax year. Personal planning includes articulating the role of the foundation in the estate plan as well as developing a strategic plan for long-term foundation management. It can also include a thorough analysis of the role of family members in management, especially if foundation employment is the career of choice for one or more family members. (Attorneys, accountants, and financial planners)

- *Managing the foundation's funds to address specific needs such as minimum distribution requirements.* This implies a partnership between the foundation manager and the foundation, not only to generate a cash flow to meet distribution requirements, but to monitor distributions and ensure funds are available on planned grant distribution dates. (Banks, investment managers, and financial planners)

- *Creating grantmaking policies and priorities.* Family foundations are taking a more active role in grantmaking. Many prefer to be proactive by targeting specific needs or expected results and calling for proposals to address those goals. Others employ a reactive grant process but improve the effectiveness of grantmaking by carefully reviewing applicants, using a standardized grant application analysis, and conducting a post-grant review. (Banks with specialized foundation units and philanthropic consultants)

- *Making grants to nondomestic entities for charitable purposes.* International grantmaking is increasingly more popular with foundations and requires a higher degree of compliance to avoid the taxable expenditure rules. There are often language barriers, customs differences, or long-distance compliance challenges that make international grants difficult to manage. (Philanthropic consultants)

- *Resolving family conflict and creating stronger relationships among family members.* Family foundations are often created to pass family values to children, to bring families closer together, or to achieve other personal family goals. When families have conflicts, these goals become illusive. Often the family requires the services of a professional counselor to identify and resolve family conflicts. (Psychologists or counselors associated with professional firms and private counseling practices)

[6] Family Counselors

Large, wealthy families are not immune from family conflict. In fact, family conflict may be accentuated by the visibility of the family, the expectations attached to that visibility, and the dollars involved. When conflict occurs, professional help may be required to address the problems so that the foundation grantmaking and management can continue. Check the resources provided in Chapter 9 for firms that provide this service. Most of the family foundation administrative firms are also able to provide referrals for counseling.

[B] Determining the Services Required

Since family members sometimes staff the family foundation, and some families already have effective legal or accounting counsel, the foundation should determine the professional services required for operation. The time to get professional counsel is when the foundation is established. Use the items above as a checklist for foundation needs, noting those services not already available to the foundation and central to the foundation's goals. Call other foundations that use professional services, obtain referrals, and compile a list of firms to interview. Then make a decision about those services best provided by third parties and select a firm that has experience, is accessible, and fits the foundation's budget.

§5.11 BOARD COMPENSATION

[A] Substantive Role of Foundation Directors

Foundation board members have a substantive role, as do the directors or trustees of all nonprofit corporations. They are charged with responsibility for establishing the foundation's mission, purpose, and direction; selecting and reviewing the performance of the foundation's CEO (where the foundation employs staff); adequately managing foundation resources (including investment, allocation, and protection of foundation assets); managing the foundation's grantmaking; complying with local, federal, and state laws; recruiting and orienting new board members; and ensuring legal and ethical integrity (including accountability to the public). In the aftermath of corporate and nonprofit scandals, there is considerably more pressure on foundations to account for their assets and expenses, and expectations that boards police and prohibit fraud and malfeasance by foundation staff and other insiders.

[B] Blurred Distinction Between Family Foundation Staff and Board Members

Family foundations have a problem that most public charities do not face: Most of the staff and board positions may be held by family members. Although the number of foundations with paid staff has increased by more than 50 percent since 1993, a survey of just over 20,000 foundations in 2005 by The Foundation Center found only 13 percent had paid staff.[84] The board members of many foundations — especially small foundations — do foundation work such as responding to grant requests, reviewing applications, and conducting site work themselves. The professional duties such as accounting, investment management, and legal work are generally performed by outside consultants or advisors, although a few foundations hire family members to perform these tasks. Using board members to perform staff roles blurs the distinction between the two and may make it seem less necessary to have policies and procedures, when in truth they are even more critical in these instances.

[C] Analyzing Family Foundation Board Payments

Foundations pay board members for reasons that range from philanthropic to personal. The most commonly cited reasons include the following:

- The need to attract highly qualified professionals with expertise related to the foundation's mission or with business credentials. The idea is that the expert or professional would not offer that expertise unless paid for his or her time.

- The need to engage a culturally and economically diverse group to guide the foundation in its focus and grantmaking. Pay may attract segments of the community that would not otherwise participate.

- The need to compensate board members for the time and substantive contribution they make to foundation management. This pay may be justified because the board member's service obviates the need to hire costly staff.

The basic premise of each of these arguments is that the foundation board member is simply (and properly) to be compensated for the time and expertise expended on behalf of the foundation.

The charities, individuals, and public representatives that oppose the practice feel that private foundations should devote more of their assets to grantmaking and less to indirect charitable purposes such as trustee salaries. (In fact, this group would likely argue that trustee salaries have no charitable purpose.) An August 2003 report from the Center for Public and Nonprofit

---

[84] Key Facts on Family Foundations, The Foundation Center (January 2006), www.fdncenter.org.

Leadership fueled the public debate.[85] The study, based on data from 1998 Form 990-PFs filed by 238 private foundations (176 large and 62 small) and interviews with those organizations, reported that the surveyed group paid $31.1 million to board members and another $13.8 to bank trustees.[86] Although the 238 in the survey group represented a fraction of the private foundations in operation in 1998, the study's compensation review led to recommendations that officer and director salaries be limited to $8,000 per individual and compensation be excluded from a private foundation's annual required distribution.[87] The report also urged regulators to focus more attention on this topic and to provide the IRS and the public with more detail by expanding the information required in the 990-PF. Key arguments for limiting or eliminating salaries include:

- Focusing foundation dollars on philanthropic purposes (and increasing the dollars distributed directly to charities);

- Eliminating self-dealing and personal benefit to foundation family members and related parties;

- Making salary payments commensurate with the work or time expended by the board member;

- Bringing foundation board member compensation into line with that of other nonprofit board members, most of whom serve without compensation.

[D] The IRS Guidelines

IRS rules limit payments made by private foundations to disqualified persons, a group that includes the foundation's major donors, most of the major donor's family members and controlled entities, and its staff and directors.[88] While most payments to, or transactions between, the foundation and disqualified persons are prohibited (and penalized with an excise tax), the regulations make an exception for compensation paid for services that are personal, reasonable and necessary to the charitable function of the foundation, and that are not excessive.[89] Traditionally, this analysis requires an evaluation of the scope of the services to be rendered, the difficulty of the job, the degree of specialty required, the amount of time devoted to the work, and the size of the foundation (making the assumption that the larger the foundation, the greater and

---

[85] Ahn, Christine, Pablo Eisenberg and Channapha Khamvongsa, Foundation *Trustee Fees: Use and Abuse*, The Center for Public and Nonprofit Leadership, Georgetown Public Policy Institute (September 2003), http://cpnl.georgetown.edu/doc_pool/TrusteeFees.pdf.

[86] *Id.*

[87] *Id.*

[88] IRC § 4941(d)(2)(E).

[89] *See* Chapter 6 for a detailed discussion on compensation and the self-dealing rules.

more extensive the responsibility). A more practical evaluation would compare the payment made to the foundation director to the amount paid to someone outside the foundation for the same services.

[E] Practical Guidelines for Family Foundations

How should the foundation or foundations you advise handle directors' compensation? Consider these six practical guidelines.

1. *Research practices of family foundations of similar size, activity, and purpose.* Use the Council on Foundations, The Foundation Center, or the Association for Small Foundations as sources, or simply network with other foundations in your state or community. Ask for copies of those foundations' salary policies to serve as drafting guidelines.

2. *Draft detailed job descriptions for staff and board members.* These should include the substantive duties attributed to the position, the qualifications required to fill the job, and the time estimated to complete the work. Include sections addressing board members filling staff roles, and salary variations when this occurs.

3. *Make a list of the reasons that compensation is not only appropriate but also critical to achieving the desired results.* For example, if the goal is to get professionals or outside business advisors to join the board to leverage the foundation's work, it may be necessary to offer compensation, especially if the foundation work requires a substantial amount of time, travel, or other time away from the individual's job. Determine alternatives to obtaining such advisors, or the cost of paying for the advice on an as-needed basis.

4. *Draft comprehensive compensation policies for staff and board when the foundation is created.* Ad hoc policies designed to address a specific individual or a specific situation are always less effective.

5. *Use a common sense test for appropriateness: Would the foundation pay the same amount to a stranger (rather than to the family member) serving as a board member or staff member?* Or to use another approach, would the family member be paid the same amount for service to an unrelated family foundation of similar size?

6. *Think about whether the foundation could discuss the payments with ease with the media or with individuals in the community who read the tax return.* If one would avoid those questions, or cannot justify a response, review both the foundation's salary policies and levels.

STEWARDSHIP PRINCIPLES FOR FAMILY FOUNDATIONS

Adopted by the Committee on Family Foundations
September 2004

Family philanthropy is "a unifying and ennobling odyssey for families with the
means and the determination to make a difference in the world around them."
— *Paul N. Ylvisaker*

INTRODUCTION

Through their philanthropy, families aspire to achieve a lasting and positive impact on society. Families' resources extend well beyond money to include leadership and reputation, time and talent, passion and commitment.

Families strive to be responsible stewards of their foundation resources, to uphold the public trust and to practice their philanthropy in ways that reflect fundamental values, including honesty, integrity, fairness and trust. As private entities operating for public purposes, family foundations must comply with federal, state and local law — but most endeavor to go further.

These Stewardship Principles and Practice Options to Strengthen Performance describe how family foundations can reflect these fundamental values in their board governance, management and grantmaking.

HOW TO USE THE PRINCIPLES

The Stewardship Principles and the Practice Options to Strengthen Performance are goals toward which to strive. They correspond to an array of philosophical and practical issues faced by all family foundations. With this document as a framework, family foundation boards and staff can discuss issues *before* they arise, enabling them to proactively develop thoughtful policy and practice that improves over time.

Family foundations can take many forms. Thus, the Practice Options to Strengthen Performance are not checklists. The degree to which a foundation can adopt individual practices will depend upon such things as:

- where it is in its life cycle;

- the requirements and restrictions in its governing documents;

- its asset size;

- whether it is staffed or unstaffed;

- cost effectiveness; and

- whether the board is composed entirely of family members or includes others.

This is not a static undertaking. As the foundation evolves, so too should the choice of Practice Options to Strengthen Performance. The most significant, ongoing reward will accrue to those foundations that employ these principles with consideration, thoughtfulness and commitment, and with the consistent evaluation and appropriate revision.

GOVERNANCE

I. **We have a governing board that establishes the mission, guides the operations, oversees the effectiveness, and ensures the ethical conduct of the foundation.**

Practice Options

A. Develop and periodically review the foundation's values and mission statement, strategies, program areas and guidelines, goals, long-(multi-year) and short- (annual) term objectives and geographic focus.
B. Dedicate sufficient human, financial and technological resources to advance the mission.
C. Plan for leadership continuity.
D. Assess the relevance and effectiveness of the foundation's grantmaking, board governance, management and investments.

II. **Authority is vested in the governing board as a whole, and each member is equipped to advance the foundation's mission.**

Practice Options

A. Identify the desired characteristics of the governing board, including size, composition, member skills and experience; consider diversity and the perspective offered by representatives from outside the family.
B. Develop bylaws that specify the term length of governing board members; the number of consecutive and/or total terms members may serve; minimum and maximum ages; roles, responsibilities and fiduciary duties; and selection and removal processes.
C. Conduct business regularly to ensure meaningful interaction, including at least one annual in-person meeting (governing board and staff if any).

D. Stay on mission; all grants are made within grantmaking guidelines. Exceptions are reviewed by the entire board and do not exceed a maximum dollar cap or percentage of total giving.

E. Provide comprehensive orientation and training for governing board members.

F. Provide continuing education on all aspects of foundation governance, including legal, fiduciary and grantmaking issues.

III. **We consider multiple strategies to further our mission.**

Practice Options

A. Learn best practice models and compare practices against others in the field.

B. Consider a range of financial support options that could include: general operating, project, capital, research, scholarship, endowment, multi-year and challenge grants, and funds to respond to emergency or other unanticipated need.

C. Use program and grant evaluation to improve outcomes.

D. Share successes, failures and lessons learned from grant and program evaluations internally and externally, as appropriate.

E. Collaborate with others who fund similar work.

F. Ensure that staff (if any) is well-qualified and receives on-going professional development.

G. Promote foundation board and staff personal giving and volunteerism (bearing in mind potential conflicts of interest).

H. Provide technical assistance to grantees and other nonprofits.

I. Invest in ways that further the mission (e.g., program-related investments, micro-credit loans, socially responsible investing, proxy voting/shareholder resolutions).

J. Convene community leaders, nonprofits and/or other funders doing similar work.

K. Engage in public policy advocacy as permitted by law.

IV. **Our governing board exercises active fiscal oversight.**

Practice Options

A. Know and ensure compliance with fiduciary duties.

B. Ensure that expenses are reasonable and in proportion to amounts spent on grants and technical assistance.

C. Expect board members to serve the foundation without compensation, recognizing:

1. that reimbursement of reasonable expenses directly related to board service does not constitute compensation;

2. that board members who perform staff functions may be compensated as staff. Like all staff, these individuals should be reasonably compensated, document time spent, and have a job description, performance objectives and evaluations.

D. Confirm that proper due diligence is performed to ensure grantees' fiscal and organizational viability and that grants are used for charitable purposes.

E. Ensure that the foundation has a written investment policy adequate for its size and complexity that includes: investment objectives, asset allocation strategy, spending and/or pay-out policy, rationale for selecting and evaluating investment managers/advisors.

F. Establish effective internal controls, systems of checks and balances, and formalized record keeping.

G. Approve an annual budget and assess the foundation's financial performance relative to the approved budget.

H. Conduct an internal review of foundation compliance with legal, regulatory and financial reporting requirements and provide a summary of the review to board members.

I. Obtain an external review of the organization's finances (in accordance with asset size) by conducting a financial review, periodic audit or annual audit (for larger foundations).

J. Establish an audit committee to oversee accounting, financial reporting, compensation practices and the external audit of the foundation.

ETHICS & ACCOUNTABILITY

V. **We recognize and act upon our obligations to multiple stakeholders: the donor and the donor's family, grantees and grantseekers, the public and governmental bodies.**

Practice Options

A. Keep abreast of the self-dealing laws; avoid self-dealing and even the appearance of self-dealing.

B. Educate the governing board and staff (if any) as to what constitutes conflict of interest:
1. document the affiliations or involvement of board members, grantmaking staff and their families with potential grantees, even if the affiliation creates no financial conflict of interest;

    2. establish and sign annually a written conflict of interest policy that identifies types of conduct or transactions that raise concerns and describes how conflicts or perceived conflicts of interest are resolved.

C.   Incorporate diverse people, perspectives, knowledge and experience into our work:
1. access pertinent data, e.g., census, regional indicators, studies;
2. include subject matter experts or community representatives as speakers at board meetings, on committees or on advisory groups;
3. appoint board members and employ staff who demonstrate the capacity to understand issues and communicate skillfully across cultural, class and other boundaries;
4. encourage board and staff to be actively involved in the community (bearing in mind potential conflicts of interest) and to bring new or underrepresented perspectives back to the foundation;
5. establish governance policies and operational and grantmaking practices;
6. develop training resources that promote inclusion and reduce discrimination.

D.   Identify and practice the elements of ethical conduct.

E.   Develop a policy to handle good-faith complaints about violations of foundation policy or the conduct of foundation board and staff.

VI. **We respect our nonprofit partners' missions and expertise and strive for relationships based on candor, understanding and fairness.**

Practice Options

A.   Develop transparent grants management processes.
1. Create clear and complete guidelines and application procedures (if unsolicited applications are accepted); consider accepting common grant applications.
2. Request only information (pre- and post-grant) that will actually be used in decision-making and corresponds appropriately to the size or purpose of the grant.
3. Specify the steps and timing of the review process.
4. Acknowledge grantseeker inquiries and submissions promptly.
5. Use grant agreement letters to outline mutual expectations.
6. Explain rationale for declined grants and give constructive feedback when appropriate.

B.   Conduct site visits when appropriate, guided by the size and purpose of the grant and the impact on the grantee.

C.   Acknowledge and minimize the effects of the imbalance of power in grantee/grantor relationships.

D. Seek feedback (including anonymous) on foundation performance from current and former grantees and denied applicants.

E. Respond to and act promptly on complaints.

VII. **We welcome public interest and communicate openly.**

Practice Options

A. Make public (on the Web and/or in print) the foundation's board of directors, mission, guidelines, grant process (including whether unsolicited proposals are accepted), finances, procedures, timetable, grantee list with amounts and purpose, etc.

B. Identify and make public a point of contact for the foundation.

C. Respond to requests for information promptly and no later than 30 days.

D. Prepare and distribute (web or print) an annual report (or letter for small foundations).

E. Train board and staff to respond to the media, legislators and other audiences.

F. Develop a proactive strategy for reaching out to the media, legislators and other audiences.

FAMILY LEGACY

VIII. **Our governing board respects donor intent and later generations' interests while also considering the demands of a changing world.**

Practice Options

Honoring Intent

A. Encourage living donors to document their intentions, while taking into account the flexibility succeeding generations may need in governing the foundation.

B. Preserve the foundation's evolution by compiling board dockets and grants made.

C. Invite senior family members to speak to the board.

D. Collect personal recollections of the foundation through interviews with donor(s) and/or senior board members (audio, video and/or written).

E. Conduct activities that provide subsequent generations the opportunity to connect with the family/foundation history.

F.   Review founding documents and donor intent or preferences periodically to assess their continued efficacy.

Recognizing Later Generations' Interests

G.   Encourage board members with interests outside the program or geographic guidelines to support them through personal giving.

H.   If not counter-indicated in the establishing documents (e.g., trusts), consider explicitly adding the flexibility to change focus areas.

I.   If competing interests hinder the foundation's mission or the family's ties, consider engaging a skilled facilitator to find common ground.

IX.   **We plan for leadership continuity.**

Practice Options

A.   Develop and implement a succession plan (with input from the family's teens and young adults) to identify, educate and prepare the next generation of family members for future board service.

B.   Inform the broader family of the foundation's work.

C.   Provide avenues for young family members to learn about and participate in the work of the foundation (or other foundations and/or the nonprofit sector) prior to serving on the board.

D.   Revisit periodically the intended lifespan of the foundation (perpetual or time-limited).

E.   Employ alternative governance structures or giving vehicles when family leadership is no longer viable or no longer desired.

APPENDIX 5-B

SAMPLE BYLAWS FOR A FAMILY FOUNDATION

Note: Bylaws may vary according to state law, the purposes of the foundation, and practical considerations of operation.

The Bylaws of the Miree Family Foundation, an Alabama nonprofit corporation (herein called the "Foundation")

ARTICLE I
OFFICES

The principal office of the Foundation in the State of Alabama shall be located in Jefferson County. The Foundation may have such other offices, either within or without the State of Alabama, as the Board of Directors may designate. The registered office and registered agent of the Foundation shall be as stated in the Articles of Incorporation of the Foundation (the "Articles") or as changed in accordance with law.

ARTICLE II
BOARD OF DIRECTORS

Section 1.   **General Powers.** The corporate powers of the Corporation shall be exercised by or under the authority, and the business affairs of the Corporation shall be managed under the direction of the Foundation's Board of Directors.

Section 2.   **Number, Tenure, and Qualifications.** The number of directors comprising the initial Board of Directors shall be ten (10) unless and until changed by resolution of the Board adopted at any regular meeting by the vote of two-thirds of the then members of the Board, provided that the Board of Directors shall consist of not less than five (5) and that no decrease shall have the effect of shortening the term of any incumbent director. The Executive Director of the foundation shall be an ex officio member of the Board of Directors. The other directors shall be elected at the annual meeting of the Foundation, as established later in these bylaws. The elected members shall serve for staggered terms of three years, except for the initial non – ex officio members whose terms shall expire at the times set out in the Articles. Except for (a) the ex officio directors, each of whose term of office as a director shall be co-extensive with the term of the office by virtue of which he or she serves as a director of the Foundation, and (b) the initial non – ex officio directors, the term of each director in office shall extend until the later to occur of (a) the adjournment of the third annual meeting of the Foundation following the annual meeting at which such director is elected or (b) the date on which his or her successor shall have been elected. No director shall be eligible for reelection to the Board of Directors of the Foundation for a period of one year following the end of his or her term of office.

At least three-quarters (75%) of the members of the Board of Directors shall be related, by blood or marriage, to John Miree, the founder of the Miree Foundation. The remaining members of the Board of Directors should be representative of the public interests served by the Foundation in its grantmaking.

Section 3.   **Meetings.** A regular meeting of the Board of Directors shall be held on the third Monday in May of each year, or on a date in the month of May as soon as practical after that date as established by the Board of Directors and published to all members. Special meetings of the Board of Directors may be called by the President or by any two directors.

Section 4.   **Notice.** Notice of any meeting shall be given at least one week prior thereto by written notice delivered personally or mailed to each director at such director's business address (except that, if such director does not have a business address, then at his or her home address), or by facsimile, or by telegram. Notice shall be deemed to be delivered when received. Any director may waive notice of any meeting. The attendance of a director at a meeting shall constitute a waiver of notice of such meeting, except where a director attends a meeting for the express purpose of objecting, at the beginning of the meeting, to the transaction of any business because the meeting is not lawfully called or convened. Any one or more directors may participate in a meeting by means of conference telephone, video teleconference, or a similar communications method allowing all persons participating to hear each other at the same time, and such participation shall constitute presence in person at the meeting for all purposes of this Article II.

Section 5.   **Election of Non–Ex Officio Directors.** Prior to each annual meeting of the Foundation, beginning with the annual meeting in calendar year 1995, the Board of Directors shall appoint a nominating committee to select and nominate for election as a director of the Corporation one or more candidates. Other nominations may be made from the floor at the annual meeting. Each vacancy in the Board of Directors created by the expiration of the term of office of a director other than an ex officio director shall be filled by the election of a director at the annual Foundation meeting as of which the term expires.

Section 6.   **Quorum.** Section 2 of this Article II shall constitute a quorum for the transaction of business at any meeting of the Board of Directors, but if less than a majority is present at a meeting, a majority of the directors present may adjourn the meeting from time to time without further notice.

Section 7.   **Vote Requirement.** No action shall be taken by the Board of Directors unless the same is authorized by the vote of a majority of the directors present at a meeting at which a quorum is present.

Section 8.   **Vacancies.** Vacancies and newly created directorships resulting from any increase in the authorized number of directors may be filled by a majority of the directors then in office, although less than a quorum, or by a sole remaining director.

Section 9.   **Committees.** The Board of Directors, by resolution adopted by a majority of the directors in office, may designate one or more committees, each of which shall consist of two or more directors, which committees, to the extent provided in such resolution, shall have and exercise the powers of the Board of Directors in the management of the Corporation and may have power to authorize the seal of the Corporation to be affixed to all papers that may require it, except that no such committee shall have the authority of the Board of Directors with reference to amending, altering, or repealing these bylaws; electing, appointing, or removing any member of such committee or any director or officer of the Foundation; amending the Articles, restating the Articles, adopting a plan of merger, or adopting a plan for consolidation with another corporation; authorizing the sale, lease, exchange, or mortgage of all or substantially all the property and assets of the Foundation; authorizing the voluntary dissolution of the Foundation or revoking proceedings therefor; adopting a plan for the distribution of the assets of the Corporation; or amending, altering, or repealing any resolution of the Board of Directors that by its terms provides that it shall not be amended, altered, or repealed by such committee. Other committees not having and exercising the authority of the Board of Directors in the management of the Foundation may be designated by a resolution adopted by a majority of the directors present at a meeting at which a quorum is present. Such committee or committees shall have such name or names as may be determined from time to time by resolution or resolutions adopted by the Board of Directors. In the absence or disqualification of a member of a committee, the member or members thereof present at any meeting and not disqualified from voting, whether or not such member or members thereof constitute a quorum, may unanimously appoint another member of the Board of Directors to act at the meeting in the place of any such absent or disqualified member. The designation of any such committee or committees and the delegation thereto of authority shall not operate to relieve the Board of Directors, or any member thereof, of any responsibility imposed upon the Board of Directors or the members thereof by law.

Section 10.   **Informal Action.** Any action required or permitted to be taken at any meeting of the Board of Directors or of any committee thereof may be taken without a meeting, if a written consent thereto is signed by all members of the Board of Directors or of such committee, as the case may be.

Section 11.   **Dissent of Director to Action of the Board.** Any director who is present at a meeting of the Board of Directors at which action on any corporate matter is taken shall be presumed to have assented to the action unless such director's dissent shall be entered in the minutes of the meeting or unless such director shall file a dissent to such action with the Secretary of the meeting before its adjournment or shall forward such dissent to the Secretary of the Foundation immediately after the adjournment of the meeting. Such right of dissent shall not apply to a director who voted in favor of such action.

ARTICLE III
OFFICERS AND AGENTS

Section 1.   **Number.** The officers of the Corporation shall be a President, one or more Vice Presidents (the number thereof to be determined by the Board of Directors), a Secretary, a Treasurer, and Executive Directors and such other officers and assistant officers as may be deemed necessary by the Board of Directors. Any two or more offices may be held by the same person, except the offices of President and Secretary.

Section 2. **Election and Term of Office.** The officers of the Corporation shall be elected annually by the Board of Directors at the annual meeting of the Board of Directors as established in Article II. If the election of officers shall not be held at such meeting, such election shall be held as soon thereafter as it conveniently may be. Each officer shall hold office until such officer's successor shall have been duly elected or until the death, resignation, or removal (in the manner hereinafter provided) of such officer.

Section 3. **Removal.** Any officer or agent elected or appointed may be removed by the persons authorized to elect or appoint such officer whenever in their judgment the best interests of the Foundation will be served thereby.

Section 4. **Vacancies.** A vacancy in any office elected or appointed by the Board of Directors because of death, resignation, removal, or otherwise may be filled by the Board of Directors for the unexpired portion of the term. A vacancy in any other office for any reason shall be filled by the Board of Directors, or any committee or superior officer to whom authority in the premises may have been delegated by these bylaws or by resolution of the Board of Directors.

Section 5. **President.** The President shall be the principal executive officer of the Corporation and, subject to the control of the Board of Directors, shall in general supervise and control all the business and affairs of the Foundation. The President shall, when present, preside at all meetings of the Board of Directors. The President may sign, with the Secretary or an Assistant Secretary, any deeds, mortgages, bonds, contracts, or other instruments that the Board of Directors has authorized to be executed, except in cases where the signing and execution thereof shall be expressly delegated by the Board of Directors or by these bylaws to some other officer or agent of the Corporation, or shall be required by law to be otherwise signed or executed; and in general the President shall perform all duties incident to the office of the President and such other duties as may be prescribed by the Board of Directors from time to time. If no Treasurer has been designated, the President shall also have the duties and powers of the Treasurer prescribed in Section 8 below.

Section 6.   **Vice Presidents.** In the absence of the President or in the event of his inability or refusal to act, the Vice President (or in the event there be more than one Vice President, the Vice Presidents in the order designated at the time of their election, or in the absence of any designation, then in the order of their election) shall perform the duties of the President, and when so acting, shall have all the powers of and be subject to all the restrictions upon the President. Any Vice President shall perform such other duties as from time to time may be assigned to such officer by the President or the Board of Directors.

Section 7.   **Secretary.** The Secretary shall (a) keep the minutes of meetings of the Board of Directors in one or more books provided for that purpose; (b) see that all notices are duly given in accordance with the provisions of these bylaws or as required by law; (c) be custodian of the corporate records and of the seal of the Foundation and see that the seal of the Foundation is affixed to all documents the execution of which on behalf of the Foundation under its seal is duly authorized; and (d) in general perform all duties incident to the office of Secretary and such other duties as from time to time may be assigned to such officer by the President or by the Board of Directors.

Section 8.   **Treasurer.** The Treasurer shall have charge and custody of and be responsible for all funds and securities of the Corporation; receive and give receipts for moneys due and payable to the Foundation from any source whatsoever, and deposit all such moneys in the name of the Foundation in such banks, trust companies, or other depositories as shall be selected from time to time by the Board of Directors; and in general perform all the duties incident to the office of Treasurer and such other duties as from time to time may be assigned to such officer by the President or by the Board of Directors.

Section 9.   **Assistant Secretaries and Assistant Treasurers.** The Assistant Secretaries and Assistant Treasurers shall perform such duties as shall be assigned to them by the Secretary or the Treasurer, respectively, or by the President or the Board of Directors.

Section 10.   **Executive Director.** The Executive Director shall be responsible for conducting the day-to-day administration and business of the Foundation and, subject to the control of the Board of Directors, shall in general supervise and control the employees of the Foundation. The Executive Director may sign, with the

President, a Secretary, or an Assistant Secretary, any deeds, mortgages, bonds, contracts, or other instruments that the Board of Directors has authorized to be executed, except in cases where the signing and execution thereof shall be expressly delegated by the Board of Directors or by these bylaws to some other officer or agent of the Corporation, or shall be required by law to be otherwise signed or executed. In addition, the Executive Director shall perform such other duties as may be prescribed by the Board of Directors from time to time.

Section 11. **Agents.** The Board of Directors may designate such agents of the Foundation as the Board of Directors may deem necessary or advisable, including but not limited to the designation (subject to the approval of the Board of Directors) of an agent to receive, deposit, and otherwise handle funds of the Foundation.

ARTICLE IV
CONTRACTS, LOANS, CHECKS, DEPOSITS, INVESTMENTS, AND EXPENSES

Section 1. **Contracts.** The Board of Directors may authorize any officer or officers or agent or agents of the Foundation to enter into any contract or execute and deliver any instrument in the name of and on behalf of the Foundation, and such authority may be general or confined to specific instances.

Section 2. **Loans.** No loans shall be made by the Foundation and no evidences of indebtedness shall be issued in its name unless authorized by a resolution of the Board of Directors. Such authority may be general or confined to specific instances. No loans shall be made by the Foundation to its directors or officers.

Section 3. **Checks, Drafts, Etc.** All checks, drafts, or other orders for the payment of money and notes or other evidences of indebtedness issued in the name of the Foundation shall be signed by such officer or officers or agent or agents of the Foundation and in such manner as shall from time to time be determined by resolution of the Board of Directors.

Section 4. **Deposits.** All funds of the Foundation not otherwise employed shall be deposited from time to time to the credit of the Foundation in such banks, trust companies, or other depositories as the Board of Directors may select.

Section 5.   **Investments.** The funds of the Foundation shall be invested in such investments as the Board of Directors or any investment manager appointed by the Board of Directors may from time to time select, giving due regard to balancing the need to preserve principal, produce income and capital gain, and achieve long-term growth for the Foundation assets.

Section 6.   **Expenses.** The Board of Directors shall pay all expenses of the Foundation, including but not limited to custodian, investment management, and accounting fees and charges, first from income (if available), and if not, from the principal assets of the Foundation.

ARTICLE V
FISCAL YEAR

The fiscal year of the Foundation shall begin on the first day of January and end on the last day of December in each year, unless the Board of Directors shall provide to the contrary by resolution duly adopted at a regular meeting of the Board.

ARTICLE VI
ACCOUNTING RECORDS; ANNUAL REPORT

Section 1.   **Accounting Records.** The Foundation shall maintain or cause to be maintained accounting records of the business and affairs of the Corporation.

Section 2.   **Annual Report.** The Foundation shall furnish to the Board of Directors and to the donors of the Foundation within 60 days of the date that the 990-PF is filed a written report of the activities and the receipts and disbursements of funds of the Foundation during such tax year.

ARTICLE VII
DIVIDENDS

No dividends shall be paid and no part of the income or profits of the Foundation shall be distributed to its directors or officers. The Foundation may pay compensation in a reasonable amount to directors, officers, and other employees for services rendered.

ARTICLE VIII
SEAL

The Board of Directors shall provide a corporate seal, which shall be circular in form and have inscribed thereon the name of the Foundation, the state of incorporation, and the words "Corporate Seal." If such a seal is not obtained, the words "Corporate Seal" following the signature of one or more officers on behalf of the Foundation shall constitute a proper affixing of the seal.

ARTICLE IX
WAIVER OF NOTICE

Whenever any notice is required to be given to any director of the Foundation under the provisions of these bylaws, the Articles, or applicable provisions of Alabama law, a waiver thereof in writing, signed by the person or persons entitled to such notice, whether before or after the time stated therein, shall be deemed equivalent to the giving of such notice.

ARTICLE X
INDEMNIFICATION

In amplification and not in limitation of the provisions of applicable law:

(a) The Foundation shall indemnify any person who was or is a party or is threatened to be made a party to any threatened, pending, or completed claim, action, suit, or proceedings, whether civil, criminal, administrative, or investigative, including appeals, by reason of the fact that such person is or was a director, officer, employee, or agent of the Foundation, or is or was serving at the request of the Foundation as a director, officer, partner, employee, or agent of another corporation, partnership, joint venture, trust, or other enterprise, whether for profit or not for profit, against expenses (other than taxes, penalties, or expenses of correction), including attorneys' fees and amounts paid in settlement, if such expenses are reasonably incurred by him in connection with such proceeding and he is successful in such defense, or such proceeding is terminated by settlement, and he has not acted willfully and without reasonable cause with respect to the act or failure to act that gave rise to the liability.

(b) Any indemnification under subsection (a) (unless ordered by a court) shall be made by the Foundation only as authorized in the specific case upon a determination that indemnification of the director, officer, employee, or agent is proper in the circumstances because such person has met the applicable standard of conduct set forth in subsection (a). Such determination shall be made (1) by the Board of Directors by a majority vote of a quorum consisting of directors who were not parties to, or who have been wholly successful on the merits or otherwise with respect to, such claim, action, suit, or proceeding, or (2) if such a quorum is not obtainable, or even if obtainable a quorum of disinterested directors so directs, by independent legal counsel in a written opinion.

(c) The indemnification authorized by this Article X shall continue as to a person who has ceased to be a director, officer, employee, or agent and shall inure to the benefit of the heirs, executors, and administrators of such a person.

ARTICLE XI
AMENDMENTS

The Board shall have power to make, alter, amend, and repeal the Bylaws of the Foundation by the affirmative vote of a majority of the trustees then in office, provided, however that notice of the proposed amendment or amendments shall have been included in the meeting notice which is given to the members of the Board and, provided, further, that no such action shall be taken that would adversely affect the qualification of the Foundation as an organization that is exempt from Federal income taxation under Code Section 501(a), or as an organization described in Code Section 501 (c)(3), contributions to which are deductible under Code Sections 170(c)(2), 2055(a)(2) and 2522(a)(2).

SAMPLE MEETING MINUTES WITH CORPORATE RESOLUTION

QUORUM ESTABLISHED. The Board of Directors of the Miree Family Foundation held its annual meeting at 2 P.M., May 15, 2005, at the Foundation offices at 1111 Crest Road, Birmingham, Alabama. All directors were present.

MINUTES APPROVED. President John Miree called the meeting to order. Minutes of the meeting of February 17, 2005, were mailed to all directors prior to the meeting, and approved upon unanimous consent.

CORPORATE RESOLUTION APPROVED. The following Resolution was adopted on the motion by Kathryn Miree, with a second by Virginia Clark, and unanimous vote of the Board of Directors:

BE IT RESOLVED, that the President and the Treasurer of the Corporation have the full power and authority to authorize the following:

(1) Open or close any bank account and designate those persons authorized to sign checks or transfer funds with regard to those accounts.

(2) Open or close any account with any other broker/dealer regarding the trading of securities, options, commodities, financial instruments, or other products that might be traded or sold by the Corporation and designate those persons authorized to execute orders in such accounts.

(3) Designate persons authorized to guarantee signatures, provide safekeeping or other custodial functions with regard to customer or Corporation securities, enter any vault or safety deposit box maintained by the Corporation for customer or Corporation securities, and transfer or cause to be transferred the name in which any security is registered.

GRANTS APPROVED. The following grants were recommended for approval by the Grants Committee. These grants were reviewed by the Board and determined to be appropriate for the

Foundation. On motion of Sean Clark, and second by Louise Blanchard, the Board approved payment by unanimous consent.

Grants Approved

AIDS Task Force of Alabama	$50,000
Alabama Institute for Deaf and Blind	$25,000
Alabama Symphony Association	$15,000
Birmingham Museum of Art	$5,000
Birmingham Zoological Society	$5,000
Community Foundation of Greater Birmingham	$10,000
McWane Center	$25,000
St. Vincent's Hospital Foundation	$10,000
The Women's Fund	$10,000
University of Alabama at Birmingham	$50,000
Total Grants Paid:	$205,000

Grants Denied

Birmingham City Schools
City of Birmingham Park System
Magic Moments
Eye Research Foundation
Jefferson County Department of Health

DIRECTORS ELECTED.   The following directors were nominated by the Nominating Committee, headed by Louise Blanchard. On motion by Virginia Clark, and second by John Miree, the directors were elected.

Governing Board

Jim Clark	Term expires May 31, 2008
Joy Drum	Term expires May 31, 2008
Maultsby Waller	Term expires May 31, 2008

Junior Board (non-voting)

Christopher Miree	Term expires May 31, 2006
Harrison Miree	Term expires May 31, 2006
Sarah Clark	Term expires May 31, 2006

OFFICERS ELECTED. The following officers were elected by unanimous consent to serve a one-year term, or until a successor is elected.

President:	John Miree
Vice President:	Kathryn Miree
Treasurer:	Virginia Clark
Secretary:	Louise Blanchard

OLD BUSINESS. There was no old business to come before the Board.

NEW BUSINESS. Budget Approved. The Finance Com-mittee presented a budget for the year 2006. On motion by Kathryn Miree, and second by Louise Blanchard.

Grant Workshop Date Set. The Grants Committee will hold its annual grant workshop for charitable organizations in the greater Birmingham area on November 8, 2005, at the Foundation offices. The committee hopes to increase attendance to 75-100 qualified charities. All Board members were encouraged to invite qualified organizations to attend.

NEXT MEETING DATE. The next meeting of the Foundation will be at 2 P.M., August 21, 2005, at the Foundation offices.

MEETING ADJOURNED. There being no further business to come before the Board, the meeting was adjourned at 5:30 P.M.

Louise Blanchard, Secretary

CORPORATE RESOLUTION
Adopted by Unanimous Consent of the Board of Directors on May 15, 2005.

The Miree Family Foundation Corporate Resolution

I, the undersigned, Secretary of The Miree Family Foundation, a nonprofit corporation organized and existing under the laws of the State of Alabama, do hereby certify that at a meeting of the Board of Directors of said Corporation duly convened and held on the 15th day of May, 2005, at which a quorum was present, and acting throughout, the following resolution was adopted, the same now is in full force and effect, and you may rely upon its remaining in such effect until you are advised otherwise by certificates executed by the Secretary of said Corporation.

BE IT RESOLVED, that the President and the Treasurer of the Corporation have the full power and authority to authorize the following:

(1) Open or close any bank account and designate those persons authorized to sign checks or transfer funds with regard to those accounts.

(2) Open or close any account with any other broker/dealer regarding the trading of securities, options, commodities, financial instruments, or other products that might be traded or sold by the Corporation and designate those persons authorized to execute orders in such accounts.

(3) Designate persons authorized to guarantee signatures, provide safekeeping or other custodial functions with regard to customer or Corporation securities, enter any vault or safety deposit box maintained by the Corporation for customer or Corporation securities, and transfer or cause to be transferred the name in which any security is registered.

I do further certify that the powers granted in this resolution are not contrary to the Articles of Incorporation or the Bylaws of said Corporation, and that said Resolution supersedes and rescinds all previous resolutions.

IN WITNESS THEREOF, I have hereunto set my hand as Secretary of said Corporation and affixed its corporate seal this the _____ day of _____, 2005.

_____
Louise Blanchard, Secretary

I, John Miree, President of The Miree Family Foundation, acting under the authority granted in the attached resolution of the Board of Directors, do hereby designate the following persons as authorized to deal with approved broker/dealers in connection with the said cash accounts and that approved broker/dealers shall accept all orders for purchases and sales and all instructions given by any of them on behalf of this Corporation as and for the action of this Corporation without further inquiry as to their authority:

John Miree	President
Kathryn Miree	Vice President
Virginia Clark	Treasurer

_____   _____
Date   Louise Blanchard, Secretary

BOARD MEMBER PROSPECTING CHECKLIST

Board Prospect	Family Member	Family Member with History of Fdn. Support	Interest in Mission of Fdn.	Experience with Fdn. Mgmt.	Experience with Invst. Mgmt.	Public Relations Contacts	Civic Contacts	Social Contacts	Other	Total
1.										
2.										
3.										
4.										
5.										
6.										
7.										
8.										
9.										
10.										
11.										

SAMPLE CONFLICT OF INTEREST STATEMENT

Note: Conflict of interest policies should be drafted to address the particular need of the family foundation. The officers, staff, and board members of the organization should sign this statement.

The following sample may be used for board members, trustees, or even advisory boards. It is perhaps most appropriate for board members or trustees who have a fiduciary duty to the organization. The IRS also provides a sample conflict of interest policy in the Form 1023 Instructions.

- As a member of the Board of Directors of XYZ Family Foundation, I, _____, am committed to XYZ Family Foundation's goal to establish and maintain the highest level of public confidence in its accountability. I have personally committed to follow the standards set out below, which are a part of XYZ Family Foundation's conflict of interest policies.

- I will conduct my activities with the Board of Directors of XYZ Family Foundation so that I do not advance or protect my own interests, or the private interests of others with whom I have a relationship, in a way that is detrimental to the interests of or to the fundamental mission of XYZ Family Foundation.

- In every instance in which I represent the XYZ Family Foundation, I will conduct my activities in a manner to best promote the interests of XYZ Family Foundation.

In all matters that come before the Board of Directors for a vote that may favorably impact my own financial interests, or the private interests of others with whom I have a financial relationship, I will reveal that relationship and abstain from a vote in the matter.

When a conflict of interest arises, or when a potential conflict of interest emerges, I will disclose that conflict or potential conflict to the President of XYZ Family Foundation or to the Chairman of its Board of Directors and seek a resolution of that issue.

Entered into on this the _____ day of _____, 20__ __.

_____ Member, Board of Directors

WORKSHEET TO SCHEDULE ANNUAL ACTIVITIES

List all foundation activities, note the completion date for each, and transfer the information to a foundation calendar. (*See* the example at Table 5–5.)

Activity/Task	*Date(s) for Activity/Frequency*
GOVERNANCE	
Appoint nominating committee	
Present slate to board for election	
Appoint committees	
Set meeting dates for committees	
Set date for board orientation	
Set date for board retreat	
Schedule review/session for strategic planning	
Review minutes of meetings, articles of incorporation, and bylaws to determine if changes are necessary	
Check minutes book to ensure all minutes are complete, signed	
Set dates for board meetings; provide notice to all board members; check to ensure quorum	Set meeting dates annually; provide notice quarterly; call to ensure quorum quarterly
ADMINISTRATIVE	
Review liability insurance; make payment to keep it up to date	
Obtain monthly values of marketable assets; send copy to accountant	
Obtain annual values for nonmarketable as sets; send copy to accountant	
Schedule audit	
Confirm contract/agreement with attorney for foundation	
GRANTMAKING	
Review application form to determine if changes are necessary	
Conduct grants workshop for eligible nonprofits; schedule time and place; send invitations	
Conduct pregrant inquiries	Quarterly
Prepare estimate for qualified distribution/ grant goals	Quarterly

Activity/Task	*Date(s) for Activity/Frequency*
Set meeting dates for grants committee; coor dinate with board meetings; provide notice; call to ensure quorum	Set meeting dates annually; publish notice quarterly
Prepare grant agreements	
Set dates for receipt of grant follow-up reports	
Prepare serial grant list	

TAX FILINGS	
Confirm contract/agreement with accountant	
File 990-PF	Due by the 15th day of the 5th month following the end of the tax year
Post 990-PF on web site; provide to clearing house web sites	
File estimated tax for foundation	
Check to see if other returns are due	
Pay property tax (real and intangible) (*Note:* Check to see if foundation is exempt from payment of these taxes; file for exemption if appropriate)	Normally due in the late fall/end of year
File 990-PF with state officials required to receive copies.	File at the same time original is filed with IRS
File employee returns	941 (tax withholding) due quarterly on April 30, July 31, October 31, and January 31; W-2s due annually on January 31; 1099s for outside/inde pendent contractors (non-employees) or interest, rent, etc., due by January 31
File 8283 if nonmarketable property of greater than $5,000 is sold or otherwise disposed of within two years of gift	Check quarterly; return due 125 days after sale or disposition

VOLUNTEER PROTECTION ACT OF 1997
Public Law 105-19 (6/18/97)
42 U.S.C. 14501

SEC. 1. SHORT TITLE.

This Act may be cited as the 'Volunteer Protection Act of 1997'.

SEC. 2. FINDINGS AND PURPOSE.

(a) FINDINGS — The Congress finds and declares that —

(1) the willingness of volunteers to offer their services is deterred by the potential for liability actions against them;

(2) as a result, many nonprofit public and private organizations and governmental entities, including voluntary associations, social service agencies, educational institutions, and other civic programs, have been adversely affected by the withdrawal of volunteers from boards of directors and service in other capacities;

(3) the contribution of these programs to their communities is thereby diminished, resulting in fewer and higher cost programs than would be obtainable if volunteers were participating;

(4) because Federal funds are expended on useful and cost-effective social service programs, many of which are national in scope, depend heavily on volunteer participation, and represent some of the most successful public-private partnerships, protection of volunteerism through clarification and limitation of the personal liability risks assumed by the volunteer in connection with such participation is an appropriate subject for Federal legislation;

(5) services and goods provided by volunteers and nonprofit organizations would often otherwise be provided by private entities that operate in interstate commerce;

(6) due to high liability costs and unwarranted litigation costs, volunteers and nonprofit organizations face higher costs in purchasing

insurance, through interstate insurance markets, to cover their activities; and

(7) clarifying and limiting the liability risk assumed by volunteers is an appropriate subject for Federal legislation because —

(A) of the national scope of the problems created by the legitimate fears of volunteers about frivolous, arbitrary, or capricious lawsuits;

(B) the citizens of the United States depend on, and the Federal Government expends funds on, and provides tax exemptions and other consideration to, numerous social programs that depend on the services of volunteers;

(C) it is in the interest of the Federal Government to encourage the continued operation of volunteer service organizations and contributions of volunteers because the Federal Government lacks the capacity to carry out all of the services provided by such organizations and volunteers; and

(D)(i) liability reform for volunteers, will promote the free flow of goods and services, lessen burdens on interstate commerce and uphold constitutionally protected due process rights; and

(ii) therefore, liability reform is an appropriate use of the powers contained in article 1, § 8, clause 3 of the United States Constitution, and the fourteenth amendment to the United States Constitution.

(b) PURPOSE — The purpose of this Act is to promote the interests of social service program beneficiaries and taxpayers and to sustain the availability of programs, nonprofit organizations, and governmental entities that depend on volunteer contributions by reforming the laws to provide certain protections from liability abuses related to volunteers serving nonprofit organizations and governmental entities.

SEC. 3. PREEMPTION AND ELECTION OF STATE NONAPPLICABILITY.

(a) PREEMPTION — This Act preempts the laws of any State to the extent that such laws are inconsistent with this Act, except that this Act shall not preempt any State law that provides additional protection from liability relating to volunteers or to any category of volunteers in the performance of services for a nonprofit organization or governmental entity.

(b) ELECTION OF STATE REGARDING NONAPPLICABILITY — This Act shall not apply to any civil action in a State court against a volunteer in which all parties are citizens of the State if such State enacts a statute in accordance with State requirements for enacting legislation —

(1) citing the authority of this subsection;

(2) declaring the election of such State that this Act shall not apply, as of a date certain, to such civil action in the State; and

(3) containing no other provisions.

SEC. 4. LIMITATION ON LIABILITY FOR VOLUNTEERS.

(a) LIABILITY PROTECTION FOR VOLUNTEERS—Except as provided in subsections (b) and (d), no volunteer of a nonprofit organization or governmental entity shall be liable for harm caused by an act or omission of the volunteer on behalf of the organization or entity if —

(1) the volunteer was acting within the scope of the volunteer's responsibilities in the nonprofit organization or governmental entity at the time of the act or omission;

(2) if appropriate or required, the volunteer was properly licensed, certified, or authorized by the appropriate authorities for the activities or practice in the State in which the harm occurred, where the activities were or practice was undertaken within the scope of the volunteer's responsibilities in the nonprofit organization or governmental entity;

(3) the harm was not caused by willful or criminal misconduct, gross negligence, reckless misconduct, or a conscious, flagrant indifference to the rights or safety of the individual harmed by the volunteer; and

(4) the harm was not caused by the volunteer operating a motor vehicle, vessel, aircraft, or other vehicle for which the State requires the operator or the owner of the vehicle, craft, or vessel to —

(A) possess an operator's license; or

(B) maintain insurance.

(b) CONCERNING RESPONSIBILITY OF VOLUNTEERS TO ORGANIZATIONS AND ENTITIES—Nothing in this section shall be construed to affect any civil action brought by any nonprofit organization or any governmental entity against any volunteer of such organization or entity.

(c) NO EFFECT ON LIABILITY OF ORGANIZATION OR ENTITY—Nothing in this section shall be construed to affect the liability of any nonprofit organization or governmental entity with respect to harm caused to any person.

(d) EXCEPTIONS TO VOLUNTEER LIABILITY PROTECTION — If the laws of a State limit volunteer liability subject to one or more of the following conditions, such conditions shall not be construed as inconsistent with this section:

(1) A State law that requires a nonprofit organization or governmental entity to adhere to risk management procedures, including mandatory training of volunteers.

(2) A State law that makes the organization or entity liable for the acts or omissions of its volunteers to the same extent as an employer is liable for the acts or omissions of its employees.

(3) A State law that makes a limitation of liability inapplicable if the civil action was brought by an officer of a State or local government pursuant to State or local law.

(4) A State law that makes a limitation of liability applicable only if the nonprofit organization or governmental entity provides a financially secure source of recovery for individuals who suffer harm as a result of actions taken by a volunteer on behalf of the organization or entity. A financially secure source of recovery may be an insurance policy within specified limits, comparable coverage from a risk pooling mechanism, equivalent assets, or alternative arrangements that satisfy the State that the organization or entity will be able to pay for losses up to a specified amount. Separate standards for different types of liability exposure may be specified.

(e) LIMITATION ON PUNITIVE DAMAGES BASED ON THE ACTIONS OF VOLUNTEERS —

(1) GENERAL RULE — Punitive damages may not be awarded against a volunteer in an action brought for harm based on the action of a volunteer acting within the scope of the volunteer's responsibilities to a nonprofit organization or governmental entity unless the claimant establishes by clear and convincing evidence that the harm was proximately caused by an action of such volunteer which constitutes willful or criminal misconduct, or a conscious, flagrant indifference to the rights or safety of the individual harmed.

SEC. 5. LIABILITY FOR NONECONOMIC LOSS.

(a) GENERAL RULE — In any civil action against a volunteer, based on an action of a volunteer acting within the scope of the volunteer's responsibilities to a nonprofit organization or governmental entity, the liability of the volunteer for non-economic loss shall be determined in accordance with subsection (b).

(b) AMOUNT OF LIABILITY —

(1) IN GENERAL — Each defendant who is a volunteer, shall be liable only for the amount of noneconomic loss allocated to that defendant in direct proportion to the percentage of responsibility of that defendant (determined in accordance with paragraph (2) for the harm to the claimant with respect to which that defendant is liable. The court shall render a separate judgment against each defendant in an amount determined pursuant to the preceding sentence.

(2) PERCENTAGE OF RESPONSIBILITY — For purposes of determining the amount of non-economic loss allocated to a defendant who is a volunteer under this section, the trier of fact shall determine the percentage of responsibility of that defendant for the claimant's harm.

SEC. 6. DEFINITIONS.

For purposes of this Act:

(1) ECONOMIC LOSS — The term 'economic loss' means any pecuniary loss resulting from harm (including the loss of earnings or other benefits related to employment, medical expense loss, replacement services loss, loss due to death, burial costs, and loss of business or employment opportunities) to the extent recovery for such loss is allowed under applicable State law.

(2) HARM — The term 'harm' includes physical, nonphysical, economic, and non-economic losses.

(3) NONECONOMIC LOSSES — The term 'non-economic losses' means losses for physical and emotional pain, suffering, inconvenience, physical impairment, mental anguish, disfigurement, loss of enjoyment of life, loss of society and companionship, loss of consortium (other than loss of domestic service), hedonic damages, injury to reputation and all other non-pecuniary losses of any kind or nature.

(4) NONPROFIT ORGANIZATION—The term 'nonprofit organization' means —

(A) any organization which is described in § 501(c)(3) of the Internal Revenue Code of 1986 and exempt from tax under § 501(a) of such Code and which does not practice any action which constitutes a hate crime referred to in subsection (b)(1) of the first section of the Hate Crime Statistics Act (28 U.S.C. 534 note); or

(B) any not-for-profit organization which is organized and conducted for public benefit and operated primarily for charitable, civic, educational, religious, welfare, or health purposes and which does not practice any action which constitutes a hate crime referred to in subsection (b)(1) of the first section of the Hate Crime Statistics Act (28 U.S.C. 534 note).

(5) STATE—The term 'State' means each of the several States, the District of Columbia, the Commonwealth of Puerto Rico, the Virgin Islands, Guam, American Samoa, the Northern Mariana Islands, any other territory or possession of the United States, or any political subdivision of any such State, territory, or possession.

(6) VOLUNTEER—The term 'volunteer' means an individual performing services for a nonprofit organization or a governmental entity who does not receive —

(A) compensation (other than reasonable reimbursement or allowance for expenses actually incurred); or

(B) any other thing of value in lieu of compensation, in excess of $500 per year, and such term includes a volunteer serving as a director, officer, trustee, or direct service volunteer.

SEC. 7. EFFECTIVE DATE.

(a) IN GENERAL—This Act shall take effect 90 days after the date of enactment of this Act.

(b) APPLICATION—This Act applies to any claim for harm caused by an act or omission of a volunteer where that claim is filed on or after the effective date of this Act but only if the harm that is the subject of the claim or the conduct that caused such harm occurred after such effective date.

APPENDIX 5-H
BOARD LIABILITY CHECKLISTS

I. Pre-Director Review

— Ask for a written list of board duties and meeting dates. How many meetings are you expected to attend? Does the organization provide board training? How many committees will you be expected to serve on, and how often do those committees meet?

— Determine why you were asked to join the board. Do you have specific expertise, fundraising ability, or other specific talents that make you an attractive board member?

— Ask for a copy of the charity's current strategic plan.

— Review the organization's last two annual reports. How clearly is the financial information presented? How well does the report communicate the charity's mission, services, and use of funds?

— Check Guidestar (*www.guidestar.org*) to review the charity's latest Form 990. Does this information correlate with information presented in the annual report? What is the relationship of the charity's expense to its expenditures on programs? How do staff salaries compare to national norms?

— Review the current list of board members. Contact several to determine if the charity believes in an active board involvement (or are board members expected to show up, vote, and not get involved) and if the board and staff have a strong, open, working relationship.

— Ask the chief executive officer (or chief financial officer) to share a written description of the board indemnification policy, directors' and officers' (D & O) policy coverage and limits, and other insurance covering the charity and its volunteers.

— Ask how the organization funds its operations. Does it rely on government grants, individual donations, fees for services, membership fees, or other revenue?

— Ask how the organization manages reserves. If it has an endowment, ask to see the most recent investment returns.

II. Annual Evaluation Checklist

— Did you attend the board's annual workshop and/or training session?

— Did you attend at least 80 percent of the scheduled board meetings?

— Did you review the minutes of each meeting you attended to ensure the board's actions were correctly reflected?

— Did you review the minutes of meetings you did not attend to learn the actions taken by the board in your absence?

— Did you participate in key decisions made by the board, asking questions, listening to the opinions of others, and voting only when you had the facts and professional input needed to make a decision?

— Did you review the charity's budget and financial statements on a monthly or quarterly basis, asking questions to clarify items you did not understand? Did you raise concerns when those figures varied from those projected and approved?

— Did you review the charity's audited financial statements? Were those prepared in a timely manner? Did you review the accompanying management letter and address all items raised as a concern?

III. Annual Management Checklist

— Has every board member been asked to sign a conflict of interest statement, agreeing to put the interests of the charity above personal interests and to reveal any conflicts of interests in matters put before the board?

— Has the board evaluated the performance of the charity's CEO? Was this performance review in writing? If there were material issues or questions, were these shared with the board?

— Is the board satisfied with the performance of staff? Did the board review the salary levels for the chief executive officers and staff, comparing those to salaries of comparable nonprofits?

— Does the board have a current strategic plan? If not, are there plans to engage in this long-term planning process?

— Has the organization made its financial statements available to the board? Has the finance committee reviewed and approved these statements?

— Is the charity operating in accordance with its budget and with its available revenues and assets?

— Did the board review (annually review) the charity's financial policies, investment management policies, gift acceptance policies, and donor data policies?

— Did the finance committee and board review the endowment's investment returns, comparing those returns to investment policy guidelines?

— Do the organization's fundraisers operate effectively and in accordance with ethical standards?

— Did staff share statistics on the charity's performance in serving the public good? For example, did it provide data on the number of individuals served, or some other measure of its programmatic effectiveness?

— Has the organization filed all tax returns with the IRS? Has it filed a copy of its 990 with the State Attorney General?

— Did the charity have an audit performed by an outside firm? Has the board received those results? Were any exceptions noted on the management letter?

— Did the charity perform an annual risk assessment? Does the charity have adequate insurance coverage based on that assessment? Does the charity have policies in place ensuring claims will be reported on a timely basis? Was director coverage reviewed and shared with the board?

— Were there lawsuits or other liabilities incurred by the charity during the year? How did the board learn of these issues?

— Does the charity have a strong nominating committee with a process designed to recruit the most effective board members? Did the committee meet and nominate new directors successfully?

CHAPTER 6

OPERATING RESTRICTIONS

Note to the Reader: One of our guiding principles in the preparation of this book was to make the text readable and understandable, even in the context of complicated and labyrinthine Internal Revenue Code concepts. For this reason, we have not attempted to include every case and ruling that has appeared since the first edition of this volume was published. Important developments have been included where they illuminate points discussed in the text or are otherwise helpful. We want this book to be helpful, but it is not intended to serve as a checklist of all cases, rulings, and other technical developments.

§ 6.01   INTRODUCTION

Unfortunately, the rules and restrictions governing private foundations have received much more attention among advisors than any other aspect of foundations, so much so that many families are discouraged from implementing plans to create a family foundation. Those few, aging advisors who remember the days before the present rules were enacted in 1969 may recall how flexible the family foundation was in those halcyon days. Indeed, there were virtually no limits to what could be done because there were no specific rules one could break. In such an atmosphere, it was probably inevitable that abuses and improprieties would occur, and reports of such abuses led Congress to create a comprehensive new set of restrictions that has survived almost without change to the current time. These restrictions are described and discussed in great detail later in this chapter.

Despite the scope and complexity of these private foundation rules, however, they still operate only to do what they were originally created to do — prevent abuses. The family that wants a family foundation for the proper reasons may find that these restrictions do not really have much impact on their operations. True, there are complications and costs involved, plus one of the most complex returns in the entire Internal Revenue Service (IRS) collection. However, the simple fact remains that the family foundation can do virtually whatever its creators want to, provided they do not enter into the basic abuse areas that led Congress to impose these rules in the first place. The reader is urged to keep this in mind as these rules and restrictions are discussed. These rules and restrictions can be tricky, and inadvertent violations are certainly possible. A foundation can safely evade most exposure to liability by avoiding questionable actions, seeking and following professional advice when issues arise, and keeping its operations simple and straightforward.

This chapter, written for the general reader, will present a nontechnical (well, not *too* technical) explanation of the major foundation restrictions, with an emphasis on how they would affect the operations of the "innocent" family foundation. The private foundation restrictions imposed by the Internal Revenue Code (IRC) are analyzed in much greater detail in Appendices 6-A through 6-F, which will give the reader the specifics of how the foundation excise taxes work and are applied.

§ 6.02   THE FOUNDATION RESTRICTIONS

[A] In General

In its hearings on the Tax Reform Act of 1969, Congress heard considerable testimony about the various ways in which foundations had allegedly been misused by their creators. Foundations were said to have provided personal benefits to creators and their families through grants, employment, and otherwise. In some cases, witnesses said, foundations would wait for years before making any distributions to charity, simply accumulating income and building up massive endowments. In other instances, foundations reportedly held substantial interests in businesses owned by their creators, thereby protecting and perpetuating control of the business by the creator and his or her family. Foundations made investments that were speculative or even risky, thereby jeopardizing the foundation's ability to continue and carry on its charitable program. The most colorful testimony of all related to the manner in which foundations were said to have made questionable or improper grants; some foundations failed to follow through with their grantees to assure that transferred funds were used for the intended purposes and that such purposes were appropriate in the first place. It is not entirely clear just how common or widespread these alleged abuses actually were, but Congress nevertheless took them quite seriously.

How, then, could all these transgressions be prevented? The approach Congress eventually adopted was a detailed set of restrictions and prohibitions, cast in the form of a system of excise taxes. These taxes were placed in Chapter 42 of the Internal Revenue Code (sections 4940 through 4948) and as a result are often called "the Chapter 42 taxes." A relatively small excise tax was imposed on the investment income of private foundations, and five separate tax provisions addressed specific problem areas. The focus of this chapter is on the *restrictions* imposed on foundation activities by several of those excise taxes. Other provisions that impose the tax on investment income and require minimum distributions are discussed in Chapter 7.

With each of the new restrictions, the forbidden behaviors were defined in detail, often excruciating detail. If a foundation engaged in the prohibited activity, the penalty in the form of an excise tax would apply. In most cases, two separate sets of penalties would apply. The first, an "initial" tax in a relatively small amount (e.g., 5 or 10 percent), would be imposed on the foundation, and a similar tax would also be imposed on the responsible foundation managers who caused or allowed the foundation to stray into forbidden territory. Thereafter, the foundation would be required to reverse or "correct" the offense, and a failure to do so would bring an "additional" tax at a much higher rate (e.g., 100 or 200 percent), with a similar penalty tax applicable to the recalcitrant foundation manager.

[B] Tough Restrictions—But Will They Affect *Your* Situation?

These penalty excise taxes are the heart of the federal regulation of private foundations. They can be quite severe and are inevitably unforgiving. Many are surprised to learn that the Internal Revenue Service has no authority to create exemptions or excuse violations that are found to be innocent or even beneficial. The very existence of these penalties has proven to be an effective deterrent to the behaviors Congress decided in 1969 to prohibit.

The Chapter 42 taxes have sometimes discouraged the creation of foundations by persons who so much as contemplate any of the forbidden categories of activity. This is often the result of advice from advisors who are affected by their perception of the Chapter 42 taxes as just too restrictive and complex to be trifled with, even if the potential foundation creator does not contemplate engaging in activities that those taxes would affect.

Many advisors overlook the fact that many of the harsh rules and restrictions applicable to foundations are narrow in their application. The tax rules that limit donors' benefits on amounts transferred to foundations are income tax rules only, and have no effect upon amounts transferred at death. There are no comparable estate tax limitations. Similarly, the operating restrictions described in this chapter may have no effect on a particular family's situation.

For example, consider the case of an individual who owns a successful business and has no heirs or other family members to whom the business may be left at his death. Before 1969, such a person might well have considered creating a private foundation to serve as the principal beneficiary of his estate and to receive and hold this business on a permanent, ongoing basis. As discussed below, however, the foundation restrictions enacted in that year include a prohibition on "excess business holdings," which limits the proportion of ownership a foundation may have in such a business. For a person in such a situation today, a private foundation is thus not a viable alternative. Instead, an individual who desires to leave his or her business to charity must either select an existing public charity or utilize one of the types of entities described Chapter 2.[1] What is equally important, however, is that this rule, awesome and unforgiving as it may be when it does apply, poses no threat whatsoever to the person who contemplates creating a foundation with publicly traded securities.

The following sections will look at each of the foundation restrictions enacted in 1969. A detailed technical explanation of each of these provisions appears in Appendices 6-A through 6-F; the following section is intended to provide an objective, "plain English" explanation of how these rules work and is not intended to serve as an attorney's reference source. Attorneys and other readers seeking the particulars on just how these restrictions apply should consult the more technical summary in the chapter appendices, where these rules are discussed in more detail. In addition, the effect of these rules and their practical

---

[1] *See* Chapter 2 for a discussion of alternatives to the family foundation.

implications are discussed throughout the book, particularly in Chapter 7, on grantmaking.

The following discussion will focus on what these rules mean to the average family foundation and how the foundation can protect itself against liability for these excise taxes. And remember that the application of these rules must be evaluated in the context of the specific client/donor under consideration.

[C] Abatement of Chapter 42 Taxes *Other Than* Self-Dealing

Section 4962(a) provides the IRS with discretionary authority to abate the automatic first-tier taxes. Abatement is permitted if the foundation establishes that the violation was due to reasonable cause, not to willful neglect, and the foundation corrects the violation.

By 1984, it became apparent that the automatic two-tier penalty structure of the Chapter 42 taxes might be more strict than necessary to enforce the private foundation restrictions, at least in certain situations. Accordingly, effective for taxable events occurring after 1984, the Tax Reform Act of 1984[2] added IRC § 4962, granting discretionary authority to the IRS to abate most first-tier Chapter 42 private foundation taxes. Abatement under § 4962 is available only if it is established to the satisfaction of the Secretary of the Treasury that the taxable event was (1) due to reasonable cause and not to willful neglect and (2) corrected within the applicable correction period for such event. If the tax has already been collected, the tax is to be credited or refunded as an overpayment. The legislative history makes it clear that a violation due to ignorance of the law will not qualify for abatement under this provision.[3]

Importantly, the discretionary authority of the IRS to abate first-tier Chapter 42 taxes does not extend to abatement of the initial taxes imposed with regard to acts of self-dealing. Section 4962(b) provides specifically that "the tax imposed by section 4941(a) (relating to initial tax on self-dealing)" is not a "qualified first tier tax of the sort subject to abatement." A parallel provision enacted in 1980, § 4961, provides for mandatory abatement of second-tier taxes where the taxable event is corrected during the correction period for such event.

For an example of how the first-tier tax abatement under § 4962(a) is applied, see Technical Advice Memorandum 200347023, in which the National Office approved abatement of foundation excise taxes under the following circumstances. Foundation X began construction of a hotel in 1985. In 1986, after the hotel opened for business, X placed the hotel in a wholly owned for-profit subsidiary. X undertook this transfer in reliance upon a written legal opinion that its ownership of the subsidiary would not result in a violation of

---

[2] Pub. L. No. 98-369.
[3] *See* H.R. Rep. No. 432 (pt. 2), 98th Cong., 2d Sess. 1472 (1984); S. Rep. No. 169 (vol. 1), 98th Cong., 2d Sess. 591 (1984).

Chapter 42 of the Code. In 1993, the Service issued a technical advice memo-randum,[4] holding that X's ownership of the subsidiary violated IRC §§4942, 4943, and 4944. X has since completed action to correct these Chapter 42 violations. In addition, in 1988, X made grants of stock to several organizations, also on the advice of counsel. The 1993 IRS technical advice memorandum also held that X failed to exercise its expenditure responsibility requirements in connection with these 1988 grants, thereby incurring liability for excise tax under IRC §4945. This situation was corrected in 1989. On these facts, the IRS National Office concluded that the initial excise taxes due under IRC §§4942, 4943, 4944, and 4945 should be abated under §4962(a).

§6.03   SELF-DEALING—WHAT YOU SHOULD, COULD, MIGHT, CAN'T, AND WOULDN'T DO

[A]   General Rule

The cornerstone of the private foundation restrictions is the prohibition on acts of self-dealing. The basic concept underlying this restriction is quite simple. The creator of a family foundation and all related family members and other interests are classified as "disqualified persons."[5] As such, they are completely prohibited from virtually all dealings with the foundation, including sales, pur-chases, exchanges, leases, and loans. Unlike public charities, which can engage in such dealings with their insiders and related parties so long as those dealings are at arm's length (i.e., there is no "excess benefit" conferred on the insiders), private foundations cannot engage in such dealings at all—period.

For this reason, the family considering and planning for a foundation would be well advised to keep in mind the basic rule that prohibits all forms of self-dealing, however benign or beneficial to the foundation. While there are excep-tions, as discussed below, the family will be better advised in most cases to adopt the flat prohibition rule as an operating standard.

Just what is self-dealing? The statutory definition in IRC §4941(d) states that any of the following actions, direct or indirect, between a foundation and its disqualified persons is an act of self-dealing that will bring liability for the tax:

- Any sale, exchange, or leasing of property;
- Any lending of money or other extension of credit;
- Any furnishing of goods, services, or facilities;
- Any payment of compensation (or payment or reimbursement of expenses) to a disqualified person, except as described below;

---

[4] TAM 9340002 (June 16, 1993).

[5] *See* §6.03[B][1] *infra.*

- Any transfer to, or use by or for the benefit of, a disqualified person of the income or assets of a private foundation; and

- Any agreement by a private foundation to make any payment to a government official, other than an agreement to employ such individual entered into 90 days before the official's government service terminates.

The operation of the tax on self-dealing depends on a number of other definitions as well, starting with the term "disqualified person." This term appears in most of the other IRC Chapter 42 taxes as well, so it is an important prerequisite to an understanding of these rules. Section § 4946(a) of the Code defines "disqualified person." Disqualified persons are discussed below in § 6.03[B][1].

While all of these definitions are important and cannot be overlooked, it is obviously the creator's family and related interests that are of paramount importance to most family foundations.

Acts of self-dealing may be direct or indirect, and this means that a family foundation must be careful to anticipate and avoid situations in which a seemingly innocent chain of events may give rise to an actual or potential violation. For example, consider this situation: A father loans $25,000 to his daughter to help her purchase a home. Later he contributes her note to the family foundation. Since the daughter is a disqualified person, this amounts to an extension of credit between her and the foundation, which violates the self-dealing rules.[6] The result is the same even if the note is secured and/or bears interest at a rate that is higher than the foundation could otherwise realize. The receipt and holding of a note pursuant to a transaction involving a decedent's estate might qualify under the exception from the self-dealing rules, as discussed below.[7] This would be the case, for example, if the father in our example bequeathed his daughter's note to the family foundation; of course, all the requirements of the exception in the Treasury Regulations, including approval of the probate court, would have to be met.

[B] Common Issues in Self-Dealing

[1] The Disqualified Person Definition

One of the key concepts in the self-dealing rules, and the other private foundation restrictions as well, is that of the "disqualified person," for it is this category of related individuals and entities that is singled out for special scrutiny.

Section § 4946(a) of the Internal Revenue Code defines "disqualified person" in general as including the following:

- A "substantial contributor" to the foundation (i.e., one who has contributed more than $5,000 to the private foundation, if such amount is more than two

---

[6] Reg. § 53.4941(d)-2(c)(1).

[7] *See* Reg. § 53.4941(d)-1(b)(3); § 6.03[C][5] *infra*, "Indirect Self-Dealing."

percent of the total contributions and bequests received by the foundation before the close of the year),[8]

- A foundation manager,

- An owner of more than 20 percent of the total combined voting power of a corporation (or the profits interest of a partnership or the beneficial interest of a trust or unincorporated enterprise) that is a substantial contributor to the foundation,

- A member of the family of any of the foregoing, and

- A corporation of which any of the above persons own more than 35 percent of the total combined voting power (or the profits interest in a partnership or the beneficial interest in a trust or estate).

In addition, a "government official" is a disqualified person for self-dealing purposes. This term is defined as including any presidential appointee; any holder of a federal elective office; most highly compensated federal employees; persons employed by the U.S. House of Representatives or Senate at a salary of $15,000 or more; most elected or appointed officials in a state, local, or District of Columbia government salaried at $20,000 or more; personal or executive assistants or secretaries to any of the foregoing; or (lest we forget) members of the Internal Revenue Service Oversight Board.[9]

> **Note:** The Regulations make it clear that not all government employees are government officials for this purpose even if the salary test is met. Under Regulations Section 53.4946-1(g)(2), a public employee holds a public office only if a significant part of his or her activities is "the independent performance of policymaking functions."

Note that, while the creator of a foundation and most of his or her family are within the category, there are some situations that are not included. A person's "family" for this purpose includes only the spouse, ancestors, children, grandchildren, great-grandchildren, and spouses of his or her children, grandchildren, and great-grandchildren.[10] This excludes some categories, such as brothers and sisters, whose participation and interaction with a foundation may be important in a given situation. By the same token, a person's nieces and nephews are excluded from the definition.[11]

Some organizations that might seem to be within the intended purview of the self-dealing rules are also excluded from the definition. The IRS Regulations state specifically that a section 501(c)(3) organization, whether a private foundation or not, is generally excluded from the definition, except for the rare category

---

[8] In the case of a trust, the creator of the trust is also a substantial contributor.

[9] *See* IRC § 4946(c), discussed in Appendix 6-A, for the precise listing.

[10] IRC § 4946(d).

[11] The IRS so ruled in Priv. Ltr. Rul. 9210029.

of section 501(c)(3) organizations organized and operated exclusively for testing for public safety.[12] Likewise, an organization wholly owned by a public charity will normally not be a disqualified person.[13] This exception for section 501(c)(3) organizations is often used by the IRS in rulings holding that an act of self-dealing does not arise upon a transfer of assets from a private foundation to one or more other private foundations in the context of liquidations, mergers, and other reorganizations.

A 2002 Tax Court decision points up the fact that only a person who falls within the technical definition of a "disqualified person" is subject to these penalties. In *Graham v. Commissioner*,[14] the trustee of a foundation, Fred Hofheinz (son of the foundation's creator), was a business associate of one Michael Graham. When Graham was indicted for federal income tax evasion, Hofheinz agreed on behalf of the foundation to buy Graham's residence, which was then worth $535,000. In exchange for the residence, the foundation agreed to pay Graham $200,000 to be used for his legal expenses, plus another $135,000, which was paid about a year later. In addition, Graham could continue to live in the residence rent-free for three years. Hofheinz felt that this was a good bargain for the foundation because the assessed value of the home for tax purposes was $630,000. As time went on (and Graham got off on a plea bargain), Hofheinz and Graham had a falling out, and the foundation began court proceedings to evict Graham from the residence.

This sounded like self-dealing to the IRS, which alleged that the foundation's purchase of the residence from Graham was a bargain sale that was sufficient to make Graham a substantial contributor (and thus a disqualified person subject to the self-dealing rules). The Tax Court disagreed, based on a detailed review of the dollar values involved. To be a substantial contributor to the foundation, his contributions would have to amount to two percent of the foundation's total contributions. In effect, Mr. Graham had made a bargain sale of the residence to the foundation. By selling the residence for less than its true value, he made a contribution of the difference. Thus, the court had to determine just how much he received from the foundation.

In addition to the initial $250,000 cash payment, the later payment of $135,000 had a present value of $131,905 at the time the parties entered into their deal. All that, plus the present value of three years' rent ($111,371), brought the total price to $493,276. This figure was $41,724 less than the $535,000 fair market value of the residence. Thus, Graham had in effect made a contribution of $41,724 to the foundation. To be a substantial contributor to the foundation, his contribution would have to amount to two percent of the foundation's total contributions, or $47,432. His actual contribution was some $5,708 less than that, so the Tax Court found that he was not a disqualified person and was thus

---

[12] Reg. § 53.4946-1(a)(8).
[13] Reg. § 53.4946-1(a)(7).
[14] T.C. Memo 2002-24 (Jan. 24, 2002).

not subject to the self-dealing rules. Accordingly, the penalties did not apply, whether or not the foundation made a good deal overall.

Obviously, this was too close for comfort, and Graham was lucky that the court accepted his view of the valuations involved. Nevertheless, there are some lessons to be learned from this case. The self-dealing rules have a broad reach, even though Mr. Graham managed to slip through the government's net. As a planning matter, the foundation took a chance in going into this private arrangement with Graham; this unconventional private arrangement with someone who was a business associate of the foundation's trustee seems questionable at best. As the IRS suggested, it seemed like self-dealing on its face, whether or not it was technically within the statute. Certainly, the foundation would have been well-advised to avoid the situation altogether. Despite this, the basic holding of the case — that Graham was not a disqualified person — does underscore the fact that not every questionable transaction with an insider will be penalized as self-dealing.

There are other situations in which such a determination may save the day on a transaction that looks (or smells) like self-dealing. For example, a notable exception to the disqualified person category is in the definition of family; while most members of a contributor's family are automatically classified as disqualified persons, his or her siblings, nieces, and cousins are surprisingly not included. This does not mean that family foundations should feel free to engage in self-dealing transactions with such family members, but it shows that the self-dealing rules do have their limits. The best advice is still what our mothers tried to teach us: Stay away from temptation and you will stay out of trouble!

[2] Compensation

One of the most frequently asked question from families considering a foundation is whether the founder's son or daughter, spouse, or other family member can be paid a salary for managing the foundation. The answer is a qualified "yes" or, more precisely, in most cases, "yes, but probably not as much as you would like." First, it is important to be sure that local law does not forbid the desired employment relationship. California and some other states have restrictions that must be checked and complied with before the tax rules described below come into play.

The Internal Revenue Code provision permitting compensation to be paid to disqualified persons states as follows:

> Except in the case of a government official . . . the payment of compensation (and the payment or reimbursement of expenses) by a private foundation to a disqualified person for personal services which are reasonable and necessary to carrying out the exempt purpose of the private foundation shall not be an act of self-dealing if the compensation (or payment or reimbursement) is not excessive.[15]

---

[15] IRC § 4941(d)(2)(E).

Thus, the services in question must be "personal services," they must be reasonable and necessary to the charitable function of the foundation, and, finally, the compensation must not be "excessive." This provision was placed in the law to make it clear that a foundation may compensate its executive director (who is by definition a disqualified person), but this permission is not without its limitations.

The key question is, How much would the foundation expect to pay a stranger (i.e., a nonfamily member) to perform the same services? Stated differently, how much would a son or daughter earn for a similar job with someone else's foundation? (And don't even think of having your foundation hire your friend's son so your friend's foundation can hire your daughter; the IRS wasn't born yesterday, and such an arrangement will eventually get both foundations in trouble.)

The scope of the services to be rendered — how difficult, how often, for how many hours or days, and so on — must be taken into account, as should the size of the foundation. If there are numerous grant applications to be reviewed and other administrative duties that require something approaching a full-time job, fairly substantial compensation may be justified. Likewise, if legal or accounting work or other services that have a demonstrable value are involved, the payment can be whatever is customary for such services. On the other hand, some family foundations receive only a few grant applications and require only occasional time for their administration. Others have a paid clerical employee or two whose work accomplishes all or most of the administration required. In such situations, little or no compensation can be justified for a family member who simply looks in occasionally.

The authors recommend that the family foundation not be viewed as providing a family member's sole source of income on an ongoing basis, whether this might be legal or not. Thus, if the founders of the family foundation envision paying a son or daughter some $100,000 per year (perhaps to put him or her on a more equal footing with a sibling who is active in the family business), they should be discouraged.

Another common question is, What about compensation for directors? The rules here are exactly the same, with another dimension in the propriety/ethics arena. The underlying principles are the same as those just discussed. Directors who are also family members can be paid whatever may be justified as reasonable for the type and amount of services rendered. Again, the duties of a family foundation director will seldom justify payment of large amounts of compensation.

But there is an additional question here: *Should* family members be paid at all for their services? The foundation is not the equivalent of a commercial enterprise, which normally has as one of its objectives the production of income for all concerned — the shareholders, the employees, and the directors. Rather, the family foundation exists to provide support, financial and otherwise, to noncommercial organizations and causes. The foundation's charitable purposes must be paramount; the presence of any substantial noncharitable purpose can be the basis for revocation of its tax-exempt status. It cannot have the provision of income to family members as any part of its purpose.

The authors urge family foundations to develop an ethic of public service for family board members so that service on the family foundation's board of directors is viewed as an uncompensated public service. When outsiders join the board, they may or may not share the family's orientation, and some compensation (and certainly reimbursement of expenses) may be in order. Also, many, perhaps most, family foundations start out with only family members and closely allied friends and advisors on the board. Not until later, when younger generations begin to dominate, do outsiders typically come on board. A number of family foundations pay compensation only to the nonfamily board members, but some pay even them only the expenses of attending meetings. This should be considered carefully before adopting a compensation policy for board members.

For current information on board compensation policies among foundations of various sizes, see the most recent data in Tables 5-7 and 5-8 or contact the Council on Foundations, The Foundation Center, or the Association of Small Foundations.

In regard to other types of compensation, such as payments for the legal services, investment management, or banking services a foundation may require, the availability of the compensation exception quoted above gets a bit cloudy. The statute states that "personal services" are permissible, and the IRS Regulations list these categories (legal, investment, and banking services) as examples of the personal services for which a family foundation may pay compensation that is not excessive. Although the Regulations refer to these as examples, the IRS appears to view these as the only types of services that are permissible for compensation of disqualified persons under the personal services exception. Surprisingly, this strict view of the personal services exception has been upheld by the Tax Court. There, in the case of *Madden v. Comissioner*,[16] a real estate operator who sought to provide property maintenance services to his family foundation took the IRS to court on this issue and lost.

For these reasons, a family foundation should approach with caution any proposal to hire disqualified persons to provide any services beyond those described above. A possible exception might be the provision of accounting services and tax return preparation, which are fairly analogous to the specific services listed in the Regulations, although even such a limited extension of the personal services exception could prove risky. In the case of any other types of services, a foundation might consider filing a request for a private letter ruling on the issue, rather than attempting to draw more extensive analogies.

---

[16] T.C. Memo 1997-395.

[3] Real Estate Sales, Exchanges, or Leases

The rules regarding real estate transactions are less complicated. The private foundation simply *cannot* sell or lease property to, buy or lease property from, or exchange property with a disqualified person, with one unsurprising exception. A disqualified person may lease property to a family foundation where the lease is rent-free and the foundation uses the property exclusively for charitable purposes. In fact, some would say that a rent-free lease exception is no exception of all.

Even when the foundation leases property free of rent from a disqualified person under this exception, self-dealing issues may arise. Particular problems surface with respect to payments and reimbursements for various types of expenditures other than rent. For example, the family foundation may not reimburse the landlord/disqualified person for such expenses as real estate taxes or insurance, for that type of payment is not within this exception. Note also that a separate provision prohibits any payment from a family foundation to a disqualified person. From this point on, the distinctions grow finer. The family foundation may pay expenses that relate directly to its interest in the property, provided it pays them directly to the service provider (who cannot be a disqualified person), rather than to the family member who is a disqualified person.

[4] Providing Goods, Services, and Facilities

In general, goods, services, and facilities cannot be provided by a disqualified person to a foundation or by a foundation to a disqualified person. There are several, relatively minor exceptions to this rule. If the goods, services, and facilities are used exclusively for charitable purposes, they may be provided *to the foundation* by a disqualified person *without charge*. In the converse situation, the foundation may provide goods, services, and facilities to a disqualified person only if the goods, services, and facilities are functionally related to the performance of the foundation's exempt purpose and the same items are provided to the general public on at least as favorable a basis. An example of the latter might be the sale of a book published by the foundation. A disqualified person could purchase the book from the foundation without committing an act of self-dealing, provided (1) the book related to an activity of the foundation and (2) the price, payment terms, and so on were no more favorable than those available to the general public.

[5] Payments for Tickets to Charity Events

The family that creates a family foundation normally uses it as a means of providing support to the various organizations in which the family is active. This often gives rise to another self-dealing issue. Beneficiary organizations receiving grants from the foundation often hold fund-raising events for which admission is charged. For the individual who pays with a personal check, part is deductible and part is not. For example, a concert or banquet may be held, with admission available to those who provide a "donation" of $500 per person, with a clear notice to attendees that the value of the entertainment, meal, or whatever is $125, so that only the balance ($375) is deductible. The family that has a foundation may feel justified in paying for its admission by means of a check from the foundation. After all, it's a charitable event, isn't it? On thinking it through, however, the family will usually understand that the self-dealing rules preclude the foundation from paying for meals, entertainment, or other goods and services provided to its disqualified person group.

What about the $375 that would be a deductible contribution if paid by the disqualified person directly? Isn't at least that part purely charitable? And for that reason, can't the foundation pay this amount as a charitable grant? No, the prohibition on self-dealing prevents this payment as well, and this, too, is understandable when thought through carefully. The IRS held that a disqualified person could not attend the event upon payment of the $125 alone; the full $500 must be paid if one wants to attend. The disqualified person receives a benefit if the family foundation pays any part of the $500 admission charge, and this violates the self-dealing rules.[17]

This principle makes it dangerous for the foundation to pay any amounts at all when admission to an event is involved. The preferable approach is to have the disqualified person pay his or her own donation/admission and have the foundation make a grant to the sponsor organization, if desired, entirely separate from the event. Sometimes the family member may view his or her attendance at an event of this type as a requirement of the job of the foundation director, so that (by analogy to the rules governing the deductibility of such expenses in a family business context) the cost is properly payable by the foundation. While that argument may have some validity in certain limited situations (e.g., where the family member is receiving an award from a community organization at the event), it is far safer to escape controversy altogether by avoiding the payment of any part of such amounts by the foundation.

This type of problem can be sidestepped by remembering a few basic truths:

- If a person has the resources and the appropriate attitude to justify a family foundation, shouldn't he or she be paying his or her own way to such events?

- The self-dealing rules are quite unforgiving, and transgressions can be very expensive.

- Remember that old standby — how would all this look in the local newspapers? Even though it *probably* won't end up there, this can be a very useful standard.

---

[17] Priv. Ltr. Rul. 9021066.

- If all of that is not sufficient, the possibility of looking both foolish and cheap should be deterrent enough.

[6] Pledges

Depending on state law and the precise facts and circumstances, a personal pledge to contribute to charity may or may not create a binding contractual obligation. The self-dealing rules preclude payment by a foundation of any obligation of a disqualified person, even a charitable pledge. This may be difficult to understand and accept, since one might expect the same result to follow from a contribution whether it is made directly to a public charity donee or indirectly from the donor to the foundation to the public charity. Notwithstanding this apparent paradox, the principle is well established, and the Regulations indicate that this is the case, at least for pledges made after April 16, 1973.[18]

To avoid running headlong into this problem, the family foundation and its disqualified persons should do whatever is necessary or appropriate on the facts to avoid any foundation payment on a personal pledge. The best way to avoid this problem is to have the foundation rather than the disqualified persons enter into the binding pledge in the first place. Thus, the family should become accustomed to making pledges of financial support to charitable organizations and other grantees *on behalf of the family foundation* in the first place, to avoid unnecessary and avoidable self-dealing issues.

[C] Exceptions to Self-Dealing

While the self-dealing rules are generally absolute and unforgiving, there are a few exceptions in the Code and Regulations that provide safe harbors for limited types of transactions.

[1] Money Loaned and Goods, Services, and Facilities Furnished to Foundation by Disqualified Person Free of Charge

In general, loans between a private foundation and a disqualified person are flatly prohibited, whether the foundation is borrowing or lending the funds in question. A special statutory exception permits a disqualified person to loan money to a private foundation, provided the loan is without interest and the proceeds are used for the foundation's tax-exempt purposes.[19]

Similarly, the furnishing of goods, services, and facilities to a private foundation by a disqualified person will normally be an act of self-dealing, but

---

[18] Reg. § 53.4941(d)-2(f)(1).
[19] IRC § 4941(d)(2)(B).

a statutory exception permits this where the goods, services, or facilities are used for charitable purposes.[20] For purposes of this exception, goods will be considered provided without charge even though the foundation pays for transportation, insurance, or maintenance charges (provided these are not directly or indirectly paid to a disqualified person).[21]

[2] Goods, Services, and Facilities Furnished to Disqualified Person by Foundation

A foundation may furnish goods, services, or facilities to a disqualified person, provided this is done on a basis no more favorable than that on which the foundation deals with the general public.[22] This exception applies only where the goods, services, or facilities in question are functionally related to the foundation's exercise of its charitable purpose under IRC § 501(c)(3).[23]

For example, if a foundation operates a museum or similar facility for which the general public is charged an admission fee of $2.00, a disqualified person may enter the facility upon payment of the same fee without violating the self-dealing prohibition. Likewise, a foundation may sell books or magazines to disqualified persons if the publication of such books or magazines is functionally related to a charitable or educational activity of the foundation and the books or magazines are made available to the disqualified persons and the general public at the same price.[24]

[3] Compensation for Certain Personal Services

A private foundation may pay reasonable compensation to its disqualified persons for personal services that are necessary to the accomplishment of the foundation's exempt purposes.[25] The compensation in question cannot be excessive, and this exception does not apply to government officials as disqualified persons. The availability of this exception and the practical implications are discussed above at § 6.03[B][2].

[4] Certain Corporate Transactions

A transaction between a private foundation and a corporation that is a disqualified person pursuant to any liquidation, merger, redemption, recapitalization,

---

[20] IRC § 4941(d)(2)(C).
[21] Reg. § 53.4941(d)-2(d)(3).
[22] IRC § 4941(d)(2)(C).
[23] Reg. § 53.4941(d)-3(b)(1).
[24] Reg. § 53.4941(d)-3(b)(2).
[25] IRC § 4941(d)(2)(E).

or other corporate adjustment, organization, or reorganization will not be an act of self-dealing, provided two tests are met:

1. All securities of the same class as those held by the foundation are subject to the same terms, and

2. Those terms provide for receipt by the foundation of no less than fair market value.[26]

[5] Indirect Self-Dealing

The prohibition on self-dealing applies to self-dealing that is entered into either directly or indirectly. Although neither the Internal Revenue Code nor the IRS Regulations spell out just what will be regarded as indirect self-dealing, the Regulations do provide several examples creating safe harbors for certain categories of transactions. Because these categories will not be classified as indirect self-dealing, they create important planning possibilities.

[a] Certain Business Transactions with Controlled Organizations

The first category of transaction excluded from indirect self-dealing is set out in a sort of transition rule for transactions that were not acts of self-dealing when they arose. This rule exempts a transaction between a disqualified person and an organization controlled by a private foundation if the following tests are met:

1. The transaction results from a business relationship that was established before such transaction constituted an act of self-dealing;

2. The transaction is at least as favorable to the organization controlled by the private foundation as an arm's-length transaction with an unrelated party; and

3. Either:

    *   The organization controlled by the foundation could engage in the transaction with someone other than a disqualified person only at a severe economic hardship to such organization, or

    *   Because of the unique nature of the product or services provided by the organization controlled by the foundation, the disqualified person could not have engaged in the transaction with anyone else or could have done so only by incurring severe economic hardship.[27]

---

[26] IRC § 4941(d)(2)(F).
[27] Reg. § 53.4941(d)-1(b)(1).

To illustrate this exception, consider the following example: The Mouse Foundation owns a controlling interest in Manufacturing Corporation. The corporation's products include a patented component that is available only from Mickey, a disqualified person with respect to the foundation. The corporation has been buying the patented component from Mickey since 1965 (before the self-dealing rules were enacted). The component is not available from other sources, and the corporation would suffer severe economic hardship if it could not continue acquiring this component from Mickey. Under this exception to the Regulations, the corporation's continued purchases from Mickey will not be an indirect act of self-dealing.[28] The same result would follow if the purchases from Mickey had commenced before the foundation acquired the stock of the corporation.

[b] Transactions During the Administration of an Estate or Revocable Trust

A very important exception applies to various transactions that arise during the administration of an estate (or a revocable trust).[29] This exception excludes from indirect self-dealing those transactions affecting a foundation's interest or expectancy in property held by an estate or a revocable trust (including a trust that has become irrevocable upon a grantor's death). This exception is available if the following tests are met:

1. The administrator or executor of the estate (or trustee of the revocable trust) possesses a power of sale with respect to the property, has the power to reallocate the property to another beneficiary, or is required to sell the property under the terms of an option subject to which the property was acquired by the estate or revocable trust;

2. The transaction is approved by the appropriate court (either by the probate court having jurisdiction over the estate or by another court having jurisdiction over the estate or trust or over the foundation);

3. The transaction occurs before the estate is considered terminated for federal income tax purposes (or, in the case of a revocable trust, before it becomes a split-interest trust subject to section 4947);

4. The amount to be received by the estate or trust equals or exceeds the fair market value of the foundation's interest or expectancy in such property at the time of the transaction, taking into account the terms of any option subject to which the property was acquired by the estate or trust; and

5. The transaction (a) results in the foundation receiving an interest or expectancy at least as liquid as the one it gave up, (b) results in the foundation

---

[28] Reg. § 53.4941(d)-1(b)(8), example 2.
[29] Reg. § 53.4941(d)-1(b)(3).

receiving an asset related to the active carrying out of its exempt purposes, or (c) is required under the terms of an option that is binding on the estate or trust.[30]

This exception can be quite useful in estate planning situations. For example, it may be possible for the founder of a foundation to give his or her heirs (who would be disqualified persons) an option to acquire business holdings, real estate, or other assets that the founder would otherwise like to leave to his or her foundation. After the founder's death, the executor of his or her estate can sell the property in question to the heirs pursuant to the option, following all the terms of this exception. The heirs thus end up holding the property, while the foundation holds an equivalent value in the form of the sale proceeds.

Moreover, if the parties comply with this exception, the exemption from self-dealing applies not only to the sale, but also to any extension of credit involved.[31] Thus, in the preceding example, the heirs could purchase the property in question from the estate using personal notes as part of the consideration paid. These notes would be distributed to and held by the foundation; although such an extension of credit would normally be a separate act of self-dealing, the foundation's holding of the notes during their terms and receipt of payments under the notes are exempt from self-dealing under this exception.[32]

[c] Grants to Intermediaries

Another exception in the Regulations excludes from indirect self-dealing certain payments to government officials made through intermediary grantees.[33] Under this exception, for example, a foundation may make a grant to another organization that is not "controlled" by such foundation, and this will not constitute indirect self-dealing even though the recipient organization uses the grant funds to fund a payment to a government official. This assumes that the foundation does not earmark the use of the grant for any named government official and that there is no agreement, oral or written, that would allow the granting foundation to cause the selection of the government official by the intermediary organization.

[d] Certain Transactions Involving Limited Amounts

Indirect self-dealing does not include certain relatively small (under $5,000) retail transactions between a disqualified person and an organization

---

[30] The last requirement, in item 5, applies only to transactions occurring after April 16, 1973.
[31] Reg. § 53.4941(d)-2(c)(1).
[32] See Priv. Ltr. Ruls. 9042030 and 9108024, approving such transactions under this exception.
[33] Reg. § 53.4941(d)-1(b)(2).

(of any sort, taxable or tax exempt) controlled by a private foundation.[34] This exception is available where:

1. The transaction in question arises in the normal and customary course of retail business engaged in with the general public;

2. The transaction is at least as favorable to the controlled organization as an arm's-length transaction with an unrelated person; and

3. The total amount involved in such transactions for any one such disqualified person in any one taxable year does not exceed $5,000. The Regulations give the following example to illustrate this rule:

> Arnold, a disqualified person with respect to the Proper Foundation, enters into a contract with the Money Corporation, which is also a disqualified person with respect to the foundation. The Proper Foundation owns 20 percent of Money's stock, and controls it under the applicable standard (in Reg. § 53.4941(d)-1(b)(5)). Money is in the retail department store business. Purchases by Arnold of goods sold by Money in the normal and customary course of business at retail or higher prices are not indirect acts of self-dealing so long as the total of the amounts involved in all of such purchases by Arnold in any one year does not exceed $5,000.[35]

Perhaps the most noteworthy aspect of this example is the implication that Arnold *would* commit an act of self-dealing if her purchases totaled more than $5,000 for any year. This demonstrates dramatically just how far the concept of indirect self-dealing may extend.

[6] Transition Rules for Certain Pre-1969 Transactions and Situations

Several special rules permit the continuation of various arrangements between foundations and disqualified persons where they originated before the effective date of the applicable provision of the Tax Reform Act of 1969. These are primarily of historical interest today and therefore are not included in this discussion.

[D] Some Practical Examples of Self-Dealing Problems and Solutions

As pointed out in the Note to the Reader at the beginning of this chapter, this Handbook does not purport to catalog and describe all rulings, cases, and other developments affecting the subjects described. Despite this, it cannot be

---

[34] Reg. § 53.4941(d)-1(b)(6).
[35] Reg. § 53.4941(d)-1(b)(8), example 7.

denied that the private letter rulings that are issued and released month after month do provide useful examples of how taxpayers have encountered and solved actual problems, with the approval of the Internal Revenue Service.

Nowhere is this more apparent than in the area of self-dealing, which tends to be the most common problem area for family foundations and their personnel. Moreover, the problem is compounded by the inflexible nature of the self-dealing rules themselves, since the IRS is not legally able to excuse exceptions for "innocent" or beneficial transactions or to allow abatement of a self-dealing excise tax otherwise due. The following sections discuss some of the self-dealing rulings that help provide solutions to potential self-dealing problems.

[1] Management Agreement Approved

Letter Ruling 200326039 involved an S corporation engaged in the business of owning and operating 35 residential condominium units in a 54-unit project. The corporation proposed to create a charitable remainder trust (CRT), with itself as the sole income beneficiary. The trustee would be Mr. D, who owns all of the voting stock of the corporation. D's daughter-in-law, C, is one of three current trustees on the condominium board. She is also the president and sole director of a property management firm (Q Co.) that serves as the manager for the project and provides management services to the S corporation on its units in the project.

D and the corporation plan to fund the trust with about half of the corporation's units in the condo and propose to do so in a complicated transaction involving a limited liability company (LLC) of which the CRT would hold a 98 percent interest. Q Co., C's management company, would own the remaining two percent. Q would be the managing member of the LLC and would continue to manage the properties for the LLC. Will this be a prohibited act of self-dealing? After all, the properties in question are in effect 98 percent owned by the CRT, and a CRT is treated as if it were a private foundation for self-dealing purposes. Accordingly, this determination is instructive for family foundations despite the fact that there was no foundation involved.

No problem, answered the IRS. It concluded that such a management agreement would not be an act of self-dealing, because the services to be provided are professional and managerial in nature and necessary to carry out the trust's exempt purposes. The Service further determined that the gift from the S corporation to the trust would not affect the trust's exempt status as a qualified CRT, because the trust will hold a controlling interest in the LLC. Moreover, and for the same reason, this arrangement will not be an improper investment restriction that would disqualify the trust.

The full ruling is much more complicated than this brief summary, and anyone considering a management agreement covering foundation assets would be well advised to read the full ruling. Although a private letter ruling is limited to the person or organization that requested it, and does not bind the IRS, it can nevertheless give important insights into how the IRS will view similar situations.

[2] No Self-Dealing in Pledge of Stock Options

In two companion rulings, Letter Rulings 200312003 and 200312004, the IRS held that a corporation's proposed pledge of stock options to its own company foundation would not violate the self-dealing rules. BigCorp is a publicly held corporation whose stock is listed on the New York Stock Exchange. It proposes to pledge to its controlled company foundation stock options to acquire its listed stock at a price equal to the closing price on the day the options are issued.

Sounds fine so far, but one should remember that when the options are exercised the holder (for now, apparently, the company foundation) is in effect buying the stock from the issuing company. Because the company, BigCorp, is a disqualified person with respect to the foundation, this sale would be a prohibited act of self-dealing.

To get around this, the parties must plan a more complicated transaction that will work in one of two ways. First, the foundation may transfer the options to one or more unrelated charitable organizations, which would be free to exercise them without worrying about self-dealing. Alternatively, the parties might arrange a "cashless" or "net exercise" transaction whereby, upon exercising the option, the foundation would receive shares equal to the net value of the options as of the date of exercise.

It would seem clear that if an unrelated party exercises the options, the self-dealing rules have no application. The IRS agreed, pointing out that the foundation might even sell the options to unrelated charities. The cashless approach, however, is not as clear — is this still a prohibited sale, or is it permissible? The IRS said that it was okay. The options were issued to the foundation free of charge, and no sale or exchange would result if the parties use the cashless approach to satisfy BigCorp's pledge. In effect, BigCorp would simply be substituting common stock for the outstanding pledge.

Note that the result would have been different if, instead of pledging the stock options, BigCorp had pledged a dollar amount to the foundation. For example, assume that BigCorp pledges $100,000 to the foundation and issues stock options as described above; when BigCorp's stock goes up and the options are worth $100,000, it issues $100,000 worth of stock to satisfy the pledge. These facts are different from those in the rulings, and BigCorp has, in effect, *sold* the stock to the foundation for $100,000. The ruling did not approve this type of transaction.

The IRS also addressed several other tax issues in these rulings. Neither the receipt of stock on a cashless exercise of the options nor the receipt of cash from another charity upon the sale of the options would be taxable as unrelated business income to the foundation. The foundation will not hold the options as a dealer holding inventory for sale to customers. Moreover, the excise tax on net investment income under Code § 4940 will not apply to any proceeds received on sale of the option. Capital gains are taxable only on "non-charitable assets susceptible to use to produce interest, dividends, rents and royalties," and these options are not in that category, said the IRS.

What about BigCorp's deduction for the contribution? The IRS covered this question too. BigCorp gets a deduction when the option is exercised. If the foundation transfers the option to an unrelated charity, that deduction is equal to the difference between the exercise price and the value of the stock. If the cashless exercise approach is used, the deduction is equal to the value of the stock transferred to the foundation.

[3] Okay for Foundation to Take Over Founder's Publication

What a foundation can and cannot do in its relationship with the donor is an ongoing problem that must be monitored very carefully. Sometimes it seems as if just about anything a foundation might do will be forbidden if it is at all beneficial to the donor. Letter Ruling 200309027 shows how some actions that seem potentially problematic may be permissible if they help carry out a foundation's charitable program. In Letter Ruling 200309027, the IRS held that a foundation would not violate the rule against self-dealing or otherwise endanger its tax-exempt status by taking over the production and dissemination of a medical publication formerly published by its founder.

The foundation was created and funded by a diversified health care company (HealthCo) that had for some time (exact time not disclosed) published and distributed free of charge an annual booklet setting forth one of the most comprehensive analyses of U.S. health statistics available, including state-by-state comparative rankings. Now HealthCo proposes to transfer its entire interest in the annual booklet to the foundation, which will publish and distribute it to health care officials, government officials, and other organizations, and to members of the general public who request it. Will this program constitute an act of self-dealing? "No," said the IRS, but it apparently was not an easy question.

The foundation had formerly sought to achieve its goals of improving the health and well-being of Americans by means of grants to established public charities. Recently, however, it undertook the direct conduct of several programs that disseminate health care information directly to the general public. It also made a one-word change in its name to distinguish itself from that of HealthCo.

The foundation's educational program includes the distribution of health-related messages through magazine ads and over the Internet. These messages try to promote improved health by presenting the public with basic facts and cautions regarding health care decisions. A recent example was a notice on how the public might prevent medical errors in dealing with doctors, pharmacies, and hospitals by learning what sorts of information they should discuss. No specific products or services, including "particularly" those of HealthCo, are recommended or mentioned in these ads.

The Service concluded that the continued publication and distribution of the statistical booklet would not be an act of self-dealing on grounds that it was a charitable and educational activity and any benefit to HealthCo would be "incidental and tenuous" within the meaning of Regulations § 53.4941(d)-2(f)(2). This conclusion was based upon a number of recent changes designed to minimize any appearance of a close connection between the foundation and HealthCo, including the change of the foundation's name, corresponding changes on the foundation's web site, and removal of a letter signed by HealthCo officers from the inside cover of the booklet. In place of that letter, the next edition of the booklet will include a statement that it is a successor to the earlier HealthCo publication, and that statement will not be included in future editions. Moreover, HealthCo will not buy or otherwise obtain copies of the booklet from the foundation and will have to download it from the foundation's web site like any other interested party. HealthCo's sales force will no longer distribute copies.

Subsequently, in Letter Ruling 200316042, the IRS issued a supplemental ruling correcting the facts in Letter Ruling 200309027. The later ruling points out that the annual statistics booklet distributed by the corporation that created the foundation was originally published by an unrelated third party from which the company bought the rights to the booklet. Perhaps more important is the amendment of the original ruling to provide that the company's transfer of its rights in the statistics booklet would not be an act of self-dealing.

As even a quick reading of this summary shows, the key to this ruling was the minimization of any impression that the foundation and HealthCo were one and the same. This in turn required elimination of a number of factors that could create that confusion. Lest there be any doubt, *any benefit* to a substantial contributor from the operations of a foundation creates serious potential problems. In this letter ruling, the parties were able (apparently with some suggestions and urging from the IRS) to fit into the exception that permits an incidental and tenuous benefit to the donor.

What lessons might this corporate foundation situation hold for family foundations? It is not at all unusual for a family to consider using a foundation to carry on a program of one sort or another that would otherwise be conducted by family members or the family business. Whether it is a family project or a grant to a local institution that is a client or customer, the need for caution is obvious. This ruling shows how far the IRS might require the family to go to separate itself from the foundation's efforts.

[4]   Investment Advisory Arrangement with Donor/Trustee Okay

In Letter Ruling 200303061, the IRS gave its blessing to an arrangement whereby a family foundation purchased investment advisory services from its founder. Mr. D was the sole contributor to his family foundation and the sole proprietor of a business providing investment advisory services, including investment strategy, research, implementation, and management services. He and the foundation entered into a contract for the services in question, which were described as "of a type of personal services that are frequently contracted for by a charitable foundation." The compensation to Mr. D was determined under a plan whereby the foundation would obtain fee schedules from at least three independent companies providing comparable services. Those rates would be averaged and applied to the assets managed by Mr. D's firm on a quarterly basis. If a significant contribution or distribution changed the amount of assets managed for a given quarter, the value of the investment portfolio would be the average daily balance for that quarter. The foundation represented that all fees to be charged to it by Mr. D's firm would be reasonable for the services provided, in accordance with industry practice, and consistent with local laws governing fiduciaries.

On these facts, the IRS ruled that the compensation to be paid to Mr. D's firm by the foundation would not be an act of self-dealing, due to the personal service's exception provided in IRC § 4941(d)(2)(E) and Regulations § 53.4941(d)-3(c)(1), and discussed in this chapter at sections 6.03[C][3] and 6.03[B][2].

[E]   Computation of Tax Due on an Act of Self-Dealing

An Internal Revenue Service ruling issued in June 2002 was largely overlooked by the private foundation community despite its potential application to foundations. Revenue Ruling 2002-43[36] deals with the excise tax on prohibited transactions between qualified plans and their disqualified persons under IRC § 4975. What is important for present purposes is that this qualified plan excise tax is similar in many respects to the private foundation tax on acts of self-dealing.

The purpose of Revenue Ruling 2002-43 is to explain how the prohibited transaction tax under § 4975 is computed when the transaction in question spans several successive tax years. That is an important issue under § 4975 because Congress changed the rate of the initial tax under that provision several times during the 1990s. Although the self-dealing tax rate has remained unchanged, the ruling provides a useful example of both how the self-dealing tax applies and how it is computed.

The facts in the ruling were as follows: On April 1, 1997, Mr. B, a disqualified person with respect to a qualified plan sponsored by his S corporation, obtained a two-year loan in the amount of $10,000 from the plan's tax-exempt trust. The loan was secured solely by Mr. B's account balance in

---

[36] 2002-28 I.R.B. 1.

Plan Y, which had a $12,000 balance at the time. The loan called for Mr. B to make substantially equal payments of principal and interest to the trust each calendar quarter. The loan bore interest at the rate of 11 percent, compounded annually, which was equal to or greater than a fair market rate of interest for such a loan at that time. Mr. B made no payments on the loan until December 31, 1999, at which time he repaid the loan, including principal and accrued interest.

Just as IRC § 4941 imposes a tax on acts of self-dealing, IRC § 4975(a) imposes an excise tax on any disqualified person who participates in a "prohibited transaction." For this purpose, § 4975(c)(1)(B) defines the term "prohibited transaction" to include any direct or indirect lending of money or other extension of credit between a plan and a disqualified person. Although there is an exception for certain secured loans to rank-and-file plan participants at reasonable rates of interest, Mr. B's loan was clearly a prohibited transaction.

Like the tax on self-dealing, the prohibited transaction tax is applied on a taxable year basis. Thus, a violation (Mr. B's loan) that continues for parts of more than one taxable year consists of several separate taxable transactions. Indeed, the Temporary Pension Excise Tax Regulations under § 4975 (Temporary Regulations § 141.4975-13) even adopt certain provisions of the Foundation Excise Tax Regulations, including the definition of the term "amount involved." The amount involved is the amount used to compute the penalty tax actually due under either IRC § 4941 or § 4945.

Regulations § 53.4941(e)-1(b)(2)(ii) provides that when the transaction involves the use of money, the amount involved is the greater of the amount paid for such use or the fair market value of such use for the period for which the money or other property is used, and the amount involved is determined for the entire period that the money is used. In addition, Regulation § 53.4941(e)-1(e)(1) provides that in the instance of a prohibited transaction that is a loan, an additional prohibited transaction is deemed to occur on the first day of each taxable year in the taxable period after the taxable year in which the loan occurred.

Thus, in the case of the loan to Mr. B, there are three separate prohibited transactions. The first prohibited transaction occurs on the date of the loan (April 1, 1997), the second prohibited transaction occurs on January 1, 1998 (the first day of the next taxable year), and the third prohibited transaction occurs on January 1, 1999. The taxable period for each of these prohibited transactions begins on the date that the prohibited transaction occurs (April 1, 1997, for the first prohibited transaction, January 1, 1998, for the second prohibited transaction, and January 1, 1999, for the third prohibited transaction). The taxable periods for all three prohibited transactions end on the date on which the prohibited transactions were corrected (December 31, 1999). The amount involved for each prohibited transaction is the interest amount, which is computed as follows:

If, instead of the qualified plan context, this had been a loan from a private foundation to a disqualified person, the result would have been virtually identical (except for the differences in tax rates).

Year	Principal	Interest Rate	Time	Amount
1997	$10,000.00	11.00%	275/365 year	$ 828.77
(4/1-12/31)				
1998	10,828.77	11.00%	1 year	1,191.16
1999	12,019.93	11.00%	1 year	1,322.19

This ruling offers several lessons about the tax on self-dealing. First, when a foundation loans money to a disqualified person (an act of self-dealing), the penalty excise tax is not figured on the basis of the loan proceeds, as one might logically guess. Rather, the amount involved is based upon the interest paid or what would have been a reasonable charge, whichever is higher. Second, the tax on self-dealing is determined on an annual basis. Thus, if a single act of self-dealing extends over more than one year, it represents a separate offense for each year. In Revenue Ruling 2002-43, Mr. B's $10,000 loan was outstanding from April 1, 1997 through December 31, 1999. This involved parts of three separate taxable years, so there were three separate taxes imposed. Moreover, the amount involved varied from $828.77 in the initial year to $1,322.19 for the final year, due to the accrued but unpaid interest.

[F] Foundation Life Insurance Plan Requires Care

May a family foundation own and pay premiums on a life insurance policy on the life of a donor? This is a question that arises occasionally (especially for people who sell life insurance). In Letter Ruling 200232036, the Internal Revenue Service held that a plan of this type could proceed without endangering the foundation's tax status, provided adequate safeguards were in place.

The founder of the foundation, Mr. F, created an irrevocable trust for the benefit of himself, his brother, and two stepchildren who were children of his ex-wife. If any beneficiary predeceased Mr. F, his or her share passed to the foundation. The trust owned a term life insurance policy on the life of Mr F; that policy was a 20-year fixed premium term policy with no cash value and not subject to any policy loan. Mr. F proposed to have the trust transfer ownership of the policy to the foundation. As part of the deal, Mr. F would also agree to pay the premiums on the policy as they came due. The foundation had as a board member an attorney who was independent of Mr. F (i.e., not subject to his control), and Mr. F gave this board member an irrevocable proxy to cast his board vote on any and all matters concerning the insurance policy (e.g., decisions regarding continuance or discontinuance of coverage and changes of beneficiary). All parties signed a binding agreement providing that if such independent attorney/board member ceased to be a director for any reason, another independent person would be elected to serve in his place and that person would hold and vote this proxy.

The Internal Revenue Service ruled that this plan would not endanger the foundation's tax-exempt status or violate any of the private foundation restrictions. Thus, neither the foundation's holding of the policy nor its payment of premiums would be an act of self-dealing or a jeopardy investment.

There are several points to note about this ruling. First, the fact that this policy had no policy loan outstanding was critical to the holding. Such a loan would have made the donation of this policy an act of self-dealing under an earlier ruling, Revenue Ruling 80-132.[37] Another earlier ruling[38] held that a foundation's payment of premiums and interest on a policy loan under similar circumstances were jeopardy investments, but this too was distinguished on factual grounds because the policy in the later ruling had no indebtedness outstanding. (Indeed, the policy involved in Letter Ruling 200232036 was a term policy, which precludes policy loans; the foundation was required to represent that it had no intention to convert this into a whole-life policy, upon which policy loans would be possible.) Thus, one should not read this ruling as suggesting that a similar transaction would be possible with a life insurance policy that *does* have a policy loan outstanding.

Another important aspect of the ruling is the extent to which the proposed plan was structured in a manner that placed the donee/foundation in complete control of the donated policy: the donor gave up all incidents of ownership and the plan included assurances that he could not subsequently use his position with the foundation to exercise any control of the policy at a later date. Again, a comparable plan that left the donor with more control over the transferred policy would be a different situation entirely.

Finally, note that the IRS examined in detail the possibility that the plan proposed might benefit anyone other than the charity. The donor attached no strings to the gift, and even though he obligated himself to make subsequent premium payments, the foundation was not required to use his contributions for premium payments or even to keep the policy in force.

Planning for charitable contributions of life insurance can be a tricky business. Virtually any attempt to squeeze out some benefit for the donor or his or her family will defeat the intended tax benefits, and the policy should be free of any indebtedness. Also, although the IRS did not discuss it in this ruling, there is an IRC provision, § 170(f)(10), that bars any deduction for a contribution to charity to be used for premiums on a policy benefiting the donor or anyone selected by the donor; it also imposes a tough penalty (100 percent of any such premiums paid) on the donee organization. Thus, careful and honest planning is necessary for charitable plans involving life insurance.

Donees and the IRS both look with skepticism and suspicion on plans that purport to use life insurance products to benefit the donor while producing a charitable deduction for the donor, and rightly so. The plan described in Letter

---

[37] 1980-1 C.B. 255.
[38] Rev. Rul. 80-133, 1980-1 C.B. 258.

Ruling 200232036 provides a useful pattern for the planner aiming to structure an effective charitable life insurance plan.

§ 6.04   JEOPARDIZING INVESTMENTS — DON'T TAKE CHANCES WITH THE FOUNDATION'S MONEY

A private foundation, like any other investor, must be careful with its investments lest losses render it unable to continue its operations. As described above, in 1969, Congress heard testimony describing instances in which private foundations were used as vehicles for speculative investments. Individuals would place funds into a private foundation, claiming an income-tax charitable deduction for the full amount transferred, and then cause the foundation to invest in some risky or speculative venture. If the investment paid off, the profits would benefit the foundation, which was exempt from tax; if the investment failed, the individual would have already received a tax deduction.

To prevent this misuse of foundations, Congress imposed a new investment rule in IRC § 4944. Under that provision, if a private foundation makes investments that financially jeopardize the foundation's ability to carry out its charitable purposes, both the foundation and its managers could become liable for excise taxes on these investments.

What investments should a private foundation avoid to minimize its exposure to this excise tax? Unfortunately, this question cannot be answered with precision. As a general matter, jeopardizing investments are those that show a lack of reasonable business care and prudence in providing for the long-term and short-term financial needs of the foundation. There is no determining factor or factors to help make this determination. The Regulations refer to several categories of investments that merit particular scrutiny[39] (e.g., margin trading, commodity futures, oil and gas working interests, options, warrants, and short sales), but no category is automatically deemed to violate this rule. Even this list of investments that bear watching may be a bit dated, since such things as commodity futures and options have become more mainstream today than was the case in 1969, and the modern prudent investor rule recognizes that investments that might be termed risky can have a place in a foundation's overall investment portfolio. This change in perspective is reflected in several rulings in which the Internal Revenue Service has held that a foundation may invest a portion of its assets in various nontraditional investments without incurring liability under IRC § 4944.[40]

---

[39] Regs. § 53.4944-1(a)(2)(i).

[40] *See, e.g.*, Priv. Ltr. Rul. 9451067 (limited partnerships holding or trading distressed real estate, commodities, and energy companies, and a hedge fund for U.S. stocks); Priv. Ltr. Rul. 9237035 (commodities trading program managed by a disqualified person); Priv. Ltr. Rul. 9320052 (investments in working oil and gas wells).

The determination of whether an investment jeopardizes the foundation's ability to carry out its purposes is made on an investment-by-investment basis, looking at the foundation's investment portfolio as a whole. For this purpose, investments are evaluated at the time they are made, and proper investments will not be considered jeopardizing investments merely because losses later result. Several IRS rulings make it clear that investment of limited portions of the foundation's entire portfolio in some more speculative investments may be permitted. For example, the investment of five percent of the portfolio in a hedge fund or a commodity futures fund may be permissible where investment of a larger proportion might not.[41]

The tax on jeopardizing investments does not apply to *program-related investments*, whose primary purpose is to accomplish a charitable purpose and for which production of income or gain is not a significant motive. An example would be student loans at low interest rates (or interest-free) and low-interest loans to small businesses owned by members of economically disadvantaged groups for whom financing at reasonable interest rates from conventional sources is not available.

The best way to avoid liability for the tax on jeopardizing investments is to approach investment decisions prudently and carefully and to rely on the advice of a qualified investment counselor. Neither the foundation nor its foundation managers will be liable for this tax if the investment in question meets certain standards. In the case of the foundation, the tax is not due if it can be shown that the investment was due to reasonable cause and not willful neglect and that the jeopardizing investment was corrected within the "correction period."[42] In the case of foundation managers, the tax will be imposed only where the manager knowingly, willfully, and without reasonable cause participated in making the jeopardizing investment. Obviously, if a foundation invests carefully and relies on investment advice from sound and proven investment professionals, it (and its managers) should avoid liability under these standards. On the other hand, investments on the basis of anonymous tips and unconventional investments are more likely to cause problems in this area. Following ordinary fiduciary standards in the selection of investments is almost certain to protect the foundation from liability for the tax under IRC § 4944.

§ 6.05 EXCESS BUSINESS HOLDINGS — MIND YOUR OWN BUSINESS (UP TO 20 OR MAYBE 35 PERCENT)

[A] In General

The Internal Revenue Code is one of the most complicated creations of its type, and section 4943 is one of the most complex provisions found therein. Like

---

[41] Priv. Ltr. Ruls. 9451067 and 9237035.

[42] *See* Appendix 6-E for a detailed discussion.

the other foundation restrictions, the concept is simple — private foundations should not be overly involved in the ownership of businesses. The limitations imposed apply to the total holdings of the foundation and all of its disqualified persons; the general limitation is that this group cannot hold in the aggregate more than 20 percent of any "business enterprise"; this increases to 35 percent if effective control of the enterprise is held by third parties outside the foundation group.[43]

Of course, disqualified persons can own as much as they desire, but if any interest in such an enterprise is transferred to a private foundation, these limitations become applicable. A *de minimis* rule permits a foundation to hold up to a two percent interest in a business enterprise, and, thereafter, the limit is the 20 or 35 percent described above, reduced by the percentage held by disqualified persons.[44] So, for example, if a foundation's disqualified persons own 50 percent of a corporation, there is no room for any permitted holding by the foundation over and above the two percent *de minimis* amount.

[1]   Two Percent *De Minimis* Rule Explained

The excess business holdings rules are complex, to say the least. Fortunately, most family foundation advisors have to remember only the 20 percent and 35 percent limitations on business holdings and, of course, the two percent *de minimis* rule. If you use these standards as your working guidelines, you need to be aware of an often-misunderstood wrinkle in the application of the two percent *de minimis* rule. Understanding this nuance can help you to steer foundations clear of legal trouble. It is important to understand that the two percent *de minimis* rule is *not* a safe harbor.

Overall, a foundation and its disqualified persons as a group may hold only a 20 percent total interest in a business before the excess business holdings prohibition of § 4943 comes into play. The 20 percent limit rises to 35 percent if it can be shown that a third person other than a disqualified person has effective control of the business. The two percent *de minimis* rule is provided by IRC § 4943(c)(2)(C), which states as follows:

> A private foundation shall not be treated as having excess business holdings in any corporation in which it [together with all related private foundations] owns not more than 2 percent of the voting stock and not more than 2 percent in value of all outstanding shares of all classes of stock.

Although the rule is expressed in terms of corporations, comparable rules apply to partnerships and joint ventures under IRC § 4943(c)(3) and the regulations. What is easy to overlook is that once the foundation owns more than two

---

[43] IRC §§ 4943(c)(2)(A) and (B).
[44] IRC § 4943(c)(2)(C).

percent of a business, then all the foundation's stock (and not merely the part in excess of two percent) is treated as excess business holdings. One might expect that the first two percent holding would always be permitted under the *de minimis* rule, but that is not the case; the protection is lost if the foundation holds more than two percent.

To demonstrate this principle, let us take the example of "Foundation A," which owns two percent of the stock in Corporation C, and its founder, F, who owns 37 percent. Together, A and F own 39 percent of C, and would normally be over the 35 percent limit. The two percent *de minimis* rule, however, applies to provide that A does not have any excess business holdings. Now let us take the same facts with one difference: A holds five percent of C. Now A and F together hold 42 percent of C, putting them well beyond the 35 percent limit. Because F holds more than two percent; however, all of its holdings are excess business holdings. A foundation advisor who does not focus on the specifics of the rule might conclude that Foundation A's first two percent is permissible under the *de minimis* rule, so that only the remaining three percent is excess business holdings, but that is not how the rule works. All five percent held by A is classified as excess business holdings.

Several private letter rulings demonstrate how the *de minimis* rule works in various situations. For example, in Letter Ruling 8412012, a foundation bought 2.05 percent of the stock of a corporation of which its disqualified persons already owned more than the permissible percentage. How much may the foundation hold without violating the excess business holdings rule? None, said the Internal Revenue Service; the entire 2.05 percent is subject to tax under § 4943. In so holding, the IRS characterized this provision as a true *de minimis* rule, not a "subtraction out" rule.

On the other hand, a foundation will always be safe if it keeps its holdings, including those of all related foundations, at or below two percent. This is demonstrated by Letter Rulings 8146075 and 8146076, in which a foundation owned 3.61 percent of the stock of a corporation in which its disqualified persons owned more than 75 percent. The foundation planned to have enough stock redeemed to reduce its holdings to not more than two percent. The IRS agreed, holding that this would be sufficient to avoid liability for the tax on excess business holdings.

[B] Business Enterprise

Obviously, some definitions are critical to this determination. A *business enterprise* may be a corporation, partnership, joint venture, or other unincorporated enterprise.[45] (Note that foundations are not permitted *any* holdings in a sole proprietorship.) In general, a business enterprise includes any trade or business or

---

[45] IRC § 4943(d)(1) and Reg. § 53.4943-3(c).

other activity that is regularly carried on for the production of income from the sale of goods or the performance of services, provided it is an unrelated trade or business under IRC § 513. Thus, the term does not include a business that is related to the foundation's exempt purpose, such as a store to sell educational materials or a snack bar on the premises of a museum owned by the foundation. In addition, the term does *not* include any of the following:[46]

1. A trade or business that obtains at least 95 percent of its gross income from passive sources;

2. A *program-related investment*, as discussed above in connection with jeopardizing investments; or

3. A *functionally related business*. This is generally any trade or business the conduct of which is substantially related to the foundation's performance of its exempt purpose or function. An example might be a snack bar or other visitor facility operated in connection with a public park maintained by a foundation.

The business interests taken into account are voting stock in the case of a corporation and capital interest or beneficial interest in the case of a partnership or other entity. A foundation may have nonvoting stock (or capital interest for holdings in a partnership or joint venture) as a permitted holding of a foundation, but only if all disqualified persons together hold no more than the 20 or 35 percent amounts described above.

Much of the complication in the excess business holdings statute results from the complex rules provided for foundation holdings in business enterprises as of the enactment of this provision in 1969. Although these are very important for the few foundations still involved with such holdings, they will not be discussed here.

[C] Five-Year Disposition Rule

Again, we see a tough rule with stiff penalties that is easily avoided by the average new family foundation. The policy of the statute is to discourage business holdings by foundations, and the safest course is to avoid any problems by deferring to the rule and not attempting to create such holdings in a foundation. Where this is desired (or where it is about to occur), there are two primary courses of action. First, it may be possible to utilize one of the alternative forms of organization described in Chapter 2, instead of a private foundation. In particular, many planners recommend creation of a supporting organization where this is an important consideration. The other possibility is to rely on the special rule that allows a foundation five years to bring its ownership (or that of disqualified persons) down to permissible levels in the case of excess business

---

[46] IRC § 4943(d)(3) and Reg. § 53.4943-10(b).

holdings created by gift or bequest.[47] The five-year period may be extended by the Internal Revenue Service for an additional five-year period if these holdings result from an unusually large gift or bequest of diverse business holdings or holdings with complex corporate structures.[48]

IRC § 4943(c)(7) allows the IRS to extend the usual five-year period for disposing of excess business holdings for an unusually large gift or bequest of diverse business holdings or holdings with complex corporate structures, provided certain tests are met. The statute requires three conditions:

1. The foundation must establish that:
    a. diligent efforts to dispose of such holdings have been made within the initial five-year period; and
    b. disposition within the initial five-year period has not been possible (except at a price substantially below fair market value) by reason of such size and complexity or diversity of such holdings;

2. Before the close of the initial five-year period:
    a. the foundation must submit to the IRS a plan for disposing of all of the excess business holdings involved in the extension; and
    b. the foundation must also submit such plan to the Attorney General having administrative or supervisory authority or responsibility over the foundation's disposition of the excess business holdings involved and submit to the IRS any response received from the Attorney General to such plan during such five-year period; and

3. The IRS must determine that the plan can reasonably be expected to be carried out before the close of the extension period.

Two private letter rulings in 2003 provide examples of circumstances under which a foundation may be granted additional time to dispose of excess business holdings.

In Letter Ruling 200332020, the IRS granted a private foundation extra time to dispose of business holdings received from the estate of the foundation's founder. The facts as stated in the ruling are confusing due to the use of letters to avoid disclosing the identity of the parties (for example, "In J you received additional shares of A which brought your ownership interest to F%"). Therefore, one should assume that the foundation received a major share of the stock of three different golf clubs. (The ruling calls these "I" clubs, but for the sake of simplicity, they will be called golf clubs here.)

The foundation was able to dispose of two of these clubs a while ago, but a deal fell through on the third club, necessitating this ruling. Several factors were cited—the club's facilities required substantial capital improvements, its com-

---

[47] IRC § 4943(c)(6).
[48] IRC § 4943(c)(7).

puter hardware and software were inadequate and outdated, and the real estate holdings used in connection with the club were not of interest to most club operators who might otherwise be interested in buying the club. The foundation submitted to the State Attorney General its plans for disposing of its holdings in the club. In addition, it represented that without the extension period requested, it would not be able to realize the true value of the club based upon the capital improvements and software conversion mentioned above. On these facts, the IRS granted the foundation an extension through August 27, 2007, of the time for disposing of its excess business holdings in the club. The ruling notes that the foundation had engaged in diligent efforts to dispose of its excess business holdings within the initial five-year period for disposition and was unable to do so by reason of the size, complexity, and diversity of its holdings in the corporation that operated the club. Moreover, the reorganization of the club's accounting department and the upgrade of its computer systems were expected to be complete by May 2003, and the foundation anticipated making various capital improvements through 2005. It expects to have a reliable record of financial, accounting, and membership information to present to buyers by May 2006. After establishing a three-year financial history, it will be in a position to market the sale of the club aggressively and secure a qualified buyer.

In Letter Ruling 200323045, the surrounding circumstances were simpler. This ruling involved a drastic drop in the value of the subject business holdings and a concern for the effect of early disposition on their value. Mr. B and his family were major shareholders in Corporation N, owning more than 50 percent of its stock. N stock is a publicly traded security listed on the NASDAQ exchange. The trading price of N stock had fluctuated widely in recent years, partly due to sales by shareholders unrelated to B. In 1996 and 1997, B contributed some N stock to his family foundation. The foundation attempted to comply with the excess business holdings rules through a systematic process of distributions of the shares to charities in an attempt to dispose of them over an extended period of time without adversely affecting the value of the securities. However, during 1998 and 1999, the market value of the shares declined dramatically so that the foundation has been unable to dispose of them without realizing a substantial adverse impact upon share price.

The foundation filed a timely plan for disposition of the shares that will result in their full disposition within the five-year extension period. From 2003 to 2007, it will distribute shares to public charities in the furtherance of its exempt purposes. It will also attempt to sell its securities when the price of the shares represents a reasonable value for them. It will dispose of the shares in smaller lots so it can avoid any adverse market impact on the stock price. By the end of the five-year period, the foundation will have disposed of all of its shares of N stock.

Based on these facts and representations, the IRS concluded that the foundation will satisfy the provisions of IRC § 4943(c)(7) and granted the foundation a five-year extension, to December 31, 2007, of the time for disposing of its excess business holdings in N.

The five-year disposition period may create other problems, however, and the foundation should consider the implications carefully before proceeding with such a plan. The business interests received by gift or bequest will normally be interests in closely held businesses, which, by definition, are illiquid and cannot be readily sold by the foundation. Often there will be little or no income to be distributed to the foundation. This sort of asset can be a problem for any holder, but for a foundation, these difficulties may be especially troublesome. These assets will be included among the assets taken into account in determining the foundation's minimum distribution requirement,[49] but there may be insufficient income from them to fund the distributions required by virtue of their inclusion. Second, and more important in most cases, the five-year period permitted (even with the potential five-year extension) may not be sufficient to find a suitable *unrelated* buyer. In many cases, the donor/creator who gave or left these interests to the foundation will have envisioned the business in question somehow passing eventually to members of his or her family, but those persons will normally be precluded by the self-dealing rules from purchasing these assets from the foundation. This need not be an insurmountable problem, but it must be anticipated and taken into account in the overall planning for the family's (and the foundation's) transition. One possibility is that the founder of the foundation can create in his or her heirs an option to purchase the business interests in question and then give these interests to the foundation subject to this option. As discussed above, an exception to the general self-dealing rules permits transfers pursuant to such an option, even where they would otherwise be precluded, but only if the applicable rules are closely followed.[50] If this is not anticipated in advance, the result can be quite disruptive to the plans and expectations of the foundation's creator.

Finally, reliance on the five-year disposition period may lead to negotiating difficulties as the foundation attempts to secure the best terms possible, but must deal with potential buyers who know that the foundation's interest *must* be sold by a date certain. Even if a five-year extension is obtained, the foundation as seller may be disadvantaged by its need to sell within a set time period, particularly when the potential buyers are limited in number.

§ 6.06 TAXABLE EXPENDITURES — LIMITS ON FOUNDATION GRANTS

As previously discussed, much of the 1969 congressional concern over foundation activities related to various grantmaking considerations. In some instances, grants had been made that Congress determined were not proper and should be prohibited. In other instances, the procedures for selecting grantees and following up on the grantees' use of grant funds were not deemed sufficient. The

---

[49] *See* Appendix 6-C for a detailed discussion of minimum distribution rules.

[50] *See* § 6.03[B] *supra.*

approach to both of these problem areas was the same. New IRC § 4945 imposed a general prohibition on grants for certain lobbying or political purposes and grants for noncharitable purposes, and it required certain procedures for grants to individuals and to organizations other than public charities. All of these categories were lumped together under the heading of "taxable expenditures," and the familiar two-stage excise tax approach was applied to foundation grants that failed to conform to the new requirements.

[A] Political Expenditures

A general prohibition in IRC § 501(c)(3) precludes any charitable organization, including any private foundation, from participating or intervening in any political campaign on behalf of (or in opposition to) any candidate for public office. This prohibition includes the publishing or distributing of statements. Despite this, Congress in 1969 found the possibility of foundation involvement in political activities to be a significant enough problem to warrant including a provision in the new restrictions imposing a two-stage penalty excise tax on foundation expenditures for such purposes. This provision, IRC § 4945(d)(2), forbids any direct or indirect expenditures made to influence the outcome of any specific public election or to carry on, directly or indirectly, any voter registration drive, except for certain nonpartisan voter activities carried on in five or more states, as described in section 4945(f).[51]

Why was it necessary to add a specific provision of this sort when IRC § 501(c)(3) already included a flat prohibition? The reason given is that the penalty under IRC § 501(c)(3), loss of exempt status, was too severe to be applied except in extreme cases, while many situations escaped any sanctions at all because of the lack of express standards and the fact that foundation grants to other organizations were often used inappropriately by the grantee organizations. Creation of this new penalty provision with a two-stage penalty allowed the IRS to impose a relatively mild monetary penalty for all of these transgressions, with a more severe penalty to follow if the foundation failed to correct the situation.

For the typical family foundation, the prohibition on political expenditures is just that — a flat prohibition that will not be broken or even stretched. A foundation is well advised to steer clear entirely of any involvement whatsoever in political campaigns. Fortunately, this is relatively easy, since, unlike the cloudy boundaries between permitted advocacy and prohibited lobbying, it is not hard to determine just when activities begin to bring a foundation to the verge of intervention in a political campaign.

The IRS has held that a foundation's attempts to influence the confirmation of a federal judicial nominee by the U.S. Senate do not constitute influencing the

---

[51] *See* Appendix 6-F for a detailed discussion of this rule.

outcome of a public election under IRC § 4945(d)(2) because federal judges are appointed, rather than elected. However, such attempts will constitute "lobbying" under section 4945(d)(1) and are prohibited under that provision instead.[52]

[B] Expenditures for Lobbying

[1] General Prohibition on Lobbying

As with political activities, IRC § 501(c)(3) includes a general prohibition whereby no significant part of an exempt charitable organization's activities may consist of "carrying on propaganda, or otherwise attempting, to influence legislation." However, in this instance, the prohibition is not absolute, for certain charitable organizations may elect under IRC § 501(h) to be subject to a set of objective standards as to their lobbying activities in lieu of the subjective and imprecise standard of section 501(c)(3), which merely says that "no substantial part" of an organization's activities may be in this category. Upon making this election, a public charity may then engage in certain amounts of activity aimed at influencing legislation, and if it exceeds the allowed amount, it will become subject to a penalty tax under IRC § 4911.

The election under IRC § 501(h) is available only for public charities, and not for private foundations. Nevertheless, the enactment of that provision in 1976 and the subsequent release of regulations on the subject have clarified the scope of activity permissible for private foundations under the taxable expenditure rules.

Section 4945(d)(1) of the Code includes as a taxable expenditure any amount paid or incurred by a private foundation for any attempt to influence "legislation," either through "grassroots lobbying" (i.e., attempting to affect the opinion of the general public or any segment thereof) or through "direct lobbying" (i.e., communicating with any member or employee of a legislative body or with any other government official or employee who may participate in the formulation of legislation). Legislation for this purpose is broadly defined and includes action by the U.S. Congress, a state legislature, any local council or similar governing body, or the public in regard to a referendum, initiative, constitutional amendment, or similar procedure. Legislative consideration of a proposed treaty submitted to the Senate for its advice and consent or of a presidential appointment submitted to the Senate for confirmation is also included. The IRS has even held that lobbying with respect to foreign laws is included as an attempt to influence "legislation" for purposes of IRC § 501(c)(3), so this is likewise forbidden under section 4945(d)(1).[53]

What sort of legislative activity is forbidden? The applicable rules are different for the two types of lobbying recognized under IRC § 4945(d)(1), grassroots lobbying and direct lobbying. Grassroots lobbying represents an

---

[52] *See* IRS Notice 88-76, 1988-2 C.B. 392.
[53] Rev. Rul. 73-440, 1973-2 C.B. 177.

attempt to affect the opinion of the general public or any segment thereof with respect to legislation where the foundation communication:

1. Refers to "specific legislation" that has already been introduced in a legislative body and a specific legislative proposal that the foundation either supports or opposes,

2. Reflects a view as to the desirability of the legislation, and

3. Encourages the recipient of the communication to take action with respect to the legislation.[54]

Thus, a passive report on pending legislation is not prohibited, as compared with a critical review of the legislation that identifies it as desirable or undesirable and urges the reader to support or oppose it by communicating with legislators.

By contrast, a direct lobbying communication is a communication made to a legislator or other government official involved in formulating legislation that:

1. Refers to specific legislation; and

2. Reflects a view on such legislation.[55]

[2]   Permissible Lobbying Activities

Despite the general prohibition, a foundation may engage in certain types of lobbying activity without running afoul of IRC § 4945.

[a]   Nonpartisan Analysis, Study, or Research

A foundation may perform nonpartisan analysis, study, or research and make the results available to the general public or to legislative officials without incurring liability for the tax imposed by IRC § 4945.[56] The emphasis here is on the nonpartisan aspect and the presentation of a balanced, unbiased point of view. The Regulations provide the following example to explain what is permitted under this exception:

> **Example:**   The Orgo Foundation establishes a research project to collect information concerning the dangers of the use of pesticides in raising crops; the ostensible purpose of the project is to examine and report information relating to the pros and cons of the use of pesticides in raising crops. The information is collected and distributed in a report analyzing the effects and costs of the use and nonuse of various pesticides under various conditions on humans, animals, and crops.

---

[54] Reg. § 56.4911-2(d)(1).
[55] Reg. § 56.4911-2(b)(1)(ii).
[56] Reg. § 53.4945-2(d).

The report also discusses the advantages, disadvantages, and economic cost of allowing the continued use of pesticides unabated, controlling the use of pesticides, and developing alternatives to pesticides. The report finally concludes that the disadvantages of using pesticides exceed the advantages and that prompt legislative regulation of the use of pesticides is needed. The project is nonpartisan analysis, study, or research, since it is designed to present information on both sides of the legislative controversy and presents a sufficiently full and fair exposition of the pertinent facts to enable the public or an individual to form an independent opinion or conclusion.[57]

By contrast, other examples in the Regulations indicate that a report will not be within the nonpartisan analysis, study, or research exception where it is designed to present information merely on one side of the legislative controversy or omits references to experimental evidence tending to dispute the foundation's point of view.

[b] Technical Advice or Assistance

A foundation may present "technical advice or assistance" to a government body, committee, or subdivision in response to a written request by such entity. This may be provided as a result of the foundation's knowledge or skill in a given area. Because such assistance or advice may be given only at the express request of a government body, committee, or subdivision, the oral or written presentation of such assistance or advice need not qualify as nonpartisan analysis, study, or research. A presentation of opinions or recommendations will ordinarily qualify under this exception only if such opinions or recommendations are specifically requested by the government body, committee, or subdivision or are directly related to the materials so requested.[58] The foundation's response must be made available to every member of the requesting body.

The Regulations provide the following example to explain what is permitted under this exception:

Example: A congressional committee is studying the feasibility of legislation to provide funds for scholarships to U.S. students attending schools abroad. The Abroad Foundation, which has engaged in a private scholarship program of this type, is asked, in writing, by the committee to describe the manner in which it selects candidates for its program. Abroad's response disclosing its methods of selection constitutes technical advice or assistance.[59]

---

[57] Reg. § 53.4945-2(d)(1)(vii), example 2.
[58] Reg. § 53.4945-2(d)(2).
[59] Reg. § 53.4945-2(d)(2)(iii), example 1.

Subsequent examples in the Regulations indicate that the Abroad Foundation may also offer its views on the advisability of adopting such a program or other aspects of the issue so long as such views are relevant to the committee's consideration of the scholarship program. Also, an unwritten request or one from a senator or a staffer (as opposed to the Senate or a committee) is not sufficient to bring this exception into play.

[c]   "Self-Defense" Lobbying

A foundation may appear before, or communicate with, any legislative body with respect to a possible decision of such body that might affect the existence of the private foundation, its powers and duties, its tax-exempt status, or the deductibility of contributions to such foundation. This exception can permit a foundation to communicate with the entire legislative body, committees or subcommittees of such legislative body, individual legislators, members of their staffs, or representatives of the executive branch who are involved in the legislative process, provided such communication is limited to the prescribed subjects. Similarly, the foundation may make expenditures in order to initiate legislation if such legislation concerns only those subjects.

[d]   Examination and Discussion of Broad Social, Economic, and Similar Problems

A foundation may expend funds for examinations and discussions of broad social, economic, and similar problems, even if the problems are of the type with which government would be expected to deal ultimately, without incurring liability for the excise tax on taxable expenditures.[60] This is permissible so long as such discussion avoids addressing the merits of a specific legislative proposal and does not directly encourage recipients to take action with respect to legislation. Examples of the sorts of topics that may be addressed under this exception are discussions of problems such as environmental pollution or population growth that are being considered by Congress and various state legislatures, but only if the discussion is not addressed to specific legislation.

[e]   Expressions of Individual Opinions by Foundation Officials

Finally, even if a foundation is precluded from expressing its views or expending its funds on behalf of a particular issue, officials and staff of the foundation may play a role in their individual capacities. The legislative history of the Tax Reform Act of 1969 suggests that IRC § 4945 was enacted to curb

---

[60] Reg. § 53.4945-2(d)(4).
[61] *See* H.R. Rep. 413 (pt. 1), 91st Cong., 1st Sess. 32 (1969).

foundation abuses and there was no expression of concern about any individual actions of foundation officials.[61]

Because there are no clear guidelines on this inherent exception to the lobbying prohibition, it is incumbent on any foundation official who seeks to rely on this principle to be certain that he or she takes adequate and careful steps to be certain that there is no basis for attributing his or her views to the foundation. The foundation's resources should not be used in the preparation of testimony or other materials used in the effort, and if any substantial time commitments are involved, the official should consider taking vacation or other leave time to devote to the project. Any invitations extended by a committee or other body should be addressed to the individual and not the foundation, and all written and oral statements should specify that the views stated are those of the individual and not those of the foundation.

[C] Restrictions on Grants to Individuals

One episode from the House Ways and Means Committee hearings on the Tax Reform Act of 1969 was particularly striking to observers. McGeorge Bundy, president of the Ford Foundation, was asked about grants made by the foundation to aides of Senator Robert F. Kennedy for travel and study after his assassination. One committee member (who repeatedly referred to the witness as "Mr. McBundy") observed that these grants sounded like termination pay, and Mr. Bundy acknowledged that this was accurate. It soon became obvious that such grants would certainly be targeted when legislation finally emerged, and that was indeed the case. Congress included in the Chapter 42 tax package a penalty tax on grants to individuals for purposes corresponding to the Kennedy aides' grants.

Section 4945(d)(3) of the Internal Revenue Code classifies grants to individuals for travel, study, or any other similar purpose as taxable expenditures unless they comply with the rules of section 4945(g), which requires that such grants:

1. Be awarded on an objective and nondiscriminatory basis;

2. Be made pursuant to a procedure approved in advance by the Commissioner; and

3. Meet one of the following provisions:

    *   Qualify as a scholarship or fellowship grant that would have been excludible from gross income under IRC § 117(a) as it stood before its 1986 amendment and be intended for study at a college or university;

    *   Qualify as a prize or award that is excludible from gross income under IRC § 74(b) (disregarding section 74(b)(3), which requires the recipient to contribute the award to charity) and be given to someone from the general public; or

    *   Have the purpose of achieving a specific objective, producing a report or other similar product, or improving or enhancing a literary, artistic,

musical, scientific, teaching, or other similar capacity, skill, or talent of the grantee.

Some grants to individuals are made for purposes other than travel or study, and these are not taxable expenditures under IRC § 4945(d)(3), regardless of whether the requirements of section 4945(g), as described above, are met. This would be true, for example, of grants to indigent persons to enable them to purchase furniture.[62] Similarly, grants that do not attempt to finance future activities or commit the recipients to any particular activity are not grants for "travel, study, or other similar purposes" and hence are not taxable expenditures.[63]

What about the common situation when a foundation grants funds to a school or other organization that then pays the funds to an individual? This foundation grant is not a grant to an individual for purposes of IRC § 4945 unless the foundation earmarks the grant funds for a particular individual or there is an agreement that permits the foundation to designate the individual recipients.[64] This is a useful format for foundation scholarship grants, with the funds granted to a school or other public charity and that entity made solely responsible for selecting the students who will receive the scholarships. So long as the foundation plays no role in such selection (including a veto privilege), the individual grant procedures of IRC § 4945(g) are not applicable.

For the family foundation that desires to make grants to individuals, there are thus two choices. Either the grants must be so arranged that they are not made for travel, study, or similar purposes (thus avoiding the requirements of IRC § 4945(g)), or the foundation must design an objective and nondiscriminatory selection system that complies with those requirements and have it approved by the Internal Revenue Service before awarding grants. If the grant program is contemplated when the foundation is formed, IRS approval may be requested on the foundation's exemption application (on Schedule H of Form 1023); otherwise, such approval must be obtained separately from the appropriate district director.

[D] Restrictions on Grants to Organizations

One of the areas of foundation misbehavior that caused concerns during congressional consideration of the Tax Reform Act of 1969 was the reported failure of many foundations to follow up and exercise control over their grantees' use of the funds received. Foundations apparently awarded grants without any means of ascertaining whether grantees actually used the funds for the purposes

---

[62] Reg. § 53.4945-4(a)(3)(i).

[63] *See, e.g.,* Rev. Rul. 75-393, 1975-2 C.B. 451, holding that cash grants to individuals in recognition of past literary achievements did not constitute section 4945(d)(3) taxable expenditures.

[64] Reg. § 53.4945-4(a)(4)(i).

for which the grants were awarded or whether grantees might be using part of the grant funds for inappropriate lobbying or political activities.

To correct this situation, Congress created a system whereby grants to other organizations would be taxable as "taxable expenditures" under IRC § 4945 unless they conformed to a set of rules designed to assure that the grant was used as intended. Although this tax provision includes a number of fairly complicated rules and definitions, it has a simple principle at its heart. To avoid liability for the penalty tax in this context, a foundation has what is a fairly straightforward choice: it may limit its grants to other organizations in one of two ways. The penalty is not applicable if the foundation either (1) makes grants only to organizations that are public charities (or exempt operating foundations, as discussed at § 6.07 below), or (2) makes grants to other organizations outside those categories and exercises *expenditure responsibility* over such grants. Although this may not always be an easy situation to explain, it is not overly difficult to understand. A family foundation will often limit its grants to public charities in any event, and, although conservative, this may not be an unreasonable approach to take as a means of eliminating most concerns about improper grants. Expenditure responsibility itself is a logical system of grant discipline that does not have to be an onerous burden for the family foundation that wishes to be more bold in its grantmaking. Whichever approach is taken with a particular grant, the foundation grants committee or staff should seek competent advice if there is any question whatsoever as to the permissibility of a grant or a grantee.

§ 6.07   GRANTS TO PUBLIC CHARITIES AND EXEMPT OPERATING FOUNDATIONS

[A] In General

Public charities include most of the familiar charitable organizations and probably comprise the largest body of family foundation grantees. The actual definition of a public charity is found in IRC § 509(a). This category includes the traditional charitable organizations — such as churches and synagogues, schools and universities, and other publicly supported entities like the American Red Cross and The Nature Conservancy — plus several less familiar categories, such as supporting organizations.

[B] Determining Grantee Status

A family foundation should obtain from every prospective grantee organization a copy of its IRS exemption letter. That letter will indicate whether the organization is or is not classified as a private foundation; if it is *not* a private foundation, it is a public charity and may receive grant funds without requiring the granting foundation to exercise expenditure responsibility. That letter will also identify the organization as an exempt operating organization if it qualifies in that category. If a prospective grantee is a public charity, its status may also be confirmed in IRS Publication 78 (also available on the IRS web site). In either case, the prospective grantee should be required to represent in writing that its status has not been modified by the IRS.

Several special rules permit grants to be made without exercising expenditure responsibility to certain categories of organizations that are not actually public charities. These include the following:

1. An entity that would qualify as a public charity except that its funds are not used within the United States or its possessions, or it was created or organized in or under the laws of a foreign country;

2. A state or local governmental entity (including a college or university); and

3. A foreign government or agency, or certain international organizations (such as the United Nations or the World Health Organization).[65]

Note that grants to these domestic and foreign governmental entities or to international organizations are excluded from the expenditure responsibility requirements only if they are made exclusively for charitable purposes.

When a foundation contemplates making a grant to an organization that is not a U.S. entity, it often faces a dilemma in that the foreign entity will usually not have a determination from the Internal Revenue Service indicating that it can qualify as a public charity. A university or museum in England or Japan is not obligated to get a determination of its status from the U.S. Internal Revenue Service, although some such institutions have done so to facilitate U.S. grants. The IRS's Publication 78 will state whether a particular foreign institution has been classified, and if its name appears there as a public charity, fine. If not, however, the Regulations provide an "equivalency" rule to enable a foundation to determine whether such a foreign organization is organized and operated in a manner substantially similar enough to that of a U.S. charitable organization that expenditure responsibility need not be exercised.[66] The granting foundation may make a "good faith determination" that the grantee organization would qualify as a public charity. Such a determination may be based on an affidavit of the grantee organization or an opinion of counsel (of either the grantor or the grantee) that the grantee qualifies as a public charity. This affidavit or opinion must set forth sufficient facts concerning the operations and support of the grantee for the Internal Revenue Service to determine that the grantee would be likely to qualify as a public charity (i.e., as an organization described in IRC §§ 509(a)(1), (2), or (3)).

---

[65] The international organizations included here are those designated by executive order under 22 U.S.C. § 288.

[66] Reg. § 53.4945-5(a)(5).

[C] Substantial or Material Changes in Support

A family foundation considering making a grant to a public charity that is relatively large in relation to the grantee's overall support must be careful not to overlook the potential effect the proposed grant may have on the status of the grantee. This is an important consideration where a prospective grantee organization establishes that its public charity status derives from the fact that it is publicly supported. This effect must be considered whenever the grantee's exemption letter classifies it as an organization that is not a private foundation because it is described either in IRC §§ 509(a)(1) and 170(b)(1)(A)(vi) or in IRC § 509(a)(2). Such an organization receives contributions from a sufficiently large group of contributors that it is not dominated by any of them under either of two fairly complex mathematical computations. In general, such an organization must have more than one-third of its support from public sources to qualify under either of these two tests. The point to be considered is whether the proposed grant may be large enough to disturb the grantee's qualification under this test or "tip" it out of public charity status.

> **Example:** The Hanson Family Foundation is considering a grant of $2,000,000 to a local food bank organization for a special project. The organization has received total support of $100,000 from 25 contributors, each of whom has contributed $4,000. Upon receiving the Hanson grant, the food bank organization would have total support of $2,100,000, of which over 95 percent has come from a single contributor, the Hanson Family Foundation. Its public support will have been reduced to a very small percentage, well below the amounts required for public charity status based on public support under either of the possible tests (IRC §§ 509(a)(1) and 170(b)(1)(A)(vi) or IRC § 509(a)(2)).

There are several ways this situation can be mitigated. It may be possible to classify the proposed grant as an "unusual grant," which may be disregarded by the recipient organization in calculating its public support fraction.[67] This is generally possible where the grant comes from an independent source that has not previously provided funds or otherwise played a role in controlling the grantee entity. Rulings are available from the Internal Revenue Service national office to clarify the status of a potential grant as an "unusual grant" for this purpose. Another way a foundation may avoid the tipping problem without the time and expense of a ruling is by timing the release of grant funds to allow the grantee organization to raise sufficient support from other sources. In the example above, the magnitude of the problem facing the Hanson Family Foundation and its proposed food bank grant is so great that an unusual grant ruling will probably be the only practical solution. If the grant will not reduce the grantee's public support fraction to so great a degree, it may be sufficient to release the

---

[67] *See* Reg. §§ 1.170A-9(e)(6)(ii) and 1.509(a)-3(c)(3) for the applicable tests.

grant funds in installments tied to the grantee's demonstration that funds have been raised from other sources.

> **Note:** Some foundations have adopted a policy of requiring public charity grantees to show that their public support meets the 331/3 percent test of IRC §§ 509(a)(1) and 170(b)(1)(A)(vi), rather than the less severe 10 percent test, since the latter test requires the organization to demonstrate facts and circumstances showing that it is operated as a public charity.[68] Such foundations have chosen this approach in order to avoid the need to make a factual determination, since it is always possible that the IRS will reach a different conclusion on the same facts. The 331/3 percent test has the advantage of relative certainty and does not require any subjective evaluation. Other foundations have a less strict rule that will permit them to make grants even if the 331/3 percent test is not met.

Where there is any significant doubt as to the continued public charity status of a potential grantee, a foundation might consider exercising expenditure responsibility, or at least reserving the right to do so as a condition of the grant for any year in which it perceives such a doubt. As we shall see, expenditure responsibility is not an onerous alternative and in fact generally represents a system of sound grantmaking procedures. Indeed, some family foundations labor under the erroneous assumption that they may make grants only to public charities or to section 501(c)(3) organizations. That is not the case, and the foundations that so limit their grantmaking may find that they can do much more to accomplish their charitable objectives and help improve conditions in their communities by reaching out to other grantees through the exercise of expenditure responsibility.

[D] Expenditure Responsibility

[1] In General

If a potential grantee is not a public charity (or another qualified grantee under the rules just described) or if its status is not sufficiently clear, a foundation may nevertheless make the grant in question without incurring liability for a taxable expenditure simply by exercising *expenditure responsibility* with respect to the grant. The purposes of the expenditure responsibility requirement are

---

[68] Under Reg. §§ 1.170A-9(e) and 1.509(a)-2(a), an organization is "publicly supported" (and thus a public charity) if at least 33⅓ percent of its total support is "normally" from governmental units, from contributions made directly or indirectly by the general public, or from a combination of these sources. Section 1.170A-9(e)(3) provides that an organization failing this 33⅓-percent-of-support test may still qualify as a "publicly supported" organization if it normally receives a substantial part (i.e., 10 percent) of its support from such sources and, on the basis of a number of factors listed in the Regulations, can establish that it is in the nature of a "publicly supported" organization. These factors include such things as the presence of a fund-raising program that is designed to attract new and additional public or governmental support on a continuous basis, the existence of a representative governing body, and the actual percentage of public support (i.e., an organization with 30 percent public support has less of a burden of proof than one with 11 percent), to name just a few.

simple and straightforward — to ensure that the foundation exerts all reasonable efforts and establishes adequate procedures to see that the grant is spent solely for the purpose for which made, to obtain full and complete reports from the grantee on how the funds are spent, and to make full and detailed reports to the IRS about such grants. Remember, the rules described below *must* be followed for grants requiring expenditure responsibility, but may be useful for other grants as well. There are generally three steps in the expenditure responsibility process:

1. A pre-grant inquiry into the grantee organization;

2. An agreement in writing concerning the details of the grant and obligating the grantee to use the funds for the purposes of the grant; and

3. Reports by the grantee to the granting foundation and by the granting foundation to the IRS concerning the use of the grant funds.

While the details can be complex, that is all that expenditure responsibility consists of — a system for assuring that grant funds are used as intended. While compliance is certainly more demanding and time consuming than not complying, these steps are nothing more than the parties might arrange among themselves to assure that grant funds are not used improperly.

[2] Pre-Grant Inquiry

Before a grant is made, the foundation should inquire about the identity and past history of the organization and its managers. The focus should be on whether there is any readily available information about the management, activities, and practices of the grantee organization that relate to the grantee's ability to use the grant as intended. This is a limited inquiry, but should be complete enough to give a reasonable person assurance that the grantee will use the grant for the proper purposes. The scope of this inquiry may vary from case to case depending on the size and purpose of the grant, the period over which it is to be paid, and the foundation's prior experience with this grantee. If initial responses create some doubt about the grantee, further inquiries may be necessary.

[3] Written Grant Agreement

Every grant for which expenditure responsibility is required must be made subject to a written commitment signed by an appropriate official of the grantee organization. That commitment must include the grantee's agreement:

- To repay any grant funds not used for the purposes of the grant;

- To submit annual reports on the use of the funds and the progress made in accomplishing the purposes of the grant;

- To maintain records of receipts and expenditures and to make its books and records available to the grantor at reasonable times; and

- Not to use any of the funds for propaganda or any other attempt to influence legislation (within the meaning of IRC § 4945(d)(1)), for electioneering or voter registration drives, or for any noncharitable purpose, and not to make any grant that does not comply with the individual grant requirements of IRC § 4945(d)(3) or the organization grant requirements of IRC § 4945(d)(4).

The agreement must also clearly specify the purposes of the grant. Comparable, but different, written agreement requirements apply to program-related investments.[69]

As comprehensive and demanding as these requirements may seem on first examination, they soon become routine once the foundation fashions a standard grant agreement form. Like any standard form, this can leave room for additions necessitated by a particular grant or grantee.

[4] Reporting Requirements

[a] Reporting to Granting Foundation

Beginning with the year in which the grant is made, and every year thereafter until the grant funds are fully spent or the grant is otherwise terminated, the grantee must file reports on the use of the grant funds, compliance with the terms of the grant, and progress made toward achieving the grant purposes. These reports must be furnished to the grantor within a "reasonable" period of time after the close of each annual accounting period.[70] A final report detailing expenditures made from the grant funds and indicating progress made toward the grant goals is due within a reasonable period after the close of the grantee's annual accounting period during which the use of the grant funds is completed. The granting foundation need not conduct any independent verification of the interim or final reports unless it has reason to doubt their accuracy or reliability.

[b] Reporting to Internal Revenue Service

With its annual return (Form 990-PF), the granting foundation must provide information with respect to each grant that is subject to expenditure responsibility, including:

- Name and address of the grantee;

- Date and amount of the grant;

---

[69] *See* Reg. § 53.4945-5(b)(4).
[70] Reg. § 53.4945-5(c)(1).

- Purpose of the grant;

- Amounts expended by the grantee;

- Whether the grantee has diverted any portion of the funds from the purpose of the grant;

- Dates of any reports received from the grantee; and

- Date and results of any verification of the grantee's reports.

In addition, the granting foundation must make available to the Internal Revenue Service copies of the grant agreement covering each expenditure responsibility grant made during the taxable year, all grantee reports received during the taxable year, and any reports made by the grantor's personnel or independent auditors.

§ 6.08   TAX ON NET INVESTMENT INCOME (IRC § 4940)

The bulk of this chapter is devoted to Chapter 42 of the Internal Revenue Code, which (as the title of the chapter suggests) imposes a number of operating restrictions on private foundations. However, one of the important provisions of Chapter 42, Code Section 4940, imposes not a restriction but rather an excise tax on the foundation's net investment income.

For a discussion of section 4940, see § 8.04 *infra*.

CHAPTER 6
APPENDICES

Most of the materials in the following appendices are adapted from Internal Revenue Service Publication 578, *Tax Information for Private Foundations and Foundation Managers*. This invaluable publication has been out of print for some time, since the last edition was released in January 1989. The authors have updated the materials in Publication 578 for post-1989 changes and simplified them to make them more readable. In addition, the authors have added commentary on practical points. These appendices provide a thorough discussion of the extremely complex tax rules governing private foundations and are designed to help the reader who wants a more detailed answer to a particular question.

DISQUALIFIED PERSONS (IRC § 4946)

Overview. A key concept in the tax rules governing private foundations, the term "disqualified person" refers to the person(s) who creates and funds the foundation, the foundation's managers, and many family members and other related interests. (*See* IRC § 4946.)

§6-A.01 GENERAL RULE

Many of the foundation rules discussed here involve the key concept of a *disqualified person*. This term refers to a set of carefully defined categories of individuals and other entities that are closely related in one way or another to a private foundation. Section 4946(a)(1) of the Internal Revenue Code (IRC) defines the following persons as disqualified persons with respect to a private foundation:

1. All "substantial contributors" to the foundation (as defined below) [IRC § 4946(a)(1)(A)];

2. All "foundation managers" of the foundation (as defined below) [IRC § 4946(a)(1)(B)];

3. Any owner of more than 20 percent of —

   a. The total combined voting power of a corporation,

   b. The profits interest of a partnership, or

   c. The beneficial interest of a trust or unincorporated enterprise that is (during the ownership) a substantial contributor to the foundation [IRC § 4946(a)(1)(C)];

4. Any "member of the family" (as defined below) of any of the individuals described in item 1, 2, or 3 above [IRC § 4946(a)(1)(D)];

5. Any corporation of which more than 35 percent of the total combined voting power is owned by persons described in item 1, 2, 3, or 4 above [IRC § 4946(a)(1)(E)];

6. Any partnership of which more than 35 percent of the profits interest is owned by persons described in item 1, 2, 3, or 4 above [IRC § 4946(a)(1)(F)];

7. Any trust, estate, or unincorporated enterprise of which more than 35 percent of the beneficial interest is owned by persons described in item 1, 2, 3, or 4 above [IRC § 4946(a)(1)(G)];

8. For purposes of the tax on self-dealing only, a "government official" (as defined below) [IRC § 4946(a)(1)(I)]; and

9. For purposes of the tax on excess business holdings only, another private foundation that either:

   a. Is effectively controlled by the same persons who control the private foundation in question or

   b. Receives substantially all of its contributions from the same persons described in item 1, 2, or 3 above, or members of their families, who made substantially all the contributions to the private foundation in question [IRC § 4946(a)(1)(H)].

§ 6-A.02   DEFINITIONS

[A]   Attribution of Ownership

In addition to the corporate stock in a corporation, profits interest in a partnership, or beneficial interest in a trust or estate that a person owns directly, indirect ownership is taken into account when determining whether the 20 and 35 percent tests described above are met. This is accomplished by IRC § 4946(a)(3) and Treasury Regulation § 53.4946-1(d), which generally apply the following rules for this purpose:

1. Stock (or profits interest or beneficial interest) owned directly or indirectly by or for a corporation (or partnership, estate, or trust) is considered owned proportionately by or for its shareholders (or partners or beneficiaries);

2. An individual is considered to own the stock (or profits interest or beneficial interest) owned directly or indirectly by or for his or her family members. (One exception: There is no double attribution through the family attribution rule. Thus, for the 35 percent ownership tests in categories 5, 6, and 7 above, stock (or profits interest or beneficial interest) is *not* treated as constructively owned by an individual solely because that individual is a member of the family of another disqualified person. For purposes of these 35 percent ownership rules, an individual will be treated as a constructive owner only if that individual himself or herself is a substantial contributor, a foundation manager, or a 20 percent owner of the combined voting power (or profits interest or beneficial interest) of a substantial contributor);

3. An individual's family includes only those persons described in "Member of the Family" below; and

4. Any stock holdings (or profits interest or beneficial interest) that have been counted once (whether because of actual or constructive ownership) in applying categories 5, 6, and 7 above may not be counted a second time.

[B]   Voting Power

Voting power for this purpose includes outstanding voting power and does not include voting power obtainable, but not actually obtained (e.g., voting power obtainable by converting securities or nonvoting stock into voting stock or by exercising warrants or options, and voting power available to preferred share-holders if dividends on preferred stock are in arrears). [Reg. § 53.4946-1(a)(6)]

[C]   Profits Interest

The profits interest of a partner is his or her distributive share of partner-ship income. [Reg. § 53.4946-1(a)(2)] However, this does not include any such interest that is obtainable, but has not been obtained by a partner. [Reg. § 53.4946-1(a)(6)]

[D] Beneficial Interest

The beneficial interest in a trust will be determined by reference to the person's actuarial interest in the trust. [Reg. § 53.4946-1(a)(4)]

[E] Substantial Contributor

A substantial contributor includes any person who meets the following two tests:

- He or she contributed or bequeathed a total amount of more than $5,000 to the foundation, and

- That amount is more than 2 percent of the total contributions and bequests received by the foundation from its creation up through the close of the tax year of the foundation in which the contribution or bequest is received from that person.

For a foundation organized as a trust, a substantial contributor also includes the creator of the trust. (*See* IRC § 507(d)(2)(A) for the full definition.)

For purposes of this 2 percent test, both the total amounts received by the foundation and the total amounts contributed and bequeathed by the person are determined as of the last day of the foundation's tax year. Each contribution or bequest is valued at its fair market value on the date it is received by the foundation. Gifts by an individual include all contributions and bequests made by that individual and his or her spouse. A determination must be made as to whether a person is a substantial contributor as of the end of each of the foundation's tax years, based on the respective totals of all contributions received and all amounts received from a particular person by that date. Status as a substantial contributor will date from the time the donor first met the $5,000 — 2 percent test. [Reg. § 1.507-6(b)(1)]

Once a person is a substantial contributor to a private foundation, generally that person remains a substantial contributor even though he or she might not be so classified if a determination were made at some later date. [Reg. § 1.507-6(b)(1)] For example, even though later contributions and bequests from other donors make a person's contributions become less than 2 percent of the total received by a private foundation, generally the person remains a substantial contributor to the foundation. However, a person ceases to be a substantial contributor as of the end of a private foundation's tax year if:

1. Neither that person nor any related persons have made any contributions to the foundation during the 10-year period ending with that tax year, and

2. Neither that person nor any related person was a foundation manager of the foundation at any time during that 10-year period; and

3. The total contributions made by that person (and related persons) are determined by the IRS to be insignificant compared to the total contributions to the foundation by one other person. For the purpose of this comparison, appreciation on contributions while held by the foundation is taken into account. (See IRC § 507(d)(2)(C), enacted in 1984.)

For purposes of this rule, a person is considered related to a substantial contributor if that person's relationship to the contributor would make that person a disqualified person with respect to the contributor, as discussed in this chapter. If the contributor is a corporation, the term "related person" also includes any officer or director of the corporation.

[F] Special Rule

A substantial contributor does not include an entity that is described in section 509(a)(1), (2), or (3) (i.e., a public charity) or any organization that is wholly owned by such an entity. [Reg. § 1.507-6(a)(2)] Also, for purposes of the tax on self-dealing, a substantial contributor does not include any other organization described in section 501(c)(3) (other than an organization with section 509 (a)(4) status); these entities are also excluded from the definition of "disqualified person." Reg. § 53.4946-1(a)(8).

The term "contribution" includes gifts and grants to the foundation as well as bequests, devises, legacies, or other transfers at death. [Reg. § 1.507-6(c)(1)]

[G] Foundation Manager

In general, section 4946(b)(1) classifies the following as *foundation managers:*

1. An officer, director, or trustee of a foundation (or other individual having powers or responsibilities similar to those of an officer, director, or trustee); and

2. For any particular act or failure to act, any employee of the foundation having final authority or responsibility (either officially or effectively) for the act or failure to act.

A person who is specifically designated as an officer under the incorporation certificate, bylaws, or other documents of the foundation or who regularly exercises general authority to make administrative and policy decisions for a foundation is considered an officer of the foundation. For any act or failure to act, a foundation employee who has authority merely to recommend particular administrative or policy decisions, but not to implement them without approval of a superior, is not an officer. Independent contractors, such as accountants, lawyers, and investment managers or advisors, acting in their capacity as such, are not considered officers of the foundation. [*See* Reg. § 53.4946-1(f)(2)]

[H] Member of the Family

A *member of the family* include: a spouse, ancestors, children, grandchildren, great-grandchildren, and spouses of children, grandchildren, and great-grandchildren. [IRC §4946(d)] Note one important departure from common understanding of this term: A person's brother or sister is not a member of his or her family for this purpose. A legally adopted child of an individual will be treated as a child by blood. [Reg. §53.4946-1(h)]

[I] Government Official

For purposes of the self-dealing rules only, a government official also is a disqualified person. Section 4946(c) provides that the term "government official" means an individual who at the time of the act of self-dealing holds any of the following offices or positions:

1. An elective public office in the executive or legislative branch of the U.S. government;

2. An office in the executive or judicial branch of the U.S. government, appointment to which was made by the president;

3. A position in the executive, legislative, or judicial branch of the U.S. government —

   a. Which is listed in Schedule C of Rule VI of the Civil Service Rules or

   b. The compensation for which is at least equal to the lowest rate prescribed for GS-16 of the General Schedule under 5 U.S.C. §5332;

4. A position under either the U.S. House of Representatives or the U.S. Senate, held by an individual who receives *gross* annual pay of at least $15,000 (including expense allowances for which no accounting need be made);

5. An elective or appointive public office in any branch of the government of any state, any possession of the United States, or any subdivision of the foregoing, or the District of Columbia, held by an individual who receives gross annual pay of at least $20,000; or

6. A position as personal or executive assistant or secretary to any of the individuals described above.

[J] Public Office

For purposes of category 5 above, a holder of a *public office* must be distinguished from a person who is merely a *public employee*. Although the determination depends on the facts and circumstances of each case, the essential element is whether a significant part of the activities of the individual is the independent performance of policy-making functions. Among the factors to be considered are whether the office is created by Congress, by a state constitution or state legislature, or by a municipality or other governmental body under powers created in it, and whether the duties to be discharged by the office are defined either directly or indirectly by the body that created it or through legislative authority. For example, the following are illustrations of positions of public employment that do not involve policy-making functions and thus are not a public office:

1. The chancellor, president, provost, dean, and other officers of a state university who are appointed, elected, or otherwise hired by a state board of regents or equivalent public body and who are subject to the direction and supervision of that body;

2. The superintendent of public schools and other public school officials who are appointed, elected, or otherwise hired by a board of education or equivalent public body and who are subject to the direction and supervision of that body; and

3. Members of police and fire departments, except for department heads who, under the facts and circumstances of the case, independently perform policy-making functions as a significant part of their activities.

[*See* Reg. §53.4946-1(g)(2)]

APPENDIX 6-B

TAXES ON SELF-DEALING (IRC § 4941)

Overview. An excise tax is imposed on virtually any dealings between a private foundation and its founders or related interests (called "disqualified persons"). It applies in two steps — an initial tax of five percent of the amount involved is imposed on the disqualified person, plus a 21/2 percent tax on the foundation manager who knowingly agreed to it. (Both of these may be escaped under certain conditions if the offense was excusable under the applicable standards.) Thereafter, if the self-dealing is not corrected within the specified period, an additional tax of 200 percent is imposed on the disqualified person, plus a 50 percent tax on the foundation manager. (*See* IRC § 4941.)

§ 6-B.01   **Tax Imposed**
      [A]   **Initial Tax**
      [B]   **Additional Tax**
      [C]   **Limits on Foundation Manager's Liability**
      [D]   **Transactions Considered Self-Dealing**
      [E]   **Definitions of Key Terms**
            [1]   **Government Officials**
            [2]   **Participation**
            [3]   **Willful**
            [4]   **Reasonable Cause**
            [5]   **Advice of Counsel**
            [6]   **Knowing**
            [7]   **Taxable Period**
            [8]   **Correction Period**

§ 6-B.02   **What Is Self-Dealing?**
      [A]   **Sales or Exchanges of Property**
      [B]   **Leases**
      [C]   **Loans**
      [D]   **Providing Goods, Services, or Facilities**
      [E]   **Paying Compensation**
      [F]   **Transfer of Use of Income or Assets**
      [G]   **Payment to a Government Official**

§ 6-B.01   TAX IMPOSED

Section 4941 of the Internal Revenue Code imposes an excise tax on certain transactions (acts of self-dealing) between a private foundation and disqualified persons.

[A] Initial Tax

Section 4941(a)(1) imposes an excise tax of 5 percent of the amount involved in the act of self-dealing on the disqualified person, other than a foundation manager acting only as a manager, for each year or part of a year in the taxable period. Section 4941(a)(2) imposes an excise tax of 21/2 percent of the amount involved on a foundation manager who knowingly participates in an act of self-dealing, unless participation is not willful and is due to reasonable cause, for each year or part of a year in the taxable period.

[B] Additional Tax

Under section 4941(b)(1), an excise tax of 200 percent of the amount involved is imposed on the disqualified person, other than a foundation manager acting only as a manager, who participated in the act of self-dealing if the act of self-dealing is not corrected within the taxable period. The additional tax will not be assessed or, if assessed, will be abated if the act of self-dealing is corrected during the correction period (described later). If an additional tax is imposed on the disqualified person under section 4941(b)(1), section 4941(b)(2) also imposes an excise tax of 50 percent of the amount involved on any foundation manager who refuses to agree to part or all of the correction of the self-dealing act.

[C] Limits on Foundation Manager's Liability

The maximum initial tax imposed on the foundation manager is $10,000, and the maximum additional tax is $10,000 for any one act. There is no maximum on the liability of the self-dealer, including one who is a foundation manager. If more than one person is liable for the initial and additional taxes imposed for any act of self-dealing, all parties will be jointly and severally liable for those taxes.

[D] Transactions Considered Self-Dealing

Under sections 4941(d)(1)(A) through (F), the following transactions are generally considered acts of self-dealing between a private foundation and a disqualified person:

1. Selling, exchanging, or leasing property;

2. Lending money or making other extensions of credit;

3. Providing goods, services, or facilities;

4. Paying compensation or reimbursing expenses to a disqualified person;

5. Transferring foundation income or assets to, or for the use or benefit of, a disqualified person; and

6. Making certain agreements to pay government officials.

[E] Definitions of Key Terms

A number of terms used in the foregoing summary must be defined before one can understand how the self-dealing prohibition operates. The following are some of those terms.

[1] Government Officials

As noted in the discussion of disqualified persons above, a government official may be a disqualified person for purposes of the tax on self-dealing. However, the tax will be imposed only if the government official knows that the act is an act of self-dealing.

[2] Participation

A disqualified person will be treated as participating in an act of self-dealing if he or she engages or takes part in a transaction, alone or with others, or directs any person to do so. Participation by a foundation manager includes silence or inaction on the manager's part where there is a duty to speak or act as well as any affirmative action by the manager. However, a foundation manager will not have participated in an act of self-dealing when the manager has opposed the act in a manner consistent with carrying out the manager's responsibilities to the private foundation. [Reg. 53.4941(a)-1(b)(2)]

[3] Willful

Participation by a foundation manager is willful if it is voluntary, conscious, and intentional. No motive to avoid the restrictions of the law or the incurrence of any tax is necessary to make the participation willful. However, participation by the foundation manager is not willful if the manager does not know that participation in the transaction is an act of self-dealing. [Reg. § 53.4941(a)-1(b)(4)]

[4] Reasonable Cause

Participation is due to reasonable cause if the foundation manager has exercised responsibility on behalf of the foundation with ordinary business case and prudence. [Reg. § 53.4941(a)-1(b)(5)]

[5]   Advice of Counsel

A person will ordinarily not be liable for the initial tax imposed for self-dealing if, after full disclosure of the factual situation to legal counsel (including in-house counsel), he or she relies on the advice of counsel as expressed in a reasoned written legal opinion that a transaction is not an act of self-dealing under the law, even if the transaction is later held to be an act of self-dealing. A written legal opinion is considered reasoned even if it reaches a conclusion that is later determined to be incorrect as long as it addresses itself to the facts and applicable law. However, an opinion will not be considered reasoned if it does nothing more than recite the facts and express a conclusion. The absence of advice of counsel will not, by itself, imply that a person participated in the act knowingly, willfully, or without reasonable cause. [Reg. § 53.4941(a)-1(b)(6)]

[6]   Knowing

A person will be considered to have participated in a transaction knowing that it is an act of self-dealing only if he or she:

1.   Has actual knowledge of enough facts so that, based only on those facts, the transaction would be an act of self-dealing;

2.   Is aware that such an act may violate the rules governing self-dealing; and

3.   Negligently fails to make reasonable attempts to learn whether the transaction is an act of self-dealing (or is actually aware that the transaction is an act of self-dealing).

[*See* Reg. § 53.4941(a)-1(b)(3)] The term "knowing" does not mean having reason to know. However, evidence tending to show that a person had reason to know of a particular fact or rule is relevant in determining whether that person has actual knowledge of the fact or rule. The IRS must bear the burden of proof that a foundation manager has knowingly participated in an act of self-dealing.

[7]   Taxable Period

The tax on self-dealing is imposed for each year or part of a year within the taxable period. Section 4941(c)(1) states that the taxable period begins on the date the act of self-dealing occurs and ends on the earliest of:

1.   The date a notice of deficiency for the initial tax is mailed;

2.   The date the initial tax is assessed; or

3.   The date correction of the act of self-dealing is completed.

An act of self-dealing "occurs" on the date all the terms and conditions of the transaction and the liabilities of the parties are fixed. For example, if a private foundation gives a disqualified person a binding option on June 17, 2001, to buy property owned by the foundation at any time before June 16, 2002, the act of self-dealing has occurred on June 17, 2001.

[8] Correction Period

The correction period starts on the day the act of self-dealing occurs and ends 90 days after a notice of deficiency for the additional tax is mailed. The correction period may be extended by:

1. Any period in which the deficiency cannot be assessed because of a petition to the Tax Court; or

2. Any period the IRS determines is reasonable and necessary.

[*See* IRC § 4963(e); Reg. § 53.4963-1(e)]

§ 6-B.02   WHAT IS SELF-DEALING?

The term "self-dealing" includes the following transactions whether direct or indirect. However, special rules applying to several particular situations are discussed under §§ 6-B.03 and 6-B.04 below.

[A] Sales or Exchanges of Property (IRC § 4941(d)(1)(A))

Any sale or exchange of property between a private foundation and a disqualified person is an act of self-dealing. For example, the sale of incidental supplies by a disqualified person to a private foundation is an act of self-dealing, regardless of the amount paid to the disqualified person. Similarly, the sale of stock or other securities by a disqualified person to a private foundation in a bargain sale is an act of self-dealing, regardless of the amount paid. However, *see* § 6-B.04 below for important special rules.

The transfer of property by a disqualified person to a private foundation is treated as a sale or exchange if the foundation assumes a mortgage or similar lien that was placed on the property before the transfer or if it takes the property subject to a mortgage or similar lien that a disqualified person placed on the property in the 10-year period ending on the date of transfer. A similar lien includes, but is not limited to, deeds of trust and vendors' liens, but does not include any other lien if it is insignificant in relation to the fair market value of the property transferred.

[B] Leases (IRC § 4941(d)(1)(A))

The leasing of property between a disqualified person and a private foundation is an act of self-dealing. *But see* § 6-B.04[E] below for important special rules.

[C]   Loans (IRC § 4941(d)(1)(B))

The lending of money or other extension of credit between a private foundation and a disqualified person is an act of self-dealing. However, this does not include the lending of money by a disqualified person to a private foundation *without interest or other charge* if the proceeds of the loan are used exclusively for charitable purposes. A loan by a disqualified person to a private foundation at below-market interest rates is treated as an act of self-dealing to the same extent as a loan at market interest rates.

An act of self-dealing occurs when a third party buys property and assumes a mortgage, the mortgagee of which is a private foundation, and later the third party transfers the property to a disqualified person who either assumes liability under the mortgage or takes the property subject to the mortgage. In this transaction, the foundation is considered to have made a loan to the disqualified person in the amount of the unpaid indebtedness on the property at the time of the transfer. [Reg. § 53.4941(d)-2(c)(1)]

The making of a promise, pledge, or similar arrangement regarding money or property to a private foundation by a disqualified person, whether by an oral or written agreement, a promissory note, or other instrument of indebtedness, is not an extension of credit before the date of maturity to the extent that it is motivated by charitable intent and is unsupported by consideration. [Reg. § 53.4941(d)-2(c)(3)] The performing of trust functions and certain general banking services by a bank or trust company, which is a disqualified person, is not an act of self-dealing if the services are reasonable and necessary in carrying out the exempt purposes of the private foundation and the compensation paid to the bank or trust company is not excessive (considering the fair interest rate for the use of the funds by the bank or trust company).

The general banking services that are not self-dealing are:

1.   Checking accounts, as long as the bank does not charge interest on any overdrafts or a service fee greater than the actual cost of processing the amount overdrawn;

2.   Savings accounts, as long as the foundation may withdraw its funds on no more than 30 days' notice without subjecting itself to a loss of interest on its money for the time the money was on deposit; and

3.   Safekeeping activities.

[*See* Reg. § 53.4941(d)-2(c)(4), applying IRC § 4941(d)(2)(E)]

The purchase of certificates of deposit that provide a reduced rate of interest if not held to maturity from a banking institution that is a disqualified person does not fall within the scope of the general banking services permitted and is an act of self-dealing.

[D] Providing Goods, Services, or Facilities (IRC § 4941(d)(1)(C))

In general, any providing of goods, services, or facilities between a private foundation and a disqualified person is an act of self-dealing. This applies to providing goods, services, or facilities such as office space, cars, auditoriums, secretarial help, meals, libraries, publications, laboratories, and parking lots. However, it is not self-dealing if a disqualified person provides the goods, services, or facilities to a foundation *without charge* and they are used exclusively for purposes specified in section 501(c)(3) of the Code. [IRC § 4941(d)(2)(C)] Also, the providing of goods, services, or facilities to a foundation manager, or to an employee or volunteer, is not an act of self-dealing if the value of the items provided is reasonable and necessary to the performance of the tasks involved in carrying out the exempt purpose of the foundation and is not excessive. [Reg. § 53.4941(d)-2(d)(2)]

Thus, for example, an act of self-dealing does not result if a private foundation provides meals and lodging that are reasonable and necessary (but not excessive) to a foundation manager. This is true whether or not the value of the meals and lodging is excludible from the manager's gross income.

[E] Paying Compensation (IRC § 4941(d)(1)(D))

The payment of compensation or reimbursement of expenses by a private foundation to a disqualified person is an act of self-dealing. *But see* § 6-B.04 below for important special rules.

[F] Transfer or Use of Income or Assets (IRC § 4941(d)(1)(E))

The transfer to, or use by or for the benefit of, a disqualified person of the income or assets of a private foundation is an act of self-dealing. For example, an act of self-dealing includes payment by a private foundation of any excise tax imposed on a disqualified person for any prohibited transactions. Similarly, the payment of premiums for an insurance policy providing liability insurance to a foundation manager for excise taxes on prohibited transactions is an act of self-dealing unless the premiums are treated as compensation to the manager. [Reg. §§ 53.4941(d)-2(f)(3), (4), (5)] In addition, the purchase or sale of stock or other securities by a private foundation is an act of self-dealing if the purchase or sale is made in an attempt to manipulate the price of the stock or other securities to the advantage of a disqualified person.

The indemnification by the foundation of its managers against reasonable expenses (other than taxes, penalties, and expenses of correction) incurred in an IRS or court proceeding involving the imposition of excise taxes on the foundation manager will not be an act of self-dealing if:

1. The manager is successful in the defense, or the proceeding is ended by settlement; and

2. The manager has not acted willfully and without reasonable cause in the act or failure to act giving rise to liability for the excise taxes.

Similarly, the indemnification of a foundation manager for reasonable expenses incurred for defense in a judicial or administrative proceeding relating to the mismanagement of funds of a charitable organization is not an act of self-dealing if the applicable preceding conditions are met. [Reg. § 53.4941(d)-2(f)(3)] The indemnification of a lender or guarantee of repayment by a private foundation of a loan to a disqualified person is treated as a use for the benefit of a disqualified person of the income or assets of a private foundation.

A grant or other payment made by a foundation to satisfy the legal obligation of a disqualified person is an act of self-dealing. Note that satisfaction of a substantial contributor's pledge of a contribution to a charitable organization can produce this result.

The fact that a disqualified person receives an incidental or slight benefit from the use by a foundation of its income or assets will not, by itself, make the use an act of self-dealing. Any public recognition a substantial contributor may receive that arises from the charitable activities of a private foundation will not in itself result in an act of self-dealing, since generally the benefit is incidental and tenuous.

Similarly, the awarding of a scholarship or fellowship grant by a private foundation to a person other than a disqualified person according to a program consistent with:

1. The requirements of the foundation's exempt status as a charitable, educational, or other similar organization;

2. The requirements for allowance of deductions for charitable contributions made to the foundation; and

3. The requirements of scholarship and fellowship grants awarded on an objective and nondiscriminatory basis under procedures approved by the IRS

will not be an act of self-dealing merely because a disqualified person indirectly receives a benefit from the grant. The awarding of a scholarship or fellowship grant by a private foundation under a program to award scholarship or fellowship grants to the children of employees of a substantial contributor will not be an act of self-dealing if these three requirements are satisfied. [See Reg. § 53.4941(d)-2(f)(2)]

[G] Payment to a Government Official [IRC § 4941(d)(1)(F)]

The agreement by a private foundation to make any payment of money or other property to a "government official" will ordinarily be an act of self-dealing. (The definition of "government official" for this purpose is discussed above under "Disqualified Persons." Certain payments to government officials are not considered acts of self-dealing, as discussed below under § 6-B.04.

§ 6-B.03   INDIRECT SELF-DEALING

An act of self-dealing is generally taxable whether it is accomplished by direct or indirect means. Nevertheless, the Regulations identify several categories of transactions that will not be treated as indirect self-dealing, thereby providing some important safe harbors for planning purposes.

[A]   Certain Business Transactions with Controlled Entities

A transaction between a disqualified person and an organization controlled by a private foundation is not indirect self-dealing if:

1. The transaction arose from a business relationship established before the transaction could be considered an act of self-dealing,

2. The transaction was at least as favorable to the organization controlled by the foundation as an arm's-length transaction with an unrelated person, and

3. Either the organization controlled by the foundation would have suffered severe economic hardship by engaging in a transaction with someone other than a disqualified person, or because of the unique nature of the product or services provided by the organization controlled by the foundation, the disqualified person could not have engaged in a transaction with anyone else or could have done so only by incurring severe economic hardship.

[*See* Reg. § 53.4941(d)-1(b)(1)]

[B]   Government Officials and Grants to Intermediaries

The term "indirect self-dealing" does not include a transaction engaged in with a government official by an intermediary organization that receives a foundation grant and that is not controlled by the grantor foundation if the foundation does not earmark the use of the grant for any named government official and there is no agreement under which the granting foundation may cause the selection of the government official by the intermediary organization. A grant by a foundation is earmarked if the grant is made under an agreement, either oral or written, that the grant will be used by any named individual. A grant by a private foundation will not be an indirect act of self-dealing, even though the foundation had reason to believe that certain government officials would receive benefits from the grant, as long as the intermediary organization exercises control in fact over the selection process and actually makes the selection completely independently of the private foundation. [See Reg. § 53.4941(d)-1(b)(2)]

[C] Transactions During the Administration of an Estate or Revocable Trust

A transaction involving a private foundation's interest or expectancy in property held by an estate (or a revocable trust, including a trust that has become irrevocable upon a grantor's death), regardless of when title to the property vests under local law, is not indirect self-dealing if:

1. The administrator, executor, or trustee has the power to sell the property or reallocate the property to another beneficiary or is required to sell the property under the terms of any option to which the property was subject when acquired by the estate or trust;

2. The transaction is approved by the probate court having jurisdiction over the estate (or by another court having jurisdiction over the estate, trust, or private foundation);

3. The transaction occurs before the estate is considered terminated for federal income tax purposes (or, for a trust, before it is considered a trust that is not tax exempt);

4. The estate (or trust) receives an amount at least equal to the fair market value of the foundation's interest or expectancy in the property, considering any option to which the property was subject when it was acquired; and

5. The transaction results in the foundation's receiving either an interest or expectancy at least as liquid as the one it gave up or an asset related to the active carrying out of its exempt purpose, or the transaction is required under the terms of any option binding on the estate or trust.

[*See* Reg. § 53.4941(d)-1(b)(3)]

[D] Transactions with Certain Organizations

A transaction between a foundation and a corporation, partnership, estate, or trust not controlled by the foundation in which disqualified persons hold no more than 35 percent of the total voting power or profits interest or beneficial interest is not an indirect act of self-dealing solely on the basis of ownership. [*See* Reg. § 53.4941(d)-1(b)(4)]

[E] Certain Transactions Involving Limited Amounts

The term "indirect self-dealing" does not include any transaction between a disqualified person and an organization controlled by a private foundation or between two disqualified persons when the foundation's assets may be affected by the transaction if:

1. The transaction arises in the normal and customary course of retail business engaged in with the general public;

2. In a transaction between a disqualified person and an organization controlled by a private foundation, the transaction is at least as favorable to the organization controlled by the foundation as an arm's-length transaction with an unrelated person; and

3. The total amount involved in all these transactions with any one disqualified person in any one tax year is no more than $5,000.

[See Reg. § 53.4941(d)-1(b)(6)]

For purposes of the foregoing rules, an organization is considered "controlled" by a private foundation if the foundation or one or more of its foundation managers acting only in their capacity as managers may, only by combining their votes or positions of authority, require the organization to engage in a transaction that, if engaged in with the private foundation, would be self-dealing. Similarly, an organization is controlled by a private foundation in the case of such a transaction between the organization and a disqualified person if the disqualified person together with certain related persons who are disqualified persons may, only by combining their votes or positions of authority with that of the foundation, require the organization to engage in such a transaction. [See Reg. § 53.4941(d)-1(b)(5)]

The controlled organization does not have to be a private foundation. It may be any kind of exempt or nonexempt organization, including a school, hospital, operating foundation, or social welfare organization. An organization will be considered controlled by a private foundation or by a private foundation and disqualified persons if the persons are able in fact to control that organization. This control may be present even if their combined voting power is less than 50 percent of the organization's total voting power or if one or more of the individuals have the right to exercise veto power over the actions of the organization relevant to any potential acts of self-dealing. However, a private foundation will not be regarded as having control over an organization simply because it exercises expenditure responsibility.

§ 6-B.04   EXCEPTIONS TO SELF-DEALING

The following transactions between a private foundation and a disqualified person are not considered self-dealing.

[A]   Providing Goods, Services, or Facilities (IRC § 4941(d)(2)(D))

A private foundation that provides goods, services, or facilities to a disqualified person does not thereby commit an act of self-dealing if the goods, services, or facilities are made available to the general public on at least as favorable a basis as they are made available to the disqualified person *and* the goods, services, or facilities are "functionally related" to the exercise or performance by a private foundation of its exempt purpose. Thus, for example, if a foundation operates a museum that is open to the general public, it may sell an admission ticket to a disqualified person without violating the self-dealing rules if the disqualified person paid no less for the ticket than a member of the general public.

The term "general public" includes those persons who reasonably would be expected to use the foundation's goods, services, or facilities. This does not apply, however, unless a substantial number of persons other than disqualified persons actually use the goods, services, or facilities. A private foundation that provides recreational or park facilities to the general public may provide those facilities to a disqualified person if they are provided to that person on a basis no more favorable than that on which they are provided to the general public. Similarly, the sale of a book or magazine to disqualified persons is not an act of self-dealing if publishing the book or magazine is functionally related to a charitable or educational activity of the foundation. The publication must be made available to disqualified persons and the general public at the same price. Moreover, if the terms of the book or magazine sale require, for example, payment within 60 days of delivery and payment is made during the 60-day period, the transaction will not be treated as a loan or extension of credit if these terms are consistent with normal commercial practices.

[B] Payment of Compensation or Reimbursement of Expenses (IRC § 4941(d)(2)(E))

The payment of compensation or reimbursement of expenses by a private foundation to a disqualified person (other than a government official) for personal services that are reasonable and necessary to carry out the exempt purpose of the private foundation is not considered an act of self-dealing if the compensation or reimbursement is not excessive. Personal services for this purpose are narrowly defined, and caution should be exercised in relying on this exception for any category beyond banking functions, investment services, and legal services. The Tax Court has held that real estate management services are not within the personal services exception. [See Madden v. Commissioner, T.C. Memo 1997-395]

Personal services include the services of a broker acting as the foundation's agent, but not the services of a dealer buying from the foundation as a principal and reselling to a third party. Furthermore, if a foundation makes a cash advance to a foundation manager or employee to cover anticipated out-of-pocket expenses, it is not an act of self-dealing if the advance is reasonable in relation to the duties and expense requirements of the foundation manager. An advance ordinarily is considered reasonable if it is not more than $500.

For example, if a foundation makes an advance to a foundation manager to cover anticipated out-of-pocket current expenses for a reasonable period (such as a month) and the manager accounts to the foundation under a periodic reimbursement program for actual expenses incurred, the foundation is not considered to have engaged in an act of self-dealing:

1. When it makes the advance,

2. When it replenishes the fund upon receipt of supporting vouchers from the manager, or

3. When it temporarily adds to the advance to cover unusual expenses expected to be incurred in carrying out a special assignment.

[C] Certain Corporate Transactions (IRC § 4941(d)(2)(F))

A transaction between a private foundation and a corporation that is a disqualified person is not an act of self-dealing if the transaction is engaged in under a liquidation, merger, redemption, recapitalization or other corporate adjustment, organization, or reorganization as long as all the securities of the same class as those held before the transaction by the foundation are subject to the same terms and the terms provide for receipt by the foundation of at least fair market value.

For securities to be considered subject to the same terms, the issuing corporation must, in connection with the transaction, make a bona fide offer on a uniform basis to the foundation and every other security holder. The fact that the foundation receives property, such as debentures, while all other persons holding securities of the same class receive cash for their interests will be evidence that the offer was not made on a uniform basis. If no other persons hold securities of the same class as the private foundation, the consideration received by the holders of other classes of securities, or the interests retained by the holders of other classes, when considered in relation to the consideration received by the foundation, must indicate that the foundation received treatment at least as favorable in relation to its interests as the holders of any other class of securities. In addition, the foundation must receive at least the fair market value of its interests.

> **Note:** Private letter rulings are available on the application of this exception, and the parties would be well advised to consider seeking such a ruling for their own transaction if there is any substantial issue respecting the application of this exception to a particular transaction.

[D] Certain Payments to Government Officials (IRC § 4941(d)(2)(G))

The following categories of payments to government officials are not considered acts of self-dealing:

1. A prize or award that does not have to be included in gross income if the official receiving the prize or award is selected from the general public. For

this purpose, the recipient may keep the prize or award and need not authorize the foundation to transfer the prize or award to a governmental unit or to another charity.

2. A scholarship or fellowship grant that is to be used for study at a recognized educational organization. For this purpose, there is no requirement that the grant recipients be limited to degree candidates, nor must the grant be limited to tuition, fees, and course-required books, supplies, or equipment. It is permissible for a recipient to use grant funds for room, board, travel, research, clerical help, or equipment that is incidental to the purposes of the grant.

3. Any annuity or other payment (forming part of a stock bonus, pension, or profit-sharing plan) from a qualified trust.

4. Any annuity or other payment under an employees' annuity plan.

5. Any contribution or gift (other than money) or services or facilities made available if the total value is not more than $25 during any calendar year.

6. Any payment made under a government employees' training program.

7. Any payment or reimbursement of travel expenses, including meals and lodging, for travel only from one point in the United States to another in connection with charitable purposes, but only if the payment or reimbursement is not more than the actual cost of transportation, plus an amount for all other traveling expenses not greater than 125 percent of the maximum payable for similar travel by U.S. government employees (without regard to any higher rates allowed in designated geographical areas).

8. A payment under any agreement to employ or make a grant to a government official for any period after the termination of government service if the agreement is entered into within 90 days before termination.

9. The cost of a government official's attendance at or participation in a conference sponsored by the foundation in furtherance of its exempt purposes, including:

   a. The official's share of the cost of the conference;

   b. Professional and other non-monetary benefits of an intellectual or psychological nature received by the official from attending or participating in the conference;

   c. Benefits to the official resulting from publication or distribution of the conference record to conference participants; and

   d. Payments, reimbursements, or reasonable advances made to the official for expenses in attending the conference.

[E] No-Rent Leases

The leasing of property by a disqualified person to a private foundation is not an act of self-dealing if the lease is without charge. The lease will be considered without charge even though the foundation agrees to pay for janitorial expenses, utilities, or other maintenance costs it incurs as long as payment is not made directly or indirectly to a disqualified person. [Reg. § 53.4941(d)-2(b)(1)] The leasing of office space by a disqualified person to a private foundation in a building with other tenants who are not disqualified persons is not an act of self-dealing if:

1. The lease is pursuant to a binding contract in effect on October 9, 1969 (or renewals thereof);

2. The lease was not a prohibited transaction under § 503(b) or any corresponding provision of prior law at the time of execution; and

3. The terms of the lease (or any renewal) reflect an arm's-length transaction.

[See IRC § 4941(d)(2)(H)]

§ 6-B.05 "AMOUNT INVOLVED" IN AN ACT OF SELF-DEALING

The excise tax on self-dealing is based on the "amount involved," which is defined in IRC § 4941(e)(2) as the greater of the amount of money and the fair market value of other property given or the amount of money and fair market value of other property received. For payments made for services performed (to persons other than government officials), the amount involved is only the excess compensation paid by the private foundation. When the use of money or other property is involved, the amount involved is the greater of either the amount paid for the use or the fair market value of the use for the period for which the money or other property is used.

For a transaction that would not have been an act of self-dealing had the private foundation received fair market value, the amount involved is the excess of the fair market value of property transferred by the foundation over the amount received by the foundation, but only if the parties have made a good-faith effort to determine fair market value. A good-faith effort to determine fair market value ordinarily will be considered made when:

1. The person making the valuation is not a disqualified person with respect to the foundation, is competent to make the valuation, and is not in a position to receive an economic benefit from the value used; and

2. The valuation is made using a generally accepted method for valuing comparable property, stock, or securities in arm's-length business transactions when valuation is a significant factor.

[See Reg. § 53.4941(e)-1(b)(1)]

For example, if a corporation that is a disqualified person undertakes a recapitalization referred to earlier under the exceptions to the self-dealing rule, but the foundation receives stock worth $95,000 in exchange for stock worth $100,000, the amount involved would be $5,000 if a good-faith effort was made to value the stock.

Note that the value of property involved in an act of self-dealing, and hence the amount involved for the tax computation, is determined differently for purposes of the two different self-dealing taxes.

1. *Initial taxes.* The fair market value of property or the use thereof, as the case may be, for purposes of the initial taxes is the value as of the date the act of self-dealing occurred.

2. *Additional taxes.* The fair market value of property or the use thereof, as the case may be, for purposes of the additional taxes is the highest fair market value during the taxable period.

[*See* IRC § 4941(e)(2); Reg. § 53.4941(e)-1(b)(3)]

§ 6-B.06   CORRECTION

When an act of self-dealing occurs and the initial tax is imposed, the parties must correct the transaction, as discussed earlier. Correction will be accomplished by undoing the transaction that constituted the act of self-dealing, to the extent possible, but in no case placing the foundation in a worse financial position than that in which it would have been had the disqualified person acted under the highest fiduciary standards. IRC § 4941(e)(3). For example, when a disqualified person sells property to a private foundation for cash, correction may be accomplished by recasting the transaction in the form of a gift by returning the cash to the foundation.

Minimum standards of correction in the case of certain specific acts of self-dealing are described below. Similar principles may be applied to other acts of self-dealing. Any action taken to correct an act of self-dealing under these standards will not be a separate act of self-dealing.

[A]   Sales by Foundation

Where a private foundation has sold property to a disqualified person for cash, undoing the transaction includes, but is not limited to, rescinding the sale if possible. However, to avoid placing the foundation in a position worse than that in which it would be if rescission were not required, the amount returned to the disqualified person may not be greater than the lesser of the cash received by the foundation or the fair market value of the property received by the disqualified person. [Reg. § 53.4941(e)-1(c)(2)]

Fair market value is determined either at the time of the act of self-dealing or at the time of rescission, whichever results in the lesser fair market value. In addition, the disqualified person must pay the foundation any net profits realized from the property during the correction period, but only to the extent the income is greater than the income received by the foundation during the correction period from the cash originally paid to the foundation.

If, before the end of the correction period, the disqualified person resells the property in an arm's-length transaction to a bona fide buyer other than the foundation or another disqualified person, rescission is not required. However, the disqualified person must pay the foundation the excess (if any) of the greater of the fair market value of the property on the date of correction or the amount realized in the arm's-length resale over the amount that would have been returned to the disqualified person if rescission had been required. In addition, the disqualified person must pay the foundation any net profits realized as described in the preceding paragraph. [Reg. § 53.4941 (e)-1(c)(2)(ii)]

[B] Sales to Foundation

Where a disqualified person has sold property to a private foundation, undoing the transaction includes, but is not limited to, requiring rescission of the sale if possible. However, to avoid placing the foundation in a worse position than it would be in if rescission were not required, the amount to be received from the disqualified person will be the greatest of:

1. The cash paid to the disqualified person;

2. The fair market value of the property at the time of the original sale; or

3. The fair market value of the property at the time of rescission.

[*See* Reg. § 53.4941(e)-1(c)(3)]

In addition, the disqualified person is required to pay the private foundation any net profit realized after the original sale from the amount received from the sale to the extent the net profit during the correction period is greater than the income received by the foundation from the property during the correction period.

If, before the end of the correction period, the foundation resells the property in an arm's-length transaction to a bona fide buyer who is not a disqualified person, no rescission is required. But the disqualified person must pay the foundation the excess (if any) of the amount that would have been paid to the foundation if the original sale had been rescinded over the amount realized by the foundation upon the resale of the property. In addition, the disqualified person must pay the foundation any net profits realized from the amount received from the original sale, described earlier.

[C] Use of Property by a Disqualified Person

If a disqualified person has used property owned by a private foundation, undoing the transaction includes, but is not limited to, terminating the use of the property. In addition, the disqualified person must pay the foundation the excess (if any) of:

1. The fair market value of the use of the property over the amount paid by the disqualified person for the use until termination; and

2. The amount that would have been paid by the disqualified person for the use of the property on or after the date of termination for the period the disqualified person would have used the property (disregarding further extensions or renewals of the period) were it not for termination, over the fair market value of the use for the period.

[*See* Reg. § 53.4941(e)-1(c)(4)]
In item 1, the fair market value of the use of the property will be the greater of the rate at the time of self-dealing and the rate at the time of correction of the act of self-dealing. In item 2, the fair market value of the use of the property will be the rate at the time of correction. The rate for the use of property other than money will be the fair rental value per period. For use of money, the rate will be the fair interest rate.

[D] Use of Property by a Private Foundation

If a private foundation has used property that is owned by a disqualified person, undoing the transaction includes, but is not limited to, terminating the use of the property. In addition, the disqualified person must pay the foundation the excess (if any) of:

1. The amount paid to the disqualified person for the use until termination over the fair market value of the use of the property; and

2. The fair market value of the use of the property, for the period the foundation would have used the property (disregarding extensions or renewals of the period) had use not been terminated, over the amount that would have been paid to the disqualified person on or after the date of termination for use during that period.

[*See* Reg. § 53.4941(e)-1(c)(5)]
In item 1, the fair market value of the use of the property will be the lesser of the rate (that is, the fair rental value per period for use of property other than money or the fair interest rate for the use of money) at the time of self-dealing and the rate at the time of correction of the act of self-dealing. In item 2, the fair rental value of the use of the property will be the rate at the time of correction.

[E] Excessive Compensation

Excessive compensation paid by a private foundation to a disqualified person for performing personal services may be corrected by repaying to the foundation any excessive amount. Termination of the employment or independent contractor relationship is not required. The excessive amount would normally be that portion of an individual's compensation that exceeds the amount that would constitute reasonable compensation for the services in question. Compensation paid may not exceed what is reasonable under all the circumstances. Reasonable compensation is only such amount as would ordinarily be paid for like services by like enterprises under like circumstances. [Reg. § 53.4941(e)-1(c)(6)]

[F] Correction of Valuation Errors

If, but for an error in the valuation of property, a transaction would not have been an act of self-dealing had the foundation received fair market value, a correction of the transaction means that the foundation is paid an amount equal to the excess of the fair market value of the property transferred over the amount that the foundation received for the property (assuming a good-faith effort to determine fair market value). In addition, the foundation must receive the amount necessary to compensate it for the loss of the use of the money or other property during the period beginning on the date the act of self-dealing occurred and ending on the date the transaction is corrected. [Reg. § 53.4941(e)-1(c)(7)]

§ 6-B.07 NUMBER OF ACTS

If a transaction is determined to be an act of self-dealing, there is generally only one act of self-dealing. If the transaction involves the leasing of property, the lending of money or other extension of credit, other use of money or property, or payment of compensation, the transaction will be treated as an act of self-dealing on the day the transaction occurs, plus an act of self-dealing on the first day of each tax year or part of a year within the taxable period that begins after the tax year in which the transaction occurs. [Reg. § 53.4941(e)-1(e)(1)(i)]

If a transaction involves joint participation by two or more disqualified persons, the transaction will be treated as a separate act of self-dealing for each individual involved. However, for purposes of terminating tax-exempt status and for purposes of determining a foundation manager's liability for penalties for repeated, willful, or flagrant disregard of self-dealing prohibitions, the transaction will be treated as only one act of self-dealing. [IRC § 4941(c)(1); Reg. § 53.4941(c)-1(a)(1)] A disqualified person and one or more members of the individual's family will be treated as one person, regardless of whether a member of the family is a disqualified person. The liability imposed on a disqualified person and one or more members of the individual's family for joint participation in an act of self-dealing is joint and several.

APPENDIX 6-C

TAXES ON FAILURE TO DISTRIBUTE INCOME (IRC § 4942)

Overview. A private foundation is generally required to make *qualifying distributions* in the forms of grants and contributions for charitable purposes in an amount at least equal to five percent of its investment assets. The failure to make distributions in such an amount will subject a foundation to a penalty excise tax. This tax applies in two steps: initial taxes of 15 percent of the undistributed income are assessed unless the failure to distribute was due to reasonable cause and not to willful neglect. Thereafter, if the failure to distribute is not corrected within the specified period, an additional tax of 100 percent of the undistributed income is imposed. [*See* IRC § 4942 and the accompanying Regulations]

§ 6-C.01   **Tax Imposed**
        [A] **In General**
        [B] **Exceptions**
            [1] **Operation Foundations**
            [2] **Incorrect Valuation of Assets**
        [C] **Definitions**
            [1] **Taxable Period**
            [2] **Allowable Distribution Period**
            [3] **Correction Period**
            [4] **Undistributed Income**
            [5] **Distributable Amount**

§ 6-C.02   **Minimum Investment Return**
        [A] **Defined**
        [B] **Assets Not Included**
        [C] **Reasonable Cash Balance**
        [D] **Valuation of Assets**
            [1] **General Rule**
            [2] **Reductions in Value for Blockage or Similar Factors**
            [3] **Unlisted Securities Effectively Controlled by Foundation and Disqualified Persons**
            [4] **Cash**
            [5] **Common Trust Funds**

§ 6-C.01   TAX IMPOSED

[A]   In General

Generally, section 4942 of the Internal Revenue Code imposes an excise tax on any *undistributed income* of a private foundation. An additional excise tax will be imposed on any income remaining undistributed at the end of the *taxable period*. The income of the foundation must be distributed as *qualifying distributions*. Private foundations must make qualifying distributions to the extent of their *minimum investment return* for the year. However, a foundation may *set aside* funds for periods up to 60 months for certain major projects. Excess qualifying distributions may be carried forward for a period of five tax years immediately following the tax year in which the excess was created. Special transitional rules apply to foundations created before May 27, 1969, but these will not be discussed here.

Like the other private foundation penalty excise taxes, the tax on undistributed income is applied in two stages:

1. *Initial tax.* An excise tax of 15 percent is imposed on the undistributed income of a private foundation that has not been distributed before the first day of the second (or any succeeding) tax year following the year earned if the first day falls within the *taxable period*. A short tax year is considered a tax year for this purpose. The initial tax may be abated if the foundation can show that the failure was due to reasonable cause and not to willful neglect and that the failure to distribute was corrected within the *correction period*. [IRC § 4942(a)]

2. *Additional tax.* If the initial tax is imposed and the undistributed income has not been distributed by the end of the taxable period, an additional tax of 100 percent of the amount remaining undistributed will be imposed. The tax will not be assessed or, if assessed, will be abated if the undistributed income is reduced to zero during the correction period. [IRC § 4942(b)]

Payment of the excise tax is required in addition to rather than instead of making the required distributions of undistributed income.

[B]   Exceptions

[1]   Operating Foundations

The tax does not apply to the undistributed income of a private operating foundation [discussed at § 2.06[A] *supra*] or to that of an exempt operating foundation [discussed at § 2.06[B] *supra*].

[2]   Incorrect Valuation of Assets

The tax also does not apply to the undistributed income of a private foundation that failed to distribute only because of an incorrect valuation of assets, provided:

1.   The incorrect valuation was not willful and was due to reasonable cause;

2.   The undistributed income is distributed as qualifying distributions during the *allowable distribution period*;

3.   The foundation notifies the IRS that the income has been distributed to correct its earlier failure to distribute; and

4.   The distribution is treated as a correction of deficient distributions for earlier tax years that would otherwise be subject to this tax.

[IRC § 4942(a)(2); Reg. § 53.4942(a)-1(b)(1)(ii)]

The foundation must be able to show it has made all reasonable efforts in good faith to value its assets according to the applicable rules. If a foundation, after full disclosure of the facts, obtains a good-faith appraisal of an asset's fair market value by a qualified appraiser (whether or not that appraiser is a disqualified person with respect to the foundation) and the foundation relies on that appraisal, then failure to properly value an asset will ordinarily be regarded as not willful and as due to reasonable cause. However, if a foundation does not obtain a good-faith appraisal, the lack of such an appraisal will not by itself imply that the foundation's failure to properly value an asset was willful and not due to reasonable cause. [Reg. § 53.4942(a)-1(b)(2)]

[C]   Definitions

[1]   Taxable Period

The *taxable period* (defined in IRC § 4942(j)(1)) begins on the first day of the tax year and ends on the earlier of either:

1.   The date a notice of deficiency for the *initial tax* is mailed or

2.   The date the *initial tax* is assessed.

[2]   Allowable Distribution Period

The *allowable distribution period* (defined in IRC § 4942(j)(2)) begins on the first day of the first tax year following the tax year in which an incorrect valuation of foundation assets occurred. The period generally ends 90 days after a notice of deficiency for the initial tax is mailed (but is extended by any period during which the deficiency cannot be assessed and by any other period that the

IRS determines is reasonable and necessary to permit a required distribution of undistributed income).

[3] Correction Period

The *correction period* begins with the first day of the tax year in which there was a failure to distribute income and ends 90 days after a notice of deficiency for the additional tax is mailed, and is extended in certain circumstances. [*See* IRC § 4963(e)]

[4] Undistributed Income

Undistributed income means the amount by which the distributable amount for any tax year exceeds the qualifying distributions made out of the distributable amount before the end of the following tax year. [*See* IRC § 4942(c); Reg. § 53.4942(a)-2(a)]

[5] Distributable Amount

The *distributable amount* is equal to the minimum investment return of a private foundation reduced by the sum of any income taxes and the tax on investment income and increased by:

1. Amounts received or accrued as repayments of amounts taken into account as qualifying distributions for any tax year,

2. Amounts received or accrued from the sale or other disposition of property to the extent that the acquisition of the property was considered a qualifying distribution for any tax year, and

3. Any amount set aside for a specific project (*see* § 6-C.03[C] below) to the extent the amount set aside was not necessary for the purposes for which it was set aside.

[*See* IRC § 4942(d); Reg. § 53.4942(a)-2(b)(1)(ii)]

If a private foundation has income from distributions from a charitable remainder trust or charitable lead trust, this income is included in the distributable amount. (Special rules apply to certain pre-1969 trusts.) As a general matter, the income portion of a distribution from such a trust is the greater of:

1. The amount of the distribution that is treated as trust income (under the governing instrument and local law that applies) and

2. The guaranteed annuity, or fixed percentage of the fair market value of the trust property as determined annually, that the private foundation is entitled

to receive for a particular tax year, regardless of when the amount is actually received.

[Reg. § 53.4942(a)-2(b)(2)]

§ 6-C.02   MINIMUM INVESTMENT RETURN

[A]   Defined

The *minimum investment return* for any private foundation is defined in IRC § 4942(e) as five percent of the excess of the combined fair market value of all assets of the foundation, other than those used or held for use for exempt purposes, over the amount of indebtedness incurred to buy these assets.

The combined fair market value of all foundation assets for this purpose includes:

1. The average of the fair market values on a monthly basis of securities for which market quotations are readily available;

2. The average of the foundation's monthly cash balances (minus cash balances excluded as cash held for charitable and related activities); and

3. The fair market value of all other assets (except assets excluded from the computation of minimum investment return or assets used for exempt purposes) for the period of time during the tax year those assets are held by the foundation. [Reg. § 53.4942(a)-2(c)(1)] For the determination of the fair market value of the assets, *see* § 6-C.02[D] below.

[B]   Assets Not Included

Certain assets are not included in determining minimum investment return. These include:

1. Future interests (such as vested or contingent remainder interests) in the principal or income of any real or personal property until all intervening interests in that property have expired or until the future interest has been constructively received by the foundation;

2. *Assets of an estate* until those assets are distributed to the foundation or the estate is considered terminated for federal income tax purposes;

3. *Present interests* in any trusts created and funded by other persons;

4. *Pledges* of money or property to the foundation, whether or not the pledges are legally enforceable; and

5. *Any assets used (or held for use) for exempt purposes.* An asset is considered used (or held for use) for exempt purposes only if it is actually

used by the foundation in carrying on the charitable, educational, or similar function that gives rise to its exempt status or if the foundation owns the asset and establishes to the satisfaction of the IRS that its immediate use in exempt functions is not practical and that definite plans exist to begin the use within a reasonable period of time. Assets held for the production of income or for investment (for example, stocks, bonds, interest-bearing notes, endowment funds, or, generally, leased real estate) are not considered used or held for use for exempt purposes even though the income from those assets is used to carry out an exempt purpose.

[*See* Reg. § 53.4942(a)-2(c)(2)]

Whether an asset is held for the production of income or for investment rather than used or held for use directly by the foundation for exempt purposes is a factual question. For example, an office building used to provide offices for employees engaged in managing endowment funds for the foundation is not considered an amount used for exempt purposes.

Where property is used for both exempt and nonexempt purposes, the property will be considered as being used entirely for exempt purposes if at least 95 percent of its total use is for exempt purposes. But if less than 95 percent of its total use is for exempt purposes, a reasonable allocation must be made between exempt and nonexempt use.

Property acquired by the foundation to be used for an exempt purpose will be considered an asset used for exempt purposes even though all or part of the property is leased for a limited and reasonable time (generally no more than one year) while arrangements are made to convert it to use for exempt purposes. Where the income-producing use continues beyond a reasonable time, the property will not be considered an asset used for exempt purposes. Instead, at the time the income-producing use becomes unreasonable, the property will be considered disposed of to the extent the acquisition was taken into account as a qualifying distribution. If the property is later used by the foundation for exempt purposes, a qualifying distribution in an amount equal to its fair market value at that time will be considered to have been made at the time the exempt use begins. [*See* Reg. § 53.4942(a)-2(c)(3)(i) for these rules]

Assets used for exempt purposes include the following items:

- Administrative assets, such as office equipment and supplies, used by foundation employees and consultants to the extent these asscts are devoted to and used directly in the administration of exempt activities;

- Real estate or the part of a building used by the foundation directly in its exempt activities;

- Physical facilities used in exempt activities, such as paintings or other works of art owned by the foundation on public display, classroom fixtures and equipment, and research facilities and related equipment, which, under the facts and circumstances, serve a useful purpose in the conduct of the exempt activities;

• Any interest in a functionally related business or in a program-related investment;

• The "reasonable cash balances" necessary to cover current administrative expenses and other normal and current disbursements directly connected with the foundation's charitable, educational, or other similar exempt activities; and

• Any property leased by the foundation in carrying out its exempt purpose at no cost, or at a nominal rent, to the lessee or for a program-related purpose, such as the leasing of renovated apartments to low-income tenants at a low rental as part of the lessor/foundation's program for rehabilitating a blighted area of a community.

[Reg. § 53.4942(a)-2(c)(3)(ii)]

[C] Reasonable Cash Balance

The reasonable cash balance that a private foundation needs to have on hand to cover current administrative expenses and other normal and current distributions for exempt purposes generally will be considered to be an amount figured on an annual basis equal to 11/2 percent of the combined fair market value of all foundation assets used in figuring minimum investment return (reduced by any acquisition indebtedness for those assets, but without reduction for the reasonable cash balance).

A foundation may exclude 1½ percent under this rule even if that is more than the average cash balance of the foundation. However, if an additional amount is necessary to pay expenses and make disbursements, that amount does not have to be included in figuring minimum investment return. All remaining cash balances will be included in the computation. If an amount in excess of the 11/2 percent figure is claimed for any year, a statement must be attached to Form 990-PF for that year explaining the reasons for the larger amount. [Reg. § 53.4942(a)-2(c)(3)(iv)]

[D] Valuation of Assets

[1] General Rule

In figuring its minimum investment return, a foundation may use any reasonable method to determine on a monthly basis the fair market value of securities for which market quotations are readily available as long as that method is consistently used. Market quotations are considered readily available if a security is:

1. Listed on the New York or American Stock Exchange or on any city or regional exchange for which quotations appear on a daily basis, including

foreign securities listed on a recognized foreign, national, or regional exchange;

2. Regularly traded in the national or regional over-the-counter market for which published quotations are available; or

3. Locally traded, for which quotations can readily be obtained from established brokerage firms.

For securities held in trust for or on behalf of a foundation by a bank or other financial institution that values those securities periodically using a computer, a foundation may determine the correct value of the securities by use of this computer pricing system if the system is acceptable to the IRS for federal estate tax purposes.

Thus, for example, a foundation that owns a stock that is regularly traded on the New York Stock Exchange may follow a consistent pattern of valuing such stock on the last trading day of each month based on its closing price for that day. Likewise, a foundation may consistently value its unlisted stock as of the 15th day of each month by getting a bona fide quote of the bid and asked prices from an established brokerage firm and by taking the mean of those prices on that day. [Reg. § 53.4942(a)-2(c)(4)]

[2] Reductions in Value for Blockage or Similar Factors

In determining the value of securities, the private foundation may establish that as a result of (1) the size of the block of securities, (2) the fact that the securities are in a closely held corporation, or (3) the fact that the sale of the securities would result in a forced or distress sale, the price at which the securities could be sold outside the usual market may be a more accurate indication of value than market quotations. In such a case, any reduction in value for all of these reasons together may not be more than 10 percent of the fair market value of the securities to which the discount applies. [IRC § 4942(e)(2)(B)(iii); Reg. § 53.4942(a)-2(c)(4)(i)(c)]

[3] Unlisted Securities Effectively Controlled by Foundation and Disqualified Persons

If the foundation owns unlisted voting securities and has (together with disqualified persons or another private foundation) effective control of the issuer, then, to the extent that the issuer's assets consist of shares of listed securities issues, the assets shall be valued monthly on the basis of market quotations. [Reg. § 53.4942(a)-2(c)(4)(iv)]

[4] Cash

For purposes of the minimum investment return, a foundation figures its cash balances on a monthly basis by averaging the amount of cash on hand on the first and last days of each month. [Reg. § 53.4942(a)-2(c)(4)(ii)]

[5] Common Trust Funds

If a private foundation owns a participating interest in a common trust fund established and administered under a plan providing for the periodic valuation of participating interests during the fund's tax year and the reporting of these valuations to participants, the valuation of the foundation's interest in the common trust fund based on the average of the valuations reported to the foundation during its tax year will ordinarily be an acceptable method of valuation for purposes of the minimum investment return. [Reg. § 53.4942(a)-2(c)(3)(iii)]

[6] Other Assets

The fair market value of assets other than those described earlier is determined annually except as described later. The valuation may be made by private foundation employees or by any other person, whether or not that person is a disqualified person. Such a valuation, if accepted by the IRS, is valid only for the tax year for which it is made. A new valuation is required for the following tax year, except that the value of an interest in real estate may be determined on a five-year basis by a written, certified, independent appraisal by a qualified person who is neither a disqualified person nor an employee of the private foundation. [Reg. § 53.4942(a)-2(c)(4)(iv)(a), (b)]

The appraisal must contain a statement to the effect that, in the appraiser's opinion, the appraised assets were valued in accordance with valuation principles regularly employed in making appraisals of such property using all reasonable valuation methods. The foundation must keep a copy of the independent appraisal for its records. If a valuation is reasonable, the foundation may use it for the tax year for which the valuation is made and for each of the four following tax years.

Any valuation of real property by a certified, independent appraisal may be replaced during the five-year period by a later five-year valuation by a certified, independent appraisal or by an annual valuation. The most recent valuation will be used in figuring the foundation's minimum investment return. The valuation must be made no later than the last day of the first tax year for which the new valuation applies. A valuation, if properly made according to the rules discussed here, will not be disturbed by the IRS during the five-year period for which it applies, even if the actual fair market value of the property changes during that period. [*See* Reg. § 53.4942(a)-2(c)(4)(iv)(b)]

Commonly accepted valuation methods must be used in making the appraisal. A valuation based on acceptable methods of valuing property for federal estate tax purposes is acceptable. An appraisal is a determination of fair market value and should not be construed in a technical sense to be peculiar to particular property or interests therein as, for example, mineral interests in real property. [Reg. § 53.4942(a)-2(c)(4)(iv)(c)]

[7] Valuation Date

An asset that is required to be valued annually may be valued as of any day in the private foundation's tax year if the foundation follows a consistent practice of valuing the asset as of that date in all tax years. A valuation of real estate determined on a five-year basis by a certified, independent appraisal may be made as of any day in the first tax year of the private foundation to which the valuation is to be applied. [Reg. § 53.4942(a)-2(c)(4)(vi)]

[8] Assets Held for Less than a Full Tax Year

If an asset is held for less than one tax year, the value of that asset is found by multiplying the fair market value of the asset by a fraction. The numerator of the fraction is the number of days in the tax year that the foundation held the asset, and the denominator is the total number of days in the tax year. [Reg. § 53.4942(a)-2(c)(4)(vii)]

§ 6-C.03 QUALIFYING DISTRIBUTIONS

[A] In General

A *qualifying distribution* is any of the following:

1. Any amount (including program-related investments and reasonable and necessary grant administrative expenses, subject to the limit discussed later) paid to accomplish religious, charitable, scientific, literary, or other public purposes. Qualifying distributions *do not include* contributions to organizations controlled by the contributing foundation or by one or more disqualified persons or to other private foundations (with certain exceptions discussed later).

2. Any amount paid to buy an asset used (or held for use) directly to carry out a charitable or other public purpose. Depreciation on these assets, however, is not considered a qualifying distribution.

3. Any qualifying amount set aside (as described below).

[*See generally* IRC § 4942(g)(1); Reg. § 53.4942(a)-3(a)(2)]

In general, a distribution to a public charity to accomplish any religious, charitable, scientific, literary, educational, or other permitted public purpose is a qualifying distribution. *See* § 6-F.03[E] in Appendix 6-F for rules on when a private foundation may rely on the public charity status of a grantee. The amount of a qualifying distribution of property is the fair market value of the property on the date the distribution is made. The amount of a qualifying distribution is determined only under the cash receipts and disbursements method.

A private foundation that bought an asset and claimed a qualifying distribution under item 2 above will be allowed a second qualifying distribution for the same asset if the asset is later given to a publicly supported charitable organization that is not controlled by the foundation and it is donated for a purpose described in item 1. The amount of the second qualifying distribution will be the difference between the fair market value of the asset on the date of the contribution and the amount of the first qualifying distribution. Rev. Rul. 79-375, 1979-2 C.B. 389.

[B] Special Rules and Definitions

[1] Borrowed Funds

If a private foundation borrows money during a tax year to make a charitable expenditure, then a qualifying distribution is considered made only at the time the borrowed funds are actually distributed for a charitable purpose. [Reg. § 53.4942 (a)-3(a)(4)(i)]

[2] Control

An organization is controlled by a foundation or by one or more disqualified persons if any of these persons may, by combining their votes or positions of authority, require the organization to make an expenditure or prevent the organization from making an expenditure, regardless of the method by which control is exercised or exercisable. In general, it is the donee, not the distribution, that must be controlled by the distributing private foundation to disqualify an otherwise qualifying distribution. If a foundation imposes budgetary procedures (e.g., requires reports on granted funds) on an organization to which it provides support, this will not by itself constitute control of the donee. The controlled organization may be a private foundation, a public charity, or any other kind of exempt or nonexempt organization. [Reg. § 53.4942(a)-3(a)(3)]

[3] Changes in Asset Use

If an asset not used or held for use for charitable, educational, or similar exempt purposes is later converted to such use, the foundation may treat the conversion as a qualifying distribution in an amount equal to the fair market value of the converted asset on the date of conversion. [Reg. § 53.4942(a)-3(a)(5)]

[4] Payment of Tax

Payment of any Chapter 42 excise tax imposed on the foundation is not considered a qualifying distribution. [Reg. § 53.4942(a)-3(a)(7)]

[C] Set-Asides

An amount that is set aside for a specific project may be treated as a qualifying distribution in the year set aside (rather than the year actually paid) if at the time of the set-aside the foundation establishes to the satisfaction of the IRS that:

1. The amount will actually be paid for the specific project within 60 months from the date of the first set-aside; *and*

2. Either of the following is met:

    a. The set-aside satisfies the *suitability test* (i.e., the project is one that can be better accomplished by a set-aside than by immediate payment); *or*

    b. The foundation satisfies the *cash distribution test.*

[IRC § 4942(g)(2)(B)(i), (ii)]

[1] Suitability Test

To satisfy the suitability test, the foundation must show that the specific project for which the amount is set aside is one that can be better accomplished by the set-aside than by the immediate payment of funds. For example, this would include situations where relatively long-term grants or expenditures must be made to assure the continuity of particular charitable projects or program-related investments or where grants are made as part of a matching-grant program. An example of a specific project is a plan to build an art museum even though the exact location and architectural plans have not been finalized. For good cause shown, the IRS may extend the period for paying the amount set aside. Note that a set-aside must be approved by the IRS, as explained later, to qualify under the suitability test; thus, if the foundation wishes to avoid the cost and inconvenience of requesting and obtaining IRS approval, it may choose the complicated, but more objective, cash distribution test (described below) instead. [Reg. § 53.4942(a)-3(b)(2)]

[2] Cash Distribution Test

The foundation satisfies the cash distribution test if:

1. The specific project for which the amount is set aside will not be completed before the end of the tax year in which the set-aside is made;

2. The foundation actually distributes for exempt purposes, in cash or its equivalent, the *start-up period minimum amount* during the foundation's start-up period; and

3. The foundation actually distributes the *full-payment period minimum amount* in each tax year of the foundation's full-payment period.

[Reg. § 53.4942(a)-3(b)(3)]

[3] Start-Up Period Minimum Amount

Generally, the start-up period consists of the four tax years following the tax year in which the foundation was created (or otherwise became a private foundation). For this purpose, a foundation is considered created in the tax year in which its distributable amount first exceeds $500. The start-up period minimum amount, the amount that a private foundation must actually distribute during its start-up period, is not less than the sum of:

1. 20 percent of its distributable amount (as defined earlier) for the first tax year of the start-up period;

2. 40 percent of its distributable amount for the second tax year of the start-up period;

3. 60 percent of its distributable amount for the third tax year of the start-up period; and

4. 80 percent of its distributable amount for the fourth tax year of the start-up period.

The *sum* of these amounts must be distributed before the end of the start-up period. There is no requirement that any part be distributed in any particular tax year of the start-up period. In general, only a distribution actually made during the start-up period is taken into account in determining whether the foundation has distributed the start-up period minimum amount. However, a distribution actually made during the tax year in which the foundation was created (the year immediately preceding the foundation's start-up period) may be treated as made during the start-up period. Also, a distribution actually made within 51/2 months after the end of the start-up period will be treated as made during the start-up period if (a) the foundation was unable to determine its distributable amount for the fourth tax year of the start-up period until after the end of the period and (b) the foundation actually made distributions before the end of the start-up period based on a reasonable estimate of its distributable amount for that fourth tax year. [Reg. § 53.4942 (a)-3(b)(4)]

[4] Full-Payment Period Minimum Amount

The foundation's full-payment period includes each tax year that begins after the end of the start-up period. The full-payment period minimum amount, the amount that the foundation must actually distribute in cash or its equivalent in each tax year of the full-payment period, must not be less than 100 percent of its distributable amount, described earlier, for that year, without regard to any carryover of excess qualifying distributions, discussed below. However, if in a given year the foundation distributes more than the full-payment period minimum amount for that year, the excess reduces the full-payment period minimum amount for the five tax years immediately following the tax year in which the excess distribution is made. The excess is applied to reduce the full-payment period minimum amount in each successive tax year of the five-year period, in order, until it is completely used up. [Reg. § 53.4942(a)-3(b)(5)]

[5] Failure to Distribute Minimum Amounts

If the foundation fails to actually distribute the start-up period minimum amount during the start-up period or, generally, if it fails to distribute the full-payment period minimum amount during a tax year of the full-payment period, then any set-aside made by the foundation during the appropriate period will not be treated as a qualifying distribution unless it was approved by the IRS under the suitability test. Also, any set-aside made after the year of such a failure to distribute a minimum amount will be treated as a qualifying distribution only if the IRS approves it under the suitability test. However, if the foundation's failure to distribute the full-payment period minimum amount during a tax year of the full-payment period is not willful and is due to reasonable cause, the foundation may correct the failure. To do so, it must distribute within the correction period (discussed earlier) cash or its equivalent in an amount not less than the difference between the full-payment period minimum amount for the tax year and the amount actually distributed during that year. The additional distribution is treated as though it had been made in the year in which it originally should have been made for purposes of meeting the cash distribution test. If a foundation fails to distribute the full-payment period minimum amount during the approprate tax year because the amount can be determined only after the end of that tax year, no "willful failure to distribute" will occur if the foundation makes an additional distribution within 51/2 months after the end of the tax year. [Reg. § 53.4942(a)-3(b)(6)]

[6] Contingent Set-Aside

If a private foundation is involved in litigation and may not distribute assets or income because of a court order, it may seek and obtain a set-aside for the purpose of making a qualifying distribution. The amount that may be set aside is equal to the part of the foundation's distributable amount that is attributable to the assets or income held under the court order that would otherwise have been distributed. If the litigation lasts more than one tax year, the foundation may seek additional contingent set-asides. The amount must actually be distributed by the last day of the tax year following the tax year in which the proceedings end. Amounts the foundation does not distribute by the end of that year will be considered gross income to the foundation for the following tax year. [Reg. § 53.4942(a)-3(b)(9)]

[7]   Seeking Internal Revenue Service Approval

Approval of a set-aside must be obtained from the IRS for the set-aside to qualify under the suitability test described above. No advance approval is required for qualification under the cash distribution test. A foundation must apply for IRS approval by the end of the tax year in which the amount is to be set aside. If the foundation fails to seek approval before that date, an otherwise proper set-aside will not be treated as a qualifying distribution. To obtain approval for a set-aside under the suitability test, the foundation must write to the Internal Revenue Service, 1111 Constitution Avenue, NW, Washington, DC 20224, Attention: EPEO, and include the following information:

1.   A statement describing the nature and purposes of the specific project and the amount of the set-aside for which approval is requested;

2.   A statement describing the amounts and approximate dates of any planned additions to the set-aside after its initial establishment;

3.   A statement of the reasons why the project can be better accomplished by the set-aside than by immediate payment;

4.   A detailed description of the project, including the estimated costs, sources of any future funds expected to be used for completion of the project, and location or locations (general or specific) of any physical facilities to be acquired or constructed as part of the project; and

5.   A statement by an appropriate foundation manager that the amounts set aside will actually be paid for the specific project within a specified period of time ending not more than 60 months after the date of the first set-aside.

[Reg. § 53.4942(a)-3(b)(7)]

[8]   Statement Required for Cash Distribution Test

Although IRS approval is not required for a set-aside qualifying under the cash distribution test, the foundation must attach to its annual return for any tax year in which amounts are set aside the following:

1. A statement describing the nature and purposes of the specific project for which amounts are set aside;

2. A statement that the amounts set aside will actually be paid for the specific project within a specified period that ends no more than 60 months after the date of the set-aside;

3. A statement that the project will not be completed before the end of the tax year in which the set-aside is made;

4. A statement showing the distributable amounts for any past tax years in the foundation's start-up and full-payment periods; and

5. A statement showing the total amount of actual payments in cash or its equivalent for exempt purposes during each tax year in the foundation's start-up and full-payment periods (including a description of any payments that are treated, according to the rules discussed earlier, as distributed during a prior tax year and of the surrounding circumstances).

The foundation must also attach to its annual return for each of the five tax years following the tax year in which the amount is set aside (and for each tax year in any extended period for paying the amount set aside) the statements described in items 4 and 5 above. [Reg. § 53.4942(a)-3(b)(7)(ii)]

[9]   Evidence of Set-Aside

A set-aside that either is approved by the IRS or meets the cash distribution test should be shown by entering a dollar amount on the books of the foundation as a pledge or obligation to be paid at a future date or dates. Any amount set aside will be taken into account in figuring the foundation's minimum investment return, and any income from the set-aside should be taken into account in figuring the adjusted net income of private operating foundations. The amount set aside need not reflect an accumulation of income, but may be a bookkeeping entry that will require funding out of corpus by the end of the set-aside period. [Reg. § 53.4942(a)-3(b)(8)]

[D] Certain Contributions to Exempt Organizations

[1] Requirements

A qualifying distribution includes a contribution to another private foundation or to another exempt organization that is controlled by the contributing foundation or by its disqualified persons if the following tests are met:

1. By the end of the following tax year, the donee organization makes a distribution equal to the full amount of the contribution, and that distribution is a qualifying distribution that is treated as being made out of corpus (or would be treated as such if the donee organization were a private foundation); and

2. The granting foundation obtains adequate records or enough other evidence from the donee organization showing that the donee organization has made a qualifying distribution. This must include the names and addresses of the recipients, the amount received by each, and evidence that the distribution is treated as being made out of corpus (or would be so treated if the donee organization were a private nonoperating foundation).

Both requirements must be met if the contribution is to be treated as a qualifying distribution. To meet the distribution requirements, the donee organization must, by the close of the first tax year after the tax year in which the contribution is received, distribute an amount equal in value to the contribution, and it must have no remaining undistributed income for the year in which the contribution was received. [Reg. § 53.4942(a)-3(c)]

[2] Characterization of Qualifying Distributions (Corpus Versus Income)

Qualifying distributions made during the tax year are characterized (i.e., as to whether made out of the prior or current year's undistributed income or the corpus) as of the close of the tax year in question except when the donee organization chooses to treat all or part of the distribution as made out of a distribution from corpus made in a designated prior tax year (*see* § 6-D.03[E] below). Once it is determined that a qualifying distribution is from corpus, that distribution will first be charged to distributions that are required to be redistributed as described earlier. [Reg. § 53.4942(a)-3(c)(2)(ii)]

To satisfy distribution requirements, a donee organization may choose to treat as a qualifying distribution from corpus for the current year any amount distributed in a prior tax year that was treated as a distribution out of corpus if:

1. That amount has not been used for any other purpose (such as a carryover of excess qualifying distributions or a prior year redistribution);

2. The corpus distribution occurred within the preceding five years; and

3. The amount distributed is not later used for another purpose.

The choice must be made by attaching a statement to the Form 990-PF filed for the tax year for which the choice is to apply. This statement must contain a declaration by the appropriate foundation manager that the foundation is making a choice under these provisions and must specify that the distribution is to be treated as having been made out of a distribution from corpus in a designated prior tax year or years. [Reg. § 53.4942(a)-3(c)(2)(iv)]

> **Example:** In 2001, the Miller Foundation, a private foundation, made a contribution out of 2000 income to the James Foundation, a private non-operating foundation. The contribution was the only one received by the James Foundation in 2001. In 2002, the James Foundation made a qualifying distribution to an art museum maintained by an operating foundation in an amount equal to the contribution received from the Miller Foundation. The James Foundation also distributed all of its undistributed 2001 and 2002 income for other charitable, educational, religious, and similar exempt purposes. The distribution to the art museum is treated as made out of corpus. The Miller Foundation's contribution to the James Foundation is a qualifying distribution out of the Miller Foundation's 2000 income if the Miller Foundation obtains adequate records or enough other evidence from the James Foundation showing the nature and amount of the distribution, the recipient's identity, and the fact that the distribution is treated as made out of corpus. If the James Foundation's qualifying distributions during 2002 had been equal only to the contribution received from the Miller Foundation and its 2002 undistributed income, the James Foundation could have chosen to treat the amount distributed in excess of its 2001 undistributed income as a qualifying distribution made out of corpus (see "Special Election" below) and thus satisfy the qualifying distribution requirements. [Reg. § 53.4942(a)-3(c)(3), example 1]

[3] Earmarking

A contribution by a private foundation to a recipient organization that the recipient then uses to make payments to a secondary recipient is not a contribution by the private foundation to the secondary recipient if the foundation does not earmark the use of the contribution for any named secondary recipient and does not keep the power to control the selection of the secondary recipient by the organization to which the foundation has contributed. [Reg. § 53.4942(a)-3(c)(4)]

[E] Treatment of Qualifying Distributions

[1] Order of Distribution

Any qualifying distribution made during the tax year will be treated as being made:

1. First, out of undistributed income of the immediately preceding tax year (if the private foundation was subject to the initial excise tax for the prior tax year) to the extent thereof;

2. Second, out of undistributed income for the current tax year to the extent thereof; and

3. Finally, out of corpus.

Distributions are taken into account in the order of time in which made. [IRC § 4942(h)(1); Reg. § 53.4942(a)-3(d)(1)]

[2] Special Election

If any qualifying distribution is not treated as being made out of undistributed income of the immediately preceding tax year, the foundation may elect to treat any part of the distribution as made out of the undistributed income of a designated prior tax year or out of corpus. This choice is made by filing a statement with the IRS during the tax year in which the qualifying distribution is made or by attaching a statement to the foundation's annual return for the tax year in which it made the qualifying distribution. The statement must contain a declaration by an appropriate foundation manager that the foundation is making this election under Treasury Regulation § 53.4942(a)-3(d)(2) and must specify whether the distribution is made out of undistributed income for a designated prior tax year (or years) or is made out of corpus. [Reg. § 53.4942(a)-3(d)(2)]

> **Example:** The Oak Foundation, a private foundation, has undistributed income of $300 for 2000 and $200 for 2001. On January 14, 2002, the Oak Foundation made its first qualifying distribution in 2002 when it set aside $700 for hospital construction. On February 22, 2002, a notice of deficiency for the initial and additional excise taxes on failure to distribute income with regard to the 2000 undistributed income was mailed to the Oak Foundation. The Oak Foundation notified the IRS in writing on March 20, 2002, that it was making a choice to apply the January 14, 2002, distribution (to the extent that it exceeded 2001 undistributed income) against the 2000 undistributed income. The Oak Foundation is liable for an initial excise tax of $45 (15 percent of $300). Because the Oak Foundation made the choice described, the $300 of undistributed income for 2000

is treated as distributed during the correction period, and no additional excise tax is imposed. Under these circumstances, the $700 distribution is treated as made first out of the undistributed income of 2001 ($200) and then out of the remaining undistributed income of 2000 ($300). The $200 remaining may be applied against the distributable amount for 2002 or may be treated as a distribution out of corpus.

[F] Carryover of Excess Qualifying Distributions

For any tax year during which the organization is a private nonoperating foundation, any excess qualifying distributions (described later) may be used to reduce distributable amounts in future tax years in the *adjustment period*.

The distributable amount for a tax year in an adjustment period will be reduced by the lesser of:

1. The excess of qualifying distributions made in prior tax years to which the adjustment period applies; and

2. The remaining undistributed income at the close of the tax year after applying any qualifying distributions made in that year to the distributable amount for the year.

If a foundation distributes more than the minimum amount required for a given year, it is allowed to carry over its excess qualifying distributions for purposes of future years' requirements. In general, an excess qualifying distribution is the amount by which the total qualifying distributions for a given tax year exceed the foundation's distributable amount for that tax year. An excess qualifying distribution for any one tax year may not be carried over for more than five subsequent tax years. [Reg. § 53.4942(a)-3(e)]

TAXES ON EXCESS BUSINESS HOLDINGS (IRC § 4943)

Overview. A private foundation is limited in its ability to hold an interest in a *business enterprise*. Generally, a foundation and its disqualified persons as a group cannot own more than a 20 percent interest (increased to 35 percent if effective control is outside that group). This tax applies in two steps. There is an initial tax of five percent of the excess business holdings (which may be abated if the excess holdings were due to reasonable cause and not to willful neglect and if they are disposed of within the *correction period*). Thereafter, if the excess holdings are not disposed of by the end of the *taxable period*, an additional tax of 200 percent of the excess holdings is imposed. [*See* IRC § 4943 and the accompanying Regulations]

§ 6-D.01   TAX IMPOSED

Generally, under section 4943 of the Internal Revenue Code, the combined holdings of a private foundation and all of its disqualified persons are limited to 20 percent of the voting stock in a *business enterprise* (defined below) that is a corporation. The 20 percent limitation also applies to holdings in business enterprises that are partnerships, joint ventures, or other unincorporated enterprises. For a partnership or joint venture, profits interest is substituted for voting stock, and, for any other unincorporated enterprise, beneficial interest is substituted for voting stock. A private foundation that has *excess business holdings* (defined below) in a business enterprise may become liable for an excise tax based on the amount of the excess holdings. There are two phases to the tax on excess business holdings:

1. *Initial tax.* An initial excise tax of five percent of the value of the excess holdings is imposed on the foundation. This tax is imposed on the last day of each tax year that ends during the taxable period (described later). The amount of the excess holdings is determined as of the day during the tax year when the foundation's excess holdings in the business were the greatest. The initial tax may be abated if the foundation can show that the excess holdings were due to reasonable cause and not to willful neglect and that the excess holdings were disposed of within the correction period (described later). [IRC § 4943(a)]

2. *Additional tax.* After the initial tax has been imposed, an excise tax of 200 percent of the excess holdings is imposed on the foundation if it has not disposed of the remaining excess business holdings by the end of the taxable period. The additional tax will not be assessed or, if assessed, will be abated if the excess business holdings are reduced to zero during the correction period (described later). [IRC § 4943(b)]

§ 6-D.02   BUSINESS ENTERPRISE

[A]   Defined

The key concept in this tax is the definition of the term "business enterprise." In general, this includes the active conduct of a trade or business, including any activity that is regularly carried on for the production of income from the sale of goods or the performance of services and that constitutes an unrelated trade or business under section 513 of the Code. The term does *not* include (1) a *functionally related business*, (2) a trade or business that obtains at least 95 percent of its gross income from passive sources, or (3) program-related investments as defined in Appendix 6-E.

[B] Functionally Related Business

A *functionally related business* is:

1. A trade or business the conduct of which is substantially related (aside from the mere provision of funds for the exempt purpose) to the exercise or performance by the private foundation of its charitable, educational, or other purpose or function constituting the basis for its exemption;

2. A trade or business in which substantially all the work is performed for the foundation without compensation;

3. A business carried on by the foundation primarily for the convenience of its members, students, patients, officers, or employees (such as a cafeteria operated by a museum for the convenience of its members, employees, and visitors);

4. A business that consists of the selling of merchandise, substantially all of which has been received by the foundation as gifts or contributions; or

5. An activity carried on within a larger combination of similar activities or within a larger complex of other endeavors that is related to the exempt purpose of the foundation (other than the need to simply provide funds for these purposes).

[*See generally* IRC § 4943(d)(1); Reg. § 53.4943-10]

[C] Gross Income From Passive Sources

Gross income from passive sources is defined for this purpose in IRC § 4943(d)(3) as including the items excluded from unrelated business income by IRC § 512(b)(1), (2), (3), and (5), plus income from the sale of goods. Thus, gross income from passive sources consists of the following categories:

1. Dividends, interest, and annuities;

2. Royalties (including overriding royalties), whether measured by production or by gross or taxable income from the property;

3. Rents from real property and from personal property leased with real property if the rents from the personal property are an incidental amount of the total rents under the lease (determined at the time the personal property is placed in service). Rents are not considered gross income from passive sources if more than 50 percent of the total rent under the lease is for personal property or if the determination of the amount of rent depends in whole or in part on the income or profits received from the leased property (unless the amount is based on fixed percentages of gross receipts or sales);

4. Gains from sales, exchanges, or other dispositions of property other than —

   a. Stock in trade or property held primarily for sale to customers in the ordinary course of business; or

   b. Gains on the lapse or termination of options written by the organization in connection with its investment activities to buy or sell securities (gains from cutting timber that upon election may be considered a sale or exchange are not considered gross income from passive sources); and

5. Income from the sale of goods if the seller does not manufacture, produce, physically receive or deliver, negotiate sales of, or keep inventories in the goods.

§ 6-D.03   EXCESS BUSINESS HOLDINGS

[A] Defined

The excess business holdings of a foundation are the amount of stock or other interest in a business enterprise that exceeds the permitted holdings. A private foundation is generally permitted to hold up to 20 percent of the voting stock of a corporation, reduced by the percentage of voting stock actually or constructively owned by disqualified persons. There are two exceptions to this rule.

First, if one or more third persons (not disqualified persons) have effective control of a corporation, the private foundation and all disqualified persons together may own up to 35 percent of the corporation's voting stock. *Effective control* means the power, whether direct or indirect, and whether or not actually exercised, to direct or cause the direction of the management and policies of a business enterprise. It is the actual control that is decisive, and not its form or the means by which it is exercisable.

Second, a private foundation is not treated as having excess business holdings in any corporation in which it (together with certain other related private foundations) owns not more than two percent of the voting stock and not more than two percent of the value of all outstanding shares of all classes of stock.

Nonvoting stock (or capital interest for holdings in a partnership or joint venture) is a permitted holding of a foundation if all disqualified persons together hold no more than 20 percent (or 35 percent, as described earlier) of the voting stock of the corporation. All equity interests that are not voting stock shall be classified as nonvoting stock. [*See* IRC § 4943(c)(1), (2)]

[B] Sole Proprietorships

A private foundation is not permitted any holdings in sole proprietorships that are business enterprises unless they were held before May 26, 1969, or acquired by gift or bequest thereafter. [IRC § 4943(c)(3)(B)]

[C]   Attribution of Business Holdings

In determining the holdings in a business enterprise of either a private foundation or a disqualified person, any stock or other interest owned directly or indirectly by or for a corporation, partnership, estate, or trust is considered owned proportionately by or for its shareholders, partners, or beneficiaries. (This rule does not apply to holdings of a charitable remainder trust or charitable lead trust). [IRC § 4943(d)(1); Reg. § 53.4943-8]

> **Example:**   Tim Jones, a foundation manager of the X Foundation, owns 50 percent of the stock of Y Corporation. (Y Corporation is not actively engaged in a trade or business.) Z Corporation is an 80 percent-owned subsidiary of Y Corporation. Therefore, 40 percent of the Z Corporation stock is considered held by a disqualified person to X Foundation. Any holding of more than 2 percent of the voting stock or 2 percent of the value of Z Corporation stock will result in all Z Corporation stock held by the foundation being treated as an excess business holding.

In making its computations, the foundation must determine its proportionate interest and those of all disqualified persons in each class of stock in relation to the proportion that the voting interest of each class has to all votes in the corporation. For example, if the foundation owns 50 percent of the coutstanding shares of a class of stock that has 60 percent of the voting rights in a corporation, the foundation's holdings in the voting stock are 30 percent.

[D]   Dispositions of Certain Excess Holdings Within 90 Days

Where a private foundation acquires excess business holdings (other than by purchase), it will not be subject to the taxes on excess business holdings if it disposes of the excess business holdings within 90 days from the date on which it knows, or has reason to know, of the event that caused it to have the excess holdings. This 90-day period will be extended to include the period during which a foundation is prevented by federal or state securities laws from disposing of the excess business holdings. This 90-day rule applies, for example, when a disqualified person acquires additional holdings in a corporation in which it also owns voting stock. The amount of holdings the foundation must dispose of is not affected by disposals by disqualified persons during the 90-day period. [Reg. § 53.4943-2(a)(1)(ii) to (v)]

[E]   Taxable Period

The taxable period begins on the first day that the foundation has excess business holdings and ends on the earlier of either:

1.   The date a notice of deficiency for the initial tax is mailed or

2.   The date the initial tax is assessed.

[IRC § 4943(d)(2)]

Example: The Yoohoo Foundation files tax returns on a calendar year basis. It acquires excess business holdings on July 7, 2001, and does not dispose of them until after the IRS mails a notice of deficiency for the initial and additional taxes on December 10, 2002. For Yoohoo's excess business holdings, the taxable period begins on July 7, 2001, and ends on December 10, 2002. Because the 2001 tax year of the foundation ended in the taxable period, the foundation is liable for a tax of five percent of the largest amount of excess holdings it had at any time during that year.

[F] Correction Period

The correction period begins on the first day that the foundation has excess business holdings and ends 90 days after a notice of deficiency for the additional tax is mailed.

This period is extended by any period during which a deficiency cannot be assessed or Tax Court proceedings are pending. In addition, the correction period may be extended by any other period the IRS determines is reasonable and necessary. [IRC § 4963(e)]

[G] Effect of Gifts or Bequests of Business Holdings

[1] In General

If there is a change in a foundation's business holdings other than by purchase by the foundation or by disqualified persons, such as through gift or bequest, and the additional holdings result in the foundation having excess business holdings, the foundation in effect has five years to reduce these holdings or those of its disqualified persons to permissible levels. The excess business holdings (or the increase in excess business holdings) resulting from the gift or bequest are treated as being held by a disqualified person rather than by the foundation itself during the five-year period beginning on the date the foundation obtains the holdings. [IRC § 4943(c)(6)]

[2] Additional Time to Dispose of Large Gifts or Bequests

The IRS may grant the foundation an additional five-year extension (beyond the initial five years) to reduce excess business holdings to permissible levels if these holdings result from an unusually large gift or bequest of diverse business holdings or holdings with complex corporate structures. To receive this extension:

1. The foundation must establish that it made diligent efforts to dispose of the holdings within the initial five-year period and could not do so (except at a price substantially below fair market value) because of the size and complexity or diversity of the holdings;

2. The foundation must submit to the IRS before the end of the initial five-year period a plan for disposing of all the excess business holdings involved in the extension; and

3. The IRS must determine that the foundation's plan for disposal can reasonably be expected to be carried out before the end of the additional five-year period.

[IRC § 4943(c)(7); Reg. § 53.4943-6]

The foundation must also submit the plan mentioned in item 2 above to the state attorney general or other appropriate official having administrative or supervisory authority or responsibility for the foundation's disposition of the excess business holdings involved. The foundation must then send to the IRS any response it receives from the attorney general (or other official) regarding its plan. Requests for extension of the period for disposition as well as the copy of any response received from state officials should be addressed to the Assistant Commissioner (Employee Plans and Exempt Organizations), Internal Revenue Service, 1111 Constitution Avenue, NW, Washington, DC 20224.

[H] Transition Rules for Business Holdings Existing on May 26, 1969

The excess business holdings rules have a general effective date of May 26, 1969. When these rules were enacted as part of the Tax Reform Act of 1969, transitional rules were provided to prevent certain holdings of a foundation as of that date that exceeded the 20 percent (or 35 percent) limit permitted under the general rules of section 4943(c)(2) from being subject to the initial tax. In effect, foundations were given time, in three phases, to dispose of their excess business holdings. A compete review of these very complex rules is now of interest primarily for historical purposes and is beyond the scope of this discussion. [For details, see IRC § 4943(c)(4) and Reg. § 53.4943-4]

TAXES ON JEOPARDIZING INVESTMENTS (IRC § 4944)

Overview. A private foundation may not make or retain investments that threaten to jeopardize its ability to carry out its charitable purpose. A failure to comply with this restriction will subject the foundation to a penalty excise tax. This tax applies in two steps: an initial tax of five percent of the amount involved in the jeopardy investment is assessed (unless the failure to distribute was due to reasonable cause and not to willful neglect), plus another five percent on the foundation manager who participated in the investment knowingly, willfully, and without reasonable cause. Thereafter, if the investment is not removed from jeopardy, an additional tax of 25 percent is imposed on the foundation, plus five percent on any foundation manager who refuses to agree to the removal from jeopardy. [*See* IRC § 4944 and the accompanying Regulations]

§ 6-E.01   TAX IMPOSED

If a private foundation makes any investments that would financially jeopardize the carrying out of its exempt purposes, both the foundation and the individual foundation managers may become liable for taxes on these jeopardizing investments under IRC § 4944. Like many of the other foundation excise taxes, these taxes apply in two stages, an initial tax and an additional tax. These taxes apply to investments of either income or principal.

1. *Initial tax.* An initial excise tax of five percent of the amount involved (the jeopardizing investment) is imposed on the foundation for each tax year, or part of a tax year, in the taxable period (described later). The foundation will not be liable for the tax if it can show that the jeopardizing investment was due to reasonable cause and not to willful neglect and that the jeopardizing investment was corrected within the correction period. [IRC § 4944(a)(1)] An initial excise tax of five percent of the amount involved is also imposed on any foundation manager who knowingly, willfully, and without reasonable cause participated in making the jeopardizing investment. [IRC § 4944(a)(2)]

2. *Additional tax.* If a private foundation incurs the initial tax and it has not removed the investment from jeopardy within the taxable period, an additional excise tax of 25 percent of the amount involved will be imposed on the foundation. The additional tax will not be assessed and, if already assessed, will be abated if the investment is removed from jeopardy within the correction period. If this additional tax is imposed on the foundation, an additional excise tax of five per-cent of the amount involved is also imposed on any foundation manager who refuses to agree to all or part of the removal from jeopardy. [IRC § 4944(b)]

§ 6-E.02   SPECIAL RULES FOR MANAGEMENT

[A] Joint and Several Liability

If more than one individual manager is liable for the excise tax on jeopardizing investments, all parties will be jointly and severally liable. [IRC § 4944(d)(1)]

[B] Limits on Liability

For any one jeopardizing investment, the maximum initial tax that may be imposed on foundation managers is $5,000, and the maximum additional tax is $10,000. [IRC § 4944(d)(2)]

[C] Willful

A manager's participation in making an investment is willful if it is voluntary, conscious, and intentional. However, it is not willful if the manager does not knowingly participate in a jeopardizing investment. [Reg. § 53.4944-1(b)(2)(ii)]

[D] Due to Reasonable Cause

A foundation manager's actions are due to reasonable cause (and hence the initial tax will not apply) if he or she has exercised responsibility on behalf of the foundation with ordinary business care and prudence. [Reg. § 53.4944-1(b)(2)(iii)]

[E] Advice of Counsel

A manager's action will be considered due to reasonable cause if the manager relies on advice of counsel expressed in a reasoned written legal opinion. In addition, a foundation manager may rely on the advice of a qualified investment counselor, given in writing in accordance with generally accepted practices, that a particular investment will provide for the long- and short-term financial needs of the foundation. [Reg. § 53.4944-1(b)(2)(v)]

[F] Participation

A foundation manager's participation in the making of an investment may consist of any manifestation of approval of the investment. [Reg. § 53.4944-1(b)(2)(iv)]

[G] Knowing

Foundation managers will be considered to have participated in making an investment knowing that it is jeopardizing the carrying out of any of the foundation's exempt purposes only if:

1. They have actual knowledge of enough facts so that, based only on those facts, the investment would be a jeopardizing investment;

2. They are aware that an investment under these circumstances may violate the provisions of federal tax law governing jeopardizing investments; and

3. They negligently fail to make reasonable attempts to learn whether the investment is a jeopardizing investment or in fact are aware that it is such an investment.

Although the term "knowing" does not mean "having reason to know," evidence that a foundation manager has reason to know of a particular fact or particular rule may nevertheless be relevant in determining whether actual knowledge of such fact or rule is present. [Reg. § 53.4944-1(b)(2)]

§ 6-E.03   JEOPARDIZING INVESTMENTS

[A]   Determining Whether an Investment Is a Jeopardizing Investment

A jeopardizing investment generally is one that shows a lack of reasonable business care and prudence in providing for the long-term or short-term financial needs of the foundation for it to carry out its exempt function. No single factor determines a jeopardizing investment, and no category of investments is treated as an intrinsic violation. However, in making this determination, the IRS Regulations indicate that careful scrutiny will be applied to:

1. Trading in securities on margin;

2. Trading in commodity futures;

3. Investing in working interests in oil and gas wells;

4. Buying "puts," "calls," and "straddles";

5. Buying warrants; and

6. Selling short.

[Reg. § 53.4944-1(a)(2)(i)]
  Note that this list was compiled in the 1970s, when such investments were less common and thus were regarded as more aggressive than might be the case today. Moreover, fiduciary investing in general has moved toward a prudent investor approach, which looks at investments on an overall portfolio basis, and away from the traditional prudent man (or prudent person) approach, which requires that each investment meet minimum standards. Under a prudent investor approach, even a fiduciary investor may appropriately invest a portion of the entire portfolio in somewhat riskier investments, which may bring a higher return if successful. The IRS has issued several private letter rulings holding that investment of minor proportions of a foundation's assets in various nontraditional investments would not incur liability under IRC § 4944. [*See, e.g.,* Ltr. Rul. 9451067 (limited partnerships holding or trading distressed real estate, commodities, and energy companies and a hedge fund for U.S. stocks); Ltr. Rul. 9237035 (commodities trading program managed by a disqualified person); Ltr. Rul. 9320052 (investments in working oil and gas wells)]
  In deciding whether the investment of an amount jeopardizes the carrying out of the exempt purposes, the determination must be made on an investment-by-investment basis, taking into account the foundation's portfolio as a whole. It is permissible for the foundation managers to take into account expected returns, risks of rising and falling prices, and the need for diversification within the investment portfolio. But to avoid the tax on jeopardizing investments, a careful analysis of potential investments must be made, and good business judgment must be exercised. [Reg. § 53.4944-1(a)(2)(i)]

Whether an investment jeopardizes the foundation's exempt purposes is determined at the time of making the investment. If the investment is proper when made, it will not be considered a jeopardizing investment even if it later results in loss. These rules do not exempt or relieve any person from compliance with any federal or state law imposing any obligation, duty, responsibility, or other standard of conduct on the operation or administration of an organization or trust. Similarly, no state law will exempt or relieve any person from any obligation, duty, responsibility, or other standard of conduct provided in these rules. [Reg. § 53.4944-1(a)(2)(i)]

The tax on jeopardizing investments does not apply to investments originally made by a person who later transferred them as gifts to the foundation. However, if the person receives any consideration from the foundation on the transfer, the foundation will be treated as having made an investment in the amount of the consideration. [Reg. § 53.4944-1(a)(2)(ii)(a)]

The tax on jeopardizing investments does not apply to investments that are acquired by the foundation as a result of a corporate reorganization, nor does the tax apply to investments made before 1970 unless the form or terms of the investments are later changed or the investments are exchanged for other investments. [Reg. § 53.4944-1(a)(2)(ii)(b)]

[B] Program-Related Investments

Program-related investments are not subject to the tax on jeopardizing investments. These are investments for which:

1. The primary purpose is to accomplish one or more of the foundation's exempt purposes;

2. The production of income or the appreciation of property is not a significant purpose; and

3. The influence of legislation or the participation in political campaigns on behalf of candidates is not a purpose.

[*See* IRC § 4944(c); Reg. § 53.4944-3(a)(1)]

In determining whether the production of income or the appreciation of property is a significant purpose of an investment, it is relevant whether investors who engage in investments only for profit would be likely to make the investment on the same terms as the private foundation. If an investment incidentally produces significant income or capital appreciation, this is not conclusive evidence that a significant purpose is the production of income or the appreciation of property. The investments, to be program related, must significantly further the foundation's exempt activities. They must be investments that would not have been made except for their relationship to the exempt purposes. The investments include those made in "functionally related" activities that are carried on within a larger combination of similar activities related to the exempt purposes. [Reg. § 53.4944-3(a)(2)]

The following are some typical examples of program-related investments:

1. Low-interest or interest-free loans to needy students;

2. High-risk investments in nonprofit low-income housing projects;

3. Low-interest loans to small businesses owned by members of economically disadvantaged groups where commercial funds at reasonable interest rates are not readily available;

4. Investments in businesses in deteriorated urban areas under a plan to improve the economy of the area by providing employment or training for unemployed residents; and

5. Investments in nonprofit organizations combating community deterioration.

If a foundation changes the form or terms of an investment and if the investment no longer qualifies as program related, the foundation then must determine whether or not the investment jeopardizes carrying out its exempt purposes. Once an investment is determined to be program related, it will continue to qualify as a program-related investment if changes in the form or terms of the investment are made primarily for exempt purposes and not for any significant purpose involving the production of income or the appreciation of property. A change made in the form or terms of a program-related investment for the prudent protection of the foundation's investment will not ordinarily cause the investment to cease to qualify as program related. Under certain conditions, a program-related investment may cease to be program related because of a critical change in circumstances, such as serving an illegal purpose or serving the private purpose of the foundation or its managers. [Reg. § 53.4944-3(a)(3)(i)]

An investment that ceases to be program related because of a critical change in circumstances does not subject the foundation making the investment to the tax on jeopardizing investments before the 30th day after the date on which the foundation (or any of its managers) has actual knowledge of the critical change in circumstances. [Reg. § 53.4944-3(a)(3)(i)]

[C] Removal from Jeopardy

A foundation removes an investment from jeopardy when it sells or otherwise disposes of it and the proceeds of the sale or other disposition are not themselves jeopardizing investments. A change by a foundation in the form or terms of a jeopardizing investment will result in the removal of the investment from jeopardy if, after the change, the investment no longer jeopardizes the carrying out of the foundation's exempt purposes. Making one jeopardizing investment and later exchanging this investment for another jeopardizing investment will be treated as only one jeopardizing investment. [Reg. § 53.4944-5(b)]

A jeopardizing investment is not removed from jeopardy by a transfer to another private foundation related to the transferor foundation unless the investment is a program-related investment in the hands of the transferee foundation. [Reg. § 53.4944-5(b)]

§ 6-E.04   TAXABLE AND CORRECTION PERIODS

[A] Taxable Period

The *taxable period* begins with the date of the investment and ends on the earliest of:

1. The date of removal from jeopardy;

2. The date a notice of deficiency for the initial tax is mailed; or

3. The date the initial tax is assessed.

It may include more than one tax year of the foundation. [Reg. § 53.4944-5(a)(1)]

> **Example:**   The Wilson Foundation has the calendar year as its tax year. It makes a jeopardizing investment on November 28, 2000, and does not remove the investment from jeopardy until January 15, 2001. The taxable period is from November 28, 2000, to January 15, 2001. It therefore is liable for a total initial tax of 10 percent of the amount invested (five percent for each tax year or part of a tax year in the taxable period).

[B] Correction Period

The *correction period* begins with the date of the investment and ends 90 days after a notice of deficiency for the additional tax is mailed. This period is extended by any period during which a deficiency cannot be assessed because of pending Tax Court proceedings and by any other period the IRS determines is reasonable and necessary. [IRC § 4963(e)(1); Reg. § 53.4963-1(e)(3)]

APPENDIX 6-F

TAXES ON TAXABLE EXPENDITURES (IRC § 4945)

Overview. An excise tax on various forms of prohibited expenditures is imposed under IRC § 4945. It applies in two steps: An initial tax of 10 percent of the amount expended is imposed on the foundation, plus 2½ percent on the foundation manager who agreed to it. (Both of these may be escaped under certain conditions if the offense was excusable under the applicable standards.) Thereafter, if the expenditure is not corrected within the specified period, an additional tax of 100 percent is imposed on the foundation, plus 50 percent on the foundation manager. [*See* IRC § 4945 and the accompanying Regulations]

§ 6-F.01   TAX IMPOSED

A private foundation that makes any *taxable expenditures*, as defined below, is liable for an excise tax on those expenditures under section 4945 of the Internal Revenue Code. Separate taxes are imposed on both the foundation and any foundation manager who knowingly and willfully agrees to the expenditures. Both an initial tax and an additional tax may be imposed.

1. *Initial tax.* The initial tax on the foundation is 10 percent of the amount expended. The foundation may avoid the tax if it shows that the expenditure was due to reasonable cause and not to willful neglect and that the expenditure was corrected within the *correction period* (as described below). In the case of a foundation manager who knowingly, willfully, and without reasonable cause agrees to the taxable expenditure, the initial tax is 21/2 percent of the amount expended, up to a maximum tax of $5,000 for any one expenditure. A foundation manager whose actions are based on the advice of counsel, given in a reasoned legal opinion in writing, is not liable for the tax. [IRC § 4945(a)]

2. *Additional tax.* If the expenditure is not corrected within the *taxable period* (as described below), an additional tax of 100 percent of the amount expended is imposed on the foundation. The tax will not be assessed or, if assessed, will be abated if the expenditure is corrected within the *correction period* (also described below). Any foundation manager who refuses to agree to part or all of the correction must pay an additional tax of 50 percent of the expenditure, up to a maximum tax of $10,000. [IRC § 4945(b)]

§ 6-F.02   FOUNDATION MANAGERS

[A]   Joint and Several Liability

If more than one foundation manager is liable for either the initial or the additional tax, all are jointly and severally liable. This means that the Internal Revenue Service may collect the full tax from any one, or several, or all of the managers who are liable for the tax. [IRC § 4945(c)(1); Reg. § 53.4945-1(c)(1)]

[B]   Initial Tax

[1]   When Imposed

The initial tax on foundation managers is imposed only in cases when the following circumstances are present:

1. The initial tax on taxable expenditures is imposed on the private foundation making the expenditure;

2. The foundation manager *knows* that the expenditure to which he or she agrees is a taxable expenditure; and

3. The agreement is *willful* and is *not due to reasonable cause*.

The tax on any particular expenditure applies only to agreements of foundation managers with authority to approve or to exercise discretion in recommending approval for expenditures by the foundation and to those foundation managers who are members of a group authorized to make or recommend those expenditures. [IRC § 4945(a)(2); Reg. § 53.4945-1(a)(2)]

[2] Definitions

[a] Agreement

A foundation manager's agreement to the making of a taxable expenditure may be found in any manifestation of approval of the expenditure that is sufficient to constitute an exercise of his or her authority to approve or to exercise discretion in recommending approval for making an expenditure by the foundation. It does not matter that the foundation manager's action may not be the final or decisive approval on behalf of the foundation, as this is not the determining factor. [Reg. § 53.4945-1(a)(2)(ii)]

[b] Knowing

A foundation manager will be considered to have agreed to an expenditure *knowing* that it is a taxable expenditure only if he or she:

1. Has actual knowledge of enough facts so that, based on these facts alone, the expenditure would be a taxable expenditure;

2. Is aware that an expenditure under these circumstances may violate the law governing taxable expenditures; and

3. Negligently fails to make reasonable attempts to determine whether the expenditure is a taxable expenditure (or is in fact aware that it is a taxable expenditure).

The term "knowing" does not mean having reason to know. However, any evidence indicating that a foundation manager has reason to know of a particular fact or rule is relevant in determining whether he or she had actual knowledge of this fact or rule. [Reg. § 53.4945-1(a)(2)(iii)]

[c] *Willful*

A foundation manager's agreement to a taxable expenditure is *willful* if it is voluntary, conscious, and intentional. It need not be based on a motive or intention to avoid the restrictions of the law or the incurrence of any tax to be willful. However, a foundation manager's agreement to a taxable expenditure is not willful if he or she does not know that it is a taxable expenditure. [Reg. § 53.4945-1(a)(2)(ii)]

[d] *Due to Reasonable Cause*

A foundation manager's actions are *due to reasonable cause* if he or she has exercised responsibility on behalf of the foundation with ordinary business care and prudence. [Reg. § 53.4945-1(a)(2)(v)]

[3] Advice of Counsel

If a foundation manager has made full disclosure of the factual situation to legal counsel (including house counsel) and relies on the advice of counsel as expressed in a reasoned written legal opinion that an expenditure is not a taxable expenditure and the expenditure is later held to be taxable, the foundation manager's agreement to the expenditure will ordinarily not be considered knowing or willful and will ordinarily be considered due to reasonable cause. A written legal opinion will be considered reasoned even if it reaches a conclusion that is later determined to be incorrect as long as the opinion addresses itself to the facts and applicable law. However, an opinion will not be considered reasoned if it does nothing more than recite the facts and express a conclusion. The absence of advice of counsel on an expenditure will not by itself give rise to any inference that a foundation manager agreed to making the expenditure knowingly, willfully, or without reasonable cause. [Reg. § 53.4945-1(a)(2)(vi)]

[C] Correction of a Taxable Expenditure

[1] In General

In most cases (other than those of inadequate reporting or failure to obtain advance approval, discussed below), a correction is accomplished by recovering the expenditure to the extent possible. When full recovery is not possible, any additional corrective action will be prescribed by the IRS. The type of additional action depends on the circumstances, and the IRS may require any of the following:

1. Withholding any unpaid funds due a particular grantee;

2. Stopping further grants to the grantee;

3. Reporting periodically to the IRS all the foundation's expenditures;

4. Improving methods of exercising expenditure responsibility (discussed below);

5. Improving methods of selecting recipients of individual grants; and

6. Taking any other actions that the IRS may prescribe in a particular case.

The foundation is not required to attempt recovery of the taxable expenditure by legal action if it appears a judgment could not be satisfied. [Reg. § 53.4945-1(d)(1)]

[2] Correction for Failure to Obtain Advance Approval

When a grant for travel, study, or the like becomes a taxable expenditure only because of a failure to obtain advance IRS approval of grant procedures, correction may be accomplished by obtaining approval of the grantmaking procedures and establishing to the satisfaction of the IRS that:

1. No grant funds have been diverted to any use not for a purpose specified in the grant;

2. The grantmaking procedures instituted would have been approved if advance approval of the procedures had been properly requested; and

3. When advance approval of grantmaking procedures is later required, the approval will be properly requested.

[Reg. § 53.4945-1(d)(3)]

[3] Correction for Inadequate Reporting

If an expenditure is taxable only because of a failure to make or obtain a full and complete report as required, correction may be made by making or obtaining the report in question. In addition, if the expenditure is taxable only because of a failure to obtain a full and complete report as required and an investigation indicates that no grant funds have been diverted to any use not for a purpose specified in the grant, correction will be accomplished if all reasonable efforts are made to obtain the report and the IRS is notified of the failure to obtain the report. [Reg. § 53.4945-1(d)(2)]

[D] Taxable and Correction Periods

[1] Taxable Period

The *taxable period* begins on the date the taxable expenditure occurs and ends on the earlier of either:

1. The date a notice of deficiency for the initial tax is mailed; or

2. The date the initial tax is assessed.

[IRC § 4945(i)(2)]

[2] Correction Period

The *correction period* begins on the date of the taxable expenditure and ends 90 days after a notice of deficiency for the *additional tax* is mailed. The period is extended for the time during which a deficiency cannot be assessed under IRC § 6213(a) (relating to pending Tax Court and other proceedings) and for any other period the IRS determines is reasonable and necessary for correction of the taxable expenditure. [IRC § 4963(e)(1)(A)]

§ 6-F.03 TAXABLE EXPENDITURES

[A] Defined

A "taxable expenditure" is defined in IRC § 4945(d) as an amount paid or incurred to:

1. Carry on propaganda or otherwise attempt to *influence legislation*;

2. Influence the outcome of any specific public *election* or carry on any voter registration drive unless certain requirements (explained below) are satisfied;

3. Make a *grant to an individual* for travel, study, or other similar purposes unless certain requirements (explained below) are satisfied;

4. Make a *grant to an organization* (other than a public charity or an exempt operating foundation, as described in § 2.06[B] *supra*) unless the foundation exercises expenditure responsibility with respect to the grant; or

5. Carry out a *noncharitable purpose* (i.e., with certain exceptions, any purpose other than a religious, charitable, scientific, literary, or educational purpose; the fostering of national or international amateur sports competition; or the prevention of cruelty to children or animals).

Each of these categories of taxable expenditures is discussed in greater detail below.

[B] Influencing Legislation

[1] What Is Influencing Legislation?

A taxable expenditure includes amounts used to attempt to influence legislation:

1. By affecting public opinion; or

2. By communicating with any member or employee of a legislative body or with any other government official or employee who may participate in formulating the legislation.

[IRC § 4945(e)]

[a] Legislation

Legislation includes *action* by Congress, any state legislature, any local council or similar governing body, or the public by way of referendum, constitutional amendment, or the like. The word "action" includes the introduction, enactment, defeat, or repeal of legislation. Actions by executive, judicial, or administrative bodies are not legislation, so expenditures made to influence action by these bodies are not attempts to influence legislation. School boards, housing authorities, sewer and water districts, zoning boards, and other similar federal, state, or local special purpose bodies, whether elective or appointive, are considered administrative rather than legislative bodies. [Reg. §§ 53.4945-2(a)(1), 56.4911-2(d)(1)]

A proposed treaty required to be submitted by the president to the Senate for its advice and consent will be considered legislation being considered by, or to be submitted imminently to, a legislative body at the time the president's representative begins to negotiate its position with the parties to the proposed treaty. [Reg. § 56.4911-2(d)(1)(i)]

[b] Jointly Funded Projects

A private foundation will not be treated as having paid or incurred any amount to attempt to influence legislation merely because it makes a grant to another organization conditioned on the recipient obtaining a matching government appropriation. In addition, it will not be treated as having made a taxable expenditure of amounts paid or incurred in carrying on discussions with government officials if:

1. The subject is a new program or an existing program jointly funded by the foundation and the government;

2. The discussions are undertaken for the purpose of exchanging data and information on the subject matter of the program; and

3. The discussions are not undertaken to make any direct attempt to persuade government officials or employees to take a particular position on specific legislative issues other than the program.

[Reg. § 53.4945-2(a)(3)]

[c] Certain Expenditures by Recipients of Program-Related Investments

Any amount paid or incurred by a recipient of a program-related investment in connection with an appearance before or communication with any legislative body on legislation or proposed legislation of direct interest to the recipient will not be attributed to the investing foundation if:

1. The foundation does not earmark its funds to carry on propaganda or otherwise attempt to influence legislation; and

2. A trade or business deduction is allowable to the recipient for this expenditure.

[Reg. § 53.4945-2(a)(4)]

[d]   Grants to Public Organizations

A grant by a private foundation to an organization other than a private foundation will not be a taxable expenditure if the grant is not earmarked to be used for, or in a manner outlined in, items 1 through 5 under § 6-F.03[A] above. In addition, a grantor foundation may not enter into an oral or written agreement with a grantee that causes the grantee to engage in any prohibited activity, nor may the grantor select the recipient of the grant. A grant is earmarked if the grant is given under an agreement, oral or written, that the grant is to be used for specific purposes. [Reg. § 53.4945-2(a)(5)]

[e]   Attempts to Affect the Opinion of the General Public

Generally, expenditures paid or incurred by a private foundation in an attempt to influence any legislation through an attempt to affect the opinion of any segment of the general public (i.e., "grass roots lobbying") are a taxable expenditure. [IRC §§ 4945(e)(1), 4911(d)(1)(A); Reg. § 56.4911-2(b)(2)(i)] Exceptions are discussed later.

[f]   Lobbying Activities

Generally, any expenditure paid or incurred by a private foundation to influence legislation through communication with any member or employee of a legislative body or with any government official or employee who may participate in the formulation of the legislation (i.e., "direct lobbying") is a taxable expenditure. [IRC § 4911(d)(1)(B); Reg. § 56.4911-2(b)(1)(i)] Exceptions are discussed later.

[2]   Exceptions to Influencing Legislation

[a]   *Nonpartisan Analysis, Study, and Research*

Engaging in nonpartisan analysis, study, or research and making the results of this work available to the general public or to government bodies, officials, or employees are not considered carrying on propaganda or otherwise attempting to influence legislation. Nonpartisan analysis, study, or research means an independent and objective exposition of a particular subject matter, including activities that qualify as educational activities. Nonpartisan analysis, study, or research may advocate a particular position or viewpoint as long as there is a sufficiently full and fair exposition of the relevant facts to enable the public or an individual to form an independent opinion or conclusion. However, a mere presentation of unsupported opinion does not qualify as nonpartisan analysis, study, or research. [Reg. § 53.4945-2(d)(1)(ii)]

[i]   **Presentation as part of a series.** Normally, whether a publication or broadcast qualifies as nonpartisan analysis, study, or research will be determined on a presentation-by-presentation basis. However, if a publication or broadcast is one of a series prepared or supported by a private foundation and the series as a whole meets the standards of nonpartisan analysis, study, or research, then any individual publication or broadcast in the series will not result in a taxable expenditure even though such individual broadcast or publication does not by itself meet the standards of nonpartisan analysis, study, or research. Whether a broadcast or publication is considered part of a series will ordinarily depend on all the facts and circumstances of each particular situation. However, for broadcast activities, all broadcasts in any period of six consecutive months will ordinarily be eligible to be considered as part of a series. If a private foundation times or channels a part of a series in a manner designed to influence the general public or the action of a legislative body for a specific legislative proposal, the expenses of preparing and distributing that part of the analysis, study, or research are a taxable expenditure. [Reg. § 53.4945-2(d)(1)(iii)]

[ii]   **Making available results of analysis, study, or research.** A private foundation may choose any suitable means, including oral or written presentations, to distribute the results of its nonpartisan analysis, study, or research, with or without charge. This may include distribution of reprints of speeches, articles, and reports; presentation of information through conferences, meetings, and discussions; and dissemination to the news media, including radio, television, and newspapers, and to other public forums. These presentations may not be limited to or directed toward persons who are interested only in one side of a particular issue. [Reg. § 53.4945-2(d)(1)(iv)]

Example 1:   The Jones Foundation establishes a research project to collect information showing the dangers of using pesticides in growing crops, including data on proposed legislation pending in several state legislatures to ban the use of pesticides. The project takes favorable positions on the legislation *without* producing a sufficiently full and fair exposition of the relevant facts to enable the public or an individual to form an independent opinion or conclusion on the pros and cons of the use of pesticides. This project is not within the exception for nonpartisan analysis, study, or research because it is designed to present information only on one side of the legislative controversy.

Example 2:   The Smith Foundation establishes a research project for the apparent purpose of examining and reporting information as to the pros and cons of the use of pesticides in growing crops. The information is collected and distributed in the form of a published report that analyzes the effects and costs of the use and nonuse of various pesticides under various conditions on humans, animals, and crops. The report also presents the advantages, disadvantages, and economic cost of allowing the continued use of pesticides unabated, of controlling the use of pesticides, and of developing alternatives to pesticides. Even if the report gives conclusions that the disadvantages of using pesticides are greater than the advantages of using pesticides and that prompt legislative regulation of the use of pesticides is needed, the project is within the exception for nonpartisan analysis, study, or research because it is designed to present information on both sides of the legislative controversy. In addition, the report presents a sufficiently full and fair exposition of the relevant facts to enable the public or an individual to form an independent opinion or conclusion.

[b]   Technical Advice or Assistance

Amounts are not taxable expenditures if they are paid or incurred in connection with providing technical advice or assistance to a government body, committee, or subdivision in response to a *written request*. Under this exception, the request for assistance or advice must be made in the name of the requesting government body, committee, or subdivision, rather than an individual member. Similarly, the response to the request must be available to every member of the requesting body, committee, or subdivision. [Reg. § 53.4945-2(d)(2)(i)]

Technical advice or assistance may be given as a result of knowledge or skill in a given area. Because this assistance or advice may be given only at the express request of a government body, committee, or subdivision, the oral or written presentation of assistance or advice need not qualify as nonpartisan analysis, study, or research. Offering opinions or recommendations will ordinarily qualify under this exception only if the opinions or recommendations are specifically requested by the government body, committee, or subdivision or are directly related to the materials requested. [Reg. § 53.4945-2(d)(2)(ii)]

> **Example 1:** A congressional committee is studying the feasibility of legislation to provide funds for scholarships to U.S. students attending schools abroad. The McCoy Foundation, which has engaged in a private scholarship program of this kind, is asked, in writing, by the committee to describe the manner in which it selects candidates for its program. The foundation's response, disclosing its methods of selection, is technical advice or assistance.

> **Example 2:** Assume the same facts given in example 1, except that The McCoy Foundation's response includes not only a description of its grantmaking procedures, but also its views regarding the wisdom of adopting such a program. Because these views are directly related to the subject matter of the request for technical advice or assistance, the amount paid or incurred for the presentation of these views is not a taxable expenditure. However, the comparable amount relating to a response that is not directly related to the subject matter of such request would be a taxable expenditure unless the presentation can qualify as making available nonpartisan analysis, study, or research.

[c]   *Decisions Affecting the Powers, Duties, and Such of a Private Foundation (Self-Defense Exception)*

Taxes on lobbying activities do not apply to amounts paid or incurred in connection with an appearance before or communication with any legislative body on a possible decision of that body that might affect the existence of the private foundation, its powers and duties, its tax-exempt status, or the deductibility of contributions to the foundation. Under this exception, a foundation may communicate with the entire legislative body; committees or subcommittees of the legislative body; individual congressmen or legislators; members of their staffs; or representatives of the executive branch who are involved in the legislative process if the communication is limited to the prescribed subjects. The foundation may even make expenditures to initiate legislation if the legislation concerns only matters that might affect the existence of the private foundation, its powers and duties, its tax-exempt status, or the deductibility of contributions to the foundation. [Reg. § 53.4945-2(d)(3)(i)]

[d]   *Examinations and Discussions of Broad Social, Economic, and Similar Problems*

Expenditures for examinations and discussions of broad social, economic, and similar problems are not taxable expenditures even if the problems are the type the government would be expected to deal with ultimately. [Reg. § 53.4945-2(d)(4)]

Similarly, the phrase "any attempt to influence any legislation" does not include public discussion, or communications with members of legislative bodies or government employees, the general subject of which is also the subject of legislation before a legislative body as long as the discussion does not address itself to the merits of a specific legislative proposal. For example, a private foundation may, without incurring the tax on taxable expenditures, present discussions of problems such as environmental pollution or population growth that are being considered by Congress and various state legislatures, but only if the discussions are not directly addressed to specific legislation being considered. [Reg. § 53.4945-2(d)(4)]

[C] Influencing Elections and Carrying On Voter Registration Drives

[1] Participation or Intervention in a Political Campaign

Taxable expenditures include amounts paid or incurred by a private foundation to influence the outcome of any specific public election or to carry on, directly or indirectly, any voter registration drive. [IRC § 4945(d)(2)] Activities that are considered participation or intervention in a political campaign include, but are not limited to:

1. Publishing or distributing written or printed statements or making oral statements on behalf of or in opposition to a candidate;

2. Paying the salaries or expenses of campaign workers; and

3. Conducting or paying the expenses of conducting a voter registration drive limited to the geographic area covered by the campaign.

[Reg. § 53.4945-3(a)(2)]

[2] Exceptions

This rule does not apply to nonpartisan activities carried on under the following conditions:

1. The organization making the expenditure is described in IRC § 501(c)(3) and is exempt from tax;

2. The organization's activities are nonpartisan, are not confined to one specific election period, and are carried on in at least five states;

3. The organization spends at least 85 percent of its income directly for the active conduct of the exempt purposes or functions for which it is organized and operated;

4. The organization receives at least 85 percent of its support (other than gross investment income) from exempt organizations, the general public, government units, or any combination of these; it does not receive more than 25 percent of its support (other than gross investment income) from any one exempt organization; and it does not receive more than 50 percent of its support from gross investment income; and

5. Contributions to the organization for voter registration drives are not subject to conditions that they may be used only in specified states or other localities of the United States or that they may be used in only one specific election period.

[*See* IRC § 4945(f); Reg. § 53.4945-3(b)(1)]

For purposes of the support test in item 4, the support received during the tax year and the four immediately preceding taxable years is taken into account. If the organization has less than four years of operational experience, the support test may be determined by taking into account all available years the organization has been in existence. [Reg. § 53.4945-3(b)(3)]

[3] Advance Ruling

An organization may obtain an advance ruling that it qualifies under the exceptions that apply to nonpartisan activities if it submits evidence establishing that it can reasonably expect to meet these tests for the year. Grantors or contributors to these organizations may rely on the advance ruling until a notice of change of status of the organization is made to the public. This does not apply, however, if the grantor or contributor was responsible for, or was aware of, the fact that the organization did not qualify under these provisions at the end of the tax year for which it obtained an advance ruling or determination letter or acquired knowledge that the IRS had given notice to the organization advising that it would be deleted from this classification. [Reg. § 53.4945-3(b)(4)]

[D] Grants to Individuals

[1] Requirements

Grants to individuals for travel, study, or other similar purposes (including loans made for charitable purposes and program-related investments as discussed in Appendix 6-E, dealing with jeopardizing investments) are taxable expenditures *unless* the following conditions are met:

1. The grant must be awarded on an objective and nondiscriminatory basis under a procedure approved in advance by the IRS; and

2. It must be shown to the satisfaction of the IRS that one of the following requirements is met:

    a.   The grant is a scholarship or fellowship and is to be used for study at an educational institution that normally maintains a regular faculty and curriculum and normally has a regularly organized body of students in attendance at the place where the educational activities are carried on. For these purposes, there is no requirement that the grant recipients be limited to degree candidates, nor must the grant be limited to tuition, fees, and course-required books, supplies, and equipment. A recipient may use grant funds for room, board, travel, research, clerical help, or equipment that is incidental to the purposes of the scholarship or fellowship grant.

    b.   The grant qualifies as a prize or award under section 74(b) if the recipient is selected from the general public. For this purpose, the recipient may keep the prize or award and need not authorize the foundation to transfer the prize or award to a government unit or to another charity.

    c.   The grant's purpose is to achieve a specific objective, produce a report or similar product, or improve or enhance a literary, artistic, musical, scientific, teaching, or similar capacity, skill, or talent of the grantee.

[*See* IRC § 4945(d)(3); Reg. § 53.4945-4(a)(3)]

[2] Advance Approval of Grantmaking Procedure

The grantmaking procedure, to be approved in advance by the Internal Revenue Service, must provide the following:

1.   The group from which the grantees are selected must be reasonably related to the purposes of the grant, and the group must be large enough to constitute a charitable class (unless, taking into account the purposes of the grant, only a few individuals are qualified to be grantees — as in the case of scientific research).

2.   The criteria used in selecting grant recipients from the potential grantees should be related to the purpose of the grant. For example, proper criteria for selecting scholarship recipients might include, among other things, past academic performance, performance on tests designed to measure ability and aptitude for college work, recommendations from instructors, financial need, and the conclusions the selection committee might draw from personal interviews.

3.   The person or persons who select recipients of grants should not be in a position to receive a private benefit, directly or indirectly, if certain potential grantees are selected over others.

4. Periodic progress reports must be made to the foundation, at least once a year, to determine whether the grantees have performed the activities the grants are intended to finance.

5. When these reports are not made or there are other indications that the grants are not being used as intended, the foundation must investigate and take corrective action.

6. The foundation must keep all records relating to all grants to individuals, including —

    a. Information obtained to evaluate grantees;

    b. Identification of grantees, including any relationship of the grantee to the foundation sufficient to make the grantee a disqualified person;

    c. Amount and purpose of each grant; and

    d. Follow-up information, including required annual reports and investigation of jeopardized grants.

However, no single procedure or set of procedures is required. Procedures may vary depending on such factors as the size of the foundation, the amount and purpose of the grants, and whether one or more recipients are involved. [Reg. § 53.4945-4(b), (c)]

[3] Renewals

A renewal of a qualified grant will not be treated as a grant to an individual subject to the above requirements if:

1. The grantor has no information indicating that the original grant is being used for any purpose other than that for which it was made;

2. The reports due under the terms of the grant have been provided; and

3. Any additional criteria and procedures for renewal are objective and non-discriminatory.

Any extension of a period over which a grant is to be paid will not by itself be regarded as a grant or a renewal of a grant. [Reg. § 53.4945-4(a)(3)(iii)]

[4] Company Scholarship Programs

[a] *Requirements*

Company scholarship programs are usually administered by company-created private foundations. These foundations may give preference in awarding scholarships to employees, the children or relatives of employees, or the children of deceased or retired employees of the company or related companies. Scholarship grants awarded by these private foundations are taxable expenditures unless the grant programs meet the requirements for individual grants (discussed above) and receive advance approval from the IRS. Company scholarship programs will not qualify if grants are essentially providing extra pay, an employment incentive, or an employee fringe benefit. Similarly, if scholarship programs are compensatory in nature, an organization administering such a program will not qualify for tax exemption because it is operated for private benefit. A private foundation administering such a program could also be involved in direct or indirect self-dealing.

Company-related scholarship programs can meet the scholarship requirements by ensuring that the scholarships awarded are for the main purpose of furthering the recipients' education, rather than compensating company employees. Certain conditions and tests must establish three facts:

1. The preferential treatment derived from employment must not have any significance beyond that of an initial qualifier;

2. The selection of scholarship grantees must be controlled and limited by substantial non-employment-related factors, including a selection committee of individuals who are independent and separate from the private foundation, its organizer, and the employer concerned; and

3. There must exist only a limited possibility that qualified employees or their children will receive scholarship grants.

[For the IRS guidelines for company foundation scholarship programs for employees and/or their children, *see* Rev. Proc. 76-47, 1976-2 C.B. 670, as amplified by Rev. Proc. 94-78, 1994-2 C.B. 833, applied by Rev. Rul. 81-217, 1981-2 C.B. 217, and clarified by Rev. Proc. 85-5, 1985-2 C.B. 717, and Rev. Proc. 81-65, 1981-2 C.B. 690]

[b]   Educational Loans

Educational loans made by a private foundation under an employer-related loan program are not taxable expenditures if the loan program:

1. Meets the applicable requirements for grants to individuals, discussed earlier; and

2. Satisfies the seven conditions and the percentage tests described below.

[For the IRS guidelines for company foundation loan programs for employees and/or their children, *see* Rev. Proc. 80-39, 1981-2 C.B. 690, as amplified by Rev. Proc. 94-78, 1994-2 C.B. 833]

The seven conditions for approval, as set forth in Revenue Procedure 76-47, 1976-2 C.B. 670, include the following items:

1. *Inducement.* The program must not be used by the employer, the private foundation, or the organizer thereof to recruit employees or to induce employees to continue their employment or otherwise follow a course of action sought by the employer.

2. *Selection committee.* Selection of loan recipients must be made by a committee of individuals who are totally independent (except for participation on this committee) and separate from the private foundation, its organizer, and the employer concerned. An individual who is a former employee of either the foundation or the employer concerned will not be considered totally independent. These committees preferably should consist of individuals knowledgeable in the field of education so that they have the background and knowledge to properly evaluate the potential of the applicants. Forwarding the selections by the independent selection committee to the employer or private foundation only for the purpose of verifying the eligibility requirements and selection criteria followed by the committee in considering the candidates and in making its selection will not disqualify the program. Any public announcement of the awards, however, must be made by the selection committee or by the foundation. The awards may be announced in the employer's newsletter if the foundation or the selection committee is clearly identified as the grantor of the awards. Loans must be awarded only in the order recommended by the selection committee. The number of loans to be awarded may be reduced, but may not be increased from the number recommended by the selection committee. Only the committee may vary the amounts of the loans awarded.

3. *Eligibility requirements.* The program must impose identifiable minimum requirements for loan eligibility. These requirements must be related to the purpose of the program and must limit the independent selection committee's consideration to those employees, or children of employees, who meet the minimum standards for admission to an educational organization for which the loans are available. No persons will be considered eligible if they would not reasonably be expected to attend such an organization, however, even if they meet the minimum standards. If an employee must have been employed for some minimum period by the employer to which the program relates to be eligible to receive a loan or to make that employee's children eligible to receive a loan, the minimum period of employment may not be more than three years. Moreover, eligibility must not be related to any other employment-related factors, such as the employee's position, services, or duties.

4. *Objective basis of selection.* Selection of loan recipients must be based only on substantial objective standards that are completely unrelated to the employment of the recipients or their parents and to the employer's line of business. Such standards as past academic performance, performance on tests designed to measure ability and aptitude for higher education, recommendations

from instructors or other individuals not related to the potential awardees, financial need, and conclusions drawn from personal interviews as to motivation and character may be used.

5. *Employment.* Once a loan has been awarded, it may not be terminated because the recipient or the recipient's parent no longer works for the employer, regardless of the reason for the termination of employment. If a loan is awarded for one academic year and the recipient must reapply for an additional loan or loans to continue studies for a later year, the recipient may not be considered ineligible for a subsequent loan simply because that individual or the individual's parent is no longer employed by the employer. If a loan is awarded for a period of more than one academic year, subject to renewal, the standards for renewal must be based only on non-employment-related factors, such as need and maintenance of scholastic standards. At the time the loan is awarded or renewed, there must be no requirement, condition, or suggestion, express or implied, that the recipient or parent is expected to perform future employment services for the foundation or the employer or to be available for future employment, even though the future employment is at the discretion of the foundation or the employer.

6. *Course of study.* The courses of study for which loans are available must not be limited to those that would be of particular benefit to the employer or to the foundation. If the courses of study for which loans are available include one or more that would be of particular benefit, a loan may not be conditioned on the recipient choosing such a course of study. The recipient must have free choice to use the loan in the pursuit of a course of study for which the loan is otherwise available that is not of particular benefit to the employer or to the foundation.

7. *Other objectives.* The terms of the loan and the courses of study for which loans are available must be consistent with a disinterested purpose of enabling the recipients to obtain an education in their individual capacities only for their personal benefit. The terms of the loan and courses of study must not include any commitments, understandings, or obligations, conditional or unconditional, suggesting that the studies are undertaken by the recipients for the benefit of the employer or the foundation or have as their objective the accomplishment of any purpose of the employer or the foundation, even though consistent with its exempt status, other than to enable the recipients to obtain an education in their individual capacities.

[c] Percentage Tests

For a program that awards loans to children of employees of a particular employer, the program meets the percentage test (as set forth in Rev. Proc. 76-47, 1976-2 C.B. 670) if the number of loans awarded under that program in any year to those children is not more than:

1. 25 percent of the number of employees' children who —

   a. Were eligible;

   b. Were applicants for such loans; and

   c. Were considered by the selection committee in selecting the recipients of loans in that year; or

2. 10 percent of the number of employees' children who can be shown to be eligible for loans (whether or not they submitted an application) in that year. For purposes of this 10 percent test, children can be shown to be eligible only if they meet the minimum eligibility requirements of the loan program and the minimum standards for admission to an educational institution for which grants or loans are available. A private foundation may include as eligible only those children who submit a written statement (or on behalf of whom a statement is submitted by an authorized representative) or for whom sufficient information is maintained to demonstrate that:

   a. The child meets the foundation's eligibility requirements; and

   b. The child has enrolled in or has completed a course of study to prepare for admission to an educational institution at the level for which loans are available and has applied, or intends to apply, to such an institution for enrollment in the immediately succeeding academic year with the expectation, if accepted by the institution, of attending the institution; or

   c. In lieu of item b above, the child is currently enrolled in an educational institution for which loans are available and is not in the final year for which awards may be made.

For a program that awards loans to employees of a particular employer, the program meets the percentage test if the number of loans awarded under that program in any year to the employees is not more than 10 percent of the number of employees who:

1. Were eligible;

2. Were applicants for such loans; and

3. Were considered by the selection committee in selecting the recipients of loans in that year.

In meeting these percentage tests, an employee or child of an employee will be considered eligible only if the individual meets all of the eligibility requirements imposed by the program. Renewals of loans awarded in earlier years will not be considered in determining the number of loans awarded in a current year. Loans awarded to children of employees and those awarded to employees will be considered as having been awarded under separate programs whether or not they are awarded under separately administered programs. [*See* Rev. Proc. 76-47, 1976-2 C.B. 670, for further guidance]

If a private foundation's employer-related program includes educational loans and scholarship or fellowship grants to the same group of eligible employees' children, the percentage tests apply to the total number of individuals receiving combined grants of scholarships, fellowships, and educational loans. If the loan program satisfies the seven conditions, but does not meet the percentage test, all the relevant facts and circumstances will be considered in determining the primary purpose of the program. A private foundation holding a ruling letter issued before September 29, 1980, may continue to rely on that ruling letter, provided the loan program fully complies with the seven conditions and the percentage tests continuously from the date on which the ruling letter was issued. Upon written request, the IRS will issue a current ruling letter affirming the qualification of the loan program under these requirements. [Rev. Proc. 80-39, 1980-2 C.B. 772]

[5] Certain Designated Grants

A foundation grant to another organization that makes payments to a qualified individual will not be treated as a grant by the private foundation to the individual if the foundation does not earmark the use of the grant for any named individual and there is no agreement (oral or written) whereby the grantor organization has any part in selecting the individual grantee. [Reg. § 53.4945-4(a)(4)(i)]

[6] Certain Grants to Public Charities

A grant by a private foundation to a public charity, other than an organization organized and operated exclusively for testing for public safety, that the grantee organization uses to make payments to an individual as a qualified grantee, will not be treated as a grant by the private foundation to the individual grantee if the grant is made for a project to be undertaken and controlled by the public charity. The public charity must also control the selection of the grantee, although the selection need not be completely independent of the private foundation. [Reg. § 53.4945-4(a)(4)(ii)]

[7] Grants to Government Agencies

[a] *Grants Earmarked to Individuals*

If a private foundation makes a grant to a government agency and the grant is earmarked for use by an individual for travel, study, or other similar purposes, the grant is not a taxable expenditure by the private foundation if the government agency satisfies the IRS in advance that its grantmaking program:

1. Is in furtherance of exempt purposes under IRC § 501(c)(3);

2. Requires the individual grantee to submit annual progress reports; and

3. Requires the organization to investigate jeopardized grants.

[Reg. § 53.4945-4(a)(4)(iii)]

[b] When Earmarked Grant to Individual Is a Taxable Expenditure

A grant by a private foundation to an individual is a taxable expenditure if:

1. The grant is earmarked to be used for a purpose described earlier under § 6-F.03;

2. The grantor foundation causes the grantee, through an oral or written agreement, to engage in a prohibited activity and the grant is in fact a taxable expenditure; and

3. The grant is made for a purpose other than a purpose of an organization organized and operated exclusively for religious, charitable, scientific, literary, or educational purposes; the fostering of national or international amateur sports competition (but only if no part of its activities involves providing athletic facilities or equipment); or the prevention of cruelty to children or animals.

A grant by a private foundation will be considered earmarked if it is given under an agreement (oral or written) that the grant will be used for specific purposes. [Reg. § 53.4945-4(a)(5)]

[8] Securing Approval of Individual Grant Procedures

In the case of a newly formed foundation, a request for approval of grant procedures may be filed as a part of the foundation's original exemption application (Form 1023, Schedule H). Otherwise, ruling requests for advance approval of procedures are to be sent to the Cincinnati Key District Office and should include the statements described earlier under "Grants to Individuals," in addition to information responsive to the seven conditions and the percentage tests described above. Note that the Regulations, in section 53.4945-4(d) (2), indicate that the request should be submitted to the district director. A number of IRS exempt-organization functions (including processing of these requests) have been centralized in Cincinnati since the issuance of the Regulations in 1972.

If, by the 45th day after a request has been properly submitted, the foundation has not been notified that the procedures are acceptable, they may be considered approved from the date of submission until receipt of actual notice from the IRS that they do not meet the requirements. Payments of remaining installments of fixed-sum grants awarded during the period the foundation's procedures were considered approved, after the foundation is notified that the procedures are unacceptable, are not taxable expenditures. [Reg. § 53.4945-4(d)]

[E] Grants to Organizations

Grants to organizations (including loans and program-related investments) are subject to special rules. These will be taxable expenditures unless *either* (1) the recipients are public charities or (2) the granting foundation exercises *expenditure responsibility* (described below) with respect to the grant. The effect is to ensure that funds granted to organizations other than public charities are used in accordance with the terms of the grant. Although the requirements are precise, they need not be onerous, as detailed below. [IRC § 4945(d)(4); Reg. § 53.4945-5(a)(1)]

[1] Reliance by Grantors on Public Charity Status of Grantees

A private foundation need not exercise expenditure responsibility with respect to a grant if the grant is made to a public charity (i.e., an organization described in IRC § 509(a)(1), (2), or (3)). If a proposed grantee organization has received an IRS determination classifying it as a public charity, the treatment of grants to the organization will generally not be affected by reason of a later revocation of the organization's classification until publication of notice of its change of status in the Internal Revenue Bulletin. In appropriate cases, however, the treatment of grants and contributions and the status of grantors and contributors to a public charity may be affected pending verification of its continued classification. Notice to this effect will be made in a public announcement by the IRS. In these cases, the effect of grants and contributions made after the date of the announcement will depend on the statutory qualification of the organization as a public charity.

The rules described in the preceding paragraph do not apply if the granting foundation:

1. Had knowledge of the revocation of the organization's public charity status; or

2. Was in part responsible for, or was aware of, the act, the failure to act, or the substantial and material change on the part of the organization that gave rise to the revocation.

A grantor or contributor will not be considered responsible for the substantial and material change if:

1. The total support received from such grantor for a taxable year is 25 percent or less of the total support received by the donee organization from all sources (excluding support provided by the grantor or contributor or related parties) for the four immediately preceding taxable years; or

2. The grant or contribution qualifies as an "unusual grant."

[Reg. §§ 1.170A-9(e)(4)(v)(c), 1.509(a)-3(c)(1)]

[2] Exercising Expenditure Responsibility

[a] *Requirements*

If the foundation is required to exercise *expenditure responsibility*, this simply means that the foundation must exert all reasonable efforts and establish adequate procedures:

1. To see that the grant is spent only for the purpose for which it is made;

2. To obtain full and complete reports from the grantee organization on how the funds are spent; and

3. To make full and detailed reports on the expenditures to the IRS.

[IRC § 4945(d)(4), (h); Reg. § 53.4945-5(b)(1)]

> **Note:** Expenditure responsibility is not required if the grantee organization meets the exception requirements described above under § 6-F.03[C].

[b] *Pre-Grant Inquiry*

If expenditure responsibility must be exercised, the foundation should conduct a limited inquiry concerning the potential grantee before the grant is made. The inquiry should deal with matters such as the identity, past history and experience, management, activities, and practices of the grantee organization and should be complete enough to give reasonable assurance that the grantee will use the grant for the purposes for which it is made. [Reg. § 53.4945-5(b)(2)(i)]

[c] *Terms of Grant*

To meet the expenditure responsibility requirements, each grant must be made subject to a written commitment signed by an appropriate officer, director, or trustee of the grantee organization. This commitment must include the following agreements by the grantee:

1. To repay any amount not used for the purposes of the grant;

2. To submit full and complete annual reports to the grantor foundation on the manner in which the funds are spent and the progress made in accomplishing the purposes of the grant;

3. To keep records of receipts and expenditures and to make its books and records available to the grantor at reasonable times; and

4. Not to use any of the funds to influence legislation, to influence the outcome of elections, to carry on voter registration drives, to make grants to individuals or other organizations, or to undertake any nonexempt activity when such use of the funds would be a taxable expenditure if made directly by the foundation.

[Reg. § 53.4945-5(b)(3)]

[d] Terms of Program-Related Investment

Similarly, to meet the expenditure responsibility requirements in making a program-related investment, a private foundation must require that each investment be made subject to a written commitment signed by an appropriate officer, director, or trustee of the recipient organization. The commitment should specify the purpose of the investment and should contain an agreement by the organization:

1. To use all amounts received from the private foundation only for the purposes of the investment and to repay any amount not used for those purposes, provided that, for equity investments, the repayment is within the limitations concerning distributions to holders of equity interests;

2. To submit, at least once a year, a full and complete financial report of the type ordinarily required by commercial investors under similar circumstances and a statement that it has complied with the terms of the investment;

3. To keep adequate books and records and to make them available to the private foundation at reasonable times; and

4. Not to use any of the funds to carry on propaganda, influence legislation, influence the outcome of any public elections, carry on voter registration drives, or, when the recipient is a private foundation, make grants that do not comply with the requirements regarding individual grants or expenditure responsibility.

[Reg. § 53.4945-5(b)(4)]

[3] Certain Grants to Foreign Organizations

Grants made to foreign organizations, other than a foreign charity that is literally described in IRC § 509(a)(1), (2), or (3), are subject to the same restrictions on use of the grants as those imposed on domestic private founda-tions. These restrictions may be phrased in appropriate terms under foreign law or custom and ordinarily will be considered sufficient if an affidavit or opinion of counsel (of the grantor or grantee) is obtained stating that, under foreign law or custom, the agreement imposes the same restrictions on the use of the grant as those imposed on a domestic private foundation. [Reg. § 53.4945-5(b)(5)]

[4] Special Rules for Grants by Foreign Private Foundations

The failure of a foreign private foundation to comply with the restrictions imposed on grants will not constitute an act or failure to act that is a prohibited transaction under IRC § 4948(c). [Reg. § 53.4945-5(b)(6)]

[5] Reports from Grantees

The granting foundation must require reports on the use of the funds, compliance with the terms of the grant, and progress made by the grantee toward achieving the purpose for which the grant was made. The grantee must make an annual accounting of the funds at the end of its accounting period and must make a final report on all expenditures made from the funds in addition to the progress made toward the goals of the grant. [Reg. § 53.4945-5(c)]

[6] Reliance on Information Supplied by Grantee

In exercising expenditure responsibility with respect to its grants, a foundation may rely on adequate records or other sufficient evidence supplied by the grantee organization showing the information that the grantor must submit to the IRS. [Reg. § 53.4945-5(c)(4)]

[7] Record-Keeping Requirements

In addition to the information required when filing a return, the granting foundation must make available to the IRS at its main office each of the following items:

1. A copy of the agreement covering each expenditure responsibility grant made during the year;

2. A copy of each report received during the tax year for each grantee on any expenditure responsibility grant; and

3. A copy of each report made by the grantor's personnel or independent auditors of any audits or other investigations made during the tax year on any expenditure responsibility grant.

[Reg. § 53.4945-5(d)(3)]

[8] Violations of Expenditure Responsibility Requirements

Any diversion of grant funds (including income from an endowment grant) to a use not specified in the grant may result in that part of the grant being treated as a taxable expenditure. If the use of the funds is consistent with the purpose of the grant, the fact that a grantee does not use funds precisely as indi-cated in the original budget projection will not create a diversion of funds. If a granting foundation determines that any part of the grant has been used for improper purposes and the grantee has not previously diverted grant funds, the foundation will nevertheless not be treated as having made a taxable expenditure if it:

1. Takes all reasonable and appropriate steps either to recover the grant funds or to ensure the restoration of the diverted funds and the dedication of the other grant funds held by the grantee to the purposes of the grant; and

2. Withholds any further payments to the grantee, after being made aware that a diversion of funds may have taken place, until it has received the grantee's assurance that future diversions will not occur and has required the grantee to take extraordinary precautions to prevent further diversions from occurring.

If a foundation is considered to have made a taxable expenditure, the amount of the taxable expenditure can be the amount of the diversion, plus any further payments, or just the amount of the further payments, depending on the measure of compliance by the foundation. [Reg. § 53.4945-5(e)(1)]

[9] Grantee's Failure to Make Reports

A failure by the grantee to make the required reports will result in the grant being treated as a taxable expenditure by the grantor unless the grantor:

1. Awarded the grant according to the expenditure responsibility require-ments discussed earlier;

2. Complied with all the reporting requirements;

3. Made a reasonable effort to get the required reports; and

4. Withholds all future payments on this grant and on any other grant to the same grantee until the report is provided.

[Reg. § 53.4945-5(e)(2)]

[10] Violations by the Grantor

In addition to the circumstances discussed earlier concerning taxable expenditures, a granting foundation will be treated as making a taxable expenditure if it:

1. Fails to make a pre-grant inquiry;

2. Fails to obtain the required written commitments described earlier; or

3. Fails to make the required reports to the IRS.

[Reg. § 53.4945-5(e)(2)]

[11] Reports to the Internal Revenue Service

The foundation is required to report to the Internal Revenue Service each year on each expenditure responsibility grant any part of which remains unexpended by the grantee at any time during the year. The required reports must be submitted with the organization's annual return (Form 990-PF or Form 5227) and must include the following information on each grant:

1. The name and address of the grantee;

2. The date and amount of the grant;

3. The purpose of the grant;

4. The amounts spent by the grantee (based on the most recent report received from the grantee);

5. Whether, to the knowledge of the grantor foundation, the grantee has diverted any funds from the purpose of the grant;

6. The dates of any reports received from the grantee; and

7. The date and results of any verification of the grantee's reports undertaken by or at the direction of the grantor foundation.

[Reg. § 53.4945-5(d)]

[12] Noncharitable Expenditures — Exceptions to Taxable Expenditures

Although expenditures for noncharitable purposes do constitute taxable expenditures, the Regulations set forth a number of examples of expenditures ordinarily not treated as taxable expenditures; these include:

1. Expenditures to acquire investments that generate income to be used to further the purposes of the organization;

2. Reasonable expenses related to acquiring these investments;

3. Tax payment;

4. Expenses that qualify as allowable deductions in figuring the tax on unrelated business income;

5. Any payments that are qualifying distributions;

6. Any deductions allowed in arriving at taxable net investment income;

7. Reasonable expenditures to evaluate, acquire, modify, and dispose of program-related investments; and

8. Business expenses of the recipient of a program-related investment.

However, payment of unreasonable administrative expenses, including wages, consultant fees, and other fees for services performed, ordinarily will be taxable expenditures unless made by the foundation in the good-faith belief that the amounts were reasonable and were consistent with ordinary business care and prudence. [Reg. § 53.4945-6(b)]

[F] Grants for Noncharitable Purposes

A private foundation cannot make a grant for any purpose other than one described in IRC § 170(c)(2)(B). Permitted purposes are religious, charitable, scientific, literary, or educational purposes; the fostering of national or international amateur sports competition (but only if no part of the activities involves providing athletic facilities or equipment); and the prevention of cruelty to children or animals. These are the purposes for which section 501(c)(3) organizations may be organized, and they must be operated exclusively for these purposes. Grants for nonpermitted purposes are taxable expenditures. [IRC § 4945(d)(5)]

Accordingly, a private foundation may not make a grant to an organization that is not described in section 501(c)(3) unless making the grant itself is a direct charitable act or a program-related investment or the grantor is reasonably assured that the grant will be used exclusively for the purposes of an organization described here. If a private foundation makes a grant (other than a transfer of assets resulting from any liquidation, merger, redemption, recapitalization, organization, reorganization, or other adjustment to any non-section 501(c)(3) organization), the grantor is reasonably assured that the grant will be used exclusively for appropriate purposes (described earlier) only if the grantee organization agrees to keep these funds in a separate fund dedicated to such purposes. In addition, the grantor must comply with the expenditure responsibility requirements discussed earlier. If a private foundation makes a transfer of assets under any liquidation, merger, or the like to any person, the transferred assets will not be considered to be used exclusively for section 170(c)(2)(B) purposes unless the assets are transferred to a section 501(c)(3) organization. [Reg. § 53.4945-6(c)]

CHAPTER 7

GRANTMAKING

Grantmaking is the essence of the family foundation and the primary benefit of selecting a private foundation over other philanthropic entities. Too often, family foundations simply divide up their available grant funds among the participating family members to be disbursed by them among charities of their choice, almost as if they held the foundation's checkbook. This is an old-fashioned approach and one which should be discouraged. The authors recommend a more professional and responsible grantmaking process, as outlined in this chapter.

§7.01   INTRODUCTION

Grantmaking is the most visible and most important function of the family foundation. This chapter deals with the rules and practical issues involved in making grants. The distributions made by the foundation represent the mission, values, and goals of the organization and the family. However, making effective grants is not easy for several reasons:

- *Family foundations are subject to restrictions in grantmaking imposed by the Internal Revenue Code.* The foundation and its managers are subject to severe penalties if the distribution rules are violated. Therefore, the grants committee and foundation board must understand the purposes for which grants can be made and the permissible recipients of those grants.

- *The foundation has the practical challenge of sorting through the grant applications it receives once the charitable public knows about the foundation.* The funds seekers may request multiyear grants for capital campaigns, start-up funds for new organizations, operating funds for existing organizations, or scholarship awards. The applicants may represent religious, health care, social services, literary, arts, or other charitable organizations. The family foundation must establish a method of prioritizing and responding to these requests.

- *The foundation is responsible for awarding, overseeing, and documenting grants in a manner that complies with fiduciary and legal duties and for reporting to the government and the public about the operation of the foundation.* This requires that the foundation collect, maintain, and evaluate information about the organizations requesting and receiving grants.

§7.02   QUALIFYING DISTRIBUTIONS

[A]   Overview of Qualifying Distributions

Private foundations, including family foundations, are required to make minimum distributions for charitable purposes each year. The first step in mastering the grantmaking process is understanding the foundation's legal obligations in grantmaking. There are three important rules:

1. *A foundation may distribute funds only for charitable purposes.* These distributions may be made to charitable organizations or to organizations that are not recognized charities.

2. *A foundation must distribute a minimum amount annually.* This figure is approximately equal to five percent of the foundation's investment assets.

3. *A foundation is required to report its activities to the Internal Revenue Service on an annual basis.* It is also required to share information about its operation with the general public upon request.

A private foundation must monitor its distributions to ensure that it makes sufficient qualifying distributions during the year to avoid an excise tax.[1] While most of the expenditures made by a foundation are considered qualifying distributions, some are not. Appropriate distributions include:[2]

- Grants made to most charitable organizations recognized by the Internal Revenue Service as section 501(c)(3) public charities;

- Grants made to noncharitable organizations or individuals for charitable purposes;

- Payments made for the foundation's reasonable and necessary administrative expenses;

- Payments made to purchase assets needed and used by the foundation in carrying out its tax-exempt purpose;

- Funds set aside for allowable distribution purposes; and

- Funds allocated to program-related investments.

[B] Outright Distributions to Certain Charitable Organizations

The most common recipient of a grant from a family foundation is a domestic (U.S.) charitable organization. While most section 501(c)(3) organizations are qualified recipients, there are section 501(c)(3)s that do not qualify. The foundation manager must understand how to clearly identify the charities that are qualified or safe harbors for distributions.

[1] Domestic Charities

[a] *Domestic Charities to Which Distributions Can Be Made*

A private foundation can safely make distributions to the following types of domestic charities: traditional charitable organizations, government organizations and agencies, private operating foundations, some private foundations,

---

[1] *See* Chapters 5 and 6 for a discussion of penalties.
[2] IRC §4942(g)(1).

and organizations controlled by the private foundation or disqualified persons to the foundation.

- *Traditional charities.* Traditional charities described in section 170(c)(2)(B) of the Internal Revenue Code (IRC) are qualified recipients when grants are made for charitable purposes. This group includes charities "organized and operated exclusively for religious, charitable, scientific, literary, or educational purposes, or to foster national or international amateur sports competition . . . or for the prevention of cruelty to children or animals."[3] This group of traditional charities does not include private foundations and charitable organizations controlled by private foundations or their disqualified persons. Disqualified persons are discussed in more detail in Chapter 6.

- *Government entities and their agencies.* The federal government, state governments, and local governments are permissible recipients so long as the distribution is for charitable purposes.[4]

- *Private operating foundations.* Private operating foundations provide or deliver charitable services, rather than making grants to organizations that provide charitable services.[5] Although the foundation is classified as "private" because it has a single source of funding rather than public support for its operations, it is treated like a "public" foundation for tax purposes because its primary function is to deliver charitable services.[6] Think of the difference this way. A private foundation will make a grant to a homeless shelter to meet the needs of homeless women; a private operating foundation will manage and staff the facility that shelters homeless women. Private operating foundations are discussed in more detail in Chapter 2 and Appendix 2-C.

- *Non-operating private foundations.* Non-operating private foundations may also be qualified recipients when the grant is spent by the grantee foundation within a specified period and is made for charitable purposes.[7] The rules are designed to prevent private foundations from shifting funds from one to another without putting the funds to charitable use. Therefore, distributions to private foundations are considered "qualifying" only if three tests are met:

   1. The receiving private foundation must distribute the funds for a purpose that meets the "qualifying distribution" test by the tax year-end of the year following the year in which the grant funds are received;

---

[3] IRC §170(c)(2)(B).

[4] Reg. §53.4945-5(a)(4).

[5] Private operating foundations are defined in IRC §4942(j)(3). There is a factual or mathematical test that defines a foundation as designed to ensure that the majority of the foundation's assets are devoted to this purpose and that income is being used for this purpose.

[6] The Treasury Regulations at §§53.4942(b)-1, -2, and -3 provide an extensive analysis of private operating foundations beyond the scope of this book.

[7] IRC §4942(g)(1)(A)(ii).

2. The receiving foundation must make this distribution in addition to any minimum distribution requirements that it has; and

3. The donor private foundation must obtain and keep records reflecting the fact that the receiving foundation has distributed the funds in a way and within a time frame that qualify.[8]

Example 1: If the McCoy Foundation received a $25,000 grant from the Miree Foundation in 2006, it must distribute the full $25,000 by the end of the 2007 tax year in addition to its annual required distributable amount. The McCoy Foundation cannot keep the money and cannot use it to meet its own distribution requirements.

Example 2: Consider a second example shown in detail at Table 7–1. The Clark Foundation, your family foundation, made a grant to the Smith Foundation, another private foundation, in 2006 in the amount of $50,000. Both foundations are on a calendar tax year ending December 31. Assume that the Smith Foundation had a minimum distribution requirement of $252,800 in 2006 and distributed only $250,000. The Smith Foundation will not be treated as having distributed any of the grant received from the Clark Foundation in 2006. In 2007, the Smith Foundation had a minimum distribution requirement of $270,000. In order to meet the distribution requirement associated with the grant from the Clark Foundation, the Smith Foundation must distribute $270,000, representing its 2007 minimum distribution requirement; $2,800, representing the prior year's deficit; and

TABLE 7-1
Analysis of Recipient Private Foundation's Distribution Requirements in Year Following Receipt of Grant from Another Private Foundation

	2006	2007
Grant received from Clark Foundation	$50,000	
Minimum distribution requirement	$252,800	$270,000
Actual distributions	$250,000	
Amount required for distribution		$270,000[*]
		$2,800[**]
		$50,000[***]
		$322,800

[*] The minimum distribution requirement for the current year
[**] The undistributed amount from the prior year
[***] The amount of the grant from the Clark Foundation

---

[8] *See* Reg. §53.4942(a)-3(c)(1)(ii) for details on the information required to document proper distribution of the funds from the receiving private foundation.

$50,000, representing the amount of the grant from the Clark Foundation for a total of $322,800.

In the event that the private foundation receiving the grant from another private foundation does not meet the distribution requirements by the close of the tax year following the grant, the distributing private foundation must add the undistributed amount to its minimum distribution requirements for that year.

- *Organizations controlled by the foundation or disqualified persons to the foundation.* Organizations controlled by the private foundation or its disqualified persons may be qualified recipients where the foundation makes a timely distribution of the funds in addition to meeting its own distribution requirements.[9] The recipient charitable organization is considered "controlled" where it can be compelled to distribute or not distribute funds because of the voting control of the private foundation or persons that are disqualified persons to the foundation.[10] The rule is designed to ensure that private foundation money is spent for charitable purposes, rather than shifted from foundation to foundation. A timely distribution is defined as use of the funds by the end of the tax year following the year of receipt of the grant.

The donor private foundation must maintain records showing that the recipient has complied with the distribution rules. If the controlled organization does not make the distributions within the appropriate time period, the granting private foundation must include the undistributed amount as an additional distribution requirement for its tax year.

[b] Determining When an Organization Is a Qualified Organization

The logical question for a family foundation grantmaker to raise is "How do you tell the difference between a qualified organization and a nonqualified organization?" The best way to sort out charitable organizations, and the safest way to document a good-faith effort to comply with the distribution rules, is to ask for the receiving organization's tax determination letter. A tax determination letter is the equivalent of a birth certificate given to a charity following review and award of tax-exempt status. The letter states the date of creation and the Code section under which the organization qualified for exempt status.

Reading the tax determination letter can be challenging for the uninitiated. There are at least three ways the Internal Revenue Code defines charities. The classifications include (1) organizations that are exempt from paying federal tax; (2) organizations that qualify for income, gift, or estate tax deductions; and (3) the form of the charitable organization.

---

[9] IRC §4942(g)(1)(A)(i).

[10] *See* §6.03[B][1] *supra* for a full discussion of how to define a disqualified person.

[i]   ***Organizations exempt from payment of federal tax.***   Organizations that are exempt for federal tax purposes are sometimes referred to as section 501(c) organizations. The section 501(c) classification is the most common reference and includes traditional charities as well as a number of organizations that are not considered charities but are simply tax exempt. Do not assume that because an entity is tax exempt, it is a qualified recipient of private foundation funds; section 501(c)(3) organizations are the only tax-exempt organizations that have charitable purposes. Table 7–2 lists the variety of organizations that are exempt from federal taxation under section 501(c).

TABLE 7-2
Types of Organizations Exempt from Income Tax Under IRC §501(c)

Code Section	Type of Exempt Organization
§501(c)(1)	Certain corporations organized by an act of Congress as an agency of the U.S. government
§501(c)(2)	Corporations organized to hold title to real property, collect income, and turn the proceeds over to an exempt organization
§501(c)(3)	Traditional charities, which are organizations that are "organized and operated exclusively for religious, charitable, scientific, testing for public safety, literary, or educational purposes, or to foster national or international amateur sports competition (but only if no part of its activities involve the provision of athletic facilities or equipment), or for the prevention of cruelty to children or animals"
§501(c)(4)	Civic leagues (social welfare organizations)
§501(c)(5)	Labor, agricultural, or horticultural organizations
§501(c)(6)	Business leagues, chambers of commerce, real estate boards, boards of trade, and professional football leagues
§501(c)(7)	Recreational or social clubs
§501(c)(8)	Fraternal benefit societies, orders, or associations
§501(c)(9)	Voluntary employees' benefit societies
§501(c)(10)	Domestic fraternal benefit societies, orders, or associations
§501(c)(11)	Teachers' retirement funds
§501(c)(12)	Benevolent life insurance associations
§501(c)(13)	Cemetery companies
§501(c)(14)	Credit unions
§501(c)(15)	Mutual insurance companies
§501(c)(16)	Corporations organized to finance crop operations
§501(c)(17)	Supplemental unemployment compensation benefit trusts
§501(c)(18)	Employee-funded pension trusts
§501(c)(19)	Veterans' organizations
§501(c)(20)	Group legal services organizations
§501(c)(21)	Black lung trusts

TABLE 7-2. CONTINUED

Code Section	Type of Exempt Organization
§501(c)(22)	ERISA trusts
§501(c)(23)	Pre-1880 veterans' organizations
§501(c)(24)	Trusts described in §4049 of ERISA
§501(c)(25)	Real estate holding companies for multiple beneficiaries
§501(c)(26)	State medical care organizations
§501(c)(27)	State workers' compensation organizations

[ii] *Organizations that qualify for an income, gift, or estate tax deduction.* Nonprofits deductible on the donor's income tax return are defined in IRC §170(c)(2)(B) while charitable entities deductible for gift tax purposes[11] and estate tax purposes[12] are found in sections 2522(a) and 2055(a), respectively. These Code sections define qualified deductions for individuals.

[iii] *Form of charitable organization.* Not all charitable organizations are created equal; the class of the charity is established in IRC §509(a). Section 509(a) begins with the premise that every charity is classified as a private foundation (generally thought of as the lowest form of charitable life because of the excise taxes on investment income and the rules and regulations attached to its operation) unless it meets one of the four exceptions listed in IRC §509(a). Those exceptions include:

- IRC §509(a)(1) These entities are *traditional charities*, such as churches, schools, hospitals, and other public charities and government units.

- IRC §509(a)(2) These charities are *publicly supported organizations*, meaning that at least one-third of the organization's income comes from public contributions, ticket sales, memberships, or related businesses and not more than one-third of its annual support comes from investment income. A community foundation is a good example of a publicly supported charity.

- IRC §509(a)(3) *Supporting organizations* are entities formed to support a public charity. For example, a supporting organization

---

[11] IRC §2522(a).
[12] IRC §2055(a).

may support a school, a museum, a hospital, or a specified group of these nonprofits. This type of entity exists solely to make grants to or in support of the specified qualified charity.

- IRC §509(a)(4) This group is reserved for *organizations that test for public safety*. It is rare that the family foundation would make a grant to a section 509(a)(4) organization.

Review the applicant's tax determination letter before making a grant to determine whether it is a traditional public charity or a private foundation that may carry more stringent grant and follow-up requirements. Traditional public charities will have a tax determination stating the organization is "not a private foundation"; the letter will then provide the tax code subsection under §509 that exempts it from private foundation status. Some public charities are not required to file for qualification as a charitable organization and are exempt because of their form. These include churches, hospitals, and certain public schools. And, of course, governments and their entities may not have tax determination letters. If the organization does not have a determination status, ask its representative to state in writing that it has no letter because it is exempt from filing. Place that letter in your files in lieu of the determination notice.

If there is a question about the tax-exempt status of an organization, you can check Internal Revenue Service (IRS) Publication 78. This publication is available on the Internet through the IRS web site[13] or by writing or calling the IRS to request a printed copy. To be safe in relying on the tax determination letter, you should also ask for a statement from the organization that the tax-exempt status has not been revoked, or changed, since the date of issuance. While the IRS publishes the list of revoked status organizations weekly in its *Internal Revenue Bulletin*, also published at its web site, most charities do not have the staff to regularly review and compare those lists to the foundation's potential grant list.

[2] Distributions for Charitable Purposes

In addition to making distributions to recognized public charities, a private foundation may make a distribution to a nonrecognized charity or individual for a charitable purpose.[14] This means that a private foundation may make a distribution to an organization or individual for religious, charitable, scientific, literary, or education purposes, or to foster amateur sports, or for the prevention of cruelty to children and animals. Where the foundation ventures beyond traditional charity, it must comply with additional administrative requirements

---

[13] The IRS web site can be located at *www.irs.gov*.
[14] Charitable purposes are defined in IRC §170(c)(2)(B).

called *expenditure responsibility*; if the foundation does not discharge expenditure responsibility, the distribution will be treated as a taxable expenditure.[15] Documenting grants to nontraditional charities can be difficult; for that reason, many private foundations have decided to make grants only to charities without the burden of expenditure responsibility.

Sometimes the foundation's corporate or trust organizing document restricts the foundation in the types of grants that it can make. For example, the document may specify that the foundation may make distributions only to qualified public charities. Review your foundation's organizing documents to make sure that the distributions you plan to make are authorized. If you choose to expand the limits authorized by your charter, see your legal counsel to draft an amendment that reflects your intentions.

[3] Distributions to Non-domestic Charities

International grantmaking is increasing as the media, the Internet, and current events make global issues more visible. The interest in funding international charitable needs is supported by the American Association of Fundraising Counsel Trust for Philanthropy's annual Giving USA study reporting that gifts to non-domestic charities from individuals, bequests, foundations, and corporations totaled $6.4 billion in 2005.[16] This figure represented a 15.6 percent increase over 2004.[17] This increased interest is likely the result of heightened visibility of global issues through media coverage, the Internet, travel access, and the country's diverse population.

[a] *Rules on Non-domestic Grantmaking*

Private foundations may make grants to foreign organizations as long as the purpose and use of those distributions fall within the scope of the charitable purposes discussed earlier. The foundation's duty to document the grants varies depending on the status of the foreign charity. Some overseas charities have qualified U.S. charities which serve OS their representatives. In these cases, making a grant is easy since the funds can be paid directly to the U.S. organization with tax-exempt status. Other charities, however, have no domestic representative. In these instances, the foundation must make a good-faith effort to document that the organization would have qualified if located in the United States and that it will spend the funds for the purposes intended.[18] Table 7–3 describes the types of foreign charities a family foundation may consider as grant recipients and the documentation required for each.

---

[15] Expenditure responsibility is discussed in more detail at §6.07[D] *supra* and later in this chapter at §7.09[B] *infra*.

[16] Blum, Debra E.and Holly Hall, *Donations to Social-Service and Environmental Groups Rose in 2005*, The Chronicle of Philanthropy, Vol. 18, No. 18 (June 29, 2006).

[17] *Id.*

[18] Reg. §53.4945-5(a)(5); Rev. Proc. 92-94, 1992-2 C.B. 507.

TABLE 7-3
Types of Foreign Charities Qualified to Receive Grant Distributions

Type of Foreign Charity	Example	Safety Factor
Qualified U.S. charity with non-U.S. programs	Red Cross	Safe, since grant is made to IRS-qualified U.S.-charity
Foreign charity that receives substantial support from U.S. citizens and is qualified by IRS as charitable organization		Safe, since grant is made to IRS-qualified charity
Organization recognized as qualified foreign charity by executive order under 22 U.S.C. §288[19]	World Health Organization, United Nations	Safe, since grant is made to qualified charity
Foreign government	England, France, China	Safe so long as grant is made only for charitable purposes and cannot be used for other purposes; get legal help in drafting the grant agreement and follow-up
Foreign charity that would qualify as public domestic charity if that foreign charity applied for exempt status[20]		Less safe; documentation of this "would have been" status is made through a good-faith determination, which can be by an affidavit from the receiving organization that it is engaged in charitable activities or by an affidavit from an attorney practicing in this area
Non-qualified organization receiving grant for charitable purposes[21]		Least safe; foundation bears the burden of establishing charitable purpose and use

Documenting and monitoring grants to foreign organizations are further complicated by language and communication barriers. Grant recipients should always be asked to sign grant agreements governing use of funds, and the foundation should monitor use of the funds. If this sounds much like exercising expenditure responsibility (as described in §§6.07[D] and 7.09 [B]),[22] it is. In an

[19] Reg. §53.4945-5(a)(4)(iii).
[20] Reg. §§53.4945-5(a)(5), 53.4942(a)-3(a)(6).
[21] Reg. §53.4945-5(b)(5).
[22] On April 18, 2001, the Council on Foundations obtained a general information letter from the IRS confirming that private foundations could exercise expenditure responsibility in making grants to nonqualified foreign charities instead of determining that the charity would qualify as a 501(c)(3) if it

Information Letter dated April 18, 2001, issued to the Council on Foundations, and in a Memorandum on International Grants and Activities issued January 31, 2005,[23] the IRS confirmed that foundations that exercise expenditure responsibility in making grants to nondomestic organizations will have met their responsibility and need not undertake an independent analysis of their potential tax status.[24] Specifically, the IRS stated that a grant from a private foundation to a foreign grantee will not be a taxable expenditure as long as:

1. The private foundation makes a good-faith determination that the foreign organization is the equivalent of a public charity. In these cases, expenditure responsibility is not required;

2. The private foundation makes a good-faith determination that the foreign organization is the equivalent of a private foundation and exercises expenditure responsibility (including obtaining records verifying that the recipient distributes the full amount of the grant by the end of the organization's next tax year);

3. The recipient is treated as neither of these types of entities, and the foundation exercises expenditure responsibility (including obtaining records verifying that the recipient distributes the full amount of the grant by the end of the organization's next tax year).

Some foundations initiate an effort to make a good-faith determination of the recipient organization's status but abandon their inquiry when they run into language or cultural differences that make the inquiry difficult. The ruling makes it clear that an exercise of expenditure responsibility will overcome the need to conduct or conclude a good-faith examination of the charity.

Foundations that have an interest in international grantmaking may need to hire a consultant or university professor familiar with the language and customs of the country in which the organizations are located to facilitate pre-grant discussions and post-grant documentation. The safest course of action for a family foundation is to make distributions only to foreign charities recognized by the IRS.

It should be noted that a foundation making foreign grants might be required to withhold tax from the amounts disbursed to the foreign grantee.[25] In 2001, the IRS amended its tax withholding rules for various kinds of foreign

---

applied for that status. For a copy of the letter, go to *http://www.cof.org/government/LegalService/ index.htm* to the item entitled "Memo — IRS Streamlines International Grantmaking."

[23] ILM 200504031.

[24] *www.cof.org/government/irsletter.pdf.* A good place to go to get the latest legal news on foundation matters is the Council on Foundations legal reference site at *http://www.cof.org/government/ LegalService/index.htm.*

[25] Reg. §§1.1441-1; 1.443-1.

payments, including grants. The amendment apparently required foundation managers to withhold taxes on *some* grants, scholarships, and prizes paid to foreign organizations and non-U.S. citizens.

This requirement came into play when grant funds were used for activities in the United States. For example, consider a foundation grant paid to a non-U.S. organization for a specific research project, with some of the grant funds to be used for travel to the U.S. for conferences, meetings with colleagues, or other project expenses within the United States. Under these circumstances, the foundation may be required to withhold taxes on the U.S.-based costs, provided it can clearly establish what portion of the grant was used for such purposes. If the foundation cannot determine the U.S. portion of the grant, a literal application of the governing law may require it to withhold taxes on the entire grant.

Where withholding is required, the foundation must normally hold back 30 percent of the grant (or 30 percent of the U.S. portion thereof, if that can be clearly established), and pay this over to the IRS. For some categories of grants, certain scholarships and fellowships, for example, this rate is reduced to 14 percent, and some tax treaties also provide for reduced rates of withholding. If a foundation is required to withhold but fails to do so, it may be subject to interest and penalties in addition to the amount of tax in question.

Even if a grant will clearly involve some U.S.-based expenditures, the withholding requirement may nevertheless be excused if one of several specific exceptions applies. These exceptions can be tricky, however. For example, some tax treaties specifically provide exemptions from the withholding requirement for various classes of payments, including certain payments to nonprofit organizations. Where a foundation wants to rely on a treaty exemption, it must obtain a completed IRS Form W-8BEN from the grant recipient. That form will not be valid unless it includes the recipient's U.S. Taxpayer Identification Number.

Another exception applies where the foreign grantee is described in IRC §501(c)(3) (or one of the other tax-exempt categories in 501(c)). Under the Regulations, however, this exemption is applicable only if the granting foundation obtains from the grant recipient a completed IRS Form W-8EXP; this Form also must include a U.S. Taxpayer Identification Number, plus either a determination letter from the IRS or an opinion from a U.S. attorney concluding that the recipient is described in Code §501(c). Unlike other foreign grant issues, the granting foundation cannot avoid the withholding problem by simply exercising expenditure responsibility.

In many cases, obviously, a foreign grantee will not have a U.S. Taxpayer Identification Number, an IRS determination letter, or other items necessary to qualify for one of these withholding exemptions. Where this is the case, the foundation may assist the grantee in filing IRS Form SS-4 to obtain a Taxpayer Identification Number or securing an opinion of counsel, but this will obviously cause delay as well as added expense.

A recent private letter ruling promises relief to some foundations faced with the possibility that a foreign grant may be subject to withholding. Priv. Ltr. Rul. 200529004 took a new approach to the subject. There, the IRS found that withholding would not be required on a grant to a foreign nonprofit non-governmental membership or organization for a specific project. That project will require participants to make presentations at a number of international conferences and seminars, including some held in the United States. The grantee would use grant funds to pay the travel and other expenses incurred in that connection. Notwithstanding the view expressed in its Regulations, the IRS held that withholding would not be required on the facts presented.

The IRS reasoned that the grant constituted a "gift" that was excludible from the recipient's income for tax purposes under IRC §102(a) and Rev. Rul. 2003-12, 2003-1 C.B. 283. Section 1441 provides for withholding on payments of taxable amounts to non-U.S. individuals and partnerships, while §1442 imposes a corresponding responsibility on payments to foreign corporations. Since these grant payments were nontaxable gifts, they were not subject to withholding under either IRC §1441 or IRC §1442. The IRS cautioned the foundation that If the grantee is a foreign trust that is not described in IRC §501(c)(3), the foundation would be required to report the grant on Form 3520 pursuant to the rules of IRC §6048(a).

Of course, Priv. Ltr. Rul. 200529004, like all private letter rulings, is specifically directed only to the foundation that requested it and, under IRC §6110(k)(3), may not be used or cited as precedent. One hopes that the IRS will amend the Regulations to clarify the applicability of withholding to foundation grants. In the meantime, a foundation which seeks to avoid withholding obligations on the basis of the principle applied in Priv. Ltr. Rul. 200529004 should be careful to conform as closely as possible to the factual assumptions specified in the ruling. Thus, the granting foundation should be sure that the grantee is a corporation or partnership, and not a trust, and that it is not engaged in a trade or business in the United States. And there should be a written grant agreement that clearly identifies the charitable objectives of the grant and ties those objectives to the charitable purposes of the granting foundation. The grant agreement should also provide that the grantee will not perform any services or provide any goods for the granting foundation in return for the grant.

[b] Compliance

What can a family foundation do to ensure that it complies with the law and to protect itself from such interest and penalties? Despite the complications involved, there are several easy steps that can help avoid trouble. First, as in so many other areas, a well-drafted grant agreement can provide a comforting measure of protection. The withholding requirement is not applicable to grants that are used exclusively for activities conducted outside the United States. A foundation can easily provide in its grant agreement that the grant funds will be used exclusively outside the United States and that no part of such funds will be expended within the United States or for travel or other uses inside the United States, and thereby ensure that withholding will not be required. Such a clause should be included routinely where the foundation regularly makes grants to nonresident aliens (i.e., non-U.S. citizens who do not live in the United States.) or to foreign corporations or trusts, for use outside the United States. (Of course, this will not help if the foundation has actual knowledge that the funds will be used in the United States despite the terms of an agreement.)

If it is clear at the outset that all or part of the grant funds in question *will* be used in the United States, the withholding requirement applies and a grant agreement will not be able to help. In this case, however, it may be feasible to make two separate grants — one for the foreign portion thereof, protected by a grant agreement specifying the exclusively foreign usage, and a second grant for the U.S. portion alone. The foundation's withholding obligation will then be limited to the second, smaller amount.

> **Example:** Family Foundation makes a grant to the physics department of a British university for a research project. Although most of the research will be conducted in a laboratory in England, the project will culminate in the presentation of a paper describing the project at a scientific conference to be held in Massachusetts. The foundation can make one grant for the project research, covered by a grant agreement specifying that the grant funds will be used exclusively for activities conducted outside the United States. A second grant would cover the costs of travel to Massachusetts for the conference, and only this amount would be subject to withholding.

Family foundations may make an occasional foreign grant without really considering whether or not they might be required to withhold taxes on all or a part of the funds paid out. If they were fully aware of their obligations, many foundations might prefer to avoid the problem by declining any grant request that might involve financing activities by foreign grantees within the United States. This would be a potentially serious limitation given the prominence of U.S. institutions in so many important program areas. The Council on Foundations has expressed its concern about this possibility and is working with IRS and Treasury Department officials to suggest reconsideration of the government's position on this issue:

> *These rules are lengthy — comprising literally hundreds of pages of Regulations — and they are also complicated. If your foundation makes foreign grants, even on an occasional basis, you may wish to have your tax adviser review these withholding requirements and determine how your grant program is affected.*

[c] The Complications in Grantmaking After September 11, 2001

The terrorist activities of September 11, 2001, and the ensuing "War on Terrorism" have impacted every aspect of life in this country — the financial markets, business and leisure travel, daily office commutes, the delivery of news, and the way we plan our business and personal lives. Not surprisingly, 9/11 and its aftermath have also affected the way family foundations make grants. Just days after the attacks on New York's World Trade Center buildings and the Pentagon, President Bush issued Executive Order 13224, prohibiting U.S. entities from providing financial and other support to terrorist organizations. This was quickly followed by passage of the United and Strengthening America by Providing Appropriate Tools Required to Intercept and Obstruct Terrorism Act of 2001 (the USA PATRIOT Act). While the primary thrust of these initiatives was to shut down financial transactions providing aid and support to terrorist units, the new laws and regulations have far reaching implications for U.S. foundations.

While U.S. laws imposed criminal penalties on individuals or companies who supported terrorist activities prior to 9/11 (for example, the Anti-Terrorism and Effective Death Penalty Act of 1996), the events of September 11, 2001, prompted an expansion of these policies through a string of executive branch, legislative, and regulatory rules aimed at financial transactions. These provisions, which imposed broad and far-reaching restrictions on financial support of known and potential terrorists, impact foundation grantmaking both in the United States and abroad. The key bodies of law and regulation are summarized below:[26]

- *Executive Order 13224.* On September 14, 2001, President Bush issued Executive Order 13224, prohibiting any individual (or entity) from funding an individual or entity associated with terrorism. The directives are broad, encompassing both intentional and inadvertent support of terrorist operations. This order, based on the President's authority under the International Emergency Economic Powers Act and the National Emergencies Act, authorized the government to freeze the assets of any individual or business in violation of the order.

- *The USA PATRIOT Act.*[27] The USA PATRIOT Act was enacted in late 2001 to add enforcement mechanisms to new and existing laws attacking terrorist financing. The USA PATRIOT Act imposes fines and criminal penalties for

---

[26] Foundations seeking more information and a more detailed explanation of Executive Order 13224, the USA PATRIOT Act, the IRS Regulations, and the Treasury's Best Practices Guidelines should consider the following online resources: Schneiderman, Martin B., "Seeking a Safe Harbor," *Foundation News and Commentary* (May/June 2004), pp. 35-41; *COF Comments to the IRS on International Grantmaking* (August 2003), available online: *www.cof.org/files/Documents/Legal/Treasury_Comments_06.03.pdf; The Handbook on Counter-Terrorism Measures: What U.S. Nonprofits and Grantmakers Need to Know*, available online: *www.cof.org/files/Documents/Publications/2004/CountertTerrorismHandbook.pdf.*

[27] Pub.L. No. 107-56, 115 Stat. 272 (2001).

any individual or entity providing support or financial resources to Foreign Terrorist Organizations (FTOs) and establishes civil actions and penalties against any entity providing terrorist support.[28]

- *Tax Law and Regulations.* The Tax Code and Regulations prohibit private foundations (and public charities) from making distributions for non-charitable purposes; these include distributions supporting terrorism. Penalties include loss of tax-exempt status, and for private foundations, excise taxes on distributions to organizations engaged in funding terrorism. In 2003, Congress amended IRC §501(p) to direct an automatic (and retroactive) suspension of a charity's tax-exempt status if it is designated as a terrorist organization.

- *Treasury's "Anti-Terrorist Financing Guidelines: Voluntary Best Practices for U.S.-Based Charities."*[29] On November 7, 2002, the U.S. Treasury Department issued a set of antiterrorist financing guidelines in the form of a set of "voluntary best practices" for U.S.-based charities designed to enable compliance with Executive Order 13224 and the USA PATRIOT Act. The guidelines suggest extensive compliance activities designed to screen the activities of the recipient organization, the individuals associated with that recipient, and even the re-distribution of funds through subcontractors or re-granting. The guidelines are not law, however. Just as difficult, compliance with the guidelines provides no guarantee of conformance or protection against asset seizure.

- *IRS Memorandum on International Grants and Activities.*[30] This legal memorandum stresses the use of expenditure responsibility for those overseas grants not made through qualified domestic charities. It provides an excellent summary of grantmaking standards.

Foundations face two major challenges in complying with the antiterrorist funding laws, both of which relate to identifying the bad guys:

1. Foundations must screen grant recipients, their staffs, their boards and other key persons against the lists of known terrorists on the Office of Foreign Assets Control's (OFAC) Specially Designated Nationals (SDN) list and other published lists of terrorist entities and individuals; and

2. The screening process must also identify individuals who are providing assistance to named terrorists or who are "otherwise associated with" named terrorists.

---

[28] Section 224 of the USA PATRIOT Act contained a December 31, 2005 sunset provision affecting most elements of the Act. On March 9, 2006, President Bush signed H.R. 3199, the USA PATRIOT Improvement and Reauthorization Act of 2005, extending the key provisions of the USA PATRIOT Act which were set to expire at the end of 2005.

[29] The full text is provided in Appendix A.

[30] ILM 200504031 dated January 26, 2004, published January 28, 2005.

Each foundation must develop its own plan to avoid problem transactions — there are no safe harbor rules protecting grantmakers. While an assumption can be made that compliance with the Treasury Department's voluntary guidelines will provide at least a good-faith defense, the Executive Order 13224, the USA PATRIOT Act, the Internal Revenue Code, and the best practices guide provide no such assurance. A foundation making a grant to an entity later determined to be a terrorist platform is likely to suffer the penalties.

While the antiterrorist legislation is generally associated with foreign grantmaking, all foundations, even those that restrict grants to qualified U.S.-based charities, are at risk of violating terrorist funding laws. The antiterrorist enforcement provisions restrict charities from making grants to organizations or individuals on published lists, those who support them, and anyone associated with them. That's a fairly wide net. Several U.S.-based charities have already been identified as terrorist organizations, raising the possibility there are other, not-yet-identified qualified charities with terrorist ties.

[d] Should the Family Foundation Make Grants to International Organizations?

Although the foundation can make cross-border grants, should it do so? The short answer is "maybe." As businesses move to a global sales and services platform, and U.S. charities takes on global issues, it is only logical that grantmaking will expand to follow those investments. Even so, foray into foreign grant programs is only appropriate when it fits the foundation's grantmaking goals and objectives, its assets, and its experience. An organization such as the Bill and Melinda Gates Foundation, with more than $24 billion in assets and years of experience in global grantmaking, can easily manage foreign programs, while a $1 million foundation without staff may be required to hire translators, consultants, and overseers to attempt a similar program.

When weighing the foundation's role in international grants, consider the following questions:

- Does the grant fit the overall goals and objectives of the foundation, and is the overseas grant the best way to accomplish these goals?

- Is a grant to a foreign organization the only way to accomplish the foundation's objectives, or is there a domestic representative that can manage the grant, or a domestic organization that will shepherd the funds? An increasing number of U.S. organizations conduct activities abroad. The foundation board members may want to serve on the board of one of these organizations to learn more about issues that arise with deployment of funds abroad.

- What is the cost ratio of the expenses for oversight and reporting (including tax or administrative advice) in relation to grant dollars?

- Would a program-related investment create a better result than a grant?

- What is the probability that the funds will be used for the intended purposes and will accomplish the expected goals?

- What is the risk the grant will be classified as a taxable expenditure? Does the foundation have the resources to make an equivalency determination or meet the expenditure responsibility rules? Can the foundation effectively monitor the use of the grant?

If the foundation can answer these questions easily, and the process is not onerous, international grants may add a new dimension to the foundation's influence. If it cannot manage the process without extensive cost and anguish, it should look for another way have an overseas impact. Either way, the foundation board and grantmaking committee will benefit from exploring the possibilities.

[e]   Managing the Risk in Cross-Border Grants

There are several ways to manage risk in cross-border grants. Consider these steps to assess the foundation's exposure and remedial actions.

- *Conduct a risk assessment of the foundation's grantmaking activities.* Begin with a review of the foundation's grant policies. (If the foundation has no policies, now is the time to develop them.) Some areas of grantmaking, such as arts, health care, and educational organizations — especially when those are local and well-known entities — may not be likely terrorist platforms. Other grants, such as those addressing international relief, aid, and health care initiatives, provide more likely potential for terrorist activities. Each foundation should adopt policies that fit its budget, staff, and oversight capabilities. This may mean restricting the geographic reach of its grants, narrowing funding purposes, limiting grants to one-year awards so that an annual review is made of the recipient charity, purchasing (and using) screening software, or hiring third-party reviews for grants above a certain size.

- *Get a legal review.* Ask legal counsel to review the foundation's grantmaking policies and grant agreement and to then make recommendations to protect the foundation. Talk to charities operating in overseas locations to get recommendations on firms and individuals with experience in the field.

- *Follow the Grant Standards published by the IRS (January 28, 2005).* This memorandum stresses the use of expenditure responsibility. Expand the foundation's grant application form to require charities to provide the names of its key employees (officers), board members, subcontractors, and re-grantees. Use a grant agreement specifying the use of the funds, prohibited uses of funds, and the duty to account.

- *Professionally screen all potential grantees.* The OFAC's SDN list is comprised of almost 150 pages of small print, far too long to check effectively by hand; when other published lists around the world are added to the review, the job becomes not only time consuming but subject to human error (see Table 7–4). Therefore, we recommend that you use commercially available screening services (see Table 7-5) to check potential grantees against known lists of terrorists. A number of software companies will do this. Services include screening of organizations, screening of contacts, and daily paper and electronic file updates when names are added to the lists. If the foundation cannot afford either the staff to perform a manual review or a subscription service, approach a local community foundation or internationally based charities to see if they would offer the service at a more reasonable cost.

- *Keep abreast of legislative changes.* If the foundation does not belong to a statewide, regional, or national foundation trade group, now may be the time to join. These organizations do an excellent job of monitoring legislation changes, reporting those requirements to members, and providing practical solutions.

In addition, Susan Cornell Wilkes and Barbara Laney Boyd offer the following tips for new cross-border grantmakers in their article *Family Foundations and International Grantmaking: Tips on How to Begin:*[31]

TABLE 7-4
Selected Lists of Terrorist Organizations and Individuals

Description	Location of List
Specially Designated Nationals – a list of named terrorist-connected individuals and entities identified in the President's Executive Order, by the Secretary of State, or by the Secretary of the Treasury	www.ofacsearch.com
OFAC Blocked Countries (sanctions program and country summaries)	www.ustreas.gov/offices/eotffc/ofac/sanctions/
Bureau of Industry and Security, Department of Commerce	www.bxa.doc.gov/
Canadian Consolidated List (organizations and individuals)	www.osfibsif.gc.ca/eng/publications/advisories/index_supervisory.asp?#Supter
FBI lists	www.fbi.gov/mostwant.htm
Interpol Most Wanted	www.interpol.int/Public/Wanted/Search/Recent.asp
United Nations Consolidated List	www.bankofengland.co.uk/sanctions/main.htm

Note: This table contains some, but not all, of the list published worldwide. It provides points of reference to major list sources and emphasizes the enormity of the search task.

---

[31] Susan Cornell, Wilkes and Barbara Laney Boyd, *Family Foundations and International Grantmaking: Tips on How to Begin*, Council on Foundations.

TABLE 7-5
Software Vendors Providing Terrorist Screening Tools[32]

Vendor	General Information
AmeriGives *www.amerigives.com*	Organizations can be checked using the OFAC list; contact checking is available for an additional charge.
Arlington Group *www.arlgroup.com*	The Arlington Group's Easygrants software checks grantee organizations (but not grantee contacts). The list of known organizations is updated regularly, and new names are passed on to clients through e-mail.
Bridger Insight *www.bridgerin-sight.* *choicepoint .com*	This software compliance firm provides OFAC and related list-checking primarily for financial institutions working to comply with Executive Order 13224 and the Patriot Act. Many grant systems are compatible with this vendor.
Bromelkamp *www.bromelkamp.com*	Bromelkamp links clients directly to Guidestar; clients can purchase Charity Check linking to OFAC information.
CreateHope *www.createhope.org*	This company, which focuses on facilitating corpo-rate philanthropy, checks organizations and contacts; services include data gathering and risk analysis.
Foundation Source *www.foundationsource.* *org*	Foundation source uses Bridger Insight to check organizations; it is planning to add contact checking capabilities in mid-2004.
4Charity *www.4charity.com*	This software checks organization and primary contact for clients using Bridger Insight.
JK Group *www.easymatch.com*	This service checks organizations and primary contacts using Bridger Insight; it also provides solicits information about officers and board members, reviews grantee records, and follows up to ensure grants were used for the purposes directed.
MicroEdge *www.microedge.com*	This software provides organization and contact checks through links to GuideStar EZ Basic and Charity Check, as well as through list export capabilities for use with other vendors.
NPO Solutions *www.nposolutions.com*	This software provides organization and contact checks through export capabilities for use with other vendors.

---

[32] This vendor list and comments were derived from an article by Martin B. Schneiderman, *Seeking a Safe Harbor, Foundation News & Commentary* (May/June 2004), pp. 38-39.

- Serve as a director of an organization operating international programs or impacting international issues;

- Locate U.S. organizations that focus on international causes;

- Consider internationally based program-related investments as a part of the foundation's investment and grantmaking strategies;

- Support educational programs about international issues;

- Make site visits to countries of interest, interviewing potential grantees;

- Fund research related to immigration and refugees in countries of interest;

- Research programs similar to those in which the foundation has an interest;

- Attend conferences on global issues; network with other foundations involved in cross-border grantmaking.

Unless the foundation was specifically created to address international issues, it is best to begin grantmaking at home. Become proficient in setting grant goals and parameters, selecting grant recipients, and analyzing grant effectiveness in an arena in which the foundation does not have language or distance barriers. When the foundation is ready to move further, it should use experienced advisors to guide the result or use one of the growing number of domestic organizations to channel grant funds. See Table 7–6.

[4] Grants to Individuals

Although personal gifts made by individuals to individuals do not qualify for income, estate, or gift tax deductions, private foundations may make grants to individuals for charitable purposes (although these distributions are complicated by extensive record-keeping and reporting requirements). Distributions to individuals fall into three broad categories: gifts made to individuals in need due to poverty or temporary distress; gifts made to individuals to conduct charitable activities; and gifts made to individuals for study, travel, or similar purposes.

[a] Gifts to Individuals in Need Due to Poverty or Temporary Distress

A private foundation may distribute monies directly to an indigent to take care of basic living needs or may distribute funds to people who are in crisis. For example, a foundation may want to provide food and shelter for the homeless after a tornado or provide money to repair a home in the event of a flood. These types of gifts require good record keeping and documentation, but do not require prior approval from the IRS.

[b] Gifts to Individuals to Conduct Activities in Furtherance of Charitable Purposes

Gifts to individuals to conduct activities in furtherance of charitable purposes may cover salary or operating costs for charitable projects, such as research for a charitable purpose. Grants to individuals also require good record keeping and documentation, but do not require prior approval from the IRS.

[c] Gifts to Individuals for Travel, Study, or Similar Purposes (Scholarships)

Family foundations that plan to make grants for scholarships must get approval for the program from the IRS prior to making the scholarship awards.[33] If the scholarship program is a central part of the foundation's charitable purpose, the approval can be requested when the foundation files for tax-exempt status. If the foundation decides to create and award scholarships after it has received tax-exempt status, it must seek approval through a private letter ruling.

TABLE 7-6
Domestic Umbrella Organizations Making Foreign Grants

Organization	Contact Information
The American Ireland Fund New York Office	30 East 29th Street, 2nd Floor New York, NY 10016 212-689-3100 *www.irlfunds.org*
CAF America	King Street Station 1800 Diagonal Road, Suite 150 Alexandria, VA 22314-2840 703-549-8931 *www.cafonline.org/cafamerica/*
Give2Asia	465 California Street, 9th Floor San Francisco, CA 94104-1832 415-743-3336 *www.Give2Asia.org*
Global Fund for Women	1375 Sutter Street, Suite 400 San Francisco, CA 94109-7640 415-202-7640 *www.globalfundforwomen.org*

---

[33] IRC §§4945(g), (d)(3); Reg. §53.4945-4.

TABLE 7-6. CONTINUED

Organization	*Contact Information*
Global Greengrants Fund	2840 Wilderness Place, Suite A Boulder, CO 80301 303-939-9866 *www.greengrants.org*
The International Community Foundation	11300 Sorento Valley Road, Suite 115 San Diego, CA 92121 858-677-2913 *www.icfdn.org*
King Baudouin Foundation United States, Inc.	Jean Paul Warmoes Executive Secretary de la KBFUS 10 Rockefeller Plaza, 16th Floor New York, NY 10020 212-713-7660 *jeanpaul@kbfus.org* *www.kbfus.org*
The Virtual Foundation	4 Mill Street P.O. Box 268 Middlebury, VT 05753 802-623-8075 *www.VirtualFoundation.org*

Scholarship programs must be structured to make grants on an objective, nondiscriminatory, and appropriate basis. The criteria for selection must be related to the purposes of the grant and should be structured to achieve the intended purposes. The foundation must also have a method to follow up and gather information about the use of the funds and the effectiveness of the program.[34]

Generally, when benefits are conferred on individuals, the group of potential recipients must be broad enough to establish that the grants are intended to further a charitable purpose, rather than simply benefiting an individual interest. The group can be smaller, however, when only a few individuals are particularly qualified to advance the charitable purpose.[35] The pool of scholarship recipients can be limited to provide for scholarships for a specific purpose, or even for a specific area of study or work.[36] The recipient pool can even be restricted to a specific gender.[37]

If a private foundation makes a grant to a government agency that is earmarked for use by an individual for purposes described in IRC §4945(d)(3), the grant may be appropriate if it is established (in advance) that the grant is

---

[34] Reg. §53.4945-4(c)(1), (d).

[35] Reg. §53.4945-4(b)(2).

[36] Rev. Rul. 76-340, 1976-2 C.B. 370; Rev. Rul. 79-131, 1979-1 C.B. 368; Rev. Rul. 77-44, 1977-1 C.B. 355.

[37] Tech. Adv. Mem. 86-13-002 (Dec. 12, 1985).

designed to further a charitable purpose, if the grant recipient is required to submit reports on the use of the funds, and if the foundation investigates jeopardized grants in accordance with the Treasury Regulations.[38]

> **Example:** State University approaches the McCoy Family Foundation to request a grant for the specific purpose of hiring a nationally known scientist to create a new science program. The McCoy Foundation considers the grant and determines that the new science program is important and the recruited scientist particularly qualified to start the program; the foundation makes the grant. This distribution is considered a grant to State University (not a grant to a specific individual), since the university, and not the foundation, selected the recipient.[39]

If the foundation restricts the grant too much, the grant may be treated as a taxable expenditure. For example, the scholarship pool cannot be limited to a specific family,[40] and the recipients cannot be restricted by race.[41] When the foundation is a corporate foundation granting scholarships to employees or their children, the pool must constitute a charitable class, the committee selecting the scholarship recipients must be independent of the employer or controlling individuals, and restrictions on the pool must be related to the charitable goals of the scholarship program.[42]

If a private foundation wants to award scholarships, it is generally easier to make a lump-sum distribution to a college, private school, or graduate school and allow that organization to screen candidates and make the awards. This shifts the approval process and record-keeping requirements from the foundation to the public charity. In addition, when scholarships are awarded by schools, decisions are made by administrators more qualified to determine need, potential for success, or evidence of past success of potential candidates. A grant made by a private foundation in this way is not considered to be a grant to individuals so long as the grant is not earmarked for a specific individual and the private foundation does not control the process.[43]

For the purpose of determining qualifying distributions, loans and outright grants are treated like scholarship grants, since both types of grants represent a transfer of funds to an individual, rather than a qualified charity.

[C] Qualified Set-asides

Sometimes a family foundation decides to make a grant for a major project that exceeds its normal distribution amount. To accommodate the larger

---

[38] Reg. §53.4945-4(a)(4)(iii).

[39] *See* the examples provided in the Regulations at §53.4945-4(a)(4)(iii).

[40] Rev. Rul. 85-175, 1985 C.B. 276.

[41] Rev. Proc. 75-50, 1975-2 C.B. 587; Rev. Rul. 71-447, 1971-2 C.B. 230; Gen. Couns. Mem. 39,082 (Dec. 1, 1983).

[42] Rev. Proc.76-47, 1976-2 C.B. 670.

[43] Reg. §53.4945-4(a)(4)(i).

distribution, the foundation may decide to set aside funds for the project in one year, even though the funds may not be spent for two or three years. Funds set aside for a future charitable purpose are considered qualifying distributions in the year that the funds are set aside (and not in the year that the funds are ultimately paid out) if the foundation demonstrates to the IRS that the funds will be paid out within five years to an organization that is a qualifying recipient *and* if the distributions meet *either* the suitability test *or* the cash distribution test.[44]

[1] The Suitability Test

The *suitability test* requires that the foundation prove that the set-aside and future distribution of funds will accomplish the objectives of the grant more effectively than the current distribution of funds.[45] Grants that meet the suitability test may include the ongoing support of a particular project, program-related investments, and even grants made as matching grants.

A set-aside ruling is not available for a grant that is simply a serial grant commitment, which is a commitment to make specific payments over a series of years. For example, if a foundation made a $300,000 pledge to a museum for a capital campaign and specified that the distributions were to be made over a five-year period, the unpaid portion of the pledge is not considered a qualified set-aside. The pledge payments are treated as qualifying distributions each year as the serial payments are made.[46]

On the other hand, if the foundation plans to hold funds to make a significant grant within the next few years to help a museum cover construction costs for a new facility, a set-aside may be more appropriate. The foundation may reserve the funds and count the reserve as a qualifying distribution, but must file for a ruling in the year the funds are set aside.

Consider these additional examples of suitable set-asides:

Example 1: The Jones Family Foundation had an interest in providing a shelter for the homeless. The foundation acquired an option on land on which to build the shelter but had not yet hired an architect, contractor, construction manager, or staff. The foundation expected to accomplish these tasks within five years and set aside $1,000,000 in 2007 and filed for a ruling. This set-aside was considered a qualifying distribution in 2007.

Example 2: The Waller Family Foundation was approached to fund a $500,000 three-year research study. The foundation's normal annual distribution was $200,000. Since the foundation board wanted to ensure that funds were available for the project in the years 2006 through 2008, it set

---

[44] IRC §4942(g)(2); Reg. §53.4942(a)-3(b).
[45] IRC §4942(g)(2)(A), (B)(i); Reg. §53.4942(a)-3(b)(1)(i), (2).
[46] Priv. Ltr. Rul. 8839003.

aside $175,000 in 2004 and 2005 and filed for a ruling. The set-asides in 2004 and 2005 were considered qualifying distributions in the year the payments were reserved.

[a] Historic Preservation Challenge Grants Qualify as Set-asides

Three 2003 private letter rulings (200318070, 200318071, and 200318072) provide additional examples of how set-asides of income for matching grant programs to restore historic sites may be qualifying distributions under §4942(g)(1). These set-asides were found to satisfy the suitability test under §4942(g)(2)(B)(I), and the facts in these rulings provide insights into just how an effective challenge grant might be structured.

In Letter Ruling 200318070, Foundation M will set aside a grant to N, a publicly supported §501(c)(3) organization that owns Property P, which is listed on the National Register of Historic Places, for restoration and renovation of that property. The purpose of the project is to restore P to its appearance at the time a "Stick style" addition was put on the property. Here, M's set-aside will cover $22.515x, or about half of the total project costs, which are estimated at $45.03x. Disbursement of M's funds is conditioned upon N's compliance with several conditions: (1) N must raise contributions of $22,515 for the project; (2) N must hire appropriate consulting and supervisory services and submit plans and specifications for M's approval; (3) N must secure M's approval of contractors, vendors, and other suppliers; and (4) N must remain tax exempt under IRC §501(c)(3) and not be in default on its other obligations under the project.

In Letter Ruling 200318071, Foundation M (presumably the same foundation as in Letter Ruling 200318070, but this is not known for sure) sought to set aside a grant to public charity N (again, apparently the same public charity). The purpose of the grant is to restore and renovate P (the same property?), which is the former site of Q and which has long been vacant. The restoration project will restore P to its appearance during its most significant time period and will include one or more museums. The estimated cost of Phase 1 of the restoration project is $78.06x, and Foundation M will provide $16x of this in a lump sum once N meets several conditions: (1) M must raise $49x in contributions for the project; (2) N and M must agree on plans, budgets, and other details of the museums on the property; (3) N and M must agree on the plans for the restoration project, and M must be satisfied that N has sufficient funding for the first phase of the restoration project; (4) N must secure M's approval of contractors, vendors, and other suppliers; and (5) N must remain tax exempt under IRC §501(c)(3) and not be in default on its other obligations under the project.

Similarly, Letter Ruling 200318072 appears to involve another set-aside for a challenge grant to public charity N to facilitate its completion of the restoration and renovation of a historic site, also known as P, which appears to be the same property again. This grant, for $5.7564x, will fund about half of the costs of Phase 2 of the restoration project. As with the other two rulings, this amount will be disbursed to N when it has raised the other half of the funds needed for Phase 2 and has met detailed requirements comparable to those in the other two rulings.

In addition, each of the rulings calls attention to three of the underlying principles of a set-aside. First, Regulations §53.4942(a)-3(b)(8) provides that any IRS-approved set-aside must be evidenced by the entry of a dollar amount on the books and records of the foundation as a pledge or obligation to be paid at a future date or dates. Moreover, any amounts set aside must be taken into account in determining the foundation's minimum investment return under Regulations §53.4942(a)-2(c)(1), and any income attributable to a set-aside must be taken into account in computing adjusted net income under Regulations §53.4942(a)-2(d).

Foundations that want to qualify funds for set-aside using the suitability test must file for a ruling from the IRS in the year of set-aside.[47] The ruling request for the suitability test should include:[48]

- The amount of money to be set aside;

- The nature and purpose of the project to be funded with the set-aside amount;

- The amounts of anticipated additional set-asides related to the project and the dates for those additions;

- The reasons that the project is best accomplished through set-aside, rather than immediate expenditure;

- A full description of the project that includes costs, sources of funds, location, and any other relevant issues; and

- A statement from a foundation manager that the set-aside amounts will be paid out in five years. If the ruling is a request for an extension, the request should state the amount of time that is required.

[2] The Cash Distribution Test

The alternative test for set-aside, the *cash distribution test*, is more a mathematical than a factual test. This test is designed to ease the distribution requirement for private foundations in the start-up years, defined as the four years following the first year the foundation is created or becomes a private foundation.[49] (A foundation is considered "created" in the tax year in which it is required to distribute an amount that exceeds $500.[50]) In effect, the distribution requirement is reduced, or phased in, during the foundation's initial taxable years for projects that will not be completed within a single taxable year.

---

[47] This means that the ruling must be requested before the end of the tax year in which the funds are set aside, rather than after the close of the tax year when the return is prepared.

[48] *See* the instructions for Form the 990-PF, page 22, in Appendix 8-D.

[49] IRC §§4942(g)(2)(A), (B)(ii)(I) to (III); Reg. §53.4942(a)-3(b)(3).

[50] Reg. §53.4942(a)-3(b)(4)(i).

The cash distribution test requires that the foundation distribute cash or a cash equivalent during the four start-up years as follows:

- 20 percent of the required distribution for the first taxable year of the start-up period;

- 40 percent of the required distribution for the second taxable year of the start-up period;

- 60 percent of the required distribution for the third taxable year of the start-up period; and

- 80 percent of the required distribution for the fourth and final year of the start-up period.

The foundation does not need to make these payments on an annual basis so long as all payments are made before the end of the start-up period. If the foundation reaches the end of the start-up period and has a good reason that the reduced payments should continue, it can petition the IRS for an extension. Consider the following examples of payment structures meeting the cash distribution test:

Example 1:   The Clark Family Foundation was established in 2000 with a contribution of $500,000; the foundation had a required distribution in 2000 of $22,000, making 2000 the year of creation. The foundation's normal required distributions were $50,000 in 2001, $55,000 in 2002, $60,000 in 2003, and $70,000 in 2004. However, the minimum distribution under the cash distribution test was $124,000, calculated as $10,000 (20 percent of $50,000) for 2001, $22,000 (40 percent of $55,000) for 2002, $36,000 (60 percent of $60,000) for 2003, and $56,000 (80 percent of $70,000) for 2004. The foundation distributed $24,000 in 2003 and $100,000 in 2004, thus complying with the requirement that the minimum amount be distributed within the four years following the date of creation.

Example 2:   The McCoy Family Foundation was established in 1994 with a contribution of $2,000; the required distribution for that year was $100. The foundation received $500,000 in 1999, resulting in a required distribution for 1999 of $25,000. Here, 1999 was considered the year of creation for the foundation. The foundation made a $25,000 distribution to a qualified environmental agency during that year.

The foundation then wanted to set aside funds during the start-up period. The foundation's normally required distributions were $27,000 in 2000, $30,000 in 2001, $35,000 in 2002, and $40,000 in 2003, for a total of $132,000. However, the foundation's minimum distribution for purposes of the cash distribution test for the years 2000–2003 was $70,400, consisting of $5,400 (20 percent of $27,000) for 2000, $12,000 (40 percent of

$30,000) for 2001, $21,000 (60 percent of $35,000) for 2002, and $32,000 (80 percent of $40,000) for 2003. The $25,000 distribution made in 1999, the year of creation, could not be used to offset this amount, since the payment did not occur in the start-up period of 2000–2003. The foundation paid $80,000 to qualified organizations in 2003, thus meeting the distribution requirements of the test.

[D] Funds Used to Acquire Assets Used by the Foundation

Qualifying distributions are not limited to grants. A family foundation may expend funds to acquire assets that it needs to operate as a tax-exempt organization. For example, the foundation staff may need computers, desks, chairs, telephones, fax machines, copying machines, and other necessary office equipment. Likewise, the family foundation may need to purchase a building to house the foundation office or to make leasehold improvements to leased space that it occupies.[51] Expenditures to support the foundation's operation for charitable purposes are considered purchases of exempt function assets and are treated as qualifying distributions in the year the funds are spent.[52]

[E] Reasonable and Necessary Administrative Expenses

The family foundation may also incur operating expenses for salaries, telephone bills, utilities, postage, printing, software maintenance, periodicals, and other usual items. An operating expense is treated as a qualifying distribution only to the extent that the expense represents a "reasonable and necessary administrative expense" used to carry out the foundation's tax-exempt purpose.[53]

Administrative fees devoted to the generation of income for the foundation are not considered qualifying distributions, although these fees are considered allowable expenditures of a foundation (i.e., such expenses are not taxable expenditures). One of the most significant allowable, but non-qualifying expense is a fee related to the generation of income. This includes a money manager's fees, the portion of a trust administration fee devoted to the investment function of the bank, and even a fee internal to mutual funds for investment management costs. (When a trust department handles both investment management and administration, the trust fee must be prorated between the administrative services related to the foundation's exempt function and the investment fee related to production of income.)

Congress has vacillated in allowing administrative expenses to be treated as qualifying distributions. For a period of time, from 1984 through the end of 1990, Congress limited administrative expenses to an amount equal to 0.65 percent of

---

[51] Priv. Ltr. Rul. 9702040.
[52] IRC §4942(g)(1)(B).
[53] IRC §4942(g)(1)(A).

the required distribution amount for the year. This limit was imposed to ensure that foundations did not pay excessive salaries and operating expenses in lieu of making distributions to charitable organizations. After a study concluding that this limit was not effective in restricting distributions and that the calculations were burdensome, the limitation was allowed to expire.[54] Current law imposes no restrictions other than the requirement that the operating expenses be reasonable and necessary to further the foundation's tax-exempt purpose.

[F] Program-Related Investments

A program-related investment (PRI) is a distribution from the foundation that is a hybrid of an investment and a charitable distribution. Although the distribution is designed to support and achieve the foundation's charitable mission, it is structured as a form of investment, such as a loan or equity investment, so there is the potential for investment return and the likelihood the funds will return to the foundation for future use. The distributions are treated as grants in the year the investment is made. When the money returns to the foundation, it must add the amount to its required distributions for the year.

[1] Defining a Program-Related Investment

Determining whether a distribution is a PRI or traditional investment is somewhat subjective. Program-related investments are not simply risky investments; they are higher risk investments that prioritize charitable objectives over economic objectives. The best question to ask is "Would the distribution have been made for any reason other than the foundation's interest in addressing a specific charitable need or meeting its exempt purpose?" If the answer is "no," then the investment is likely a PRI.

The IRS has established the following standards to determine whether an investment is program-related:[55]

- *The distribution must be made primarily for charitable purposes (meaning that return on the investment is secondary to the programmatic goals).* Subordinating the investment purpose does not mean that the foundation cannot expect, and in fact receive, a return on its money. In some cases, the investment return is far better than anticipated. However, the success of the PRI does not doom its classification or mean that investment return was a higher priority than the charitable use of the funds.[56]

---

[54] The limitation expired for tax years beginning after December 31, 1990. The report used to review the effectiveness of the limitation was entitled *Private Foundation Grant-Making Administrative Expenses Study.*

[55] IRC §4944(c); Reg. §53.4944-3.

[56] Reg. §53.4944-3(a)(2)(ii).

- *The investment would not ordinarily have been made in the private sector because of the risk.* Program-related investments are often made in instances in which conventional financing is not available because of the risk involved. The investment's high-risk profile is another indicator that the loan's purpose was related to charity rather than return. Even though the investment is generally risky and the principle may be in danger of loss, PRIs are specifically excluded from classification as jeopardizing investments.

- *There is a relationship between the foundation's funding goals and the purpose for which the investment is used.* The PRI should reflect the mission of the foundation as evidenced by its mission statement or past funding history.

- *The funds are not used to lobby or support lobbying.*

[2]   Types of Program-Related Investments

Program-related investments generally take one of three forms:

1.   *Loans.* Loans are the most common form of PRI. These loans may be at market interest rates or lower, and may or may not be secured.

    Example 2:   The Miree Foundation made a $1 million 10-year loan to the YWCA at less than market rates to provide the capital to build a new building. The Miree Foundation supports affordable housing and program services for women and children but could not ordinarily afford to make a grant as large as $1 million; the YWCA could not build the building without the less-than-market rates; and at the end of the 10-year term, the funds will be returned (assuming the YWCA can amortize the loan) for reinvestment in the community.

    Example 2:   Honda, a large for-profit company, was interested in establishing a car production plant in Talladega, Alabama, an area of high unemployment. Honda had difficulty raising sufficient funds because the area in which the plant was to be located was not well developed. The Miree Family Foundation made a below-market-rate loan to Honda for the purpose of building its plant. The purpose of the loan was to improve the unemployment rate and reduce the poverty of the citizens of Talladega County. Since the foundation would not have made the loan except for its interest in building the economic opportunities in the area by building the community's infrastructure, the loan was treated as a PRI.

2.   *Loan guarantees.* Alternatively, the foundation may issue a loan guarantee, allowing the benefited charity to achieve credit when it otherwise would not qualify.

Example: The Miree Foundation may choose to guarantee the $1 million loan to the YWCA rather than actually make the loan. Loan guarantees are not treated as distributions for grant purposes unless the loan defaults or the funds are set aside in a separate fund to guarantee repayment.

3. *Equity investments.* Equity investment is a broad term used to describe ownership of an asset that supports a charitable goal. This type of PRI can range from purchase of stock in a closely held company designed to build affordable housing and promote community development, to the purchase of bank stock to provide capital for loans to rebuild an inner-city neighborhood, to the purchase of land to allow a new plant to be built that will bring jobs to the area. The common link in each of these projects is a charitable purpose, even though there is also potential for economic benefit.

Once an investment is classified as program-related, it retains that character unless the foundation makes changes to the investment for the purpose of generating a higher return.[57] Consider these examples.

Example 1: The Boys and Girls Club of Birmingham planned to build a new program center in a downtown area but had not been able to obtain conventional financing because it did not generate enough annual income to amortize the loan at standard rates. The Miree Foundation made a 10-year loan at less than market rate to the Boys and Girls Club because one of the foundation's funding priorities was to build infrastructure in disadvantaged neighborhoods. This loan was considered to be a PRI and a qualifying distribution, since it advanced the exempt purpose of the foundation.

Example 2: Expanding the facts in example 1, assume that at the end of the 10-year period, the Boys and Girls Club asked the Miree Foundation to extend the term of the loan. This change would not endanger the loan's classification as a PRI, since the purpose in the change of terms was to further the original exempt purpose of the loan, rather than to increase the investment return on the loan.

[3] Using Program-Related Investments as Part of a Grants Program

Using PRIs as part of a grants strategy requires that the foundation and its board have a long-term perspective of the role of the foundation. Program-related investments can be used for purposes as diverse as community development projects, science and health care endeavors, building purchases, renovations, and equipment purchases. Most PRIs are structured for seven- to 10-year terms, requiring the foundation to look well down the road in its grantmaking objectives.

---

[57] Reg. §53.4944-3(a)(3).

Program-related investments fit best when traditional grants will not achieve a charitable goal. For example, a charitable organization (or a group of organizations) may simply need a bit of help to get started and will produce sufficient income to amortize debt after several years of operation. On the other hand, perhaps the dollars required for a project exceed the foundation's normal grant range; in this case, the foundation may make a loan, or a combination of a loan and a grant.

Family foundations that use PRIs normally limit their commitment to a percentage of assets. A survey published in 1998 by Brody, Weiser, Burns, a consulting firm based in Connecticut, reported that the Ford, Mott Foundation and MacArthur Foundations, for example, typically committed one to two percent of their assets to PRIs.[58] These foundations, with average PRIs of $300,000 to $1,250,000, have been able to diversify the range and impact of their grants with this practice.[59]

[4] Practical Issues

Program-related investments may not be appropriate for every foundation. As stated previously, using this approach requires a clearly defined mission and well-designed system of allocating grant funds. In addition, PRIs require more sophisticated policies and practices. The foundation's grantmaking policies should limit PRIs to a percentage of its overall activity; it should have the ability to perform pregrant/investment and post-grant/investment inquiries, monitor the progress of the investments, and analyze the results; and it should have a review mechanism that allows it to make changes, if necessary.

Even when the foundation can achieve these operating objectives, there may be practical reasons to avoid PRIs:

1. *The money "invested" is no longer available for grants or traditional investments.* This means that the foundation must find another way to fuel its long-term growth and required distributions.

2. *The size of the foundation affects its ability to use program-related investments.* Some foundations may be able to afford to make $1,000 PRIs, while others may be able to afford to make $1 million PRIs. But the practical result is that smaller foundations may have so many demands on their grant funds, or commitments to specific projects, that it makes no sense to use this strategy.

---

[58] Frances Brody, and John Weiser, *Introduction to Program-Related Investments, www.brody-weiser.com/articles/IntroPRI2.html.*

[59] For insight into the process, go to the MacArthur Foundation's web site at *www.macfound.org/programs/pri/pri_guidelines.htm* to view grantmaking guidelines and an application form.

3. *There's more paperwork and potentially higher administrative costs.* Program-related investments are subject to expenditure responsibility. This means the foundation is required to conduct a pre-grant inquiry and to document the use of the funds. Consequently, there is a higher degree of liability for the foundation manager and board members if these duties are not handled properly.

4. *There is always the risk the foundation's funds will not be returned.* The equity investment may fail. The charity may default on the loan. Again, a smaller foundation may not be able to afford the "hit" to its assets and may be limited to small amounts. The best approach is to treat the funds as a distribution and ensure the foundation has sufficient resources to continue to be effective in the event the investment goes bad.

Some foundations treat PRIs as a recoverable grant. They distribute the funds requiring repayment at the end of a set time period and classify the grant as a PRI on the return. If the funds are not returned, the distribution is reclassified as a grant.

[5] Special Requirements

Program-related investments are subject to expenditure responsibility. This means that the foundation engaging in such a program must have sufficient staff, policies, and procedures to ensure that oversight takes place. The certification and reporting requirements to meet expenditure responsibility are described in detail in §7.08[B].

In the final analysis, family foundation boards should be alert to opportunities to use PRIs rather than grants. Program-related investments are an option that may expand the foundation's influence in the charitable sector in a time when traditional grant funds are tight. Consideration of the option alone is also productive. A discussion of PRIs encourages a healthy analysis of the value of the foundation's investments in the charitable sector and a thoughtful consideration of the results of its grantmaking.

[6] A Practical Example

A letter ruling issued in 2002 provides a useful, real-world example of how a PRI enabled a foundation to accomplish its charitable purpose through loans to real estate developers.

In Letter Ruling 200222034, a private operating foundation (Foundation E, for environment) proposed to enter into favorable deals with for-profit real estate developers in an effort to encourage the protection of environmentally sensitive land. Foundation E will make below-market or interest-free loans to the developers to enable them to buy environmentally sensitive undeveloped land in areas subject to development pressures. The terms of the arrangement call for the developer to give a conservation easement to protect a portion of the land purchased (including a commitment to improve the environmental quality of the land by planting forest or vegetative buffers, restoring wetlands, etc.), then develop and sell the rest of the land, subject to the terms of the easement. The loans are to be paid back to Foundation E within $3\frac{1}{3}$ years, and if the developer fails to transfer the easement, interest at 18 percent will be due for the full term of the loan. Foundation E will (1) approve the selection of the land, (2) treat the loans as PRIs, and (3) exercise expenditure responsibility with respect to the loans. Moreover, none of the developers receiving loans from Foundation E will be disqualified persons.

The Internal Revenue Service approved this program, holding that it would not endanger the exemption of Foundation E or incur penalty excise taxes under the self-dealing rules (IRC §4941), the restrictions on jeopardy investments and excess business holdings (IRC §§4943 and 4944), or the prohibition on taxable expenditures (IRC §4945). In effect, the IRS found that this program would further a charitable purpose in preserving environmentally sensitive land for the benefit of present and future generations. Just as receiving and maintaining conservation easements over such land is charitable, so too is assisting in the creation of such easements charitable. Any benefit to the developers in receiving below-market interest rates on the loans and charitable deductions upon giving the easements to qualified charities is incidental to the accomplishment of E's charitable purposes. This is a creative approach that could be an effective way for a family foundation to achieve environmental goals. (**Note:** Advisors should be sure to read the full ruling before proceeding with a plan of this type, and may even want to seek a ruling on their own plan before proceeding.)

[G]   Grants to Donor-Advised Funds May Be Advantageous

Donor-advised funds have come on strong in the last few years as a vehicle for family philanthropy.[60] The donor-advised fund is generally thought of as an alternative to a family foundation, especially for the family that is willing to trade the complete control of a foundation for the ease and economy of a fund. However, there are some situations in which a family may want to consider using a donor-advised fund in conjunction with its family foundation to help solve a particular problem.

> **Note:**   As this goes to press, the Senate Finance Committee is considering legislation that would set forth specific rules for donor-advised funds and their grantmaking programs. One proposal would prohibit grants from private foundations to donor-advised funds. The committee is concerned

---

[60] *See* the discussion in §2.05[C] regarding the manner in which a family may consider using a donor-advised fund as a less expensive choice when contemplating the creation of a family foundation.

that some foundations may use such grants to circumvent the minimum distribution requirement by keeping funds "on ice" in a donor-advised fund rather than distributing them to an active charitable organization. Another proposal would preclude grants from donor-advised funds to foundations, on the grounds that such a transfer would facilitate evasion of the strict limitations on contributions to foundations. Enactment of such rules would obviously affect the uses of donor-advised funds discussed below.

First, let us review just what the donor-advised fund is and how it works. Such a fund may be formed by an existing charity, such as a community foundation or a university, or it may be a freestanding public charity with no significant other operations. For tax purposes, a contribution to the fund is a contribution to a public charity, so the most favorable deduction treatment is applicable and none of the foundation restrictions and limitations apply. The gift is complete when given to the fund, and the fund normally creates an account in the name of the donor. The amounts in this donor account are then distributed to charitable donees on the basis of grant recommendations suggested by the donor. This is where the family foundation and the donor-advised fund differ significantly.

With a family foundation, the members of the family have complete control over the amounts, timing, and recipients of the distributions, as well as the management of investments and other operational details. With a donor-advised fund, however, these matters, including distributions, are under the control of the fund's trustees or directors; the donor and his or her family have the right to offer suggestions and recommendations as to how the amounts in their account will be managed and disposed of, but the officers of the donor-advised fund may accept or reject that advice. Of course, if the recommendation is for a routine distribution to a qualified charity, they will seldom refuse the donor's suggestions.

Consider how this sort of arrangement may be helpful to a family that has its own foundation. First, remember that the foundation has to meet a minimum distribution requirement. It must make distributions (in the form of "qualifying distributions") every year equal in general terms to five percent of its net investment assets. These distributions must be made by the close of the following year. Thus, a foundation that is required to distribute $35,000 for 2004 has until the end of 2005 to make those distributions. If its distributions exceed the required amount, it may carry the excess over to reduce the amounts it must distribute for the next five years. (For full details, see Appendix 6-E, §6-D.03[F].)

It is a good idea for a foundation to plan its distributions well in advance, and likewise it is generally not a good idea to cut things too close by distributing only the bare minimum required. By leaving distributions to the last possible minute at the end of the foundation's taxable year, then trying to distribute only the smallest amount that will meet the applicable requirement, a foundation leaves itself open to possible errors and unnecessary penalties.

No matter how carefully a foundation is run, however, it may find itself with undistributed funds on hand as the year-end deadline approaches. Intended grantees may delay returning grant agreements, or details concerning a project to be funded may remain unresolved, to name just a few potential ways such a situation may arise. Sometimes a foundation in this position may find that a grant to a donor-advised fund will enable it to avoid potential problems of this sort without disrupting its intended grant program. For tax purposes, the amount distributed to the donor-advised fund will be a grant to a public charity, a qualifying distribution. And even though the funds are effectively granted at that point, the foundation and its managers can continue their discussions and other pregrant steps with the ultimate grantee until the distribution is ready to proceed. At that time, they can advise the donor-advised fund to proceed with the funding and give the funds in question to the ultimate grantee.

This can be an effective solution to a problem that emerges at the end of the year when a family foundation discovers that it has to distribute a significant sum by year-end and it hasn't yet made appropriate grant arrangements. This problem may arise for any number of reasons: someone may have simply forgotten to schedule sufficient grant activity; grants already approved may have been delayed by the grantee's failure to supply documentation; or the board may have deemed it appropriate to withhold a grant. Whatever the reason, the foundation may have to act quickly to distribute the amounts in question.

Another context in which a donor-advised fund may prove helpful is with longer-term grant arrangements in which later distributions are dependent on the grantee's performance or other contingencies that are critical to the overall project. Such distributions may have to be withheld or redirected, disrupting the foundation's grant projections, if the results achieved by the grantee call for reconsideration of the grant project. That reconsideration may require more time than is available where the foundation had contemplated making distributions in support of the project by an approaching year-end. A grant to a donor-advised fund enables the foundation to distribute the funds once and for all, thereby meeting its distribution requirement, while maintaining some flexibility to withhold funds or redirect them if the project as originally conceived is thwarted.

Example: The XYZ Family Foundation wants to help a local hospital establish a drug abuse treatment program. The overall costs are estimated at $800,000, beginning with the expense of adapting and equipping an existing suite of offices in the hospital. That will take about a year, after which the facility must be staffed before operations commence. The project is near and dear to the XYZ family because of their experience when a family member was treated in such a facility, and they are intent upon helping plan and design every detail of the facility and the program. While the family are eager to have such a facility located right there in their suburban community, the hospital administration is less enthusiastic, although receptive. The foundation has available funds to commit to the project, but the family is concerned that unexpected developments, such as a personnel change in the hospital administration, might derail the project. The amounts needed to launch this project will satisfy the foundation's distribution requirement for several years, and there are no other major projects currently contemplated. The foundation's cash flow estimates have been based on an assumption that this hospital project will proceed as the family desires.

Solution: XYZ Foundation discusses the plan and its concerns with its local community foundation, which finds the project to be both desirable and feasible, and agrees to assist. The Foundation grants $400,000 to the community foundation to be used as initial funding for the hospital's drug treatment facility and an amount sufficient to move the project forward according to schedule. Plans call for the community foundation to provide another $400,000 in the following year if things proceed as planned. These grants will assure the Foundation's compliance with the minimum distribution requirement. However, if at any time the hospital administration should withdraw its support (apparently a real possibility), the community foundation will place the remaining grant funds in its donor-advised fund to be disbursed for other projects in the community, based in part on suggestions and recommendations from the Foundation or its directors. All parties hope and expect that the drug treatment facility will go forward to completion. However, with the assistance of the community foundation, XYZ Foundation can provide the necessary funding without worrying that factors such as a withdrawal of support by the hospital administration may require it to make major changes in its grantmaking program. Its compliance with the minimum distribution requirement is assured as it enters this major project, and it will not need to develop alternative plans on short notice if the project proves impractical at a later date.

Of course, a family foundation should not use a donor-advised fund as a regular intermediary for its grants. The added level of administration and expense would make this a solution to be used sparingly, that is, where it is clear that the donor-advised fund adds some element that is important to the foundation. In many cases, there will be other, indirect advantages gained by proceeding with such an arrangement; this is especially true where the foundation can select a donor-advised fund operated by the local community foundation. In addition to serving as a mere intermediary, a community foundation is often in a position to provide additional assistance with the proposed grant. It will normally have a knowledgeable staff that can provide information based on experience with local charities, and can often provide other advice and assistance that will prove helpful. Building a working relationship with the community foundation in this manner can enable a family foundation to become a more effective grantmaker.

§7.03   TAXABLE EXPENDITURES — GRANTS YOU MUST NOT MAKE

The Tax Reform Act of 1969 introduced sweeping changes for private foundations designed to compel foundations to distribute funds to qualified charities and to penalize foundations for distributions that might have an individual benefit. These forbidden distributions, called "taxable expenditures," were accompanied by penalties on the foundation and the foundation's managers. There are five types of taxable expenditures:

1. Distributions made to influence legislation;

2. Distributions made as political contributions;

3. Certain distributions made to individuals;

4. Certain grants made to organizations; and

5. Distributions for noncharitable purposes.[61]

[A]   Distributions Made to Influence Legislation

Private foundations are not generally permitted to make distributions for lobbying, or attempts to influence legislation. While public charities are allowed to get involved in lobbying so long as their activities are not a substantial part of the activities of the organization,[62] private foundations have two additional restrictions.[63] A private foundation may not pay or incur expense to influence legislation by communicating with the public about a legislative issue, nor can it pay for direct communications with legislators or individuals involved in enacting a specific law.[64]

Private foundations may make distributions to organizations that are involved in lobbying so long as the foundation's grant is not used for that purpose. For example, the Waller Family Foundation made a grant to the Child Welfare League to pay for a computer network. The Child Welfare League is involved in lobbying for child welfare issues in Alabama. The Waller Foundation grant was not considered a taxable expenditure because it was not earmarked for legislative activities and it was smaller than the Child Welfare League's budget for nonlobbying activities.[65] The burden is on the private foundation — in this example, the Waller Foundation — to show that it reviewed the recipient's budget to determine that the grant is within the appropriate range.[66]

---

[61] IRC §4945(d). Taxable expenditures are also addressed in Chapter 6.

[62] IRC §501(c)(3).

[63] §§4945(d)(1), (e)(1), (e)(2); Reg. §53.4945-2(a)(1).

[64] Reg. §§56.4911-2(b)(1)(ii), (d)(1)(ii).

[65] Reg. §53.4945-2(a)(6)(ii).

[66] Reg. §53.4945-2(a)(6)(iii).

Private foundations may also make distributions to facilitate conversations with lawmakers or government officials under limited circumstances.[67] These conversations are appropriate where the foundation and the government official or lawmaker meet to discuss a program that may be jointly funded by the foundation and the government so long as these conversations are not designed to get the government official or legislator to take a particular legislative position on anything outside the program under discussion.

Finally, private foundations may get involved in educational conferences, research activities, and other forums to share ideas on charitable topics so long as the activities are nonpartisan and are not directly related to the legislative activities.[68] Foundations can even distribute or pay for the distribution of information about a particular study or research so long as the information is unbiased and represents an objective analysis of the issue or result.[69]

The foundation should not take chances. Seek the help of legal counsel before making distributions for an activity that could be considered lobbying at the legislative level or propagandizing at the public level. The penalties for the foundation and its managers are too great to venture a wrong guess.

[B] Distributions Made as Political Contributions

Private foundations may not make political contributions. There are two types of prohibited political distributions:

1. *Foundations may not finance or conduct activities intended to influence the outcome of a public election.*[70] The Internal Revenue Code uses the words "participation or intervention" in a political campaign to describe the prohibited activity. This phrase has been interpreted to mean paying salaries for campaign workers, distributing (or paying to publish) written materials to speak for or against a candidate, paying for a voter registration drive in the area covered by the campaign, and making a direct contribution to a candidate. Many of these activities not only are considered a taxable expenditure by the foundation, but may violate federal campaign and election laws as well.

2. *Foundations may not finance or conduct a voter registration drive for a specific election.*[71] Expenditures for voter registration are not taxable expenditures so long as the activities are ongoing, do not target a specific election period, involve activity in at least five states, and represent a small part of the foundation's expenditures.[72] Contributions cannot be earmarked

---

[67] Reg. §53.4945-2(a)(3).

[68] IRC §4945(e); Reg. §53.4945-2(d)(1)(i).

[69] Reg. §53.4945-2(d)(1)(ii).

[70] IRC §4945(d)(2); Reg. §53.4945-3(a)(2).

[71] IRC §4945(d)(2); Reg. §53.4945-3(a)(2).

[72] These expenditures cannot represent more than 15 percent of the foundation's distributions.

to conduct voter registration. The foundation must also meet a relatively complicated source-of-funding test.[73] A private foundation interested in using funds for voter registration should use legal counsel to obtain a ruling from the IRS that the activity contemplated by the foundation is appropriate and will not be considered a taxable expenditure.

[C] Certain Distributions Made to Individuals

Grants to individuals are considered taxable expenditures unless the foundation has met the requirements of an advance ruling where scholarships are involved or of expenditure responsibility when distributions to reduce poverty, to relieve the effects of disaster, or to further charitable purposes are involved.[74]

Note that these rules do not apply to awards for past achievements. In Revenue Ruling 77-380,[75] the IRS held that grants made by a private foundation to individuals primarily in recognition of past achievement, with the funds being unrestricted and not earmarked for subsequent travel or study, were not taxable expenditures within the meaning of IRC §4945(d)(3).

The IRS applied the same reasoning in Letter Ruling 200318075, which involved a foundation focused on educational institutions, medical research, hospitals, and health care for children that proposed to start a new awards program to recognize past accomplishments by individuals in the areas of medicine and science. The objective of the program is to identify and recognize outstanding individuals who have demonstrated success in mentoring the next generation of physicians and scientists and who have the highest reputations for integrity and ethics. A nationwide network of 12 nominators from the medical and science communities would independently and anonymously recommend potential recipients of the awards, with each nominator submitting two nominations each year to a selection committee comprising six nationally recognized individuals in the medical and scientific communities. The selection committee will meet each year to screen the nominations and make recommendations to the foundation's Board of Directors, which will then choose the recipients from those recommendations.

Up to four awards will be made in the first year, and the recipients would be asked to provide a year-end letter outlining the effect of the award on his or her life or career. Except for this letter, no future services would be required of any recipient.

The foundation sought approval of this award process in accordance with IRC §4945(g). Under IRC §4945(d)(3), any amount paid or incurred by a private foundation as a grant to an individual for travel, study, or other similar purposes by such individual will generally be taxed as a "taxable expenditure," unless such grant satisfies the requirements of §4945(g). Those requirements include an objective and nondiscriminatory selection procedure approved in advance by the IRS.

---

[73] IRC §4945(f).

[74] See §7.02[B][4], *supra* for a full discussion of this issue.

[75] 1977-2 C.B. 419.

The IRS pointed out, however, that the grants to be awarded in the proposed program are for past achievement and are not intended to finance any future activity of the recipient. Consequently, there are no conditions or requirements to be met subsequent to receiving the awards, and the awards are not grants to individuals for travel, study, or similar purposes by such individuals. Accordingly, these awards for past achievement are made for purposes other than stated in §4945(d)(3) and are not subject to advance approval under §4945(g).

[D] Certain Grants Made to Organizations

Distributions to qualified organizations for charitable purposes constitute the bulk of distributions from family foundations. "Charitable" purposes are defined in IRC §170(c) as religious, charitable, scientific, literary, or educational purposes; the fostering of national or international amateur sports; and the prevention of cruelty to children and animals. A grant made to accomplish a goal that is not charitable is not permitted, even if the grant is made to a public charity. The rules relating to permissible distributions for charitable purposes are discussed above in §7.02[B].

[E] Distributions for Noncharitable Purposes

By definition, distributions from private foundations that do not fit within a clearly defined charitable purpose are considered to be taxable expenditures. The foundation manager's job is to avoid these distributions by examining each expenditure to ensure that it fits within a permissible category outlined earlier in this chapter and, if necessary, that the foundation has exercised appropriate expenditure responsibility.

> **Example:** In a letter ruling requested by a private foundation in 1998, the foundation proposed to implement a grant program to make distributions to ministers to allow them to reduce or pay in full their outstanding educational loan balances related to entering the ministry. The foundation's goal was to encourage ministers to perform their religious work without having to worry about generating sufficient income to discharge these debts. Ministers applying for grants were required only to be active in the ministry, to have outstanding debt related to obtaining a master of divinity degree, and to work for a church in the state in which the foundation was located. The foundation planned to select recipients in an objective and nondiscriminatory manner, but it did not want to require that the ministers stay in the ministry, to document the financial need (to prioritize the award of grants based on need), or to require follow-up on the use of the funds. The IRS found that such grants would not be qualifying distributions, and therefore would be taxable expenditures, because:

- The grant program did not require the recipient to document the use of the funds, so there was no way to establish that the funds were used for a charitable purpose or that they represented a qualifying distribution for an exempt purpose;

- The grant program did not require follow-up or record keeping, so the program did not comply with the documentation and record-keeping requirements established in the Internal Revenue Code; and

- The program was not tailored to either needy ministers or a specific objective (such as getting ministers to remain in the ministry), so that it was not certain the program would advance religion.[76]

The most important lesson here is that a good idea related to an apparently charitable purpose is not enough. The foundation must comply with the IRS Regulations in order to make a qualifying distribution for an exempt purpose. Perhaps the other lesson here is to always file for a letter ruling if you have invented a new way to solve an old problem.

§7.04   CALCULATING THE REQUIRED DISTRIBUTION

[A]   Background

A principal purpose of the Tax Reform Act of 1969 was to ensure that individuals who controlled family and other private foundations did not accumulate funds allocated for charitable purposes. Prior to 1969, private foundations were required to distribute only a "reasonable amount." With enactment of the Tax Reform Act of 1969, the distribution rules defined what was "reasonable" by proscribing a minimum investment return.

While the distribution formula is termed a "minimum investment return," the current calculation has little to do with the actual return on the foundation's investments. The history of the distribution rule may provide some insight into the rule's purpose and name.

The distribution requirement established in the Tax Reform Act of 1969 was six percent of the foundation's assets. The Treasury was given the right to adjust that figure as economic conditions changed. The figure fluctuated between 5.25 percent and six percent over the next eight years until the law was amended in 1976 to require that foundations distribute the greater of five percent of the assets or net investment income.[77] At the same time, the Treasury's right to adjust the figure was eliminated. The rule was changed to its current form by the Economic Recovery Act of 1981, and requires a private foundation to distribute five percent, regardless of the actual income generated by its investments.[78]

---

[76] Priv. Ltr. Rul. 9927047.

[77] Tax Reform Act of 1976.

[78] Bruce Hopkins and Jody Blazek provide a detailed review of these changes in *Private Foundations: Tax Law and Compliance* 198-200 (John Wiley and Sons 1997).

[B]   The Formula

[1]   General Rule

The general rule is that the foundation must distribute 5 percent of the average market value of its investment assets.[79] The formula has two elements. First, the foundation must calculate a minimum investment return, which is roughly 5 percent of the average market value of its investment assets adjusted by several factors. Second, the foundation must determine its qualifying distributions, which are those payments made for exempt purposes. The foundation must make qualifying distributions equal to the required distributable amount; if it fails to pay out the required distributable amount within 12 months after the close of the tax year, an excise tax is imposed. This section provides greater detail on the determination of the distributable amount.

[2]   Assets Used to Calculate the Required Distribution

The first step in calculating the required annual distribution is the computation of the minimum investment return. This figure, computed in Part X of Form 990-PF, is based on the market value of the foundation's investment assets. Investment assets are defined as stocks, bonds, real estate, and other assets held for investment purposes. Excluded from this calculation are the following items:[80]

- *Cash reserve.* A cash reserve equal to 11/2 percent of the foundation's total assets may be excluded from the calculation. This reduction may be used whether the foundation has this amount of cash on hand or not.[81] When the foundation needs to maintain more than 11/2 percent as a cash reserve for operations, it can make the case for a larger reserve on its 990-PF.

- *The assets used by the foundation to carry out its tax-exempt purpose.* These assets include furniture, equipment, supplies, and other fixed assets. They also include buildings, such as historical properties, research and education facilities, and even property offered to other charities at nominal rent so long as the facilities are related to its tax-exempt purpose. Note that assets maintained on foundation property for the specific use of the foundation's investment managers, such as computers, resource materials, or software, are included as investment assets, since those assets are used to produce the foundation's income. The foundation may be required to apportion an asset partially as an

---

[79] A distribution requirement of 5 percent of the foundation's assets is in keeping with modern portfolio theory, in which assets are invested for total return (appreciation and income), rather than current income only.

[80] Reg. §53.4942(a)-2(c)(2).

[81] Reg. §53.4942(a)-2(c)(3)(iv).

investment asset and partially as a tax-exempt-purpose asset. Have your accountant make this calculation.

- *Indebtedness.* The calculation excludes indebtedness used by the foundation to acquire its assets.

- *Program-related investments.* Program-related investments or functionally related businesses may be excluded.

- *Assets held for future use.* Assets held for future use (similar to set-asides in that the property is earmarked for a future use, such as building a building or staffing a new office[82]) may be excluded.

Once the foundation's investment assets are calculated (*see* Table 7-7), the market value of the remaining assets is multiplied by five percent to get the minimum investment return.

After the minimum investment return is established for a specific year, the foundation will generally need to make several adjustments:

- The figure may be reduced by tax on investment income for the year;

- The figure is increased by the prior year's qualifying distributions that have been returned;

- The figure is increased by the amount of income distributions from IRC §4947 (a)(2) trusts, which are split-interest trusts;

- The foundation may have underpayments for prior years, in which case the current year payments should be increased by the amount of the prior years' underpayments; and

- The foundation may have overpayments from prior years; those overpayments may be used to reduce the current year's distribution obligation (overpayments from prior years may not be credited once those credits are five years old or older).

TABLE 7-7
Example of Determination of Investment Assets — Minimum Investment Return

The McCoy Family Foundation	
Investment assets:	$5,400,000
Noninvestment assets:	$75,000
Foundation indebtedness:	($100,000)
Amount subject to calculation:	$5,300,000 ($5,400,000 investment assets – $100,000 foundation indebtedness; noninvestment assets are excluded from the calculation)

---

[82] Reg. §53.4942(a)-2(c)(3)(i).

Do not panic about mastering the details of the computation. The computation for most foundations is fairly straightforward and does not involve noninvestment assets, debt, program-related investments, or assets held for future use. In any event, the foundation's accountant will make the computation of the investment assets on the foundation's annual tax return, and the figure computed in this way will govern the amount that must be distributed by the close of the next tax year.

[3] Effect of Short Tax Year

The foundation may prorate the required distribution when it has a short tax year (such as the start-up year of the foundation or a year in which it changes its tax year-end). When the foundation has a short year, the distributable amount is five percent of the average market value of the assets multiplied by a fraction, the numerator of which is the number of days in the foundation's short year and the denominator of which is the number of days in a full year.

> **Example:** Assume that the Miree Family Foundation was established on April 15, 2006, with a contribution of $500,000. The foundation uses a calendar year. The average market value of the investment assets of the foundation for 2006 was $450,000. The distribution is calculated by creating a formula as follows: ($450,000 × 5%) × 261/365 = $16,089.04.

Short years are not an issue in the last year of the foundation, since generally all, or a substantial portion, of the assets of the foundation are distributed for charitable purposes.

[4] Penalty for Failure to Distribute

The foundation has a full tax year after the close of the tax year to make a distribution of the funds.[83] For example, if the foundation's required distribution for 2006 was $50,000 and the foundation distributed only $40,000 in 2006, the foundation must distribute the remaining $10,000 by the end of the 2006 tax year to meet the distribution requirement. If the foundation still has undistributed income after the close of the 2007 tax year, a 15 percent excise tax will be imposed on the foundation for each year, or part thereof, that it fails to distribute the required amount.[84] As an additional penalty, the foundation will face a 100 percent excise tax on the undistributable amount if it fails to distribute the income within 90 days of receiving a deficiency notice from the Internal Revenue Service. At this point, the foundation's managers should be concerned about personal liability unless there is some reasonable explanation for the failure to comply.

---

[83] IRC §4942(j)(2).

[84] The foundation does not have 12 months in which to correct the underpayment, but only a period through the close of the next tax year. This distinction is critical when the foundation makes a decision to change its tax year-end, since this change normally results in a short tax year.

This grace period, extending the time for the mandatory payment through the end of the following tax year, is helpful since the foundation may not be able to compute the current year's distribution requirement with accuracy until well after the close of the year-end accounting period. The minimum investment return calculation is complicated and requires, among other things, a market valuation on the last day of the tax year. Brokerage statements, appraisals, and other asset valuation may not be produced for several days or weeks after that close. The easiest way to avoid a penalty is to make sure that the foundation distributes at least the prior year's undistributed amount during the tax year. This figure is located on Form 990PF on page 8, line 6(f).

In some cases, the foundation has distributed in excess of the required amount. Excess distributions can be carried forward for five years; if not used within the five years, the ability to use the excess to reduce current distributions is lost. Excess distribution amounts are also found on Form 990PF on page 8, line 9.[85]

If the foundation fails to distribute the required amount by the end of the tax year following the year in which the underpayment was incurred, there is still potential relief under limited circumstances. First, the IRS may waive the excise tax where the foundation can meet the abatement test.[86] The abatement test requires the following:

- The foundation did not willfully fail to distribute, and there was reasonable cause for the error (where the error is improper valuation, the burden is on the foundation to show that it made its best effort to value the assets correctly);[87]

- The deficiency is corrected within 90 days of the IRS notice;

- The foundation informs the IRS by submitting the revalued asset information and calculation on its 990-PF; and

- The additional distribution is treated as a distribution in the year of deficiency.

The IRS may also waive the excise penalty where the foundation fails to make sufficient qualifying distributions due to some other reasonable (rather than willful) error so long as the foundation corrects the problem within the specified amount of time.

It is easy enough to avoid a penalty by making regular distributions of the approximate required amount. Here are some tips for avoiding the excise tax on the failure to distribute or for meeting the abatement test in the event that you do run afoul of the rules:

1. Make sure that you have an accurate and dependable valuation method so that the values used to compute your distribution requirements are correct.

---

[85] The amount that is lost as carryforward is shown on the 990-PF on page 8, line 8. Foundations should use carryforward in planning distributions where the foundation's goal is to grow the assets and meet only minimum distribution requirements.

[86] IRC §4942(a)(2).

[87] Reg. §53.4942(a)-1(b)(2).

2. Use the 990-PF to monitor potential penalties for the failure to distribute. The tax return shows the calculated underpayment for the tax year on page 8, line 6(f). Generally, the excise tax can be avoided so long as the prior year's underpayment is distributed in the current tax year. Note the excess distributions that can be carried over to the next tax year on page 8, line 9.

3. Keep required distributions as current as possible so that the foundation is not forced to make distributions to organizations that are not priorities simply to meet the distribution requirements.

4. Do not work too hard to make a distribution equal to the exact amount required. A foundation working to the dollar may find it has underdistributed or overdistributed upon final calculation. There is much work required for but no benefit obtained from a perfectly calculated distribution figure.

[5] Creating a Rough Estimate

The foundation manager should develop a worksheet to estimate the distribution amount to guide the grants committee and board in setting distribution amounts for meetings and to project the cash flow needed from the foundation investments. Form 7-1 provides a simple worksheet to use for computation purposes. Complete and distribute this worksheet with the grants package for each meeting to guide the committee in determining the size and number of awards that should be awarded in the grant cycle.

If the foundation has a more complicated balance sheet, you may prefer to use the more detailed worksheet shown at Form 7-2. While these current year calculations will still not be perfect (because you will not have the final monthly valuations to determine investment asset value until the year ends), pinpoint accuracy is not critical. Penalties are not imposed for the failure to distribute the required amount in the year due; penalties are imposed only if the foundation fails to distribute the underdistributions from prior years. The purpose of the forms is to provide a comfortable working estimate to guide the grantmaking process.

[C] Valuation of Assets

The most important element of calculating the foundation's distribution requirements is determining the value of its investment assets. The assets must be valued regularly using the methods detailed below:

• *Marketable assets.* Assets such as cash and securities should be valued monthly. Ask the brokerage firm or trust company that holds the foundation's assets to generate a monthly statement for this purpose.

• *Nonmarketable assets.* Assets such as real estate, closely held stock, or other miscellaneous assets should be valued using a method accepted for estate tax or charitable gift valuations.[88] Table 7-8 sets out the valuation cycles for the most common types of assets.

---

[88] Reg. §53.4942(a)-2(c)(4)(iv)(a).

FORM 7-1   Simple Worksheet for Rough Estimate of Required Distribution

Family Foundation Worksheet to Determine Rough Estimate of Required Distribution in Current Tax Year

(1) Determine average value of investment assets

January Market Value $_____

February Market Value $_____

March Market Value $_____

April Market Value $_____

May Market Value $_____

June Market Value $_____

July Market Value $_____

August Market Value $_____

September Market Value $_____

October Market Value $_____

November Market Value $_____

December Market Value $_____

Total $_____/#months_____ = $_____

   Note: These calculations will often be made early in the year. Where only three or four months of valuation figures are available, use the market values for those months and divide by the number of months used to get an average.

(2) Multiply (1) $_____ × 5% = $_____

(3) Reduce (2) by

grants made to date   − $_____

and serial grant commitments − $_____

add prior year underpayments + $_____

or subtract prior year overpay- − $_____
ments

to get the required distribution $__ _____

Date:_____ Prepared by:_____

FORM 7-2   Detailed Worksheet for Determination of Required Distribution

Family Foundation Worksheet to Determine Estimate of Required Distribution in Current Tax Year

(1) Determine average value of investment assets (do not include program-related investments, foundation assets used in tax-exempt purpose, set-asides, or assets held for future use)

January Market Value	$_____
February Market Value	$_____
March Market Value	$_____
April Market Value	$_____
May Market Value	$_____
June Market Value	$_____
July Market Value	$_____
August Market Value	$_____
September Market Value	$_____
October Market Value	$_____
November Market Value	$_____
December Market Value	$_____
Total	$_____ /#months_____ = $_____

Note: These calculations will often be made early in the year. Where only three or four months are available, use the market values for those months and divide by the number of months used to get an average.

(2) Reduce average investment figure by the following:

Cash reserve of 11/2% of investment assets	– $_____
Foundation indebtedness	– $_____
Balance	$_____

(3) Multiply (2) $_____ × 5% = $_____

Note: If short year, multiply this amount by a fraction, the numerator of which is the number of days in the tax year and the denominator of which is the number of days in the full year.

(4) Reduce (3) by

grants made to date	– $_____
and serial grant commitments	– $_____
add prior year underpayments	+$_____
or subtract prior year overpayments	– $_____
to get the required distribution	$_____

Date: _____   Prepared by:_____

TABLE 7-8
Required Valuation Frequency for Foundation Assets

Type of Asset	Frequency of Valuation	Source of Valuation
Cash or cash equivalents (such as money market funds)	Monthly	Monthly bank statement
Marketable securities (such as stocks, bonds, and mutual funds traded on a public exchange or market)	Monthly	Bank, trust company, or brokerage statement of assets
Real estate	5 years	Independent real estate appraiser
Other assets	Annual	Independent appraiser

Think about the valuation requirements and request monthly statements when you establish relationships with money managers, custodians, and bankers. Statements should be sent to the foundation manager as well as the foundation accountant. If monthly statements are not available, the alternative is to re-create the monthly cash and securities balances through a manual calculation. Bank statements can be used to determine monthly cash balances, and the *Wall Street Journal*, the Internet, and other financial publications can be used to piece together the month-end values for the securities held by the foundation.

§7.05   SETTING A DISTRIBUTION POLICY

Family foundations must set policies and procedures for awarding grants prior to the first grant committee meeting. Policies, which are discretionary and vary greatly from family to family, should reflect the foundation's mission, its goals, and a certain realism about the limits of the foundation's size. The types of policies that should be set include:

1. The cycle on which grants will be reviewed;

2. The charitable areas in which the foundation will make grants; and

3. The types of grants the foundation will make.

[A]   The Grant Review Cycle

The cycle on which the foundation considers and awards grants is purely discretionary. Some foundations meet as often as quarterly, while others meet only once or twice a year. Considerations for setting the grant cycle include:

• *The number of grants for review.* When the foundation receives numerous grant applications, more frequent meetings may help make grant review meetings manageable. For example, if the foundation receives 30 or 40 applications a year, no more than two meetings should be required. If the foundation receives a hundred or more applications in a year, then quarterly meetings may be more appropriate.

- *The location of the board members.* Grant meetings are more effective when committee members can meet in person. Other options include telephone conferences and teleconferences. The foundation bylaws establish the meeting methods that are sufficient for making decisions. Obviously, if the foundation prefers to have attendance of its members and those members are scattered geographically, the meetings might be scheduled less frequently than for a foundation with local participants.

- *The need to be timely in meeting needs of requesting charitable organizations.* Frequent meetings allow a timely review and award of grants. When the foundation meets annually, many requests for funding may become moot as organizations are forced to seek funds elsewhere in order to accomplish their goals on a timely basis.

[B] Grant Purposes

Next, the foundation should determine its charitable areas of grantmaking interest. Some foundations make grants for any qualified charitable purpose, while others focus on specific priorities. Charitable giving can be segregated into broad charitable categories and then further segmented into subgroups of those broad charitable interests.

Broad charitable purposes include the arts, education, health care, religion, social and human services, and the environment. Each of these categories can be further divided into as many as a dozen subsegments of service. Table 7-9 provides more detail about the many charitable options of interest to family foundations.

The foundation need not restrict its grantmaking to any segment of charitable interest; that is one of the advantages of the private foundation form. However, the foundation should track its giving to determine its effectiveness in meeting its mission and in creating change in the community. Over time, the foundation may find that it does have particular segments that represent priorities. It may even decide to narrow its grant-making to those areas or simply to treat those areas as preference items.

[C] Forms of Grants

[1] Single-Year Grants or Multiyear Grants

There is much debate over whether a foundation should make single-year grants, which are commitments made for the current funding year, or multiyear grants, which are commitments made in the current year to commit funds over a period of years. The periodic payments may be based on the availability of funds to the foundation or on a set schedule requested by the recipient organization. The family foundation may find that a combination of each type of grant is most effective.

TABLE 7-9
Areas of Charitable Interest and Subsegments

Arts	Education	Health Care	Social and Human Religion	Services	Environment
culture	preschool	general health care	infrastructure—places of worship	housing/shelter	natural resource preservation
media/communications	elementary school	rehabilitation	religious education	food/nutrition	pollution control
museums	secondary school	health care for the poor	community care	transportation	beautification projects
visual arts	trade school	health care education	outreach	crime/courts	animal protection
performing arts	college education	mental health	scholarships for clergy and lay persons	legal services	wildlife preservation
historical societies	graduate/professional school	medical research	other	recreation	humane societies
other	adult education	Other		youth development	zoos/aquariums
	libraries			employment/jobs	botanical gardens/activities
	student organizations			multiple services	environmental education
	other			other	other

The foundations that make grant commitments on a single-year basis usually do so to maintain control over distributable dollars. The foundation board may realize that distribution dollars are limited and unexpected projects may arise that require funding. The board does not want to get caught in a position of wanting to fund a project and having no money to do so.

Other foundations restrict grantmaking to single grant commitments because they want to maintain control over the organization using the funds. If a school approaches a foundation for multiyear funding for a school antismoking program, for example, the foundation may require that the school return each year to provide a report of progress to date and to repeat its case for continued support. This allows the funding organization to put restrictions or performance requirements on the grant recipient.

Foundations generally fund multiyear grants because the recipient organization needs the full dollar commitment in order to move ahead with the project, although it may not need the actual dollars from the grant more often than annually. Multiyear funding is seen most often in capital campaigns where large dollar commitments are required to construct buildings or provide program start-up funding.

There are some dangers to multiyear commitments. The big commitments are attractive to foundations, since the foundation generally wants to make as much of an impact as possible. If the foundation cannot afford to make the payment in a single year, the multiyear commitment is an obvious solution. The danger arises when the foundation makes a continuing series of multiyear grants because the cumulative effect of the commitments may be to dry up discretionary funds. Consider the example shown in Table 7-10. In this example, the McCoy Family Foundation, has approximately $5,000,000 in investment assets in 2004 and is growing at the rate of five percent. However, multiple long-term commitments reduce discretionary funds.

The best advice is to incorporate both forms of grants into your award process, but limit the number of years to which the foundation will commit as well as the total number of dollars subject to future commitment. For example, you may choose to limit grants to no more than three years and future years' commitments to no more than 30 percent of each year's estimated distribution requirement. Pick a formula that is simple to administer, but keeps you focused on the need to ensure you will have funds to distribute each year.

Also consider maintaining a serial grant chart, much like the one shown in Table 7-10; distribute this chart at each grant meeting. The chart will provide decision makers with a snapshot of future commitments so that the group will appreciate the impact of additional commitments on future discretionary funds.

[2] Matching or Challenge Grants

The value of the matching or challenge grant is that it allows the foundation to leverage the value of its dollars and ensures that the recipient organization will work to raise funds from a variety of sources. Since foundations have limited

TABLE 7-10
The Effect of Multiple Multiyear Grants on Available Discretionary Funds

	2004	*2005*	*2006*
Amount estimated available for distribution	**$250,000**	**$262,500**	**$275,625**
$150,000 grant, over 3 years, to Museum for addition to building	$50,000	$50,000	$50,000
$30,000 grant, over 3 years, to Boy Scouts	$10,000	$10,000	$10,000
$75,000 grant, over 3 years, to United Way for new programs	$25,000	$25,000	$25,000
$100,000 grant, over 4 years, to Zoo for capital funds project		$25,000	$25,000
$100,000 grant, over 2 years, to University for capital campaign		$50,000	$50,000
$75,000 grant, over 3 years, to Girl Scouts			$25,000
$75,000 grant, over 3 years, to Library for expansion			$25,000
Funds remaining for distribution after serial grant commitments:	**$250,000 – 85,000**	**$262,500 – 160,000**	**$275,625 – 210,000**
	$165,000	**$102,500**	**$65,625**

funds, this method of grantmaking serves as an impetus to the requesting organization to keep pushing to get the big payoff. Some foundations place a priority on matching or challenge grants (interchangeable terms).

There are two usual forms of these grants. The first is the corporate match made by an individual's employer to match a personal contribution made by the employee. For example, if Kathryn Miree worked at AllSouth Bank, which had a $1 for $1 matching program, and she made a gift of $1,000 to the Alabama Symphony, her employer, AllSouth Bank, would also make a contribution of $1,000. Matching grants are made by employers to encourage philanthropy. The same arrangement can be used by a family foundation to encourage family members to make gifts to charitable organizations.

Another form of matching grant is called a challenge grant. The purpose of a challenge grant is to use the award to encourage others to make contributions. The grant can be structured in several ways. The foundation may make a grant of a specific amount, but withhold the award until the charity receiving the grant has raised an equal amount, a double amount, or an amount based on any ratio established by the foundation from other sources. For example, funds may be matched $1 for $1, meaning that the foundation will grant the organization $50,000 for a project when the organization has raised $50,000 from other sources. Or the foundation may agree to make the final $1,000,000 payment of a large campaign once the charity has raised the remaining funds. The foundation can structure the grant in any way that provides the greatest incentive.

[3] Start-up Grants

[a] An Overview

Family foundations are often asked to fund start-ups, which are organizations that have just begun engaging in formal, organized nonprofit work. These organizations may be three to six months old, or they may be volunteer groups that have operated informally for several years and are now formalizing the charitable missions. Start-up grants are designed to provide financial stability for the new charity, allowing it time to establish itself without devoting all its resources to fundraising or enduring the uncertainty associated with reaching the end of the financial road before the organization has visibility. Start-up grants are generally multiyear grants and may involve level funding for each of the grant years or steadily decreasing amounts over the commitment term.

Start-up grants are attractive to foundations because of their impact. A $50,000 grant to a 50-year-old charity with a $25 million budget is important, but it is not the factor keeping its doors open. On the other hand, a $50,000 start-up grant creates a new nonprofit where none existed before.

[b] The Growing Number of Start-ups

The most obvious question to ask about a new charity is "Is the charity necessary, or are there already charities addressing this need?" The number of new nonprofits has been steadily increasing, showing a significant flurry after September 11. The growth in the number of tax-exempt entities from 1994 to 2004 as reported in the *IRS Data Book* from 2004 and previous years is shown in Table 7-11.

While new charities are required to file a Form 1023 with the Internal Revenue Service stating their charitable purpose, their governance structure, their budget for a three-year period, and other operating particulars, the IRS does not ask if the charity serves a unique and critical role in the community. The foundation is in a far better position to raise that question. Most often, the foundation is familiar with the community needs, other charities that address those needs, the board of the new charity (and its potential to follow through and be successful), and even potential executive staff of the new charity.

TABLE 7-11
Growth of the Number of Traditional Charities, 1994–2004

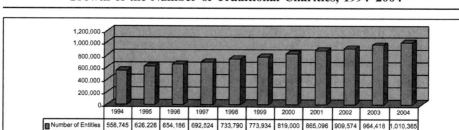

	1994	1995	1996	1997	1998	1999	2000	2001	2002	2003	2004
Number of Entities	558,745	626,226	654,186	692,524	733,790	773,934	819,000	865,096	909,574	964,418	1,010,365

[c] *Grantmaking Policies for Start-ups*

A foundation of any size has limited grant dollars. Grantmakers generally have two goals: to achieve a specific mission or purpose designed to further the foundation's mission and to ensure the foundation's grant dollars are applied to charitable purposes. If a foundation provides $100,000 to fund a start-up operation, it does not want to watch that nonprofit go out of business, taking the foundation's $100,000 with it.

Assessment of start-up charities is difficult since the organization is new and has no track record. There are no financial histories. The staff is untested. The strategic plan and operation have not had an opportunity to be implemented or to show results. Therefore, the foundation must devise its own method of determining the appropriateness of the grant. The best way to make consistently good decisions about start-ups is to adopt grantmaking policies. On the most basic level, the foundation should decide if philosophically it feels its grant dollars are better spent with start-ups or with existing organizations and if it will fund start-ups. It must decide whether it will consider and make grants for start-ups and, if so, under what conditions.

Of course, even with policies, there are no guarantees — every start-up has some level of risk and perhaps a higher likelihood of failure than ongoing charitable operations face. Consider raising the following questions, then filtering the answers with a healthy dose of subjective judgment.

1. When was the nonprofit organized? Review the charity's Form 1023, and ask to see the tax determination letter. Compare the revenue and expense projections to the history to date. If the charity has not yet prepared or filed Form 1023 (generally, the Form must be filed within 15 months of the charity's creation), the foundation may want to wait until the charity has taken this step.

2. Read the board and committee minutes to date. How many of the charity's board members were in attendance? What does it reveal about the charity's ability to think strategically, to respond to unanticipated problems, and to stay on mission?

3. What type of professional team has the charity assembled? Do they have sound legal, accounting, and programmatic advice?

4. Has the organization adopted strong internal financial, personnel, and operating policies?

5. Who provided the initial funding, and where will the organization find its long-term funding?

6. Has the charity received other foundation grants? If so, how has the charity handled those funds?

7. Does the chief executive have experience in the field and experience with start-ups? How about other key staff members?

[d]   *Funding Options*

Note strengths and weaknesses in the interview process. Use these to determine the charity's potential for survivability and success. Foundations that have experience with start-ups find this an easier analysis than foundations that make such grants only occasionally.

Once the foundation has made an assessment, it has the following funding options:

1. Make the requested grant and ask for a report on use of the funds at the end of the grant term;

2. Make the grant but require that the charity address obvious problems as a condition of acceptance;

3. Make a contingent grant — that is, award the grant once the charity has achieved certain benchmarks or corrected obvious problems;

4. Award a grant, and bring in consultants to help the organization build its infrastructure and operating effectiveness;

5. Do not make the grant but provide specific advice or suggestions for improvement or set benchmarks for funding. Encourage the charity to reapply when it has achieved those benchmarks;

6. Do not make the grant, and do not encourage the charity to return.

[D]   Grant Recipients

The foundation should decide how it will define appropriate grant recipients. Earlier in this chapter, the concept of qualifying distributions was discussed in detail. The safest distributions are those to qualified, public, domestic charitable organizations recognized by the Internal Revenue Service. Many foundations choose to limit grantmaking to these organizations.

Other grants are permissible, however, and each foundation should make a decision about whether grants requiring greater administration will be allowed. These include:

- Program-related grants;

- Grants to individuals for poverty or relief;

- Grants to individuals for scholarships; and

- Grants to foreign organizations without a domestic representative.

[E] Geographic Limitations

Finally, the foundation must determine if it will limit the geographic scope of its grantmaking. Typical limitations are:

- Grants made in the immediate community;

- Grants made in the metropolitan statistical area (MSA) consisting of multiple counties;

- Grants made in the state;

- Grants made within a group of states (a region);

- Grants made in a country (such as the United States); and

- Grants made in a continent.

Most family foundations limit the geographic scope of grants to some degree, but this is purely a function of foundation mission and dollars available for funding. If your foundation intends to limit the scope of its grantmaking, publish these limits in your marketing materials and in your grant application.

[F] Grants to Individuals and Scholarships

The foundation should make a decision about whether it will make grants to individuals since the most common form of individual grants, scholarship awards, requires prior approval from the IRS. A scholarship fund may seem a logical extension of the foundation's grantmaking for family foundations that focus on education. After all, making a grant to an individual to fund his or her education is the most direct and personal application of a charitable grant that exists. However, like many activities associated with private foundations, conducting a scholarship program is not as easy as it appears.

[1] The Issues in Awarding Scholarships

The two biggest hurdles in operating a scholarship program are compliance and management. These challenges can be overcome with planning and appropriate staff support.

The most intimidating aspect of scholarship grantmaking is compliance with IRS regulations. The general rule is that scholarship grants may be awarded to students for study or travel so long as the awards are made on an objective and nondiscriminatory basis. The foundation must establish scholarship policies and procedures consistent with its charitable purposes and submit them to the IRS for approval prior to making awards. This approval is sought as a part of the foundation's application for tax-exempt status if scholarship awards are a part of its initial goals. When foundations decide to offer scholarships after receiving exempt status, they must file a separate application for approval.

In addition to complying with the regulatory requirements, the foundation must be able to manage the administrative details. These include putting together a scholarship award committee, setting up application and award records, creating brochures, advertising the availability of the funds, evaluating candidates, selecting recipients, and monitoring students involved in the program. Although these requirements are not necessarily difficult, they do require staff with knowledge of the process to do it well. Also, although record keeping is easily accomplished with organization and staff, selecting the best scholarship candidate (without experience in the education field or scholarship administration) is much tougher.

[2] Administrative Duties for Scholarship Funds

The foundation is responsible for the following administrative duties when managing a scholarship program:

- Draft guidelines for award of scholarships;

- Advertise and distribute those guidelines to the potential scholarship pool to let them know about the scholarship awards;

- Receive and analyze scholarship applications to select the individuals with the greatest potential (that most closely match the foundation's goals). This means handling correspondence, requesting additional information when required, verifying information provided, and ranking applications;

- Determine financial need, if the scholarship is based on need;

- Select and notify the award winners. The foundation must also notify applicants that did not receive awards;

- Distribute the funds, together with the appropriate letter outlining the conditions of the grant;

- Review scholarship renewal applications, if multiyear scholarships are available;

- Follow through to determine that the funds were used for the purposes specified;

- Prepare annual report to the board.

[3] Assessing the Foundation's Needs

The most important step in determining how the foundation should structure its scholarship program is making a list of its objectives in awarding scholarships and the amount of personal time family members want to invest in the process.

The first step is establishing objectives. Is the foundation's goal to attract out-of-state students to a state private or public educational institution? Is it to provide incentives for disadvantaged students? Is it to encourage girls to become more involved in science or math? Any of these purposes is appropriate, so long as the process of awarding the funds is objective and nondiscriminatory.

Next, the foundation should consider the time board members can invest and available staff and budget resources.

- Are family members interested in reviewing applications and awarding scholarships? If not, are they willing to hire specialized help to coach the foundation board?

- Does the foundation have sufficient funds to award scholarships on an ongoing basis and cover the administrative expenses (or will the administrative costs substantially reduce the number of scholarships that can be awarded)?

- What is the ratio of administrative costs of internal administration compared to the scholarship dollars awarded?

[4] The Options

Once objectives, strengths, and limitations are established, it is time to look at the alternative forms the program may take. Family foundations have great flexibility in designing a scholarship program that fits its goals, budget, and staff. The most common choices include a scholarship fund inside the private foundation, a fund at a community foundation or scholarship administration entity, or a direct distribution to an institution of higher or secondary education and allowing that school to distribute the funds. There are advantages and disadvantages to each:

- *Family foundation managed fund.* Large foundations often choose to manage the scholarship process themselves. These foundations hire staff with experience in managing scholarship programs, create committees consisting of individuals with experience in evaluating applications and knowledge of the foundation's goals, and handle compliance with the supervision of attorneys or accountants. The advantage is control of the process. The downside is the cost of the process and the burden of compliance.

- *Community foundation or scholarship administration company.* Some foundations choose to use their community foundation to manage scholarship selection and administration. The family foundation distributes funds to the community foundation and enters into an agreement setting the parameters for awards. The community foundation then takes responsibility for advertising, reviewing, selecting candidates, and record keeping. As an alternative to a community foundation, some foundations use nonprofit administrative firms. Good examples are the Center for Scholarship Administration in South Carolina and the Citizens Scholarship Foundation of America in Minneapolis/St. Paul, Minnesota. This process allows the foundation to meet its goals without taking on the liability for compliance, reduces cost to a manageable level, and can even be structured to allow family involvement in the selection process.

- *Direct grant to an educational organization.* If the foundation's goal is to attract students to a particular school or institution, the simplest option is to make a grant to the school to establish a scholarship fund. The school is in the best position to evaluate students (since it already awards scholarships on a regular basis), make awards, and handle the paperwork, and the foundation (or the donor) can be recognized with each award. The benefit is the professional expertise achieved by giving the funds to the school. The clearest disadvantage is that the awards will not benefit students who do not attend the school.

[5]   Determining Which Option Is Best for the Foundation

Selecting the best scholarship option is difficult without the advice of counsel. The foundation's attorney or consultant is the best resource. Community foundations and scholarship administration firms are also good resources for working through the management duties. If the donor creating the foundation has any interest in scholarships, the decision should be made in the planning process. The donor may find that there are greater tax advantages to making gifts for scholarships directly to a public charity (such as the community foundation or the school) to take advantage of the more advantageous deduction rules. Or, if the decision is made to house the scholarship funds inside the private foundation, application for the process can be handled with the exemption application.

Once the decision on scholarship structure is made, it should be reviewed periodically. The foundation may make an initial decision to operate the fund on its own, determine that administration and compliance require too much time and money, then move the fund to a public charity. On the other hand, the foundation may begin by making a scholarship fund grant to an educational institution and later decide that form is too limited. Rather than continuing to build the corpus at the school, the foundation may decide to administer scholarship grants on its own.

Scholarships can make a significant difference in the lives of students who receive them. To make every dollar count, the foundation should select the option that is the most effective in terms of cost, time, and results. It should follow the rules and pay particular attention to the paperwork. Moreover, it should not hesitate to make a change if other options do a better job of achieving its objectives.

§7.06   CREATING AND DISTRIBUTING THE GRANT APPLICATION FORM

[A]   Purpose of Grant Application Form

The grant application form is an important management tool for the foundation. The form has four purposes:

1. *The grant application form adds organization and structure to the application process.* Without guidance, grant applications may range from one to over 100 pages. Some applications will contain little of the information needed to make a decision, while others will obscure the important facts with information you do not need. A form also adds efficiency to the process of assembling the grant requests for review and brings consistency to that review so that the grants committee can compare apples to apples and make decisions based on established criteria.

2. *The form communicates the foundation's funding objectives clearly to the applicants.* The application form should clearly communicate the foundation's restrictions in grantmaking as well as the information required for grant submissions. A clear statement of funding goals should reduce the number of unqualified applications and provide solid direction on how to assemble the grant application to those organizations new to the process.

3. *The form communicates limitations to grantees.* A clearly worded application conveys limits or conditions in grants made by the foundation. This may save applicants and the foundation time in reviewing ineligible submissions.

4. *The form protects the foundation in its compliance efforts.* A well-designed form ensures that the foundation will collect the information necessary to meet its legal obligation to make grants only for appropriate purposes. It is a checklist for the applicant as well as the foundation manager.

[B] Information Needed for Decision Making

[1] Asking the Right Questions

While the Securities and Exchange Commission requires that public companies provide information on earnings, expenses, executive compensation, board structure, committee structure, and other performance-oriented factors, there are not yet similar standards for nonprofits. Charities are required to make their Form 990, which contains some of this information, available each year, but much is left to the imagination. Ask the following questions, which can easily be incorporated into a grant application form, before considering a request for a grant.

- *What is the charity's mission?* The charity should have a clear vision of its role in the charitable community and should have adequate resources to achieve that mission.

- *What services does the charity provide?* Ask the charity to describe the services it provides which represent a budget allotment of five percent or more. The following questions will help the foundation place the request for grant into the context of the other work it does.

- *What is the geographic area served by the organization?*

- *What is the budget for the most recent year-end?* Consider whether the budget is consistent with the charity's stated goals and objectives.

- *Provide five years of fund-raising data.* Consider whether the annual income is well diversified (grants, individual donations, fund-raising activities) and whether the number of donors and amount of annual revenue are growing. Determine if the charity has a qualified, competent fund-raising staff.

- *What year was the organization established?* Additional scrutiny should be applied for a newly established entity. (See §7.05.)

- *What is the number of employees for each of the past three years?* Is this number steady, growing, or going up and down?

- *Provide the name of the accounting firm that performs the charity's audit and a copy of the most recent audited financial statement.* How many years has this firm been employed as the charity's independent auditor? Does the firm have board connections or other relationships to the charity?

- *Describe the project to be funded by the grant, and provide a budget for the project.* The project budget should be compared to the organization's overall budget to ensure costs for personnel and overhead are in line with the relationship of the project to the budget.

- *Provide a statement describing the impact or expected outcomes of the project, including the number of individuals served and the time line for completion.*

- *Provide a list of other project funders (as well as outstanding requests for funding).*

- *Provide a copy of the foundation's exemption letter, with an affidavit stating that the exemption has not been modified or revoked.*

- *Attach a copy of the most recent annual report.*

- *Provide a list of the current board members of the charity, as well as the volunteers who will be involved with the project.* Note the number of years each one has been in that position. Get a sense of whether the board turns over frequently, whether members are appointed for life (both of which may signal problems), or whether they seem to have a solid term progression.

- *Supply a list of previous grants received from foundations, a brief description of the project, and a statement about the success of the project.* Review whether the projects were completed (and if so, whether they were completed on time) and ensure the projects had the anticipated outcome.

The foundation's grant application form should list the information required about the applicant organization and the project for which the organization seeks funds. Use the questions above, and the information provided in Table 7-12, to develop an inquiry that yields the most important information to the individuals making grant decisions.

TABLE 7-12
List of Information Needed from Grant Applicants

Item to Be Attached	Detail	Rationale
One-page cover letter	The letter should explain the project, the amount requested, and the time line on which the funds are needed.	This one-page letter is an easy way for the applicant to summarize the request in as succinct a manner as possible. It is also an easy way for the grant decision makers to get a focus on the request before reading the entire application.
Application form	The instructions should make it clear whether there is a structured form that must be used or whether the applicant can create an unstructured request that incorporates specific information. This information might include: • A project description, • The goals of the project, • A description of the manner in which the success of the project will be measured, • A budget for the project, • A schedule of when the requested funds are needed, • Sources of potential funding for the project (funds contributed by the organization, by the board, from individual contributors, from government grants or other foundation grants, etc.), • A list of other organizations to which the applicant is applying for a grant, and • A budget for the organization (or annual report).	Place the responsibility for making the case for the grant on the requesting organizations. There are many organizations with great ideas that have not worked through the more practical issues. It is also important to set goals to Measure the success of a project.

TABLE 7-12   CONTINUED

Item to Be Attached	*Detail*	*Rationale*
Required attachments	Required attachments may include: • The tax determination letter for the organization, • A statement that the organization's tax determination letter has not been rescinded or otherwise changed since the date of issue, and • A list of board members of the applicant organization, including the name, occupation, and address of each.	The tax determination letter is a critical piece of information needed to determine the form and legitimacy of the application; this step is essential in exercising care in grantmaking. Certification that the tax status of the applicant has not changed is also prudent. You can also check the *Internal Revenue Service Bulletin* and IRS Publication 78.
Optional attachments	You may also want to follow the requesting organization to give you additional information about the organization, including: • A brochure about the organization, • A brochure about the project, or • Other relevant items not to exceed "x" pages.	You have to balance the "need to know" with the practical need to be able to read and handle the materials.
Do not attach	The application instructions should clearly define information that will not be considered in the grant determination process. Examples include: • Videos about the organization or the project and • Requests for personal appearances before the foundation.	You will be surprised by the ingenuity and apparent resources of some of the request ing organizations. If you are not clear to describe the format of the request, you will be overwhelmed with extraneous information.

[2]   Developing Other Information

The foundation should also verify data provided by grantseekers and do independent research on the organization, especially if the grant is large. Go to Guidestar (*www.guidestar.org*) and review the charity's Form 990. Check the salaries paid to the top executives, the fund-raising costs, and the charity's balance sheet. Ask more questions if any of these figures appear unusual or out of line.

The most effective way to guard against fraud or misuse of foundation funds is to research potential grant recipients carefully before writing the organization a check. Information is readily available through a variety of sources. The sources in Tables 7-13, 7-14, and 7-15, organized by online resources, trade

TABLE 7-13
Online Charity Research Sites

Name	Contact Information	Comments
Charity navigator	www.charitynavigator.org	The organization maintains a searchable database with ratings of more than 3,700 charities.
Give.org	www.give.org	This site, sponsored by the BBB Wise Giving Alliance, provides information for donors, businesses, and charities about charitable organizations. The site includes an online Charity Reporting and Evaluation System.
Guidestar	www.guidestar.org	This searchable database is built on the list of exempt organizations listed in IRS Publication 78. It provides web sites, pdf files of 990s, and selected financial profiles. Guidestar also offers subscription services for salary research, grant research, and charity evaluation.
NASCO (National Association of State Charity Officials)	http://www.nasconet.org/agencies	This site lists the state offices that regulate charitable organizations in the United States with the links to those officials.
American Institute of Philanthropy	http://www.charitywatch.org/	This site contains charity ratings, information on charities, tips on giving wisely, and other data to support donors in giving in an informed manner.

TABLE 7-14
Charitable Trade Groups

Name	Contact Information	Comments
BBB Wise Giving Alliance	4200 Wilson Boulevard, 8th floor Arlington, VA 22203 703-276-0100 www.bbbonline.org	This organization resulted from the merger of the National Charities Information Bureau and the Council of BBB's Foundation and its Philanthropic Services.
Center on Nonprofits & Philanthropy	The Urban Institute 2100 M Street NW Washington, DC 20037 202-833-7200 www.urban.org	This division of The Urban Institute conducts research and provides information to the public about nonprofits maintained by the National Center for Charitable Statistics. (See listing below.)
Evangelical Council for Financial Accountability	440 West Jubal Early Drive, Suite 130 Winchester, VA 22601 540-535-0103 www.ecfa.org	ECFA's mission is to improve accountability for Christian organizations to elevate public trust. The site has information on its more than 1,000 members.

TABLE 7-14. CONTINUED

Name	Contact Information	Comments
Independent Sector	1200 Eighteenth Street NW, Suite 200 Washington, DC 20036 202-467-6100 *www.independentsec-tor.org*	Independent Sector conducts extensive research on the nonprofit sector. The web site contains good information and links for those researching philanthropic issues.
National Center for Charitable Statistics	The Urban Institute 2100 M Street NW Washington, DC 20037 866-518-3874 *http://nccsdataweb. urban.org/FAQ/index. php?category=90*	This organization develops and distributes data on nonprofits and their activities.

TABLE 7-15
Miscellaneous Resources

Source	Comment
Attorney General's Office	The State Attorney General is charged with representing the charitable interests in the state. Do not start with this source, but check with this office if you have concerns about or want to report fraud or malfeasance.
Better Business Bureau (in the area the charity is located)	The Better Business Bureau maintains files on charities that are involved in fraud or that fail to meet donor expectations.
Community Foundation	The local community foundation may be an excellent resource for information on local organization, grant management, and board operation. Some family foundations use the community foundation to do grant review (for a fee).
IRS Publication 78	For a bottom-line answer on whether a specific charity is recognized as a tax-exempt entity, check IRS Publication 78, *www.irs.org*.
Public Library	Public libraries with research areas often have extensive information about charitable organizations. Some have microfiche with 990 information.

associations, and miscellaneous sources, are quick and easy to use. Use these for an initial review of the legitimacy of an organization to ensure the information given in the sources matches information provided by the charity and to unearth any complaints filed by other foundations or donors. Do not rely on the charity's web site alone — any organization can create a web site and represent itself in an attractive fashion.

With larger grants it may also be important to make a subjective review of the charity. Are there adequate safeguards in place to avoid fraud? Is the charity adequately staffed and structured to honor commitments to the foundation and to its donors?

For smaller grants or charities employing a less formal process, interview the grant applicants on the phone or on site and raise the same questions. Those organizations that are well run, have policies and procedures to prevent fraud, have a strategic growth process, and will be able to answer the questions easily. Those with less structure, who intend to engage in planning after receipt of the grant, will struggle to provide answers. Asking these questions in advance of funding puts the charity on notice that it must be accountable to receive the funds, and focus its board and staff on program goals, desired outcomes, and follow-through.

[C] The Structured Application Form

A structured application form is preferred by organizations that want to quickly assess relevant information and limit the information provided by the applicant. When referred to in this book, a structured form is defined as a preprinted form or a form that can be downloaded from the foundation's web site. The applicant must complete each of the lines and boxes of the form and must restrict responses to the space provided. This space is limited to encourage brief, focused responses. Many government grant applications are published in this format, although most family foundation applications are not.

The advantages and disadvantages of the structured grant application form are detailed in Table 7-16. A sample structured grant application form is provided at Appendix 7-C.

TABLE 7-16
Advantages and Disadvantages of a Structured Grant Application

Advantage	Disadvantage
1. The information is set out in a familiar, comparable format. The grants committee can quickly review application and find the information that is important in making the decision.	1. Limiting the way that information is presented may limit the information you receive. The applicant may have an exciting or innovative idea that is not easily distilled to a 2-inch-by-4-inch box on a form.
2. It is easy to list the information required for consideration; missing information can be quickly identified.	
3. The applicants are forced to be succinct and to limit the information to its most important elements. Without limits, applicants may be tempted to provide too much information, making the key points difficult to distill.	

TABLE 7-16.   CONTINUED

Advantage	Disadvantage
4. The form makes it easier for some applicants to apply for the grant. Some applicants are sophisticated with large staffs, while others have staff inexperienced in filing requests for funds. Applicants requesting grant funds for the first time may find it difficult to draft an unstructured proposal.	
5. The grant requests are easy to copy and distribute.	

TABLE 7-17
Advantages and Disadvantages of an Unstructured Grant Application

Advantage	Disadvantage
1. The applicant has the opportunity to make the case for the grant in the most effective way possible.	1. The proposals may be more difficult to review and compare. The length and way in which the information is organized may make it challenging for an administrator to review the request and determine that the relevant information is attached. The proposal structure may also make it time consuming for a committee member/board member to find information that he or she needs to make a decision.
2. The applicants can incorporate photos or attachments to add depth to the proposal.	2. The proposal may be too short or organized in a way that is difficult to understand.

[D]   The Unstructured Application Form

The unstructured application form is the most common format for family foundations. While the form is unstructured in that it does not restrict applicants to boxed responses, it does contain a list of specific information to be included. The foundation will generally list the information set out in Table 7-12 and instruct the applicants to include it somewhere in their applications.

Place a limit on the pages in the application when using an unstructured form. While most applicants do not have the time to draft lengthy proposals, others will cover you with a hundred pages or more if allowed. A limit of 20 or 25 pages is generally a generous allowance. Think about the task of the grant committee members. If the committee member receives 40 requests, each of which is 20 pages in length, he or she will have 800 pages to review prior to the meeting date.

The advantages and disadvantages of this form are the reverse of those listed for structured applications. *See* Table 7-17. A sample unstructured grant application form is provided at Appendix 7-B.

These forms are not a matter of science, but a matter of convenience. Use the format that works best for your family, and do not be afraid to mix the two forms to get the best results.

§7.07   SELECTING GRANT RECIPIENTS

The grant committee must organize the grant selection process to make effective decisions with the least amount of frustration. Defining the process and criteria for decision making also eliminates one common area for family battles.

[A]   Before the Meeting

1. *Make sure that the foundation sets priorities and parameters for awarding grants before reviewing requests.* These decisions, which may be guided by the above discussion, should be handled at a separate meeting of the foundation governing board. The board members will have a difficult time setting boundaries on a case-by-case basis as applications are reviewed.

2. *Set a deadline for receipt of applications at least one month in advance of the meeting at which grants are awarded.* Review the grant applications to determine whether the information is clear, complete, and consistent with foundation guidelines. Eliminate the applications that do not fit the parameters for the foundation.

3. *Prepare a financial worksheet for the grant committee members to guide them in the amount that can be distributed.* The sheet should recap the estimated distribution amount for the year, reduced by the grants made to date and the serial grants committed for payment later in the year. The figure that remains represents the distribution figure for the year. Worksheets for calculating payments are provided in §7.04[C].

4. *Prepare a grants worksheet to use when considering individual grants.* For each grant to be reviewed in the meeting, the sheet should list the purpose, the amount requested, the time over which the funds are needed, and the grants awarded to the applicant in earlier years and should provide a space to make notes. A sample grants worksheet is included at Appendix 7-G.

5. *Mail the grant package to the committee members at least two weeks in advance of the meeting.* Include the financial worksheet, the grants worksheet, and a copy of each grant. Ask the committee members to review each request, call the foundation manager with any questions, and do any personal research on the requesting organization that is appropriate.

[B] At the Meeting

1. *Begin by reviewing the amount of money available for distribution and reaching consensus on the maximum to be distributed.* If there is any unusual issue, such as the potential for excessive serial grants, raise that issue in advance, and reach a resolution on how the issue will be handled.

2. *Consider and take action on the grant requests.* There are at least three actions that can be taken on each grant request. The request can be denied. The request can be granted in full or in part. Or the request can be held pending a decision until more information is gathered or until year-end.

   When the foundation has many grants to consider, look for ways to streamline the process so that discussion can be focused on the relevant grants. One technique used by some foundations is to begin with a poll of the group to determine if there are any firm "no's" before discussion. Begin with the first member and ask him or her to call out the requests that should be denied. (It is a good idea to start with the junior members of the board, or the newest members of the board, to avoid undue influence or domination by elders or long-term members.) Move around the table recording the negative votes. Eliminate the grant requests receiving a "no" majority, and discuss only those grants remaining.

3. *Keep a running tally of grants awarded during the deliberation process.* This enables the committee to have a focus on the dollars remaining for distribution.

4. *Conclude the meeting with a reading of the amounts awarded and a total of those grants.*

[C] After the Meeting

[1] Administrative Follow-up After the Meeting

1. *Prepare minutes of the meeting, including a list of approved grants and amounts, as quickly as possible after the meeting.* Send this list to all grant committee members to confirm the meeting decisions.

2. *Have the minutes approved by the full board.* This should be done as quickly as possible.

3. *Prepare and mail the checks for grants awarded together with a grant agreement.* Also notify organizations that did not receive grants. Sample letters for use in notifying applicants that a grant has been awarded or denied are included at Appendices 7-H and 7-I, respectively.

4. *Set up a tickler system to remind the foundation administrator to confirm the return of grant agreements four to six weeks after mailing.* Set up any follow-up notices for further action where required.

5. *Establish a list of grants with expenditure responsibility, since the grantees must file follow-up reports on the use of the grants.*

6. *Record the grant awards in the foundation's database.* Be sure to record multiyear grant payment dates in a tickler system to prompt payment on a timely basis.

[2] Six Nice Ways to Say "No" to Grantseekers

Family foundations, especially those that have been in existence long enough to be included in the most popular searchable foundation databases, are often inundated with requests for funds. Even those foundations with relatively low profiles are likely to receive more requests for funding than the foundation can or should fund. This means the foundation will have many times it needs to say no to charities seeking funds.

The easiest way to turn down a grant request is to send a letter saying "no" with as little explanation as possible. There are times a foundation administrator may be tempted to print several hundred "no" letters, seal them in envelopes, and simply address them as grant requests that rate a "no" response arrive in the mail. That process is quick and easy, requires little thought, and invites no discussion. It does not, however, reduce future requests from the grant applicant, assist the grantseeker in doing a better job on the next application, or further philanthropy in the community.

As with any aspect of foundation management, there is a way to decline grant requests that furthers the foundation's mission. The foundation will create a much greater philanthropic impact if it takes the time to write a letter that effectively communicates the problem with the request. Consider the most common scenarios in which a grant request is declined.

1. *"No, We Do Not Take Unsolicited Grant Requests"*

One of the great advantages to a private foundation is the board's right to fund any charities or charitable purposes it selects. Many families use private foundations to make grants to organizations where they serve on the board, attend church, use the services, or have other personal interests. These foundations may have limited funds and therefore no interest or ability to consider outside requests. The best way to convey this message is to tell the grantseeker clearly that the foundation initiates and selects its own grants, and unsolicited grant applications are not accepted. Saying this clearly should prompt the grantseeker to remove the foundation from the potential donor list.

2. *"No, Your Request Does Not Fit Our Guidelines"*

Sometimes grantseekers make mass application to every foundation in a grant resource directory without bothering to determine if the foundation has limitations (purpose, sector, location, etc.). In some cases, the family foundation has not effectively communicated those limits, while in others the grantseeking charity has not researched available information. In either instance, the foundation should clearly communicate those limits in its response denying the request. The foundation should include a copy of the grant guidelines with the denial letter to underscore the point. With any luck, clear communication of guidelines will keep the applicant from repeating the mistake and will allow it to make a record of the restrictions in its files.

3. *"No, We Have Funded You the Last Five Years"*

Some charities look at foundations as ongoing sources of operating funds. Family foundations may have favorite charities that merit an annual grant, but most active grantmaking foundations place limits on the number of years they will make grants to a single organization. Multiyear limits are set for two reasons. First, the foundation has a finite pool of funds and generally wants to create the greatest possible impact with those funds. Allocating funds to the same organization year after year limits its scope. Second, charities that receive funds every year, even if they are creative in the requests underlying those grants, begin to budget foundation revenue in their operating budget. This dependence on the foundation grant removes the incentive to diversify its funding base.

The foundation should clearly communicate the foundation's policy on multiyear funding in its written grant policies, in the grant agreement awarding the first year's grant, and in the no letter sent when the charity has reached the multiyear limit. Because these charities are generally favorites of the foundation, it is always helpful to let the applicant know when it is appropriate to reapply. Some foundations require a one-year break, while other foundations have two- to five-year break requirements.

4. *"No, You Did Not Meet the Requirements of Follow-up with Your Last Grant"*

Most active grantmaking foundations use grant agreements when making distributions. These agreements require the charity to use the funds for the purpose intended, to submit a written report on the use and impact of the grant funds (within a specified period of time), and to return any funds not used for the project specified. When charities accept grants but fail to comply with the requirements, the foundation should not continue to fund the entity. Many times these noncompliant charities do not take grant requirements seriously until they are turned down for subsequent grants. The foundation should be clear with the funds seeker to underscore the importance of the grant requirements and encourage compliance in relationships with other foundations.

5. *"No, You Need to Develop Your Request and Submit Additional Information"*

Most grantmakers publish grant applications or provide grantseekers with a list of information required for consideration of a grant. If the foundation does not publish written guidelines, it often provides this information to grantseekers over the telephone. When a charity submits a grant request in letter form, or in a canned format (one format sent to tens or hundreds of foundations) that either does not contain the information requested or does not relay it in the manner required for consideration, the foundation should instruct the charity to resubmit the request in the required format and should supply the applicant with the grant guidelines. Many times the charity will apply so late in the grant cycle it is impossible to resubmit the application in a timely manner. When rejecting the request and instructing the organization to resubmit, the foundation should be clear about deadlines for current and future grant meetings.

6. *"No, We Suggest You Do [X, Y, or Z] and Resubmit"*

One of the real advantages to consideration of unsolicited grant requests is the board's exposure to the many charitable initiatives in the community. The foundation develops a great perspective on capital campaigns, community initiatives, and start-up charities. The foundation may observe duplicative efforts or the potential for collaboration. When it sees the opportunity to leverage its grants — or leverage charitable activities — it may choose to respond to a grant request by requesting the charity to make contact with another organization engaged in a similar effort. For example, when a local foundation in the Southeast realized two homeless shelters in the city planned capital campaigns for the same three-year period, it encouraged them to engage in a joint campaign and to collaborate on housing facilities. This effort reduced campaign expenses and created efficiencies in construction and management.

The foundation will receive fewer inappropriate grant requests if it registers its grant requirements and limitations with Guidestar and the major foundation resource directories. (See Table 7–18, listing the major publishers and contact

TABLE 7-18
Foundation Resource Guides — Whom to Contact
(This list is not comprehensive but is designed to provide contact information for the key directory publishers.)

Publisher	*Publications*	*Contact Information*
The Foundation Center	• The Foundation Directory • Guide to US Foundations, Their Trustees, Officers and Donors • The Foundation 1000 • The PRI Directory: Charitable Loans and Other Program Related Investments by Foundations • Foundation Grants to Individuals	79 Fifth Avenue New York, NY 10003-3076 212-620-4230 *www.fdncenter.org*

TABLE 7-18.   CONTINUED

Publisher	Publications	Contact Information
The Taft Group	• National Directory of Nonprofit Organizations • Foundation Reporter • Prospector's Choice	Thompson-Gale 27500 Drake Street Farmington Hills, MI 48331 800-877-4253 *www.galegroup.com/taft.htm*
Guidestar	• The National Database of Non-profit Organizations • Salary Search Grant Explorer, Data Services; • Analyst Reports; Compensation Reports	4801 Courthouse Street, Suite 220 Williamsburg, VA 23188 757-229-4631 *www.guidestar.org*
IRS	• Publication 78, Cumulative List of Organizations	*www.irs.gov*
State Foundation Directories	• State and Local Funding Directories: A Bibliography (most states have one or more sources of information about statewide foundations)	The Foundation Center, *http://fdncenter.org/getstarted/topical/sl_dir.html*

information.) Some of these services allow foundations to make entries and changes on their own initiative, while others survey grantmakers periodically, soliciting this information. Although it may seem unappealing to seek out resource directory publishers (and thereby increase the foundation's public profile), the foundation should remember that the publishers already know the foundation exists and have the foundation's name, contact information, and Form 990-PF from the public IRS files. Once the foundation has been identified, the foundation resource center has only two choices: it can deduce the foundation's interests by reading the list of grants shown in its 990-PF, or it can use the more accurate information provided by the foundation. A clear articulation of the foundation's policies will provide guidance to grantseekers who take the time to do the research and will cut down on the number of "no" letters and responses required.

It takes little time to master the art of saying "no". The foundation should create five or six basic form letters that can be personalized as interest and time allow. Taking the time to say "no" focuses the foundation on grants analysis, provides guidance to the grantseeker on how to improve, and ultimately improves the quality of grants made in the community.

[D]   Pacing the Foundation's Grantmaking

Sometimes a foundation gets into the habit of funding the same organizations each year, or makes so many multiyear commitments that it has few discretionary funds for distribution. This problem is exacerbated in years in which the foundation's asset values drop, resulting in a lower required distribution amount. This problem is not uncommon. When the foundation board gives up all discretion over grantmaking, reserving little or no funds for its discretionary distributions and new projects, the board may find it difficult to remain enthusiastic or focused on the process.

The best way to pace your grantmaking, especially in difficult investment markets, is to establish good habits during the strong markets. This means following a few simple steps:

1. *Set clear goals for grantmaking.* There are few foundations that are large enough to solve all the problems in the world. Even the Bill and Melinda Gates Foundation (with assets of approximately 26.8 billion [2004 annual report value]) focuses its grantmaking on "sharing advances in health and learning with the global community" — narrow areas of need that are important to them and reflect their personal values.

2. *Target your distributable amount before the year begins.* It helps to know in advance how much one must distribute and to decide what one will distribute. This formula involves an understanding of the minimum distribution rules, undistributed amounts from prior years, and any multiyear commitments made by the foundation. Divide this amount by the number of grant meetings for the year, weighting the funds into those grant cycles that attract the highest number of grants.

3. *Establish clear policies for multiyear grants.* Will the foundation make three-year or five-year grants, or will it require those seeking long-term funding to return annually and reapply? The policies should distinguish those projects that are start-up and may not be able to move into year 1 without a three- or five-year commitment from those where the foundation's commitment is not critical to moving forward. It is also a good idea to limit the sum of all multiyear grants to a fraction of the foundation's average annual distributions. For example, some foundations limit multiyear grants to no more than 25 percent or one-third of their total funds.

4. *Avoid annual grants to the same charities.* Charities that receive a distribution every year, without writing a grant request and describing how prior-year funds were used, receive the message that the foundation wants to be part of its operating budget and that it is not concerned about the use of the funds. The foundation's policies should limit the number of years an organization receives funding, prioritize organizations that have not received multiyear funding, or in some way require a year-to-year analysis of need. There will always be exceptions, of course. The foundation may decide to team with other local foundations to fund a specific project or new service in the community. These projects should be the exception rather than the rule.

5. *Analyze the dispersal of grant awards at the end of each year.* Calculate the percentage of grants that represent multiyear commitments. Review the schedule of grants committed for subsequent years. Make a list of organizations that have received funding in three, four, five, or more years in the last 10. Divide the grants by sectors and compare the grants awarded to the foundation's mission statement. This studied review is the only way to make an objective analysis of the foundation's grantmaking habits.

Clear policies and objectives, limitations on certain types of grants, and specific guidance for the grants committee are the only way to stay on track and ensure the foundation will have some annual and long-term flexibility to meet its charitable objectives. Review your foundation's policies and you may find you have control of your grantmaking dollars and results.

§7.08   THE GRANT AGREEMENT

A grant agreement is a document that establishes the terms for use of the grant. A grant agreement is necessary for distributions requiring expenditure responsibility, such as grants to individuals or to organizations not recognized as tax exempt by the Internal Revenue Service. The document is evidence that the foundation has complied with the Regulations. The agreement is recommended, however, for all grants, since the agreement establishes a system of accountability and increases the likelihood that the funds will be used for the purposes intended.

The grant agreement lists the purposes for which the grant must be used, sets reporting standards, and requires that unused funds be returned to the foundation. A sample grant agreement is provided at Appendix 7-E.

§7.09   MONITORING THE USE OF GRANT FUNDS

[A]   The Basic Duty of Fiduciary Care

Foundation board members serve in a fiduciary role and must exercise care in making grant decisions, distributing foundation funds, and following up on grants. The best way to meet this fiduciary responsibility is to establish a series of procedures. These recommendations are mandated for grants requiring expenditure responsibility, but are recommended for all grants to comply with both the spirit and the letter of the law.

• *Use a grant application.* The grant application solicits the information needed to ascertain that the applicant meets the basic requirements for funding. These include the tax determination letter evidencing the organization's IRS status, the project goals, and the project budget.

- *Conduct on-site visits.* Where the foundation has the time and staff, it should conduct on-site visits. These visits may be conducted prior to the award of grant to learn more about an unfamiliar charity or as part of the follow-up after award to ensure funds have been used for designated purposes. A written report should be prepared following the site visit and placed in the foundation's files.

- *Require a grant agreement.* The grant agreement establishes standards for use of the grant funds, sets a schedule for reporting on use of those funds, and requires the return of unused funds. Without a reporting and response mechanism, grant recipients may receive funds for a project, decide not to proceed with the project, and simply keep the money and apply it to another use.

- *Require a follow-up report.* The grant agreement should require that the grant recipient file a report on the use of the funds that includes:

  — The goals of the project, the benchmarks for success, and the results achieved during the period;

  — The lessons learned in the project, including any unanticipated result;

  — A list of any outstanding project elements;

  — A description of any variances in the project and the reasons for those variances;

  — The implementation process and the individuals and agencies involved;

  — The future of the project, including goals and sources of future funding;

  — Certification that the funds were used for the purposes intended; and

  — Detail on unused funds, including the amount and the approximate date of the use or return of those funds.

A sample follow-up report outline is provided at Appendix 7-F.

[B] Complying with Expenditure Responsibility Rules

[1] In General

The IRS requires that foundations exercise a higher duty of care, called "expenditure responsibility," when making distributions to organizations that are not considered traditional charities. Grants requiring exercise of expenditure responsibility include:

- Grants to organizations that are not section 501(c)(3) organizations, such as chambers of commerce, trade organizations, or organizations without a formal structure;

- Grants to foreign organizations; and

- Program-related investments.

Distributions made to the above-named organizations without the exercise of expenditure responsibility will be treated as taxable expenditures.[89] Grants made to organizations to carry on nonpartisan activities that are not confined to one election period and are carried on in five or more states are specifically excluded from expenditure responsibility.

Some foundations refuse to make grants that require expenditure responsibility because of difficulty in complying with the rules. Actually, the expenditure responsibility requirements are not onerous and evidence good fiduciary practice. The exercise of expenditure responsibility requires only that the foundation exercise care and diligence in award and review of the grant, and does not require that the foundation ensure that the organization spends the funds as directed.[90] The three steps in the process are (1) a pre-grant inquiry, (2) a written agreement governing expenditure of the funds, and (3) a follow-up report. Each of these is discussed below.

[2] Pre-Grant Inquiry

The foundation is required to review the applicant and its management prior to making the grant. The purpose of the review is to assess the reliability of the recipient in using the funds for charitable purposes. Create a checklist that includes:

- The tax status of the organization;

- The history of the organization and its management;

- The length of time that the organization has operated; and

- The organization's prior experience in managing grant funds.

The scope of the review may vary with each organization. For example, the McCoy Family Foundation may make an annual grant to a community food bank that is not an organized, traditional charity. In 1998, the first year the grant was made, the foundation made extensive inquiries about the history of the organization, reviewed audited statements of its use of funds, and talked to other foundations that had made grants to the organization in prior years. The food bank complied with all requests for reports on the use of funds and has been managed by the same staff since 1998. In subsequent years, the McCoy Foundation reduced its level of inquiry, relying instead on its personal experience and

---

[89] IRC §4945(d)(4); Reg. §53.4945-5(a)(1).
[90] IRC §4945(h); Reg. §53.4945-5(b)(1).

the continued compliance of the food bank with the foundation's requests. The foundation's reliance on actual experience in the years after 1998 was sufficient to meet the review requirements of the IRS.[91]

The foundation is also entitled to rely on the information supplied and the records maintained by the grant recipient as long as the records are signed by the appropriate officer.[92] It is important, however, for the foundation to clearly mark grants requiring expenditure responsibility, take the steps required to evidence responsible grantmaking, maintain proper internal records, and report to the IRS on a timely and complete basis.

[3] Written Agreement with Receiving Organization

The foundation must require that the recipient agree to use the funds for the specified charitable purpose. This agreement must be in writing and signed by someone with authority to bind the organization, such as an officer, director, or trustee. The agreement must require that the recipient:[93]

- Use the funds for the purpose intended and return the funds not used for that purpose;

- Provide full reports on how the funds were used;

- Keep accurate records of receipts and expenditures and make those records available to the foundation upon request; and

- Make no expenditure to carry on propaganda, attempt to influence legislation, influence the outcome of a public election, carry on a voter registration drive, make a grant that is for purposes other than allowed for private foundations, or spend the funds for a noncharitable purpose.

[4] Follow-up Report

The third element of expenditure responsibility is the preparation of a follow-up report by the grant recipient (and its receipt by the foundation making the grant). The report should state that the funds were used for the purpose intended, provide detail on the use of the funds, state that the organization complied with the terms of the grant agreement, and include information on how the funds furthered the charitable purpose intended by the grant. The report should be made at the end of each fiscal year in which the funds were received and used. If use of the funds extends over several years, a report should be issued each year, including a final report after the project is complete.[94]

---

[91] Reg. §§53.4945-5(b)(2)(i), (ii).
[92] Reg. §53.4945-5(c)(4).
[93] Reg. §53.4945-5(b)(3).
[94] Reg. §53.4945-5(c)(1).

[5] Foundation Reporting Requirements

When a family foundation makes a grant requiring expenditure responsibility, it must attach a report on award, terms, and use of the grant to Form 990-PF. The report must contain:[95]

- The name and address of the organization receiving the funds subject to expenditure responsibility;

- The date of the grant;

- The amount of the grant;

- The purpose of the grant;

- The amount spent by the receiving organization, including the dollar amount and the purpose of the expenditure;

- A statement that the funds have not been spent for purposes other than the purpose for which the grant was awarded;

- The dates of the reports filed by the recipient; and

- A description of any verification activities conducted by the foundation.

The foundation can write an original report for the tax return or file the report submitted by the recipient so long as the report contains the required information. The simplest way to handle this is to require the grant recipient to draft the report to the foundation in a format that will suffice for the tax return.

In addition to filing a report with the 990-PF, the foundation must maintain records documenting its compliance with the oversight rules. These include a copy of the grant agreement signed by the appropriate representative of the foundation, a copy of all reports filed by the recipient reporting on the use of funds, and a copy of any audits of the use of the funds made by foundation staff or third-party auditors hired for that purpose.[96]

[6] Special Rules for Grants to Private Foundations for Endowments

Where a private foundation makes a grant to an exempt private foundation for endowment purposes, meaning that the funds will be retained by the recipient rather than spent, the grantmaking foundation must obtain reports on the use of principal and income from the recipient foundation for the year of award and the succeeding two tax years to ensure that the funds are used for the purpose intended. The purpose of the review is to ensure that the income and principal of the endowment is spent only for charitable purposes. If the recipient is in

---

[95] Reg. §53.4945-5(d)(2).
[96] Reg. §53.4945-5(d)(3).

compliance through the three-year period and it appears that it has a process to ensure ongoing compliance, no further reports are required.[97]

[7] Additional Requirements for Program-Related Investments

Program-related investments have special expenditure requirements. The recipient of the program-related investment funds must execute a written agreement, signed by an officer, director, or trustee with authority to bind the organization, stating that:[98]

- It will use the funds only for the purpose of the designated investment;

- It will return or repay any portion of the funds not used for the designated investment (where the family foundation takes an equity position in the investment, state law on corporations and stockholders may affect the extent to which assets may be returned);

- It will provide full financial reporting (such as that required of commercial investors in like circumstances) and a statement that it has honored the terms of the investment;

- It will keep detailed records of transactions and make those records available to the foundation; and

- It will not use any of the funds to carry on propaganda, attempt to influence legislation, influence the outcome of a public election, carry on a voter registration drive, or make a distribution that would not comply with the requirements for private foundation grants.

[8] Rules Related to Foreign Organizations and Foreign Private Foundations

The written grant agreement used for grants to foreign organizations must bind the foreign recipient organization to the same restrictions placed on private foundations in the spending of funds.[99] These agreements are more difficult to draft in foreign countries because of the language barriers. The restrictions may be phrased in terms reflecting local language usage and custom as appropriate, but must be accompanied by an affidavit or opinion of counsel of the family foundation or the recipient stating that the agreement imposes restrictions on the use of funds that are substantially equivalent to those imposed on domestic private foundations.[100]

---

[97] Reg. §53.4945-5(c)(2).

[98] Reg. §53.4945-5(b)(4).

[99] Reg. §53.4945-5(b)(5), citing the requirements placed on domestic private foundations under IRC §4945(d).

[100] Reg. §53.4945-5(b)(5).

§7.10   PERFECTING AND ENFORCING GRANT INTENT

As family foundations work strategically to focus grants on specific out-comes and grant accountability, the grant agreement assumes an increasingly important role. Without a clear written directive on use of the funds, the foundation may miss an opportunity to tie grant use to outcomes, may have difficulty exhibiting and forcing accountability, and may have little recourse to enforce directives when charitable recipients choose to use the funds for other purposes.

Why should foundations be concerned about enforcing grant intent? With-out clear written direction, grant funds may be misapplied. Sometimes, this occurs as a result of poor communication. Sometimes, memories fade with time or individuals involved in negotiating the grant are replaced with those who were not party to the conversation. Sometimes, the charitable environment changes so that current needs overshadow grant goals. Or in a real lapse of accountability, those making decisions about the use of the funds are simply not aware of the grant requirements. (Rarely are the funds misapplied with the intention of violating the grant terms.) In each case, a clearly written grant agreement with reporting requirements could resolve the issues.

[A]   What Could Possibly Go Wrong? Case Studies in Erosion of Grant Intent

A review of court cases reveals foundation grantees get off track for a variety of reasons and experience myriad results. These cautionary tales offer an effective way to explore problems experienced by other foundations and avoid making them your own.

[1]   Carl H. Herzog Foundation

The Carl H. Herzog Foundation filed to recover a portion of a $250,000 grant made to the University of Bridgeport designated for medical education scholar-ships claiming the University had used the funds for another purpose. The court did not allow the lawsuit to move forward finding the foundation had no standing to sue. The court suggested the foundation might have had an actionable claim if the foundation had included language in a written agreement granting them the right to enforce the restrictions through litigation. "At common law, a donor who has made a completed charitable contribution, whether as an absolute gift or in trust, had no standing to bring an action to enforce the terms of his or her gift or trust unless he or she had expressly reserved the right to do so."[101] Further, the court stated such a written directive is "enforceable at the suit of the attorney general...."

---

[101] *Carl J. Herzog Foundation, Inc. v. University of Bridgeport*, 243 Conn. 1, 699 A.2d 995 (1997).

[2] The L. B. Research and Education Foundation

In 2002, the L. B. Research and Education Foundation made a $1 million grant to the UCLA Foundation to create an endowed chair in Cardiothoracic Surgery governed by a written grant agreement specifying the criteria for the chair holder. The grant agreement required ongoing reporting and had a "gift over" provision providing for the transfer of funds in the event the UCLA Foundation did not meet its obligations. Shortly thereafter, the UCLA Foundation used the fund for individuals the L.B. Research and Education Foundation did not feel met the terms of the agreement, and the donor-Foundation sued. While the lower court dismissed the lawsuit stating the L. B. Research and Education Foundation had no standing to sue, the appeals court reversed that decision determining the arrangement was contractual, and that even if not contractual the plaintiff had a "special interest" that allowed it standing, and the Attorney General's power to enforce charitable trusts under California law (the defendants had argued the arrangement was a charitable trust rather than contractual) was not exclusive.[102]

[3] The Catherine B. Reynolds Foundation and the Smithsonian

The Catherine B. Reynolds Foundation conflict with the Smithsonian resulted in the rescission of the grant commitment. The Catherine B. Reynolds Foundation made a $38 million pledge to the Smithsonian for the National Museum of American History. The Foundation was quite clear about the gift's goals. The exhibit was designed to recognize the power of a single individual to influence lives and to inspire other Americans to make their mark. Specifically, the exhibit was designed to recognize individuals who received the Nobel Prize, had invented something of great importance, had achieved success in the arts or sciences, or had conducted a significant public service.[103] When Ms. Reynolds was asked about the type of individuals to be honored, she suggested Oprah Winfrey, Sam Donaldson, Dorothy Hamill, and Martha Stewart as those typical of influential individuals.

The terms of the gift were negotiated and agreed to in a written document signed by the Foundation and the Smithsonian. Following the gift's announcement, however, many of the Smithsonian curators — and much of the public — objected strenuously to the stated goals and the rights the Foundation had retained to stay involved. As an example, the Foundation reserved the right to appoint a number of the initial board members who would select recipients,

---

[102] *L. B. Research and Education Foundation v. The UCLA Foundation et. al.,* Cal. App. No. B176151 (6/14/2005). The opinion is available at http://www.courtinfo.ca.gov/opionions/documents/B176151.PDF.

[103] Lewis, Nicole Controversy Over Donor's Role Causes Smithsonian to Lose $36.5 Million, *The Chronicle of Philanthropy,* Vol. 14, Issue 9 (Feb. 21, 2002).

although the Museum had the final say over those honored. In addition, Ms. Reynolds name would be added to the front of one of the Museum's buildings.

The gift stirred such a controversy and criticism that the Catherine B. Reynolds Foundation withdrew the bulk of its gift ($1.5 million had already been spent for planning.) Shortly after that, the American Association of Museums issued a set of ethical guidelines to be used by its 3,000 members in acceptance of gifts. These guidelines are designed to ensure gifts comply with the law, gift purposes are consistent with the museum's mission, that museum officials control content and integrity of exhibitions, that no individual benefits at the expense of an organization's mission or reputation, that transactions are open to the public, and that a donor understands how the gift will be used.[104]

[B] The Grant Agreement

While a written grant agreement is a requirement for foundation distributions requiring expenditure responsibility — such as grants to private non-operating foundations, private operating foundations and organizations without IRC Section 501(c)(3) status — the authors recommend a written document for all foundation grants. Quite simply, a written grant agreement provides a platform that allows the foundation to set standards for use of the funds, detail reporting requirements, and outline permissible deviations from the specified purpose of the grant. A grant agreement may also preserve the foundation's remedies in the event the funds are not used or used for other than intended purposes.

Working through a well-designed grant agreement is tantamount to working with a checklist. Every aspect of the grant and its use should be discussed and agreed upon. Consider the following checklist as a guideline in creating an effective gift document:

1. *Amount of the grant and the timing of the funding.* For example, the grant award may be $100,000 payable on award; the grant award may be $100,000 payable over two years in equal payments on April 1 2005, 2006; or it may be an award of $50,000 with a potential award of an addition $50,000 if certain conditions (specified in the agreement) are met.

2. *Grant purpose and permissible deviations.* Clearly specify the purposes for which the funds may be spent. If funds can only be spent for specific elements of a project — such as the purchase of books and teaching supplies but not office space or similar overhead or purchase of vehicles but not ongoing maintenance — spell out those restrictions. If the funds can be applied for other purposes, the grant agreement should specify the conditions under which the charity can deviate, whether permission is required, and if so, who must approve the deviation.

---

[104] Lipman, Harvy, Museum Group Issues Guideline on Ethics, *The Chronicle of Philanthropy*, Vol. 15, Issue 4 (Nov. 28, 2002). These guidelines can be viewed at www.aam-us.org.

3. *Grant goals.* Detail the gift goals (number of individuals served, number of teachers hired, the publication of a needs assessment) or incorporate by reference the grant proposal detailing expected outcomes.

4. *Recognition and publicity (if any) to be provided for the grant.* If the grant is made with the expectation of ongoing recognition — such as the naming of a building, program, scholarship or chair — the agreement should detail this obligation and the timing for that recognition. Or, if the foundation expects the charity to publicly announce the gift in its annual report, on its website, or through a press release, those requirements should be listed as well. While the latter requirement is unusual, public information about the grant may be designed to encourage others in the community to focus on the need or to follow suite with similar grants.

5. *Grant accounting and reporting.* Specific requirements on grant accounting (internal expenditure and alignment) and grant reporting (external communication of those results) must be specified at the outset of the grant so that the recipient can (i) verify it can meet those requirements and (ii) create internal accounting codes that allow it to segregate grant expenditures from other budgeted items. In addition, the foundation should require the grantee to file a written report by a specified date that contains a description of the grant purpose, detail on the expenditure of funds, the current status of the grant (the date the grant funds were expended, or the expected date of completion of the grant), and the charitable impact of the grant. The foundation may also specify additional requirements (number of individuals served, other charities participating in the grant project, or other specifics).

6. *Return of funds.* The grant agreement should clearly direct the return of grant funds that are not used for the specified purposes and the timeline for that return.

7. *Reservation of right to sue.* Check state law to determine appropriate language that preserves the right for the foundation to file suit in the event the recipient charity fails to honor the grant agreements and/or uses the funds for purposes outside the specified grant purpose.

Good grants are a matter of strategy and planning; the grant agreement is the tool that preserves and enforces those objectives and manages the conflicts inevitable over time. It's hard to see a downside. Family foundations should get in the habit of requiring grantees to execute an agreement prior to receipting for funds and should put administrative procedures in place that prompt grant monitoring and follow-up. If the foundation issues so many grants each year this process is burdensome, begin the exercise for all grants over a certain size or for specified project purposes. Once the foundation gains experience, it can easily extend the grant agreement requirement to other grants. At the end of the day, the foundation will make more effective grants, will document its accountability and should avoid the cautionary tales experienced by other foundations.

[C]   What To Do If the Recipient Does Not Comply With Grant Terms

Sometimes in the course of the monitoring the use of the funds, the foundation will learn that the recipient organization has either used the funds for a purpose not covered by the grant agreement or that it has not used the funds at all. A distribution used for an inappropriate purpose will not constitute a taxable expenditure so long as the foundation has taken reasonable steps to ensure the appropriateness of the grant in accordance with the IRS requirements and has maintained appropriate records of its actions. What should and can the foundation do at this point?

1. The foundation should make no further grants to the recipient or to related entities until it is certain, through reasonable review, that future funds will be expended for appropriate purposes. It should be a rare occasion when the foundation continues to fund an organization that has spent funds inappropriately, since an improper grant of funds subjects the foundation and its managers to penalties for taxable expenditures.

2. The foundation should invoke the terms of the grant agreement and require that the recipient return funds expended for inappropriate purposes. In the event that the recipient does not comply with this request, the foundation should seek legal counsel to review options open to the foundation to recover the funds. The grant agreement represents a contract on which legal action can be based.

§7.11   EVALUATING THE EFFECTIVENESS OF GRANTS

The foundation has a fiduciary duty, a legal duty, and a practical interest in evaluating the effectiveness of its grants. The only way to measure success is to establish measurable expectations at the award of the grant. The grant application should elicit the specific goals of the project. For example, if the program provides a service, the foundation should know the number of individuals that will be served with the funds. If the applicant plans to construct a building, the foundation should know the total budget and the time-line for fund-raising and construction. If the nonprofit plans to provide insurance for uninsured children, the application should reflect the number of children to be served and the date the funds will be used.

Sometimes the grant objectives are difficult to measure. The nonprofit may use a grant to place counselors in schools with the long-term goal of reducing teenage pregnancy, smoking, and drug use. Evaluation may require building baseline data about those health issues and collecting data from hospitals and clinics for a period of time.

Grants can be effectively evaluated in several ways. Consider the following options:

- *Question the recipient.* One of the most common, and practical, methods of program evaluation is to ask the recipient to analyze the results of the grant. This can be done through use of a grant evaluation form that the recipient must return with a certification that the funds have been used for the purposes intended. A sample form is provided at Appendix 7-F.

- *Hire a consultant.* Sometimes it makes sense for the foundation to hire a consultant to perform this function, especially if future grants depend on the success of the initial project. Look for consultants with expertise in the nonprofit sector and with experience in program evaluation. These consultants generally have a background as a program officer in a public or private charity, or may have served in a corporate capacity in administering grants for a foundation. Expect these consultants to cost from $50/hour to $200/hour.

- *Hire a graduate student.* Many graduate students are interested in nonprofit and public welfare issues. These individuals may not have as much practical experience with evaluation, but may have the skills to develop models. This solution is often less expensive than hiring professional consultants.

- *Use a local community foundation or large private foundation that already performs these services.* Community foundations often have staff with the sole responsibility of evaluating applications and fund use. Some foundations offer evaluation services to other foundations for a fee. This is an excellent way to get expertise as well as to build a relationship with a foundation that offers resources in nonprofit management, strategic planning, and financial management.

Grantmaking is complicated but rewarding. The foundation should put a manageable process in place that ensures compliance with its fiduciary and legal obligations. The family can then focus on making grants to organizations that fulfill its mission and reflect its charitable goals.

§7.12 COLLABORATIVE GRANTMAKING

Collaborative grantmaking is frequently used to leverage results. The John D. and Catherine T. MacArthur Foundation sets aside a portion of its funds for its programs on "Human and Community Development" and "Security and Sustainability," encouraging nonprofits to apply for grants to address these issues. The Peninsula Community Foundation in San Mateo, California, offers collaborative grants to teams consisting of teachers, administrators, or community experts interested in developing new learning opportunities for children. The Ms. Foundation in New York maintains a fund to facilitate Youth-Led Social Change. These foundations are a few of the many public and private grantmaking organizations that allocate funds to priority projects.

All of these grants are forms of collaborative grantmaking, one of the most compelling methods of addressing specific charitable needs. Collaborative grantmaking allows a foundation to be proactive and focus its grant funds on charitable projects that achieve specific goals. The practice has value for foundations of all sizes, but particularly for the thousands of smaller foundations in this country managed by families.

[A]   Why Collaborate?

The greatest benefit in collaboration is the ability to focus and leverage the foundation's available grant funds. The goal can be as simple as providing health care for public school children in the county, to increasing affordable housing, to providing music lessons. Whatever the goal, the distinguishing factor is that the foundation on its own cannot achieve the result.

Collaboration may achieve results in several ways. It may encourage existing nonprofits to refocus their work or to work with other nonprofits to achieve the goals targeted by the foundation. In other instances, the goal may be to generate community interest for a specific project, call attention to a critical need (such as the need for health care for public school children referenced above), or attract shared funding. It will also tie the initiating foundation's mission to the project's objectives, generating long-term attention to both the family and the cause.

[B]   Articulating the Project Goals

Family foundations best suited to collaborate are those that have a clear mission statement and a list of objectives. These may have been developed through a family meeting, an active grants committee, or some other consensus-building process. This articulation of goals is often adopted only by larger foundations when in fact it is the smaller foundations — those with the smallest pots of money — that benefit the most from having this clear direction.

If the foundation has never tackled this process as part of its grantmaking, begin by establishing the foundation's charitable area(s) of focus, such as education, health care, science, or public welfare. If the foundation has more than one focus, the board may further divide the distributable funds by percentage, setting aside a portion for the discretionary distributions by board members.

Next, identify the geographic focus of the foundation's grantmaking. At the end of the process, the foundation board should have a clear idea of the amount of funding the foundation can contribute to the process and the geographic area of focus.

Finally, establish a time line for the project. How pressing is the need? Is it likely to be addressed in one financial infusion, or will it take a long time (or large sums of money) to achieve the result? The foundation may need to research the need and proposed solution to resolve this issue.

[C]   Identifying Funders and Program Managers

Once the foundation's goals and financial abilities are established, it is time to research potential funding sources and charities that address the foundation's goals. Contact the community foundation in the targeted geographic area and meet with its organization's grants manager to learn more about funds available from the foundation as well as other potential funders in the community. Many community foundations allocate a portion of funds annually to collaborative projects. If the project relates to human services and welfare, contact the United Way. That organization also serves as a funds manager for projects requiring multiple agency or public funding and has a wealth of information about organizations that address the area of the foundation's focus. Check with church foundations. Many maintain a community ministries area responsible for distribution of funds in the local community. At every step, get input on community organizations that provide the service that is the focus of the foundation's mission.

The research should give the foundation a clear picture of how to proceed. If the community foundation has a pool of funds available to address the issue, the foundation can add to the available funds and participate in the process. Joining in existing projects allows many foundations to use their limited funding most effectively and allows them to draw on the expertise and staffing of larger community charities.

[D]   Attracting Additional Funds

If there are no funds available, the foundation can issue a Request for Proposal from local charities currently addressing these services. Convene a meeting of potential project managers, outline the proposed project, and detail the funds available to project managers addressing the need. Establish measurable standards for success and encourage multiple agencies to combine their efforts, if appropriate. If foundation funds do not cover the cost, consider reaching out to other private foundations and the community foundation for funding. Again, research improves the results of the effort. Use the state foundation listing (usually found at the public library) to identify other foundations with similar interests. Use the search capabilities on *guidestar.com* to identify potential funders (and grant administrators). Conduct searches on the Internet to identify similar projects in other communities. Contact those responsible for the projects to get insights on funding, management, and potential outcomes.

[E] Follow-through

The foundation should set goals for the project, measurable by objective standards. If the foundation joins an existing project, study the reports of the agency coordinating the project to understand the dynamics of collaborative funding and how results are reported. Board members should determine whether coordinating project work creates the expected results. If the foundation coordinates the effort, provide ongoing feedback to other funders, analyze results, and set goals for future projects.

Try collaborative grantmaking with your foundation. Collaborative grantmaking allows foundations to effect change in the community or the world with limited funding. All that is required is board focus, research on potential funders and managing agencies, and convening the key parties in order to reach a consensus on anticipated outcomes. These steps build not only better communities but also stronger family foundation boards.

§7.13 STRATEGIES FOR GRANTMAKING IN YEARS WITH LIMITED DOLLARS

Family foundations, regardless of size, seek ways to maximize assets. The following strategies allow the foundation to coax more impact from grant dollars:

1. *Focus the foundation's grantmaking on specific areas of charitable need.* The foundation's grantmaking will have more impact if it is concentrated in a few areas of charitable need rather than scattered across every area of need. Placing limitations on grants, whether by geography, area of need, and even size, occurs at every grantmaking meeting. Making decisions about grant scope and focus before the grantmaking meeting has several benefits. First, it allows the family to set its priorities before its objectiveness is skewed by specific requests for funding. Second, it allows the foundation to focus its grants on specific, well-conceived priorities. Third, it allows the foundation to become an expert in the area, researching the needs, potential solutions, and available resources. Finally, it associates the foundation more closely with a specific charitable field, making the foundation a powerful advocate for change.

2. *Use accountability to increase the effectiveness of the foundation's grants.* Although grantmaking is by definition a risky business, the chance of success is improved through direction and oversight. The foundation should begin by using a grant application form that requires applicants to provide a budget for the project and to detail the standards for measuring

the grant's impact. Issue the grant subject to a grant agreement, requiring the recipient to use the funds for the purpose requested, file a grant report when the funds have been spent, and return any funds not used.

3. *Allocate a portion of the foundation's grant dollars to training and advocacy.* Sometimes the key service providers (or potential service providers) need help in becoming more effective. Consider providing the services of a strategic planning consultant to the organization as part of a grant award. Provide an annual training workshop for all nonprofits serving the foundation's focus area. This allows the foundation grantmakers to meet the nonprofit providers, and for those providers to meet each other. In addition, it allows the foundation to take potential grant recipients through a careful analysis of needs and to collaborate on solutions.

Spend grant dollars to educate the community. Conduct a needs assessment in the foundation's focus area and present the results to the community through a newspaper supplement. If the foundation works on a regional, national, or international basis, choose a publication that most effectively reaches the audience that can act or contribute to address the need.

4. *Collaborate with organizations with similar programmatic interests.* Leverage the foundation's dollars by joining with other community funders. If the foundation cannot identify likely partners, ask grant recipients for the names of other family foundations providing funding, work with the community foundation to identify other potential funders, or post a request for foundation (or other) partners in a nonprofit forum. The inquiries may prompt additional organizations to get involved.

5. *Make foundation distributions as loans rather than grants when appropriate.* An interest-free loan, a form of program-related investment, has real benefits to the recipient and to the foundation. From the recipient's perspective, the loan allows it to start a new program or initiate an important project at a time when funding may have diminished. It can then repay the loan in whole or in part when its revenue stream improves. In some cases, the organization may even use the loan to increase its fund-raising capacity, thus establishing a more stable basis for future growth. From the foundation's perspective, the distribution produces an immediate impact and will ultimately be returned to the foundation for future use.

6. *Make renewable — rather than serial — grants.* Many family foundations have found it difficult to meet past obligations for multiyear grants made in years in which grant capacity was expanding at a steady rate. In some cases, these multiyear commitments have increased beyond available grant funds, meaning the foundation may be forced to either sell assets to meet commitments or renegotiate grant terms to defer payments to later years. At a minimum, it dries up funds available for new grants. Rather than make firm commitments for multiyear grants, the foundation should

consider making renewable grants requiring nonprofits to return each year, report their progress, and apply for another grant installment. This provides the foundation greater flexibility and increases accountability.

If these six strategies do not fit one's family foundation, the foundation should find other ways to maximize grant dollars using focus, accountability, and control. In the final analysis, it is most important that the foundation have a strategy fitting its objectives. Careful management of grant funds will maximize the impact of grant dollars and further the foundation mission.

U.S. DEPARTMENT OF THE TREASURY ANTI-TERRORIST FINANCING GUIDELINES: VOLUNTARY BEST PRACTICES FOR U.S.-BASED CHARITIES

Table of Contents

Compliance with these guidelines shall not be construed to preclude any criminal or civil sanctions by the Department of the Treasury or the Department of Justice against persons who provide material, financial, or technological support or resources to, or engage in prohibited transactions with, persons designated pursuant to the Antiterrorism and Effective Death Penalty Act of 1986, as amended, or the International Emergency Powers Act, as amended.

I. Governance: The charity should have an adequate governing structure.

A. Governing Instruments: The charity should operate in accordance with governing instruments, e.g., charter, articles of incorporation, bylaws, etc. The governing instruments should:

1. delineate the charity's basic goal(s) and purpose(s);

2. define the structure of the charity, including the composition of the board, how the board is selected and replaced, and the authority and responsibilities of the board;

3. set forth requirements concerning financial reporting, accountability, and practices for solicitation and distribution of funds; and

4. state that the charity shall comply with all applicable federal and state laws.

B. Board of Directors: The charity should be governed by a board of directors consisting of at least three members.

1. The board should be an active governing body, meeting at least three times annually with the majority of members attending in person.

2. The board should be an independent governing body, exercising effective and independent oversight of the charity's operations.

    (a) The charity should establish a conflict of interest policy for board members and employees. The policy should establish procedures that must be followed if a board member or employee has a conflict of interest or a perceived conflict of interest.

    (b) The charity should not engage in transactions with entities in which a board member has a conflict of interest.

    (c) The charity whose directly and/or indirectly compensated board members constitute more than one-fifth (20%) of the total voting membership of the board or of the executive committee will not be considered to have an independent governing body.

3. The board should maintain records of all decisions made. These records should be available for public inspection.

II. Disclosure/Transparency in Governance and Finances

A. Board of Directors

1. The charity should make publicly available a list of its board members and the salaries they are paid.

2. The charity should maintain records containing additional identifying information about its board members, such as home address, social security number, citizenship, etc.

3. The charity should maintain records containing identifying information for the board members of any subsidiary or affiliate receiving funds from the charity.

B. Key Employees

1. The charity should make publicly available a list of its five highest paid employees (the key employees) and the salaries and/or direct or indirect benefits they receive.

2. The charity should maintain records containing additional identifying information about its key employees, such as home address, social security number, etc.

3. The charity should maintain records containing identifying information for the key employees of any subsidiary or affiliate receiving funds from the charity.

C. *Distribution of Funds*

1. The charity should publicly identify any subsidiaries and/or affiliates that receive funds from the charity.

2. The charity should provide upon request an annual report. The annual report should describe the charity's purpose(s), programs, activities, tax exempt status, the structure and responsibility of the governing body of the charity, and financial information.

3. The charity should provide upon request complete annual financial statements. The financial statements should present the overall financial condition of the charity and its financial activities in accordance with generally accepted accounting principles and reporting practices.

D. *Solicitations for Funds*

1. The charity should clearly state its goals and purposes so that anyone examining its disbursement of funds can determine whether the charity is adhering to those goals.

2. Solicitations for donations should accurately and transparently tell donors how and where their donations are going to be expended.

3. The charity should substantiate on request that solicitations and informational materials, distributed by any means, are accurate, truthful, and not misleading, in whole or in part.

III. Financial Practice/Accountability

A. The charity should have a budget, adopted in advance on an annual basis that is overseen by the board.

B. The board of the charity should appoint one individual to serve as the financial/accounting officer who is ultimately responsible for the day to day control over the money of the charity.

C. If the charity's total annual gross income exceeds $250,000, the board of the charity should select an independent certified public accounting firm, which serves as an auditor and reviews the finances of the charity and issues a yearly audited financial statement. The yearly audited financial statement should be available for public inspection.

D. *Receipt and Disbursement of Funds*

1. The charity should account for all funds received and disbursed in accordance with generally accepted accounting principles and the requirements of the Internal Revenue Code. The charity should maintain records of the salaries it pays and the expenses it incurs.

2. The charity should include in its accounting of all charitable disbursements the name of each recipient and the amount disbursed.

3. The charity, after recording, should promptly deposit all received money into the bank account maintained by the charity. In particular, all cash donations should be promptly deposited into the charity's bank account.

4. The charity should make disbursements by check or wire transfer, but not in cash.

IV. **Anti-Terrorist Financing Procedures:** The charity should take the following steps before any charitable funds are distributed to foreign recipient organizations.

A. The charity should collect the following basic information about a foreign recipient organization:

1. The foreign recipient organization's name in English, in the language of origin, and any acronym or other names used to identify the foreign recipient organization;

2. The jurisdictions in which the foreign recipient organization maintains a physical presence;

3. The jurisdiction in which the foreign recipient organization is incorporated or formed;

4. The address and phone number of any place of business of the foreign recipient organization;

5. The principal purpose of the foreign recipient organization, including a detailed report of the recipient's projects and goals;

6. The names and addresses of organizations to which the foreign recipient organization currently provides or proposes to provide funding, services, or material support, to the extent known, as applicable;

7. The names and addresses of any subcontracting organizations utilized by the foreign recipient organization;

8. Copies of any public filings or releases made by the foreign recipient organization, including most recent official registry documents, annual reports, and annual filings with the pertinent government, as applicable;

9. The foreign recipient organization's existing sources of income, such as official grants, private endowments, and commercial activities.

B. The charity should conduct basic vetting of potential foreign recipient organizations as follows:

1. The charity should be able to demonstrate that it conducted a reasonable search of public information, including information available via the

internet, to determine whether the foreign recipient organization is or has been implicated in any questionable activity.

2. The charity should be able to demonstrate that it verified that the foreign recipient organization does not appear on any list of the U.S. Government, the United Nations, or the European Union identifying it as having links to terrorism or money laundering. The charity should consult the Department of the Treasury's Office of Foreign Assets Control Specially Designated Nationals List, which will identify entities designated by the U.S. Government as Foreign Terrorist Organizations or as supporters of terrorism. The charity also should consult the U.S. Government's Terrorist Exclusion List maintained by the Department of Justice, the list promulgated by the United Nations pursuant to U.N. Security Council Resolutions 1267 and 1390, the list promulgated by the European Union pursuant to EU Regulation 2580, and any other official list available to the charity.

3. The charity should obtain the full name in English, in the language of origin, and any acronym or other names used, as well as nationality, citizenship, current country of residence, place and date of birth for key staff at the foreign recipient organization's principal place of business, such as board members, etc., and for senior employees at the recipient's other locations. The charity should run the names through public databases and compare them to the lists noted above.

4. The charity should require foreign recipient organizations to certify that they do not employ or deal with any entities or individuals on the lists referenced above, or with any entities or individuals known to the foreign recipient organization to support terrorism.

C. The charity should review the financial operations of the foreign recipient organization as follows:

1. The charity should determine the identity of the financial institutions with which the foreign recipient organization maintains accounts. The charity should seek bank references and determine whether the financial institution is: (i) a shell bank; (ii) operating under an offshore license; (iii) licensed in a jurisdiction that has been determined to be non-cooperative in the international fight against money laundering; (iv) licensed in a jurisdiction that has been designated by the Secretary of the Treasury to be a primary money laundering concern; and (v) licensed in a jurisdiction that lacks adequate anti-money laundering controls and regulatory oversight.

2. The charity should require periodic reports from the foreign recipient organization on its operational activities and use of the disbursed funds.

3. The charity should require the foreign recipient organization to undertake reasonable steps to ensure that funds provided by the charity are not ultimately distributed to terrorist organizations. Periodically, the foreign recipient organization should apprise the charity of the steps it has taken to meet this goal.

4. The charity should perform routine, on-site audits of foreign recipient organizations whenever possible, consistent with the size of the disbursement and the cost of the audit.

SAMPLE STRUCTURED AND UNSTRUCTURED GRANT INSTRUCTIONS AND GUIDELINES

THE MIREE FAMILY FOUNDATION

INSTRUCTIONS FOR GRANT APPLICATION AND GRANT GUIDELINES

About the Foundation

The Miree Family Foundation is a private foundation established in 1998 to make grants to domestic § 501(c)(3) organizations in Jefferson County, Shelby County, and St. Clair County, Alabama, in furtherance of health care. The mission of the foundation is improve the quality of health care of the citizens of Jefferson, Shelby, and St. Clair counties through development of health care facilities, through education of its citizens, and by expansion of health care access.

The foundation is governed by a board of eight directors serving three-year terms. These directors make the final decision on all grants and expenditures made by the foundation.

Grants Made by the Foundation

The foundation makes grants to qualified charitable organizations that address the following areas of interest:

- Health care for the elderly,
- Substance abuse prevention,
- Health care education for minorities,
- Provision of prescription medications to those who cannot afford them, and
- Environmental health care.

The foundation gives priority to projects that involve joint efforts of multiple agencies and to projects that provide immediate health care access to individuals who are unable to afford basic medical care.

The foundation will make its grants in the following forms as appropriate for the project proposal and the project time line. Be specific about the form of grant you are requesting.

- One-time grants, which are single-year grants for a specific purpose;
- Multiyear grants, which are commitments for funding to be paid in increments over a period no longer than three years;
- Start-up program grants; and
- Challenge or matching grants. (Note that grant proposals that have matching funds available are given preference over proposals without matching funds. All capital projects in excess of $100,000 must have other sources of funding to cover at least 50 percent of the project.)

Grants That the Foundation Will Not Make

The foundation will not make the following types of grants. Any request for funding for these purposes will be denied:

- Grants to individuals for any purpose;
- Grants to religious organizations for religious purposes;
- Grants to domestic organizations for funds spent outside of Alabama;
- Grants to international organizations that do not have a qualified domestic § 501(c)(3) representative;
- Grants to private foundations (other than operating foundations);
- Grants to endowments or other discretionary funding pools;
- Grants for dinners, balls, or other ticketed events;
- Grants for political purposes;
- Grants for lobbying activities; and
- Grants for purposes outside of the foundation's funding priorities as listed in the prior section.

Application Procedure

Applicants must use the foundation form in applying for a grant. [*When unstructured grant request forms are used, this sentence should be changed to instruct applicants to include all required information on the application for grant.*] These applications must be delivered to the foundation, or postmarked, by the following dates:

Meeting Date	Deadline for Submission of Grant Request
March	January 31
June	April 30
September	July 31
December	October 31

Grant applications must contain:

- A one-page cover letter summarizing the project, the amount requested, and the time table for the project;
- A completed grant application; and
- All attachments listed on the application form.

The foundation will notify you if additional information is required for your grant application package. The foundation reserves the right to hold consideration of incomplete grant requests until the next grant consideration date at the discretion of the foundation president.

Applications for grant should be delivered as follows:

Mail Delivery	Overnight Delivery	Hand Delivery
P.O. Box 11111	1111 Crest Road	1111 Crest Road
Birmingham, AL 11111	Birmingham, AL 11111	Birmingham, AL 11111

Form of Proposal

Applicants must submit eight copies of the grant proposal. These proposals should be bound in a secure, but nonbulky fashion. Do not submit grant proposals in three-ring notebooks or other large packages.

All proposals are limited to 20 pages in length. This page limit does not include required attachments.

Frequency of Application

The foundation receives numerous grant requests and is unable to fund all projects, even though those projects may be well-designed and well-conceived. Applicants may make only one application per year, whether successful in receiving a grant or not.

Other Requirements

Organizations receiving funds from the Miree Family Foundation must provide a certified statement that the funds received from the foundation have been used for the purpose intended. This statement, which must be signed by the nonprofit's accounting firm and chief financial officer, must be filed with the foundation no later than 18 months after the date such funds are awarded.

SAMPLE STRUCTURED GRANT APPLICATION FORM

THE MIREE FAMILY FOUNDATION
GRANT APPLICATION FORM

Applicant Organization's Name:_____

Address:_____

City/State/Zip:_____

Name of Person Submitting Request: _____

Title of Person Submitting Request:_____

Phone:_____Fax:_____ E-mail:_____

Area of Charitable Service:

☐ Arts   ☐ Health care   ☐ Religious

☐ Education   ☐ Social/human services   ☐ Environmental

Mission (Describe the purpose of your organization):

Services provided by your organization (list all services that represent five percent or more of your budget):

Area served by organization (circle all that apply):

[Your city], USA   [Your state], USA   Outside USA (specify):

[Your county], USA   United States   _____

Year organization established: _____ Year received tax-exempt status: _____

Number of employees: _____ Budget for most recent year end: $ _____

Name of accounting firm that handles audit and review of funds: _____ _____

Contact name: _____ Contact phone: _____

Can the foundation contact the accounting firm for additional information? ☐ yes ☐ no

PROJECT DESCRIPTION

Describe your proposed project. Include (i) the purpose and goals of your project; (ii) the statement of need for your project; (iii) the class of individuals served by the project, the number of individuals served by the project, and the location of those individuals; and (iv) the way in which you will measure the success of your project. You may use this space and attach up to one additional page if necessary.

PROJECT PLAN

Describe the implementation process for your project. Be sure to include information on key staff and volunteer project managers.

Describe the evaluation process for your project, including expected outcomes. Outline (i) the evaluation process, (ii) the individuals responsible for measuring and reporting the outcome of the project, (iii) the statistical manner in which results will be calculated, and (iv) a description of how the project will be funded in future years.

BUDGET INFORMATION

Applicant year end: _____ Time period for budget below: _____

Amount requested: _____ Time period for payment: _____

Budget Detail	Budget for Project	Annual Budget for Organization
Salaries	$ _____	$ _____
Payroll taxes	$ _____	$ _____
Fringe benefits	$ _____	$ _____
Office space	$ _____	$ _____
General overhead	$ _____	$ _____
Travel	$ _____	$ _____
Consultants/professional fees	$ _____	$ _____
Postage	$ _____	$ _____
Office supplies	$ _____	$ _____
Marketing/communications	$ _____	$ _____
Capital expenditures	$ _____	$ _____
Total	$ _____	$ _____

Revenue Detail	Revenue for Project	Annual Revenue for Organization
Individual contributions	$ _____	$ _____
Corporate contributions	$ _____	$ _____
Foundation grants	$ _____	$ _____
Government grants	$ _____	$ _____
Membership income	$ _____	$ _____
Special events	$ _____	$ _____
In-kind support	$ _____	$ _____
Other (specify) _____	$ _____	$ _____

List other foundations that have been asked to fund this project, the amounts requested, and the current status. Add an additional page if necessary.

Foundation	Amount Requested	Status
_____	$ _____	_____
_____	$ _____	_____
_____	$ _____	_____

ATTACHMENTS REQUIRED

—— IRS tax determination letter showing that you are a recognized public charity and that you are not a private foundation.

—— Affidavit from a representative of your organization stating that the IRS has not revoked your tax-exempt status or changed that status since the issuance of the tax determination letter.

—— A copy of the most recent audited financial statement of your organization.

—— A copy of the organization's most recent annual report, if available.

—— A list of the organization's board of directors or trustees, showing name, corporate title, volunteer title, address, work telephone, and home telephone.

Statement from Applicant Organization's Chief Executive Officer and Chief Volunteer Officer:

We do hereby certify that the information provided in this grant application is accurate and complete to the best of our ability and knowledge. We further acknowledge that if awarded a grant from the Miree Family Foundation, we will provide certification to the Miree Family Foundation that the funds have been used for the purposes for which the grant was awarded. We will make this certification within the time specified in the grant agreement.

_____   _____

Chief Executive Officer of Applicant/Provide Name and Title   Date

_____   _____

Chief Volunteer Officer of Applicant/Provide Name and Title   Date

Appendix 7-D

SAMPLE UNSTRUCTURED GRANT APPLICATION FORM

MIREE FAMILY FOUNDATION

GRANT APPLICATION INSTRUCTIONS

Applications for grant should include the following information. The applicant may arrange this information in any order considered to best make the case to the foundation for funding the project.

I. The Organization

A.   List the name, address, and tax ID number of the requesting organization. If the funds will be used for the benefit of another organization, clearly state the name, address, tax ID number, and relationship of the secondary organization.

B.   List the name of the person responsible for this grant application and the use of the funds. Provide title, telephone, fax, and e-mail address of the responsible party.

C.   State the mission of your organization.

D.   List all services provided by your organization that represent five percent or more of your budget.

II. The Project

A.   Describe your proposed project. Include (i) the purpose and goals of your project; (ii) the statement of need for your project; (iii) the class of individuals served by the project, the number of individuals served by the project, and the location of those individuals; and (iv) the way in which you will measure the success of your project.

B.   Describe the implementation process for your project. Be sure to include information on key staff and volunteer project managers.

C.   Describe the evaluation process for your project, including expected outcomes. Outline (i) the evaluation process, (ii) the individuals responsible for measuring and reporting the outcome of the project, (iii) the statistical manner in which results will be calculated, and (iv) a description of how the project will be funded in future years.

D.   Describe the geographic scope of your project.

E.   Describe the time line for the project. This should include a statement of when the project will begin and when it will be completed.

III. The Budget

A.   State the amount requested for the project.

B.   Provide a time line of when the funds are needed.

C.   List other sources of funding for the project, including applications submitted to other foundations. Show the status of all funding requests for these foundations.

D.   Provide the name of the accounting firm that prepares the organization's annual audit, a contact name, and a contact number. State in the application that it is, or is not, permissible to contact your accountant for additional information if needed.

E.   State the tax year-end of the organization.

F.   Provide a budget for the project in as much detail as possible.

G.   Provide a budget for the organization (state tax year for which budget is provided) in as much detail as possible.

Note: A budget information form is attached. Organizations may use this form to supply budget information, or the information may be provided in a form desired by the organization.

Attachments Required

——   IRS tax determination letter showing that you are a recognized public charity and that you are not a private foundation.

——   Affidavit from a representative of your organization stating that the IRS has not revoked your tax-exempt status or changed that status since the issuance of the tax determination letter.

——   A copy of the most recent audited financial statement of your organization.

——   A copy of the organization's most recent annual report, if available.

——   A list of the organization's board of directors or trustees, showing name, corporate title, volunteer title, address, work telephone, and home telephone.

Statement from Applicant Organization's Chief Executive Officer and Chief Volunteer Officer:

We do hereby certify that the information provided in this grant application is accurate and complete to the best of our ability and knowledge. We further acknowledge that if awarded a grant from the Miree Family Foundation, we will provide certification to the Miree Family Foundation that the funds have been used for the purposes for which the grant was awarded. We will make this certification within the time specified in the grant agreement.

_____   _____

Chief Executive Officer of Applicant/Provide Name and Title   Date

_____   _____

Chief Volunteer Officer of Applicant/Provide Name and Title   Date

Budget Information Form

Applicant year end: _____ Time period for budget below: _____

Amount requested: _____ Time period for payment: _____

Budget Detail	Budget for Project	Annual Budget for Organization
Salaries	$_____	$_____
Payroll taxes	$_____	$_____
Fringe benefits	$_____	$_____
Office space	$_____	$_____
General overhead	$_____	$_____
Travel	$_____	$_____
Consultants/professional fees	$_____	$_____
Postage	$_____	$_____
Office supplies	$_____	$_____
Marketing/communications	$_____	$_____
Capital expenditures	$_____	$_____
Total	$_____	$_____

Revenue Detail	Revenue for Project	Annual Revenue for Organization
Individual contributions	$_____	$_____
Corporate contributions	$_____	$_____
Foundation grants	$_____	$_____
Government grants	$_____	$_____
Membership income	$_____	$_____
Special events	$_____	$_____
In-kind support	$_____	$_____
Other (specify)_____	$_____	$_____

List other foundations that have been asked to fund this project, the amounts requested, and the current status. Add an additional page if necessary.

Foundation	Amount Requested	Status
_____	$_____	_____
_____	$_____	_____
_____	$_____	_____

SAMPLE GRANT AGREEMENT

GRANT AGREEMENT BETWEEN XYZ CHARITABLE ORGANIZATION AND THE MIREE FAMILY FOUNDATION

The Miree Family Foundation (hereinafter referred to as the Foundation) has awarded a grant in the amount of $ _____ to _____ (hereinafter referred to as the recipient) pursuant to the recipient's application for grant filed for the Foundation's _____ grant cycle. The purpose of this grant is to _____

_____

In accepting this grant, the recipient agrees to the following terms and conditions:

1. The recipient will use the grant funds only for the purpose(s) detailed in the grant request, as restricted by any award letter issued by the Foundation and attached to this agreement as an exhibit.

2. The recipient will provide a report on the use of these funds using the attached grant review form by December 31, 20_____, or within six months of receipt of funds, whichever is later. The recipient must report receipt of funds and expenditures of those funds in a manner consistent with general accounting principles. This report may relate to the specific use of the Foundation grant, or it may represent the project receipts and expenditures to include other grantmaking organizations. Records of receipts and disbursements must be maintained by the recipient for at least four years from the date of grant.

3. The recipient will return all funds constituting this grant that are not used for the purpose of the grant by December 31, 20_____, or within six months of receipt of funds, whichever is later. In the event that the project for which the funds are requested is not complete by that date, the recipient should inform the Foundation in writing of this fact and request an extension of time. In analyzing the use of its funds, the Foundation considers its grant to be the last grant made, so that additional funds remaining at the end of the project will be considered the property of the Foundation. In the event that other foundations have made a similar request, the Foundation at a minimum requires that the funds remaining be divided on a pro rata basis based on the financial contributions to the project of other funding sources requesting prioritization.

4. The recipient will notify the Foundation immediately if there is a change in grant status of the recipient or if the proposed project is canceled or delayed.

5. No portion of these funds will be used for any purpose other than the purpose stated in the application for grant. Further, no portion of these funds will be used to carry on propaganda or otherwise attempt to influence legislation, to influence the outcome of a public election, to carry on a voter registration drive, to make a grant that does not comply with I.R.C. § 4945(d) (3) or (4) (attached to this agreement), or to finance an activity for any purpose other than the charitable purposes stated in I.R.C. § 170(c)(2)(B) (attached to this agreement).

6. The recipient will provide a full report on the use of the funds within 18 months of the date of receipt of the grant. The report must be signed by an officer, director, or trustee with the

authority to make such certification. A reporting form is provided as an attachment to this agreement.

_____   _____
Chief Executive Officer, Foundation   Chief Executive Officer, Recipient

_____   _____
                                             Chief Volunteer Officer, Recipient

_____   _____
Date   Date

Appendix 7-F

SAMPLE GRANT FOLLOW-UP FORM

THE McCOY FAMILY FOUNDATION

GRANT REPORT FORM

Please complete all information and return this form to the McCoy Family Foundation no later than 18 months following receipt of the award. When multiyear grants are involved, the grant agreement may specify a different schedule of reporting; please check that agreement to determine the date that this report must be filed.

Organization name:_____

Address: _____

Person responsible for grant administration: _____

Title: _____ Phone:_____

Describe the measurable goals for the project, including benchmarks for success:

Report the organization's success in reaching those goals, including data indicating that you met these goals. Additional sheets may be attached if necessary.

Provide a short narrative of the implementation of this project, including the involvement of other agencies or organizations.

Provide a summary of the lessons learned from this project, including any unanticipated positive or negative results.

Is the project for which you received funds complete? Y/N
If yes, when was the project completed? _____ What portion of the grant funds provided by the McCoy Family Foundation were used for the project? _____

If no, when do you expect the project to be completed? _____

Provide a description of the outstanding elements and the cost for those elements?

What portion of the Foundation funds remain to be spent? _____ Do you expect to spend all of these funds to complete the project? Y/N If no, please provide detail on the portion to be returned and the expected date of return of those funds.

Does this project require ongoing funding? Y/N

If yes, please describe how funds will be raised to fund its continued operation.

I certify that the [*recipient organization*] has not used any portion of these funds for any purpose other than the purpose stated in the application for grant. Further, no portion of these funds has been or will be used to carry on propaganda or otherwise attempt to influence legislation, to influence the outcome of a public election, to carry on a voter registration drive, to make a grant that does not comply with I.R.C. Ï 4945(d)(3) or (4), or to finance an activity for any purpose other than the charitable purposes stated in I.R.C. Ï 170(c)(2)(B).

_____   _____

Chief Executive Officer, Foundation   Chief Executive Officer, Recipient

_____   _____

                                            Chief Volunteer Officer, Recipient

_____   _____

Date   Date

APPENDIX 7-G

McCOY FAMILY FOUNDATION SAMPLE GRANT WORKSHEET FOR MEETING

Organization Requesting Grant	Purpose of Grant	Amount Requested	Prior Grant History	Comments/ Award
The Nature Conservancy	To purchase wilderness area in Alabama	$250,000	1995 — $75,000 1997 — $90,000 1998 — $20,000	$750,000 needed to complete purchase; Waller Foundation and Miree Foundation willing to contribute similar amount. Award:
United Way of Washington, D. C.	To establish operating endowment	$300,000	1990 — $10,000 1991 — $10,000 1992 — $12,000 1993 — $14,000 1997 — $20,000 1998 — $20,000	Award:
Maryland Symphony Orchestra	To create conductor's chair	$1,000,000	$0	Award:
Boys and Girls Club of Greater Washington	To construct new facility in down-town area	$150,000	$0	Total cost of the project is $2.5 million. Award:
Smithsonian Museum	To fund celebration of opening of new wing	$50,000	1995 — $100,000 1998 — $25,000	Award:
Georgetown University School of Law	To fund chair in taxation at the law school	$1,500,000	1994 — $25,000 1997 — $25,000 1998 — $25,000	Award:

Organization Requesting Grant	Purpose of Grant	Amount Requested	Prior Grant History	Comments/ Award
Boy Scouts	Annual campaign	$2,500	1991 — $2,000	
			1992 — $2,000	
			1993 — $2,000	
			1994 — $2,500	
			1995 — $2,500	
			1996 — $2,000	
			1997 — $2,000	
			1998 — $2,500	
			1999 — $2,500	Award:

Total Grants Requested $3,252,500

APPENDIX 7-H

SAMPLE "YES" LETTER AWARDING GRANT

[*Date*]

Mr. Lucky Recipient
Executive Director
Healthcare Miracles
111 Healthcare Way
Birmingham, AL 12345

Re: McCoy Family Foundation

Dear Mr. Recipient:

Enclosed you will find a check in the amount of $50,000 representing a grant to Healthcare Miracles awarded by the McCoy Family Foundation at its June meeting. This grant is for the purpose of providing nurses for school health-care clinics as detailed in your grant application of March 31, 2001.

This grant is made to Healthcare Miracles subject to the following requirements:

- You must sign the enclosed grant agreement evidencing receipt of the check and agreeing to abide by the terms in its issue.

- You must report to the Foundation on the use of the funds; this reporting must be made within 18 months of receipt of these funds.

- These funds must be used only for the purposes specified. Any funds not used for this specific project must be returned to the Foundation as soon as practical.

Congratulations on your award. Please contact Ms. Foundation Manager at 205-111-2234 if you have any questions about the use of these funds or the requirements of the Foundation.

Yours very truly,

Jeffrey T. McCoy
Foundation President

APPENDIX 7-1

SAMPLE "NO" LETTER DENYING GRANT

[*Date*]

Mr. Notso Fortunate
Executive Director
Food for All
111 Harvest Way
Birmingham, AL 54321

Re: Miree Family Foundation

Dear Mr. Fortunate:

The Miree Family Foundation has reviewed your request for funding for [*insert purpose of project*]. I regret that the Foundation is unable to fund your request at this time. The Foundation receives numerous requests for assistance. Unfortunately, the number of requests received by the Foundation far exceeds its available funds. Many worthwhile projects such as yours cannot be funded.

While we are unable to assist you in this project, we wish you every success in securing your funding from other sources.

Yours very truly,

Virginia M. Miree
President

CHAPTER 8

FOUNDATION ADMINISTRATION

§ 8.01   INTRODUCTION

Family foundations are often operated in the same haphazard manner as many of us manage our personal lives. We begin with great resolve and determination to do things right, but end up spending our time on the more interesting issues. Foundation administration is probably not high on anyone's list of interesting issues, and yet proper administration is an essential element of the board's fiduciary duty and the key to the foundation's effectiveness in fulfilling its mission.

The concept of fiduciary responsibility is at the heart of this chapter. The foundation board has the duty and responsibility to manage the foundation's assets for the public good. Fiduciary duties include the obligation to keep accurate records, to comply with laws and regulations, to protect and grow the trust assets, and to put the foundation's interests above personal interests. These principles form the basis for a discussion of the foundation manager's administrative duties.

§ 8.02   RECORD KEEPING AND ACCOUNTING

Record keeping involves keeping accurate records of the foundation's receipts, expenses, grantmaking activities, and regulatory filings. Record keeping is a ministerial function that can be delegated to third parties and supervised or can be staffed by the foundation. In either instance, the foundation is advised to invest in a good set of filing cabinets and software to keep the information organized and at hand.

[A]   Making the Case for Good Records

Individuals do not create foundations for the joy of keeping records. Yet, in the new realm of nonprofit accountability, good records may be the foundation's most important liability management tool. There are at least five compelling reasons to keep good records:

1. *Documenting compliance with state and federal law.* The majority of private foundations are organized as nonprofit corporations. While state laws differ, most require evidence that the corporation is functioning within legal parameters, including conducting regular meetings, maintaining a certain number of directors, and filing regular reports with state regulators. Evidence of these activities include minutes of meetings, minutes or properly executed documents giving authority to individuals who transact business in the foundation's name and properly recorded business decisions (for example, to buy or sell property or purchase insurance).

Foundations, of course, must comply with an extensive list of tax and employee benefit laws requiring the filing of 990-PFs (Tax Return of Private Foundation), 941 (Employer's Quarterly Tax Return), W-2 (Wage and Tax Statement), 1099-INT, 1099 MISC, 1099-R, and up to 22 other forms listed by the IRS. Foundations should maintain these returns for the IRS audit period for filing returns and paying taxes. Five years is a recommended minimum record retention period, but always check with your accountant when setting policy;

2. *Evidence of exercise of fiduciary judgment.* Foundation board members must make regular decisions on investment management, salaries, and budgets. For example, the Prudent Investor Rule, applicable to fiduciary investment in most states, requires fiduciaries to consider current economic conditions, spending policies, risk, and the interests of current and future beneficiaries when investing the foundation's assets. Say a foundation's directors went through this process a few years ago and decided to invest in Enron, which as we know later lost its entire value because of company mismanagement. Despite this ultimate "proof" that a bad investment was made, the decision makers should be protected, if they are sued as long as they have documentation of the board's evaluative process supporting the investment.

3. *Help in avoiding recurring discussions or disagreements.* There is nothing more frustrating, or divisive to family relationships, than having the same disagreement every year. The conflict may revolve around board structure, the location of the meetings, or how to involve younger children. Once these difficult issues are raised, discussed, and resolved, a clear set of minutes records the decision and helps the family avoid having to thrash through the same issue at the next meeting.

4. *Recording due diligence in grantmaking.* Foundations should exercise due diligence in grantmaking as a matter of policy and effectiveness. When grants are made to individuals, to non-501(c)(3) entities, or to other restricted groups, the due diligence, in the form of expenditure responsibility, is required by law. Private foundations must pay excise taxes for taxable distributions if they cannot document that distributions were made for charitable purposes. These records are more critical than ever under the terms of the USA Patriot Act, especially with regard to its prohibition against distributions to terrorist organizations.

5. *Building family history.* Meeting minutes and good historical records in general reflect the founder's goals, the family's history, and the foundation's evolution. It is difficult to reconstruct the past, and make decisions about the future, without the details gleaned from accurate records. As time passes and the original founder's descendants take over a foundation's management, such records may prove invaluable.

[B] Recommended and Required Records — And How Long to Keep Them

[1] Types of Records

Foundations should file the information in the manner that is most accessible and useful to those accessing and using it. Start the process by identifying the types of information that must be filed and determining the frequency and purposes of access. Then establish a system that works best for your foundation. The following records need to be filed:

1. *IRS filings.* Section 8.07 below lists potential IRS filings in detail. However, the most common filings are listed here:

   - Form 1023. The foundation must file Form 1023 to obtain tax-exempt status. The form contains a description of the foundation's purpose and mission, a three-year anticipated budget, information about the founders and original board, and other key information. Once the application is approved, the foundation is obligated to allow anyone to inspect it or to supply a copy to those who make a request. (See § 8.09 on public disclosure below).

   - *Tax determination letter.* The IRS issues a tax determination letter, confirming the tax-exempt status of the foundation, at the conclusion of its review of Form 1023 (assuming that the review is successful). This letter may be requested by donors or any organizations contributing funds to the foundation.

   - *Form 990-PF.* The foundation, as a taxpayer, is responsible for filing an annual information return, described in more detail later in this chapter. Three years of these returns must also be made available to the public on request.

   - *Excise tax estimates.* The foundation must file Form 8109 to pay estimated excise tax on its income. If the foundation is subject to excise taxes for violation of the prohibited transaction rules, it must file Form 4720.

2. *Employee records.* The foundation may have employees; if so, detailed records on those employees, their benefit packages, and tax forms should be maintained. Federal, state, and local tax reporting records must also be maintained.

3. *Financial asset records.* The foundation may hold its financial assets in several locations. Accurate records are important to generate tax-reporting information as well as to monitor and account for those assets. Records may include:

   - *Bank accounts.* Foundations may operate one or more bank accounts as well as holding investment assets at one or more custodians.

- *Stocks, bonds, mutual funds, and other investment assets.* The foundation should maintain complete records of transactions, asset values, and fees or distributions paid from those assets.

- *Reports from outside managers.* When outside investment managers are employed to manage investment assets or unusual assets such as timber, oil and gas, or real estate, periodic reports of income and performance should be maintained.

- *Appraisals and monthly valuations.* Appraisals and monthly valuations should be maintained for the purposes of determining the foundation's distributable amount and reporting annual asset value. When monthly asset statements are generated, it is a good idea to send a copy to the accountant for the foundation as well, so that two sets of valuations are maintained (in the event that one set is lost).

- *Contracts, agreements, deeds, insurance binders, and other legal documents.* The foundation should keep records of all legal documents evidencing agreements between the foundation and third parties.

4. *Account for receipts and expenditures for foundation administration.* The foundation should keep detailed records and documentation of expenses and receipts. Talk to the foundation accountant to determine how to organize or segregate this information so that it is easy to review and incorporate in the annual return.

5. *Grant records.* One of the most difficult tasks for the foundation administrator is to manage the information that accumulates over years of grantmaking. Keep full grant proposals for grants that are awarded through the period of the follow-up report; once the grant is finished, and the information on use of the funds is complete, the original proposal can be thrown away. If you prefer to retain extensive files, scan the information into a record-keeping system that allows later review. Always retain the tax determination letter, the grant follow-up report, and any other elements of the proposal that may be helpful for future projects.

6. *Files on grantseekers.* If you have space, it is useful to maintain resource files with basic information on nonprofits within your foundation's grantmaking scope. Include the nonprofit's tax determination letter, annual report, newspaper clippings, capital campaign information, board list, or any other data that may be helpful in answering questions, developing history, or assessing the needs of the organization.

7. *Minutes.* Writing minutes is one of the less glamorous roles of foundation management. However, minutes record key activities and provide important protection for the foundation's managers by documenting decisions about grants, salaries, contracts, insurance, legal authority for board action,

officer appointments, and grant awards. The secretarial role should be assigned to a board member who understands the importance of a sound record and has been trained to do the job. (The elements of good minutes are set out in Table 8–1 *see also* Chapter 5, § 5.02[B].)

TABLE 8-1
The Elements of Good Minutes

Date, time, and location of meeting	Record the date, time, and location of the meeting. If the meeting was scheduled by written notice, attach a copy to the records. If the record was called in another manner (as set out in the bylaws or trust document), note that method.
The attendees	List the participants in the meeting and the method of participation. For example, some members may attend in person, while others may attend by teleconference or telephone.
Committee reports	Record committee reports, recommended action and resolution, or further action directed by the board, and attach all committee reports as an appendix. Key committees include the grants committee, the investment committee, and the governance committee. The actions requiring board action should be clearly noted and handled as an action item (see below).
Action items	All action items should be clearly marked so that they are easily identified in the minutes. Use the words "Action Item" at the beginning of the paragraph. Note the individual who made the motion and the second. Summarize the key issues discussed in resolution and the final determination. Attach a copy of the resolution and any amendments to the minutes.
Old business	Summarize and list separately all old business items raised at the meeting requiring resolution or further discussion. This is especially helpful if there is a three- to six-month break between meetings.
New business	Summarize and list separately all new business raised at the meeting requiring resolution or further discussion in later meetings.
Next meeting date	Clearly note the next meeting date, if set, and the location of the meeting.
Adjournment	Note time of adjournment and those present at adjournment. If the quorum was lost during the meeting, the time of that loss of quorum should be noted.

[2]   The Retention Period

Documents have varying degrees of importance to the foundation. Some are required by law, others help the foundation operate more effectively and efficiently, and still others build family values and history. Therefore, the specific documents retained by your foundation and the length of time you keep them is subject to discretion. A checklist of key documents and recommendations on retention periods is shown in Table 8-2.

[3]   Policies and Procedures on Record Retention

The foundation should adopt policies and procedures on recordkeeping and retention just as it does for investment management, fiscal management, audits, and other key functions. These policies should specify not only the records to be retained, but the individual responsible, the retention period, and the form (electronic, paper, original, copy) in which they should be retained.

TABLE 8-2
Recommended Records and Retention Periods

Document Type	Document	Comments	Recommended Retention Period
Governance	Articles of incorporation and by-laws	Required if the foundation is organized as nonprofit a corporation under state law.	Perpetual; amendments should be retained with originals.
Governance	Trust document (including any amendments)	Applicable if the foundation is organized in trust form.	Perpetual; if amendments are made (generally with court approval), and new trustees are appointed, copies should be retained with the original.
Governance	Meeting minutes (including committee minutes)	Include all meeting attachments, including the agenda and supporting documents and reports.	Perpetual records are the most effective; use electronic storage methods such as scanning to manage space requirements.
Governance	Resolutions passed by the board	For example, keep resolutions authorizing a specific individual to make investment	Retain as long as the resolution is applicable, and longer if there are applicable statutory

TABLE 8-2.   CONTINUED

Document Type	Document	Comments	Recommended Retention Period
		decisions, or write checks.	for periods fraud or other legal claims based on the authority; check with legal counsel to establish retention policies.
Governance	Detail of board history	Maintain a list of board members for each year; this will assist the foundation in appointing new members and educating new members about the foundation's history.	Perpetual. Note: This compilation is not legally required, but will make the foundation's governance easier to manage.
Tax	Form 1023 Application for Tax-Exempt Status; retain all amendments, such as approval to award Scholarships	Form 1023 is the most accurate record of the foundation's original goals and objectives.	Perpetual; required for public disclosure purposes.
Tax	Tax determination letter	This establishes the foundation's tax-exempt status.	Perpetual
Tax	Form 990-PF	Do not overlook the value of the annual informational tax return for historical perspective.	Five years recommended (three years for public disclosure and audit purposes, and five years for minimum distribution purposes); always check with your accountant.
Administrative	Contracts executed by the foundation	Contracts include investment management contracts, software contracts, insurance documents, leases, etc.	Contracts should be retained for the period covered by the contract, and by any statutory period following the contract period in which the contract can be enforced;

TABLE 8-2.   CONTINUED

Document Type	Document	Comments	Recommended Retention Period
			seek advice of counsel for the limits established by state law.
Administrative	Employee person-nel files	Records include the application for em-ployment, resume, annual employee re-views, documents setting and increas-ing salary and bene-fits.	Retain for the length of thc employee term; check with counsel for advice on retention past that date.
Grantmaking	Grant application, grant award letter, and grant follow-up document for grants awarded by the foundation; all documents relat-ing to exercise of expenditure responsibility	These documents chronicle the foun-dation's care in awarding and moni-toring grants.	Retain the grant documents through satisfactory com-pletion of the proj-ect; retain grant letter and follow-up documents throughperiod of potential IRS audit, i.e., five years.
Grantmaking	Tax determination letters for chari-ties receiving grants	Maintain permanent files for charities within foundation's scope that apply for grants. The tax de-termination letter is key, since it estab-lishes the charity's tax-exempt status, without which ex-penditure responsi-bility or a similar evaluative process is required.	Retain tax determi-nation letters as long as the founda-tion's audit period (if the charity was awarded a grant) or as long as the po-tential grantee fits within the founda-tion's scope. Do not retain annual re-ports, board lists, and other data that are quickly out of date.
Grantmaking	Grant records for charities consid-ered	Record the nonprofit name, grant purpose, and grant amount of all charities that fit within the foundation's scope and are considered for grant on the founda-tion's data system.	Retain as long as practical and possi-ble. There is likely a time period — 25 to 50 years — beyond which the data has no relevance. If the foundation has limits

TABLE 8-2.   CONTINUED

Document Type	Document	Comments	Recommended Retention Period
		This provides valuable long-term perspective.	for data storage, look for ways to retain the data off-site so that access is available.
Financial	Copies of bank re-cords, receipts for expenditures, stocks, bonds, mutual funds and other investment assets, appraisals, and monthly asset valuations	These documents track the use and management of the foundation's funds, information critical for accountability.	At least five years, or longer if required for historical pur-poses; check with legal counsel and accountant to determine if this retention period should be longer to address state or federal law issues.
Financial	Investment perfor-mance reports showing invest-ment turns for quarterly and an-nual periods	Investment perfor-mance records are important documents to establish the foun-dation's exercise of invest-ment discretion, and to monitor managers.	At least 10 years, if practical, to main-tain a long-term investment per-spective and to track changes in the foundation's asset allocation over time.

The policies should include a disaster recovery plan. Certainly we are all more attuned to the potential for disaster after the events of September 11, 2001; however, terrorist attacks are not the only threat. There are natural disasters such as hurricanes, floods, tornados, and earthquakes, as well as man-made disasters like fire, nuclear disaster, theft, or accidental loss. Technological disasters also loom, in terms of both loss of data (computer crashes) and destruction of data (a computer virus).

Disaster recovery plans have three primary elements. First, the policies describe the protected documents (specific documents and the time period involved). Second, they address the method of data recovery. This normally involves regular electronic data backup on site (if the foundation maintains its own data), through a third party (if the foundation uses a vendor's system), or through old-fashioned copying and filing if documents cannot be retained in other ways. Third, the plan should address storage. Backup copies of electronic and written documents should generally be kept at an off-site location to ensure that if the foundation offices suffer a disaster, the alternate site might be safe.

Paper and electronic data can both mount up in a hurry. The foundation should periodically review its documents, purging those that have either outlived their usefulness or have been preserved in another manner. For example, the foundation may maintain written minutes, investment records, and grant applications in original paper form for five years. Thereafter, they may have those documents scanned and retained on a compact disc. (*Caution:* Pay attention to the format in which you preserve data. Tapes, compact discs, and even paper are not designed to last forever. The foundation may need to transfer data from one medium to another as new technology becomes available.)

[C] Selecting a Record-Keeping System

The foundation should establish a record-keeping system that is sophisticated enough to manage multiple years worth of information and produce reports when needed, but easy enough to handle internally. The factors guiding the selection of an accounting system include the size of the foundation, the extent (number and form) of its grants, the staff available to input and access the information, and the funds available to pay for the system.

There are two basic ways that the foundation can approach record keeping. The foundation can purchase standard home office/business software available through any computer retailer. Options include products such as Microsoft Access for database management, ACT! for contact management, and Quick-Books for financial accounting and check generation. These products can be easily customized to reflect your foundation's needs. Ask your accounting firm for guidance in selecting the programs you need or help in customizing your purchase to meet your needs.

Alternatively, the foundation may purchase more complex software that handles everything. Record keeping is much easier if the foundation has software that integrates budgeting, balance-sheet functions, accounting functions, fund raising (where appropriate), and grantmaking. This software is especially important for large foundations (defined for this purpose as foundations of $10 million or more) because of the complexities of the tasks and the numerous entries involved. Integrated software allows the foundation administrator to enter key records once and have those records posted to the appropriate place in the ledger or database. This software generally incorporates report formats for common functions such as budget reports, tax reports, and grantmaking as well as features that allow you to easily design your own reports.

Keep in mind that the foundation assets will generally be held at a brokerage firm or bank. The software you use should allow easy coordination with asset reports from custodians. You will be required to report the market value of assets at the end of the fiscal year and should instruct the custodian to generate a report on that date. Banks and trust companies generate statements at month end and can easily accommodate this request. If you use a brokerage firm for custody, however, you may find that month-end statements are produced on another, less consistent schedule. For example, for many years a major national brokerage firm generated statements on the each Friday of each month except December, when statements were cut off at year end. The same firm now generates broker-age statements on the last business day of the month. Year-end statements at brokerage firms are normally generated only on December 31.

Ask your foundation's custodian to describe its monthly statement cycle. The Treasury Regulations do not specify a valuation cycle for private founda-tions; they only specify that the method be consistent. Also request that the custodian generate an annual statement for the foundation's fiscal year-end. If the custodian is unable to accommodate these requests, you should look for another custodian or be prepared to generate the information through a more expensive manually calculated system.

If your trust company or brokerage firm handles many foundations, it may be able to recommend an accounting package that bridges, or links, the transac-tion information and pricing to the custodial software. Without a bridge you will need to manually input the information into your accounting system in order to update your financial statements.

Many banks and trust companies provide a full range of services, including asset custody, bill paying, grant distribution (check writing, grant agreements, and tracking), and tax reporting. Fiduciary accounting systems have several advantages over brokerage or off-the-shelf systems:

- Fiduciary software accommodates a detailed transaction description for each entry. This makes it easy to track distributions to specific organizations.

- *Fiduciary software generally has a double cash entry option.* A double cash accounting system is one that makes income and principal distinctions on earned income, other receipts, and sales and keeps an ongoing tally of these balances for historical purposes. The double cash accounting feature also allows the foun-dation board to monitor the amount of principal distributed to meet expenses and required distributions.

- *Fiduciary record-keeping systems can be set to fiscal years to reflect the foun-dation's tax accounting period.* They can also generate detailed tax reports for year-end tax reporting purposes.

Brokerage firms are excellent custodians, but may not offer the range of accounting functions offered by traditional fiduciaries such as banks. While brokerage firms can generate detailed reports of receipts, disbursements, and securities transactions, the transactions carry limited descriptions. Brokerage firm systems generally operate with single cash accounting and generate tax reports for calendar year-ends. On the plus side, a brokerage firm generally charges no fee for these services. To decide which option works best for the foundation, consider the services needed, the cost of those services, and the staff available.

When selecting a software package, remember that bigger is not necessarily better. Although the best software system is generally one that integrates finan-cial accounting and reporting, fund raising, and administration and has report generation features, an integrated software package can be expensive and may be more muscle than your family foundation needs. Table 8-3 provides a checklist of functionality options that you may need.

TABLE 8-3
Checklist of Software Functionality Options for Foundation Accounting Software

Software Function	Type of Activity	Comments
Financial reporting and accounting	General ledger	
	Payroll	
	Check writing*	Important because it allows you to generate a check and entry with one input.
	Billing/accounts receivable	
	Accounts payable	
Income*		
	Distributions*	Detailed history of transactions, including description of recipient and purpose of grant.
	Budgets	Modeling, projections, comparative analysis.
	Cost allocation	Allocate expenses (and split expenses) among fund raising, investment management, and grants administration (at time of recording entry and edit functions).
	Tax reporting*	Fiscal and calendar year capabilities.
Fund raising	Gift acceptance/acknowledgment Pledges	
	Donor records	
Administrative	Grants administration*	
	Nonprofit grant seeker index	Capability to record profile of nonprofit grant seekers, including name of chief

TABLE 8-3. CONTINUED

Software Function	Type of Activity	Comments
		contact, nonprofit type, address, phone, fax, e-mail, web site, purpose for which funds are requested, date of request, general memo.
	Tickler function	For serial grants, actions to be taken by administrator or board, scheduled meeting dates, other activities.
Report writing	FASB 116, FASB 117	The FASB rules require that you segregate restricted fund balances and that you report commitments for grant payments.
	Tax reporting*	
	Grant history	The grants committee needs to see a funding history for each grant seeker (number of years grants requested, number of years grants received, purposes and amounts for which grants received), the areas of foundation funding on a year-to-year basis (arts, education, health care, social services, etc.), serial grants committed for future years, and other information.

*Functions that can be handled either by a foundation's internal software or by an outside fiduciary, such as a bank, trust company, or brokerage firm.

Table 1-3, in Chapter 1, *supra* lists vendors and contact information for advanced accounting systems. This list is not intended to be an endorsement or recommendation for these products, but offers a place to start your search.[1]

§ 8.03   BUDGETING

Budgeting is the process of setting limits on expenses, setting goals for grantmaking, and anticipating income from contributions and investment growth.

---

[1] *Contributions* newspaper publishes an annual software directory called *The National Technology Buyer's Guide* that is extremely helpful in identifying vendors and options. Vendor contact information is listed in Table 1-3 in Chapter 1, *supra.*

The budgeting process is a matter of discipline, which allows the board to set priorities in spending.

[A]   Selecting a Tax Year-End

The family foundation may select a fiscal or calendar year-end at the time it is established. This year end can be changed in subsequent years if needed. It is generally easier to select a calendar year-end simply because it coincides with most accounting and reporting systems and allows you to coordinate foundation reporting with personal reporting.[2]

However, there are times that it is beneficial to use a fiscal year. Considerations in selecting a tax year-end include:

- Anticipated grant cycles of the foundation. Grant cycles are particularly important in the early years of the foundation. The foundation is required to distribute five percent of its average market value during the tax year, but it has until the close of the following tax year to make up any deficiencies. The foundation may want to select a fiscal year-end that delays payment of initial grants for as long as possible to allow foundation assets to generate revenue and to give the board time to develop a process to make decisions.

- *Anticipated cash flow*. Cash flow impacts the selection of the tax year, since the foundation may need time to invest its funds to generate sufficient cash flow to make grant distributions and cover start-up expenses. For example, the foundation may hold unusual assets such as undeveloped real property, unmarketable assets that must be sold, closely held stock that pays dividends annually, or installment notes. Look at the practical issues of getting through the tax year and meeting distribution requirements in order to get the best feel for the appropriate tax year-end.

- *Conduit foundation status*. The foundation that plans to qualify as a conduit foundation may find it useful to adopt a fiscal year ending on November 30. Such a foundation is required to distribute contributions it receives by a definite date — the 15th day of the third month after the close of its taxable year in which the contributions are received. A November 30 fiscal year will enable it to receive contributions in December and delay the time by which these amounts must be distributed until February 5 of the second subsequent year, even though

---

[2] Foundation tax returns are not due on the same date as personal tax returns. Individual returns are due three months and 15 days following the close of the tax year, or April 15. IRC § 6072(a). Private foundation returns are due four months and 15 days following the close of the tax year. Reg. § 1.6033-2(e). Therefore, if the foundation is using a calendar year-end, the tax return is due on May 15.

the donor will reflect the resultant tax benefit on the return filed within a few months.[3]

- *Other special issues.* The foundation may have special issues, such as the coordination of the foundation's year end with those of the organizations that it supports or an organization with a project that does not need funding until a later date. Or the foundation may prefer to use a fiscal year-end because the accounting and audit fees are cheaper and the accountant's response quicker in the off-season.

The bottom line is that you have a choice, and you should select the tax year end that best fits the foundation's needs.

[B] The Essential Budget Pieces

While many of the traditional budget line items are self-explanatory, this section provides a detailed discussion of those that are important to family foundations. A budget worksheet is provided at Appendix 8-A. Keep this worksheet in front of you as you move through an explanation of the most common budget elements.

[1] Receipts

A foundation has three primary sources of receipts: contributions made to the foundation, investment income, and realized capital gains. In addition, the foundation may receive a return of program-related investment funds or unused grants. The return of funds should be treated separately since those funds will increase the foundation's distribution requirements for the year.

Contributions to family foundations are rare, or at least irregular, since the foundation is generally established by family members or even one family member through a single funding. The foundation does not solicit contributions from the public. When founders or family members plan to make regular contributions, you can reflect those contributions as receipts to the extent they are anticipated.

Investment income, the income generated by foundation assets, is easier to estimate. The investment income of the foundation depends on the asset allocation of the investment portfolio. The easiest way to project income for the budget is to use the projected income figures shown on the custodian's monthly asset report.

Capital gains are more difficult to estimate and consist of two types of gains. The first is realized capital gain (or loss) on the sale of assets; the second is unrealized gain (or loss), representing the appreciation or depreciation in assets. The foundation's asset allocation is built on anticipated total return — meaning the total of earned income, realized gain, and unrealized gain. The investment markets, however, are unpredictable. Growth may reflect the

---

[3] *See* the discussion of this option at §2.06[C], *supra* and the examples set forth there.

averages in some years, but dramatically miss them in others. The foundation may want to budget anticipated growth, but with caution, since the foundation investment returns may not meet expectations.

[2]   Disbursements

Disbursements fall into three basic categories: administrative expenses, grants, and taxes. Administrative expenses include:

- *Leased space*. The foundation will generally lease, rather than own, its offices. Some family foundations are run from the grantor's corporate office, from home, or from a separate physical location. If the foundation is using corporate space or home space, then the foundation may not incur expense. If the foundation leases separate space, it should budget the costs of the space, leasehold improvements, taxes, and other costs allocated in the lease agreement. Of course, the foundation cannot lease space from a disqualified person unless the lease is rent-free.

- *Utilities.* The costs of electricity, gas, water, phone, and Internet connections are included here.

- *Office equipment and furnishings*. Large foundation offices incur expense for office furniture and furnishings, copiers, fax machines, telephone systems, computers, and other necessary equipment.

- *Administrative costs*. Administrative costs generally refer to the costs of record keeping and accounting. They include software costs, bank fees, trust fees, and other miscellaneous fees.

- *Training and conferences*. Training is necessary to use software, to improve management and office skills, and to learn more about the nonprofit world. Conferences represent opportunities to attend sessions on family foundation issues and to network with similar organizations.

- *Staff*. Staff costs vary widely among family foundations.[4] This expense may include full-time secretarial and grant management employees or part-time workers. Some foundations are small enough that administration is handled by the donor's corporate office staff, while others are so active that one or more full-time employees are required. When budgeting include the costs of benefits, including medical coverage and retirement benefits, if appropriate.

- *Professional expenses*. All family foundations will incur some professional expense for attorneys, accountants, consultants, and/or investment managers. Include annual entries for attorneys' fees, accounting fees, and investment management. Consulting fees should be budgeted as anticipated unless annual use of a consultant for grantmaking direction or regular advice is planned.

---

[4] *See* an extensive discussion of staffing and salaries in Chapter 5, *supra*.

- *Professional associations.* There are a number of organizations that may help provide support and counsel to family foundations. These associations have membership fees, and many have annual meetings. Get materials from all of them and talk to a few members who are active to determine which is best for you. A list of trade associations that address family foundation issues is provided in Chapter 1. You may also plan to attend the annual meetings for these associations; if so, include the costs of registration, travel, lodging, and meals.

- *Publications.* The foundation may find help from industry publications. The most common of these is the *Chronicle of Philanthropy*, a biweekly newspaper for the philanthropic world. Others have smaller circulations. Almost all of them carry advertisements for software, conferences, staff, and other management resources that may be of interest. Contact the publication, ask for a trial subscription if available, and retain the publications that are useful or interesting to you. A list of publications is provided in Chapter 1.

- *Marketing.* Marketing costs should be low, since family foundations do not generally expect to solicit or receive contributions from the public and so do not publish general brochures or annual reports. Family foundations with specific social agendas may want to publicize activities and grants simply to make the community more aware of needs and to inspire other organizations to support the issue. If you do plan to publicize your activities, make contact with a professional public relations and/or marketing firm if you need this service and develop a relationship. Make sure that the firm you choose has experience working with nonprofit organizations.[5]

- *Grants.* Grant expenditures are the key function of the family foundation. The foundation is required to distribute a minimum of five percent of its assets annually, but may make distributions of any amount up to the entire value of its assets. This is a tricky issue that requires discipline. There will always be more needs and requests for distributions than the foundation can meet. If the foundation chooses to distribute more than five percent, it will impact the investment asset allocation, since it will be distributing principal as well as earned income. And if it consistently distributes an amount such as eight percent or 10 percent or more of its assets, the foundation may slowly decrease in size, thereby decreasing the annual amount that it is capable of distributing.

  Set a distribution goal, communicate that to your investment manager, and stick with it as closely as possible. Special circumstances may arise that require additional distributions or early distributions in a year. However, keeping an eye on a specific goal instills discipline in grantmaking.

- *Taxes.* Finally, the family foundation must pay excise taxes on investment income. Although the foundation is exempt from income tax, it must pay an

---

[5] *See* Chapter 9 for more information on public relations and marketing issues.

excise tax of two percent of its income, defined as revenue from assets, capital gains, and other income.[6] This excise tax can be reduced to one percent if the foundation distributes an increasing percentage of its assets in grants. The best way to budget this line item is based on the required minimum distribution, based on prior years' experience, and current asset value. The foundation may be subject to additional excise taxes if the foundation or its managers violate the prohibited transaction rules. Proper management should avoid unnecessary tax.

A budget worksheet is provided at Appendix 8-A. Use this form, or the forms incorporated in your software, to create a budget for your foundation.

§ 8.04   THE TAX ON NET INVESTMENT INCOME

[A] Introduction

As pointed out above, one consideration that must be kept in mind in budgeting for a family foundation is the necessity of making timely payments of taxes due, which necessitates having sufficient cash balances on hand. Although a foundation is exempt from tax under section 501(c)(3), that exemption does not protect it from all federal taxes. As part of the system of excise taxes imposed on private foundations under the Tax Reform Act of 1969, Congress included an excise tax on foundations' net investment income.[7]

The original purpose of this was to provide a source of federal revenues to pay for the increased audit burden that the Internal Revenue Service was expected to bear under the rules enacted in 1969. The resultant excise tax was thus billed as an "audit fee" or "user charge" rather than as an income tax. In practice, however, that plan was not carried out, even though the proceeds far exceeded the audit and enforcement costs for all exempt organizations, not just for foundations.

The tax is imposed on the net investment income of a foundation, which includes its capital gains on the sale of assets held for investment purposes or for the production of income. The basic rate of tax is two percent, but the rate may be reduced to one percent for years in which the foundation's distributions are sufficiently in excess of the minimum distribution requirement. A foundation that qualifies as an exempt operating foundation (as defined in IRC § 4940(d)(2), and discussed at Section 2.06[B] above) is exempt from the tax on net investment income.

[B] Net Investment Income

The tax imposed by IRC § 4940 applies to the foundation's "net investment income," which is defined in IRC § 4940(c) as "gross investment income" plus "capital gain net income," "less any applicable deductions."

---

[6] IRC § 4940 and the Regulations thereunder.
[7] IRC § 4940(a).

[1] Gross Investment Income

Gross investment income is defined in § 4940(c)(2) as the gross amount of income from interest, dividends, rents, payments with respect to securities loans (as defined in IRC § 512(a)(5)), and royalties, not including any unrelated business taxable income. This includes such investment income derived from the conduct of an exempt charitable activity, such as interest on a program-related loan.

IRC § 4940(c)(5) provides specifically that neither interest on state and local bonds nor payments of expenses and interest allocable to tax-exempt income are taken into account in determining net investment income.

At one time the IRS took the position that net investment income of a foundation included distributions from trusts and estates. This position was impliedly rejected in *Ann Jackson Family Foundation v. Comm'r*.[8] In 2004, the IRS announced its intention to amend the Regulations (Regs. § 53.4940-1(d)(2)) to provide specifically that a private foundation's net investment income does not include such income.[9]

[2] Capital Gains and Losses

The gains subject to tax under IRC § 4940 are the foundation's capital gain net income — the excess of includible capital gains over includible capital losses. Any capital gains and losses from the sale or other disposition of property held for investment purposes or for the production of income must be taken into account. Likewise included are capital gains from mutual funds, and gains and losses from the disposition of property used in an unrelated trade or business, but only to the extent not included in the computation of unrelated business income.

The Regulations provide that property will treated as held for investment purposes, even though the foundation disposed of it immediately upon its receipt, if it is the kind of property that generally produces interest, dividends, rents, royalties, or capital gains through appreciation.[10] This position was challenged in *Friedman Foundation v. Comm'r*,[11] but the Tax Court upheld the regulation as a permissible interpretation of the statute. That holding has been criticized, however, and in appropriate circumstances another taxpayer may decide to litigate the issue.[12] For example, the Fifth Circuit held in *Zemurray Foundation v. U.S.*[13] that gain from the sale of timberland was not subject to tax under § 4940 where it was not economically prudent to use the land in a way that would produce interest, dividends, rents, or royalties. The IRS has apparently

---

[8] 15 F.3d 917 (9th Cir. 1994), *aff'g* 97 T.C. 534 (1991).

[9] Notice 2004-35, 2004-19 I.R.B. 889.

[10] Reg. § 53.4940-1(f)(1).

[11] 71 T.C. 40 (1978). *See also* Greenacre Foundation v. U.S., 762 F.2d 965 (Fed. Cir. 1985).

[12] *See* Richardson and Jewett, *Is Stock Donated to a Foundation and Resold Right Away a Taxable Investment Asset?*, 50 J. Taxation 10 (1979).

[13] 755 F.2d 404 (5th Cir. 1985).

accepted the holding of this case that gains from the sale of assets that are not of the type which will normally produce income will not be investment income.[14]

Gains and losses from the disposition of property used for the exempt purposes of the foundation are not included in figuring the tax under § 4940. Gains and losses from such property will not be subject to tax even if the foundation incidentally receives income (such as rents, dividends, or interest) that is subject to the tax. For example, a foundation that maintains historic buildings that are open to the public and charges employees rent for residing in such buildings must include such rent in its net investment income, but any gain or loss resulting from the sale of these buildings is not subject to the tax.[15]

If property is used for both investment purposes and exempt purposes (such as a building in which the foundation conducts both its charitable program and its investment management), an allocation must be made. Only the gain or loss allocable to the investment function is taken into account under IRC § 4940.

Capital losses from the disposition of investment property may be used to offset capital gains from such property during the same tax year, but only to the extent of the gains. No carryovers or carrybacks of excess losses are allowed.

The basis used for computing gain or loss is determined under the normal tax rules governing basis, with one exception. The basis for property that was held by the foundation on December 31,1969, will not in any event be less than the value of that property on that date, plus or minus any post-1969 adjustments.

[C]   Deductions

In computing net investment income, deductions are allowed for all of the ordinary and necessary expenses paid or incurred for the production or collection of gross investment income or for the management, conservation, or maintenance of property held for the production of income, with two modifications.[16] First, the depreciation deduction is limited to the straight line method; and second, although depletion is allowed, the percentage depletion method of IRC § 613 is not available.

An expense which serves both an investment purpose and a charitable purpose must be allocated between the two categories, and only the investment portion is deductible. *See* Rev. Rul. 75-410, 1975-2 C.B. 446, where the IRS ruled that fees paid for an annual audit of its financial records were not fully deductible for this purpose because the audit examined income and expenses attributable to both investment activities and distributions; only the part of the audit fee attributable to examination of investment income and expenses was held to be deductible.

---

[14] *See, e.g.*, Priv. Ltr. Ruls. 8903090,8846005, and 8752033, involving the sale of donated stock options, and Technical Advice Memorandum.8852001, involving the sale of stock warrants.

[15] Reg. § 53.4940-1(f)(1).

[16] IRC § 4940(c)(3).

[D]   Rate of Tax

The basic tax rate under IRC § 4940 is two percent. However, in 1984 Congress added § 4940(e) to the Code, reducing the tax rate from two percent to one percent for foundations that meet two requirements:

1.   The foundation's qualifying distributions (as defined in IRC § 4942(g), discussed at Section 7.02 above) for the year are at least equal to a minimum amount. That amount is equal to the sum of (a) the assets of the foundation for the tax year multiplied by its average percentage payout for the five preceding taxable years, plus (b) one percent of the foundation's net investment income for the tax year; and

2.   The foundation was not liable for the tax under IRC § 4942 on a failure to meet minimum distribution requirements for any of the preceding five taxable years.

If the foundation's qualifying distributions for the current year equal or exceed the amount calculated in item (1) above and it also meets the standard in item (2) for the year, its tax on net investment income under IRC § 4940 for the year is assessed at one percent rather than two percent.

In the case of a foundation that is a successor, by merger or otherwise, to another foundation, the experience of that predecessor is taken into account for purposes of the five-year average computation described above.[17]

[E]   Returns and Payment of Tax

The foundation reports its tax liability on its Form 990-PF. Since 1987, foundations have been required to make quarterly payments of estimated tax, in the same manner as corporate estimated tax payments. If the tax shown on the foundation's tax return is over $500, a penalty is due for any underpayment of such estimated tax. This penalty is imposed under IRC § 6655(a) at a rate three percentage points higher than the federal short-term rate determined under IRC § 6621(b).

§ 8.05   MANAGING THE GRANTMAKING PROCESS

[A]   Grant Models

Grantmaking, discussed in detail in Chapter 7, is the central function of the family foundation. Therefore, it is logical that the grantmaking function is the largest administrative task managed by the foundation, and the one that benefits the most from organization and attention to detail. It is important to understand how grantmaking works in order to manage the process. There are three grant models.

---

[17] IRC § 4940(e)(6).

1. *Proactive model.* In this model, the board determines the public issues to be addressed, identifies the organizations that can meet these needs, and asks those organizations to submit grant proposals to address and solve the issues. The foundation board then reviews the proposals and selects the one or two that meet the identified need. This model is rare.

2. *Reactive model.* In this model, the foundation opens its doors for business and waits for nonprofit organizations to find it and submit requests for grants. In the early years, there is often a paucity of grant requests, since few nonprofits are aware of the existence of the foundation. As the charitable world becomes aware of the foundation and the foundation's profile is listed in foundation directories, the number of requests will increase dramatically. The foundation board then reviews the requests, prioritizes them based on the foundation's mission and the funds available, and distributes grants as appropriate. More and more family foundations are moving to this model.

3. *Traditional family foundation model.* The family members in this model identify charitable organizations that they want to support personally and make grants to those organizations. Although the foundation may receive a number of unsolicited grant requests, those are not generally considered.

All approaches are effective. The authors recommend that the foundation be open to requests for funding from the community for several reasons. First, it is a good way to remain aware of critical charitable community initiatives. Second, the foundation's dollars may be spent in more coordinated and powerful ways if they are contributed as part of a larger effort. Third, the ability to participate in community campaigns may give the foundation and family more visibility, if that is desired. All require good administrative management in order to maximize the effectiveness of the distribution of dollars.

[B] Managing the Application Process

Managing the grantmaking process begins with keeping good records. The family foundation may receive grant requests from hundreds of organizations. These grant seekers will be a mix of first-time applicants, repeat applicants, and applicants with purposes beyond the scope of the foundation mission. The foundation should have a process for screening these applicants and responding promptly to them, saying either "We're sorry, but your grant falls outside the scope of our funding" or "We have received your grant request and have put it in line for consideration at our next meeting in _____."

In the event that the applicant has not submitted the appropriate form or all the necessary information, reply by providing the organization with an application package and a deadline for return. Responding promptly and letting the applicant know the time line for decision making will cut down on the number of phone calls that you will get with inquiries about the status of the request.

It is also a good idea to record all grant requests in your database, whether the requests are immediately denied, denied after consideration, deferred until a later date, or granted, in order to create a historical picture of the interest in your foundation. At a minimum, record the name of the requesting organization, the date of the request, the amount requested, the purpose of the request, and the disposition. If the grant is to be deferred until a later meeting, set up a tickler to remind you to include it later. The information should be entered in a database so that the foundation can generate a report for the meeting when those grants being considered as well as a list of rejected applications for the board's information. This information will help the foundation identify areas of need in the community as well as trends in grant requests. Or the information may identify communication problems that need to be addressed.

> **Example:** A well-established foundation suddenly began to receive a number of requests for scholarships from individuals attending a local university. The first dozen requests were unusual because the foundation had not previously received requests for that purpose. By the time the foundation had received two dozen requests the administrator knew that something or someone was generating that interest. The source was finally traced to a local university's student aid office. The foundation had been incorrectly listed as one of the top prospects for individual scholarship funds. As soon as the foundation's name was removed from the list, the flood of scholarship requests stopped.

Although it is not necessary to permanently retain all grant applications, it is recommended that you keep the full application on file until the project for which the funds were awarded is complete. This will allow you to make sure the funds were used for the intended purposes (especially if expenditure responsibility is involved). From a practical perspective, the paper will accumulate rapidly. Scan the papers you need to retain for electronic storage; throw the rest away.

[C] Records of Awards

The foundation must maintain a record of grant awards for a number of reasons:

- The foundation can generate the list of details about the year's grants for the 990-PF annual tax return.

- The foundation can sort the data in preparing for grant meetings. Among the pieces of information that a foundation grant committee member should have in considering a grant are the number of times that an applicant has been awarded a grant, the dates of those awards, and the cumulative total of the awards.

- The foundation should be able to generate historical grantmaking activity for board training, for policy purposes, and for personal information. Once the data is structured in a format that makes it easily accessible, the information can be analyzed in a variety of forms that may prove helpful to the foundation board.

- The foundation can generate a list of information and types of funding for the annual report, if applicable. Few family foundations generate an annual report, but the trend for the more public and the larger private foundations is to do so. The annual report may focus on the grants made, or the areas of funding, but the purpose is generally to make the foundation and its role in the community visible.

Begin good record keeping from the outset. It may not be much of a problem to manually assemble a history of grants when the foundation has one or two years of history. However, putting together a five-year or 10-year history of grants by hand is a daunting job.

[D] The Need for Periodic Reminders

The foundation administrator should also have the ability to generate periodic activity reminders related to grants and meeting schedules. These include:

- *Dates of payment of serial grants.* Where grants are structured in three-, four- or even five-year increments, the administrator must have a solid system to make sure that grants are paid at the right times each year. Serial grant obligations also represent a liability of the foundation and must be reported as such. These grant obligations should be tied to a report that is provided to the board members in grant meetings so that the board has a clear picture of funding commitments made for future years.

- *Reminders of information due.* If payment of a grant is contingent upon your foundation receiving a progress report or financial update from the recipient organization, the foundation administrator should create a tickler to trigger that request for information.

- *Dates of deferred or irregular payment periods.* A grant may be awarded during a spring grant meeting, although the first payment may be deferred until January 1 of the following year, or six months after the award, or some other time-linked period. In other cases, grants are payable upon the happening or completion of an event. While the nonprofit will generally be quick to let the foundation know when this event has occurred, the foundation should schedule periodic follow-ups to determine the status of payment.

- *Due dates for grant use/audit forms.* The foundation should require that grant recipients report to the foundation on the use of the funds and certify that all funds have been used for the purposes intended. Most follow-ups are due within a specified time period from grant, such as after six or 12 months after award or by the organization's tax year-end, whichever is later. Since many organizations are on a nonstandard grant cycle and since there are 12 potential year-ends for the receiving organization, the foundation administrator should have a system for generating reminders that the reports are due.

- *Meeting dates.* The foundation administrator should establish deadlines for grant applications, dates for mailing materials to trustees, and meeting dates and then set ticklers as reminders for these dates.

- *Other activities.* The administrator may also find it useful to establish ticklers to prompt requests for month-end statements of asset values and tax reports, to remind him or her of tax return filing dates and estimated tax payment dates, or to highlight any other activities requiring prompt action.

[E] Who Does the Work?

Family foundations may be staffed or unstaffed depending on the foundation's resources, the foundation's mission, and the family members with the time and interest to do the work. The foundation may choose to hire an executive director and/or chief operating officer to handle all of the management of the foundation, including managing administrative or secretarial staff. Salaries may range from $25,000 a year for a part-time employee to as much as $150,000 a year for an experienced professional.

The foundation may also hire professional advisors and/or consultants to handle specific duties. Attorneys and accountants may manage the legal and accounting affairs of the foundation. Consultants may assist with software management or grants analysis. Investment managers may manage foundation assets. Banks and trust companies can also provide some of these services, such as receipt, analysis, and review of grant applications; preparation of grant worksheets for meetings; check generation; correspondence with grantseekers; and tax return filings. Finally, there are some specialty financial services firms that manage family foundations and family offices.

The foundation board should be practical in analyzing responsibilities and assigning those to staff, professionals, or consultants to ensure that the work is done. Most family members have neither the time nor the inclination to handle secretarial tasks, data input and report production, and interaction with grantseekers. *See* Chapter 5 for more detail on staffing and salaries.

[F] Expenses

The cost of administration varies widely depending on whether the foundation uses inside staff, outside advisors, or family. The Council on Foundations[18]

---

[18] Council on Foundations, 1828 L Street NW, Washington, DC 20036, 202-466-6512.

conducted a study of foundations in 1997, published in 1998,[19] which provided insight into the costs incurred by family foundations for charitable administrative expenses. The results, reflecting input from 187 respondents, were segmented by foundation size and calculated in three ways: as a percentage of noncharitable use assets (investment assets), as a percentage of grants, and as a percentage of total payout.[20] The mean and median for each of these categories are shown in Table 8-4.

TABLE 8-4
Average Costs for Administration as Reported in 1997
Survey of Family Foundations

Type of Analysis	Median Range for Various Asset Sizes (%)	Mean Range for Various Asset Sizes (%)
Expenses as percentage of nonchari-table use assets	0.35–0.65 all 0.47	0.49–0.77 all 0.63
Expenses as percentage of grants	6.84–13.6 all 9.79	11.94–19.22 all 14.65
Expenses as percentage of total payout	4.98 to 10.85 all 8.04	7.61–12.51 all 10.06

§ 8.06 INVESTMENT MANAGEMENT

Investment management is a key responsibility of the foundation board because the return on investments is the primary source of funding for grants. Most family foundations are funded with a single contribution, or with multiple contributions from a single donor, and do not receive ongoing public support. Therefore, the return on investment must be sufficient to meet the foundation's five percent distribution requirement and accomplish the foundation's goals.

Investment management may be difficult because the decision makers on the board or investment committee bring strong personal opinions to the table. Most board members are inclined to manage the foundation's assets in the same way they would manage their personal or business assets. Instead, the foundation assets should be managed in accordance with fiduciary standards and so as to best meet the needs and long-term mission of the foundation.

[A] The Standard of Care

While there is no federal legislation that governs foundation investment management other than the requirement that the assets be managed in a way so

---

[19] Foundation Management Series (Council on Foundations 9th ed. 1998).
[20] *Id.* at 42-46.

as not to jeopardize the foundation's ability to carry out its tax-exempt status,[21] there are three bodies of state law that may govern the board's conduct. These include the Restatement (Third) of Trusts: Prudent Investor Rule; the Uniform Prudent Investor Act, established by the National Conference of Commissioners on Uniform State Law,[22] and the Uniform Management of Institutional Funds Act,[23] governing management of funds held for nonprofit purposes.[24] Boards are not always ready to hear a lecture on investment duties, but it is important for the board to understand its responsibility and attendant liability.

[1] Restatement (Third) of Trusts: Prudent Investor Rule

The Restatement (Third) of Trusts: Prudent Investor Rule sets the standard of conduct for most trustees. This standard is applicable to family foundations organized in trust form and governed by trustees and to those individuals or organizations that serve as trustees of pension plans, charitable remainder trusts, revocable trusts, or other trust documents. The original standard for a trustee's conduct, called the prudent man rule, was defined in *Harvard College v. Amory*.[25] There the court stated:

> All that can be required of a trustee to invest is that he shall conduct himself faithfully and exercise a sound discretion. He is to observe how men of prudence, discretion and intelligence manage their own affairs, not in regard to speculation, but in regard to the permanent disposition of their funds, considering the probable income, as well as the probable safety of capital to be invested. . . . [26]

The old prudent man rule judged the fiduciary on the results of individual investment decisions, rather than the performance of the portfolio as a whole; it

---

[21] IRC § 4944.

[22] *See* Appendix 8-F for the full text of the Uniform Prudent Investor Act (UPIA). The Act has been adopted in part or in full by many states. Many states have amended the model act to some degree in adoption.

[23] *See* Appendix 8-G for the full text of the Uniform Management of Institutional Funds Act (UMIFA). This Act may have been adopted in part or in full by your state. Many states have amended the model act to some degree in adoption.

[24] The Uniform Management of Institutional Funds Act incorporates the same principles and was designed to govern funds permanently set aside for charitable purposes. UMIFA allows expanded investment options beyond the legal list; gives the fiduciary the ability to hold contributed assets or sell them; allows the fiduciary to pool investments in a common fund, pool, or investment partnership; and allows the fiduciary to delegate investment management to independent advisors. Considerations in making investments should include an analysis of the long- and short-term needs of the nonprofit in carrying out its purpose, current financial needs, anticipated financial needs, expected total return on investments, and general economic conditions.

[25] 26 Mass. (9 Pick.) 446 (1830).

[26] *Id* at 46.

set rigid rules on issues such as diversification of assets; and it placed a premium on generation of income. Fiduciaries were held strictly accountable for violation of the rules, even when actions were taken with the approval of the governing document or at the encouragement of the beneficiary, meaning that fiduciaries had no incentive to take chances that might increase the growth rate of assets.

For example, state law generally provided the fiduciary with a "legal list" of investments, which was a list of types of assets such as U.S. government obligations, insured bonds, and certificates of deposit that were deemed to be safe. If the governing document did not expand the legal list, the fiduciary was not permitted to purchase stocks, mutual funds, common trust funds, or any asset not listed. If the governing document did expand the fiduciary's powers to invest in assets beyond the legal list, the fiduciary could be held liable if the investment did not succeed.

The prudent man rule also required that the trustee diversify or stand accountable for the loss if he failed to do so. Consider the strict application of this principle in the Alabama case of *First Alabama Bank v. Spragins.*[27] In Spragins, First Alabama Bank served as trustee under the will of the former president and chairman of the board of the bank. The stock of First Alabama Bank represented 70 percent of the total estate. The will specifically relieved the trustee from the duty to diversify; in addition, the family agreed to hold the stock. Over the period of administration, the stock increased in value. However, the bank stock did not appreciate to the degree that the overall equity markets advanced. The family filed suit against the trustee, alleging that the bank had violated its duty by failing to diversify the stock. In spite of the clear language in the will, the court held that the beneficiaries suffered a loss and ruled that the executor was liable and assessed damages based on a return that could have been achieved if the assets were invested in the general securities market. While the court agreed that the trust document governed the duties and obligations of the trustee, it did not agree that the trust language could "be applied here to lessen the duty imposed by the "prudent person" standard."[28]

In 1990, the American Law Institute recommended a new standard for trustee conduct with the publication of the Restatement (Third) of Trusts: Prudent Investor Rule.[29] The drafting committee lamented the strict, court-driven interpretation of the prudent man standard, stating that "[k]nowledge, practices, and experience in the modern investment world have demonstrated that arbitrary restrictions on trust investments are unwarranted and often counterproductive."[30] The new rule eliminated the rigidity created through court interpretation of the prudent man rule and allowed the fiduciary flexibility and discretion in exercising judgment in investment matters.[31]

---

[27] 475 So. 2d 512 (Ala. 1985), *on rehearing*, 515 So. 2d 962 (Ala. 1987).

[28] *Id.* at 516.

[29] Restatement (Third) of Trusts: Prudent Investor Rule (American Law Institute 1992).

[30] *Id.* at 4.

[31] *Id.* at ix.

Under the prudent investor rule, the fiduciary is judged on the decision-making process employed at the time the investment decision is made, rather than on an after-the-fact analysis of performance. The focus is on the total portfolio and its investment strategy, rather than each individual portfolio asset. Finally, the emphasis on production of income and preservation of principal is replaced by a measurement of total return (total of income and capital appreciation) of the portfolio—looking at real return after inflation; this can also be stated as the duty to balanced risk and return. Finally, the trustee is allowed to delegate investment management so long as he or she monitors the process effectively. The prudent investor rule actually places more responsibility on the fiduciary to make reasoned decisions, since it removes the safety of the "legal list" and other rules that provide a safe harbor. However, the change has greatly enhanced the ability to manage investments and does protect the trustee who is diligent in managing the process.

While the Restatement (Third) of Trusts: Prudent Investor Rule is designed to govern the actions of trustees, the drafting committee observed that the standards might also be appropriate for directors and officers of charitable corporations, since "the duties of the members of the governing board of a charitable corporation are generally similar to the duties of the trustee of a charitable trust."[32]

[2] Uniform Prudent Investor Act

The Uniform Prudent Investor Act (UPIA) was drafted and approved by the National Conference of Commissioners on Uniform State Law in 1994 and approved by the American Bar Association in February 1995. The Act is basically a codification of the Restatement (Third) of Trusts: Prudent Investor Rule recommended for adoption in all states to bring uniformity to trust investment law. The UPIA contained the five major changes advanced by the Restatement:

1. The measure of the trustee's prudence in investing is determined by a review of the entire portfolio, rather than individual assets;

2. The trustee's primary role in investing is to balance risk and return;

3. There are no prohibited investments; the trustee is allowed to invest in those assets appropriate for the needs of the trust (balancing risk and return);

4. While diversification is evidence of exercise of prudence, there is no strict requirement that the trustee diversify. Rather, this is an element of the overall balancing of risk and return; and

5. Delegation of investment management is permitted.

---

[32] *Id.* at 190. The committee also commented, "[A]bsent contrary statute or other provision, the prudent investor rule applies to investment of funds held for charitable corporations." *Id.* at 190-191.

The law was intended to govern the conduct of trustees as well as that of other fiduciaries, such as executors, conservators, and guardians. However, in recommending the standards, the drafting committee noted that "the standards of the Act can be expected to inform the investment responsibilities of directors and officers of charitable corporations." At least 28 states have adopted the UIPA in some form.[33]

[3] Uniform Management of Institutional Funds Act

The Uniform Management of Institutional Funds Act (UMIFA) was drafted and recommended for enactment by the National Conference of Commissioners on Uniform State Law in 1972. The uniform law was developed because nonprofit corporations and institutions had no specific directives governing investment conduct. Fearing that the only applicable standard was the prudent man rule, directors often structured investments conservatively using investments considered "safe," with a premium on production of income.[34] The Act applies to incorporated or unincorporated charitable organizations, including some government organizations; it specifically excludes trusts.[35] While UMIFA was recommended in 1972, well before the development of the Restatement (Third) of Trusts: Prudent Investor Rule and the UPIA, it contains many of the same prudent investor standards. Key elements of UMIFA are these:

- The nonprofit institution is allowed to use appreciation (realized and unrealized); directors and officers are urged to take a total return approach, looking at income and appreciation;

- Investments are not restricted to specific types of assets. The directors and officers are allowed to invest in an unlimited range of assets;

- Delegation of investment responsibility is permitted. This duty may be delegated to employees or third-party managers;

- The standard of prudence is to be a standard of business care and prudence, rather than the fiduciary standard set out in the prudent man rule;

- Restrictions imposed by donors can be released by the donor. If the donor is no longer alive, the institution can ask a court of competent jurisdiction to release the restrictions so long as the court is not asked to convert an endowment to a non-endowment.

---

[33] Alaska, Arizona, Arkansas, California, Colorado, Connecticut, Florida, Hawaii, Idaho, Illinois, Maine, Massachusetts, Michigan, Minnesota, Missouri, Nebraska, New Jersey, New Mexico, New York, North Dakota, Oklahoma, Oregon, Rhode Island, Utah, Vermont, Virginia, Washington, and West Virginia. Also, some states, such as Alabama, have adopted the prudent investor rule, but did so before 1994 when the UPIA was promulgated.

[34] Uniform Management of Institutional Funds Act, National Conference of Commissioners on Uniform State Law (1972), prefatory note.

[35] UMIFA § 1(1) and comments.

TABLE 8-5
STATUS OF STATE ADOPTION OF UNIFORM MANAGEMENT OF
INSTITUTIONAL FUNDS ACT

States That Have Adopted UMIFA in Whole or in Part

State	*Code Section*	*State*	*Code Section*
Alabama	§§ 16-61A-1 to 16-61A-8	Montana	§§ 72-30-101 to 72-30-207
Arkansas	§§ 28-69-601 to 28-69-611	Nebraska	§§ 58-601 to 58-609
California	Probate Code §§ 18500 to 18509	Nevada	§§ 164.500 to 164.630
Colorado	§§ 15-1-1101 to 15-1-1109	New Hampshire	§§ 292-B:1 — 292-B:9
Connecticut	§§ 45a-526 to 45a-535	New Jersey	§§ 15:18-15 to 15:18-24
Delaware	Tit. 12, §§ 4701 to 4708	New Mexico	Art. 9 §§ 46-9-1 to 46-9-12
District of Columbia	§§ 44-1601 to 44-1604	New York	NPC §§ 102, 512, 514, 522
Florida	Title XLVIII § 1010.10	North Carolina	§§ 36B-1 to 36B-10
Georgia	§§ 44-15-1 to 44-15-9	North Dakota	§§ 15-67-01 to 15-67-09
Hawaii	§§ 517D-1 to 517D-11	Ohio	§§ 1715.51 to 1715.59
Idaho	§§ 33-5001 to 33-5008	Oklahoma	Title 60 §§ 300.1 to 300.10
Illinois	760 ILCS 50/1 to 560 ILCS 50/10	Oregon	§§ 128.310 to 128.355
Indiana	§§ 30-2-12 to 30-2-12-13	Rhode Island	§§ 18-12-1 to 18-12-9
Iowa	§§ 540A.1 to 540A.9	South Carolina	§§ 34-6-10 to 34-6-80
Kansas	§§ 58-3601 to 58-3610	South Dakota	§§ 55-14-1 to 55-14-7
Kentucky	§§ 273.510 to 273.590	Tennessee	§§ 35-10-101 to 35-10-109
Louisiana	§§ 9:2337.1 to 9:2337.8	Texas	Property Code §§ 163.001 - 163.009

TABLE 8-5.   CONTINUED
States That Have Adopted UMIFA in Whole or in Part

State	Code Section	State	Code Section
Maine	Title 13 §§ 4100 to 4110	Utah	§§ 13-29-1 to 13-29-10
Maryland	Est. & Tr., §§ 15-401 to 15-409	Vermont	Tit. 14, §§ 3401 to 3407
Massachusetts	Chapter 180A, §§ 1 to 11	Virginia	§§ 55-268.1 to 55-268.10
Michigan	§§ 451.1201 to 451.1210	Washington	§§ 24.44.010 to 24.44.900
Minnesota	§§ 309.62 to 309.71	West Virginia	§§ 44-6A-1 to 44-6A-8
Mississippi	§§ 79-11-601 to 79-11-617	Wisconsin	§§ 112.10 to 112.10(7)(b)
Missouri	§§ 402.010 to 402.225	Wyoming	§§ 17-7-201 to 17-7-205

States That Have Not Adopted UMIFA

Alaska, Pennsylvania

Arizona

The Act advanced by the National Conference of Commissioners on Uniform State Laws in 1972 has now been adopted by 47 states and the District of Columbia, as shown in Table 8-5.

The Uniform Law Commissioners, realizing the current version of the Act needed revisions, considered a new version of the Uniform Management of Institutional Laws Act at its 2005 Annual Meeting in Pittsburgh in late July. The 2005 UMIFA Draft expands on the release or modification of donor gift restrictions in Section 6. The 2005 Draft allows changes under 4 circumstances:

1. *Donor Release*: "With the donor's consent in a record," the charity can release a restriction in whole or in part, so long as the gift is still used for the organization's charitable purposes.[36]

2. *Doctrine of Deviation*: If a modification to a gift agreement/document will enhance the furtherance of the donor's purposes, or a restriction is "impracticable or wasteful and impairs the management or investment of the fund," the charity can ask a court to modify the restriction. The Attorney

---

[36] UMIFA 2005, Section 6(b).

General must be notified and allowed to be heard, and the modification must reflect the donor's "probable intention."[37]

3. *Doctrine of Cy Pres*: If the purpose or restriction becomes "unlawful, impracticable, impossible to achieve, or wasteful," the court may use the cy pres doctrine to modify the fund purposes. The Attorney General must be notified and allowed to be heard.

4. *Small Funds*: For funds with a value less than $25,000 that have been in place more than 20 years, court action is not required if the charity determines a restriction is "unlawful, impracticable, impossible to achieve, or wasteful" so long as the charity waits 60 days after notice to the state Attorney General of the intention to make the change, and the change is designed to be a good faith reflection of the expressed charitable purposes.[38]

The new Uniform Management of Institutional Funds Act must be considered by the Uniform Law Commissioners at two annual meetings before receiving final approval and published for consideration by state legislatures. It was first considered by the Commissioners at the July 2005 and will be considered a second time for final review and approval in the 2006 annual meeting.[39] The outcome of that meeting was not available at date of publication.

[4]   Comparing the Standards

At the heart of all these standards of conduct is the prudent investor rule, requiring that the board exercise the care that "a prudent investor would, by considering the purposes, terms, distribution requirements, and other circumstances" and that the fiduciary "exercise reasonable care, skill and caution."[40] Defining the standard of care is difficult, although it is easier to explain by reviewing the evolution of the rule.

The rules governing the board's conduct in investing foundation assets in accordance with the rule can be summarized as follows:[41]

- *Nonprofit directors and trustees must analyze and make decisions about the relationship of risk and return in the portfolio.* This analysis requires a sophisticated knowledge of the markets and an allocation of assets to the stock and

---

[37] UMIFA 2005, Section 6(c).

[38] UMIFA 2005, Section 6(e).

[39] *National Law Group Wraps Up 114th Annual Meeting*, The National Conference of Commissioners on Uniform State Laws, http://www.nccusl.org/Update/DesktopModules/NewsDisplay.aspx?ItemID=143 (July 28, 2005).

[40] UPIA § 2(a) (1994).

[41] These concepts are summarized in the introductory remarks of the drafting committee in Restatement (Third) of Trusts: Prudent Investor Rule 5-6.

bond sectors reflecting the current and long-term goals of foundation investment as well as the degree of volatility that the directors or trustees find comfortable. There are few foundation board members with this expertise, so reliance on knowledgeable investment advisors is customary;

- *Nonprofit directors and trustees are generally required to diversify, since sound diversification is a critical element of risk management.* This requires that the fiduciaries have some understanding of basic market returns and principles. This also means that the fiduciary must look at issues such as concentrations of stock; the balance of stocks, bonds, and cash; and diversification within the sectors of the equity market;

- *Trustees must be conscious of costs in the portfolio and must limit them to justified expenses; this standard is not addressed in UMIFA, but may be seen as a basic responsibility of a nonprofit to manage its assets wisely.* Costs are but one element of management, but are singled out by the prudent investor rule as an area of concern. Management costs can range from 0.10 to five percent of the asset market value. Some assets, such as small cap stocks, foreign stocks, or venture capital offerings, carry higher cost ratios. Other funds, such as index funds, cost little. The fiduciary must have a knowledge of the average costs for such transactions and management and must be able to articulate the value added for additional fees where those fees fall well outside of normal standards.

- *Trustees have an additional responsibility to balance competing interests. Income beneficiaries and remaindermen may have different goals, and the fiduciary's duty is to be impartial and to generate income, while preserving the purchasing power of the assets.* This concept has application when considering the current and future needs of charitable beneficiaries of the foundation, since most family foundations are designed to be perpetual. The beneficiaries of those organizations are nonprofit organizations, the public served by those organizations, the individuals and organizations that benefit from grants or distributions currently, and the institutions or organizations that may benefit from those services in the future. Balancing current and future needs requires consideration of the anticipated life and mission of the foundation.

- *Under all standards, delegation of investment duties may be prudent.* This concept has enormous impact on fiduciaries. A history of this rule provides some context. Fiduciaries or trustees have two types of duties: ministerial duties and discretionary duties. Ministerial duties include preparing tax returns, collecting income, and making repairs, or duties that are generally exercised to carry on the daily activities of the organization. The trustee is not always capable of performing each ministerial detail, and so long as care is exercised in the delegation of the duties and the organizing documents do not prohibit delegation, agents can be engaged. Of course, when agents are employed, the fiduciary is under a duty to use reasonable care in selecting them, instructing them, and monitoring their progress. However, discretionary duties (such as investment management) require ongoing supervision and exercise of judgment. Examples of discretionary functions include determining which assets to sell or purchase, when to sell or purchase them, and the price at which to sell or purchase them and making discretionary distributions of grants. The prudent investor rule recognizes that many of the aspects of investment management, though discretionary, are not within the skill set of trustees or directors. In those instances, the role of the fiduciary is to hire professional assistance, to set standards for that conduct, to monitor the activities of the agent, and to make changes in that agent where necessary.

The prudent investor rule requires that trustees and directors spend more time formulating and administering policy than in the past but provides them with greater protection from the court when they do so. Effective policy making requires both an understanding of the factors affecting the investment markets and discipline.

Table 8-6 compares the standards of the prudent man rule, Restatement (Third) of Trusts: Prudent Investor Rule, Uniform Prudent Investor Act, and Uniform Management of Institutional Funds Act.

TABLE 8-6
Comparison of Fiduciary and Institutional Investment Standards

	Prudent Man Rule	*Restatement (Third) of Trusts: Prudent Investor Rule*	*Uniform Prudent Investor Act*	*Uniform Management of Institutional Funds Act (1972)*
Priority on making assets income producing	Yes	No	No	No
Investments restricted to specific assets	Yes, through legal list and court interpretation	No	No	No
Analysis of "prudence" made by examining performance of individual assets	Yes	No, entire portfolio	No, entire portfolio	Business standard of conduct, portfolio
Primary role of investment manager	Select asset that is safe, produces income	Balance risk and return	Balance risk and return	Balance risk and return
Delegation of duties permitted	No	Yes	Yes	Yes

TABLE 8-6 CONTINUED

	Prudent Man Rule	Restatement (Third) of Trusts: Prudent Investor Rule	Uniform Prudent Investor Act	Uniform Management of Institutional Funds Act (1972)
Can remove restrictions on income/ principal distributions, restrictions on investment assets	No	No	No	Yes
Diversification required	Yes	No	No	No

[B] Writing the Investment Policies

[1] Policies Should Be in Writing

Investment policies should be reduced to writing for four purposes:

- *To ensure that the board takes the time to review the issues and make a decision on the critical points.* Board members may be more likely to go through the discussion if it is necessary to adopt the policies;

- *To codify the consensus of opinion of the board on the total return goals and the risk tolerance appropriate for the foundation investments developed in the meeting.* This written record of consensus will serve as a platform for a regular (at least annual) discussion of that opinion;

- *To provide clear instructions for the investment manager.* A record of instructions on goals and restrictions is an important part of the communication with and accountability system for the foundation's investment manager, whether internal or external; and

- *To meet the requirements of the prudent investor rule or Uniform Management of Institutional Funds Act.* Written policies help protect the board from liability.

There is no need to have complicated, lengthy, or difficult-to-interpret policies. It is more important to put thought into the issues such as asset allocation, spending policy, and limits on investments and then reduce the results to a form that the board can understand and implement. A sample set of investment policies is provided at Appendix 8-B. The following sections discuss key provisions.

[2] Spending Policy

The spending policy sets out the expected spending rate of the foundation. The spending policy generally expresses the percentage of the foundation's assets that will be spent on grants and administrative expenses during the year. Setting a goal for spending is important because the spending rate impacts the cash flow and need for liquidity from the investments. For example, if the foundation assets generate 3.5 percent in income and the foundation distributes five percent in grants and spends 2.5 percent in expenses, the foundation must use the assets themselves to make up the four percent shortfall. The foundation investment manager must either have this amount available in cash or sell assets (stocks or bonds) to raise the cash. An untimely sale of investment assets may negatively impact long-term performance.

The spending policy can be expressed in a combination of ways. The advantage of the formulas below is that they communicate the specific dollar amount required during the year so that the manager can plan.

- *A dollar amount (e.g., $50,000 or $100,000).* This formula is the most straightforward, since it expresses a specific need for funds based on a budgeted spending amount.

- *A percentage amount based on a specific valuation date (e.g., six percent of the market value of the assets on the first day of the tax year).* The advantage of this formula is that it allows the foundation to budget a specific figure that is based on current assets.

- *A more complicated formula (e.g., six percent of the average market value of the last 16 quarterly end market values).* This formula provides some stability to the spending amount, since short-term fluctuations in value are evened out through the averaging process.

However formulated, the policy sets direction for spending, alerts the money manager to the cash needs, and provides consistency in budgeting from year to year.

[3] Investment Objectives

The investment policies should state the investment objectives of the funds. The board must begin by prioritizing preservation of capital, growth of assets, need for current income, and need for future income and then express that conclusion in a statement.

Example 1: The investment goal for the foundation assets is to balance the need to achieve long-term growth in the funds with the current production of income.

Example 2: The investment goal for the foundation assets is to produce an ever-increasing stream of income and increase the underlying assets by an average of five percent per year.

Example 3: The investment goal for the foundation assets is to maximize the income from the invested funds and preserve the capital through investment in assets with a minimum of risk.

[4] Risk Tolerance

Risk should be addressed as clearly and openly as possible.[42] If the members of the investment committee do not reach consensus on how to measure risk, the policies may be constantly adjusted to react to minor variations in the market. As shown earlier, constant change will have a negative impact on the overall investment portfolio.

The most common measurement of risk is standard deviation, which is a statistical measurement of variances from the norm. When the performance in your portfolio has a standard deviation (either positively or negatively) from the norm, this means that the portfolio is exposed to more risk or less risk than the norm. One of the common industry measures of risk variance is the beta. The beta of a stock or a portfolio is a measure of its volatility compared to an index for that stock or portfolio, with the index represented by a beta of 1. Therefore, if your portfolio's beta is 0.5, it is only half as volatile as the index and therefore less risky. If your portfolio's beta is 2, it is twice as volatile as the index and therefore more risky. Ask your money manager to explain this in more detail and include a measurement of your portfolio's beta in your regular investment reports.

Another way to control risk is diversification. You should set limits on the percentages of assets held in any one stock and in any one sector within the class. These limits are normally expressed as a percentage of the total market value of the portfolio. A form that may be used to poll the board on risk attitudes and begin this discussion is included in Appendix 8-C.

[5] Asset Allocation Bands

The policies should set target asset allocation bands for each asset class. The policies should set the percentages of equities, fixed income, and cash that make up the portfolio. Some policies go further and set bands within asset classes. For example, the equity band may be divided so that 30 percent of all equities are invested in international securities, 50 percent are invested in large cap growth stocks, and 20 percent are invested in small cap growth stocks.

The investment policies should allow for variances to established percentages. The policy might state, for example, that the ratios are 60 percent equities, 25 percent fixed income, and five percent cash, but that the percentages can vary within five percent on either side of those figures. This allows for some move-

---

[42] *See* § 8.06[B], *supra* for a discussion of the key factors.

ment in the market without the requirement that the investment manager constantly buy and sell to stay at the exact percentage limits.

Finally, the polices should set benchmarks for the performance of each asset class. (The most common benchmarks for asset classes are set out in Table 8–10 *infra*.) Setting a benchmark for an asset class is the best way to ensure that the foundation communicates expectations to the investment manager and assures there will be a method for consistent evaluation.

A recently published study of family foundation assets at 1999 year-end provides excellent insight into foundation investments at the height of the bull market of the 1990s. The average asset allocation for family foundations of various sizes at the time of the study is shown in Table 8-7. The full survey is available from the Council on Foundations.

[6] Restrictions on Types of Equity Holdings

The policies should set restrictions on the types of equity investments that are permitted. Can the portfolio hold international holdings subject to currency fluctuations? Can the portfolio hold American depository receipts? Are small cap stocks permissible? Are there any social investing restrictions, for example, restrictions on companies that sell tobacco, alcohol, or firearms? Can the portfolio hold mutual funds? Are initial public offerings appropriate? Are privately held issues appropriate? If the policies do not restrict the manager from investment in risky equity forms, the foundation may have its assets exposed to greater risk than anticipated.

TABLE 8-7
Council on Foundations Investment Study of Family
Foundation Asset Allocation Models

Family Foundation Size	*Stocks*	*Bonds*	*Real Estate (Equity)*	*Cash*	*Program-Related Investments*	*Other*
Under $5 million	69.6%	12.5%	0.2%	13.4%	0.0%	4.4%
$5 to $10 million	74.0%	18.1%	0.6%	6.1%	0.3%	0.9%
$10 to $25 million	70.3%	16.2%	1.0%	8.4%	0.5%	3.6%
$25 to $50 million	68.5%	21.0%	0.2%	3.5%	0.1%	6.8%
$50 to $100 million	70.7%	21.8%	0.1%	3.8%	0.1%	3.6%
$100 to $250 million	62.9%	22.0%	0.0%	7.0%	0.2%	7.9%
$250 to $500 million	68.1%	17.1%	6.1%	2.4%	0.0%	6.3%
$500+ million	68.9%	20.1%	0.7%	2.3%	0.3%	7.7%
All	69.3%	17.9%	0.7%	7.2%	0.2%	4.8%

Note: Totals may exceed 100% due to rounding.

[7] Restrictions on Types of Fixed-Income Investments

The policies should provide guidelines about the types of fixed-income investments that are permissible. What is the average duration of the bonds? Bonds receive quality ratings from market rating services expressed as AAA, AA, A, BBB, BB, B, and so on. Generally, A (or A– in some ratings) and BBB (or B+ in some ratings) bonds are considered "investment quality," indicating that the bonds are relatively secure from default. What is the minimum quality bond the foundation will hold? What should the manager do if the bonds fall in quality? Are derivatives appropriate? How about collateralized mortgage obligations? What are the quality requirements for the cash?

[8] Review Cycle

The policies should address the review process used to evaluate the success of the investment policies and investment manager. The review policy should articulate the frequency of the review cycle and the review standards.

Example: The foundation investments shall be reviewed on a quarterly basis through a written performance report showing the performance by asset class and as a composite. The investment manager shall make a personal investment analysis presentation to the foundation on an annual basis, or more frequently if requested. The three-year investment goal of the foundation is to exceed the composite benchmark returns for the portfolio.

[9] Investment Horizon

The board must reach a consensus on the investment horizon for the assets. Although the long-term investment horizon for a foundation is perpetual (since the foundation is designed to exist without a set termination date), the investment cycle should be short enough to make changes if objectives are not met. However, as discussed earlier in this chapter, the market may suffer extreme fluctuations in the short term, so that a one-year or shorter horizon is also inappropriate. The most appropriate investment horizon is probably in the three- to five-year time span. This is long enough to measure performance versus benchmarks, but short enough to correct problems (if they exist) before they have a long-term negative impact.

[10] Making Changes in Investment Managers

The policies should provide direction on when and how changes are made in investment managers in the event that the results do not meet expectations.[43] Sometimes policies require that the investment manager perform in the upper 33

---

[43] *See* § 8.06[F], *infra* for a discussion of when to fire your investment manager.

percent (or 25 or 50 percent) of their peer group for the one-year or five-year period (or both). Other managers are required to perform within 200 basis points of the composite benchmarks for the portfolio. Do not set a standard that will result in firing your manager on a frequent basis. Gear the performance expectations for the manager to a cycle that approximates the investment horizon.

The sample policies provided at Appendix 8-D can be adapted to fit your needs. Take the time to work through the policies, reach consensus on each issue, and modify the text to reflect those decisions. Adopting the policies without discussion is not meaningful, helpful, or responsible.

[C] Selecting an Investment Manager

Most foundation boards are not trained or experienced enough to manage the foundation's investments. The most effective approach is to set policies at the board level and hire professionals to make investment decisions. However, this still means that the board will need a method of selecting and managing an investment manager.

Investment management is a commodity offered by banks, brokerage firms, mutual funds, boutique managers, and other sources. The key to hiring the most effective manager for your foundation is to use discipline in the selection process. Follow these steps:

1. Begin with the *development of a written spending policy*. The distributions required from the invested funds — whether income or principal — have a critical impact on the underlying asset allocation of the portfolio.

2. *Develop written investment policies* to communicate your spending rates, asset allocation structure, and any restrictions that may apply to an investment manager. Do not begin the investment manager search until you know what you are looking for. This may appear self-evident, but many organizations choose a manager first and then write the policies to fit the manager.

3. *Include members of the investment committee*, especially those with experience in investment matters or the development of policies, in the search. You can include firms represented by your board members. However, make sure that all participants follow the guidelines and that the interested parties do not vote.

4. *Get references* from the investment management firm and then call the references to ask about performance results, responsiveness of the firm, and understanding of nonprofit issues. Talk to other nonprofits and family foundations to see which firms they use. Find out how the manager operates, how accessible the firm is, and whether the firm delivers the products and services as agreed. Look for investment management firms with experience, with an understanding of the tax-exempt world, and with the flexibility to address your individual concerns.

5. *Develop a format for interviewing the investment manager* and then call for proposals. Ask the managers to come to you. Any managers who are unable to move through this process will not be responsive to you over time.

The questions shown in Table 8-8 may be helpful in interviewing a manager or in designing a request for proposal (RFP).

Set a deadline for submission of the responses to your questions, and ask the investment firm to provide enough copies of the report for all members of the investment committee or board. Make an initial review of the materials and narrow the selection to three to five firms that you believe fit your criteria. Then invite those firms to make presentations to your investment committee or board, and select the one that has solid, consistent long-term performance; a working knowledge of foundations and your objectives; and individuals that have personalities that mesh well with those of your board.

The job is not finished when the investment manager is hired. The board has a fiduciary duty to monitor investment performance on an ongoing basis. Use the following guidelines to keep the group focused and the manager attentive:

1. *Ask the manager to provide quarterly reports for review by your investment committee.* These reports should show:

   • Current positions, with cost and market values;

   • Performance for the current period against selected benchmarks for the current period;

   • Performance for the 1-, 3-, 5-, and 10-year periods against selected benchmarks for that period (this number will obviously be restricted to the number of years that the manager has been involved with your account);

   • A list of sales and purchases during the period; and

   • The manager's ranking within the universe of other like managers.

2. *Ask the manager to make a personal presentation of the report on an annual basis.* Create a forum in which you can educate the members of your investment committee as well as getting to understand the performance and philosophy of the manager.

TABLE 8-8
Investment Manager Interview Questions

Question	Things to Look For
1. How long has the firm been in the investment management business?	There are so many new firms that the easiest way to begin to screen is through experience. Many organizations will not use a manager with less than five years of experience; some organizations require 10 years of experience.
2. How would you classify your style of management?	Managers come in all styles. Is the manager a balanced manager? If so, the manager should describe the philosophy that governs the balancing. Is the manager a large cap value manager? Of a small cap growth manager? Each style has a different level of risk and return associated with it. In your risk assessment, you will select a risk exposure. Do not select a manager that does not manage at the risk level you select.
3. What is the average asset allocation (stocks, fixed income, cash) of your portfolio?	This answer should confirm the style described in question 2.
4. What benchmark is most appropriate to measure your management style? How did your portfolio perform against that benchmark?	For example, small cap growth stocks are generally measured against the Russell 2000, rather than the S & P. The two indices, while both equity indices, perform very differently. Make sure that your manager's performance compares favorably with the appropriate benchmark.
5. Ask to see 1-, 3-, 5-, and 10-year performance figures. Make sure that those figures are through the most recent quarter end. And then ask the following questions: Is the performance representative of the broader group of accounts that are managed? Is the performance net or gross of fees?	You will find it difficult to compare apples to apples unless you are specific about what you want to see. Ask these questions, and make sure that you compare each of the managers for the same time period. Make sure that the manager does not show you the performance of one portfolio. Ask him or her for the average size of the portfolios that make up a composite figure.
6. Ask to see the quarterly returns for as many periods as possible. Compare them to the quarterly returns for the benchmark.	Review the quarterly returns against the benchmark to see more about the total return figures. If you see the manager's returns vary too widely from the benchmark returns, this generally means that the manager is taking more risk than the benchmark.
7. Ask to see a copy of the performance reports that they will provide you.	You want to make sure that the reports make sense and provide you with useful comparative data.
8. Ask the manager to provide you	Most nonprofits will set a standard that the manager

TABLE 8-8. CONTINUED

Question	*Things to Look For*
with a report showing his or her performance among his or her peer group.	must be in the top 25 percent or top 33 percent of the peer group for a certain period — for example, the last three years. You must set this standard yourself. However, be sure to get the manager to provide these data and to source the data.

3. *After the review, discuss the performance, the presentation, and the responsiveness of the manager, and compare the performance to the standards set in the investment guidelines.* Has the manager fallen below the benchmarks set in your written investment policies? For how long?

4. *Review the results for the year.* If the manager has failed to meet the nonprofit's expectations, monitor the results and consider firing the manager if necessary.[44]

5. *Establish a method for making changes.* Make sure that the investment policies do not require action at the end of each and every quarter if the manager fails to meet investment targets. Review results each quarter, but set longer-term performance goals. Frequent movement from manager to manager is damaging, since there is enormous risk in moving in and out of positions in the market on short time lines.

[D] Monitoring Investment Performance

Your investment manager should provide quarterly reports with performance information. The performance report should include quarterly results as well as one-year, three-year, and five-year results. These figures should include composite numbers for the account (performance of all assets) as well as performance figures for each asset class. Each return figure should have a comparative index (as established in your investment policies or in an agreement with the manager) that represents the index closest to the style of management of the asset manager. In other words, if the equity portion of the portfolio is designed to mirror a large cap growth style, then the performance report should show not only the equity portfolio performance, but also the performance of the index, such as the Barra Large Cap Growth Index. There are hundreds of possible indices that may be used by managers for comparative purposes; the most commonly used measures are shown at Table 8–9. If your investment manager selects an index that is not on this list, ask him or her to explain that index and why it is more appropriate for your portfolio.

---

[44] *See* § 8.06[F], *infra* for a detailed discussion of when to fire your manager.

Ask the manager to make a personal appearance to explain the performance results at least annually. This ensures that the manager knows that the foundation wants to stay informed and makes the manager continually accountable to the foundation board.

[E] When to Fire Your Investment Manager

There are a number of factors that may indicate that it's time to consider firing your investment manager. These include:

TABLE 8-9
Selected Market Indices for Stocks and Bonds

Index Name	Description
LARGE CAP STOCKS	
Dow Jones Industrial Average	The Dow Jones Industrial Average is a price-weighted index of 30 large cap stocks selected by Dow Jones. This is the most commonly quoted index, although it is not indicative of the performance of the larger domestic equity market.
NASDAQ	The National Association of Securities Dealers Automated Quotation System (NASDAQ) handles trades in 4,000 large to mid-cap stocks and 1,000 small-cap stocks. This exchange, created in 1971 with 2,500 companies, was mandated by the Securities and Exchange Commission as a way to handle transactions fairly for investors in smaller securities issues, and was implemented by the National Association of Securities Dealers.
Standard & Poor's 500 Composite Stock Index	The S & P 500 is designed to reflect the broad performance of domestic large cap equity markets. S & P selects stocks representative of an industry with certain liquidity and stability requirements.
Barra Growth	The Barra Growth Index is a measure of the performance of the growth stocks comprising the S & P 500.
Barra Value	The Barra Value Index is a measure of the performance of the value stocks comprising the S & P 500.
Russell 3000	The Russell 3000 Index includes the 3,000 largest domestic companies by market capitalization.
Wilshire 5000	This index includes almost all U.S. stocks, currently holding over 7,000 (not 5,000) domestic stocks.

TABLE 8-9. CONTINUED

Index Name	*Description*
MID-CAP STOCKS	
Standard & Poor's 400 Mid-Cap Index	This index of 400 stocks is selected to represent the key industries in the mid-cap sector. Stocks representative of their industry are selected based on market capitalization.
Wilshire 4500	This index, with about 6,900 stocks, consists of the Wilshire 5000 without the S & P 500 stocks. Roughly two-thirds of the stocks in the index are mid-cap stocks.
SMALL CAP STOCKS	
Standard & Poor's Small Cap 600	These 600 stocks are selected by S & P to represent small cap industry groups. Companies are selected by market cap and liquidity.
Russell 2000	This index is the Russell 3000 with the largest 1,000 companies removed.
INTERNATIONAL EQUITIES	
Morgan Stanley Capital International Europe, Australia, Far East Index (MSCI EAFE)	This index, consisting of 1,000 stocks, is designed to measure the performance of 21 non-U.S. stock exchanges.
FIXED INCOME	
Lehman Brothers Aggregate Bond Index (LB Aggregate Bond)	This index consists of taxable bonds — government, high-quality corporate, and mortgage-backed securities.
J.P. Morgan Government Bond Index	This index measures the performance of leading government bond markets in issues available to investors. The return is based on total return (income and principal growth) in U.S. currency.

- *Failure to meet the index for periods of one year or more.* Your investment horizon, or the period in which you expect to achieve your investment results, should be at least three to five years. Equity investments are very volatile and will not generate positive returns each year. Bonds are also volatile and can have years in which returns are negative. However, a good manager will perform slightly better than the index in positive years and slightly less negatively than the index in negative years. Managers that vary two percent, three percent, or more from the index — either positively or negatively — may not be meeting your goals.

When the manager underperforms by two percent or more, this means the manager's strategy is not working. If it continues, this will cost your foundation growth. Where the foundation growth wildly exceeds the index, this may also be cause for concern. While few of us worry when our managers strongly outperform the index, this may be a sign that the management style is more risky than your comfort level. While this overperformance may be cause for celebration in good years, it can just as easily lead to much lower than average performance in later years.

- *A change in a key employee in the management firm.* Many times the results and philosophy that made you select the firm change when a key decision maker leaves. Your contract with the investment manager should require that the firm inform you of such changes. Evaluate each situation on its merits, but take the time to evaluate the impact on the overall performance. You may decide to wait to make a decision until the firm has managed your funds for several quarters with new management in place.

- *A style drift or dramatic change in style.* The manager should be able to describe his or her investment philosophy and that of the firm. Often this will be expressed in terms of the capitalization of the stocks the firm uses (small cap, mid-cap, large cap) together with the underlying philosophy (growth, value, or some extended description of those basics). With bonds, the philosophy may be described in terms of risk (ratings, corporate or government) as well as duration (akin to the average maturity of the bonds). When that style changes dramatically, the manager may be changing styles to "catch up" in terms of performance.

It is a good idea to conduct a manager search every three years or so, even when your manager is performing to expectations. This is a healthy way to ensure that your manager remains responsive as well as getting a feel for other services available and their costs.

[F] Choosing a Professional Fiduciary

[1] Services Provided

The foundation may want to use a professional fiduciary, such as a bank or trust company, to assist in investment management or administration. Selecting the right fiduciary can also be difficult. The place to begin is by determining which services you need. The basic services include:

- *Custodial/safekeeping services.* The foundation should identify a single institution that can take physical custody of all of the assets.

- *Income/principal accounting.* Income and principal accounting may be important in tracking principal spending or in dealing with any restrictions in spending set out in the foundation document. For example, some documents limit spending to earned income unless distributions are required to meet the minimum distribution requirements set by the IRS.

- *Master trust accounting.* Master trust accounting is important for larger foundations that plan to allocate investment management to several firms, but roll the balances together for investment review, reporting, and analysis purposes. Master trust software provides detailed accounting and reporting at several levels. For example, large foundations may employ one money manager for large cap value equity, another for small cap growth, and still another for fixed-income management. These management pools should be segregated so that managers have access only to assets that they manage and so that performance for that manager's funds can be measured separately. However, the foundation must combine these assets to get a single asset statement, to do tax reporting, and to develop a performance figure or market value for the full account. Master trust accounting is simply a way of segregating assets for accounting purposes and then combining those assets in a master account for reporting purposes.

- *Clearing for securities transactions.* The fiduciary must be able to clear securities transactions for internal as well as for outside trades. For example, the fiduciary may be serving as investment manager and custodian for a portion of the foundation's assets and must be able to clear those investment trades. The fiduciary may be serving only as custodian for other assets where an outside manager is making the decisions. Where outside managers are involved, trades will be initiated by the investment manager, but the delivery of assets and payment for those assets will take place at the fiduciary office. Make sure that you ask the fiduciary to detail the clearing costs. The costs are generally set as a specified fee per transaction, but may be structured as a percentage of the trade.

- *Providing statements to interested parties.* It is important that the family members and board members receive copies of transaction and asset statements on a regular basis. Ask to review a sample statement. Make sure that you can read and understand the statements. Do not expect income and principal accounting to look the same as single cash accounting. You will find that all double cash accounting statements take a little work. But some are clearer than others are. If you prefer single cash accounting, ask the fiduciary if the option is available.

- *Writing checks.* The fiduciary can make distributions of grants, expenses, and salaries if needed. The advantage to you is that the bank does the busywork and you are left with good records. In addition, the information will be available for tax reporting purposes. The downside is that the foundation will still need to have a process of listing and approving payments to be made and will likely have to reenter all of the information on its data system in order to track grants and distributions.

- *Investment management.* Fiduciaries provide a wide range of investment options to their trust customers. Although most fiduciaries have long been viewed as too conservative or as poor money managers, the larger banks and trust companies have very competitive results. Do not overlook your fiduciary when considering investment managers. Invite the fiduciary to join the RFP process in your search for the investment management team. Consider the fiduciary on the same basis that other managers are considered. There is an advantage to the nonprofit concentrating management in one fiduciary at one location.

- *Management of special assets.* Some banks specialize in management of timber, oil and gas, real property, or closely held business interests. If your foundation has a difficult-to-manage asset and you need help, look for a fiduciary that can provide that service in addition to meeting your administrative needs.

In choosing a fiduciary, look for banks and trust companies that have special charitable management units. These special units can be extremely valuable, especially to the smaller foundation, since the officers are generally knowledgeable in investment management and have participated in many investment review searches. The trust staff can help the board through the process of establishing risk tolerance, setting long-term goals, and adopting written spending and investment policies. In addition, the trust charitable units have personnel with experience with a variety of gift forms and the grantmaking process. While the trust officers cannot share confidential information with the nonprofit, the officers can share general observations on success in the application process.

The types of companies that provide fiduciary services are set out in Table 8-10.

[2] Selecting the Trustee

The selection of the trustee is similar to the selection of the other professionals. The foundation must begin by determining its needs. Use the list of services outlined above as a starting point, and list, in order of priority, the services that are required. In addition, note those services that are not important. You should get pricing on only the services that are needed.

TABLE 8-10
Types of Fiduciaries

Type of Firm	Comments
Banks/independent trust companies	Banks and trust companies are regulated by state and/or federal agencies, provide a high level of care, and have sophisticated reporting (statement) capabilities. They charge a fee for safekeeping services.
Brokerage firms	The SEC and other regulatory bodies regulate brokerage firms. Brokerage firms are also audited. Brokerage firms do not charge a fee for services, but their statements are far more limited. These firms have SIPC insurance; ask them to provide you with information on those limits.
Insurance companies	Some insurance companies can provide custody through an affiliated brokerage company.

Incorporate the list of needs in a request for proposal, and submit the RFP to a variety of fiduciary institutions. Present the RFP questions in a clear, concise manner so that the responses are easily compared. Take special care in collecting pricing information. Some fiduciary fees are based on the market value of assets and include all services in the fee. Other fiduciaries charge based on transactions. The nonprofit will get the best estimates on cost if the types and numbers of transactions as well as the market values are included on the RFP.

Request biographical information for the individuals that provide administrative and investment management services. Also ask for information on the length of service of each fiduciary manager.

Choose the three or four fiduciaries that look the best in the written responses to the RFPs. Invite those fiduciaries to the nonprofit to make a presentation. Make a list of required services and score each applicant. Proper use of a scoring sheet will eliminate the tendency to choose the best salesperson. Remember, the person selling the account may not be the person administering the account.

Once a fiduciary is selected, evaluate performance on a regular basis. Make the requests and needs of the nonprofit clear. Communicate problems quickly. And if the institution is not responsive or cannot provide the service, consider a change to another fiduciary.

[G]   Costs of Investment Management and Administration

Management costs vary widely depending on the type of services and the amount of money under management. Use Table 8-11 as a rough guide for costs. 100 BP (basis points) = 1%.

Make sure that you know what you are paying for. Investment management firms generally charge higher fees than banks and trust companies, and they do not have the accounting software or the ability to manage the custody assets. Therefore, the costs are greatly affected by how the combination of services is purchased. Banks and trust companies are used for these services most often because of their ability to provide the full complement of services in a cost-effective manner.

TABLE 8-11
Estimated Costs for Investment and Custodial Services

Type of Service	Less than $1,000,000	$1,000,000–$5,000,000	Over $5,000,000
Custody only	20 BP	10–15 BP	8–10 BP
Custody and administration	75–100 BP	50–75 BP	35–60 BP
Investment management only	100–300 BP	100–250 BP	75–125 BP
All services	100–300 BP	50–25 BP	35–100 BP

[H]   Social Investing

Some family foundations carry their mission into their investments. That is, they deploy funds for investment purposes that reflect the foundation's broader social, moral, or ethical goals and objectives. Social investing is a visible element of portfolio management. The Social Investment Forum reported that $2.16 trillion dollars were allocated to social investments in 1999 through one of three methods: screened portfolios, shareholder advocacy, or community investments.[45] There are also indices used to benchmark social investments. Two of the most popular are the Domini 400 Social Investment Index and the Calvert Index.[46]

The overall goal of social investing is to support those companies that meet certain standards and to avoid investment in those companies that do not. Most of the prohibited activities involve the sale of tobacco, alcohol, gambling, or firearms. However, a company might also make the non-social list if it engages in activities that produce environmental damage, uses low-paid contract labor overseas, or is primarily a defense contractor. For example, Dow Chemical is avoided by many social investors because of Union Carbide's disastrous gas leak in Bhopal, India, in 1984. Walmart was excluded from the Domini 400 Social Index in 2001 because the Domini felt the company had failed to respond to concerns about human rights violations in its overseas labor practices. The prohibited activities that violate the standards vary from foundation to foundation, and are often influenced by world events. In the 1980s, to oppose apartheid, many companies and foundations avoided investing in companies that did business in South Africa.

The biggest issues related to social investing are practical ones. It is difficult to define social investing and identify investment firms that use this approach. Charitable organizations may define social investing in a way that relates to the foundation's interests. If the foundation focuses on environmental funding, for example, it may want to exclude companies that violate environmental standards, or invest in companies that are innovative in this area. DuPont, for example, is a company that has been recognized for its efforts to conduct its business in a manner that respects the environment. Other investors avoid companies that pay excess compensation to executives or have poor records for race and gender balance on corporate boards. Still others avoid companies known as the "sin stock" — which are companies that sell firearms, tobacco, or alcohol. In short, it is sometimes difficult for a foundation to define its social investment standards.

Once those standards have been defined, it is difficult to be sure when a company meets or violates the standards set by the foundation. Mergers between companies may mean that a company generally perceived as noncontroversial

---

[45] The Social Investment Forum, *Socially Responsible Investing in U.S. Tops Two Trillion Dollar Mark, www.socialinvest.org/areas/news/1999-trends.htm*, November 4, 1999.

[46] Domini is an investment firm found at *www.domini.com*. Investors can obtain a profile of each of the companies used in the index at the Domini site under the tab marked "Domini funds." The index is maintained and reported at KLD Research & Analytics, a research firm serving social investors at *www.kld.com*. The Calvert Index can be found at *www.calvertgroup.com*.

may have a division that fails to meet the foundation's standards. For example, a company such as Sara Lee Corporation — associated with frozen desserts, lunch meats, and bakery products — also owns Hanes, Playtex, DIM, Bali, Just My Size, and L'eggs (intimate apparel, hosiery, socks, and knitwear), Hillshire Farms, Jimmy Dean, Ball Park, and Bryan (smoked sausages and meats), Champion (athletic wear), Superior Coffee (coffee products), and Kiwi (shoe care). Some of these products may be manufactured in countries guilty of human rights violations, or, the company may lobby Congress on matters in violation of the foundation's policy. It is difficult to become familiar with a company and all of its holdings and policies without extensive research.

Finally, the foundation must consider whether it is giving up return by limiting itself to investment firms that invest in socially responsible companies (a more limited universe). This matter has been widely debated without resolution. In truth, there are a number of investment managers and mutual funds that specialize in the area that have achieved returns comparable to other non-social investing models.[47]

The best advice for a family foundation interested in exploring social investing is to get an education on methods of approaching social investing, set objectives for its social investing, and work with an investment manager or mutual fund using similar goals and objectives with a long-term track record and solid investment results. Table 8-12 provides a sampling of Internet resources with information about socially responsible investment managers and mutual funds.

TABLE 8-12
Socially Responsible Investment Internet Resources

Site Name	*Site Location*	*Comment*
The Green Money On-Line Guide	*www.greenmoney journal.com*	Index of socially responsible mutual funds, community investment profiles (including investing in nonprofit activities), and corporations that operate in a manner consistent with social investment principles.
The Philanthropic Initiative	*www.tpi.org*	The Philanthropic Initiative periodically posts excellent articles on social investing at this site.
The Social Investment Forum	*www.socialinvest.org*	The Social Investment Forum is a membership organization designed to promote social investing. The web site provides information to guide investors interested in social investing principles, maintains copies of news releases, and allows access to independent studies conducted by the forum.

[47] For more information on managers and mutual funds adhering to a social investment screening policy, go to *www.greenmoneyjournal.com* or *www.socialinvest.org*. These sites rate and review managers and also provide commentary on and a history of social investing.

TABLE 8-12. CONTINUED

Site Name	Site Location	Comment
SocialFunds. com	www.socialfunds.com	This site is designed to encourage individual investors to make socially responsible investments. It provides information on corporate practices (searchable), reports on socially responsible mutual funds, daily market indices (including the DSI 400 and Calvin indices), and issues news releases on the topic.
Domini 400 Social Index	www.domini.com	Domini, a research firm focusing on social investments, has created an index for socially responsible investments. The firm's web site provides a profile of each of the 400 companies in its index in a searchable form. The index is reported and researched by Kinder, Lindenburg, Domini & Company (KLD) at www.kld.com. The index has 10 years of history.
Calvert Social Index	www.calvertgroup. com	This investment firm maintains a broader index for socially responsible investments consisting of 1,000 companies. This is a much younger index created in April 2000.
GoodFunds.com	www.goodfunds.com	This financial planning and investment management firm specializes in socially responsible investing and provides services that allow the foundation to establish avoidance screening criteria (i.e., tobacco, gambling, alcohol, weapons) as well as qualitative screening and analysis (i.e., domestic and international labor practices, environmental practices, public disclosure). The firm provides overall investment policy guidance such as asset allocation and spending policies.
Pax World Funds	www.paxworld.com	Pax World Funds runs balanced, equity, and money market mutual funds investing in companies "which not only present financial opportunity but also produce goods and services that improve the quality of life." Pax World is actively involved in shareholder activism and proxy voting to reflect its socially responsible goals.

Use these steps to adopt a social investing policy:

1. Articulate the foundation's goals and objectives. Consider human rights, animal rights, environmental goals, arms, alcohol, tobacco, gambling, or other issues.

2. Consider the expected benefits of the policy. Is the foundation providing leadership to the community and other nonprofits? Does it expect to effect change in a company's social policy? Does it expect to improve its investment return? Reduce these goals to writing so that they can be communicated to the foundation's investment manager and results can be measured at year-end.

3. Quantify the assets available for investment. Determine whether the policy will apply to equities, to fixed income, or to a portion of its equities or fixed income. The investment committee should determine the dollar figure and the asset allocation for the investment pool before investing the funds.

4. Seek help from a qualified investment advisor. The foundation's investment manager should be able to provide input on the services provided by the firm or should refer the foundation to other qualified managers. If the assets are less than $500,000, consider a mutual fund that reflects the foundation's social objectives. If the assets exceed $500,000 (some may require as much as $1 million to $2 million), then an individually managed portfolio may be appropriate.

5. Monitor results and make changes as you would with any investment policy. Monitoring results is particularly important for social investment policies, since those policies should reflect the broad programmatic goals of the foundation.

§ 8.07   IRS FILING REQUIREMENTS

The family foundation is a taxpayer and is required to file an annual tax return. This return, the 990-PF, requires the foundation to provide extensive information about its investments, income, expenses, directors, and activities. A copy of the current 990-PF is included in Appendix 8-D.[48] All foundations are required to file the 990-PF from the time that the Form 1023 application for exemption is filed, even if the foundation has no income or assets.

The IRS publishes good instructions for completion of the form. Foundation administrators should also get IRS Publication 578, Tax Information for Private Foundations and Foundation Managers, which provides guidance on foundation activities.[49]

[A]   Where to Get Foundation Tax Forms

The Internal Revenue Service has made most of the tax forms for 2001 and later years (including new Schedule B, described below) available on its web

---

[48] The form is available through the IRS web site at *www.irs.gov.*

[49] All government tax forms and publications can be ordered by calling 1-800-829-3676. There is no charge for these items.

site, *www.irs.gov.* The IRS sends Form 990-PF packages directly to most foundations that filed returns for the preceding year, and those packages include Schedule B. However, if you go to the IRS web site for your forms, note that Schedule B is listed there as a separate form and is not included with Form 990-PF. Thus, even though Schedule B is a mandatory inclusion for the foundations required to file it, persons who go to the IRS web site for these forms must scroll down the list to separately access Schedule B and Form 990-PF to which it will be attached.

While the foundation's accountant, not the foundation manager, generally prepares the 990-PF, the foundation board is responsible for the information contained in that return. The return also contains information on distribution requirements, which are central to the grantmaking of the foundation.

A summary of the key elements of the 990-PF follows:

- Analysis of revenue of the foundation (Part I);

- Analysis of administrative expenses, with particular emphasis on compensation of officers, directors, trustees, and employees (Part I);

- Balance sheet of assets and liabilities (Part II);

- Analysis of changes occurring in net assets or fund balances over the year (Part III);

- Summary of the realized capital gains and losses (Part IV);

- Calculation to determine if the tax on net investment income can be reduced from two percent to one percent (Part V);

- Calculation of the excise tax due on the foundation's investment income (Part VI);

- Disclosure of the foundation activities during the year (Part VII-A);

- Disclosure of the foundation activities that trigger the excise tax for prohibited transactions (i.e., self-dealing, failure to distribute income, excess business holdings, investments that jeopardize charitable purposes, taxable expenditures) (Part VII-B);

- Information about officers, directors, trustees, and foundation managers, including compensation, benefits, and expense allocations (this section also requires that you reveal the names and addresses of employees paid more than $50,000 and the five highest-paid independent contractors for professional services) (Part VIII);

- Description of the foundation's charitable activities, including statistics on the number of organizations receiving grants, number of people receiving benefits from grants, number of conferences and research papers, and so on (Part IX-A);

- Information about the foundation's program-related investments, if any (Part IX-B);

- Calculation of the minimum investment return (a calculation of the required five percent distribution) (Part X);

- Calculation of the distributable amount (a calculation deducting certain expenses or taxes from the five percent distributable amount) (Part XI);

- Calculation of the foundation's qualifying distributions (a calculation of the distributions made by the foundation that qualify as distributions for the purposes of the five percent requirement) (Part XII);

- Record of undistributed income (a listing of undistributed amounts from prior years and the current year, incorporating overdistributions that qualify for current year; this section is used to verify the amount that must be distributed in the current year to avoid a tax on failure to distribute) (Part XIII);

- Information specific to private operating foundations, if applicable (Part XIV);

- Supplementary information on large contributors, related parties, and the individual to whom grant applications should be addressed (Part XV);

- Listing of all grants paid during the current year or approved for future payment (Part XV);

- Analysis of revenue-producing activities, such as program services, fees, membership dues, assessments, investment income, and other income (Part XVI-A);

- Explanation of the relationship of the revenue-producing activities to the exempt purpose of the foundation (Part XVI-B); and

- Information on transfers to noncharitable tax-exempt organizations (Part XVII).[50]

If the foundation owes tax, it must deposit its estimated tax using the Electronic Federal Tax Payment System or Form 8109, Federal Tax Deposit Coupon.

In addition, the foundation may be required to file the following returns:

- *Form 990-W* — estimated tax on unrelated business taxable income and on investment income for private foundations,

---

[50] Earlier 990-PFs contained a Part XVIII relating to the now-repealed requirement that foundations satisfy public inspection requirements by publishing a notice in a newspaper of general circulation in the county in which the primary office of the foundation was located. Although the federal requirement for newspaper publication of the availability of foundation returns has been repealed, be sure to check state requirements. New York adopted a requirement of newspaper publication — reportedly in response to lobbying by newspaper interests — in mid-2000.

- *Form 990-T*—unrelated business taxable income (for income in excess of $1,000 from businesses conducted by the nonprofit that are unrelated to its exempt purpose),

- *Form 4720*—return of excise taxes on charities and persons (for excise taxes on self-dealing, failure to distribute income, excess business holdings, jeopardizing investments, and political or noncharitable expenditures);

- *Form W-2/Form W-3/Form 941*—employee returns; and

- *Form 8282*—Donee Information Return, must be filed if a nonmarketable asset contributed to the foundation is sold or disposed of within two years of receipt. The return must be filed within 125 days of the sale or disposal.

In the 990-PF instructions, the IRS lists other tax forms that the foundation may be required to file. These include Forms 1041, 1041-ES, 1096, 1099-INT, -MISC, -OID, and -R, 1120, 1120-POL, 1128, 2220, 2758, 4506-A, 4720, 5500, 5500-C/R, 8109, 8282, 8275, 8275-R, 8300, and 8718. Table 8–13 sets out a summary of these forms, their purposes, and when they must be filed. These returns and instructions can be downloaded from the Internet at *www.irs.treas.gov* or ordered from the Internal Revenue Service by calling 1-800-TAX-FORM (1-800-829-3676).

The 990-PF is due by the 15th day of the fifth month following the close of the foundation's tax year.[51] If the return is not filed on a timely basis, a penalty of 0.5 percent of the unpaid tax will be assessed for each month or part of a month in which the tax is unpaid, not to exceed 25 percent of the tax due.[52] The IRS can waive this tax if there was reasonable cause for the failure to file. All private foundations are required to send returns to the Internal Revenue Service Center in Ogden, Utah 84201-0027.

TABLE 8-13
Tax Forms Potentially Applicable to Private Foundations

Form	Name	Purpose
990-PF	Return of Private Foundation or Section 4947(a)(1) Nonexempt Charitable Trust Treated as a Private Foundation	This is the annual tax return of the foundation
990-T	Exempt Organization Business Income Tax Return	This return is used by exempt organizations to report and pay taxes on income in excess of $1,000 that is unrelated to

---

[51] Reg. § 1.6033-2(e). *See also* Instructions for Form 990-PF, Par. F, pp. 4-5.
[52] IRC § 6651(a)(1). *See also* Instructions for Form 990-PF, Par. N, p. 5.

TABLE 8-13.   CONTINUED

Form	Name	Purpose
		the nonprofit's trade or business.
990-W	Estimated Tax on Unrelated Business Taxable Income for Tax-Exempt Organizations	This form is used to pay estimated tax on unrelated business taxable income and investment income for private foundations.
941	Employer's Quarterly Federal Tax Return	This form is used to report income, Social Security, and Medicare taxes withheld by an employer as well as Social Security and Medicare taxes paid by an employer.
W-2	Wage and Tax Statement	This form must be filed for each employee of the foundation.
W-3	Transmittal of Wage and Tax Statements	This form serves as the cover when filing the W-2's with the Internal Revenue Service.
1041	U.S. Income Tax Return for Estates and Trusts	Some section 4947(a)(1) trusts must file a trust tax return in addition to the 990-PF; if the trust does not have taxable income, however, it can check a box on the 990-PF and avoid the 1041 filing.
1041-ES	Estimated Income Tax Return for Estates and Trusts	This return is used to pay estimated tax for organizations that must pay tax and are required to file the 1041.
1096	Annual Summary and Transmittal of U.S. Information Returns	This form is used to transmit paper Forms 1099, 1098, 5498, and W-2G to the IRS.
1099-INT	1099 for Interest Income	This is an informational return used to report payments of interest income, foreign tax on interest withheld, or federal income tax withheld for

TABLE 8-13.   CONTINUED

Form	Name	Purpose
		individuals. This form is not required for payments to corporations, tax-exempt organizations, IRAs, U.S. agencies, states, the District of Columbia, U.S. possessions, or registered securities or commodities dealers.
1099 MISC	1099 for Miscellaneous Income	This is an informational return used to report payments of miscellaneous Income to individuals.
1099-OID	1099 for Original Issue Discount (OID) Income	This form is used to report original issue discount income to individuals.
1099-R	1099 for Distributions from Pensions Annuities, Retirement or Profit-Sharing Plans, IRAs, Insurance Contracts, etc.	This is an information return used to report distributions from annuities, insurance products, or retirement plans.
1120	U.S. Corporation Income Tax Return	This return is filed by non-exempt taxable private foundations organized as a corporation that owe tax; the foundation must also file the 990-PF.
1120-POL	U.S. Income Tax Return for Certain Political Organizations	This return is filed by foundations that make political expenditures in excess of $100 in a year where net investment income exceeds $100 in a year.
1128	Application to Adopt, Change, or Retain a Tax Year	This form is used to request a change in tax year-end for the foundation.
2758	Application for Extension of Time to File Certain Excise, Income Information, and Other Returns	This form is used to file for an extension for excise tax, income tax, information, and certain other returns.
2220	Underpayment of Estimated Tax by Corporations	This form is required where a foundation owes a penalty and is used to calculate the penalty due.

TABLE 8-13.   CONTINUED

Form	Name	Purpose
4506-A	Request for Public Inspection or Copy of Exempt Organization Tax Form	This form is used to request a copy of a tax return or application for exemption for a tax-exempt entity.
4720	Return of Certain Excise Taxes on Charities and Other Persons Under Chapters 41 and 42 of the Internal Revenue Code	This form is used to calculate excise taxes due on self-dealing, failure to distribute income, excess business holdings, jeopardizing investments, and political or non-charitable expenditures.
5500	Annual Return/Report of Employee Benefit Plan	This form is filed to report activity in an employee benefit plan where the plan has 100 or more participants.
5500-C/R	Return/Report of Employee Benefit Plan	This form is filed to report activity in an employee benefit plan where the plan has less than 100 participants.
8109	Federal Tax Deposit Coupon	This form is used to make federal tax deposits for income, Social Security, and Medicare taxes paid and withheld.
8282	Donee Information Return	This return is used the report the sale, exchange, consummation, or other disposal of nonmarketable property gifted to the charity with a value at the time of contribution of $5,000 or more (requiring the donor to first file Form 8283).
8275	Disclosure Statement	This statement is attached to Form 990-PF to disclose positions or issues not adequately disclosed on the tax return; see Form 8275-R below, which is used to specifically report positions or issues

TABLE 8-13.   CONTINUED

Form	Name	Purpose
		counter to Treasury Regulations.
8275-R	Regulation Disclosure Statement	This form is used to report positions taken on a tax return that are contrary to Treasury Regulations. It can also be used for disclosure relating to the preparer penalties for income tax understatements where the understatements are due to a position contrary to the Regulations.
8300	Report of Cash Payments over $10,000 Received in a Trade or Business	This form is used to report detail on receipts of cash of $10,000 or more, including the identity of the person, the form of the deposit (currency, cashier's check, foreign currency, etc.), and the nature of the transaction.
8718	User Fee for Exempt Organization Determination Letter Request	This form accompanies the payment of a user's fee when applying for tax-exempt status for the foundation.

Eventually, foundation returns will be filed electronically. In February 2004, the IRS, in partnership with software developers, tax professionals and state charity officials, released a new electronic version of Form 990-PF. Initially, electronic filing for foundations is voluntary. To participate in 2005 and thereafter, a foundation simply files its return through an Approved IRS 990 e-file Provider. A list of such providers, with links to their web sites, appears on the IRS web site at *www.irs.gov/efile/businesses*. Foundations that file at least 250 returns, including income tax, excise tax, information and employment tax returns, during a calendar year, will be required to file Form 990-PF electronically for 2006 and subsequent tax years. For more details, see IRS Publication 4453, Form 990, IRS E-file for Charities and Non-Profits, available on the IRS website, and Temp. Reg. *§ 301.6033-4T*.

Since 2001, Form 990-PF has included a new schedule for foundations to complete. Beginning with their 2000 returns, public charities filing Forms 990 or 990-EZ were required to include a preprinted form, Schedule B, to report contributions of $5,000 or more from any one contributor. Private foundations have been required for some time to prepare and attach to Form 990-PF a schedule setting forth similar information, but for 2001 and thereafter the Schedule B preprinted form is to be used for this purpose.

Schedule B asks for the names and addresses of those contributors contributing over $5,000, their aggregate contributions, and the type of contribution. Additional information is required for noncash contributions: a description of the property, its estimated value, and the date of the contribution. If a foundation received no contributions of $5,000 or more from any one individual, it need not file Schedule B. However, it is important for foundations that received no contributions over $5,000 to check the box on Form or 990-PF indicating specifically that Schedule B is not required to be filed. If this box is left blank, the IRS computers will look for Schedule B, and, if it is not found, follow-up action is likely. No one wants to hear from the IRS if it is not necessary, so it is important for foundations to be sure their returns *either* include Schedule B or contain a checked box indicating that Schedule B is not required.

§ 8.08   STATE FILING REQUIREMENTS

[A]   The State Attorney General

States also regulate the activities of private foundations through the state attorney general's office and through taxation. The state attorneys general represent the public beneficial interests of the foundation. States are involved in two ways. First, they establish standards for corporations and charitable entities that conduct business or activities in the state. These activities may include incorporating in the state, locating an office in the state, maintaining employees in the state, owning property or placing property (through a checking account) in the state, and soliciting contributions in the state. In many states, a private foundation is required to register with the state to request a state tax exemption letter. Most attorney general offices have a special division for charitable interests, which is responsible for monitoring all nonprofits doing business in the state and ensuring that the nonprofits operate for the public good.[53]

Second, the IRS requires that foundations with assets of $5,000 or more (at any time during the tax year) file a copy of the 990-PF (and Form 4720, if applicable) with the attorney general of every state in which it reports or is registered, the state in which the principal office is located, and the state in which the foundation was created (through trust or incorporation) at the same time that the foundation files the 990-PF with the IRS.[54] In addition, the foundation must

---

[53] A complete list of State Attorneys General can be found on the National Association of Attorneys General website at http://www.naag.org/ag/full_ag_table.php.

[54] IRC § 6033(c)(2); Reg. § 1.6033-3(c)(1).

provide a copy of the 990-PF or Form 4720 to any state that requests this information.[55]

When a foundation is refused recognition as a tax-exempt organization, loses its exemption, or has a tax deficiency and the determination is final (meaning that all administrative review is complete), the Internal Revenue Service is required to notify the state attorney general and the principal tax officer of the states in which the foundation's principal office is located and in which the foundation was incorporated (or in which it was created if it is in trust form).[56] Notice is provided by sending the state officers a copy of the notice sent to the foundation containing the determination.[57] State officers are then entitled to inspect the foundation's returns, filed statements, records, reports, and any other information relating to the determination. State officers are not entitled to inspect reports of informers (or any information that would identify those informers and put them in jeopardy), material that the Commissioner determines would prejudice proper administration of the revenue laws, or information not normally available to states under the disclosure laws of IRC § 6103.[58]

[B]   Local Issues

If the foundation is involved in selling goods or services, it must also determine if state or local filings are required to report (or pay tax on) this activity. If the foundation owns property, it may be entitled to file for an exemption from payment of that property tax if the property is devoted to exempt use.

§ 8.09   DISCLOSURE REQUIREMENTS

[A]   Form 990 PF

Form 990-PF is considered a public document.[59] Not only will the IRS make the document available to those who request it, but also the foundation must make the return available for inspection at the foundation's offices, or at an appropriate substitute location, or provide the person requesting the return with a copy of the information. Form 990-PF's are voluntarily made available through some foundation web sites and will ultimately be made available to everyone through the IRS web site.

---

[55] Reg. § 1.6033-3(c)(1).

[56] Reg. § 301.6104(c)-1(a)(1).

[57] Reg. § 301.6104(c)-1(a)(2).

[58] Reg. § 301.6104(c)-1(b).

[59] Exceptions include information that relates to the national defense and information that relates to a trade secret, patent, or other special process. For more information, *see* Reg. § 301.6104(a)(5).

In June 1999, the IRS amended the public disclosure requirements and issued final regulations outlining compliance with those requirements.[60] Prior to the changes, private foundations were required to publish notice of availability of the tax return in a local paper with general circulation in the county where the main office was located. The notice, which had to be published by the date that the return (or extensions) were due, had to provide the name and address of the contact person in the main office and state that the return was available at the office for inspection within 180 days of the date of publication. A copy of this notice was required to be filed with the 990-PF.

Under the new disclosure requirements, all exempt organizations, including private foundations, must make their applications for exemption and attachments (a foundation is not required to provide the application if the Internal Revenue Service has not yet recognized it as exempt[61]) and their last three annual returns available for public inspection (without charge) at their principal, regional, and district offices.[62] The annual information return includes an exact copy of the return, any amended return, and all schedules, attachments, and supporting documents. If the foundation does not have a permanent office, it can make the information available at a public location of its choice.[63] Private foundations, as a part of this disclosure, must provide the names and addresses of contributors to the organization; charities other than private foundations are not required to provide this information.[64]

The foundation must comply with the request to publicly inspect the information within a reasonable time, generally defined as not more than two weeks from the date of request, and at a reasonable time during the day. Or it may mail a copy of the requested information to the individual requesting it within two weeks in lieu of inspection at the foundation's offices.[65] The foundation cannot charge a fee for the privilege of inspecting the returns.

If the foundation receives a request for copies of the information, the time prescribed by the Internal Revenue Service for compliance with the request depends on its form.[66] If a request is made in person at the foundation offices, copies must be provided on the day requested. If the request places an unusual burden on the foundation, the copies must be provided on the first business day after the circumstances creating the unusual burden cease to exist or within five business days of the request, whichever occurs first. If the request for copies is made in writing (i.e., by letter, fax, e-mail), the foundation must mail the requested documents within 30 days of receiving the request (or if the foundation requires payment for the copies in advance, within 30 days from receipt of payment). The foundation may charge a fee

---

[60] IRC § 6104(d); Prop. Reg. § 301.6104(e)-1.

[61] Reg. § 301.6104(d)-1(b)(3)(iii)(A).

[62] IRC § 6104(b), Reg. § 301.6104(d)-1.

[63] Reg. § 301.6104(d)-1(c)(2).

[64] IRC § 6104(d)(3).

[65] Reg. § 301.6104(d)-1(c)(2).

[66] Prop. Reg. § 301.6104(d)-1(d).

for copies of the requested returns, but this fee may not exceed the per-page charge charged by the Internal Revenue Service to provide copies.[67]

There are two exceptions to the requirement that the foundation provide copies of its application for exemption or its annual returns. A tax-exempt organization is not required to comply with requests for copies if the documents have been made widely available to the public. First, the organization can post the information on the Internet either through its own Web site or through another organization's web site that provides a database of information on tax-exempt organizations (such as Guidestar at *www.guidestar.org* and the Economic Research Institute at *www. eri-nonprofitsalaries.com*).[68] Second, the foundation is not required to respond when the request for copies is part of a harassment campaign.[69]

[B]   IRS Tax Shelter Disclosure Regulations May Apply to Foundations

While tax shelters and foundations are seldom thought of as having much in common, in February 2003, the Internal Revenue Service issued regulations under § 6011 of the Internal Revenue Code requiring a wide variety of taxpayers to disclose various types of tax-motivated transactions, register confidential corporate tax shelters, and maintain lists of potentially abusive tax shelters. Surprisingly, transactions involving the private foundation excise taxes are specifically included within the disclosure portion of this framework.

Here is how the system works. A taxpayer who has participated in a "reportable transaction" is required to report the fact to the IRS on Form 8886. Reportable transactions are defined in the regulations to include six specific categories of transactions, all of which are sufficiently dodgy that a reasonable person would probably know he or she was getting into a potentially questionable area. That is the theory of the regulations, which are designed to help the IRS combat abusive tax shelters more effectively. The six categories specified in the regulations are as follows:

1. Confidential transactions — deals offered to a taxpayer under conditions of confidentiality;

2. Transactions with "contractual protection" — where the taxpayer is entitled to a refund if the tax consequences do not work out as promised;

3. Loss transactions — deals that produce a loss deduction of $10 million or more for corporations, or $2 million for individuals, trusts, or S corporations;

4. Transactions with a significant ($10 million) difference between book income and taxable income;

---

[67] Reg. § 301.6104(d)-1(d)(3)(i).
[68] Reg. § 301.6104(d)-2.
[69] IRC § 6104(d)(4).

5. Transactions producing a tax credit of more than $250,000 if the underlying asset that produces the credit is held for 45 days or less; and

6. "Listed" transactions — those determined by the IRS to be tax avoidance transactions and identified as such by a published announcement. This builds in flexibility by allowing the IRS to move swiftly to shut down new forms of tax shelter activity as they arise rather than go through a lengthy period of audit activity involving particular taxpayers.

The rules governing these transactions are highly detailed — almost 100 pages in the original typewritten document — and set forth a very complex structure. This brief summary only scratches the surface.

What is worth noting is that there is a specific provision (Regulations § 53.6011-4) specifically declaring that any listed transaction that involves a private foundation excise tax under Chapter 42 of the Code must be disclosed under these rules. It is not clear what this provision is aimed at, but foundation advisors should keep it in mind when asked to evaluate a plan that aims to avoid a self-dealing tax, reduce the tax on net investment income, etc.

Advisors should also be aware of various companion measures in these regulations that impose similar requirements. For example, a person who is a "material advisor" with respect to a "potentially abusive tax shelter" must maintain (and furnish to the IRS) a list of such plans and a list of the plan participants, including their tax identification numbers. Similarly, promoters of certain types of corporate tax shelters must register with the IRS. The applicable definitions are quite broad, and substantial penalties are imposed for noncompliance. These rules are nominally effective for transactions after February 28, 2003, but may apply retroactively in certain cases.

§ 8.10   CONDUCTING AN ANNUAL REVIEW

It is important to conduct an annual review of the foundation's structure, activities, and future objectives to determine what changes are needed to operate effectively. In addition to any improvements in administration and effectiveness, the annual review provides a framework that enables the foundation to detect and correct serious problems that may otherwise continue unabated.

[A]   Independent Audit

The foundation may want to consider a periodic independent audit to ensure the foundation is operating in accordance with IRS guidelines and generally accepted accounting practices.

A 2003 federal case involving an accountant's actions with respect to an Arkansas family foundation provides an instructive, if extreme, example of the type of wrongdoing that may occur without the knowledge of the foundation or its principals. The case is *United States v. Frost*,[70] which affirmed the conviction of a certified public accountant for a number of offenses, including wire fraud, mail fraud, money laundering, filing false tax returns, making a false declaration before a grand jury, and obstruction of justice, all arising out of his involvement with a family foundation.

The CPA, H.G. "Jack" Frost Jr., worked for Harvey Jones, and a number of Jones family entities, including the Jones Investment Company and the Harvey and Bernice Jones Charitable Trust (a family foundation). He and Harvey's wife, Bernice Jones, were the trustees of the trust, and they were paid for their services by the Jones Investment Company. After Harvey's death, Frost continued to work exclusively for the Jones entities. Without Bernice's consent, Frost withdrew money from the foundation and invested it in oil wells, and the royalty payments were paid to him. He also wired money from the foundation to his personal account, invested the funds, and wrote checks to himself from the foundation for compensation. Frost stipulated that although checks drawn on the trust checking account required the signatures of both trustees, he forged Bernice's signature on a number of invoices and checks. Over the four-year period from 1993 to 1997, Frost received $1,110,708 from the investment company and another $1,852,246 from the foundation.

The court quickly disposed of Frost's contention that the evidence against him was insufficient, holding:

> Frost devised a scheme to defraud the Trust, he intended to defraud the Trust, and he used the mails and wires to implement his scheme. This case does not represent a simple misunderstanding as to how Frost was to be compensated for his services.[71]

Frost's main contention on appeal was that nothing in either Arkansas law or the trust instrument required the consent of both trustees before one could be compensated by the trust for services rendered to the trust. The court rejected this suggestion that the government, having proved beyond a reasonable doubt each element of the offense, must also prove a violation of Arkansas law. In addition, the court went on to find that "[i]f Arkansas law did control this point, however, we would hold that Frost was required to obtain the authorization of Bernice Jones before compensating himself from the Trust account."[72]

Fortunately, this is not a typical situation; nevertheless, there are some lessons here for the typical family foundation. Family members should be aware of how funds, especially funds in checking accounts, are handled. Who has signature authority? How closely are invoices and other bills and disburse-

---

[70] 321 F.3d 738 (8th Cir. 2003).
[71] *Id.* at 741.
[72] *Id.*

ments examined? The board of directors or the trustees should know the answers to these questions and take steps to be sure that a scheme like this can never get started.

[B]   Family and Administrative Assessment

- Locate the minutes from the prior year, make sure those minutes are complete, and insert them in the foundation's minute book.

- Review the foundation's bylaws. Make changes if necessary to reflect changes in direction, board membership, or meeting practices.

- Review board membership. If terms expire and new members are to be elected, convene the nominating committee.

- Review committees. Ask family members to express personal interests for committee work, and accommodate those interests to the extent possible.

- Schedule a family meeting. Use this annual meeting to review the previous year's activities, the role of family members, and goals for the coming year. A family meeting is an excellent way to share values, surface important issues, and determine roles for the coming year.

[C]   Investment Review

- Review the foundation's investment results for the prior year, and compare those results to the standards established in the investment policies. Consider these results against three-year and five-year indices, and make the decision to fire or retain the investment firm or make other adjustments to investment policies as appropriate.

- Review the foundation's asset allocation and make a decision to retain or adjust those ratios. Changes in economic indicators or positive or negative returns in the investment markets may signal the need for change or may offer opportunities for the coming year.

[D]   Liability Management

- Review state law to see if changes have occurred that may positively or negatively affect the foundation's insurance coverage.

- Check the foundation's insurance coverage to ensure it is up-to-date. Has the foundation acquired new property or new board members, or engaged in activities representing a direct delivery of its services?

- Determine that foundation employees and assets are fully covered. Pass on changes in foundation structure to the insurance carrier.

[E] Grantmaking

- Check the foundation's 990-PF to ensure the foundation is current in its grantmaking obligation. Take the figure reflecting an overdistribution or underdistribution from the return and use it in the annual grant calculation.

- Make an initial calculation of the foundation's grant target for the year.

- Check to ensure that all follow-up reports for grants (especially those requiring expenditure responsibility) have been received. Contact those organizations that have not complied and set a date for compliance.

- Review the foundation's grant priorities. If changes are appropriate, make those changes on the foundation's web site, in the foundation's marketing materials, and on the foundation's grant application form.

- Review the foundation's mission statement. Update or edit it, as appropriate.

- Schedule a grantwriting training session for nonprofits in the community. Share the foundation's goals and objectives, explain the grantmaking form, and establish grantmaking cycle deadlines.

[F] Taxation

- Check to make sure the foundation's tax returns are current. Make sure that the foundation board members all receive copies of the most recent 990-PF. Ask each to read the return and raise questions about items that are unfamiliar.

- Have the 990-PF available for distribution on request. If the foundation posts its 990-PF on the Internet, send the most recent copy to the web master for publication.

[G] Marketing

- Prepare materials needed for the foundation's annual report. (If the foundation is audited, this should follow the audit.)

- Review the foundation's web site and consider ways in which it can be expanded or made more effective. Add helpful links for grantseekers and those who want to learn more about the foundation and its philosophy. If the foundation does not have a web site, consider its appropriateness for the overall marketing plan.

§8.11 MANAGING CONFLICT OF INTEREST ISSUES

The private foundation self-dealing rules[73] were put in place in 1969 as a part of the sweeping changes made to the Internal Revenue Code to prevent abuse or personal benefit to the donors and family who created them. The rules are extremely

---

[73] IRC §§ 4940-4948.

effective in preventing (or punishing) individual benefit from the foundation by imposing sanctions and excise taxes on foundations and managers for violations. Examples may include the purchase or sale of assets involving disqualified persons and the foundation, taking a higher than appropriate salary for services, or taking a fee for services for professional work not specified in the regulations.[74]

With a statutory prohibition against personal benefit, is a conflict of interest policy necessary or appropriate? The answer is "absolutely" for several reasons. First, a conflict of interest policy highlights self-dealing issues that may not be apparent to board members. Second, it helps improve the public's perception of private foundations and their operation. Third, it establishes strong ethical values for foundation operation that carry over into the foundation directors' private lives.

The foundation's board members will likely be visible and active in their community and should avoid not only conflicts of interest but also the appearance of conflict. Consider the following potential problems:

- The board member or member's immediate family may serve on the board of an organization requesting a grant from the foundation.

- The board member or member's immediate family may be employed by an organization requesting a grant from the foundation.

- The board member or member's immediate family may be a vendor of an organization requesting a grant.

- The board member or member's immediate family may own an interest in a potential vendor doing business with the foundation.

These relationships should be revealed to the full board before decisions are made. Conflicts representing self-dealing issues should be identified and the potential conflict discussed. If there is a possibility that the action will trigger the self-dealing excise tax, the foundation should consult its legal counsel. Situations involving potential conflict or the appearance of conflict should also be discussed in full and a decision made with full knowledge of that information. In some cases, the board member may need to abstain from voting on the matter and the minutes should reflect this decision.

Asking board members to sign a conflict of interest policy as they begin board service is an excellent way to emphasize the importance of their role and the potential for problems.[75] Talk about the policy at each board meeting and encourage members to reflect and report potential problems. Discuss the issues openly and resolve them fairly. The process will have a powerful effect on the integrity of the foundation's board, effectiveness of its operation, and public perception of its activities.

---

[74] *See* Chapter 6 for a complete discussion of the self-dealing rules.

[75] A sample Conflict of Interest Statement is included in Appendix 5-D, and can also be found in the Instructions for IRS Form 1023.

FAMILY FOUNDATION BUDGET WORKSHEET

Budget Line Item	Year One	Year Two
INCOME		
Contributions:		
Earned income:		
Interest		
Dividends		
Other		
Realized gains:		
TOTAL INCOME		
NET		
EXPENSES		
Lease space:		
Space		
Tenant improvements		
Taxes		
Utilities:		
Electricity		
Water		
Telephone		
Internet		
Office equipment/furnishings:		
Office furniture		
Copy machine		
Fax		
Telephone		
Computers		
Other		

Administration:		
Staff		
Employee benefits		
Training		
Professional expenses:		
Attorney		
Accountant		
Investment manager		
Consultant		
Miscellaneous:		
Insurance		
Professional associations		
Conferences		
Meals/travel/entertainment		
TOTAL EXPENSE	($)	($)

Appendix 8-B

ASSET ALLOCATION QUESTIONNAIRE

1. **Which of the following statements best describes your investment objectives for your endowment assets? Circle one:**

   A. *Income*   Maximum current income. Need to grow funds is negligible.

   B. *Income & Growth*   Modest current income. Some emphasis on capital preservation and limited capital appreciation.

   C. *Balanced*   Equally balanced need for current income, capital appreciation, and capital preservation.

   D. *Long-Term Growth*   Moderate capital appreciation and low level of current income.

   E. *Aggressive Growth*   Maximum capital appreciation and negligible current income.

2. **Which of the following investment objectives best describes your preference or attitude toward investment volatility and risk? Circle one:**

   A. *Income*   Low risk, conservative income-oriented, low volatility.

   B. *Income & Growth*   Moderate risk, consistent returns, income-oriented limited capital appreciation.

   C. *Balanced*   Exposure to higher level of volatility with expectations of growth, with income as secondary objective.

   D. *Long-Term Growth*   Little concern for volatility, high expectations, can tolerate periodic negative returns, low level of income.

   E. *Aggressive Growth*   Maximum capital growth, no concern for periodic volatility, can tolerate negative returns, negligible income.

3. **What investment horizon is most appropriate for these managed assets? Circle one:**

Greater than 10 years

5–10 years

2–5 years

Less than 2 years

4. **Are there any stocks, industries, and/or sectors in which the portfolio should be prohibited from investing?**
   If yes, what type of stocks do you feel you should avoid? _____
   _____
   _____

5. **Please indicate the portfolio that represents the maximum gain or loss trade-off that you are willing to accept during one investment year. (Assume an initial investment portfolio of $200,000.) Circle one:**

A. *Income*	$200,000	$210,000
	-0-	15%
B. *Income & Growth*	$190,000	$220,000
	25%	110%
C. *Balanced*	$180,000	$240,000
	210%	+120%
D. *Long-Term Growth*	$170,000	$260,000
	215%	+130%
E. *Aggressive Growth*	$160,000	$280,000
	220%	+140%

APPENDIX 8-C

TAX ON NET INVESTMENT INCOME (IRC § 4940)

Overview. An excise tax of two percent on net investment income applies to most private foundations except exempt operating foundations. [*See* IRC § 4940 and the Regulations thereunder.] This tax is reduced to one percent in certain situations where the foundation makes distributions in excess of the minimum requirements, as discussed below. A foundation must report this tax on Form 990-PF, Return of Private Foundation. Payment of the tax is subject to estimated tax requirements. For more information concerning payment of estimated tax, *see* the Instructions for Form 990-PF in Appendix 3-B.

§ 8-C.01   NET INVESTMENT INCOME

The tax is two (or one) percent of *net investment income*. Net investment income is the amount by which the sum of *gross investment income* and *capital gain net income* exceeds the allowable deductions. Tax-exempt interest on governmental obligations and related expenses are excluded.

[A]   Gross Investment Income

Gross investment income is the total income from interest, dividends, rents, payments with respect to securities loans (as defined in IRC § 512(a)(5)), and royalties (including overriding royalties) received by a private foundation from all sources. [IRC § 4940(c)(2)] It does not include unrelated business income, but it does include interest, dividends, rents, and royalties received from assets devoted to charitable activities. Thus, for example, interest received on a student loan would be includible in the gross investment income of a private foundation making such a loan.

[B]   Capital Gains and Losses

[1]   Capital Gain Net Income

Capital gain net income consists of the excess of includible capital gains over includible capital losses. A private foundation must include any capital gains and losses from thesale or other disposition of property held for investment purposes or for the production of income. [IRC § 4940(c)(4)(A)] This includescapital gain dividends received from mutual funds. If the foundation sells or otherwise disposes of property used in the production of income that is subject to the unrelated business income tax, any gain or loss from the sale of that property must be included in net investment income, but only to the extent that it is not included in figuring the tax on unrelated businessincome. Property is treated as held for investment purposes, even though the property is disposed of by the foundation immediately upon its receipt, if it is the kind of property that generally produces interest, dividends, rents, royalties, or capital gains through appreciation. [Reg. § 53.4940-1(f)(1)]

[2]   Property Used for Exempt Purposes

Gains and losses realized on the disposition of property used for the exempt purposes of the foundation are not includedin figuring the tax on net investment income. If the foundation uses property for its exempt purposes, but also incidentally receives income from the property that is subject to the net investment income tax, any gain or lossfrom the sale or other disposition of the property is not subject to the tax. Thus, for example, a tax-exempt private foundation that maintains historic buildings that are open to the public and requires some employees to live in these buildings and charges them rent must include such rent in its net investment income, but any gain or loss resulting from the sale of these buildings is not subject to the tax. [Reg. § 53.4940-1(f)(1)]

Where property is used both for exempt purposes and for investment purposes (e.g., a building in which the foundation conducts both its charitable program and its investment activities), that part of the gain or loss from the sale or other disposition of the property that is allocable to the investment use of the property must be taken into account in figuring the tax on net investment income.

[3] Losses

Capital losses from the sale or other disposition of investment property may be subtracted from capital gains incurred in the sale or disposition of other investment property during the same tax year, but only to the extent of the gains. If the capital losses are greater than the capital gains, the excess may not be subtracted from gross investment income, nor may the losses be carried back or forward to other tax years, regardless of whether the foundation is a corporation or a trust. [Reg. § 53.4940-1(f)(3)]

[4] Basis

The basis for determining gain from the sale or other disposition of property is the greater of:

1. The fair market value of the property onDecember 31, 1969, plus or minus any post-1969 adjustments; or

2. The basis of the property determined under normal basis rules (i.e., actual basis).

For purposes of determining gain on property received by gift, the basis of the property is its basis in the hands of the donor at the time of the gift. For purposes of determining a loss, the basis of property received by gift is the lesser of the donor's basis at the time of the gift or the fair market value at the time of the gift. [Reg. § 53.4940-1(f)(2)]

[C] Deductions

[1] General

In determining net investment income, a private foundation may deduct from gross investment income all the ordinary and necessary expenses paid or incurred for the production or collection of gross investment income or for the management, conservation, or maintenance of property held for the production of income, subject to the modifications given later. Expenses include the part of the foundation's operating expenses (such as compensation, outside professional fees, interest, and rent) that is paid or incurred for the production or collection of gross investment income. The amount paid as tax on net investment income may not be deducted. [Reg. § 53.4940-1(e)(1)(i)]

If any expenses, including salaries and compensation, are incurred for both investment purposes and exempt purposes, they must be allocated between the investment activities and the exempt activities. Expenses paid or incurred for exempt functions are not deductible in figuring net investment income. Also, any expenses that are taken into account in figuring the tax on unrelated business income may not be deducted in figuring net investment income. No deduction is allowed for any expense that was not incurred for the purposes stated earlier. Thus, no deduction is allowed for charitable contributions, net operating losses, or any of the special deductions for corporations. [Reg. § 53.4940-1(e)(1)]

[2] Deduction Modifications

The following modifications must be made to otherwise allowable deductions in arriving at net investment income:

1. Depreciation is allowed only on the basis of the straight-line method;

2. Depletion is allowed only on the basis of the cost depletion method;

3. The basis used in figuring depreciation or depletion is the basis determined under normal basis rules, without regard to the fair market value on December 31, 1969 (*see* § 6-B.01[B][4] *supra*); and

4. Deductions for expenses paid or incurred in any tax year for the production of gross investment income earned as an incident to a charitable function cannot exceed the income from that function that is includible as gross investment income for the year. For example, when rental income is incidentally realized in a given year from historic buildings open to the public, the deductions paid or incurred in that year for the production of that income are limited to the amount of rental income includible as gross investment income for the year.

[Reg. § 53.4940-1(e)(2)]

§ 8-C.02   REDUCTION IN TAX RATE

Under IRC § 4940(e), the tax rate on net investment income is reduced from 2 percent to 1 percent for a private foundation that meets both of the following distribution requirements:

1. The foundation must make *qualifying distributions* during the tax year at least equal to the sum of (a) the *assets* of the foundation for the tax year

multiplied by its *average percentage payout* for the *base period* and (b) one percent of the foundation's net investment income for the tax year.

2. The foundation must not have been liablefor any of the penalty excise taxes in Chapter 42 of the Code for any year of the base period.

Qualifying distributions for this purpose are the same as those for purposes of the tax on failure to distribute income, discussed and described in Appendix 6-D.

The *assets* of the foundation for any tax year are the excess of the total fair market value of all its assets (except those used directly in carrying out the foundation's exempt purpose) over the acquisition indebtedness with respect to those assets.

The *average percentage payout* is the average of the percentage payouts for each of the tax years in the foundation's base period. For each tax year, the percentage payout is figured by dividing the qualifying distributions made during the year by the foundation's assets for that year. If, for any tax year in the foundation's base period, the foundation's tax rate on net investment income is reduced to one percent by meeting these distribution requirements, the qualifying distributions made by the foundation during that year must be reduced by the amount of such reduction in tax.

The *base period* for any tax year consists of the five tax years preceding that year. A private foundation that has not been in existence for five tax years has a base period consisting of the tax years during which it has been in existence.

APPENDIX 8-D

SAMPLE ENDOWMENT FUND INVESTMENT POLICIES

INVESTMENT OBJECTIVES

To achieve a moderate capital appreciation on investments held for endowment and to protect those assets for the long-term use of the XYZ Charitable Organization and its programs, while achieving a moderate level of current income.

To pool the various endowed funds for investment purposes to achieve efficiency in costs and management. Although funds may be pooled for investment purposes, underlying fund balances directed to specific programs shall be accounted for individually in reporting balances and in assigning expenses and distributions for the specific program oragency.

To provide a steady stream of funding to provide for the XYZ Charitable Organization and designated programs for which the endowment is held. Projected distributions shall be _____ of the beginning market value of the endowment fund. This distribution amount is set as an outside range for distributions and shall not be considered a required distribution. Distributions from the endowed funds shall be made at the direction of the authorized Trustees of the XYZ Charitable Organization.

INVESTMENT GUIDELINES

The principal of the pooled endowment assets shall be divided as follows:

Equity Investments:	___%
Fixed-Income Investments:	___%
Cash	___%

Investment holdings may vary within five percent of either side of these ranges. Additions to the fund shall be invested in like ratios as quickly as possible upon receipt. Where gifts are received as stock, or as in-kind contributions, those gifts should be sold as quickly as possible upon receipt and the proceeds thereof invested in a likemanner, provided, however, that there may be some exceptions where the donor of a particular gift makes a gift subject to certain direction relating to sale or retention.

The following guidelines shall apply to each type of investment.

Equity Investments

The portion of the portfolio committed to equity investments shall be assigned to a professional equity manager(s) selected by the Trustees.

These investments may consist of domestic or international equity holdings and may include American depository receipts (for securities in non-U.S. corporations).

To the extent possible, equity holdings should not contain holdings in companies whose earnings are generated primarily by alcohol, tobacco, gambling, or manufacture of commercial firearms.

Portfolios may contain cash as part of an asset allocation strategy of a manager.

Fixed-Income Investments

The portion of the endowment funds committed to fixed income may be assigned to a professional investment manager or may be managed by the Trustees within the guidelines set out in this section.

The investments will be limited to domestic fixed-income instruments to include certificates of deposit, U.S. government agency instruments, Treasury instruments, A or better rated corporate bonds, A-1 or P-1 rated commercial paper, or money market funds.

The average maturity of the holdings of the portfolio shall be seven to 10 years, with a portion of the portfolio maturing periodically over the term.

The portfolio shall not hold any collateralized mortgage obligations or derivatives of any form.

Cash

Receipts of income, donations, or maturities shall be moved to money market funds as quickly as possible to await distribution or reinvestment.

INVESTMENT REVIEW

The Trustees shall be responsible for the annual review of the assets and the investment performance of the investment managers. This review shall be based on a performance report prepared by an organization other than the investment manager used to manage the funds and shall focus on the performance of the funds relative to other managers with similar goals and similar allocations.

Review of investment performance shall be based on an investment horizon of _____ (__) years. The Trustees are responsible for the regular review of the investment objectives and investment guidelines and for the retention of the investment managers.

Appendix 8-E
990-PF AND INSTRUCTIONS

[Note: A full-sized version of the following form and instructions can be viewed at www.irs.gov/pub/irs=pdf/iggopf.pdf *and* www.irs.gov/pub/irs=pdf/fggopf.pdf, *respectively.]*

Department of the Treasury
Internal Revenue Service

2005

Instructions for Form 990-PF

Return of Private Foundation or Section 4947(a)(1) Nonexempt Charitable Trust Treated as a Private Foundation

Section references are to the Internal Revenue Code unless otherwise noted.

What's New

Private Foundations now have the option to file electronically. See *e-file* for Charities & Nonprofits on the IRS website at *www.irs.gov/efile/index.html.*

For tax year 2006, certain private foundations will be required to file electronically. See Regulations section 301.6033-4T for more information.

Cat. No. 11290Y

Reminder

Form 990-PF, Part I, was revised in 2004 to reflect Notice 2004-35, 2004-19, I.R.B. 889, regarding distributions received by private foundations from split interest trusts. Distributions received by a private foundation from an estate or trust, including split interest trusts, will not retain its character in the hands of the private foundation for the purposes of computing the private foundation's net investment income. Also, Part XI was revised in 2004 to reflect Notice 2004-36, 2004-19, I.R.B. 889, concerning the treatment of certain distributions from split interest trusts described in section 4947(a)(2). Distributions from split interests trusts, are no longer included in figuring a private foundation's distributable amount.

For prior years within the statute of limitations, and for which a refund of Section 4940 taxes paid is requested, private foundations must file an amended Form 990-PF. Write "Filed pursuant to Notice 2004-35" at the top of the first page.

To request a refund of section 4942 taxes paid, a private foundation must file an amended Form 990-PF and an amended Form 4720, Return of Certain Excise Taxes on Charities and Other Persons Under Chapters 41 and 42 of the Internal Revenue Code, for each year with a schedule showing the corrected amount of section 4942 liability. The front page of the returns should be marked "Filed pursuant to Notice 2004-36." See *General Instruction L* of Form 990-PF for more information on filing amended returns.

Photographs of Missing Children

The Internal Revenue Service is a proud partner with the National Center for Missing and Exploited Children. Photographs of missing children selected by the Center may appear in instructions on pages that would otherwise be blank. You can help bring these children home by looking at the photographs and calling 1-800-THE-LOST (1-800-843-5678) if you recognize a child.

Phone Help

If you have questions and/or need help completing this form, please call 1-800-829-4933. This toll-free telephone service is available Monday through Friday.

How To Get Forms and Publications

Internet

You can access the IRS website 24 hours a day, 7 days a week at *www.irs.gov* to:
● Download forms, instructions, and publications,
● Order IRS products online,
● See answers to frequently asked tax questions,
● Search publications online by topic or keyword,
● Send us comments or request help via email, or
● Sign up to receive local and national tax news by email.

CD-ROM

Order Pub. 1796, Federal Tax Products on CD-ROM, and get:
● Current year forms, instructions, and publications,
● Prior year forms, instructions, and publications,
● Frequently requested tax forms that may be filled in electronically, printed out for submission, and saved for recordkeeping, and
● The Internal Revenue Bulletin.

Buy the CD-ROM on the Internet at *www.irs.gov/cdorders* from the National Technical Information Service (NTIS) for $25 (no handling fee), or call 1-877-CDFORMS (1-877-233-6767) toll free to buy the CD-ROM for $25 (plus a $5 handling fee).

By Phone and In Person

You can order forms and publications by calling 1-800-TAX-FORM (1-800-829-3676). You can also get most forms and publications at your local IRS office.

Use these electronic options to make filing and paying easier.

IRS E-Services Make Taxes Easier

Now more than ever before, businesses can enjoy the benefits of filing and paying their federal taxes electronically. Whether you rely on a tax professional or handle you own taxes, the IRS offers you convenient programs to make taxes easier.
● You can *e-file* your Form 990-PF; Form 940 and 941 employment tax returns; Form 1099 and other information returns. Visit *www.irs.gov/efile* for details.
● You can pay taxes online or by phone using the free Electronic Federal Tax Payment System (EFTPS). Visit

www.eftps.gov or call 1-800-555-4477 for details. Electronic Funds Withdrawal (EFW) from a checking or savings account is also available to those who file electronically.

General Instructions

Purpose of form. Form 990-PF is used:
● To figure the tax based on investment income, and
● To report charitable distributions and activities.

Also, Form 990-PF serves as a substitute for the section 4947(a)(1) nonexempt charitable trust's income tax return, Form 1041, U.S. Income Tax Return for Estates and Trusts, when the trust has no taxable income.

A. Who Must File

Form 990-PF is an annual information return that must be filed by:
● Exempt private foundations (section 6033(a), (b), and (c)),
● Taxable private foundations (section 6033(d)),
● Organizations that agree to private foundation status and whose applications for exempt status are pending on the due date for filing Form 990-PF,
● Organizations that made an election under section 41(e)(6),
● Organizations that are making a section 507 termination, and
● Section 4947(a)(1) nonexempt charitable trusts that are treated as private foundations (section 6033(d)).

TIP *Include on the foundation's return the financial and other information of any disregarded entity owned by the foundation. See Regulations sections 301.7701-1 through 3 for information on the classification of certain business organizations including an eligible entity that is disregarded as an entity separate from its owner (disregarded entity).*

Other section 4947(a)(1) nonexempt charitable trusts. Section 4947(a)(1) nonexempt charitable trusts that are not treated as private foundations do not file Form 990-PF. However, they may need to file Form 990, Return of Organization Exempt From Income Tax, or Form 990-EZ, Short Form Return of Organization Exempt From Income Tax. With either of these forms, the trust must also file Schedule A (Form 990 or 990-EZ), Organization Exempt Under Section 501(c)(3) (Except Private Foundation), and Section 501(e), 501(f), 501(k), 501(n), or Section 4947(a)(1) Nonexempt Charitable Trust Supplementary Information. (See Form 990 and Form 990-EZ instructions.)

B. Which Parts To Complete

The parts of the form listed below do not apply to all filers. See *How to avoid filing*

an incomplete return on this page for information on what to do if a part or an item does apply.
● Part I, column (c), applies only to private operating foundations and to nonoperating private foundations that have income from charitable activities.
● Part II, column (c), with the exception of line 16, applies only to organizations having at least $5,000 in assets per books at some time during the year. Line 16, column (c), applies to all filers.
● Part IV does not apply to foreign organizations.
● Parts V and VI do not apply to organizations making an election under section 41(c).
● Part X does not apply to foreign foundations that check box D2 on page 1 of Form 990-PF unless they claim status as a private operating foundation.
● Parts XI and XIII do not apply to foreign foundations that check box D2 on page 1 of Form 990-PF. However, check the box at the top of Part XI. Part XI does not apply to private operating foundations. Also, if the organization is a private operating foundation for any of the years shown in Part XIII, do not complete the portions that apply to those years.
● Part XIV applies only to private operating foundations.
● Part XV applies only to organizations having assets of $5,000 or more during the year. This part does not apply to certain foreign organizations.

How to avoid filing an incomplete return.
● Complete all applicable line items,
● Answer "Yes," "No," or "N/A" (not applicable) to each question on the return,
● Make an entry (including a zero when appropriate) on all total lines, and
● Enter "None" or "N/A" if an entire part does not apply.

Sequencing Chart To Complete the Form

You may find the following chart helpful. It limits jumping from one part of the form to another to compute an amount needed to complete an earlier part. If you complete the parts in the listed order, any information you may need from another part will already be entered.

Step	Part	Step	Part
1	IV	8	XII, lines 1–4
2	I & II	9	V & VI
3	Heading	10	XII, lines 5–6
4	III	11	XI
5	VII-A	12	XIII
6	VIII	13	VII-B
7	IX-A – X	14	XIV – XVII

C. Definitions

1. A private foundation is a domestic or foreign organization exempt from income tax under section 501(a); described in section 501(c)(3); and is other than an organization described in sections 509(a)(1) through (4).

Form 990-PF Instructions

In general, churches, hospitals, schools, and broadly publicly supported organizations are excluded from private foundation status by these sections. These organizations may be required to file Form 990 (or Form 990-EZ) instead of Form 990-PF.

2. A nonexempt charitable trust treated as a private foundation is a trust that is not exempt from tax under section 501(a) and all of the unexpired interests of which are devoted to religious, charitable, or other purposes described in section 170(c)(2)(B), and for which a deduction was allowed under a section of the Code listed in section 4947(a)(1).

3. A taxable private foundation is an organization that is no longer exempt under section 501(a) as an organization described in section 501(c)(3). Though it may operate as a taxable entity, it will continue to be treated as a private foundation until that status is terminated under section 507.

4. A private operating foundation is an organization that is described under section 4942(j)(3) or (5). It means any private foundation that spends at least 85% of the smaller of its adjusted net income (figured in Part I) or its minimum investment return (figured in Part X) directly for the active conduct of the exempt purpose or functions for which the foundation is organized and operated and that also meets the assets test, the endowment test, or the support test (discussed in Part XIV).

5. A nonoperating private foundation is a private foundation that is not a private operating foundation.

6. A foundation manager is an officer, director, or trustee of a foundation, or an individual who has powers similar to those of officers, directors, or trustees. In the case of any act or failure to act, the term "foundation manager" may also include employees of the foundation who have the authority to act.

7. A disqualified person is:

a. A substantial contributor (see *instructions for Part VII-A, line 10, on page 19*);

b. A foundation manager;

c. A person who owns more than 20% of a corporation, partnership, trust, or unincorporated enterprise that is itself a substantial contributor;

d. A family member of an individual described in a, b, or c above; or

e. A corporation, partnership, trust, or estate in which persons described in a, b, c, or d above own a total beneficial interest of more than 35%.

f. For purposes of section 4941 (self-dealing), a disqualified person also includes certain government officials. (See section 4946(c) and the related regulations.)

g. For purposes of section 4943 (excess business holdings), a disqualified person also includes:

i. A private foundation that is effectively controlled (directly or indirectly)

by the same persons who control the private foundation in question, or

ii. A private foundation to which substantially all of the contributions were made (directly or indirectly) by one or more of the persons described in a, b, and c above, or members of their families, within the meaning of section 4946(d).

8. An organization is controlled by a foundation or by one or more disqualified persons with respect to the foundation if any of these persons may, by combining their votes or positions of authority, require the organization to make an expenditure or prevent the organization from making an expenditure, regardless of the method of control. "Control" is determined regardless of how the foundation requires the contribution to be used.

D. Other Forms You May Need To File

- Form W-2, Wage and Tax Statement.
- Form W-3, Transmittal of Wage and Tax Statements.
- Form 941, Employer's Quarterly Federal Tax Return.

These forms are used to report social security, Medicare, and income taxes withheld by an employer and social security and Medicare taxes paid by an employer.

If income, social security, and Medicare taxes that must be withheld are not withheld or are not paid to the IRS, a trust fund recovery penalty may apply. The penalty is 100% of such unpaid taxes.

This penalty may be imposed on all persons (including volunteers, see below) whom the IRS determines to be responsible for collecting, accounting for, and paying over these taxes, and who willfully did not do so.

This penalty does not apply to any volunteer, unpaid member of any board of trustees or directors of a tax-exempt organization, if this member:

- Is solely serving in an honorary capacity,
- Does not participate in the day-to-day or financial activities of the organization, and
- Does not have actual knowledge of the failure to collect, account for, and pay over these taxes.

However, this exception does not apply if it results in no person being liable for the penalty.

Form 990-T, Exempt Organization Business Income Tax Return. Every organization exempt from income tax under section 501(a) that has total gross income of $1,000 or more from all trades or businesses that are unrelated to the organization's exempt purpose must file a return on Form 990-T. The form is also used by tax-exempt organizations to report other additional taxes including the

additional tax figured in Part IV of Form 8621, Return by a Shareholder of a Passive Foreign Investment Company or Qualified Electing Fund.

Form 990-W, Estimated Tax on Unrelated Business Taxable Income for Tax-Exempt Organizations (and on Investment Income for Private Foundations). Use of this form is optional. It is provided only to aid you in determining your tax liability.

Form 1041, U.S. Income Tax Return for Estates and Trusts. Required of section 4947(a)(1) nonexempt charitable trusts that also file Form 990-PF. However, if the trust does not have any taxable income under the income tax provisions (subtitle A of the Code), it may use the filing of Form 990-PF to satisfy its Form 1041 filing requirement under section 6012. If this condition is met, check the box for question 13, Part VII-A, of Form 990-PF and do not file Form 1041.

Form 1041-ES, Estimated Income Tax for Estates and Trusts. Used to make estimated tax payments.

Form 1096, Annual Summary and Transmittal of U.S. Information Returns. Used to transmit forms 1099, 1098, 5498, and W-2G to the IRS. Do not use it to transmit electronically or magnetically.

Form 1098-C, Contributions of Motor Vehicles, Boats, and Airplanes. Information return for reporting contributions of qualified motor vehicles, boats, and airplanes from donors.

Forms 1099-INT, MISC, OID, and R. Information returns for reporting certain interest; miscellaneous income (e.g., payments to providers of health and medical services, miscellaneous income payments, and nonemployee compensation); original issue discount; and distributions from retirement or profit-sharing plans, IRAs, SEPs or SIMPLEs, and insurance contracts.

Form 1120, U.S. Corporation Income Tax Return. Filed by nonexempt taxable private foundations that have taxable income under the income tax provisions (subtitle A of the Code). The Form 990-PF annual information return is also filed by these taxable foundations.

Form 1120-POL, U.S. Income Tax Return for Certain Political Organizations. Section 501(c) organizations must file Form 1120-POL if they are treated as having political organization taxable income under section 527(f)(1).

Form 1128, Application To Adopt, Change, or Retain a Tax Year. Form 1128 is used to request approval from the IRS to change a tax year or to adopt or retain a certain tax year.

Form 2220, Underpayment of Estimated Tax by Corporations. Form 2220, is used by corporations and trusts filing Form 990-PF to see if the foundation owes a penalty and to figure the amount

Form 990-PF Instructions

-3-

8-91

of the penalty. Generally, the foundation is not required to file this form because the IRS can figure the amount of any penalty and bill the foundation for it. However, complete and attach Form 2220 even if the foundation does not owe the penalty if:
• The annualized income or the adjusted seasonal installment method is used, or
• The foundation is a "large organization," (see *General Instruction O*) computing its first required installment based on the prior year's tax.
If Form 2220 is attached, check the box on line 8, Part VI, on page 4 of Form 990-PF and enter the amount of any penalty on this line.

Form 4506-A, Request for Public Inspection or Copy of Exempt or Political Organization IRS Form. Used to request a copy of an exempt or political organization's return, report, notice, or exemption application.

Form 4720, Return of Certain Excise Taxes on Charities and Other Persons Under Chapters 41 and 42 of the Internal Revenue Code. Is primarily used to determine the excise taxes imposed on:
• Acts of self-dealing between private foundations and disqualified persons,
• Failure to distribute income,
• Excess business holdings,
• Investments that jeopardize the foundation's charitable purposes, and
• Making political or other noncharitable expenditures.

Certain excise taxes and penalties also apply to foundation managers, substantial contributors, and certain related persons and are reported on this form.

Form 5500, Annual Return/Report of Employee Benefit Plan. Is used to report information concerning employee benefit plans and Direct Filing Entities.

Form 8109, Federal Tax Deposit Coupon. Used by business entities to make federal tax deposits.

Form 8282, Donee Information Return. Required of the donee of "charitable deduction property" that sells, exchanges, or otherwise disposes of the property within 2 years after the date it received the property. Also required of any successor donee that disposes of charitable deduction property within 2 years after the date that the donor gave the property to the original donee. (It does not matter who gave the property to the successor donee. It may have been the original donee or another successor donee.) For successor donees, the form must be filed only for any property that was transferred by the original donee after July 5, 1988.

Form 8275, Disclosure Statement. Taxpayers and tax return preparers should attach this form to Form 990-PF to disclose items or positions (except those contrary to a regulation—see *Form 8275-R* below) that are not otherwise adequately disclosed on the tax return. The disclosure is made to avoid parts of the accuracy-related penalty imposed for disregard of rules or substantial understatement of tax. Form 8275 is also used for disclosures relating to preparer penalties for understatements due to unrealistic positions or for willful or reckless conduct.

Form 8275-R, Regulation Disclosure Statement. Use this form to disclose any item on a tax return for which a position has been taken that is contrary to Treasury regulations.

Form 8300, Report of Cash Payments Over $10,000 Received in a Trade or Business. Used to report cash amounts in excess of $10,000 that were received in a single transaction (or in two or more related transactions) in the course of a trade or business (as defined in section 162).

Form 8718, User Fee for Exempt Organization Determination Letter Request. Used by a private foundation that has completed a section 507 termination and seeks a determination letter that it is now a public charity.

Form 8822, Change of Address. This form is used by taxpayers to notify the IRS of changes in individual and business mailing addresses.

Form 8868, Application for Extension of Time To File an Exempt Organization Return. This form is used by an exempt organization to request an automatic 3-month extension of time to file its return and also to apply for an additional (not automatic) 3-month extension if the initial 3-month extension is not enough time.

Form 8870, Information Return for Transfers Associated With Certain Personal Benefit Contracts. Used to identify those personal benefit contracts for which funds were transferred to the organization, directly or indirectly, as well as the transferors and beneficiaries of those contracts.

Form 8899, Notice of Income from Donated Intellectual Property. Use this form to report income from qualified intellectual property.

E. Useful Publications

The following publications may be helpful in preparing Form 990-PF:
• Publication 525, Taxable and Nontaxable Income,
• Publication 578, Tax Information for Private Foundations and Foundation Managers,
• Publication 583, Starting a Business and Keeping Records,
• Publication 598, Tax on Unrelated Business Income of Exempt Organizations,
• Publication 910, IRS Guide to Free Tax Services, and

• Publication 1771, Charitable Contributions—Substantiation and Disclosure Requirements.
• Publication 3833, Disaster Relief, Providing Assistance Through Charitable Organizations.

Publications and forms are available at no charge through IRS offices or by calling 1-800-TAX-FORM (1-800-829-3676).

F. Use of Form 990-PF To Satisfy State Reporting Requirements

Some states and local government units will accept a copy of Form 990-PF and required attachments instead of all or part of their own financial report forms.

If the organization plans to use Form 990-PF to satisfy state or local filing requirements, such as those from state charitable solicitation acts, note the following.

Determine state filing requirements. Consult the appropriate officials of all states and other jurisdictions in which the organization does business to determine their specific filing requirements. "Doing business" in a jurisdiction may include any of the following:
• Soliciting contributions or grants by mail or otherwise from individuals, businesses, or other charitable organizations,
• Conducting programs,
• Having employees within that jurisdiction, or
• Maintaining a checking account or owning or renting property there.

Monetary tests may differ. Some or all of the dollar limitations that apply to Form 990-PF when filed with the IRS may not apply when using Form 990-PF instead of state or local report forms. IRS dollar limitations that may not meet some state requirements are the $5,000 total assets minimum that requires completion of Part II, column (c), and Part XV; and the $50,000 minimum for listing the highest paid employees and for listing professional fees in Part VIII.

Additional information may be required. State and local filing requirements may require attaching to Form 990-PF one or more of the following:
• Additional financial statements, such as a complete analysis of functional expenses or a statement of changes in net assets,
• Notes to financial statements,
• Additional financial schedules,
• A report on the financial statements by an independent accountant, and
• Answers to additional questions and other information.

Each jurisdiction may require the additional material to be presented on forms they provide. The additional information does not have to be submitted with the Form 990-PF filed with the IRS.

-4-   **Form 990-PF Instructions**

If required information is not provided to a state, the organization may be asked by the state to provide it or to submit an amended return, even if the Form 990-PF is accepted by the IRS as complete.

Amended returns. If the organization submits supplemental information or files an amended Form 990-PF with the IRS, it must also include a copy of the information or amended return to any state with which it filed a copy of Form 990-PF.

Method of accounting. Many states require that all amounts be reported based on the accrual method of accounting.

Time for filing may differ. The time for filing Form 990-PF with the IRS may differ from the time for filing state reports.

G. Furnishing Copies of Form 990-PF to State Officials

The foundation managers must furnish a copy of the annual return Form 990-PF (and Form 4720 (if applicable)) to the attorney general of:
- Each state required to be listed in Part VII-A, line 8a,
- The state in which the foundation's principal office is located, and
- The state in which the foundation was incorporated or created.

A copy of the annual return must be sent to the attorney general at the same time the annual return is filed with the IRS.

Other requirements. If the attorney general or other appropriate state official of any state requests a copy of the annual return, the foundation managers must give them a copy of the annual return.

Exceptions. These rules do not apply to any foreign foundation which, from the date of its creation, has received at least 85% of its support (excluding gross investment income) from sources outside the United States. (See *General Instruction S* for other exceptions that affect this type of organization.)

Coordination with state reporting requirements. If the foundation managers submit a copy of Form 990-PF and Form 4720 (if applicable) to a state attorney general to satisfy a state reporting requirement, they do not have to furnish a second copy to that attorney general to comply with the Internal Revenue Code requirements discussed in this section.

If there is a state reporting requirement to file a copy of Form 990-PF with a state official other than the attorney general (for instance, the secretary of state), then the foundation managers must also send a copy of the Form 990-PF and Form 4720 (if applicable) to the attorney general of that state.

Form 990-PF Instructions

H. Accounting Period
- File the 2005 return for the calendar year 2005 or fiscal year beginning in 2005. If the return is for a fiscal year, fill in the tax year space at the top of the return.
- The return must be filed on the basis of the established annual accounting period of the organization. If the organization has no established annual accounting period, the return should be on the calendar-year basis.
- For initial or final returns or a change in accounting period, the 2005 form may also be used as the return for a short period (less than 12 months) ending November 30, 2006, or earlier.

In general, to change its accounting period the organization must file Form 990-PF by the due date for the short period resulting from the change. At the top of this short period return, write "Change of Accounting Period."

If the organization changed its accounting period within the 10-calendar-year period that includes the beginning of the short period, and it had a Form 990-PF filing requirement at any time during that 10-year period, it must also attach a Form 1128 to the short-period return. See Rev. Proc. 85-58, 1985-2 C.B. 740.

I. Accounting Methods

Generally, you should report the financial information requested on the basis of the accounting method the foundation regularly uses to keep its books and records.

Exception. Complete Part I, column (d) on the cash receipts and disbursements method of accounting.

J. When and Where To File

This return must be filed by the 15th day of the 5th month following the close of the foundation's accounting period. If the regular due date falls on a Saturday, Sunday, or legal holiday, file by the next business day. If the return is filed late, see *General Instruction M.*

In case of a complete liquidation, dissolution, or termination, file the return by the 15th day of the 5th month following complete liquidation, dissolution, or termination.

To file the return, mail or deliver it to:

Internal Revenue Service Center
Ogden, UT 84201-0027

Private Delivery Services. You can use certain private delivery services designated by the IRS to meet the "timely mailing as timely filing/paying" rule for tax returns and payments. These private delivery services include only the following.

- DHL Express (DHL): DHL "Same Day" Service, DHL Next Day 10:30 AM, DHL Next Day 12:00 PM, DHL Next Day 3:00 PM, and DHL 2nd Day Service.
- Federal Express (FedEx): FedEx Priority Overnight, FedEx Standard Overnight, FedEx 2day, FedEx International Priority, FedEx International First.
- United Parcel Service (UPS): UPS Next Day Air, Ups Next Day Air Saver, UPS 2nd Day Air, UPS Next Day A.M., UPS Worldwide Express Plus, and UPS Worldwide Express.

The private delivery service can tell you how to get written proof of the mailing date.

If you use a private delivery service, use the following address for filing the return:
Internal Revenue Service
1973 N. Rulon White Blvd.
Ogden, UT 84404

K. Extension of Time To File

A foundation uses Form 8868 to request an extension of time to file its return.

An automatic 3-month extension will be granted if you properly complete this form, file it, and pay any balance due by the due date for Form 990-PF.

If more time is needed, Form 8868 is also used to request an additional extension of up to 3 months. However, these extensions are not automatically granted. To obtain this additional extension of time to file, you must show reasonable cause for the additional time requested.

L. Amended Return

To change the organization's return for any year, file an amended return, including attachments, with the correct information. The amended return must provide all the information required by the form and instructions, not just the new or corrected information. Check the "Amended Return" box in G at the top of the return. See the *instructions for line 9 of Part VI on page 19.*

If the organization files an amended return to claim a refund of tax paid under section 4940 or 4948, it must file the amended return within 3 years after the date the original return was filed, or within 2 years from the date the tax was paid, whichever date is later.

State reporting requirements. See *Amended returns* under *General Instruction F.*

Need a copy of an old return or form? Use Form 4506-A to obtain a copy of a previously filed return. You can obtain blank forms for prior years by calling 1-800-TAX-FORM (1-800-829-3676).

-5-

M. Penalty for Failure To File Timely, Completely, or Correctly

To avoid filing an incomplete return or having to respond to requests for missing information, see *General Instruction B*.

Against the organization. If an organization does not file timely and completely, or does not furnish the correct information, it must pay $20 for each day the failure continues ($100 a day if it is a large organization), unless it can show that the failure was due to reasonable cause. Those filing late (after the due date, including extensions) must attach an explanation to the return. The maximum penalty for each return will not exceed the smaller of $10,000 ($50,000 for a large organization) or 5% of the gross receipts of the organization for the year.

Large organization. A large organization is one that has gross receipts exceeding $1 million for the tax year.

Gross receipts. Gross receipts means the gross amount received during the foundation's annual accounting period from all sources without reduction for any costs or expenses.

To figure the foundation's gross receipts, start with Part I, line 12, column (a), then add to it lines 6b and 10b, then subtract line 6a from that amount.

Against the responsible person. The IRS will make written demand that the delinquent return be filed or the information furnished within a reasonable time after the mailing of the notice of the demand. The person failing to comply with the demand on or before the date specified will have to pay $10 for each day the failure continues, unless there is reasonable cause. The maximum penalty imposed on all persons for any one return is $5,000. If more than one person is liable for any failures, all such persons are jointly and severally liable for such failures (see section 6652(c)).

Other penalties. Because this return also satisfies the filing requirements of a tax return under section 6011 for the tax on investment income imposed by section 4940 (or 4948 if an exempt foreign organization), the penalties imposed by section 6651 for not filing a return (without reasonable cause) also apply.

There are also criminal penalties for willful failure to file and for filing fraudulent returns and statements. See sections 7203, 7206, and 7207.

N. Penalties for Not Paying Tax on Time

There is a penalty for not paying tax when due (section 6651). The penalty generally is $1/2$ of 1% of the unpaid tax for each month or part of a month the tax remains unpaid, not to exceed 25% of the unpaid

tax. If there was reasonable cause for not paying the tax on time, the penalty can be waived. However, interest is charged on any tax not paid on time, at the rate provided by section 6621.

Estimated tax penalty. The section 6655 penalty for failure to pay estimated tax applies to the tax on net investment income of domestic private foundations and section 4947(a)(1) nonexempt charitable trusts. The penalty also applies to any tax on unrelated business income of a private foundation. Generally, if a private foundation's tax liability is $500 or more and it did not make the required payments on time, then it is subject to the penalty.

For more details, see the discussion of Form 2220 in *General Instruction D*.

O. Figuring and Paying Estimated Tax

A domestic exempt private foundation, a domestic taxable private foundation, or a nonexempt charitable trust treated as a private foundation must make estimated tax payments for the excise tax based on investment income if it can expect its estimated tax (section 4940 tax minus allowable credits) to be $500 or more. The number of installment payments it must make under the depository method is determined at the time during the year that it first meets this requirement. For calendar-year taxpayers, the first deposit of estimated taxes for a year generally should be made by May 15 of the year.

Although Form 990-W is used primarily to compute the installment payments of unrelated business income tax, it is also used to determine the timing and amounts of installment payments of the section 4940 tax based on investment income. Compute separately any required deposits of excise tax based on investment income and unrelated business income tax.

To figure the estimated tax for the excise tax based on investment income, apply the rules of Part VI to your tax year 2006 estimated amounts for that part. Enter the tax you figured on line 10a of Form 990-W.

The Form 990-W line items and instructions for large organizations also apply to private foundations. For purposes of paying the estimated tax on net investment income, a "large organization" is one that had net investment income of $1 million or more for any of the 3 tax years immediately preceding the tax year involved.

Penalty. A foundation that does not pay the proper estimated tax when due may be subject to the estimated tax penalty for the period of the underpayment. (See sections 6655(b) and (d) and the Form 2220 instructions.)

Special Rules

Section 4947(a)(1) nonexempt charitable trusts. Form 1041-ES should be used to pay any estimated tax on income subject to tax under section 1. Form 1041-ES also contains the estimated tax rules for paying the tax on that income.

Taxable private foundations. Form 1120-W should be used to figure any estimated tax on income subject to tax under section 11. Form 1120-W contains the estimated tax rules for paying the tax on that income.

P. Tax Payment Methods for Domestic Private Foundations

Whether the foundation uses the depository method of tax payment or the special option for small foundations, it must pay the tax due (see Part VI) in full by the 15th day of the 5th month after the end of its tax year.

Depository Method of Tax Payment

Some foundations (described below) are required to electronically deposit all depository taxes, including their tax payments for the excise tax based on investment income.

Electronic Deposit Requirement

The foundation must make electronic deposits of all depository taxes (such as employment tax or the excise tax based on investment income) using the Electronic Federal Tax Payment System (EFTPS) in 2006 if:
• The total deposits of such taxes in 2004 were more than $200,000, or
• The foundation was required to use EFTPS in 2005.

If the foundation is required to use EFTPS and fails to do so, it may be subject to a 10% penalty. If the foundation is not required to use EFTPS, it may participate voluntarily. To enroll in or get more information about EFTPS, call 1-800-555-4477. To enroll online, visit *www.irs.gov*.

Depositing on time. For deposits made by EFTPS to be on time, the foundation must initiate the transaction at least 1 business day before the date the deposit is due.

Deposits With Form 8109

If the foundation does not use EFTPS, deposit estimated tax payments and any balance due for the excise tax based on investment income with Form 8109, Federal Tax Deposit Coupon. If you do not have a preprinted Form 8109, use Form 8109-B to make deposits. You can get this form only by calling 1-800-829-4933. Be sure to have your employer identification number (EIN) ready when you call.

-6-

Form 990-PF Instructions

Do not send deposits directly to an IRS office; otherwise, the foundation may have to pay a penalty. Mail or deliver the completed Form 8109 with the payment to an authorized depositary, such as, a commercial bank or other financial institution authorized to accept federal tax deposits.

Make checks or money orders payable to the depositary. To help ensure proper crediting, write the foundation's EIN, the tax period to which the deposit applies, and "Form 990-PF" on the check or money order. Be sure to darken the 990-PF box on the coupon. Records of these deposits will be sent to the IRS.

For more information on deposits, see the instructions in the coupon booklet (Form 8109) and Pub. 583, Starting a Business and Keeping Records.

Special Payment Option for Small Foundations

A private foundation may enclose a check or money order, payable to the United States Treasury, with the Form 990-PF or Form 8868, if it meets all of the following requirements:

1. The foundation must not be required to use EFTPS,
2. The tax based on investment income shown on line 5, Part VI of Form 990-PF is less than $500, and
3. If Form 8868 is used, the amount entered on line 3a of Part I or line 8a of Part II of Form 8868 must be less than $500 and it must be the full balance due.

Be sure to write "2005 Form 990-PF" and the foundation's name, address, and EIN on its check or money order.

 Foreign organizations should see the instructions for Part VI, line 9.

Q. Public Inspection Requirements

A private foundation must make its annual returns (including any amended returns) and exemption application available for public inspection.

Definitions

Annual returns. An annual return is an exact copy of the Form 990-PF that was filed with the IRS including all schedules, attachments, and supporting documents. It also includes any amendments to the original return (amended return).

By annual returns, we mean any annual return (defined above) that is not more than 3 years old from the later of:

1. The date the return is required to be filed (including extensions), or
2. The date that the return is actually filed.

Exemption application. An application for tax exemption includes (except as described later):

Form 990-PF Instructions

• Any prescribed application form (such as Form 1023 or Form 1024),
• All documents and statements the IRS requires an applicant to file with the form,
• Any statement or other supporting document submitted in support of the application, and
• Any letter or other document issued by the IRS concerning the application.

An application for tax exemption does not include:
• Any application for tax exemption filed before July 15, 1987, unless the private foundation filing the application had a copy of the application on July 15, 1987, or
• Any material that is not available for public inspection under section 6104.

Who Must Make the Annual Returns and Exemption Application Available for Public Inspection?

The foundation's annual returns and exemption application must be made available to the public by the private foundation itself and by the IRS.

How Does a Private Foundation Make Its Annual Returns and Exemption Application Available for Public Inspection?

A private foundation must make its annual returns and exemption application available in 2 ways:
• By office visitation, and
• By providing copies or making them widely available.

Public Inspection by Office Visitation

A private foundation must make its annual returns and exemption application available for public inspection without charge at its principal, regional, and district offices during regular business hours.

Conditions that may be set for public inspection at the office. A private foundation:
• May have an employee present,
• Must allow the individual conducting the inspection to take notes freely during the inspection, and
• Must allow an individual to make photo copies of documents at no charge but only if the individual brings photocopying equipment to the place of inspection.

Determining if a site is a regional or district office. A regional or district office is any office of a private foundation, other than its principal office, that has paid employees whose total number of paid hours a week are normally 120 hours or more. Include the hours worked by part-time (as well as full-time) employees in making that determination.

What sites are not considered a regional or district office. A site is not considered a regional or district office if:

1. The only services provided at the site further the foundations exempt

-7-

purposes (e.g., day care, health care, or scientific or medical research), and
2. The site does not serve as an office for management staff, other than managers who are involved only in managing the exempt function activities at the site.

What if the private foundation does not maintain a permanent office? If the private foundation does not maintain a permanent office, it will comply with the public inspection requirement by office visitation requirement by making the annual returns and exemption application available at a reasonable location of its choice. It must permit public inspection:
• Within a reasonable amount of time after receiving a request for inspection (normally, not more than 2 weeks), and
• At a reasonable time of day.

Optional method of complying. If a private foundation that does not have a permanent office wishes not to allow an inspection by office visitation, it may mail a copy of the requested documents instead of allowing an inspection. However, it must mail the documents within 2 weeks of receiving the request and may charge for copying and postage only if the requester consents to the charge.

Private foundations with a permanent office but limited or no hours. Even if a private foundation has a permanent office but no office hours or very limited hours during certain times of the year, it must still meet the office visitation requirement. To meet this requirement during those periods when office hours are limited or not available, follow the rules above under, *What if the private foundation does not maintain a permanent office?*

Public Inspection—Providing Copies

A private foundation must provide copies of its annual returns or exemption application to any individual who makes a request for a copy in person or in writing unless it makes these documents widely available.

In-person requests for document copies. A private foundation must provide copies to any individual who makes a request in person at the private foundation's principal, regional, or district offices during regular business hours on the same day that the individual makes the request.

Accepted delay in fulfilling an in-person request. If unusual circumstances exist and fulfilling a request on the same day places an unreasonable burden on the private foundation, it must provide copies by the earlier of:
• The next business day following the day that the unusual circumstances end, or
• The fifth business day after the date of the request.

Examples of unusual circumstances include:
• Receipt of a volume of requests (for document copies) that exceeds the private foundations daily capacity to make copies,
• Requests received shortly before the end of regular business hours that require an extensive amount of copying, or
• Requests received on a day when the organization's managerial staff capable of fulfilling the request is conducting official duties (e.g., student registration or attending an off-site meeting or convention) instead of its regular administrative duties.

Use of local agents for providing copies. A private foundation may use a local agent to handle in-person requests for document copies. If a private foundation uses a local agent, it must immediately provide the local agent's name, address, and telephone number to the requester.

The local agent must:
• Be located within reasonable proximity to the principal, regional, or district office where the individual makes the request, and
• Provide document copies within the same time frames as the private foundation.

Written requests for document copies. If a private foundation receives a written request for a copy of its annual returns or exemption application (or parts of these documents), it must give a copy to the requester. However, this rule only applies if the request:
• Is addressed to a private foundation's principal, regional, or district office,
• Is delivered to that address by mail, electronic mail (email), facsimile (fax), or a private delivery service approved by the IRS (see *Private Delivery Services* on page 5 for a list), and
• Gives the address to which the document copies should be sent.

How and when a written request is fulfilled.
• Requested document copies must be mailed within 30 days from the date the private foundation receives the request.
• Unless other evidence exists, a request or payment that is mailed is considered to be received by the private foundation 7 days after the postmark date.
• If an advance payment is required, copies must be provided within 30 days from the date payment is received.
• If the private foundation requires payment in advance and it receives a request without payment or with insufficient payment, it must notify the requester of the prepayment policy and the amount due within 7 days from the date it receives the request.
• A request that is transmitted to the private foundation by email or fax is considered received the day the request is transmitted successfully.

• Requested documents can be emailed instead of the traditional method of mailing if the requester consents to this method.

A document copy is considered as provided on the:
• Postmark date,
• Private delivery date,
• Registration date for certified or registered mail,
• Postmark date on the sender's receipt for certified or registered mail, or
• Day the email is successfully transmitted (if the requester agreed to this method).

Requests for parts of a document copy. A person can request all or any specific part or schedule of the annual returns or exemption application and the private foundation must fulfill their request for a copy.

Can an agent be used to provide copies? A private foundation can use an agent to provide document copies for the written requests it receives. However, the agent must provide the document copies under the same conditions that are imposed on the private foundation itself. Also, if an agent fails to provide the documents as required, the private foundation will continue to be subject to penalties.

Example. The ABC Foundation retained an agent to provide copies for all written requests for documents. However, ABC Foundation received a request for document copies before the agent did.

The deadline for providing a response is referenced by the date that the ABC Foundation received the request and not when the agent received it. If the agent received the request first, then a response would be referenced to the date that the agent received it.

Can a fee be charged for providing copies? A private foundation may charge a reasonable fee for providing copies. Also, it can require the fee to be paid before providing a copy of the requested document.

What is a reasonable fee? A fee is reasonable only if it is no more than the per-page copying fee charged by the IRS for providing copies, plus no more than the actual postage costs incurred to provide the copies.

What forms of payment must the private foundation accept? The form of payment depends on whether the request for copies is made in person or in writing.

Cash and money order must be accepted for in-person requests for document copies. The private foundation, if it wishes, may accept additional forms of payment.

Certified check, money order, and either personal check or credit card must be accepted for written requests for document copies. The private foundation, if it wishes, may accept additional forms of payment.

Other fee information. If a private foundation provides a requester with notice of a fee and the requester does not pay the fee within 30 days, it may ignore the request.

If a requester's check does not clear on deposit, it may ignore the request.

If a private foundation does not require prepayment and the requester does not prepay, the private foundation must receive consent from the requester if the copying and postage charge exceeds $20.

Private foundations subject to a harassment campaign. If the IRS determines that a private foundation is being harassed, it is not required to comply with any request for copies that it reasonably believes is part of the harassment campaign.

A group of requests for a private foundation's annual returns or exemption application is indicative of a harassment campaign if the requests are part of a single coordinated effort to disrupt the operations of the private foundation rather than to collect information about it.

See Regulations section 301.6104(d)-3 for more information.

Requests that may be disregarded without IRS approval. A private foundation may disregard any request for copies of all or part of any document beyond the first two received within any 30-day period or the first four received within any 1-year period from the same individual or the same address.

Making the Annual Returns and Exemption Application Widely Available

A private foundation does not have to provide copies of its annual returns and/or its exemption application if it makes these documents widely available. However, it must still allow public inspection by office visitation.

How does a private foundation make its annual returns and exemption application widely available? A private foundation's annual returns and/or exemption application is widely available if it meets all four of the following requirements:

1. The internet posting requirement— This is met if:
• The document is posted on a World Wide Web page that the private foundation establishes and maintains, or
• The document is posted as part of a database of like documents of other tax-exempt organizations on a World Wide Web page established and maintained by another entity.

2. Additional posting information requirement—This is met if:
• The World Wide Web page through which the document is available clearly informs readers that the document is available and provides instructions for downloading the document;

Form 990-PF Instructions

• After it is downloaded and viewed, the web document exactly reproduces the image of the annual returns or exemption application as it was originally filed with the IRS, except for any information permitted by statute to be withheld from public disclosure; and

• Any individual with access to the Internet can access, download, view, and print the document without special computer hardware or software required for that format (except software that is readily available to members of the public without payment of any fee) and without payment of a fee to the private foundation or to another entity maintaining the web page.

3. Reliability and accuracy requirements—To meet this, the entity maintaining the World Wide Web page must:

• Have procedures for ensuring the reliability and accuracy of the document that it posts on the page;

• Take reasonable precautions to prevent alteration, destruction, or accidental loss of the document when posted on its page; and

• Correct or replace the document if a posted document is altered, destroyed, or lost.

4. Notice requirement—To meet this, a private foundation must notify any individual requesting a copy of its annual returns and/or exemption application where the documents are available (including the Internet address). If the request is made in person, the private foundation must notify the individual immediately. If the request is in writing, it must notify the individual within 7 days of receiving the request.

Penalties

A penalty may be imposed on any person who does not make the annual returns (including all required attachments to each return) or the exemption application available for public inspection according to the section 6104(d) rules discussed above. If more than one person fails to comply, each person is jointly and severally liable for the full amount of the penalty. The penalty amount is $20 for each day during which a failure occurs. The maximum penalty that may be imposed on all persons for any 1 annual return is $10,000. There is no maximum penalty amount for failure to make the exemption application available for public inspection.

Any person who willfully fails to comply with the section 6104(d) public inspection requirements is subject to an additional penalty of $5,000 (section 6685).

Requirements Placed on the IRS

A private foundation's annual returns and approved exemption application may be inspected by the public at an IRS office for your area or at the IRS National Office in Washington, DC.

To request a copy or to inspect an annual return or an approved exemption application, complete Form 4506-A. Generally, there is a charge for photocopying.

Also, the IRS can provide a complete set of Form 990-PF returns filed for a year on CD-ROM. A partial set of Form 990-PF returns filed by state or by month is also available. Call 1-877-829-5500 or write to the address below for details.

Internal Revenue Service
TE/GE Customer Account Services
P.O. Box 2508
Cincinnati, OH 45201

R. Disclosures Regarding Certain Information and Services Furnished

A section 501(c) organization that offers to sell or solicits money for specific information or a routine service to any individual that could be obtained by the individual from a Federal Government agency free or for a nominal charge must disclose that fact conspicuously when making such offer or solicitation.

Any organization that intentionally disregards this requirement will be subject to a penalty for each day the offers or solicitations are made. The penalty is the greater of $1,000 or 50% of the total cost of the offers and solicitations made on that day.

S. Organizations Organized or Created in a Foreign Country or U.S. Possession

If you apply any provision of any U.S. tax treaty to compute the foundation's taxable income, tax liability, or tax credits in a manner different from the 990-PF instructions, attach an explanation.

Regulations section 53.4948-1(b) states that sections 507, 508, and Chapter 42 (other than section 4948) do not apply to a foreign private foundation that from the date of its creation has received at least 85% of its support (as defined in section 509(d), other than section 509(d)(4)) from sources outside the United States.

Section 4948(a) imposes a 4% tax on the gross investment income from U.S. sources (such as, income from dividends, interest, rents, payments received on securities loans (as defined in section 512(a)(5)), and royalties not reported on Form 990-T of an exempt foreign private foundation. This tax replaces the section 4940 tax on the net investment income of a domestic private foundation. To pay any tax due, see the instructions for Part VI, line 9.

Taxable foreign private foundations and foreign section 4947(a)(1) nonexempt

charitable trusts are not subject to the excise taxes under sections 4948(a) and 4940, but are subject to income tax under subtitle A of the Code.

Certain foreign foundations are not required to send copies of annual returns to state officials, or comply with the public inspection and notice requirements of annual returns. (See General Instructions G and Q.)

T. Liquidation, Dissolution, Termination, or Substantial Contraction

If there is a liquidation, dissolution, termination, or substantial contraction (defined below) of the organization, attach:

• A statement to the return explaining it,
• A certified copy of the liquidation plan, resolution, etc. (if any) and all amendments or supplements that were not previously filed,
• A schedule that lists the names and addresses of all recipients of assets, and
• An explanation of the nature and fair market value of the assets distributed to each recipient.

Additional requirements. For a complete corporate liquidation or trust termination, attach a statement as to whether a final distribution of assets was made and the date it was made (if applicable).

Also, an organization must indicate:
• That it has ceased to exist, check the "Final Return" box in G at the top of page 1 of the return, or
• Is terminating its private foundation status under section 507(b)(1)(B), see General Instructions U and V, or
• Is voluntarily terminating its private foundation status under section 507(a)(1) and owes a termination tax, send the notice (and tax payment, if applicable) required by Rev. Rul. 2003-13, 2003-4 I.R.B. 305, and Rev. Rul. 2002-28, 2002–20, I.R.B. 941 (2002-1 C.B., 941) to the Manager, Exempt Organizations Determinations, at the address given in General Instruction U.

Relief from public inspection requirements. If the organization has terminated its private foundation status under section 507(b)(1)(A), it does not have to comply with the notice and public inspection requirements of their return for the termination year.

Filing date. See General Instruction J for the filing date.

Definitions. The term substantial contraction includes any partial liquidation or any other significant disposition of assets. However, this does not include transfers for full and adequate consideration or distributions of current income.

-9-

8-97

A significant disposition of assets does not include any disposition for a tax year if:

1. The total of the dispositions for the tax year is less than 25% of the fair market value of the net assets of the organization at the beginning of the tax year, and

2. The total of the related dispositions made during prior tax years (if a disposition is part of a series of related dispositions made during these prior tax years) is less than 25% of the fair market value of the net assets of the organization at the beginning of the tax year in which any of the series of related dispositions was made.

The facts and circumstances of the particular case will determine whether a significant disposition has occurred through a series of related dispositions. Ordinarily, a distribution described in section 170(b)(1)(E)(ii) (relating to private foundations making qualifying distributions out of corpus equal to 100% of contributions received during the foundation's tax year) will not be taken into account as a significant disposition of assets. See Regulations section 1.170A-9(g)(2).

U. Filing Requirements During Section 507(b)(1)(B) Termination

Although an organization terminating its private foundation status under section 507(b)(1)(B) may be regarded as a public charity for certain purposes, it is considered a private foundation for filing requirement purposes and it must file an annual return on Form 990-PF. The return must be filed for each year in the 60-month termination period, if that period has not expired before the due date of the return.

Regulations under section 507(b)(1)(B)(iii) specify that within 90 days after the end of the termination period the organization must supply information to the IRS establishing that it has terminated its private foundation status and, therefore, qualifies as a public charity. Send the information to:

Internal Revenue Service
TE/GE Customer Account Services
P.O. Box 2508
Cincinnati, OH 45201

If information is furnished establishing a successful termination, then, for the final year of the termination period, the organization should comply with the filing requirements for the type of public charity it has become. See the Instructions for Form 990 and Schedule A (Form 990 or 990-EZ) for details on filing requirements. This applies even if the IRS has not confirmed that the organization has terminated its private foundation status by the time the return for the final year of the termination is due (or would be due if a return were required).

The organization will be allowed a reasonable period of time to file any private foundation returns required (for the last year of the termination period) but not previously filed if it is later determined that the organization did not terminate its private foundation status. Interest on any tax due will be charged from the original due date of the Form 990-PF, but penalties under sections 6651 and 6652 will not be assessed if the Form 990-PF is filed within the period allowed by the IRS.

V. Special Rules for Section 507(b)(1)(B) Terminations

If the organization is terminating its private foundation status under the 60-month provisions of section 507(b)(1)(B), special rules apply. (See *General Instructions T and U.*) Under these rules, the organization may file Form 990-PF without paying the tax based on investment income if it filed a consent under section 6501(c)(4) with its notification to the TE/GE Customer Account Services at the Cincinnati address given in *General Instruction U* of its intention to begin a section 507(b)(1)(B) termination. The consent provides that the period of limitation on the assessment of tax under Chapter 42, based on investment income for any tax year in the 60-month period will not expire until at least 1 year after the period for assessing a deficiency for the last tax year in which the 60-month period would normally expire. Any foundation not paying the tax when it files Form 990-PF must attach a copy of the signed consent.

If the foundation did not file the consent, the tax must be paid in the normal manner as explained in *General Instructions O and P.* The organization may file a claim for refund after completing termination or during the termination period. The claim for refund must be filed on time and the organization must supply information establishing that it qualified as a public charity for the period for which it paid the tax.

W. Rounding, Currency, and Attachments

Rounding off to whole-dollars. You may round off cents to whole dollars on your return and schedules. If you do round to whole dollars, you must round all amounts. To round, drop amounts under 50 cents and increase amounts from 50 to 99 cents to the next dollar. For example, $1.39 becomes $1 and $2.50 becomes $3.

If you have to add two or more amounts to figure the amount to enter on a line, include cents when adding the amounts and round off only the total.

Currency and language requirements. Report all amounts in U.S. dollars (state conversion rate used). Report all items in total, including amounts from both U.S. and non-U.S. sources. All information must be in English.

Attachments. Use the schedules on Form 990-PF. If you need more space use attachments that are the same size as the printed forms.

On each attachment, write:
- "Form 990-PF,"
- The tax year,
- The corresponding schedule number or letter,
- The organization's name and EIN, and
- The information requested using the format and line sequence of the printed form.

Also, show totals on the printed forms.

Specific Instructions

Completing the Heading

The following instructions are keyed to items in the Form 990-PF heading.

Name and Address

If the organization received a Form 990-PF package from the IRS with a peel-off label, please use it. If the name or address on the label is wrong, make corrections on the label. The address used must be that of the principal office of the foundation.

Include the suite, room, or other unit number after the street address. If the Post Office does not deliver mail to the street address and the organization has a P.O. box, show the box number instead of the street address.

A—Employer Identification Number

The organization should have only one employer identification number. If it has more than one number, notify the Internal Revenue Service Center at the address shown under *General Instruction J.* Explain what numbers the organization has, the name and address to which each number was assigned, and the address of the organization's principal office. The IRS will then advise which number to use.

B—Telephone Number

Enter a foundation telephone number (including the area code) that the public and government regulators may use to obtain information about the foundation's finances and activities. This information should be available at this telephone number during normal business hours. If the foundation does not have a telephone, enter a telephone number of a foundation official who can provide this information during normal business hours.

-10-

Form 990-PF Instructions

D2—Foreign Organizations

If the foreign organization meets the 85% test of Regulations section 53.4948-1(b), then:

• Check the box in D2 on page 1 of Form 990-PF,

• Check the box at the top of Part XI,

• Do not fill in Parts XI and XIII,

• Do not fill in Part X unless it is claiming status as a private operating foundation, and

• Attach the computation of the 85% test to Form 990-PF.

E—Section 507(b)(1)(A) Terminations

A private foundation that has terminated its status as such under section 507(b)(1)(A), by distributing all its net assets to one or more public charities without keeping any right, title, or interest in those assets, should check the box in E on page 1 of Form 990-PF. See *General Instructions Q* and *T.*

F—60-Month Termination Under Section 507(b)(1)(B)

Check the box in F on page 1 of Form 990-PF if the organization is terminating its private foundation status under the 60-month provisions of section 507(b)(1)(B) during the period covered by this return. To begin such a termination, a private foundation must have given advance notice to TE/GE at the Cincinnati address given on page 10 and provided the information outlined in Regulations section 1.507-2(b)(3). See *General Instruction U* for information regarding filing requirements during a section 507(b)(1)(B) termination.

See *General Instruction V* for information regarding payment of the tax based on investment income (computed in Part VI) during a section 507(b)(1)(B) termination.

H—Type of Organization

Check the box for "Section 501(c)(3) exempt private foundation" if the foundation has a ruling or determination letter from the IRS in effect that recognizes its exemption from federal income tax as an organization described in section 501(c)(3) or if the organization's exemption application is pending with the IRS.

Check the "Section 4947(a)(1) nonexempt charitable trust" box if the trust is a nonexempt charitable trust treated as a private foundation. All others, check the "Other taxable private foundation" box.

I—Fair Market Value of All Assets

In block I on page 1 of Form 990-PF, enter the fair market value of all assets the foundation held at the end of the tax year.

Form 990-PF Instructions

 This amount should be the same as the figure reported in Part II, column (c), line 16.

Part I—Analysis of Revenue and Expenses

Column Instructions

The total of amounts in columns (b), (c), and (d) may not necessarily equal the amounts in column (a).

The amounts entered in column (a) and on line 5b must be analyzed in Part XVI-A.

Column (a)—Revenue and Expenses per Books

Enter in column (a) all items of revenue and expense shown in the books and records that increased or decreased the net assets of the organization. However, do not include the value of services donated to the foundation, or items such as the free use of equipment or facilities, in contributions received. Also, do not include any expenses used to compute capital gains and losses on lines 6, 7, and 8 or expenses included in cost of goods sold on line 10b.

Column (b)— Net Investment Income

All domestic private foundations (including section 4947(a)(1) nonexempt charitable trusts) are required to pay an excise tax each tax year on net investment income.

Exempt foreign foundations are subject to an excise tax on gross investment income from U.S. sources. These foreign organizations should complete lines 3, 4, 5, 11, 12, and 27b of column (b) and report only income derived from U.S. sources. No other income should be included. No expenses are allowed as deductions.

Definitions

Gross investment income. Gross investment income is the total amount of investment income that was received by a private foundation from all sources. However, it does not include any income subject to the unrelated business income tax. It includes interest, dividends, rents, payments with respect to securities loans (as defined in section 512(a)(5)), royalties received from assets devoted to charitable activities, income from notional principal contracts (as defined in Regulations section 1.863-7), and other substantially similar income from ordinary and routine investments excluded by section 512(b)(1). Therefore, interest received on a student loan is includible in the gross investment income of a private foundation making the loan.

Net investment income. Net investment income is the amount by which the sum of gross investment income and the capital gain net income exceeds the allowable deductions

discussed later. Tax-exempt interest on governmental obligations and related expenses are excluded.

Investment income. Include in column (b) all or part of any amount from column (a) that applies to investment income. However, do not include in column (b) any interest, dividends, rents or royalties (and related expenses) that were reported on Form 990-T.

For example, investment income from debt-financed property unrelated to the organization's charitable purpose and certain rents (and related expenses) treated as unrelated trade or business income should be reported on Form 990-T. Income from debt-financed property that is not taxed under section 511 is taxed under section 4940. Thus, if the debt/basis percentage of a debt-financed property is 80%, only 80% of the gross income (and expenses) for that property is used to figure the section 511 tax on Form 990-T. The remaining 20% of the gross income (and expenses) of that property is used to figure the section 4940 tax on net investment income on Form 990-T. (See Form 990-T and its instructions for more information.)

Investment expenses. Include in column (b) all ordinary and necessary expenses paid or incurred to produce or collect investment income from: interest, dividends, rents, amounts received from payments on securities loans (as defined in section 512(a)(5)), royalties, income from notional principal contracts, and other substantially similar income from ordinary and routine investments excluded by section 512(b)(1); or for the management, conservation, or maintenance of property held for the production of income that is taxable under section 4940.

If any of the expenses listed in column (a) are paid or incurred for both investment and charitable purposes, they must be allocated on a reasonable basis between the investment activities and the charitable activities so that only expenses from investment activities appear in column (b). Examples of allocation methods are given in the instructions for Part IX-A.

Limitation. The deduction for expenses paid or incurred in any tax year for producing gross investment income earned incident to a charitable function cannot be more than the amount of income earned from the function that is includible as gross investment income for the year.

For example, if rental income is incidentally realized in 2005 from historic buildings held open to the public, deductions for amounts paid or incurred in 2005 for the production of this income may not be more than the amount of rental income includible as gross investment income in column (b) for 2005.

-11-

8-99

Expenses related to tax-exempt interest. Do not include on lines 13–23 of column (b) any expenses paid or incurred that are allocable to tax-exempt interest that is excluded from lines 3 and 4.

Column (c)—Adjusted Net Income

 Nonoperating private foundations should see item 1 under Nonoperating private foundations on this page to find out if they need to complete column (c).

Private operating foundations. All organizations that claim status as private operating foundations under section 4942(j)(3) or (5) must complete all lines of column (c) that apply, according to the general rules for income and expenses that apply to this column, the specific line instructions for lines 3–27c, the Special rule, and Examples 1 and 2 below.

General rules. In general, adjusted net income is the amount of a private foundation's gross income that is more than the expenses of earning the income. The modifications and exclusions explained below are applied to gross income and expenses in figuring adjusted net income.

For income and expenses, include on each line of column (c) only that portion of the amount from column (a) that is applicable to the adjusted net income computation.

Income. For column (c), include income from charitable functions, investment activities, short-term capital gains from investments, amounts set aside, and unrelated trade or business activities. Do not include gifts, grants, or contributions, or long-term capital gains or losses.

Expenses. Deductible expenses include the part of a private foundation's operating expenses that is paid or incurred to produce or collect gross income reported on lines 3–11 of column (c). If only part of the property produces income includible in column (c), deductions such as interest, taxes, and rent must be divided between the charitable and noncharitable uses of the property. If the deductions for property used for a charitable, educational, or other similar purpose are more than the income from the property, the excess will not be allowed as a deduction but may be treated as a qualifying distribution in Part I, column (d). See Examples 1 and 2 below.

Special rule. The expenses attributable to each specific charitable activity, limited by the amount of income from the activity, must be reported in column (c) on lines 13–26. If the expenses of any charitable activity exceed the income generated by that activity, only the excess of these expenses over the income should be reported in column (d).

Examples.
1. A charitable activity generated $5,000 of income and $4,000 of expenses. Report all of the income and expenses in column (c) and none in column (d).

2. A charitable activity generated $5,000 of income and $6,000 of expenses. Report $5,000 of income and $5,000 of expenses in column (c) and the excess expenses of $1,000 in column (d).

Nonoperating private foundations. The following rules apply to nonoperating private foundations.
• If a nonoperating private foundation has no income from charitable activities that would be reportable on line 10 or line 11 of Part I, it does not have to make any entries in column (c).
• If a nonoperating private foundation has income from charitable activities, it must report that income only on lines 10 and/or 11 in column (c). These foundations do not need to report other kinds of income and expenses (such as investment income and expenses) in column (c).
• If a nonoperating private foundation has income that it reports on lines 10 and/or 11, report any expenses relating to this income following the general rules and the special rule. See Examples 1 and 2 above.

Column (d)—Disbursements for Charitable Purposes

Expenses entered in column (d) relate to activities that constitute the charitable purpose of the foundation.

For amounts entered in column (d):
• Use the cash receipts and disbursements method of accounting no matter what accounting method is used in keeping the books of the foundation;
• Do not include any amount or part of an amount that is included in column (b) or (c);
• Include on lines 13–25 all expenses, including necessary and reasonable administrative expenses, paid by the foundation for religious, charitable, scientific, literary, educational, or other public purposes, or for the prevention of cruelty to children or animals;
• Include a distribution of property at the fair market value on the date the distribution was made; and
• Include only the part entered in column (a) that is allocable to the charitable purposes of the foundation.

Example. An educational seminar produced $1,000 in income that was reportable in columns (a) and (c). Expenses attributable to this charitable activity were $1,900. Only $1,000 of expense should be reported in column (c) and the remaining $900 in expense should be reported in column (d).

Qualifying distributions. Generally, gifts and grants to organizations described in section 501(c)(3), that have been determined to be publicly supported charities (for example, organizations that are not private foundations as defined in section 509(a)), are qualifying distributions only if the granting foundation does not control the public charity.

 The total of the expenses and disbursements on line 26 is also entered on line 1a in Part XII to figure qualifying distributions.

Alternative to completing lines 13–25. If you want to provide an analysis of disbursements that is more detailed than column (d), you may attach a schedule instead of completing lines 13–25. The schedule must include all the specific items of lines 13–25, and the total from the schedule must be entered in column (d), line 26.

Line Instructions

Line 1—Contributions, gifts, grants, etc., received. Enter the total of gross contributions, gifts, grants, and similar amounts received.

Schedule B (Form 990, 990-EZ, or 990-PF). If money, securities, or other property valued at $5,000 or more was received directly or indirectly from any one person during the year, complete Schedule B and attach it to the return. If the foundation is not required to complete Schedule B (no person contributed $5,000 or more), be sure to check the box on line 2.

To determine whether a person has contributed $5,000 or more, total only gifts of $1,000 or more from each person. Separate and independent gifts need not be totaled if less than $1,000. If a contribution is in the form of property, describe the property and include its fair market value.

The term "person" includes individuals, fiduciaries, partnerships, corporations, associations, trusts, and exempt organizations.

Split-interest trusts. Distributions from split-interest trusts should be entered on line 1 of column (a). They are a part of the amount on line 1.

Substantiation requirements. An organization must keep records, required by the regulations under section 170, for all its charitable contributions.

Generally, a donor making a charitable contribution of $250 or more will not be allowed a federal income tax deduction unless the donor obtains a written acknowledgment from the donee organization by the earlier of the date on which the donor files a tax return for the tax year in which the contribution was made or the due date, including extensions, for filing that return. However, see section 170(f)(8) and Regulations section 1.170A-13 for exceptions to this rule.

The written acknowledgment the foundation provides to the donor must show:

-12-

Form 990-PF Instructions

1. The amount of cash contributed,
2. A description of any property contributed,
3. Whether the foundation provided any goods or services to the donor, and
4. A description and a good-faith estimate of the value of any goods or services the foundation gave in return for the contribution, unless:

a. The goods and services have insubstantial value, or

b. A statement is included that these goods and services consist solely of intangible religious benefits.

Generally, if a charitable organization solicits or receives a contribution of more than $75 for which it gives the donor something in return (a quid pro quo contribution), the organization must inform the donor, by written statement, that the amount of the contribution deductible for federal income tax purposes is limited to the amount by which the contribution exceeds the value of the goods or services received by the donor. The written statement must also provide the donor with a good-faith estimate of the value of goods or services given in return for the contribution.

Penalties. An organization that does not make the required disclosure for each quid pro quo contribution will incur a penalty of $10 for each failure, not to exceed $5,000 for a particular fundraising event or mailing, unless it can show reasonable cause for not providing the disclosure.

For more information. See Regulations section 1.170A-13 for more information on charitable recordkeeping and substantiation requirements.

Line 2. Check this box if the foundation is not required to attach Sch. B.

Line 3—Interest on savings and temporary cash investments.

In column (a). Enter the total amount of interest income from investments of the type reportable in Balance Sheets, Part II, line 2. These include savings or other interest-bearing accounts and temporary cash investments, such as money market funds, commercial paper, certificates of deposit, and U.S. Treasury bills or other government obligations that mature in less than 1 year.

In column (b). Enter the amount of interest income shown in column (a). Do not include interest on tax-exempt government obligations.

In column (c). Enter the amount of interest income shown in column (a). Include interest on tax-exempt government obligations.

Line 4—Dividends and interest from securities.

In column (a). Enter the amount of dividend and interest income from securities (stocks and bonds) of the type reportable in Balance Sheets, Part II, line 10. Include amounts received from

payments on securities loans, as defined in section 512(a)(5). Do not include any capital gain dividends reportable on line 6. Report income from program-related investments on line 11. For debt instruments with an original issue discount, report the original issue discount ratably over the life of the bond on line 4. See section 1272 for more information.

In column (b). Enter the amount of dividend and interest income, and payments on securities loans from column (a). Do not include interest on tax-exempt government obligations.

In column (c). Enter the amount of dividends and interest income, and payments on securities loans from column (a). Include interest on tax-exempt government obligations.

Line 5a—Gross rents.

In column (a). Enter the gross rental income for the year from investment property reportable on line 11 of Part II.

In columns (b) and (c). Enter the gross rental income from column (a).

Line 5b—Net rental income or (loss). Figure the net rental income or (loss) for the year and enter that amount on the entry line to the left of column (a).

Report rents from other sources on line 11, Other income. Enter any expenses attributable to the rental income reported on line 5, such as interest and depreciation, on lines 13–23.

Line 6a—Net gain or (loss) from sale of assets. Enter the net gain or (loss) per books from all asset sales not included on line 10.

For assets sold and not included in Part IV, attach a schedule showing:
• Date acquired,
• Manner of acquisition,
• Gross sales price,
• Cost, other basis, or value at time of acquisition (if donated) and which of these methods was used,
• Date sold,
• To whom sold,
• Expense of sale and cost of improvements made subsequent to acquisition, and
• Depreciation since acquisition (if depreciable property).

Line 6b—Gross sales price for all assets on line 6a. Enter the gross sales price from all asset sales whose net gain or loss was reported on line 6a.

Line 7—Capital gain net income. Enter the capital gain net income from Part IV, line 2. See Part IV instructions.

Line 8—Net short-term capital gain.

 Only private operating foundations report their short-term capital gains on line 8.

Include only net short-term capital gain for the year (assets sold or exchanged that were held not more than 1 year). Do not include a net long-term capital gain or a net loss in column (c).

Do not include on line 8 a net gain from the sale or exchange of depreciable property, or land used in a trade or business (section 1231) and held for more than 1 year. However, include a net loss from such property on line 23 as an Other expense.

In general, organizations may carry to line 8 the net short-term capital gain reported on Part IV, line 3. However, if the foundation had any short-term capital gain from sales of debt-financed property, add it to the amount reported on Part IV, line 3, to figure the amount to include on line 8. For the definition of "debt-financed property," see the Instructions for Form 990-T.

Line 9—Income modifications. Include on this line:

1. Amounts received or accrued as repayments of amounts taken into account as qualifying distributions;
2. Amounts received or accrued from the sale or other disposition of property to the extent that the acquisition of the property was considered a qualifying distribution for any tax year;
3. Any amount set aside for a specific project (see explanation in the instructions for Part XII) that was not necessary for the purposes for which it was set aside;
4. Income received from an estate, but only if the estate was considered terminated for income tax purposes due to a prolonged administration period; and
5. Amounts treated in an earlier tax year as qualifying distributions to:

• A nonoperating private foundation, if the amounts were not redistributed by the grantee organization by the close of its tax year following the year in which it received the funds, or
• An organization controlled by the distributing foundation or a disqualified person if the amounts were not redistributed by the grantee organization by the close of its tax year following the year in which it received the funds.

Lines 10a, b, c— Gross profit from sales of inventory. Enter the gross sales (less returns and allowances), cost of goods sold, and gross profit or (loss) from the sale of all inventory items, including those sold in the course of special events and activities. These inventory items are the ones the organization either makes to sell to others or buys for resale.

Do not report any sales or exchanges of investments on line 10.

Do not include any profit or (loss) from the sale of capital items such as securities, land, buildings, or equipment on line 10. Enter these amounts on line 6a.

Do not include any business expenses such as salaries, taxes, rent, etc., on line 10. Include them on lines 13–23.

Attach a schedule showing the following items: Gross sales, Cost of goods sold, Gross profit or (loss). These items should be classified according to type of inventory sold (such as books, tapes, other educational or religious material, etc.). The totals from the schedule should agree with the entries on lines 10a–10c.

In column (c), enter the gross profit or (loss) from sales of inventory shown in column (a), line 10c.

Line 11—Other income. Enter the total of all the foundation's other income for the year. Attach a schedule that gives a description and the amount of the income. Include all income not reported on lines 1 through 10c. Also, see the instructions for Part XVI-A, line 11.

Include imputed interest on certain deferred payments figured under section 483 and any investment income not reportable on lines 3 through 5, including income from program-related investments (defined in the instructions for Part IX-B).

Do not include unrealized gains and losses on investments carried at market value. Report those as fund balance or net asset adjustments in Part III.

In column (b). Enter the amount of investment income included in line 11, column (a). Include dividends, interest, rents, and royalties derived from assets devoted to charitable activities, such as interest on student loans.

In column (c). Include all other items includible in adjusted net income not covered elsewhere in column (c).

Line 12—Total. In column (b). Domestic organizations should enter the total of lines 3–11. Exempt foreign organizations, enter the total of lines 3, 4, 5, and 11 only.

Line 13—Compensation of officers, directors, trustees, etc.

In column (a). Enter the total compensation for the year of all officers, directors, and trustees. If none was paid, enter zero. Complete line 1 of Part VIII to show the compensation of officers, directors, trustees, and foundation managers.

In columns (b), (c), and (d). Enter the portion of the compensation included in column (a) that is applicable to the column. For example, in column (c) enter the portion of the compensation included in column (a) that was paid or incurred to produce or collect income included in column (c).

Line 14—Other employee salaries and wages. Enter the salaries and wages of all employees other than those included on line 13.

Line 15—Contributions to employee pension plans and other benefits. Enter the employer's share of the contributions the organization paid to qualified and nonqualified pension plans and the employer's share of contributions to employee benefit programs (such as insurance, health, and welfare programs) that are not an incidental part of a

pension plan. Complete the return/report of the Form 5500 series appropriate for the organization's plan. (See the Instructions for Form 5500 for information about employee welfare benefit plans required to file that form.)

Also include the amount of federal, state, and local payroll taxes for the year, but only those that are imposed on the organization as an employer. This includes the employer's share of social security and Medicare taxes, FUTA tax, state unemployment compensation tax, and other state and local payroll taxes. Do not include taxes withheld from employees' salaries and paid over to the various governmental units (such as federal and state income taxes and the employee's share of social security and Medicare taxes).

Lines 16a, b, and c—Legal, accounting, and other professional fees. On the appropriate line(s), enter the amount of legal, accounting, auditing, and other professional fees (such as fees for fundraising or investment services) charged by outside firms and individuals who are not employees of the foundation.

Attach a schedule for lines 16a, b, and c. Show the type of service and amount of expense for each. If the same person provided more than one of these services, include an allocation of those expenses.

Report any fines, penalties, or judgments imposed against the foundation as a result of legal proceedings on line 23, Other expenses.

Line 18—Taxes. Attach a schedule listing the type and amount of each tax reported on line 18. Do not enter any taxes included on line 15.

In column (a). Enter the taxes paid (or accrued) during the year. Include all types of taxes recorded on the books, including real estate tax not reported on line 20; the tax on investment income; and any income tax.

In column (b). Enter only those taxes included in column (a) that are related to investment income taxable under section 4940. Do not include the section 4940 tax paid or incurred on net investment income or the section 511 tax on unrelated business income. Sales taxes may not be deducted separately, but must be treated as a part of the cost of acquired property, or as a reduction of the amount realized on disposition of the property.

In column (c). Enter only those taxes included in column (a) that relate to income included in column (c). Do not include any excise tax paid or incurred on the net investment income (as shown in Part VI), or any tax reported on Form 990-T.

In column (d). Do not include any excise tax paid on investment income (as reported in Part VI of this return or the equivalent part of a return for prior years) unless the organization is claiming status

as a private operating foundation and completes Part XIV.

Line 19—Depreciation and depletion.

In column (a). Enter the expense recorded in the books for the year.

For depreciation, attach a schedule showing:
• A description of the property,
• The date acquired,
• The cost or other basis (exclude any land),
• The depreciation allowed or allowable in prior years,
• The method of computation,
• The rate (%) or life (years), and
• The depreciation this year.

On a separate line on the schedule, show the amount of depreciation included in cost of goods sold and not included on line 19.

In columns (b) and (c). A deduction for depreciation is allowed only for property used in the production of income reported in the column, and only using the straight line method of computing depreciation. A deduction for depletion is allowed but must be figured only using the cost depletion method.

The basis used in figuring depreciation and depletion is the basis determined under normal basis rules, without regard to the special rules for using the fair market value on December 31, 1969, that relate only to gain or loss on dispositions for purposes of the tax on net investment income.

Line 20—Occupancy. Enter the amount paid or incurred for the use of office space or other facilities. If the space is rented or leased, enter the amount of rent. If the space is owned, enter the amount of mortgage interest, real estate taxes, and similar expenses, but not depreciation (reportable on line 19). In either case, include the amount for utilities and related expenses (e.g., heat, lights, water, power, telephone, sewer, trash removal, outside janitorial services, and similar services). Do not include any salaries of the organization's own employees that are reportable on line 15.

Line 21—Travel, conferences, and meetings. Enter the expenses for officers, employees, or others during the year for travel, attending conferences, meetings, etc. Include transportation (including fares, mileage allowance, or automobile expenses), meals and lodging, and related costs whether paid on the basis of a per diem allowance or actual expenses incurred. Do not include any compensation paid to those who participate.

In column (b). Only 50% of the expense for business meals, etc., paid or incurred in connection with travel, meetings, etc., relating to the production of investment income, may be deducted in figuring net investment income (section 274(n)).

In column (c). Enter the total amount of expenses paid or incurred by officers, employees, or others for travel, conferences, meetings, etc., related to income included in column (c).

Line 22—Printing and publications. Enter the expenses for printing or publishing and distributing any newsletters, magazines, etc. Also include the cost of subscriptions to, or purchases of, magazines, newspapers, etc.

Line 23—Other expenses. Enter all other expenses for the year. Include all expenses not reported on lines 13–22. Attach a schedule showing the type and amount of each expense.

If a deduction is claimed for amortization, attach a schedule showing:
• Description of the amortized expenses;
• Date acquired, completed, or expended;
• Amount amortized;
• Deduction for prior years;
• Amortization period (number of months);
• Current-year amortization; and
• Total amount of amortization.

In column (c). In addition to the applicable portion of expenses from column (a), include any net loss from the sale or exchange of land or depreciable property that was held for more than 1 year and used in a trade or business.

A deduction for amortization is allowed but only for assets used for the production of income reported in column (c).

Line 25—Contributions, gifts, grants paid.

In column (a). Enter the total of all contributions, gifts, grants, and similar amounts paid (or accrued) for the year. List each contribution, gift, grant, etc., in Part XV, or attach a schedule of the items included on line 25 and list:
1. Each class of activity,
2. A separate total for each activity,
3. Name and address of donee,
4. Relationship of donee if related by:
   a. Blood,
   b. Marriage,
   c. Adoption, or
   d. Employment (including children of employees) to any disqualified person (see *General Instruction C* for definitions), and
5. The organizational status of donee (e.g., public charity—an organization described in section 509(a)(1), (2), or (3)).

You do not have to give the name of any indigent person who received one or more gifts or grants from the foundation unless that individual is a disqualified person or one who received a total of more than $1,000 from the foundation during the year.

Activities should be classified according to purpose and in greater detail than merely classifying them as charitable, educational, religious, or scientific activities. For example, use

identification such as: payments for nursing service, for fellowships, or for assistance to indigent families.

Foundations may include, as a single entry on the schedule, the total of amounts paid as grants for which the foundation exercised expenditure responsibility. Attach a separate report for each grant.

When the fair market value of the property at the time of disbursement is the measure of a contribution, the schedule must also show:
• A description of the contributed property,
• The book value of the contributed property,
• The method used to determine the book value,
• The method used to determine the fair market value, and
• The date of the gift.

TIP *The difference between fair market value and book value should be shown in the books of account and as a net asset adjustment in Part III.*

In column (d). Enter on line 25 all contributions, gifts, and grants the foundation paid during the year.
• Do not include contributions to organizations controlled by the foundation or by a disqualified person (see *General Instruction C* for definitions). Do not include contributions to nonoperating private foundations unless the donees are exempt from tax under section 501(c)(3), they redistribute the contributions, and they maintain sufficient evidence of redistributions according to the regulations under section 4942(g).
• Do not reduce the amount of grants paid in the current year by the amount of grants paid in a prior year that was returned or recovered in the current year. Report those repayments in column (c), line 9, and in Part XI, line 4a.
• Do not include any payments of set-asides (see *instructions for Part XII, line 3*) taken into account as qualifying distributions in the current year or any prior year. All set-asides are included in qualifying distributions (Part XII, line 3) in the year of the set-aside regardless of when paid.
• Do not include current year's write-offs of prior years' program-related investments. All program-related investments are included in qualifying distributions (Part XII, line 1b) in the year the investment is made.
• Do not include any payments that are not qualifying distributions as defined in section 4942(g)(1).

Net Amounts

Line 27a—Excess of revenue over expenses. Subtract line 26, column (a), from line 12, column (a). Enter the result. Generally, the amount shown in column (a) on this line is also the amount by which net assets (or fund balances) have

increased or decreased for the year. See the instructions for *Part III, Analysis of Changes in Net Assets or Fund Balances.*

Line 27b—Net investment income. Domestic organizations, subtract line 26 from line 12. Enter the result. Exempt foreign organizations, enter the amount shown on line 12. However, if the organization is a domestic organization and line 26 is more than line 12 (such as, expenses exceed income), enter zero (not a negative amount).

Line 27c—Adjusted net income. Subtract line 26, column (c) from line 12, column (c) and enter the result.

Part II—Balance Sheets

For column (b), show the book value at the end of the year. For column (c), show the fair market value at the end of the year. Attached schedules must show the end-of-year value for each asset listed in columns (b) and (c).
• Foundations whose books of account included total assets of $5,000 or more at any time during the year must complete all of columns (a), (b), and (c).
• Foundations with less than $5,000 of total assets per books at all times during the year must complete all of columns (a) and (b), and only line 16 of column (c).

Line 1—Cash—Non-interest-bearing. Enter the amount of cash on deposit in checking accounts, deposits in transit, change funds, petty cash funds, or any other non-interest-bearing account. Do not include advances to employees or officers or refundable deposits paid to suppliers or others.

Line 2—Savings and temporary cash investments. Enter the total of cash in savings or other interest-bearing accounts and temporary cash investments, such as money market funds, commercial paper, certificates of deposit, and U.S. Treasury bills or other governmental obligations that mature in less than 1 year.

Line 3—Accounts receivable. On the dashed lines to the left of column (a), enter the year-end figures for total accounts receivable and allowance for doubtful accounts from the sale of goods and/or the performance of services. In columns (a), (b), and (c), enter net amounts (total accounts receivable reduced by the corresponding allowance for doubtful accounts). Claims against vendors or refundable deposits with suppliers or others may be reported here if not significant in amount. (Otherwise, report them on line 15, Other assets.) Any receivables due from officers, directors, trustees, foundation managers, or other disqualified persons must be reported on line 6. Report receivables (including loans and advances) due from other employees on line 15.

Line 4—Pledges receivable. On the dashed lines to the left of column (a), enter the year-end figures for total pledges receivable and allowance for doubtful accounts (pledges estimated to be uncollectable). In columns (a), (b), and (c), enter net amounts (total pledges receivable reduced by the corresponding allowance for doubtful accounts).

Line 5—Grants receivable. Enter the total grants receivable from governmental agencies, foundations, and other organizations as of the beginning and end of the year.

Line 6—Receivables due from officers, directors, trustees, and other disqualified persons. Enter here (and on an attached schedule described below) all receivables due from officers, directors, trustees, foundation managers, and other disqualified persons and all secured and unsecured loans (including advances) to such persons. Disqualified person is defined in *General Instruction C.*

Attached schedules. (a) On the required schedule, report each loan separately, even if more than one loan was made to the same person, or the same terms apply to all loans made.

Salary advances and other advances for the personal use and benefit of the recipient and receivables subject to special terms or arising from transactions not functionally related to the foundation's charitable purposes must be reported as separate loans for each officer, director, etc.

(b) Receivables that are subject to the same terms and conditions (including credit limits and rate of interest) as receivables due from the general public from an activity functionally related to the foundation's charitable purposes may be reported as a single total for all the officers, directors, etc. Travel advances made for official business of the organization may also be reported as a single total.

For each outstanding loan or other receivable that must be reported separately, the attached schedule should show the following information (preferably in columnar form):

1. Borrower's name and title,
2. Original amount,
3. Balance due,
4. Date of note,
5. Maturity date,
6. Repayment terms,
7. Interest rate,
8. Security provided by the borrower,
9. Purpose of the loan, and
10. Description and fair market value of the consideration furnished by the lender (e.g., cash—$1,000; or 100 shares of XYZ, Inc., common stock— $9,000).

The above detail is not required for receivables or travel advances that may be reported as a single total (see *(b)* above); however, report and identify those totals separately on the attachment.

Line 7—Other notes and loans receivable. On the dashed lines to the left of column (a), enter the combined total year-end figures for notes receivable

and loans receivable and the allowance for doubtful accounts.

Notes receivable. In columns (a), (b), and (c), enter the amount of all notes receivable not listed on line 6 and not acquired as investments. Attach a schedule similar to the one for line 6. The schedule should also identify the relationship of the borrower to any officer, director, trustee, foundation manager, or other disqualified person.

For a note receivable from any section 501(c)(3) organization, list only the name of the borrower and the balance due on the required schedule.

Loans receivable. In columns (a), (b), and (c), enter the gross amount of loans receivable, minus the allowance for doubtful accounts, from the normal activities of the filing organization (such as scholarship loans). An itemized list of these loans is not required but attach a schedule showing the total amount of each type of outstanding loan. Report loans to officers, directors, trustees, foundation managers, or other disqualified persons on line 6 and loans to other employees on line 15.

Line 8—Inventories for sale or use. Enter the amount of materials, goods, and supplies purchased or manufactured by the organization and held for sale or use in some future period.

Line 9—Prepaid expenses and deferred charges. Enter the amount of short-term and long-term prepayments of expenses attributable to one or more future accounting periods. Examples include prepayments of rent, insurance, and pension costs, and expenses incurred in connection with a solicitation campaign to be conducted in a future accounting period.

Lines 10a, b, and c—Investments— government obligations, corporate stocks and bonds. Enter the book value (which may be market value) of these investments.

Attach a schedule that lists each security held at the end of the year and shows whether the security is listed at cost (including the value recorded at the time of receipt in the case of donated securities) or end-of-year market value. Do not include amounts shown on line 2. Governmental obligations reported on line 10a are those that mature in 1 year or more. Debt securities of the U.S. Government may be reported as a single total rather than itemized. Obligations of state and municipal governments may also be reported as a lump-sum total. Do not combine U.S. Government obligations with state and municipal obligations on this schedule.

Line 11—Investments—land, buildings, and equipment. On the dashed lines to the left of column (a), enter the year-end book value (cost or other basis) and accumulated depreciation of all land, buildings, and

equipment held for investment purposes, such as rental properties. In columns (a) and (b), enter the book value of all land, buildings, and equipment held for investment less accumulated depreciation. In column (c), enter the fair market value of these assets. Attach a schedule listing these investment fixed assets held at the end of the year and showing, for each item or category listed, the cost or other basis, accumulated depreciation, and book value.

Line 12—Investments—mortgage loans. Enter the amount of mortgage loans receivable held as investments but do not include program-related investments (see *instructions for line 15*).

Line 13—Investments—other. Enter the amount of all other investment holdings not reported on lines 10 through 12. Attach a schedule listing and describing each of these investments held at the end of the year. Show the book value for each and indicate whether the investment is listed at cost or end-of-year market value. Do not include program-related investments (see *instructions for line 15*).

Line 14—Land, buildings, and equipment. On the dashed lines to the left of column (a), enter the year-end book value (cost or other basis) and accumulated depreciation of all land, buildings, and equipment owned by the organization and not held for investment. In columns (a) and (b), enter the book value of all land, buildings, and equipment not held for investment less accumulated depreciation. In column (c), enter the fair market value of these assets. Include any property, plant, and equipment owned and used by the organization to conduct its charitable activities. Attach a schedule listing these fixed assets held at the end of the year and showing the cost or other basis, accumulated depreciation, and book value of each item or category listed.

Line 15—Other assets. List and show the book value of each category of assets not reportable on lines 1 through 14. Attach a separate schedule if more space is needed.

One type of asset reportable on line 15 is program-related investments. These are investments made primarily to accomplish a charitable purpose of the filing organization rather than to produce income.

Line 16—Total assets. All filers must complete line 16 of columns (a), (b), and (c). These entries represent the totals of lines 1 through 15 of each column. However, organizations that have assets of less than $5,000 per books at all times during the year need not complete lines 1 through 15 of column (c).

 The column (c) amount is also entered on the entry space for I on page 1.

Line 17—Accounts payable and accrued expenses. Enter the total of accounts payable to suppliers and others and accrued expenses, such as salaries payable, accrued payroll taxes, and interest payable.

Line 18—Grants payable. Enter the unpaid portion of grants and awards that the organization has made a commitment to pay other organizations or individuals, whether or not the commitments have been communicated to the grantees.

Line 19—Deferred revenue. Include revenue that the organization has received but not yet earned as of the balance sheet date under its method of accounting.

Line 20—Loans from officers, directors, trustees, and other disqualified persons. Enter the unpaid balance of loans received from officers, directors, trustees, and other disqualified persons. For loans outstanding at the end of the year, attach a schedule that shows (for each loan) the name and title of the lender and the information listed in items 2 through 10 of the instructions for line 6 on page 15.

Line 21—Mortgages and other notes payable. Enter the amount of mortgages and other notes payable at the beginning and end of the year. Attach a schedule showing, as of the end of the year, the total amount of all mortgages payable and, for each nonmortgage note payable, the name of the lender and the information specified in items 2 through 10 of the instructions for line 6. The schedule should also identify the relationship of the lender to any officer, director, trustee, foundation manager, or other disqualified person.

Line 22—Other liabilities. List and show the amount of each liability not reportable on lines 17 through 21. Attach a separate schedule if more space is needed.

Lines 24 Through 30—Net Assets or Fund Balances

Organizations that follow SFAS 117. If the organization follows SFAS 117, check the box above line 24. Classify and report net assets in three groups—unrestricted, temporarily restricted, and permanently restricted—based on the existence or absence of donor-imposed restrictions and the nature of those restrictions. Show the sum of the three classes of net assets on line 30. On line 31, add the amounts on lines 23 and 30 to show total liabilities and net assets. This figure should be the same as the figure for Total assets on line 16.

Line 24—Unrestricted. Enter the balances per books of the unrestricted class of net assets. Unrestricted net assets are neither permanently restricted nor temporarily restricted by donor-imposed stipulations. All funds without donor-imposed restrictions must be classified as unrestricted, regardless

of the existence of any board designations or appropriations.

Line 25—Temporarily restricted. Enter the balances per books of the temporarily restricted class of net assets. Donors' temporary restrictions may require that resources be used in a later period or after a specified date (time restrictions), or that resources be used for a specified purpose (purpose restrictions), or both.

Line 26—Permanently restricted. Enter the total of the balances for the permanently restricted class of net assets. Permanently restricted net assets are (a) assets, such as land or works of art, donated with stipulations that they be used for a specified purpose, be preserved, and not be sold or (b) assets donated with stipulations that they be invested to provide a permanent source of income. The latter result from gifts and bequests that create permanent endowment funds.

Organizations that do not follow SFAS 117. If the organization does not follow SFAS 117, check the box above line 27 and report account balances on lines 27 through 29. Report net assets or fund balances on line 30. Also complete line 31 to report the sum of the total liabilities and net assets/fund balances.

Line 27—Capital stock, trust principal, or current funds. For corporations, enter the balance per books for capital stock accounts. Show par or stated value (or for stock with no par or stated value, total amount received upon issuance) of all classes of stock issued and, as yet, uncancelled. For trusts, enter the amount in the trust principal or corpus account. For organizations continuing to use the fund method of accounting, enter the fund balances for the organization's current restricted and unrestricted funds.

Line 28—Paid-in or capital surplus, or land, building, and equipment fund. Enter the balance per books for all paid-in capital in excess of par or stated value for all stock issued and uncancelled. If stockholders or others gave donations that the organization records as paid-in capital, include them here. Report any current-year donations you included on line 28 in Part I, line 1. The fund balance for the land, building, and equipment fund would be entered here.

Line 29—Retained earnings, accumulated income, endowment, or other funds. For corporations, enter the balance in the retained earnings, or similar account, minus the cost of any corporate treasury stock. For trusts, enter the balance per books in the accumulated income or similar account. For organizations using fund accounting, enter the total of the fund balances for the permanent and term endowment funds as well as balances of any other funds not reported on lines 27 and 28.

Line 30—Total net assets or fund balances. For organizations that follow SFAS 117, enter the total of lines 24

through 26. For all other organizations, enter the total of lines 27 through 29. Enter the beginning-of-year figure in column (a) on line 1, Part III. The end-of-year figure in column (b) must agree with the figure in Part III, line 6.

Line 31—Total liabilities and net assets/fund balances. Enter the total of lines 23 and 30. This amount must equal the amount for total assets reported on line 16 for both the beginning and end of the year.

Part III—Analysis of Changes in Net Assets or Fund Balances

Generally, the excess of revenue over expenses accounts for the difference between the net assets at the beginning and end of the year.

On line 2, Part III, re-enter the figure from Part I, line 27(a), column (a).

On lines 3 and 5, list any changes in net assets that were not caused by the receipts or expenses shown in Part I, column (a). For example, if a foundation follows FASB Statement No. 12 and shows an asset in the ending balance sheet at a higher value than in the beginning balance sheet because of an increased market value (after a larger decrease in a prior year), include the increase in Part III, line 3.

If the organization uses a stepped-up basis to determine gains on sales of assets included in Part I, column (a), then include the amount of step-up in basis in Part III. If you entered a contribution, gift, or grant of property valued at fair market value on line 25 of Part I, column (a), the difference between fair market value and book value should be shown in the books of account and as a net asset adjustment in Part III.

Part IV—Capital Gains and Losses for Tax on Investment Income

Use Part IV to figure the amount of net capital gain to report on lines 7 and 8 of Part I.
- Part IV does not apply to foreign organizations.
- Nonoperating private foundations may not have to figure their short-term capital gain or loss on line 3. See the rules for *Nonoperating private foundations* on page 12.

Private foundations must report gains and losses from the sale or other disposition of property:
- Held for investment purposes, or
- Used to produce unrelated business income; however, only include in net investment income the part of the gain or loss that is not included in the computation of its unrelated business taxable income.

Property held for investment purposes. Property is treated as held for investment purposes if the property is of a type that generally produces interest, dividends, rents, or royalties, even if the foundation disposes of the property as soon as it receives it.

Charitable use property. Do not include any gain or loss from disposing of property used for the foundation's charitable purposes in the computation of tax on net investment income. If the foundation uses property for its charitable purposes, but also incidentally derives income from the property that is subject to the net investment income tax, any gain or loss from the sale or other disposition of the property is not subject to the tax.

However, if the foundation uses property both for charitable purposes and (other than incidentally) for investment purposes, include in the computation of tax on net investment income the part of the gain or loss from the sale or disposition of the property that is allocable to the investment use of the property.

Program-related investments. Do not include gains or losses from the sale or exchange of program-related investments as defined in the instructions for Part IX-B.

Losses. If the disposition of investment property results in a loss, that loss may be subtracted from capital gains realized from the disposition of property during the same tax year but only to the extent of the gains. If losses are more than gains, the excess may not be subtracted from gross investment income, nor may the losses be carried back or forward to other tax years.

Basis. The basis for determining gain from the sale or other disposition of property is the larger of:

1. The fair market value of the property on December 31, 1969, plus or minus all adjustments after December 31, 1969, and before the date of disposition, if the foundation held the property on that date and continuously after that date until disposition, or

2. The basis of the property on the date of disposition under normal basis rules (actual basis). See Code sections 1011–1021.

The rules that generally apply to property dispositions reported in this part are:
• Section 1011, Adjusted basis for determining gain or loss;
• Section 1012, Basis of property—cost;
• Section 1014, Basis of property acquired from a decedent;
• Section 1015, Basis of property acquired by gifts and transfers in trust; and
• Section 1016, Adjustments to basis.

To figure a loss, basis on the date of disposition is determined under normal basis rules.

The completed Form 990-PF in Package 990-PF, Returns for Private Foundations or Section 4947(a)(1) Nonexempt Charitable Trusts Treated as Private Foundations, contains an example of a sale of investment property in which the gain was computed using the donor's basis under the rules of section 1015(a).

Part V—Qualification Under Section 4940(e) for Reduced Tax on Net Investment Income

This part is used by domestic private foundations (exempt and taxable) to determine whether they qualify for the reduced 1% tax under section 4940(e) on net investment income rather than the 2% tax on net investment income under section 4940(a).

Do not complete Part V if this is the organization's first year. A private foundation cannot qualify under section 4940(e) for its first year of existence, nor can a former public charity qualify for the first year it is treated as a private foundation.

A separate computation must be made for each year in which the foundation wants to qualify for the reduced tax.

Line 1, column (b). Enter the amount of adjusted qualifying distributions made for each year shown. The amounts in column (b) are taken from Part XII, line 6 of the Form 990-PF for 2000–2004.

Line 1, column (c). Enter the net value of noncharitable-use assets for each year. The amounts in column (c) are taken from Part X, line 5, for 2000–2004.

Part VI—Excise Tax Based on Investment Income (Section 4940(a), 4940(b), 4940(e), or 4948)

General Rules

Domestic exempt private foundations. These foundations are subject to a 2% tax on net investment income under section 4940(a). However, certain exempt operating foundations described in section 4940(d)(2) may not owe any tax, and certain private foundations that meet the requirements of section 4940(e) may qualify for a reduced tax of 1% (see the *Part V instructions*).

Exception. The section 4940 tax does not apply to an organization making an election under section 41(e)(6). Enter "N/A" in Part VI.

Domestic taxable private foundations and section 4947(a)(1) nonexempt charitable trusts. These organizations are subject to a modified 2% tax on net investment income under section 4940(b). (See *Part V and its instructions* to find out if they meet the requirements of section 4940(e) that allows them to use a

modified 1% tax on net investment income.) However, they must first compute the tax under section 4940(a) as if that tax applied to them.

Foreign organizations. Under section 4948, exempt foreign private foundations are subject to a 4% tax on their gross investment income derived from U.S. sources.

Taxable foreign private foundations that filed Form 1040NR, U.S. Nonresident Alien Income Tax Return, or Form 1120-F, U.S. Income Tax Return of a Foreign Corporation, enter "N/A" in Part VI.

Estimated tax. Domestic exempt and taxable private foundations and section 4947(a)(1) nonexempt charitable trusts may have to make estimated tax payments for the excise tax based on investment income. See *General Instruction O* for more information.

Tax Computation

⚠ *Line 1a only applies to domestic exempt operating foundations that are described in section 4940(d)(2) and that have a ruling letter from the IRS establishing exempt operating foundation status. If your organization does not have this letter, skip line 1a.*

Line 1a. A domestic exempt private foundation that qualifies as an exempt operating foundation under section 4940(d)(2) is not liable for any tax on net investment income on this return.

If your organization qualifies, check the box and enter the date of the ruling letter on line 1a and enter "N/A" on line 1. Leave the rest of Part VI blank. For the first year, the organization must attach a copy of the ruling letter establishing exempt operating foundation status. As long as the organization retains this status, write the date of the ruling letter in the space on line 1a. If the organization no longer qualifies under section 4940(d)(2), leave the date line blank and compute the section 4940 tax in the normal manner.

Qualification. To qualify as an exempt operating foundation for a tax year, an organization must meet the following requirements of section 4940(d)(2).
• It is an operating foundation described in section 4942(j)(3).
• It has been publicly supported for at least 10 tax years or was a private operating foundation on January 1, 1983, or for its last tax year ending before January 1, 1983.
• Its governing body, at all times during the tax year, consists of individuals less than 25% of whom are disqualified individuals, and is broadly representative of the general public, and
• It has no officer who was a disqualified individual at any time during the tax year.

Form 990-PF Instructions

Line 2—Section 511 tax. Under section 4940(b), a domestic section 4947(a)(1) nonexempt charitable trust or taxable private foundation must add to the tax figured under section 4940(a) (on line 1) the tax which would have been imposed under section 511 for the tax year if it had been exempt from tax under section 501(a). If the domestic section 4947(a)(1) nonexempt charitable trust or taxable private foundation has unrelated business taxable income that would have been subject to the tax imposed by section 511, the computation of tax must be shown in an attachment. Form 990-T may be used as the attachment. All other filers, enter zero.

Line 4—Subtitle A tax. Domestic section 4947(a)(1) nonexempt charitable trusts and taxable private foundations, enter the amount of subtitle A (income) tax for the year reported on Form 1041 or Form 1120. All other filers, enter zero.

Line 5—Tax based on investment income. Subtract line 4 from line 3 and enter the difference (but not less than zero) on line 5. Any overpayment entered on line 10 that is the result of a negative amount shown on line 5 will not be refunded. Unless the organization is a domestic section 4947(a)(1) nonexempt charitable trust or taxable private foundation, the amount on line 5 is the same as on line 1.

Line 6a. Enter the amount of 2005 estimated tax payments, and any 2004 overpayment of taxes that the organization specified on its 2004 return to be credited toward payment of 2005 estimated taxes.

 Line 6a applies only to domestic organizations.

Trust payments treated as beneficiary payments. A trust may treat any part of estimated taxes it paid as taxes paid by the beneficiary. If the filing organization was a beneficiary that received the benefit of such a payment from a trust, include the amount on line 6a of Part VI, and write, "Includes section 643(g) payment." See section 643(g) for more information about estimated tax payments treated as paid by a beneficiary.

Line 6b. Exempt foreign foundations must enter the amount of tax withheld at the source.

Line 6d. Enter the amount of any backup withholding erroneously withheld. Recipients of interest or dividend payments must generally certify their correct tax identification number to the bank or other payer on Form W-9, Request for Taxpayer Identification Number and Certification. If the payer does not get this information, it must withhold part of the payments as "backup withholding." If the organization files Form 990-PF and was subject to erroneous backup withholding because the payer did

not realize the payee was an exempt organization and not subject to this withholding, the organization can claim credit for the amount withheld.

 Do not claim erroneous backup withholding on line 6d if you claim it on Form 990-T.

Line 8—Penalty. Enter any penalty for underpayment of estimated tax shown on Form 2220. Form 2220 is used by both corporations and trusts.

Line 9—Tax due. Domestic foundations should see *General Instruction P.*

All foreign organizations should enclose a check or money order (in U.S. funds), made payable to the United States Treasury, with Form 990-PF.

Amended return. If you are amending Part VI, be sure to combine any tax due that was paid with the original return (or any overpayment credited or refunded) in the total for line 7. On the dotted line to the left of the line 7 entry space, write "Tax Paid w/ O.R." and the amount paid. If you had an overpayment, write "O.R. Overpayment" and the amount credited or refunded in brackets.

If you file more than one amended return, attach a schedule listing the tax due amounts that were paid and overpayment amounts that were credited or refunded. Write "See Attachment" on the dotted line and enter the net amount in the entry space for line 7.

Part VII-A—Statements Regarding Activities

Each question in this section must be answered "Yes," "No," or "N/A" (not applicable).

Line 1. "Political purposes" include, but are not limited to: directly or indirectly accepting contributions or making payments to influence the selection, nomination, election, or appointment of any individual to any federal, state, or local public office or office in a political organization, or the election of presidential or vice presidential electors, whether or not the individual or electors are actually selected, nominated, elected, or appointed.

Line 3. A "conformed" copy of an organizational document is one that agrees with the original document and all its amendments. If copies are not signed, attach a written declaration signed by an officer authorized to sign for the organization, certifying that they are complete and accurate copies of the original documents.

Note. If you are filing electronically, send a conformed copy of the changes to the IRS at the address listed in *General Instruction U.*

Line 6. For a private foundation to be exempt from income tax, its governing instrument must include provisions that require it to act or refrain from acting so as not to engage in an act of self-dealing

(section 4941), or subject the foundation to the taxes imposed by sections 4942 (failure to distribute income), 4943 (excess business holdings), 4944 (investments which jeopardize charitable purpose), and 4945 (taxable expenditures). A private foundation may satisfy these section 508(e) requirements either by express language in its governing instrument or by application of state law that imposes the above requirements on the foundation or treats these requirements as being contained in the governing instrument. If an organization claims it satisfies the requirements of section 508(e) by operation of state law, the provisions of state law must effectively impose the section 508(e) requirements on the organization. See Rev. Rul. 75-38, 1975-1 C.B.161, for a list of states with legislation that satisfies the requirements of section 508(e).

However, if the state law does not apply to a governing instrument that contains mandatory directions conflicting with any of its requirements and the organization has such mandatory directions in its governing instrument, then the organization has not satisfied the requirements of section 508(e) by the operation of that legislation.

Line 8a. In the space provided list all states:

1. To which the organization reports in any way about its organization, assets, or activities, and
2. With which the organization has registered (or which it has otherwise notified in any manner) that it intends to be, or is, a charitable organization or that it is, or intends to be, a holder of property devoted to a charitable purpose.

Attach a separate list if you need more space.

Line 9. If the organization claims status as a private operating foundation for 2005 and, in fact, meets the private operating foundation requirements for that year (as reflected in Part XIV), any excess distributions carryover from 2004 or prior years may not be carried over to 2005 or any year after 2005 even if it does not meet the private operating foundation requirements. See the *instructions for Part XIII.*

Line 10—Substantial contributors. If you answer "Yes," attach a schedule listing the names and addresses of all persons who became substantial contributors during the year.

The term "substantial contributor" means any person whose contributions or bequests during the current tax year and prior tax years total more than $5,000 and are more than 2% of the total contributions and bequests received by the foundation from its creation through the close of its tax year. In the case of a trust, the term "substantial contributor"

Form 990-PF Instructions

-19-

also means the creator of the trust (section 507(d)(2)).

The term "person" includes individuals, trusts, estates, partnerships, associations, corporations, and other exempt organizations.

Each contribution or bequest must be valued at fair market value on the date it was received.

Any person who is a substantial contributor on any date will remain a substantial contributor for all later periods.

However, a person will cease to be a substantial contributor with respect to any private foundation if:

1. The person, and all related persons, made no contributions to the foundation during the 10-year period ending with the close of the taxable year;
2. The person, or any related person, was never the foundation's manager during this 10-year period; and
3. The aggregate contributions made by the person, and related persons, are determined by the IRS to be insignificant compared to the aggregate amount of contributions to the foundation by any other person and the appreciated value of contributions held by the foundation.

The term "related person" includes any other person who would be a disqualified person because of a relationship with the substantial contributor (section 4946). When the substantial contributor is a corporation, the term also includes any officer or director of the corporation. The term "substantial contributor" does not include public charities (organizations described in section 509(a)(1), (2), or (3)).

Line 11—Public inspection requirements and website address. All domestic private foundations (including section 4947(a)(1) nonexempt charitable trusts treated as private foundations) are subject to the public inspection requirements. See *General Instruction Q* for information on making the foundation's annual returns and exemption application available for public inspection.

Enter the foundation's website address if the foundation has a website. Otherwise, enter "N/A."

Line 13—Section 4947(a)(1) trusts. Section 4947(a)(1) nonexempt charitable trusts that file Form 990-PF instead of Form 1041 must complete this line. The trust should include exempt-interest dividends received from a mutual fund or other regulated investment company as well as tax-exempt interest received directly.

Part VII-B—Activities for Which Form 4720 May Be Required

The purpose of these questions is to determine if there is any initial excise tax due under sections 170(f)(10), 4941–4945, and section 4955. If the

answer is "Yes" to question 1b, 1c, 2b, 3b, 4a, 4b, 5b, or 6b, complete and file Form 4720, unless an exception applies.

Line 1—Self-dealing. The activities listed in 1a(1)–(6) are considered self-dealing under section 4941 unless one of the exceptions applies. See Publication 578, Tax Information for Private Foundations and Foundation Managers.

The terms "disqualified person" and "foundation manager" are defined in *General Instruction C.*

Line 1b. If you answered "Yes" to any of the questions In 1a, you should answer "Yes" to 1b unless all of the acts engaged in were "excepted" acts. Excepted acts are described in Regulations sections 53.4941(d)-3 and 4 or appear in Notices published in the Internal Revenue Bulletin, relating to disaster assistance.

Line 2b—Taxes on failure to distribute income. If you answer "No" to question 2b, attach a statement explaining:
- All the facts regarding the incorrect valuation of assets, and
- The actions taken (or planned) to comply with section 4942(a)(2)(B), (C), and (D) and the related regulations.

Line 3a. A private foundation is not treated as having excess business holdings in any enterprise if, together with related foundations, it owns 2% or less of the voting stock and 2% or less in value of all outstanding shares of all classes of stock. (See "*disqualified person*" under *General Instruction C.*) A similar exception applies to a beneficial or profits interest in any business enterprise that is a trust or partnership.

For more information about excess business holdings, see Pub. 578 and the instructions for Form 4720.

Line 4—Taxes on investments that jeopardize charitable purposes. In general, an investment that jeopardizes any of the charitable purposes of a private foundation is one for which a foundation manager did not exercise ordinary business care to provide for the long- and short-term financial needs of the foundation in carrying out its charitable purposes. For more details, see Pub. 578 and the regulations under section 4944.

Line 5—Taxes on taxable expenditures and political expenditures. In general, payments made for the activities described on lines 5a(1)–(5) are taxable expenditures. See Pub. 578 for exceptions.

A grant by a private foundation to a public charity is not a taxable expenditure if the private foundation does not earmark the grant for any of the activities described in lines 5a(1)–(5), and there is no oral or written agreement by which the grantor foundation may cause the grantee to engage in any such prohibited activity or to select the grant recipient.

Grants made to exempt operating foundations (as defined in section

4940(d)(2) and the instructions to Part VI) are not subject to the expenditure responsibility provisions of section 4945.

Under section 4955, a section 501(c)(3) organization must pay an excise tax for any amount paid or incurred on behalf of or opposing any candidate for public office. The organization must pay an additional excise tax if it does not correct the expenditure timely.

A manager of a section 501(c)(3) organization who knowingly agrees to a political expenditure must pay an excise tax unless the agreement is not willful and there is reasonable cause. A manager who does not agree to a correction of the political expenditure may have to pay an additional excise tax.

A section 501(c)(3) organization will lose its exempt status if it engages in political activity.

A political expenditure that is treated as an expenditure under section 4955 is not treated as a taxable expenditure under section 4945.

For purposes of the section 4955 tax, when an organization promotes a candidate for public office (or is used or controlled by a candidate or prospective candidate), amounts paid or incurred for the following purposes are political expenditures:
- Remuneration to the individual (or candidate or prospective candidate) for speeches or other services,
- Travel expenses of the individual,
- Expenses of conducting polls, surveys, or other studies, or preparing papers or other material for use by the individual,
- Expenses of advertising, publicity, and fundraising for such individual, and
- Any other expense that has the primary effect of promoting public recognition or otherwise primarily accruing to the benefit of the individual.

See the regulations under section 4945 for more information.

Line 5b. If you answered "Yes" to any of the questions in 5a, you should answer "Yes" to 5b unless all of the transactions engaged in were "excepted" transactions. Excepted transactions are described in Regulations section 53.4945 or appear in Notices published in the Internal Revenue Bulletin, relating to disaster assistance.

Line 6b. Check "Yes" if, in connection with any transfer of funds to a private foundation, the foundation directly or indirectly pays premiums on any personal benefit contract, or there is an understanding or expectation that any person will directly or indirectly pay these premiums.

Report the premiums it paid and the premiums paid by others, but treated as paid by the private foundation, on Form 8870 and pay the excise tax (which is equal to premiums paid) on Form 4720.

For more information, see Form 8870 and Notice 2000-24, 2000-17 I.R.B. 952 (Notice 2000-24, 2000-1, C.B., 952.)

Part VIII—Information About Officers, Directors, Trustees, Foundation Managers, Highly Paid Employees, and Contractors

Line 1—List of officers, directors, trustees, etc. List the names, addresses, and other information requested for those who were officers, directors, and trustees (or any person who had responsibilities or powers similar to those of officers, directors, or trustees) of the foundation at any time during the year. Each must be listed whether or not they receive any compensation from the foundation. Give the preferred address at which officers, etc., want the Internal Revenue Service to contact them.

Also include on this list, any officers or directors (or any person who had responsibilities or powers similar to those of officers or directors) of a disregarded entity owned by the foundation who are not officers, directors, etc., of the foundation.

If the foundation (or disregarded entity) pays any other person, such as a management services company, for the services provided by any of the foundation's officers, directors, or trustees (or any person who had responsibilities or powers similar to those of officers, directors, or trustees), report the compensation and other items on Part VIII as if you had paid the officers, etc., directly. But see Announcement 2001-33, 2001-17 I.R.B., 1137, 2001-1 C.B. 1137.

Show all forms of compensation earned by each listed officer, etc. In addition to completing Part VIII, if you want to explain the compensation of one or more officers, directors, and trustees, you may provide an attachment describing the person's entire 2005 compensation package.

Enter zero in columns (c), (d), and (e) if no compensation was paid. Attach a schedule if more space is needed.

Column (b). A numerical estimate of the average hours per week devoted to the position is required for the answer to be considered complete.

 Phrases such as "as needed" or "as required" are unacceptable entries for column (b).

Column (c). Enter salary, fees, bonuses, and severance payments received by each person listed. Include current year payments of amounts reported or reportable as deferred compensation in any prior year.

Column (d). Include all forms of deferred compensation and future severance payments (whether or not funded or vested, and whether or not the deferred compensation plan is a qualified

plan under section 401(a)). Include payments to welfare benefit plans (employee welfare benefit plans covered by Part I of Title 1 of ERISA, providing benefits such as medical, dental, life insurance, apprenticeship and training, scholarship funds, severance pay, disability, etc.) on behalf of the officers, etc. Reasonable estimates may be used if precise cost figures are not readily available.

Unless the amounts are reported in column (c), report, as deferred compensation in column (d), salaries and other compensation earned during the period covered by the return, but not yet paid by the date the foundation files its return.

Column (e). Enter both taxable and nontaxable fringe benefits, expense account and other allowances (other than de minimis fringe benefits described in section 132(e)). See Publication 525, Taxable and Nontaxable Income for more information. Examples of allowances include amounts for which the recipient did not account to the organization or allowances that were more than the payee spent on serving the organization. Include payments made in connection with indemnification arrangements, the value of the personal use of housing, automobiles, or other assets owned or leased by the organization (or provided for the organization's use without charge).

Line 2—Compensation of five highest-paid employees. Fill in the information requested for the five employees (if any) of the foundation (or disregarded entity that the foundation owns) who received the greatest amount of annual compensation over $50,000. Do not include employees listed on line 1. Also enter the total number of other employees who received more than $50,000 in annual compensation.

Show each listed employee's entire compensation package for the period covered by the return. Include all forms of compensation that each listed employee received in return for his or her services. See the *line 1 instructions* for more details on includible compensation.

Line 3—Five highest-paid independent contractors for professional services. Fill in the information requested for the five highest-paid independent contractors (if any), whether individuals or professional service corporations or associations, to whom the organization paid more than $50,000 for the year to perform personal services of a professional nature for the organization (for example, attorneys, accountants, and doctors). Also show the total number of all other independent contractors who received more than $50,000 for the year for performing professional services.

Part IX-A—Summary of Direct Charitable Activities

List the foundation's four largest programs as measured by the direct and indirect expenses attributable to each that consist of the direct active conduct of charitable activities. Whether any expenditure is for the direct active conduct of a charitable activity is determined, generally, by the definitions and special rules of section 4942(j)(3) and the related regulations, which define a private operating foundation.

Except for significant involvement grant programs, described below, do not include in Part IX-A any grants or expenses attributable to administering grant programs, such as reviewing grant applications, interviewing or testing applicants, selecting grantees, and reviewing reports relating to the use of the grant funds.

Include scholarships, grants, or other payments to individuals as part of an active program in which the foundation maintains some significant involvement. Related administrative expenses should also be included. Examples of active programs and definitions of the term "significant involvement" are provided in Regulations sections 53.4942(b)-1(b)(2) and 53.4942(b)-1(d).

Do not include any program-related investments (reportable in Part IX-B) in the description and expense totals, but be sure to include qualified set-asides for direct charitable activities, reported on line 3 of Part XII. Also, include in Part IX-A, amounts paid or set aside to acquire assets used in the direct active conduct of charitable activities.

Expenditures for direct charitable activities include, among others, amounts paid or set aside to:

1. Acquire or maintain the operating assets of a museum, library, or historic site or to operate the facility;
2. Provide goods, shelter, or clothing to indigents or disaster victims if the foundation maintains some significant involvement in the activity rather than merely making grants to the recipients;
3. Conduct educational conferences and seminars;
4. Operate a home for the elderly or disabled;
5. Conduct scientific, historic, public policy, or other research with significance beyond the foundation's grant program that does not constitute a prohibited attempt to influence legislation;
6. Publish and disseminate the results of such research, reports of educational conferences, or similar educational material;
7. Support the service of foundation staff on boards or advisory committees of other charitable organizations or on public commissions or task forces;
8. Provide technical advice or assistance to a governmental body, a

governmental committee, or subdivision of either, in response to a written request by the governmental body, committee, or subdivision;

9. Conduct performing arts performances; or

10. Provide technical assistance to grantees and other charitable organizations. This assistance must have significance beyond the purposes of the grants made to the grantees and must not consist merely of monitoring or advising the grantees in their use of the grant funds. Technical assistance involves the furnishing of expert advice and related assistance regarding, for example:

a. Compliance with governmental regulations,

b. Reducing operating costs or increasing program accomplishments,

c. Fundraising methods, and

d. Maintaining complete and accurate financial records.

Report both direct and indirect expenses in the expense totals. Direct expenses are those that can be specifically identified as connected with a particular activity. These include, among others, compensation and travel expenses of employees and officers directly engaged in an activity, the cost of materials and supplies utilized in conducting the activity, and fees paid to outside firms and individuals in connection with a specific activity.

Indirect (overhead) expenses are those that are not specifically identified as connected with a particular activity but that relate to the direct costs incurred in conducting the activity. Examples of indirect expenses include: occupancy expenses; supervisory and clerical compensation; repair, rental, and maintenance of equipment; expenses of other departments or cost centers (such as accounting, personnel, and payroll departments or units) that service the department or function that incurs the direct expenses of conducting an activity; and other applicable general and administrative expenses, including the compensation of top management, to the extent reasonably allocable to a particular activity.

No specific method of allocation is required. The method used, however, must be reasonable and must be used consistently.

Examples of acceptable allocation methods include:

• Compensation that is allocated on a time basis,

• Employee benefits that are allocated on the basis of direct salary expenses,

• Travel, conference, and meeting expenses that are charged directly to the activity that incurred the expense,

• Occupancy expenses that are allocated on a space-utilized basis, and

• Other indirect expenses that are allocated on the basis of direct salary expenses or total direct expenses.

Part IX-B—Summary of Program-Related Investments

Program-related investment. Section 4944(c) and corresponding regulations define a program-related investment as one that is made primarily to accomplish a charitable purpose of the foundation and no substantial purpose of which is to produce investment income or a capital gain from the sale of the investment. Examples of program-related investments include educational loans to individuals and low-interest loans to other section 501(c)(3) organizations.

General instructions. Include only those investments that were reported in Part XII, line 1b, for the current year. Do not include any investments made in any prior year even if they were still held by the foundation at the end of 2005.

Investments consisting of loans to individuals (such as educational loans) are not required to be listed separately but may be grouped with other program-related investments of the same type. Loans to other section 501(c)(3) organizations and all other types of program-related investments must be listed separately on lines 1 through 3 or on an attachment.

Lines 1 and 2. List the two largest program-related investments made by the foundation in 2005, whether or not the investments were still held by the foundation at the end of the year.

Line 3. Combine all other program-related investments and enter the total on the line 3 Amount column. List the individual investments or groups of investments included (attach a schedule if necessary).

 The total of lines 1 through 3 in the Amount column must equal the amount reported on line 1b of Part XII.

Part X—Minimum Investment Return

Who must complete this section? All domestic foundations must complete Part X.

Foreign foundations that checked box D2 on page 1 do not have to complete Part X unless claiming status as a private operating foundation.

Private operating foundations, described in sections 4942(j)(3) or 4942(j)(5), must complete Part X in order to complete Part XIV.

Overview. A private foundation that is not a private operating foundation must pay out, as qualifying distributions, its minimum investment return. This is

generally 5% of the total fair market value of its noncharitable assets, subject to further adjustments as explained in the instructions for Part XI. The amount of this minimum investment return is figured in Part X and is used in Part XI to figure the amount that is required to be paid out (the distributable amount).

Minimum investment return. In figuring the minimum investment return, include only those assets that are not actually used or held for use by the organization for a charitable, educational, or other similar function that contributed to the charitable status of the foundation. Cash on hand and on deposit is considered used or held for use for charitable purposes only to the extent of the reasonable cash balances reported in Part X, line 4. See the *instructions for lines 1b and 4 below.*

Assets that are held for the production of income or for investment are not considered to be used directly for charitable functions even though the income from the assets is used for the charitable functions. It is a factual question whether an asset is held for the production of income or for investment rather than used or held for use directly by the foundation for charitable purposes.

For example, an office building that is used to provide offices for employees engaged in managing endowment funds for the foundation is not considered an asset used for charitable purposes.

Dual-use property. When property is used both for charitable and other purposes, the property is considered used entirely for charitable purposes if 95% or more of its total use is for that purpose. If less than 95% of its total use is for charitable purposes, a reasonable allocation must be made between charitable and noncharitable use.

Excluded property. Certain assets are excluded entirely from the computation of the minimum investment return. These include pledges of grants and contributions to be received in the future and future interests in estates and trusts. See Pub. 578, chapter VII, for more details.

Line 1a—Average monthly fair market value of securities. If market quotations are readily available, a foundation may use any reasonable method to determine the average monthly fair market value of securities such as common and preferred stock, bonds, and mutual fund shares, as long as that method is consistently used. For example, a value for a particular month might be determined by the closing price on the first or last trading days of the month or an average of the closing prices on the first and last trading days of the month. Market quotations are considered readily available if a security is any of the following:

• Listed on the New York or American Stock Exchange or any city or regional exchange in which quotations appear on

Form 990-PF Instructions

a daily basis, including foreign securities listed on a recognized foreign national or regional exchange,
• Regularly traded in the national or regional over-the-counter market for which published quotations are available, or
• Locally traded, for which quotations can be readily obtained from established brokerage firms.

If securities are held in trust for, or on behalf of, a foundation by a bank or other financial institution that values those securities periodically using a computer pricing system, a foundation may use that system to determine the value of the securities. The system must be acceptable to the IRS for federal estate tax purposes.

The foundation may reduce the fair market value of securities only to the extent that it can establish that the securities could only be liquidated in a reasonable period of time at a price less than the fair market value because of:
• The size of the block of the securities,
• The fact that the securities held are securities in a closely held corporation, or
• The fact that the sale of the securities would result in a forced or distress sale.

Any reduction in value allowed under these provisions may not be more than 10% of the fair market value (determined without regard to any reduction in value).

Also, see Regulations sections 53.4942(a)-2(c)(4)(i)(b), (c), and (iv)(a).

Line 1b—Average of monthly cash balances. Compute cash balances on a monthly basis by averaging the amount of cash on hand on the first and last days of each month. Include all cash balances and amounts that may be used for charitable purposes (see line 4 below) or set aside and taken as a qualifying distribution (see *Part XII*).

Line 1c—Fair market value of all other assets. The fair market value of assets other than securities is determined annually except as described below. The valuation may be made by private foundation employees or by any other person even if that person is a disqualified person. If the IRS accepts the valuation, it is valid only for the tax year for which it is made. A new valuation is required for the next tax year.

5-year valuation. A written, certified, and independent appraisal of the fair market value of any real estate, including any improvements, may be determined on a 5-year basis by a qualified person.

The qualified person may not be a disqualified person (see *General Instruction C*) with respect to the private foundation or an employee of the foundation.

Commonly accepted valuation methods must be used in making the appraisal. A valuation based on acceptable methods of valuing property

Form 990-PF Instructions

for federal estate tax purposes will be considered acceptable.

The appraisal must include a closing statement that, in the appraiser's opinion, the appraised assets were valued according to valuation principles regularly employed in making appraisals of such property, using all reasonable valuation methods. The foundation must keep a copy of the independent appraisal for its records. If a valuation is reasonable, the foundation may use it for the tax year for which the valuation is made and for each of the 4 following tax years.

Any valuation of real estate by a certified independent appraisal may be replaced during the 5-year period by a subsequent 5-year certified independent appraisal or by an annual valuation as described above. The most recent valuation should be used to compute the foundation's minimum investment return.

If the valuation is made according to the above rules, the IRS will continue to accept it during the 5-year period for which it applies even if the actual fair market value of the property changes during the period.

Valuation date. An asset required to be valued annually may be valued as of any day in the private foundation's tax year, provided the foundation values the asset as of that date in all tax years. However, a valuation of real estate determined on a 5-year basis by a certified, independent appraisal may be made as of any day in the first tax year of the foundation to which the valuation applies.

Assets held for less than a tax year. To determine the value of an asset held less than 1 tax year, divide the number of days the foundation held the asset by the number of days in the tax year. Multiply the result by the fair market value of the asset.

Line 1e—Reduction claimed for blockage or other factors. If the fair market value of any securities, real estate holdings, or other assets reported on lines 1a and 1c reflects a blockage discount, marketability discount, or other reduction from full fair market value because of the size of the asset holding or any other factor, enter on line 1e the aggregate amount of the discounts claimed. Attach an explanation that includes the following information for each asset or group of assets involved:

1. A description of the asset or asset group (e.g., 20,000 shares of XYZ, Inc., common stock),
2. For securities, the percentage of the total issued and outstanding securities of the same class that is represented by the foundation's holding,
3. The fair market value of the asset or asset group before any claimed blockage discount or other reduction,
4. The amount of the discount claimed, and

-23-

5. A statement that explains why the claimed discount is appropriate in valuing the asset or group of assets for section 4942 purposes.

In the case of securities, there are certain limitations on the size of the reduction in value that can be claimed. See the *instructions for Part X, line 1a.*

Line 2—Acquisition indebtedness. Enter the total acquisition indebtedness that applies to assets included on line 1. For details, see section 514(c)(1).

Line 4—Cash deemed held for charitable activities. Foundations may exclude from the assets used in the minimum investment return computation the reasonable cash balances necessary to cover current administrative expenses and other normal and current disbursements directly connected with the charitable, educational, or other similar activities. The amount of cash that may be excluded is generally $1\frac{1}{2}\%$ of the fair market value of all assets (minus any acquisition indebtedness) as computed in Part X, line 3. However, if under the facts and circumstances an amount larger than the deemed amount is necessary to pay expenses and disbursements, then you may enter the larger amount instead of $1\frac{1}{2}\%$ of the fair market value on line 4. If you use a larger amount, attach an explanation.

Line 6—Short tax periods. If the foundation's tax period is less than 12 months, determine the applicable percentage by dividing the number of days in the short tax period by 365 (or 366 in a leap year). Multiply the result by 5%. Then multiply the modified percentage by the amount on line 5 and enter the result on line 6.

Part XI—Distributable Amount

If the organization is claiming status as a private operating foundation described in section 4942(j)(3) or (j)(5) or if it is a foreign foundation that checked box D2 on page 1, check the box in the heading for Part XI. You do not need to complete this part. See the *Part XIV instructions* for more details on private operating foundations.

Section 4942(j)(5) organizations are classified as private operating foundations for purposes of section 4942 only if they meet the requirements of Regulations section 53.4942(b)-1(a)(2).

The distributable amount for 2005 is the amount that the foundation must distribute by the end of 2006 as qualifying distributions to avoid the 15% tax on the undistributed portion.

Line 4. Enter the total of recoveries of amounts treated as qualifying distributions for any year under section 4942(g). Include recoveries of part or all (as applicable) of grants previously made; proceeds from the sale or other

8-111

disposition of property whose cost was treated as a qualifying distribution when the property was acquired; and any amount set aside under section 4942(g) to the extent it is determined that this amount is not necessary for the purposes of the set-aside.

Line 6—Deduction from distributable amount. If the foundation was organized before May 27, 1969, and its governing instrument or any other instrument continues to require the accumulation of income after a judicial proceeding to reform the instrument has terminated, then the amount of the income required to be accumulated must be subtracted from the distributable amount beginning with the first tax year after the tax year in which the judicial proceeding was terminated. (See the *instructions for Part VII-A, line 6*.)

Part XII—Qualifying Distributions

"Qualifying distributions" are amounts spent or set aside for religious, educational, or similar charitable purposes. The total amount of qualifying distributions for any year is used to reduce the distributable amount for specified years to arrive at the undistributed income (if any) for those years.

Line 1a—Expenses, contributions, gifts, etc. Enter the amount from Part I, column (d), line 26. However, if the borrowed funds election applies, add the total of the repayments during the year to the amount from Part I, column (d), line 26, and enter it on line 1a.

Borrowed funds. If the foundation borrowed money in a tax year beginning before January 1, 1970, or later borrows money under a written commitment binding on December 31, 1969, the foundation may elect to treat any repayments of the loan principal after December 31, 1969, as qualifying distributions at the time of repayment, rather than at the earlier time that the borrowed funds were actually distributed, only if:

1. The money is used to make expenditures for a charitable or similar purpose, and
2. Repayment on the loan did not start until a year beginning after 1969.

On these loans, deduct any interest payment from gross income to compute adjusted net income in the year paid.

Election. To make this election, attach a statement to Form 990-PF for the first tax year beginning after 1969 in which a repayment of loan principal is made and for each tax year after that in which any repayment of loan principal is made. The statement should show:
• The lender's name and address,
• The amount borrowed,
• The specific use of the borrowed funds, and

• The private foundation's election to treat repayments of loan principal as qualifying distributions.

Line 1b—Program-related investments. Enter the total of the "Amount" column from Part IX-B. See the *Part IX-B instructions* for the definition of program-related investments.

Line 3—Amounts set aside. Amounts set aside may be treated as qualifying distributions only if the private foundation establishes to the satisfaction of the IRS that the amount will be paid for the specific project within 60 months from the date of the first set-aside and meets 1 or 2 below.

1. The project can be better accomplished by a set-aside than by the immediate payment of funds (suitability test), or
2. The private foundation meets the requirements of section 4942(g)(2)(B)(ii) (cash distribution test).

Set-aside under item 1. For any set-aside under 1 above, the private foundation must apply for IRS approval by the end of the tax year in which the amount is set aside. Send the application for approval to the:

    Internal Revenue Service
    TE/GE EO - Determinations
    P.O. Box 2508
    Cincinnati. OH 45201

The application for approval must give all of the following information:
• The nature and purposes of the specific project and the amount of the set-aside for which approval is requested,
• The amounts and approximate dates of any planned additions to the set-aside after its initial establishment,
• The reasons why the project can be better accomplished by the set-aside than by the immediate payment of funds,
• A detailed description of the project, including estimated costs, sources of any future funds expected to be used for completion of the project, and the location(s) (general or specific) of any physical facilities to be acquired or constructed as part of the project, and
• A statement of an appropriate foundation manager that the amounts set aside will actually be paid for the specific project within a specified period of time ending within 60 months after the date of the first set-aside; or a statement explaining why the period for paying the amount set aside should be extended and indicating the extension of time requested. (Include in this statement the reason why the proposed project could not be divided into two or more projects covering periods of no more than 60 months each.)

Set-aside under item 2. For any set-aside under 2 above, the private foundation must attach a schedule to its annual information return showing how the requirements are met. A schedule is required for the year of the set-aside and

for each subsequent year until the set-aside amount has been distributed. See Regulations section 53.4942(a)-3(b)(7)(ii) for specific requirements.

Line 5—Reduced tax on investment income under section 4940(e). If the organization does not qualify for the 1% tax under section 4940(e), enter zero. See *Parts V and VI of the instructions.*

Part XIII—Undistributed Income

If you checked box D2 on page 1, do not fill in this part.

If the organization is a private operating foundation for any of the years shown in Part XIII, do not complete the portions of Part XIII that apply to those years. If there are excess qualifying distributions for any tax year, do not carry them over to a year in which the organization is a private operating foundation or to any later year. For example, if a foundation made excess qualifying distributions in 2003 and became a private operating foundation in 2005, the excess qualifying distributions from 2003 could be applied against the distributable amount for 2004 but not to any year after 2004.

The purpose of this part is to enable the foundation to comply with the rules for applying its qualifying distributions for the year 2005. In applying the qualifying distributions, there are three basic steps.

1. Reduce any undistributed income for 2004 (but not below zero).
2. The organization may use any part or all remaining qualifying distributions for 2005 to satisfy elections. For example, if undistributed income remained for any year before 2004, it could be reduced to zero or, if the foundation wished, the distributions could be treated as distributions out of corpus.
3. If no elections are involved, apply remaining qualifying distributions to the 2005 distributable amount on line 4d. If the remaining qualifying distributions are greater than the 2005 distributable amount, the excess is treated as a distribution out of corpus on line 4e.

If for any reason the 2005 qualifying distributions do not reduce any 2004 undistributed income to zero, the amount not distributed is subject to a 15% tax. If the 2004 income remains undistributed at the end of 2006, it could be subject again to the 15% tax. Also, see section 4942(b) for the circumstances under which a second-tier tax could be imposed.

Line 1—Distributable amount. Enter the distributable amount for 2005 from Part XI, line 7.

Line 2—Undistributed income. Enter the distributable amount for 2004 and amounts for earlier years that remained undistributed at the beginning of the 2005 tax year.

Form 990-PF Instructions

Line 2b. Enter the amount of undistributed income for years before 2004.

Line 3—Excess distributions carryover to 2005. If the foundation has made excess distributions out of corpus in prior years, which have not been applied in any year, enter the amount for each year. Do not enter an amount for a particular year if the organization was a private operating foundation for any later year.

Lines 3a through 3e. Enter the amount of any excess distribution made on the line for each year listed. Do not include any amount that was applied against the distributable amount of an earlier year or that was already used to meet pass-through distribution requirements. (See the instructions for line 7.)

Line 3f. This amount can be applied in 2005.

Line 4—Qualifying distributions. Enter the total amount of qualifying distributions made in 2005 from Part XII, line 4. The total of the amounts applied on lines 4a through 4e is equal to the qualifying distributions made in 2005.

Line 4a. The qualifying distributions for 2005 are first used to reduce any undistributed income remaining from 2004. Enter only enough of the 2005 qualifying distributions to reduce the 2004 undistributed income to zero.

Lines 4b and 4c. If there are any 2005 qualifying distributions remaining after reducing the 2004 undistributed income to zero, one or more elections can be made under Regulations section 53.4942(a)-3(d)(2) to apply all or part of the remaining qualifying distributions to any undistributed income remaining from years before 2004 or to apply to corpus.

Elections. To make these elections, the organization must file a statement with the IRS or attach a statement, as described in the above regulations section, to Form 990-PF. An election made by filing a separate statement with the IRS must be made within the year for which the election is made. Otherwise, attach a statement to the Form 990-PF filed for the year the election was made.

Where to enter. If the organization elected to apply all or part of the remaining amount to the undistributed income remaining from years before 2004, enter the amount on line 4b.

If the organization elected to treat those qualifying distributions as a distribution out of corpus, enter the amount on line 4c.

 Entering an amount on line 4b or 4c without submitting the required statement is not considered a valid election.

Line 4d. Treat as a distribution of the distributable amount for 2005 any qualifying distributions for 2005 that remain after reducing the 2004 undistributed income to zero and after

electing to treat any part of the remaining distributions as a distribution out of corpus or as a distribution of a prior year's undistributed income. Enter only enough of the remaining 2005 qualifying distributions to reduce the 2005 distributable amount to zero.

Line 4e. Any 2005 qualifying distributions remaining after reducing the 2005 distributable amount to zero should be treated as an excess distribution out of corpus. This amount may be carried over and applied to later years.

Line 5—Excess qualifying distributions carryover applied to 2005. Enter any excess qualifying distributions from line 3, which were applied to 2005, in both the Corpus column and the 2005 column. Apply the oldest excess qualifying distributions first. Thus, the organization will apply any excess qualifying distributions carried forward from 2000 before those from later years.

Line 6a. Add lines 3f, 4c, and 4e. Subtract line 5 from the total. Enter the net total in the Corpus column.

Line 6c. Enter only the undistributed income from 2003 and prior years for which either a notice of deficiency under section 6212(a) has been mailed for the section 4942(a) first-tier tax, or on which the first-tier tax has been assessed because the organization filed a Form 4720 for a tax year that began before 2004.

Lines 6d and 6e. These amounts are taxable under the provisions of section 4942(a), except for any part that is due solely to improper valuation of assets to which the provisions of section 4942(a)(2) are being applied (see *Part VII-B, line 2b*). Report the taxable amount on Form 4720. If the exception applies, attach an explanation.

Line 6f. In the 2005 column, enter the amount by which line 1 is more than the total of lines 4d and 5. This is the undistributed income for 2005. The organization must distribute the amount shown by the end of its 2006 tax year so that it will not be liable for the tax on undistributed income.

Line 7—Distributions out of corpus for 2005 pass-through distributions.

1. If the foundation is the donee and receives a contribution from another private foundation, the donor foundation may treat the contribution as a qualifying distribution only if the donee foundation makes a distribution equal to the full amount of the contribution and the distribution is a qualifying distribution that is treated as a distribution of corpus. The donee foundation must, no later than the close of the first tax year after the tax year in which it receives the contributions, distribute an amount equal in value to the contributions received in the prior tax year and have no remaining undistributed

income for the prior year. For example, if private foundation X received $1,000 in tax year 2004 from foundation Y, foundation X would have to distribute the $1,000 as a qualifying distribution out of corpus by the end of 2005 and have no remaining undistributed income for 2004.

2. If a private foundation receives a contribution from an individual or a corporation and the individual is seeking the 50% contribution base limit on deductions for the tax year (or the individual or corporation is not applying the limit imposed on deductions for contributions to the foundation of capital gain property), the foundation must comply with certain distribution requirements.

By the 15th day of the 3rd month after the end of the tax year in which the foundation received the contributions, the donee foundation must distribute as qualifying distributions out of corpus:

a. An amount equal to 100% of all contributions received during the year in order for the individual contributor to receive the benefit of the 50% limit on deductions, and

b. Distribute all contributions of property only so that the individual or corporation making the contribution is not subject to the section 170(e)(1)(B)(ii) limitations.

If the organization is applying excess distributions from prior years (for instance, any part of the amount in Part XIII, line 3f) to satisfy the distribution requirements of section 170(b)(1)(E) or 4942(g)(3), it must make the election under Regulations section 53.4942(a)-3(c)(2). Also, see Regulations section 1.170A-9(g)(2).

Enter on line 7 the total distributions out of corpus made to satisfy the restrictions on amounts received from donors described above.

Line 8—Outdated excess distributions carryover. Because of the 5-year carryover limitation under section 4942(i)(2), the organization must reduce any excess distributions carryover by any amounts from 2000 that were not applied in 2005.

Line 9—Excess distributions carryover to 2006. Enter the amount by which line 6a is more than the total of lines 7 and 8. This is the amount the organization may apply to 2006 and following years. Line 9 can never be less than zero.

Line 10—Analysis of line 9. In the space provided for each year, enter the amount of excess distributions carryover from that year that has not been applied as of the end of the 2005 tax year. If there is an amount on the line for 2001, it must be applied by the end of the 2006 tax year since the 5-year carryover period for 2001 ends in 2006.

Form 990-PF Instructions

-25-

8-113

Part XIV—Private Operating Foundations

All organizations that claim status as private operating foundations under section 4942(j)(3) or (5) for 2005 must complete Part XIV.

Certain elderly care facilities (section 4942(j)(5)). For purposes of section 4942 only, certain elderly care facilities may be classified as private operating foundations. To be so classified, they must be operated and maintained for the principal purpose explained in section 4942(j)(5) and also meet the endowment test described below.

If the foundation is a section 4942(j)(5) organization, complete only lines 1a, 1b, 2c, 2d, 2e, and 3b. Enter "N/A" on all other lines in the Total column for Part XIV.

Private operating foundation (section 4942(j)(3)). The term "private operating foundation" means any private foundation that spends at least 85% of the smaller of its adjusted net income or its minimum investment return directly for the active conduct of the exempt purpose or functions for which the foundation is organized and operated (the Income Test) and that also meets one of the three tests below.

1. Assets test. 65% or more of the foundation's assets are devoted directly to those activities or functionally related businesses, or both. Or 65% or more of the foundation's assets are stock of a corporation that is controlled by the foundation, and substantially all of the assets of the corporation are devoted to those activities or functionally related businesses.

2. Endowment test. The foundation normally makes qualifying distributions directly for the active conduct of the exempt purpose or functions for which it is organized and operated in an amount that is two-thirds or more of its minimum investment return.

3. Support test. The foundation normally receives 85% or more of its support (other than gross investment income as defined in section 509(e)) from the public and from five or more exempt organizations that are not described in section 4946(a)(1)(H) with respect to each other or the recipient foundation. Not more than 25% of the support (other than gross investment income) normally may be received from any one of the exempt organizations and not more than one-half of the support normally may be received from gross investment income.

See regulations under section 4942 for the meaning of "directly for the active conduct" of exempt activities for purposes of these tests.

Complying with these tests. A foundation may meet the income test and either the assets, endowment, or support test by satisfying the tests for any 3 years

during a 4-year period consisting of the tax year in question and the 3 immediately preceding tax years. It may also meet the tests based on the total of all related amounts of income or assets held, received, or distributed during that 4-year period. A foundation may not use one method for satisfying the income test and another for satisfying one of the three alternative tests. Thus, if a foundation meets the income test on the 3-out-of-4-year basis for a particular tax year, it may not use the 4-year aggregation method for meeting one of the three alternative tests for that same year.

In completing line 3c(3) of Part XIV under the aggregation method, the largest amount of support from an exempt organization will be based on the total amount received for the 4-year period from any one exempt organization.

A new private foundation must use the aggregation method to satisfy the tests for its first tax year in order to be treated as a private operating foundation from the beginning of that year. It must continue to use the aggregation method for its 2nd and 3rd tax years to maintain its status for those years.

Part XV—Supplementary Information

Complete this part only if the foundation had assets of $5,000 or more at any time during the year. This part does not apply to a foreign foundation that during its entire period of existence received substantially all (85% or more) of its support (other than gross investment income) from sources outside the United States.

Line 2. In the space provided (or in an attachment, if necessary), furnish the required information about the organization's grant, scholarship, fellowship, loan, etc., programs. In addition to restrictions or limitations on awards by geographical areas, charitable fields, and kinds of recipients, indicate any specific dollar limitations or other restrictions applicable to each type of award the organization makes. This information benefits the grant seeker and the foundation. The grant seekers will be aware of the grant eligibility requirements and the foundation should receive only applications that adhere to these grant application requirements.

If the foundation only makes contributions to preselected charitable organizations and does not accept unsolicited applications for funds, check the box on line 2.

Line 3. If necessary, attach a schedule for lines 3a and 3b that lists separately amounts given to individuals and amounts given to organizations.

Purpose of grant or contribution. Entries under this column should reflect the grant's or contribution's purpose and

should be in greater detail than merely classifying them as charitable, educational, religious, or scientific activities.

For example, use an identification such as:
• Payments for nursing service,
• For fellowships, or
• For assistance to indigent families.

⚠️ *Entries such as "grant" or "contribution" under the column titled Purpose of grant or contribution are unacceptable.* See Completed Example of Form 990-PF found in Package 990-PF, Returns for Private Foundations, for additional examples that describe the purpose of a grant or contribution.

Line 3a—Paid during year. List all contributions, grants, etc., actually paid during the year, including grants or contributions that are not qualifying distributions under section 4942(g). Include current year payments of set-asides treated as qualifying distributions in the current tax year or any prior year.

Line 3b—Approved for future payment. List all contributions, grants, etc., approved during the year but not paid by the end of the year, including the unpaid portion of any current year set-aside.

Part XVI-A—Analysis of Income-Producing Activities

In Part XVI-A, analyze revenue items that are also entered in Part I, column (a), lines 3–11, and on line 5b. Contributions reported on line 1 of Part I are not entered in Part XVI-A. For information on unrelated business income, see the Instructions for Form 990-T and Pub. 598.

Columns (a) and (c). In column (a), enter a 6-digit business code, from the list in the Instructions for Form 990-T, to identify any income reported in column (b). In column (c), enter an exclusion code, from the list on page 29, to identify any income reported in column (d). If more than one exclusion code is applicable to a particular revenue item, select the lowest numbered exclusion code that applies. Also, if nontaxable revenues from several sources are reportable on the same line in column (d), use the exclusion code that applies to the largest revenue source.

Columns (b), (d), and (e). For amounts reported in Part XVI-A on lines 1–11, enter in column (b) any income that is unrelated business income (see section 512). In column (d), enter any income earned that is excluded from the computation of unrelated business taxable income by Code section 512, 513, or 514. In column (e), enter any related or exempt function income; that is, any income earned that is related to the organization's purpose or function which constitutes the basis for the organization's exemption.

Also enter in column (e) any income specifically excluded from gross income other than by Code section 512, 513, or 514, such as interest on state and local bonds that is excluded from tax by section 103. You must explain in Part XVI-B any amount shown in column (e).

Comparing Part XVI-A with Part I. The sum of the amounts entered on each line of lines 1–11 of columns (b), (d), and (e) of Part XVI-A should equal corresponding amounts entered on lines 3–11 of Part I, column (a), and on line 5b as shown below:

Amounts in Part XVI-A on line . . .	Correspond to Amounts in Part I, column (a), line . . .
1a–g	11
2	11
3	3
4	4
5 and 6	5b (description column)
7	11
8	6
9	11 minus any special event expenses included on lines 13 through 23 of Part I, column (a)
10	10c
11a–e	11

Line 1—Program service revenue. On lines 1a–g, list each revenue-producing program service activity of the organization. For each program service activity listed, enter the gross revenue earned for each activity, as well as identifying business and exclusion codes, in the appropriate columns. For line 1g, enter amounts that are payments for services rendered to governmental units. Do not include governmental grants that are reportable on line 1 of Part I.

Report the total of lines 1a–g on line 11 of Part I, along with any other income reportable on line 11.

Program services are mainly those activities that the reporting organization was created to conduct and that, along with any activities begun later, form the basis of the organization's current exemption from tax.

Program services can also include the organization's unrelated trade or business activities. Program service revenue also includes income from program-related investments (such as interest earned on scholarship loans) as defined in the instructions for Part IX-B.

Line 11. On lines 11a–e, list each "Other revenue" activity not reported on lines 1 through 10. Report the sum of the amounts entered for lines 11a–e, columns (b), (d), and (e), on line 11, Part I.

Line 13. On line 13, enter the total of columns (b), (d), and (e) of line 12.

Form 990-PF Instructions

You may use the following worksheet to verify your calculations.

Line 13,	Part XVI-A . . . . _____
Minus:	Line 5b, Part I . . . . _____
	Note: *If line 5b, Part I, reflects a loss, add that amount here instead of subtracting.*
Plus:	Line 1, Part I . . . . _____
Plus:	Line 5a, Part I . . . . _____
Plus:	Expenses of special events deducted in computing line 9 of Part XVI-A . . . . _____
Equal:	Line 12, column (a), of Part I _____

Part XVI-B—Relationship of Activities to the Accomplishment of Exempt Purposes

To explain how each amount in column (e) of Part XVI-A was related or exempt function income, show the line number of the amount in column (e) and give a brief description of how each activity reported in column (e) contributed importantly to the accomplishment of the organization's exempt purposes (other than by providing funds for such purposes). Activities that generate exempt-function income are activities that form the basis of the organization's exemption from tax.

Also, explain any income entered in column (e) that is specifically excluded from gross income other than by Code section 512, 513, or 514. If no amount is entered in column (e), do not complete Part XVI-B.

Example. M, a performing arts association, is primarily supported by endowment funds. It raises revenue by charging admissions to its performances. These performances are the primary means by which the organization accomplishes its cultural and educational purposes.

M reported admissions income in column (e) of Part XVI-A and explained in Part XVI-B that these performances are the primary means by which it accomplishes its cultural and educational purposes.

Because M also reported interest from state bonds in column (e) of Part XVI-A, M explained in Part XVI-B that such interest was excluded from gross income by Code section 103.

Part XVII—Information Regarding Transfers To and Transactions and Relationships With Noncharitable Exempt Organizations

Part XVII is used to report direct and indirect transfers to (line 1a) and direct and indirect transactions with (line 1b) and relationships with (line 2) any other noncharitable exempt organization. A "noncharitable exempt organization" is an organization exempt under section 501(c) (that is not exempt under section 501(c)(3)), or a political organization described in section 527.

For purposes of these instructions, the section 501(c)(3) organization completing Part XVII is referred to as the "reporting organization."

A noncharitable exempt organization is "related to or affiliated with" the reporting organization if either:
• The two organizations share some element of common control, or
• A historic and continuing relationship exists between the two organizations.

A noncharitable exempt organization is unrelated to the reporting organization if:
• The two organizations share no element of common control, and
• A historic and continuing relationship does not exist between the two organizations.

An "element of common control" is present when one or more of the officers, directors, or trustees of one organization are elected or appointed by the officers, directors, trustees, or members of the other. An element of common control is also present when more than 25% of the officers, directors, or trustees of one organization serve as officers, directors, or trustees of the other organization.

A "historic and continuing relationship" exists when two organizations participate in a joint effort to achieve one or more common purposes on a continuous or recurring basis rather than on the basis of one or more isolated transactions or activities. Such a relationship also exists when two organizations share facilities, equipment, or paid personnel during the year, regardless of the length of time the arrangement is in effect.

Line 1—Reporting of certain transfers and transactions. Generally, report on line 1 any transfer to or transaction with a noncharitable exempt organization even if the transfer or transaction constitutes the only connection with the noncharitable exempt organization.

Related organizations. If the noncharitable exempt organization is related to or affiliated with the reporting organization, report all direct and indirect transfers and transactions except for contributions and grants it received

Unrelated organizations. All transfers to an unrelated noncharitable exempt organization must be reported on line 1a. All transactions between the reporting organization and an unrelated noncharitable exempt organization must be shown on line 1b unless they meet the exception in the specific instructions for line 1b.

Line 1a—Transfers. Answer "Yes" to lines 1a(1) and 1a(2) if the reporting organization made any direct or indirect transfers of any value to a noncharitable exempt organization.

A "transfer" is any transaction or arrangement whereby one organization transfers something of value (cash, other assets, services, use of property, etc.) to another organization without receiving something of more than nominal value in return. Contributions, gifts, and grants are examples of transfers.

If the only transfers between the two organizations were contributions and grants made by the noncharitable exempt organization to the reporting organization, answer "No."

Line 1b—Other transactions. Answer "Yes" for any transaction described on line 1b(1)–(6), regardless of its amount, if it is with a related or affiliated organization.

Unrelated organizations. Answer "Yes" for any transaction between the reporting organization and an unrelated noncharitable exempt organization, regardless of its amount, if the reporting organization received less than adequate consideration. There is adequate consideration when the fair market value of the goods and other assets or services furnished by the reporting organization is not more than the fair market value of the goods and other assets or services received from the unrelated noncharitable exempt organization. The exception described below does not apply to transactions for less than adequate consideration.

Answer "Yes" for any transaction between the reporting organization and an unrelated noncharitable exempt organization if the "amount involved" is more than $500. The "amount involved" is the fair market value of the goods, services, or other assets furnished by the reporting organization.

Exception. If a transaction with an unrelated noncharitable exempt organization was for adequate consideration and the amount involved was $500 or less, answer "No" for that transaction.

Line 1b(3). Answer "Yes" for transactions in which the reporting organization was either the lessor or the lessee.

Line 1b(4). Answer "Yes" if either organization reimbursed expenses incurred by the other.

Line 1b(5). Answer "Yes" if either organization made loans to the other or if

the reporting organization guaranteed the other's loans.

Line 1b(6). Answer "Yes" if either organization performed services or membership or fundraising solicitations for the other.

Line 1c. Complete line 1c regardless of whether the noncharitable exempt organization is related to or closely affiliated with the reporting organization. For purposes of this line, "facilities" includes office space and any other land, building, or structure whether owned or leased by, or provided free of charge to, the reporting organization or the noncharitable exempt organization.

Line 1d. Use this schedule to describe the transfers and transactions for which "Yes" was entered on lines 1a–c above. You must describe each transfer or transaction for which the answer was "Yes." You may combine all of the cash transfers (line 1a(1)) to each organization into a single entry. Otherwise, make a separate entry for each transfer or transaction.

Column (a). For each entry, enter the line number from line 1a–c. For example, if the answer was "Yes" to line 1b(3), enter "b(3)" in column (a).

Column (d). If you need more space, write "see attached" in column (d) and use an attached sheet for the description. If making more than one entry on line 1d, specify on the attached sheet which transfer or transaction you are describing.

Line 2—Reporting of certain relationships. Enter on line 2 each noncharitable exempt organization that the reporting organization is related to or affiliated with, as defined above. If the control factor or the historic and continuing relationship factor (or both) is present at any time during the year, identify the organization on line 2 even if neither factor is present at the end of the year.

Do not enter unrelated noncharitable exempt organizations on line 2 even if transfers to or transactions with those organizations were entered on line 1. For example, if a one-time transfer to an unrelated noncharitable exempt organization was entered on line 1a(2), do not enter the organization on line 2.

Column (b). Enter the exempt category of the organization; for example, "501(c)(4)."

Column (c). In most cases, a simple description, such as "common directors" or "auxiliary of reporting organization" will be sufficient. If you need more space, write "see attached" in column (c) and use an attached sheet to describe the relationship. If you are entering more than one organization on line 2, identify which organization you are describing on the attached sheet.

Signature

The return must be signed by the president, vice president, treasurer, assistant treasurer, chief accounting officer, or other corporate officer (such as tax officer) who is authorized to sign. A receiver, trustee, or assignee must sign any return that he or she is required to file for a corporation. If the return is filed for a trust, it must be signed by the authorized trustee or trustees. Sign and date the form and fill in the signer's title.

If an officer or employee of the organization prepares the return, the Paid Preparer's space should remain blank. If someone prepares the return without charge, that person should not sign the return.

Generally, anyone who is paid to prepare the organization's tax return must sign the return and fill in the Paid Preparer's Use Only area.

If you have questions about whether a preparer is required to sign the return, please contact an IRS office.

The paid preparer must complete the required preparer information and:
- Sign it in the space provided for the preparer's signature (a facsimile signature is acceptable), and
- Give the organization a copy of the return in addition to the copy to be filed with the IRS.

If the box for question 13 of Part VII-A is checked (section 4947(a)(1) nonexempt charitable trust filing Form 990-PF instead of Form 1041), the paid preparer must also enter his or her social security number or, if applicable, PTIN and employer identification number in the spaces provided. Otherwise, do not enter the preparer's social security or employer identification number.

Privacy Act and Paperwork Reduction Act Notice. We ask for the information on this form to carry out the Internal Revenue laws of the United States. You are required to give us the information. We need it to ensure that you are complying with these laws and to allow us to figure and collect the right amount of tax. Section 6109 requires return preparers to provide their identifying numbers on the return.

You are not required to provide the information requested on a form that is subject to the Paperwork Reduction Act unless the form displays a valid OMB control number. Books or records relating to a form or its instructions must be retained as long as their contents may become material in the administration of any Internal Revenue law. The rules governing the confidentiality of Form 990-PF are covered in Code section 6104.

The time needed to complete and file this form will vary depending on individual

Form 990-PF Instructions

circumstances. The estimated average time is:

Recordkeeping . . . .   140 hr., 37 min.

Learning about the law or the form . . . .   28 hr., 15 min.

Preparing the form . . . . . .   33 hr., 39 min.

Copying, assembling, and sending the form to the IRS   32 min.

If you have comments concerning the accuracy of these time estimates or suggestions for making this form simpler, we would be happy to hear from you. You can write to the Internal Revenue Service, Tax Products Coordinating Committee, SE:W:CAR:MP:T:T:SP, 1111 Constitution Ave. NW, IR-6406 Washington DC, 20224. Do not send the tax form to this address. Instead, see *When and Where To File* on page 5.

Exclusion Codes

General Exceptions

01— Income from an activity that is not regularly carried on (section 512(a)(1))

02— Income from an activity in which labor is a material income-producing factor and substantially all (at least 85%) of the work is performed with unpaid labor (section 513(a)(1))

03— Section 501(c)(3) organization— Income from an activity carried on primarily for the convenience of the organization's members, students, patients, visitors, officers, or employees (hospital parking lot or museum cafeteria, for example) (section 513(c))

04— Section 501(c)(4) local association of employees organized before May 27, 1969— Income from the sale of work-related clothes or equipment and items normally sold through vending machines; food dispensing facilities; or snack bars for the convenience of association members at their usual places of employment (section 513(a)(2))

05— Income from the sale of merchandise, substantially all of which (at least 85%) was donated to the organization (section 513(a)(3))

Specific Exceptions

06— Section 501(c)(3), (4), or (5) organization conducting an agricultural or educational fair or exposition— Qualified public entertainment activity income (section 513(d)(2))

07— Section 501(c)(3), (4), (5), or (6) organization—Qualified convention and trade show activity income (section 513(d)(3))

08— Income from hospital services described in section 513(e)

09— Income from noncommercial bingo games that do not violate state or local law (section 513(f))

10— Income from games of chance conducted by an organization in North Dakota (section 311 of the Deficit Reduction Act of 1984, as amended)

11— Section 501(c)(12) organization— Qualified pole rental income (section 513(g)) and/or member income (described in section 501(c)(12)(H))

12— Income from the distribution of low-cost articles in connection with the solicitation of charitable contributions (section 513(h))

13— Income from the exchange or rental of membership or donor list with an organization eligible to receive charitable contributions by a section 501(c)(3) organization; by a war veterans' organization; or an auxiliary unit or society of, or trust or foundation for, a war veterans' post or organization (section 513(h))

Modifications and Exclusions

14— Dividends, interest, payments with respect to securities loans, annuities, income from notional principal contracts, other substantially similar income from ordinary and routine investments, and loan commitment fees, excluded by section 512(b)(1)

15— Royalty income excluded by section 512(b)(2)

16— Real property rental income that does not depend on the income or profits derived by the person leasing the property and is excluded by section 512 (b)(3)

17— Rent from personal property leased with real property and incidental (10% or less) in relation to the combined income from the real and personal property (section 512(b)(3))

18— Gain or loss from the sale of investments and other non-inventory property and from certain property acquired from financial institutions that are in conservatorship or receivership (sections 512(b)(5) and (16)(A))

19— Gain or loss from the lapse or termination of options to buy or sell securities or real property, and on options and from the forfeiture of good-faith deposits for the purchase, sale, or lease of investment real estate (section 512(b)(5))

20— Income from research for the United States; its agencies or instrumentalities; or any state or political subdivision (section 512(b)(7))

21— Income from research conducted by a college, university, or hospital (section 512(b)(8))

22— Income from research conducted by an organization whose primary activity is conducting fundamental research, the results of which are freely available to the general public (section 512(b)(9))

23— Income from services provided under license issued by a federal regulatory agency and conducted by a religious order or school operated by a religious order, but only if the trade or business has been carried on by the organization since before May 27, 1959 (section 512 (b)(15))

Foreign Organizations

24— Foreign organizations only—Income from a trade or business NOT conducted in the United States and NOT derived from United States sources (patrons) (section 512(a)(2))

Social Clubs and VEBAs

25— Section 501(c)(7), (9), or (17) organization—Non-exempt function income set aside for a charitable, etc., purpose specified in section 170(c)(4) (section 512(a)(3)(B)(i))

26— Section 501(c)(7), (9), or (17) organization—Proceeds from the sale of exempt function property that was or will be timely reinvested in similar property (section 512(a)(3)(D))

27— Section 501(c)(9) or (17) organization— Nonfunction income set aside for the payment of life, sick, accident, or other benefits (section 512(a)(3)(B)(ii))

Veterans' Organizations

28— Section 501(c)(19) organization— Payments for life, sick, accident, or health insurance for members or their dependents that are set aside for the payment of such insurance benefits or for a charitable, etc., purpose specified in section 170(c)(4) (section 512(a)(4))

29— Section 501(c)(19) organization— Income from an insurance set-aside (see code 28 above) that is set aside for payment of insurance benefits or for a charitable, etc., purpose specified in section 170(c)(4) (Regs. 1.512(a)–4(b)(2))

Debt-Financed Income

30— Income exempt from debt-financed (section 514) provisions because at least 85% of the use of the property is for the organization's exempt purposes. (**Note:** *This code is only for income from the 15% or less non-exempt purpose use.*) (section 514(b)(1)(A))

31— Gross income from mortgaged property used in research activities described in section 512(b)(7), (8), or (9) (section 514(b)(1)(C))

32— Gross income from mortgaged property used in any activity described in section 513(a)(1), (2), or (3) (section 514(b)(1)(D))

33— Income from mortgaged property (neighborhood land) acquired for exempt purpose use within 10 years (section 514(b)(3))

34— Income from mortgaged property acquired by bequest or devise (applies to income received within 10 years from the date of acquisition) (section 514(c)(2)(B))

35— Income from mortgaged property acquired by gift where the mortgage was placed on the property more than 5 years previously and the property was held by the donor for more than 5 years (applies to income received within 10 years from the date of gift (section 514(c)(2)(B))

36— Income from property received in return for the obligation to pay an annuity described in section 514(c)(5)

37— Income from mortgaged property that provides housing to low and moderate income persons, to the extent the mortgage is insured by the Federal Housing Administration (section 514(c)(6)). (**Note:** *In many cases, this would be exempt function income reportable in column (e). It would not be so in the case of a section 501(c)(5) or (6) organization, for example, that acquired the housing as an investment or as a charitable activity.*)

38— Income from mortgaged real property owned by: a school described in section 170(b)(1)(A)(ii); a section 509(a)(3) affiliated support organization of such a school; a section 501(c)(25) organization; or by a partnership in which any of the above organizations owns an interest if the requirements of section 514(c)(9)(B)(vi) are met (section 514(c)(9))

Special Rules

39— Section 501(c)(5) organization—Farm income used to finance the operation and maintenance of a retirement home, hospital, or similar facility operated by the organization for its members on property adjacent to the farm land (section 1951(b)(8)(B) of Public Law 94-455)

40— Annual dues, not exceeding $127 (subject to inflation), paid to a section 501(c)(5) agricultural or horticultural organization (section 512(d))

Trade or Business

41— Gross income from an unrelated activity that is regularly carried on but, in light of continuous losses sustained over a number of tax periods, cannot be regarded as being conducted with the motive to make a profit (not a trade or business)

Other

42— Receipt of qualified sponsorship payments described in section 513(i)

43— Exclusion of any gain or loss from the qualified sale, exchange, or other disposition of any qualifying brownfield property (section 512(b)(18)[(19)])

-30-   Form 990-PF Instructions

Index

Form **990-PF**

Department of the Treasury
Internal Revenue Service

Return of Private Foundation
or Section 4947(a)(1) Nonexempt Charitable Trust
Treated as a Private Foundation

Note: *The organization may be able to use a copy of this return to satisfy state reporting requirements.*

OMB No. 1545-0052

2005

For calendar year 2005, or tax year beginning _____ , 2005, and ending _____ , 20 ____

G Check all that apply: ☐ Initial return   ☐ Final return   ☐ Amended return   ☐ Address change   ☐ Name change

Use the IRS label. Otherwise, print or type. See Specific Instructions.	Name of organization		A Employer identification number
	Number and street (or P.O. box number if mail is not delivered to street address)	Room/suite	B Telephone number (see page 10 of the instructions) ( )
	City or town, state, and ZIP code		C If exemption application is pending, check here ► ☐

D 1. Foreign organizations, check here . . ► ☐

H Check type of organization: ☐ Section 501(c)(3) exempt private foundation
☐ Section 4947(a)(1) nonexempt charitable trust   ☐ Other taxable private foundation

2. Foreign organizations meeting the 85% test, check here and attach computation . ► ☐

I Fair market value of all assets at end of year *(from Part II, col. (c), line 16)* ► $ _____

J Accounting method: ☐ Cash   ☐ Accrual
☐ Other (specify) _____
(Part I, column (d) must be on cash basis.)

E If private foundation status was terminated under section 507(b)(1)(A), check here . ► ☐

F If the foundation is in a 60-month termination under section 507(b)(1)(B), check here . ► ☐

Part I — Analysis of Revenue and Expenses *(The total of amounts in columns (b), (c), and (d) may not necessarily equal the amounts in column (a) (see page 11 of the instructions).)*

		(a) Revenue and expenses per books	(b) Net investment income	(c) Adjusted net income	(d) Disbursements for charitable purposes (cash basis only)
Revenue	1 Contributions, gifts, grants, etc., received (attach schedule)				
	2 Check ► ☐ if the foundation is **not** required to attach Sch. B				
	3 Interest on savings and temporary cash investments				
	4 Dividends and interest from securities . . .				
	5a Gross rents				
	b Net rental income or (loss) _____				
	6a Net gain or (loss) from sale of assets not on line 10				
	b Gross sales price for all assets on line 6a _____				
	7 Capital gain net income (from Part IV, line 2) .				
	8 Net short-term capital gain				
	9 Income modifications				
	10a Gross sales less returns and allowances				
	b Less: Cost of goods sold. .				
	c Gross profit or (loss) (attach schedule) . . .				
	11 Other income (attach schedule).				
	12 **Total.** Add lines 1 through 11				
Operating and Administrative Expenses	13 Compensation of officers, directors, trustees, etc.				
	14 Other employee salaries and wages				
	15 Pension plans, employee benefits				
	16a Legal fees (attach schedule).				
	b Accounting fees (attach schedule)				
	c Other professional fees (attach schedule) . .				
	17 Interest.				
	18 Taxes (attach schedule) (see page 14 of the instructions)				
	19 Depreciation (attach schedule) and depletion .				
	20 Occupancy				
	21 Travel, conferences, and meetings.				
	22 Printing and publications				
	23 Other expenses (attach schedule).				
	24 **Total operating and administrative expenses.** Add lines 13 through 23				
	25 Contributions, gifts, grants paid				
	26 **Total expenses and disbursements.** Add lines 24 and 25				
	27 Subtract line 26 from line 12:				
	a Excess of revenue over expenses and disbursements				
	b **Net investment income** (if negative, enter -0-)				
	c **Adjusted net income** (if negative, enter -0-) .				

For Privacy Act and Paperwork Reduction Act Notice, see the instructions.   Cat. No. 11289X   Form **990-PF** (2005)

Part II	Balance Sheets	Attached schedules and amounts in the description column should be for end-of-year amounts only. (See instructions.)	Beginning of year	End of year	
			(a) Book Value	(b) Book Value	(c) Fair Market Value

Assets

		(a)	(b)	(c)
1	Cash—non-interest-bearing			
2	Savings and temporary cash investments			
3	Accounts receivable ▶			
	Less: allowance for doubtful accounts ▶			
4	Pledges receivable ▶			
	Less: allowance for doubtful accounts ▶			
5	Grants receivable			
6	Receivables due from officers, directors, trustees, and other disqualified persons (attach schedule) (see page 15 of the instructions)			
7	Other notes and loans receivable (attach schedule) ▶			
	Less: allowance for doubtful accounts ▶..............................			
8	Inventories for sale or use.			
9	Prepaid expenses and deferred charges			
10a	Investments—U.S. and state government obligations (attach schedule)			
b	Investments—corporate stock (attach schedule) . . .			
c	Investments—corporate bonds (attach schedule)			
11	Investments—land, buildings, and equipment: basis ▶			
	Less: accumulated depreciation (attach schedule) ▶....................			
12	Investments—mortgage loans			
13	Investments—other (attach schedule)			
14	Land, buildings, and equipment: basis ▶..............................			
	Less: accumulated depreciation (attach schedule) ▶....................			
15	Other assets (describe ▶.....................................)			
16	**Total assets** (to be completed by all filers—see page 16 of the instructions. Also, see page 1, item I)			

Liabilities

		(a)	(b)	(c)
17	Accounts payable and accrued expenses			
18	Grants payable			
19	Deferred revenue.			
20	Loans from officers, directors, trustees, and other disqualified persons			
21	Mortgages and other notes payable (attach schedule) . .			
22	Other liabilities (describe ▶ ....)			
23	**Total liabilities** (add lines 17 through 22).			

Net Assets or Fund Balances

		(a)	(b)	(c)
	Organizations that follow SFAS 117, check here ▶ ☐ **and complete lines 24 through 26 and lines 30 and 31.**			
24	Unrestricted			
25	Temporarily restricted			
26	Permanently restricted			
	Organizations that do not follow SFAS 117, check here ▶ ☐ **and complete lines 27 through 31.**			
27	Capital stock, trust principal, or current funds			
28	Paid-in or capital surplus, or land, bldg., and equipment fund			
29	Retained earnings, accumulated income, endowment, or other funds			
30	**Total net assets or fund balances** (see page 17 of the instructions)			
31	**Total liabilities and net assets/fund balances** (see page 17 of the instructions)			

Part III	Analysis of Changes in Net Assets or Fund Balances

1	Total net assets or fund balances at beginning of year—Part II, column (a), line 30 (must agree with end-of-year figure reported on prior year's return).	1	
2	Enter amount from Part I, line 27a.	2	
3	Other increases not included in line 2 (itemize) ▶	3	
4	Add lines 1, 2, and 3	4	
5	Decreases not included in line 2 (itemize) ▶	5	
6	Total net assets or fund balances at end of year (line 4 minus line 5)—Part II, column (b), line 30. .	6	

Form **990-PF** (2005)

Form 990-PF (2005)   Page **3**

Part IV — Capital Gains and Losses for Tax on Investment Income

(a) List and describe the kind(s) of property sold (e.g., real estate, 2-story brick warehouse; or common stock, 200 shs. MLC Co.)	(b) How acquired P—Purchase D—Donation	(c) Date acquired (mo., day, yr.)	(d) Date sold (mo., day, yr.)
1a			
b			
c			
d			
e			

(e) Gross sales price	(f) Depreciation allowed (or allowable)	(g) Cost or other basis plus expense of sale	(h) Gain or (loss) (e) plus (f) minus (g)
a			
b			
c			
d			
e			

Complete only for assets showing gain in column (h) and owned by the foundation on 12/31/69

(i) F.M.V. as of 12/31/69	(j) Adjusted basis as of 12/31/69	(k) Excess of col. (i) over col. (j), if any	(l) Gains (Col. (h) gain minus col. (k), but not less than -0-) or Losses (from col.(h))
a			
b			
c			
d			
e			

2 Capital gain net income or (net capital loss) { If gain, also enter in Part I, line 7 / If (loss), enter -0- in Part I, line 7 } **2**

3 Net short-term capital gain or (loss) as defined in sections 1222(5) and (6):
If gain, also enter in Part I, line 8, column (c) (see pages 13 and 17 of the instructions). If (loss), enter -0- in Part I, line 8 . . . . **3**

Part V — Qualification Under Section 4940(e) for Reduced Tax on Net Investment Income

(For optional use by domestic private foundations subject to the section 4940(a) tax on net investment income.)

If section 4940(d)(2) applies, leave this part blank.

Was the organization liable for the section 4942 tax on the distributable amount of any year in the base period? ☐ Yes ☐ No
If "Yes," the organization does not qualify under section 4940(e). Do not complete this part.

1 Enter the appropriate amount in each column for each year; see page 18 of the instructions before making any entries.

(a) Base period years Calendar year (or tax year beginning in)	(b) Adjusted qualifying distributions	(c) Net value of noncharitable-use assets	(d) Distribution ratio (col. (b) divided by col. (c))
2004			
2003			
2002			
2001			
2000			

2 **Total** of line 1, column (d) **2**

3 Average distribution ratio for the 5-year base period—divide the total on line 2 by 5, or by the number of years the foundation has been in existence if less than 5 years **3**

4 Enter the net value of noncharitable-use assets for 2005 from Part X, line 5 . . . . **4**

5 Multiply line 4 by line 3 . . . . **5**

6 Enter 1% of net investment income (1% of Part I, line 27b) **6**

7 Add lines 5 and 6 . . . . **7**

8 Enter qualifying distributions from Part XII, line 4 . . . . **8**

If line 8 is equal to or greater than line 7, check the box in Part VI, line 1b, and complete that part using a 1% tax rate. See the Part VI instructions on page 18.

Form **990-PF** (2005)

Form 990-PF (2005)   Page **4**

Part VI	**Excise Tax Based on Investment Income (Section 4940(a), 4940(b), 4940(e), or 4948—see page 18 of the instructions)**

1a Exempt operating foundations described in section 4940(d)(2), check here ▶ ☐ and enter "N/A" on line 1.
     Date of ruling letter: .... **(attach copy of ruling letter if necessary—see instructions)**
  b Domestic organizations that meet the section 4940(e) requirements in Part V, check   **1**
     here ▶ ☐ and enter 1% of Part I, line 27b . . . .
  c All other domestic organizations enter 2% of line 27b. Exempt foreign organizations enter 4% of Part I, line 12, col. (b)
  2 Tax under section 511 (domestic section 4947(a)(1) trusts and taxable foundations only. Others enter -0-)   **2**
  3 Add lines 1 and 2. . . . .   **3**
  4 Subtitle A (income) tax (domestic section 4947(a)(1) trusts and taxable foundations only. Others enter -0-) .   **4**
  5 **Tax based on investment income.** Subtract line 4 from line 3. If zero or less, enter -0- . . .   **5**
  6 Credits/Payments:
  a 2005 estimated tax payments and 2004 overpayment credited to 2005   **6a**
  b Exempt foreign organizations—tax withheld at source **6b**
  c Tax paid with application for extension of time to file (Form 8868)   **6c**
  d Backup withholding erroneously withheld. **6d**
  7 Total credits and payments. Add lines 6a through 6d **7**
  8 Enter any **penalty** for underpayment of estimated tax. Check here ☐ if Form 2220 is attached.   **8**
  9 **Tax due.** If the total of lines 5 and 8 is more than line 7, enter **amount owed** . . . . ▶   **9**
 10 **Overpayment.** If line 7 is more than the total of lines 5 and 8, enter the **amount overpaid**. . . ▶   **10**
 11 Enter the amount of line 10 to be: **Credited to 2006 estimated tax** ▶ | **Refunded** ▶ | **11**

Part VII-A	**Statements Regarding Activities**

                                                                                       Yes | **No**

1a During the tax year, did the organization attempt to influence any national, state, or local legislation or did
     it participate or intervene in any political campaign? **1a**
  b Did it spend more than $100 during the year (either directly or indirectly) for political purposes (see page
     19 of the instructions for definition)? **1b**
       *If the answer is "Yes" to **1a** or **1b**, attach a detailed description of the activities and copies of any materials
       published or distributed by the organization in connection with the activities.*
  c Did the organization file **Form 1120-POL** for this year? **1c**
  d Enter the amount (if any) of tax on political expenditures (section 4955) imposed during the year:
     (1) On the organization. ▶ $ _____ **(2)** On organization managers. ▶ $ _____
  e Enter the reimbursement (if any) paid by the organization during the year for political expenditure tax imposed
     on organization managers. ▶ $ _____
  2 Has the organization engaged in any activities that have not previously been reported to the IRS? . .   **2**
     If "Yes," attach a detailed description of the activities.
  3 Has the organization made any changes, not previously reported to the IRS, in its governing instrument, articles
     of incorporation, or bylaws, or other similar instruments? *If "Yes," attach a conformed copy of the changes* .   **3**
 4a Did the organization have unrelated business gross income of $1,000 or more during the year? . . .   **4a**
  b If "Yes," has it filed a tax return on **Form 990-T** for this year? **4b**
  5 Was there a liquidation, termination, dissolution, or substantial contraction during the year?. . . .   **5**
     If "Yes," attach the statement required by General Instruction T.
  6 Are the requirements of section 508(e) (relating to sections 4941 through 4945) satisfied either:
     • By language in the governing instrument, or
     • By state legislation that effectively amends the governing instrument so that no mandatory directions
       that conflict with the state law remain in the governing instrument? **6**
  7 Did the organization have at least $5,000 in assets at any time during the year? *If "Yes," complete Part II, col. (c), and Part XV.*   **7**
 8a Enter the states to which the foundation reports or with which it is registered (see page 19 of the
     instructions) ▶ ....
  b If the answer is "Yes" to line 7, has the organization furnished a copy of Form 990-PF to the Attorney
     General (or designate) of each state as required by *General Instruction G? If "No," attach explanation* .   **8b**
  9 Is the organization claiming status as a private operating foundation within the meaning of section 4942(j)(3)
     or 4942(j)(5) for calendar year 2005 or the taxable year beginning in 2005 (see instructions for Part XIV on
     page 26)? *If "Yes," complete Part XIV* **9**
 10 Did any persons become substantial contributors during the tax year? *If "Yes," attach a schedule listing their names and addresses.*   **10**
 11 Did the organization comply with the public inspection requirements for its annual returns and exemption application?   **11**
     Web site address ▶ ....
 12 The books are in care of ▶ .... Telephone no. ▶ ....
     Located at ▶ .... ZIP+4 ▶ ....
 13 Section 4947(a)(1) nonexempt charitable trusts filing Form 990-PF in lieu of **Form 1041**—Check here . . . . . ▶ ☐
     and enter the amount of tax-exempt interest received or accrued during the year . . . ▶ | **13**

                                                                                         Form **990-PF** (2005)

Part VII-B Statements Regarding Activities for Which Form 4720 May Be Required

			Yes	No
File Form 4720 if any item is checked in the "Yes" column, unless an exception applies.				

1a During the year did the organization (either directly or indirectly):

   (1) Engage in the sale or exchange, or leasing of property with a disqualified person? ☐ Yes ☐ No

   (2) Borrow money from, lend money to, or otherwise extend credit to (or accept it from) a disqualified person? . . . . ☐ Yes ☐ No

   (3) Furnish goods, services, or facilities to (or accept them from) a disqualified person? ☐ Yes ☐ No

   (4) Pay compensation to, or pay or reimburse the expenses of, a disqualified person? ☐ Yes ☐ No

   (5) Transfer any income or assets to a disqualified person (or make any of either available for the benefit or use of a disqualified person)? . . . . ☐ Yes ☐ No

   (6) Agree to pay money or property to a government official? (**Exception.** Check "No" if the organization agreed to make a grant to or to employ the official for a period after termination of government service, if terminating within 90 days.) . . . . ☐ Yes ☐ No

b If any answer is "Yes" to 1a(1)–(6), did **any** of the acts fail to qualify under the exceptions described in Regulations section 53.4941(d)-3 or in a current notice regarding disaster assistance (see page 20 of the instructions)? . . **1b**
Organizations relying on a current notice regarding disaster assistance check here . . . . . ▶ ☐

c Did the organization engage in a prior year in any of the acts described in 1a, other than excepted acts, that were not corrected before the first day of the tax year beginning in 2005? **1c**

2 Taxes on failure to distribute income (section 4942) (does not apply for years the organization was a private operating foundation defined in section 4942(j)(3) or 4942(j)(5)):

a At the end of tax year 2005, did the organization have any undistributed income (lines 6d and 6e, Part XIII) for tax year(s) beginning before 2005? . . . . ☐ Yes ☐ No
If "Yes," list the years ▶ 20 ..... , 20 ..... , 20 ..... , 20 .....

b Are there any years listed in 2a for which the organization is **not** applying the provisions of section 4942(a)(2) (relating to incorrect valuation of assets) to the year's undistributed income? (If applying section 4942(a)(2) to **all** years listed, answer "No" and attach statement—see page 20 of the instructions.) **2b**

c If the provisions of section 4942(a)(2) are being applied to **any** of the years listed in 2a, list the years here.
   ▶ 20 .... , 20 .... , 20 .... , 20 .....

3a Did the organization hold more than a 2% direct or indirect interest in any business enterprise at any time during the year? . . . . ☐ Yes ☐ No

b If "Yes," did it have excess business holdings in 2005 as a result of **(1)** any purchase by the organization or disqualified persons after May 26, 1969; **(2)** the lapse of the 5-year period (or longer period approved by the Commissioner under section 4943(c)(7)) to dispose of holdings acquired by gift or bequest; or **(3)** the lapse of the 10-, 15-, or 20-year first phase holding period? *(Use Schedule C, Form 4720, to determine if the organization had excess business holdings in 2005.)* **3b**

4a Did the organization invest during the year any amount in a manner that would jeopardize its charitable purposes? **4a**

b Did the organization make any investment in a prior year (but after December 31, 1969) that could jeopardize its charitable purpose that had not been removed from jeopardy before the first day of the tax year beginning in 2005? **4b**

5a During the year did the organization pay or incur any amount to:

   (1) Carry on propaganda, or otherwise attempt to influence legislation (section 4945(e))? ☐ Yes ☐ No

   (2) Influence the outcome of any specific public election (see section 4955); or to carry on, directly or indirectly, any voter registration drive? . . . . ☐ Yes ☐ No

   (3) Provide a grant to an individual for travel, study, or other similar purposes?. . . ☐ Yes ☐ No

   (4) Provide a grant to an organization other than a charitable, etc., organization described in section 509(a)(1), (2), or (3), or section 4940(d)(2)? . . . . ☐ Yes ☐ No

   (5) Provide for any purpose other than religious, charitable, scientific, literary, or educational purposes, or for the prevention of cruelty to children or animals? . . ☐ Yes ☐ No

b If any answer is "Yes" to 5a(1)–(5), did **any** of the transactions fail to qualify under the exceptions described in Regulations section 53.4945 or in a current notice regarding disaster assistance (see page 20 of the instructions)? **5b**
Organizations relying on a current notice regarding disaster assistance check here . . . . . ▶ ☐

c If the answer is "Yes" to question 5a(4), does the organization claim exemption from the tax because it maintained expenditure responsibility for the grant? . . . . ☐ Yes ☐ No
If "Yes," attach the statement required by Regulations section 53.4945–5(d).

6a Did the organization, during the year, receive any funds, directly or indirectly, to pay premiums on a personal benefit contract? . . . . ☐ Yes ☐ No

b Did the organization, during the year, pay premiums, directly or indirectly, on a personal benefit contract? . **6b**
If you answered "Yes" to 6b, also file Form 8870.

Form 990-PF (2005) Page **6**

Part VIII | Information About Officers, Directors, Trustees, Foundation Managers, Highly Paid Employees, and Contractors

1 List all officers, directors, trustees, foundation managers and their compensation (see page 21 of the instructions).

(a) Name and address	(b) Title, and average hours per week devoted to position	(c) Compensation (If not paid, enter -0-)	(d) Contributions to employee benefit plans and deferred compensation	(e) Expense account, other allowances

2 Compensation of five highest-paid employees (other than those included on line 1—see page 21 of the instructions). If none, enter "NONE."

(a) Name and address of each employee paid more than $50,000	(b) Title and average hours per week devoted to position	(c) Compensation	(d) Contributions to employee benefit plans and deferred compensation	(e) Expense account, other allowances

Total number of other employees paid over $50,000 . . . . ▶

3 Five highest-paid independent contractors for professional services—(see page 21 of the instructions). If none, enter "NONE."

(a) Name and address of each person paid more than $50,000	(b) Type of service	(c) Compensation

Total number of others receiving over $50,000 for professional services . . . . ▶

Part IX-A | Summary of Direct Charitable Activities

List the foundation's four largest direct charitable activities during the tax year. Include relevant statistical information such as the number of organizations and other beneficiaries served, conferences convened, research papers produced, etc.	Expenses
1	
2	
3	
4	

Form **990-PF** (2005)

Part IX-B Summary of Program-Related Investments (see page 22 of the instructions)

Describe the two largest program-related investments made by the foundation during the tax year on lines 1 and 2.	Amount
1	
....	
....	
2	
....	
....	

All other program-related investments. See page 22 of the instructions.

3 ....

....

Total. Add lines 1 through 3 . . . . ▶

Part X Minimum Investment Return (All domestic foundations must complete this part. Foreign foundations, see page 22 of the instructions.)

1	Fair market value of assets not used (or held for use) directly in carrying out charitable, etc., purposes:		
a	Average monthly fair market value of securities	1a	
b	Average of monthly cash balances	1b	
c	Fair market value of all other assets (see page 23 of the instructions)	1c	
d	**Total** (add lines 1a, b, and c)	1d	
e	Reduction claimed for blockage or other factors reported on lines 1a and 1c (attach detailed explanation) . . . . [1e]		
2	Acquisition indebtedness applicable to line 1 assets	2	
3	Subtract line 2 from line 1d	3	
4	Cash deemed held for charitable activities. Enter 1½% of line 3 (for greater amount, see page 23 of the instructions)	4	
5	**Net value of noncharitable-use assets.** Subtract line 4 from line 3. Enter here and on Part V, line 4	5	
6	**Minimum investment return.** Enter 5% of line 5	6	

Part XI Distributable Amount (see page 23 of the instructions) (Section 4942(j)(3) and (j)(5) private operating foundations and certain foreign organizations check here ▶ ☐ and do not complete this part.)

1	Minimum investment return from Part X, line 6	1	
2a	Tax on investment income for 2005 from Part VI, line 5 . . . . . [2a]		
b	Income tax for 2005. (This does not include the tax from Part VI.) . . [2b]		
c	Add lines 2a and 2b	2c	
3	Distributable amount before adjustments. Subtract line 2c from line 1	3	
4	Recoveries of amounts treated as qualifying distributions	4	
5	Add lines 3 and 4	5	
6	Deduction from distributable amount (see page 24 of the instructions)	6	
7	**Distributable amount** as adjusted. Subtract line 6 from line 5. Enter here and on Part XIII, line 1	7	

Part XII Qualifying Distributions (see page 24 of the instructions)

1	Amounts paid (including administrative expenses) to accomplish charitable, etc., purposes:		
a	Expenses, contributions, gifts, etc.—total from Part I, column (d), line 26	1a	
b	Program-related investments—total from Part IX-B	1b	
2	Amounts paid to acquire assets used (or held for use) directly in carrying out charitable, etc., purposes	2	
3	Amounts set aside for specific charitable projects that satisfy the:		
a	Suitability test (prior IRS approval required)	3a	
b	Cash distribution test (attach the required schedule)	3b	
4	**Qualifying distributions.** Add lines 1a through 3b. Enter here and on Part V, line 8, and Part XIII, line 4 .	4	
5	Organizations that qualify under section 4940(e) for the reduced rate of tax on net investment income. Enter 1% of Part I, line 27b (see page 24 of the instructions)	5	
6	**Adjusted qualifying distributions.** Subtract line 5 from line 4	6	

Note: *The amount on line 6 will be used in Part V, column (b), in subsequent years when calculating whether the foundation qualifies for the section 4940(e) reduction of tax in those years.*

Form **990-PF** (2005)

Part XIII **Undistributed Income** (see page 24 of the instructions)

		(a) Corpus	(b) Years prior to 2004	(c) 2004	(d) 2005
1	Distributable amount for 2005 from Part XI, line 7				
2	Undistributed income, if any, as of the end of 2004:				
a	Enter amount for 2004 only				
b	Total for prior years: 20 ___ , 20 ___ , 20 ___				
3	Excess distributions carryover, if any, to 2005:				
a	From 2000				
b	From 2001				
c	From 2002				
d	From 2003				
e	From 2004				
f	**Total** of lines 3a through e				
4	Qualifying distributions for 2005 from Part XII, line 4: ▶ $ _____				
a	Applied to 2004, but not more than line 2a				
b	Applied to undistributed income of prior years (Election required—see page 25 of the instructions)				
c	Treated as distributions out of corpus (Election required—see page 25 of the instructions)				
d	Applied to 2005 distributable amount . .				
e	Remaining amount distributed out of corpus				
5	Excess distributions carryover applied to 2005 *(If an amount appears in column (d), the same amount must be shown in column (a).)*				
6	**Enter the net total of each column as indicated below:**				
a	Corpus. Add lines 3f, 4c, and 4e. Subtract line 5				
b	Prior years' undistributed income. Subtract line 4b from line 2b				
c	Enter the amount of prior years' undistributed income for which a notice of deficiency has been issued, or on which the section 4942(a) tax has been previously assessed				
d	Subtract line 6c from line 6b. Taxable amount—see page 25 of the instructions .				
e	Undistributed income for 2004. Subtract line 4a from line 2a. Taxable amount—see page 25 of the instructions				
f	Undistributed income for 2005. Subtract lines 4d and 5 from line 1. This amount must be distributed in 2006				
7	Amounts treated as distributions out of corpus to satisfy requirements imposed by section 170(b)(1)(E) or 4942(g)(3) (see page 25 of the instructions)				
8	Excess distributions carryover from 2000 not applied on line 5 or line 7 (see page 25 of the instructions)				
9	**Excess distributions carryover to 2006.** Subtract lines 7 and 8 from line 6a . .				
10	Analysis of line 9:				
a	Excess from 2001 . .				
b	Excess from 2002 . .				
c	Excess from 2003 . .				
d	Excess from 2004 . .				
e	Excess from 2005 . .				

Form **990-PF** (2005)

8-127

Form 990-PF (2005)   Page **9**

Part XIV   Private Operating Foundations (see page 26 of the instructions and Part VII-A, question 9)

1a   If the foundation has received a ruling or determination letter that it is a private operating foundation, and the ruling is effective for 2005, enter the date of the ruling . . . . ▶

b   Check box to indicate whether the organization is a private operating foundation described in section ☐ 4942(j)(3) or ☐ 4942(j)(5)

2a Enter the lesser of the adjusted net income from Part I or the minimum investment return from Part X for each year listed	Tax year	Prior 3 years			(e) Total
	(a) 2005	(b) 2004	(c) 2003	(d) 2002	
b 85% of line 2a					
c Qualifying distributions from Part XII, line 4 for each year listed					
d Amounts included in line 2c not used directly for active conduct of exempt activities . .					
e Qualifying distributions made directly for active conduct of exempt activities. Subtract line 2d from line 2c . . .					
3 Complete 3a, b, or c for the alternative test relied upon:					
a "Assets" alternative test—enter:					
(1) Value of all assets					
(2) Value of assets qualifying under section 4942(j)(3)(B)(i)					
b "Endowment" alternative test—enter ⅔ of minimum investment return shown in Part X, line 6 for each year listed . .					
c "Support" alternative test—enter:					
(1) Total support other than gross investment income (interest, dividends, rents, payments on securities loans (section 512(a)(5)), or royalties) . .					
(2) Support from general public and 5 or more exempt organizations as provided in section 4942(j)(3)(B)(iii) . .					
(3) Largest amount of support from an exempt organization					
(4) Gross investment income					

Part XV   Supplementary Information (Complete this part only if the organization had $5,000 or more in assets at any time during the year—see page 26 of the instructions.)

1   **Information Regarding Foundation Managers:**

a   List any managers of the foundation who have contributed more than 2% of the total contributions received by the foundation before the close of any tax year (but only if they have contributed more than $5,000). (See section 507(d)(2).)

b   List any managers of the foundation who own 10% or more of the stock of a corporation (or an equally large portion of the ownership of a partnership or other entity) of which the foundation has a 10% or greater interest.

2   **Information Regarding Contribution, Grant, Gift, Loan, Scholarship, etc., Programs:**

   Check here ▶ ☐ if the organization only makes contributions to preselected charitable organizations and does not accept unsolicited requests for funds. If the organization makes gifts, grants, etc. (see page 26 of the instructions) to individuals or organizations under other conditions, complete items 2a, b, c, and d.

a   The name, address, and telephone number of the person to whom applications should be addressed:

b   The form in which applications should be submitted and information and materials they should include:

c   Any submission deadlines:

d   Any restrictions or limitations on awards, such as by geographical areas, charitable fields, kinds of institutions, or other factors:

Form **990-PF** (2005)

Part XV Supplementary Information (continued)

3 **Grants and Contributions Paid During the Year or Approved for Future Payment**

Recipient Name and address (home or business)	If recipient is an individual, show any relationship to any foundation manager or substantial contributor	Foundation status of recipient	Purpose of grant or contribution	Amount
a *Paid during the year*				
Total . . . . ▶ 3a				
b *Approved for future payment*				
Total . . . . ▶ 3b				

Form **990-PF** (2005)

Part XVI-A Analysis of Income-Producing Activities

Enter gross amounts unless otherwise indicated.

	Unrelated business income		Excluded by section 512, 513, or 514		(e)
	(a) Business code	(b) Amount	(c) Exclusion code	(d) Amount	Related or exempt function income (See page 26 of the instructions.)
1 Program service revenue:					
a					
b					
c					
d					
e					
f					
g Fees and contracts from government agencies					
2 Membership dues and assessments					
3 Interest on savings and temporary cash investments					
4 Dividends and interest from securities . . .					
5 Net rental income or (loss) from real estate:					
a Debt-financed property					
b Not debt-financed property					
6 Net rental income or (loss) from personal property					
7 Other investment income					
8 Gain or (loss) from sales of assets other than inventory					
9 Net income or (loss) from special events. . .					
10 Gross profit or (loss) from sales of inventory .					
11 Other revenue: a					
b					
c					
d					
e					
12 Subtotal. Add columns (b), (d), and (e) . . .					

13 **Total.** Add line 12, columns (b), (d), and (e) . . . . **13** _____

(See worksheet in line 13 instructions on page 27 to verify calculations.)

Part XVI-B Relationship of Activities to the Accomplishment of Exempt Purposes

Line No. ▼	Explain below how each activity for which income is reported in column (e) of Part XVI-A contributed importantly to the accomplishment of the organization's exempt purposes (other than by providing funds for such purposes). (See page 27 of the instructions.)

Part XVII Information Regarding Transfers To and Transactions and Relationships With Noncharitable Exempt Organizations

		Yes	No
1 Did the organization directly or indirectly engage in any of the following with any other organization described in section 501(c) of the Code (other than section 501(c)(3) organizations) or in section 527, relating to political organizations?			
a Transfers from the reporting organization to a noncharitable exempt organization of:			
(1) Cash	1a(1)		
(2) Other assets	1a(2)		
b Other transactions:			
(1) Sales of assets to a noncharitable exempt organization	1b(1)		
(2) Purchases of assets from a noncharitable exempt organization	1b(2)		
(3) Rental of facilities, equipment, or other assets	1b(3)		
(4) Reimbursement arrangements	1b(4)		
(5) Loans or loan guarantees	1b(5)		
(6) Performance of services or membership or fundraising solicitations	1b(6)		
c Sharing of facilities, equipment, mailing lists, other assets, or paid employees	1c		

d If the answer to any of the above is "Yes," complete the following schedule. Column **(b)** should always show the fair market value of the goods, other assets, or services given by the reporting organization. If the organization received less than fair market value in any transaction or sharing arrangement, show in column **(d)** the value of the goods, other assets, or services received.

(a) Line no.	(b) Amount involved	(c) Name of noncharitable exempt organization	(d) Description of transfers, transactions, and sharing arrangements

2a Is the organization directly or indirectly affiliated with, or related to, one or more tax-exempt organizations described in section 501(c) of the Code (other than section 501(c)(3)) or in section 527? . . . . . . ☐ Yes ☐ No
b If "Yes," complete the following schedule.

(a) Name of organization	(b) Type of organization	(c) Description of relationship

Under penalties of perjury, I declare that I have examined this return, including accompanying schedules and statements, and to the best of my knowledge and belief, it is true, correct, and complete. Declaration of preparer (other than taxpayer or fiduciary) is based on all information of which preparer has any knowledge.

Sign Here

| Signature of officer or trustee | | Date | Title | |

Paid Preparer's Use Only

Preparer's signature		Date	Check if self-employed ▶ ☐	Preparer's SSN or PTIN (See **Signature** on page 28 of the instructions.)
Firm's name (or yours if self-employed), address, and ZIP code ▶			EIN ▶	
			Phone no. ( )	

Form **990-PF** (2005)

UNIFORM PRUDENT INVESTOR ACT

§ 1. PRUDENT INVESTOR RULE.

(a) Except as otherwise provided in subsection (b), a trustee who invests and manages trust assets owes a duty to the beneficiaries of the trust to comply with the prudent investor rule set forth in this [Act].

(b) The prudent investor rule, a default rule, may be expanded, restricted, eliminated, or otherwise altered by the provisions of a trust. A trustee is not liable to a beneficiary to the extent that the trustee acted in reasonable reliance on the provisions of the trust.

§ 2. STANDARD OF CARE; PORTFOLIO STRATEGY; RISK AND RETURN OBJECTIVES.

(a) A trustee shall invest and manage trust assets as a prudent investor would, by considering the purposes, terms, distribution requirements, and other circumstances of the trust. In satisfying this standard, the trustee shall exercise reasonable care, skill, and caution.

(b) A trustee's investment and management decisions respecting individual assets must be evaluated not in isolation but in the context of the trust portfolio as a whole and as a part of an overall investment strategy having risk and return objectives reasonably suited to the trust.

(c) Among circumstances that a trustee shall consider in investing and managing trust assets are such of the following as are relevant to the trust or its beneficiaries:

(1) general economic conditions;

(2) the possible effect of inflation or deflation;

(3) the expected tax consequences of investment decisions or strategies;

(4) the role that each investment or course of action plays within the overall trust portfolio, which may include financial assets, interests in closely held enterprises, tangible and intangible personal property, and real property;

(5) the expected total return from income and the appreciation of capital;

(6) other resources of the beneficiaries;

(7) needs for liquidity, regularity of income, and preservation or appreciation of capital; and

(8) an asset's special relationship or special value, if any, to the purposes of the trust or to one or more of the beneficiaries.

(d) A trustee shall make a reasonable effort to verify facts relevant to the investment and management of trust assets.

(e) A trustee may invest in any kind of property or type of investment consistent with the standards of this [Act].

(f) A trustee who has special skills or expertise, or is named trustee in reliance upon the trustee's representation that the trustee has special skills or expertise, has a duty to use those special skills or expertise.

§ 3. **DIVERSIFICATION.** A trustee shall diversify the investments of the trust unless the trustee reasonably determines that, because of special circumstances, the purposes of the trust are better served without diversifying.

§ 4. **DUTIES AT INCEPTION OF TRUSTEESHIP.** Within a reasonable time after accepting a trusteeship or receiving trust assets, a trustee shall review the trust assets and make and implement decisions concerning the retention and disposition of assets, in order to bring the trust portfolio into compliance with the purposes, terms, distribution requirements, and other circumstances of the trust, and with the requirements of this [Act].

§ 5. **LOYALTY.** A trustee shall invest and manage the trust assets solely in the interest of the beneficiaries.

§ 6. **IMPARTIALITY.** If a trust has two or more beneficiaries, the trustee shall act impartially in investing and managing the trust assets, taking into account any differing interests of the beneficiaries.

§ 7. **INVESTMENT COSTS.** In investing and managing trust assets, a trustee may only incur costs that are appropriate and reasonable in relation to the assets, the purposes of the trust, and the skills of the trustee.

§8. REVIEWING COMPLIANCE. Compliance with the prudent investor rule is determined in light of the facts and circumstances existing at the time of a trustee's decision or action and not by hindsight.

§9. DELEGATION OF INVESTMENT AND MANAGEMENT FUNCTIONS.

(a) A trustee may delegate investment and management functions that a prudent trustee of comparable skills could properly delegate under the circumstances. The trustee shall exercise reasonable care, skill, and caution in:

(1) selecting an agent;

(2) establishing the scope and terms of the delegation, consistent with the purposes and terms of the trust; and

(3) periodically reviewing the agent's actions in order to monitor the agent's performance and compliance with the terms of the delegation.

(b) In performing a delegated function, an agent owes a duty to the trust to exercise reasonable care to comply with the terms of the delegation.

(c) A trustee who complies with the requirements of subsection (a) is not liable to the beneficiaries or to the trust for the decisions or actions of the agent to whom the function was delegated.

(d) By accepting the delegation of a trust function from the trustee of a trust that is subject to the law of this State, an agent submits to the jurisdiction of the courts of this State.

§10. LANGUAGE INVOKING STANDARD OF [ACT]. The following terms or comparable language in the provisions of a trust, unless otherwise limited or modified, authorizes any investment or strategy permitted under this [Act]: "investments permissible by law for investment of trust funds," "legal investments," "authorized investments," "using the judgment and care under the circumstances then prevailing that persons of prudence, discretion, and intelligence exercise in the management of their own affairs, not in regard to speculation but in regard to the permanent disposition of their funds, considering the probable income as well as the probable safety of their capital," "prudent man rule," "prudent trustee rule," "prudent person rule," and "prudent investor rule."

§11. APPLICATION TO EXISTING TRUSTS. This [Act] applies to trusts existing on and created after its effective date. As applied to trusts existing on its effective date, this [Act] governs only decisions or actions occurring after that date.

§ 12. UNIFORMITY OF APPLICATION AND CONSTRUC-TION. This [Act] shall be applied and construed to effectuate its general purpose to make uniform the law with respect to the subject of this [Act] among the States enacting it.

§ 13. SHORT TITLE. This [Act] may be cited as the "[Name of Enacting State] Uniform Prudent Investor Act."

§ 14. SEVERABILITY. If any provision of this [Act] or its application to any person or circumstance is held invalid, the invalidity does not affect other provisions or applications of this [Act] which can be given effect without the invalid provision or application, and to this end the provisions of this [Act] are severable.

§ 15. EFFECTIVE DATE. This [Act] takes effect

. . . .

§ 16. REPEALS. The following acts and parts of acts are repealed:

(1)

(2)

(3)

UNIFORM MANAGEMENT OF INSTITUTIONAL FUNDS ACT

An Act to establish guidelines for the management and use of investments held by eleemosynary institutions and funds.

[Be it enacted . . .]

§ 1 [Definitions] In this Act:

(1) "institution" means an incorporated or unincorporated organization organized and operated exclusively for educational, religious, charitable, or other eleemosynary purposes, or a governmental organization to the extent that it holds funds exclusively for any of these purposes;

(2) "institutional fund" means a fund held by an institution for its exclusive use, benefit, or purposes, but does not include (i) a fund held for an institution by a trustee that is not an institution or (ii) a fund in which a beneficiary that is not an institution has an interest, other than possible rights that could arise upon violation or failure of the purposes of the fund;

(3) "endowment fund" means an institutional fund, or any part thereof, not wholly expendable by the institution on a current basis under the terms of the applicable gift instrument;

(4) "governing board" means the body responsible for the management of an institution or of an institutional fund;

(5) "historic dollar value" means the aggregate fair value in dollars of (i) an endowment fund at the time it became an endowment fund, (ii) each subsequent donation to the fund at the time it is made, and (iii) each accumulation made pursuant to a direction in the applicable gift instrument at the time the accumulation is added to the fund. The determination of historic dollar value made in good faith by the institution is conclusive.

(6) "gift instrument" means a will, deed, grant, conveyance, agreement, memorandum, writing, or other governing document (including the terms of any institutional solicitations from which an

institutional fund resulted) under which property is transferred to or held by an institution as an institutional fund.

§ 2. [**Appropriation of Appreciation**] The governing board may appropriate for expenditure for the uses and purposes for which an endowment fund is established so much of the net appreciation, realized and unrealized, in the fair value of the assets of an endowment fund over the historic dollar value of the fund as is prudent under the standard established by § 6. This section does not limit the authority of the governing board to expend funds as permitted under other law, the terms of the applicable gift instrument, or the charter of the institution.

§ 3. [**Rule of Construction**] Section 2 does not apply if the applicable gift instrument indicates the donor's intention that net appreciation shall not be expended. A restriction upon the expenditure of net appreciation may not be implied from a designation of a gift as an endowment, or from a direction or authorization in the applicable gift instrument to use only "income," "interest," "dividends," or "rents, issues or profits," or "to preserve the principal intact," or a direction which contains other words of similar import. This rule of construction applies to gift instruments executed or in effect before or after the effective date of this Act.

§ 4. [**Investment Authority**] In addition to an investment otherwise authorized by law or by the applicable gift instrument, and without restriction to investments a fiduciary may make, the governing board, subject to any specific limitations set forth in the applicable gift instrument or in the applicable law other than law relating to investments by a fiduciary, may:

(1) invest and reinvest an institutional fund in any real or personal property deemed advisable by the governing board, whether or not it produces a current return, including mortgages, stocks, bonds, debentures, and other securities of profit or nonprofit corporations, shares in or obligations of associations, partnerships, or individuals, and obligations of any government or subdivision or instrumentality thereof;

(2) retain property contributed by a donor to an institutional fund for as long as the governing board deems advisable;

(3) include all or any part of an institutional fund in any pooled or common fund maintained by the institution; and

(4) invest all or any part of an institutional fund in any other pooled or common fund available for investment, including shares or interests in regulated investment companies, mutual funds, common

trust funds, investment partnerships, real estate investment trusts, or similar organizations in which funds are commingled and investment determinations are made by persons other than the governing board.

§ 5. [Delegation of Investment Management] Except as otherwise provided by the applicable gift instrument or by applicable law relating to governmental institutions or funds, the governing board may (1) delegate to its committees, officers or employees of the institution or the fund, or agents, including investment counsel, the authority to act in place of the board in investment and reinvestment of institutional funds, (2) contract with independent investment advisors, investment counsel or managers, banks, or trust companies, so to act, and (3) authorize the payment of compensation for investment advisory or management services.

§ 6. [Standard of Conduct] In the administration of the powers to appropriate appreciation, to make and retain investments, and to delegate investment management of institutional funds, members of a governing board shall exercise ordinary business care and prudence under the facts and circumstances prevailing at the time of the action or decision. In so doing they shall consider long and short term needs of the institution in carrying out its educational, religious, charitable, or other eleemosynary purposes, its present and anticipated financial requirements, expected total return on its investments, price level trends, and general economic conditions.

§ 7. [Release of Restrictions on Use or Investment]

(a) With the written consent of the donor, the governing board may release, in whole or in part, a restriction imposed by the applicable gift instrument on the use or investment of an institutional fund.

(b) If written consent of the donor cannot be obtained by reason of his death, disability, unavailability, or impossibility of identification, the governing board may apply in the name of the institution to the [appropriate] court for release of a restriction imposed by the applicable gift instrument on the use or investment of an institutional fund. The [Attorney General] shall be notified of the application and shall be given an opportunity to be heard. If the court finds that the restriction is obsolete, inappropriate, or impracticable, it may by order release the restriction in whole or in part. A release under this subsection may not change an endowment fund to a fund that is not an endowment fund.

(c) A release under this section may not allow a fund to be used for purposes other than the educational, religious, charitable, or other eleemosynary purposes of the institution affected.

(d) This section does not limit the application of the doctrine of *cy pres*.

§ 8. [**Severability**] If any provision of this Act or the application thereof to any person or circumstances is held invalid, the invalidity shall not affect other provisions or applications of the Act which can be given effect without the invalid provision or application, and to this end the provisions of this Act are declared severable.

§ 9. [**Uniformity of Application and Construction**] This Act shall be so applied and construed as to effectuate its general purpose to make uniform the law with respect of this Act among those states which enact it.

§ 10. [**Short Title**] This Act may be cited as the "Uniform Management of Institutional Funds Act."

§ 11. [**Repeal**] The following acts and parts of acts are repealed:

(1)

(2)

(3)

CHAPTER 9

SPECIAL ISSUES

§ 9.01   DIFFERENCES OF OPINION

[A]   Reasons for Conflict

Family foundations are created for many purposes. The foundation may be designed to develop philanthropic responsibility in younger generations, to perpetuate the family name in the community, or to establish a flexible mechanism for charitable giving. In many cases, there is also an unspoken goal — to create a forum to bring family members together to heal rifts and relationships.

Unfortunately, a family foundation is more likely to perpetuate than to change the dynamics of a family's relationships. In fact, the foundation may amplify problems with family relationships by simply offering one more setting in which the family members move through their accustomed roles. The conflicts, where they exist, generally result from poor communication, controlling behavior of one or more family members, or pressure to conform to certain standards.[1]

The following conflicts may seem familiar:

- A family member consistently omitted from important family decisions may feel similarly deprived if not allowed input in setting foundation priorities or reaching grant decisions. She reacts by voting against the preferences of specific family members or by loudly protesting each decision.

- A patriarch or older sibling who has dominated most family decisions may become annoyed when quieter family members (or those outside the immediate family) are empowered to vote and do not consistently endorse his goals. He responds by forcing his result, shouting down or cutting off the weaker members.

- An older generation board member may favor arts grants, while a younger generation member may prefer environmental causes. As the older generation family member tries logic-based persuasion, the younger family member rolls her eyes.

Conflicts may be avoided by making a conscious effort to examine the personality and goals of each member of the family and to create foundation management roles that build on individual strengths.

[B]   The Dynamics of Family Conflict

[1]   Behavioral Patterns

Family relationships are based on learned patterns of behavior that are not likely to change when the family meets as a foundation board. Behavioral patterns are driven by strong emotions, including:

---

[1] Mary F. Whiteside, Craig E. Aronoff, and John L. Ward, How Families Work Together, Family Business Leadership Series No. 4 (Marietta, Ga. 1993).

- *Love*, which occurs between spouses, between siblings, between a parent and child, and between family members and those outside the family;

- *Jealousy*, which is often found among siblings, between parent and child, or between family members of second or third relation;

- *Respect*, for a parent, for a sibling, or for a cousin;

- *Fear*, of losing control, of losing influence, or of being outperformed;

- *Anger*, at a classification as a "failure," at the inability to have more input in the family company, or at the inability to exact more money from parents or a controlling uncle; and

- *Condemnation*, for the failure to conform, for lifestyle choices, for previous mistakes, or for the unwillingness to take up a specific profession or business.

These strong emotions are further complicated by factors unique to family relationships. These include the need for a parent's approval, the need to be the center of attention, and the need to be in control. Every family can identify the sibling, cousin, aunt, or uncle that demands to be the focus of every gathering. These patterns are hard to break for those that exercise control and for those that are under control.

Add to this natural turmoil the fact that families are no longer easy to define. Multiple marriages generally result in multiple spouses and sets of children. And while most of us find a way to maintain a level of civility with our immediate family members, these restraints do not always apply to spouses of siblings or step-relations.

Family dynamics are further complicated by money. Some members of the family may have more money than others. While the impact of wealth varies from family to family, the most frequent observation is that the individual with the most money generally controls the lives of others within his or her sphere of influence. Since this wealthy family member may also be the founder of the foundation, board meetings may represent just one more forum in which the "have-nots" or "have-lesses" are forced to meet the expectations of the holder of wealth.

The money issues can be even more divisive where the family depends on a family business as its primary source of income. Sons, daughters, or cousins may be a part of this business and may be frustrated with a lack of control, inability to advance, or failure to bring home a higher salary. The foundation board structure may simply reinforce the sense of helplessness and lack of control. For these reasons, the family foundation may serve as an accelerant for smoldering issues rather than a panacea for family problems.

> **Example:** Consider the story of the Clark Family Foundation. Ed Clark, age 65, established a general contracting company in his late twenties. While he started the company doing much of the labor himself, he quickly moved to

more substantive projects and added staff to do the work. The company grew, branching out into construction of large office buildings across the country. The company thrived because of Ed's ability to manage risk and leverage company assets. Ed's sons John and Ben joined the company after graduation, but neither lasted more than five years before leaving to join other contracting firms. The departures had much to do with their father's hard-driving management style. He gave instructions; he asked for and wanted little input; he was quick to criticize when something went wrong. Each son's departure was accompanied by little fanfare, but left Ed puzzled.

Ed established the Clark Foundation last year in the hope that it would provide some common ground for his family to work together to fund projects of mutual interest in the community. Each of his sons was appointed to the board, together with his daughter, Kate, and one of Kate's adult sons. In the first meeting, however, it became clear that Ed was still in charge. Ed presented a list of recommended distributions, making a detailed explanation of the merits of each recipient. There was little discussion. The board ratified his decisions and left the room. Ed again was puzzled.

This family foundation did not serve to solve communication problems because the family did not function any more effectively as a foundation than as a corporation. The reason was clear. Ed was in charge, and the safest way for others to participate was to quietly agree. In order for Ed's family to begin to work together, Ed will need to develop a more open and deliberative environment in which the family members can impact the outcome.

Time provides some relief for these established roles and inherent conflicts. While the factors driving the relationship do not change, the dynamics of the relationships shift over time. Family members die, age, marry, divorce, succeed, and fail. These changes give rise to new struggles as emerging leaders seek control.

The best way to create new dynamics is to create an environment that does not reinforce the old roles. This requires that each family member give thought to his or her own behavioral patterns and attempt to understand why family members behave as they do.

[2] Who's in Charge?

Birth order and gender are two of the most powerful influences on control in the family.[2] By understanding the forces at play, family members may be able to communicate more effectively. Marty Carter, a family counselor who works with families and family foundations to facilitate communication, feels that understanding the impact of birth order is important in understanding how a

---

[2] Deanne Stone, *Family Issues* 58-59 (Council on Foundations 1997).

family will work together on a foundation board.[3] She offers the following insights into the traits of the eldest, middle, and youngest children.

[a]   The Eldest Child

Firstborn children tend to be cooperative, compliant, high achieving, competitive, and eager to please authority figures. They are comfortable with clear expectations and possess a need to do things decently and in the right order. First-borns may not have a well-developed sense of humor. They can be highly anxious when things are not perfect and are irritated when younger siblings are more relaxed and easygoing.

[b]   The Middle Child

The middle children may be the easiest to work with. These children have been dominated by older siblings but have had the opportunity to command younger siblings. The exposure to both experiences makes them more sensitive to the responsibilities and consequences of power. These children are generally more relaxed, less competitive, and skilled at mediation and compromise, making them excellent foundation managers.

[c]   The Youngest Child

The youngest children may grow up in a world where things are handled for them, especially if there are a number of children in the family. This means the last-born may be less responsible and less accountable. These children pay less attention to demands of authority figures and may be more creative because they design their own answers and solutions to problems. Sometimes the youngest is spoiled and self-indulgent. He or she fights for the right to be the "baby."

Where a youngest child marries another youngest child, the relationship can be even more difficult. Neither spouse wants responsibility and fights to retain the role as the "baby." Consider the resolution of a classic conflict in the Chatham Family Foundation.

> **Example:**   Jonathan Chatham, a successful businessman, has five grandsons ranging in age from 17 to 32. He created the Chatham Family Foundation in the hope that his grandchildren would become interested in philanthropy and work collaboratively on a Junior Foundation Board. These grandsons are the children of Jonathan's son, Sam, and his wife, Doris. Both Sam and Doris are last-borns of their sibling pools.

---

[3] Marty Carters, Family Communications, Jefferson, Maine, 207-549-3959.

The Junior Board meetings were chaotic and disruptive. The grand-children were unable to agree, to make decisions, or to compromise. Although Sam and Doris attended each meeting, they failed to provide leadership or suggestions to resolve disputes. The family agreed to partici-pate in a family meeting to develop standards for behavior to encourage effective meetings. While the family adopted the new rules, these standards were not used, the parents failed to enforce the rules, and the meetings continued to flounder.

During the next few months, Sam and Doris changed jobs, requiring each to travel. It became apparent that when one parent was at home, meetings went smoothly, and the behavioral standards were enforced. This was true at every meeting at which only one parent attended, regard-less of which parent was involved. Where both parents attended, however, the meetings broke down, and chaos returned.

The problem stemmed from the fact that both Sam and Doris were the youngest and had difficulty operating with authority. The counselor sug-gested that the parents decide which parent was in charge, leaving the other safely in the "baby" role. This helped to successfully rearrange this life pattern, so that they served as effective parents and advisors to the Junior Foundation Board. Understanding the dynamics of the birth order of youn-gest marrying youngest helped to move this family from chaotic to productive meetings.

[3] The Factors Governing Relationships

Psychologists have published volumes of work on the factors that govern the way individuals relate to each other. If you have ever raised a child, you know that each individual is born with certain deeply rooted personality traits. These traits can be tempered or embellished, but can rarely be changed.

Think about the personality differences within a single family. One person is very methodical, detail oriented, and slow to judgment. Another makes decisions quickly. Still another is confident, forms opinions based on the facts available, and make decisions quickly. These personalities may have difficulty working together unless they are willing to understand and accommodate each other's behavior patterns.

Isabel Briggs Myers and Katharine Cook Briggs developed a test based on Carl Jung's theory that personality traits are inherited. This test, called the Myers-Briggs Type Indicator (MBTI),[4] was designed to help a person to under-stand more about his or her personality and the personalities of those around him or her. The MBTI is often used in corporate environments to help managers relate to employees in a more effective way, to create teams of employees that

---

[4] Established by Consulting Psychologists Press, 3803 East Bayshore Road, Palo Alto, CA 94303, 800-624-1765, *www.cpp-db.com/index.html*.

are more effective, and to develop leadership. It also has application in any arena in which individuals want to develop a better understanding of how to relate to and work with one another. The MBTI is not designed to favor one personality preference over another. Instead, it acknowledges these preferences and simply provides insight on how persons learn and relate to others.

Most people take the time to observe and learn something about those around them as they become a part of a workplace or boardroom. These same individuals may not extend that courtesy to family, relying instead on the dynamics and roles established over years as a family unit. We begin by assuming that our family must be just like us. We expect they have the same values, the same goals, the same opinions about money, and the same attitudes about time management. That utopia rarely exists.

The MBTI is a tool that can explain behavior and offer ways to make positive changes in relationships. Most psychological firms, especially those that specialize in the corporate workplace, can administer the test. The results are valuable because they affirm the preferences of the individual and reveal much about how the individual relates to the family group. It may also explain why a son picked a particular career, a daughter married a particular type of man, or a grandson is always late.

There are four key preferences measured by the test. The results are scaled to reflect whether an individual is strongly at one end or the other of the spectrum or somewhere in between.

- *Introvert versus extrovert.* This measure governs an individual's preference to work alone or with others. It may also provide an indicator of whether individuals draw energy and ideas from the world outside or from themselves. Look at your workplace and your family, and you will generally be able to sort people you know into one of these two groups.

- *Intuition versus sensation.* This trait governs how an individual gathers information or learns. A person who learns through intuition gathers the facts, but then projects those facts into possibilities, while a person who learns through sensation relies on his or her senses — sight, sound, touch, smell, hearing — and makes decisions grounded in those facts. Consider the saying "He can't see the forest for the trees." This statement is representative of a complaint by an intuitor about a sensor.

- *Thinking versus feeling.* This measure describes how an individual internally processes the information after it is gathered to make decisions. Those classified as thinkers process the available facts in an objective, sometimes critical, long-term manner, while those who are feelers process information subjectively, tempered by a short-term perspective and personal values. A thinker might be described by a feeler as someone who is guided by his or her head, rather than his or her heart.

- *Judging versus perceiving*. This preference reflects a measurement of how individuals structure or organize their lives. Those that weight judging are very ordered, value control of their schedules, and plan their day or life in a predictable way. Those that prioritize perception are more likely to be spontaneous and resist calendars that tie them to commitments and an ordered way of life. The conflict between those who judge and those who perceive can sometimes be the most frustrating. J's can yell at P's for hours on end and still fail to reach closure or get a commitment on an issue.

> **Example:** Consider the story of the Blanchard Foundation. Jan Blanchard is the program director and trustee for the Blanchard Family Foundation, located in Boston. Jan, an ENFP (Extrovert/Intuition/Feeling/Perceiving), has worked diligently to bring grant proposals to the board for approval; the board has failed to support the proposals. Her older sister, Delores Blanchard, is a trustee of the foundation who teaches accounting at a nearby private college. Delores, an ISTJ (Introvert/Sensation/Thinking/Judging), leads the charge in challenging Jan's proposals. Each meeting devolves into a predictable, noisy conflict between the two.
>
> The MBTI provides an answer for the conflict. Jan's proposals reflect her creativity, her passion, and her insight into the issues addressed by the grant. Delores, however, responds only to facts. She wants to see logical and analytical data accompanied by measurable assessments of need and results. Her opposition of the projects had little to do with her feelings for Jan, but had everything to do with analyzing the information in a way that was meaningful to her.
>
> Once Jan understood more about the way that her sister gathered information, processed information, and made decisions, she was able to rewrite the presentations to include the information Delores needed. This produced a spirit of cooperation rather than confrontation in the decision-making process.

[C] Alternatives in Resolving Conflict

Conflict resolution must begin with a commitment to examine the underlying issues and a determination to create positive patterns of behavior. Alternatives range from using common courtesy and establishing rules of engagement at board meetings to hiring a family counselor to help the family move through the issues. Four options for resolving conflict are discussed in more detail below.

[1] Set Rules for Communication

Basic rules of civility should apply in the family foundation boardroom just as they do in other places in society. These rules include:[5]

---

[5] Stone, *supra* note 2, at 103-110.

- Maintaining respect for others when talking and listening;

- Speaking only when you have something to contribute;

- Listening to the thoughts and ideas of others;

- Including everyone at the table in the conversation;

- Talking directly to other board members, rather than speaking about them as if they were not present or ignoring their interest in an issue;

- Offering only your own opinions in a discussion, rather than using opinions of those outside the room or elsewhere at the table to form your vote;

- Preparing for a meeting so that you are informed on all issues;

- Speaking about specific issues; and

- Speaking and offering information that is honest.

The rules of communication help avoid patterns of behavior in which the loudest or the most powerful individual sets the tone for discussion and establishes options to be considered. The rules do not eliminate the differences of opinion; they simply allow a respectful way for each family member to be heard.

There are foundations that believe these communication rules are so important, and so easily forgotten, that the rules are printed on placemats in front of each board member. This simple solution provides a way to prioritize these courtesies without calling those to task who violate the rules.

[2] Set Rules for Conduct of Business

Foundations do not operate effectively when board members are not prepared. Make sure all board members receive information about upcoming meetings and upcoming grant requests well in advance of the meeting date. Encourage them to make calls to agencies, to staff, and to other board members to gather information prior to the meeting. Ensure that the meeting is conducted in a manner that is inclusive. Some foundations operate in a formal fashion, employing Robert's Rules of Order, while others conduct meetings with a family dinner atmosphere. Either option works so long as the meeting format is comfortable for participants and allows everyone to contribute and play a part.

[3] Set Rules to Avoid Deadlock

Find a way to compromise and to resolve disputes. There are many options in reaching decisions, limited only by creativity and common sense. Consider the following:

- If the decision relates to operation, budgeting, governance, or a function governed by a committee, send the disputed issue back to the committee where the proposal originated. Ask the committee to do further work or research and make a new recommendation that accommodates the issues raised in the full meeting.

- If the decision relates to funding, set target goals for distribution of funds by category. For example, a percentage of the distribution for the year may be allocated to the environment, or to women's issues, or to health care, or to social welfare. Assign each board member on the distribution committee responsibility for a particular sector. Make that sector chief responsible for gathering information and researching alternatives. Then also give that individual the tie-breaking vote for a grant in that area.

  The concept of dividing funding into areas at the outset may also stop fundamental conflicts on grant priorities. Each family member comes to the table with a different interest. Individuals that are part of the same family, and were raised with the same experiences, may nonetheless have diametrically opposed views on issues such as rights of women and children, civil rights, and how to best address the needs of the poorest in our society.

- If the conflict relates to board representation, establish qualifications for board members, board terms, and perhaps an application procedure. Establishing qualifications for membership, such as attendance at meetings, duties required, training required, committee work required, or any achievable tangible factor, raises the standards for membership and adds meaning to the election process. Avoid using birth order as the sole determinant of board position, since it excludes rather than includes family members and does nothing to raise expectations of those who do participate.

[4] Call for Help When Needed — Better Yet, Don't Wait Until You Have to Call for Help

Sometimes the operation of the family foundation reaches a standstill. Everyone is frustrated. When the foundation board does nothing but fight and has lost its focus on its mission or its ability to deliberate effectively and inclusively, it is time for professional help. Consider the following sources of help.

Family counselors are perhaps the most effective option. These individuals operate as consultants or as part of a psychology practice and are experienced in understanding, articulating, explaining, and resolving family conflicts. Do not be afraid to pull an outsider into the family circle. Family relationships are sometimes so established that the family cannot see the issues that are the most divisive. There are counselors and psychologists that specialize in this area.

Marty Carter, a counselor with extensive experience working with families, offered the following observation about the role of the family counselor:

> In the last several years I have found myself moving from a consultant who comes in when a fire truck is needed, to a resource that functions as a

combination of a coach, guide and adventurer. The focus has shifted from "this family needs a shrink" to providing a facilitator to articulate visions and goals.[6]

Example: The Boysen Foundation provides insight into the role of the counselor. The Boysen Foundation was established in the 1950s and has now grown to $25,000,000. The third generation of the Boysen family, representing three branches of the founding family, had reached a deadlock on whom to appoint as board members and officers for the coming year. Two members of the third generation, Natalie and Jacob, were active in the foundation, but expressed interest in turning leadership over to the next generation. Natalie and Jacob were always at odds, and it soon became clear that neither was willing to be the first to resign. Unintentionally, other members of the family began to line up behind their mother/aunt and father/uncle.

TABLE 9-1
Resources for Managing Family and Foundation Issues

Resource	*Contact Information*
Family Philanthropy Advisors Diane Neimann, President	1818 Oliver Avenue South Minneapolis, MN 55405-2208 612-377-8400 (phone) 612-377-8407 (fax) *www.users.quest.net/~famphiladv*
Family Communications Marty Carter	682 South Clary Road Jefferson, Maine 04348 207-549-3959 (phone) *martyzcarter@verizon.net*
Family Firm Institute	200 Lincoln Street #201 Boston, MA 02111 617-482-3045 (phone) *www.ffi.org*

With the assistance of a family counselor, Natalie and Jacob were willing to admit that they were tired of the conflict and willing to try another approach. The counselor suggested that the spouses of the third generation join the board, adding new input, energy, and balance. At a retreat, the family members realized that change comes through commitment, rather than coercion. They compromised by creating two funds within the foundation, allowing each group to make the types of distributions important to them.

Foundation consultants can help the family work through personal conflicts by returning the group to focus on why and how the foundation should function.

---

[6] Marty Carter, Family Communications, Jefferson, Maine, in interview with Kathryn Miree, June 2000.

Think in terms of a family retreat in which the group has a facilitator to help the family work through mission, purpose, and operation in a meaningful way. The outside facilitator is an important element of this exercise. Select someone who is experienced in family foundation work and strategic planning and who is willing to help the group focus on its strengths and weaknesses. Table 9-1 lists resources for help in working through family issues.

[5] What If Your Fellow Directors Are Taking the Foundation Off Track?

Two 2002 cases demonstrate a few of the problems that can arise when the directors of a nonprofit charitable organization fail to take action to stop corporate actions that threaten to take the organization off its charitable course. Although both involve application of the laws of a particular state, they nevertheless serve as reminders of the importance of board scrutiny and oversight.

[a] Pursuing Public versus Private Purposes

The first such case, *Summers v. Cherokee Children & Family Services, Inc.*,[7] involved an attempt by the Tennessee Attorney General (AG) to bring about the involuntary dissolution of two charitable corporations formed to provide child welfare services under governmental programs. The essence of the AG's case was that these charities had abandoned their charitable purposes and were devoted to private gain. The founder and executive director of both entities, Willie Ann Madison, was shown to have engaged in various deals with the corporations, including leases of property.

For example, in one such instance, Willie Ann and her husband bought an office building for $275,668, which they leased to one of the corporations for an initial rental of $49,000 per year for five years. Within two months, the rent was "renegotiated" to $72,000 per year, and three years later, another renegotiation raised the rent retroactively to $210,000 per year. The latter lease reflected rental of 20,000 square feet, but the building contained only 9,700 square feet, and only 7,680 of that was office space.

The directors of the corporations included a number of family members, such as Willie Ann's father and her pastor. Her husband was the corporations' accountant, and as presiding elder of her church, was also the immediate supervisor of the pastor/director. Two of her children were employees, as were her nephew, her stepson, and her husband's nephew. (It should be noted that these were ostensibly public charities and not family foundations.) There were also reports of generous compensation, numerous bonuses, and loans to Willie Ann, her family, and her real estate entities.

---

[7] 2002 Tenn. App. LEXIS 699 (Sept. 26, 2002).

The record also showed a number of transactions with board members and their related entities. [*Note*: These were not private foundations, so the self-dealing rules did not apply.] One director justified a number of related-party transactions as follows:

> If they were giving their time to serve on the volunteer Board I think it would be unkind if they had a business and you needed something they had, I think it would be unkind not to purchase from them.

The Board members were described as "less than vigilant or probing in examining corporate activities and in remaining knowledgeable about the corporation." They relied primarily on Willie Ann for information and for recommendations, which they seldom questioned. Not surprisingly, several directors testified that they were not familiar with their duties and obligations as directors.

The Court of Appeals of Tennessee found that the record led to the inevitable conclusion that the corporations were operated for the benefit of Willie Ann, her family, and other insiders. It rejected the corporations' contention that the "business judgment rule" precluded the AG from second-guessing the Board's decisions in managing the corporations. Although the business judgment rule does generally apply to nonprofit corporations, it has no application to a situation where a corporation is alleged to have abandoned its public purpose and is pursuing private gain. That rule applies only to situations where a corporation's directors have acted in good faith in the exercise of honest judgment in pursuit of corporate purposes. Therefore, the court upheld the lower court decision appointing a receiver for the assets of the corporations and ordering their dissolution.

[b]   *Director versus Director*

The second of the 2002 cases, *Judith Lundberg ex rel. Orient Foundation v. Graham Colemen et al.*,[8] involved an attempt by one director of a nonprofit charitable corporation to bring a derivative action on behalf of the corporation against her fellow directors. The Orient Foundation is a Washington nonprofit corporation formed in 1982 to raise funds for cultural heritage projects worldwide. Despite its name, it is a public charity and not a private foundation. In 1983, a separate entity known as the Orient Foundation (U.K.) was established as a registered charity in the United Kingdom. The directors of both entities were Judith Lundberg (a U.S. person) and three U.K. residents. The U.K. corporation has a wholly owned subsidiary, Orient Films, Ltd. U.K., and there is also an Orient Foundation, India.

---

[8] 2002 Wash. App. LEXIS 2435 (Oct. 7, 2002).

In 1998, a rift developed between Judith and her U.K. colleagues concerning expenditures and interactions among the various entities. She sought information from them and made a number of complaints that resulted in investigations by both the Charity Commission in the United Kingdom and the U.K. Inland Revenue (the equivalent of the Internal Revenue Service). In the course of all these inquiries, Judith discovered what she believed to be serious breaches of fiduciary obligations with respect to the Washington nonprofit corporation. Accordingly, she brought a lawsuit on behalf of the corporation in Washington against the three directors who reside in the United Kingdom, seeking damages, an accounting, and removal of the U.K. directors.

The Court of Appeals of Washington held, affirming the trial court, that a single or minority director of a Washington nonprofit corporation does not have the ability to bring a legal action on behalf of the corporation. Although Washington law specifically gives this right to the shareholder of a business corporation, the legislature did not extend a comparable right to directors of nonprofit corporations. Similarly, the Revised Model Nonprofit Corporation Act, from which the Washington law is derived, gives directors and members of nonprofit corporations standing to bring derivative suits, but the Washington legislature chose not to adopt this provision.

The court noted that the State Attorney General was the only party with standing to bring this suit, and, despite the involvement of that office in filing an *amicus* brief, the Attorney General was not a party to the suit. Accordingly, the court advised Ms. Lundberg to take her case to the legislature.

Of course, both of these are state court cases, and the result is likely to vary from one state to another. It is important for a family foundation advisor to be familiar with the rules applicable to his or her foundation clients and to avoid situations like the ones described above. Read together, these cases underscore the obligations of a nonprofit director and the importance of paying attention to those obligations and to the business of the entity. Today, more than ever, the press is likely to seize on situations like the facts described in the Tennessee case above and report on the shortcomings and abuses in vivid detail. After the Enron scandal and all the subsequent corporate abuses, both the media and the public are more likely to ask, "Where were the directors when all this happened?" Some people seem to regard appointment to a nonprofit board as more of an honor than a duty, but that is not the case. Mark Twain could have been thinking of such a director when he wrote of the fellow who was tarred and feathered and ridden out of town on a rail; asked later about the event, he stated: "Well, if it hadn't have been for the honor, I would rather have walked."

In addition, the Washington case shows how even a vigilant director may encounter obstacles in doing what he or she perceives as the right thing. Obviously, the involvement of the state attorney general may be necessary in some states (such as Washington) if court action is warranted. It seems likely that the Tennessee Attorney General would have stepped in much earlier if presented with evidence of the sort described in the recent opinion, and the directors could have notified that office if they were even aware of what was going on in "their" corporation. With a family foundation, the self-dealing rules make many of these abuses doubly improper, and most foundation directors are (or should be) sensitized to such violations. Indeed, those rules present the Internal Revenue Service as another possible source of outside help to the director who cannot get the foundation to stop or correct improper acts.

Presumably one important function of a director is to be observant enough to know when questionable activities are taking place, to ask questions, even if they are embarrassing, and to see that the situation is corrected before state officials must step in. Although the director who brought the Washington lawsuit tried to do this, her attempts were thwarted by local law. It is not always easy to be a good director!

[D] Restructuring to Resolve Family Differences

Letter Rulings 200323046 and 200323047 show how it is possible to restructure a series of family foundations to resolve family differences. The late Mr. A created two foundations — one (Foundation X) was a nonprofit corporation established in one state during his lifetime, and the other (Foundation Z) was a charitable trust created under his will pursuant to the laws of a different state. The trustees of X were three grandchildren of A, a nephew, and two unrelated persons, while A's son, his daughter, and her husband, plus one unrelated individual, were the trustees of Z. A's will also created a family trust and established an Audit Committee to select an auditor and perform various other functions with respect to Z and the family trust.

Numerous disputes between the trustees of X, the trustees of Z, and the Audit Committee gave rise to considerable litigation in various state and federal courts. To resolve these disputes, the parties proposed to reorganize and restructure the foundations. A new foundation (New Foundation) was created by the court, with four of Z's trustees plus another person selected by them serving as its directors. Z's current assets and liabilities ($100x) were transferred to the New Foundation. Two trustees of X became the new trustees of Z, and the current Z trustees resigned. X then transferred to Z assets worth $100x and additional assets to New Foundation. The X trustees, the Z trustees, and the Audit Committee all executed a settlement agreement, with the approvals of the attorneys general of the two applicable states. The agreement was conditioned upon New Foundation's qualifying as a § 501(c)(3) organization and receipt of a ruling from the IRS approving the transaction.

The settlement contemplated that A's adult lineal descendants and their spouses will attend biennial family meetings at which all of the foundations will make presentations about their philanthropic work and practices. These presentations were to be made during the charitable "business" portions of the meetings, which would also include the election of members of the Audit Committee. The costs of the charitable "business" portion of these meetings (such as meeting space rent, audiovisual tools, duplicating costs, and food costs) were to be divided among the various foundations and family trusts according to an agreed-upon set of percentages, and such costs were not envisioned to be significant in amount. The individual attendees would pay their own travel costs (transportation, meals, lodging, etc.) for attending the meetings.

The settlement also provided for a series of summer intern positions to be awarded to four 16- to 22-year-old descendants of A. The interns were to be chosen objectively on their merit from applicants, with each descendant eligible to be an intern only once. The interns would be paid no more than reasonable compensation and no less than the legally required minimum wage. Moreover, the interns would be required to contribute to the charitable activities of the foundation for which they were working to prepare them for the leadership roles they would likely have with one or more of these foundations during their lifetimes. X would pay the salaries and benefits of up to three summer interns, and New Foundation would pay the salaries and benefits of potentially one summer intern.

The IRS ruled that the settlement would not violate any of the private foundation prohibitions in Chapter 42 of the Code. The various asset transfers would all go to § 501(c)(3) organizations, which are specifically excluded from disqualified person status, so these transfers would not be acts of self-dealing. New Foundation would be treated as the successor to Z for purposes of Chapter 42 as provided in Regulation § 1.507-3(a)(9)(i), since it would be controlled by the former Z trustees and would receive all of Z's assets and liabilities. The IRS reached this conclusion despite the fact that the restructuring plan would have assets transferred from X to Z just after Z's assets were transferred to New Foundation. Although this presented an issue as to whether Z had transferred "all of its assets" to New Foundation as required by Regulation § 1.507-3(a)(9)(i), the IRS was satisfied that the settlement, the changes in Z's board of directors and its program, and the other facts and circumstances all indicated that New Foundation was a continuation of the old Z. Furthermore, the settlement passed muster under the self-dealing and taxable expenditure rules of IRC §§ 4941 and 4945 as well.

§ 9.02   THE NEXT GENERATION

[A]   The Constant Struggle to Engage the Next Generation

Most family foundation creators intend that family foundations will continue for generations with family involvement. Many are successful, as shown in the partial listing of family foundations who self-identified in a study conducted in 2000.[9] Table 9-2 lists a number of large family foundations now in the second or third generation (there are, of course, many more).

TABLE 9-2
Large Family Foundations 25 or More Years Old[10]

Foundation	Location	Date Established	Assets in 2004
Lilly Endowment	Indiana	1937	$8,585,049,346
David and Lucile Packard Foundation	California	1964	$5,328,293,452
McKnight Foundation	Minnesota	1953	$2,073,754,860
Brown Foundation	Texas	1951	$1,322,156,535
W. M. Keck Foundation	California	1954	$1,307,546,774
William Penn Foundation	Pennsylvania	1945	$1,185,344,692
Ahmanson Foundation	California	1952	$890,412,590
Meadows Foundation	Texas	1948	$842,877,031
Horace W. Goldsmith Foundation	New York	1955	$837,631,585
Conrad N., Hilton Foundation	Nevada	1964	$764,031,944
Surdna Foundation	New York	1917	$681,880,246
J.A. & Kathryn Albertson Foundation	Idaho	1966	$552,008,821
Arthur S. DeMoss Foundation	Florida	1955	$397,695,511
Buffett Foundation	Nebraska	1964	$80,741,033

[1] What Can Go Wrong?

Sometimes, family foundations lose family involvement after one or two generations. This may happen because family members die out, or because older generations are unwilling to involve or accept input from younger family members. In truth, getting lower generations involved is a challenge.

Consider these three common scenarios (these are real situations, although the names have been changed; the stories, however, are universal):

---

[9] A copy of the report, *Family Foundations: A Profile of Funders and Trends*, can be ordered for $19.95 from The Foundation Center, 79 Fifth Avenue, New York, NY 10003-3076, by phone at 800-424-9836, or from the Foundation Center's web site, *www.fdncenter.org*.

[10] The research is published in *Foundation Giving* (The Foundation Center 2001). The Foundation Center is located at 79 Fifth Avenue, New York, NY 10003-3076, information updated to include asset value reported on 2004 990-PF.

1. *Out of state, out of mind.* John Threadgill created a family foundation following the sale of his manufacturing business in 1995. His wife, Mary, works with him to manage the foundation, which makes grants to educational institutions for need-based four-year college scholarships for community children. The Threadgills have been delighted with the outcome and impact of their grants, and hope to add additional assets at their deaths. However, they worry about who will handle the scholarships when they're gone. They would like to involve their children — who now live in other states — but the kids appear to have no interest in the foundation work. Is there any way to get the children engaged?

2. *The grant fight of the titans (or rather, the generations).* The Smithing Family Foundation — a $50 million foundation established 25 years ago by Tom and Jan Smithing — now has three generations of family members involved in governance. The foundation originally focused on arts and education groups in a five-county area in Pennsylvania. Increasingly, however, the second and third generations are advocating grants to organizations outside the five-county area for charitable purposes that include environmental issues and international human rights. Grant meetings have become a real battle ground and promise to damage family relationships if the struggle continues. Some family members have stopped attending meetings altogether simply to avoid the conflict. How can this family reach consensus on its grantmaking goals and objectives?

3. *Who's in charge here (the patriarch; everyone else is losing interest)?* Sanford McMann built his company from the ground up. He started the family-owned steel fabrication plant when he was in his 30s and built it into an international supplier. Ten years ago he funded the McMann Family Foundation with the sale of a family business subsidiary to a Japanese corporation. Sanford credits his business success to hard work and his continuing day to day involvement in the nuts and bolts details. He runs his family and the foundation with the same hands-on, take-charge personality that characterizes his business style. However, he's puzzled by the reticence of his children and grandchildren to get involved with foundation management. He's hired planners and consultants to make foundation management easy, all the family members need to do is to show up and approve the grant decisions. How can he get his family involved?

These scenarios have one thing in common. The unengaged family members lack ownership in the foundation's mission, policies, and operation. Fortunately, the problem can be overcome with analysis, intervention, and planning.

Engaging family members in the work of the foundation and encouraging them to contribute personally has many benefits:

• *Giving breeds ownership of the foundation.* Family members who feel ownership are more likely to engage in setting goals, to carefully review grant requests, to evaluate the impact of the foundation's grants, and to take personal interest in the more routine board duties such as investment management and budgeting.

- *Additional contributions increase the foundation's long-term philanthropic impact.* Although most foundations experienced double-digit internal growth during the 1990s as a result of dramatic returns in the investment markets, foundations have lost asset value over the last three years because of negative investment returns. In addition, inflation has taken a toll on the purchasing power of the remaining assets. Building foundation assets through gifts ensures the foundation's ability to maintain — and eventually increase — its grantmaking and impact.

- *Giving encourages other family members to get involved.* When a member of the next generation makes a gift, it sets the tone for siblings, cousins, and children. When all of the next generation members make a gift, it sets the pace and example for the following generation, and with each additional donor, the foundation moves closer to a foundation truly representing the family.

[2] Tips For Effective Engagement

[a] Set Goals for Family Involvement

The first step in devising a plan for family involvement is to be clear about the goals. Think broadly about the founder's purposes and objectives in creating the foundation. Did the founder have a specific charitable goal? Did he or she have visions of the family's role? Or was the foundation created as a way to defer decisions about charitable distributions until a future date? Be honest about the answers. They will explain much about the foundation's structure and design.

Then consider whether those objectives have changed since the foundation was established. What are the current goals for charitable mission and family involvement? Write these down, prioritizing those goals that are most important.

Next, make a list of all potentially involved family members. Include their names, ages, occupations, and permanent residences. Organize the information in a family tree format to distinguish first, second, and third (or more) generations. Circle current members of the foundation board. Highlight board officers. Review the results. Are there branches that are underrepresented on the current board? Are there branches that are overrepresented? Are there other obvious trends? If the representation is skewed, does this form the basis for lack of interest by some family members? Think about how the current structure came to exist.

[b] Make Sure the Foundation's Governance
Structure Fits the Family Goals

Once the goals are established and the structure is charted, review the foundation's governance structure to determine if changes are required. For example, if the second generation has three branches, yet only one of the three branches is represented on the board, it may be necessary to apportion board seats among the three branches in the bylaws to maintain balance.

Also check term limits. Does the governance structure allow uninvolved family members to assume board roles? If board members have life appointments, it will be difficult to involve new participants without adding board seats or establishing terms and term limits that encourage turnover. Some boards limit terms to three years and require rotation after two terms. This allows new members to assume board responsibilities, ensures ongoing change in the board dynamics, and encourages the introduction of new ideas and energy levels. The goal in moving members off the board is not to drive them away from the foundation, but to allow everyone a voice. Retiring members need not cease all involvement; these experienced foundation managers can always take responsibility as a committee chair, take on a special project such as marketing or web site design, or may even assume a critical role in strategic planning or risk assessment. Other foundations have an unlimited number of board seats. The design should comport with state law and reflect the family's structure and politics.

When designing board structure and governance, consider setting aside a certain percentage of the board seats for younger generations. This ensures younger family members will always have a place at the board table.

[c] Involve Family Members in Foundation Work as Early as Possible

The single most effective strategy for family involvement is to get younger generations involved as early as possible and to engage them in meaningful work. There are at least three ways to pull children into foundation work: the junior board, committee work, the family workshop and site visits, discussed in more detail in the following sections.

[d] Place a Premium on Communication

Communication among family members is often taken for granted, and suffers as a result. The individual or couple who created the foundation should write a brief history of the foundation's origins, how it was established, and why the foundation form was selected. This should include insight into personal goals and objectives, and the vision for the foundation as it moved through the second, third, and lower generations. The document should also acknowledge the change that is certain to result with new laws, additional family members, and the shift in societal needs.

Take minutes that reflect family personalities, priorities, and involvement. Share the minutes with family members as appropriate. *Caution:* Foundation minutes may be subject to public review and scrutiny of lower generations. Take care to omit incidents or comments that are too personal or would not withstand public scrutiny.

Conduct family foundation meetings at family gatherings. Talk about the work of the foundation; allow junior family members to attend meetings. Encourage parents to talk to their children about the foundation's focus and distributions. Create a page for family members on the foundation's web site and allow any family member to access information about the foundation's grants and work.

Sometimes family communication is so poor that an outside facilitator is required to get the conversation moving and to engage the key players. Family counselors, family philanthropy consultants, and psychologists are available to help families identify barriers and establish meeting protocols that give everyone a voice.

[e] Expand the Foundation's Grantmaking to Incorporate New Interests

Every individual's charitable interests change over time. Someone may focus on humanitarian and health care needs in his younger years, the arts and education in midlife, and health care and fundamental needs in later life. This shift is understandable since most individuals give to charities where they are involved or use the services. For this reason, there are often generational differences in charitable grantmaking interests. Rather than force younger generations to embrace another generation's priorities, these differences should be acknowledged and accommodated whenever possible.

Consider changes to grantmaking policy that:

- *Accommodate grants to organizations located in a family member's community.* If the foundation has policies restricting grants to arts and education organizations, allow a percentage of the foundation's grants to be distributed to arts and education organizations in other states. In all cases, require the family members to develop the baseline information required for a grant. (This teaches the family member about the need for accountability in the foundation's operation.)

- *Accommodate and reflect grantmaking priorities of younger generations.* All policies affecting grants and priorities should be managed through the grants committee. All grants should reflect the foundation's mission. If the objectives established by the younger generations stretch beyond that mission, involve the family members in a review and restatement of the foundation's mission through a strategic planning process.

[f] Use Training to Build Knowledge and Interest

Board service is a learned not a genetic trait. We are taught manners, social skills, the art of conversation, and a variety of educational topics. Board skills are no different. Schedule annual training that establishes member expectation and provides the training to meet those expectations. Training elevates the importance of the foundation work and provides a forum for discussion of its primary elements.

[3] Practical Barriers to Participation

It is easy to identify several barriers to participation. First, philanthropy is a concept that is taught rather than intuited. Children and grandchildren — especially in the early years — think more about acquiring than distributing assets. When asked to participate in charitable grantmaking, they have few benchmarks to assist them in making good decisions. Second, charitable interests vary by generation. The arts, education, and religious interests of the first generation may give way to the environmental and international welfare concerns of the next. Finally, children may be saddled with a family stereotype or hierarchy that is hard to overcome. "Little Joey," who sank the family sailboat at age 14, still lives with that image at age 44.

The key to longevity and effective family involvement is to get subsequent generations involved as early as possible. Early activity allows the new family participants to focus on the role of the foundation and to understand how the grantmaking of the foundation reflects family values. This interaction allows experienced board members to teach those of the next generation how to handle their role and responsibilities as trustees or board members. With planning, the family foundation can be structured to give each board member a meaningful role and to provide family members with an opportunity to pursue areas of interest. The most common ways of developing involvement are through the use of a junior board, a family workshop, creative committee work, and a program evaluation team. For resources, see Table 1-2 in Chapter 1, *supra*.

[B] The Junior Board

A junior board is simply a younger group that serves in an advisory role in the distribution of grants. The board is designed to get children involved early in the process and to find a role for children too young to serve as trustees or board members. Normally, a junior board is assigned a specific amount of income to distribute and is given a list of potential organizations qualified to receive a distribution. The junior board is then responsible for conducting research, holding its own grant meetings, and making recommendations on how the limited pool of funds will be distributed.

The goal is to begin to make the junior board members aware of needs, help them focus on the benefits of receiving a foundation grant, and educate them on the balancing process required to allocate funds. This training should build community values, educate children about needs and resources, and help move them from an inward focus to an outward community focus. It also provides a meaningful way for children to interact with older generations and to begin to assert their ideas.

Since the purpose of the exercise is to teach children about how to make grants and to get them actively involved in the foundation's work, the group should receive direction and training from members of the board. The leadership can do as much or as little of the research as appropriate for the age of the junior members, but the more the younger group is allowed to do, the more they will learn. There is a wealth of information on charitable organizations on the Internet, and some of the junior members may be more skilled than senior members in using this resource.

Many grantors create family foundations for the specific purpose of passing philanthropic values to children. Once members of the younger generation have participated in several years of the junior board experience, they are far more capable of making a contribution to the full board.

[C]   The Family Workshop

A family workshop is an activity similar to a corporate or nonprofit workshop except that the family workshop focuses on the management of the family foundation, rather than a corporation. The workshop offers a method to bring the family together for the specific purpose of addressing the foundation and its objectives, strategic planning for future years of the foundation, and even issues related to transfer of family assets. These sessions have the most impact on older nonboard family members, but can also be structured to include sessions for the very young where appropriate.

These workshops are most effective when a professional facilitator is used. Using the patriarch or matriarch to conduct the sessions may not move the family beyond its current comfortable relationships. While you can employ a strategic planning firm, you are far more likely to succeed if you use facilitators trained in managing family conflicts and family transfers. This may mean using a combination of a psychologist and financial planner or a firm that specializes in this field.

Make sure that you set clear goals and objectives for the session and that you share those goals prior to the meeting. You may also find that the facilitator uses a questionnaire to solicit input from the participants prior to the session.

[D]   Committee Work

Sometimes a "child" is in his 40s or 50s and still struggling to find his place or role in the family foundation. In these cases, simply serving on the board may not be enough to ensure participation and respect. The lower generation family member may have no more voice than he does in running the family business or making other family decisions. It is important to understand that it is as hard for the parent or grandparent as it is for the child or grandchild to break out of this behavior pattern.

A creative use of committees may solve the problem. Many smaller foundations do not use committees; all should. Since most foundations spend the majority of their meeting hours dispersing grants, the important work of strategic planning, investment management, or budgeting is forgotten. Create committees that perform or provide oversight for these critical functions. Assign lower generations responsibility in running the committee and reporting results and recommendations at board meetings. Determine the skill sets of the younger family members who need to get involved, and match committee assignments with those skills.

This accomplishes two objectives. First, it gives the child a meaningful way to get involved. (The more involved he is, the greater the interest in participating and continuing the family foundation.) Second, it gives older generations a new perspective on the skills and contribution of younger generations, helping to overcome stereotypes and create new levels of confidence and respect.

[E] The Program Evaluation Team

Sometimes lower generations serve as directors, attend all the meetings, do whatever is asked of them, but evidence no interest in the work of the foundation. In these cases, it is important to find a way to get them engaged. The single most effective way to generate excitement is to make a site visit to potential recipients to evaluate their grant request or to document spending of grant funds.

There are at least four benefits to using younger family members as a part of a program evaluation team. First, assigning family members to program evaluation is an excellent way to develop information on potential or current grant recipients, train future board members about how to evaluate programs, and help future board members build a base of knowledge about the nonprofit community. Second, service on the evaluation team allows the younger generation to meet the nonprofit community leaders. Third, the process increases the information available to foundation grantmakers. And fourth, evaluation improves fiduciary accountability.

Make sure that your evaluation team members are sent out with training, with questionnaires to guide their research, and with direction on learning objectives. Have the family members prepare the reports for the grants committee, complete with observations and recommendations. Then allow the younger members to report their findings to the grants committee or the full board. Allow them to listen to the grant award deliberations and decision making (or participate if they are full board members). Being a part of this process reinforces the concept of responsible grantmaking, gives members of the younger generation a role, and shows them how to evaluate community needs and resources.

Each family and family foundation is different. The talents, ages, and personalities of the family members are different. Look for ways to integrate family into the foundation management process, educate family about the issues, and build an interest in future participation.

[F] Introducing the Giving Concept

Once a child is engaged in foundation work, focus him or her on its long-term impact. Suggest that the child include the foundation in the child's own annual giving. Ask the child to include the foundation in his or her estate planning. Educate the child on opportunities to give. Set expectations and provide suggestions on how to follow through. The concept of adding to the foundation may not occur naturally, especially if the founder has made a significant initial contribution. The idea must be introduced and cultivated.

Take a lesson from fundraisers who understand the two critical rules for generating a gift. First, one must ask the potential donor to make the gift; hints do not work. This means the founder must be clear with subsequent generations about opportunities and obligations. Second, one must cultivate the donor — sometimes for many years — before the gift will result. The founder who encourages children and grandchildren to engage in building the foundation must be patient and accept the fact that he or she may not live to see the transfer. It takes many years for individuals to mature to the point where they consider thoughtful gifts and to reach a stage of economic ability to make significant gifts.

§ 9.03 PUBLIC RELATIONS — GETTING THE MESSAGE OUT

[A] Benefits of a Public Relations Program

Marketing and public relations may seem to be unusual concepts for the family foundation. After all, family foundations are insular. They make decisions on governance based on family dynamics and generally do not look to the broad community for leadership. They seek additions to the foundation from sources internal to the family and have no obligation to raise money from the public. Furthermore, they make grantmaking decisions based solely on personal preferences within the IRS guidelines. So why does the foundation need a public image?

Increasingly, private foundations are turning to the public to report activities and assets and solicit grant requests. The Foundation Center, which annually surveys the 20,000 largest foundations, has measured a more than 40 percent increase in the number of foundations issuing publications from 1992 to 2001, although those that report are still in the minority.[11] Of the grantmakers that did

---

[11] Josefina Atienza and Leslie Marino, *Foundation Reporting — Update on Public Reporting Trends of Private Community Foundations* (The Foundation Center 2002).

report to the public through an annual report, web site, or other publication, most were large foundations. In the 2002 survey, the Foundation Center estimated that only 5.8 percent of the total 56,600 grantmaking foundations produced publications, but those grantmakers accounted for 64.4 percent of total foundation assets and 60.2 percent of total foundation giving in 2000.[12]

There is a good case to be made for a solid public relations program for the family foundation:

- *A good public relations message can shape a positive public perception of family foundations.* The public has mixed feelings about private foundations. There is strong sentiment in some sectors that the mega-foundations — such as the Bill and Melinda Gates Foundation, with assets of $28.8 billion[13] — are too large and distribute too little. This mistrust is easy to understand because the foundations are large and the public has no input into management or policy. Recent articles in the *Chronicle of Philanthropy* report that lawmakers have been urged to look at policy that would force a private foundation to distribute more, or all, of its assets. The more open that a foundation is to public scrutiny, and the more that is understood about its goals and objectives, the easier it will be to establish the concept of private foundations as an important national resource.

- *A well-designed public relations campaign may help the foundation maximize its goals.* Family foundations often focus on the community, and more specifically on particular issues within that community. The foundation is in a unique position to award challenge or matching grants to community nonprofits in order to encourage other contributions for the purpose designated in the grant. Through publicity, the foundation can also call attention to important community issues addressed by the grant award. Also, through funding a needs assessment, the foundation can define the underlying factors giving rise to the problem. The foundation cannot fund and solve community problems on its own. It must build support and allies in the community. A public relations effort offers a way to leverage foundation dollars to accomplish goals larger than the foundation can fund.

- *Such a program can encourage others to become philanthropists.* One of the most powerful marketing tools in the nonprofit world is the use of donor testimonials or stories. These stories are important because they provide a way for potential donors to identify with the donor telling the story. They often inspire others to take action on the basis that they, too, can accomplish goals similar to the donor telling the tale. Use stories about your family and your contributions and your goals to help others in the community to understand more about making charitable gifts.

---

[12] *Id.*

[13] Reported asset size as in 2004 Annual Report, <*www.gatesfoundation.org*>.

Example: Consider the story of Oseola McCarty, a poor black woman from Mississippi; without an education, she washed clothes for a living. Ms. McCarthy saved a portion of her earnings, invested those funds, and made a gift of $150,000 to the University of Southern Mississippi. These funds were to be used specifically for scholarships to provide other poor, black students with the opportunity to attend school and become economically viable. Her statement, as reported by the university, was: "I want to help somebody's child go to college . . . . I just want it to go to someone who will appreciate it and learn. I'm old and I'm not going to live always." This story drew worldwide attention because it made the point that anyone and everyone could be a philanthropist. Wealth was not necessary to make a significant impact on the community.

The family foundation is in a position to spread the same message. Through news releases, public interest stories, or even the foundation's annual report, talk about how and why the foundation was established. Place the emphasis on the personal goals and objectives of the donor and the donor's family, rather than the tax incentives for the gift. Get other potential donors in the community to stop and think about similar possibilities and goals.

- *A public relations program will reinforce the family's legacy and leadership.* Many families establish foundations because it is important to be perceived as a leader in the community or because the foundation may provide a position of power and control in the decision making in the community. These goals can be reinforced through ongoing communication about the foundation, its leadership, and its grants.

- *Such a program can project a favorable image for the family itself.* Good work reflects well on the workers, and this is a sort of benefit that is regarded as incidental and therefore permissible.

The decision to publicize the foundation should be a decision made by the board as part of its overall mission and goals. Your foundation may choose to operate quietly in the community. Or it may choose to operate in a very public fashion to encourage greater understanding of the family's mission and goals and of the operation of foundations in general. Make the decision based on your comfort level and objectives.

[B]   Deciding How to Position the Foundation

Positioning the foundation in the community should be handled in a manner similar to positioning any nonprofit. You must first determine your goals. Consider the objectives and alternatives listed in Table 9-3.

Take an organized approach to setting goals and developing strategies to meet those goals. Develop a way of gathering information to measure results. For example, if your goal is to increase the number of applications, measure the number of new applications received and the number of new qualified applications received. These figures can be compared to results in past years and serve as a basis for ongoing measurement. If the goal is to measure publicity, count the number of mentions of the foundation in print, electronic, and Internet media locations. Hire a clipping service if necessary. Record the context and length of all mentions and the source of the information used in the publicity. You can then measure progress from year to year as well as measuring the most effective means of communicating your message.

TABLE 9-3
Options in Positioning the Family Foundation

Goal	*Options*
1. The foundation wants to publicize the grants made by the foundation in order to encourage a wider variety of grant applications.	• Publish a press release announcing the new grant cycle. • Publish a public interest story about the results of a recent grant. • Mail a letter to qualified charities informing them of how to obtain a grant application. • Add a grant application to the foundation's web site, with information on how and when to apply; Consider electronic applications for grants.
2. The foundation wants to call attention to a particular need in the community.	• Make media contacts through a press release with details about the need. • Conduct a needs assessment related to the issue; call a press conference to announce the results; distribute printed materials to the media and non-profits addressing the need to focus on the issue.
3. The foundation wants to create a change in the way that education/health care/homeless care/women and children [*insert the issue important to the foundation*] *is* handled in the community.	• Conduct a needs assessment to determine problems and to determine the community resources available to meet the needs; call a press conference to announce the results; distribute printed materials to the media and nonprofits addressing the need; post the results on the foundation's web site. • Assemble a group of community leaders that can solve the problem; provide leadership in working through the issue. Use press releases and printed materials to raise public awareness of the issues.
4. The foundation wants to associate the foundation's	• Send family members with oversized checks to board meetings to make grant awards.

grantmaking with the family members involved in managing the foundation.	• Prepare a press release about the foundation's grant cycle, anniversary year, additional contributions, and names of board members; post the information on the foundation's web site. • Create an annual report with detail about family involvement; post a copy of the report on the foundation's web site. • Sponsor special events with awards to organizations that have accomplished the most with the use of grant awards; use family members to make the awards.
5. The foundation wants to encourage more philanthropy in the community.	• Make family members available to speak at civic clubs, board meetings, and annual meetings related to philanthropy. • Use family members to distribute checks; prepare a three-minute talk on why the foundation was created and how others can accomplish the same goals.
6. The foundation wants to organize a consortium of charities to address a particular issue in the community.	• Conduct a needs assessment or use a current assessment to determine key constituencies and agencies that address the need; contact agencies and provide leadership and funding to accomplish goals; post the results on the foundation's web site. • Conduct public meetings to address needs and solicit participation in solving problems. • Publish a white paper addressing the issues and possible solutions; distribute it to media and appropriate constituencies; publish the information on the foundation's web site.
7. The foundation wants to serve as a poster child for all family foundations in order to raise public awareness of family foundations and the good those foundations accomplish.	• Require that agencies that receive funds publicly announce grants from the foundation, accompanied companied by a prepared statement on the foundation. • Publish an annual report; circulate the report widely; post the report on the foundation's web site. • Offer to appear as speakers at civic clubs, nonprofit grant recipient board meetings, and other public forums to highlight the foundation's grant policies and results.
8. The foundation wants to encourage the creation of more family foundations.	• Offer to appear as speakers at civic clubs, nonprofit grant recipient board meetings, and other public forums to highlight the foundation's grant policies and results. • Include information on how and why the foundation was created in the foundation's annual report; post the information on the foundation's web site. • Initiate discussions with peers about the purpose and function of the foundation.

[C] The Process of Positioning the Foundation

The process of positioning the foundation requires the development of a strategic plan that most effectively accomplishes your goals and objectives. The most common methods of marketing include use of the electronic and print media, direct mail, the Internet, registration with foundation clearinghouses, and public appearances and meetings. Your method of marketing will depend on your geographic scope, the funds available for marketing, and your goals.

1. *Use electronic and print media to deliver your message.* Develop a list of contact names and numbers of all media outlets. These can be easily obtained from the chambers of commerce located in the areas that you want to reach. These lists generally include:

    - Daily, weekly, and monthly newspapers;

    - Radio stations;

    - Television stations; and

    - Internet news and information sites.

    Identify the name, telephone number, fax number, and e-mail address of the individual responsible for covering nonprofit organizations. Make sure that these individuals receive press releases, annual reports, and any special reports produced by the foundation.

2. *Use direct mail to spread your message.* Develop a database with names of key contacts in the community you serve. These may include the media names identified above, but should also include key community leaders, leaders of nonprofit agencies that receive grants from the foundation, and leaders of nonprofit agencies that perform services of the type for which the foundation makes grants. These individuals should receive copies of the foundation's annual report, white papers, needs assessments, and other information of interest to the public.

3. *Use the Internet to spread your message.* The Internet is a cost-effective and powerful way to distribute information about the foundation, especially where the foundation is serving a large geographic area. The Internet allows the foundation to easily distribute information to the public. Make sure that the information can be found through search engines and that it is in a format that can be easily downloaded and printed.
    Designing and building the web site can be challenging. The site must look professional, since it will represent the foundation to the public. Use a professional firm that has experience and history to help you in the process. This will cost money, but will save valuable time and ensure that your site has a professional, easy-to-use appearance. Thousands of potential donors may have their first contact with your organization through this

medium. In addition, a web site provides you with a cost-effective way to make the foundation's tax returns available to the public.

If cost is an issue, consider these options in hiring someone to design and build your site:

- *Check availability on the board.* Is there someone that can provide this service?

- *Check local schools and universities.* Is there a class looking for a civic project?

- *Check local providers.* Get estimates and a list of services. There are many affordable young web site builders in the market.

- *Check organizations that provide support.* For example, at one time, the Resource Center for Nonprofit Organizations, located in Birmingham, Alabama, offered development of a web site at a cost of $50 as a benefit of membership. Organizations that took advantage of this opportunity received their own address as a subsite of the domain for the Resource Center, *www.nonprofital.org*. For $50, the participant received three pages and four free updates.

If all else fails, turn to volunteers for development of the site. A volunteer or student who works at no cost generally works on his or her own schedule. This "free" process allows little control over the timing or quality of the work.

4. *Make contact with your state legislators and congressional representatives.* Make sure that the lawmakers in the community you serve are aware of your foundation and the positive results that it creates in the community. While private foundations may not engage in lobbying, you may communicate with those individuals making laws that govern charitable giving and regulate charitable grantmaking. Your communications about the positive impact of your foundation on the community may be the only information they get on the benefits to the community.

5. *Register with foundation clearinghouses.* There are a number of nonprofit organizations dedicated to collecting and disseminating information about foundations. The information is designed to help grantmakers locate nonprofits that address needs targeted by their foundations, to help grant seekers find foundations that fund specific needs, and to help researchers analyze foundation activity.

If your foundation wants to maintain a low profile, you need do nothing. These organizations receive annual lists of new foundations. If your organization is large enough, they will find you to solicit information about your operations. If your foundation wants to quickly move into the public view, you can contact these agencies to ensure listing. The most common alternatives are listed in Table 9-4. All of these can be located by using a search engine on the Internet with such key words as "family foundations" "grants from foundations." These may change often, especially the independent sites noted, so refresh your information periodically.

TABLE 9-4
Foundation Clearinghouses

Name	Address	Comments
Council on Foundations	1828 L Street, NW Washington, DC 20036 202-466-6512 (phone) 202-785-3926 (fax) *www.cof.org*	The Council on Foundations is a nonprofit membership organization of grantmaking foundations and corporations
The Foundation Center	79 Fifth Avenue New York, NY 10003-3076 212-620-4230 (phone) 212-807-2426 (fax) *www.fdncenter.org*	The Foundation Center is the largest nonprofit serving as a clearinghouse for information on domestic foundations; it is generally the starting place for those looking for information. The only limitation of the Foundation Center is that it focuses most of its attention on larger foundations. Its publications include *Foundation Giving: Yearbook of Facts and Figures on Private, Corporate and Community Foundations.*
Guidestar	*www.guidestar.org*	Guidestar is an Internet site that provides information on all charities, including foundations. Guidestar is in the process of upgrading its information to include more detail. Your foundation can provide information on directors, finances, and funding goals by contacting the site.
Local State Directories	Various	Contact your public library to determine if there is a foundation listing in your state. Many states provide this service through either a library or a funded source. In every instance, however, the library should have a copy of the most recent report.

National Center for Family Philanthropy	1818 N Street NW, Suite 300 Washington, DC 20036 202-293-3424 (phone) 202-293-3395 (fax) *www.ncfp.org, ncfp@ncfp. org*	This organization was established in 1997 to support families engaged in philanthropy. It offers publications, networking, and support services.

[D] Public Disclosure and Its Impact on the Foundation

Family foundations are often formed for very personal — and private — reasons. Donors may want to organize their giving, teach children about philanthropy, create a permanent family presence in the community, or simply distance themselves from personal solicitations. Some may even choose the family foundation form to achieve privacy. Those that do may be surprised to learn that foundations are not really private.

[1] The Disclosure Requirements

Although public charities have long been subject to public disclosure requirements, private foundations were subject to less extensive and burdensome requirements. Under the old rules, foundations were required to publish notice that their annual tax return was available for inspection for 180 days. In addition, they had to allow inspection of and provide copies of the foundation's exemption application to those that requested it.

The Tax and Trade Relief Extension Act of 1998[14] eliminated the publication rules and subjected private foundations to the public disclosure requirements imposed on public charities. These rules, designed to enhance oversight and provide greater public accountability, direct private foundations to make the following information available upon request:[15]

- Copies of Form 1023, the foundation's application for exemption. (Since foundations in existence for many years may not have the application, this requirement is applicable to private foundations that filed an exemption application before July 15, 1987, only if they had a copy on July 15, 1987);

- Copies of three years of Form 990-PF and Form 4720 (filings related to unrelated business income or excise taxes); and

- Contributors' names, addresses, and the amounts they donated to the foundation.

In at least one respect, the rules are more onerous for private foundations than public charities. Whereas private foundations are required to provide a

---

[14] Pub. L. No. 105-277, § 1004(b)(1) (Oct. 20, 1998).

[15] IRC § 6104(a)(1)(A); Reg. § 301.6104(d)-1(a). *See* § 8.08 for more detail on disclosure requirements.

contributor's name, address, and contribution amount, public charities are required only to reveal contribution amounts. This puts family foundation contributors who want to protect their privacy in a vulnerable position.

There is one further complication for family foundations. Many are small and do not have the extensive staff employed by larger public charities. Furthermore, they may not have offices available to the public and likely do not conduct foundation business on a daily basis, making compliance more cumbersome.

In comments provided when the final regulations were adopted, the IRS assumed a positive attitude about the burden of the rules. They felt that the cost of compliance — both in time expended and dollars required — would be minimal. They assumed each private foundation would receive one request annually and that it would take 30 minutes and $10 to respond. Since there are no published statistics on the number of requests made since these rules went into effect, it is difficult to gauge the accuracy of these estimates. The IRS comments did not address the privacy issues.

[2] How to Comply

Compliance expectations and timetables vary depending on whether the requestor makes a request in person or in writing and whether he or she wants to examine the documents or requests copies of them.

- *Requests made for public inspection.* If the foundation has a permanent office, it is required to allow the individual who wants to review the return to examine the copies, take notes, and make copies if the office has photocopying equipment. If the foundation does not have a permanent office, it must make the material available at a reasonable location that it selects within a reasonable amount of time, generally considered no more than two weeks. Or, it may mail the copies to the individual requesting the information within two weeks of the time it receives the request.[16]

- *Requests for copies.* When a request for copies is made in person at the foundation's office, the foundation is generally required to respond on the same day unless circumstances exist that place an unusual burden on it; in those cases, the foundation should comply by the next business day after the unusual circumstances cease. When the request is made in writing (including mail, e-mail, facsimile, or private delivery service), the foundation must comply within 30 days of the request. The foundation may charge a reasonable fee for the copies (that cannot exceed the IRS fee for copies). If it requires payment for copies in advance, it must comply within 30 days of receiving payment.[17]

---

[16] Reg. § 301.6104(d)-1.
[17] *Id.*

As an alternative to both of these options, the foundation can post copies on the World Wide Web. This rule, called the "widely available exception,"[18] has been available to public charities and recognizes the growing public access to information posted on the Internet. If the charity has a web site, it can post the information on that site. If it does not maintain a web site or chooses not to post it in that location, public forums such as Guidestar (*www.guidestar.org*) will also post returns.

It is unusual to find a charity that has posted its application for exemption on the Internet; foundations may want to post only their 990-PF and hold the exemption application for review upon request. Family foundations may also want to be guarded about posting names and addresses of contributors on the Internet, again distributing that information on a request-only basis.

[3] When to Refuse to Provide Information

While the spirit of the rules is to enhance accountability and oversight, there are three instances in which a foundation may refuse to comply. First, a foundation may refuse if it has made the information available through the widely available exception described above. Second, a foundation may refuse if the request is part of a harassment campaign.[19] Finally, the foundation may apply to the Secretary of the Treasury for an exception to the disclosure rules if the information requested would adversely affect the foundation because it relates to a trade secret, patent, process, style of work, or apparatus belonging to the foundation or if the information would adversely affect the national defense.[20]

Failure to provide requested copies of returns for reasons other than those listed can result in a fine of $20 a day with a maximum penalty per return of $10,000. Failure to comply with a request for its application for exemption is set at $20 per day with no maximum amount. Both fines are imposed on the foundation. In addition, the individual who willfully fails to comply with a request for inspection or copies can be assessed a penalty of $5,000 for each return or application.[21]

[4] The Bottom Line

From a practical perspective, large foundations (such as the Bill and Melinda Gates Foundation) are more likely to engender public and press curiosity than small to midsized entities. Less visible foundations may not receive requests for information unless the foundation is involved in controversial projects, made distributions to questionable charities, or made payments appearing to provide personal benefit. However, all foundations need to know and comply with the rules. Indeed, compliance and publication build public confidence in private foundations, demystify their activities, and assign value to the private sector capital they provide.

---

[18] Reg. § 301.6104(d)-2.
[19] Reg. § 301.6104(d)-3.
[20] IRC § 6104(a)(1)(D).
[21] IRC §§ 6652(c)(1)(C), (D); 6685.

The best advice to family foundations is to honor requests within the time limits and under the conditions set out in the regulations. If the request seems inappropriate, call your foundation counsel and get a second opinion. Keep records of requests and the time it takes to comply. If the laws are revisited, this information may prove helpful in providing input to new regulations. And finally, look for ways to tell the public about the impact your foundation has on the community.

Table 9–5 summarizes the disclosure requirements for private foundations.

TABLE 9-5
Public Disclosure Requirements for Private Foundations

Issues	*Exemption Application*	*990-PF (3 Years) Including Contributors' Names, Addresses, and Amounts*
Family foundation required to provide upon request for inspection or copy[*]	Yes[**]	Yes
Response Time for Public Inspection		
• If foundation has a primary office	As soon as practical	As soon as practical
• If foundation does not have a primary office	Within a reasonable time (no more than two weeks); or may mail within two weeks	Within a reasonable time (no more than two weeks); or may mail within two weeks
Response Time for Copies		
• When request is made in person at the foundation's office	Same day, unless the request places an unusual burden on the Foundation	Same day, unless the request places an unusual burden on the foundation
• When request is made in writing (including mail e-mail, facsimile, private delivery service) — no fee requiredin advance	Within 30 days of receipt	Within 30 days of receipt
• When request is made in writing (including mail, e-mail, facsimile, private delivery service) — copy fee required in advance	Within 30 days of receipt of fee	Within 30 days of receipt of fee

• Penalties for Failure to Comply	\$20 per day/no maximum[***]	\$20 per day/maximum penalty of \$10,000 per return

[*] Foundations that post this information on the World Wide Web are not required to comply with inspection and copy files. In addition, the foundation need not comply if the request is part of a harassment campaign. Finally, the foundation can apply for an exception to the disclosure rules of the information would damage the foundation or national defense.

[**] This is not applicable to foundations formed before July 15, if they had a copy on that date.

[***] Individuals who willfully fail to comply can be assessed a penalty of \$5,000 per document.

[5] Other Disclosure Issues for Trustees and Board Members

Foundation board and staff must be prepared to answer questions from the press and public about the information reported on these annual filings. Consider the following typical questions that may be raised by the media:

- How do you determine which organizations will receive funding?

- How do organizations apply for funds from your foundation?

- When is the grant application deadline?

- Do you have a grant form for application?

- When do you make decisions about grants? Who makes those decisions?

- Can we attend the grants meeting to make a personal proposal?

- Do you fund organizations without tax-exempt status?

- Why does the foundation continue to hold assets, rather than distributing those assets to meet critical needs?

- Does a member of your family receive compensation from the foundation? Why is that appropriate?

- Why does the board consist solely of family members? Shouldn't you broaden your board to include representation by individuals who have an understanding of nonprofit needs?

- How can you justify the ongoing expenses of the foundation? Wouldn't it be easier to distribute the funds outright and save those annual costs?

- Why does your foundation focus primarily on arts/education/social welfare/ women/AIDS [*insert the foundation focus*]?

Many of these questions can be answered through publication of a grant application package. However, other questions require a response that reflects personal goals, objectives, and attitudes. Think through your answer carefully before responding. Remember that most individuals and even media representatives raising the questions do not understand private foundations and their purposes. Foundation actions that are well within the spirit and letter of the law may seem inappropriate to the observer who knows little.

Consider this example. Imagine that Jerry McCoy founded the McCoy Center for the Disabled. The center is a qualified public charity, operating to meet the needs of the disabled in the county. The center may have been named after Mr. McCoy to reflect the board's appreciation of his role in establishing the entity. Let us further assume that Mr. McCoy has established a family foundation named the McCoy Family Foundation and that his board has decided that 90 percent of all distributions from the McCoy Family Foundation will be made to the McCoy Center for the Disabled. This direction of funds to an entity bearing the same name as the foundation and the effective bar against funding other qualified organizations may prove frustrating and confusing for other nonprofits, leading to questions about appropriateness. Answers to questions should anticipate that those who ask may or may not understand the operation of a private, as opposed to a public, foundation and should incorporate basic principles in the answer.

The best policy is to anticipate the most common questions and ensure that you have an answer. If you are surprised with a question you have not considered, defer an answer until you've had some time to collect your thoughts. It is also advisable to answer all questions posed to you by the media as quickly and as accurately as possible unless there is a clear reason — such as advice of counsel or your public relations manager — that you should not do so.

[E] What to Do When the Foundation Must Impart Bad News (Such as Limited Grant Funds)

Many foundations struggled to meet grantseekers' expectations in 2003. According to a survey of the country's 134 largest foundations conducted by the *Chronicle of Philanthropy* (reported in the March 6, 2003, issue), assets of the country's largest private foundations decreased significantly for the third year in a row, signaling a potential decrease in funds available for grantmaking. The large foundations surveyed by the newspaper reported a collective decrease of $19.7 billion in assets, translating into a decrease in grants of at least $985 million in required distributions. That decrease came at a bad time for charities already suffering from a decline in public contributions and counting on foundations to keep their operating budgets intact.

The third straight year of decreases in foundation assets — due largely to sustained negative investment returns — prompted some foundations to make changes in their policies.

- *Some foundation boards adopted more conservative asset allocation policies to combat the potential for continued erosion of assets.* While these boards may have reduced or eliminated their stock exposure, replacing those assets with short-term fixed income, the policy may dampen long-term investment returns.

- *Other foundations embraced a more conservative spending policy to rebuild assets.* Many foundations steadily increased grant distributions through the 1990s — often exceeding the required five percent distribution. The David and Lucile Packard Foundation, for example, suffered an asset decline of $8.2 billion (63 percent) since 1999, and planned to give away $50 million less in 2003 than in 2002. These foundations cut back on the cumulative grant total and reduced the number of organizations funded. (It is important to note that some foundations, such as the John D. and Catherine T. MacArthur Foundation, took the opposite approach, increasing spending to meet the increased need.)

- *Some foundations were hesitant to award grants for periods longer than one or two years.* Too many foundations were caught overextended coming into the asset downturn. These entities had made so many multiyear grant commitments that discretionary grants were suspended until the serial obligations were fulfilled. Going forward, these foundations will likely be more cautious about making long-term commitments, creating uncertainty for charities that depend on these types of grants to meet capital campaign or major project goals.

- *Some foundations may significantly reduce funds for start-up projects and new charities.* In an environment in which fewer grant funds are available, family foundations may not be willing to make the riskier grants to start-up programs and new charities, preferring to stick with well-established charities with a reputation for accountability.

Family foundations (indeed, all foundations) periodically receive public criticism for "hoarding" charitable funds. This objection is based on the fact that an individual (the foundation founder) makes a charitable contribution to a foundation, receives an income tax deduction for the contribution, but continues to hold the contributed funds inside the foundation rather than apply them to a direct charitable use. Congress acknowledged these objections when it imposed the minimum distribution rules and other restrictions on private foundations in the 1969 Tax Reforms, which were designed to force foundation boards to distribute funds for charitable purposes. (Ironically, many of the same charities objecting to foundation asset pools are struggling to build their own endowments to avoid future fluctuations in income.)

What does this mean for the family foundation? Most families create foundations to create a positive impact on the community and a favorable image for the family. Negative publicity or criticism for undistributed funds is not the intended outcome. The best way to address these issues before they become a problem is to anticipate concerns from the nonprofit community and develop an effective communications strategy.

The grant allocation process is mysterious to many applicants. What the foundation intends as a focused and methodical method of meeting its stated charitable goals may be perceived by grantseekers — especially those with little experience — as arbitrary. A solid communications strategy that allows the foundation to communicate priorities, to describe and coach the application process, and to publicize final decisions will improve the foundation's relationship with the charitable community.

TABLE OF CASES

References are to sections and appendices.

TABLE OF STATUTES

References are to sections and appendices.

TABLE OF TREASURY REGULATIONS

References are to sections and appendices.

TABLE OF LETTER RULINGS, REVENUE PROCEDURES, AND REVENUE RULINGS

References are to sections and appendices.

73-440, 1973-2 C.B. 177	6.06[B][1]
75-393, 1975-2 C.B. 451	6.06[C]
76-340, 1976-2, C.B. 370	7.02[B][4][c]
77-380, 19977-2 C.B. 419	7.03[C]
77-44, 1977-1 C.B. 355	7.02[B][4][c]
79-131, 1979-1 C.B. 368	7.02[B][4][c]
79-375, 1979-2 C.B. 389	App. 6-D.03[A]
80-132, 1980-1 C.B. 255	6.03[F]
80-133, 1980-1 C.B. 255	6.03[F]
80-207	2.05[D]
80-305, 1980-2 C.B. 71	2:06[C], [D]
81-217, 1981-2 C.B. 217	App. 6-G.03[D][4][a]

81-43	2.05[D]
85-175, 1985 C.B. 276	7.02[B][4][c]
2002-28, 2002-20 I.R.B. 941	2.08[D], [G], [H]
2003-13, 2003-4 I.R.B. 305	2.08[D], [G], [H]
2003-43, 2002-28 I.R.B. 1	6.03[E]

TAM

9340002	6.02[B]
9730002	2.05[D]
200347023	6.02[B]

INDEX

References are to sections and appendices.

Substantial contributor, App. 6-A.02[E]
Succession, 5.04[C][5], [6], 9.02
Suitability test, App. 6-C03[C][1],
　　[7], 7.02[C][1]
Support test, 2.06[A][2][c], App. 2-B.01[E]
Supporting organizations
　category one, App. 2-A.02
　category two, App. 2-A.03
　converting to, 2.08[C]
　definition, App. 2-A.01
　generally, 2.05[D], [G]
　Type 3, integral part test, 2.05[D]

T

Tax determination letter, 8.02[B]
Tax disadvantages
　carryover problems, 2.03[B][2]
　lower percentage limitations, 2.03[B][1]
　reduced deductions for property
　　contributions, 2.03[B][3]
　special rules, 2.03[B][4]
　state income tax issues, 2.03[B][5]
Tax-exempt organizations, 7.02[B][1][b]
Tax-exempt status, 3.03
Tax returns, 8.07
Tax year-end, 8.03[A]
Taxable expenditures
　correction, App. 6-F.02[C]
　correction period, App. 6-F.02[D][2]
　defined, App. 6-F.03[A]
　distributions for non-charitable purposes,
　　App. 6-F.03[E][12], [F], 7.03[E]
　foundation managers, App. 6-F.02
　generally, 5.05[A][3][c][iii]
　grants to individuals. See Grants to
　　individuals
　grants to organizations. See Grants to
　　organizations
　influencing legislation, 6.06[B], App. 6-
　　F.03[B], 7.03[A]. See also
　　Influencing legislation
　penalty tax, 5.05[A][3][c], App. 6-F.01
　political expenditures, 6.06[A],
　　App. 6-F.03[C], 7.03[B]
　taxable period, App. 6-F.02[D][1]
　types, 7.03
Taxation
　advantages of family foundation, 2.02[A]
　annual review of compliance, 8.10[E]

charitable lead trusts, 4.03[B]
charitable remainder trusts, 4.02[F], [G]
debt-financed income, 3.01[A][6]
disadvantages of family foundation,
　　2.03[B]. See also Tax disadvantages
excise taxes, 8.03[B][2]. See also Excise
　　taxes
filing requirements, 8.07
Form 990-PF, 8.07, App. 8-E
generation-skipping transfer tax, 4.03[F]
insurance benefits, 5.05[B][5]
on net investment income, 8.04
property tax, 8.08[B]
receipt, 3.02[F]
Seeking tax-exempt status (Form 1023),
　　3.03[A], App. 3-B
state income tax issues, 2.02[B][5]
state tax qualification, 3.03[B]
substantiation, 3.02[F], App. 3-A
tax returns, 8.07
tax shelter disclosure requirements, 8.09[B]
termination tax, 2.08[B]
unrelated business income, 3.01[A][6]
where to get forms, 8.07[A]
Termination of foundation, 2.08
　public charity, transfer of assets to,
　　2.08[H]
　termination tax, ways to avoid, 2.08[H]
　tax on, 2.08[B]
Third party, 5.05[A][3][b]
Timing the market, 8.05[A][2]
Tocqueville, Alexis de, 1.01[A]
Trade associations, 1.03
Traditional charities, 7.02[B][1][a]
　growth of number of, 7.05[C][3][b]
Traditional family foundation model, 8.05[A]
Trust. See Form of entity
Trustees, 5.05[A][3][a]. See also Board of
　　directors

U

Umbrella insurance, 5.05[B][4]
Uniform Management of Institutional Funds
　　Act (UMIFA), 8.06[A][3], App. 8-G
Uniform Prudent Investor Act (UPIA),
　　8.06[A][2], App. 8-F
Unrelated business income, 3.01[A][6]
Unstructured application form, 7.06[D],
　　App. 7-B, 7-D